For Reference

Not to be taken from this room

THE CAMBRIDGE
ANCIENT HISTORY

VOLUME X

THE CAMBRIDGE
ANCIENT HISTORY

SECOND EDITION

VOLUME X
The Augustan Empire, 43 B.C.–A.D. 69

edited by

ALAN K. BOWMAN
Student of Christ Church, Oxford

EDWARD CHAMPLIN
Professor of Classics, Princeton University

ANDREW LINTOTT
Fellow and Tutor in Ancient History,
Worcester College, Oxford

CAMBRIDGE
UNIVERSITY PRESS

Published by the Press Syndicate of the University of Cambridge
The Pitt Building, Trumpington Street, Cambridge CB2 1RP
40 West 20th Street, New York, NY 10011-4211, USA
10 Stamford Road, Oakleigh, Melbourne 3166, Australia

First published 1996

Printed in Great Britain by
Woolnough Bookbinding Ltd, Irthlingborough, Northants.

A catalogue record for this book is available from the British Library

Library of Congress Catalogue card number: 75-85719

ISBN 0 521 26430 8 hardback

SE

CONTENTS

PART I NARRATIVE

PART IV ROMAN SOCIETY AND CULTURE UNDER THE JULIO-CLAUDIANS

BIBLIOGRAPHY

NOTE ON THE BIBLIOGRAPHY

The bibliography is arranged in sections dealing with specific topics, which sometimes correspond to individual chapters but more often combine the contents of several chapters. References in the footnotes are to these sections (which are distinguished by capital letters) and within these sections each book or article has assigned to it a number which is quoted in the footnotes. In these, so as to provide a quick indication of the nature of the work referred to, the author's name and the date of publication are also included in each reference. Thus 'Syme 1986 (A 95) 50' signifies 'R. Syme, *The Augustan Revolution*, Oxford, 1986, p. 50', to be found in Section A of the bibliography as item 95.

MAPS

TEXT-FIGURES

TABLES

STEMMATA

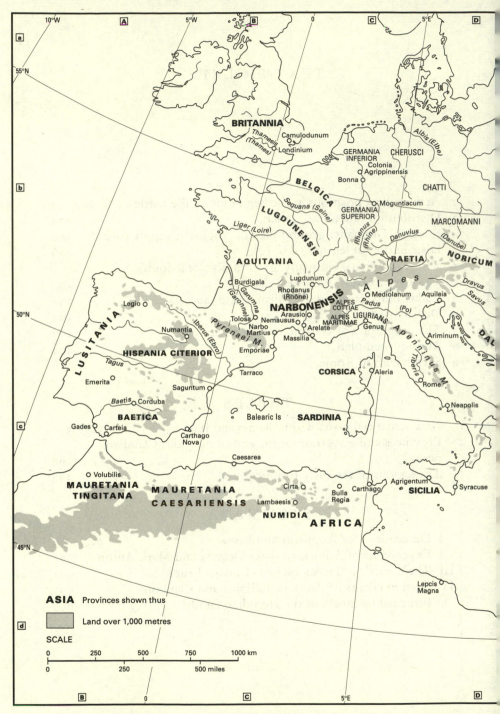

Map 1. The Roman world in the time of Augustus and the Julio-Claudian emperors.

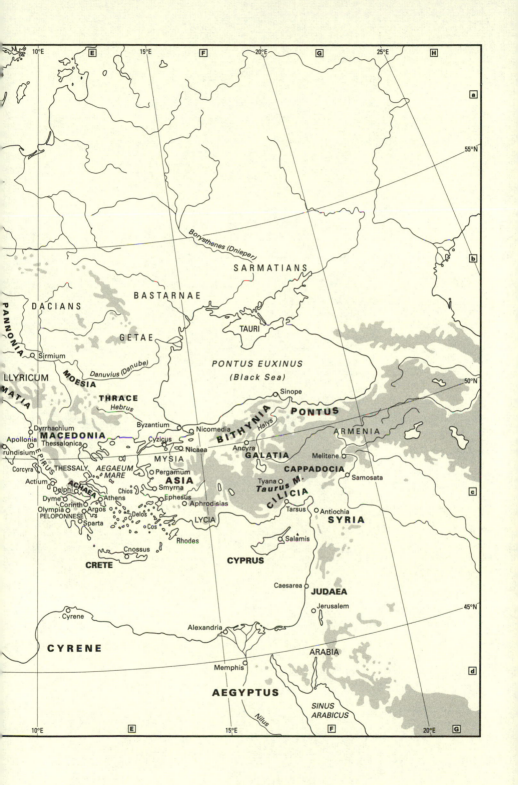

PREFACE

The period covered in this volume begins a year and a half after the death of Iulius Caesar and closes at the end of A.D. 69, more than a year after the death of Nero, the last of the Julio-Claudian emperors. His successors, Galba, Otho and Vitellius had ruled briefly and disappeared from the scene, leaving Vespasian as the sole claimant to the throne of empire. This was a period which witnessed the most profound transformation in the political configuration of the *res publica*. In the decade after Caesar's death constitutional power was held by Caesar's heir Octavian, Antony and Lepidus as *tresviri rei publicae constituendae*. Our narrative takes as its starting-point 27 November 43 B.C., the day on which the Lex Titia legalized the triumviral arrangement, a few days before the death of Cicero, which was taken as a terminal point by the editors of the new edition of Volume IX. By 27 B.C, five years after the expiry of the triumviral powers, Octavian had emerged as *princeps* and Augustus, and in the course of the next forty years he gradually fashioned what was, in all essentials, a monarchical and dynastic rule which, although passed from one dynasty to another, was to undergo no radical change until the end of the third century of our era.

If Augustus was the guiding genius behind the political transformation of the *res publica*, his influence was hardly less important in the extension of Roman dominion in the Mediterranean lands, the Near East and north-west Europe. At no time did Rome acquire more provincial territory or more influence abroad than in the reign of the first *princeps*. Accretion under his successors was steady but much slower. Conquest apart, the period as a whole is one in which the prosperity resulting from the *pax romana*, whose foundations were laid under the Republic, can be properly documented throughout the empire.

It is probably true that there is no period in Roman history on which the views of modern scholars have been more radically transformed in the last six decades. It is therefore appropriate to indicate briefly in what respects this volume differs most significantly, in approach and coverage, from its predecessor and to justify the scheme which has been adopted, particularly in view of the fact that the new editions of the three volumes covering the period between the death of Caesar and the death of Constantine have to some extent been planned as a unity.

As far as the general scheme is concerned, we have considered it essential to have as a foundation a political narrative history of the period, especially to emphasize what was contingent and unpredictable (chs. 1–6). The following chapters are more analytical and take a longer view of government and institutions (chs. 7–12), regions (chs. 13–14), social and cultural developments (chs. 15–21), although we have tried on the whole to avoid the use of an excessively broad brush. Interesting and invaluable though it was in its day, we have not been able to contemplate, for example, a counterpart to F. Oertel's chapter (1st edn ch. 13) on the 'Economic unification of the Mediterranean region'. We are conscious, however, that in the absence of such chapters something of value has been lost and we urge readers not to regard the first edition as a volume of merely antiquarian interest; the chapters of Syme on the northern frontiers (12) and Nock on religious developments (14), to name but two, still have much to offer to the historian.

The profound influence of Sir Ronald Syme's *The Roman Revolution*, published five years after the first edition of *CAH* Volume x, is very evident in the following pages, as is that of his other, prosopographical and social studies which have done so much to re-write the history of the Roman aristocracy in the first century of the Empire. No one will now doubt that the historian of the Roman state in this period has to take as much account of the importance of family connexions, of patronage, of status and property relations as of constitutional or institutional history; and to see how these relations worked through the institutions of the *res publica*, the *ordines*, the army, the governmental offices and provincial society.

The influence of another twentieth-century classic, M. I. Rostovtzeff's *Social and Economic History of the Roman Empire*, first published in 1926, was perhaps less evident in the pages of the first edition of *CAH* Volume x than might have been expected. That balance, it is hoped, has been redressed. Rostovtzeff's great achievement was to synthesize, as no-one had done before, the evidence of written documents, buildings, coins, sculpture, painting, artefacts and archaeology into a social and economic history of the empire under Roman rule which did not adopt a narrowly Romanocentric perspective. The sheer amount of new evidence accruing for the different regions of the empire in the last sixty years is immense. It is impossible for a single scholar to command expertise and knowledge of detail over the empire as a whole, and regional specialization is a marked feature of modern scholarship. The present volume recognizes this by incorporating chapters on each of the regions or provinces, as well as Italy, a scheme which will also be adopted in the new edition of Volume xi. As far as these surveys of the parts of the empire are concerned, the guiding principle has been that the chapters in the present volume should attempt to describe the developments which were the preconditions for the achievements, largely beneficial, of the 'High Empire', while the corresponding chapters in Volume xi will describe more statically, *mutatis mutandis*, the state of the different regions of the Roman world during that period.

Something must be said about the apparent omissions and idiosyncrasies. We have not thought it necessary to write an account of the sources for the period. The major literary sources (Tacitus, Suetonius, Cassius Dio, Josephus) have been very well served by recent scholarship and this period is not, from the point of view of the literary evidence, as problematical as those which follow. The range of documentary, archaeological and numismatic evidence for different topics and regions has been thought best left to individual contributors to summarize as they considered appropriate.

The presence in this volume of a chapter on the unification of Italy might be thought an oddity. Its inclusion here was a decision taken in consultation with the editors of the new edition of Volume ix, on the ground that the Augustan period is a good standpoint from which to consider a process which cannot really be considered complete before that, and perhaps not fully complete even by the Augustan age. Two of the chapters (those on Egypt and on the development of Roman law) will have counterparts in Volume xii (A.D. 193–337), but not in Volume xi; in both cases the accounts given here are intended to be generally valid for the first two centuries A.D. The treatment of Judaea and of the origins of Christianity posed difficulties of organization and articulation, given the extensive overlap of subject-matter. We nevertheless decided to invite different scholars to write these sections and to juxtapose them. It still seems surprising that the first edition of this volume contains no account of the origins and early growth of Christianity, a phenomenon which is, from the point of view of the subsequent development of civilization, surely the most important single feature of our period. Some degree of overlap with other standard works of reference is inevitable. We have, however, deliberately tried to avoid this in the case of literature by including a chapter which is intended as a history of literary activity in its social context, rather than a history of the literature of the period as such, which can be found in *The Cambridge History of Classical Literature*, Vols. i and ii.

Each contributor was asked, as far as possible, to provide an account of his or her subject which summarizes the present state of knowledge and (in so far as it exists) orthodoxy, indicating points at which a different view is adopted. It would have been impossible and undesirable to demand uniformity of perspective and the individual chapters, as is proper, reflect a rich variety of approach and viewpoint, Likewise, we have not insisted on uniformity of practice in the use of footnotes, although contributors were asked to avoid long and discursive notes as far as possible. We can only repeat the statement of the editors in their preface to Vol. VIII, that the variations reflect the different requirements of the contributors and their subject-material. It will be noted that the bibliographies are much more extensive and complex than in earlier volumes of *The Cambridge Ancient History*; again a reflection of the greater volume of important work which has been produced on this period in recent years. Most authors have included in the bibliographies, which are keyed by coded references, all, or most, of the secondary works cited in their chapters; others have included in the footnotes some reference to books, articles and, particularly, publications of primary sources which were not considered of sufficient general relevance to be included in the bibliographies. We have let these stand.

Most of the chapters in this volume were written between 1983 and 1988 and we are conscious of the fact that the delay between composition and publication has been much longer than we would have wished. The editors themselves must bear a share of the responsibility for this. The checking of notes and bibliographies, the process of getting typescripts ready for the press has too often been perforce relegated because of the pressure of other commitments. Contributors have, nonetheless, been given the opportunity to update their bibliographies and we hope that they still have confidence in what they wrote.

There are various debts which it is a pleasure to acknowledge. Professor John Crook was involved in the planning of this volume and we are much indebted to his erudition, sagacity and common sense. We very much regret that he did not feel able to maintain his involvement in the editorial process and we are the poorer for it. For the speedy and efficient translation of chapters 14*c*, 14*d* and 20 we are indebted, respectively, to Dr G. D. Woolf, Dr J.-P. Wild (who also provided valuable bibliographical guidance) and Edward Champlin. Mr Michael Sharp, of Corpus Christi College, Oxford and Mr Nigel Hope rendered meticulous and much-appreciated assistance with the bibliographies. David Cox drew the maps; the index was compiled by Barbara Hird.

To Pauline Hire and to others at Cambridge University Press involved in the supervision and production of this volume, we offer thanks for patience, good humour and ready assistance.

A.K.B
E.J.C
A.W.L

CHAPTER 1

THE TRIUMVIRAL PERIOD

CHRISTOPHER PELLING

I. THE TRIUMVIRATE

On 27 November 43, the Lex Titia initiated the period of absolute rule at Rome. Antony, Lepidus and Octavian were charged with 'restoring the state', *triumviri rei publicae constituendae*: but they were empowered to make or annul laws without consulting Senate or people, to exercise jurisdiction without any right of appeal, and to nominate magistrates of their choice; and they carved the world into three portions, Cisalpine and Further Gaul for Antony, Narbonensis and Spain for Lepidus, Sicily, Sardinia and Corsica for Octavian. In effect, the three were rulers. Soon there would be two, then one; the Republic was already dead.

Not that, at the time, the permanence of the change could be clear. As Tacitus brings out in the first sentence of the *Annals*, the roots of absolute power were firmly grounded in the Republic itself: there had been phases of despotism before – Sulla and Caesar, and in some ways Pompey too – and they had passed; the cause of Brutus and Cassius in the East was not at all hopeless. But what was clear was that history and politics had changed, and were changing still. The triumviral period was to be one of the great men feeling their way, unclear how far (for instance) a legion's loyalty could simply be bought, whether the propertied classes or the discontented poor of Rome and Italy could be harnessed as a genuine source of strength, how influential the old families and their patronage remained. At the beginning, there was a case for a quinquevirate, for Plancus and Pollio had played no less crucial a role than Lepidus in the manoeuvrings of mid-43. But Lepidus was included, Plancus and Pollio were not; and Lepidus owed that less to his army than to his clan and connexions. In 43 those seemed to matter; a few years later they were irrelevant, and so was he. Money too was a new, incalculable factor. In 44–43 the promises made to the troops reached new heights; and there was certainly money around – money of Caesar himself; money from the dead dictator's friends, men like Balbus and Matius; money that would be minted in plenty throughout the Roman world – no wonder that so many hoards from the period have been found, some of them vast.[1] But would that money ever find its way to the

---

[1] Crawford 1969 (B 318) 117–31, 1985 (B 320) 252.

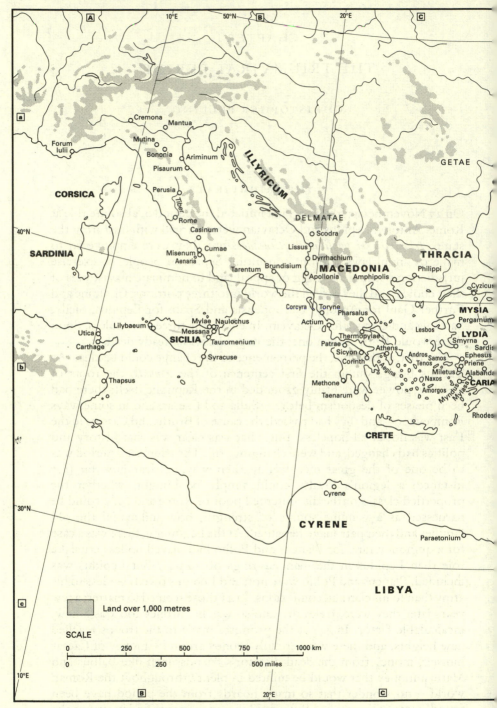

Map 2. Italy and the eastern Mediterranean.

legionaries? They did not know; no one knew. The role of propaganda was also changing. Cicero had been one master of the craft – we should not, for instance, assume that the *Philippics* were simply aimed at a senatorial audience; they would have force when read in the camps and market-places of Italy. But what constituency was worth making the propagandist's target? The armies, certainly: they were a priority in 44–43. But what of the Italians in the municipalities? Could they be won, and would they be decisive? Increasingly, the propaganda in the thirties turned in their direction, and they were duly won for Octavian. But was he wise to make them his priority – did they matter much in the final war? One may doubt it, though they certainly mattered in the ensuing peace. But it was that sort of time. No one knew what sources of strength could be found, or how they would count. The one thing that stood out was that the rules were new.

The difference is even harder for us to gauge than for contemporaries, simply because of our source-material. No longer do we have Cicero's speeches, dialogues and correspondence to illuminate events; instead we have only the sparsest of contemporary literary and epigraphic material, and have to rely on much later narratives – Appian, who took the story down to the death of Sextus Pompeius in his extant *Civil Wars* (he told of Actium and Alexandria in his lost *Egyptian History*); Cassius Dio, who gave a relatively full account of the triumviral period in Books XLVII–L; and Plutarch's fine *Lives* of *Brutus* and *Antony*. Suetonius too had some useful material in his *Augustus*; so does Josephus. The source-material used by these authors is seldom clear, though Asinius Pollio evidently influenced the tradition considerably, and so did Livy and the colourful Q. Dellius; but all the later authors may well have used other, more recherché material. Still, all are often demonstrably inaccurate, and there is indeed a heavy element of fiction throughout the tradition. Octavian's contemporary propaganda, doubtless repeated and reinforced in his *Autobiography* when it appeared during the twenties, spread stories of the excesses and outrages of Antony and Cleopatra; then the later authors, especially Plutarch, elaborated with romance, evincing sometimes more sympathy for the lovers, but scarcely more accuracy. And all these authors naturally concentrated on the principals themselves – Brutus, Cassius, Octavian, Sextus, Antony and Cleopatra. We are given very little idea of what everyday political life in Rome was like, how far the presence of these great men smothered routine activity and debate in the Senate, the courts, the assemblies and the streets. The triumvirs controlled appointments to the consulship and to many of the lower offices, but some elections took place as well; we just do not know how many, or how fiercely and genuinely they were contested.[2] The plebs and

2 Cf. Frei-Stolba 1967 (c 92) 80–6; Millar 1973 (c 175) 51–3.

the Italian cities did not always take the triumvirs' decisions supinely; but we do not know how often or how effectively the triumvirs were opposed in the Senate, or how much freedom of speech and action senators asserted in particular areas. We hear little or nothing of the *equites*: we cannot be sure that they were so passive or uninfluential. We no longer hear of showpiece political trials; it does not follow that they never happened. Everything in the sources is painted so starkly, in terms of the actions and ambitions of the great persons themselves. We have moved from colour into black and white.

II. PHILIPPI, 42 B.C.

At Rome the year 42 began momentously. Iulius Caesar was consecrated as a god.[3] Roman generals were used to divine acclamations in the East, and divine honours had been paid in plenty to Caesar during his lifetime: but a formal decree of this kind was still different. Octavian might now style himself *divi filius* if he chose;[4] and the implications for his prestige were, like so much else, incalculable. But a more immediate concern was the campaign against Brutus and Cassius in the East, a war of vengeance which the consecration invested with a new solemnity. Antony and Octavian were to share the command. The triumvirs now controlled forty-three legions: probably forty were detailed to serve in the East, though only twenty-one or twenty-two actually took part in the campaign and only nineteen fought at Philippi.[5] Lepidus would remain in control of Italy, but here too Antony's influence would be strong: for two of his partisans were also to stay, Calenus in Italy and Pollio in the Cisalpina, both with strong armies.

A preliminary force of eight triumviral legions, under C. Norbanus and L. Decidius Saxa, crossed the Adriatic early in the year: but the Liberators' fleets soon began to operate in the Adriatic, eventually some 130 ships under L. Staius Murcus and Cn. Domitius Ahenobarbus, and it would evidently be difficult to transport the main army. A further uncertainty was furnished by the growing naval power of Sextus Pompeius. His role in the politics of 44–43 had been slight, but he had appeared on the proscription list, and now it must have seemed inevitable that he would be forced into the Liberators' camp. By early 42 he had established himself in control of Sicily, his fleet was growing formidable, and he was already serving as a refuge for the disaffected, fearful and destitute of all classes. Many of the proscribed now swelled his strength. But Octavian sent Salvidienus Rufus to attack Sextus' fleet,

---

[3] Dio XLVII.18.3–19.3; cf. Weinstock 1971 (F 235) 386–98; Wallman 1989 (C 243) 52–8.
[4] He did not choose for some time: the title first appears on coins of (probably) 40/39 (*RRC* 525).
[5] Brunt 1971 (A 9) 484–5; Botermann 1968 (C 36) 181–204.

and a great but indecisive battle ensued outside the Straits of Messana. After this Sextus' contribution was slight, and the Liberators gained very little benefit from potentially so valuable an ally. By summer, the main triumviral army managed to force its crossing.

In Macedonia the news of the proscriptions and Cicero's death had sealed C. Antonius' fate: he was at last executed, probably on Brutus' orders.[6] Brutus himself had been active in Greece, Macedonia, Thrace and even Asia through the second half of 43, raising and training troops and securing allies and funds. He finally began his march to meet Cassius perhaps in the late summer, more likely not until early 42.[7] Cassius himself was delayed far away in the East till late in 43: even after Dolabella's defeat in July, there was still trouble to clear up – in Tarsus, for instance, where he imposed a fine of 1,500 talents, and in Cappadocia, where unrest persisted until Cassius' agents murdered the king Ariobarzanes and seized his treasure in summer 42. The troubles were doubtless exacerbated by the harshness of Cassius' exactions, but the wealth of the East was potentially the Liberators' greatest asset (extended though they were to support their army, the triumvirs' position was even worse), and Cassius naturally wanted to exploit it to the full. It was perhaps not until winter, when the triumvirs had united and there were already fears that the first of their troops were crossing to Greece, that Cassius began the long westward march.[8] He and Brutus met in Smyrna in the spring of 42. Between them they controlled probably twenty-one legions, of which nineteen fought in the decisive campaign.[9]

The story went that they differed over strategy, Brutus wishing to return quickly to Macedonia, Cassius insisting that they first needed to secure their rear by moving against Rhodes and the cities of Lycia.[10] Cassius had his reasons, of course. Lycia and Rhodes were temptingly wealthy, and there were even some strategic arguments for delay: with the Liberators dominating the sea, the triumviral armies might be destroyed by simple lack of supplies. But still he was surely wrong. Philippi is a very long way east, and the battles there were fought very

---

[6] Plut. *Brut.* 28.1, *Ant.* 22.6, probably right on chronology and responsibility; cf. esp. Dio XLVII.24.3–6.

[7] Plut. *Brut.* 28.3 and Dio XLVII.25.1–2 agree that this march began after C. Antonius' death, but the chronology is very insecure.

[8] Cf. App. *BCiv.* IV.63.270–1; Dio XLVII.32.1; Plut. *Brut.* 28.3. So long a winter march is hard to believe, but the sources clearly connect the beginning of the march with news of the proscriptions and related events; there does not in any case seem time for it in late summer or autumn 43; yet it cannot have been as late as spring 42, for that would not leave time for the campaigns in southern Asia Minor.

[9] Brunt 1971 (A 9) 485–8; Botermann 1968 (C 36) 204–11.

[10] App. *BCiv.* IV.65.276–7; cf, Plut. *Brut.* 28.3–5; contrast Dio XLVII.32, defensively stressing their unanimity.

late in the year. The friendly states in Macedonia and northern Greece, who had welcomed Brutus with some spontaneity the previous year and whose accession Cicero had so warmly acclaimed in the *Tenth Philippic*, were by then lost, and their wealth and crops were giving vital support to the triumvirs, not the Liberators. Rhodes and Lycia had strong navies, but Cassius and Brutus had very little to fear from them: the Liberators would dominate the sea in any case. It would surely have been better to move west quickly, provide better bases for their fleet in the Adriatic, and seek to isolate the advanced force on the west coast of Greece – to play the 48 campaign over again, in fact; and those eight unsupported legions of Norbanus and Saxa would have been hopelessly outmatched. The Liberators' brutal treatment of Rhodes and Lycia did nothing for their posthumous moral reputation. Perhaps it also cost them the war.

Cassius moved against Rhodes, Brutus against Lycia, and both won swift, total victories: in particular, the appalling scenes of slaughter and mass suicide in Lycian Xanthus became famous. Perhaps 8,500 talents were extorted from Rhodes; the figure of 150 talents for Lycia is hard to believe.[11] The other peoples of Asia were ordered to pay the massive sum of ten years' tribute, although the region had already been squeezed dreadfully in the preceding years. Some of the money was doubtless paid direct to the legionaries, some more was kept back for further distributions during the decisive campaign: in the event the army stayed notably loyal, though this was doubtless not only for crude material reasons. The campaigns were rapid, but it was still June or July before Brutus and Cassius met again at Sardis, and began the northward march to the Hellespont, which they crossed in August.

Norbanus and Saxa had marched across Macedonia unopposed, and took up a position east of Philippi, trying to block the narrow passes; but the much larger force of Brutus and Cassius outflanked them, and reached Philippi at the beginning of September. Norbanus and Saxa fell back upon Amphipolis, where they linked with the main army under Antony: Octavian, weakened by illness, was following some way behind. Brutus and Cassius then occupied a strong position across the Via Egnatia. Within a few days Antony came up and boldly camped only a mile distant, in a much weaker position in the plain. Octavian, still sick, joined him ten days later. Despite the strength of their position, the Liberators at first sought to avoid a battle. They controlled the sea, the triumvirs' land communications to Macedonia and Thessaly were exposed, and Antony and Octavian would find it difficult to maintain a long campaign. But Antony's deft operations and earthworks soon began to threaten the Liberators' left, and Cassius and Brutus decided to

[11] Plut. *Brut*. 32.4.

accept battle. There was not much difference in strength between the two sides: the triumviral legions had perhaps nearly 100,000 infantry, the Liberators something over 70,000; but the Liberators were the stronger in cavalry, with 20,000 against 13,000.[12]

Cassius commanded the left, Brutus the right, facing Antony and Octavian respectively. The battle began on Cassius' wing, as Antony stormed one of his fortifications. Then Brutus' troops charged, apparently without orders; but they were highly successful, cutting to pieces three of Octavian's legions and even capturing the enemy camp. Cassius fared much worse: Antony's personal gallantry played an important part, it seems, and he in turn captured Cassius' camp. In the dust and the confusion Cassius despaired too soon, and in ignorance of Brutus' victory he killed himself. So ended this first battle of Philippi (early October 42). On the same day (or so it was said) the Liberators won a great naval victory in the Adriatic, as Murcus and Ahenobarbus destroyed two legions of triumviral reinforcements.

Then there were three weeks of inaction. The first battle had done nothing to ease the triumviral problems of supply, and Antony was forced to detach a whole legion to march to Greece for provisions. But Brutus was under pressure from his own army to fight again; he was a less respected general than Cassius, and after the first battle he feared desertions; and he also soon found his own line of supplies from the sea threatened, for Antony and Octavian occupied new positions in the south. He felt forced to accept a second battle (23 October). His own wing may again have won some success, but eventually all his lines broke. The carnage was very great; and Brutus too took his own life. With him died the republican cause. Several of the surviving nobles also killed themselves, some were executed, others obtained pardon; a few fled to Murcus, Ahenobarbus, or Sextus Pompeius. Most of the troops came over to the triumvirs.[13]

Antony had long been known as a military man, but until now his record was not especially lustrous. His wing had played little part at Pharsalus, he had been absent from most of Caesar's other battles, and the outcome at Mutina had been shameful. All that was now erased. Octavian had given little to this victory; he had indeed been absent from the first battle – hiding in the marsh, and not even his friends could deny it.[14] Before the fighting the forces had appeared equally matched: it was Antony's operations that forced the battles, his valour that won the day. He took the glory and the prestige. Now and for years to come, the world saw Antony as the victor of Philippi.

[12] Cf. esp. App. *BCiv.* IV.108.454; Brunt 1971 (A 9) 487.
[13] App. *BCiv.* IV.135.568–136.576, V.2.4–9; Dio XLVII.49.3–4; Brunt 1971 (A 9) 488.
[14] Agrippa and Maecenas, Pliny, *HN* VII.148.

III. THE EAST, 42–40 B.C.

Antony's strength was reflected in the new division of responsibility and power. His task would be the organization of the East; he was also to retain Further Gaul, and take Narbonensis from Lepidus; he would lose only the Cisalpina, which was to become part of Italy. Italy itself was nominally left out of the reckoning, but Octavian was to be the man on the spot, with the arduous and unpopular task of settling the veterans in the Italian cities. He was also to carry on the war against Sextus Pompeius; he would retain Sardinia; and he too was to gain at Lepidus' expense, taking from him both provinces of Spain. Lepidus himself would be allowed only Africa; and there was some doubt even about that.[15] Already, clearly, he was falling behind his colleagues. Antony was also to keep the greater part of the legions. A large number of the troops in the East had served their time, and were to be demobilized; the rest, including those who had just come over from Brutus and Cassius, were to be re-formed into eleven legions. Antony was to take six of these, Octavian five; he was also to lend Antony a further two. The position concerning the western legions is more obscure, but there too Antony's marshals seem to have controlled about as many legions as Octavian.[16] Antony promised that Calenus would transfer to Octavian two legions in Italy to compensate for the two he was now borrowing: but such promises readily foundered. The legions stayed with Calenus.

In Antony's lifetime two generals had successfully invaded Italy from their provinces, Sulla from the East and Caesar from Gaul. Both Gaul and the East would now fall to Antony. The menace was clear. The case of Gaul is particularly interesting. So much of the fighting and diplomacy of the last two years had been, in one way or another, a struggle for Gaul: and the province's strategic importance was very clear.[17] With hindsight, we always associate Antony with the East; Octavian's propaganda was to make great play with his oriental degeneracy. But nothing suggests that Antony yet planned any extended stay in the East. Naturally, he eyed its riches and prestige; he *might* of course have to play Sulla over again; but it was just as likely that he would return peaceably, as Pompey had returned in the sixties, to new power and authority in the West. In that case, and in the likely event of the triumvirs eventually falling out, Gaul would prove vital. Its governor would be Calenus, with eleven legions: Antony could rely on him. And, even if the Cisalpina were technically part of Italy, that too

---

[15] App. *BCiv.* v.3.12 and Dio XLVIII.1.3 (cf. XLVIII.22.2) suggest some equivocation.
[16] Cf. Brunt 1971 (A 9) 493–7.
[17] '. . . Galliaeque quae semper praesidet atque praesedit huic imperio', Cic. *Phil.* v.37; cf. esp. *Phil.* v.5, XII.9, 13, XIII.37.

would not be out of Antony's control: Pollio was to be there, and he too
had veterans under his command. The trusty Ventidius would also be
active in the West, perhaps in Gaul, perhaps in Italy.[18] In the event
Antony's possession of Gaul came to nothing, for Octavian took it over
bloodlessly on Calenus' death in 40. It was that important historical
accident that would turn Antony decisively towards the East. But, for
the moment, possession of Gaul kept all his important options free.

The East came first. Its regulation would be a massive task, but a
rewarding one; and it also offered the possibility of a war against Parthia.
King Orodes had helped Cassius and Brutus,[19] and vengeance was in
order; indeed, the republican commander Labienus was still at the
Parthian court. No one yet knew what to expect of that; but, whether or
not Parthia attacked Roman Asia Minor again, a Roman general could
always attack Parthia, avenging Crassus' defeat, tickling the Roman
imagination and enhancing his own prestige. He might even appear a
second Alexander, if all went well: that always had a particular appeal to
Roman fancy.

Antony spent the winter of 42/1 in Greece, where he made a parade of
his philhellenism.[20] In spring 41 he crossed to Asia; it seems that he
visited Bithynia, and presumably Pontus too, before returning to the
Aegean coast.[21] At Ephesus, effectively Asia's capital, he was greeted as a
god – such acclamations were by now almost routine in the East;[22] but
exuberance soon turned sour, as Antony addressed representatives of the
Asian cities and announced his financial demands. Yet again, the East
found it had to fund both sides in a Roman civil war: and this time vast
sums were needed to satisfy the legions – perhaps 150,000 talents if all the
promised rewards were to be paid.[23] That was well beyond even the
East's resources, especially after the exactions of Dolabella, then Cassius
and Brutus. Antony eventually demanded nine years' tribute from Asia,
to be paid over two years;[24] and he would be fortunate if the province
could manage that. Asia's normal tribute was probably less than 2,000
talents a year.[25] Even allowing for contributions from the other eastern
provinces and for extra sums from client kings and free cities,[26] Antony
could scarcely hope for more than 20,000 talents, the amount which Sulla
raised in a similar levy after the Mithridatic War. And not all of that
could be spent on rewards. There were the running costs of Antony's

---

[18] App. *BCiv.* v.31.121 with *MRR* II 393.   [19] App. *BCiv.* IV.59.257, 63.271, 88.373, 99.414.
[20] Plut. *Ant.* 23.   [21] Joseph. *AJ* XIV.301–4; cf. Buchheim 1960 (C 49) 11–12.
[22] Plut. *Ant.* 24.4 with Pelling 1988 (B 138) *ad loc.*
[23] App. *BCiv.* v.5.21 makes Antony claim that he needs 'money, land and cities' for twenty-eight
legions, comprising 170,000 men μετὰ τῶν συντασσομένων: there were also the cavalry and 'another
mass of another army'. The figure 170,000 may be realistic for the total of triumviral troops,
including those in the West (οἱ συντασσόμενοι ?), owed money, land, or both: but 'another mass of
another army' is obscure. Cf. esp. Brunt 1971 (A 9) 489–94, Keppie 1983 (E 65) 60–1.
[24] App. *BCiv.* v.6.27.   [25] Broughton 1938 (E 821) 562–4 estimated it as 1,600 talents.
[26] Cf. App. *BCiv.* v.6.27.

army and staff; there was a fleet to build, for Murcus, Ahenobarbus and Sextus were still worryingly strong;[27] there were preparations to be made for war with Parthia. The troops were still calling for their rewards a year later.[28]

Yet there was generosity, too, in Antony's dispensations. He pardoned virtually all the supporters of Brutus and Cassius, excepting only those who had participated in the tyrannicide itself; that was more merciful than many expected.[29] The states that had suffered worst from the Liberators, Lycia and Rhodes, were excused from the levies; later he extended a similar clemency to Laodicea and Tarsus. Rhodes was indeed given some new territory – Andros, Tenos, Naxos and Myndus.[30] From mainland Greece the Athenians soon sent an embassy, and they too were favoured: they gained control of several islands, including Aegina. Antony was clearly favouring the great cultural centres. Such ostentatious philhellenism doubtless came naturally to him, but it might also prove politically valuable, and not merely in certain circles at Rome: in the East itself it had become fashionable for monarchs to show their enthusiasm for the great cities of the past by benefactions, and they might applaud Antony when he showed similar indulgence. It was also probably now, and in line with the same cultural policy, that he granted various privileges and immunities to 'the worldwide association of victors in the festival games' – an association which, it seems, included artists and poets as well as athletes.[31] Antony spent the rest of summer 41 in touring the eastern provinces, imposing further levies and beginning to reorganize the administration after the disruption of the war: Antony himself could refer to Asia's need to recover from its 'great illness'.[32] The range and deftness of his dispositions were eventually to be peculiarly impressive, but as yet there was only time for a few piecemeal measures. The highest priority had to be the regions furthest to the east, for they would be vital if it came to war with Parthia. Syria was particularly sensitive. Its cities had greeted Cassius with enthusiasm, and he had supported tyrants who were (it seems) disturbingly sympathetic to Parthia:[33] most of them clearly had to go. So, probably, did Marion, tyrant of Tyre.[34] Herod of Judaea was similarly compromised by his

[27] App. *BCiv.* v.55.230.   [28] Dio XLVIII.30.2.

[29] Dio XLVIII.24.6 – perhaps guesswork, but as often intelligent.

[30] Possibly Amorgus too: cf. *IG* XII 5.38 and XII *Supp.* p. 102 no. 38, with Schmitt 1957 (E 872) 186 n. 2; *contra*, Fraser and Bean 1954 (E 828) 163 n. 3.

[31] E J² 300, *RDGE* 57; but it is possible that these privileges were not granted till 32: see *RDGE ad loc.* and Millar 1973 (C 175) 55, 1977 (A 59) 456. Cf. also the triumviral inscription from Ephesus concerning travel-privileges for 'teachers, sophists and doctors': Knibbe 1981 (C 138).

[32] In his letter to the Jews, Joseph. *AJ* XIV.312.

[33] According to App. *BCiv.* v.10.39, 42, they fled to the Parthian king after their deposition: not improbable, cf. Buchheim 1960 (C 49) 27.

[34] Tyrant in 42 when he invaded Galilee (Joseph. *BJ* 1.238–9, *AJ* XIV.298); but Antony's letter in 41 (next note) is addressed only to the magistrates and council (*AJ* XIV.314). Cf. Weinstock *RE* XIV 1803.

support for Cassius, but here Antony knew better than to play into the hands of the anti-Roman nobility. Herod and his brother Phasael were recognized as 'tetrarchs'; Judaea even recovered some territory it had lost to the Phoenician cities.[35] And Egypt, with all its wealth, would inevitably be important. Momentously, Antony summoned its queen to meet him in Cilicia.

Plutarch and Shakespeare have immortalized the famous meeting on the Cydnus – the marvellous gilded barge, the purple sails, Cleopatra's display as Aphrodite; and, delightfully, much of the description is likely to be true.[36] The queen's relations with Antony swiftly became more than diplomatic: their twins were born only a year later; and he spent the winter of 41–40 with her in Alexandria – a winter of careless frolics, so the story later went.[37] But there were bloody elements too. Cleopatra was still insecure on her throne, threatened by her sister Arsinoe; Antony had Arsinoe dragged from sanctuary in Ephesus and murdered. Tyre had to surrender Serapion, the admiral who had betrayed Cleopatra's fleet to Cassius and Brutus; Arados was forced to give up a pretender to the Egyptian throne. Later writers naturally dwelt on the infatuation which forced Antony to such gruesomeness; but he could reasonably feel that it made political sense to favour Cleopatra in this way. He was regularly to favour strong, talented rulers, people like Polemo in Pontus or Herod in Judaea, people on whom he felt he could rely; and he could certainly rely on Cleopatra. Any infatuation was clearly under control; at least, for the present. In the spring of 40 he left her, and did not return for nearly four years.

For by the spring Alexandria was no place for Antony. Worrying news had been arriving about disorder in Italy, and now there was a more immediate threat in Asia Minor itself. During 41 Antony had probably been preparing for an *offensive* war against Parthia – by the end of the season he had indeed taken the border town of Palmyra in Syria. It seems that Parthia, naturally enough, responded by gathering a force in Mesopotamia to meet the evident threat. But, after Antony had departed to Alexandria for the winter, the Parthians decided to seize the moment and attack Roman Asia Minor themselves;[38] and, far from waging a glorious campaign of vengeance, Antony had to hasten to put up what defence he could. The Parthian command was shared between the crown-prince Pacorus and Q. Labienus himself, son of that famous commander of Caesar who went over to Pompey at the beginning of the civil war. Brutus and Cassius had sent him to seek aid from Orodes, and

[35] Tyre, Sidon, Antioch and Aradus: cf. Joseph. *AJ* xiv.304–23, quoting verbatim Antony's letters to the Jews and to Tyre.   [36] Plut. *Ant.* 26, with Pelling 1988 (B 138) *ad loc.*

[37] Plut. *Ant.* 28–9; cf. App. *BCiv.* v.11.43–4.

[38] Dio xlviii.24.6–8, explicitly placing the decision after Labienus had heard of Antony's 'departure to Egypt'.

he had still been at the Parthian court when news of Philippi arrived. Wisely, he stayed where he was; and we need not doubt that he played an important role in persuading Orodes to attack now, when he rightly gauged that Antony might be vulnerable. It is easy but unfair to see Labienus as a latter-day Coriolanus, a renegade turning against his country through pique. In fact, republicans had long since been playing for Parthian support. Pompey had sought an alliance with Orodes against Caesar;[39] a few years later the Parthians had been helping the republican troops of Q. Caecilius Bassus against Caesarians in Syria;[40] Parthian contingents had even fought in the Philippi campaign.[41] Over in the West, men could equally toy with the notion of exploiting Gallic nobles in a Roman civil war; might they not show themselves worthier champions of liberty than the Romans themselves?[42] Doubtless there was hypocrisy in such proud phrases; but it was not confined to Labienus. He was indeed largely welcomed by the Roman garrisons in Syria,[43] and apparently in Asia too.[44]

The campaign began in the early spring of 40. Labienus – now styling himself Q. LABIENUS PARTHICUS IMPERATOR[45] – and Pacorus swiftly overran Syria: it had fallen before Antony could even reach Tyre, then he anyway found it necessary to sail west to Italy. The Parthian successes continued. Pacorus took Palestine, and installed the pretender Antigonus on the throne; Phasael was taken captive, then contrived to kill himself; Herod fled to Rome. Meanwhile Labienus swept through Cilicia and onward to the Ionian coast. The Carian cities of Alabanda and Mylasa fell to him, and Stratoniceia and Aphrodisias clearly suffered terribly;[46] so perhaps did Miletus;[47] Lydia too was overrun.[48] Labienus met no effective resistance till 39, and by then northern Asia Minor had also felt his power; his agents were raising money even from Bithynia.[49]

And Antony could do nothing about it; for by now the news from Italy was even more alarming.

---

[39] Plut. *Pomp.* 76.4; in general, cf. Timpe 1962 (C 236) 114–16.

[40] *MRR* II 308.   [41] Above, p. 10 and n. 19.

[42] Plancus in Cic. *Fam.* x.8.3 and 6, with n. in D. R. Shackleton Bailey's commentary.

[43] Dio XLVIII.25.2 implies that the garrisons were composed of old partisans of Brutus and Cassius, though this is scarcely credible in so sensitive an area: cf. Brunt 1971 (A 9) 497.

[44] Strab. XVI.2.24–5 (660C); cf. Brunt 1971 (A 9) 497.

[45] So on coins, EJ² 8, *RRC* 524: cf. Strab. XIV.2.24–5 (660C); Plut. *Ant.* 28.1; Dio XLVIII.26.5. Plutarch and Strabo both take *Parthicus imperator* together, 'commander of the Parthians'; Dio more plausibly takes *Parthicus* as an assumed cognomen, implying that Labienus had himself acclaimed *imperator* by his troops *and also* took the cognomen *Parthicus*. Cf. Crawford 1974 (B 319) 529; Wallmann 1989 (C 243) 232–4.

[46] Dio XLVIII.26.3–4; Strab. XIV.2.24–5 (660C); Tac. *Ann.* III.62.2; *RDGE* 27 (Stratoniceia) and 59–60 (Mylasa); Reynolds 1982 (B 270) docs. 11, 12, and probably 7 and 13 (Aphrodisias).

[47] Rehm 1914 (B 267) 128–9.   [48] Plut. *Ant.* 30.2.   [49] Strab. XII.8.7–9 (574C).

IV. PERUSIA, 41–40 B.C.

Even before Philippi, eighteen Italian cities had been marked down to provide land for the triumvirs' veterans; and it fell to Octavian to organize the settlement. It was a hateful task, involving widespread confiscation and intense misery for the dispossessed, who received no compensation: a hideous climax to a half-century of rural violence and horror. Virgil's *Eclogues*, especially the first and ninth, leave a moving imprint of a small farmer's suffering. But the tiniest holdings were eventually exempted, and so, often, were the largest: in particular, senators' estates were excluded; and, as in most of the cities some *veteres possessores* managed to hold on to their property, one may assume that the most influential local citizens often secured exemption. That left a great range of the middling well-off who were dispossessed, some who farmed at not much more than subsistence level, others who were quite wealthy people with slaves and fine villas. Their holdings were replaced by the standardized chequer-boards of the new allotments, usually it seems of up to 50 *iugera* for an ordinary soldier and perhaps 100 *iugera* or more for an officer. Eighteen cities turned out to be too few, and perhaps as many as forty were eventually involved. The most usual method was to extend the confiscations into the territory of a neighbouring town, as, famously, into Virgil's Mantua when nearby Cremona could offer too little land: 'Mantua, vae miserae nimium vicina Cremonae'.[50]

It all came at a time when Italy was anyway torn by famine, as Sextus grew stronger and his fleet prevented the vital corn-ships from coming to port. (Ahenobarbus' and Murcus' ships were doing the same, though still acting independently of Sextus.) Unsurprisingly there were violent protests, from landowners, from the magnates in the country-towns, from the urban plebs, even from the veterans themselves: they were becoming anxious at the slow pace of the settlement, and also concerned to protect the holdings of their own families and those of their dead comrades. There was soon rioting throughout Italy, with clashes between the new colonists and those they threatened; armed bands were roving the countryside. It was to take years for the disorder to settle.[51]

Antony's brother L. Antonius was consul in 41, and far from helping Octavian he served as a rallying-point for the discontented. Initially he was perhaps opposed by Antony's wife Fulvia,[52] but she soon lent her

---

[50] Virg. *Ecl.* IX.28. On the settlements cf. esp. Gabba 1970 (B 55) lix–lxviii, 1971 (C 93); Brunt 1971 (A 9) 290–1, 294–300, 328–31, 342–4; Schneider 1977 (D 231) 213–28; Keppie 1983 (E 65) 58–69, 87–133, and (on Cremona) 190–2.

[51] App. *BCiv.* IV.25.104 (43/2 B.C.), v.18.72–3 (now), 132.547 (still in 36 B.C.); Dio XLVIII.9.4–5, XLIX.15.1; cf. esp. Gabba 1970 (B 55) lxvi, Brunt 1971 (A 9) 291.

[52] App. *BCiv.* v.19.75; cf. Plut. *Ant.* 30.1. But the role of Fulvia remains hard to estimate; she was dead by the time of the Brundisium treaty, and by then, as Dio XLVIII.28.3 shrewdly remarks, it was in everyone's interest to blame her for the war.

full support. To the dispossessed they urged resistance in the name of liberty and the established laws.[53] Perhaps we need not take their own commitment to freedom too seriously,[54] but it is interesting that they thought the slogans worth airing; and, indeed, old republicans were regularly to find Antony's cause more appealing than Octavian's.[55] The veterans were encouraged to believe that all would be well once Antony returned: their debt of duty to the great man became another slogan. L. Antonius even, rather absurdly, took the cognomen *Pietas*.[56] There were charges, too, that Octavian was favouring his own veterans above Antony's in the distributions, and demands that the Antonian settlements should be supervised by Antony's own partisans.[57] The charges seem to have been conspicuously untrue: the Antonian colonies turned out to be the more numerous and the more strategically based.[58] But Octavian still felt it best to accede to the demand for Antonian commissioners, whatever might have been said at Philippi about his freedom to organize the settlement as he chose. That agreement of Philippi was indeed looking increasingly frail. The other Antonian marshals were less blatant than the consul Antonius, but they too were adding to the tension. Calenus never gave the promised two legions; Pollio blocked the route of Salvidienus Rufus as he tried to march with six legions to Spain.

At first Antony, far off in the East, thought it best to send no clear response, though he certainly knew what was going on. Everyone made sure of that, with Octavian sending confidential messengers and the colonies too taking care that their plight was known.[59] He had probably not planned or encouraged the troubles himself: it was a nice judgment whether he really stood to gain more than lose by the exchanges. Now he might naturally relish Octavian's embarrassment, but he could hardly come out openly against him; Octavian after all was merely pursuing his part of a shared bargain. Besides, Antony could not let his own veterans down, or allow Octavian to win more of their gratitude. He might need them again soon. A studied vagueness about his own views would indeed make sense, allowing him to exploit the outcome whichever way it went: there were times in antiquity when the slowness and unreliability of communications could be useful. But the consequences were very unfortunate. Unsure of his wishes, confused by various reports and

---

[53] App. *BCiv.* v.19.74, 30.118, 39.159–61, 43.179–80; cf. Dio xlviii.13.6; Suet. *Aug.* 12.1 (misdating).

[54] For a different view, Gabba 1971 (C 93) 146–50; Roddaz 1988 (C 201).

[55] Some indeed fought for Antonius and died when Perusia fell: Roddaz 1988 (C 201) 339–41.

[56] EJ² 7, Dio xlviii.5.4 cf. Wallmann 1989 (C 243) 82–4.

[57] App. *BCiv.* v.14.55; Dio xlvii.14.4; cf. Keppie 1983 (E 65) 59–60.

[58] Keppie 1983 (E 65) 66–7.

[59] App. *BCiv.* v.21.83, 52.216, 60.251; cf. Dio xlviii.27.1.

missives,[60] his supporters in Italy were bewildered. Just as on several occasions in 44 and 43, army officers and the veterans themselves pressed for a compromise,[61] and so did two senatorial embassies to L. Antonius; but in the summer of 41 it came to war.

L. Antonius occupied Rome with an army, then marched north, hoping to link with Pollio and Ventidius. Operations in Etruria were complex and confused, but in the autumn L. Antonius was forced into Perusia and besieged by Octavian, Agrippa and Salvidienus Rufus. Still unsure of Antony's wishes, Pollio and Ventidius decided not to intervene. Plancus, arriving from the south, made the same choice. That made thirteen Antonian legions which stood by, inactive; L. Antonius himself had no more than eight.[62] The siege wore on, bitterly. Both sides occupied idle moments by adding obscene graffiti to their sling-bullets, musing on Antonius' baldness, Octavian's backside, and Fulvia's private parts; Octavian himself wrote some peculiarly rude elegiacs at Fulvia's expense.[63] The city eventually fell, amid scenes of dreadful bloodshed, in the early spring of 40. L. Antonius' veterans were spared: interestingly, their old comrades on Octavian's side interceded for them.[64] Antonius himself was received honourably by Octavian, and indeed was sent to govern Spain (he died soon afterwards). Fulvia was allowed to flee to Athens. The ordinary dwellers of Perusia were not so fortunate. All the town-councillors except one were killed. Octavian's enemies soon elaborated the story, with talk of a human sacrifice of 300 senators and knights at the altar of *Divus Iulius*;[65] but the unembroidered truth was horrifying enough. The city itself was given over to Octavian's troops to plunder, and it burnt to the ground. A few years later the Umbrian Propertius chose to conclude his first book of witty love elegies with a disquieting and unexpected coda, two short stark poems on the suffering of the Perusine war (I.21, 22).

If a generation before Pompey had seemed an *adulescentulus carnufex*, Octavian was surely emerging as his equal. But he had not let the veterans down, and he had emphatically established his control of Italy. Soon, indeed, he would seem master of the entire West, when Calenus died in the summer of 40 and he swiftly occupied Gaul as well. Calenus' legions seem to have come over fairly readily, and so did two legions of Plancus in Italy. Perhaps they felt Octavian was now the more reliable champion of their interests.[66]

60 Cf. App. *BCiv.* v.29.112 (a letter which Appian sensed might have been forged), 31.120.
61 App. *BCiv.* v.20.79–23.94.
62 App. *BCiv.* v.50.208, cf. 24.95, 29.114–30.115; Brunt 1971 (A 9) 494–6.
63 *ILLRP* 1106–18; cf. Hallett 1977 (C 109). Mart. XI.20 quotes Octavian's verses.
64 App. *BCiv.* v.46.196–47.200.
65 Suet. *Aug.* 15.1; cf. Dio XLVIII.14.4: but App. *BCiv.* v.48.201–2 makes clear that senators and knights were spared. In general, Harris 1971 (E 55) 301–2.
66 Cf. Dio XLVIII.20.3; Aigner 1974 (C 3) 113.

No wonder Antony was concerned. He hurried back to Italy in the midsummer of 40; and he arrived in some strength.

V. BRUNDISIUM AND MISENUM, 40–39 B.C.

As relations had worsened, both Antony and Octavian had thought of wooing Sextus to their side. He was indeed worth wooing: Murcus had recently joined him, and Sextus' combined fleet now numbered something like 250 ships.[67] Now, in the summer of 40, Octavian married Scribonia, the sister of Sextus' associate and father-in-law L. Scribonius Libo. But Sextus was always particularly distrustful of Octavian, and preferred to look to Antony: indeed, Antony's mother Iulia had fled confidently to Sextus after Perusia's fall, which may suggest that there was already some secret understanding. Sextus sent a prestigious escort, including Libo, to accompany her to Antony, and took the opportunity to offer him an alliance. Antony replied in measured but encouraging terms: if it came to war with Octavian, he would welcome Sextus as his ally; if he and Octavian made their peace, he would try to reconcile Octavian with Sextus as well. The understanding was sufficiently strong for Sextus to raid the Italian coast in Antony's support;[68] and a little later he occupied Sardinia and displaced Octavian's governor M. Lurius.

Octavian's ruthlessness in Italy, and perhaps his uncompromising response to L. Antonius' proclamations of freedom, had a further sequel. Domitius Ahenobarbus was also persuaded by the consul Pollio to join Antony, and his seventy ships joined Antony's two hundred as they sailed towards Brundisium. The alignments of early 43 had been paradoxically reversed. Republicans and Antony, with Sextus in the background, now stood together to confront the isolated Octavian; Brundisium might well turn out a Mutina in reverse, except that both Antony and Octavian were now much stronger. But, as in 43 but this time before serious bloodshed, Antony and Octavian were to find it prudent to come to terms.

There was some initial military activity. Brundisium, guarded by five of Octavian's legions, would not admit Antony's fleet, and was laid under siege; meanwhile Sextus was still continuing his raids on the coast. Octavian sent Agrippa to the town's aid, and himself swiftly followed; his troops were numerically superior[69] but reluctant, and some of them turned back. There was some skirmishing; Antony had the better of it. But by now deputations of each army were urging compromise, and it was not at all clear that either side would fight. The two men's friends began to discuss terms, with Maecenas negotiating for Octavian, Pollio

[67] App. *BCiv.* v.25.100; Vell. Pat. II.77.3.
[68] Dio XLVIII.20.1–2, clearly dating to midsummer..   [69] Brunt 1971 (A 9) 497.

for Antony, and L. Cocceius Nerva as something of a neutral. Lepidus, unsurprisingly, was not represented. (He had been notably ineffectual in Italy during the Perusine War, and by now he was out of the way in Africa.) Thus was reached the Treaty of Brundisium (September 40).

The agreement closely duplicated the compact of Philippi, except for the important change that followed from Calenus' death. Octavian's occupation of Gaul was now recognized; he was also to have Illyricum. Antony was no longer simply entrusted with the organization of the East, he was also recognized as its master. The division of the world was correspondingly neater, with Antony controlling the East and Octavian the West: Scodra in Illyria was given unprecedented prominence as the dividing-point of the dominions. Lepidus might retain Africa, for what that was worth. Antony was to avenge Crassus by carrying through the Parthian War, Octavian to assert his claim to Sardinia and Sicily by expelling Sextus – unless (an interesting qualification) Sextus came to some agreement. There was also to be an amnesty for republican supporters. The consulships for the next few years were allocated; there was also a reallocation of legions, with Antony receiving some recompense for Calenus' army.[70]

This division of East and West was less clear-cut than it appeared. For instance, eastern as well as western states could address petitions to Octavian, and Octavian could answer them with authority;[71] he even sent ἐντολαί, a 'commission' (the Latin *mandata*), to Antony to restore loot to Ephesus.[72] But, rough though it was, the division had momentous consequences. First, Antony faced a more exclusively eastern future. If it came to war, he could no longer think of fighting the campaign of 49 over again, descending from the Alps as a new Iulius Caesar into a quavering Italy. Secondly, Octavian's position in Italy was a priceless asset. In 42 it might have seemed an embarrassment, with all those veterans to settle; but he had ridden that storm. Italy was now supposed to be shared by both men, open to each for his recruiting. But Octavian was there, Antony was not. It proved steadily more possible for Octavian to pose as the defender of Roman and Italian traditions against the monstrous portent of a degenerate Antony, declining into eastern weakness and eastern ways. The control of Italy, in 42 a sign of Octavian's inferiority, became an important element in his final success.

The new accord of Antony and Octavian was confirmed by a further

---

[70] Cf. App. *BCiv.* v.66.279, with Gabba 1970 (B 55) *ad loc.*; Brunt 1971 (A 9) 498.

[71] Cf. the correspondence with Rhosus (EJ² 301, *RDGE* 58) and with Ephesus, Samos and Aphrodisias (Reynolds 1982 (B 270) docs. 10, 12, and probably 6 and (if correctly dated and interpreted) 13, with pp. 39–40); Millar 1973 (C 175), esp. 56; Badian 1984 (B 208).

[72] Reynolds 1982 (B 270) doc. 12; Millar 1973 (C 175) 56. At *Antony and Cleopatra* 1.1.20–2 Cleopatra spoke truer than Shakespeare knew: 'Fulvia perchance is angry; or who knows If the scarce-bearded Caesar have not sent His powerful mandate to you: "Do this, or this …".'.

bond, one which was to add richness to the latter romantic legend. Antony was now a widower, Fulvia having conveniently died in Greece. Octavia, the sober sister of Octavian, was to be his new bride. The great dynastic marriage was to seal the union of the dominions. There was no need to complicate the matter with any thoughts of Cleopatra.

Italy rejoiced at the treaty. It is probably wrong to connect Virgil's *Fourth Eclogue* with this: it was more likely written earlier, in the miserable days of late 41, and was designed to greet Pollio as he entered his consulship on the first day of 40. But more mundane celebration is clear enough. On 12 October the magistrates of Casinum erected a monument to mark the accord, a *signum Concordiae*.[73] Coins too were struck in celebration, one for instance showing a head of *Concordia* and two hands around a *caduceus* (a symbol of concord) with the inscription M.ANTON.C.CAESAR.IMP.[74] Both Antony and Octavian celebrated *ovationes* as they entered Rome a few weeks later. But the festivities again swiftly soured. For one thing, the impoverished triumvirs again imposed unprecedented taxes.[75] Just as serious, Sextus - who could reasonably feel let down by the treaty's terms – was maintaining his pressure. There was fighting in Sardinia within a few weeks of the accord, with Octavian's general Helenus recapturing the island, then in his turn expelled by Sextus' admiral Menodorus. Sextus had by now taken over Corsica as well, and penetrated to Gaul and Africa;[76] and his blockade of the Italian corn-ships was more effective than ever. By November Rome was again reduced to famine, and Antony and Octavian were confronted by violent popular riots. Both men also had troubles of their own, and the atmosphere was heavy with strain and suspicion. Antony executed his agent Manius, who had been very active in the Perusine War. Still more striking, Octavian recalled his general Salvidienus Rufus from Gaul, and had him killed. This extraordinary man had been consul designate for the following year, the first man since Pompey to be awarded a consulship before even entering the Senate: now his fall was just as abrupt. It was said that he had been plotting with Antony earlier in the year – indeed, that Antony frankly admitted it. That strains belief; but the truth is wholly elusive.[77]

Salvidienus' killing was prepared by the passing of the *senatus consultum ultimum*. The triumvirs' own extraordinary position was itself sufficient to authorize such emergency action; but, as usual with the *s.c.u.*, it was moral rather than legal justification which was really in point. The Senate's moral backing was still worth having, and this was one of several occasions when the triumvirs paraded a certain constitutiona-

[73] *ILLRP* 562a.   [74] *RRC* 527–9, especially 529.4a; cf. Wallmann 1989 (C 243) 80–2.
[75] App. *BCiv.* v.67.282 with Gabba's note; Dio XLVIII.31, XLVIII.34.2; cf. Nicolet 1976 (D 104) 95.
[76] App. *BCiv.* v.67.280; Dio XLVIII.30.   [77] Syme 1939 (A 93) 220 and n. 6.

lism. For instance, Octavia's marriage to Antony was technically difficult, for she had not completed the legal term of mourning after the death of her first husband, Marcellus: a dispensation was scrupulously secured from the Senate.[78] And Herod was to be recognized as king of Judaea: Antony and Octavian had agreed it – but the formal decision was deferred to the Senate, with Antony himself joining in the debate; a solemn procession to the Capitol followed, led by the consuls.[79] At some time during 39 the triumvirs also secured a senatorial decree to ratify all their past and future acts:[80] constitutionalism again, though of a rather quizzical kind. Like L. Antonius two years earlier, they evidently felt that traditionalist public sentiment was worth impressing.

But peace would surely impress people more. The Brundisium agreement had explicitly envisaged the possibility of coming to terms with Sextus as well. But it was not clear if Sextus himself would agree: there seems to have been some difference of view among his supporters, who were very disparate. The pirate-admiral Menodorus, we are told, pressed Sextus to continue the war, Staius Murcus and others took the opposite view; and here too the issues were fogged by suspicion, with Sextus by now deeply distrustful of Murcus. Murcus duly died, mysteriously. But Sextus still saw the force of his advice: he himself had always been realistic about his chances in a full-scale war. There was a preliminary meeting of negotiators at Aenaria in spring, 39. Scribonius Libo, once again emerging in a context of conciliation, represented Sextus. Octavian, Sextus and Antony then met at Cape Misenum in full summer, perhaps as late as August,[81] and terms were agreed. Sextus was to retain Corsica as well as Sicily and Sardinia, and take the Peloponnese as well; he was to hold this dominion for five years. Consulships were agreed for every year till 32: Libo was promised 34 and Sextus 33, just after the expiry of his quinquennium. For the present, he could have an augurship. In return for all this, he was to raise his blockade of Italy and remove his troops, to undertake to build no more ships and to receive no more runaway slaves, to guarantee Rome's corn supply, and to 'keep the sea free of pirates'. His supporters were to be allowed to return to Italy, with an amnesty for the proscribed: they were to receive some compensation for their vanished property. His slave supporters were to be freed, and his free soldiers were to receive the same rewards on retirement as those of the triumvirs. These last concessions were ones that Antony and Octavian were doubtless very ready to grant: they would placate many of Sextus' supporters, and,

[78] Plut. *Ant.* 31.5; cf. Buchheim 1960 (C 49) 40–1.

[79] Joseph. *BJ* 1.282–5, *AJ* xiv.381–5. Other grants too were made by the Senate: freedom, it seems, for Stratoniceia, Miletus and Aphrodisias–Plarasa (Reynolds 1982 (B 270) doc. 8).

[80] App. *BCiv.* v.75.318; Dio xlviii.34.1; Reynolds 1982 (B 270) doc. 8 with p. 39: cf. Millar 1973 (C 175) 53–4.   [81] Reynolds 1982 (B 270) 70–1.

if it came again to war, he would not find it easy to recall them to arms.[82]
There was also some more constitutionalist talk, this time more grandly
of 'restoring the Republic': in eight years' time, perhaps.[83]

The agreement was celebrated by a banquet on Sextus' galley – once
again rich material for later legend, with tales of the swashbuckling
Menodorus eyeing the cable and thinking of cutting it, to make Sextus
master of the world.[84] The agreement was indeed a precarious one,
though for less romantic reasons – largely because it diminished and
threatened Octavian distinctly more than Antony. It also freed Antony
to return to the East. He left Rome shortly after 2 October 39,
accompanied by Octavia.[85] He was not to see the city again.

VI. THE EAST, 39–37 B.C.

During the summer of 39 news from the East had been reaching Rome.
It was astoundingly good. A year earlier Antony had despatched
Ventidius to try to recover Asia Minor:[86] and it seems that Ventidius
took Labienus by surprise, forced him to flee eastwards, and finally
trapped and defeated him near the Taurus range, perhaps at the Cilician
Gates (midsummer 39). Labienus himself fled to Cilicia, but was
overtaken there and presumably killed. Later in the summer Ventidius
won another great victory at Mt Amanus over Phranipates, the satrap of
the newly conquered Syria. Phranipates was killed, and the rest of the
Parthian forces fell back beyond the Euphrates. Ventidius had done
magnificently, and by the autumn of 39 it was already time for the Senate
to reward certain states for their resistance to Labienus – Stratoniceia,
Aphrodisias-Plarasa, and (now or a little later) Miletus.[87] The war
seemed over. Indeed, there was uncomfortably little left for Antony to
do himself.

Still, after spending the winter in Athens he prepared to depart
eastwards in the spring of 38. There were a few preliminaries to take care
of. The Parthian evacuation made this a sensible time to reorganize some
parts of the East, at least provisionally; this time he concentrated on a
great swathe from north to south of central Asia Minor. Twenty-five
years earlier Pompey had ascribed a considerable tract of western Pontus
to Bithynia, but allowed control to remain largely with the cities he had
fostered: Antony now reversed the process, weakening the cities and

---

[82] It is suggestive that the offer of compensation was made directly to the proscribed, and was
apparently more acceptable to them than to Sextus: App. *BCiv.* v.71.301–2.

[83] App. *BCiv.* v.73.313.   [84] Plut. *Ant.* 32; cf. App. *BCiv.* v.73.310; Dio XLVIII.38.

[85] Reynolds 1982 (B 270) doc. 8 line 26, with her commentary.

[86] On the date, Pelling 1988 (B 138) 206; Wallmann 1989 (C 243) 234.

[87] Stratoniceia: *RDGE* 27. Aphrodisias-Plarasa: Reynolds 1982 (B 270) docs. 8 and 9, cf. doc. 6
lines 28–9, 10 line 2, with her commentary. Miletus: *Milet* I 3 nr. 126 lines 23–5 with pp. 252–3,

establishing a new strong kingdom of Pontus.[88] It was to be ruled by Darius, a descendant of Mithridates Eupator. Deiotarus of Galatia had died, and his possessions in Pontus were assigned to Darius; however, Deiotarus' grandson Castor was recognized as king of Galatia, and he was also allowed the interior of Paphlagonia.[89] So far Antony was following the traditional Roman policy of supporting kings from the old regal families; thus also Lysanias was confirmed as king of Ituraea.[90] And so far he was not especially concerned with rewarding past loyalties: Lysanias for one had taken the Parthian side.[91] But he also had new, able favourites of his own. Amyntas, once Deiotarus' secretary, was given Pisidia; Polemo of Laodicea-ad-Lycum, whose father Zeno was one of the few who resisted Labienus, received a dominion combining the western part of Cilicia with some parts of Lycaonia.[92] Like Ituraea and parts of Pontus, these were rough, unpacified regions: the new kings evidently had work to do. It was also probably now that Cleopatra was given Cyprus and a region of eastern Cilicia: she too perhaps had a task, for Cilicia and Cyprus were peculiarly rich in timber, and she was presumably to build ships to replenish Antony's fleet.[93] Herod of Judaea also received some further backing. Ventidius and his lieutenant Poppaedius Silo had apparently not tried very hard to displace the rival claimant Antigonus for the throne:[94] he had more pressing concerns. Stronger support could now be given. It seems that Antony began, rather oddly, by recognizing Herod as 'king of the Idumaeans and Samarians': possibly he acknowledged that Jerusalem was for the moment beyond recovery, and granted him this new title in provisional compensation.[95]

It was also now that Antony entered on a new religious policy, and began to insist more emphatically on his identification with Dionysus:[96] a god of liberation and eastern conquest, of course, as well as of vitality and exhilarating release. In Athens, he was duly celebrated as θεὸς Νέος

Magie 1950 (E 853) 1282 n. 15. If Reynolds 1982 (B 270) doc. 7 refers to the Labienus war (cf. lines 3–4 with her commentary), rewards were also voted to Rhodes, Lycia, Laodicea and Tarsus. On the campaign in general cf. Sherwin-White 1984 (A 89) 303–4.

[88] App. *BCiv.* v.75.319; cf. esp. Buchheim 1960 (c 49) 49–51; Hoben 1969 (E 840) 34–9.

[89] Cf. esp. Hoben 1969 (E 840) 116–19.   [90] Cf. Dio XLIX.32.5; Buchheim 1960 (c 49) 18–19.

[91] Joseph. *AJ* XIV.330, *BJ* 1.248.

[92] App. *BCiv.* v.75.319 with Gabba 1970 (B 55) *ad loc.*; on the date, Buchheim 1960 (c 49) 51–2. The realm extended as far as Iconium (Strab. XII.5.3–6.2 (568C)); cf. Mitford 1980 (E 860) 1242. For Zeno's resistance to Labienus cf. Strab. XIV.2.24–5 (660C).

[93] Cf. Joseph. *AJ* XIV.392–7, 406, *BJ* 1.288–92, 297; Buchheim 1960 (c 49) 67.

[94] Strab. XIV.5.2–3 (669C), 671, 685: cf. R. Meiggs, *Trees and Timber in the Ancient Mediterranean World* (Oxford, 1982) 117. On the date cf. the inscription published by Pouilloux 1972 (c 189), attesting an Egyptian στρατηγός of 'Cyprus and Cilicia' in 38–7; Mitford 1980 (E 860) 1293–4.

[95] App. *BCiv.* v.75.319 with Gabba 1970 (B 55) *ad loc.*; Buchheim 1960 (c 49) 66–7.

[96] Dio XLVIII.39.2.

Διόνυσος, in 39/8,[97] and he and Octavia were hailed as θεοὶ Εὐεργεταί.[98]
There were even perhaps hints of a divine marriage between Antony-
Dionysus and the city's goddess Athena;[99] he issued *cistophori* representing himself as Dionysus;[100] and stories were later told about his
extravagant Dionysiac displays – a platform above the theatre, decorated
with Dionysiac tambourines and fawnskins, where he drank with his
friends all day; then torchlit Dionysiac processions to the Acropolis.[101]
Some of the detail is surely fantastic, but the general policy makes sense.
His future now more clearly lay in the East; eastern states often
worshipped their rulers; and he would be the greatest master of all.
Divinity was the only comfortable status.

In spring 38 Antony made a rapid visit to Brundisium, where
Octavian had invited him for talks about the worsening situation in
Italy; but Octavian did not arrive. Antony issued a public letter of
rebuke, and crossly sailed back. This irritating distraction must have
delayed his departure to the East (that may even, in part, have been
Octavian's intention), but Antony still reached Syria, with an army, by
midsummer. He arrived to discover that Ventidius' triumphs had
continued. The winter of 39/8 had been spent in consolidation: there was
little sign, for instance, of any more energetic support for Herod, who
had returned to Judaea during the summer and linked with Silo's troops.
By the autumn he was encamped against Jerusalem, but Silo was still
unco-operative, and his army soon scattered to its winter billets. In the
spring Ventidius recalled Silo to Syria, anticipating a further attack from
Pacorus. It soon came, but Ventidius had time to occupy a strong
position at Gindarus, north east of Antioch in the Cyrrhestica region of
Syria. As at the Cilician Gates the previous year, the Parthians attacked
rashly; as at Mt Amanus, their leader fell, and they were wholly routed.[102]
Ventidius most effectively brought many of the Syrian cities over by
sending around Pacorus' head on a stake.

Now there was little left to do. It was even possible to support Herod
more openly, and Ventidius sent two legions and 1,000 cavalry to his
help. (They turned out to be notably ineffective.) Otherwise there was
only a pocket of resistance in Commagene, whose wealthy king

---

[97] *IG* II² 1043. 22–3.   [98] Agora inscription published by Raubitschek 1946 (F 202) 146–50.

[99] Dio XLVIII.39.2; Sen. *Suas.* 1.6.7 (the story has evidently been embroidered, but probably has at
least some basis). It need not follow that Octavia herself was regarded as Athena incarnate, as
Raubitschek 1946 (F 202) thought.

[100] Cf. especially Mannsperger 1973 (C 171) 384–6. Here Dionysiac types were admittedly
standard: Crawford 1974 (B 319) II 743 n.4.   [101] Socrates of Rhodes, *FGrH* 192 F 2.

[102] Dio XLIX.19–20 with Reinhold 1988 (B 150) *ad loc.*; cf. Sherwin-White 1984 (A 89) 304–6. The
similarities to the events of 39 are in fact suspicious, and the same stories may have been used by
historians for two different campaigns. But it is likely enough that Ventidius tried to repeat his
waiting game, and just possible that Pacorus fell into the trap.

Antiochus was recalcitrant, refusing to surrender the Parthian survivors who had fled to him. Ventidius besieged him in Samosata, then Antony arrived to take over the campaign. Antiochus was eager to negotiate, but Antony refused; yet the siege proved more difficult than he expected, and he later, rather ingloriously, accepted terms.[103] Ventidius returned to Rome, and celebrated the triumph he richly deserved on 27 November 38; he died a little later, and was given a state funeral. Antony returned to Athens, where he spent the winter of 38/7. He had little more to fear from the Parthians in Asia Minor; it might even be time to think of carrying the war into Parthia itself, the richest way of winning glory that could be imagined. But first events in the West were again calling for attention.

VII. TARENTUM, 37 B.C.

The pact of Misenum was fragile. Antony, now a wary ally of both Sextus and Octavian, was the man who could preserve it: but he was soon away in the East, and the uneasy division of the West between Sextus and Octavian began to show strain. Signs of a rift emerged only a few months after the pact, when in autumn 39 Octavian divorced Scribonia, the bride he had married when courting Sextus' favour the previous year. (A few months later he married Livia instead: a love-match, perhaps, as people said[104] – but she certainly linked him to another great clan, and that was not imprudent.) And the Italian famine continued, with pirates continuing to ravage the shore of Campania and harry the grain ships: Octavian publicly blamed Sextus. Antony too was contributing to the instability, prevaricating about the surrender of the Peloponnese to Sextus. During the winter of 39/8 matters came to a head. Sextus' admiral Menodorus went over to Octavian and gave him control of Sardinia and Corsica, three legions and sixty ships. War between Octavian and the outraged Sextus naturally followed, and in spring 38 there were two great sea-battles, one off the coast of Cumae near Naples and one in the Straits of Messana. Both were considerable victories for Sextus, but he still followed his distinctive defensive policy, and did not press home his advantage. Octavian retired safely to Campania.

Antony must have heard of this with mixed feelings. He will not have been dismayed to see Sextus and Octavian assiduously weakening one another; but one of them might win, and an undisputed master of the

---

[103] Plut. *Ant.* 34.5–7. The terms clearly gave the city over to the Romans (Joseph. *AJ* xiv.447, *BJ* 1.322; Oros. vi.18.23). Cf. Sherwin-White 1984 (A 89) 306 and n.24.

[104] Suet. *Aug.* 62.2 with Carter 1982 (B 24) *ad loc.*; Dio xlviii.34.3.

West was a disconcerting prospect. Before the two battles in the spring
of 38, he had been worried enough to make the journey back to
Brundisium, despite his urgency to move to the eastern front; at this
point he was still pressing Octavian to avoid a breach with Sextus.[105]
Octavian had then avoided a meeting, but after his defeats stood in much
greater need of Antony's support. In Autumn 38 Octavian sent Maecenas to seek a pledge of help against Sextus. We are told that Antony gave
it;[106] and indeed the odds now favoured Sextus, so that moderate aid to
Octavian might seem the best way to preserve the balance of power. But
Antony's pledge doubtless carried its conditions, and relations were very
strained.

Octavian had further problems too. There had been trouble in Gaul
since the previous year, which had culminated in a full-scale revolt in
Aquitania. By the end of 38 this had been dealt with by Agrippa, but this
merely replaced one embarrassment with another: Agrippa's glory
contrasted too obviously with Octavian's own defeats, and Agrippa
tactfully went without a triumph.[107] And Octavian's control of Italy was
not beyond reproach. Public life was unusually disordered, with a
shortage of candidates for some offices, while in other cases magistrates
were hastening to resign their offices: in 38 there were no less than sixty-
seven praetors.[108] And the popular riots were continuing, including
some support of a new favourite, a certain M. Oppius. Predictably, he
soon died.[109] Any pretence of normality was wearing very thin.

Another meeting was clearly needed. Antony sailed for Italy in early
spring 37: he was accompanied by 300 ships. The menace was unmistakable. Perhaps he claimed he was coming to help Octavian against
Sextus;[110] if so, he was naturally disbelieved, and it seems that the
townsfolk of Brundisium refused to admit the fleet.[111] Bewildered and
nervous, they doubtless trusted that Octavian would applaud them.
Antony sailed to Tarentum instead, and Octavian travelled there to meet
him. Lepidus was again unrepresented. Negotiations were slow, and it
was perhaps late July or August before agreement was reached.[112] The
questions were indeed delicate: it was certainly not clear that it was in

[105] App. *BCiv.* v.79.336.   [106] So App. *BCiv.* v.92.386.

[107] Dio XLVIII.49.2–3; cf. App. *BCiv.* v.75.318, 92.386.

[108] Dio XLVIII.43.1–3, cf. XLVIII.53.1–3, XLIX.16.2, XLIX.43.7; Frei-Stolba 1967 (C 92) 83.

[109] Dio XLVIII.43.1, XLVIII.53.4–6; App. *BCiv.* IV.41.172–3.

[110] So App. *BCiv.* v.93.386–95.398. For the divergences between this account and Plut. *Ant.* 35.1
and Dio XLVIII.54 cf. Pelling 1988 (B 138) 213–14.   [111] Plut. *Ant.* 35.1.

[112] The treaty is normally put a little later, in September or October, but the grounds for this are
slight. A July/August date would be late enough to rule out a resumption of the Parthian War until
36 (cf. Plut. *Ant.* 35.8); Octavian's delay of the war against Sextus (App. *BCiv.* v.95.396) was
probably one of the treaty's terms, and tells nothing of its date. It is hard to think that even
protracted negotiations would have dragged on into September.

Antony's interests to support Octavian at all emphatically against Sextus. The mediation of Octavia, it was said, was crucial[113] – possibly romantic fiction once again, but she may indeed have played a part.

Finally Antony agreed to back Octavian against Sextus, who was stripped of his priesthood and his promised consulship. Octavian was to carry through the war, but it was agreed that he should delay his attack on Sextus to the following year: it was doubtless Antony who pressed for this, for it offered him the hope of synchronizing his invasion of Parthia with this further war in Italy. The propaganda possibilities were clear: while Sextus and Octavian were refusing to let the civil wars die, Antony would be doing what Roman generals should always have done, advancing the empire and spilling foreign blood. It was all to work out rather differently. They further agreed that Octavian would give Antony 20,000 men and 1,000 elite troops in return for 120 men-of-war and ten skiffs.[114] The deal made sense, for Octavian vitally needed reinforcements for the fleet which Sextus had damaged so badly, while Antony had recently been unable to recruit Italian troops. But, from his viewpoint, there was one drawback. He left the ships there and then. Octavian merely promised the troops. They never came.

There was a further problem, of a constitutional sort. The triumvirate had formally expired at the end of 38, leaving the triumvirs' position uncomfortably vague. Probably nobody knew whether their power was now illegal. The triumvirate was an irregular magistracy: to which regular magistracy should it be regarded as analogous? To the consulship, which had a fixed term of one year, but *formally* ended when the consuls abdicated their office on the last day? On the one hand, the term had passed; on the other, the triumvirs had not abdicated.[115] Or perhaps it was closer to a provincial governorship, normally assigned by *senatus consultum*, which continued until a successor was appointed and arrived? Here there were no successors. In some ways the vast task *rei publicae constituendae* left the triumvirs more closely analogous to a dictator, who was similarly appointed for a specified purpose and held his office until he abdicated on completion of the task: now the *res publica* was certainly not yet *constituta*. But the early, traditional dictatorship had also had a maximum duration of six months, and that had been scrupulously observed:[116] what would have happened had a dictator outstayed that

---

[113] App. *BCiv*.93.390–1, 96.397; Dio XLVIII.54.3; and especially Plut. *Ant.* 35. Wallmann 1989 (C 243) 181–2 thus explains Octavia's prominence on coins of 37–36 celebrating the accord (*CRR* 1256, 1262, 1266).

[114] App. *BCiv*. v.95.396–7; cf. (with slightly different, less credible numbers) Plut. *Ant.* 35.7; Brunt 1971 (A 9) 502.

[115] The constitutional puzzle certainly exercised the minds of contemporaries: cf. the elaborate treatment of similar issues at Livy, III.36.9, 38.1, 54.5–6 (decemvirs not laying down their office when their term expired; the decemvirate was an irregular magistracy like the triumvirate); IX.33–4 (similar behaviour by a censor).   [116] Cf. Mommsen 1887 (A 65) II.1³ 161.

period? No one knew. Admittedly, the more recent (and very uneasy) precedents of Sulla and Caesar furnished a dictatorship without any such legal maximum term.[117] But those dictatorships had been voted in those terms, without any time-limitation. Now it was precisely the specification of a limit which differentiated the triumvirate: how crucial was this difference, and who was to say? Perhaps the closest analogy was to those few provincial commands assigned by *lex* rather than *s.c.*, such as Caesar's command in Gaul. That *had* carried a fixed term – but the events of 51–50 had shown that the legal implications of its expiry were tangled and unclear. Were further confusion required, it was offered by the triumvirs' provincial commands. They had assigned these to themselves by virtue of their triumviral powers, but had also had them ratified by *s.c.*; it was not at all clear that their provincial *imperium* lapsed when their triumviral powers lapsed.[118] The analogy with a regular proconsul, assigned a province by *s.c.*, was close.

In short, the legal position was hopelessly confused. Perhaps it did not matter very much: the realities of power were clear enough. But the events of 51–50 had shown that legal issues could be important, at least in propaganda terms; and, anyway, the triumvirs had recently been making a show of their constitutionalism. It would certainly be comfortable to give their status more clarity. Reassuringly, the triumvirate was now formally renewed for another five years, very probably to expire on the last day of 33,[119] and a little later this was ratified by the people of Rome.[120] But the constitutional tangle was to return.

VIII. THE YEAR 36 B.C.

While Antony and Octavian had been engaged at Tarentum, their lieutenants had been busy. Agrippa, consul in 37, had considerably strengthened Octavian's fleet; he had also recruited vast numbers of new seamen – 20,000 slaves were freed to allow them to serve.[121] Most impressively of all, he had constructed the *portus Iulius* in Campania by linking the shallow Lucrine lake by a canal to the much deeper Avernus, then removing the dyke separating the Lucrine lake from the sea. The work was completed by two tunnels connecting the Avernus with

---

[117] Cf. Mommsen 1887 (A 65) II.1³ 703–5, 714–16. Caesar's dictatorship had originally been annual, then formally extended to ten years and then 'for life': *MRR* II 272, 285 n.1, 294–5, 305, 317–18.   [118] Cf. p. 20 and n.80; Girardet 1990 (C 97).   [119] See Endnote pp. 67–8.

[120] Thus App. *Ill.* 28.80, ... καὶ ὁ δῆμος ἐπεκεκυρώκει. There is no inconsistency here (as is often suggested) with *BCiv.* v.95.398, where the triumvirs agree the renewal οὐδὲν ἔτι τοῦ δήμου δεηθέντες. In *BCiv.* Appian is simply contrasting the procedure in 37 with that of November 43, when the triumvirs needed a *lex* to establish them in office (*BCiv.* IV.7.27). Their powers now authorized them (it could be claimed) to renew their own term: it still suited their current policy to obtain ratification for their acts from the Senate (cf. p. 20 and n. 80) or, as here, the people.

[121] Suet. *Aug.* 16.1; cf. Brunt 1971 (A 9) 508.

Cumae and the beach.[122] Sextus had recently been concentrating his attacks on the Campanian coast:[123] now the tunnels would allow Agrippa to convey supplies safely, while the double lake would afford a protected expanse of water for training crews.

In the East, meanwhile, Herod at last received effective aid. C. Sosius, Antony's governor of Syria and Cilicia, first subdued the Aradians (a Syrian people who were still disaffected), then arrived in Palestine. The war had been dragging on through 38, with Antigonus having much the better of it; Herod himself had been absent for a good part of the summer, pressing Antony at Samosata for more energetic help. In late 38 two legions had been sent ahead under Herod's direct command (a most irregular procedure): he promptly won a considerable victory at Isana. The rest of Judaea, except for the capital, quickly fell to him, and in spring 37 he resumed the siege of Jerusalem itself. Sosius' new force then arrived, and in July the city fell, very bloodily.[124] Herod became king; Antigonus was captured, and when Antony returned to the East he yielded to Herod's pressure and had him publicly executed at Antioch.

Herod was not specially loved by his countrymen, but his decisive victory still added to the stability of the East. What is more, the Parthian threat seemed to have disappeared. Indeed, there was a new dynastic crisis within Parthia itself. Orodes abdicated in late 38 or 37, and from his thirty sons he unwisely selected Phraates as successor, who promptly killed his father, all his brothers, and his son. The Parthian nobility soon revolted: the prospects for a Roman invasion had seldom been better.

But there was no time to exploit the crisis in 37: Antony did not arrive back in the East until autumn. He spent the winter at Antioch, continuing his new administrative arrangements, and this time the reorganization was more extensive. In 39 he had already given hints of what was to come, when he had strengthened the kingdom of Pontus and begun to favour new men like Amyntas and Polemo. Now these policies were taken much further, and the East began to fall into a number of large client kingdoms, each ruled by an efficient and loyal prince. The newly enlarged kingdom of Pontus would more or less do, but the king would not; Darius was replaced by Polemo, who in his small dominion of 39 had evidently proved himself worthy of promotion.[125] Castor in Galatia was similarly replaced. (It is possible that Darius and Castor had both conveniently died; but the coincidence is suspicious, and it is more likely that both were deposed.) Castor's son Deiotarus

---

[122] For the details, Paget 1968 (D 218) 163–9; Roddaz 1984 (C 200) 95–114.

[123] Dio XLVIII.46.1; Strab. v.4.3–5 (243C).   [124] For the date, Schürer 1973 (E 1207) I.284–6.

[125] The territorial extent of Polemo's realm is not precisely clear, but it was evidently similar to that of Darius: cf. Hoben 1969 (E 840) 42–4.

Philadelphus was allowed to inherit Paphlagonia,[126] but Galatia passed to Amyntas;[127] and the realm was greatly expanded, to include parts of Pamphylia and Polemo's former domain in Lycaonia.[128] The old boundaries of Cappadocia would serve adequately, but there had been dynastic unrest there for years. On Ariobarzanes' death in 42 the kingdom should have passed to his brother Ariarathes, a man of dubious loyalty to Rome; Antony preferred a certain Archelaus Sisines from Pontic Comana, and probably made his favour clear from the outset.[129] But in 42–41 it was not yet time to overthrow the legitimate heir in favour of an outsider. By 37–36 Antony's policy of favouring such men was more securely established, and Archelaus was duly confirmed as king.[130] Not that the great kings controlled everything: for instance, the priest-kings in southern Pontus, at Comana, Megalopolis and Zela, were retained and strengthened; several other minor princes were created, Cleon in Mysia, Adiatorix in Heraclea Pontica; in Upper Cilicia Tarcondimotus, a pirate in his youth, was encouraged in his small kingdom.[131] But it was Amyntas, Polemo and Archelaus who along with Herod would keep Asia Minor safe. It was a wise policy, and Antony chose his men well. The system, together with most of the individual kings, was to be continued by Octavian after Antony's fall: Archelaus, for instance, reigned for a full fifty years.[132]

Another monarch, too, had her realm increased. Cleopatra was given parts of coastal Phoenicia and Nabataean Arabia, and also the rich balsam woods around Jericho in Judaea.[133] Lysanias of Ituraea was executed, and she took over his kingdom along with some adjoining territory;[134] perhaps she had her dominion in Cilicia extended, and, now or earlier, she also became mistress of Crete and Cyrene.[135] Not all of this

---

[126] Possibly at first jointly with his elder brother Deiotarus Philopator. Cf. Strab. XII.3.40–2 (562C); Hoben 1969 (E 840) 118–19.

[127] Strabo. XII.6.2–7.1 (569C); Hoben 1969(E 840) 123–4.   [128] Cf. Levick 1967 (E 851) 25–6.

[129] App. *BCiv.* V.7.31 (of 41 B.C., συνέπραξεν ἐς τὴν βασιλείαν: cf. Buchheim 1960 (C 49) 55–6, observing Appian's careful phrasing.

[130] Dio XLIX.32.3: on the date cf. Buchheim 1960 (C 49) 59.

[131] Strab. XII.3.6–8 (543C), 3.33–5 (558C), 3.37–8 (560C), 8.7–9 (574C), XIV.5.16–21 (676C), with Pelling 1988 (B 138) *ad loc.*; cf. Magie 1950 (E 853) 435–6, 1240, 1285–7, and on Antony's policy in general Bowersock 1965 (C 39) 42–61.   [132] Tac. *Ann.* II.42.2.

[133] Plut. *Ant.* 36.3–4 and Dio XLIX.32.3–5 agree in placing these grants in 37–36. Joseph. *AJ* XV.94–5 appears to place the gifts of parts of Phoenicia, Arabia and Judaea in 34, but he himself seems to associate these gifts with that of Lysanias' domain, which certainly belongs in 37–36: he is clearly combining several different phases of Cleopatra's past. Cf. for the date Buchheim 1960 (C 49) 69–73; for the Arabian grant Bowersock 1983 (E 990) 40–4; for the balsam woods Schürer 1973 (E 1207) 198–300.

[134] Porphyry *FGrH* 260 F.2.17; Dio XLIX.32.5; Joseph. *AJ* XV.92, *BJ* 1.440. The adjoining territory probably included Canatha (Joseph. *AJ* XV.112, *BJ* 1.366), Hippos and Gadara (Joseph. *AJ* XV.217, *BJ* 1.396); possibly also Damascus, where Cleopatra's portrait appears on coins (though that need not be decisive). Cf. Bicknell 1977 (C 29) 339.

[135] Dio XLIX.32.5; cf. Grant 1946 (B 322) 55–8; Buttrey 1983 (B 315) 24–7.

served Rome's interests – for instance, now or in 34 both Herod and
Malchus of Arabia leased back from Cleopatra the land she now gained.
The rent was vast, 200 talents apiece: Cleopatra rather than Rome was
clearly the beneficiary of that arrangement. But the grants still fitted
Antony's policy of strengthening loyal monarchs, and so far nothing
suggests that Antony was favouring her unduly. Amyntas and Polemo
did better out of this reorganization than she did, and indeed Antony
now as later refused to give her parts of Judaea, Phoenicia, Syria and
Arabia which she coveted.[136] But he seems to have advertised their union
in other ways. She travelled to meet him in Syria in late 37; in 36 she bore
him another son, Ptolemy Philadelphus. He also acknowledged
paternity of the twins born in 40. This was not yet clearly a marriage – at
least, not in Roman eyes, though Egyptians themselves may not have
known quite what to make of it.[137] But it was still a scandal, and one
which left Antony peculiarly vulnerable to Octavian's propaganda. The
Parthian War afforded Antony the chance of a propaganda triumph, one
which might impress Italian sentiment much more than Octavian's continuation of the civil war with Sextus.[138] That was now compromised.

Why did Antony do it? Perhaps Cleopatra needed her position within
Egypt strengthened (we know little of the internal history of her reign,
but Ptolemies were often insecure on their thrones); but this seems an
extreme method. More likely, Antony was hoping to strengthen his own
position in the East, at least within Egypt itself. This festive connexion
with an eastern queen – almost indeed a sacred marriage of Dionysus-
Osiris and Isis – might be as popular there as it turned out to be
unpopular in Italy. Glamour was important to Cleopatra in articulating
her style of leadership; it was a style which Antony could naturally share;
and eastern support would be crucial if it came to war with Octavian –
that, surely, was already clear. But it is still surprising that he risked
outraging Italian opinion quite so much; was Italy yet such a lost cause?
Perhaps he thought he was doing nothing more outrageous than Caesar
had done; Caesar had even installed Cleopatra at Rome; but Caesar did
not have a master of propaganda to oppose him, and Antony should
have sensed the danger. We rarely see Antony's political naivety so
clearly, and it does remain quite possible that the personal factor was
indeed important, with Cleopatra leading Antony against his political
judgment. Not that he was infatuated beyond control: his refusal of the
territory she desired is enough to show this; and he was shortly to leave
her again, for a Parthian War which (he must have expected) would keep
them apart for several years. But romance could still have been there.

Still, romance did not impede the preparations for Parthia. The signs

---

[136] Joseph. *AJ* xv.79, 91–4, 95, 258; cf. 24–5, 74–9.
[137] Pelling 1988 (B 138) 219–20.   [138] See above, p. 26.

of unrest at the court continued to come; in 37 or early 36 one Monaeses, from a great Parthian family, arrived with promises of a wider defection among the nobility. Monaeses' role is hard to gauge, and possibly he was playing a double game;[139] still, his news was not implausible, given Phraates' barbarity – Parthians might after all be as ready to exploit Roman help in their internal conflicts as the Roman Labienus had been to exploit the Parthians. There was obviously much to be said for striking quickly; but Crassus' fate in 53 had shown the vulnerability of a Roman force in the open plains of Mesopotamia, and Antony preferred a plan on the lines of the one which (it seems) Iulius Caesar was intending to follow in 44[140] – to take the slower northern route through Armenia into Media Atropatene, a rougher and hillier terrain where the Parthian cavalry would be less effective. The long-standing bad feeling between the kings of Armenia and Media (both named Artavasdes) offered the further possibility of exploiting one against the other. Presumably the Armenian Artavasdes would be the Romans' natural ally as they attacked his Median enemy, and it seems that he was already urging Antony on;[141] but both kings were very uncertain quantities. In 37 or early 36 P. Canidius Crassus made a firmer understanding with the Armenian Artavasdes, then passed on in the spring to defeat the Iberi and Albani: this remarkably swift campaign protected what would now become the Roman rear left. In the event the rear would be more exposed than it now seemed, but that was because of Artavasdes' unreliability; and, without a much more extensive campaign, that was a risk the Romans had to take.

Antony had by now sent to Phraates demanding the return of the eagles captured at Carrhae: a firm statement that, whatever Octavian might be saying at Rome, Antony's agreed task of 'avenging Crassus' was still incomplete.[142] Phraates of course refused – the insecure new monarch could hardly make so humiliating a concession – and Antony's muster continued. He first marched with his Syrian army to Zeugma. That might suggest that he was planning to follow Crassus' policy and strike direct at Mesopotamia, but that strategy would only work if the advance was to be unopposed. In fact Phraates swiftly concentrated the Parthian army in Mesopotamia. That ruled out Crassus' plan, and

---

[139] Cf. Plut. *Ant.* 37.1–2 with Pelling 1988 (B 138) *ad loc.*; Dio XLIX.23.5, XLIX.24.3 with Reinhold 1988 (B 150) *ad loc.* Phraates won Monaeses back suspiciously quickly; Hor. *Carm.* III.3.9–12 may even indicate that he entrusted him with an important command. Possibly Monaeses' 'desertion' was simply a signal to Phraates that he would go over to Rome unless restored to authority.

[140] Suet. *Iul.* 44; cf. Bengtson 1974 (C 22) 4–9, Malitz 1984 (C 169) 56–7.

[141] Dio XLIX.25.1. In 54–3 he had advised Crassus similarly (Plut. *Crass.* 19, 22.2).

[142] That had been agreed at Brundisium (see above, p. 18). The strong stress in the tradition that Ventidius had *already* avenged Crassus (Plut. *Ant.* 34.3; Dio XLIX.21.2; Val. Max. VI.9.9; Flor. II.19.7; Tac. *Germ.* XXXVII.4) probably reflects an idea contemporary with the events themselves, and one which Octavian would have found welcome: cf. Buchheim 1960 (C 49) 39; Timpe 1962 (C 236) 114–19; Wallmann 1989 (C 243) 236, 238–9, 263–4.

Antony struck north instead towards Armenia. There he linked with Canidius' army, perhaps at the plateau of Erzerum, perhaps at Artaxata;[143] he was also joined by contingents from the allied kings, including Polemo.[144] As Armenia had evidently been selected as the mustering-point some months before, Antony must always have expected that the northern route would turn out to be the only practicable one; otherwise, indeed, Canidius' preliminary campaign would make little sense; and it looks as if the Zeugma exercise had been no more than an elaborate feint.[145] In all Antony had perhaps sixteen legions and a mass of auxiliaries,[146] and Artavasdes of Armenia supplied a large contingent of cataphracts and lighter-armed cavalry, perhaps as many as 16,000.[147] It was a vast army indeed, distinctly greater than that with which Caesar had conquered Gaul.

Antony was later accused of wrecking the campaign for Cleopatra's sake. He had begun it too late in the season, they said, because he had dallied too long at Alexandria; then he had conducted the invasion itself too hurriedly, eager to return to her side.[148] But the points were hardly fair. The muster in Armenia was perhaps in June or July; what with Canidius' preliminary campaign and the long preliminary marches,[149] it was astounding it could be so soon. Perhaps there was still a case for waiting till 35, keeping the army concentrated in the East ready for an early strike in the spring;[150] but there was also the Parthian dynastic crisis to consider, as well as the chance of outflanking the Parthian army by a swift advance now – a ploy in which Antony very nearly succeeded. Of course Parthia would not fall in a single campaign: Iulius Caesar had planned on three years,[151] and that was reasonable. But it was also reasonable to hope for a solid victory or so in Media, bolstering the morale of the Roman army and Phraates' internal enemies; then, if necessary, Antony could withdraw and winter in Armenia (though hardly at Cleopatra's side). Antony's strategy made sense.

---

[143] Erzerum: Kromayer 1896 (C 142) 82. Artaxata: Sherwin-White 1984 (A 89) 311.

[144] Polemo: Plut. *Ant.* 38.6; Dio XLIX.25.4. Other kings: Plut. *Ant.* 37.3.

[145] So Kromayer 1896 (C 142) 100–1; *contra*, Sherwin-White 1984 (A 89) 309–10.

[146] Brunt 1971 (A 9) 503–4, Sherwin-White 1984 (A 89) 311 n.37.

[147] So Plut. *Ant.* 50.3, though at 37.3 he wrote of '6,000' at the initial muster in Armenia. Strab. XI.14.9–12 (530C) speaks of 6,000 cataphracts 'besides the other cavalry', which may explain Plutarch's confusion; or both Plutarch's figures may be right, if the mass of the cavalry joined Antony in eastern Armenia after the muster; or 16,000 perhaps represented the paper strength, 6,000 the force which materialized (Sherwin-White 1984 (A 89) 311 n.37).

[148] Livy, *Per.* 130: cf. Plut. *Ant.* 37.5–38.1 with Pelling 1988 (B 138) *ad loc.* The criticism probably derived from Q. Dellius, an eyewitness of the campaign (Strab. XI.13.1–4 (523C)) and no friend of Cleopatra.

[149] It was some 1,000 Roman miles from Zeugma to the Median border (Strab. XI.13.4–6 (524C); Plut. *Ant.* 38.1), itself a march of three to four months, and Antony's troops first had to march from Antioch.

[150] So Plut. *Ant.* 38.1, perhaps from Dellius; Sherwin-White 1984 (A 89) 316–17 thinks the point fair.   [151] Dio XLIII.51.2.

But it went wrong. Things started well, and he drove deep into Media. He indeed reached the capital Phraata[152] before the main Parthian force could double back from Mesopotamia. The Median king Artavasdes had left his royal family in residence at Phraata: he at least was evidently taken by surprise by Antony's strategy and speed. But to get there in time Antony had to rush on ahead of his own siege-engines. That was an evident gamble, though not dissimilar to the risks Caesar himself had famously taken in Gaul and in the Civil War, and the swift arrival of a formidable army might indeed have carried the unprotected city. But it did not, and a siege was necessary. Without the engines, it was a curiously amateurish job.[153] And, crucially, the engines never arrived, for Phraates' cavalry overtook the wagon-train and destroyed it, together with its accompanying two legions.[154] Polemo himself was captured, though not killed – he would be more useful alive when it came to negotiations.[155] Artavasdes of Armenia promptly despaired of Antony's cause, and withdrew with his force: a severe loss, for the heavy Armenian cataphracts would have been particularly useful in defence. A series of engagements followed, with Antony successful in the most substantial of them;[156] but the swift Parthian cavalry fled most effectively, and Antony could not follow it up.

Before long Antony was forced to abandon the siege; and, predictably, his retreat turned out to be intensely difficult, with sickness and famine as great a problem as the harrying Parthian archers. The resilience and the valour of Antony and his army became famous, and the comparison with Xenophon's Ten Thousand was an obvious one.[157] Eventually, after an epic final night-time march across the foothills of the Kūh-e-Sahand range,[158] the army reached the Talkheh, then the Araxes and Armenia. The retreat had taken twenty-seven days, and even now safety could not be taken for granted, given Artavasdes' earlier treachery. But Antony successfully made terms with him, and by mid-winter the remains of the army had reached Cappadocia: there were further

---

[152] The city's site is uncertain: according to Dellius (cit. Strab. XI.13.1–4 (523C)) it was 2,400 stades, i.e. some 480 km, from the Armenian border. Its conventional location at Taht-i-Soleiman is not at all likely, and it was probably much further east, near Maragheh. Cf. Schippman 1971 (F 220) 338–47; Bengtson 1974 (C 22) 29–30. Much of the standard topographical reconstruction of this campaign is in need of correction (it is mainly still based on Rawlinson 1841 (E 866) 113–17): cf. now Sherwin-White 1984 (A 89) 311–21 and Pelling 1988 (B 138) 220–43.

[153] Plut *Ant.* 38.4; Arr. *Parth.* fr. 95R.

[154] Vell. Pat. II.82.2; cf. Livy, *Per.* 130; Plut. *Ant.* 38.5 (10,000 men).

[155] Plut *Ant.* 38.6; Dio XLIX.25.4; cf. below, p. 38.

[156] Plut. *Ant.* 39, though the account has implausible elements: cf. Pelling 1988 (B 138) *ad loc.*

[157] It is embellished by Plutarch (cf. Pelling 1988 (B 138) 221), but perhaps originates with Dellius: so Jacoby on *FGrH* 197 F 1.

[158] Presumably the western rather than the eastern foothills, if Phraata was near Maragheh (cf. n. 152): cf. the map in Pelling 1988 (B 138) 230; Sherwin-White 1984 (A 89) 318 and n.53.

deaths in this final section of the march. The total losses in the campaign were indeed catastrophic, some third of the entire army.[159]

So ended Antony's great attempt to emulate Alexander. Ironically, his best military qualities had seldom been clearer – his energy, his enterprise, his inspirational leadership; and yet it was disastrous. Plutarch later did well to make this campaign the centrepiece of his *Life*, but not only for those reasons. This was indeed the turning-point of the triumviral period. Till now Antony's military prestige and power had far outstripped Octavian, and he had consequently been the stronger partner in their diplomatic exchanges. This campaign should have raised his supremacy beyond challenge.

But instead the victories were being won elsewhere, and by Octavian. His war with the popular favourite Sextus was a delicate one to fight: it could much too easily seem Octavian's personal vendetta. Indeed, even while he was fighting it disturbances at Rome required urgent attention;[160] there were grumblings in the veteran colonies too;[161] Etruria was particularly restive.[162] Octavian could not afford to lose or delay – for all he knew, Antony was carrying all before him in Parthia – but the events of 38 had shown how formidable an enemy Sextus could be.[163] Now Agrippa's preparations were magnificent, but Sextus had been preparing too, and by 36 he had some 350 ships.[164] Just as he had in 38, Octavian even sent to Lepidus in Africa for help. In 38 Lepidus had made no response, content to leave Octavian with his own problems.[165] This time he decided to come in force. He eventually arrived with twelve legions and 5,000 cavalry, with a further four legions following as reinforcements (two were destroyed by Sextus' fleet before they could land).[166] Perhaps Lepidus already had clear plans of his own, perhaps not; he at least knew that the great battle for the West should not be fought without him.

By July 36 Octavian was able to launch a triple-pronged attack on Sextus in Sicily. He would attack from the north and Statilius Taurus from the east; Lepidus would attack the western coast. The plan was good. The campaign itself was to show how difficult Sextus would find it to stretch his forces to meet several threats. But Octavian's forces were beset by storms; so many ships were lost that there were thoughts of delaying the campaign to 35. At first only Lepidus managed to land in strength, and he laid Sextus' lieutenant L. Plinius Rufus under siege in

---

[159] Plut. *Ant.* 50.1, 51.1, cf. Vell. Pat. 1.82.3; Flor. 1.20.10; Livy, *Per.* 130.

[160] App *BCiv.* v.99.414, 112.470.   [161] App. *BCiv.* v.99.414.

[162] Dio xlix.15.1; cf. App. *BCiv.* v.132.547. Octavian had spent some time there in 38. Dio xlviii.46.2–3.   [163] See above, p. 24.

[164] Flor. 11.18.9; 300 fought at Naulochus (App. *BCiv.* v.118.490, 120.499). Cf. Brunt 1971 (A 9) 507–8, Hadas 1930 (C. 108) 123.   [165] Dio xlviii.46.2.

[166] Cf. App. *BCiv.* v.98.406, 104.430–2; Vell. Pat. 11.80.1; Brunt 1971 (A 9) 499.

Lilybaeum. In the east there were naval battles, with first Agrippa successful off Mylae, then Sextus defeating Octavian himself off Tauromenium. Sextus' victory was more emphatic than Agrippa's, but at least Octavian established bridgeheads both by Cape Tyndaris and near Tauromenium: Sextus' resistance on land was surprisingly half-hearted, particularly at Tauromenium.[167] Octavian soon had twenty-one legions on the island,[168] besides Lepidus' army; Sextus had only ten.[169] He was soon hemmed into the island's north-east corner, a triangle bounded by Mylae and Tauromenium, and Mylae itself fell soon afterwards. And now even Lepidus himself was approaching, rather tardily. His part in the whole campaign is indeed enigmatically lackadaisical: it is odd that he did not move eastwards earlier – that was clearly where he was needed, and perhaps expected.[170] The sequel was to show him dissatisfied with his subordinate role. Was he perhaps content to let Octavian and Sextus weaken one another in the east, hoping by a last minute arrival to claim the authority he felt he deserved? The events of 44/3 had shown his capacity to bide his time before a decisive change of front.[171] If Octavian distrusted him, it was not without reason.[172]

Sextus' last hope was to pit everything on a battle at sea. Perhaps unwisely, Octavian accepted battle (there was possibly even a formal challenge and acceptance, agreeing time, place and numbers):[173] but the risk came off. The battle was fought off Naulochus (3 September 36), with 300 ships on either side. Agrippa, not Octavian, took command. By now brawn rather than skill was dominant in naval warfare, and Agrippa's heavier ships and more sophisticated grappling equipment carried the day. Only seventeen of Sextus' ships escaped. Sextus himself fled: his only slender hope lay with Antony in the East.

His land forces came over to Octavian with little demur. Plinius Rufus had moved eastwards to Messana, presumably following Lepidus. By now he had command of a large portion of Sextus' army, comprising eight legions.[174] It was clear that they would surrender: but to whom? Agrippa and Lepidus appeared before the city: Agrippa insisted that they wait for Octavian, but Lepidus overrode him. His forces indeed linked with those of Plinius, and together they sacked Messina. Lepidus now seemed in control of the combined force, some twenty-two legions. He had not been so powerful for years. Now if ever was the time to assert

---

[167] App. *BCiv.* v.110.457–9, with Gabba 1970 (B 55) *ad loc.*

[168] App. *BCiv.* v.116.481; Brunt 1971 (A 9) 498.   [169] Brunt 1971 (A 9) 499–500.

[170] App. *BCiv.* v.103.427 with Gabba 1970 (B 55) *ad loc.*   [171] Cf. *CAH* IX² 471, 482.4.

[172] Dio XLIX.8.3–4 even suggests that Lepidus was in secret league with Sextus, and that Octavian suspected as much (cf. XLIX.1.4). That is implausible, and probably influenced both by Octavian's propaganda and by Dio's tendency to guess at motivation; but some distrust is possible enough.

[173] App. *BCiv.* v.116.489 with Gabba 1970 (B 55) *ad loc.*; cf. Gabba 1977 (C94).

[174] App. *BCiv.* v.122.505 with Gabba 1970 (B 55) *ad loc.*

himself, to show how unfairly he had been excluded from all those diplomatic dealings at Brundisium, Misenum and Tarentum. He laid claim to all Sicily, though he magnanimously offered to exchange Sicily and Africa for all his former portion, Narbonensis and Nearer and Further Spain.[175] At first Octavian's friends remonstrated gently, then Octavian himself more fiercely; Lepidus was adamant. The legions were unamused. But the delusion could not last. Octavian entered his camp, almost unaccompanied – though there was a sizeable force of cavalry just outside. The troops at least knew where the balance of power lay: with only a little scuffling, they joined Octavian. Lepidus was allowed to keep his property and his life, and he even remained *pontifex maximus*. But Octavian stripped him of membership of the triumvirate and his provincial command.[176] There were no thoughts of consulting Antony first. Octavian took over Africa and Sicily into his own domain. Lepidus retired into exile and anonymity.

That effectively concluded the elimination of Sextus and Lepidus. Antony and Octavian remained; and Antony was beginning to look a little tattered.

IX. 35–33 B.C.

Politics now looked simpler: the reckoning would surely come, and we might expect Antony and Octavian to spend the next few years in preparation. But it was not quite like that. Octavian, it is true, seems to have seen the future clearly enough. He soon intensified his battle to win Italian public opinion, with fierce propaganda against Cleopatra and Antony; he may even have been in contact with Antony's enemy Artavasdes of Armenia (unless that charge is simply a fiction of Antony's propaganda);[177] and he was soon battle-hardening his troops in Illyricum, suggestively close to the dividing-line with Antony's dominion. But Antony was slow to respond. He may have talked of joining Octavian in an Illyrian campaign[178] – in self-defence, that would have been no bad ploy, if it were practicable: but really his focus lay on the East – indeed, on the *far* East, and for several years he was preoccupied with vengeance on the perfidious Armenian king Artavasdes. Of course an Armenian success would do something to mend the shame of the Parthian débâcle, but in Roman eyes Armenia lacked the glamour of Parthia; a new Alexander should be more glorious than that, and Armenia could only be the beginning; but a clearer-sighted man would have realized that now Parthia itself was a lost cause. With Octavian preparing in the West, there simply would not be time for the years a

175 Cf. *CAH* ix² 486.   176 *MRR* ii 400.
177 Dio xlix.14.6.   178 App. *BCiv.* v.132.549.

second Parthian invasion would demand. Yet in 33 nearly all Antony's legions were still in the extreme east of his domain; only then, very slowly, did they begin the long march west. War with Octavian was scarcely foremost in Antony's mind. Perhaps he was peaceable, content by now to share the world; perhaps he was simply naive. But it is clear which of the two was seeking the breach, and which had his thoughts elsewhere.

The fall of Sextus involved both in temporary embarrassments. Octavian found himself with forty-five legions, but confronted by a mutiny. Uncomfortably enough, his troops were beginning to believe his own propaganda. He had concluded the civil wars and brought peace on land and sea, so he said:[179] well, in that case there was no need for further service, and they demanded immediate demobilization. That would hardly do. Octavian knew he would need them again soon. But at least the longest-serving could be released, those who had fought for Octavian since Mutina and Philippi, some 20,000 men.[180] There were delays, but land was found for most of them, largely in Italy but partly in Gaul.[181] The others were promised 500 denarii, and, rather surprisingly, soon received it;[182] they were also induced to expect lucrative spoils in Illyricum – not very plausible for any who knew the land, but probably few did, and the ploy passed. Octavian could now return to Rome and acclaim. He celebrated an *ovatio*, and the other honours included a grant of tribunicial sacrosanctity,[183] interestingly presaging a conspicuous feature of his later constitutional façade. And there was more talk of restoring the Republic when Antony returned – how could he refuse, now Octavian had ended the civil wars? Peace and security would shortly be restored at home as well: Calvisius Sabinus was appointed to put down Italian brigandage, and a police force of some sort was established in Rome itself.[184] There was even a remission of some taxes, and the regular magistrates were ostentatiously allowed more freedom.[185] This was not the first time that the triumvirs had portrayed themselves as champions of Roman tradition, even a sort of constitutional normality.[186] But Octavian was beginning to steal the mask for his own.

In Antony's case, the embarrassment was Sextus himself. In the winter of 36/5 he arrived at Mytilene, hoping to ally himself with Antony; when

---

[179] App. *BCiv.* v.128.530, 130.540–2, 132.546–8; cf. Dio xlix.15.2.

[180] App. *BCiv.* v.129.534 ('since Mutina or Philippi'); Dio xlix.14.1 specifies those who had served 'since Mutina or for ten years'; cf. Reinhold 1988 (B 150) *ad loc.*; Brunt 1971 (A 9) 331; Keppie 1983 (E 65) 69–73. Some of them soon re-enlisted: Dio xlix.34.3.

[181] Keppie 1983 (E 65) 70–3; cf. Dio xlix.34.4.

[182] Dio xlix.14.2, with Reinhold 1988 (B 150) *ad loc.*; App. *BCiv.* v.129.536.

[183] See Endnote, p. 68.

[184] App. *BCiv.* v.132.547; cf. Suet. *Aug.* 32; Dio xlix.15.1; Palmer 1978 (C 184) 320–1.

[185] App. *BCiv.* v.130.540, 132.548; Dio xlix.15.3; cf. Nicolet 1976 (D 104) 95.

[186] See above, pp. 19–21, 27.

he heard of the Parthian disaster, he began to intrigue against him instead. Either way, he was a problem. Not that he was very strong: he was raising troops again, but even at the end he had little more than three legions and a handful of ships.[187] But he would be an awkward ally: with Italy being encouraged to celebrate his downfall, it might now seem to be Antony rather than Octavian who was refusing to let the civil wars die. And it would be awkward to kill him too. There were enough people in Rome who still recalled wistfully the hopes they had placed in him:[188] Octavian himself, outrageously, was later to make capital of this, and attack Antony for his faithless treatment of him.[189] Antony appointed M. Titius to take charge of the problem. Titius' father had been among the proscribed who fled to Sextus, and Titius himself had been spared by Sextus when captured by Menodorus in 40.[190] Antony probably selected Titius precisely because of these earlier favours, to smooth any dealings which proved necessary. But in the event no dealing proved possible, for Sextus' faithlessness became too apparent. By the spring of 35 the pursuit was tying up the governors of both Asia and Bithynia, C. Furnius and Domitius Ahenobarbus, as well as a sizeable fleet; King Amyntas too was involved. That was too much. When Sextus was finally captured by Amyntas in Phrygia, he was brought to Titius in Miletus and executed there. Antony may or may not have authorized his death. If he did, he covered his tracks: some said that Plancus, not he, had given the order; other stories were told of two letters, one ordering the execution and one countermanding it, which of course arrived in the wrong sequence.[191]

Antony himself was more concerned with Armenia. He was clearly determined to exact vengeance from Artavasdes; and he doubtless considered he was being prudent as well as vindictive, for he still dreamed of a second Parthian campaign. (He was indeed to embark on one two years later.) For this a secure Armenia was essential; but that could never be, as long as Artavasdes was king. Matters now took an unexpected turn, for an envoy arrived in Alexandria from the *Median* Artavasdes, Antony's enemy of the previous year: an envoy in fact of peculiar distinction, King Polemo himself. Antony's designs on Armenia would seem no surprise, and Median Artavasdes offered Antony an alliance. Antony accepted, and set out from Egypt during the summer.

[187] App. *BCiv.* v.137.571, 138.574.

[188] There was a popular demonstration against Titius, Vell. Pat. ii.79.6.

[189] Dio l.1.4; cf. App. *BCiv.* v.127.525.

[190] Dio xlviii.30.5–6. Titius was later unfairly represented as Sextus' personal enemy: cf. App. *BCiv.* v.140.584 with Gabba 1970 (b 55) *ad loc.*, 142.589–90. But Dio xlix.18.3 more shrewdly suggests that Sextus had hopes of Titius' goodwill.

[191] Dio xlix.18.4–5 with Reinhold 1988 (b 150) *ad loc.*; App. *BCiv.* v.144.598–600. But Velleius, as ever a faithful follower of Octavian's line, has no doubts: 'iussu M Antonii', ii.79.5 (cf. 87.2).

Perhaps he pretended that he was attacking the Parthians; but his immediate goal was surely Armenia.[192]

For the present it came to nothing, for a different sort of crisis supervened. Octavia arrived in the East. Whatever people were saying about her husband and Cleopatra, she was still his wife. (Her journey indeed demonstrates that *Italians* at least could not yet think of Antony as married to Cleopatra: otherwise she would surely have divorced him by now.)[193] It may well be that Octavian himself had encouraged his sister in the mission, as some suspected;[194] it was certainly deeply embarrassing to Antony – and not just because of Cleopatra, who was away from Antony's company at present, tactfully at home in Alexandria.[195] The real problem was that Octavia was bringing with her 2,000 elite troops from her brother, besides money and supplies to replace those lost in Parthia, and perhaps some Italian cavalry.[196] Octavian in fact owed Antony far more than this, all the 20,000 troops that he had promised at Tarentum in return for Antony's 140 ships.[197] Those ships had been most useful in the war against Sextus, and since then Octavian had returned half of them; but that was hardly enough.[198] It would be a triumph for Octavian if Antony accepted the troops, but insulting to Octavia if he refused – and probably politically damaging as well, for Octavian was soon to show himself adept at building propaganda from his sister's maltreatment.[199] Sensibly, Antony accepted. But that was all the annoyance he was prepared to take from Octavia's presence for the moment, and he told her to stay in Athens, perhaps even to return to Rome.[200] He himself retired to Alexandria for the winter of 35/4. (It was evidently too late in the season to resume the Armenian expedition.) Cleopatra was more congenial company than Octavia; Octavian could make of that what he wished. In fact, he would make a great deal.

In early 34 Antony turned to Armenia again. First, during the winter, came diplomacy: he sent Dellius to ask the Armenian Artavasdes for the king's daughter, pretending he wished to marry her to his son Alexander Helios. She would of course make a splendid hostage. Artavasdes was shrewd enough to refuse. In the spring Antony appeared suddenly at

[192] So Dio XLIX.33.3, possibly conjecturing, but intelligently.

[193] Cf. above, p. 30; Plut. *Ant.* 36.5 with Pelling 1988 (B 138) *ad loc.*, 53.9–10, 54.3.

[194] Plut. *Ant.* 53.1.

[195] Despite the implications of Plut. *Ant.* 53.5–9: cf. Pelling 1988 (B 138) *ad loc.*

[196] App *BCiv.* v.138.575 – unless these 'cavalry' are the same as the 200 'elite troops', cf. Gabba 1970 (B 55) *ad loc.*

[197] See above, p. 26.

[198] Their use against Sextus: cf. App. *BCiv.* v.98.406; Dio XLIX.1.1, 5.1. Their return: App. *BCiv.* v.129.537, 139.577; Dio XLIX.14.6.

[199] His attacks on this front probably began as early as winter 35/4; cf. Plut. *Ant.* 54.1.

[200] To stay in Athens: Plut. *Ant.* 53.2. To return to Rome: Dio XLIX.33.4.

Nicopolis on the Armenian border, and sent for the Armenian king to discuss a new Parthian campaign; Artavasdes again refused. While Dellius travelled once more to ask Artavasdes to a conference, Antony himself marched quickly on Artaxata; Artavasdes was finally forced by his own nobility and soldiers to come to Antony, despite his suspicions of such curious friendliness. Antony took him captive, and quickly occupied the whole country: he left his troops there for the winter, and within a year at least sixteen legions would be there.[201] His enemies, first among them Octavian, might claim that the victory was all dishonourable, won through perfidy; his friends would retort that Artavasdes' own treachery justified it quite sufficiently.[202] At least, it was something to restore Antony's paling prestige. On coins he could celebrate a conquest at last: ARMENIA DEVICTA.[203]

Artavasdes himself was conveyed to Alexandria. The thing could be done in style: his chains were silver, or perhaps gold.[204] And the victory merited celebration. A great Dionysiac procession took place in Alexandria in late 34, as was only fitting for Antony as Dionysis-Osiris, and amply precedented in the city. Not everything went according to plan: Artavasdes and his fellow captives refused to pay obeisance to Cleopatra. But it was still a ceremony in which Antony could bask.

Unfortunately, it was also uncomfortably close to a Roman triumph, which itself had many Dionysiac associations;[205] and it was all too easy for Octavian to represent it as a sacrilegious transfer of the Roman ceremony to Egypt.[206] And that was not all. At around the same time, perhaps indeed at the same ceremony,[207] came the 'Donations of Alexandria'. In the Alexandrian Gymnasium were set up high golden thrones for himself and Cleopatra, and lower ones for their children: and he declared Cleopatra monarch (along with her son Caesarion) of Egypt, Cyprus and Koile Syria. Armenia, Media and – when conquered – Parthia were to fall to their six-year-old son Alexander Helios; Libya and Cyrene to his twin Cleopatra Selene; and Ptolemy Philadelphus, still only two, was to have Phoenicia, Syria and Cilicia. Then the children appeared themselves, Alexander with Median clothes and head-dress, Ptolemy with the distinctive Macedonian boots, cloak and cap – but

---

201 Dio XLIX.40.3; Plut. *Ant.* 56.1: cf. below, p. 48.

202 'Octavian claimed that Antony's treacherous arrest had brought great discredit on the Roman people', Dio L.1.4: cf. Tac. *Ann.* 11.3.1 with Goodyear's commentary; Vell. Pat. 11.82.3; Fadinger 1969 (B 42) 150–1. The emphasis on Artavasdes' treachery probably originates with Dellius: cf. Strab. XI.13.4–6 (524C); Dio XLIX.25.5; Plut. *Ant.* 50.3–7 with Pelling 1988 (B 138) *ad loc.*

203 *RRC* 543, of about 32 B.C.

204 Silver: Dio XLIX.39.6. Gold: Vell. Pat. 11.82.3, with Woodmann 1983 (B 203) *ad loc.* Cf. Dio XLIX.40.3.   205 Cf. Versnel 1970 (A 97), especially 20–38, 235–54, 288–9.

206 That is the emphasis of Plut. *Ant.* 50.6–7; cf. Vell. Pat.11.82.4 with Woodmann 1983 (B 203) *ad loc.*; Grant 1974 (C 101) 161–2; Reinhold 1988 (B 150) on Dio XLIX.40.3–4; Wallmann 1989 (C 243) 288–91.   207 As Dio XLIX.40–1 implies.

Alexander had a regal tiara too, and Ptolemy a diadem.[208] It was all show. The gestures made no difference to the administration of the East.[209] But it was a show with style, and it doubtless went down very well in Alexandria.

It was still an extraordinary thing to do, and Octavian clearly relished it. Just as in 36 when he flaunted his liaison with Cleopatra, Antony surely underestimated the dangers of such behaviour before the Roman public: and once again we see a substantial political error centring on Cleopatra – perhaps indeed inspired by her persuasion. At that time, Antony was still concerned about Italian opinion. He responded to Octavian's constitutional talk by writing grandly himself to the Senate about restoring the Republic.[210] But the antics in Alexandria belied the republican pretence. The gestures may have meant little, but if they meant anything they meant a dynastic succession: Antony was indeed a second Hercules, but in fathering a new race of monarchs, and fathering them from a foreign woman. He would even issue coins with his head on one side and Cleopatra's on the other. It was unthinkable, a foreign woman on a Roman coin![211] True, his Roman children were not forgotten either: at around this time he was issuing coins with his head and that of his eldest son Antyllus, his principal heir in Roman law.[212] But there too the suggestions were all too close to a dynasty; and that was not the Roman way.

Still, one should not overstate the damage. Octavian certainly fastened on this, and Antony's friends in Rome were certainly discomfited:[213] that is enough to demonstrate its unwisdom. But still in early 32, when he sought ratification in Rome for his *acta*, the Antonian consuls Sosius and Ahenobarbus believed they could hush up the affair of the Donations, some fifteen months earlier:[214] hardly credible, if they had been as public and spectacular as our sources Plutarch and Dio suggest.

Other propaganda mattered more. Of course, Antony and Octavian had been exchanging public abuse for years, with particular ferocity during the early stages in 44–43 and the Perusine War of 40.[215] But

---

[208] Plut. *Ant.* 54.8, with Pelling 1988 (B 138) *ad loc.*

[209] Pelling 1988 (B 138) 249–50, on Plut. *Ant.* 54.4–9 (*contra*, Wallmann 1989 (C 243) 291–6). Even the association of Caesarion in the monarchy was not new: that dates back to 37–36 (Samuel 1971 (C 206)).

[210] Dio XLIX.41.6, cf. Suet. *Aug.* 28.1. This offer may have been included in the dispatch to the Senate which arrived in early 32 (see below, p. 49); so e.g. Fadinger 1969 (B 42) 119–28, 195–206; Gray 1975 (C 102) 17–18; but Dio's language does not fix it so precisely.

[211] Especially *RRC* 543, the ARMENIA DEVICTA coin (see above, p. 40), but also some more minor local issues: cf. Buttrey 1953 (B 314) 54–86 (esp. 84), 95; Wallmann 1989 (C 243) 251–2, 255.

[212] *RRC* 541: cf. Wallmann 1989 (C 243) 251–2.   [213] Dio XLIX.41.4.   [214] Dio *ibid.*

[215] Scott 1933 (C 212) collects the material; for subtler treatment, with illuminating modern parallels, cf. Kennedy 1984 (C 134), Watson 1987 (B 192) and especially Wallmann 1989 (C 243). On artistic questions Zanker 1987 (F 632) is outstanding.

during the last few years Octavian had rather been directing his fire at Sextus – the champion of the slaves and pirates, or so Octavian could pretend.[216] With Sextus' fall, the propaganda battle with Antony recommenced, and they were soon exchanging public letters and manifestos. Part of it was simply the competition to outbid one another in constitutionalist protestation; but much was more personal. That of course followed the traditions of Roman invective, but it also suited the times. To be successful, propaganda needs to find a willing public, with prejudices it can subtly mirror and exploit. Now it was easy to see civil war and fraternal bloodshed as the index of the collapse of the old virtues. The public was ripe for believing what it was told about Antony's morality, and for thinking that it mattered. By winter 35/4 Octavian was probably making capital out of his sister's treatment: surely she was entitled to a divorce – but she was of course too noble to seek one.[217] Then there was all the eastern degeneracy, the debauchery, the infatuation (as of course it must be) with Cleopatra. All could be painted in the most lurid colours. Horace's ninth *Epode*, written a few years later in 31, gives some of the flavour:

> Future generations will not believe it – a Roman soldier,
> bought and sold, carrying stakes and bearing arms for a woman,
> even bringing himself to serve under withered eunuchs! And amid
> the army's standards the sun glimpses a shameful mosquito net.
>
> (Hor. *Epodes* IX. 11–16)

Tales could be told of Antony anointing Cleopatra's feet in public, or reading love-letters as he delivered judgments – even springing from his tribunal to hang on to Cleopatra's litter as she passed![218] Antony's entourage too came in for picturesque attack: stories were told of a banquet where Plancus danced, naked and painted, as a sea-god.[219] And Cleopatra herself: she evidently wished to rule in Rome – why, her favourite form of oath was 'so may I give my judgments on the Capitol'! But Rome might then be nothing: were they not scheming to move the capital to Alexandria?[220]

[216] Cf. above, p. 20; Wallmann 1989 (c 243) 163–77, 185–220. Even after Sextus fell, this public front was maintained: cf. *RG* 25.1, 'mare pacavi a praedonibus', and 27.3, 'bello servili'; and in late 36 Octavian made a great show of restoring his 'slaves' to their owners for punishment (*RG* 25.1; App. *BCiv.* v.130.544–5 with Gabba 1970 (b 55) *ad loc.*; Dio XLIX.12.4–5).

[217] Plut. *Ant.* 54.1, 57.4, with Pelling 1988 (b 138) *ad loc.* In 35 sacrosanctity was extended to include Livia and Octavia (Dio XLIX.38.1 with Reinhold 1988 (b 150) *ad loc.*; cf. Endnote 2): that was doubtless a related ploy. Octavian's women should have a solemnity to offset the awesome but shameless Cleopatra.

[218] Plut. *Ant.* 58.9–11, the stories of Octavian's friend Calvisius Sabinus: Plutarch did not believe them, 59.1.   [219] Vell. Pat. II.83.2.

[220] Dio L.4.1–2, 5, 26.5; Vell. Pat. II.82.4; Livy, *Per.* 132; cf. Prop. III.11.31–50, esp. 46; Hor. *Carm.* 1.37.5–12; Ov. *Met.* xv.826–8; Scott 1933 (c.212) 43–4; Fadinger 1969 (b 42) 115–18, 163. Augustus himself included such material in his *Autobiography*, published in the twenties: cf. fr. 16M.

Antony of course responded. Octavian's battle-record was frivolous and cowardly; now his treatment of Lepidus was outrageous. What had happened to Antony's share of Sicily? Or to the troops he was owed? Now Octavian had found land for all his own troops, what would be left for Antony's? And Octavian's behaviour was pretty outlandish too: he had had his affairs with consular wives, indeed his friends were carefully inspecting unclothed matrons and virgins to pick for his pleasure; and had people not heard of that strange banquet of the twelve gods, when Octavian had taken the role of Apollo?[221] It was not just Antony who dealt in foreign marriages, either; Octavian had offered his daughter Iulia to Cotiso, king of the Getae – indeed, promised to take Cotiso's own daughter in return.[222] (One wonders what Livia might have said to that.) Octavian was much too fond of gaming, too.[223] But many of Antony's lines, far too many, had to be defensive. He wrote a work *de sua ebrietate*, *On his own drunkenness*, for instance[224] – presumably less entertaining than it sounds, not a tippler's memoir but an earnest insistence that he was less drunken than Octavian alleged. But the attacks on Cleopatra were clearly the most damaging. In a public letter of 33 he remonstrated with Octavian:

What has changed your view towards me? Because I'm screwing the queen? Is she my wife? [Of course not!][225] And I've been doing it for nine years anyway. And what about you? Is Livia the only woman you screw? I bet, when you read this, you'll just have been inside some Tertulla or Terentilla or Rufilla or Salvia Titisenia – or all of them. Does it matter where and in whom you have your erections?   (Suet. *Aug.* 69)

The tone as well as the content has its point. This is the broad, coarse language of the soldier, the thoroughly masculine Roman. A man like this would not waste his time with effeminate mosquito nets.

There was another medium, too, that of visual art: and here Antony found it even more difficult to hold his own. Particularly striking was the treatment of the gods. Antony might have his Dionysus, and a few years earlier he had been emphasizing Hercules. Both could seem all too appropriate to an Italian audience. That Dionysiac blend of excess, drunkenness and eastern menace was hardly reassuring. And Hercules, it was recalled, had fallen unmanned before Omphale: a suggestive model for Antony, indeed, and one that duly recurs in contemporary art. Octavian countered with more comfortable gods, especially Apollo with

---

[221] Battle-record: Suet. *Aug.* 10.4, 16.2; cf. Charlesworth 1933 (c 60) 174–5. Lepidus, Sicily and settlements: Plut. *Ant.* 55; cf. Dio L.1.3–4, 20.2–3. Apolline banquet: Suet. *Aug.* 69.1, 63.2, 70; cf. Charlesworth 1933 (c 60); Wallmann 1989 (c 243) esp. 268–74.   [222] Suet. *Aug.* 69.2.

[223] Suet. *Aug.* 71.   [224] Pliny, *HN* xiv.148; cf. Scott 1929 (c 211); Geiger 1980 (c 96).

[225] This punctuation and interpretation is clearly right: cf. Kraft 1967 (c 140) and Carter 1982 (B 24) *ad loc.*

his civilized order, discipline, calm and restraint. Here too Octavian found a willing audience: Apolline themes, portrayed with delicate restraint, swiftly become favourites in private dwellings, sometimes in rooms which would not be open to any public gaze: that must reflect genuine Italian taste, a spontaneous welcoming of the new moral climate. But it was not just Apollo. On beautifully minted coins, Venus, Jupiter, Hermes and Victoria were all shown in association with Octavian. If the gods were taking sides, no one could doubt which divine entourage was the weightier.[226] And here Antony could do little to reply: religion worked differently in the East, and he could hardly be more than Dionysus incarnate. A plurality of gods would simply blur the picture, and no wonder that even Hercules was dropping from view.

So propaganda flourished. At whom was it all aimed? Really, at everyone, or at least everyone in Italy. We might expect the veteran colonies to be most important: after all, the veterans had refused to fight one another in 40,[227] and the recent mutiny had shown that Octavian's control of them was insecure. Doubtless they did matter, and Antony's coarse language would strike a particular chord with them; but perhaps they mattered less than we naturally assume. For one surprising omission from the catalogue of propaganda themes is the memory of Iulius Caesar himself. Was Antony or Octavian his true heir? In 44–43 that theme had been vital.[228] Now there was certainly a little of this: Antony for instance made something of Caesarion – Caesar's *true* son, as he claimed in a letter to the Senate (not merely adopted, like Octavian);[229] while Octavian toyed publicly with the idea of invading Britain again, and – very slowly – was building a temple to Divus Iulius in the Forum Romanum.[230] Still, this is surprisingly little. To judge from the propaganda now, Caesar was out of date; just as there had been no particular concern to portray the war with Sextus as a rehash of the old civil war, with a young Caesar and a young Pompey reliving their fathers' destinies. Yet surely, in the colonies themselves, Caesar's name was no irrelevance, and his veterans would not have been impervious to the battle-cry. Soldiers would surely be less moved by all this talk of oriental excess: Caesar too had had his women; soldiers, and their captains, were simply like that. Those themes had more appeal for the propertied classes of the Italian towns, where traditional morality was strong. These,

---

[226] Hercules and Omphale: the Arretine cup in the Metropolitan Museum, New York (*CVA* Metr. Mus. IV B F Pl. 24): Zanker 1987 (F 632) 65–7. Cf. Prop. III.11.16–20; Plut. *Ant.* 90(3).4.Coins: Zanker 1987 (F 632) 61–5; cf. Wallmann 1989 (C 243) 273–4 and (on Apollo) Mannsperger 1973 (C 171).   [227] See above, p. 17. Cf. Wallmann 1989 (C 243) 151–2, 159–61, 219–20, 339–43.

[228] Cf. *CAH* IX² 471–8.   [229] Suet. *Iul.* 52.2; cf. Dio XLIX.41.2, L.1.5.

[230] Britain: Dio XLIX.38.2 with Reinhold 1988 (B 150) *ad loc.*; Virg. *G.* 1.30, III.25; Hor. *Epod.* VII.7. The temple was not finished till 29 B.C., though celebrated on coins as early as 36 (*RRC* 540; cf. Weinstock 1971 (F 235) 399–400; Zanker 1987 (F 632) 44).

probably, were the people whom Augustus was to eye a few years later with his moral legislation,[231] and a constituency to which he was always alert. Even the Senate, the rich, the cultured would not be unmoved by the themes; we might expect them to be more sophisticated – after all, they turned out too sophisticated to stomach the moral reforms – and it is true that many of the most republican and traditional stayed loyal to Antony;[232] but even the most urbane find propaganda hard to escape, if it is repeated often and insistently enough, and if it appeals sufficiently sharply to their pre-existent assumptions and prejudices. More senators eventually took Octavian's part than Antony's.[233]

Octavian anyway knew better than to bludgeon the cultured too crudely. 'Propaganda' is too crass a word to apply to the literary production of his followers. Horace, for instance, was hardly disloyal. When he was writing an *Epode*, the tone would be appropriately Archilochean and abusive. But he was also writing his *Satires*, where Lucilius had set the generic pattern of personal attack and derision; yet, very self-consciously, Horace turned away from the tradition, dwelling instead on the delicate portrayal of his life and his values, especially the value of friendship. Remarkably, Antony and Cleopatra escape attack; Horace's personalia are different, warmer and more intimate. If Octavian is in the background, the suggestions are gentle ones: these are his friends, and this is how they live. A few years earlier Virgil too had complimented Octavian in the first *Eclogue* – 'deus nobis haec otia fecit' (1.6), and there can be little doubt that the god is Octavian. Coming so early in the first poem, that is almost an informal dedication of the whole collection. But the tone is anything but bluntly propagandist. The final emphasis of the first *Eclogue* rests more on the emptiness faced by the dispossessed Meliboeus; and the whole book explores the different registers of tragedy one found in the Italian countryside, an idyllic land now wracked by a devastation for which, if one thought about it, Octavian himself took much of the blame. In the late thirties Virgil was at work on the *Georgics*, and there too he wrote warmly of Octavian. But once again the tone is often sombre, dwelling on the vast work that was needed to restore the beauty that had been marred and lost.[234] As in the first *Eclogue*, Octavian can certainly offer hope: 'hunc saltem everso iuvenem succurrere saeclo|ne prohibete' (*G.* 1.500–1). But still not all of these are the emphases Octavian would have favoured himself. Guided doubtless by Maecenas, he was already seeing the value of a patronage which was notably loose and free, and the poets responded with writing

---

[231] See below, ch. 18 pp. 883–93.   [232] See below, pp. 49–50.   [233] See below, p. 53.

[234] That is a suggestion even of the proem to the third *Georgic*, where Virgil promises Octavian a poetic temple in the manner of Pindar. The 'temple' will be in Mantua. After *G.* ii.198–9, and indeed *Ecl.* ix.27–9 (see above, p. 14), Mantua's suggestions are tragic; its idyllic description at *G.* ii.12–15 must now seem bland, with the tragedy artificially muted.

which meshed with his propagandist themes without always crudely echoing them. He already knew better than to confuse independence with subversion: knowledge which he was to retain for many years to come.

And, all this while, what was Octavian doing himself? He was in Illyricum, winning some glory for himself with cheap foreign blood. There had been campaigns there a few years earlier: in 39 Pollio had been involved with the Parthini in the south, and possibly with the Delmatae as well,[235] at the same time an army of Octavian had apparently been active somewhere in the country.[236] But little had been achieved, and there was still plenty for Octavian to do. And, of course, Illyricum bordered Antony's dominion. It was not very likely that it would be strategically valuable if it came to war; at least, not unless Illyricum could be fully conquered, and that would hardly be practicable in the time. A civil war would probably be fought in Greece, and Greece would still be reached most readily by the sea-crossing from Italy. But, when war came, at least Octavian's troops would not have far to go. He could reasonably hope to make inroads into Antony's territory before Antony himself could return.

The campaigns themselves are described elsewhere in this volume.[237] By summer 33 Octavian was back in Rome, sporting the eagles which Gabinius had lost in 48 and the defeated Delmatae had now returned.[238] The achievements were modest but real, and Illyricum had certainly served its purpose: Octavian had secured his excuse for keeping his soldiers in arms, the men had been battle-hardened, and Octavian himself looked far more soldierly at the end than at the beginning. Why, he had even contrived to be wounded, though not always very satisfactorily: at Setovia, for instance, he was struck by a stone on the knee. And he might seem something of a disciplinarian as well. On one occasion he had gone so far as to order a decimation of his own troops.[239] During his brief winter stays at Rome Octavian could inveigh against Antony, and contrast his own energy with Antony's sloth.[240] Now

---

[235] This is disputed, and is connected with the difficult question of Pollio's own political position during those years. For different views cf. Syme 1937 (D 67); Bosworth 1972 (C 34); and Woodman 1983 (B 203) on Vell. Pat. II.78.2.

[236] App. *BCiv.* v.80.338; Vell. Pat. II.78.2; it is possible, but not perhaps very likely, that Octavian's army and Pollio's were one and the same (cf. Bosworth 1972 (C 34) 466–7; Woodman 1983 (B 203) on Vell. Pat. II.78.2). App. *BCiv.* v.75.320 records an expedition sent by Antony against the Parthini in late 39; that campaign, *pace* Bosworth 1972 (C 34) 466, is much more likely to be identical with Pollio's.   [237] See below, pp. 172–3, 549–50.

[238] App. *Ill.* 28.82; *RG* 29.1. On the date of Octavian's return cf. Schmitthenner 1958 (C 304) 215–16.

[239] Decimation was in fact rather in fashion: instances had been ordered by Caesar in 49 (Dio XLI.35.5, if that can be trusted), Domitius Calvinus in 39 (Dio XLVIII.42.2), and Antony in 36 (Plut. *Ant.* 39.9, Dio XLIX.27.1). But in each of those cases the punishment was rather more clearly deserved than on this occasion.   [240] Cf. Plut. *Ant.* 55.1, App. *Ill.* 16.46.

people might actually believe him. And in Rome itself celebration could be marked in other ways. It might be by triumphs. Admittedly, in 34 the Antonian Sosius celebrated his triumph over Judaea, possibly the most brilliant of them all – and celebrated it on, of all days, 3 September, the anniversary of Naulochus, when men's thoughts should have been with Octavian. For this to be allowed, Antony must still have had his influential friends. But at least Octavian's men could outdo Antony in *numbers* of triumphs: in 36 Domitius Calvinus over Spain, in 34 Statilius Taurus over Africa and Norbanus Flaccus over Spain, in 33 Marcius Philippus and Claudius Pulcher over Spain and L. Cornificius over Africa.[241] And in the Roman way triumph led to buildings *ex manubiis*, from the spoils of conquest. In the late thirties Domitius Calvinus was rebuilding the Regia, while in the Campus Martius Statilius Taurus was building a stone amphitheatre and Marcius Philippus restoring a temple of Hercules Musarum; on the Aventine Cornificius was rebuilding the temple of Diana. And it was not just the triumphators: Paullus Aemilius, apparently Octavian's partisan, completed and dedicated his Basilica in 34. Antony's followers responded. Domitius Ahenobarbus too built a temple of Neptune; Sosius planned a splendid temple to Apollo in the Circus, vainly hoping to impugn Octavian's exclusive claim on the god; but on their own they could hardly compete with Octavian's men. And though Octavian himself made a point of delaying his acceptance of an Illyrian triumph (he eventually celebrated it in 29), he certainly joined in the craze for construction: in 33 he rebuilt the Porticus Octavia, and put Gabinius' eagles on display there; in 32 he restored Pompey's theatre; work was also proceeding on the temples of Divus Iulius, Palatine Apollo and Jupiter Feretrius; and particular energy was spent on the Mausoleum, the material guarantee of Octavian's own eternal glory.[242] All of this would visibly attest the restoration of Rome's glory; nearly all pointed to Octavian. He was already turning Rome from brick to marble.

Sewerage mattered too; that fell to trusty Agrippa. He organized an extensive scheme of cleaning and repair; indeed, during these years he carried out a massive overhaul of the whole water supply.[243] In 34, it seems, he restored one aqueduct, the Aqua Marcia, then in 33 the Aqua Iulia; he also repaired others, the Aqua Appia and the Anio Vetus; and reservoirs and ornamental fountains were built all over the city. As aedile in 33 – an odd but significant appointment for so distinguished a man – Agrippa fostered the people in other ways, with spectacular games, free distributions of salt and olive oil, free admission to the baths, and a scattering of vouchers in the theatre for clothing, money and other

[241] *IItal* XIII 1 342–3, 569–60.
[242] On all this cf. below, pp. 785–9, and Shipley 1931 (F 571), Zanker 1987 (F 632), 73–80.
[243] For the details, Roddaz 1984 (C 200) 148–52.

things.[244] A more dignified step was Agrippa's revival of the *lusus Troiae*,[245] later to be celebrated in the *Aeneid* (v. 545–603). Octavian had been alert for some time to the possibilities of a tasteful antiquarianism. As early as 43 he had been hinting at a link with Romulus,[246] and in 38 there had been some ritual at the *casa Romuli* on the Palatine:[247] nor, probably, was it coincidence that he chose to live so close to the *casa Romuli* himself.[248] His traditionalism was gathering style. To emphasize the point, astrologers and magicians were expelled from the city.[249] They were altogether too unroman.

And Antony? His thoughts were still far away. In 33 he planned a second Parthian campaign, this time with his new ally Artavasdes of Media: they were now more closely linked, with Alexander Helios betrothed to the king's daughter Iotape. Iotape had indeed been safely transported to Alexandria – an additional stimulus to loyalty, perhaps. In the spring of 33 Antony and Artavasdes met on the Araxes. All, or almost all, of Antony's eastern army was already in Armenia, a full sixteen legions.[250] In 36, the need to concentrate his troops had delayed the invasion till uncomfortably late in the year; now, he was in a much better position for an early attack. But such thoughts were already out of date, and finally even Antony came to realize it. The defence of the eastern frontier was left to the Median king and to Polemo, to whom he now gave Lesser Armenia.[251] Antony's own troops began the 2,500-km march back to the Ionian coast. At last, he had 'turned to the civil war'.[252]

X. PREPARATION: 32 B.C.

Almost certainly, the second term of the triumvirate expired on 31 December 33.[253] This time there would evidently be no question of renewing it, even as the duovirate it had now become. This would not leave the legal position of Antony and Octavian unsupportable,[254] but it was certainly embarrassing, and more embarrassing for Octavian than for Antony. Octavian had lately been making so much of his respect for Roman tradition and the Roman republican constitution; and Octavian would be in Italy, where legal questions could awaken more interest. In the East Antony simply ruled – as god, monarch, proconsul, or triumvir, it hardly mattered. In Italy , it might. And Octavian's position was delicate in other ways, for if the triumvirate had expired the consuls might matter more; and the consuls of 32 were to be C. Sosius and Cn.

[244] Dio XLIX.42–3 with Reinhold 1988 (B 150) *ad loc.*; cf. Roddaz 1984 (C 200) 145–57.
[245] Dio XLIX.43.3.   [246] Suet. *Aug.* 95.   [247] Dio XLVIII.43.4.
[248] Suet. *Aug.* 72, with Carter 1982 (B 24) *ad loc.* He acquired the house in 42/1.
[249] Dio XLIX.43.5.   [250] Plut. *Ant.* 56.1; cf. Dio XLIX.40.2, see above, p. 40; Brunt 1971 (A 9) 504.   [251] Dio XLIX.44.2.   [252] Plut. *Ant.* 53.12.   [253] See Endnote, p. 67.   [254] See above, pp. 26–7.

Domitius Ahenobarbus – not merely Antonians but peculiarly impressive ones, particularly Domitius with his record of republican political commitment and all the weight of an ancient family. Nor was he the only old republican to prefer Antony to Octavian. So did Cato's grandson, L. Calpurnius Bibulus, and there were others too.[255] Not that the issue would be decided simply by the credentials of one's Roman followers. It would depend on martial strength: and Antony's army and Antony himself were infinitely more formidable a force than anything Octavian had yet confronted. In retrospect, we too readily think of Octavian as already marked out for victory. History may have been on his side, but many of the crucial factors were not. Since 37 Octavian had certainly done much to redress the odds, which till then had heavily favoured Antony: Octavian's politics had been much the shrewder, his campaigns the more triumphant; his supporters increasingly included persons of family and achievement.[256] But to a measured observer those odds were still on Antony.

The pleasantries soon started. The consuls were armed with a dispatch from Antony, recounting his *acta* and asking for ratification – something he did not legally need,[257] but knew it was tactful to seek; it may also have included some further offer to lay down the triumvirate.[258] True, in January little was heard of all this; the experienced Domitius held the *fasces*, and thought some of the *acta* better suppressed. But on 1 February[259] Sosius took over the *fasces* and launched a public attack on Octavian. Most interestingly, his motion of censure was vetoed by a tribune: the institutions of the Republic might seem alive once more. If that suggests that the motion would otherwise have passed, it is eloquent testimony for the degree of senatorial sympathy Antony still enjoyed. But the inference is precarious. The motion was an extreme step; if Sosius had doubted whether it would pass, a prearranged veto would have been a shrewd device.

For the moment, Octavian himself was sensibly absent from the city. But a few weeks later he responded with a show of force in the Senate: he was surrounded by an armed guard, and, whatever his legal status, he took his seat on a chair of state between the consuls. Rome was accustomed to violent displays, but this was not the sort of tradition that Octavian wished to be seen reviving; still, it was immediately effective, for the consuls fled to Antony. Many senators, possibly several

[255] Syme 1939 (A 93) 222, 239, 266–70, 282; Syme 1986 (A 95) 206–7, 264.
[256] Syme 1939 (A 93) 234–42.
[257] All the triumviral acts had already been ratified in advance: cf. above, p. 20 with n.80.
[258] Cf. p. 41 and n. 210.
[259] Cf. Gray 1975 (C 102) 17; Reinhold 1988 (B 150) on Dio L.2.3. For the alternative view, that Sosius launched an attack on 1 January, cf. Fadinger 1969 (B 42) 195 n.1.

hundred,[260] accompanied them. Antony organized them into a 'counter-senate', reflecting his claim that the constitution was on his side. In the presence of the consuls, driven out by arrant force, the claim was not ridiculous. But their flight left Italy an open field for the completion of Octavian's propaganda, and his final transformation of a selfish war into a national crusade. It was a travesty, of course. The consuls might after all have been more useful in Rome itself, providing a visible reminder that there was more to Antony's side than eastern effeminacy.

They found Antony in Ephesus,[261] organizing the transport of his troops to Greece. It was a massive task. His army was eventually more than 100,000 strong, at least as large as for the Parthian campaign.[262] He had clearly been recruiting in the East, presumably both native orientals and resident Italians.[263] His fleet numbered 800, nearly 300 of them transports;[264] but that was surely not enough to carry the whole army, and they must have crossed the Aegean in several waves. Shortly Antony and his staff moved to Samos. As usual on campaign, there was time to kill: Cleopatra and Antony characteristically did so in style. The festivities became famous.[265] They also, of course, afforded a further diet for Octavian to feed his public.

Antony also faced a more serious choice. It still seemed likely that the campaign would start before the end of 32. Should Cleopatra stay for it, or should she return to Egypt? Domitius Ahenobarbus and others urged Antony to send her away, Canidius Crassus said she should remain – so the story went, and probably it was more than a story, for Domitius had just been in Rome and knew what Octavian was making of Cleopatra there. Other experienced politicians, including Plancus, clearly took the same view. Equally Canidius, soon to command the land-army, would naturally stress the importance of Cleopatra's military aid – at least 200 ships (presumably including crews), and vast financial support as well.[266] It was not at all an easy choice, for there was also the question of the troops' and allies' morale. Just as Octavian encouraged Italians to see the war as a crusade against the East, so many easterners surely saw it as a

[260] Syme 1939 (A 93) 278 and others state that there were more than 300: this is because RG 25.3 claims 'more than 700 senators' serving under Octavian's colours in the Actium war, and the Senate's total strength was more than 1,000. The inference is most precarious.

[261] Plut. Ant. 56.1–3; cf. ZPE 14 (1974) 257–8, an inscription honouring Domitius as patron of Ephesus and Samos.

[262] Plut. Ant. 61 with Pelling 1988 (B 138) ad loc.; Brunt 1971 (A 9) 503–7. Most of those troops would have joined Antony by the spring of 32.

[263] Brunt 1971 (A 9) 507, Levick 1967 (E 851) 58–60. Already in 38 some cohorts included 'many recruits from Syria', Joseph. AJ XIV.449, BJ 1.324.   [264] Plut. Ant. 56.2, cf. 61.5.

[265] Plut. Ant. 56.6–57.1: doubtless elaborated, but some of the detail (e.g. the gift of Priene to the 'Artists of Dionysus') seems too circumstantial for sheer fiction. It was perhaps now that Antony also granted privileges to 'the worldwide association of victors at the festival games' (above, p. 11 and n. 31).   [266] Plut. Ant. 56.2.

chance to avenge themselves on Rome.[267] Such men would fight for their queen, not for a Roman general. Cleopatra had to stay.

By early summer the slow western journey had reached Athens.[268] The time was coming for decisiveness, and Antony sent a note of divorce to Octavia. Perhaps he had little choice. When war came, it was inconceivable that Octavia could remain his wife, demurely tending the house and family of a public enemy (for such he would very likely be declared). Octavian had, it seems, been publicly urging his sister to divorce her lecherous and unfaithful husband for some time;[269] Octavia would hardly continue to refuse. At Athens the prospect was already the subject for public jokes.[270] One could already foresee the grave and sorrowful speech where Octavia announced her decision – a moving and elegant culmination for her brother's propaganda. Far better for Antony to initiate the matter himself; far better to get it over with now.

Octavia had to be dismissed, Cleopatra had to stay. Both steps made sense; but both were hard decisions, which fuelled Octavian's attacks and alienated valuable Italian support. In earlier days, with Pompey and with Brutus and Cassius, the better cause had managed to draw on eastern support without losing its solid Roman respectability. This was different. Even to Antony's most valued captains, Octavian's derision might seem to have a core of truth. The womenfolk symbolized something deeper. Antony *did* look more like a champion of the East, an uncomfortable figurehead. Opinions might differ on what to do about it. The most influential figure was Domitius, by now it seems leader of a sort of 'Roman party'.[271] He confined himself to public rudeness to Cleopatra:[272] that was harmless enough. Others were more decisive. Plancus was Antony's most senior consular;[273] Titius, Plancus' nephew and the slayer of Sextus, was consul designate.[274] It was about now[275] that both fled to Octavian, who was doubtless delighted: with every Roman who transferred allegiance, especially men as distinguished as

---

[267] Cf. Tarn 1932 (C 233) 135–43, suggesting that *Sib. Or.* III.350–61 dates to this period. That oracle looks forward with joy to Rome's humiliation and Asia's triumph, and might seem to be casting back much of Octavian's propaganda in his face. But sadly, the dating is insecure, cf. Nikiprowetzky 1970 (B 131), esp. 144–50, 201–2.

[268] Eus. *Chron.* II.140 dates Antony's divorce of Octavia to May – June 32; Plut. *Ant.* 57 says that the divorce note was sent from Athens, probably rightly.   [269] See above, p. 42.

[270] Someone scrawled under a statue of Antony, ''Οκταουία καί 'Αθηνᾶ 'Αντωνίῳ: res tuas tibi habe' (the normal formula of divorce), Sen. *Suas.* 1.6. Cf. above, p. 23, for talk of a divine marriage of Antony and Athena.

[271] Suet. *Ner.* 3.2.   [272] Vell. Pat. II.84.2.   [273] Syme 1939 (A 93) 267.

[274] *ILS* 891 (Miletus). He was eventually cos. suff. in 31, but he owed that to Octavian; he may originally have been designated for a different year.

[275] Samos honoured Titius as a benefactor, so he was probably still with Antony then: cf. *IGRR* IV 1716, *MDAI (A)* 75 (1960) 149d. Dio L.3.2 seems to put their defection after the divorce, though that may be only his conjecture; Plut. *Ant.* 58.4 connects it with the issue whether Cleopatra should remain.

this, the lines of East and West became more plain. Still, Plancus and Titius as yet had no followers, or none of which we hear. Antony's men might be troubled, but most stayed firm.

Plancus derided Antony in the Senate; not everyone was impressed,[276] and a more sensational ploy was needed. The two renegades suggested that Antony's will, which rested with the Vestal Virgins, might repay study. It was illegal, as it happened, to open the will of a living man; no matter – Octavian opened it, alone and unsupervised.[277] Its provisions were extraordinary: when Antony died he was to be buried in Alexandria; Caesarion was recognized as Caesar's son (though it is hard to say why this quite fitted in Antony's will); vast gifts were to be made to the children borne by Cleopatra to Antony. It was all exactly what Octavian might have wished for. Why, he might almost have written it himself. Perhaps indeed he did, at least in part:[278] the Vestals would not know the will's contents, and Octavian could claim what he wished. And he was skilful enough to allege provisions which Antony, eager to retain his eastern support, would find as uncomfortable to deny as to admit.

Even Antony's preparations, worryingly massive as they were, could be turned to account. Perhaps by early August, his force was on the west coast of Greece.[279] Was he intending to invade Italy, the natural climax of such treachery to Rome?[280] That was desperately unlikely, in fact. Octavian firmly held Tarentum and Brundisium, the two great harbours of southern Italy, and it would be no easy matter for Antony to transport large quantities of troops in several waves and land them on hostile beaches.[281] Roman civil wars were always fought in Greece, for precisely this reason: it was natural for one side to flee to exploit the resources of the East, but then virtually impossible to force a passage back to a defended Italy.

Still, the Italian public were not strategists. They feared what they were told to fear. Evidently they needed a champion, and it could only be Octavian; but his status was still uncertain. He was no longer calling himself triumvir (Antony, incidentally, had no such compunctions);[282] though it would be hard to doubt that Octavian retained his vast provincial *imperium*, he wanted something more, something which would clearly justify him as the defender of Rome and its traditions, and

---

[276] Cf. the cutting remark of one Coponius, Vell. Pat.II.83.3.

[277] Just as, alone and unsupervised in a temple, he found equally convenient material a few years later: the truth (so he claimed) about the consular status of old Cornelius Cossus. Cf. Livy IV.20.5–11 with Ogilvie 1965 (B 135) *ad loc.* and below, ch. 2 p. 80.

[278] Cf. e.g. Syme 1939 (A 93) 282 n.1; Crook 1957 (C 68) 36–8; *contra*, Johnson 1978 (C 128); Wallmann 1989 (C 243) 310–13.   [279] Kromayer 1898 (C 143) 57.

[280] Cf. Livy, *Per.* 132; Dio L.9.2; Vell. Pat. II.82.4; Plut. *Ant.* 58.1–3 with Pelling 1988 (B 138) *ad loc.*

[281] Cf. Plut. *Ant.* 62.3; Hermocrates at Thuc. VI.34.5. The strategic position is set out masterfully by Kromayer 1898 (C 143) 57–67.   [282] *MRR* II 417–18, cf. *RRC* 545–6.

render this the most moral of civil wars. The propertied classes of Italy came to his rescue. For much of summer 32 he was organizing an oath to follow his personal leadership:[283] it was to be taken throughout Italy, and indeed all the western provinces (that probably meant little more than the Roman citizens in each).

Of its own free will, all Italy swore allegiance to me, and demanded me as its general for the war I won at Actium; the Gallic and Spanish provinces, Africa, Sicily and Sardinia took the same oath.   (*Res Gestae* 25.2)

The oath did nothing to improve Octavian's legal status, but its moral implications were extraordinary. It was taken to him personally. There were a few civilian precedents,[284] but the nearest analogies were in fact military, the oath taken by soldiers to their general: and it was appropriate that Italy and the provinces were 'demanding Octavian as their general' for the war. Besides the backing it gave Octavian, this was also one way of preparing Italy psychologically for conflict. There were doubtless others too – for instance, the *Res Gestae* passage goes on to speak of more than 700 senators 'serving under Octavian's colours',[285] and such language probably goes back to the events themselves. Of course, there had been appeals to *consensus Italiae*, the united sentiment of all Italy, many times before.[286] Now, as usual, the public's feelings were doubtless more complex. For one thing, Italy was growling at Octavian's new financial exactions, severe even by the standards of the last twenty years.[287] And it would be naive to think that the oath was wholly voluntary. Some communities were indeed 'excused' from taking it, for instance Antony's own veteran colonies.[288] Still, the claim of harmony was not mere hypocrisy. A great many senators, for instance, seem to have come over to Octavian during these final stages;[289] and it seems likely that only a few of Antony's colonists exploited Octavian's dispensation.[290] In 40 the veterans had refused to fight one another, but this time it would be different. At last, Italy was almost solid for Octavian.

[283] Cf. esp. von Premerstein 1937 (A 74) and, briefly, Brunt and Moore 1967 (B 215) on *RG* 25.2; Syme 1939 (A 93) 284–92; Herrmann 1968 (C 117) 78–89; Linderski 1984 (C 164); Girardet 1990 (C 97) 345–50. The evidence for the oath's dating is set out by von Premerstein 1937 (A 74) 41; Syme 1939 (A 93) 284–5 suggests, probably rightly, that the Italian cities took the oath not simultaneously but in sequence.

[284] Von Premerstein 1937 (A 74) 27–36; for important qualifications, Herrmann 1968 (C 117) 50–89.

[285] *RG* 25.3, cf. n.260 above. The phrase is often taken to imply that all the senators accompanied Octavian on his campaign: that need not follow.   [286] Syme 1939 (A 93) 285–6.

[287] Plut. *Ant.* 58.2; Dio L.10.4–5, 16.3, 20.3, LIII.2.3; Pliny, *HN* XXXVII.10; cf. Syme 1939 (A 93) 284; Nicolet 1976 (D 104) 95; Yavetz 1969 (A 110) 25–6.

[288] Especially Bononia, Suet. *Aug.* 17.2; but it seems that even here Octavian made attempts to win them over (Dio L.6.3).

[289] Cf. Wallmann 1976 (C 242).   [290] Dio L.6.3, cf. LI.4.6 with Keppie 1983 (E 65) 76.

The time for action was approaching, though the summer was wearing on, and it did not now look as if the decision would be reached this year. That was in Octavian's interests, in fact: Antony had his vast army ready, backed by all the wealth of the East; Octavian's treasury was worryingly empty.[291] But Octavian's political preparations, at least, were almost complete, and in late summer he could declare war. That too should be done in the right style. War was declared on Cleopatra alone: she after all was the real enemy. And it was declared in the most Roman of fashions: Octavian disinterred, perhaps even fabricated, an ancient fetial rite – a picturesque affair of casting a spear into a symbolically hostile patch of land.[292] Not of course that Antony was ignored: he was stripped of the consulship he was to hold the next year, and also of 'the rest of his power'[293] – presumably the triumvirate which he was still claiming and, on one possible view, he still held. But he was not yet declared a public enemy. The moment for that would soon come.[294] For Antony would surely stand by Cleopatra: and then, would he not be a self-confessed enemy of Rome?

XI. ACTIUM, 31 B.C.

During winter 32/1 Antony's force stood ready in Greece. His main fleet was in the harbour of Actium; but Greece's western coast is pitted by natural harbours, and it was best to defend them all. Pockets of ships were distributed fairly widely – in Methone, for instance, Leucas, Corcyra, Taenarum and probably Corinth.[295] Antony himself wintered in Patrae, with yet another contingent of ships and men. The next summer would clearly see the critical campaign, and he could still be sanguine. True, Italy was lost, and lost more conclusively than he would have hoped; that was disappointing. But he could reasonably reflect that, once Octavian had survived the buffeting of the Perusine War, he would always have the advantage there. In Italy Octavian was the man in possession: far less adept politicians would have been able to capitalize on that. Anyway, the politics were virtually over. Antony might still go through the motions of offering to resign the triumvirate, after he had won his victory (as he now had to specify): two months later, or possibly six.[296] It all hardly mattered now.

---

[291] Cf. p. 53 and n. 287.

[292] Dio L.4.4–5 with Reinhold 1988 (B 150); cf. Livy, 1.32.4 with Ogilvie 1965 (B 135) *ad loc.*; Rich 1976 (A 81) 56–7, 105–6; Wiedemann 1986 (F 237).

[293] τὴν ἄλλην ἐξουσίαν πᾶσαν, Dio L.4.3 with Reinhold 1988 (B 150) *ad loc.*; cf. Plut. *Ant.* 60.1.

[294] Antony certainly was declared a *hostis* at some point (App. *BCiv.* IV.45.193, cf. IV.38.161; Suet. *Aug.* 17.2): probably later in 32 or in early 31 rather than after Actium, as Fadinger 1969 (B 42) 245–52 argues.

[295] Cf. Dio L.11–13; Oros. VI.19.6–7; Strab. VIII.4.1–4 (359C); Vell. Pat. II.84.1, Plut. *Ant.* 67.5; Kromayer 1898 (C 143) 60.   [296] Dio L.7.1–2.

In military terms Antony still looked ahead. He had been unable to recruit in Italy, but not all orientals were weaklings, and his forces were probably the larger, possibly 100,000 infantry against Octavian's 80,000. The cavalry was equally matched, but Antony's fleet of 500 men-of-war was more numerous than Octavian's and – almost as important – his were the larger ships.[297] The way naval battles were now fought, bulk was likely to count; certainly, it had counted at Naulochus. Antony's side was also the wealthier. Octavian's exactions had doubtless done something to replenish his treasury, but he could still hardly compete: for one thing, he had already had to give his troops a precautionary donative.[298] Last of all, there was Antony himself, still surely more effective a general than Octavian despite those Illyrian victories. Antony knew how little those meant. True, he must have heard impressive things of Agrippa, who was still virtually untried when last Antony was in the West; he might prove a worthier adversary. But, everything considered, Antony still looked to be the winner.

It was clear what his strategy should be. Invading Italy was not an option, for sound military reasons.[299] Antony would have to wait for Octavian to come to him, just as Pompey had waited in 49–48; and, again like Pompey, he would hope to harass Octavian's fleet during the crossing, when the ships would be terribly cumbersome, with cavalry, legionaries and baggage on board. Even if they could land, they might find it hard to support themselves if Antony could maintain his expected superiority at sea. The lesson of 48 was again there to be learnt, when Caesar had certainly found it very difficult to establish himself with sufficient numbers of troops.[300] It might still be disconcerting that Pompey had finally lost, and then in the next civil war the eastern side had lost again; but Antony could still reflect that Pompey should really have won at Dyrrhachium, while Brutus and Cassius had fought their battle too far east.[301] The eastern side should strategically be the stronger. Sulla was the more telling precedent.

Once again, it all went wrong.[302] The danger in Antony's position was simply the necessity to divide his army and fleet among so many harbours. These various forces could reasonably be expected to reinforce one another if threatened; besides, the main force at Actium could be expected to harry any invasion fleet as it sailed down the Adriatic, if any target further south were chosen for its landing. But Agrippa was

---

[297] Plut. *Ant.* 61 with Pelling 1988 (B 138) *ad loc.*; Brunt 1971 (A 9) 501–7. Legend doubtless exaggerated the superior size of Antony's ships (perhaps as early as Hor. *Epod.* 1.1–2), cf. e.g. Prop. III.11.44, IV.6.47–50; Plut. *Ant.* 62.2; Vell. Pat. II.84.1 with Woodman 1983 (B 203) *ad loc.*: Octavian's were the massive galleys which had defeated Sextus in 36. But Antony's doubtless were bigger still.   [298] Dio L.7.3.   [299] See above, p. 52.

[300] Caes. *BCiv.* 3.7–8, 14, 23–6; cf. *CAH* IX² 432.   [301] *CAH* IX² 432; see above, pp. 6–7.

[302] For the early stages of the Actium campaign cf. esp. Kromayer 1899 (C 144) 4–28.

too quick. Surprisingly early in the 31 season, he struck with an advance force and took Methone, then launched surprise attacks elsewhere on the coast, even as far north as Corcyra. Meanwhile Octavian himself managed to cross, surprisingly unimpeded, to the mainland north of Corcyra; within a few days he had reached Actium, and occupied the tactical strongpoint in the area, the hill of Mikalitzi. Soon Octavian had linked his camp by earthworks to the harbour of Gomaros. We do not even hear of any resistance, which is astounding. Perhaps there were operations which our sources omit, perhaps the Actium land-force had been called away to meet one of Agrippa's sudden threats elsewhere. Anyway, the first tricks had fallen to Octavian, and they turned out to be decisive.

Antony soon arrived himself from Patrae, and pitched camp near Punta on the southern coast of the bay. Octavian naturally tried to bring him to battle before he could concentrate the rest of his fleet or army; Antony naturally declined. When his troops arrived from their various stations, Antony established a new camp on the northern side of the straits, near Preveza. Only the plain of Nicopolis now separated the two armies, but it was Octavian who refused a land-battle. Antony tried strenuously to cut Octavian off from the river Louros in his rear, vital to his water supply, and there was clearly a series of cavalry battles in the northern plain: the most substantial was won by Statilius Taurus and the renegade Titius, by now one of Octavian's commanders. Then, once again, a contribution of Agrippa was crucial. His fleet took the island of Leucas, just south west of the mouth of the harbour; this afforded Octavian a safer anchorage than Gomaros, and made it difficult for Antony's other scattered ships to reinforce him. A little later Agrippa also took Patrae, where there were still ships, and Corinth. Antony was now under virtual blockade.

The analogy with 48 must again have been felt. This was Dyrrhachium over again, but the roles were strangely reversed: it was now the eastern force under Antony which, like Caesar then, was cut off on the coast by a stronger army and fleet. Antony naturally thought of breaking out to the interior of Greece: that was what Caesar had done, and had gone on to win at Pharsalus. Octavian had already sent his own men into Greece and Macedonia, while Antony sent Dellius and Amyntas into Macedonia and Thrace[303] – to seek mercenaries, according to our source Dio, but probably their brief was a wider one. Soon Antony himself set out to overtake them. While he was away Sosius tried to break out at sea, but was beaten by Agrippa. On his return Antony lost another cavalry battle. By now it looked very bleak. Allied kings had been killed – Bogud of Mauretania at Methone, Tarcondimotus[304] with Sosius. Others were

---

[303] Dio L.13.4.   [304] See above, p. 29.

defecting. Deiotarus Philadelphus of Paphlagonia had gone to Octavian some time since, and at some point he was joined by Rhoemetalces of Thrace;[305] now the much more valuable Amyntas went too. That was cheering to Horace,[306] and doubtless to Octavian too. Antony's position was becoming desperate. Provisions were failing: disease was rife — particularly, perhaps, malaria and dysentery, worsened by the shortage of supplies and water. Antony had no option but to withdraw all his troops to the southern bank, but that is even more waterless than the north, and the deaths went on.

Romans too were defecting. The most dispiriting was that of Domitius Ahenobarbus, already mortally ill. Dellius too, notorious for picking the right moment to change sides, realized that it was now: with him he took Antony's battle-plans. Not that they were hard to divine. The break-out to the interior was a serious option, and it seems to have been urged by the land-commander Canidius Crassus. But it would have meant abandoning the fleet; and even if the army could break out to Thessaly, even if Octavian obliged by offering battle there rather than relying on attrition, Antony's army was so wasted by disease that it would barely be able to fight. Realistically, the battle had to be fought at sea. Later romantic fiction would represent this as a crazed decision, influenced by Cleopatra:[307] but that is absurd. Antony had already done all he could on land; only now, in late summer, did he decide that a naval battle was the only option left.[308]

At the outset of the campaign Antony's fleet had outnumbered Octavian's, but Agrippa had destroyed some of his squadrons, while others had been unable to force their way through to join the Actium fleet. And there was a manning problem as well, for death and desertion had reduced Antony's numbers considerably. By now he had no hope at all of matching Octavian's numbers: otherwise, indeed, he would have forced on the sea-battle earlier. He eventually put to sea with perhaps 200 or 250 ships, while Octavian had 400 or more.[309] Antony simply burnt the remainder of his ships: better that than to allow them to fall into Octavian's hands.

Antony's chances of victory were evidently very poor. The most he could realistically hope for was to break out with as many ships and men as possible, and this seems to have been in his mind from the beginning:

---

[305] [Plut.] *Mor.* 207A.

[306] 'At huc frementes uerterunt bis mille equos|Galli canentes Caesarem' (*Epod.* IX.17–18). That *Epode* seems to be a dramatic recreation of the moods of a spectator of the campaign: cf. Nisbet 1984 (B 132) 10–16.   [307] Plut. *Ant.* 62.1, 63.8, 64.

[308] The outstanding modern discussions of the battle are by Kromayer 1899 (C 144); Tarn 1931 (C 232); and Carter 1970 (C 51). For further discussion and argument for the views presented here, cf. Pelling 1986 (C 186) and 1988 (B 138) 272–89, esp. 278–9.

[309] Kromayer 1899 (C 144) 30–2; Brunt 1971 (A 9) 508: Pelling 1988 (B 138) 268, 276, 287–8.

he shipped his treasure-chest, for instance, an extraordinary thing to do unless he was planning flight; he also gave orders to carry sails, which was most unusual for an ancient battle. He could keep his mind a little open, perhaps: he knew he could not break out without a fight, sea-battles were often unpredictable, and if things went surprisingly well then of course he would try to fight it out to the end. The weather might even be rough – it had been for the last few days before the battle – and that might add some further unpredictability: his galleons might better survive a buffeting than Octavian's slightly lighter ships. Still, the chance of a break-out in force was always the more likely option. He may not have told too many of his own troops: it would of course be highly damaging to morale, for most of them would have to be left to the victor's mercy. One need not doubt their surprise and dismay when, in mid-battle, they realized the truth.[310] But his own mind must have been clear enough. He must also have known that the break-out was not going to be easy. Outflanking Octavian's superior numbers would be impossible, and the only way was to drive a wedge through the centre. Even if that could be done, a flight southwards involved a technical difficulty. The island of Leucas juts out just south of Actium, and with prevailing winds from the west and north west it would be hard to clear it under sail.[311] The best hope was to join the battle as far out to sea as he could (Octavian would in fact be unlikely to resist this, for he too would want open waters to exploit his superior numbers and manoeuvrability); and if possible to delay it till the afternoon, when the wind typically veers from west to west-north-west.

That indeed is exactly what happened. On the morning of 2 September 31, Antony's fleet took up its station outside the harbour mouth. Cleopatra's squadron of sixty ships rested behind his centre, ready (it seems) for a concentrated strike on any weak point in Octavian's line – a sort of maritime Panzer-tactic, in fact. Octavian's much longer line moved to hem them in. Then, most eerily, for hours nothing happened. Antony was waiting for afternoon; Octavian would be content to wait much longer, for it was Antony, not he, who needed to break the blockade by battle. Around midday there was at last some movement of both fleets to seaward; but still, no real action. The first decisive move came in early afternoon, for both northern wings – Antony's right and Octavian's left under Agrippa – began to drift further north. It is not clear who started it. Perhaps it was Agrippa, as our principal source Plutarch suggests: now that both fleets were in more open sea, he could reasonably begin an outflanking move. More likely it was Antony, trying to entice Octavian into leaving a critical gap in the centre of his line. Anyway, gaps began to open, at least in Antony's line and perhaps

<hr />

[310] Memorably described by Plut. *Ant.* 66.6–8.   [311] Carter 1970 (C 51) 215–27.

in Octavian's too. Cleopatra's squadron seized the moment: she hoisted sail and bore down on the enemy. It is hard to say which side was the more startled. The squadron forced its way through, perhaps surprisingly easily;[312] Antony himself moved from his massive flagship to a quinquereme and followed. So did others, but perhaps not very many. It is hard to think that even a hundred ships escaped; these had some legionaries on board, perhaps one hundred apiece – but the bulk of the fleet, and over three-quarters of the army, remained.

Once Antony and Cleopatra had sailed away, the rest of their fleet saw little point in the battle. Some galleons made their way back to the harbour in a peculiarly undignified way, backing water in a halting crab-like movement to port.[313] There was perhaps a little fighting, but nothing very fierce. The whole battle produced only 5,000 casualties, an amazingly small number by the standards of a sea-battle. Octavian did his best to make it a little more spectacular: a few ships were fired;[314] and he took the ostentatious precaution of spending the night on board ship.

But it was hard to disguise the truth. The Battle of Actium was a very lame affair. Such as it was, Antony and Cleopatra arguably won it: at least, they achieved all they could reasonably have hoped. But they had so decisively lost the campaign that the success made little difference. There was some talk of the surviving army saving itself on land, and some forlornly set out for Macedonia;[315] but it was all highly unrealistic. They soon went over to Octavian, who gave generous terms.[316] The Battle of Actium delayed the end for a year; nothing more.

XII. ALEXANDRIA, 30 B.C.

Antony had concentrated almost, but not quite, all of his legions for the Actium campaign. The exception was a force of four legions under L. Pinarius Scarpus in Cyrene, left probably to protect Egypt from political disorder, for like most of the Ptolemies Cleopatra had many internal enemies. Anyway, they were now Antony's only hope, and the remains of his fleet crossed not to Alexandria but to Paraetonium, the nearest port to Pinarius' force. But, all too predictably, the hope proved ill founded: Pinarius swiftly declared for Octavian; and the dispirited Antony returned to Alexandria. Cleopatra had already been there for

[312] Or so Plut. *Ant.* 66.5–6 suggests: that is not necessarily reliable (cf. Pelling 1988 (B 138) on *Ant.* 65–6), but the low casualty figures do suggest that there was no fierce fighting.

[313] Hor. *Epod.* IX.19–20, 'hostiliumque navium portu latent|puppes sinistrorsum citae', a striking epigram. These were probably the remains of Antony's right, whose northern movement would have left them uncomfortably far from the harbour mouth. Cf. Pelling 1986 (C 186).

[314] Augustan poets made the most of this. It was the best they could do. Cf. Hor. *Carm.* 1.37.13, 'vix una sospes navis ab ignibus ...'; and Virg. *Aen.* VIII.694–5; then Dio L.34, whose battle-description is as usual wholly unreliable. [315] Dio LI.1.4; cf. Plut. *Ant.* 67.8.

[316] Plut. *Ant.* 68.2–5, with Pelling 1988 (B 138) *ad loc.*; Keppie 1983 (E 65) 79–80.

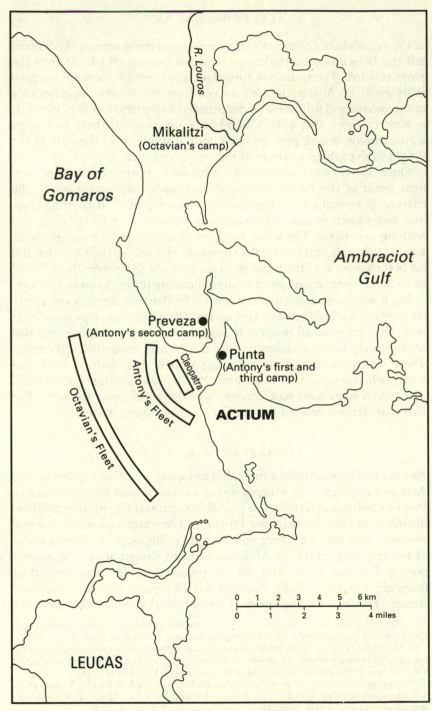

Fig. 1. Actium: fleet positions at the beginning of the battle

some time, acting decisively. Many of the suspected nobles were murdered, and Artavasdes too was hauled from his captivity and executed. She also plundered extensively to gather money for the armies: hopelessly enough, for by now no money was likely to retain their loyalty.

Depressing news continued to arrive throughout the winter. The intelligent princes Antony had encouraged in Asia Minor were alert enough to know they should change sides. Amyntas had already gone at Actium, and Herod of Judaea shortly followed his example.[317] So did lesser men, for instance the sons of Tarcondimotus of Cilicia;[318] we do not hear when Archelaus and Polemo declared for Octavian, but that too was probably soon during the winter.[319] Octavian himself had spent some time in Samos and Ephesus after the end of the Actium campaign, and was beset by embassies, for instance from Rhosus and probably Mylasa;[320] for the cities too recognized who was their master now. By the end of 31 Octavian had effectively taken over Asia Minor, with his own man Q. Didius as governor of Syria. The loyalty Antony had always inspired still paid some slight dividends, for some gladiators were so determined to join him that they fought their way from Cyzicus through Galatia and Cilicia to Syria.[321] But that was the only good news, and that was not much.

At the end of the year Octavian returned briefly to Italy, where there was a little trouble. Doubtless the financial discontent had not disappeared, though there were now some remissions; but a more immediate problem was presented by a large body of veterans, both his own and those who had come over to him after the battle. They had been sent back to Brundisium, and, just as their comrades had after Naulochus,[322] they were insisting on their dispensability: for everyone knew that the war was virtually concluded. They wanted immediate demobilization, and that meant land. The obvious way to find it was to expropriate Antony's Italian partisans, yet it seems that there were precious few of those.[323] Agrippa had been sent back to Italy soon after Actium, apparently because problems were already looming. Maecenas was already there.[324] Octavian himself could afford only a month in Italy, and

[317] Herod secured formal pardon from Octavian in Rhodes in spring, 30; but he had already given help to Q. Didius in resisting the Antonian gladiators. [318] Dio L.7.4; cf. above, pp. 29, 56.

[319] Soon after Actium Archelaus was explicitly excused from any reprisals, along with Amyntas (Dio LI.2.1). That suggests that he had gone over at once. Polemo, away on the eastern frontier, would take longer to hear of Actium, but nothing suggests that he delayed for long.

[320] RDGE 58.III (= EJ² 301) and perhaps 60 (= EJ² 303); cf. Millar 1973 (C 175) 58. Perhaps Samos too: Reynolds 1982 (B 270) doc. 13, with Badian 1984 (B 208) 168–9.

[321] There they reluctantly made terms with Didius. Most soon met their deaths.

[322] See above, p. 37.   [323] See above, p. 53.

[324] It is just possible that Maecenas himself was at Actium, as Eleg. ad Maec. 45–8 implies: so Wistrand 1958 (B 200) 16–19. If so, he returned very soon afterwards. But Dio LI.3.5 seems clearly to suggest that Maecenas had been left in charge at Rome during the campaign, and that is more likely to be right; so Syme 1939 (A 93) 292; cf. Woodman 1983 (B 203) on Vell. Pat. II.88.2.

proceeded no further than Brundisium: large numbers of senators and
knights, and many of the city plebs, poured forth from Rome to meet
him. He was also met, somewhat less obsequiously, by the veterans. He
made a show of asserting discipline, but in fact largely capitulated: those
'who had served him throughout' – probably that means those who had
fought on his side at Actium – were to get land, the others (probably the
Antonians) only money. Even this meant settling perhaps 40,000 or
more.[325] Where was the land to come from? Italy was quaking. The risk
was all too clear that the trauma of the Perusine War would return. There
was only one alternative, to buy the land rather than seize it, and that was
what Octavian chose. Of course he did not have the money; but the
treasure of Egypt beckoned, and the soldiers and the sellers of land had
to be content with promises. There continued to be rumblings during
Octavian's absence, including a mysterious 'conspiracy' led by young M.
Lepidus, the former triumvir's son.[326] But Italy would have to wait.
Quite evidently, the final defeat of Antony and Cleopatra had to come
first. Egypt's spoils were needed now.

It took a long time for Octavian's forces to reach Alexandria. With
Syria safe, he might perhaps have shipped them to the Phoenician ports;
but that too would take time, for they would need to travel in several
waves, and Octavian preferred to march them overland from the Ionian
coast. It was July before they approached Egypt. By then Antony and
Octavian had been exchanging embassies for some time.[327] Octavian
offered nothing, though it does seem that he was more encouraging to
Cleopatra. For one thing, he was worried that she might destroy her
treasure, which Octavian needed so vitally: she was already making a
great show of piling it together and packing it round with inflammable
flax and tow. There was even some talk of allowing her children
(presumably the younger ones, not the embarrassing Caesarion) to retain
the throne, provided always that she surrendered Antony or killed him.
All that was not unthinkable. Alexandria had seen mysterious deaths
before; Rome had appointed many a surprising client king. Cleopatra
herself may well have taken the proposals seriously, more seriously than
Antony would have wished: certainly, Octavian's messengers seem to
have been able to reach her and talk to her privately – very odd, unless
she was giving them some encouragement. But such an outcome was
never very likely, and it may be that Octavian never intended more than
to sow mutual suspicions, or restrain Cleopatra from premature hopeless
suicide. By July it was clear that it would be fought out to the end.

[325] Dio LI.4.2–8 with Reinhold 1988 (B 150) ad loc.; Keppie 1983 (E 65) 73–82, especially 85.
[326] Vell. Pat. II.88, cf. Livy, Per. 133; Dio LIV.15.4; Suet. Aug. 19.1: probably in 30 rather than 31
(as App. BCiv. IV.50.217 clearly implies), even though inierat at Vell. Pat. II.88.1 cannot give the
precise dating that Woodman claims. Cf. Wistrand 1958 (B 200).
[327] Plut. Ant. 72–3 with Pelling 1988 (B 138) ad loc.; Dio LI.6–8.

Octavian planned a simple pincer movement. Cornelius Gallus had taken over and reinforced Pinarius' legions, and he would attack from the west while Octavian's own troops completed their long journey from the east. Oddly, Antony himself moved to the western front (and was pretty ineffective there); yet the east was clearly the more important front. Octavian's difficult desert march to Pelusium turned out to be wholly unopposed, and Pelusium itself fell quickly, perhaps by treachery. Soon Octavian's army appeared before Alexandria itself. On 31 July there was a cavalry battle, which went quite well for Antony; but the storming of the city itself was clearly imminent.

During the night of 31 July came a most curious event, or so the story was later told – a mysterious sound of divine music, a strange procession as Dionysus himself abandoned the city.[328] What really happened is not beyond conjecture. There was an ancient Roman custom, the *evocatio* of the gods of an enemy city before a battle: the Roman general would call them out and invite them to take up a new friendly Roman home. The rite was probably enacted before the fall of Carthage in 146;[329] it was also used in the routine capture of a Cilician town, Isaura Vetus, in 75 B.C.[330] Octavian was always sensitive to the use he could make of antique custom. The fall of Alexandria would be the greatest conquest of an enemy city since Carthage itself, and Cleopatra was the greatest threat to Rome since Hannibal. Octavian was the man who had solemnly recalled the old fetial formula for declaring war; he would hardly neglect an opportunity like this, and *evocatio* is exactly what we should expect. Antony had played Dionysus-Osiris for long enough. Now he was indeed to be deserted by his god.

On 1 August Octavian attacked, and Alexandria fell. First came a naval fiasco in the harbour: Antony's whole fleet deserted to Octavian. Then came an infantry exchange, which Octavian once again won decisively. Antony returned to the palace, and he died. Plutarch and after him Shakespeare tell the story magnificently – the false news that Cleopatra is dead, the slow removal of the armour, the slave who kills himself rather than strike his lord, the bungled death-blow, the wretched writhing as Cleopatra and her maids haul him into the mausoleum. At least we can believe that in the tumult Antony heard confused reports, and he may well have falsely believed that Cleopatra had taken her own life: it was the natural thing to do. But in fact Octavian's men took her captive first, and she lived on for nine more days.[331]

Octavian himself entered Alexandria without resistance, and in a careful speech announced his forgiveness of the city. But his mercy had

[328] Plut. *Ant.* 75.
[329] Macrob. *Sat.* III.9.6; Serv. *ad Aen.* XII.841; doubted by Rawson 1973 (F 203).
[330] Hall 1972 (B 240); Le Gall 1976 (D 210).
[331] For the date of her death (probably 10 August) cf. Skeat 1953 (C 219) 98–100.

its bounds. He took the treasure, of course. Caesarion was hunted down and killed; so was Antyllus, Antony's eldest son; there were other victims too, including Cassius Parmensis, the last of Iulius Caesar's assassins, and Canidius Crassus, the general of the Actium campaign. But many were spared, including Cleopatra's other children – at least for the present.[332] They were being kept for the triumph, and the taunts of the Roman crowd. And so, it seems, was Cleopatra herself: but here Octavian's plan went astray.

The story of her death is still more extraordinary than Antony's, and very hard to estimate. The ancient sources, especially Plutarch and Dio,[333] had no doubt that Octavian was trying to prevent her suicide, and used threats to her children to ensure that she stayed alive. This was, of course, to make certain that she would be displayed humiliatingly at his triumph in Rome; and, for the ancient sources, it was when Cleopatra realized the horror of this fate that she finally determined to kill herself. She bathed herself, and dressed in her finest regal attire – a strange version of the bathing and dressing that were important parts of a real funeral. Then she clasped the asp to her arm; she took her seat on the regal throne, flanked by the devoted maids Iras and Charmion who chose to join their mistress in death. The guards burst in to find them there in their tableau of death; Cleopatra had won her final marvellous victory. And it was the most appropriate of deaths, for the double cobra was an old Ptolemaic symbol, the *uraeus*: on a Ptolemaic head-dress the cobras would rear up, as if to strike any enemy of the throne.[334] Now Cleopatra's very life had become hostile to her. It was right for the royal cobra to strike.

The version goes back very close to the events themselves. In outline it had taken shape by the time Horace wrote his Cleopatra *Ode* a few years later.[335] But modern scholars are sceptical.[336] They point to the advantages to Octavian of having her dead: even as it was, trouble continued in Egypt for some months,[337] and it would have been more perilous if Cleopatra had remained a potential figurehead. Would it not be better for Octavian to remove her? If actual murder was too crude, then at least he

---

[332] Cleopatra Selene survived to marry Juba of Mauretania; Alexander Helios walked in the triumph of 29, but is not heard of after that and was probably murdered. Ptolemy Philadelphus is not mentioned at the triumph, and probably died even sooner.

[333] The same tradition is reflected by Flor. II.21.9–10 and Oros. VI.19.18. It probably owes its currency to Livy, who had a taste for such final scenes (cf. his Sophoniba, XXX.12–15) and certainly dwelt on the importance to Cleopatra of the triumph (fr. 54, οὐ θριαμβεύσομαι).

[334] Cf. esp. Griffiths 1961 (C 105), Nisbet and Hubbard 1970 (B 133) on Hor. *Carm.* 1.37.

[335] 1.37.

[336] Cf. esp. Nisbet and Hubbard 1970 (B 133) on Hor *Carm.* 1.37. It is often stated confidently that Octavian ordered or connived in her suicide; cf. e.g. Grant 1974 (C 101) 224–7; Huzar 1978 (C 122) 227; Syme 1939 (A 93) 298–9 is only a little more cautious.

[337] Dio LI.17.4 with Reinhold 1988 (B 150) *ad loc.*; Strab. XVII.1.52–3 (819C).

could leave poison, or indeed cobras, pointedly available – a glamorous equivalent of the revolver on the officer's table. Yet such a view raises more difficulties than it solves. It leaves it unclear why Octavian should have allowed her to live on for those nine days; we are even told that he foiled two earlier suicide attempts.[338] Octavian must have known his mind well before the city was taken. In the turmoil of the first day Cleopatra could readily have died, and it would have been easy to portray it as suicide, doubtless by a barbaric method. Octavian would have spoken regretfully of the mercy he would have shown: that sort of scene was to become commonplace in the early Principate. But the implications of the story we have are very different, and much less flattering to Octavian. No one could escape the inference that he was trying to keep her alive against her will, but was outwitted. Octavian was usually a more accomplished propagandist than this. It is surely better to assume that, if he kept her alive at all, he genuinely did want her for the triumph, just as his supporters wished.[339] Some of the details may well be fictional[340] – perhaps the famous story of the basket of figs, for instance. But, at least in outline, her splendid, serene, triumphant death is probably history, not legend.

XIII. RETROSPECT

Why did Antony and Cleopatra lose? Of course one can point to their political errors, and Octavian's greater shrewdness. There was Antony's insensitivity to the western crisis, which misled him into keeping his legions on the eastern frontier for too long; there was the indelicacy with which he flaunted his liaison with Cleopatra; there were the Donations of Alexandria – pure spectacle, but once again so damaging before an Italian audience. On the other side, there was Octavian's adept manipulation of Italian public opinion, exploiting propaganda with greater power and insight than had ever been done before. It is so easy to isolate these facts that we naturally assume they were decisive. They certainly made a difference: how big a difference, one may doubt. It remains true that, with Antony so confined to the East, Italy would have favoured Octavian overwhelmingly in any case; it remains true that, once all the politics had been played out, at the beginning of the 31 campaign Antony still looked as if he would win. The East was as solid for him as the West for Octavian, and the military factors were on his side. Octavian

---

[338] Plut. *Ant.* 79.3–4, 82.4–5.

[339] Cf. esp. Prop iv.6.63–6. If it were too dangerous to let her live longer than the triumph, she could of course be removed then: a tawdry execution would not be necessary, but an accident might happen a little later, or a wasting disease. These things could be managed.

[340] Though some may not: cf. Pelling 1988 (B 138), 318–23.

certainly outwitted Antony in their political exchanges; but it was not this that finally brought the victory.

Perhaps it is easier to isolate the decisive moments. One is obvious, the autumn of 36, when Antony was failing in Parthia and Octavian was crushing Sextus: a suggestive contrast for the Italian public to ponder, and also a startling one – victory could not have been expected to dwell with the weak unmilitary Octavian rather than Antony, the greatest captain of the world. But there are at least two more turning-points. One, rather inconspicuously, was the death of Calenus in 40. It was that which robbed Antony of Gaul, and turned him so firmly eastwards; and, in the longer term, that gave Octavian not merely Gaul but also the whole West. And Calenus' death was just an accident, just Antony's bad luck. The second was the first stage of the Actium campaign itself, with Octavian's swift unimpeded crossing and, more important, Agrippa's series of debilitating thrusts on Antony's scattered forces. It was then that, within a few weeks, Antony started to look the loser rather than the winner; thereafter, the fighting simply ran its course. The true history of those few weeks remains hard to grasp. *Why* was Antony so dilatory in his resistance? *Why* was Octavian able to take over the decisive land station at Actium so easily? We shall never know; perhaps once again luck played a great part. But those few weeks decided the future of the Mediterranean world.

Octavian's greater political shrewdness should suggest a different reflection. Antony and Cleopatra might well have won the Actium campaign. If they had, the task of settling the world would in some ways have been easier for them. Their marriage – for marriage, unequivocally, it would then have been – would provide a most attractive register to describe and suggest a new harmony of West and East. That would be particularly true in any culture which thought of its royalty as gods: this would be a divine marriage, a most certain guarantee of the world's prosperity. But such cultures were the cultures of the East: Antony and Cleopatra would be both gods and monarchs, and the fate of Iulius Caesar made clear how sensitive such topics were in Rome. Antony had shown his statesmanship in other ways, especially in his penetrating judgment of the individuals he raised to power in the East, and in the style and range of his settlement. But his failure to appease Italian sentiment would surely have turned out to be a decisive flaw. The union of the Greco-Roman world was always a precarious thing, and it is hard to think that it could have survived the continuing dominion of Cleopatra and Antony. Looking a generation ahead, one could see what might happen: two worlds, not one, with Antyllus (perhaps) succeeding to some sort of control in the West, and Caesarion a more traditional monarch in the East. Or rather, that was the best that could be hoped for;

a further debilitating series of revolts and civil wars, once again fought out in Italy and Greece, was just as likely. And no one could see what would emerge at the end.

Enthusiasm for Octavian comes less naturally to us now than fifty years ago. 'Because he stood for something more than mere ambition he could draw a nation to him in the coming struggle'[341] – one would not write that now. We admire the political shrewdness which forwarded ambition so well, but we admire it grudgingly: we have seen too many similar leaders since, and what they have meant for the world. Now the story is once again told, not as Octavian's triumph, but as the tragedy of Antony and Cleopatra. But, still, they could not have coped with success, and Octavian could: his mastery of Italian propaganda may not have won him the war, but it did much to win the ensuing peace. For Rome, the right man won.

ENDNOTE: CONSTITUTIONAL QUESTIONS

1. THE TERMINAL DATE OF THE TRIUMVIRATE

This is notoriously disputed. For thorough discussion of the evidence and bibliography, reaching opposite conclusions, cf. esp. Fadinger 1969 (B 42) 98–133, Gabba 1970 (B 55) lxviii–lxxix.

The Lex Titia of 27 November 43 established the triumvirate for five years: its terminal date was 31 December 38 and the term was more precisely five years and a little over a month. It was renewed for a further term, but not until the conference of Tarentum in 37 (above, p. 27). The disputed question is the terminal date fixed at the time of this renewal, whether 31 December 33 or 31 December 32.

At *RG* 7.1 Augustus claims to have held the triumvir *per continuos annos decem/* συνεχέσιν ἔτεσιν δέκα (cf. Suet. *Aug.* 27.1): i.e. clearly, from 27 November 43 to 31 December 33: cf. Brunt – Moore *ad loc*. I agree with those who regard this as decisive. Thus the Fasti Capitolini, inscribed under Augustus, include the triumvirs before the consuls in their entry for 1 January 37 (rather than 36): the second five-year term had retrospectively been fixed as beginning then. App. *Ill.* 28. 80 shows that Appian regarded the triumvirate as due to end at the end of 32 rather than 33: δύο γὰρ ἔλειπεν ἔτη τῇ δευτέρᾳ πενταετίᾳ τῆσδε τῆς ἀρχῆς [of 1 January 33], but that seems to be his own misinterpretation: even though in *Ill.* Appian is in general drawing on Augustus' *Autobiography*, it would not be surprising if Augustus was delicately vague in that work about his status in 32, and it would be in Appian's manner to fill out the gap with his own explanation. *BCiv.* v.95.398, ἐπεὶ δὲ ὁ χρόνος ἔληγε τῆς ἀρχῆς ... [of Tarentum], perhaps implies that Appian wrongly thought that the triumvirs still held office in 37, when in fact this had *already* expired (cf. Dio XLVIII.54.6): in that case he would naturally assume that the five-year renewal would last from 36 to the end of 32. As Antony and Octavian were due to assume the consulship on 1 January 31, it was tempting to infer that the triumvirate was due to expire on the previous day, and that perhaps misled Appian. But such extensions usually went in five-year terms, and at Tarentum the triumvirs' first priority was to legalize their current position retroactively and therefore to backdate the new term to 1 January 37.

The oddity is in fact not that they renewed their term only to December 33 (that is explained sufficiently by the taste for five-year terms and the need for retrospective recognition in 37); but that at Misenum, when they completed their consular lists for the following years, they had fixed on 31 rather than 32 as the date for their own consulship. They might then already have anticipated that a second quinquennium would expire in 33 rather than 32. But that may well have been Antony's choice: he was in a strong position at both Brundisium and Misenum, and the Antonians Ahenobarbus and Sosius were due to be consuls in 32. Antony may well have been content to rely on them to support him and embarrass Octavian in a crucial year.

2. OCTAVIAN'S 'TRIBUNICIAL SACROSANCTITY'

Dio XLIX.15.5–6 clearly implies that Octavian was granted this in 36: 'they [the people] voted him ... protection from insult in word or deed (τὸ μήτε ἔργῳ μήτε λόγῳ τι ὑβρίζεσθαι): anyone who committed such an outrage was to fall liable to the same penalties as in the case of a tribune'. (On the terminology cf. Bauman 1981 (C. 20)). He also received the right to sit on the tribunician bench, *ibid.*; the following year sacrosanctity was extended to Octavia and Livia, Dio XLIX.38.1. But App. *BCiv.* v.132.548 says that in 36 'they' elected Octavian δήμαρχος ἐς ἀεί, i.e. presumably gave him *tribunicia potestas*, 'encouraging him, it seems, to replace his previous ἀρχή [the triumvirate] with this permanent one': Oros. VI.18.34 also attests a grant of full *tribunicia potestas* in 36. At LI.19.6 Dio says that Octavian was voted *tribunicia potestas* in 30; then, oddly enough, at LIII.32.5–6 he records a similar vote in 23. In fact Augustus certainly counted his *trib. pot.* from 23 (*RG* 4.4), and the easiest resolution of the evidential tangle seems to be to assume that Dio XLIX.15.5–6 is right about sacrosanctity. The misinterpretation of Appian and Orosius is then unsurprising. Dio LIII.32.5 will then correctly record the final vote to confer *trib. pot.* in 23, and LIII.32.6 makes it clear that the honour was then accepted. At LI.19.6 Dio specifies only an *offer* of *trib. pot.* in 30; at LI.20.4 he says that Octavian accepted 'all but a few' of the honours voted on that occasion – admittedly surprising phraseology, if the *trib. pot.* was among those he rejected, but perhaps not impossible (Dio elsewhere tends to present catalogues of honours voted as if they were generally accepted). So Last 1951 (C 153).

Some prefer to assume that Octavian *provisionally* accepted *trib. pot.* in 36, but only on condition that both he and Antony laid down the triumvirate; on this view the proposal lapsed when Antony refused, but Octavian managed to preserve sacrosanctity from the original offer: cf. e.g. Schmitthenner 1958 (C 304) 191 n.2, Palmer 1978 (C 184) 322–3. That is possible. Some, e.g. von Premerstein 1937 (A 74) 260–6, suggest that Octavian accepted full *trib. pot.* in 36, then renounced it at some time (probably early 27) before re-accepting it in 23; but in that case it is odd that this first *trib. pot.* is never mentioned in contemporary documents, nor its renunciation in the literary sources. Others, e.g. Kromayer 1888 (C 141) 40, Grant 1946 (B 322) 446–53, Jones 1960 (A 47) 10, 94–5, Reinhold 1988 (B 150) 229–30, prefer to assume that Octavian was allowed the tribunician *ius auxilii* in 30: this rests on Dio LI.19.6, where Dio connects the *ius auxilii* with the conferring of *trib. pot.*, a notice which that view anyway has to reject or explain in the way outlined above; and it was anyway 'not a Roman habit of thought to decompose the *potestas* itself' in this manner (Last 1951 (C 153) 101).

CHAPTER 2

POLITICAL HISTORY, 30 B.C. TO A.D. 14

J. A. CROOK

I. INTRODUCTION

With the victory of Iulius Caesar's heir there began – though it is
apparent only to historical hindsight – both a distinct phase in the history
of Europe, the 'Augustan Age', and a distinct epoch in the standard
divisions of world history, the 'Roman Empire'. That fact has always
constituted a problem for historians, from the earliest writers about
Augustus until now, in that Augustus was both an end and a beginning.
The temptation is for chronological narrative to be given up – for time,
as it were, to stop – at the beginning of the Principate (whether that be
put in 27 or 23 or 19 B.C. or in some other year), giving way to thematic
accounts of 'institutions' of the Roman Empire as initiated by its
'founder'. Augustus did, indeed, 'found' the Roman Empire; but the
danger of succumbing to the thematic temptation is that it makes the
institutions he initiated look too much the product of deliberation and
the drawing-board, whereas they need to be seen as arising, incomplete
and tentative, out of the vicissitudes of a continuing political story. That
story will be told in the present chapter.[1]

The sources of evidence for the reign of Augustus, subsequent to the
'triumviral' period narrated in chapter 1 above, are too multifarious to be
described generally here,[2] yet in some ways they are far from satisfactory
all the same, and the Augustan beginnings of many institutions of the
Roman Empire remain hard to detect. The narratives we have are also of
such a kind as to lure people into placing too much emphasis on minor
turbulences. One or two features of the evidence need to be brought to
the reader's attention. The first is that the only full-scale ancient
chronological narrative of Augustus' reign that has come down to us is
the relevant part (Books LI–LVI) of the *Histories*, in Greek, by Cassius
Dio, a consular senator of the Severan age.[3] We are fortunate that, for a

---

[1] To be read in conjunction with the military story told in ch. 4.
[2] On the main literary sources see *CAH* x[1] 866–76. Epigraphic documents: Ehrenberg and
Jones, 2nd edn 1955 (B 227) (the paperback reprint of 1976 and 1979, containing important addenda)
(EJ[2]). Translations: *AN*. Select sources in English: Chisholm and Ferguson 1981 (A 16).
[3] Millar 1964 (B 128); Manuwald 1979 (B 121).

good deal of the period, the full narrative written by Dio survives, as opposed to the Byzantine abridgements of him with which historians of the post-Augustan period have mostly to be content; but there are a number of small gaps, due not to any sinister cause but to the mere loss of leaves from a codex, where we are reduced either to the abridgements or to nothing of Dio at all.[4] The loss thus caused to the detailed picture of the last twenty years of the reign is disproportionately great, leaving all too much room for conjecture and making inevitable some imbalance of emphasis upon the first half of the reign.

A second feature of Dio's *Histories* about which notice must be given is the peculiarity of Book LII. It consists almost entirely of an artificial debate, set in 29 B.C., between Agrippa and Maecenas, as advisers to the future Augustus, on the relative merits of a 'democratic' or a 'monarchic' state; the speech of Maecenas advocating the latter is enormously the longer.[5] The prevailing view, here accepted, is that the Maecenas-speech, at least, is a *démarche* composed by Dio in the hope of influencing the policy of government in his own age, and cannot be used as direct evidence for what was intended or was the case at the time when it is supposed to have been spoken.

The two major literary sources, apart from the *Histories* of Dio, are Suetonius' lives of Augustus and Tiberius: the *Lives* are immensely important, but they are organized thematically rather than chronologically.[6] In any case, Suetonius and Dio being non-contemporary sources, the question arises what *their* sources may have been, and how reliable. Of contemporary material there survive today Augustus' own *Res Gestae* (as well as other important inscriptions and papyri), the relevant parts of the *Roman History* of Velleius Paterculus,[7] and Strabo's *Geography*. We know that there was much more: Augustus wrote an autobiographical fragment (going down only to 25 B.C.), and there were collections of his letters and sayings; Agrippa, too, wrote memoirs, and we hear of various contemporaries and near-contemporaries who may have narrated the events of the reign – though not a word of them survives.[8] Livy continued his *History* down to 9 B.C.; but of that work we possess only the so-called *Periochae* or 'Tables of Contents', and to the important question whether Livy was the main source of the narrative of Dio for

---

[4] 6–5 B.C. excerpt only; 4–3 B.C. no Dio at all; 2 B.C. begins with excerpt, becomes full again, but ends with excerpt; 1 B.C., A.D. 1 and 3, excerpt only; A.D. 8, nothing except a scrap of excerpt at the end; A.D. 9, full Dio except for a gap after the 'Varian disaster', where there is only excerpt; summer A.D. 13 to summer A.D. 14, excerpt only.

[5] Millar 1964 (B 128) 102–18; McKechnie 1981 (B 116); Espinosa Ruiz 1982 (C 84).

[6] Wallace-Hadrill 1983 (B 190) 10–15; Gascou 1984 (B 59) 390–6.

[7] Vell. Pat. II.88–123, ed. Woodman 1983 (B 203), with commentary.

[8] E.g. Aufidius Bassus; Servilius Nonianus (on whom Syme in *Hermes* 92 (1964) 408–14 = Syme 1970 (B 178) 91–109).

the Augustan period as he had been for the previous period, the answer seems to be that he was probably not.[9] That leaves the historian of Augustus in the uncomfortable position that his main narrative source is itself dependent upon an unknown and lost source as to whose credentials no judgment can be made.

Of the inscriptions, abundant and of the first importance, though all call for careful interpretation, only one group would really baffle the reader without a word of explanation: the lists known as the Fasti and the Calendars.[10] The Fasti are chronological lists, on stone, of the annual Roman consuls or of those who celebrated triumphs, from early times, the bare lists being sometimes accompanied by brief annotations of other events. The most important surviving set, which includes both consuls and *triumphatores*, is called the Fasti Capitolini, and was inscribed on an Augustan triumphal arch at the southern end of the Forum Romanum.[11] It is crucial to realize that those Fasti are not, as we have them, age-old primary material but a learned compilation, set up entire at a single moment, not for a historical but for a propaganda purpose. Sets of consular Fasti were also erected in the municipalities, who added their local magistrates, and some corporations kept such lists: the *vicomagistri* furnish a good consular list down to A.D. 3. The Calendars were lists of festivals and other events organized under the days of the year;[12] there was no doubt an official Roman set, but the ones that, in more or less fragmentary states, have come down to us belonged to municipalities or corporations or even private persons. The most useful are the Fasti Praenestini, from the *forum* of Praeneste: they, too, were a learned construction, the work of the antiquarian Verrius Flaccus, the tutor of Augustus' grandsons, Gaius and Lucius Caesar.

The quantity of new information available today that was not in the possession of those who wrote on Augustus in the first edition of the *Cambridge Ancient History* is small, consisting of a few inscriptions and papyri – not but what some of those are of high significance. But an enormous enlargement of the historian's task in handling the evidence for the Augustan age has resulted from three conceptual developments. Scholars have come, first, to see that the physical monuments – buildings, art-objects, coins – are central and not merely corroboratory evidence: they were, to the Romans, speaking monuments, and they spoke politically.[13] Secondly, that appreciation is part of a wider enlargement of perspective, in that we are required to view symbolism

9 Manuwald 1979 (B 121).
10 Texts in EJ²; edition, Degrassi 1947 and 1963 (B 224) XIII, fascs. 1 and 2.
11 Latest arguments, Coarelli 1985 (E 19) II 263–308.
12 Ovid's *Fasti* is a versification of the calendar material for half a year.
13 Hölscher 1984 (F 424); Hannestad 1986 (F 409); Simon 1986 (F 577); Zanker 1987 (F 632).

and myth-making as an integral function of all societies, and a nation's political symbols and images as essential to the understanding of any segment of its history. Finally, there stretches a vast field, on whose battles scarcely any historian has been competent to be more than an onlooker – the works of the famous figures of Augustan literature. A present trend amongst literary specialists is to see those writings as through-and-through political, whether as propaganda for the political regime or as in more or less covert resistance against it, asserting either 'Augustan values' or those of the 'alternative society'. The historian cannot avoid the challenge to regard that material also as central rather than peripheral, though his sense of the impossibility of mastering all the evidence is thereby greatly aggravated.[14]

II. 30–17 B.C.

Actium, though it is convenient to historians as a punctuation mark (Dio says we should date the years of the new ruler's 'monarchy' from 2 September 31 B.C.),[15] and was convenient to the victor as a symbol, was not quite the end of civil war. A campaign had to be mounted for Egypt,[16] and 1 August 30 B.C., *Aegypto capta*, is the real ending date, with the deaths of Antony and Cleopatra following hard upon it.

Caesar[17] now had, at just under thirty years of age, all the power there was, but not yet – if ever – was there a 'happy ever after', for there was no necessary acquiescence. The presuppositions of republican political life did not disappear overnight, and though many had gone and many survivors leapt on to the winning bandwagon, opposition did not instantly die away. That fact has received much emphasis in recent scholarship, to the point of finding in 'opposition' the key to most of what happened down to 17 B.C.,[18] but it is best not to exaggerate: such opposition had no sufficient base of power to force Caesar to take or refrain from any action. It is, perhaps, a matter of the right language to use, for there were certainly considerations that he had to face. Victory cast into his lap, along with it, all current problems and all future policies. He held power as long as he satisfied the various elements in the body politic – the armies, mostly wanting demobilization on good terms,[19] his supporters who had made victory a reality, the plebs of Rome, too large, politicized and volatile to ignore,[20] and the surviving governing class, without whom an empire could not be maintained. And

---

[14] Literature of the age discussed in ch. 19 below. [15] Dio LI.1.2. [16] Ch. 1 above, pp. 59–65.
[17] He will always be so named in this chapter, until he becomes Augustus.
[18] Especially Sattler 1960 (D 63) and Schmitthenner 1962 (C 305).
[19] A major politico-agrarian problem; see Brunt 1971 (A 9) 332–42.
[20] N. Purcell, *CAH* IX[2], ch. 17.

there were pre-existing structures to which, for the very sake of power, he must relate himself, and which could not be wished away, such as career expectations and *clientelae*.

A career reward for an important supporter may be the banal explanation of the first momentous decision taken after Cleopatra's death, with which our tale begins. Egypt was a new responsibility. The question was, how that land should be governed; the answer, that it should be a province of the Roman empire, but with an *eques*, not a senator, as its governor. The choice may, at the time, have been obvious: simply, the member of the victorious junta who had successfully handled the Egyptian campaign and who deserved a major reward. That Gaius Cornelius Gallus[21] was only an *eques* was perhaps of secondary or no consideration. Like Dio and Tacitus,[22] with hindsight we seek a principle for the consigning of Egypt, ever after, to an *eques*: the crucial importance of its corn for Rome and the need to deny its resources to opponents. But Gallus was the man on the spot, and Upper Egypt, the old traditional part of the Double Kingdom, recalcitrant to the Ptolemies and wooed by Cleopatra, had to be integrated militarily with the rest. Meanwhile, the royal treasure-house was seized, which meant the end of shortage of funds and enabled promised payments to be made for the land bought for discharged veterans.

At Rome, tight control was exercised on behalf of his absent chief by another member of the triumphant junta, also an *eques*, Gaius Maecenas. He scotched an alleged plot by Lepidus, the son of the deposed triumvir, to assassinate Caesar – an unconvincing story indeed, given that Caesar was across the seas. Anyone looking for what was usurpatory and unconstitutional about the new rulers who had vaulted into power need look no further, for there is no sign that Maecenas had any formal authority at all, and there were perfectly valid consuls in office: 'non mos, non ius', yet.[23] And though certain new constitutional powers were voted to the absent Caesar, the 'Vote of Athena' or power of pardon,[24] the *auxilii latio* or power, like a tribune , to come to the aid of citizens in the city of Rome,[25] and the power to 'judge when called upon'[26] (which scholars seize upon in the search for a constitutional basis for the emperor as judge), they are best seen either as marks of honour, simply – for 30 B.C., with Caesar away from Rome, was hardly a time for constitution-making – or else as giving him some judicial standing in the East, in relation to former partisans of Antony, or of himself.[27] (Cf. ch. 1. Endnote 2.)

[21] Boucher 1966 (C 37).   [22] Dio LI.17.1; Tac. *Ann.* II.59.3.   [23] Tac. *Ann.* III.28.1.

[24] Jones 1960 (A 47) 95.

[25] Dio LI.19.6 says all powers of a tribune, for life. That may have been offered; Caesar accepted (only) 'most' of what was offered, LI.20.4.   [26] ἔκκλητον δικάζειν.

[27] His partisans in the cities may have been calling for support.

For Caesar showed no sign of hurry to reach the hub of things. He entered upon his fifth consulship of 29 B.C., as he had done his fourth the year before, in absence from Rome, still in the East, where there was need for diplomatic activity and reflection (no doubt) on policy, and where a major decision was forced on him about cult of himself as the new liberator, peace-bringer and benefactor.[28] Caesar was bombarded with offers of official cult, in line with what was customarily offered in the hellenistic world. Dio tells us what he decided: for the Roman citizens in the East, temples of Rome-plus-the-divine-Iulius at Ephesus and Nicaea were to be the prescribed limit of official cult; for the non-Romans, temples of Rome-plus-himself at Pergamum and Nicomedia.[29] That, Dio says, was the precedent for the subsequent general pattern; like the prefecture of Egypt, and much else, what came to be settled policy sprang from a quick decision made in a particular context.

The Senate, at its first meeting of 29 B.C., excogitated further honours for the still absent victor: the right to use Imperator as his permanent first name,[30] formal approval of his eastern diplomatic arrangements, and, on 11 January, the closing of the gates of Janus in sign that Rome was at total peace. (We can all notice, with Dio,[31] that campaigns were going on in Spain, Gaul and Africa, but the Romans meant peace as far as they were concerned, and the 'business-as-usual' foreign triumphs by which the aspiring leaders of the Republic brought themselves to prominence, and which had gone on, significantly, all through the triumviral period, were still going on.)

Caesar came leisurely home. In August he was back on Italian soil (Virgil and Maecenas read the *Georgics* to him at Atella);[32] and on 13, 14 and 15 August he celebrated the only three triumphs he was ever to celebrate: for his Dalmatian campaigns of 35-33 B.C., for Actium, and for Egypt. His sister's son Marcus Claudius Marcellus, and his stepson, Tiberius Claudius Nero, coeval, born in 42 B.C., rode with the triumviral carriage. There were gladiatorial and beast shows, a distribution of 400 sesterces per person to everybody 'from the booty', and a present to discharged soldiers of 1,000 sesterces per head. On 18 August came another ceremony: the dedication, on their completion, of two structures in the Forum Romanum proclaiming the glory of the *gens Iulia*,[33] the temple of *divus Iulius* at the southern end and the new senate-house, the Curia Iulia, at the northern. The new Curia housed the statue of Victory from Tarentum and the statue of 'Venus rising' by Apelles, purchased by Caesar expressly; and outside the new temple were placed

---

[28] Habicht 1973 (F 154) 55-64.   [29] Dio LI.20.6-9.
[30] So *de facto* on coins already in the triumviral period.   [31] Dio LI.20.5.
[32] Donatus, *Life of Virgil*, from Suetonius' *Lives of the Poets* (ed. Rostagni 1956 (B 153) 89).
[33] Transformation of the Forum Romanum, Simon 1986 (F 577) 84-91.

the *rostra* captured at Actium, to face the *rostra* at the other end of the Forum (in their new Caesarian location). Noting these details is not to descend into triviality; they are the first of many examples to come of political statements made through visual monuments.

Caesar and the chief among all his collaborators, Agrippa, were granted *censoria potestas*, the authority possessed by censors, with which, in 28, being both also the *consules ordinarii* of the year, they carried out the first solemn lustration of the Roman people since 70 B.C. They also carried out a revision of the senate-list, *lectio senatus*, which obliged numerous senators to resign. It was the first of several purges of the curial order, but one should be aware of incautious inferences from the story that Caesar and Agrippa wore breastplates under their togas at that *lectio*. Of course, assassination was always a possibility, but the idea that the purge in 28 B.C. was for the rooting out of irredentist Antonians is simplistic, because such enemies were hardly to be scotched merely by excluding them from the Curia. The Senate had, notoriously, been grossly enlarged by the introduction of people whom the rest of that body regarded as socially unworthy, and in the restoration of the *status quo ante* which – as will be seen – was afoot, a return to a normalized Senate was in the interest of the senatorial order itself. Furthermore, if Caesar was going to set up a committee chosen by lot from the senators to play some role in the preparation of public business,[34] it would need first to shed its unsuitables. Dio mentions here (it is the first of many new regulations governing senatorial affairs) a new rule that senators might only leave Italy-Sicily with Caesar's permission: hitherto the Senate itself had been the licensing authority.[35]

It was in 28 B.C. that some of the slowly maturing plans began to take shape. There faces us in the end that unavoidable topic, the constitution of the Principate: it will be dealt with in chapter 3, but in the present chronological account what happened can best be described as 'business as usual after alterations', which was what all Rome wanted and expected. 'In my sixth and my seventh consulship, after I had extinguished the fires of civil war, in accordance with the wishes of all [Greek version: 'of my fellow citizens'] having taken control of all things, I transferred the *res publica* [Greek version: not *politeia* but *kyrieia*, 'supreme authority'] from my power into the arbitrament of the Roman Senate and people.'[36] It can be noted at once that there was no such thing as 'the constitutional settlement of 27 B.C.': 'In my sixth (28) and my seventh (27) consulship ...', says Augustus.[37] The process was conceived of as a steady return to normality after years of abnormality. In 28

[34] Crook 1955 (D 10) 11.   [35] Dio LII.42.6; Mommsen 1888 (A 65) III 912–13.
[36] RG 34.1.   [37] And cf. Tac. *Ann.* III.28, *sexto demum consulatu.*

Caesar shared the consular *fasces*, month by month, with his colleague, in the traditional manner (after all, he was now in Rome and so able to do so), and he announced that the rulings of the triumvirs –including his own, and presumably insofar as not already validated – would be abolished as from the end of the year.[38] What was occurring was what Antony and Caesar, as triumvirs, had promised would occur. They had envisaged it for their intended joint consulate of 31 B.C.:[39] it had been regrettably delayed by civil war, so Caesar implied, but now here it was; and nobody at Rome can have expected that the 'dynasts' would reserve to themselves *no* special place in the restored order. The difference was that there was now only one 'dynast' left, which was, needless to say, no small difference.

But first, the year 28 had other excitements for the Roman public. To begin with, no less than three 'business-as-usual' proconsular triumphs, in May, July and August; then in September the first celebration of 'Actian Games' in Rome; and in October the completion of the white marble temple of Apollo on the Palatine.[40] Potent symbolism lay in that: Actian Apollo to be the presiding genius of a new age, a synthesis of Greece and Rome, of arms and arts, his shining temple standing prominent, housing famous original statues and flanked by libraries, and connecting with – so as to be virtually a part of – the house of Caesar. The ever-recurring paradox of all this story comes out in those symbols: the effort of Caesar, on one plane, to restore the 'Scipionic' Rome of past glories, matched, on another plane, by the rapid growth, also by his efforts, of new concepts and structures, of a 'parallel language'.[41] The paradox is yet more apparent if the view of some modern writers be accepted that Caesar's huge Mausoleum beside the Tiber was already finished by 28 B.C. and was a great symbol; but that may not be right,[42] and there is disagreement about what it is supposed to have symbolized. Certainly, the Mausoleum was not redolent of modest aspirations, but the late-republican Romans were competitive about tombs, and it was perhaps just an ace of trumps in that competition.[43]

Caesar was absent from his 'Actian Games': he was ill. Scepticism is common amongst historians about the illnesses that punctuated the first forty years of Caesar's life: they were, it is supposed, psychological reactions to tense situations, or even fraudulent and calculated. The scepticism is fuelled by the fact that after 23 B.C. he lived to a great age in

---

[38] Dio LIII.2.5. Grenade equates that announcement with the edict quoted by Suetonius, *Aug.* 28.2. Unconvincing.   [39] App. *BCiv.* v.73.313.
[40] Propertius II.31; Simon 1986 (F 577) 19–25; Zanker 1987 (F 632) 52–73 and 242–5.
[41] Concept borrowed from C. Nicolet 1976 (A 66) ch. 9, 'les langages parallèles'.
[42] Reliance is placed on Suet. *Aug.* 100.4; but it was *recens* when Virgil wrote *Aen.* VI.873 and still unfinished when Marcellus was placed in it.   [43] For the competition see Zanker 1987 (F 632) 27.

essentially sound health,[44] by the lack of success of medical historians in diagnosing, from the vague evidence, what, if anything, was seriously the matter with him, and by the fact that he is known to have staged one crisis, when Tiberius threatened retirement – and Tiberius was undeterred. Nevertheless, doubt is hypersceptical. Illness and early death stalked the corridors of power in antiquity.[45] Iulius Caesar was epileptic; Pompey was ill every year,[46] and very gravely ill at Naples in 50 B.C.; as for our Caesar, he nearly died in his teens, and in 42 he was ill at Dyrrhachium and at Philippi, and there were rumours of his death. In 33 he was ill in Dalmatia. His illness in 28 went on after the Games all through the winter, for he was still not recovered in May the following year. In 26 illness overtook him at Tarraco after the first Spanish campaign, and may have been continuous through 25 and 24; for he was ill at Rome in June 24, and very likely continued so right down to his resignation of the consulship in July 23: then, notoriously, he was thought to be at death's door again. And, surely, he thought himself so: hence the building of the Mausoleum, and the autobiography, afterwards abandoned, and the early versions of the *Res Gestae*. Caesar's precarious condition, and his own belief in it, must be borne in mind when we think of 'constitutional settlements': it really was possible that the whole story would end abruptly, and he must hasten to leave something stable behind.

At the beginning of 27 B.C., all special powers being abolished, Caesar and Agrippa were joint consuls once again. On the Ides of January, in a careful consular speech in the Curia, Caesar handed the whole Roman state back into the hands of the Senate and people, for them to decide the nature of its future government: that was the gesture of fulfilment of the promise. It does not seem likely that the Senate's response was other than carefully prepared and stage-managed:[47] it was to grant to Caesar what the Senate had traditional authority to grant, a *provincia*. But that *provincia*, 'Caesar's province', gave him nevertheless an overwhelming role in the new order, because of its size: Spain, Gaul and Syria (plus, indeed, Egypt, which, having not existed as a province at all until 30 B.C., may not have been thought of as any of the Senate's business to grant), on a ten-year maximum tenure. Caesar made no gesture to resign the consulship, which lay with the people to grant; and if he chose to continue to offer himself annually for election to it, no doubt he would be regularly elected: he would hold his vast *provincia* either as consul, or, if he ever dropped the consulship, as proconsul. No change at all needed to be made in the traditional arrangements for the rest of the provinces of the Roman world. Strabo, indeed, states – implying that it was at this

---

[44] Though he remained hypochondriacally fussy about himself all his life, and often had throat infections.   [45] Syme 1986 (A 95) 20–5.   [46] Cic. *Att.* VIII.2.3.   [47] *Contra*, Dio LIII.11.

time – that Caesar received 'headship of the hegemony' and was made arbiter of peace and war for life, but reasons for limiting the significance of that claim will be given in chapter 3 below.[48]

The formal authority Caesar thus took for himself was vast, indeed, and in its totality un-republican; nevertheless, it was a way of expressing his overwhelming predominance in encouragingly familiar concepts – sovereignty vested in Senate and people, and no political structure incompatible with *mos maiorum*. And not a colossal confidence trick, for who, amongst those who mattered, could have been taken in? Rather – if Caesar turned out to have made the right political guess – what most people badly wanted to believe; and, furthermore, experimental and with a fixed term. And finally, if he died, the traditional *res publica* would be standing in place, inviolate.

But at once comes the counterpoint and the paradox. For on 16 January Caesar was heaped with new honours proposed by his adherents, above all with the name 'Augustus'; and that was a fantastic novelty, the impact of which is blunted for us by two millennia of calling him by that name. No human person had been called it before, and its symbolic range was very large. The sources preserve a tale that Caesar, or some of his advisers, or both, had first thought of 'Romulus'.[49] Some scholars doubt, others think that 'Augustus' was a second-best imposed by the strength of opposition; but it came to the same thing, for they all knew their Ennius: '... since famous Rome was founded with august augury'. There were other insignia: the 'civic crown' of oak-leaves 'in honour of the salvation of the citizens'; the shield proclaiming Augustus' special qualities, *virtus, clementia, iustitia* and *pietas erga deos patriamque*[50] (expressing, of course, what was *wanted* of the ruler); the laurels placed on either side of his house doorway.[51] As children of a different culture we might be impatient with those insignia, as politically trivial; but in a society in which, to be a great man, you had to be acknowledged and proclaimed as such, the names and crowns and dedications had power, carrying symbolic messages both ways, of what was granted and what was expected.

In Sextilis (or August) Augustus, in poor health again, went off, first to Gaul and then to Spain. In fact, for fifteen years he kept up virtually a regime of three-year trips to the provinces alternating with two-year stays in Rome,[52] and Suetonius remarks that Augustus saw personally every Roman dominion except Africa and Sardinia.[53] We need not

---

[48] Strab. XVII.3.25 (840C).   [49] Suet. *Aug.* 7.2; Dio LIII.16.6–8.

[50] Text of the copy from Arles, EJ² 22; picture, Earl 1968 (C 81) pl. 38.

[51] Livy, *Per.* 134 gives also the change of the name of the month Sextilis to 'Augustus'; but other evidence suggests a much later date for that change.

[52] Gardthausen 1891 (C 95) I 806.   [53] Suet. *Aug.* 47.

attribute to him the passion for personal oversight – and for tourism –
that motivated Hadrian over a hundred years later. Escape from
opposition, at least in the sense of letting experiments simmer, may be
more relevant; the desire, also, to foster the impression of 'business-as-
usual': the governor goes to his province and Senate and people are
sovereign at Rome. Nevertheless, already and at once, the *res publica* was
stamped with that hallmark of a changed world, 'ubi imperator, ibi
Roma', 'where the ruler is, there is Rome'. There was only one ruler
now, and the world must make its way to where he was.

'Business-as-usual' included a triumph, in September, for Marcus
Valerius Messalla Corvinus (the patron of Tibullus and perhaps of Livy),
ex Gallia, but before that, in July, one for Marcus Licinius Crassus, *ex
Thracia et Getis*. Crassus (a grandson of Iulius Caesar's triumviral
colleague), who had been a partisan of Sextus Pompeius and then of
Mark Antony, but, in spite of that, *consul ordinarius* in 30 B.C., requested
the further honour of dedicating *spolia opima* for having personally killed
an enemy chief. Augustus had it disallowed, on a probably trumped-up
ground:[54] no one was to be allowed military honours greater than the
ruler himself could ever conceivably have – indeed, before long not even
triumphs would be permitted to any except members of the 'divine
family'. But use of this incident to infer a 'challenge to the usurping
authority' by an unreconciled Antonian, and a 'crisis of the new order' is
altogether out of proportion. Crassus celebrated a full triumph, and the
fact that he 'disappears from history' afterwards does not warrant
sinister suspicions. What is more, the history of his campaigns, far from
being suppressed, must have been written up by somebody, for Dio has a
disproportionately long account of them.[55]

Another disappearance at about this time, however, might be
regarded as more of a tragedy: the suicide, in 26,[56] of the poet, soldier,
and part-architect of Augustus' victory, Gaius Cornelius Gallus, first
prefect of Egypt. Recent new – or newly evaluated – evidence[57] has led to
revisions of the older story, that it was because he got above himself for
his undoubtedly successful campaigns to unify Egypt that he forfeited
the *amicitia* of Augustus. But whatever the reason, he did forfeit it, and
the protection it afforded, and laid himself open to a senatorial declaration that he was liable to prosecution. Suetonius states that Augustus
was distressed by Gallus' suicide and had not desired it;[58] so modern
interpreters have urged that Gallus fell, not to the malice of his old chief,
but to that of the 'opposition', to whom the consignment of Egypt to an

---

[54] Livy, IV.20.5 (who plainly (32.4) did not believe Augustus' case).

[55] Dio LI.23.2–27; and observe Livy *Per.* 134–5.

[56] Dio LIII.23.4–7. Syme 1986 (A 95), 32, following Jerome, argues for 27.

[57] Hartmann 1965 (B 241); Volkmann 1965 (B 295); Boucher 1966 (C 37); Daly and Reiter 1979 (C
74); Hermes 1977 (B 82).   [58] Suet. *Aug.* 66.2.

eques had been an outrage and who seized upon some Achilles' heel of Gallus to destroy him. There is a puzzle of evidence here, whose pieces do not all fit; but it may be that we can legitimately see the Senate emboldening itself to declare – now that the favourite had fallen from grace – that a prefect of Egypt was not exempt from prosecutions to which other governors were liable. And perhaps it is not too fanciful to guess that the fall from grace was because Gallus had had further career pretensions, such as entry into the Senate with high standing. At any rate, insofar as there was a display of opposition in the incident it quite failed to unnerve Augustus, who continued to entrust Egypt to *equites* (and did not let them rise further).

The story here being challenged, that of attacks upon the usurping junta by an increasingly powerful and bold opposition, leading to disintegration of the 'Party' and forcing upon the ruler a rethinking of his entire position that bore fruit in 23 B.C., is held to embrace even Augustus' Spanish war – its purpose political propaganda and its goal not achieved.[59] Northern Spain had been a useful triumph-hunting ground for years, down to 26 B.C., but it seems probable that it was now to be definitively annexed for its precious metals. That proved a hard task: Augustus had intended to lead a victorious campaign in person, and he had Marcellus and Tiberius with him as military tribunes, but he was ill at Tarraco and the war had to be carried forward – to no properly conclusive end – by legates. The illness gives a better key to these years: Augustus doubted his own long survival. *Timor mortis*, rather than fear of the opposition, was what preoccupied him.

His consular colleagues in Rome in 27 and 26 were Marcus Agrippa and Titus Statilius Taurus, reliable men. It can therefore hardly have been out of a sense of insecurity that in 26, from Spain, he promoted another experiment, the appointment of a prefect of the city, the respected *triumphator* Messalla Corvinus.[60] The post had a remote republican history: in the dim past a prefect had been appointed by the consuls if both had to be absent on campaign, to see to the government of the city, and Iulius Caesar had appointed several prefects simultaneously in his absence. The prefecture was destined to become a regular post under the Principate, with responsibility for policing Rome, for which the urban cohorts were at the prefect's disposal; it came, in fact, to be the crown of a senatorial career. But in 26 there was a sitting consul, and Messalla, having accepted, gave up the post after six days.[61] The oddity is, if he thought it was a breach of *mos maiorum*, why he accepted in

---

[59] Schmitthenner 1962 (C 305). See also ch. 1 above and ch. 4 below.
[60] Syme 1986 (A 95), chs. 15 and 16, and, on the prefecture of the city, esp. 211–12.
[61] 'Claiming that he did not understand the job-description', Tac. *Ann.* VI.11; 'Embarrassed by the job', Sen. *Apocol.* 10; 'Unconstitutional position', Jerome, *Chron. sub ann.* 26.

the first place. Scholars suggest that pressure from his peers caused him to resign – another 'victory for the opposition' – or that he realized he was being manipulated by the ruler into acquiescing in a sinister novelty. It may be suggested, rather, that Augustus intended the post as an addition to the 'honours list' and Messalla accepted it as such and then learnt (from someone like Livy? We must remember that the Romans did not know much about their ancient history) how historically anomalous it was. There is no sign that he forfeited Augustus' esteem by his resignation, and the post was not, at that time, proceeded with. Statilius Taurus, according to Tacitus, took it, and with success, but hardly immediately, for he was consul; and it is by no means certain that Augustus ever intended that prefecture as a permanent post.

Agrippa, in his chief's absence, was engaged in the creation of a new complex of public structures and leisure-spaces in the Campus Martius. It was part of the stage-by-stage capture of the public spaces of Rome for the symbolism of the new ruler, as well, of course, as the cultivation of the plebs and the continuation of Agrippa's own populist image, inaugurated by his astonishing aedileship in 33 B.C.[62] The new complex comprised, particularly, the Saepta Iulia, the great covered hall for voting (a project of Iulius Caesar), new baths with an attached park, and a new temple, the Pantheon.[63] Now the precedents for such a temple as that were hellenistic and monarchical, and scholars detect a whiff of opposition again, for we are told that Agrippa wished to call his structure Augusteum and place in it a statue of Augustus, so implanting direct cult of the ruler in Rome itself. Augustus declined, and if he was not under pressure he was certainly, in the matter of cult, feeling every step of the way; his absence will have helped to save embarrassment.

The creation of public spaces advertising the triumphant glory of Rome was proceeding also in newly conquered lands – in, for example, the major new cities of Colonia Augusta Praetoria (Aosta) and Colonia Augusta Emerita (Mérida), both of them settlements of retired soldiers. A second closing of the gates of Janus signalized the all-too-incomplete victory in Spain.[64] Meanwhile, to Tarraco flocked the world's embassies: Parthians, Scyths, Indians, delegations from Greek cities. There could be no doubt where policy was being made; and that was the reverse of the coin, the disadvantage of absence, for not even a pretence could there be made of senatorial involvement. Incidentally, Augustus' wife, Livia Drusilla, was always at his side, whether on tour or at home. But there was no son of that marriage, a fact which remains a mystery.

[62] Zanker 1987 (F 632) 144–8.

[63] Not like the Hadrianic rotunda to be seen today, and facing in the opposite direction. Coarelli 1983 (F 116).

[64] Dio dates the closing to 25 B.C., LIII.27.1; and that is certainly before Augustus got back to Rome.

Hence the major preoccupation of the sick ruler at Tarraco was: what happens if I die tomorrow? The answer arrived at, of immense significance (and hardly what Livia Drusilla can have advised), was to marry his two nearest blood relations to each other, his daughter Iulia, aged fourteen, to his sister's son, Marcellus, aged seventeen. In 24 B.C. Marcellus was admitted to the Senate with the rank of one who had already held the praetorship and with the promise of an early consulship, and in 23, to enhance his popular image, he was made aedile and Augustus contributed to make his aedilician games especially noteworthy.[65] We ought not to be puzzled at the paradox of a regime carefully founded on the ostensible principle of election to offices, all of whose successive rulers, including the high-minded Marcus Aurelius, thought in exclusively dynastic terms about the succession. Paradox it is, but not novel; on the contrary, rooted in the mentality of the governing class of the Republic, whose young hopefuls had in each generation to compete for the people's votes to obtain office and so 'stay in the club', but felt themselves entitled by descent to be the competitors, and whose major families expected the highest honours for their sons. Augustus' solution, then, was, *mutatis mutandis*, a traditional one: to see that his natural dynastic successors were placed in the appropriate positions of office. The one idiosyncrasy was his very strictly 'genetic' concept of the succession: it was the blood of his family that was to prevail over all. It is easy to perceive the difficulty, namely that he had to make, and be seen to be responsible for, the choices that, in the Republic, the *populus Romanus* had made. Tiberius, for example, the son of Livia Drusilla, coeval with Marcellus: what of him? He must play second fiddle. In 24 he was elected quaestor for 23 – a step behind Marcellus – and allowed to stand for further offices five years ahead of normal. Or what of Agrippa, the main architect of victory, guarantor of stability, and focus of plebeian support? He had, at all events, no son. If mortality were to strike Augustus now, he alone could conceivably carry on the regime as they had planned it. Would he do so faithfully in the name of Marcellus and Iulia? Well, he presided over the marriage ceremonies, which suggests that he supported the solution – except that Augustus was never sensitive to the feelings of those closest to him.

Augustus struggled home at the end of 25. He entered on his tenth consulship on the road from Spain to Rome; and on that day, 1 January 24 B.C., the Senate took an oath to uphold his *acta*, and it was announced that he would make a present to the plebs of 400 sesterces per person. Whereupon the Senate, according to Dio, 'released him from all compulsion of the laws',[66] which meant, goes on Dio, that Augustus was

[65] The *vela*, Prop. III.18.13. Crinagoras, Poems X and XI, ed. Gow and Page 1968 (B 65).
[66] Dio LIII.28.2.

to be 'master of himself and the laws and do what he liked and not do what he did not like'. Now Dio remarks elsewhere[67] that the emperor is 'absolved from the laws' – which was proper constitutional doctrine by his day. If that, plus 'doing what he liked', was proclaimed as the prerogative of Augustus as from 1 January 24 B.C., it is that date, not 31 nor 29 nor 27 nor 23 nor 19 nor 2 B.C., that would have to count as the start of formal constitutional autocracy at Rome, for both the great doctrines of the High Empire, 'the emperor is dispensed from the laws' and 'what is pleasing to the emperor has the force of statute', are inherent in what Dio says. Scholars do not so count it, and they are right not to; for even those who deduce from the *lex de imperio Vespasiani* that the second of those doctrines did apply already to Augustus[68] are usually constrained by parity of reasoning to admit that that same *lex* shows that Augustus was not, in general, 'dispensed from the laws'.[69] Such prerogatives could not have been granted by the Senate alone, and it is best to treat the alleged grant just as a proposal, made in Augustus' absence and in contemplation of his illness, that never got beyond the Senate. Constitutional redefinition was on the way, but it was to take a quite different turn.

The year 23 B.C., Augustus' fortieth, was a year of crisis, because Augustus almost died and Marcellus did die. Numerous historians at the present time re-date two events placed by Dio in the year 22 B.C., the 'trial of Marcus Primus' and the 'conspiracy of Caepio and Murena'.[70] They place them in 23, and claim that those events, coupled with the assumed disgruntlement of Agrippa with the promotion of Marcellus, were the culmination of the long tale of increasingly bold and successful opposition, nearly brought the whole regime down to disaster, and forced upon Augustus a constitutional retreat. The illness of Augustus is seen as a feint, a sharp incentive to the 'Party' to pull itself together. That transposition (with all the inferences that it carries with it) is, on methodological grounds, not adopted in what follows.[71]

Early in the year 23, Augustus did not expect to survive. There were, no doubt, people who rejoiced, and to whom the ruler's unexpected and rapid recovery was deeply disappointing. But at the crisis he handed state papers to his fellow-consul and his private signet to Agrippa. That was a scrupulously correct procedure. And he had not given the dynastic signal of adoption to Marcellus, not even in his will – as he was anxious to assure people.[72] Upon recovery, in fact, he hastened to redefine powers, and, first of all, those of Agrippa. A law was passed conferring

---

[67] Dio LIII.18.1.   [68] See ch. 3 below, pp. 118–20.

[69] And historians, from Dio onwards, are wrong if they think the two doctrines 'come close to the same thing'.   [70] Dio LIV.3.

[71] Badian 1982 (C 14) argues cogently against it.   [72] Dio LIII.31.1.

upon Agrippa an *imperium proconsulare*, probably with a term of five years:[73] not for action, but for eminence next to Augustus (and certainly not *maius*, for not even Augustus had that yet). Agrippa, with his new *imperium*, sailed off promptly to the East, to no particular activity, settling his headquarters at Lesbos and governing Syria through his own legates. Already in antiquity historians thought up explanations of this odd conduct: Agrippa had taken himself off, or been sent off by the very grant of proconsular *imperium*, in rage and humiliation, or in loyal co-operation, in order not to be in the path of the rising star, Marcellus. 'Crisis' historians, nowadays, prefer to see him sent to 'hold the East' because of the strength of opposition to the regime. Better than any of those explanations is to see in Agrippa's departure an experiment with the concept of double-harness at the top, one ruler in the West and one in the East. Augustus was, presumably, convalescent, and no one could know that he was destined never to be seriously ill again. Moreover, there was plague at Rome.

In any case, the new formula for Agrippa was only the first stage in a bigger reformulation, the 'constitutional settlement' of 23 B.C. On 1 July Augustus laid down his eleventh consulship, and must then have made it plain that in subsequent years he would not normally be a candidate for the office; for alternative formulae were adopted for giving him the various powers that he was relinquishing by giving up the consulship. But let us here be clear about the difference between powers and power. Augustus was not engaged in taking or declining or modifying the latter: factual power was not in question; he had that, totally, as long as he satisfied the general interest of governing class, plebs and armies. What was being taken or declined or modified was the expression of that power, which would settle expected boundaries of its use, of the behaviour of the ruler, and the scope to be allowed for a *modus vivendi* under his power. Not, then, retreats and compromises in a struggle over power, but in order to get the most acceptable *modus vivendi*. And in 23 the prime need was to restore to full availability the highest social prize of the aristocracy, the consulship,[74] which had been monopolized for years, as to one place, by Augustus, and twice also, as to the other, by Agrippa.[75] 'Business-as-usual' was what the aristocracy wanted as the price for their co-operation. Suetonius records, undated, a proposal by Augustus for there to be three consuls in any year when he was one, which was turned down:[76] the proposal tends to be associated with 19 B.C., but it might belong here in 23 – tried out, perhaps, on the senatorial

---

[73] Roddaz 1984 (C 200) 339–51 has a full discussion; it is not in Dio. Essential now is EJ² 366, the Greek fragment of Augustus' funeral oration for Agrippa, with the additional fragment published by Gronewald 1983 (B 370) 61–2.   [74] Dio LIII.32.3.

[75] Agrippa never took another after 23.   [76] Suet. *Aug.* 37.

steering committee and greeted with too much dismay. The alternative was for the ruler to relinquish the highest office.

Instead (or at least at the same time) Augustus received the grant, annually renewable but for life, of the official powers possessed by tribunes of the plebs, *tribunicia potestas*. We can argue that he needed the tribunician power so as, constitutionally, to be able to summon the Senate and to introduce legislation, and Augustus certainly so employed it. Some historians, regarding it as the principal cloak for autocracy, designate it as 'vague' and 'all-embracing': that is not right, for, unlike *imperium*, which was indeed vague, *tribunicia potestas* was a bundle of specifically defined powers. That is corroborated by the fact that an addition had to be made:[77] the Senate granted Augustus the right to make a formal motion at any session (a right that had not been part of the power of tribunes in the Republic). Tacitus looked in a different direction for the prime significance of the tribunician power: 'Augustus invented it as the title of highest pre-eminence, in order not to assume the name of king or dictator, and yet to have an appellation that would make him stand above all other *imperia*'.[78] Tacitus thus saw it as a distinction rather than a power, and the same inference can be drawn from two other considerations, first that it came to be used as the chronological marker of the reign,[79] and, second, that it came to be the ultimate honour conferred on those chosen to be partners in the ruler's responsibilities – the sign of a 'colleague in rule', *collega imperii*. Also, of course, in an age attuned to symbols, tribunician power implied a relationship of protectorate over the common people; though how far that impressed them is doubtful, and what they were hoping for was, as we shall see, something much more full-blooded.

The *imperium* of Augustus was redefined: it became *imperium maius*, which gave him prevailing authority over any other provincial governor in any case of conflict. It was, however, only proconsular *imperium*, giving him no authority in the home sphere such as he had possessed as consul (though, simply for practical convenience, he was allowed to have it 'once for all' in the sense of not having to drop it every time he entered the sacred *pomerium* of Rome and resume it every time he departed).[80] Some interpret the redefinition as compensating Augustus for the total *maius imperium* over the Roman world traditionally possessed by consuls; but not all historians are agreed as to the reality, in practice, of the consular *maius imperium*, and, once again, not the least importance of the new device was to function as a distinction, keeping Augustus' *imperium* one stage higher than the new *imperium* of Agrippa.

---

[77] Dio LIII.32.5; Talbert 1984 (D 77) 165.

[78] Tac. *Ann.* III.56.2. 'Title of highest pre-eminence' must be an echo of an official description; the Greek for it can be seen in the oration for Agrippa, EJ² 366, lines 11–12.

[79] Though not immediately: Lacey 1979 (C 147).   [80] Dio LIII.32.5.

'Constitutional settlement' is, then, too schematic a description of the changes of 23 B.C.; but it is only fair to add that the two elements, *imperium proconsulare maius* and *tribunicia potestas*, proved a very stable formula for the executive authority of Roman emperors for a long time to come.

So much for paper arrangements; in the world beyond the drafting-board nature and chance play their part: disease and death, fire, flood and famine affect the stability of regimes. The years 23 and 22 B.C. were plague years all over Italy. Marcellus died (we do not know whether of plague), and there was no child of his marriage; that was a blow to Augustus' first attempt to create a succession, though the less urgent in that the ruler himself seemed out of danger. More urgent was the condition of the plebs of Rome, whose goodwill Agrippa had fostered. Along with its huge growth in numbers the plebs, overwhelmingly of freedman status, had acquired some political force.[81] It is exaggerated to suppose that Augustus was either dependent on it or could ever have based power mainly upon it, but it had huge 'nuisance-value' and had to be managed and prevented from developing popular leaders. Along with plague went grave food shortage,[82] and the commons were angry and disillusioned, calling upon the ruler to undo the careful paperwork and take official powers more plenary than he had ever yet had.

The year 22 B.C. was, in fact, fraught with ills. The statutory court for treason had to be convened for more than one case.[83] The trial of Marcus Primus, proconsul of Macedonia, for making war on the Odrysae of Thrace unprovoked and without authority, his claim to have done so at the behest of 'Augustus or Marcellus', the appearance of Augustus at the tribunal to deny any such instruction, the question by defence counsel what standing he had to intervene, and his reply that his justification was 'the public interest': all that is a well-known story.[84] The matter was, no doubt, serious, especially as the resulting conviction of Primus was not unanimous; but it may have been accorded a significance beyond its deserts by being transposed to 23 B.C. It belongs, rather, to the category of 'famous repartees', Augustus' reply being reminiscent of that of Pericles, that moneys had been spent 'for a necessary purpose'.[85]

But there was also a conspiracy by two persons, presumably to attempt what nature had failed to achieve.[86] One was a wholly unknown Fannius Caepio,[87] the other a certain Murena (so Dio calls him),[88] connected with a group close to the ruler: he was the brother, or half-brother, of Maecenas' wife, Terentia[89] and of Augustus' other equestrian

---

[81] See *CAH* IX,[2] ch. 17.   [82] Note the *frumentatio* recorded in *RG* 15.1.
[83] Its composition was, presumably, at least half non-senatorial.   [84] Dio LIV.3.1–3.
[85] Plut. *Per.* 23.1.   [86] Dio LIV.3.4–8; Vell. Pat. II.91.2.   [87] Syme 1986 (A 95) 40, n.47.
[88] Referred to in different sources as Licinius Murena and Varro Murena; doubtless he was also a Terentius, but he was not the mystery man in the consular Fasti for 23. Syme 1986 (A 95) 387–9.
[89] With whom Augustus was supposed to be having a liaison.

friend, Gaius Proculeius, and he was also the very defence counsel who had sought to embarrass Augustus at the trial of Marcus Primus. There is no reason to think that the charge was merely trumped up by Augustus.[90] There was a formal trial for treason,[91] and a conviction, but, again, short of unanimous. The sinister part of the tale is that the convicted men were not permitted to slip away into exile in the traditional way but apprehended and put to death.[92] Perhaps they failed to depart instantly enough. Maecenas is said by Suetonius to have given the nod to his wife to warn her brother to flee,[93] and commonly supposed to have lost his confidential standing with Augustus from that moment (though it is not clear that he did lose it abruptly, and Terentia hardly needed her husband as a go-between for information). Augustus celebrated his delivery from the plot (presumably to knife him) as a victory, and was furious at the lack of unanimity of the condemnation.

Disease and hunger led to demonstrations in Rome. Augustus had set out for eastern parts (we shall see why), but the disorders were too great to ignore, and Agrippa was away, so he hurried back. He was offered the dictatorship,[94] by the Senate under heavy pressure from the city plebs, which was thinking of Iulius Caesar; he was offered the powers of a censor for life; he was offered a consulship that would be 'annual yet perpetual', like his tribunician power. He made, like Iulius Caesar at the Lupercalia, a histrionic scene of public refusal.[95] He cannot have been scheming to get those offices, any one of which amounted to formal constitutional supremacy, though those who believe that the arrangements of 23 B.C. were a retreat imposed by opposition also believe that Augustus engineered the public outcry to give him the excuse to recover constitutional ground. If scheming is in question it would be more plausible to suppose that he schemed for a chance to refuse them. Or were opponents trying to manoeuvre him into a false step that would justify tyrannicide? Perhaps all was straightforward on both sides, for the context was that of demands that somebody, somehow, should produce bread, and Augustus did accept *cura annonae*, charge of the corn supply, and it is altogether too subtle to think that that authority was a disguise for total supremacy and that the shortage itself was engineered for that. Bread appeared quickly enough,[96] and for the future a not very radical experiment was embarked on to improve the distribution of the free ration: a new annual committee of senior senators, *praefecti frumenti dandi*.

In September 22 B.C. Augustus got away from Rome, and was away

---

[90] The story at Suet. *Aug.* 56.4 implies that it had shaken him badly.

[91] Perhaps separate trials: young Tiberius was prosecutor of Caepio.

[92] Dio's '. . . on the grounds that they intended to flee' is probably just a mistake natural to one of his century.   [93] Suet. *Aug.* 66.3.

[94] Twice, he says in the *Res Gestae*.   [95] Dio LIV.1.4–5; Suet. *Aug.* 52.

[96] Augustus probably just leant heavily on hoarders: cf. *Dig.* 48.12.2 on the *lex Iulia de annona*.

three whole years. Agrippa was in the eastern lands, no prefect of the city
was appointed, and the urban plebs was not satisfied: the consuls had a
rebellious populace on their hands. The people in *comitia* refused to elect
more than one consul for 21 B.C.; equally, Augustus, writing from
Samos, refused to take the vacant place. Only at the beginning of 21 did
the people obediently elect a second consul.

What had taken the ruler to the East was a major policy issue, and he,
not Agrippa, must be the one to achieve a hoped-for diplomatic coup. So
Agrippa was available to change places with him, to return to Rome,
and, momentously, to marry the widow Iulia. (Tiberius, the stepson, was
not offered that hand: he was intended for a career of great public service,
indeed, but not to reach the summit of all things.) If Agrippa's presence,
briefly, in Rome was also supposed to calm plebeian agitation and
prevent the now open consulship from falling into wrong hands, his
success was limited, for in 20 B.C. the *comitia* again declined to elect more
than one consul, Gaius Sentius Saturninus, who, in early 19 B.C., found
himself facing, alone, the rise of a 'people's champion', a certain Marcus
Egnatius Rufus.

The garbled tale of Egnatius Rufus[97] may be not unfairly boiled down
to this: he was a senator who, as aedile, had won the favour of the Roman
plebs by organizing a fire service; that had taken him straight to the
praetorship, emboldened by which he stood in 19 B.C. for the consulship.[98] That conduct counts, in our sources, as one of the 'canonical' list
of conspiracies against Augustus;[99] it is puzzling why. For Augustus was
in the East (and Agrippa was, in a single year's campaign, finally
conquering the Cantabrians in Spain), and the problem, whatever it was,
was dealt with firmly and successfully by the consul and the Senate. The
consul refused Egnatius' candidature, and when a popular uprising
occurred it was suppressed, in accordance with a *senatus consultum
ultimum*, and the aspiring popular leader executed. The naive guess is
probably right, that the plebs had found a new Clodius, and the fact was
dangerous – but to the whole elite, not just to the ruler, so they closed
ranks. If Augustus was hoping, as some authors think, that the political
agitations of the plebs would lead to an enlargement of his own powers,
he would not want his position to seem to be dependent on a
demagogue; and if he just feared the plebs would be seduced away from
him and Agrippa, he had a yet more obvious motive for wanting
Egnatius removed. In any event, neither he nor Agrippa saw any need to
rush home.[100]

---

[97] The sources are muddled, not least chronologically: Dio LIII.24.4–6 (under 26 B.C.); Vell. Pat.
II.91.3–4, with the notes of Woodman 1983 (B 203).
[98] The vacant one of 19? It sounds, rather, as if the consul was presiding over ordinary elections,
which would have been those for 18.   [99] Suet. *Aug.* 19.1.
[100] Agrippa's Aqua Virgo was opened on 9 June, but he can hardly have completed the clinching
Spanish campaign quickly enough to be present.

Augustus' eastern sojourn claimed striking achievements. The background of affairs in the kingdoms of Parthia and Armenia is described in chapter 4 below.[101] The first result of Augustus' intervention in 20 B.C. was a diplomatic agreement with the government of Parthia, the only substantial territorial power on Rome's horizon. It was no doubt welcome to both sides, and established a treaty relationship as between equal powers and an official frontier. Moreover, legionary standards captured from Marcus Crassus and from Mark Antony were handed back to the Romans. Augustus succeeded brilliantly in exploiting the fact, for home consumption, as a victory of arms, which it was not. An opportunity also offered itself for Tiberius Claudius Nero, the stepson, to gain diplomatic or military credit by installing a Roman supporter on the throne of Armenia – which proved easy, because the monarch of the moment had been assassinated before Tiberius arrived. But it was the 'return of the standards' that became a corner-stone of the ideology of a reinvigorated Rome resuming her historic right to 'spare the conquered and defeat the proud'.[102]

Augustus made many other political dispositions in the eastern provinces, for example depriving cities of their status as 'free' cities and promoting others, quite irrespective (as Dio points out) of the nature of provinces such as Asia and Bithynia, which were technically *provinciae populi Romani* governed by proconsuls.[103] It was done by the authority of his *imperium maius*. Also, according to Dio,[104] he sent the Senate a letter stating a policy strangely like the instructions that Tacitus says he left behind in A.D. 14: 'to keep the empire within bounds'. That is surprising at this juncture, in view of the huge expansion that was to come: perhaps it was a justification for treaty relations with Parthia and the continued use of 'client kings' in the East.

Augustus voyaged home via Athens, whither Virgil journeyed in his honour (and died in his entourage at Brundisium on the way back: a heavy year for Roman poetry, which saw the death of Tibullus also). The magistrates and Senate proceeded to Campania to meet the returning ruler, a gesture that became a precedent;[105] and he appointed, *proprio motu*, a second consul for the empty place, thus both resolutely declining to change course but also cutting a Gordian knot by pure *auctoritas*: it was not, apparently, challenged.

An altar to Fortuna Redux, 'Fortune the Bringer Home', was erected at the Porta Capena and a ceremony of *reditus*, return, was enacted, of which much is made in the Res *Gestae*.[106] A triumph, however, Augustus

---

[101] Pp. 158–63.
[102] Virg. *Aen.* VI.853. Cf. Prop. IV.6.83, Horace's *Carmen Saeculare*, and the breastplate of the statue of Augustus from Prima Porta, Simon 1986 (F 577) 52–7.   [103] Dio LIV.7.4–5.
[104] Dio LIV.9.1.   [105] First, actually, in 30 B.C., Dio LI.4.5.
[106] *RG* 11; the Fasti Amiternini and Oppiani have it also, under 12 Oct.

refused, accepting instead *ornamenta triumphalia*, the insignia without the ceremony.[107] Triumphs were to be quite rare, partly because independent proconsular commands, a prerequisite of a triumph, died out and partly because triumphs competed, as public spectacle, with the ruler's own image-making: Agrippa led the abstinence. In March 19 B.C. Lucius Cornelius Balbus held a full, formal triumph for campaigns in Africa, and that was the last to be recorded in the Fasti Triumphales and the last to be held by anyone outside the 'divine family': for others, *ornamenta triumphalia* became the usual limit of honours. It may have been at that time that the arch was built next to the temple of Divus Iulius which had on its inner walls the pageant of Roman history represented by the Fasti Capitolini and Fasti Triumphales;[108] the ideology of military success and hegemony was the very breath of Rome: it was to be channelled in the interest of the ruler.

Dio gives a list of further constitutional grants to Augustus in 19 B.C.: an 'overseership of morality' (*praefectura morum* would have been the Latin), a censorial authority, a grant that most scholars interpret as the consular power for life, and the right to enact any laws he might wish, presumably without submitting them to the *comitia*, and to call them *leges Augustae*.[109] Was that the successful outcome of a Machiavellian policy of 'reculer pour mieux sauter'? Had the popular agitations given Augustus the all-embracing formal authority he coveted, under an at last acceptable formula? Though widely believed, that is probably not right; the context will suggest an alternative view. In the *Res Gestae*, Augustus strenuously denies receiving all-embracing formal authority: but what he did proceed to in the years that followed was a programme of legislation, particularly such as he hoped would restore traditional standards of the Roman people. The intention so to legislate must have been known in advance, through the deliberations of the senatorial sub-committee. *Praefectura morum*, we may guess, was a suggestion mooted for the formal authority on which Augustus should proceed, censorial power another, the right to enact *leges Augustae* another; all politely rejected, but somehow the offers have got into the record as accepted.[110] The 'consular power' is a more complex, and certainly a controversial, question. Most scholars, nowadays,[111] are only too happy to believe that Augustus accepted it for life in 19 B.C., because it serves to provide formal justification for certain actions he took, for which they can see no other. There is, however, no explicit statement but Dio's and Dio,

[107] Dio says he celebrated an ovation, but see Abaecherli Boyce 1942 (A 1).

[108] For the date, and the argument that the Fasti were on a 'Parthian arch', see Coarelli 1985 (E 19) 11.   [109] Dio LIV.10.5–6.

[110] Rejection of magistracy of *curator morum*, *RG* 6.1 (Greek only); of censorial power, implicit in *RG* 8; only Dio mentions *leges Augustae*, and Augustus' reference to his laws at *RG* 8.5 gives no hint. Suetonius was misled: *Aug.* 27.5.   [111] Following Jones 1960 (A 47) 13–15.

properly read, is saying something different: '... and the power of the consuls he took for life, to the extent of using the twelve *fasces* always and everywhere and sitting on a magisterial chair between the consuls at any time'.[112] In the *Res Gestae* Augustus informs the reader of revisions of the Senate list carried out 'by consular power': he surely means *ad hoc* grants, and so implies that he did not possess it permanently. What Dio is telling us about is not a power but an honour; for some 'social' rule was bound to be invented, now that Augustus no longer held, every year, one of the two highest offices of the state, about where, on formal occasions, he should be placed in relation to those two officers and what insignia he should have: we remember how the idea of three consuls did not appeal and was dropped.

In fact, those who like to see the first third of Augustus' reign punctuated by 'constitutional settlements' might better look to 18 than to 19 B.C. (though what is to be seen in 18 gives no comfort to any belief that he had acquired some kind of 'total power' in 19.) In 18 B.C. Augustus' *provincia* ran out: something certainly had to be done about that, and it was, in fact, renewed for the modest term of five years. Simultaneously, Agrippa's proconsular *imperium* was renewed for the same five years, and in addition he received the tribunician power for five years.[113] In that development there is constitutional novelty in plenty: an original and experimental arrangement based on a collegiate conception of the rulership. Agrippa and Iulia now had a son, and another baby was due, so dynasty was once again assured. The past decade had been uncomfortable for the ruler and his regime; now, with a good measure of optimism and militarism, Rome was to resume her role of conqueror and mistress of the world.

So the years 18 and 17 were marked by a programme of social reform, public and private, including a second revision of the Senate list, and by a great festival of Rome, to proclaim regeneration and traditional values, the *ludi saeculares* of 17 B.C.

Details of Augustus' social laws of this phase are treated in chapters 3 and 18 below.[114] He did not accept the offer to promulgate statutes as *leges Augustae*, but proposed them to the people by virtue of his tribunician power, so that they were *leges Iuliae*. In general, they were concerned with two themes, first the fairer and smoother running of the organs of state and law, and, second, family and birth-rate – of the *ordines*, the upper class, which was what Augustus thought mattered. Under the first heading the major element was the pair of *leges Iuliae iudiciorum publicorum*

---

[112] Dio LIV. 10.5, exactly analogous to '... for life, to the extent of not having to relinquish...' at LIII.32.5; see above p. 86.
[113] Dio LIV.12.4. Agrippa's *imperium* was not made *maius* until 13 B.C., Dio LIV.28.1 (and that is the correct inference from the *laudatio*, EJ² 366).   [114] Pp. 732–3, 883–93.

et privatorum, virtually a code for the organization of the courts of justice (and including, probably, a regulation *de vi* that reaffirmed the ancient citizen right of *provocatio*). Others were a *lex Iulia de ambitu* and a *lex Iulia de collegiis*.[115] The package proclaimed that the traditional system of public life was to run as before, at a better level of efficiency. The *lectio senatus* of 18 B.C. was in the same vein. It was an attempt to reduce the Senate to nearer its old pre-Sullan number of 300, though Augustus did not succeed in getting it below double that figure. More important, a senatorial *census* was laid down for the first time – a minimum property rating for a man to enter or stay in the august body.[116] Augustus wanted an old-fashioned Senate, whose members were to continue to hold virtually all major executive positions in the state, the legionary commands and provincial governorships, as well as receiving new commissions from time to time.

The second heading of the legislation of 18 and 17 B.C., the *lex Iulia de adulteriis* establishing a new criminal court for sexual offences that included extra-marital intercourse of men with freeborn women as well as adultery, and the *lex Iulia de maritandis ordinibus*, which provided bonuses for those with children and penalties for those not, is castigated nowadays as having imported the freedom-denying arm of the law into what had hitherto been matters of private morality and family concern. That, indeed, it did, but the perspective is erroneous unless it be observed that interference by the state in matters of private conduct was no novelty, but part of the age-old tradition of the Republic, which had comitial trials for *stuprum*, sumptuary laws, the Oppian and Voconian laws, and above all the surveillance of the censors, with their *nota* for all sorts of conduct disapproved of by society.[117] No more than the Greeks did the Romans believe that there was any sphere of private morality separable from the interests of the community at large. Augustus was taking over both the mantle of ancient Greek legislators and the Roman censorial role that he had been offered, but not under the formal title. That is not to say that all of the elite class found the laws to their taste, although Augustus claims in the *Res Gestae* that the Senate was in favour of his measures.[118]

Augustus and Agrippa were in Rome. Iulia had borne a second son, and the two little boys, Augustus' grandsons, were now formally adopted as his sons, taking the names Gaius and Lucius Caesar – which served plain notice upon the stepsons, Tiberius Claudius Nero and his brother Nero Claudius Drusus, as to what the future could *not* hold for

[115] Whether we should add, on the basis of the *Tabula Irnitana* (Gonzalez 1986 (B 235) 150), a *lex Iulia municipalis* standardizing the constitutions of the municipalities of Italy, is a matter of continuing debate.
[116] Discrepancy in the sources: Suet. *Aug.* 41.1 gives 1,200,000, Dio LIV.17.3 gives 1,000,000 sesterces. [117] Underestimated by Dixon 1988 (F 26A) 71. [118] *RG* 6.2 (the Greek text).

them, though it would be more than a decade before the boys could come into their political inheritance.

The celebration of a new *lustrum* – indeed, far more, a new *saeculum* of Rome – came, in triumphal mood, on 31 May 17 B.C.,[119] and Horace's official Ode for the occasion, the *Carmen Saeculare*, cannot be bettered as a compendium of the ideology set before the Roman people. It is the fashion of our age to undercut official triumphalism, and there is plenty of reason in the present case. Many of the governing class exhibited irreconcilable dissatisfaction with the attempt to regulate their conduct: Augustus had been up against the plebs, but now he was up against its betters. Dio (and it must come from his source) stresses the *un*-popularity of Augustus at this time, and even makes 18 B.C. the beginning of plots against him and against Agrippa,[120] whose status was resented. So if, as we are commonly taught, Augustus' greatest skill was the political tact whereby he experimented to fit his *de facto* supremacy into a framework of what people wanted it to seem to be, he had not, in the decade down to the *ludi saeculares*, reaped much fruit of that alleged skill – or so we might think until we notice the consuls of 16 B.C.[121]

III. 16 B.C. – A.D. 14

The consuls of 16 B.C. were young nobles (and similarly in the years that followed, so all was right in *that* relationship, at least). That particular pair were also related to Augustus. Publius Cornelius Scipio was the son of his former wife Scribonia by an earlier marriage, and so half-brother to Iulia, and Lucius Domitius Ahenobarbus was married to Augustus' niece Antonia, one of the two women of that name, the daughters of Octavia and Mark Antony, who carried the great enemy's genes deep into the heart of the 'divine family'.[122] The 'divine family' was the most distinctly Augustan innovation of all, his way of reconciling the high aristocracy. It was powerful both as fact and as concept. Practically, it secured a cadre of collaborators at the highest level; psychologically, it was the exemplar of Augustus' moral programme; and symbolically it was the 'parallel language' of dynasty and court taking over from elective republicanism. (As a matter of fact, for the second half of the year 16, the plebeian Lucius Tarius Rufus took over from P. Scipio; and that well illustrates the historian's peril in pretending to interpret the politics of the age, for we do not know why. Was it because Rufus could not be denied an honour and had to be fitted in? Or was Scipio ill, or

---

[119] Pighi 1965 (B 263) 107–30, plus 131–6, shown by Cavallaro 1979 (B 217) to belong to the Augustan *ludi*.   [120] Dio LIV.15.1.   [121] Syme 1986 (A 95) 53–63.
[122] For all such persons see, now, Syme 1986 (A 95), via the index.

incompetent, or dissident? Many stories could be told, and a 'crisis of 16 B.C.' invented; but it would all be idle conjecture.)

In any case, the main theme of Augustus' second decade was different. Towards the end of the year 16 Augustus and Agrippa left Rome, for opposite ends of the empire, each for three years – according, as it were, to pattern. Rome was left to the consuls, plus Titus Statilius Taurus as 'prefect of the city and Italy'.[123] Agrippa's role in the East was not military: he exercised imperial policy in half the empire as *collega imperii*, dealing, for example, with the affairs of the remote client kingdom of the Crimea,[124] and confirming the right of the Jews of the Diaspora to their ancestral laws and customs.[125] More in need of interpretation is Augustus' purpose in the West. His departure was hastened by the flurry caused by a legionary standard lost on the Rhine,[126] for rebuffs to Roman military prestige could not be allowed. According to Dio, some said he left Rome in order to consort with Maecenas' Terentia with less scandal, others that it was to avoid general unpopularity. But maybe a main theme was already emerging: imperial expansion in northern Europe, of which the two efficient stepsons would be the principal agents. Augustus was inexhaustible in experiments with the material at any time to hand: three centuries later, under Diocletian and his successors, the Roman empire would be ruled by two 'Augusti' and two 'Caesares', and the experiment of Augustus' second decade looks as if based on some such idea – save for the awkward and ominous difference that the two 'Caesares' due to be groomed for succession were a different pair of brothers entirely from the ones who were to share the present burdens.

Certain things that were done can be seen as preparatory. The generation of soldiers who had been recruited after Actium must now be pensioned off, so a big phase of veteran settlement occurred in Gaul and Spain; and it is no surprise that, connected with the discharges and new recruitments, the term of service was now[127] officially established at a minimum of sixteen years for legionaries and twelve for the praetorian guard. Thus, out of the needs of the time, emerged the formal establishment of the Roman army as a professional service (for 'other ranks', not officers). And at roughly the same time Lugdunum seems to have begun to function as a major government mint, coining gold and silver; new money was going to be needed to pay legions campaigning in

---

[123] Dio LIV.19.6: Dio's Greek implies that title: it was probably a formal, even if not a standing, office. [124] Dio LIV.24.4–6.

[125] Rajak 1984 (E 1194) favours the authenticity of the texts cited by Josephus, but minimizes their scope.

[126] The 'Lollian Disaster', 16 B.C. (or 17, as argued by Syme, see 1986 (A 95) 402, n.116).

[127] Dio LIV.25.5 puts it in 13 B.C.

north and west. Gaul was subjected to a census, and detested both the tax and the procurator.

The first big movement[128] was the subjugation by the brothers, Tiberius Nero and Nero Drusus, of Raetian and Vindelician Switzerland (not without mass deportations) and the bloodless incorporation of the kingdom of Noricum. Augustus took an imperatorial salutation; the stepsons could have neither triumph nor ovation, for they were only *legati Augusti*, but at least Horace accorded them proud celebration, as he did also for the return of Augustus to Rome in 13 B.C.[129] And in relation to that *reditus* a magnificent new way was invented to advertise the 'divine family': on 4 July 13 B.C., by decree of the Senate, there was inaugurated a sacred precinct and altar of the 'Augustan Peace' in the north part of the Campus Martius; it was not dedicated till 10 January 9 B.C. Its famous frieze is an imaginary depiction of a procession of the 'divine family' and the members of the great priesthoods to an inaugural celebration; contemporaries will probably have been able to identify every figure.[130] Both the frieze and the independent panels of the Ara Pacis are eloquent with all the themes of Augustan ideology, not the least striking emphasis being upon children, the 'young hopefuls', the key to future glory.[131]

To the Ara Pacis we now have to add, as an element – perhaps the major element – in a complex architectural ensemble, the enormous public sundial and astronomical clock created, also, in the north part of the Campus.[132] Its gnomon, 30 m high (with plinth), was one of the two obelisks brought from 'captured Egypt';[133] the paved ground under the feet of pedestrians was itself the sundial; and the equinoctial line on the ground passed through the Ara Pacis and subtended a right angle to the Mausoleum by the Tiber. There has been detected a whole wealth of symbolism about the birth and conception of Augustus in relation to renewal and peace, adding significance to one of the best-known inscriptions of the period, the letter of the proconsul of Asia and decrees of the Joint Council of the province inaugurating a new calendar for Asia based on Augustus' birthday, which is celebrated as 'giving a new look to the cosmos'.[134]

Of course, both the rulers returned to Rome in 13 B.C., for their

---

128 A prelude consisted of campaigns by Publius Silius in the Alpine foothills.

129 Hor. *Carm*. IV.4 and 14; IV.5 and 2, lines 41–60.

130 *Contra*, however, Zanker 1987 (F 632) 128. There are still many disagreements about the identity of individual figures: see, e.g., the next note.

131 Zanker 1987 (F 632) 219, contests the view that two of the little boys are barbarian captives, and thinks that they are, after all, Gaius and Lucius Caesar.

132 Buchner 1982 (F 306); Zanker 1987 (F 632) 149–50. Unmentioned in the *Res Gestae*: had it already been discovered that the 'clock was wrong'? (Pliny, *HN* XXXVI.72–3).

133 EJ² 14. The other was placed on the *spina* of the Circus Maximus. Their transport and erection were a tremendous technological feat.   134 EJ² 98.

official powers lapsed and required renewal. Needless to say, they were duly renewed, for a cautious five years, including Agrippa's tribunician power.[135] A tiresome complication is added to the story of official powers by Dio's statement that the *cura morum* of Augustus was renewed in 12 B.C. for five years;[136] for, if Augustus possessed it at all, he had had it, on Dio's own account, for five years from 19 B.C., and its renewal should have occurred two years sooner. In the *Res Gestae* it is asserted that the offer of a *cura morum* was made again in 11 B.C., but declined. There was, however, a revision of the Senate list in 11 B.C., performed by virtue of *censoria potestas*; perhaps Dio's garbled tale is an echo of that temporary grant. A much more significant constitutional fact is that in 13 B.C. Agrippa's *imperium* was, at last, defined as *maius*.[137] For a brief span he and Augustus had equal formal authority as rulers of the Roman world; it was a joint rule of two colleagues, the one superior to the other only in *auctoritas*. We notice the immense significance of that experiment all too little because fate decreed that it should be so brief; for in March 12 B.C., only a few days after another great ceremony, stressed in the *Res Gestae*, the solemn assembly of the Roman people at which, at long last, Augustus became *pontifex maximus*,[138] Agrippa died.[139] Catastrophe following hard on the heels of triumph is an obstinate motif in the story of the age.

But the engine of Roman imperialism, having been turned on, was not allowed to falter: Tiberius Nero and Nero Drusus embarked at once on their great joint *aristeia* of 12–9 B.C. in the north, and Augustus set himself at Aquileia and other northern towns, to be in touch with the grand strategy. Tiberius already knew, before he left for Illyricum, what he was going to have to do: divorce Agrippa's daughter, Vipsania, by whom he had a son, and marry Iulia, Agrippa's widow. The marriage took place in 11 B.C., and caused all parties untold misery: lives sacrificed to duty. Augustus was relentless in his demand for co-operation, from high as from low, and there are straws in the wind, by the middle of the reign, that not even those well-disposed in general were keen to co-operate on his stern terms. Hence various experiments to get the Senate to work properly, and to encourage the elite not to turn their backs on public service, which belong in this decade.[140]

To celebrate the second year of the northern campaigns, in which Drusus, the younger stepson but the favourite of the ruler and the public,[141] had the more spectacular part, both he and Tiberius were voted ovations and *ornamenta triumphalia*, and in their honour there was a

---

[135] Dio LIV.28.1.   [136] Dio LIV.30.1.   [137] Dio LIV.28.1; see above, n.113.

[138] *RG* 10. The former triumvir Lepidus had never been deprived of that priestly office, and had remained a senator until his death, though not permitted to live in Rome.

[139] The consular *Fasti* of 12 B.C. are strange: Syme deduces plague.

[140] See ch. 3 below, pp. 124–5.   [141] Tac. *Ann.* 11.41.3, *favor vulgi.*

distribution of 400 sesterces per head and games were held.[142] But then Octavia died, Augustus' sister and Antony's widow, who had given and inspired devotion. Drusus spoke the laudation, as her son-in-law.

For the third year, 10 B.C., Augustus accompanied the headquarters to Gaul, where the 'Altar at the Confluence of Rhône and Arar' was dedicated as a focus in the West for cult of the ruler, and, on the selfsame day, the future emperor Claudius was born, son of Drusus and the younger Antonia. (The prevailing view, drawing an inference from Dio, is that the dedication was in 12 B.C. It involves a strained interpretation of Suetonius' 'selfsame day'; and Augustus could not have been present at Lugdunum in that year, whereas in 10 we have corroboration from a papyrus that he was.)[143] In the winter Drusus did not return to Rome, but entered upon his consulship of 9 B.C. in absence; and in that year he carried Roman arms to the river Elbe. Those were noteworthy military achievements: Augustus and both his stepsons took imperatorial salutations, Tiberius celebrated the ovation voted to him, and Drusus was due to celebrate his. Whereupon death struck again: Drusus, the darling of all, died, in his consular year, aged 29, on 24 September – there is no record of any suffect consul being created to fill the brief vacancy. Tiberius made all speed, and, according to Dio, just managed to greet his brother before he died.[144] For Tiberius above all it was a catastrophe: as a united force they had had much to achieve.

Augustus did not permit the expansion in Germany to pause; he simply transferred Tiberius to that front. Nevertheless, to him also Drusus' departure was a bad blow, coming so soon upon those of Agrippa and Octavia; it may not be fanciful to detect a growing rigidity in Augustus' attitudes and proceedings, now that he was deprived of the personalities from whom he had derived support and counsel. But there is a remarkable further tale that the reader must be asked to estimate, for it plays quite a part in recent accounts: 'republicanist' opposition on the part of the stepsons. It derives from Suetonius, who says that Drusus at some time wrote to Tiberius 'about forcing Augustus to restore liberty'; there was plainly some historical source that gave Drusus that colouring.[145] Conspiracies are mentioned by Dio at the end of his account of the year 9 B.C., and in the very next year a new rule was made that slaves could be compulsorily purchased by the state so as to make them available as witnesses against their former masters in cases of treason. Have we, then, uncovered the 'crisis of 9 B.C.'? There were those who believed that Augustus suspected Drusus and had him poisoned; also, that none other than Tiberius had reported the treasonable correspon-

---

[142] L. Piso also had *ornamenta triumphalia* for a *Bellum Thracicum*, probably in 11 B.C.
[143] Dio LIV.32.1; Suet. *Claud.* 2.1; *POxy* 3020, col. 1, line 4. Absence of Augustus is, admittedly, not impossible: in 9 B.C., for example, he was at Ticinum and cannot have attended the consecration of the Ara Pacis.   [144] Dio LV.2.1.   [145] Suet. *Tib.* 50.1; *Claud.* 1.4.

dence to his stepfather. Suetonius, however, who records all that, gives one reason for hesitating, namely that there is so much evidence that Drusus was a favourite of Augustus: he had a place in the ruler's will, for instance. Antiquity was given to novelettes about poisoning; we do not have to accept that tale, and the conspiracies alluded to by Dio are unrelated. But it may be a fact that the brothers had discussed the kind of *res publica* they would like to serve under, and that Tiberius had undertaken to lay their views before Augustus while he was heavily reliant on them. We can imagine how, with Drusus gone, the sole effect would be to make Augustus reluctant to leave things to Tiberius.

The year 8 B.C. was twenty years from that sixth consulship when Augustus had begun handing the *res publica* back to the Senate and people: *vicennalia*, it would have been called in a later century, and it was, if mutedly, celebrated (though hand in hand with celebration went, again, loss: Maecenas first, and Horace shortly after). A 'census was completed, by consular *imperium* (a special, conceivably celebratory, grant), with a revision of the Senate list and – a rare curiosity – an extension of the *pomerium* of Rome.[146] Now, too, the month Sextilis was renamed 'Augustus'.[147] The anniversary was accompanied, as it had to be, by another formal renewal of Augustus' powers, for – surprisingly but perhaps also in celebration – a further complete decade; what did not accompany it was any acknowledgement of Tiberius as *collega imperii*: no love existed there, and no trust, and other possibilities were nearly in sight.

Yet the campaign of Tiberius in 7 B.C. was triumphant, leaving Germany 'practically ready to become a province of the Roman empire',[148] and permitting the discharge of large numbers of legionaries over the next few years.[149] Tiberius, who was, that year, consul for the second time, celebrated a full, formal triumph, and afterwards laid the foundation of a temple of Concord in the Forum Romanum, his thoughts perhaps still upon the lost partnership.

There were relatively everyday tasks and problems of government, not necessarily trivial. One such was an accusation, astonishingly, of *ambitus*, electoral bribery, against all the magistrates, presumably of the year 8. Augustus took care not to peer into that too closely, but he did make new rules to reduce bribery at the consular elections in the future. The very fact that it occurred shows that there was still popular choice, but it is principally a pointer to something else. What was amiss was that for twenty years Augustus had insisted on the being, in the old tradition, only two consuls a year (barring emergencies); but the office was still

---

[146] Boatwright 1986 (C 33).   [147] Dio LV.6.6. See n. 51 above.
[148] Vell. Pat. II.97.4; but see ch. 4 below, pp. 181–3.
[149] The *Res Gestae* record troop discharges in 7, 6, 4, 3 and 2 B.C.

eagerly sought after and fought over, as the crown of a social career, and soon Augustus experimented again, dividing the year into two halves, with two 'ordinary' consuls followed by two 'suffect' consuls, a system that became regular from 5 B.C.

Natural disasters, too, never ceased to punctuate the history of the biggest conurbation in the ancient world, and governments never did enough. There was a very grave fire in 7 B.C., just before the funeral games in memory of Agrippa. Augustus took occasion to reorganize the local structure of the city into fourteen official 'regions', with a devolution down to the 265 *vici* or 'blocks', the latter to be responsible for fire precautions. It did not prove adequate.

His coeval generation dying away, Augustus was obliged to place reliance on the younger folk. For Herod the Great and his dynastic problems and brutal treatment of his sons, Augustus had the greatest contempt,[150] but that turned into a terrible irony. In the year 6 B.C. Tiberius Nero received a renewal of *imperium*, plus tribunician power for five years, which proclaimed him to the world as *collega imperii*; and at that very moment he declared his wish to retire from state responsibilities and took himself off to Rhodes. Augustus staged a bit of illness to detain him, but it did not work. The historian Velleius, adulatory of Tiberius, exaggerates the consequences of his retirement into a sort of paralysis of the *res publica*,[151] and the loss of the full text of Dio for those years contributes to a possibly false picture; but it was undeniably major trouble in high politics.

The modern, as well as the ancient, interpretation is that it was dynastic trouble. Gaius and Lucius Caesar were of an age to begin their progress into the limelight (and 'above themselves' already, according to Dio, who writes that in 6 B.C. the people 'chose' Gaius as consul and Augustus had to step in and quash it: a demonstration, perhaps).[152] In 5 B.C. Gaius was made a *pontifex* and designated consul for A.D. 1, and a new title was invented for him, *princeps iuventutis* or honorary president of the order of *equites*, and a distribution of money was made in his honour; in 4 B.C. he had a seat on the great *consilium* called to settle the fate of Judaea upon the death of Herod. In 2 B.C. Lucius was made an *augur* and designated consul for A.D. 4, and became joint *princeps iuventutis*. What is more, the coinage was the medium for a course of advertisement for the pair such as neither Drusus nor Tiberius had been accorded.[153] So, then, Tiberius moved downstage, and the questions that gather about Agrippa's departure seventeen years earlier repeat themselves. Did he go in self-effacing co-operation or in rage and frustration? Scholars have conjured up binary opposites, a Claudian faction led by

150 Macrob. *Sat.* II.4.11.   151 Vell. Pat. II.100.1.
152 Dio LV.9.1–2.   153 Zanker 1987 (F 632) 218–26.

Livia Drusilla on behalf of her sons (now reduced to one) and a Julian, led by Iulia on behalf of hers, whose opposition was destined to tear at the vitals of the regime until Augustus' death, and beyond. That picture may be not so much wrong as a bit too simple. First, there could never have been any doubt, from the moment that Gaius and Lucius were adopted, that if Augustus, and they, survived long enough for them to grow to manhood they would be his chosen successors; Tiberius Nero and Nero Drusus could never have expected a role greater than that of Agrippa. Again, it was in 6 B.C., before the formal elevation of the youths began, that Tiberius retired; that elevation looks more like the ruler's instant response to, than the cause of, Tiberius' desertion. And finally, you hardly make a man *collega imperii* to kick him out: rather, to try to keep him. The latter end of Tiberius' Rhodian sojourn was certainly an unofficial exile; but there is a wider story to which his initial retirement belongs, the story of people's growing unwillingness to work with and for Augustus, and to play their roles in the drama according to his script. Tiberius Nero, with the independent spirit he had shared with his brother (and shared, to their mutual cost, with his wife, Augustus' daughter), saw himself type-cast as *collega imperii*, the new Agrippa, and rebelled. To Agrippa, his status as *collega imperii* had been an insurance for the succession of his sons, and part, anyway, of a lifelong collaboration. For Tiberius it was neither: therefore, Augustus must carry on alone.

The impression of a political standstill is doubtless false, but not much can be done to compensate. One important experiment of 4 B.C. serves to help fill the gap: it is known only from an inscription.[154] By a *senatus consultum* of that year, on a proposal from Augustus, a novel, expedited procedure became available to provincials alleging extortion by Roman magistrates, in all but the gravest (i.e. capital) cases. It probably was genuinely quicker; on the other hand it contained an unadvertised advantage for senatorial governors by enabling them to be tried by a committee of their peers instead of the mainly non-senatorial juries of the *quaestio repetundarum*.

But 2 B.C. was a year of crisis – or so it has been called. Certainly it contained paradox enough to satisfy any novelist. It began with a tremendous burst of ceremony, symbolism and festivity. Augustus was sixty; he was *consul ordinarius* (he had taken the consulship in 5 B.C. to preside over the début of Gaius Caesar, and now did the same for Lucius); and on 5 February he was officially designated *pater patriae*, 'Father of the Nation'. The title crowns the *Res Gestae*, and Suetonius quotes the very words in which it was bestowed and accepted.[155] It was not (though historians recently have tried to make it) a constitutional

[154] EJ² 311, v.   [155] Suet. *Aug.* 58.2.

statement, nor a symbol that the state was ultimately governed by the concept of *patria potestas*, nor an ingeniously invented jurisprudential basis for equating attacks on the 'divine family' with treason against the state.[156] It was an honour – an extension of the title *parens patriae* that had been accorded to Marius, to Cicero, and to Iulius Caesar, a supremely high public decoration.

Augustus' *quid pro quo* was (besides a distribution of money) some very grand consular games – a new set, the *ludi Martiales*. The name was not fortuitous, for on 12 May[157] the two young Caesars dedicated the most symbolic and triumphalist of all the Augustan public buildings, the temple of Mars Ultor at the far end of the new Augustan Forum, where those long-ago recovered standards would repose permanently. With its porticoes, friezes and caryatids, and the statues of all the Roman *triumphatores*,[158] the Augustan Forum is the building that must be most attentively listened to. Its emphasis is, actually, not so much on the 'divine family' (and we may be inclined to guess why not) as on victory and the long, successful tale of Roman imperialism: hard, bold, assertive, confident – and for constant public use, especially for law-courts.[159] And, in celebration of the celebration, another marvellous entertainment was provided, the 'naval battle of the Greeks and Persians', in a specially constructed artificial lake beside the Tiber; that, too, is recalled with pride in the *Res Gestae*.

So it was a many-sided paradox that, later in that year, Iulia, the daughter of Augustus, was deported to the island of Pandateria. Her mother Scribonia went with her into exile. Multiple adulteries were the charge against Iulia, or the excuse.[160] Tacitus says that Augustus chose to treat those adulteries as treason,[161] implying that he did not believe Iulia's offence to have been treason; but modern historians have woven here a tale of a major attempt at a *coup d'état*. It ought to be allowed, in any case, that immorality at the heart of that 'divine family' that Augustus wanted as the paradigm for his society was a blow to pride and optimism in the year of the title *pater patriae*; and, further, that Iulia, like Tiberius, was committing the crime of repudiating her role in the scenario as composed by her father. That might be enough and to spare. It is the involvement, as the foremost among Iulia's alleged lovers, of Iullus Antonius that, to some detective minds, has suggested more.[162] He was either executed or forced to commit suicide: the other named men

[156] *Contra*, respectively, Salmon 1956 (C 204); Lacey 'Patria Potestas', in Rawson 1986 (F 54) 121–44; Bauman 1967 (F 640) 235–9.   [157] For this date, rather than in August, Simpson 1977 (F 578).

[158] Zanker n.d. [*c.* 1968] (F 625); Zanker 1987 (F 632) 215. It had been long in building: Macrob. *Sat.* II 4.9. Forum dedicated earlier than temple: Degrassi 1945 (F 346).

[159] Suet. *Aug.* 29.1–2; tablets from Puteoli, Camodeca 1986 (F 311).   [160] Dio LV. 12.10–16.

[161] Tac. *Ann.* III.24.2.   [162] It did not to Tacitus, *Ann.* IV.44.5; but cf. Sen. *De Brev. Vit.* 4.5.

involved incurred mere banishment,[163] an inadequate reaction if they had been part of a treasonable conspiracy. They were members of families of the nobility, indeed,[164] and one of them had been consul in 9 B.C., as Iullus was in 10; but hardly of prominence or stature, apart from him, to justify a picture of a 'faction of the nobility' opposed to the 'radical' Tiberius. Iullus is different: son of Antony and Fulvia, spared after Actium, half-brother of the Antonias, he had become a favoured court figure. As praetor he had given the games for Augustus' birthday in 13 B.C.; he had reached the consulship in 10 B.C. and Dio's epitome states that he was allegedly out for *monarchia*. Actium reversed and revenged: was that the idea?

The greatest sobriety of judgment is needed here. One matter for pause is what fate we are to suppose Iullus and Iulia had in store for Gaius and Lucius Caesar. Were they to perish in the bloodbath? Was Iulia to sacrifice her sons? Or was the whole scheme designed to bolster their succession against Tiberius Nero? But they were secure as things were, and it was Tiberius who lived in eclipse and danger. And was Iullus to be content with prominence as a mere caretaker for Iulia's sons, an alternative Tiberius? Not, of course, that the craziness of a proposal is proof that people did not entertain it.

In 2 B.C. prefects of the praetorian guard were appointed for the first time, and some are tempted to relate that novelty to the alleged state of emergency; but caution will suggest hesitation. First, they were a pair, and mere *equites* at that; secondly, this was certainly not the moment of creation of the praetorian guard, which already existed. It is not known what commanding officer the guard had before 2 B.C. – quite probably Augustus himself, with no intermediary; in which case it is hard to see the establishment of a pair of equestrian prefects as strengthening the ruler's control in face of a crisis.

This is usually held to have been the season of Ovid's *Ars Amatoria*. That chronology has been challenged,[165] but Dio records some other activities of the 'smart set' that were capable of making Augustus' blood boil.[166] The simple man's alternative, about this story, is therefore still the best: morality uppermost in the ruler's stern plan for triumphant Rome; revelations – perhaps, indeed, made by enemies – of a fast-living set, with Iulia and Iullus at its centre; humiliation and rage of the ruler matching the psychological climate of resistance to his relentless imperatives.

The social imperatives were evident in that year in another context. The suffect consuls, Lucius Caninius Gallus and Gaius Fufius Geminus,

---

[163] The epitome of Dio says others were executed, and on a charge of conspiracy, but names no names.   [164] Syme 1986 (A 95) 91.   [165] Syme 1978 (B 179).   [166] Dio LV.10.11.

put through the *comitia* a law setting limits to the number of slaves an individual master might free by testament; and that may well have a relationship to another change attributed to 2 B.C. whereby the number of recipients of the free corn ration was cut down to 200,000. Too much foreign blood in the citizen body, and too many layabouts!

Phraates IV of Parthia had just, after a long reign, been murdered, and succeeded, by his favourite son, who, with anti-Roman zeal, had assisted in the ejection of the king of Armenia, all that while a Roman nominee. There was an irritable international correspondence, and an air in Rome as of the prelude to a Parthian war; but Augustus repeated almost exactly the successful formula of twenty years before.[167] Tiberius Nero had been his envoy then, and could have been so again, but he was in retirement: indeed, since all his formal powers had run out, and no attempt had been made to renew them, he was – like his wife – an exile. In any case, the occasion could be used to give Gaius Caesar his first impressive role in the official drama; so in 1 B.C., invested with an *imperium* for the whole East, he set out, amidst a cloud of diplomatic advisers and to the strains of eager poetasters.[168] There was no state of war, so no hurry; in A.D. 1,[169] when he entered *in absentia* upon his long-prearranged consulship, Gaius was engaged in some sort of campaign in Nabatean Arabia.[170] The hopes he carried with him (along with his brother, who died, however, in A.D. 2 at Massilia of some non-sinister cause) are revealed in a letter of Augustus to him written in September, A.D. 2: '... with you two playing your part like true men and taking over the sentry-post from me'.[171] The great diplomatic exchange of courtesies duly took place, on an island in the Euphrates,[172] followed, as it were canonically, by the march to set a Roman protégé again on the Armenian throne. This time it was not a formality. At an unknown place, Artagera, Gaius received a stab-wound, though it seemed to heal, and both he and Augustus took imperatorial salutations.[173] And then occurred the strangest event in the whole tale. Tiberius Nero had just been permitted to return to Rome, a mere private citizen, with a question-mark upon his future;[174] and now Gaius wrote home to say that *he* was going to retire into private life and contemplation.[175] He was 23. People said at the time, and they were very likely right, that Gaius was a mortally sick man, and, to Augustus'

---

[167] See above, p. 90.

[168] A propemptic effusion: Antipater, Poem 47 (Gow and Page 1968 (B 65)). Cf. Ov. *Ars Am.* I.171.   [169] The year immediately following 1 B.C.   [170] Romer 1979 (C 301).

[171] Gell. *NA* xv.7.3 (there was a collection of Augustus' 'Letters to his Grandson'). At Pisa, after his death, in an *elogium* (EJ² 69) he is called 'already designated *princeps*'.

[172] Velleius was present, and describes it, II.201.

[173] In A.D. 3, by Syme's reckonings (1979 (C 230)).

[174] Bowersock 1984 (C 40) speculates about the divided allegiance in the East between Tiberius and Gaius Caesar.   [175] Dio LV.10a.8.

culminating dismay, in A.D. 4 he died; in so short an interval were both the young hopefuls gone. But one can imagine, even before that, the effect of the letter of resignation: 'You too, son'. Like Tiberius and like Iulia: this was the canker that had rotted Augustus' third decade, that the people of his choice did not want to tread his path of duty. When, in A.D. 3, his constitutional powers were again renewed (and for a full decade) there could be no word of Tiberius Nero or of Gaius Caesar, for both were sulking in their tents; there was no *collega imperii*.

But in A.D. 4 Augustus, alone, implacable[176] and indefatigable, with imperialism and social reform still on his agenda, bowed to political necessity. Tiberius Nero was rehabilitated *faute de mieux*, received tribunician power for ten years,[177] and was appointed to command in Germany,[178] though apparently even then not with a general *imperium maius*. The dynastic goal was still the old one. Augustus' nearest relatives, apart from his daughter, were now her surviving three children, her daughters Iulia and Agrippina and her son Agrippa, the so-called 'Postumus'; and the goal determined the action. On 26 June A.D. 4 Augustus adopted Tiberius and Agrippa as his sons – 'for the sake of the *res publica*', he is supposed to have said in Tiberius' case[179] (though we cannot recapture the tone of that remark, whether of bleak resignation or of confident affirmation). For Tiberius, the choice was power and the chance of new military glory, even if only, still, as a caretaker, over against eclipse and perhaps worse. As for Agrippa, he must not be treated as just peripheral to the story.[180] The ancient writers all describe him as truculent and retarded;[181] he may have become so, or this may be no more than the official story by which his later exile and elimination were justified. But in A.D. 4 he was a still viable, if eleventh-hour, replacement for his deceased brothers. In any case, that was not the full extent of the ruler's scheme. For, at the same time, Tiberius adopted his own nephew, Nero Claudius Germanicus, son of the adored Drusus, to count as brother to his own son, the second Drusus. Germanicus was married to Agrippina, so it was their children who would carry the Julian inheritance – an exceedingly efficient way of repairing the badly torn 'divine family'.

Legislatively, A.D. 4[182] was the year of the Lex Aelia Sentia, the most

---

[176] He did, under popular pressure, allow his daughter to change her place of exile as far as Rhegium.   [177] So Dio LV.13.2. Suetonius is wrong.
[178] See ch. 4 below; Wells 1972 (E 601) 158–61. Not a new war: there had been activity all the while. Domitius Ahenobarbus, who reached the Elbe, and Marcus Vinicius had both won *ornamenta triumphalia*.   [179] Vell. Pat. II.104.1; Suet. *Tib.* 21.3.   [180] Levick 1976 (C 366) ch. 4.
[181] Vell. Pat. II.112.7; Tac. *Ann.* 1.5; Suet. *Aug.* 65.1; Dio LV.32.1–2.
[182] The 'conspiracy of Gnaeus Cornelius Cinna Magnus', placed in this year by Dio LV.14–22.1 (cf. Sen. *Clem.* 1.9) is a moral fiction. The Lex Valeria Cornelia of A.D. 5 is described in ch. 3 below, p. 127.

far-reaching of the statutes regulating slavery and freedom from slavery;[183] also of important improvements in the administration of justice,
notably the addition of a fourth *decuria* of persons liable for jury
service.[184] Militarily, Tiberius' campaigns in Germany in A.D. 4, 5 and 6
were, as twelve years before, grand successes:[185] in A.D. 5 Roman armies
reached the Elbe again, and in A.D. 6 the pincers were set to close on a
great prize, the Bohemian kingdom of Maroboduus.

It was the last moment of imperial optimism in Augustus' reign. What
was left, looked at narrowly, takes on a colouring of disaster and
disillusion, not least – though not only – in the military sphere, where it
hurt hardest: the historical irony of that letter to Gaius Caesar becomes
very acute. So before plunging into the gloom it is as well to remind
ourselves that Augustus had succeeded in establishing a political order
that survived, with modifications, for some centuries and a territorial
hegemony that expanded for another hundred years and for two
centuries lost nothing that it had included at his death.

The forces were poised against Bohemia when the shock came, the
news that all Illyricum was in rebellion. Tiberius' efforts of fifteen years
before had not proved lasting. Bohemia had to be abandoned, and
Tiberius to return to the front he had known, to battle for three heavy
years against a national uprising.[186] And it was not the only trouble of
those years.[187] We hear of cities in revolt, and proconsuls having to be
appointed instead of chosen by the lot and to have their tenures
prolonged. The wild Isaurians in Asia Minor were in ferment, and
Cossus Cornelius Lentulus won *ornamenta triumphalia* for operations in
Africa against the Gaetulians. Sardinia had to be redesignated as a part of
the 'province of Caesar' because of a recrudescence of the corsairs. There
was once again a Judaean problem: Archelaus, who had received the
lion's share on the death of Herod, had been denounced by his people
and exiled to Gaul, and Rome had to take Judaea over as an equestrian
province.[188]

Resources were strained. The very nature of the professional army
came into question, its recruitment and its cost, especially that of
providing for time-expired soldiers. Augustus attempted to cut the cost
by lengthening the term of service.[189] He also put to the Senate the
problem of funding an overall increase in state income,[190] met a stony
silence, and so, in A.D. 6, imposed on Roman citizens a death-duty of 5

[183] See ch. 18 below, pp. 893–7.   [184] Suet. *Aug.* 32.3; Bringmann 1973 (D 249).
[185] Vell. Pat. II.105–7; and see ch. 4 below, pp. 183–4.
[186] Five legions were very nearly cut to pieces in A.D. 7, with severe loss of junior officers: Vell.
Pat. II.112.6.   [187] Dio LV.28.1–4.
[188] Dio LV.27.6; Joseph. *BJ* II.111 and 117.   [189] Dio LV.23.1.
[190] He also set up a committee of consular senators to review expenditure in the public sector.
Plus ça change. . .

per cent on the estates of the moderately rich and upwards, if left to any but their families.[191] Its purpose was to fund a new Military Treasury to provide the retirement payments to the soldiers. Augustus primed it with 170 million sesterces of his own money,[192] but the death-duty was the first direct taxation of Roman citizens since 167 B.C., and was regarded by the rich, who paid it, with outrage.

The years A.D. 6 and 7 have the fairest claim of all the years of Augustus' reign to be called 'crisis' years, for upon military and financial anxieties, and widespread disaffection, there supervened natural catastrophes and dynastic discords. Nature did her best to prove that none of the problems of the great conurbation had been even halfway solved: food shortages led to rationing, and there was another bad fire. A new fire service was established, since the devolution solution had proved inadequate: thus began the *vigiles* of the imperial period, under an equestrian prefect.[193] But the plebs was disgruntled: there was a spate of revolutionary talk, and flysheets circulated at night.[194] According to Dio, a certain Publius Rufus was thought to have instigated those things, but to have had more powerful hidden backers – a story with repercussions that will emerge.

In A.D. 7 Germanicus, quaestor that year, was sent to Illyricum with troop reinforcements for Tiberius. They included not only the products of a rare levy of citizens at Rome,[195] but also slaves purchased by the government and manumitted to enable them to be enrolled.[196] Dio transmits a story that Augustus suspected Tiberius of dragging his feet and sent Germanicus to stir things up: Tiberius had actually said he had soldiers in plenty, and sent some back.[197] We may well suspect political manoeuvrings behind these facts, but they remain obscure. At the elections there were riots, and Augustus, impatient with the proprieties, nominated all the magistrates himself – the only time: he had worked at full stretch for fifty years, and crisis was taking its toll. He began to give up public appearances, and appointed a committee of senior senators to take over the hearing of embassies.

There is a view amongst historians[198] that in Augustus' last decade all was done to the tune of Tiberius, who returned to Rome after each annual campaign. That would be not unlikely, though the arguments tend to be circular and it was normal for commanders-in-chief to return to Rome between campaigning seasons. The question whether it was Tiberius' tune that was being played is certainly very relevant to the next item in the tale of 'passion and politics'. No doubt it ought to have been

---

[191] Dio LV.25.5.   [192] RG 17.
[193] Dio LV.26.4–5. A new 2 per cent tax on sales of slaves was instituted to fund the new service.
[194] Dio LV.27.2–3.   [195] EJ² 368.   [196] Dio LV.31.1.
[197] Vell. Pat. II.113.   [198] Already stated by Dio LV.27.5.

young Agrippa's privilege to be quaestor and take the troops to Germany; instead, probably in A.D. 6,[199] he was removed from Rome to Surrentum, and in A.D. 7 he was repudiated by Augustus and deported to the island of Planasia. In A.D. 8 his sister also, young Iulia, suffered banishment, never to return.[200] Scholars deduce treason again, at the heart of the 'divine family': a story going back to 23 B.C., of thirty years of crisis in the 'Party', of the Julian faction's last bid against the, otherwise, now inexorable accession of the hated Claudian. Some speculations on those lines are too close to fiction, but there is a case. Why the exile of Agrippa? He was alleged to have been, or turned into, a cretinous thug; but Germanicus' brother Claudius, spastic and eccentric, though kept out of the limelight, was neither repudiated nor banished: his star was yet to rise. Agrippa, too, had been denied the limelight, being accorded no title of *princeps iuventutis* and no permission to stand early for office. Was that at Tiberius' behest? Had Agrippa less than mildly suggested that it was not good enough? Suetonius carries a story about a person (of low status) who 'in the name of young Agrippa put out to the public a most bitter letter about him' (Augustus).[201] But those who rush to make use of the tale fail to notice its ambiguities: it is not clear whether the biographer meant 'on Agrippa's behalf' or 'pretending it was written by Agrippa', nor whether the letter was supposed to have been a private one that was wrongly made public – and if so to whom it was addressed – or a letter actually addressed to the public.

As for Iulia, the official account was, again, adultery, though with only one partner, Decimus Iunius Silanus – who was merely told that he was no longer a friend of the emperor, which he took as dismissal from Rome.[202] She, by contrast, was banished, implacably, for life (and it turned out to be twenty years); she was supported financially – this we must take into account – by Livia Drusilla.[203] No less to be taken into account is the identity of Iulia's husband: he was Lucius Aemilius Paullus, who appears in Suetonius' canon of conspirators against Augustus.[204] He is there linked with one Plautius Rufus, who reminds historians (though it is a thin point) of the Publius Rufus who is supposed to have spread the revolutionary pamphlets in A.D. 6. Were husband and wife convicted of conspiracy? And of joint, or separate, conspiracies? It has been common to suppose that Paullus was executed, but a strong case has been made against that.[205] If he was only banished, that is insufficient punishment for conspiracy; and Iulia's offence is better seen as what it was stated to be. Augustus insisted on the child she bore

[199] Vell. Pat. II.112.7.
[200] Ovid, too, had to go, and he, too, was never to be allowed back home.
[201] Suet. *Aug.* 51.1.   [202] Unlike Ovid, he was allowed back by Tiberius, Tac. *Ann.* III.24.
[203] Tac. *Ann.* IV.71.4.   [204] Suet. *Aug.* 19.1; Syme 1986 (A 95) ch.9.
[205] Syme 1986 (A 95) 123–5.

not being allowed to live, and the sharp-eyed Tacitus found no other cat to let out of the bag. Nor is either Iulia named in Suetonius' canon of conspirators.

But yet another mysterious set of facts adds fuel to the hypothesis of conspiracy. There were two – or in an ironical sense perhaps three – attempts to achieve a break-out for Agrippa. In Suetonius' conspiracy-list 'Audasius and Epicadus had intended to spirit Iulia the daughter and Agrippa the grandson from the islands where they were held to the armies.'[206] There is something amiss with the tale, because by the time Agrippa was sent to his island 'Iulia the daughter' had left hers. Perhaps it is a mere slip for 'Iulia the granddaughter'; but the elder Iulia was still in exile and still a potential focus for dissidence, so the error may be different. In any case, the story reinforces the view that Agrippa was in banishment because he was dangerous; and the danger was to Tiberius. The second story is how, immediately upon Augustus' death, Agrippa's slave Clemens went hotfoot to Planasia but arrived too late, the *primum facinus novi principatus* having already occurred – and how, two years later, he obtained a following by passing himself off as Agrippa, was arrested and put to death, and care was taken not to probe deeply into what were suspected to be his powerful backers 'in the house of the *princeps*' and amongst senators and *equites*.[207] That story finds credence amongst historians; the third, ironical indeed if true, still divides them. It is that Augustus, shortly before his death, visited Agrippa in his exile and they were reconciled.[208] Whether true or not, that tale, too, points in a consistent direction: Agrippa was politically of high significance. And it may well be that in conjuring up a conspiracy against Augustus (or Tiberius) in the years A.D. 6 to 8 historians have tried to be too clever. The *cui bono* of the elimination of Iulia's children was Tiberius, and they may have been the victims rather than the authors of a deadly dynastic struggle.

On the return of Tiberius from Illyricum at the beginning of A.D. 9 there was a ceremony of *reditus* in his honour in the Saepta; and resentment, not on the part of the plebs but of its betters, spilt over: the *equites* protested against the rules of the *lex Iulia de maritandis ordinibus*, with their penalties upon the childless. Old Augustus read the assembled populace in the Forum a furious lecture about childlessness;[209] and while Tiberius travelled back to the front for what was to prove the conclusive campaign against the rebels in Dalmatia, a Lex Papia Poppaea was put to the assembly by the suffect consuls. It modified the statute of twenty-five

[206] Suet. *Aug.* 19.2.   [207] Tac. *Ann.* 11.39–40.

[208] Tac. *Ann.* 1.5.1 (a 'rumour'); Dio LVI.30.1. Dismissed by Syme 1986 (A 95) 415. Part, perhaps, of a propaganda campaign against Tiberius and Livia.

[209] Dio LVI.1–9 invents two speeches; Suet. *Aug.* 34 with 89, 2 and Livy, *Per.* 59.

years earlier: Dio and Suetonius, however confusing and incompatible their accounts, give an impression that concessions were made, whereas Tacitus speaks expressly to the contrary.[210] For the unmarried, at any rate, one should not underestimate the public ignominy in which the legislation sought to place them: if the *ordo equester* (being, presumably, the biggest concentration of wealthy *caelibes*) thought they had influence with the aged ruler, they were sharply rebuffed.

When, late in A.D. 9, with the great rebellion crushed, Tiberius and Germanicus returned to Rome, full triumphs were voted to Augustus and Tiberius, and Germanicus was voted *ornamenta triumphalia*, praetorian standing, and permission to stand for the consulship ahead of normal.[211] But no triumphs ensued, for, five days later, the mood of congratulation was shattered by the yet more unimaginable blow of the 'disaster of Varus';[212] three legions lost, and everything beyond the Rhine lost with them. The optimism of Roman conquest had, as in Illyricum, proved unjustified, *imperium sine fine* unattainable. Augustus' nerve very nearly broke, and we are told he had thoughts of suicide. The defeat laid bare the slender military base on which the empire rested; the Illyricum campaign had already stretched manpower to the limits. Conscription was applied, and stepped up, and there are tales of people executed for refusing the levy. All veterans were recalled, freedmen again enrolled. It was a question whether the Roman people would stand it: fear of a *tumultus* in Rome led to drafting of an extra military force, and the ruler's personal German bodyguard was held no longer safe.[213]

Tiberius had to take on Germany. He toiled for three more hard years,[214] with nothing to show for all of them that could be treated triumphally; when his ceremony of *reditus* finally took place,[215] and his celebration of a full triumph, it was labelled not as 'over the Germans' but as the postponed triumph 'over Illyricum'. There was to be no *provincia Germania*.

In the year 12 Germanicus was consul. He was emerging as the new 'limelight personality': Dio has surprisingly much about his part in the Illyrian and German campaigns, which suggests that someone must have been writing them up.[216] However, his consular year was anything but cheerful. Natural disaster played its part again: the Tiber in spate, the Circus flooded and the *ludi Martiales* displaced. A new, sinister, note is

---

[210] Dio LVI.10; Suet. *Aug.* 34; Tac. *Ann.* III.28.3–4.

[211] Numerous subordinate commanders got *ornamenta triumphalia* for their services during the critical campaigns: Messalla Messallinus, M. Lepidus, C. Vibius Postumus, M. Plautius Silvanus.

[212] A 'set piece' in Velleius, II.117.2–119; another in Dio, LVI.18–22.2.   [213] Dio LVI.23.

[214] A vexed problem of chronology plagues these years, crystallizing round the question whether Tiberius' triumph was in A.D. 12 or 13 (we know at least the day: 23 October).

[215] Of which the Gemma Augustea is the visual monument: Simon 1986 (F 577) 156–61 and Pl. 11.   [216] Dio LVI.11 and 15.

heard, of seditious literature burnt and authors punished. Dates are uncertain, but this year is quite likely that of the banishment of the abrasive, witty barrister Cassius Severus,[217] for having 'defamed men and women of the highest status with licentious writings' – not, to judge from Tacitus' phrase, the ruler himself; but the offence was treated, for the first time, under the law of treason. One of Cassius' sarcasms related to the burning, by decision of the Senate, of the writings of a fellow-barrister, Titus Labienus, who wrote history, it seems, with a 'republicanist' flavour: he committed suicide.[218] And Ovid's books had been withdrawn from the libraries. The deterioration is evident: an anxious, touchy government and a subservient Senate.

In A.D. 13 the constitutional powers of Augustus and Tiberius were renewed again for ten years, and the *imperium* of Tiberius was at last declared equal to that of Augustus:[219] he was *collega imperii*. He had saved the sum of things, twice, he was fifty-six, and his duty was now quietly to take over, with Germanicus, his adopted son, and Drusus, his original son, as the hopefuls for the succession. The senatorial sub-committee that prepared business for the full Senate, which Augustus had always used as his sounding-board, was given a revised membership and new powers, enabling it to pass resolutions equivalent to formal *senatus consulta*; Tiberius, Germanicus and Drusus joined it as regular members.[220] The purpose was stated to be to relieve Augustus of regular attendance at the Senate, but one can see how it could be an organ for quiet transition. Not that Augustus was 'going downhill': paradoxically, the very next thing we hear in Dio, when upper-class fretfulness over the iniquities of the death-duty became vocal again, displays the hand of the old manipulator still on the helm of policy. Augustus challenged the senators, individually, to suggest any better way of raising the necessary revenue, and then put in hand apparent preparations to institute an even stiffer scheme (a land-tax on *solum Italicum*), whereupon they decided to keep the devil they knew.[221]

Augustus and Tiberius began a census, with a special grant of consular *imperium*, and completed the *lustrum* in the next year on 11 May. Augustus travelled as far as Beneventum with Tiberius, who was on his way to Illyricum. Velleius has it that Tiberius' journey was 'to consolidate in peace what he had conquered in war',[222] which is an admission that there was not anything needing the attention of Tiberius in Illyricum; but the two *collegae imperii* could not sit in Rome together. As

---

[217] Tac. *Ann.* 1.72.3 with the notes of Goodyear 1981 (B 62).   [218] Sen. *Controv.* x *Praef.* 4–8.

[219] Vell. Pat. II.121.1 with the note of Woodman 1983 (B 203); Suet. *Tib.* 20–21.1. There can be no certainty just when Tiberius received that grant.

[220] Dio LVI.28.2–3; Crook 1955 (D 10) 14–15. Cf. EJ² 379, which may have some genuine documentary basis.   [221] Dio LVI.28.4–6.   [222] Vell. Pat. II.123.1.

in Marcus Agrippa's distant day, they must operate apart; yet, evidently, it was no longer wise for Tiberius to be many days' journey away. Augustus, on his way home, spent a few days at Capri, which he had acquired from the city of Naples, in exchange for Ischia, because he and Tiberius liked it.[223] He attended local games at Naples, and struggled as far as an old family property at Nola, where, on 19 August, he died.

Transmission, both constitutional and dynastic, had been taken care of. There was a *collega imperii* in place, and he should not have too many problems, for all that three members of the 'divine family', Augustus' nearest blood-relations, lived in exile – one, poor fellow, too dangerous to be left.[224] Factual power would depend on whether the system had become sufficiently ingrained in Roman political life to survive, without seriously imaginable alternative, the rule of successors less skilful and less ruthless than Augustus; and in that respect his long reign had helped to make success somewhat more likely than not. In the course of the more than forty years since Actium a new age of European history had, in fact, managed to struggle into being, but our narrative has at least shown how far its genesis was from any kind of blueprint.

[223] Suet. *Aug.* 92.2 Dio LII.43.2.
[224] Pani 1979 (C 185) has acute, if over-stated, analysis of the dynastic situation.

CHAPTER 3

AUGUSTUS: POWER,
AUTHORITY, ACHIEVEMENT

J. A. CROOK

I. POWER

Rome's tradition of government, down to Iulius Caesar, was characterized by distributed power and multiple sources of decision. That was
never to return. From 30 B.C. onwards, the whole Roman world found
itself in the grasp of a single ruler, possessing all power and making all
decisions, except insofar as he might choose to leave some of them to
others. We are insistently bidden to penetrate behind the 'façade' to the
'reality' of Augustus' power, and some advantage is to be gained if, to
begin with, we separate the power – its extent and sources and the
functions it was used to accomplish – from the authority, which was the
dress in which the power was clothed. But we must remember that such a
separation is, in the long run, artificial, because, in the actual political life
of a nation, power and its formalizations are inextricably linked, and
where authority is entrenched recourse to power is unnecessary.

Tacitus, in a paragraph which, if its hostility of tone be discounted,
remains the most masterly succinct statement of what Augustus did,
writes thus: '. . . he laid aside the title of triumvir and paraded himself as
consul and as content with the tribunician authority for looking after the
commons. The soldiery he enticed with gifts, the people with corn, and
all alike with the charms of peace and quiet; and thus he edged forward
bit by bit (*insurgere paulatim*), taking into his hands the functions of
Senate, magistrates, laws.'[1] Both as to the use of power, and its spheres of
application, and as to its translation into constitutional terms, *insurgere
paulatim* describes what occurred with profound insight. What did not
change or develop was the ruler's hold on actual coercive power: he
possessed that, totally, from the start, and never let a particle of it slip
from his hands. Power, he had; functions, he increasingly took over;
formulations of that power and those functions he carefully fostered. But
one aspect deserves to be stressed from the outset: initiative. All policy
was decided by Augustus, as far as we know.[2] In making decisions he
naturally listened to representations from, and took advice from,
appropriate quarters, and, for all we know, he may have put into practice

[1] Tac. *Ann.* 1.2.1.   [2] Millar 1977 (A 59) 616.

policies proposed to him by others, though the state of the evidence makes that difficult to demonstrate. But, apart from what he might choose to leave to others, for example to the Senate, he presided over the withering away of independent sources of initiative.

Those who urge the historian to look behind the 'façade' and confront the 'reality' of Augustus' power mostly imply that he should acknowledge that Augustus' ultimate possibility of coercion lay in control of the army. That is a truism, and scarcely penetrates far enough, for we have still to ask, especially in the case of that first sole Roman ruler, how he was able to control the army. The Roman Republic had had no post of Commander-in-Chief of the Armed Forces; and, until it began to change in the crucible of the late Republic, the army had been a conscript force recruited by the consuls *ad hoc*, allotted by the the Senate to those whose *provinciae* required armies, and swearing an oath of obedience to each commander set to lead them. The triumviral age had been the culmination of changes: nevertheless, it was the achievement of Augustus to create a volunteer, professional army, its size determined by himself, 'depoliticize' it,[3] and establish for it an ethos of loyalty to himself and the 'divine family'. That result was not accomplished in a day. One of the reasons why Augustus' formal authority cannot be detached from his actual power is that armies can only with difficulty and exceptionally be recruited and held without a legitimate claim. Augustus was, in the first years after 30 B.C., consul, and the *provincia* he was given from 27 B.C. entitled him to overall command of the troops within it (which was most of the troops, and their oath of obedience was necessarily to him). Although for a time there continued to be independent proconsuls with their own *auspicia*, they did not command enough forces to be a serious counterpoise to those commanded by Augustus. Perhaps the crucial fact in the whole story is that, in Augustus' first decade, Roman citizens were tired of civil war, which had brought no advantage to the ordinary soldier; that generation mostly wanted peace and discharge, and would not have been available for recruitment by a mere new pretender in a struggle against Augustus for power. By the time that war-weariness had worn off, he had succeeded in building a new army loyal to himself, and could offer it enough reward to make service worth while.

But, though legitimacy is important, the most direct influence on soldiers is that of their immediate commanding officers. It was those people's loyalty that Augustus needed to secure. The Republic had had no professional officer class with a distinct ideology or solidarity: commanding troops was something that every member of the governing class must do, but none could or wished to do for more than sporadic periods. Augustus, then, had no army lobby either to oppose him or to

[3] Raaflaub 1980 (C 190).

be coaxed into supporting him. His formal powers gave him the right to choose his *legati* for his *provincia*, which included most of the areas of military activity, and the formally independent commands soon withered away; beyond that, his ability to control who commanded the armies remained simply a part of his general patronage of those who sought high office in the state. So two things were needful to enable Augustus to keep control of the army: he had to satisfy the aspirations of the political class, and to be a reliable paymaster to the troops.

That consideration leads to the second 'brute fact' about the power of Augustus, his overwhelming predominance in resources. The figures he gives in the *Res Gestae* suffice to show that the resources he directly had and personally controlled, from the start (once the Ptolemaic fortune passed into his hands), made it inconceivable for any alternative paymaster to arise, capable of supporting any notable army against him. The *imperium* that he caused to be bestowed on himself supplied the formal right to receive out of public revenue the cost of the major part of the armies; but beyond that, though he did not need to mingle the state's revenues officially with his private fortune, he took care to account for, and budget in the light of, the whole resources of the state.

A third aspect of Augustus' *de facto* power, and that which has received most emphasis recently, is his role as the universal patron, the sole source of benefits.[4] Already in preparation for war upon Antony and Cleopatra he had obtained from Italy and the provinces of the West an oath of personal allegiance, which was to become a standard element in the position of the ruler.[5] For a time, recently, historians urged us to see it as an oath of 'clientship' and describe Augustus as the universal *patronus* in as formal a sense as a former owner was *patronus* of his freedmen. That notion has been shown to have been too schematic,[6] and, besides, the practical importance of the oath, beyond its original context, cannot be judged. Nevertheless, patronage played a great role in the ruler's position, and its workings can be seen, already under Augustus, in various spheres. The leading families of the Republic had cultivated clientships all over the Roman world, especially in the East and in Spain and Africa; and numerous documents of the triumviral period show the 'dynasts' of the civil wars using their clients as agents in the control of cities and regions.[7] 'So-and-so, my friend' (*philos, amicus*) might be the key figure in a locality. And when there was only one 'dynast' left it was his 'friends' around the world who kept cities and regions in line with his wishes, and could expect rewards such as the grant of Roman citizenship. (One category of such supporters were the 'client kings',[8] who, even if

---

[4] Saller 1982 (F 59) esp. ch. 2.   [5] Herrmann 1968 (C 117).   [6] Saller 1982 (F 59) 73–4.
[7] Bowersock 1965 (C 39) ch. 3, and texts in Reynolds 1981 (B 270) nos. 10–12.
[8] Braund 1984 (C 254).

originally Antony's men, soon submitted to the patronage of the victor of Actium.)

But how far the upper class of Rome as a whole depended for their careers, henceforward, on the patronage of the ruler is, at least for Augustus' time, dificult to determine. It cannot be ascertained how minutely he supervised entry into the *militiae* that formed the base of every public career. After those first steps, civil promotion depended, as before, on election. We know that Augustus was prepared to promote specific candidates openly by his own canvas and vote; and he could grant the *latus clavus* or see that a man did not lack the senatorial *census*. In so far as he created new executive posts, such as the praetorian prefectures, he nominated to them as he chose. But he did not have to control the whole promotion system in painful detail. The Roman state had never had high governmental or executive posts held for life or till retirement: there were no Chancellorships or the like. Nor did Augustus establish any such posts. The structure of public careers remained sporadic and gentlemanly in character: offices were held on short tenures, and none created any kind of fief. That was in one way an advantage to the ruler, but it precluded him, even if he had wished otherwise, from dominating areas of political life through the promotion of his *amici* to permanencies.

Historians have, since the 1930s, very readily applied to this period the notion of a dominant 'Party'.[9] Augustus began his career, certainly, as a *dux partium*; when he became sole ruler, we are told, it was through the 'Party' that he continued to dominate the political world, his biggest problems, consequently, being those involved in holding the 'Party' together. That analysis is too closely based on the modern experience; and as soon as one attempts to locate the alleged 'Party' one is confronted with either too many people or too few. The obvious place to look is at the 'Friends of the Ruler', *amici principis* (and *renuntiatio amicitiae*, such as happened to Cornelius Gallus, is then described as 'expulsion from the Party'). But the *amici principis* are too broad a group, for although Augustus' few close collaborators were, of course, *amici principis*, that category could also include jurists, philosophers, doctors and poets; in fact, it is hard to say where *amicitia* ended and *clientela* began. And if we include Augustus' well-wishers in the cities of the empire, we are soon in danger of ascribing to the 'Party' more or less everyone who is not known to have been an opponent of the regime – at which point the concept ceases to be helpful. Neither is any structural organization to be seen such as is nowadays associated with the idea of a 'Party', or would have held Augustus' adherents in the Roman world together politically. Of his handful of close associates, and how he bound them to him, there

[9] The most cogent account in terms of 'Party' is Béranger 1959 (c 27).

will be more to say later; it is not at a 'Party' that we shall be looking, but at a dynastic network.

The fact that one finds it impossible not to speak of Augustus 'doing' this or 'deciding' that or 'establishing' the other is a reflection of blunt reality. It was he who decided what campaigns should be waged and when, and by armies of what size. As overall commanders of the main enterprises he appointed whom he chose. He decided policy towards Parthia, and the disposal of Judaea (though in that case we have in Josephus a window through which to watch him taking public advice).[10] It was he who settled, not who should be consuls, but, much more importantly, how many consuls and praetors there should be each year, and from what minimum ages men might hold office. The campaign to legislate for morality was his campaign. And as he took over functions, such as responsibility for food supply, security and fire-fighting in the capital, so his executive hold grew on more and more aspects of public life. Of power, that is to say of initiative and its important counterpart, the power to prevent things being done, Augustus held the essential reins from the beginning, and the rest he took over.

II. AUTHORITY

So the whole Roman world had a single ruler. The Greek-speaking part of that world , used to rulers and their ideology, saw no complications. By the time of, let us say, Hadrian or Marcus Aurelius, the ruler's total power was equally taken for granted in Rome, Italy and the West, and descriptions and justifications of it in Roman terms were available without embarrassment or hesitation. It was due to Augustus that that came to be so, because he combined a conservative cast of mind, and a vision of himself as restorer of Rome's erstwhile greatness and stability, with the ruthless determination to turn his power into a transmissible system. The descriptions and justifications of the power of the Roman ruler run, for that reason, on two parallel tracks: conformity to *mos maiorum* and creation of 'charisma'.

It was suggested in chapter 2 above that accounts of the traditional elements in Augustus' position in terms of a 'hoax', a 'cloak', or a 'veneer', masking 'brute power', though common, are seriously inadequate. The better concept is 'legitimization': 'political power and legitimacy rest not only in taxes and armies, but also in the perceptions and beliefs of men'.[11]

The narrative in chapter 2 showed how the main constitutional elements of the imperial system, *imperium proconsulare maius* and *tribunicia*

---

[10] Joseph. *BJ* II. 25 and 81: *AJ* XVII.229 and 301; Crook 1955 (D 10) 32.
[11] Hopkins 1978 (A 45) 198.

potestas, arose as solutions to particular political situations rather than out of any global vision. What is more, by no means every element of the eventual system was in place by Augustus' death: some of the cogs were added by his successors, and some of what were, during all his time, still experiments, hardened into fixity under his successors. Whether the inventive brain was that of Augustus alone, we cannot be sure. It is possible that the conventions of ancient historiography, aggravated by the self-advertising genius of Augustus, may have caused the suppression from the record of people whose ideas and influences helped to create the imperial system. But little can be done to put that record straight. A final preliminary is to observe that one may judge the product to have been a remarkable achievement without, necessarily, admiring it wholeheartedly.

The Roman Republic – to repeat – had had, by tradition and convention, multiple points of decision-making: votes of the *comitia*, resolutions of the Senate, edicts of magistrates, interventions of tribunes, verdicts of criminal juries, *sententiae* of lay judges in the civil courts. The most fundamental long-term political trend of the imperial age of Roman history is the dwindling of that multiplicity until decision-making was, by formal rule even, in the hands of the emperor or of those to whom he might delegate authority. When it is asked how far Augustus carried Rome along that path – the path to 'the emperor is dispensed from the laws' and 'what is pleasing to the emperor has the force of statute' – two contrasting answers are given by historians, and debate is not over.

One answer was implied in the narrative of chapter 2, where Augustus was described as keeping, and brilliantly utilizing, the old republican unwritten 'rule-book' and its well-tried terminology, and rejecting offers of powers formally inconsistent with that; but modern scholarship has repeatedly emphasized that there appear to exist a whole set of counterfactuals to that picture, which would lead to the view that, in fully formal terms, Augustus' constitutional position was quite different, and quite revolutionary. One source, above all, poses the problem: the so called *lex de imperio Vespasiani*, the surviving second bronze tablet of an inscription on which were set out the constitutional powers conferred on the emperor Vespasian.[12] The sixth surviving clause reads: ' . . . and that, whatever he judges to be in accordance with the interest of the state and the solemnity (*maiestas*) of divine and human and public and private affairs, he shall have the right and power to do and perform, as the divine Augustus, and Tiberius Iulius Caesar Augustus, and Tiberius Claudius Caesar Augustus Germanicus, had'. If that sentence be taken at its face value, the consequences for the picture so far given of

[12] EJ² 364; Brunt 1977 (C 335).

Augustus' formal position are devastating, for in that event it must be admitted that he had, all the time, in the most formal sense,[13] total constitutional power. That conclusion is particularly welcome to legal historians, as an explanation of how it was that Augustus seems to have been accepted as the head of the legal order, which no concatenation of executive or initiative powers (which is what *imperium* and *tribunicia potestas* were) could have achieved. Numerous further pieces can be fitted into the picture, especially the remark in Gaius' *Institutes*[14] that ' . . . it has never been doubted that it [a decision by the emperor, *constitutio principis*] has the force of statute', and the statement in Suetonius' *Life of Caligula* that Caligula received *en bloc*, at his accession, the 'right and arbitrament of all matters'.[15] Strabo's claim that Augustus had the arbitrament of peace and war[16] is another item for the dossier. And scholars have found, in phrases from the sources here and there, possible titles for the supremacy Augustus is supposed to have received – 'care of the *res publica*', 'headship of the common weal', 'Principate', or just *imperium*.

Augustus told the world how he wished it to think about this in the *Res Gestae*. Minimizing his formal powers, and insisting on his rejection of powers contrary to *mos maiorum*, he asserted that what he predominated in was *auctoritas*,[17] the predicate of 'being accepted as a top person' that the 'chief men' (*principes viri*) of the Republic had been said to possess, by which the things he commanded were done simply because it was he who commanded them. Some historians have tried to show that unofficial *auctoritas* was turned – by some step that has eluded us – into an official power of legislation, or that it replaced *imperium* as the formal statement of total power, or that by an edict of 28 B.C. Augustus received a formal 'Principate' that carried all else with it.[18]

There is no compatibility between the two pictures, and no compromise will accommodate both; it is necessary to choose. The choice made in chapter 2 and in the present account, of the more old-fashioned, 'minimalist' – and at present heterodox – picture of the 'Augustan constitution' imposes some immediate caveats and clarifications. First, to repeat: neither picture is an account of *de facto* power; both are accounts of descriptions, justifications, legitimizations, of power. To choose the first is not, therefore, to imply that Augustus finished up any the less the *de facto* ruler of Rome; it is to say that he and his contemporaries clothed his rule in concepts that were not yet of the monolithically monarchical kind familiar to the Severan emperors and their contempor-

---

[13] *Ius* and *potestas*.   [14] Gai. *Inst.* 1. 5.   [15] Suet. *Calig.* 14.1.   [16] Strab. XVII.3.25 (840C).
[17] The Greek is ἀξίωμα. The Latin word that stood in that place was not known until discovery of the Antioch-in-Pisidia copy of the *RG* (published 1927), and Mommsen's guess was *dignitas*.
[18] Respectively, Magdelain 1947 (C 167); Grant 1946 (B 322); Grenade 1961 (C 103).

aries two hundred years later. Secondly it imposes the duty to offer an alternative account of at least three texts, but especially of the sixth clause of the *lex de imperio Vespasiani*, the so-called 'discretionary clause'.[19]

The difficulty about believing that clause to mean, baldly, what it seems to imply – that is, that Augustus already had total, formal power to act at will – is that it would have made otiose the whole of the rest of the document, including the grants of the major specific powers that presumably occupied the missing first tablet. Proper significance needs, instead, to be given to its position in the list of regulations: it belongs to a closing group, in which the seventh clause grants the new ruler exemption from certain statutes and the eighth validates retrospectively his actions before becoming ruler. That position establishes for the sixth clause its natural and appropriate role as a grant of residual emergency powers.[20] It is, in any case, erroneous to invoke the 'discretionary clause' as a prop for the ruler's legislative authority, for it gives him power to do things, whereas legislation is only in a truistic sense the 'doing' of things: it is the creation of rules, an altogether broader activity.

Gaius, writing an elementary law-book in the second century A.D., sounds uncomfortable in his protestation (if it is his) that 'no one has doubted' that a *constitutio principis* has the force of statute. Such was certainly correct doctrine in his own day, and perhaps we should simply infer from his embarrassment that he knew that earlier constitutional statements had not taken that form. But Gaius' passage is in a more parlous state still, for it continues by giving a reason for the principle that a *constitutio principis* has the force of statute which is deficient in logic: '... because the emperor receives his *imperium* by statute'. The *non sequitur* is so blatant as to cast doubt whether Gaius could have penned such an absurdity. It bears, too, the marks of an unintelligent echo of Ulpian's account, quoted in Justinian's *Digest*, of what is there called the 'royal law', *lex regia*;[21] it is in all probability an intrusion into the real text of Gaius, which will simply have stated the rule about imperial pronouncements that prevailed in his day.

The third text is that of Strabo. He was a contemporary and a serious author; but his assertion that Augustus received 'headship of the hegemony' and 'the power of war and peace for life' comes at the end of his *Geography*. That is not a work of legal science, and he is not making a constitutional statement. (He is, in fact, detailing the division of the provinces into 'people's provinces' and 'Caesar's provinces'; and that

---

[19] The view here argued for is mentioned, but dismissed, by Brunt 1977 (C 335) 113.

[20] For my negative argument, see Jolowicz and Nicholas 1972 (F 660) 365–6; for my positive argument, see Hammond 1959 (A 43) 306, n. 59; de Martino 1974 (A 58) fasc. I, 501–2.

[21] *Dig.* 1.4.1 pr., Ulpian, I *Inst.*: 'Quod principi placuit legis habet vigorem: utpote cum lege regia, quae de imperio eius lata est, populus ei et in eum omne suum imperium et potestatem conferat.'

was actually accomplished not by virtue of any great overriding power of Augustus, but, in all probability, in a senatorial debate.)[22]

The case, then, for Augustus having been granted a formal 'constitutional monarchy' does not prevail over the account, derived from Dio and elsewhere, of his receiving at different stages a concatenation of particular powers; and when Dio himself says that it was from the beginning 'unalloyed monarchy'[23] he is not giving a description but making a comment.

In any case, there is still more to be said about the constitutional forms in which the ruler's power was expressed. They interacted with the 'brute realities' by creating boundaries of normal conduct: the clothing helped to define the role. And the separate powers had a further usefulness: they could be applied piecemeal in the gradual promotion of the ruler's principal collaborator to the position of *collega imperii*. The pedantic precision of their use in that way can be observed in the papyrus fragment of a Greek translation of Augustus' funeral laudation of Agrippa: ' ... tribunician power for five years in 18 B.C. on the basis of a *senatus consultum*, and again in 13 B.C., plus, in a statute, that no man's authority should be greater than yours in any province to which the public weal of Rome might hale you'.[24] That careful formulation helps to corroborate the case that has been argued here, that the ruler's own powers were described in terms of a concatenation rather than by some global formula.

Auctoritas is the aspect of the forms (in the sense that it could be given a name and is appealed to in the *Res Gestae*) that lay closest to the actuality. It was personal to the individual ruler, and if he lacked or lost it his rule was in peril. He possessed it partly by force of personality, partly by the 'brute fact' that he held the reins of power; yet at the same time it was by possessing *auctoritas* that he held those reins, for, insofar as he possessed it, he had only to command to be obeyed. Inscriptions recording that things were done 'by order of Augustus', *iussu Augusti*,[25] ought not to cause perplexity: they are the reflection of *auctoritas*, for the people concerned were content to state that they had done things because Augustus told them to. *Auctoritas* was, furthermore, the link between the conformity to *mos maiorum* (for it had been predicated of republican *principes viri*) and the creation of 'charisma' (because it was predicated of the ruler as an individual): it could pave the way for the insertion of the ruler's personality in the permanent, extra-constitutional consciousness of the people.

But legal historians are quite right, that it is above all for the ruler's role as an issuer of norms, regulations to be obeyed generally and for the future, that we need to seek the constitutional basis, because that role is

[22] Lacey 1974 (C 146).   [23] Dio LII.I.I.   [24] EJ² 366.   [25] EJ² 283; 368.

not explicable in terms of the 'blunt realities' of power. Augustus' word, though it was as well to obey it in the instant case, did not 'have the force of statute'. He was offered, as a special grant, the right to make *leges Augustae*, but turned it down; instead he put bills before the *comitia* by virtue of his tribunician power, and they became *leges Iuliae*.[26] He could summon and put motions to the Senate, but the resulting decisions were *senatus consulta*.[27] His edicts would lapse unless validated, at least tacitly, by his successors (though is was probably not doubted that they would be).[28] The *responsa prudentium*, 'opinions of the jurists' (the jurists of the late Republic had sought normative status for their *responsa*,[29] which came, in the imperial period, to count as an official source of law) continued to depend on the *auctoritas* of the individual jurist. Augustus, besides himself giving some *responsa*,[30] is said to have 'decided that they [the jurists] should give their opinions *ex auctoritate eius*'.[31] There are reasons for being extremely unsure what exactly that meant or what resulted from it. Some scholars see it as a takeover by the ruler of the interpretation of the law, which is very implausible; others think it just gave certain favoured jurists a status somewhat like that of English Queen's Counsel. In any case, what supported the privilege was not *imperium* or *potestas*, but, properly, *auctoritas*, Augustus' *auctoritas* supplementing, as it were, that of the particular jurist.

The ruler in the imperial period had the role, also, of supreme and ultimate judge. In the Republic there had been no supreme judge or court of the Roman state, and decisions both of the criminal and of the civil courts were inappellable. So it has again to be asked what part Augustus played in that important development, and by what constitutional authority. Under him the civil courts continued to function in the standard way, and so did the criminal *quaestiones*, with, even, an addition, the adultery court; and for the organization of them all the important pair of statutes *de iudiciis* was passed.[32] But besides that, there existed already judicial appeal to the ruler as a supreme court and jurisdiction by the ruler at first instance, in the form of pure *cognitio*: there is not much evidence, and it is anecdotal at that, but historians mostly, and rightly, accept that at least tentative beginnings can be perceived under Augustus.[33] Attempts to derive that *extra ordinem* jurisdiction of

---

26 And after the one great burst of 'Julian Laws' there are very few certain cases of even those.

27 Not until the second century A.D. was the *oratio principis* in the Senate treated as *per se* normative.

28 For normative-looking edicts of Augustus see EJ² 282, and, in the law, *Dig.* 16.1.2 pr. and 28.2.26.   29 Frier 1985 (F 652) 186–7.

30 E.g. *Dig.* 23.2.14.4. See also the new fideicommissary jurisdiction, *Inst. Just.* II.25 pr. and 23.1.   31 Pomponius at *Dig.* 1.2.2.49. On *ius respondendi* see, especially, Wieacker 1985 (F 706).

32 Essential still: Girard 1913 (F 653). On the *decuriae*, see Bringmann 1973 (D 249) 235–42.

33 Suet. *Aug.* 33; Val. Max. VII.7.3–4; Dio LV.7.2.

Augustus from republican precedents and his traditional constitutional powers[34] all fail, at least in part, however hard scholars press into service the early grants of 'judging when called upon' and the 'vote of Athena',[35] or seek to extract a judicial power from his proconsular *imperium* or – for those who believe in its existence – his consular *potestas*. It seems necessary to posit some formal legislative basis for Augustus' jurisdiction; and as that is unlikely to have been a statute of which no hint survives in the sources, a reasonable guess, in a situation of admitted uncertainty, is that something may have been contained in the *leges de iudiciis*. Be that as it may, the emergence of the ruler as supreme judge and head of the legal order is the principal formal difference between the Republic and the Empire.

III. ACHIEVEMENT

1. Governing class

However one may qualify or re-phrase, the late Republic was running into an imbalance between the growing scale of its responsibilities as a world power and the organization needed to meet them,[36] and, with further growth of empire, some initiatives would have had to be taken, though they did not need to be massive or revolutionary. The organs of government of the Roman empire are treated in various chapters below, but we must here consider what part Augustus played in their development.

To call the Senate an 'organ of government' brings out vividly the change it had to undergo, for it had been, not an 'organ', but the government itself. To an extent, that continued to be so.[37] There was no 'dyarchy': just as Augustus' *imperium maius* entitled him to determine things all over the empire, so *senatus consulta* could be of universal application. And the Senate gained (like Augustus) one completely new role, as a court of law.[38] Nor need it be doubted that Augustus' repeated efforts to reduce the size and purify the social composition of the Senate were motivated by his desire for that body to retain a responsible role in public affairs. The sub-committee he set up to prepare senatorial business with him will have improved, not diminished, the chance of the Senate to maintain a hold on serious matters of state, as well as for the ruler to propose initiatives and gauge reactions.[39] As individuals, the senators remained the holders of virtually all the top offices of state – in principle,

---

[34] The principal attempt is that of Jones 1960 (A 47) ch. 5.
[35] Dio LI.19.7; and see ch. 2 above, p. 74.   [36] Though *contra*, Eck 1986 (C 82).
[37] Brunt 1984 (D 27).   [38] Ov. *Tr.* II.131–2; Dio LV.34.2; and see ch. 12 below, pp. 408–9.
[39] Crook 1955 (D 10) 9–10.

all home magistracies, all legionary legateships and all governorships of provinces, save for the one major exception, Egypt, and a few minor ones. (Nor was Egypt any harbinger of change: no further major province, nor any other legionary command, became equestrian till Severan times.) Senators also retained charge of the state treasury, and supplied, exclusively, the personnel of a number of new administrative committees: *praefecti frumenti dandi* from 22 B.C.; *curatores viarum* from 20 B.C., *curatores aquarum* from 11 B.C.; *praefecti aerarii militaris* from A.D. 6; *curatores operum publicorum* (not datable); *curatores frumenti*[40] for acquiring grain in A.D. 6 and 7; the consular commission on expenditure, A.D. 6; the consular committee to take over embassies, from A.D. 8. The consuls were also charged with a new jurisdiction over *fideicommissa*, testamentary trusts. Finally, experimental but with a future of high prestige, there was the prefecture of the city.

An important advance on tradition, however, was that Augustus created in the senatorial order something closer to a hereditary peerage.[41] Suetonius informs us that Augustus permitted the sons of senators to wear the 'broad stripe', *latus clavus*,[42] and Dio that in 18 B.C. he imposed a minimum property qualification upon candidates for office, which settled at 250,000 drachmas – a million sesterces. Dio states, indeed, that Augustus' original minimum was 100,000 drachmas (400,000 sesterces), but that was just the 'equestrian' rating that everybody had to have to serve as an officer, the necessary preliminary to all political office. So 18 B.C. should date the inception of a specifically senatorial *census*.[43] Sons of senators could, henceforward, automatically stand for the offices that – still, alone – gave entrance to the order. Suetonius does not say that others could only do so as a *beneficium* of the ruler, thus giving him sole control over access to the order, but the power may have been employed to keep out 'gatecrashers'.[44] As for the property qualification, the figure was presumably chosen with an eye to getting a senatorial order of the desired size, for there were plenty of people – and not only senators – much richer than the minimum.

But Augustus' struggle was uphill, because he could not bring himself to accept the inevitability of apathy. To put it in a homely form, if you say to people 'I am the ruler, but please, everybody, carry on exactly as usual', they won't. The honorific and social position was still a goal, and legionary and provincial commands were still sought after, but the requirement of residence to attend formal meetings was thought a

[40] Dio LV.26.2; 31.4.

[41] Nicolet 1976 (D 53); Chastagnol 1973 (D 31) and 1975 (D 33). Both Mommsen and Willems had, in their day, pointed this out.

[42] Suet. *Aug.* 38.2; Suetonius does not necessarily imply that (for example, owing to a 'crisis of recruitment') they were forced to enter the Senate.

[43] Dio LIV.17.3; Suet. *Aug.* 41.1, with Carter's note.   [44] As in 36 B.C., Dio XLIX.16.1.

nuisance. Hence the changes that had to be made in the rules of senatorial procedure.[45] The 'acts of the Senate' ceased to be published,[46] and it is possible that that was intended actually to encourage freedom of oral debate; but principally the changes were by way of securing proper levels of attendance:[47] increased fines for absence, fixing of regular sessions of the Senate fortnightly on specified days, and – in capitulation, really – lowering of the quorum needed to pass valid *senatus consulta*.

Recently, in line with the general theme of 'opting out' whose repercussions on the 'divine family' were seen in chapter 2 above, historians have discerned a 'crisis of recruitment' in the governing class, especially in the Senate. In 13 B.C. the Senate itself, in Augustus' absence, alarmed at the situation, appointed men from the equestrian order to the lowest set of senatorial posts, the 'vigintivirate' (allowing them to remain *equites*), and obliged ex-quaestors over forty to draw lots for the tribunate; and on his return Augustus compelled some people with the requisite *census* to enter the Senate. In the following year there was again a shortage for the tribunate, and *equites* were forced into it, with a choice, at the end, which order to stay in. In A.D. 5 (and often, says Dio) people were unwilling to be aediles, and compulsion was used. Suetonius alleges that the additional *decuria* was necessitated by avoidance of jury-service, and Dio records the difficulty of getting people to offer their daughters as Vestal Virgins.[48] We can, then, agree as to the phenomenon, provided that a careful distinction be made. For the people at the lower end of the elite group, the sort who in the Republic would not have got beyond quaestorian rank and would have remained *senatores pedarii*, in the new dispensation the rank was not worth the trouble and expenditure. But the top was unaffected; praetorships and consulships were still sought after and fought over, hence Augustus' need to pass a *lex de ambitu* and make a rule, in 8 B.C., requiring deposits from candidates for office.[49] In 23 B.C. he had declared that only ten praetors were needed annually, and the figure was kept at that for a few years; but there was pressure, and they were restored to twelve. And in A.D. 11, there being sixteen candidates, all were let in.[50] As for the consulship, both its relinquishment by Augustus from 23 B.C. and the introduction of a second pair each year, which was regular from 5 B.C., must be seen as a response to the number of men eagerly surging up through the system and wanting the social reward: the age at which *nobiles* might reach the consulship was actually lowered.[51] So it is no wonder that in the Augustan marriage-laws one of the privileges achieved by the possession of children was priority in the candidature for office.

[45] Talbert 1984 (D 77) 222–4, following Rotondi, posits a *lex Iulia de senatu habendo* of 9 B.C.
[46] Suet. *Aug.* 36.1. [47] Dio LIV.18.3 and 35.1; LV.3. [48] Suet. *Aug.* 32; Dio LV.22.5.
[49] Dio LV.5.3. [50] Dio LVI.25.4. [51] Syme 1986 (A 95) 51–3.

The election to magistracies was plainly not intended by Augustus to go simply by his fiat. There was insistence on giving people the vote, as in the arrangements for the decurions of the twenty-eight Italian *coloniae* to have a kind of 'postal vote';[52] and Agrippa's new Saepta and Diribitorium must have been intended and used for actual voting and vote-counting, even if also for exhibitions. That might not be very significant: by Pliny's time, elections by the people in the Campus, though they still happened, were just a piece of pageantry. But to the extent to which, in Augustus' day, the ruler still needed to influence them, that state had not yet arrived. We are told how he gave presents to his own tribes and canvassed personally for his preferred candidates.[53] One of his privileges was that of 'commendation' of candidates for the higher offices, who were then 'candidates of Caesar' and automatically elected: Augustus seems to have used it sparingly, and not at all (as far as we know) for the consulship. He did not 'give' consulships to people, though we have seen in chapter 2 how he caused special arrangements to be made for the young hopefuls of the 'divine family'. Dio asserts that Augustus often chose the urban praetor himself[54] (not, it appears, the peregrine praetor, who shared the civil jurisdiction, which shows that this is nothing to do with a 'grip on the law'); doubtless what that means is that he decided which of the annually elected praetors should have the hierarchically senior position.[55] As for governors of provinces, those of Augustus' own *provincia* were, properly, his to choose: it was an immense hold on promotion to the really significant jobs. The proconsulships of the 'provinces of the Roman people', were, in principle, still determined by the lot. Some scholars are minded to show that they were somehow picked with an eye to particular talent or suitability or experience.[56] The attempt results in very little, but some manipulation of the lot is plausible, for ensuring, for example, that Africa got a soldier when needed, and we know that the lot was abandoned in at least one period of emergency.

In any case, it is a merit of recent scholarship to have pointed out that, in the Empire just as in the Republic, public responsibilities were not specialized (not even, by and large, the military ones, for every gentleman had to do some soldiering). Provided candidates seemed loyal and ordinarily competent, it did not greatly matter who received which office, and there was little need to gerrymander the system in detail, except, perhaps, negatively, to exclude men not competent enough – or too competent. The great, overriding campaign commands were just put, unashamedly, in the hands of members of the 'divine family';

---

[52] Suet. *Aug.* 46; cf. EJ² 301 II, 2.   [53] Suet. *Aug.* 40.2; 56.1.   [54] Dio LIII. 2.3.

[55] People who became *collegae imperii* seem to have held, as praetors, the urban praetorship.

[56] Szramkiewicz 1975–6 (D 75).

otherwise, the important criteria were, really, social, and it is best to view the whole as an honours system, positions of distinction graded in a traditional ladder up which the socially ambitious could move. Its other importance was as a 'brokerage' system in the distribution of the ruler's *beneficia*, because it was those who rose in the order whose recommendations carried weight, and who could obtain favours for the people or cities who were their *clientes*.[57]

The only other 'order' that mattered was that of the *equites*, and to them Augustus looked for some administrative personnel, without whom he would have had to expand the traditional magistracies and so dilute the senatorial *crème de la crème*. The wealthy class of newly united Italy was ready to be brought into the scheme of things. We have learnt better, however, than to see Augustus as 'inventing the Roman civil service' or harnessing to his regime the skills of a 'business class'. He used individuals of different kinds and skills and backgrounds, and did not create for them a *cursus honorum* in imitation of that of the senators: that was a later development. He did take steps to give the order a stronger collective image, with a formal 'entrance examination' and an annual equestrian parade, and, when Gaius and Lucius Caesar were old enough, making them its honorary presidents. From the funeral honours for Germanicus[58] we learn of a Lex Valeria Cornelia of A.D. 5, by which a new electoral committee of senators and select *equites* was interposed between candidature for office and the *comitia*, choosing a list of persons *destinati*, to be added, probably, to any *commendati*, to be put before the assembly of the people. It was allowed for that there might still be more candidates presenting themselves independently, but maybe from then on the assembly was virtually a rubber stamp. The significance of the new committee has been variously assessed; one view is that it had a political purpose, to encourage, by allowing some *equites* a say in the process, the rise to office of 'new men' favourable to Tiberius. But the more sober, and now prevailing, view is that it was an 'honour', a further special mark of distinction for the equestrian order.[59]

When it came to the offices opened to the *equites*, there was, in Augustus' conception, no 'ladder'.[60] The order maintained, in any case, its traditional role as a principal source for the manning of the standard jury-courts and the filling of junior army officerships. The most significant of the new functions were for experienced military *equites*: the prefectures of small provinces and of the naval squadrons, and the census

---

[57] Saller 1982 (F 59) 94–111 and 73–8.

[58] The *rogatio Valeria Aurelia* of A.D. 19. Sources: *Tabula Hebana*, EJ² 94a; *Tabula Siarensis*, J. González 1984 (B 234); Rome fragment, *CIL* VI 31199; perhaps also the *Tabula Ilicitana*, EJ² 94b (or the latter may come from similar honours for Drusus in A.D. 23).   [59] Brunt 1961 (C 47).

[60] Dismantling of the 'ladder' began with Sherwin-White 1939 (D 65).

officerships in the provinces. Above all, of course, stood the prefecture of Egypt and Alexandria itself. The first three prefects performed important military tasks; quite a number of other prefects are known by name from Augustus' reign, but we hear little of their activities, they had short terms of office, and they were socially not of high consequence.[61] *Equites* were also employed in new procuratorial, that is financial, offices (though such offices might go to freedmen, such as the notorious Julius Licinus).[62] The equestrian offices in the capital arose only relatively late, in the process of experimentation: the two praetorian prefects first in 2 B.C., the *praefectus vigilum* in A.D. 6, the *praefectus annonae* not before A.D. 7.[63] The stimulus may not have been so much growing confidence in the equestrians as dissatisfaction with experiments using senatorial committees.[64]

In the imperial period there is a civil service, purely executive, staffed by 'slaves of Caesar' and 'freedmen of Augustus' (until its headships begin to go to *equites*, and then we really are in a different world). There are, especially, a number of central posts occupied by freedmen, the secretaryships of correspondence, accounts, and petitions being the principal: and for a period in the first century A.D. holders of some of those posts had powerful personal influence on the rulers. Augustus' part in initiating the system is hard to estimate because of shortage of evidence, but historians, probably rightly, tend to conclude from that shortage that the beginnings, under him, were slight and unsystematic. To his last instructions, leaving behind a military and financial handbook to the empire, he 'appended also the names of the freedmen and slaves who could be called to account',[65] which suggests a precursor of the Department of Accounts; but the floodtide of correspondence was yet to come,[66] and the regular answering of, at any rate, legal petitions a later development. Certainly, there is no sign of any such persons having political influence on Augustus. Naturally, there was also a large personnel, greater than, though not different in kind from, that of the republican *principes viri*, of household servants, and with the rise of a 'court' (to which we shall come) it was destined to become very large indeed. But Augustus treated his servants sternly,[67] and no sign is yet to be detected of the influence of chamberlains or the like, let alone of the ruler's inaccessibility behind layers of personnel.

Our focus has shifted from the way Augustus secured the personnel he needed to the extent of their influence upon him. The 'Party' has been

---

[61] Brunt 1975 (E 906).   [62] Dio LIV. 21.3–8.

[63] It is likely that the *praefectus vehiculorum* also goes back to Augustus, though not yet epigraphically attested so early: Suet. *Aug.* 49.3.

[64] Eck 1985 (C 82).   [65] Suet. *Aug.* 101.4.

[66] Though for a trace of a precursor of *ab epistulis* see Suet. *Aug.* 67.2, with Kienast 1982 (C 136) 262.   [67] Suet. *Aug.* 67; 74.

adduced, and the *amici principis* were his obvious channel of advice; but it is practically impossible to attribute any particular action to the influence of a specific individual, except in a few cases of personal patronage. Crucially lacking, of course, are the files, letters, memoirs and diaries from which historians of the modern age extract such information. In accordance with *mos maiorum*, Augustus brought in persons of standing, of his choice, when public decisions had to be seen to be made; they can be observed, listed hierarchically, in the minutes of formal meetings.[68] It is also quite certain that Augustus used *amici* of his choice, according to their talents and the matter in hand, as his informal *consilium*, summoned according to need.[69] Doubtless they did exercise influence; someone must have been involved, for example, in the orchestration of the imperial symbolism (a subject to which we shall come). Doubtless, too, the senatorial probouleutic sub-committee was not always on the mere receiving end. But that is all that can be said.[70] There were *éminences grises*: Maecenas and Sallustius Crispus were sources of confidential information and privy to secret plans, and people, no doubt rightly, believed that they could get what they wanted;[71] but we do not actually know what items of policy sprang from their brains.[72] Livia Drusilla, always at her husband's side, may have had the greatest influence of all; in her case, the less people knew, the more – and worse – they guessed. Prosopography has, to be sure, given vivid life to a number of powerful personalities of the age whom we may well guess to have been immensely influential: M. Lepidus, M. Valerius Messalla Corvinus, L. Calpurnius Piso, consul of 15 B.C., Cn. Cornelius Lentulus, consul of 14 B.C., Paullus Fabius Maximus, consul of 11 B.C., and plenty of others. But the most characteristic means whereby Augustus obtained the co-operation of, and promoted to high responsibilities, the people of his choice, was their incorporation in the ramifications of the 'divine family'.[73] Complex family alliances were not in the least contrary to tradition, but when such an alliance revolved round just one *princeps vir* instead of many, the quantitative change became qualitative, and an imperial court was in the making. To the ideological aspects of the 'divine family' we shall return; its practical aspect was that the greatest commands and the most spectacular diplomatic missions went – and were held for as long as the ruler thought necessary – to the closest members of his family and then, as it were, spread outwards. It is likely that, insofar as they were experienced enough, those men were also Augustus' principal counsel-

---

[68] *EJ*² 379, lines 34–40. [69] Crook 1955 (D 10) ch. 3.
[70] Policy about codicils was suggested by the jurist Trebatius Testa, *Inst. Just.* II. 25.
[71] Hor. *Sat.* 1.9.43–56; II.6.38–58.
[72] Crispus may have been solely responsible for the elimination of Agrippa Postumus.
[73] For the process, and the people, see Syme 1986 (A 95).

lors and collaborators; hence the political tragedy of Augustus' unwillingness to trust Tiberius and Tiberius' withdrawal from collaboration with Augustus.

2. Policy

What, with hindsight, historians analyse as Roman 'policy' was often, simply, the Roman government's pragmatic reaction to situations. (The 'spread of citizenship', with the founding of new coloniae, is, as far as Augustus is concerned, a case in point, because veterans had to be settled somewhere.) There are, nonetheless, one or two areas in which it is proper to speak of, and needful briefly to review, Augustus' 'policy'. He had a military and imperial policy: that is assessed in chapter 4 below. He had a financial and budgetary policy and a social and demographic policy. He also had an ideology, the most important part of the whole story.

A degree of financial policy and initiative greater than that of the Republic was forced upon Augustus by the need for a permanent military budget. What was needed was relatively exact housekeeping – and the Res Gestae was evidently composed by someone who relished exact figures. A 'statement of accounts' of the empire, such as was left by Augustus to his successor, had already been available to be handed to his fellow-consul in 23 B.C., when he thought he was dying.[74] The general basis of taxation from the republican time was not seriously changed, except for the introduction, quite late on, of the estate duty, vicesima hereditatium, to feed the new account for meeting army discharge gratuities. However, a full property and poll census of the provinces was put in hand, gradually and over many years; it was imposed particularly on newly acquired regions, where it was regarded as the principal sign of subjection and was a major cause of unrest. Besides army pay, another costly item was the supply of free corn at Rome (though much of the taxation for that came in in kind). Augustus did not invent the policy of 'bread and circuses'; in fact, probably after the great food panic of A.D. 6, he was minded to abolish the frumentatio (his motive being not economic but social, namely the very conservative belief that free corn at Rome lured citizens away from the admirable activity of peasant farming). But he concluded that abolition was politically inexpedient.[75] The main economic fact, however, that determined policy was the enormous, and ever-growing, wealth of the ruler himself; the patrimonium could serve as an alternative treasury, and enabled Augustus to practise a kind of deficit financing on the main accounts, with himself making up the shortfall from his private fortune. Chapters 15 to 18 of the Res Gestae tell the story:

[74] Dio LIII.30.2.   [75] Suet. Aug. 42.3.

'... four times I helped the state treasury with my money'; '... from the year of the Lentuli [18 B.C.], when the public revenues were insufficient, I gave subventions of corn and cash from my own granary and bank to sometimes 100,000 people and sometimes many more'. The ruler thus imposed on himself, as the richest citizen, a kind of super-liturgy, which enabled him – as the ancient liturgical principle always enabled the payer – to take on the role of super-benefactor.[76]

Except for that part of the taxation of the provinces that was paid in kind, the Roman empire had a money economy. In particular, the armies were paid in cash, and so were the principal officials. Governors of provinces received large salaries (which was an important innovation of Augustus),[77] and equestrian officialdom was from the start a salaried service. As in every respect, so in that of coinage the Roman imperial system relied on the continuance of local government and practice, and so the cities of the Roman world went on issuing, for everyday use, their own, mostly bronze, coinages. The gold and, above all, the silver coinages, for major payments, passed into the control of Rome, the ruler. Numismatists tell us that under Augustus there came into being a 'world coinage'. There was less of policy about that than just the way things worked out (and the only actual Augustan change in the currency system was, surprisingly, in the non-precious metal currency of Rome, which became bimetallic):[78] huge coinages had been issued in the triumviral period, to pay the rival armies, so there was much in circulation; the government opened and closed mints at different times and places, as and when the need was perceived for specific quantities of new coin. The total production was, undeniably, enormous.[79]

The aspect of Augustus' activity, however, that most plainly deserves the name of 'policy' is that which is commonly called his 'social policy', since it evidently sprang from passionate personal concern: he doggedly fought his own elite over it. The impression given by much recent writing is that Augustus was both revolutionary, in trying to mould the morality and demography of a society by legislation, and at the same time grossly illiberal and reactionary in the rules he sought to impose. As was pointed out in chapter 2 above, there stood behind Augustus a strong republican tradition of the state's interference in the behaviour of the citizens, through legislation, the courts, and, above all, the censorship.[80] As to the illiberality, it has often been characteristic of dictators and the like to treat what part, at least, of the citizenry regard as freedoms of personal choice as signs of decadence, and try to curb them, and Augustus is easily tarred with that brush; but the debate about the state's

[76] Not only in the capital: Suet. *Aug.* 47.1; Dio LIV.23.7–8.   [77] Dio LIII.15.4.
[78] *Sestertii* and *dupondii* of brass (*orichalcum*), *asses* and *quadrantes* of copper.
[79] Sutherland 1976 (B 356) ch. 4, and ch. 8 below, pp. 316–19.   [80] See ch. 2 above, p. 93.

role in relation to morality and family is perennial, and we should beware of imposing a current standard too crudely. Augustus shared with Cicero[81] the belief in a superior early and middle Republic, whose victories had been based on better morals and solider family virtues, and he strove to re-create that idealized past.

The legislation relating to slaves and former slaves (freedmen and freedwomen) occurs relatively late in Augustus' reign, and was not part of the 'package' of the *leges Iuliae*.[82] Proposed by consuls, it may well have been with the approval or even at the initiative of the Senate; for the governing class had a tradition (as can be seen in 'sumptuary laws') of restraining their richer members from stepping too far out of line.[83] The astute may even detect, in the Lex Aelia Sentia, some competing pressures, for example, between the drastic regulation of the number and kind of persons who could be elevated to Roman citizenship by the mere process of being liberated by a Roman owner, and, on the other hand, the even-handed provisions governing conduct between freed people and their former owners.[84] The *leges Iuliae de adulteriis* and *de maritandis ordinibus* and the Lex Papia Poppaea are the group that represent a moral commitment evinced by Augustus from the beginning,[85] and never given up. The curious title of the *lex Iulia de maritandis ordinibus* seems to relate only to those parts of the big statute that restricted the right to full Roman marriage between certain status classes, for example between the senatorial order and freed persons and between all freeborn persons and the usual classes of 'people of low repute' (*infames*); but its best-known feature is the pressure that it placed on citizens to marry and re-marry, backed by rewards for those with at least three children and penalties for the childless. The rewards included priority in the competition for public office, and the penalties included severe public marks of disesteem for the unmarried; but the system was made to turn a good deal on how far people were allowed to take inheritances, and those rules did not apply as between close kin, nor below a modestly high property rating. It is fair to infer that it was the birth-rate in the upper ranks of society that Augustus cared about (less so to infer that the true purpose of the legislation was different from what lies on its face, such as the preservation of estates).[86] It is, of course, true that Augustus did not dispose of proper demo-

---

[81] Cic. *Marcell.* 23.

[82] The Lex Iunia, which created the status of 'Junian Latins', bears the title *Iunia Norbana* in *Inst. Just.* 1. 5.3, and should be dated to A.D. 19 accordingly. If it had been part of the early batch of Augustus' laws it would have been a Lex Iulia like the rest.

[83] For *leges sumptuariae* of Julius Caesar and of Augustus in the old republican tradition, see Rotondi 1912 (F 685) 421 and 447 and Gell. *NA* 11.24.14–15.

[84] Accusation of ingratitude against freedmen, *Dig.* 40.9. 30 pr.; but if patron fails to support freedman he loses rights, *Dig.* 38.2.33; and if he obliges freedman or freedwoman to agree not to marry he loses rights, *Dig.* 37.14.15.

[85] The standard view; challenged by Badian 1985 (F 4).   [86] So Wallace-Hadrill 1981 (F 73).

graphic knowledge about the trend of the birth-rate and what needed to
be achieved to change it; but he probably thought he knew quite enough,
and the upper class he could, if unsystematically, observe. His legislation
was not going to produce waves of stout yeomen (unless by imitation of
their betters), but what he might achieve was a stable officer class. That
such was his aim is corroborated by two other new legal rules that will
have had importance mainly for the better-off: first, the introduction of
peculium castrense, the fund comprising what a *filius familias* earned from,
or acquired in connexion with, his military service, which he could
control independently of his *paterfamilias*; and, secondly, the rule that a
paterfamilias was not allowed to disinherit a *filius familias* during his
military service.[87]

Augustus was, then, probably telling in the *Res Gestae* the simple truth
about what he conceived his legislation to have been for: 'By new
statutes passed on my initiative I restored many good examples of our
forbears that were disappearing from the current age, and I personally[88]
handed on to posterity examples of many things for them to imitate'.
That does not mean that it was particularly successful or that it was
without pernicious consequences, of which perhaps the worst was that
the marriage laws conjured up a fiscal interest in escheated estates that
had not existed before.

3. Ideology

The act of creative policy, however, that was Augustus' abiding legacy
to Rome was the bringing into being of an ideology of rule, parallel to
the careful traditionalism of most of what has been spoken of so far –
surprising, in that it manifests itself quite early in Augustus' reign, and
multifaceted, so that to describe it even summarily involves consideration of many phenomena, of which the 'imperial cult' is only one.
Glorification of the personality of the ruler, advertisement of his role,
proclamation of his virtues, pageantry over his achievements, visual
reminders of his existence, and the creation of a court and a dynasty:
those are, *par excellence*, the things that make A.D. 14 different from 30 B.C.

It is a difficult question how far the pattern of ideas and symbols that
pervades the culture of Augustus' age was 'orchestrated'. Scholars do
make such a claim,[89] and, however great the need to resist exaggeration,
at least some of the broad lines of the pattern must have been someone's
deliberate contrivance. Augustus was probably entirely sincere when he

[87] Respectively, *Tit. Ulp.* 20.10; *Dig.* 28.2.26.
[88] *RG* 8, 5. The Greek version says 'I gave myself as an example'.
[89] They are influenced by Weinstock 1971 (F 235). See, e.g., Gros 1976 (F 397) esp. ch. 1; Zanker 1987 (F 632) 110–13; 215.

said he wanted to be remembered as the creator of the 'best possible condition' (*optimus status*), and in his delight when the crew and passengers of a ship from Alexandria put on festal dress and poured libations and cried that 'because of him they had their livelihood, because of him they sailed the seas, they enjoyed freedom and prosperity through him';[90] but into that broad river flowed many channels, some the result of more deliberate channelling than others.

The public cult of the ruler bulks large in the ideology of the Roman empire. Augustus began it – though Iulius Caesar and Antony would have done the same. Cult means, strictly, performing acts of worship to the ruler as a god, but, broadly conceived, it is about people's perceptions and descriptions of the ruler and his role, and also about the practical business of securing and rewarding adherents in positions of importance in the cities and regions. The cult of the ruler as founder, saviour and benefactor was well established in the Greek-speaking world, and such honours had been bestowed, from time to time, on Roman commanders in the late Republic; even 'Roma', as a divinity, had come to be an object of cult in the East.[91] But it was the rival claims of the triumvirs to influence in the cities that raised the stakes in the game,[92] and hence the cult and symbolism of the ruler were promoted and financed in the East by Augustus and by his wealthier supporters.[93] In Rome, the plebs had offered worship to Scipio, Marius and Iulius Caesar, but its betters had been too strongly *principes inter pares* for that, and Augustus behaved carefully. A gesture used by his successors, but no doubt deriving from him,[94] was the refusal of public divine honours for his person in his lifetime: we have seen how he declined to allow Agrippa's temple in the Campus to be called 'Augusteum'. On the other hand, there were by now many Roman citizens about the world: the colonizations of Iulius Caesar had made a big difference. For them, the answer was an official cult of 'Rome and Augustus'. The West and North (except for Provence, southern Spain and Africa, long the home of *cives Romani*) were still under conquest and first-stage reorganization, and had no traditions offering precedent: Augustus promoted there major centres of cult and ceremony, the 'Altar of the Three Gauls' at Lugdunum and the 'Altar of the Ubii' at Cologne. For the Roman plebs there was yet another expedient in this rich fund of devices, the setting of a new cult of the *genius*, or 'abiding spirit', of the ruler amongst the little tutelary gods of the 'blocks' of urban Rome, the *lares compitales*: their cult was in the charge of the 'block leaders', *magistri vicorum*.[95] Those *magistri* were

---

[90] Suet. *Aug.* 28.2; 98.2.   [91] Mellor 1975 (F 186).   [92] Reynolds 1982 (B 270) nos. 7, 8 and 12.
[93] Millar 1984 (D 102). The 'Common Councils' certainly pre-existed, but they were turned into a principal focus of the cult.   [94] Charlesworth 1939 (F 115).
[95] Simon 1986 (F 577) 97–103; Zanker 1987 (F 632) 135–8.

freedmen; Augustus took account more globally of the fact that large numbers of Roman citizens were actually of that status, promoting another novelty: *collegia* of freedmen devoted to the cult of the ruler came into being in the cities under the title of 'Augustales', forming a freedman elite parallel to the municipal elites of the freeborn.[96]

No account on the scale here available can do justice to this vast subject. The antiquarian revival of cults, temples and ceremonies in Rome, and the harnessing of the major priesthoods to the new order, are part of the story;[97] so, too, the inclusion of Augustus' *genius* in oaths sworn by the divinities; so, too, the additions to the religious calendar celebrating his important dates. We have been bidden, rightly, to develop an imagination for the enormous visual impact of it all, with images of the ruler everywhere, in endless profusion, both actual and portrayed on the coinage. In summary, the whole complex was meant to serve as an ecumenical unifying force: citizens and non-citizens, classes and statuses, language- and culture-groups enmeshed in a common, though varied, symbolic network, and the cult acts of Gallic magnates, leading bourgeois of Asia, successful freedmen in the *municipia*, the plebs of Rome, and the legions,[98] all focussed on the ruler, legitimizing his rule on the charismatic plane, while ministering at the same time to their own desire for social prominence.

The 'divine family' must return into consideration here, from a more conceptual viewpoint. Should we, for example, see Livia Drusilla as an 'empress', or Gaius and Lucius Caesar as 'princes'? Did Augustus inhabit a 'palace', and was he surrounded by a 'court'? The best answer to all those questions would be 'hardly, yet', and, as in the constitutional sphere, comparison with the Severan or Diocletianic age shows how far there was to go. Yet transition was certainly occurring, as can be neatly seen in the matter of Augustus' house.[99] Its nucleus was the house of the republican orator, Hortensius, on the south-western slope of the Palatine, and it remained modest in type and scale, though neighbouring properties were added to it[100] to an extent that is yet uncertain (and the well-known 'House of Livia' presumably came to count as part of it). But the symbolic significance of the dwelling was played upon with insistence.[101] Augustus' temple of Apollo was built not merely adjacent to it but connecting directly with it. Then, in 27 B.C., the civic crown of oak was placed permanently above its doorway, and laurels were planted to flank the entrance.[102] When Augustus became *pontifex maximus* in 12

---

[96] Duthoy 1978 (E 37).

[97] Augustus was, besides *pontifex maximus*, a member of all the major priestly colleges; and their role on the Ara Pacis is evident.   [98] Kienast 1982 (C 136) 211, with n. 168.

[99] Coarelli 1985 (E 20) 129–33.   [100] Suet. *Aug.* 72.1.

[101] Wiseman 1994 (F 81) esp. 101–8.   [102] *RG* 34, 2.

B.C., a shrine of Vesta was consecrated in the house.[103] After a fire on the
Palatine in A.D. 2 or 3, in which the house of Augustus and the temple of
the Magna Mater suffered badly, a public subscription was got up, of
which Augustus graciously accepted part; but he then declared the house
public property, as being the residence of the *pontifex maximus*.[104] A few
years later, Ovid, describing how his books from exile might approach
the ruler, shows – if we discount a degree of understandable sycophancy
– how much more than a mere house the 'Caesaris domus', though still
so called, had become.[105]

The association of the ruler's family with him took no long time to
develop.[106] We have seen the 'divine family' on exhibition in the frieze of
the Ara Pacis of 13 B.C., and can see it at a later stage in the inscriptions
recorded in the Codex Einsiedlensis as coming from statues that adorned
a gateway at Ticinum, dated to Augustus' thirtieth tribunician power,
A.D. 7-8.[107] Honours, even cult, were paid in the cities to members of the
family besides Augustus. To what extent the group associated, or even
lived, together is uncertain;[108] but there sound like the makings of a
'court' when we hear of Augustus' views about the younger members
appearing for dinner with their elders and whether young Claudius
could be allowed to make public appearances,[109] and there is rather more
evidence about the education of the 'princes' and other youngsters who
belonged to the charmed circle.[110] The house of a *princeps vir* of the
republican time had never been solely a haven of privacy, so it was not
new for the ruler to live his life in the public gaze, but Augustus wanted
his *domus* to serve as a universal exemplar of the values he aimed to
promote.

Most of the evidence about imperial insignia and ceremonial[111]
concerns developments later than Augustus: till well after his day,
accessibility of the ruler and primacy *inter pares* remained the ideal. The
orb and sceptre carried by the 'emperor', the sacred fire carried before the
'empress', belong to an ideology that was to lead to the remote and
hieratic emperorship of late antiquity, and hardly began before the
middle of the second century A.D. Yet some seminal elements can already
be traced, for example, in the oak-leaf crowns and laurel wreaths, and the
symbolism of victory-on-the-orb on the coinage and elsewhere; and

103 The Calendar for April 28, in EJ.   104 Dio LV.12.4–5.
105 Ov. *Tr*, 1.i.69–70; III.i.33–40. The formal approach was by then, it seems, from the northern
side, via the Forum Romanum.
106 Beginning with the grant of tribunician sacrosanctity to Livia and Octavia, the wives of the
triumvirs, in 35 B.C.   107 EJ² 61.
108 Agrippa was offered a home there in 25 B.C., after his own had burnt down, Dio LIII.27.5; but
it is not clear that that was more than temporary.   109 Suet. *Aug.* 64.3; *Claud.* 4.1–6.
110 Wallace-Hadrill 1983 (B 190) 177–80; Kienast 1982 (C 136) 253–63.
111 Alföldi 1971 (F 246) and 1980 (F 247).

Augustus was accorded the right to wear at any time the triumphal costume, which was the dress of Jupiter himself, and included a sceptre.

In any case, ceremonial in a wider sense was of the first importance. Augustus was a supreme showman (or someone was on his behalf), and made a perpetually inventive use of the 'parallel language' to maintain himself and his achievements in the public consciousness. The games and shows are one part of the story, valuable to him to establish a relationship to his plebs, to preside over its pleasures and expose himself to its demonstrations. Augustus provided generously, adding *ludi Actiaci* and *ludi Martiales* to the traditional regular series; and there were regular games on his birthday from 11 B.C. onwards. Triumphs, the irregular spectacle *par excellence*, reserved after 19 B.C. for members of the 'divine family', were pretty rare, but they were complemented by the great funerals, often also with games: Marcellus, Octavia, Agrippa, Drusus. As for the posthumous honours for Gaius and Lucius Caesar, their complexity and comprehensiveness are revealed in detail by inscriptions[112] (which show, incidentally, that such ceremonies were not laid on only at Rome, but took place in the municipalities and provinces).

The reign was punctuated by other colourful excitements; Augustus' pride in them is attested by the attention given to them in the *Res Gestae*. There was the journey of Senate and people to Campania to meet the returning ruler in 19 B.C., with the ceremonies at the altar of Fortuna Redux: 'returns' became a standard occasion for pageantry. The *ludi saeculares* in 17 B.C., the thronged assembly for Augustus' assumption of the role of *pontifex maximus* in 12 B.C., the full triumph of Tiberius in 7 B.C., the successive installations of Gaius and Lucius as *principes iuventutis*, reached a culmination in 2 B.C. with the bestowal of the title *pater patriae* on Augustus and the dedication of the temple of Mars Ultor, accompanied by gladiatorial combats and the long-remembered 'Naval Battle of the Greeks and Persians'. Perhaps creativity ran out after 2 B.C., but activity did not, for the games of A.D. 8 in honour of Germanicus and (astonishingly) Claudius were notable, and it must not be forgotten that it was intended for Augustus and Tiberius to hold full triumphs after the defeat of the Pannonian rebellion in A.D. 9, and Tiberius did celebrate one on 23 October of A.D. 12 or 13. The whole was, in any event, a remarkable calendar of novelties to keep the images of victory and peace simultaneously before the public eye.

Commonly related to the process of image-building are the legends and pictures on the Augustan coinage. It is wise to be cautious about calling them 'propaganda', not least because much uncertainty and disagreement persists as to whom the coinage was supposed to influence

---

[112] EJ² 68–9, and the material in n. 58 above.

and who decided on the types and legends.[113] Gold coinage, and even silver, down to the denarius (the 'tribute-money') will not often have been in the hands of ordinary people; and some of the best-known 'speaking' types and legends are portentously rare and must have been struck in relatively tiny issues, while, conversely, some very large emissions have relatively uninformative material on them. New money probably went first to the troops, so the influence of the coins may have been intended primarily for them; certainly, an explosion of vivid and dramatic, plainly propaganda, types is a feature of the years after Julius Caesar's assassination, and they were part of the armoury of the triumvirs and Sextus Pompeius. In the new age after Actium that momentum was maintained for a while, but it then diminished. Augustus' 'saving of the citizens' and the crown of oak leaves, and the Shield of the Virtues, achieved celebration, as did festivals and buildings and cult – Fortuna Redux, the *ludi saeculares*, Actian Apollo, the Altar of the Three Gauls and the temple of Rome and Augustus at Pergamum. The collegiality of Augustus and Agrippa was also given some emphasis. But the only specific promotional campaign run by the official coinage was bestowed on Gaius and Lucius Caesar (though the successes of Tiberius late in the reign did not go quite without mark). At least, however, the Augustan coinage was, even in terms of types, as well as scale, a world-coinage, with Lugdunum and Nemausus, Ephesus and Pergamum, all striking to recognizably similar effect, and as a dissemination of the image of the ruler that was tremendous.

Buildings also (to return to that important theme) were part of the image-making.[114] The public heart of the city of Rome was transformed: everyone knows how Augustus boasted that he had 'taken over a Rome of brick and left a Rome of marble',[115] and Ovid, justifying the *soignée* look for ladies, exclaims 'Before, all was country plainness: now Rome is of gold'.[116] The transformation was not just in grandeur, but in symbolic orientation towards the ruler. It is, indeed, unfair to see the programme solely in that context: improvement and amenity went hand in hand with symbolism. Sewers and water supply, markets and porticoes, theatres and an amphitheatre, improvements to the race-course, parks, baths and libraries now adorned Rome, and Agrippa's part was the more brilliant in that it combined the prosaic and the charismatic. But improvement stopped short when it paid no dividends in prestige (and when Agrippa was no longer there), so that some of the recurrent scourges of the plebs – floods, fires and collapses – were tackled with less than total commitment. About the transformation of Augustus' house enough has

---

[113] Consigliere 1978 (c 64); Sutherland 1976 (b 356); Levick 1982 (b 338); Wallace-Hadrill 1986 (b 362).   [114] See the references in ch. 2, n. 13 above.

[115] Suet. *Aug.* 28.3. Carrara marble had just come into use.   [116] Ov. *Ars Am.* III.113.

been said, and about his new Forum; but even the Forum Romanum took on the symbolism of the ruler and his divine ancestry, and Jupiter Tonans on the Capitol stole some of the limelight of the Capitoline god himself.[117] Agrippa adorned the middle Campus, Augustus the northern part, with the Mausoleum, the Ara Pacis and the Horologium. Buildings were erected by, or in the name of, many members of the 'divine family'; as for the republican tradition by which triumphing generals embellished the capital and built roads 'out of spoils' (*ex manubiis*), Augustus was keen for it to continue, and for a while it did, endowing Rome with such important structures as Asinius Pollio's Atrium Libertatis, with the first Roman public library, Cn. Domitius Calvinus' marble rebuilding of the Regia, T. Statilius Taurus' amphitheatre in the Campus and the major temples of C. Sosius (Apollo Sosianus in the Campus) and C. Cornificius (Diana on the Aventine). That tradition only died out because the triumphs and the independent commands on which they rested died out: the last major such building was the theatre of Balbus, and he was, precisely, the last person outside the 'divine family' to celebrate a full triumph.

It hardly needs saying that building programmes advertising the ruler were not confined to the capital. Nor, in the Roman world in general, were they confined to structures erected at government expense, for there was a great mass of building on local and private initiative, as the municipal wealthy responded to the stability of the 'Augustan Peace'. Much was, however, inspired from the centre, such as the Augustan arches that still stand in testimony to the construction of roads, city-walls and harbours, and other imposing structures still to be seen – the Pont du Gard, the Maison Carrée, the public buildings of Mérida: enough for the imagination to grasp how new a visual world had been created by A.D. 14. In the Roman Forum stood the Golden Milestone,[118] and the Chorographic Map of Agrippa stood in his sister Vipsania's portico.[119]

Of such elements was composed the great assault on the psychology of a generation. A consistent ideology is conveyed, an 'Augustan synthesis', the visual monuments being echoed by the literary monuments: it may be summarily spelt out, under three or four heads. First, this is a 'new age', *novum saeculum* – the keystone of Virgil's *Aeneid*,[120] the theme of the *ludi saeculares* and of the architectural transformation of Rome. It is an age in which the Hellenic and Roman cultural heritages are to be no longer enemies but partners,[121] a partnership symbolized by Actian Apollo, the god combining arms and arts, with his temple and libraries on the Palatine. The gift of the new age is the 'Augustan Peace'; and the

---

[117] On the Forum Romanum, Simon 1986 (F 577) 84–91; on Jupiter Tonans, Zanker 1987 (F 632) 114. [118] Dio LIV. 8.4. [119] Strab. II.5.17 (120C); Pliny, *HN* III.17.
[120] Virg. *Aen.* VI.791–853. [121] Bowersock 1965 (C 39) ch. 10.

prerequisite of that peace is the ruler's untiring devotion to his *cura*, by reason of his *virtus, clementia, iustitia* and *pietas*. But it demands an answering devotion from others, a willingness to constitute a nation of stern morality and stable family life: that comes out best in the most overtly moralizing of all the literary monuments, the *Carmen Saeculare* of Horace. And amongst the duties demanded is untiring militarism. For Roman victory and supremacy to be maintained the Romans must keep faith with their long history. That is the message of the Fasti Triumphales and the busts of Rome's heroes in the porticoes of the Augustan Forum, of the triumphal arches placed about the Roman world, and of the importance attached to the 'return of the standards' in the symbolic nexus. Virgil's 'Be it thy care, O Roman, to rule the peoples with thy sway' is the formal repudiation of the Epicureanism of Lucretius: 'Better to obey in quiet than wish to rule things with your sway and control kingdoms.'[122]

4. Resistance

The 'Augustan synthesis', thus summarized, is a rich diet and a heady brew; historical therapy demands that it be countered, in conclusion, by more astringent and sobering reflections. The historian must ask how successful the mystique was. To what extent can we perceive scepticism, rejection, an alternative ideology,[123] a revolutionary temper, even? 'Resistance' is an insistent modern theme;[124] how much of it is to be found beneath the confident surface of the 'Augustan synthesis'?

A distinction can properly be made between political and ideological dissent within the Roman people (which is really our theme) and the resistance of conquered peoples to Roman imperialism. Of the latter there was enough and to spare, but the only question about it needing to be raised here is how Augustan rule was viewed in the Greek half of Rome's dominions. For the Greek world too, was a conquered world. Most of it, indeed, had been conquered already under the Republic, and the 'intellectual opposition' (a well-worn topic)[125] was rather to Rome in general than to the Augustan rearrangements – though it was them that Alexandria long bitterly resented.[126] By and large, the ruling classes, to whom the Augustan effort was mainly addressed, were glad of the 'Augustan Peace', which perpetuated their own local predominance; and there was no shortage of leading families eager for Roman citizenship. If

---

122 Virg. *Aen.* VI.851; Lucr. V.1129–30.
123 D'Elia 1955 (B 41); La Penna 1963 (B 102).
124 See the collections of papers in Pippidi 1976 (A 72A) and Yuge and Doi 1988 (A 111).
125 Bowersock 1965 (C 39) ch. 8.
126 Hence the 'Acts of the Pagan Martyrs': for the Augustan items that may belong to them, see Musurillo 1954 (B 381) no. 1; *POxy* 3020; *POxy* 2435, verso (= EJ² 379).

they did not 'rally to the support of the Principate',[127] they did not rally against it. The two expatriate Greek intellectuals in Rome of the Augustan time of whose writings the most survives today, Dionysius of Halicarnassus and Strabo of Amaseia, were enthusiastic supporters; if the rest of the Greek world was cooler, it was not estranged.

Coming, however, to Roman opposition to Augustus, we should first remember that there were conspiracies, numerous, it appears,[128] and spanning his whole reign. Heads of state are, notoriously, at the mercy of plain and simple assassination attempts by individuals, but it was – presumably – Augustus' triumph not to bring upon himself a conspiracy of an entire section of the governing class, as Iulius Caesar had done. As to conspiracy by factions within the 'divine family', reasons have been given for wariness in the face of some sensational hypotheses; in so far as such conspiracies existed, they seem to have been directed against the succession of Tiberius, and, in the end, by him against residual rivals.

More generally, however, we have to do with what was described earlier as resistance to playing the game by Augustus' rules and subscribing to the Augustan ethic. Modern studies place emphasis on the 'crisis of recruitment' of the senatorial class and Augustus' continual battle against the apathy of senators towards attendance in the Curia; they invite attention, too, to the 'crisis of recruitment' of the armed forces in the last decade of the reign. And, lastly, recent studies of Augustan Latin literature have dwelt upon the themes of resistance to tyranny, revolt against crude demands for panegyric and conformity, and covert undermining of the official ethic and promotion of an alternative ideology of 'love, not war' – with the fates of Cornelius Gallus, at one end, and Ovid, at the other, as the real, and damning, historical symbols of the 'Augustan Peace'.

As to the 'crisis of recruitment' in the governing elite, something has been already said, and a distinction has been insisted on: from the top parts of the *cursus honorum* and the valuable and prestige-enhancing offices of state there was no such flight, and leading dignitaries from the provinces would soon be eager for a place in the system. In the case of the armies, conscription was certainly needed at the military crisis, which shows that the envisaged system was over-stretched; the reduction of the legions to twenty-five after the Varian disaster may have brought the size of the citizen army into balance with what the recruiting possibilities were as well as what the treasury could afford. Already in A.D. 5 the length of service of legionary rank-and-file was raised from sixteen to twenty years, because time-expired soldiers were not staying on;[129] that implies that there were not plenty of citizens queuing to take over from

---

127 Bowersock 1965 (c 39) 104; he is talking specifically about A.D. 6.
128 Suet. *Aug.* 19.1; Dio LIV.15.1.   129 Dio LV.23.1.

them. But the undoubted eventual decline of recruitment in Italy was a very long-term process, hardly to be attributed to discontent with Augustus. He did not, after all, find himself constrained to raise the pay of the troops, he gave only two army donatives, and he was able to impose a prohibition of *iustum matrimonium* upon serving soldiers.[130] At his death the northern armies were just about to mutiny; but they had not, nor had the rest, simply melted away.

Finally, as to social and moral attitudes, in literature and life: Augustus proposed, in certain matters, standards stiffer than those to which part, at least, of the leading class were accustomed. Resistance to the legislation about sexual behaviour, marriage, celibacy and childlessness (and to the direct taxation of *cives Romani*!) was vociferous. On the other hand, the very practical case of high-status people engaging in theatrical and gladiatorial performances, and of the attempts by the Senate as well as Augustus to prohibit such conduct,[131] brings out the feature that the elite had motives for maintaining its own cohesion by drawing the bounds of accepted standards more tightly. Nevertheless, we can appreciate why, more than anything else, it was Augustus' daughter who broke the spell of Augustus' vision – the candid and caustic Iulia, who did every bit of her duty in her dynastic role but refused to bound her life with demure domesticity.

Some *bons mots* of Iulia survived, as did some of her father's[132] – and of his opponents. It is not right to imply (though that is sometimes done) that the voice of opposition was somehow suppressed from the historical record, for plenty of it has come down to us, not only in anecdotes but in whole passages in the chief historians where editors point out that the writer is 'following a hostile source'.

And the poets?[133] They have been seen by some as purveyors of propaganda, drafted in detail by someone for them to versify: for how else could their images correspond so well with those of the visual monuments? Patronage certainly demanded its *quid pro quo*, and it was open and explicit in that age: the frankest statement is the preface of Vitruvius' *De Architectura*.[134] We must beware of hypocrisy: we find no difficulty about accepting that the epigrammatists Crinagoras and Antipater wrote to order for the 'divine family' and others, or that the panegyrist of Messalla or the writer of the *Consolatio ad Liviam* were *clientes*, so why should we doubt it of the patriotic purple passages in the *Aeneid*, the 'Roman Odes' of Horace, the *Carmen Saeculare*, or Propertius'

---

130 Campbell 1978 (D 172) esp. 153–4.
131 Illuminated by the new bronze from Larinum, *AE* 1978, 145; see Levick 1983 (C 369).
132 Julia: Macrob. *Sat.* II.5; Augustus, *ibid.* II.4.   133 See ch. 19, below.
134 Vitr. *De Arch.* Praef. 2–3. Vitruvius was the only one to whom Augustus is known to have been direct patron.

celebrations of Roman legend? Tibullus, precisely because he never belonged to the crucial *salon*, could stay cool and aloof from the Augustan mystique, and Ovid was able to take on the role of cynic and 'debunker' for the same reason, while Propertius trod a complicated middle ground. It is in Ovid and Propertius that we meet most explicitly the 'alternative life style', the cult of the clandestine love-affair, the theme of *militia amoris*, or 'love, the true enlistment', and the cry that 'there shall no soldier be born of thee and me'.[135] Yet even among the 'establishment' poets there occurred *recusatio*, the elegant refusal of commissions: Augustus never got the simply conceived epic of his *Res Gestae* that he would have liked, nor the revival of good old native drama.[136] A recent tendency goes further, detecting concealed sniping even in the most panegyrical works. Is fulsomeness of praise, then, a form of deliberate 'overkill'? Is the *Aeneid*, actually, a condemnation of Augustan triumphalism (since it is, admittedly, not a naive affirmation)? Some recent claims may come to be thought exaggerated: what it is certainly important not to forget is that, with the exception of Ovid, the minds and hearts of the major poets – and of Livy – were formed before Augustus ever became Augustus, *and so were his mind and heart*. Their praise of peace and the unity of Italy and Rome's mission, their vision of the 'new age', grew out of the experiences of the late Republic and the triumviral age, and Augustus, their coeval, was the fortunate inheritor of those sentiments: he did not have to drum them up. It may be that all of them, *including himself*, as time went on, came to perceive only too well the price that had to be paid for the 'Augustan Peace'.

For the Augustan creation perpetuated some of the ruthlessness of its origins. Certainly, in the 'police states' that we nowadays know, the ordinary folk as well as their betters are under fear and compulsion – the informer in the pub and the apartment block, the exclusion of the dissident from employment and of his children from education, the bloody suppression of meetings and arrest of popular leaders. The Augustan regime did not possess the apparatus of ideological tyranny to operate on that global scale, though every provincial governor's duty of 'maintaining the peace' included keeping a sharp eye on public meetings, and both abroad and in Rome the *collegia* were anxiously controlled. In Rome, too, the Egnatius episode shows that the government would not tolerate a successful demagogue; and the city was heavily policed at the crisis of A.D. 6.

But if we stick to the ambience of the governing elite at the political centre, there, particularly, though not exclusively, in Augustus' later years, things were done that we do associate with the behaviour of 'police states': the widening of the range of offences counting as treason

[135] Prop. II.7.14.   [136] If that is what he wanted, as argued by La Penna 1963 (B 102).

(with the inevitable encouragement of informers); banishments and exiles without trial; the sudden courier and the enforced suicide; the suppression of literature and the banning, and worse, of authors. And those things were a legacy: they formed part of the apparatus of rule of Augustus' successors, used from time to time as *raison d'état* demanded.

Yet, though they were a characteristic, they were not the dominant characteristic, nor even the dominant ultimate weakness, of Augustus' creation. The work known as the *Dialogus*, attributed to Tacitus, contains, through the mouth of an 'opposition' writer, a well-known expression of the view that the ending of the creative phase of, at least, Roman eloquence was directly due to the loss of freedom.[137] That was not the only view then,[138] nor need it be now; but historians are not wrong to perceive a general loss of momentum supervening on the Augustan triumphs. The late Republic had been moving fast; the very fact of Augustus' rule, let alone his ideals and policies, applied a brake that brought his whole society to a relative standstill. The 'New Age' was conceived of as a 'return to the Age of Saturn', not a great leap into the future; and just as the Greek literature of the age swung back from 'Asianism' to 'Atticism', so did the visual arts return from Hellenistic 'baroque' to serene Classicism and even a curious cult of the Archaic.[139] It is likely that to most of the upper classes in the Roman world, in most respects, that result was welcome rather than otherwise, for their interest was in stability, and Augustus had to fit in with their career ambitions and social expectations as much as they with his proddings and exhortations. Certainly, his revolution was no social revolution: the maintenance, and strengthening, of status hierarchy was high on its priorities,[140] and some historians have seen its principal historical effect as the consolidation of the 'slave society'. Be that as it may, 'it is a fair criticism of the new order, that its temptation was to be static in high matters',[141] and stability is, of the political virtues, the least heart-warming to read about.

5. An estimate

Tacitus offers an appraisal of Augustus, in contrasting paragraphs: what can be said in his favour and what against.[142] For Tacitus, as for many historians after him, the bad outweighed the good. Nevertheless, whether for good or ill, Tacitus lived in a political world of which Augustus had been the principal architect; and for an estimation of

---

[137] K. Heldmann, *Antike Theorien über Entwicklung und Verfall der Redekunst* VI.1, Munich, 1982, esp. 271–86.

[138] It is not even the only view in the *Dialogus*; and in 'On the Sublime', ch. 44, expressed more broadly, it is rejected by the author of that work himself; see Heldmann, *Antike Theorien* VI.2.

[139] Literature: Gabba 1982 (B 57); visual arts: Simon 1986 (F 577) 110–36, with the illustrations.

[140] Rawson 1987 (F 56).   [141] Adcock, *CAH* x¹ 606.   [142] Tac. *Ann.* I.9–10.

Augustus' achievement, for good or ill, it is as necessary to look at what followed him as at what preceded him. For we can then see that his was not a 'blueprint' creation, but experimental, and that it underwent much further change. Neither was it in all respects successful, even in his own time and terms:[143] there was more propaganda than reality about some of the military enterprises, and the programme of social reform probably had little good effect and certainly had some bad. As for the subsequent changes, some represent practical breakdowns in his scheme of things. For instance, the transmission of power broke down with Nero, and it is doubtful whether Augustus envisaged the rise of any of the new equestrian officials to formal political influence, and virtually certain that he would have been appalled at the political power of freedmen.

But if we look from the political world of Cicero to that of Tacitus, we ought to be able to discern what structures Augustus left (in principle, at least, and for good or ill) to the Roman world after him. First, the ideology, as well as the reality, of a single ruler (supported, it might be, by a *collega imperii*). Secondly, a system for the transmission of power and authority, namely dynasty, by birth or adoption, coupled with the bringing of the chosen successor into proper relation with the legitimizations of power as early as possible, which, though sometimes nullified in practice, was always, in principle, revived and never supplanted. Thirdly, a rule of law – for the ruler was not, in principle, 'above the law' – intended normally to prevail, although *raison d'état* overrode it all too readily in crises.[144] Fourthly, the preservation of strict social hierarchy, the leading role being still assigned to the senatorial order, the governing class of the empire remaining a tiny elite. Fifthly, unchanged also from the Republic, the principle of 'government without bureaucracy',[145] by which the local management of the vast empire was left to the municipalities and imperial administration could remain unprofessionalized and economical of manpower and cost. Sixthly, by contrast, armed forces that were, in the lower ranks, professional. They were composed partly of Roman citizens and partly of non-citizens, and by careful budgeting they were supported on a scale enabling them to achieve some modest further expansion of Rome's dominions down to the time of Trajan – though they were destined, in the 'Year of the Four Emperors', to be the vehicle of renewed civil war. Lastly, it would be unfair to rob Augustus of his part in turning the city of Rome into a monumental imperial capital.

'Achievement', however, may seem too biographical a term in which

---

[143] Raaflaub 1980 (C 190), and see ch. 4, below.

[144] Nero's remark, in the course of murdering Britannicus (Suet. *Ner.* 33.2), 'So I'm supposed to be frightened of the Lex Iulia', illustrates the consciousness of the rule of law in the very moment of flouting it. [145] Garnsey and Saller 1987 (A 34) ch. 2.

to estimate the place of Augustus in history: more neutrally, we could substitute 'results' or 'effects', and the observed effects may have had a multiplicity of causes, amongst which Augustus was only one. He stands between what we recognize (or have created for our own convenience) as two ages of European history, the Roman Republic and the Roman Empire. But was he, after all, the 'architect' of the Empire? Or was he just the culminating 'dynast' thrown up by the 'Roman Revolution',[146] a process of change that began with Sulla, or even the Gracchi, and had its own momentum, so that even if Antony had won at Actium or Augustus had died in 23 B.C. the Roman Republic would still have been succeeded by the Roman Empire? What specific contribution is it possible to attribute to Augustus within that massive historical process? Perhaps just this much (if only by slipping back into biography): if Julius Caesar or Antony had been the culminating dynast there would, very likely, still have been a Roman Empire, but it would, very likely, have had a different face. The characteristic structure of the Empire, in which so much of what was new was based so firmly on what was old, is likely to have owed something to the particular cast of mind of its first ruler – narrow, pragmatic and traditionalist. Augustus was equated, in his time, with most of the gods of the Roman pantheon; today, we might think him best fitted by one he was not equated with, Janus, as he steered the Roman world into the future with his eyes fixed on the values of the past. Plutarch records a saying of his (it matters little whether *vero* or *ben trovato*): when somebody told him that Alexander, after his conquests, had been at a loss what to do next, Augustus said he was surprised that Alexander had not realized that a greater job than acquiring empire was getting it into shape when you had acquired it.[147] The shape of the Roman Empire was his contribution.

[146] See the studies in the bibliography, A 82A.
[147] Plut. *Apophthegmata reg. et imp.* 207D, τὸ διατάξαι τὴν ὑπάρχουσαν.

CHAPTER 4

THE EXPANSION OF THE EMPIRE
UNDER AUGUSTUS

ERICH S. GRUEN

The contemporaries of Augustus delivered high praise for conquest and empire. The poet of the *Aeneid* has Jupiter forecast a Roman rule that will know no bounds of time or space, and Anchises' pronouncement from the underworld previews Augustus extending imperial power to the most remote peoples of the world. Livy characterizes his city as *caput orbis terrarum* and its people as *princeps orbis terrarum populus*. Horace asserts that the *maiestas* of the *imperium* stretches from one end of the world to the other.[1]

The phrases echo sentiments and expressions of the Roman Republic. Militarism marked much of its history. And the exploits of the conqueror were envied, honoured and celebrated. Those precedents stimulated and helped shape the character of the Augustan years. Wars dominate the era, victories were repeatedly gained (or claimed), and the humbling of external foes became a prime catchword of the regime.

The successes of Augustus abroad suggest a drive to consolidate the empire, to create a united dominion under Roman rule.[2] The *princeps*, it can be argued, conceived a broad-gauged military strategy, based on economy of force, which, through a combination of mobile troops and loyal dependencies, provided both for internal security and frontier stability.[3]

Theoretical formulations in retrospect, however, fail to catch the dynamics of a volatile situation. And they slight the diversity of geographical, political, diplomatic and cultural considerations that faced Augustus in the vast expanse of the Roman world. One need not assume that the *princeps* had a structured blueprint for empire. Nor did his actions adhere to a uniform pattern imposed on all sectors of the *imperium Romanum*. Different circumstances in different areas provoked a variety of responses, sometimes cautious, sometimes bold, occasionally calculated, often extemporaneous. Augustus was less concerned with a systematic plan for world dominion than with a systematic construct of his image as world conqueror.

---

[1] Virg. *Aen.* 1.278–9; Livy, XXI.30.10, XXIV.58.8; Hor. *Carm.* IV.15.13–16.
[2] Cf. Kienast 1982 (C 136) 366–70, 406–20.   [3] Luttwak 1976 (A 57) 13–50.

I. EGYPT, ETHIOPIA AND ARABIA

The deaths of Antony and Cleopatra left Octavian as master of Egypt. He would not permit that land to slip from his grasp again. Its wealth and resources in the hands of a rival would constitute a serious menace, and its role as a granary could be critical. Egypt became a province in 30 B.C., but no ordinary province. Octavian took full responsibility for governance. He appointed an equestrian prefect to administer the nation, and allowed no Roman senator or high-ranking *eques* even to visit it without his authorization. The *princeps* reckoned Egypt a place apart and kept close surveillance over its affairs.[4]

The prefect of Egypt supervised collection of revenue in the highly centralized fiscal system, exercised judicial duties, and commanded the three legions and auxiliary troops stationed in the country.[5] The forces seem adequate for the preservation of security and the entrenchment of Roman control.

Yet Octavian did not content himself with the acquisition of Egypt. His first appointee as *praefectus Aegypti*, C. Cornelius Gallus, both poet and military man, pressed for expansion from the start. He quelled revolts in Heroonpolis, east of the Delta, and in the Thebaid. That was an appropriate and expected part of the job. But Gallus had no intention of stopping there. He took his forces southward, beyond the First Cataract of the Nile, where, so he claimed, neither Roman nor Egyptian arms had ever penetrated before. Gallus received representatives of the king of Ethiopia, accepted the king under his protection, and installed a dynast to rule over Triacontaschoenus, evidently as buffer zone between the realms of Egypt and Ethiopia. All this had been accomplished by the spring of 29 B.C. when Gallus erected a trilingual inscription in Latin, Greek and hieroglyphics to celebrate his exploits.[6] The prefect's penchant for self-display eventually proved fatal. He had images of himself set up all over Egypt and a record of his achievements inscribed even on the pyramids. Such *hybris*, combined with a host of other alleged misdeeds, brought about Gallus' recall, *renuntiatio amicitiae* by Augustus, accusation, conviction and suicide perhaps in 26 B.C.[7] But nothing in the charges raised objections to Gallus' pushing Roman authority beyond the First Cataract and obtaining the homage of Ethiopian princes. Augustus may have frowned on his prefect's over-zealousness in taking personal credit for Roman expansion – but he did not disavow the

---

[4] Tac. *Ann.* 11.59; *Hist.* 1.11; Dio LI.17.1–3. See the recent treatments, with bibliography, by Geraci 1983 (E 924) 128–46 and 1988 (E 926), who rightly questions the common idea that Augustus treated Egypt as a 'private preserve'. It was considered as one among Rome's revenue producing provinces; Vell. Pat. 11.39.2; Strab. XVII.1.12 (797C); Tac. *Ann.* XV.36; Huzar 1988 (C 277) 370–9.
[5] On his position, see Geraci 1983 (E 924) 163–76; Huzar 1988 (C 277) 352–62; and below, ch. 14*b*.
[6] *ILS* 8994, 8995; Strab. XVII.1.53 (819C).   [7] Dio LIII.23.5–7; Suet. *Aug.* 66.

expansionism. Installation of a client prince and acceptance of the Ethiopian ruler under Roman protection appealed to the pride – and probably stemmed from the policy – of Augustus.

The intentions of the *princeps* emerge with greater clarity in the actions of the next prefect, Aelius Gallus. First-class testimony survives from the pen of his friend and confidant Strabo. Augustus instructed his prefect to investigate the peoples and topography of Ethiopia and to explore the situation in Arabia. The plan formed a prelude to Gallus' invasion of Arabia Felix, the land of the Sabaeans in the north-west corner of the Arabian peninsula. The economic advantages did not escape Augustus' notice: the Sabaeans were key suppliers or middlemen in the lucrative commerce of spices, gems and perfumes from the East. Gallus' invasion may have had in view some Roman involvement in that traffic. But the move forms part of a larger pattern. Roman power was to extend into both Arabia and Ethiopia and the Sabaeans would be the first step. Augustus expected to coerce them into alliance, or to add to his reputation as conqueror.[8]

As it happened, Aelius Gallus' venture proved calamitous, and the plan abortive. Numerous vessels were wrecked in a long and unnecessary voyage from Arsinoe in 26 or 25 B.C. Worse followed when the troops marched into the interior of Arabia from Leuke Kome, a six month trek to Marib, major city of the Sabaeans. There were victories, or alleged victories, along the way, but also disease and death. And the siege of Marib ended in failure: lack of water dictated the abandonment of the whole campaign. The humiliated Roman legions returned through the desert, recrossed the Red Sea and made their way back to Alexandria. Interested sources did their best to obscure the ignominy. The *Res Gestae* of Augustus speaks only of advance into Arabia, to the land of the Sabaeans and the town of Marib. Not a word about the outcome. And Strabo, though he does not conceal the failures, places the blame on the treacherous Nabataean minister Syllaeus who purportedly misdirected and sabotaged the Roman enterprise.[9] The fault, however, lay with Aelius Gallus, or perhaps with Augustus.

The *princeps* nevertheless refused to be deflected from his scheme. Arabia no longer seemed inviting, but Ethiopia still beckoned. Augustus' new prefect of Egypt, P. Petronius, headed the invasion in 25 or 24 B.C., an undertaking whose groundwork had been prepared by Aelius

[8] Strab. 11.5.12 (118C); XVI.4.22 (780C); XVII.1.53–4 (819–21C); Jameson 1968 (E 939), on the chronology and motives; cf. Bowersock 1983 (E 990) 46–7; Sidebotham 1986 (C 311), 592–3; 1986 (C 310) 120–4, 138–40; Desanges 1988 1(C 263) 4–7. On Roman commerce in the East, see Raschke 1978 (C 298) 650–76; Schmitthenner 1979 (C 306) 104–6.

[9] Aug. RG 26.5; Strab. XVI.4.23–4 (780–2C); XVII.1.53 (819C); von Wissmann 1978 (C 326) 313–18; Isaac 1980 (E 1015) 889–901; Bowersock 1983 (E 990) 46–9; Sidebotham 1986 (C 311); 1986 (C 310) 124–30; Desanges 1988 (C 263) 7–12.

Gallus. In Strabo's version, Ethiopians took the initiative, crossed the First Cataract, and attacked the towns of Syene, Philae and Elephantine, thus provoking retaliation by Petronius. There may be truth in that: the Ethiopians perhaps learned that they had been marked out as next victims, thus anticipating Rome and taking advantage of the temporary absence of Roman forces (they were with Aelius Gallus in Arabia). Petronius' assault, in response, was vigorous and effective. His troops drove the Ethiopians out of the places they had seized, pushed them well back into their own territory, regained the cities and trophies captured by the Ethiopians, and penetrated all the way to Napata, chief northern city of the kingdom, which they stormed and destroyed. Only the forbidding terrain prevented further advance. This was much more than a retaliatory campaign. Petronius installed a garrison at Primis between the First and Second Cataracts, dispatched Ethiopian prisoners to Augustus as token of new conquest, and imposed tribute upon the people as sign of Roman rule.

An Ethiopian attempt to break the yoke came a year or two later, under the energetic queen Candace: an attack on the garrison at Primis which brought Petronius back swiftly from Alexandria. The second campaign re-established Roman supremacy in a hurry in 22 B.C. Candace sought terms, and Petronius sent her representatives to the *princeps* at Samos, where he magnanimously offered a remission of tribute.[10]

Peaceful relations prevailed thereafter. Petronius' campaigns had secured the southern borders of Egypt, rendering that land largely invulnerable to external menace. But this was no mere defensive mission. Roman suzerainty now extended over the Dodecaschoenus, the zone between the First and Second Cataracts. And Augustus boasted in the *Res Gestae* of military conquest stretching to Napata: Roman power now reached almost to the great Ethiopian city of Meroe.[11]

Aelius Gallus' ill-fated expedition had thwarted Roman aims in Arabia Felix. But Augustus maintained interest in the Nabataean Arabs and even meddled in the internal affairs of that kingdom. Intrigue and rivalry between the Nabataeans and the realm of Herod the Great in Palestine kept the *princeps* repeatedly involved in hearing and judging competitive claims. Augustus briefly considered adding the Nabataeans to the dominion of Herod, but decided instead to confirm Aretas IV on the throne *c.* 8 B.C. After the death of Herod in 4 B.C., however, Rome may actually have annexed Nabataea for a short time, subjecting it to direct rule before relinquishing it again to Aretas. The latter act can be

[10] Strab. XVII.1.53–4 (819–21C); Dio LI.5.4–6; Pliny, *HN* VI.181; see Jameson 1968 (E 939) 72–6, 79–82; Török 1988 (E 976) 275–9. On the name P. Petronius, see Bagnall 1985 (E 889). Additional bibliography in Burstein 1988 (C 258) 16–20, who argues that the tribute was first imposed by Cornelius Gallus and that Augustus' remission of it represented abandonment of his aggressive policies in the region.   [11] Aug. *RG* 26.

associated with a military expedition by C. Caesar, grandson of the *princeps*, in A.D. 1, who fought a campaign in or near Arabia, out of which perhaps came the reinstatement of Aretas as Roman client king over the Nabataeans.[12] Augustus kept in touch with affairs of the Near East – and made certain to manifest Roman authority in the area.

II. ASIA MINOR

The Greek East had been a mainstay for Antony. But the battle of Actium, followed in the next year by the suicides of Antony and Cleopatra, tipped the balance decisively. Rulers and dynasts in the hellenistic world faced a crisis. Earlier support for Antony, once a source of authority, now became a perilous liability. The new shape of the East would be at the command of Octavian, a fact that prompted hasty shifts of allegiance and spread alarm among the leadership.

Octavian, however, knew better than to conduct a wholesale overturn of the old order. Men of experience and established influence could be valuable instruments in preserving stability in the Greek world. They served to illustrate the conqueror's clemency, to deliver a comforting sense of continuity, and to transmit the advantages of loyalty to the new regime.[13]

Octavian confirmed the ex-Antonian Polemo in place in Pontus. The king subsequently gained formal recognition as friend and ally of Rome.[14] He had to yield up Armenia Minor, but only because Octavian wished to award it to another ex-Antonian, Artavasdes of Armenia.[15] Polemo collaborated loyally and faithfully with the Augustan regime. When rebellion broke out in the Bosporan kingdom, headed by an obscure usurper named Scribonius, Agrippa, who oversaw Rome's eastern interests in Syria, commissioned Polemo to restore the situation in 14 B.C. Polemo carried out the task, though it required Agrippa's forces to intimidate the rebels. The Pontic dynast, with Augustus' approval, went on to marry Dynamis, widow both of Scribonius and the previous Bosporan king, and to add the Bosporan realm to his own holdings.[16] The combination of royal houses and kingdoms evidently appealed to Augustus: it permitted him to hold the allegiance of a broad area under a tested client prince. As it happened, the marriage soon foundered. Dynamis regained control of her dominion on the Bosporus, Polemo selected a new bride, Pythodoris from Tralles, and hostilities resumed between the kingdoms. Polemo fell in battle while endeavour-

---

[12] Pliny, *HN* 11.168, VI.160; Strab. XVI.4.21 (779C), with the discussion of Bowersock 1983 (E 990) 53–6; cf. Romer 1979 (C 301) 204–8; Sidebotham 1986 (C 310) 130–3. On the Nabataean kingdom in this period, see Negev 1978 (C 292) 549–69. Gaius' martial accomplishments are celebrated in *ILS*, 140, lines 9–12; EJ² 69.   [13] See Levick's account below, ch. 14a.
[14] Strab. XII.8.16 (578C); Dio LIII.25.1.   [15] Dio LIV.9.2.   [16] Dio LIV.24.4–6

ing to regain the Bosporan realm in 8 B.C., and his wife Pythodoris inherited power in Pontus.[17] Augustus remained aloof from the contest, hoping to encourage stability without intervention. Dynamis obtained recognition as friend and ally of the Roman people. The *princeps* preferred to endorse continuing regimes rather than to undermine or destabilize them. Dynastic ties unravelled between Pontus and the Bosporan kingdom, but gained new strength between Pontus and Cappadocia when Polemo's widow Pythodoris wed Archelaus of Cappadocia, thus linking the two kingdoms.[18] That arrangement too was doubtless orchestrated by Augustus, thereby to bind together the royal houses of Anatolia as surrogates for Roman suzerainty.

Archelaus, beneficiary of Antony, kept his throne through the favour of Caesar Octavianus. Indeed, he would soon increase his holdings with Roman encouragement. Archelaus obtained Cilicia Tracheia, parts of the coast, and Armenia Minor by 20 B.C., a move to build a more solid shield against Parthia.[19] The king experienced less success with his subjects, some of whom lodged an accusation against him in Rome – to no avail.[20] And at some point Augustus was induced to install an overseer in Cappadocia.[21] Nevertheless, Archelaus' connexions and machinations kept him on his throne through the reign of Augustus.[22]

Deiotarus Philadelphus ruled Paphlagonia with Antony's approval, switched sides at Actium, and earned the gratitude of the conqueror. Octavian confirmed him in power.[23] The kingdom may have been enlarged later with parts of Phazemonitis. Deiotarus enjoyed an untroubled dominion until his death in 6 B.C.[24]

Amyntas of Galatia too changed allegiance hastily before Actium, and profited. He remained sovereign in his realm and received further territorial grants in Pisidia, Lycaonia, Isauria and Cilicia Tracheia.[25] The new dominions brought added responsibilities. Amyntas undertook to subjugate the fiercely independent and troublesome mountain tribes sheltered in the Taurus range and menacing the southern fringes of Galatia. The king made admirable headway, up to a point, capturing a number of mountain fastnesses. But terrain favoured the guerrillas. Amyntas fell victim to the formidable tribe of the Homonadenses and

---

[17] Strab. XI.2.11 (495C); XII.3.29 (556C); Hoben 1969 (E 840) 47–53; Sullivan 1980 (E 879) 915–22; Roddaz 1984 (C 200) 463–8.

[18] Strab. XII.3.29 (556C); XII.3.37 (559–60C); Pani 1972 (C 295) 140–2; Cimma 1976 (D 120) 293, n. 8.

[19] Joseph. *AJ* XV.105; Strab. XII.1.4 (535C); XII.2.7 (537C); XII.2.11 (540C); XIV.5.6 (671C); Dio LIV.9.2; Hoben 1969 (E 840) 182–7.

[20] Suet. *Tib.* 8; Dio LVII.17.3; Pani 1972 (C 295) 107–11.

[21] Dio LVII.17.4–5. Perhaps during Archelaus' trial; Romer 1985 (C 302) 76–84.

[22] Cf. Pani 1972 (C 295) 131–45; Sullivan 1980 (E 880) 1149–61; Romer 1985 (C 302) 84–100.

[23] Strab. XII.3.41 (562C).   [24] Magie 1950 (E 853) 1283–4.

[25] Strab. XII.6.3–5 (569C); XIV.5.6 (671C).

was executed in 25 B.C.[26] Augustus moved swiftly and decisively. He would leave no vacuum in central Anatolia that might tempt marauders or rebels. Galatia was annexed as a Roman province. The region encompassed Isauria, Pisidia, Lycaonia and part of Pamphylia, in addition to Galatia proper. It would henceforth come under the supervision of a Roman governor.[27] Reasons for Augustus' sudden shift of policy are not easy to discern. Amyntas had sons but Augustus ignored their claims. It would be hazardous to infer that the *princeps* had a long-standing and deliberate design to convert client states into provinces, once their rulers had prepared them for incorporation. Nor would provincialization of the land provide the glory of imperial expansion that came with conquest. An *ad hoc* decision seems more likely. Death of the king at the hands of rebellious tribes threatened the region and challenged the efficacy of Roman overlordship. Augustus would now make a display of direct Roman rule. The new province included a number of military colonies dispatched by Augustus to Pisidia. The annexation of Galatia served to solidify the area, overawe recalcitrant mountaineers, and provide a buttress for client princes in Pontus, Paphlagonia and Cappadocia, as well as for the provinces of Bithynia and Asia.

Augustus had no commitment to provincialization as a matter of policy. In fact, he detached the area of Cilicia Tracheia from Galatia and bestowed it upon Archelaus, the loyal ruler of Cappadocia.[28] When circumstances called for it, he would alter arrangements and reorganize territory accordingly. The death of Deiotarus Philadelphus in 6/5 B.C. gave occasion for incorporating his realm into the province of Galatia. Three years later came a further addition to the province, the region of Pontus Galaticus.[29] A preserved oath of allegiance from Gangra underscores the new order: the inhabitants swore fealty to Augustus and included his name among the gods and goddesses by whom the oath was sanctioned.[30] Improvisation rather than elaborate design appears to characterize Roman decisions in Asia Minor. The Homonadenses had brought about the demise of Amyntas and provided the impetus for provincialization. Yet Roman governors of Galatia, whose appointments began in 25 B.C., conducted no campaign against that people for two decades. The tribe had presumably been quiescent in the mean time. It can be inferred that Augustus ordered an offensive only when the Homonadenses stirred trouble again. The legate P. Sulpicius Quirinius headed forces that engaged the mountaineers, perhaps *c.* 5–3 B.C.,

---

[26] Magie 1950 (E 853) 1303–4; Levick 1967 (E 851) 26–8; Hoben 1969 (E 840) 130–8.
[27] Dio LIII.26.3; Strab. XII.5.1 (567C); XII.6.5 (569C); XII.8.14 (577C); Levick 1967 (E 851) 30–2.
[28] Strab. XIV.5.6 (671C); Dio LIV.9.2.
[29] Magie 1950 (E 853) 465–6, 1328–9; Sherk 1980 (E 875) 960–1.   [30] *OGIS* 532.

gradually reducing their strongholds and starving out the defenders, a lengthy and arduous process.[31] One other uprising demanded Rome's attention a few years later: the turbulent Isaurians challenged her authority and had to be quelled in A.D. 6. The province had now been effectively pacified.[32]

Elsewhere in Asia Minor petty dynasts ruled in cities or lesser principalities. Some had served the cause of Antony and were removed, others kept in place. And even where Augustus deposed a dynast he might subsequently restore the dynasty. He left tyrannies in power in Mysia, at Caranitis and Amasia, and in the Bosporan kingdom. He removed rulers from Hierapolis Castabala in Cilicia Pedias and from Olba in Cilicia Tracheia, only to reinstate the ruling houses later. At Pontic Comana he overthrew one Antonian supporter and replaced him with another. Tarsus, where Octavian replaced a client of Antony with one of his own partisans, was exceptional rather than representative. And in Commagene, Augustus expelled more than one dynast before turning the principality back to a previous ruling line.[33] The *ad hoc* character of these dispositions stands out clearly. Some changes took place after Actium, and some dynasties suffered interruption. In general, however, Augustus preferred continuity or reverted to earlier dynastic houses which could bring experience and promote stability.

III. JUDAEA AND SYRIA

Syria held Rome's principal military installation in the East. Three, later four, legions were stationed there, a show of strength to Parthia, and a garrison to intervene at need in Asia Minor or Palestine. Expansionism was not the aim here, rather the maintenance of order and the entrenchment of control. Internal security took precedence.

Syria had become a Roman province after Pompey's campaigns in the 60s and remained a centre for implementation of eastern policy. Antony of course controlled it in the 30s, and Octavian made certain to establish his dominion there shortly after the fall of his rival. The governor of Syria, Q. Didius, was among those who made timely transfer to Octavian after Actium; and Octavian himself spent some time in Syria in late 30 B.C. His presence alone underscored the importance of the area.[34] In the settlement of 27 B.C. Augustus acquired formal responsibility for the province of Syria and thereby for Rome's defence system in the East. The *princeps* kept close surveillance on the region through his appoin-

---

[31] Strab. XII.6.5 (569C); Tac. *Ann.* III.48.2. Levick 1967 (E 851) 32–41, sees long-range design on Augustus' part; cf. 203–14.   [32] Dio LV.28.3; Sherk 1980 (E 875) 970.

[33] References and discussion in Bowersock 1965 (C 39) 46–51, 57–8. On Commagene, see Sullivan 1977 (E 878) 775–83.   [34] Dio LI.7.1–2, LV.18.1.

tees. Roman troops quelled an uprising of the Ituraeans in Lebanon. And the loyalty of minor dynasts like Dexandros at Apamea helped keep the region under control.[35] Augustus gave his chief deputy M. Agrippa general supervision of the East based on Syria in 23 B.C., an office he discharged for ten years, though usually *in absentia*, with trusted legates in place.[36] A similar duty seems to have been exercised by Augustus' grandson Gaius, in association with his eastern expedition *c.* 1 B.C., thus reaffirming the central significance of Syria for Rome's position in the East.[37]

On the Syrian flanks Augustus relied on client princes to serve as buffers and to cushion the province. The petty kingdoms of Emesa and Ituraea provided protection against Bedouin tribes from the desert.[38] And supervision over much of Palestine was entrusted to a remarkable man, Herod the Great.

The extensive testimony of Josephus affords a more intimate glimpse into the affairs of Herod than we possess for any other dependent ruler. Herod has thus become the client prince *par excellence*, a prime exhibit for the relationship between Rome and vassal kings.

This half-Jewish Idumaean had been a chief beneficiary of Antony, confirmed and supported in his authority by the triumvir. And he sided loyally with Antony right down to Actium itself. Herod was not at Actium, engaged instead in fighting with the Nabataeans. But for Herod, as for so many others, the battle represented a decisive turning point. No pretence of hidden sympathies for Octavian was possible. Herod sought out Octavian in Rhodes in 30 B.C. and took a straightforward line: the same sort of unswerving fidelity he had shown to Antony he could now offer to Antony's conqueror; he could be trusted to serve Octavian's interests – as he served his own. Octavian recognized the mutual benefits inherent in this relationship, reaffirmed Herod's royal status and expanded his holdings along the coast, in Samaria, in the Decapolis and around Jericho. Herod put his loyalty on display by visiting Octavian in Egypt and accompanying the Roman on his return trip as far as Antioch.[39] The events of 30 B.C. set a pattern for the relationship between *princeps* and client king.

Herod discharged or anticipated obligations. He supplied soldiers for Aelius Gallus' campaign in Arabia *c.* 26 B.C., refounded and renamed cities in Augustus' honour, dispatched two of his sons to Rome for their education in 23 B.C., and had his subjects swear an oath of allegiance to

---

[35] Crushing of the Ituraeans: *ILS* 2683; Dexandros and in general, Rey-Coquais 1978 (E 1054) 47–9. [36] Dio LIII.32.1; Joseph. *AJ* XVI.3.3.

[37] Oros. VII.3.4. For the evidence on Roman governors of Syria under Augustus, see Schürer 1973 (E 1207) 253–60.

[38] Augustus appears to have deposed and later restored the dynasty of Emesa; Sullivan 1977 (E 1065) 210–14.   [39] Joseph. *AJ* XV.183–201, 218; *BJ* 1.386–97.

the emperor.[40] And the king profited. Augustus enlarged his territorial holdings twice more in the decade after Actium: in 23 B.C. Herod's friendship with the *princeps'* son-in-law and chief helpmate M. Agrippa only enhanced his status further. The king orchestrated an elaborate tour and a lavish reception for Agrippa during his stay in the area in 15 B.C. and performed numerous services for him on a mission to Asia Minor.[41] The tighter the bonds, however, the greater the dependency. The kingdom of Herod was evidently not liable for tribute to Rome.[42] The obligations were subtler and more ambiguous, and thereby, in some ways, more demanding. Augustus gave to Herod some responsibility for supervision in Syria, thus, no doubt, to co-ordinate efforts with the *princeps'* legate in that province.[43] He also awarded to Herod the privilege of appointing his own successor.[44] The *princeps* presumably intended that gesture as a sign of esteem and an encouragement to independent behaviour. But the very fact that such a privilege had to be explicitly articulated is the most telling indicator of the true relationship. And the outcome only intensified subordination. Herod more than once thrust upon Augustus the burden of adjudicating disputes within the royal family. The sordid tale of intrigues in the court, domestic discord, and Herod's morbid suspicions which led to the execution of three sons need not be recounted here. The pertinent fact is that Herod declined to settle matters even in his own household without seeking the emperor's directions. His reign was long and memorable – but always precarious. Conflict between Herod and the Nabataeans led to recriminations in Rome, as the king alternately fell out of and was restored into the favour of Augustus.[45]

Herod's will, twice rewritten during his lifetime, drew Augustus still further into the affairs of the realm after the Idumaean's death in 4 B.C. The document parcelled Herod's holdings among three sons. But it also provided for vast sums of money for Augustus, Livia, the imperial children, *amici* and freedmen, and it further specified that none of the provisions could take effect without ratification by the *princeps*.[46]

[40] Troops for Aelius Gallus: Joseph. *AJ* xv.317; the naming of Sebaste and Caesarea: Joseph. *AJ* xv.296, xv.339; the sending of sons to Rome: Joseph. *AJ* xv.342; oath of allegiance: Joseph. *AJ* xvii.42.

[41] Territorial acquisitions: Joseph. *AJ* xv.343–8, 360; *BJ* 1.398–400; Dio LIV.9.3; cf. Bietenhard 1977 (E 988) 238–40. Herod and Agrippa: Joseph. *AJ* xv.350, xv.361, xvi.12–16, xvi.86; *BJ*, 1.400. Cf. Schalit 1969 (E 1206) 424–6; Smallwood 1976 (E 212) 86–90; Braund 1985 (C 254) 79–80, 85; Roddaz 1984 (C 200) 450–5.

[42] As argued by Schürer 1973 (E 1207) 1.399–427; *contra*, Applebaum 1977 (E 1074) 373. But note the cash gift on a trip to Rome in 12 B.C.; Joseph. *AJ* xvi.128.

[43] Joseph. *AJ* xv.360; *BJ* 1.399.   [44] Joseph. *AJ* xv.343, xvi.129.

[45] Smallwood 1976 (E 1212) 96–104; Schürer 1973 (E 1207) 320–6; Schalit 1969 (E 1206) 563–644; Bammel 1968 (E 1083) 73–9; Piatelli (E 1189) 323–40; Bowersock 1983 (E 990) 49–53; Baumann 1983 (E 1091) 221–37; and see below ch. 15*d*.

[46] Joseph. *AJ* xvii.146, xvii.188–90, 195; *BJ* 1.646, 1.664–5, 1.669.

Herod's privilege of appointing a successor had thus been transformed into a recommendation rather than a directive; Augustus would have the final say. That clause invited discord. The sons of Herod brought conflicting claims to Rome, complicated by a separate Jewish delegation which requested abolition of the monarchy. Augustus decided matters with even-handedness: he endorsed Herod's territorial dispositions, in effect dividing his realm into three parts, but withheld the royal title from all three sons. Archelaus would rule Judaea, Samaria and Idumaea as ethnarch, Antipas and Philip obtained the designation of tetrarch, the one over Galilee and Peraea, the other over Batanaea, Trachonitis and Auranitis. The will and its sequel allowed Augustus both to exercise beneficence and to re-assert his ultimate authority.[47] Further, the *princeps'* chief appointee in the East, P. Quinctilius Varus, the governor of Syria, intervened with force to quell a Jewish rebellion which had arisen in the wake of Herod's death. The limits of autonomy gained clear expression.[48]

What Augustus gave he could also take away. The precedent of asking the emperor to redress grievances created in Palestine had been firmly set in the reign of Herod. A logical step followed in A.D. 6. Complaints registered in Rome against the misrule of Archelaus led Augustus to depose the Herodian dynast, banish him to Gaul, and convert his domain into a Roman province. The smaller principalities under Antipas and Philip remained 'autonomous', but the key districts of Judaea, Samaria and Idumaea would now come under direct Roman rule, governed by an equestrian prefect and under the general surveillance of the imperial legate in Syria. A census directed by the Syrian legate P. Sulpicius Quirinius marked the new order in A.D. 6. It signalled the imposition of Roman taxes and the official subordination of Judaea.[49]

Consolidation rather than expansion characterized Augustan policy in Syria and Palestine. Syria contained the major Roman garrison in the East and provided the pivot for the defence of Rome's position and enforcement of her authority. The history of Judaea under Augustus exposed the fragility of 'independence' for client states which served as buffers for Roman interests. Herod earned imperial favour by tying his realm more closely to the emperor, thus bolstering power but increasing dependence. The transition from client kingdom to province represented a logical stage in the development. Taxation and direct rule only formalized a continuing process of implementing Roman authority in the East.

[47] Joseph. *AJ* XVII.219–49, XVII.300–23; *BJ* II.14–38, II.80–100; Braund 1984 (C 254) 139–42.
[48] Joseph. *AJ* XVII.250–99; *BJ* II.39–79.
[49] Joseph. *AJ* XVII.342–4, XVII.354–5; *BJ* II.111–13, II.117; Dio LV.27.6; Pani 1972 (C 295) 133–7. The census of Quirinius is wrongly dated to the reign of Herod by Luke 2:1–5. On the new province, see Smallwood 1976 (E 1212) 144–56; Ghiretti 1985 (E 1119) 751–66.

IV. ARMENIA AND PARTHIA

M. Antonius had invested heavily in warfare against Parthia. Contests with the great eastern power entailed substantial costs in men and prestige. Parthia had inflicted defeat upon Roman armies, and Rome's influence in Armenia had proved ephemeral. The humiliation left deep scars. Standards of the Republic's army captured at Carrhae and hostages taken in Antony's abortive campaign remained in Parthian hands.[50] After Antony's demise, the burden of restoring Rome's honour rested with the victor of Actium. But Octavian resisted the temptation to retaliate. More urgent tasks of consolidation took priority after Actium. And the restraint set a pattern: the *princeps* recognized that prudent diplomacy and discreet display of force were preferable to expensive and hazardous ventures across the distant Euphrates. Indirect suzerainty in Armenia and a *modus vivendi* with Parthia represented the means to preserve prestige and protect security.

Octavian exercised caution from the outset with Parthia. Dynastic rivalry, as so often, plagued the Parthian ruling houses. Even before Actium Phraates IV and the pretender to his throne Tiridates both sought to enlist Octavian's assistance in their respective causes. Octavian wisely refrained from taking action. After Actium, when Phraates expelled his rival, Tiridates sought refuge in the Roman province of Syria. Octavian permitted him to reside there, a useful card to play in diplomatic games with Parthia, while also maintaining amicable relations with Phraates at an official level.[51] In similar fashion, he declined the request of the Armenian ruler Artaxias to restore his brothers, held as hostages in Rome. They too would serve as insurance and potential counter-weight. And he installed the Mede Artavasdes as king of Armenia Minor, thus to provide further check on any Armenian aspirations.[52]

A reserved cordiality toward Parthia continued through the next decade. In the mid 20s Tiridates left Syria and made his way to Augustus, having in tow the young son of Phraates IV, whom he had managed to kidnap. Phraates sent envoys to the emperor, asking for the surrender of Tiridates and the release of his son. Tiridates, in turn, advertised himself as *philorhomaios* and promised unswerving loyalty as client king if Rome should put him on the Parthian throne. Augustus again delivered an even-handed decision. He would neither turn over the rebel for punishment nor promote his designs on Parthia. Tiridates remained in Rome, his wants amply provided for, and his ambitions circumscribed by Augustus' needs. Phraates got his son back – a magnanimous gesture

---

[50] On Antony and Parthia, see above, ch. 1.
[51] Dio LI.18.2–3.   [52] Dio LI.16.2, LIV.9.2; Strab. XII.3.29 (555C); Magie 1950 (E 853) 443.

by Augustus – but no more. Amicable relations held, so long as the *princeps* could make the decisions.[53]

Restraint and quiet diplomacy kept the peace during the 20s. Other matters occupied Augustus' attention: the working out of constitutional arrangements and the entrenchment of Rome's position in the West. But the *princeps* did not rest content with the *status quo* in the East. Parthia's retention of standards and captives taken from Roman armies remained an open sore and an implicit denial of Rome's omnipotence. The year 20 B.C. proved to be the year of reckoning. Augustus travelled personally to the East, adjudicated disputes, made territorial dispositions and settled internal quarrels in cities of Greece, Asia Minor and Syria. He further exhibited the authority of the suzerain by reassigning lands to dynasts in Cilicia, Emesa, Judaea, Commagene and Armenia Minor.[54] The *princeps'* presence in the Near East may have provided the occasion for upheaval in Armenia. The citizenry, or a significant portion thereof, rose against Artaxias II, protégé of the Parthian monarch, and requested a new ruler, namely Artaxias' brother Tigranes, then resident in Rome. Augustus, who had given refuge to the brothers for just such a contingency, readily complied. The emperor directed his stepson Tiberius to install Tigranes at the head of a Roman army. Mobilization alone sufficed. The Armenians assassinated Artaxias, and Tiberius could deliver Tigranes to a vacant throne without use of force.[55] Presentation of the event in Rome, however, simulated military victory. The coinage blared slogans of *Armenia capta* or *Armenia recepta*.[56]

In the East Augustus affected war but practised diplomacy. The celebrated arrangement with Phraates IV in 20 B.C. cannot be disassociated from the *princeps'* presence in Syria and the settlement in Armenia. Phraates yielded up at last the standards and captives held for a generation as Parthian prizes, thereby allowing Augustus to claim credit for wiping out a long-standing stain on Roman honour.[57] Negotiations had brought about that result. Phraates evidently received assurances of non-interference in his own realm (the pretender Tiridates is not heard from again), while Parthia acknowledged the Roman interest in Armenia. The king allegedly supplied hostages to Rome as well. An informal accord arose from the bargaining, perhaps even an overt acceptance that the Euphrates would serve as boundary between the zones of

---

[53] Just. *Epit.* XLII.5.6–9; Dio, LIII.33.2; Aug. *RG* 32.1. Chronology is uncertain; cf. e.g., Debevoise 1938 (A 19) 136–7, Ziegler 1964 (C 327) 147, and, esp., Timpe 1975 (C 320) 157–60. On Tiridates' coinage, see Timpe, 1975 (C 320) 155–7. [54] Dio LIV.7, LIV.9.1–3.
[55] Dio LIV.9.4–5; Vell. Pat. II.94.4; Aug. *RG*, 27.2; Tac. *Ann.* II.3; Strab. XVII.1.54 (821C); Joseph. *AJ* XV.105.
[56] *BMCRR*, II nos. 301–8; cf. Hor. *Epist.* I.12.26–7; Vell. Pat. II.94.4; Chaimont 1976 (A 15) 73–5.
[57] Aug. *RG* 29.2; Vell. Pat. II.91.1; Dio LIV.8.1–2; Ov. *Fast.* V.579–84; Suet. *Aug.* 21.3; Suet. *Tib.* 9.1.

influence.[58] But here again Augustus proclaimed victory, conquest and martial supremacy for consumption at home. The *Res Gestae* declared that he had 'compelled' the Parthians to surrender trophies and beg for Roman friendship. The Senate offered to vote a triumph, and a triumphal arch was erected in the Forum. Numismatic representations repeatedly called attention to *signis receptis*. And the central scene of the cuirass on the Prime Porta statue depicted the transfer of the standards.[59] Augustus made the most of his diplomatic success. A compact of mutual advantage and mutual agreement took on the glow of military mastery.

A sign of continuing cordiality between Rome and Parthia came in 10 B.C. Phraates IV sent four sons to live in Rome. The gesture did not signify deference or subordination, as sometimes portrayed; rather, it provided a means whereby the Parthian king could defuse opposition at home and stabilize his hold on the throne. Augustus was pleased to comply. He could both grant a favour to Phraates and take possession of potentially valuable instruments of diplomacy.[60]

Relations between the empires remained smooth and undisturbed for nearly two decades after Phraates relinquished the standards. Trouble arose, as so often, in the client state and buffer region of Armenia. The death of Augustus' appointee Tigranes II *c.* 7 B.C. ushered in a turmoil of which our sources preserve only a few confused fragments. A struggle for the throne evidently gripped Armenia, pitting Tiridates III against another Roman nominee Artavasdes, and prompting the *princeps* to dispatch Tiberius to settle affairs. But Tiberius, for motives that remain forever hidden, abandoned his commission and took up residence in Rhodes. Rome's influence over subsequent events in Armenia suffered sharp decline.[61]

The situation in Parthia soon complicated matters, dealing Roman interests a further blow. Phraates IV perished, perhaps murdered, in 2 B.C., and his successor Phraates V (or Phraataces) took the occasion to meddle in Armenia.[62] Augustus could not permit Rome's prestige in the East to suffer further deterioration. His own prestige at home was at

---

[58] Aug. *RG* 29.2; Strab. XVI.1.18 (748–9C); Vell. Pat. II.100.1; Oros. VI.21.24. Parthia's acknowledgment of Roman interest in Armenia: Suet. *Aug.* 21.3; cf. Vell. Pat. II.100.1; Eutrop. VII.9. The Euphrates as boundary: Strab. XVI.1.28 (748C). Hostages to Rome: Suet. *Aug.* 21.3; Eutrop. VII.9; Oros. VI.21.29.

[59] Aug. *RG* 29.2; Dio LIV.8.1–3; *BMCRE* Augustus, nos. 410, 412, 414–19, 421–3. The propaganda may be reflected also in the report that Phraates gave up the standards out of fear of a Roman invasion; Dio LIV.8.1; Just. *Epit.* XLII.5.10–11.

[60] Tac. *Ann.* II.1; Strab. XVI.1.28 (748–9C); Aug. *RG* 32.2; Vell. Pat. II.94.4; Joseph. *AJ* XVIII. 41–2; Suet. *Aug.* 21.3. Cf. Braund 1984 (C 254) 12–13, rightly stressing that they should not be considered hostages.

[61] Dio LV.9.4–5; Tac. *Ann.* II.4. The record is sparse and frustrating on this period. Numismatic testimony helps only slightly; Chaumont 1976 (A 15) 75–7.

[62] Dio. LV.10.18; Vell. Pat. II.100.1.

stake. The *princeps* then staged a public demonstration to reassure the citizenry that Roman power would again make itself felt, undiminished, in the lands of the East. Augustus' grandson (and adopted son and heir) Gaius took command of troops to head for the Euphrates, intimidate Parthia, and settle accounts in Armenia. The young prince received a handsome send-off. Elaborate pageantry marked the occasion, with talk in the air of conquest, vengeance against Parthia, new triumphs and spoils for the imperial house, and expansion of the Roman empire.[63]

Augustus' intentions, in fact, were rather more modest. But public perception, as ever, counted. Gaius took an extensive detour, to Arabia and elsewhere, in part to add to his distinctions, primarily to show the flag.[64] News of his achievements and of his arrival in Syria had the desired effect. Tigranes III of Armenia sent a conciliatory message to the *princeps*, seeking Roman endorsement for his claims on the throne, and received a friendly response. Phraataces also prepared to negotiate. His letter to Rome probed for an accommodation, but simultaneously requested the return of his brothers, now under the *princeps'* protection. Augustus fired off a sharp reply, demanding that Parthia refrain from interference in Armenia and leaving off the royal title in his address, a deliberate affront — not a slight on Parthian sovereignty but on Phraataces' legitimacy. The king responded in kind: his letter addressed the *princeps* merely as Caesar and identified himself as 'King of Kings'. The exchange of messages plainly directed itself to a domestic constituency — on both sides. The whole sequence of events supplied more show than substance. No fighting was necessary, not even a hostile confrontation. The encounter, when it came, was amicable and fruitful. It too had been carefully programmed in advance. In A.D. 2 Gaius and Phraataces, each with impressive and equal entourage, met on an island in the Euphrates. Mutual pledges and a recognition of formal equality ensued. The king dined with Gaius on Rome's side of the river and then Phraataces hosted a banquet on the Parthian side. The scene was well orchestrated. Phraataces now officially acknowledged Rome's interests in Armenia and dropped his request for restoration of his brothers. Augustus, in effect, consented to leave Phraataces undisturbed, renewed *amicitia*, and implicitly designated the Euphrates as a frontier between spheres of influence. But his retention of the Parthian princes left the critical diplomatic leverage in his hands.[65]

The arrangement in A.D. 2 ought to have settled matters. But

[63] Ov. *Ars Am.* 1.177–86, 1.201–12; cf. Dio LV.10a.3; Hollis 1977 (B 86) 65–73; Syme 1978 (B 179) 8–11. Gaius' appointment is recorded also by Tac. *Ann.* 11.4; Dio LV.10.18–19; Vell. Pat. 11.101.1.

[64] Cf. Romer 1978 (C 300) 187–202, 1979 (C 301) 203–8.

[65] Dio LV.10.20–1, LV.10a.4; Vell. Pat. 11.101.1–3. Among modern discussions, see e.g., Ziegler 1964 (C 327) 53–6; Chaumont 1976 (A 15) 77–80; Romer 1979 (C 301) 203–4, 208–10; Pani 1972 (C 295) 45–6; Cimma 1976 (D 120) 324–8.

Armenian affairs followed their own path, regardless of agreements
between Rome and Parthia. Tigranes III died, probably in A.D 3, setting
off a chain of events no longer recoverable in detail or in precise
sequence. Gaius installed a new ruler, the Mede Ariobarzanes, thus to
reiterate Rome's role in the indirect governance of that client kingdom.
But Armenian nationalist sentiment resisted once more, and upheaval
followed in which Gaius himself suffered a wound that would prove
fatal. Two or three more changes of rulers came in Armenia during the
lifetime of Augustus. The *princeps* claimed credit for the appointments,
but the real extent of his influence cannot be ascertained. Internal
struggles for power in that land reduced it for a time to anarchy.[66]

Comparable struggles for the throne occurred in Parthia during the
final decade of Augustus' reign. The *princeps* neither promoted nor
abetted them, but he did profit from them. In the midst of this turmoil, *c.*
A.D. 6, a delegation of Parthian leaders arrived in Rome to seek release of
Vonones, one of the sons of Phraates IV who had resided in Rome for
the past decade and a half, in order to install him as Parthian ruler. The
prospect appealed to Augustus who sent off Vonones with handsome
gifts – as if setting his own appointee on the throne of Parthia.[67]
Augustus welcomed the opportunity to have an indirect hand in
ordering Parthian affairs – or at least to appear to be doing so. In fact, the
Roman connexions and upbringing proved to be more a liability than an
asset for Vonones. The Parthians themselves eventually found him
unacceptable, summoned Artabanus of the Arsacid line to the throne,
and expelled Vonones in A.D. 12. Augustus, who had played only a
passive role in the installation of Vonones, took no steps to support him.
It was not part of Rome's policy to provoke Parthia; rather she aimed to
maintain her interests in Armenia and to keep Parthian influence on the
far side of the Euphrates. Those aims could even be seen as advanced by
the flight of Vonones: he made his way to Armenia and there took the
throne made vacant by recent upheavals. So, the Parthian prince, raised
in Rome, now held the crown in Armenia.[68] Such was the situation, quite
acceptable from the Roman vantage-point, at the death of Augustus.
The reliance on diplomacy, with occasional brandishing but only rare
exercise of force, continued as standard policy throughout most of the
Julio-Claudian era.

The pattern of the emperor's policy in that region maintained
consistency throughout. He pursued the twin goals of hegemony via

---

[66] Aug. *RG* 27.2; Tac. *Ann.* 11.4; Vell. Pat. 11.102.2; Flor. 11.32; Dio LV.10a.5–7. See the
reconstructions of Chaumont 1976 (A 15) 80–3, with numismatic testimony; Pani 1972 (C 295) 55–
64; Cimma 1976 (D 120) 328–9.

[67] Aug. *RG* 33; Tac. *Ann.* 11.2; Joseph. *AJ* XVIII.43–6; cf. Suet. *Tib.* 16.

[68] Joseph. *AJ* XVIII.47–50; Tac. *Ann.* 11.2–4.

client rulers in Armenia and amicable relations, including mutually acknowledged spheres of influence, with Parthia.[69] The behaviour was marked by restraint, but the public posture was one of aggressiveness. So Augustus presented endorsement of a client king as capture of Armenia, recovery of the standards as Parthian submission, and the assignment of Gaius as an imperialist venture. The *princeps* knew the limits of Rome's effective authority in the East and kept within them. But keeping up appearances was no less important than keeping within limits. Augustus projected the image of a conqueror who extended Roman sovereignty to the East.

V. SPAIN

The reputation of the *princeps* also played a major part in determining the extension of imperial power to north-west Spain. That region, home of the fierce Cantabrians and Asturians, remained outside Rome's control, despite more than two centuries of Roman presence in the Iberian peninsula. Augustus led his forces in person, the last time he was to do so. The matter was evidently deemed to be of high importance.

The campaigns proved long and arduous, as so often in Spain. Augustus headed the effort in one year only, 26 B.C., but resistance continued at intervals until 19 B.C., perhaps even beyond. The *princeps* was determined to subjugate the area.

Strategic motives do not account for the thrust. Roman commanders regularly claimed triumphs in Spain – six of them had been awarded in the decade just prior to Augustus' invasion itself. Raids by the Cantabrians upon neighbouring tribes might have supplied a pretext. But hardly enough to warrant the emperor's own presence at the head of the army. Nor do economic motives provide an answer. Spanish mines and other resources had long been exploited by Rome; the wealth of the north west was an afterthought rather than an incentive.[70] Our sources offer little by way of explanation: Cantabrian harassment of neighbours, Augustus' intent to regulate affairs in Spain, or simply irritation that after 200 years a corner of the peninsula still held itself independent of Roman rule.[71] Concrete goals take second place here; propaganda counted for more.

The provinces of Spain (Baetica was soon to be removed) were among the overseas territories assigned to Augustus at the beginning of the year

[69] Sherwin-White 1984 (A 89) 322–41, sees a more menacing posture by Augustus toward Parthia.   [70] Cf. Flor. 11.33.60.

[71] On the triumphs, see Fasti Triumph. for the years 36, 34, 33,32, 28, and 26; *IItal* XIII p. 570; cf. also Dio LI.20.5; *ILS* 893. Raids by Cantabrians: Flor. 11.33.47; regulation of affairs: Dio LIII.22.5; subjugation of independent peoples: Oros. VI.21.1. For discussions of these motives, see Schmitt-henner 1962 (C 305) 43–53; Santos Yanguas 1982 (E 237) 7–10, with further literature.

27 B.C. He announced his resolve to bring them firmly under Roman authority. Since most of the peninsula already fell in that category, the intended targets were plainly the Cantabrians and Asturians. Tales made the rounds of their ferocious nature and fanatic resistance to any infringement on autonomy. Augustus threw open the gates of Janus' temple, a symbolic means to proclaim a crusade against the foe. And his personal leadership of the army would reinforce martial credentials, a check on actual or potential rivals with military claims of their own.[72] As the opening of the gates declared Augustus' purpose, so their closing advertised its accomplishment. The *princeps* made certain to have that ceremony conducted to commemorate his success in 25 B.C., only the fourth time in Roman history that Janus' gates were shut – but the second time in five years.[73] The occasion in 29 had marked official termination of civil war; this time the ritual signified pacification of the empire. Augustus declined to celebrate a triumph, a display of *moderatio*, but accepted a more enduring distinction: the privilege of wearing garlands and triumphal dress on the first day of every year.[74] He plainly intended to make the event memorable, a fact underscored by the composition and publication of Augustus' own autobiography. The work concluded with the successful close of the Cantabrian War.[75] It memorialized a capstone of the *princeps'* career. In light of later accomplishments, the *bellum Cantabricum et Asturicum* may not have seemed so momentous. Augustus gives it only brief mention in the *Res Gestae*, among a number of regions which he brought to submission.[76] The earlier and more emphatic presentation, however, is reflected in the Livian tradition and picked up by Velleius Paterculus: after two centuries of bloodshed in that violent and savage land, Caesar Augustus' campaigns imposed a lasting peace that not only crushed armed resistance but even wiped out brigandage.[77] The conquest of north-west Spain rounded off control of the entire peninsula.

As in the case of Parthia, battlefield exploits in Spain did not match their publicity in Rome. Confusion in the sources prevents a confident reconstruction of events, geography, or chronology. It is clear, in any case, that Augustus' personal intervention was anything but decisive. The *princeps* was at Tarraco at the beginning of 26 B.C., there to inaugurate his eighth consulship.[78] He participated in the campaign of that year, but in what area and for how long remain unknown. Florus

---

[72] The distribution of provinces in Dio LIII.12.4–5; cf. Syme 1934 (C 313) 300. Augustus' announced resolve for subjugation: Dio LIII.13.1. The ferocity of the foe: Strab. III.4.17–18 (164–5C); Oros. VI.21.8. The opening of the gates: Oros. VI.21.1.

[73] Dio LIII.26.5; Oros. VI.21.11; Aug. *RG* 13.

[74] Dio LIII.26.5; cf. Flor. II.33.53; Barnes 1974 (C 253) 21.   [75] Suet. *Aug.* 85.1.

[76] Aug. *RG* 26.2–3; cf. 29.1.

[77] Livy, XXVIII.12.12; Flor. II.33.59; Vell. Pat. II.90.2–4.   [78] Suet. *Aug.* 26; Dio LIII.23.1.

and Orosius record only Roman victories in Cantabria, with the *princeps* directing a three-pronged attack from the base camp at Segisamo: the Romans inflicted a defeat on their foes at Bergida (or Velleia), starved them out at Mt Vindius and captured the city of Aracelium (or Racilium). Names of the sites and their locations have long been disputed. Nor is it clear whether the campaign of 26 confined itself to Cantabria or included Asturia. The question connects to a further one: did the three Roman assaults occur serially or simultaneously? No definitive answers are possible.[79] Cassius Dio's account, however, discloses setbacks: the Romans made little headway under Augustus, illness felled the *princeps* who withdrew to Tarraco, and successes came only through the exertions of C. Antistius Vetus, legate of Tarraconensis.[80] Augustus, it may be safely surmised, did not return to the battlefield after the campaigning season of 26 B.C. Roman forces penetrated into Asturia and gained a dramatic victory over besieged and desperate Spaniards at Mt Medullius in 26 or 25.[81] A concerted assault by the Asturians followed in 25, nearly overwhelming Roman forces in the region, thwarted only by a last-minute betrayal of their plan and a march to the rescue by the army of P. Carisius, legate of Lusitania. Carisius' capture of the Asturian stronghold Lancia concluded the fighting. Romans had gained the upper hand, but the struggle had been bloody and the cost in lives heavy.[82]

The victories prompted Augustus to direct the closing of Janus' doors, an announcement of thorough pacification, and generated the award of triumphal honours. The *princeps* even authorized the establishment of a veteran colony, *colonia Augusta Emerita* (Mérida), to mark the settled status of the land.[83] An ode of Horace welcomed home the returning conqueror, comparing him to Hercules and rejoicing in a new security.[84] But the conquest was superficial and the celebration premature. Both Cantabrians and Asturians exploded into revolt as soon as Augustus left the province in 24, thus exposing the fragility of his achievement. The legate of Tarraconensis, L. Aelius Lamia, resorted to brutality in suppressing the rebellion.[85] Two years later the Cantabrians

---

[79] Flor. II.33.48–50; Oros. VI.21.3–5. Among numerous scholarly discussions, see Magie 1920 (C 285) 325–39; Syme 1934 (C 313) 293–317; Schuten 1943 (E 238); Horrent 1953 (C 276) 279–90; Schmitthenner 1962 (C 305) 54–60; Syme 1970 (C 314) 83–103; a recent summary of scholarship in Santos Yanguas 1982 (E 237) 16–26. See also Santos 1975 (C 303) 531–6; Lomas Salmonte 1975 (E 230) 103–27; Solana Sainz 1981 (E 239) 97–119; Tranoy 1981 (E 244) 132–44; Martino 1982 (C 287) 41–104.   [80] Dio LIII.25.5–8; cf. Flor. II.33.51; Suet. *Aug.* 81.

[81] Flor. II.33.50; Oros. VI.21.6–8. The location of Mt Medullius, whether in Asturia or in Callaecia, is uncertain; Santos Yanguas 1982 (E 237) 18–26; Martino 1982 (C 287) 105–24.

[82] Flor. II.33.54–8; Oros. VI.21.9–10; Dio LIII.25.8. For the deployment and identification of the legions, see testimony collected by Lomas Salmonte 1975 (E 230) 135–9; Jones 1976 (E 226) 48–51; Solana Sainz 1981 (E 239) 120–42; Santos Yanguas 1982 (E 237) 26–45.   [83] Dio LIII.26.1.

[84] Hor. *Carm.* III.14; cf. IV.14.50. A darker interpretation of the poem by Sholz 1971 (C 307) 123–37.   [85] Dio LIII.29.1–2. For the legate's name, see *AE* 1948, 93.

rose against their new governor, C. Furnius, and the Asturians against the increasing cruelty of Carisius, bringing still more ruthless repression and subjugation.[86] Yet another insurrection by the redoubtable Cantabrians in 19 B.C. provoked the dispatch of M. Agrippa himself who subdued them, but only at heavy cost and severe losses, declining even to accept the triumph voted him at Augustus' urging.[87] Agrippa's campaign which flushed the Cantabrians out of their strongholds and compelled them to settle in the plains finally brought a measure of stability to the region.[88] The *princeps* was able to make a more peaceful tour of Spain in 15–14 B.C., organizing colonial foundations and exhibiting generosity.[89]

Here as elsewhere propaganda and reality diverged. Augustus entered Spain to claim victory and announce pacification. And so he did. His autobiography saluted the achievement, Velleius Paterculus embellished it, the tradition followed by Florus and Orosius reiterated it. The conquest of north-west Spain rounded off Roman suzerainty in the Iberian peninsula. But the real victory did not match Augustus' boast. It came slowly, a bloody and brutal process that endured well beyond the *princeps'* declaration of success. The Ara Pacis was duly decreed to herald Augustus' return from Spain. Not, however, in 25 B.C. when Janus' doors were closed and triumphal honours bestowed; rather in 13 B.C. after more than a decade of intermittent insurrection, costly casualties and terrorism.

VI. AFRICA

In Africa entrenchment of control rather than expansionism predominated. The region served as an important granary for Rome and its security held a place on the imperial agenda. The *provincia Africa*, once the realm of Carthage, had been in Roman hands for a century. Iulius Caesar added to the empire's holdings, annexing the kingdom of Numidia, henceforth Africa Nova, with the former province becoming Africa Vetus.[90] The fall of Sextus Pompeius in 36 B.C. brought both provinces under Octavian's authority. He strengthened Roman presence in both, sending new settlers to Carthage in 29 B.C. and to Cirta in 26 B.C.[91] Confidence in their security allowed him to transfer responsibility for the area, whether as one or as two provinces, to the Senate in the dispositions of 27 B.C.[92]

---

[86] Dio LIV.5.1–3.   [87] Dio LIV.11.2–6; cf. Roddaz 1984 (C 200) 402–10.
[88] A minor rising was quelled in 16 B.C.; Dio LIV.20.3.
[89] Dio LIV.23.7, LIV.25.1, LIV.43.3; Aug. *RG* 12.2.
[90] Dio XLVIII.9.4; App. *BCiv.* IV.53; Pliny, *HN* v.4.25.
[91] Carthage: Dio LII.43.1; App. *Pun,* 136; Cirta: *AE* 1955, 202.   [92] Dio LIII.12.4.

Not that calm had descended altogether. Nor did Rome abandon aggression and content herself with consolidation. A series of proconsuls earned triumphs *ex Africa*, five of them in the period 24–19 B.C.[93] Details of the campaigns escape us for the most part, as do motives, location and the identity of the foe. Evidence does not permit characterization of them either as defence of the frontier or as extension of empire. The southern boundaries of the provinces were fluid. One can hardly draw a distinction between protection of Roman interests and intimidation of semi-nomadic tribes. The *legio III Augusta* remained as a continuing presence even after the Senate took official responsibility in 27 B.C. Of the triumphs recorded, details survive only for the campaign of L. Cornelius Balbus who gained his reward in 19 B.C. Balbus, a friend and loyal lieutenant of Augustus and a man experienced in Africa, drove deeply into the territory of the Garamantes, the restive Berber people who dwelled south of the Roman province. Pliny describes the triumph, with a catalogue of the towns and tribes whence came the spoils displayed by Balbus. The extent of his victories indicates carefully planned campaigns with a number of columns to penetrate the present Fezzan and its environs. Balbus' well-earned triumph suggests a systematic thrust to intimidate the Berber. And Augustus could take credit for his subordinate's accomplishment. Virgil's homage to the *princeps'* imperialism makes special mention of the subjugation of the Garamantes.[94]

The intimidation apparently took effect. Two decades passed with no evidence of trouble from the nomadic or semi-nomadic tribes on the fringes of the province. The stationing of *legio III Augusta* at Ammaedara no doubt helped to keep matters under control.[95] Troubles did not recommence until *c.* A.D. 2: another *imperator*, L. Passienus Rufus, gained triumphal honours for victories in Africa.[96] The triumph presupposes rebellion and upheaval. And other fragmentary evidence confirms it: the Gaetulians and Musulamii in the region of the Syrtes engaged in guerilla warfare against Roman rule and against Rome's commanders, until subdued in A.D. 6 by Cossus Cornelius Lentulus who would pass to his son the commemorative title of Gaetulicus.[97] It may have been during these same years that the Garamantes rose again, together with the

---

[93] Fasti Triumph. for the years 34, 33, 28, 21, 19.

[94] Virg. *Aen.* VI.792–5. The conquests of Balbus are recorded by Pliny, *HN* v.35–7. See the exhaustive reconstruction by Desanges 1957 (C 262) 1–43; cf. Romanelli 1959 (E 760) 176–81; Rachet 1970 (C 297) 70–4; Gutsfeld 1989 (E 742) 26–30.

[95] Cf. Romanelli 1959 (E 760) 186–7; Rachet 1970 (C 297) 74.

[96] Vell. Pat. II.116.2; cf. *ILS* 120, 8966.

[97] Vell. Pat. II.116.2; Flor. II.31.40; Dio LV.28.3–4; Oros. VI.21.18. L. Cornelius Lentulus may have been among the Roman generals who perished at the hands of the rebels; Just. *Inst.* II.25. See, in general, Romanelli 1959 (E 760) 181–6; Bénabou 1976 (E 715) 61–5; Gutsfeld 1989 (E 742) 31–9.

Marmarides, providing occasion for another Roman military success, that of Sulpicius Quirinius, who with modesty uncharacteristic of *imperatores*, declined the honorific name of Marmaricus.[98] Testimony is thin and woefully inadequate. But it is plain that the stability imposed by Balbus' successes did not endure through the reign of Augustus. Native resistance to Roman rule resurfaced when opportunity arose, a periodic rejection of the *pax Augusta*.

Roman influence, limited on the southern borderlands, spread along the Mediterranean coast of Africa. The ruler of Mauretania, Bocchus, died in 33 B.C. and Octavian took charge of his kingdom, keeping it out of the hands of any native prince and transforming it into a direct Roman dependency.[99] Precisely how the region was administered in subsequent years remains obscure. Mauretania does not appear among the provinces enlisted on Octavian's side in 32 B.C., nor among those assigned in the settlement of 27 B.C.[100] The nature of its governance eludes inquiry, but Rome directly or indirectly, took responsibility for it. In 25 B.C., however, the arrangement gave way to a new solution: Augustus turned the realm over to Juba II, son of the former king of Numidia whose dominion had been annexed by Caesar.[101] The transfer had perhaps been anticipated from the start, or else Augustus gradually recognized the undue burden of extending Roman resources to administer north Africa all the way to the Atlantic. In any event, the scholarly Juba, now accorded a new throne and assigned new duties, accepted the role of loyal and dependent client.[102]

The *princeps*, however, did not pin his faith entirely upon the client king in Mauretania. Nor exclusively on military force in the border regions of Africa Vetus and Africa Nova. Augustus embarked on a systematic policy of colonization. In addition to restocking Carthage and Cirta, he planted three or four colonies in Africa Vetus, at least two in Africa Nova, and twelve in Mauretania. And he further settled veterans and other colonists in rural districts, the *pagi* outside the towns.[103]

Roman presence in north Africa increased markedly under Augustus. A garrison at Ammaedara, military action in the frontier zones, a dependent ruler in Mauretania and, perhaps, twenty colonial foundations all reinforced that presence. The need to secure an area which

---

[98] *SEG* ix.6.63; Flor. II.31.41. The date is quite uncertain; Rachet 1970 (C 297) 77, n. 4.

[99] Dio XLIX.43.7.   [100] Aug. *RG* 25.2; Dio L.6.3–4, LIII.12.4–7.

[101] Dio LIII.26.2; Strab. VI.4.2 (288C); XVII.3.7 (828C). It is unlikely, despite Dio, LI.15.6, that Numidia had been restored to Juba II in the meantime and was now exchanged for Mauretania. See the arguments of Romanelli 1959 (E 760) 156–8; Ritter 1987 (C 299) 137–42.

[102] On Mauretania between 33 and 25 B.C., see Pavis d'Escurac 1982 (C 296) 219–25; Mackie 1983 (E 753) 333–42 – highly conjectural. On Juba, see Romanelli 1959 (E 760) 162–74; Pavis d'Escurac 1982 (C 296) 225–9.

[103] Evidence and discussion in Romanelli 1959 (E 760) 187–226; Bénabou 1976 (E 715) 50–7; Kienast 1982 (C 136) 395–7; Pavis d'Escurac 1982 (C 296) 229–30; Mackie 1983 (E 753) 332–58.

served as an important source of grain supplied prime motivation. But the measures also provoked resentment and retaliation, guerrilla warfare and disruption by native peoples. The shoring up of Roman authority had at the same time generated challenges to that authority and stirred sentiments that would lead to even more explosive reaction in the reign of Augustus' successor.

VII. THE ALPS

The Alps loomed over northern Italy, a haven for fierce tribes and violent folk who might menace the Roman hold on Gaul and disrupt communications from Italy. For Augustus, ready access through that barrier and containment of restive tribes who could obstruct movement were important desiderata. And he made certain to achieve those goals. That larger motives held – a prelude to comprehensive conquests in the Balkans and Germany – would be a hasty conclusion and premature judgment.

The young triumvir recognized early the importance of controlling the Little and Great St Bernard passes, the routes to Helvetia and the Upper Rhine. His officer Antistius Vetus attacked the Salassi in 34 B.C., tough warriors who inhabited the higher reaches and represented constant danger to that region. Initial efforts miscarried, as the Salassi first surrendered and then expelled a Roman garrison with scorn and glee. The imperial legate Valerius Messalla retaliated a few years later, but success again was short-lived. Subjugation of the recalcitrant Salassi came only in 25 B.C. when Augustus' appointee Terentius Varro forced them to capitulate and sold the able-bodied into slavery. The military colony of Augusta Praetoria (Aosta) soon rose on the site of Varro's camp and facilitated Roman access to central Gaul.[104]

Determination to command the Alps did not slacken thereafter. Military installations gradually multiplied in strategic places during the next decade: Zurich, Basel, Vindonissa, Oberwinterthur and elsewhere.[105] That provincial penetration prepared the way for outright conquest.

Campaigns began in earnest in 17 or 16 B.C. when P. Silius Nerva, proconsul of Illyricum, subdued two Alpine tribes, the Camunni and the Vennii, the first at least and perhaps both in the region between Como and Lake Garda.[106] Roman sources, of course, held the enemy respon-

---

[104] App. *Ill.* 17; Dio XLIX.34.2, XLIX.38.3, LIII.25.2–5; Strab. IV.6.7 (205–6C).

[105] Wells 1972 (E 601) 40–6; Frei-Stolba 1976 (E 616) 350–5.

[106] Dio LIV.20.1. Debate continues over the identity and location of the Vennii. If they are identified with the Vennonetes of the upper Rhine, then Silius' assaults were quite wide-ranging; cf. van Berchem 1968 (E 605) 4–7; Wells 1972 (E 601) 63–6. But the matter remains uncertain; Overbeck 1976 (E 633) 665–8; Kienast 1982 (C 136) 295; Waasdorp 1982/3 (E 639) 39–40.

sible for provoking the conflict. More probably, it represents a stage in Augustus' drive to bring the Alpine regions under Roman dominion. It can hardly be coincidence that a two pronged assault followed in the next year of 15 B.C., headed by the *princeps*' stepsons. Tiberius marched eastwards from Gaul, Drusus northwards through the Brenner and Reschenscheideck passes to the valley of the Inn. Blame was once again fastened upon the foe: Dio describes the Raeti of the central Alps as savages who plundered Gaul and northern Italy, preyed upon travellers, and murdered all male captives, even unborn babies divined to be male.[107] But the Roman purpose went beyond retaliation. Silius' campaign had served as prelude; Drusus and Tiberius then carried out a systematic design, moving into Raetia from two directions and with various columns emerging at different points simultaneously.[108] Augustus determined to clear out hostile elements in the central Alps and to extend Roman control throughout the Alpine regions. The brothers achieved their goals, subduing the formidable Raeti and Vindelici of eastern Switzerland, the Tyrol and southern Bavaria.[109] Roman dominion in the Alps would be secure.

The victories of Augustus' stepsons were followed in 14 B.C. by subjugation of the Ligurians and annexation of the Maritime Alps.[110] The native dynast Cottius gained recognition as *praefectus* to rule over the Cottian Alps in Roman interest.[111] Occupation of strategic sites in the lands of the Raeti and Vindelici came in subsequent years. Augustus stationed two legions in the area and appointed an equestrian prefect to make Raetia an administrative unit of the empire, thus bringing under control all the major passes of the central Alps and allowing Roman influence to stretch through the Voralpenland to the Danube. Strabo attests to peaceful acquiescence by the once savage tribes in Roman rule and taxation a generation later.[112]

The Alpine campaigns in 16 and 15 B.C. included fighting against peoples further east, branches of the Norici, inhabitants of the *regnum Noricum* that linked Raetia to Pannonia.[113] That fighting later served as pretext for Roman occupation of Noricum. At what point the region became formally annexed remains in dispute. But a Roman presence in the land under Augustus and as consequence of the Alpine conquests admits of little doubt. Noricum, a generally peaceful acquisition,

---

107 Dio LIV.22.1–2; cf. Flor. II.22.   108 Dio LIV.22.3–4; Vell. Pat. II.95.1–2.

109 Dio LIV.22.3–4; Vell. Pat. II.95.1–2; Strab. IV.6.9 (206C); Suet. *Aug.* 21; *Tib.* 9; Flor. II.22; Livy, *Per.* 138; *Consolatio ad Liviam*, 15–16, 175, 385–6. Cf. the discussion of Christ 1957 (C 259) 416–28; Waasdorp 1982/3 (E 639) 40–7; Schön 1986 (E 635) 43–56. A summary in Drack and Fellmann 1988 (E 608) 22–5.   110 Dio LIV.24.3.   111 *ILS* 94. On his family, see Letta 1976 (C 283) 37–76.

112 Strab. IV.6.9 (206C). For the occupation and administration of Raetia, see Wells 1972 (E 601) 67–89; Overbeck 1976 (E 633) 668–72; Laffi 1975–6 (E 627) 406–20.

113 Dio LIV.20.2; Strab. IV.6.8–9 (206C); Flor. II.22 (inaccurate).

supplied a vital communication between the forces in Raetia and the army of Illyricum.[114] Roman influence now spread all along the middle Danube.

What prompted pacification of the Alps? A long-range imperialist plan is often conjectured: the Alpine campaigns merely set the stage for major offensives against Germany, the expansion of Roman power across both the Rhine and the Danube to effect the subjugation of that land all the way to the Elbe.[115] Perhaps. But that ambitious scheme need not have been in prospect at the time of the Alpine conquests. Other motives sufficed. The opening of the Great St Bernard and the route through Helvetia gave swifter access from Italy to the Rhine and thus greater protection to Gaul. Reduction of Raetia and occupation of Noricum provided essential links between legions on the Rhine and the armies of Illyricum.[116] The Upper Danube as yet contained no fortresses, a zone of influence, not a fixed frontier.[117] Ease of communications rather than the prospect of further expansion may have been the immediate stimulus.

Concrete objectives coincided with political motives and public relations. Augustus utilized the Alpine campaigns to hone the talents and advance the claims of his stepsons. The advertisement of victory came in varied forms and reached a wide constituency. Horace sang of the exploits in two *carmina*, celebrating Drusus' routs of Alpine tribes and Tiberius' decisive conquest of the Raeti.[118] The *Consolatio ad Liviam*, composed later in the reign of Augustus, also extolled the accomplishments of the brothers and the thorough defeat of the barbarians.[119] A monument was erected to commemorate these events, the Tropaeum Alpium, installed at La Turbie in the Maritime Alps and listing no fewer than forty-five tribes brought under subjection by the *princeps*.[120] And Augustus boasts in the *Res Gestae* that he had pacified the Alps all the way from the Adriatic to the Tuscan Sea – adding the questionable corollary that every campaign had been legitimate and justified.[121] The *princeps*, as ever, cultivated the image of the successful and rightful conqueror.

VIII. THE BALKANS

Strategy and politics combined to motivate Roman action in Illyricum. Octavian recognized the region's importance at an early stage and led the

---

[114] Vell. Pat. II.39.3; Dio, LIV.20.2; Festus, *Brev.* 7. Alföldy 1974 (E 652) 52–6, is too confident in setting annexation in 15 B.C.; so also Winkler 1977 (E 709) 197–9; Kienast 1982 (C 136) 297. By contrast, Kneissl 1979 (C 280) 261–72, goes too far in denying any occupation before Claudius.

[115] See, esp., Kraft 1973 (A 53) 1, 181–208; cf. also Wells 1972 (E 601) 70; Kienast 1982 (C 136) 297.

[116] Cf. van Berchem 1968 (E 605) 8–9; Christ 1977 (C 260) 188–9.

[117] Christ 1957 (C 259) 425–7.   [118] Hor. *Carm.* IV.4.17–18, IV.14.7–19.

[119] *Consolatio ad Liviam* 15–16, 175, 384–6.   [120] Pliny, *HN* III.136–8.   [121] Aug. *RG* 26.3.

campaigns in person during the triumviral period. That proved to be just a prelude. Major expansion took place between 13 and 9 B.C., and then the imposition of a new and more permanent arrangement after suppression of the Pannonian revolt in A.D. 9. Augustus prepared the ground for two provinces, Dalmatia and Pannonia, extended Roman control to the Danube, and secured the land route between northern Italy and the Balkans.

The result had not been forecast from the outset. Octavian's thrust into Illyricum from 35 to 33 B.C. had more specific ends in view. He looked to his own needs – and to those of his soldiers. The rugged lands across the Adriatic would provide good training and discipline, a hardening of the sinews that might otherwise grow soft with idleness.[122] Weapons would now be trained on the barbarian, a conspicuous turning away from the civil strife that exhausted and demoralized the troops. They could look forward to enrichment from the spoils of the enemy, so Octavian alleged. Campaigns against foes of the empire would restore morale to the forces and allow their commander to claim leadership in the national interest instead of a factional struggle.[123] The memoirs of the *princeps* expounded at length on the Illyrian adventure, reproduced in part by the historian Appian a century and a half later. They provided due justification for the war: Illyrians had periodically plundered Italy, they had damaged the cause of Iulius Caesar, had destroyed the armies of Gabinius and Vatinius in the 40s, and held the captured standards of Roman legions – enough reason for retaliation and restoration of national honour.[124] A harsher assessment comes from the pen of Cassius Dio, drawing on a tradition outside Augustus' memoirs. Dio notes correctly that no Illyrian provocation prompted the war: Octavian lacked legitimate complaint and sought pretext to give practice to his legions against a foe whose resistance was likely to be ineffective.[125]

Neither the cynical judgment nor the self-serving explanation gets to the heart of the matter. Octavian needed to enhance his military reputation, an effort to match the accomplishments of his partner and rival Antony. It is no accident that Octavian took conspicuous personal risks and twice suffered injury in Illyricum. Those badges of courage could be useful. And upon completion of the contest he delivered a speech to the Senate making pointed contrast between Antony's idleness and his own vigorous liberating of Italy from incursions by savage peoples.[126]

Larger strategic considerations have also been postulated. Perhaps Octavian sought to secure Italy to the north east in order to prevent a

---

122 Vell. Pat. II.78.2.   123 App. *BCiv.* v.128.
124 App. *Ill.* 12–13, 15, 18; *BCiv.* v.145; cf. Dio XLIX.34.2.   125 Dio XLIX.36.1
126 App. *Ill.* 16, 27; Suet. *Aug.* 20; Pliny, *HN* VII.148; Flor. II.23; Dio XLIX.35.2.

march by Antony via that route, as had once been contemplated by Philip V and Mithridates, or else to seize the area in preparation for a future offensive against his fellow triumvir. Or perhaps Octavian already contemplated a broad strategic design that would push the borders of Illyricum to the Danube and forge a link with imperial defences on the Rhine.[127] But military conflict with Antony was not yet imminent in 35; nor had any eastern ruler yet employed such a path to invade Italy. As for the eventual push to the Danube, Augustus himself ascribes that plan to the campaigns of his stepson Tiberius more than two decades later. Octavian had more immediate needs: establishment of a military reputation through punishment of tribes that had sullied Roman honour. He could thus contrast solid accomplishment with the sloth of Antony. Octavian would unfurl the Roman standards regained from the barbarian. And he would suggest even greater conquests in store for the future: victories in Illyria, it was reported, might lead to bold offensives against Dacians and Bastarnae.[128] Not that Octavian actually considered such offensives at this time. But here, as elsewhere, he sedulously advanced the pose of the conqueror.

Actual accomplishments in the Illyrian War of 35 to 33 B.C. were modest. Octavian opened the fighting in 35 B.C. with a thrust against the Iapodes, bringing their forces to surrender, and besieging their principal city and citadel at Metulum which was soon destroyed by fire.[129] Roman armies pressed on to assault Segesta (Siscia) at the confluence of the Save, blockade the city, and force it to submission. Octavian could take pride in the achievement and returned to Rome for the winter, intending to resume operations in Illyria in the following spring.[130] That next season, however, saw him transfer attention to Dalmatia. Talk of advance against Dacia was evidently given up – or never meant seriously. Octavian did not intend to go beyond the Save. Instead, he could earn further laurels by punishing the tribes that had defeated Roman armies and held Roman standards. The *princeps'* forces stormed the Dalmatian stronghold of Promona and destroyed Synodium at the edge of the forest where Gabinius' troops had been cut down. Early in the next year, 33 B.C., the chastened and desperate Dalmatians, cut off from outside supplies, yielded up themselves and the Roman standards, pledged payment of arrears in tribute, and vowed obedience to Roman power. Other tribes also offered submission, and Octavian brought the three-year Illyrian War to a conclusion.[131]

Territorial gains were relatively limited. But territory had not been the

---

[127] On the motives, see Syme 1971 (E 702) 17, 137; Wilkes 1969 (E 706) 48–9. A healthy scepticism is expressed by Schmitthenner 1958 (C 304) 193–200.

[128] Aug. *RG* 29.1, 30.1; App. *Ill.* 22; Strab. VII.5.2 (313C).   [129] App. *Ill.* 18–21.

[130] App. *Ill.* 22–4; Dio XLIX.37.1–XLIX.38.1.

[131] App. *Ill.* 25–8; Dio XLIX.38.3–4, XLIX.43.8; Strab. VII.5.5 (315C).

objective. Octavian had driven as far as Siscia on the Save and displayed Roman power to the Dalmatians, thus retaliating against peoples who had raided Roman territory or vanquished Roman troops in the past. What mattered was the presentation of events in Rome. Octavian spoke to the Senate and rattled off the names of nearly thirty tribes which his forces had coerced into submission, surrender and payment of tribute. He proudly set up the recovered standards in the portico of Cn. Octavius, thus linking his success to earlier republican victories. And he elevated the prestige of his family through the award of statues and the privilege of tribunician sacrosanctity for Livia and Octavia. Propaganda value, as so often, counted for more than tangible achievement.[132]

Another barbarian people also held Roman standards in their possession: the Bastarnae on the Lower Danube. They had captured the trophies from a defeated Roman army thirty years before. Octavian would restore Roman honour here as well. The proconsul of Macedonia, M. Licinius Crassus, marched north in 29 B.C. to engage the Bastarnae who, it was reported, had crossed the Haemus mountain range and had overrun parts of Thrace wherein dwelt allies of Rome. Crassus conducted campaigns over a two year period, driving back the Bastarnae, gaining victories over other Thracian tribes from the lower Danube, including the Moesi, the Getae and perhaps the Dacians, slaying a prince of the Bastarnae in hand to hand combat, and regaining the Roman eagles. He celebrated a well-earned triumph in 27 B.C.[133] Nothing suggests that these campaigns actually extended the boundaries of Macedonia. But the punishment of unruly tribes and the recovery of lost military emblems served to demonstrate and reinforce Roman authority.

Major advance in the region awaited a decade and a half. The provincial distributions of 27 B.C. assigned responsibility for Dalmatia and Macedonia to the Senate, two separate and independent proconsular commands. That formal situation remained unchanged through the 20s and for some years thereafter. But the advantages of a link between these domains and a push to the Danube that would control the land route from northern Italy to the lands of the East became increasingly evident. Restive Pannonian tribes attacked Istria in 16 B.C., Thracians ravaged Macedonia, and an uprising in Dalmatia had to be quelled in the same year. The Pannonians rose again in 14 B.C., calling forth yet another *ad hoc* suppression.[134] Augustus now made plans in earnest for subjugation.

---

[132] Announcement of tribes subjugated: App. *Ill.* 16–17. The standards: App. *Ill.* 28; cf. Dio XLIX.43.8. Honours for Livia and Octavia: Dio XLIX.38.1. The political implications are rightly noted by Schmitthenner 1958 (C 304) 218–20, 231–3. Useful summaries of the campaigns can be found in Mócsy 1962 (E 675) 538–9; Wilkes 1969 (E 706) 49–57. Further bibliography in Roddaz 1984 (C 200) 140–5.

[133] The campaigns are recorded in detail by Dio LI.23–7; cf. Flor. II.26; Livy, *Per.* 134–5; Danov 1979 (E 660) 123–7. For the triumph, see *ILS* 8810.   [134] Dio LIV.20.2–3, LIV.24.3.

M. Vinicius, probably proconsul of Illyricum, undertook operations in 14 B.C., but Augustus soon entrusted overall direction of the war to Agrippa with broad powers, a *maius imperium*, in the following year.[135]

The *princeps* obviously took the matter very seriously. After Agrippa died in 12 B.C., he appointed his stepson and new son-in-law Tiberius to the post. More than just suppression of tribal incursions was at stake here. Roman forces advanced against the peoples between the Save and the Drave, presumably the war-like Breuci. Tiberius, with the aid of the Scordisci who had already been brought under Roman authority, earned triumphal honours for a vigorous campaign against Pannonians in 12 B.C. and then continued against both Dalmatians and Pannonians in 11. The operations evidently gave Rome control of the Save valley and allowed for the initial penetration of Bosnia.[136] Parallel campaigns were conducted in Thrace where L. Piso subjected hostile tribes in three years of fighting and secured Roman mastery by 11 B.C.[137] The Augustan regime had now made a major commitment in the Balkans. The former proconsular command of Illyricum came directly under Augustus' authority, to be governed by the *princeps'* legates. It encompassed an area that would soon stretch from the Adriatic to the Danube.[138] Tiberius led campaigns for two more seasons in 10 and 9, reducing tribes that resisted domination, pacifying the region, and winning an *ovatio*. Augustus himself paid signal tribute to his stepson's achievements in the *Res Gestae*: he had subjugated the previously unconquered peoples of Pannonia and extended the frontier of Illyricum to the banks of the Danube.[139]

Evidence largely fails for the next fifteen years. Those years, it may be presumed, constituted the time of real pacification, the securing of the middle Danube, and the intimidation of tribes beyond it in order to assure control of the frontier. Augustus' legate Sex. Appuleius completed coercion of the Pannonians in 8 B.C. Excursions across the Danube followed in subsequent years: L. Domitius Ahenobarbus resettled the Hermunduri as a check on the Marcomanni and even brought his troops to the far side of the Elbe; epigraphic testimony records another Augustan legate, perhaps M. Vinicius, who routed the Bastarnae and entered into relations with a number of trans-Danubian tribes; Aelius Catus transplanted 50,000 Getae from the far side of the

---

[135] Vell. Pat. II.96.2; Flor. II.24.8; Dio LIV.28.1.

[136] Dio LIV.31.2–4, LIV.34.3; Vell. Pat. II.96.3; Flor. II.24.8; Suet. *Tib.* 9; Festus, *Brev.* 7; Frontin. *Str.* II.1.15.

[137] Vell. Pat. II.98.1–2; Dio LIV.34.5–7; Flor. II.27; Danov 1979 (E 660) 129–31. On Roman connexions with friendly Thracian dynasts, see Sullivan 1979 (E 698) 189–204.

[138] Dio LIV.34.4.

[139] Aug. *RG* 30.1; Dio LIV.36.2, LV.2.4; cf. Vell. Pat. II.90.1. On the operations from 16 to 9 B.C., see Syme 1971 (E 702) 18–22; Mócsy 1962 (E 675) 540–1; Wilkes 1969 (E 706) 63–5.

Danube to Thrace, where they took on the name of Moesians; and Cn. Cornelius Lentulus successfully drove Dacians and Sarmatians back from the vicinity of the Danube, thus to solidify further Rome's hold on the river.[140] A legionary command was installed in Moesia during these years.[141] Augustus boasts hyperbolically of smashing the Dacians and compelling them to submit to Roman orders, a claim echoed but modified by Strabo.[142] The situation seemed secure.

But that confidence proved to be premature. In A.D. 6 Tiberius assembled troops for a decisive thrust against the Marcomannic leader Maroboduus in Bohemia. The Roman *imperator* summoned recruits from the ostensibly compliant Illyrians for the purpose. The assemblage itself, however, gave the indigenous forces a sense of their own strength and numbers. National pride came to the surface, intensified by resentment at harsh exactions of tribute by Roman officials and the fierce spirit of a new generation of Illyrian warriors. Bato, a chieftain of the Daesitiates in central Bosnia, took the lead in whipping up hostility. And the rising of the Daesitiates was soon matched by rebellion of the Breuci in Pannonia, headed by Pinnes and another Bato. Thus erupted the great Pannonian revolt which would endure from A.D. 6 to 9 and nearly shake the empire to its foundations. Suetonius labelled it, without much exaggeration, the most serious external threat to Rome since the war with Hannibal.[143]

The rebels assaulted legionary detachments and massacred Roman merchants. The Breuci headed for the key Roman garrison at Sirmium and would have taken it but for the timely arrival of A. Caecina Severus, legate of Moesia who turned back the Pannonian threat while suffering heavy losses. Tiberius immediately cancelled operations against Maroboduus and dispatched the Illyrian legate M. Valerius Messalla to secure the other critical Roman fortress at Siscia which guarded the route to north-eastern Italy. The rebel forces in Pannonia and Dalmatia had been slow to combine efforts; otherwise, the entire Roman position in Illyricum might have collapsed. As it was, the insurgents controlled most of the territory from the Save to the Adriatic and had gathered forces, so it is reported, of 200,000 infantry and 9,000 cavalry. Caecina Severus returned to his own *provincia* of Moesia to protect it against incursions of Dacians and Sarmatians. Sirmium was still vulnerable, and

---

[140] Appuleius: Cassiod. *Chron.* II.35; Ahenobarbus: Dio LV.10a.2; Tac. *Ann.* IV.44; M. Vinicius (?): *ILS* 8965; cf. Syme 1971 (E 702) 26–39; Mócsy 1962 (E 675) 543–4; Aelius Catus: Strab. VII.3.10 (303C); Lentulus: Flor. II.28–9; Tac. *Ann.* IV.44; Aug. *RG* 31.2; Syme 1971 (E 702) 40–72.

[141] Dio LV.29.3, LV.30.4; Syme 1971 (E 702) 50–8.

[142] Aug. *RG* 30.2; Strab. VII.3.11, VII.3.13 (304–5C). Defeat of the Dacians may have been spurred by a Dacian invasion of 10 B.C.; Dio LIV.36.2.

[143] Suet. *Tib.* 16. For the origins and occasion of the conflict, see Dio LV.28.7, LV.29.3, LVI.16.3. A less satisfactory account in Vell. Pat. II.109.5–110.5. Cf. Dyson 1971 (A 25) 250–3.

Tiberius could not afford to move far or fast from his base at Siscia. Grave anxieties gripped Rome. Augustus, now severely alarmed, ordered extraordinary levies, impressed veterans back into service, imposed new taxes, called upon the patriotic instincts of senators and *equites*, and enrolled freedmen into the ranks as reinforcements for the army of Illyricum. The *princeps* sent recruits with Velleius Paterculus who would then gain an eyewitness's view of the war for his future history, dispatched additional troops with a trusted member of his own household, young Germanicus the nephew of Tiberius, and even moved his personal entourage to Ariminum where he could keep in closer touch with developments.[144]

Rebuilding of the Roman position began in earnest in A.D. 7. Reinforcements from Italy brought Tiberius' army up to five legions. M. Plautius Silvanus led two legions from the east and joined forces with Caecina's army of Moesia. Both commanders, together with the Thracian cavalry under Rhoemetalces, now headed west to link with Tiberius. They survived near calamity at the Volcaean Marshes, an ambush by troops under the combined leadership of the two Batos. Old-fashioned discipline, as Velleius describes it, repaired ranks that were broken, stemmed panic, and turned defeat into victory.[145] By the winter of A.D. 7/8 an immense assemblage of ten legions had converged at Siscia, swollen further by seventy auxiliary cohorts, fourteen cavalry units, and no fewer than 10,000 veterans recalled to the colours from Italy – the largest military concourse since the civil wars. Yet the giant gathering once effected, Tiberius almost immediately dissolved it again, escorting the reinforcements from Moesia and the east back to Sirmium.[146] A perplexing decision. Perhaps the assemblage had been Augustus' idea, the product of impatience and anxiety, without consultation of Tiberius.[147] More likely, it was a tactic of intimidation: such a concentration of power could overawe the resistance of rebels.

The manoeuvre achieved its end. In the following year, without further show of force, the Pannonians offered full surrender and received terms. A final flurry occurred late in the year, when the Dalmatian chieftain Bato captured and killed his treacherous Breucian namesake and rekindled revolt among the Pannonians. But the Roman garrison at Sirmium under Silvanus crushed the uprising and restored order. The Save valley was once again safely in Roman hands.[148]

Dalmatia remained to be reduced in A.D. 9. Tiberius returned to Rome in the winter, but three commanders held responsibility for completing the reconquest: M. Lepidus, left as legate in Siscia, Silvanus at Sirmium

[144] Dio LV.29.3–31.4, LV.34.3; Vell. Pat. II.110.3–112.2.
[145] Vell. Pat. II.112.3–6; Dio LV.33.3.   [146] Vell. Pat. II.113.1–3.
[147] So Koestermann 1953 (C 281) 362–3.   [148] Vell. Pat. II.114.4; Dio LV.33.1–2, LV.34.4–7.

and Germanicus on the Dalmatian coast itself. But the combination
proved inadequate. The inexperienced Germanicus made little headway,
and Augustus sent back Tiberius himself to resume command. That
decision sealed the fate of Dalmatia. Lepidus forced his way through
hostile territory to join with Tiberius. And the redoubtable Bato, though
eluding capture and resisting siege, finally came to terms – and was
spared by the admiring Tiberius.[149]

Four bloody years had been consumed in suppressing this mighty
challenge to Roman authority.[150] Military success, as usual, would be
translated into political distinction. Augustus exploited the victory to
bestow honours on his family. Germanicus made public announcement
of the result. The *princeps* and his stepson both celebrated triumphs in
A.D. 10 and received triumphal arches in Pannonia, as well as other
distinctions. Germanicus gained triumphal insignia and praetorian rank.
And even Tiberius' son Drusus, though he played no part in the war,
obtained the right to attend the Senate and to hold praetorian status as
soon as he reached the quaestorship.[151] The geopolitical consequences,
however, were greater still. The process of consolidation and organization lay in the future. But conquest was complete. Roman power
extended to the middle Danube, a critical link in the connexion that now
ran from northern Italy through the Balkans to the provinces of the East.
At some time after A.D. 8 the *princeps* set in place the two great military
commands that would become the new provinces of Dalmatia and
Pannonia.[152] It was a solid and enduring achievement.

IX. GERMANY

The confrontation of Rome and Germany created high drama in the time
of Augustus – and heated debate in the modern era. What were the
objectives of Rome's crossing the Rhine, how far did she intend to go,
and how firm a hold did she expect to exercise? The penetration of
Germany was no isolated event. It must be considered in close conjunction with Roman presence in Gaul.

Caesar had conquered Gaul but had not fully pacified it. Octavian
took the matter in hand, an item of the first priority in consolidation of
the western empire. In the early 30s B.C. he commissioned his most
trusted collaborator, M. Agrippa, to campaign against rebellious
peoples in Aquitania in the south west and against tribes in the north

---

[149] Dio LVI.11–16; Vell. Pat. II.115.1–4. See the analysis of Koestermann 1953 (C 281) 368–76;
Wilkes 1965 (E 705) 111–25.

[150] On the war, in general, see the thorough treatment of Koestermann 1953 (C 281) 345–78; also
Mócsy 1962 (E 675) 544–8; Wilkes 1969 (E 706) 69–77.

[151] Dio LVI.17.1–3.   [152] Cf. Braunert 1977 (C 255) 215–16.

east.[153] Unrest persisted. The years 31 to 28 B.C. witnessed three uprisings requiring Roman military action: against the Morini, the Treviri and the Aquitani, each issuing in triumphs or imperial salutations for the victorious commanders.[154] Those episodes drove home the lesson that the policing of Gaul could not be divorced from control of Germanic tribes across the Rhine. Caesar had experienced the problem, having faced large scale migrations by Germans like the Sugambri, the Usipetes and the Tencteri who dwelled near the river and who felt the pressure of the potent Suebi.[155] It is noteworthy and revealing that Gallic disturbances in the 30s and early 20s B.C. repeatedly involved assistance or provocation from peoples across the Rhine. Agrippa had to fight on the other side of the river; the Treviri got support from trans-Rhenane tribes; and the Suebi came to the aid of the Morini.[156] Augustus effected a settlement in Gaul in 27 B.C., conducting a census and perhaps implementing the tripartite division of the land.[157] But administrative arrangements did not avert upheaval. The legate M. Vinicius brought an army against Germans in retaliation for their murder of Roman citizens who practised trade in their lands.[158] Agrippa returned to Gaul in 20 and 19 B.C. and encountered a familiar scene: conflicts among the Gauls compounded by intervention of the Germans.[159] The situation had changed little from the time of Caesar's Gallic Wars a generation earlier. The Rhine was an artificial and largely ineffectual barrier. Germanic peoples dwelled on both sides of the river. It represented at best a frontier zone rather than a demarcated border. And harassment of Roman Gaul by trans-Rhenane intruders was a continual menace.

Diplomatic measures proved unsatisfactory. Rome reached friendly accords with the Chatti and perhaps others, thereby to use them as counter-weight to other peoples who might enter the Roman province.[160] To no avail. In 17 or 16 B.C. Sugambri, Usipetes and Tencteri spilled over the Rhine, plundered Gallic territory, ambushed Roman forces, and inflicted an ignominious defeat on the legate M. Lollius.[161] The *princeps* himself hastened to Gaul in 16 B.C. to repair the damage. The cost in prestige outweighed any material losses. By the time Augustus reached Gaul, the Germans had withdrawn and there was no one to fight. A peaceful settlement followed.[162] But it is no accident that

[153] App. *BCiv*. v.92; Dio XLVIII.49.2–3; Eutrop. VII.5; Roddaz 1984 (C 200) 66–75.
[154] Dio LI.20.5, LI.21.5–6; App. *BCiv*. IV.38; Tib. 1.7.3–12, II.1.31–6; *ILS* 895; *CIL* I².50, 77.
[155] Caes. *BGall*. IV.1ff; cf. Timpe 1975 (C 321) 125–9.
[156] Dio XLVIII.49.2–3, LI.20.5, LI.21.6.
[157] Dio LIII.22.5; Livy, *Per*. 134; cf. Drinkwater 1983 (E326) 20–1, 95.   [158] Dio LIII.26.4–5.
[159] Dio LIV.11.2. On Agrippa's activities, see Roddaz 1984 (C 200) 383–402.
[160] Dio LIV.36.3; Timpe 1975 (C 321) 135–9.
[161] Dio LIV.20.4–5; Vell. Pat. II.97.1; Suet. *Aug*. 23; Tac. *Ann*. I.10; Obsequens, 71.
[162] Dio LIV.19.1, LIV.20.6; Vell. Pat. II.97.1; Suet. *Aug*. 23.

Augustus appeared in the region, prepared to lead forces in person. A Roman defeat, however minor, could not be tolerated. It was essential to present a bold face to the public. Hence the appearance of the emperor in the field. The image of Roman authority had to be advanced.

Augustus stayed in the West for three years.[163] That period marks the beginning of a more aggressive Roman posture to assure ascendancy in Gaul and to intimidate tribes across the Rhine. It represents a logical time for establishment of legionary forts on the river. Six camps eventually arose on the lower and middle Rhine: Fectio, Noviomagus, Vetera, Novaesium, Oppidum Ubiorum and Moguntiacum.[164] Once again the close association of this development with new administrative arrangements to strengthen Roman governance in Gaul is plain.[165]

The *princeps'* stepson Drusus took over in Gaul when Augustus returned to Rome in 13 B.C.[166] In the following year Drusus launched the first four major offensives against tribes on the far side of the Rhine. The campaigns have stimulated speculation on Roman motives and intentions for conquest to the Elbe or beyond. It would be more prudent to recognize the continued connexion between suppression of Gallic unrest and the terrorizing by Rome of Germanic peoples who had contributed or might contribute to that unrest. The sources make the connexion explicit. Drusus established an altar of Augustus at Lugdunum (see p. 98 above for the view that this was in 10 B.C.), thereby to rally Gallic loyalty to the regime. But his conduct of a census, presumably associated with financial exactions, sparked new upheaval, aggravated by interference from German tribes on both sides of the Rhine.[167] Drusus' campaigns in Germany, therefore, grew out of familiar circumstances. They intensified pressure on the Germans in order to strengthen the Roman dominion in Gaul.

The campaigns spread over four years, gathering in momentum, and displayed might to the barbarian to an extent not previously experienced. Drusus began in 12 B.C. with assaults on the Sugambri whom he caught on the Gallic side of the Rhine and on the Usipetes across the river. He proceeded to an amphibious operation along the North Sea coast, gaining the Frisii as allies and invading the land of the Chauci.[168] Notable advances came in the following year. Drusus subdued the Usipetes, bridged the Lippe, and passed through the land of the

---

    163 Dio LIV.25.1.

    164 For the archaeological evidence – which cannot fix specific dates – see Wells 1972 (E 601) 94–148; cf. Schönberger 1969 (E 591) 144–7.

    165 On Augustus' activities in Gaul, see Frei-Stolba 1976 (E 615) 355–65.   166 Dio LIV.25.1.

    167 Livy, *Per.* 139; Dio LIV.32.1; *ILS* 212.11, lines 36–9; Timpe 1975 (C 321) 142; Dyson 1975 (C 266) 155–6.

    168 Dio LIV.32.1–3; Livy, *Per.* 139. The campaign probably included a defeat of the Bructeri on the Ems; Strab. VII.1.3 (290C).

Sugambri into that of the Cherusci as far as the Weser river. The coming of winter again induced him to return to the Rhine, but not before he installed a garrison on the junction of the Lippe and the Eliso, perhaps at Haltern, and another near the Rhine in the region of the Chatti. The achievements earned Drusus triumphal honours.[169]

Augustus himself accompanied Drusus to Gaul in winter 11/10 B.C., there to inspect the altar at Lugdunum and to observe the German situation. The linkage between defeat of Germans and consolidation of Gaul remained close. Another season in 10 B.C. saw Drusus gain further victories over the Sugambri and Chatti who abandoned lands awarded them in an earlier diplomatic settlement by Rome.[170]

More far reaching successes marked the fourth and final campaign in 9 B.C. Drusus commenced the invasion, it appears, from Moguntiacum, attacked the Chatti once more, defeated the Marcomanni on the upper Main after stiff resistance, turned northward to the realm of the Cherusci, crossed the Weser again, and got as far as the Elbe. That, however, proved to be the terminus. Drusus turned back, suffered the misfortune of a broken leg, and died *en route* to the Rhine.[171] What stayed his advance at the Elbe is unspecified. But Augustan policy demanded that the best face be placed upon the events. Drusus, like Alexander the Great at the Hyphasis, set up trophies at the Elbe to signify progress rather than setback. And a story conveniently surfaced that Drusus was halted by a vision delivering divine pronouncement about the fate of the mission.[172] The gods, not any Roman failures, accounted for withdrawal. And elaborate honours were showered upon the memory of Drusus and his deeds.[173] Whatever the reality of the situation, Augustus, here as elsewhere, insisted on the appearance of success.

What had been accomplished? Drusus' campaigns had been invasions rather than conquests, the Germans intimidated rather than subdued. But these were more than hit and run raids. Drusus left tangible reminders of Roman power. Cassius Dio reports two garrisons planted in 11 B.C.; Florus, with obvious exaggeration, speaks of numerous forts and guard posts installed all along the Maas, the Weser and the Elbe.[174] Archaeology discloses the existence of important legionary bases at Haltern and Oberaden on the Lippe, and other garrisons elsewhere, but does not permit a precise chronology that would fix them to the time of

[169] Dio LIV.33.1–5; Livy, *Per.* 140; Flor. II.30.23; Suet. *Claud.* 2.1. On Haltern, see Wells 1972 (E 601) 163–211.

[170] Dio LIV.36.3–4; Oros. VI.21.15; Livy, *Per.* 141. A speculative reconstruction by Timpe 1967 (C 316) 296–300.

[171] Dio LV.1.2–5; Flor. II.30.23–7; Strab. VII.1.3 (291C); Livy, *Per.* 141; Suet. *Claud.* 1.2.

[172] Dio LV.1.3; cf. Suet. *Claud.* 1.2. On the tale and its significance, see Timpe 1967 (C 316) 289–306.   [173] Dio LV.2.1–3; Livy, *Per.* 142; Suet. *Claud.* 1.3–5; Tac. *Ann.* 11.7.

[174] Dio LIV.33.4; Flor. II.30.26.

Drusus' incursions.[175] Nor can one assume that the garrisons signalled a permanent and a full-scale occupation. Tiberius rushed to the scene upon the death of his brother and, if Tiberius' panegyrist Velleius Paterculus is to be believed, he overran all of Germany as victorious commander in 8 B.C. without sustaining any losses. Other sources supply some specifics: Tiberius induced all Germans but the Sugambri to agree to peace terms, but Augustus then refused to embrace a peace without the Sugambri – a convenient pretext to keep options open and maintain a presence in Germany. Tiberius proceeded to deport 40,000 Germans to the Gallic side of the Rhine.[176] The exhibition of Roman power is clear, a necessary demonstration in the wake of Drusus' death. But it is rash to speak of Germany organized as a province of the empire, with Roman authority extended to the Elbe.[177] In fact, even Velleius, who would hardly minimize Tiberius' accomplishment, speaks only of reducing Germany 'almost to the form of a tributary province'. And Florus acknowledges that Germans were defeated rather than subdued.[178] Rome held only selected portions of German soil.[179] As so often, the appearance of Roman success outstripped the reality of Roman control.

The need to maintain a posture of strength in Germany continued to mark Augustan policy. An altar to Augustus was erected among the Ubii who had settled on the Rhine bank, at what later became Colonia Agrippina (Cologne). Appointment of a priest to the cult from the Cherusci was clearly meant to signal German allegiance to the *princeps* and his regime.[180] Periodic Roman military incursions gave repeated reminders of the empire's authority. Tiberius snuffed out some minor troubles in 7 B.C.[181] At some time before A.D. 1 L. Domitius Ahenobarbus undertook a more significant venture. He took troops from the Danube, encountered the tribe of the Hermunduri whom he settled on the upper Main, an area evacuated by the Marcomanni, crossed the Elbe without any resistance, made alliance with people on the further bank of that river, and planted a new altar to Augustus on the site, a symbol that loyalty extended even to that distant region. The idea that this expedition prepared the way for a Roman invasion of Bohemia is unnecessary conjecture. It supplied a means to reassert Roman influence without taking undue risks. Domitius even became embroiled in intra-tribal disputes among the Cherusci. But he made sure to winter his men back in

---

[175] Schönberger 1969 (E 591) 147–9; Wells 1972 (E 601) 161–233.
[176] Dio LV.6.2–3; Suet. *Aug.* 21; *Tib.* 9; cf. Tac. *Ann.* II.26, XII.39.
[177] As, e.g., Wells 1972 (E 601) 156–7; Kienast 1982 (C 136) 300–1.
[178] Vell. Pat. II.97.4; Flor. II.30.29–30. Florus' claim, II.30.22, that Augustus sought to make Germany a province in order to honour Julius Caesar is not to be taken seriously.
[179] Dio LVI.18.1; cf. Christ 1977 (C 260) 189–98.
[180] Tac. *Ann.* 1.39, 1.57.2.   [181] Dio LV.8.3.

the safer quarters on the Rhine.[182] Domitius' successor M. Vinicius found it necessary or advantageous to engage in hostilities with German peoples beginning in A.D. 1, a massive war, so it is described. The sources preserve no record of location or details. But Vinicius did obtain triumphal honours and a public decree inscribed with his exploits.[183] The presentation at home of continued success and ascendancy in Germany remained consistent.

An ostensibly more vigorous expedition was launched in A.D. 4. Tiberius had come back into his stepfather's good graces, gained adoption by him, and was forthwith appointed to Germany. His *laudator* Velleius Paterculus describes the events with excessive adulation. Tears of joy allegedly filled the eyes of soldiers in greeting the much decorated commander under whom many had already served in various sectors of the empire. Tiberius, so Velleius reports, subdued the Cananefates, Attuarii and Bructeri, regained dominion over the Cherusci, crossed the Weser, and set up winter quarters at the source of the Lippe.[184] Velleius waxes even more rhetorical on the second campaigning season in A.D. 5: Tiberius' armies traversed all of Germany, beat down the Chauci once again, snapped the power of the fearsome Langobardi, and then capped his success by having his fleet sail up the Elbe. In two years, according to Velleius, Tiberius had been victorious everywhere, his army unscathed. The victories left nothing unconquered in all Germany except the Marcomanni.[185] Exaggeration is patent. The outbursts of Velleius do not warrant full confidence. Among other things, he calls Tiberius the first Roman general to reach the Elbe and the first to winter in Germany.[186] Cassius Dio provides a curt and sober assessment: Tiberius advanced to the Weser and the Elbe, but accomplished nothing worthy of record.[187] Only peace treaties resulted, whereas the legate got triumphal honours and the *princeps* and his son were hailed as *imperatores*.[188] The contrast between appearance and reality persists.

An assault on the Marcomanni was next on the Roman agenda. They had abandoned their ancestral lands in the Main valley under pressure of Drusus' attacks in 9 B.C. and had now carved out a kingdom under their formidable ruler Maroboduus.[189] The realm sat in an area bordering on

[182] Dio LV.10a.2–3; Tac. *Ann.* IV.44. The conjecture on Domitius' purpose in Syme 1934 (C 312) 365–6. The starting-point of his expedition remains in dispute; Syme 1934 (C 312) 365–6; Timpe 1967 (C 317) 280–4; Wells 1972 (E 601) 158–9; Christ 1977 (C 260) 181–3.   [183] Vell. Pat. II.104.2.

[184] Vell. Pat. II.104.3–105.3.

[185] Vell. Pat. II.106.1–3, II.107.3, II.108.1. Similarly, Aufidius Bassus, in Peter, *HRR*, II, 96, 3.

[186] Vell. Pat. II.105.3, II.106.2.

[187] Dio LV.28.5; cf. Timpe 1967 (C 317) 284–88. Note that after the campaigns of A.D. 5 Tiberius evidently returned to winter quarters on the Rhine; Vell. Pat. II.107.3.   [188] Dio LV.28.6.

[189] Vell. Pat. II.108.1–2; Strab. VII.1.3 (290C); Tac. *Germ.* 42; cf. Flor. II.30.23–4; Dio LV.1.2. On Maroboduus, see Dobias 1960 (C 264) 155–66.

regions subject to or linked with Rome: Pannonia, Noricum and neighbouring German tribes. Maroboduus brought some of these tribes under his authority, and induced others into alliance. He made no moves to threaten Rome, but his position and his prestige represented an embarrassment.[190] The Roman high command designed a two-pronged operation in A.D. 6. Tiberius was to lead the army of Illyricum from Carnuntum on the Danube, and the legate Sentius Saturninus would bring the Rhine legions from the west through the land of the Chatti, thus to close the vice on Maroboduus.[191] The plan never came to fruition. News of a Pannonian revolt arrived to panic Augustus and cancel the assault on Bohemia when the two Roman armies were within days of effecting a junction.[192] Peace negotiations ensued instead, and Maroboduus became a friend and ally of Rome. The outcome, of course, was interpreted differently by each party, as suited respective tastes. Maroboduus represented the agreement as putting him on equal terms with his opponents.[193] From the Roman vantage-point, however, the Marcomannic prince had been obliged to keep the peace.[194] That version appropriately accommodated public opinion.

The great rebellion in Pannonia pinned down the bulk of Rome's forces for more than three years from A.D. 6 to 9. Germany was surprisingly quiet during those years. Maroboduus held to his treaty, and the rest of the land seemed untroubled. Five legions remained in the Rhine command, but the hand of Rome, it appears, was felt only lightly in Germany. Roman authority extended to parts of the nation, but by no means to all. The process of urbanization, establishment of markets, and encouragement of peaceful assemblies that came with Roman presence advanced without apparent resistance.[195] The new legate P. Quinctilius Varus, related by marriage to the houses of Augustus and Agrippa, was a man more accustomed to peace than to war, more comfortable with administration than with fighting.[196] Varus' activities, therefore, concentrated on the imposition of rules, the exercise of judicial powers, and the collection of revenues – a practice not hitherto implemented in Germany. Cassius Dio appropriately notes that Varus acted *as if* the Germans were subject peoples. Other sources, eager to blame the legate for future calamity, stress his combination of greed and ineptitude.[197] The actions provoked a subversive movement among the Germans, nourished perhaps as much by scorn as by resentment. Their leaders

---

[190] Vell. Pat. II.108.2–109.4; Strab. VII.1.3 (290C).
[191] Vell. Pat. II.109.5; cf. Tac. *Ann.* II.46.   [192] Vell. Pat. II.110.1–3; Dio LV.28.7.
[193] Tac. *Ann.* II.46, II.63.   [194] Tac. *Ann.* II.26; cf. II.45.
[195] Dio LVI.18.1–2. On this passage, see the astute remarks of Christ 1977 (C 260) 194–8, as against Timpe 1967 (C 317) 288–90; 1970 (C 319) 81–90.
[196] Vell. Pat. II.117.2. For his relationship to the imperial family, *PKöln* 1.10, *AE* 1966, 425.
[197] Dio LVI.18.3; Vell. Pat. II.117.2–118.1; Flor. II.30.31.

despised the symbols of Roman authority, the rods, axes and togas – and the emptiness that they masked.[198]

Details of the insurrection can here be omitted. A young warrior from the ruling house of the Cherusci, Arminius, inspired and headed the rebels. They lulled Varus into complacency, then lured him into an ambush. In the vicinity of the Teutoburg Forest in September, A.D. 9 Varus lost his life and Rome lost three legions, a disaster unparalleled in the Augustan years.[199]

The news shocked and dispirited the *princeps*. Augustus reportedly let his hair and beard grow for months as a sign of mourning, and more than once broke into the celebrated lament 'Varus, give me back my legions!'[200] Those histrionics buttress the common view that Varus' defeat marked the major turning point in Augustus' German policy: the plan to pacify all of Germany to the Elbe was given up and the empire's borders were withdrawn to the Rhine.[201] It might be more revealing, however, to point to the continuities than to stress the caesura. Augustus made no public move to surrender Germany. Quite the contrary. The *princeps* forthwith dispatched Tiberius, fresh from his victory in the Pannonian War, to resume command of forces on the Rhine. Indeed those troops were soon built up with reinforcements from elsewhere to reach a total of eight legions, a far larger army than had been gathered in that region before. Augustus would not give even a suggestion of retreat. Tiberius reconfirmed allegiance in Gaul, distributed armies and fortified garrisons.[202] The veteran commander knew better than to venture much beyond the Rhine in A.D. 10 and 11. He restricted himself to cautious raids and demonstrations. But the demonstrations themselves were important. In the presentation of Velleius Paterculus, they were vigorous offensive manoeuvres and aggressive warfare – and that is doubtless the impression that Augustus wished to deliver.[203] Evidence fails on the years A.D. 12 and 13, but Roman troops clearly did not huddle behind a Rhine frontier. Forces remained in or were sent to the land of the Chauci.[204] And Augustus appointed young Germanicus, who had served with Tiberius on the Rhine in A.D. 11, to supreme command in the region in A.D. 13. This was no mere holding action. Germanicus would lead vigorous offensive campaigns into the interior of Germany. Tacitus pinpointed the motive with accuracy: war on the Germans derived less

[198] Tac. *Ann.* 1.59.

[199] Vell. Pat. II.118.2–119.5; Dio LVI.18.4–22.2; Tac. *Ann.* 1.57–61; Suet. *Aug.* 23; *Tib.* 17. The account of Florus, II.30.32–8, is unreliable. On the site of the battle, see Koestermann 1957 (C 282) 441–3. On Arminius, see Timpe 1970 (C 319) 11–49; Dyson 1971 (A 25) 253–8. Tacitus' description of Arminius as *liberator Germaniae* (*Ann.* II.88) does not imply that Rome had previously annexed the land as a province.   [200] Suet. *Aug.* 23.2; Oros. VI.21.27.   [201] Cf. Flor. II.30.39.

[202] Vell. Pat. II.120.1; Dio LVI.23.2–4. The eight Rhine legions are listed in Tac. *Ann.* 1.37.

[203] Vell. Pat. II.120.1–2, II.121.1; LVI.24.6, LVI.25.2–3; Suet. *Tib.* 18.   [204] Tac. *Ann.* 1.38.

from desire to extend the empire or to achieve tangible gain than to wipe out the disgrace of Varus' defeat.[205] The *princeps* would not allow that calamity to stain Rome's reputation.

The campaigns of Germanicus after the death of Augustus belong to a later discussion. Suffice it here to point out that those campaigns in A.D. 15 and 16 follow a long familiar pattern rather than mark a conspicuous break with the past. They exemplify once again the repeated discrepancy between achievement and advertisement. Germanicus engaged naval and land forces, brought armies across the Weser, claimed major victories – and accomplished very little.[206] Despite, or rather in consequence of, that fact, he enjoyed lavish honours. Germanicus celebrated a handsome triumph and his legates received *ornamenta triumphalia*. The triumph specified as defeated tribes the Cherusci, Chatti, Angrivarii, and all other peoples dwelling west of the Elbe – assertions that went well beyond tangible reality.[207] When Tiberius recalled Germanicus in A.D. 16, the young general expressed disappointment, and claims were made that another season's campaigning would have brought the war to an end.[208] Whatever the plausibility of those claims, they were bound to be made – nor did Tiberius dispute them. Rome halted offensive operations across the Rhine. But she also let it be known that she could have subjugated Germany in a year, had she wished.[209]

Definition of a general Augustan 'policy' on Germany would be difficult to formulate and probably pointless to attempt. To designate it either as 'defensive' or as 'imperialistic' risks oversimplification.[210] And it would be erroneous to consider Roman actions in Germany as following a static plan.

Initial thrusts across the Rhine in the early Augustan years stemmed from the need to police and pacify Gaul. Rome experimented with both diplomacy and warfare, intimidating hostile tribes or winning the allegiance of some to neutralize others. A shocking defeat suffered by Lollius provoked sterner measures, not to satisfy imperialist urgings but to restore imperial prestige. Legions were brought up to the Rhine and forts installed at key sites along the river. Augustus himself returned to Gaul to implement administrative changes and dramatize the import-

---

[205] Tac. *Ann.* 1.3.6; cf. Vell. Pat. 11.123.1. The motive is confirmed by Strab. vii.1.4 (291–2C).

[206] On Germanicus' campaigns, see Koestermann 1957 (c 282); cf. the analysis by Telschow 1975 (c 315) 148–82.

[207] Tac. *Ann.* 1.55.1, 1.72.1, 11.41.2–4; Strab. vii.1.4 (291C); Timpe 1968 (c 318) 41–77.

[208] Tac. *Ann.* 11.26.

[209] Strab. vii.1.4 (291C), written after Augustus' death, implies that the *princeps* never relinquished claims on Germany west of the Elbe.

[210] For an extensive rehearsal of opinions through the early twentieth century, see Oldfather and Canter 1915 (c 294) 9–20, 35–81. A more recent survey by Christ 1977 (c 260) 151–67. Add also Welwei 1986 (c 323) 118–37.

ance he attached to the area. Defence of the Gallic provinces and
expansion into Germany were complementary rather than contrasting
policies. The *princeps'* stepsons, first Drusus, then Tiberius, carried
Roman standards into the lands of the barbarian over the next several
years, in campaigns that included impressive victories, advance to the
Elbe, deportations of peoples, and the planting of garrisons at selected
locations. No obvious ultimate goal had been announced or probably
formulated. The successes represented more than a display of might, but
rather less than the organization of a province. Altars at Cologne and on
the Elbe signified German loyalty to the *princeps*, and Domitius' crossing
of the Elbe to enlist new peoples in Roman *amicitia* put on show Rome's
ability to influence events wherever she wished in that vast land. The
garrisons in the interior implied that Roman presence would be neither
brief nor superficial. But generals continued to withdraw the main body
of their forces to the Rhine after almost every campaigning season.
Augustus preferred to exhibit power than to put it to risk.

Tiberius' appointment to Germany in A.D. 4 signalled the restored
confidence of the *princeps* in his newly adopted son and gave him the
opportunity to add further laurels to his reputation. The campaigns were
more notable for enhancement of prestige than for solid accomplishment. Conquest of the Marcomanni would have provided something
solid but had to be abandoned for pressing needs elsewhere. As
substitute came a movement toward more systematic application of
judicial and financial authority by the new legate Varus. But the changes
engendered reaction and calamity. Augustus had to adjust accordingly.
If he could not replace Varus' three legions, he could shift forces from
elsewhere in the empire to the Rhine. His appointment of Tiberius and
Germanicus in the years that followed the Varian disaster served to
controvert any suggestion of Roman weakness. And their campaigns
proposed to show that Rome could resurrect her influence in Germany
whenever circumstances required it.

Despite shifts in behaviour and action, continuities prevailed: the
emphasis on Rome's international authority and her ascendancy over all
rivals. That emphasis emerges in the swift retaliation after each challenge, the timely appearance of the *princeps* and his stepsons, the
establishment of garrisons, the promotion of the imperial cult, the
expeditions (however brief and temporary) to the Elbe, triumphal
honours and imperial salutations repeatedly awarded, the display of
Roman magisterial symbols, the introduction of administrative regulations, and the drive to compensate publicly for every setback. Reference
to Germany in the *Res Gestae* suitably completes the picture. Augustus
ignores precision for propaganda: he includes Germany with Gaul and

Spain as evidence for his pacification of Europe from Gades to the Elbe.[211]

X. IMPERIAL IDEOLOGY

Assessment of Augustus' imperial policy has long divided scholars. Was he a relentless expansionist or a prudent leader who set bounds to the empire? Did he conduct aggressive imperialism or a defensive policy? Was he military conqueror or bringer of peace?

Pax Augusta has become the conventional characterization of the new order introduced by the *princeps*.[212] Repetition by moderns, however, obscures the fact that the phrase rarely surfaced in the age of Augustus himself. It finds voice occasionally in dedications offered by individuals or officials in Italian or provincial towns.[213] But it does not represent a slogan emanating from the government.

Augustus, it is often alleged, placed limits on the extension of territory and advised that the empire be held within fixed bounds. But evidence for that conclusion is slim and dubious. Recovery of the standards from Parthia in 20 B.C. induced the *princeps* to announce that the realm could remain at its present extent – a posture that, at best, was only temporary and brief.[214] He issued instructions directing generals not to pursue enemies beyond the Elbe, but that too was a temporary restraint designed to allow concentration on another conflict, not a delineation of boundaries.[215] More significant, or so it would seem, was a document read to the Senate after Augustus' death and purporting to contain his advice that the empire be held within its present frontiers.[216] The authenticity of that item remains in doubt. Tiberius may have had cause to seek posthumous Augustan sanction for policies he intended to promote. And the statement attributed to Augustus by Dio that he had never added possessions from the barbarian world is preposterous.[217]

The martial accomplishments of Augustus belie any systematic policy of limits or leanings toward pacifism. The *princeps'* appointees penetrated beyond the First Cataract in Egypt, extended influence to Ethiopia and invaded Arabia. He converted Judaea into a province, rattled sabres at Parthia, and maintained an indirect hegemony in Armenia. Roman forces subjugated north-west Spain and carried campaigns against tribes in north Africa. Augustus or his surrogates fought Dalmatians and Pannonians, mounted a force against the Marcomanni, and laid the

[211] Aug. *RG* 26.2.   [212] Cf e.g., Stier 1975 (A 91) 18–42; Fears 1981 (C 267) 884–9.
[213] *ILS* 3787, 3789; *IGRR* IV 1173; cf. Weinstock 1960 (F 617) 47–50.
[214] Dio LIV.9.1; cf. LIII.10.4–5.   [215] Strab. VII.1.4 (291C).
[216] Tac. *Ann.* I.11.4; Dio LVI.33.5–6.
[217] Dio LVI.33.6. Suetonius' assertion that Augustus had no ambition for empire or martial glory (*Aug.* 21.2) is nonsense. On these matters, see now Ober 1982 (C 293) 306–28.

groundwork for Roman provinces along the Danube. He routed Alpine peoples, opened passes in the mountains, reduced Raetia, and occupied Noricum. Romans crossed the Rhine, established garrisons in Germany, and dispatched armies to the Elbe. The record of conquest eclipsed that of all predecessors. The regime thrived on expansionism – or at least the reputation of expansionism.

Augustus left the impression of aggressiveness even where he had no intent to undertake aggression. Britain is a prime example. On three occasions, so Cassius Dio reports, the *princeps* let it be known that he was on the point of mounting an expedition against that remote island: in 34, 27 and 26 B.C. Each time other pressing needs conveniently intervened to postpone the venture: a rising in Dalmatia, unsettled conditions in Gaul, and the Cantabrian War respectively.[218] In the eyes of contemporaries in the 30s and 20s, the invasion of Britain was a sure thing – as was its conquest. Repeated allusions in the poems of Virgil, Horace and Propertius attest to that public perception.[219] Augustus could later abandon the idea altogether by producing a plausible justification: British kings had sent embassies, made offerings on the Capitol, and formally acknowledged the *princeps'* authority. It was as good as a conquest – and much cheaper.[220] Britain could subsequently be ignored, a matter of policy, as Augustus explicitly characterized it.[221] The earlier projection of an aggressive pose had equally been a matter of policy.

Reputation held pre-eminent place in the realm of Augustus. The precedents of the Republic helped shape the ideology of the Principate – not so much in constitutional matters as in the image of martial success. *Pax* rarely made an appearance as symbol of Republican aspirations. *Victoria* predominated as a numismatic slogan, triumphs represented the most coveted prizes, expansion of territory elicited ringing phrases from orators who trumpeted Roman mastery of the world.[222] That is the proper context for comprehending the imperial posture of Augustus.[223]

Defeat of Antony and Cleopatra placed unprecedented power in the hands of the victor. He may have sought to bind up the wounds of the civil war, but he also made certain to commemorate the victory – and to institutionalize reminders of it. Two new cities rose as memorials to the achievement, each bearing the imposing designation of Nicopolis, one on the site of Octavian's camp at Actium, the other to mark the battle

[218] Dio XLIX.38.2, LIII.22.5, LIII.25.2.

[219] Virg. *Ecl.* 1.67; *G.* 1.29, III.25; Hor. *Epod.* VII.7; *Carm.* 1.21.13, 1.35.29, III.4.34, III.5.2–4, IV.14.47; Prop. II.27.5, IV.3.7; cf. Momigliano 1950 (C 290) 39–41.

[220] Strab. IV.5.3 (200C). These embassies need to be kept distinct from the arrival of British refugee princes as suppliants at the court of Augustus; *RG* 32.1.   [221] Tac. *Agr.* XIII.

[222] E.g. Cic. *Leg. Man.* 53; *Mur.* 22; *Off.* 1.38, II.26; *Phil.* VIII.12. For *Victoria* as a symbol, see Fears 1981 (C 268) 773–804. On Republican attitudes toward militarism and conquest, see Harris 1979 (C 273) 10–41; cf. Brunt 1978 (C 257) 162–72; Jal 1982 (C 279) 143–50.

[223] On what follows, see the fuller treatment in Gruen 1986 (C 271) 51–72.

near Alexandria that completed the conquest. At Epirote Nicopolis the conqueror sponsored games, enlarged the temple of Apollo, erected a trophy, and displayed a huge inscription to memorialize the victory.[224] And in 29 B.C. Octavian celebrated a triple triumph, a spectacular event that stretched over three days, to signal his successes in Illyria, Actium and Alexandria.[225] The monuments and the ceremonies spelled out these messages clearly: they exalted not *pax* but the *gloria* of the conqueror.

Those celebrations set a pattern for the imagery, both written and visual, that characterized the self-representation of the *princeps* and his government. The *Res Gestae* makes the point without ambiguity. Augustus reels off his victories abroad and the distinctions which they earned him at home: *ovationes*, triumphs, salutations as *imperator*, the annexation of Egypt, advance against Ethiopia and Arabia, recovery of eastern provinces and captured standards, defeat of Pannonians and Dacians, pacification of the Alps, Gaul, Spain and Germany, and extension of the Illyrian frontier to the Danube.[226] He summarized the achievement with a claim that he had pushed the boundaries of every province as a lesson to peoples who did not acknowledge the *imperium* of Rome.[227] The *princeps* does indeed boast of bringing *pax*. But it is a *pax* achieved by victories. And he declared that the temple of Janus had been closed three times during his reign – a fact that signalled not permanent peace but repeated subjugation of enemies and pacification of empire.[228] The *Res Gestae* provides no apologia or justification. Augustus takes for granted the legitimacy of Roman conquest and expansionism.[229] The preamble of the document itself sums up the contents quite pointedly: 'The achievements of the divine Augustus whereby he subjected the world to the power of the Roman people.'

The poets of the era reinforce that impression. It need not be surmised that they wrote at Augustus' behest; nor, conversely, that their writings either provoked the *princeps*, exceeded his intent, or subtly criticized his ambitions.[230] One can, however, postulate with confidence that ideas and attitudes repeatedly voiced by the poets evoke the prevailing atmosphere of public discussion.

---

[224] Epirote Nicopolis: Strab. VII.7.5–6 (324–5C); X.2.2 (450C); Pliny, *HN* IV.1.5; Paus. X.38.4; Dio LI.1.2–3, LIII.1.4–5; Suet. *Aug.* 18; the inscription: Oliver 1969 (B 259) 178–82; Carter 1977 (B 216) 227–30; Alexandrian Nicopolis: Strab. XVII.1.10 (795C); Dio LI.18.1; see Hanson 1980 (C 116) 249–54.   [225] Suet. *Aug.* 22; Dio LI.21.5–9.

[226] Aug. *RG* 26.2–5, 27.1, 27.3, 29.1–2, 30.1–2; cf. Nicolet 1988 (A 69) 28–40.

[227] Aug. *RG* 26.1. The passage is interpreted, rather too strictly, by Braunert 1977 (C 255) 207–17, to imply that Augustus created no new provinces. See Vell. Pat. II.39.3.

[228] Aug. *RG* 13; cf. Dio LIV.36.2.

[229] The only exception is a claim that the Alps were subdued without bringing an unjust war on any tribe; *RG* 26.3.

[230] For various views, see e.g., Meyer 1961 (C 288); Brunt 1963 (C 256) 170–6; Seager 1980 (C 309) 103–11; Williams 1990 (C 325) 258–75. Recent bibliographies in Doblhofer 1981 (C 265) 1922–6; Little 1982 (B 111) 352–70. See esp., Johnson 1973 (B 93) 171–80; Griffin 1984 (C 269) 189–218.

Virgil's verses supply pertinent illustrations. The *Georgics* portray the *princeps* as heir to Rome's hardiest warriors of the past: Decius, Camillus, Scipio and Marius. Actium made him victor in the furthest bounds of the East; Parthia is reckoned as already defeated and humbled; Octavian thunders on the banks of the Euphrates, imposing laws upon compliant peoples.[231] The *Aeneid* forecasts world dominion in the age of Augustus. Jupiter promises imperial holdings without limits. And the shield of Aeneas depicts the *princeps* as sitting in proud splendour while long rows of conquered peoples from Africa to the Euphrates pass in array before him.[232]

Comparable indications recur in the songs of Horace. The poet urges that Roman arms no longer be trained on fellow-citizens but be directed against foreign foes. He takes for granted Roman offensive thrusts against Parthians, Gauls, Scythians, Arabs and Britons. The drive for expansionism is simply a given. Horace foresees a universal dominance for his nation.[233] Parthia is the principal target: Augustus will avenge Roman honour, regain the standards lost by other generals, lead conquered Parthians in triumph, and annex the land to Rome's empire.[234] The *princeps* did indeed obtain the standards in 20 B.C. but without battle, trophies, or triumphs. Horace, however, presents the outcome as fulfilment of his own prediction: Parthians are stripped of their spoils, bend to the dictates of Rome, and venerate Augustus. Capture of the standards is juxtaposed to the exercise of Roman sway throughout the world.[235] Whatever his personal predilections, Horace accurately reflects the dominant propaganda of the era.

Reflection can be found also in the lines of Propertius. The convention of the *recusatio* conveniently served the purpose. By disclaiming competence to sing of Augustus' martial feats, Propertius also calls attention to those feats. The poet alludes to victories abroad, kings led in triumph, distant lands trembling and obedient to the authority of the *princeps*.[236] Like Horace, Propertius projects campaigns to the extremities of empire and visualizes a humiliation of Parthia.[237] And when the standards were returned to Rome, Propertius duly represents the result as a Parthian confession of defeat.[238]

The cynical Ovid, both playful and serious, describes the heady excitement in Rome on the eve of young C. Caesar's departure to the East in 2 B.C. His *Ars Amatoria* characterized the intent of the

---

[231] Virg. *G.* II.169–72, III.30–3, IV.559–62.

[232] Virg. *Aen.* I.278–9, III.714–18; cf. I.286–90, VI.791–800, VII.601–15.

[233] Hor. *Epod.* VII.3–10; *Sat.* II.1.10–15; *Carm.* I.12.49–57, I.29.1–5, I.35.29–40, III.3.45–58, III.4.25–36.   [234] Hor. *Carm.* I.2.51–2, I.12.53–4, I.29.4–5, II.9.18–22, III.3.43–4, III.5.2–12.

[235] Hor. *Epist.* I.12.27–8, I.18.56–7, II.1.256; *Carm.* IV.14.41–52, IV.15.6–8, IV.15.21–4; *Carm. Saec.* 53–6.   [236] Prop. II.1.25–36, II.10.13–18; cf. IV.4.11–12.

[237] Prop. II.10.13–14, II.14.23–4, III.4.1–9, III.9.54, III.12.3, IV.3.7–10, IV.3.35–40, IV.3.63–9.

[238] Prop. IV.6.79–80.

expedition: Augustus to add to his dominions, Parthia to pay the price for her misdeeds, Crassus' shades to be avenged. The poet even envisions the future triumph of Gaius, bringing in its train captive Asians from exotic parts of the world.[239] Gaius, in fact, never returned from that venture, and no triumph was earned. Ovid therefore recalls the language of his predecessors: recovery of the standards sufficed to make the point and Augustus had already coerced the Parthians into humble compliance.[240] The *Metamorphoses* and the *Fasti* speak of the subjugation of barbarian peoples and the deep penetration of Roman power. Jupiter surveys a world where Roman dominion is universal. The earth lies under the heel of the conqueror.[241] Even in the poems from exile, late in Augustus' reign, Ovid's praise of the *princeps* places stress upon victory, the garnering of military laurels, the conquest of Pannonia, Raetia and Thrace, surrender by Armenia and Parthia, awe-struck Germany, and imperial holdings now at their greatest reach.[242]

The public manifestations of the regime tell much the same story. Coins, inscriptions and monuments converge in transmitting the picture of Roman might and dominance. *Victoria*, whether as bust or as figure, occurs frequently on the coinage, especially with the globe that exemplified world rule. Other martial symbols also prevail: triumphal chariots, the *ornamenta triumphalia*, trophies, a triumphal arch, the temple of Mars Ultor, victory laurels.[243] Annexation, acquisition, or military reprisals are regularly on display. The numismatic legends trumpet *Aegyptus capta*, *Armenia capta*, *Asia recepta* and *signa recepta*.[244] The inscribed trophy that recorded Augustus' pacification of the Alpine regions listed the names of nearly fifty tribes that had been subjected to Roman power.[245]

The city of Rome exhibited striking monuments that transmitted the image of conqueror, master and guarantor of security through force. As early as 29 B.C. Octavian installed a statue of Victory in the Curia Iulia. A triumphal arch commemorated his successes abroad.[246] Two years later the Senate appropriately voted Augustus the privilege of placing laurel trees before his residence and setting an oak crown above them – a gesture that symbolized his role both as perpetual victor over enemies and as saviour of citizens.[247]

The Forum Augustum gave the most visible and prominent display of Augustan ideology. The imposing temple of Mars Ultor, vowed by

[239] Ov. *Ars Am.* 1.177–228.   [240] Ov. *Fast.* v.579–94.
[241] Ov. *Met.* xv.820–31, xv.877; *Fast.* 1.85–6, 1.717, 11.684, iv.857–62.
[242] Ov. *Tr.* 11.1.169–78, 225–32, 111.12.45–8.
[243] E.g. *BMCRE* Augustus, nos. 1, 68, 77–8, 101–2, 217–19, 224, *et al.*
[244] E.g. *BMCRE* Augustus, nos. 10–19, 40–4, 56–9, 332, 410–23, 647–55, 671–81, 703.
[245] Pliny, *HN* 111.136–7.   [246] Dio li.22.1–2; Zanker 1972 (F 626) 8–12.
[247] Dio liii.16.4.

Augustus after Philippi but not completed until 2 B.C., held conspicuous place. It would be the locus of assemblage for the Senate for all declarations of war or award of triumphs, and the symbolic starting-point for every general to lead his troops abroad. The Forum Augustum served as repository for weapons of all sorts and for arms seized as booty from the defeated foes of Rome.[248] The statue of the *princeps* himself stood in the centre of the Forum, set in a triumphal chariot which contained record of his conquests.[249] The flanks of the Forum held two rows of statues. In the niches of one side Augustus installed representatives of the great men of Rome's past, with inscribed *elogia* attesting, among other things, to military achievements and triumphal honours. Opposite that array of heroes stood the figures of Aeneas and all the representatives of the Julian line.[250] The *princeps* thus linked himself and his family to a gallery of republican *duces*, *triumphatores* and *summi viri*, as heir to the grandest martial traditions of the state.

Other items add to the impression. Among them the commanding statue of Augustus at Prima Porta takes pride of place. An elaborately engraved cuirass calls forth the martial image. The centrepiece of the breastplate displays the transfer of captured standards by the Parthians to Rome, emblematic of Roman supremacy in the East. And the figures of female barbarians in the middle zone of the cuirass, dejected and submissive, represent Roman humbling of the Celtic peoples of the West. Triumphal symbolism predominates. The mother earth figure, reclining at the bottom with cornucopiae and babies, projects prosperity and the bountifulness of the land. As is clear, the new and prosperous age depends upon armed force and constitutes the fruits of victory.[251] The Prima Porta figure signifies conquest of the empire and world-wide rule assured by the continual vigilance of the *princeps*.

The celebrated Ara Pacis, it might be thought, forms a counterpoint to this presentation. Not necessarily so. The altar, in fact, strikes a balance that parallels other verbal and visual productions of the Augustan era: a juxtaposition of the rewards of peace with the military success that made them possible. The Senate voted to consecrate the Ara Pacis in 13 B.C. as memorial to Augustus' return in that year from the subjugation of Spain and the pacification of Gaul.[252] The panel of Aeneas on the west side of the altar has him offering sacrifice to the Di Penates, a scene that evidently celebrates his homecoming, just as the monument itself celebrated Augustus' homecoming. But that panel is balanced by

[248] Ov. *Fast.* v.550–62; Suet. *Aug.* 29.2; Dio LV.10.2–3.

[249] Aug. *RG* 35.1; Vell. Pat. II.39.2.

[250] Ov. *Fast.* v.563–6; Suet. *Aug.* 31.5; Dio LV.10.3; *SHA. Alex. Sev.* 28.6; Zanker 1968 (F 625); Frisch 1980 (B 231) 91–8; Zanker 1988 (F 633) 210–14; Luce 1990 (C 284) 123–38.

[251] On the Prima Porta statue, see esp. Kähler 1959 (F 441); Zinserling 1967 (F 636) 327–39; Pollini 1978 (F 531) 8–74; Zanker 1988 (F 633) 183–92.   [252] Aug. *RG* 12.2.

another, featuring the partially preserved Mars, father of the twins Romulus and Remus, and pre-eminent god of war. A similar balance occurs on the eastern panels of the Ara Pacis. One depicts a female deity with the attributes of fertility and bountifulness, calling attention to the blessings of a tranquil time. But its corresponding panel contains the goddess Roma resting, as often, on a pile of arms. The imagery takes on meaning in combination. The accomplishment of peace is inseparable from success in war.[253]

That association is reinforced by a recent discovery. Close connexion held between the Ara Pacis and the Egyptian obelisk that stood as the *gnomon* of the colossal sundial, the *Solarium Augusti*. The shadow of the obelisk pointed squarely at the centre of the Ara Pacis on 23 September, the birthday of Augustus himself.[254] The obelisk itself was set up to memorialize Augustus' subordination of Egypt to the control of the Roman empire. The collective message dramatically linked peace with military authority and imperial expansion.

XI. CONCLUSION

A survey of territorial expansion under Augustus tempts conclusions about strategic designs, empire-wide policy, and imperialist intent. It has been claimed, for example, that Augustus adopted and refined a military system of hegemonic rule, resting on a combination of client states and an efficiently deployed armed force stationed in frontier sectors but mobile enough for transfer wherever needed.[255] Many reckon the push to the north as a carefully conceived and sweeping plan that linked the Alpine, Balkan and German campaigns, and aimed to establish a secure boundary of the empire that ran along the line of the Danube and the Elbe.[256] Others, however, consider Augustus a determined imperialist, bent on expansion everywhere and motivated by dreams of world conquest. Only the Pannonian revolt and the defeat of Varus obliged him to check his ambition and bequeath a defence policy to his successor.[257]

Yet the very idea of an all-encompassing scheme, whatever its form,

---

[253] Bibliography on the Ara Pacis is immense. Among the more important publications, see Moretti 1948 (F 505); Toynbee 1953 (F 597) 67–95; Kähler 1954 (F 439) 67–100; Hanell 1960 (F 405) 31–123; Simon 1967 (F 576); Borbein 1975 (F 294) 242–66; Pollini 1978 (F 531) 75–172; Torelli 1982 (F 596) 27–61; Zanker 1988 (F 633) 172–83, 203–6. de Grummond 1990 (C 272) 663–77, unconvincingly identifies the female deity with Pax.

[254] See the meticulous calculations of Buchner 1976 (F 304) 319–65; 1983 (F 307) 494–508.

[255] Luttwak 1976 (A 57) 13–50, 192.

[256] See the list of scholars in Oldfather and Canter 1915 (C 294) 9–10, and note, esp., Syme 1934 (C 312) 351–4; Kraft 1973 (A 53) 181–208.

[257] Brunt 1963 (C 256) 170–6; Wells 1972 (E 601) 1–13; Moynihan 1986 (C 291) 149–62; Nicolet 1988 (A 69) 41–8.

misconceives the diversity and flexibility of Augustus' foreign ventures. No uniform plan or articulated goal guided his acts. Location, circumstances and contingencies determined decisions.

The eastern realms provoked varied responses. In Asia Minor and Judaea Augustus cultivated client princes, generally keeping in place those already established, regardless of prior allegiances. But he was not averse to deposing dynasts (e.g. in Commagene), intervening in royal dispensations (as with Herod), or even converting principalities into provinces (Galatia and Judaea) when unexpected developments called for it. Principal garrisons of Roman power in the East stood in Egypt and Syria – but for very different purposes. Egypt held a special place for Augustus, its economic resources a mainstay of empire and its territory a staging-ground for military adventures in Ethiopia and Arabia. Troops in Syria, by contrast, served to signal stability rather than advance, a means of showing the flag and discouraging Parthian ambitions. The *princeps* kept a hand in the dynastic affairs of Armenia and a careful watch on vicissitudes in the royal house of Parthia. Recovery of the standards took priority in policy and propaganda. But dealings with Parthia relied on diplomacy – alternate displays of resolve and negotiated settlements – rather than force. The kingdom supplied occasions for posturing, not a menace against which to devise a strategy.

Different motives and different actions prevailed in the West. The *princeps* or his generals conducted vigorous campaigns in Illyria and Spain in the 30s and 20s B.C. Strategic purposes, however, played at best a secondary role. Octavian used the Illyrian adventure to shore up his reputation *vis-à-vis* Antony, and brought north-west Spain under subjection to demonstrate Roman might throughout the Iberian peninsula. Roman involvement in north Africa had still a different character (or characters): the *princeps* experimented with client kings, warfare and colonial foundations at various times and places in that area – with no consistent results.

The great northern campaigns may assume coherent shape in retrospect – but hardly at the time. Divergent aims dictated action, Roman response occurred as often as Roman initiative, political and ideological purposes frequently took precedence over strategic goals. Control of the Alpine regions facilitated communications between the Rhine forces and the troops in Illyricum. The push to the Danube held out many advantages: the disciplining of recalcitrant tribes which had damaged Rome's repute, military laurels for members of Augustus' family, and opening of a land route from northern Italy to the eastern dependencies. The heaviest fighting, however, came in reaction to rebellion rather than as part of an imperial scheme. Advancement against Germans derived from security and administrative needs in Gaul. Strikes across the Rhine advertised Roman might and authority without establishing a permanent presence. Prestige may have counted for more than strategy. Exhibitions of force occurred after the Varian disaster as before.

Diversity stands out far more boldly than uniformity. There was uniformity, however, in one key respect. The *princeps* need not have felt commitment to relentless conquest and indefinite extension of territory and power. But he did feel commitment so to represent his aspirations.

Representation and reality often diverged. Augustus made certain to maintain consistency in the former. Pragmatic considerations might on occasion dictate restraint or withdrawal. And defeat could sometimes mar the achievement. But the public posture remained uniform: a posture of dynamism, success and control. Aelius Gallus' calamitous campaigns in Arabia were covered over in the *Res Gestae* which reports only Roman advance in the area; and aggressive thrusts served to compensate for the setbacks. Bloodless negotiations allowed Augustus to recover the standards from Parthia and diplomacy provided an acceptable settlement in Armenia; but the regime made menacing gestures, and the propaganda proclaimed defeat for Parthia and subjection for Armenia. The closing of Janus' doors and triumphal honours awarded after a campaign in north-west Spain belied the superficiality of that achievement – to be followed by another decade of brutal fighting in the region and some heavy losses for Rome. Modest successes in Illyria during the triumviral period became exaggerated in report and announcement so as to elevate Octavian's reputation at the expense of his rival. Victories and the honours of victory marked advance to the Danube and even encouraged the mounting of a campaign against the Marcomanni; the Pannonian revolt, however, shattered the illusion of Roman mastery and required an enormous commitment of resources to restore control. Conquest of the Alps may have had strategic ends, but it also served to advertise the prowess of Augustus' stepsons and to summon public acclaim for the imperial house. Similarly, Drusus' thrusts across the Rhine called forth magnificent honours, out of proportion to solid accomplishments, and the termination of his advance at the Elbe was explained away as the consequence of divine intervention. In comparable fashion Tiberius obtained high honours for victories in Germany, and his panegyrist Velleius rhapsodized about his successes, though little of substance was accomplished. And when disaster did strike, in the form of Varus' crushing defeat, the *princeps* strove to stress continuity, appointing Tiberius and then Germanicus to resume aggressive campaigns across the Rhine, as if to deny any setback or interruption.

The imperial policy of Augustus varied from region to region, adjusted for circumstances and contingencies. Aggression alternated with restraint, conquest with diplomacy, advance with retreat. Acquisitions and annexations occurred in some areas, consolidation and negotiation in others. The insistence upon reputation, however, was undeviating. The regime persistently projected the impression of vigour, expansionism, triumph and dominance. Augustus reiterated the aspirations and professed to eclipse the accomplishments of republican heroes. The policy may have been flexible, but the image was consistent.

CHAPTER 5

TIBERIUS TO NERO

T. E. J. WIEDEMANN

I. THE ACCESSION OF TIBERIUS AND THE NATURE OF POLITICS UNDER THE JULIO-CLAUDIANS

Political history explores the ways in which the men (and very occasionally women) who wielded power over others chose to exercise that power. In every system of government there are dozens, if not hundreds, of individuals who have to use their initiative about the exercise of power in particular circumstances, or about the best way to implement decisions taken by their superiors. But Rome under Augustus and his successors was a monarchy: every exercise of political power had ultimately to be answered for to the emperor. The emperor's authority could not publicly be challenged (anyone who successfully did so would become the new emperor). The political history of the Principate is therefore primarily an account of the relationship between the reigning emperor and the other individuals and groups who played a role in public life. Although some of the political figures of the Julio-Claudian period were descended from families that had been powerful under the Republic, it does not follow that the 'republican' aristocracy still wielded independent power. Such men – like the 'new men' who were prepared to put their military or rhetorical skills at the service of the Caesars – had only as much power as the emperor allowed them, and only for as long as the emperor needed to make use of them. They had a place in public life only because, and insofar as, they had the *princeps'* favour; they were what in Latin would be called his *amici*, friends. He who lost the emperor's friendship lost the basis for his public existence – and the effect of that was that his public life (and sometimes his personal existence) came to an end, whether he was a patrician or a *novus homo* or a freedman or even a close relative of the emperor himself.[1]

From Augustus on, as Cassius Dio noted, politics had ceased to be 'public'. Important political choices no longer needed to be debated, or voted on, in public, but only in the private *consilium* of the emperor and

---

[1] For the nature of politics under the Principate, see chs. 2 and 3 above; Wickert 1974 (A 102) (with bibliography, pp. 5–8); Millar 1977 (A 59); Levick 1985 (C 371). Standard narrative histories of this period: H.H. Scullard, *From the Gracchi to Nero* (London, 1st edn. 1959); Garzetti 1974 (A 35).

his *amici*. Consequently historians, ancient as well as modern, lack public records of how decisions came to be taken by the emperor, or of the different views held by his *amici*. As in modern dictatorships, the absence of reliable information meant that the decision-making process was portrayed through rumours, jokes, anecdotes, and the hostile reminiscence of bitter and disillusioned men (and women) who hated the establishment largely because they felt it had not given them the rewards they deserved. The actions of emperors often baffled contemporaries; and what is baffling is liable to be dismissed as lunatic, or condemned as monstrous. Hence, as the poet Claudian was to write later,

> The annals speak of the crimes committed by the men of old,
> And the stains will remain for ever. Who will not for all eternity
> Condemn the monstrous actions of the House of Caesar,
> Nero's dreadful murders, the disgusting cliffs of Capri,
> Inhabited by an aged pervert?[2]

The most fascinating source of such information about the Julio-Claudians is to be found in the surviving portions of Tacitus' *Annals*. They cover the periods A.D. 14-29, 31-37 and 47-66. Archaeology and epigraphy may provide additional evidence to supplement the disappointingly meagre accounts of life outside the metropolis in the ancient literary sources; but the *Annals* are the point of departure for political history. There are other accounts by ancient writers; although often based on the same sources, they are sometimes not so reliable because of their particular literary format, but we can use them to modify the more obviously tendentious interpretations in Tacitus. Tacitus was writing a century after the death of Augustus, and many of his preoccupations were as much with the actions and attitudes (especially towards the Senate) of Trajan and Hadrian, under whom he lived, as with those of the Julio-Claudians.[3]

The relationship between emperor and Senate is a major concern of other senatorial writers beside Tacitus. The language in which they tend to express that concern is that of a contrast between 'tyranny' and 'freedom' (*libertas*), concepts inherited from the late Republic. But this republican vocabulary should not mislead us into treating the history of the Julio-Claudian period as similar to that of the Republic – as a chronicle of the magistracies and honours achieved by politicians as the result of competition with one another. There was competition, but it was for the emperor's favour. It was the emperor who took the decisions.

---

[2] Cassius Dio on secret politics: LIII.19. The *consilium*: ch. 7 below. Claudian, *IV Cons. Hon.*, 8.311–15.

[3] Furneaux's edition of Tacitus' *Annals* remains the most accessible; for commentaries, see Koestermann 1963–8 (B 98); Goodyear 1972 and 1981 (B 62). On Tacitus, Syme 1958 (B 176) remains basic; among others, see Christ 1978 (B 28).

In recent years historians have stressed that imperial 'policy' was often purely passive, that the decisions taken by emperors were often made in response to the actions of others. The emperor's most important activity was the exercise of *gratia*; as the most powerful of patrons, he was expected to distribute favours to senators and the plebs, to Romans and provincials who came and asked for them. The story of how imperial responses to such initiatives changed the nature of Mediterranean culture and society is traced in other chapters of this volume. We should be sceptical about earlier views of the emperors as great visionaries who sought to impose upon their officials policies of administrative central-ization, the systematic spreading of Roman culture, the systematization of Roman law, justice for provincials (let alone slaves), and even, as was once believed, a positive attitude towards agriculture, trade and indus-try. Nor should we put too much emphasis on the emperor's need to be a successful showman, like the leader of a modern mass democracy; an emperor certainly had to advertise his popularity, but that popularity itself was based on the care he took for his people as patron of rich and poor alike, *pater patriae*. But not all imperial policies were passive responses to the demands of others. Every emperor needed to have a minimal policy – to stay in command of the political process; to maximize his own prestige; and to maintain in his own hands the choice of whom to hand his power on to after his death. These aims had applied to Augustus as much as they applied to his Julio-Claudian successors.[4]

The events which followed the death of Augustus at Nola in Campania on 19 August A.D. 14 became a paradigm for the smooth transfer of power from an emperor to his successor; few future emperors found themselves in total control with as little difficulty as Tiberius did. Nevertheless the moment at which monarchical power is transferred from one man to his successor is a critical point at which the different elements that constitute a political system can be seen most clearly. Although Tacitus' record of these events at the opening of the *Annals* betrays his concern about the accessions of much later emperors (Trajan in 97 and Hadrian in 117), it reveals the control that a new emperor had to exercise over, first and foremost, the imperial household, the *domus Caesaris*; and then over the soldiers of the praetorian guard, magistrates, the Senate and people of Rome, and the Roman armies in the provinces.

Although the *domus Caesaris* was in law just another Roman house-hold, it gave its head (Lat. *paterfamilias*) access to material resources,

---

[4] For imperial 'policy' as a response to initiatives from others, esp. Millar 1977 (A 59). Patronage: Wallace-Hadrill 1989 (F 75), esp. chs. 3 and 6. Showmanship: Cizek 1972 (C 340) (and below, on Nero). Succession in pre-industrial states: J. Goody (ed.) *Succession to High Office*, Cambridge, 1966, p. 113: 'The Baganda firmly maintain that it is dangerous to publish in advance the choice of a successor, as he will surely commit murder to hasten his succession.'

services (via procurators managing estates throughout the empire) and informal social control on a scale with which no other household could compete. The emperor's *domus* contained not just those of his descendants who were under his legal control (*in potestate*), a definition much narrower than that of the word 'family' in English, but also their chattels and estates, including slaves (Lat. *familia*), and dependants: freedmen, provincial magnates (including 'client kings'), and also those Roman *amici* who regarded themselves as owing their personal or political lives to the present Caesar or his predecessors. In this sense, every ex-magistrate had to consider that he had a personal duty to ensure the well-being of the current head of the imperial household.

Tiberius was Augustus' stepson; notwithstanding his marriage to Augustus' daughter Iulia, it was not his birthright to succeed Augustus as 'Caesar'. But in A.D. 4 he had been formally adopted by Augustus as his son. The grant of *tribunicia potestas* awarded then and renewed in A.D. 13 together with a grant of *imperium maius* meant that there was no doubt as to who would rule Rome after Augustus. Some of the men who might have been Tiberius' rivals had been disgraced along with Iulia in 2 B.C.; others were sent into exile in connexion with the fall of her daughter, Iulia the Younger, in A.D. 8. At the moment of Augustus' death, Tiberius was the only man who could seriously be considered as his political successor.[5] But there was someone else with a legitimate claim to a share in Augustus' personal estate: his grandson Agrippa Postumus, whom Augustus had adopted at the same time as Tiberius. Although Roman law gave a *paterfamilias* wide rights to dispose of his property as he pleased, it was customary for sons (together with the widow and daughters who were still *in potestate*) to inherit equal portions of the estate. Anyone who wished to disinherit a son had to do so explicitly in his will; even if he had been explicitly disinherited, a son could still appeal against the will as 'undutiful' (*querella inofficiosi testamenti*). Although Postumus had been sent into exile by his adoptive father, there is no clear evidence that he had been disinherited: in terms of Roman private law, he had the same claim to be 'Caesar' as Tiberius. However weak his political influence, the existence of Agrippa Postumus as an exile on the island of Planasia threatened the smooth transfer of power; it gave Tiberius' opponents the option of making use of him.

This made it imperative for Tiberius as heir to step into the *persona* of Augustus immediately that he died. He had to be on the spot to be recognized as the new *paterfamilias*, but Augustus' final illness came suddenly. Earlier in the year, the seventy-six-year-old emperor had still

---

[5] Tiberius has attracted numerous biographers, among them Seager 1972 (C 392); Levick 1976 (C 366). Cf. Pippidi 1965 (C 385); Rogers 1943 (C 388); Syme 1974 (C 398). On the events of 2 B.C. and A.D. 8, Meise 1969 (C 375), chs. 2 and 3; Syme 1974 (C 229).

been in good health; on 11 May, he had completed a census revision, with Tiberius as his colleague. Early in August Tiberius left Augustus in Campania to return to the army in Pannonia. He hastened to Nola as soon as he heard that Augustus was ill, possibly in response to a summons by the emperor himself. Tacitus reports a rumour that when Tiberius reached Nola, he found Augustus already dead, and that Livia kept the truth hidden in order to facilitate the transfer of power to her son (more suggestive of the role played by Plotina at Hadrian's accession in A.D. 117). Tiberius himself claimed that he had spoken to Augustus before he died.

Tiberius' first reported action after Augustus' death was to write to all the Roman armies (not just his own in Pannonia). He did not style himself Augustus, since that was a title that had been bestowed by the Roman Senate, and he had no right yet to use it. But there was no need to wait for the Senate to confirm the manifest fact that following Augustus' death, Tiberius had become the new head of the imperial household. The next thing that happened was that Agrippa Postumus was put to death. Augustus had suggested that Postumus' rowdy character made him entirely unsuitable for public responsibility. But Tacitus reports rumours, presumably put about by those who did not wish to see Tiberius succeed, that the emperor had visited his exiled grandson at Planasia in the year before his death, and planned to reinstate him. Later, one of his freedmen pretended to be the dead Postumus, suggesting that there were those who might be expected to back his claims against Tiberius. He had to be killed. The fact that Postumus' name was not mentioned at all in Augustus' will suggests that the execution had been arranged by Augustus before his death, to facilitate Tiberius' accession; it might have been ordered by Livia, purporting to act for Augustus, for the same reason (or out of 'stepmotherly spite', as Tacitus would have it); or by Tiberius himself. It was probably carried out by one of Augustus' advisers, Gaius Sallustius Crispus (a grand-nephew of the historian), as soon as he heard of the emperor's death. When Tiberius heard of the execution, he denied responsibility and said that the action would have to be answered for to the Senate. No further discussion occurred.[6]

By inheriting the imperial household, the *domus Caesaris*, Tiberius controlled greater material resources than were available to any other Roman, either in a private capacity or as a magistrate. Caesar owned property throughout the empire; he commanded procurators in every province to look after his interests (even when they conflicted with those of the governor, whether pro-magistrate or legate), and consequently was served by a more effective network for gathering information than

[6] On the accession, Timpe 1962 (c 403). Tiberius writes to armies: Dio LVII.2.1. Postumus: Jameson 1975 (c 126). The 'false Postumus': Tac. *Ann.* II.39.

was available to anyone else, including the magistrates at Rome. He also inherited the loyalty and gratitude which every Roman in public life owed to his predecessor in return for the patronage which Augustus had bestowed (and which Tiberius ensured would not be forgotten: see the *Res Gestae Divi Augusti*). That this made Tiberius the undisputed ruler of Rome from the moment of Augustus' death was beyond question. That fact was symbolically recognized by the oath to protect him and the rest of the *domus* whose *paterfamilias* he had now become, taken as soon as they heard the news by the consuls, and the prefects of the praetorian guard and of the corn supply, and then administered to the Senate, the equestrian *ordo* and the Roman people. Similar oaths were subsequently sworn by communities elsewhere in the empire; a copy of an oath to Tiberius and his whole household taken by the cities of Cyprus survives. This oath illustrates the dependence of groups as well as individual magistrates on the head of the imperial family as the source of patronage, honour and decision-making. But – unlike the *sacramentum*, the military oath taken by a soldier to the emperor as his commander-in-chief – its force was private and personal, not public or constitutional. An emperor's power and influence as Caesar may be distinguished from the public powers conferred upon him by the Senate and people, the organs who alone had the right to grant him *imperium*, the power to command. Later imperial candidates realized that the moment they controlled the imperial household, the award of public titles and offices by Senate and people would be a formality; in A.D. 14, in the absence of any historical precedent, the distinction was very clear, and Tiberius took pains to act with complete constitutional propriety. He could not take public acquiescence in his accession for granted. Velleius Paterculus refers to fears of disorder, confirmed by the posting of large numbers of troops at Augustus' funeral.[7]

Tiberius accompanied Augustus' body on its ceremonial return to Rome, just as twenty-two years before he had accompanied the body of his brother Drusus on its long journey back from northern Germany. The ceremonial procession, and the funeral itself, were to set precedents for the treatment of other members of the imperial family after their deaths. The public funeral was decreed at a meeting of the Senate early in September, convoked by Tiberius in virtue of his *tribunicia potestas* rather than his *imperium*. This does not mean that Tiberius thought that the *imperium maius* he had been granted in the previous year did not suffice to make him a legitimate emperor; but it does suggest that there was uncertainty about whether Augustus' responsibility (referred to in Tacitus as his *cura* or *munera*) for governing the empire had lapsed at his

---

[7] *EJ*² 105 = *AN* 551. Cf. Price 1984 (F 199) (and ch. 16 below). Fears for stability: Vell. Pat. II.124.

death. Augustus' will was read to the Senate. It confirmed Tiberius as principal heir; he was awarded two thirds of Augustus' property, and the remaining third went to Livia. Historians have made much of the opening words of the will, stating that Augustus wanted Tiberius to be his heir because 'a cruel fate' had taken away his own (adopted) sons (and natural grandsons) Gaius and Lucius. This was not a calculated or even unintended insult to Tiberius, suggesting that he was only a second best as successor, but an explanation for why Augustus had adopted as his son and instituted as his heir someone from outside the Julian family. These words can only have been intended to strengthen further the legitimacy of Tiberius' position as head of the *domus Caesaris* – particularly since no mention was made of Agrippa Postumus.

On 17 September, after the funeral, there was a second meeting of the Senate, at which it was reported that Augustus' spirit had been seen rising to heaven in the form of an eagle while the body was being cremated. If the Senate chose to believe this testimony, it would be powerful evidence in favour of the proposition that Augustus had now joined the Olympians; the Senate chose to believe, and accepted the consequence, that a cult ought to be formally established by the Roman state to worship the new god.

Turning next to the matters of this world, the Senate had to give its opinion on what was to happen to Augustus' responsibilities now that he had departed the scene. Tacitus does not explicitly tell us what motion was debated. It cannot have been to advise the people to grant Tiberius *imperium*, since he already had that; nor to define his *provincia*, since that had presumably been done when he was given *maius imperium* to equal that of Augustus in A.D. 13. Probably the point at issue was whether Tiberius should be asked to undertake the whole of Augustus' *cura*, his oversight of political (and especially foreign and military) affairs.[8] Tiberius pointed out that these responsibilities were vast; he wondered whether there was any case for sharing them. Tacitus tells us that one of the senators, Asinius Gallus, was quick to agree with this suggestion.

At this point in his narrative Tacitus reports a story that Augustus had once suggested that, apart from Tiberius, there were other persons who were 'capable of being emperor', *capaces imperii*. He names them as M. Lepidus, Asinius Gallus and L. Arruntius (or alternatively Cn. Piso). Tacitus does not give us the exact context of this statement; it may have been invented by an earlier historian. It may be more than a coincidence that two of those named were the fathers of men who were later themselves to lay claim to the Principate. The son of Marcus (rather than Manius, as printed in most editions of Tacitus since the seventeenth century) Aemilius Lepidus (cos. A.D. 6) was first trusted, and then

[8] Liebeschuetz 1986 (C 163); cf. Tac. *Ann.* I.11: 'partem curarum'.

executed, by Caligula; Lucius Arruntius (also cos. A.D. 6) was the son of one of Octavian's commanders at Actium, and adopted as his own son Camillus Scribonianus, who was to rebel against Claudius in 42; and various Julio-Claudian emperors felt themselves threatened by men called Piso. Whatever lies behind the anecdote, it raises the question what the source would be from which an alternative leader might derive his authority. Tacitus' account is intended to suggest that at the beginning of Tiberius' reign, there still existed political figures whose power was independent of the backing of the *princeps*. The fourth man named was the Asinius Gallus who took up Tiberius' question as to whether the *cura* borne by Augustus ought to be divided. He was the son of Asinius Pollio, one of the early generals of Octavian during the 40s and 30s B.C., but by no means a constant and unquestioning supporter. Virgil had dedicated the Fourth ('Messianic') *Eclogue* to Pollio; and Gallus is said to have told the literary critic Asconius Pedianus that he himself was the promised Messiah. According to Tacitus, it was Augustus' opinion that Gallus was incapable of exercising imperial power, but avid for it. Tiberius could not forget that after Augustus had forced him to divorce Vipsania, a woman he genuinely loved, in favour of Augustus' own daughter Iulia (and that was not a happy marriage), it was Gallus who married Vipsania.[9]

Gallus had implied that Tiberius could not shoulder Augustus' responsibilities alone. Tiberius could not conceal his displeasure; Gallus backtracked by pretending that he had made the point only in order to prove that imperial power could not in fact be divided. The episode raises the question of Tiberius' honesty in claiming that he did not want the imperial office. Contemporary evidence shows that Tiberius himself was worried about his reputation for disguising his real intentions, *dissimulatio*, a quality without which he might well have failed to live through Augustus' reign.[10] Later emperors at their accession went through a pretence of rejecting the offer of imperial power; in Tiberius' case, such a *recusatio imperii* might have been misunderstood because there was no precedent for it. If Tiberius was genuine in not wishing to take on all Augustus' responsibilities, this is hardly likely to have been because he was afraid that his claims would be disputed by one, or possibly several, other candidates. Velleius Paterculus tells of the fear and uncertainty that filled Rome at the time of Augustus' death; not everyone believed that the transfer of power would run smoothly. But Velleius also makes it clear that the three main concentrations of legions, in Spain, the Balkans, and on the Rhine, were all in the hands of generals

---

[9] 'Capaces imperii': Tac. *Ann.* 1.13.2. Gallus: Oliver 1947 (C 382); Shotter 1971 (C 393). On M. Lepidus, Syme 1970 (B 178).

[10] On the *Tabula Siarensis* and Tiberius' *dissimulatio*: González 1984 (B 234); Zecchini 1986 (B 301).

loyal to Tiberius. In Spain there was Marcus Lepidus (the consul of A.D. 6), who had been Tiberius' legate in putting down the Pannonian revolt between A.D. 6 and 9; in Pannonia, Tiberius had his own legates, in particular Iunius Blaesus, and Germany was governed by Tiberius' adopted son Germanicus. Tiberius had nothing to fear from any of these generals; the soldiers themselves were not to transfer their allegiance without trouble, but that was a question of discipline, not of high politics. Even if Tiberius had already heard of the mutinies in the Pannonian army which broke out as soon as the troops heard of the death of Augustus, the commander to whom they had taken their oaths of military service, it does not follow that such a threat of rebellion would have been a real reason for declining the imperial office.

The Senate duly confirmed Tiberius' succession to the *cura* bestowed on his predecessor (and also granted him the title Augustus). Tiberius' were not the only powers the Senate was required to confirm. On the occasion when Augustus had adopted Tiberius into the Julian household, he had also made him adopt Germanicus, the son of Tiberius' younger brother Drusus and of Antonia, daughter of Mark Antony and Augustus' sister Octavia. This formally made Germanicus Tiberius' eldest son. Tiberius, in A.D. 14, was fifty-five. Should anything happen to him, it would be Germanicus who would succeed as head of the *domus Caesaris.*

The same session of the Senate also proposed to vote honours to Livia; Tiberius expressed reservations about these, possibly because he was embarrassed by suggestions that he derived his position from his mother's influence over Augustus. Other decisions relating to the extent of Tiberius' *cura* for the state were taken at the same meeting; in particular, Tacitus says that Tiberius proclaimed a change in the procedures for nominating candidates for magistracies. In future, the list of nominations would be discussed by the Senate; four of the praetorships would be filled by persons recommended by Tiberius, the other places would be open to any candidates selected by the Senate (though clearly the support of the *princeps* would be decisive here too). Formally, the list would then go before the *comitia centuriata* for approval, just as had happened in republican times; but competition for the votes of the people now became a pure formality for candidates for the praetorship (as it had been for candidates for the consulship since the time of Julius Caesar). Candidates needed the support only of the emperor and of the Senate. An important effect of this was to make it unnecessary for quaestors and aediles who had an eye on a praetorship to win the favour of the Roman plebs by putting on spectacular games. The giving of games was one of the principal ways in which those who participated in public life advertised their prestige. The poverty of such spectacles under Tiberius is an aspect of the concentration of power in the hands of the *princeps*, to the detriment both of the senatorial elite and of the people.[11]

Apart from the imperial household, the Senate and the people, the emperor also had to control the army: as we have seen, Tiberius' first act after Augustus' death was to inform every provincial army. Tacitus describes in great detail the mutinies of the two most powerful groups of legions, on the Rhine and the Danube; but we should not assume that they were a serious threat in the same way as apparently similar events were in A.D. 69 and A.D. 97. Augustus' death gave the Roman conscripts serving in Pannonia and Germany an opportunity to express their long-repressed resentment at their terms of service. The Roman soldier's oath of loyalty was not only to the *res publica*, but to the individual *imperator* who had called him up for that particular campaign. This was the first time in almost half a century that an *imperator* had died and needed to be replaced by a new one – albeit one who had seen many years' service both in Pannonia and Germany. It was an appropriate occasion to demand improvements in conditions of service. Tacitus describes these events as a complete collapse of discipline, and maximizes both the moral disgrace and the potential danger to Tiberius. He and other historians following the same sources (probably Pliny the Elder's *Histories of the German Wars* and the younger Agrippina's memoirs) agree that the Pannonian mutiny was comparatively easy to control. The mutiny on the Rhine was politically more significant because of the presence there of Germanicus, whom these sources wish to represent as a potential alternative emperor.[12]

Tacitus' account of the unrest among the Pannonian legions includes a speech encapsulating the soldiers' (largely legitimate) grievances, such as long terms of service, often over twenty years, low pay and the deduction of money to buy exemption from unpleasant duties, and the quality of the land allotments granted to soldiers by the *aerarium militare* on completion of their period of service. The speech is attributed to Percennius, said to have been a professional claque-manager for the Roman theatre-audiences before having been called up during the emergency levy that followed the destruction of Varus' three legions just five years previously. The Pannonian commander, Quintus Iunius Blaesus (cons. A.D. 10; uncle of the praetorian prefect L. Aelius Seianus) was unable to prevent his soldiers from looting civilian settlements. Although he promised to send his son, a tribune, to Rome at the head of a delegation to request improved terms of service, he was only able to

---

[11] Elections: Levick 1967 (c 365).
[12] On the military *sacramentum*: Campbell 1984 (D 173), pp. 19ff. Mutinies: Schmitt 1958 (c 391); Sutherland 1987 (B 358) ch. 16.

reimpose discipline when Tiberius' son Drusus arrived on the scene with two praetorian cohorts commanded by Sejanus (now described as co-prefect of the guard along with his father, Lucius Seius Strabo). Tacitus describes Tiberius' decision to send his son as though it was a response to a major threat; but we should remember that the theme of civil discord is basic to the *Annals*.

The story told by Tacitus implies that the mutineers were by no means inclined to accept Drusus' promise to refer their complaints to Tiberius as their commander, and through him to the Senate. But a coincidental eclipse of the moon on the night of 25-6 September served them as an excuse to back down, enabling Drusus to execute the two ringleaders and return to Rome without even bothering to await the return of the soldiers' delegation to Tiberius.

The legions on the Lower Rhine, under the command of Aulus Caecina Severus, also used the death of the *imperator* to whom they had sworn their military oath as an occasion to express their discontent about the unremitting military operations which Augustus had imposed upon them for so many years. One theme which runs through Tacitus' account of the politics of Tiberius' reign is the conflict between the widow and children of Germanicus on the one hand, and Tiberius and his direct descendants on the other. Even if this analysis (probably going back to the younger Agrippina's memoirs) were correct, it would be wrong to accept the implication that Germanicus was a rival or a threat to Tiberius during his lifetime. On the contrary, there is epigraphical and other evidence that Germanicus was recognized as Tiberius' successor by men who had no wish to show disloyalty to Tiberius himself. When Ovid, in exile at Tomi on the Black Sea, addressed Germanicus as a *princeps*, he will hardly have assumed that he would be understood to want Germanicus to be emperor in Tiberius' place.[13]

According to Tacitus, the major difference between the mutinies in Pannonia and on the Rhine was that some of the soldiers on the Rhine offered to make Germanicus emperor if he acceded to their demands. We may be sceptical about how serious this offer was; an anecdote about a soldier who was prepared to help kill Germanicus himself is just as likely to be authentic. Whatever the political significance of the mutiny, it is clear from Tacitus' account that (some) soldiers who had completed long terms of service had to be discharged, and that in return the legions on both the lower and the upper Rhine were prepared to take the military oath to their new *imperator*. But the arrival at Ara Ubiorum (Cologne) of a delegation of senators sent by Tiberius led to renewed outbreaks of insubordination, since the soldiers correctly feared that Tiberius would

---

[13] Ov. *Fast.* 1.19. G. Herbert-Brown, *Ovid and the Fasti* (Oxford, 1994), ch. 5. An Ephesian inscription describes Germanicus and Drusus together as the 'New Dioscuri' (*SEG* IV.515).

use the authority of the Senate as an excuse to reject the newly won concessions. The legate Lucius Munatius Plancus, who had been consul in the previous year, was humiliated; and Germanicus ostentatiously sent his wife and children (including the two-year-old Gaius, often dressed in 'little boots' – hence his later name Caligula) away to safety at Trier. Tacitus suggests that the mutiny was now so serious that Germanicus should have called on the upper Rhine legions to suppress it by force; in fact he seems to have been able to restore order without difficulty at Cologne, and Caecina was able to do the same for the two legions stationed at Xanten (when Germanicus inspected the bodies of those executed, he claimed to be appalled at the catastrophe). The mutinies on the Rhine and in Pannonia were not unimportant, but they were by no means the threat either to Rome or to Tiberius that Tacitus, or his sources, imply. Spectacular though the mutinies may have been, they were an expression of Augustus' failure, or inability, to provide for the real costs of his military policy, rather than a threat to Tiberius.

II. THE REIGN OF TIBERIUS[14]

In the autumn of A.D. 14, and during the following two summers, Germanicus employed his legions on a series of campaigns east of the Rhine. Both archaeological and literary evidence indicates that there was no serious attempt to expand the territory under direct Roman control. These campaigns were fought for reasons of prestige, both for Rome – whose reputation for military success had to be re-established after the Varus disaster of A.D. 9 – and for Germanicus himself. The fact that Germanicus received the news of Augustus' death while organizing a census of the Gallic provinces suggests that Augustus himself had planned these campaigns; they did not contradict the advice he allegedly appended to his summary of the resources of the empire, that its borders should not be expanded. Augustus' advice to his heir to restrict the opportunities for commanders to acquire military *gloria* was not intended to apply to Tiberius' own adopted successor. Tacitus' belief that historiographical literature required long military narratives, coupled with his desire to heroize Germanicus, gave him the opportunity for an epic account of a visit to the site of the defeat of Varus' army and the reburial of the corpses of the slain, and of a heroic retreat through the north German marshes. This does not hide the fact that Germanicus achieved nothing of permanence – and probably did not intend to.[15]

We should not accept Tacitus' suggestion that Tiberius was jealous of any successes Germanicus might achieve, and therefore recalled him

---

[14] Tiberius' reign: see n. 5 above. The main narrative sources are: Tac. *Ann.* I–VI; Suet. *Tib.*; Dio, LVII–LVIII; Vell. Pat. II.123–31, with Woodman 1977 (B 202).   [15] Koestermann 1957 (C 362).

after two years. He wanted to make it clear to the Germans that Augustus' death did not mean the end of Roman military efforts on the northern frontiers. He also wanted Germanicus to win enough glory to make his *virtus* manifest; consequently he awarded his adopted son and successor a full triumph, the highest mark of military distinction, in A.D. 17. In the following year Tiberius made Germanicus' position as his designated successor explicit by sharing his third consulship with him.

It was because of a genuine concern that his successor should have the experience required of a ruler that Tiberius sent Germanicus on a tour of the eastern half of the empire in this year. There were precedents from the Augustan period: Agrippa, Tiberius himself, and Gaius Caesar had all ruled the east of the empire for a time when they had been heirs-apparent. Some practical tasks had to be performed. King Archelaus of Cappadocia had died at Rome in A.D. 17 (of natural causes, but exacerbated by the hostility shown by his *patronus* Tiberius). In order to help solve the shortage of funds for military pay, Tiberius wanted Cappadocia integrated into the empire as a province (see ch. 14*a*). Germanicus was also to oversee the fiscal administration of Palmyra, and inspect earthquake damage suffered by several cities of Asia in A.D. 17. As his adviser Tiberius appointed Cnaeus Calpurnius Piso – who had been his colleague as consul in 7 B.C. – to accompany him as legate of Syria. Tacitus insinuates that the intention was to use Piso to control Germanicus. If we abandon the idea that Tiberius and Germanicus mistrusted each other, then Piso's task as a trusted *amicus* of the *domus Caesaris* was simply to give support and advice. But Piso's advice was irksome to Germanicus; it may be that he restrained Germanicus from engaging in unnecessary military adventures against the Parthians to enhance his own glory. In any case, Piso's bad temper was notorious. Germanicus avoided further advice from Piso by travelling to Egypt (from which Roman senators were excluded), where his attempts to win popularity by opening the grain reserves may have had the effect of exacerbating a grain shortage at Rome. Tiberius was displeased, and Piso misinterpreted his displeasure as permission to quarrel with Germanicus. Germanicus formally renounced the *amicitia* between Piso and the *domus Caesaris*. Piso had no option but to leave Syria. Unfortunately Germanicus died soon after (10 October A.D. 19), and Piso (despite the warnings of his *consilium*) thought he could return to take control of his province again. If Germanicus had acted provocatively, Piso's reaction was simply treasonable; he was arrested and sent to Rome to be tried before the Senate on the charge of having waged war on a province of the Roman people. Agrippina, bearing the ashes of her husband to Rome with her, saw to it that he was also accused of having had Germanicus poisoned; the charge was pressed by Publius Vitellius, who had been one of Germanicus' generals in Germany and whose brothers were to be loyal supporters of Germanicus' son Caligula and brother Claudius. There was no evidence to support it. But despite Tiberius' efforts to ensure that the affair was handled openly and fairly, Piso's suicide was later taken as a sign that he had done away with Germanicus – on Tiberius' orders.[16]

The death of Germanicus meant that Tiberius' other son, his natural son Drusus, was now the heir-apparent. That is suggested by coins celebrating the birth of Drusus' twin sons in A.D. 19/20 (only one, known as Tiberius Gemellus, was to survive). Drusus' position was fully confirmed when Tiberius shared his fourth consulship with him in A.D. 21; and in April 22 he was formally granted *tribunicia potestas*. Agrippina may have felt that Fortune had cheated her of the chance of becoming an emperor's wife, but she was not justified in laying the blame for this on Tiberius; nor is there evidence that she did so at this stage. It was in the memoirs of her daughter, Agrippina the Younger, that the picture of Germanicus as a new Alexander, poisoned in his prime, was created, and Tiberius attacked for failing to mourn him properly – though we may note that Tiberius made a point of his *moderatio* in mourning all his relatives, as in other respects; Seneca refers to the restraint he had shown when he had to arrange the obsequies for his own brother, Drusus, in 9 B.C.[17]

This *moderatio* did not imply restraint in protecting himself against those foolish enough to think that they had a claim to be emperor in his place. Accusations of sorcery were brought against Marcus Scribonius Libo, a great-grandson of Pompey and grand-nephew of Scribonia, who had been Augustus' wife and the mother of the elder Iulia; he was convicted (3 September A.D. 16), and on his aunt's advice killed himself.[18] And despite insinuations to the contrary, Tiberius exercised his *cura* over the provinces efficiently – taking care that too much military virtue should not be displayed by provincial governors. The need to suppress a rebellion in the province of Africa led by a romanized military leader called Tacfarinas brought into the open the question of whom the emperor could trust, and whom he could not. The proconsul of Africa was the only man apart from the *princeps* who commanded a legion under his own *imperium* (though the emperor would take the credit for his victories, too). Tiberius asked the Senate to appoint an extraordinary commander. Two candidates were proposed, both presumably known

[16] Koestermann 1958 (C 363); Hennig 1972 (C 353); Sutherland 1987 (B 358) ch. 19. On Tiberius' own network of patronage in the East, Levick 1971 (C 156). Piso's temper: Sen. *Ira* 1.18.3ff. Egypt: EJ² 320, 379 = *AN* 557, 558. Funeral honours for Germanicus: González 1984 (B 234).
[17] Drusus' twins: EJ² 91. *Moderatio*: Levick 1976 (C 366); Sutherland 1987 (B 358), ch. 23.
[18] Libo: Weinrib 1967 (C 411)

to be loyal servants of the *princeps*: Marcus Lepidus and Iunius Blaesus (suffect consul in A.D. 10). Perhaps out of deference to Blaesus' nephew Sejanus, Tiberius' trusted praetorian prefect, Lepidus withdrew his candidature. Blaesus would not misuse the *ornamenta triumphalia* he was awarded for the expected victory.

Gaul, too, suffered from rebellion at this time, because of heavier taxation to pay for the army and perhaps also as a result of the cessation of military activity involving Gallic units in Roman operations against Germany. Tacitus' account mentions the leaders as Florus and Sacrovir, and implies that druids were involved. But he describes the crisis very much in terms of Vindex's uprising in A.D. 68, criticizing Tiberius for failing to go in person to defeat the rebels as though he was behaving as thoughtlessly as Nero did in 68.

One of the roots of Tiberius' later reputation for failing to exercise the responsibilities of an emperor was his own emphasis on *moderatio*, including a willingness to allow a plurality of opinions to be aired in the Senate when what senators wanted him to do was give a clear indication of what his own *sententia* was. Another was his lack of interest in spectacles – when the people of Trebia asked him what to do with money their city had been left, he told them to build a road rather than a theatre. Most crucially, he was physically absent from Rome. Augustus had often been away from the capital, but that was to take command of wars or to supervise provincial affairs. Tiberius went to Campania, where rich Romans had traditionally spent their holidays. His reasons may sometimes have been valid – between A.D. 21–22 he spent twenty months away from Rome, probably to avoid a period of pestilence. When his mother fell ill, Tiberius returned at once.[19]

But Tiberius' absences resulted in a failure to control proceedings in the Senate. That was one of the elements responsible for the series of accusations of treason, *maiestas*, which made his reign so distasteful to later senatorial historians. For ambitious men with rhetorical ability, such prosecutions were the most effective way to get to the top now that Tiberius' policy of military retrenchment made it more difficult for 'new men' to demonstrate their *virtus* in the military field. A successful prosecutor would manage to eliminate a personal enemy, win acclaim for his rhetorical ability, receive at least one quarter of the goods of the convicted, and gain the emperor's gratitude – possibly resulting in appointment to the highest offices. While Tiberius remained in Rome, he did his best to restrain *delatores* in order to minimize the insecurity they created. Tacitus suggests, and coins confirm, that Tiberius made much of his self-restraint, *moderatio*, in rejecting the weapon of *maiestas-*

---

[19] Trebia: Suet. *Tib.* 31. Tiberius' absences from Rome: Syme 1986 (A 95) 24; Stewart 1977 (F 583), Orth 1970 (C 384), Houston 1985 (C 357). Livia: Sutherland 1987 (B 358) ch. 20.

accusations against senators during these years. The emperor could intervene to exercise the imperial virtue of *clementia*; in A.D. 22 he allowed Decimus Iunius Silanus to return from the exile that had been forced upon him when Augustus had revoked his *amicitia* because of Decimus' association with the younger Iulia during the crisis of A.D. 8. Tiberius did not, however, feel that Decimus could be allowed to return to public life.[20]

Another important effect of Tiberius' absences from the capital was to increase the importance of Aelius Sejanus, now the sole praetorian prefect, as the channel of communication between senators and the emperor. During these years Sejanus greatly strengthened his police powers in Rome by concentrating the praetorian cohorts in a single, permanent camp (one of the first military camps to have a permanent stone wall). There is no reason to believe that the immediate objective was anything more sinister than to impose better discipline on the soldiers; but the camp was also a suitable place to keep political prisoners.

The death of Drusus on 14 September A.D. 23 ended for the time being any hopes Tiberius had of leaving his power in the hands of a son, natural or adopted, who would be old enough and experienced enough to rule. Perhaps Drusus would not have been an ideal emperor. Like his father, he was a heavy drinker; it was said that he had once physically attacked Sejanus during a drinking party. The story was one of the arguments later advanced in support of allegations that Sejanus had poisoned Drusus, but these inventions postdated Sejanus' fall; the two had been loyal colleagues and friends for many years, and the summer of A.D. 23 was another particularly unhealthy one. Tiberius made a point of being present in Rome to give the funeral speech.

The question of the succession was now open again. By early A.D. 23, two of Germanicus' sons had already come of age; to strengthen their position, their mother Agrippina asked Tiberius to provide her with a new husband. It is possible that she had Asinius Gallus in mind. One of his sons, Asinius Saloninus, had been betrothed to a daughter of Germanicus, but died in A.D. 22, before the marriage could take place; two other sons of Gallus were consuls during these years, C. Asinius Pollio in 23, and Marcus Asinius Agrippa in 25 (but he died in the following year). Tiberius would not allow Nero and Drusus to come under the protection of such a powerful stepfather, particularly one whom he loathed.

The emperor's concern that Germanicus' sons might replace him was

[20] Bauman 1974 (F 641). Nero cut rewards to one fourth: Suet. *Ner.* 10. *Dig.* 37.14.10 (Antistius Labeo) on the accused's immediate exclusion from the emperor's *amicitia*. *Moderatio* and *clementia*: n. 17 above.

shared by the praetorian prefect Sejanus. Sejanus' own interest in
Tiberius' survival was illustrated by an incident in A.D. 26.[21] While
Tiberius was on his way to his villa at Capri, part of the ceiling of a grotto
near Terracina collapsed on the imperial party during a dinner. Sejanus
threw himself upon Tiberius, convincing him of the genuineness of his
loyalty. In the previous year Tiberius had had doubts about Sejanus: he
refused a request that he should be allowed to marry Drusus' widow
Livilla (Livia Iulia). Sejanus may have been a loyal supporter of the
dynasty, like his father and perhaps grandfather before him, but that did
not give him sufficient status to rank with the republican nobility. Even
his wife's family had only been consular for one generation. In Tiberius'
opinion, Sejanus would not have had the political influence needed to
protect Tiberius Gemellus against the claims of Agrippina's children. In
any case, he had every intention of remaining alive for many years to
come, and was supported in this by the prognostications of his personal
astrologer Thrasyllus.

Tiberius had been 66 in the previous November. At an age when other
Roman senators could look forward to retiring from public life, he saw
no escape from the responsibilities inherited from Augustus. It is not
surprising that he should have preferred to stay away from Rome, even
for the funeral of his mother Livia in A.D. 29. The question of the
succession will have been a major source of conflict between mother and
son; Tiberius Gemellus was Livia's great-grandson, but so (through
Drusus) were Agrippina's three sons, and Augustus had clearly indicated in his will that the succession should ultimately go to them. So long
as Livia was alive, she could protect them against Tiberius' displeasure.
Livia's funeral oration was given by Gaius Caligula, whom Livia had
taken into her own *domus*. Soon after the funeral, Sejanus had Agrippina,
Nero and Drusus arrested. Caligula had not been allowed to don the *toga
virilis* yet, and consequently could not be treated as a political threat. He
moved to the house of his grandmother the younger Antonia, who
protected the interests of the supporters of her son Germanicus as well as
she could during the years of Sejanus' supremacy.

Following her funeral, Livia was awarded full divine honours by the
Senate, similar to those awarded to her husband on his death (there were
minor differences, as protocol required; for instance the image of the
divus was carried by a four-horse chariot, while the *diva Augusta* had to be
satisfied with two horses). Her will was notable for the enormous legacy
she bestowed on the young Servius Sulpicius Galba (born 3 B.C.); a
relative of Livia's, Livia Ocellina, was his stepmother and had adopted
him. Tiberius was understandably upset by the size of the legacy – 50
million sesterces – and apparently held back even the revised sum of

500,000 he was prepared to countenance. Galba's elder brother (cos. A.D. 22) had already attracted his disfavour, and was later forced to commit suicide (c. A.D. 36). Livia's legacy demonstrated both her displeasure at her son and a belief that Galba was worthy of holding a central position on the public stage. After Livia's death, Galba had the support of Antonia (and later of Caligula). His wife was probably the daughter of M. Aemilius Lepidus, *capax imperii*, the consul of A.D. 6; another of Lepidus' daughters married Drusus, son of Germanicus. Galba himself had already won the praetorship (it is not certain in what year he held it, but we are told of the tightrope-walking elephants he presented at the Floralia). In A.D. 33, he was *consul ordinarius*. It is not surprising that Tiberius, having worked out his horoscope, should have said that the young Galba was destined to be emperor one day.

Although Tacitus insinuates that one of Tiberius' main motives for leaving Rome had been to avoid his mother, her death made him no more willing to return. His absence did not mean that he ceased to control the empire; but it allowed Sejanus to monopolize the information and advice about events in the capital on the basis of which Tiberius' decisions were taken. Sejanus had already made clear to the emperor his readiness to marry Drusus' widow Livilla, and thus immediately become the stepfather of Tiberius' grandson and intended successor, and in due course perhaps the father of further children who would be eligible for imperial office. So long as Sejanus' stepson, or his own children, were still too young for this office, he could fulfil the role that Augustus had intended Tiberius to play for Germanicus. Tiberius understood this ambition, though it is not clear whether he was now prepared to allow the marriage.[22] What he did do was appoint Sejanus, although he was not a senator, *consul ordinarius* for A.D. 31, and he publicly demonstrated the extent to which the praetorian prefect was 'partner of his labours' by holding his own fifth consulship as Sejanus' colleague. His third consulship had been held with Germanicus, his fourth with Drusus: in both cases this was a way of indicating who was the heir-apparent. Sejanus' election was held on the Aventine hill, traditionally associated with the urban plebs, and the gifts and shows granted on this occasion were for them a welcome contrast to the neglect which Tiberius' electoral reforms had occasioned, since such bids for popularity now normally had little point.[23]

For Tiberius, the public recognition of another potential successor could only increase his freedom of manoeuvre *vis-à-vis* the children of

[22] Only a late source, John of Antioch (*FHG* IV.570) states that Tiberius 'called him his child [ie., son-in-law] and successor'.

[23] Syme 1956 (B 288). The *inprobae comitiae* are mentioned in *ILS* 6044 = EJ² 53 = *AN* 101. On Sejanus, Meise 1969 (C 375) ch. 4; Hennig 1975 (C 354); Woodman 1977 (B 202).

Agrippina. For Sejanus, on the other hand, the elimination of Agrippina's children as candidates was essential for the success of his dynastic
ambitions. Nero and Drusus were accused of plotting against the
emperor by a relative of Sejanus, Cassius Longinus (probably Lucius,
who was *consul ordinarius* in A.D. 30, rather than his brother Gaius, the
famous jurist (see ch. 21), who was a suffect consul in the same year). The
fact that the Cassii Longini were related to the Caesaricide Cassius did
not make them republicans, though that was what Gaius was to be
accused of by Nero after the conspiracy of Piso many years later. The
threat posed by Nero and Drusus to Tiberius and to the succession of
Gemellus (with or without Sejanus as his stepfather) was real. Even after
the elimination of Sejanus, Tiberius took no steps to release Drusus from
prison. It is likely that Agrippina and her sons, seeing the danger that
Sejanus represented, thought it necessary to plan for Tiberius' removal
before Sejanus' position had become unchallengeable.

It was Germanicus' mother the younger Antonia, the young men's
grandmother, who warned Tiberius in a letter delivered to him personally through her freedman M. Antonius Pallas that Sejanus' consolidation of his power was not just aimed against Agrippina and her
children, but beginning to threaten Tiberius' own chances of political
survival. With Sejanus as protector of Tiberius' heir, and no other
candidates for the Principate surviving, Tiberius' own role would have
been played out. And given that it was Sejanus who was responsible for
Tiberius' personal security, Antonia must have pointed out to him that
Sejanus would have no further interest in keeping Tiberius alive once
Agrippina and her offspring no longer existed. It was a powerful
argument, and Tiberius summoned Germanicus' remaining son, Gaius
Caligula, to the safety of his household at Capri. He did not prevent
Sejanus from executing Nero.

In over seventeen years as emperor, Tiberius had not ordered the
execution of one single senator. The old man's well-planned and efficient
elimination of Sejanus on 18 October A.D. 31 consequently came as a
great shock to Rome. His agent was another equestrian public servant,
Sutorius Macro, prefect of the urban *vigiles*: he brought two letters from
Tiberius. One was read out to the Senate in Sejanus' presence; it was
lengthy and impenetrable (in Juvenal's words, 'grandis et verbosa') and
only after a long time did it come to the point: Sejanus was denounced as
a traitor. While the Senate, and Sejanus himself had been kept guessing,
Macro took command of the praetorians, authorized by Tiberius' second
letter. Sejanus had expected to be granted *tribunicia potestas* as Tiberius'
colleague. Instead he found himself stripped of his office and arrested.
He was executed the same day; so were his wife and daughter. It was

claimed that eight years before, Sejanus and Livilla had together poisoned Tiberius' son, Livilla's husband Drusus.

Sejanus' fall enabled a number of figures who had been supporters of Germanicus to return to the centre of the political stage, under the protection of the younger Antonia. Some of them were to give support to the regimes of her grandson Caligula, and then her son Claudius. Lucius Vitellius, who was to become Claudius' principal adviser and the father of another later emperor, was *consul ordinarius* in A.D. 34, and in 35 a suffect consulship was held by his friend Valerius Asiaticus from Vienne, whose son was to be betrothed to the emperor Vitellius' daughter, and whose grandson was to be a powerful figure into the next century (M. Lollius Paulinus Decimus Valerius Asiaticus Saturninus, cos. A.D. 94, cos. II A.D. 125). Flavius Sabinus (*praefectus urbi* under Nero, Otho and Vitellius, and the brother of Vespasian), entered the Senate in A.D. 34 or 35. Galba has already been mentioned; his successor as suffect consul in A.D. 33 was Lucius Salvius Otho, whose father, a *novus homo*, had reached the praetorship early in Tiberius' reign as a result of the favour of Livia. Otho's daughter had once been betrothed to Germanicus' son Drusus; his elder son Lucius Titianus was to reach the consulship in 52, become proconsul of Asia, and like his father, *promagister* of the Arval Brethren; his younger son became emperor.[24]

On the other hand the overthrow of Sejanus did not make any difference to Tiberius' hostility to Agrippina herself. Neither she nor Drusus were released from prison or exile, and they both died in A.D. 33. Her daughters could be made harmless without being killed. In 33, Tiberius married Drusilla to Lucius Cassius Longinus, and Germanicus' youngest daughter, Iulia Livilla, to the powerful and loyal Marcus Vinicius; his grandfather, the consul of 19 B.C., had been one of Tiberius' early generals in Illyricum and won the *ornamenta triumphalia* for his services in Germany. The father, *consul ordinarius* in A.D. 2, was highly regarded as an orator; Vinicius himself had been consul in A.D. 30 (the year in which Velleius Paterculus dedicated his history to him), and perhaps was among those who felt insulted, if not threatened, by Sejanus' predominance. By entrusting Livilla to him, Tiberius was marking him out as someone to whom the empire too might be entrusted; and indeed (despite Caligula's banishment of Livilla in 39)

---

[24] The prosopography of individuals' careers and family relationships often has to be based on epigraphical evidence and chance remarks in literature. Many questions remain unresolved (e.g. the relationship to each other and to the Caesars of different Scribonii and Pisones). Family background was an essential element of imperial biography, but even Suetonius' lives (*Galba, Otho, Vitellius* and *Divus Vespasianus*) contain unreliable or ambiguous statements. For Valerius Asiaticus, cf. Tac. *Hist.* 1.59; for the clients of Germanicus and Antonia the Younger, see Gallotta 1988 (C 348); Kokkinos 1992 (C 364).

Vinicius was powerful enough to be the major contender for the succession after Caligula's removal in 41. The third daughter, Agrippina the Younger, had already been married in A.D. 28, to Cn. Domitius Ahenobarbus (cos. A.D. 32). Through his mother Antonia the Elder, he was the grandson of Mark Antony and Augustus' sister Octavia. It is hardly surprising that the couple avoided having children so long as Tiberius was alive. Only in the last year of Tiberius' life was Ahenobarbus exiled on a charge of incest with his sister, Domitia Lepida. Tiberius also forced Asinius Gallus to end his life in A.D. 33, after three years of house-arrest. Tiberius' hatred for him went much further back than Gallus' association with Agrippina and alleged support for Sejanus. Nevertheless three of his sons survived to take office again under Caligula (Servius Asinius Celer, cos. 38, executed in 47; Asinius Gallus, banished in 46; and Asinius Pollio, proconsul of Asia 38/39).

Tacitus notes that the attacks on Sejanus and Livilla in the Senate were led by 'men with the great names Scipio, Silanus, Cassius'. If Tacitus wished to imply that the political significance of these men derived from their republican ancestry, that was not the whole story. Their links with the *domus Caesaris* mattered as much, if not more. These men, and others, used the freedom provided by Tiberius' absence from Rome to indulge in an orgy of recrimination, accusing their personal opponents of having been associated with Sejanus. Some of those who suffered were no doubt indeed close associates of Sejanus – though it is interesting that even his uncle, Quintus Iunius Blaesus, was not formally condemned and executed, but committed suicide after Tiberius renounced his *amicitia*. Blaesus' two sons even survived until 36. Indeed, some of those keenest to attack Sejanus' memory were related to him: the grandfather of the two Cassii, Quintus Aelius Tubero, had been Sejanus' stepfather. The trials of the next few years were certainly not the result of any plan by Tiberius to round up those who had participated in Sejanus' 'conspiracy' against him: there had been no such conspiracy.

But it suited other political figures to suggest that there had. The charge of association with Sejanus was used as a cover for political, family and personal hatreds in such a way as to give the impression that there must have been a major conspiracy organized by Sejanus in which half the Senate had been involved. Rumour exaggerated his power to such an extent that it was even said that Tiberius had given instructions that, if Sejanus' supporters in the praetorian guard posed a threat, Germanicus' children might have to be released from prison to act as a rallying-point for those loyal to the dynasty. But the minute number of those directly convicted of being Sejanus' associates suggests that they were not executed for being conspirators, but because they might resent the way in which a loyal servant and his wife and daughter had been dealt with by Tiberius. Had Sejanus managed to remove all the offspring of Germanicus, he might have been a real threat to Tiberius. As it was, the conspirator was not Sejanus, but Tiberius.

Tacitus blames Tiberius for the deaths of a considerable number of people accused of *maiestas* (as he does for virtually any other death during these years, whether from sickness or old age, like that of Manius Lepidus, or by suicide like that of L. Arruntius). If Tiberius was to blame, then it was by omission: his absence from Rome lifted any restraint on *delatores* who made use of treason-accusations to attack their personal rivals or simply to enrich themselves. *Maiestas*-accusations at this time had the great advantage to the accuser that they were based on the accused's dissatisfaction with an emperor; hence those accused lost the emperor's *amicitia* the moment they were charged, and that meant that their public careers (and usually their lives) came to an immediate end. One of the first to suffer this fate was C. Annius Pollio, accused in A.D. 32; he had been suffect consul in 21 or 22. His son Lucius Annius Vinicianus was accused with him, but was to survive to become consul suffect, probably under Caligula, and important enough to be considered an imperial candidate after Caligula's assassination. But not all treason-accusations resulted in conviction. One who survived was C. Appius Iunius Silanus (cos. 28).

Tiberius' main concern during these years continued to be to ensure the succession of his grandson Tiberius Gemellus. His astrologer seems to have persuaded him that he would survive to see Gemellus old enough to succeed him. Consequently there was no danger in honouring Caligula: he was made a member of the college of augurs and a pontifex and in 33 he held the office of quaestor. At some time during these years, Tiberius tried to bring Caligula more firmly under his control by marrying him to Iunia Claudilla, the daughter of his old supporter Marcus Silanus (cos. A.D. 15). Also in 33, Tiberius' granddaughter Livia Iulia was remarried; her husband was the relatively insignificant Gaius Rubellius Blandus (cos. suff. A.D. 18, and grandson of Tiberius' rhetoric teacher). Tiberius will have assumed that they and their descendants would represent no threat to Gemellus, though many years later Nero was to be sufficiently frightened of their son Rubellius Plautus to have him killed in A.D. 62. Together with Domitius Ahenobarbus, Marcus Vinicius and Cassius Longinus, Blandus was publicly honoured as one of the emperor's grandsons-in-law, *progeneri Caesaris*. When large areas of Rome were destroyed by fire in A.D. 36, the four of them were appointed to supervise the distribution of aid on Tiberius' behalf.[25]

Tiberius continued to carry out his other duties as *princeps* with equal efficiency. Not only did he help those members of the Roman plebs

[25] Blandus: Syme 1982 (C 401) *Progeneri Caesaris*: Tac. *Ann.* VI.45.3.

whose houses had been destroyed by fire, he intervened to avoid a major crisis of credit in A.D. 33, apparently caused by a shortage of coin; although the economic significance of Tiberius' actions has been grossly overestimated by modern historians applying anachronistic economic models to antiquity, it was thought to be part of an emperor's duties to ensure that the wealthy could feel secure in the possession of their property. In another respect too Tiberius' reign was a period when the security of those with property increased, through the continuing development of Roman jurisprudence by the so-called 'schools' of jurists whose legal opinions were backed by the emperor's authority. In comparison, Tiberius' own absence from the courtrooms of Rome will have made little difference, though it made life more difficult for those who sought privileges (and would have to travel to Campania) and was a major reason for the emperor's increasing unpopularity. Claudius attacked 'the constant absence of my uncle' in a surviving edict.[26]

It is less clear how much attention he devoted to providing good government for provincials; although he was credited with telling Aemilius Rectus, a later prefect of Egypt, that 'good governors shear their sheep, they do not strip them', there is no reason for believing that he took a personal interest in initiating accusations against governors for corruption, or that the reason why he left his legates in charge of the same province for years on end was that this would make them less greedy. Poppaeus Sabinus served as legate of Moesia from A.D. 11 until 35. Tiberius himself complained to the Senate about the unwillingness of consulars to accept their obligation to govern distant provinces. Nevertheless the old emperor was clearly afraid that change might mean trouble; Augustus too had kept governors on in their respective commands after the crisis of A.D. 9. One reason why a legate might be left in charge of an army was that Tiberius feared that he would rebel if he tried to recall him: the governor of the upper Rhine army, Lentulus Gaetulicus, is reported to have come to an unofficial arrangement whereby he promised to cause no trouble for Tiberius so long as he was not recalled. Gaetulicus must have calculated, rightly, that Tiberius' reign would soon be over. But where the good of the Republic required it, Tiberius was still capable of taking decisions. In A.D. 35 Lucius Vitellius was sent to Syria as legate, to intervene in the affairs of Armenia by imposing a Roman nominee, Tiridates, on the throne.[27]

Despite his firm belief that he would live for another ten years,

---

[26] Finance and credit: Rodewald 1976 (B 348); Sutherland 1987 (B 358) ch. 24. Jurisprudence: chs 12 and 21 below. Note Sejanus' relationships with Aelius Tubero and the Cassii; and his son Decimus Capito Aelianus may have been adopted by C. Ateius Capito. Claudius blames the 'absentia pertinaci patrui mei' for failure to resolve the citizen status of the Anauni: *ILS* 206.
[27] Provinces: Orth 1970 (C 384); Rectus: Dio LVII.10.5.

Tiberius died on 16 March A.D. 37 at Misenum, while on a journey back to the capital. The following day was the feast of the Liberalia, traditionally one of the days suitable for bestowing the *toga virilis* on a boy. If Tiberius had intended to perform this ceremony for Gemellus before presenting him to the Senate and people at Rome as his heir, then his death was remarkably opportune for Caligula. The inevitable rumour had it that Caligula and Macro helped Tiberius on his way by smothering him with a pillow. In any case Gemellus was still a child, and in no position to stop Caligula from taking command of the *domus Caesaris*.

III. GAIUS CALIGULA[28]

The popular rejoicing that greeted the news of Tiberius' death was not just a reaction against an unpopular *princeps* who in his last years had failed to provide Rome with his presence and consequently with the public shows and other *beneficia* that a Roman ruler owed his supporters. There was also a positive welcome for the Principate of Caligula, the surviving son of Germanicus, a man who had been destined by Augustus to be head of the *domus Caesaris* only to be robbed of his expectations by premature death. On 18 March, two days after Tiberius' death, the Senate met and acclaimed Caligula, and Caligula alone, as emperor. Caligula and Macro hastened to Rome ahead of Tiberius' body; they arrived on 28 March, and Caligula attended a meeting of the Senate which confirmed his position (there is no need to assume that he had made a pretence of refusing the imperial acclamation of 18 March).[29] It was probably at this point that Tiberius' will was produced; in accordance with normal Roman custom, he had instituted his two grandsons, natural and adopted, as equal heirs. But the *domus Caesaris* was not a normal household; its formal division between the two brothers – which was what the will required – would have had disastrous political results, even if it had been possible in practice. There was no precedent at Rome for one household to be headed by two *patresfamilias*. Only in the time of Marcus Aurelius and Lucius Verus in the 160s A.D. would the position of 'Caesar' become sufficiently recognizable as a public office to make the concept of a college of equal emperors feasible. In any case Gemellus was still a child and could hold no public office. Caligula alone was recognized as Tiberius' heir. As a standard justification for the setting aside of the will, it was declared that Tiberius had been insane.

---

[28] Tacitus does not survive for Caligula: we have Dio LIX and Suet. *Calig.* The *acta* of the Arval Brethren survive for the period January 38 to June 40 (=*GCN* 1–11). Caligula's personality continues to attract interpretations in terms of psychosis. The most far-reaching attempt at a rehabilitation remains Balsdon 1934 (C 331). For a conservative account, see Barrett 1989 (C 333).

[29] Timpe 1962 (C 403); for date of acclamation and *recusatio*, Jakobson and Cotton 1985 (C 358).

Communities and officials in East and West swore their loyalty to
Caligula and to his *domus*. Caligula's speech at Tiberius' funeral on 3
April emphasized that he was Germanicus' son, and proclaimed a return
to the style of Augustus. Although the dead emperor's apotheosis was
duly reported, as Augustus' had been, he was too unpopular for the
Senate to grant him divine honours. (The mint at Lyons erroneously
struck *aurei* and denarii depicting Tiberius as divine.) Caligula promised
formally to adopt Gemellus and honoured him as *princeps iuventutis*. This
both labelled him as too young to be a serious alternative to Caligula, and
removed any justification his supporters might have for resentment
against the emperor.[30]

The immediate requirement if the new regime was to establish itself
was the distribution of *beneficia* to Romans of all classes. Tiberius' will
had promised the praetorians a donative of 500 sesterces each; by giving
them twice as much, Caligula set the precedent that the loyalty of the
guard should be bought by their new *imperator*, instead of being
rewarded by the old one at his death. The fact that sesterces representing
the emperor addressing his praetorian cohorts appear to have been ·
produced throughout his reign suggests that these donatives were
repeated. Caligula also demonstrated his care for the people; inscriptions
confirm that 75 sesterces were distributed to the entire citizen population
of Rome on 1 June and 19 July. In pointed contrast to Tiberius, Caligula
spared no expense in providing the plebs with games; the very first
privilege he requested from the Senate was for permission to exceed the
statutory number of gladiators. He is also said to have returned the right
to elect praetors to the *comitia*. What that meant in practice was that
potential candidates for the praetorship – notably the aediles – would try
to win popularity by putting on much more lavish games than they had
needed to under Tiberius. Caligula also inaugurated a grandiose programme of public building, on the Palatine hill and elsewhere, to make
up for Tiberius' years of neglect. It will have been these plans, rather
than the distributions of cash (which cannot have come to more than 150
million sesterces) that lie behind the accusation that Caligula squandered
the 2.7 billion sesterces reported to have been left by Tiberius.

At the same time, Caligula did what he could to win the support of the
upper classes; he refused the title *pater patriae* on the grounds that he was
too young, recalled exiles, and made a public show of burning Tiberius'
private papers without (he claimed, falsely) having read the contents. An
early *sestertius* with the legend 'For Citizens Saved' advertises his claim to
have restored the security of the law. The backlog of legal business for

---

30 Oaths: *GCN* 32 = *AN* 562, from Aritium in Lusitania: 11 May 37; *GCN* 33 = *AN* 563, from
Assus in the Troad. Tiberius' funeral: Dio LIX.3.7. The inscription on Gemellus' tomb shows that
no formal adoption in fact occurred: *ILS* 172.

which Tiberius' absence from Rome was blamed was tackled by adding a fifth panel of jurors and allowing magistrates' sentences to be carried out without the need for imperial confirmation.[31]

The new emperor's policy towards client kings should also be seen primarily as an attempt to ensure that the network of hellenistic rulers which was an integral part of the Roman empire had close personal links with the reigning Caesar. The fact that some of them were related to Caligula through Antony, and some had been brought up together with him in the house of Antonia the Younger, also helped to bind them and their territorial resources to him; but the great-grandson of Antony had no grand plan to resolve the conflict between East and West.[32] The three Thracian princes, Cotys, Polemo and Rhoemetalces, to whom he granted the kingdoms of Lesser Armenia, Pontus and eastern Thrace, were probably cousins. The son of the last king of Commagene was given back his father's kingdom, plus the taxes extracted by the Romans over the intervening twenty years. The Jewish prince Marcus Iulius Agrippa (usually known as Herod Agrippa I) was also presented with extensive domains. We should be sceptical of later accusations that these kings trained Caligula in the ways of oriental (ie. hellenistic) despotism.

Caligula was particularly keen to draw attention to his family relationships in order to stress that (by implication, unlike Tiberius) he deserved loyalty because he was a Caesar by descent and not just by adoption. He went in person to bring back to Rome the ashes of his exiled mother and brother Nero for interment in the mausoleum built for the Caesars by Augustus. Coins show his mother Agrippina and grandfather Agrippa, his brothers Nero and Drusus on horseback, and his sisters Agrippina, Drusilla and Iulia Livilla holding the attributes of 'Security', 'Concord' and 'Good Fortune'. The three sisters were given the honours due to Vestal Virgins. Caligula's uncle, Claudius (who had not been adopted into the imperial household), was honoured as befitted Germanicus' brother; he became Caligula's colleague in his first consulship, held from 1 July to 31 August (so as not to impair the respect due to the regular consuls). The memory of Livia was also honoured: Caligula began the construction of a temple and cult, voted but never undertaken at her death. When his grandmother Antonia died on 1 May, the prestige of the imperial family was emphasized again by the grant of similar honours.

The losers were those who had supported Tiberius. It is hardly

[31] ADLOCVT COH, OB CIVES SERVATOS. For Caligula's coinage, cf. Sutherland 1987 (B 358) chs. 26–9; GCN 81–6. Congiaria: Fasti Ostienses = GCN 31 = AN 174. Building programme: Thornton 1989 (F 594). The 2.7 billion sesterces was perhaps the value of the patrimonium: Suet. Calig. 37.3.

[32] Ceauşescu 1973 (C 337) (at a time when Rumania was seeking to play a similar role as mediator between East and West). Cf. Sherk 42; Braund 1984 (C 254) 41–6; Sullivan 1985 (E 1224) (Judaea).

surprising that Gemellus was soon required to commit suicide on the charge of having taken an antidote, ie. implicitly accusing Caligula of wanting to poison him. Caligula executed Tiberius' long-term associate Marcus Iunius Silanus (cos. A.D. 15), the father of his deceased wife Iunia Claudilla, and presumably a supporter of Gemellus. Caligula accused him of attempting a coup while he was away, possibly during his trip to recover his mother's ashes. Macro, too, soon met his end: Caligula had no intention of making the mistake of being as dependent upon him as Tiberius had been on Sejanus. It is interesting that while later tradition accuses Caligula of having been too friendly with client kings, there are no references to his being under the influence of his freedmen or even prefects: Caligula did not shift the responsibility for his own actions onto others.

The way in which Caligula built up support and eliminated potential opposition shows that the new emperor had learnt a great deal from Tiberius. These executions also suggest that attempts to divide his reign into a 'good' beginning followed by unremitting atrocities, or even lunacy, are misplaced. It is useless to date the turning-point to before the death of Antonia (two months after his accession), an illness in the autumn of A.D. 37 which is supposed to have affected his brain, or the death of his sister Drusilla on 10 June 38. (According to the ancient sources, Drusilla was so dear to him that he was accused of incest with her, and modern historians have suggested that she was a 'restraining influence' on him.) We cannot judge how genuine Caligula's affection for his sisters was; but it is clear that he knew from the start that their children, and their husbands, were his rivals. We are told that when his sister Agrippina and her husband, Cnaeus Domitius Ahenobarbus, had a son on 15 December 37, Caligula insultingly suggested that he be named after Claudius. The death of Ahenobarbus in 39 meant that Agrippina and her child – the later Nero – were not an immediate threat.

Drusilla was married to Lucius Cassius Longinus; Caligula gave her instead to Marcus Aemilius Lepidus, member of one of the wealthiest surviving republican dynasties, long associated with Augustus' family.[33] His father (cos. A.D. 6) was one of those allegedly described by Augustus as suitable for imperial office (see p. 204f. above); he was related to the younger Iulia's husband Aemilius Paullus, exiled in A.D. 8; and his sister Aemilia Lepida had been the wife of Caligula's brother Drusus. Caligula trusted Lepidus to the extent that they were said to have been homosexual lovers, and more significantly he gave his seal-ring to Lepidus during his serious illness in A.D. 37 – the customary sign that Lepidus, as Drusilla's husband, was to administer the household if Caligula were to die without issue.

[33] Syme 1970 (B 178) ch. 4; 1986 (A 95); *PIR*.

When Drusilla died, Caligula had her deified (23 September 38). There was nothing un-Roman about her cult: as a Julian, she was associated with Venus, the ancestor of the Iulii. The title 'Panthea' associated her with the Magna Mater, but that cult too (notwithstanding its hellenistic origins) had been at home in Rome for over two centuries. And there was nothing 'oriental' about the new goddess' elephant-drawn *biga* (male *divi* like Augustus had their image drawn by a *quadriga* of elephants), nor about the requirement that Roman women should swear by Drusilla (Claudius made the women of his household swear by the *diva* Livia).

The deification of Drusilla raises the question of whether Caligula had a 'religious policy', wanting to be adored as a god in the style of hellenistic monarchs. 'Emperor-worship' can no longer be dismissed as an irrational oriental superstition (see ch. 16 for a discussion of the various cults); if Caligula saw himself, or his office, as divine, then this was an attempt to express the reality of his position as a mediator between the Roman community and the world of the gods. It was not fantastic to express this position as analogous to that of Hercules, the man whose labours made him divine (and, like later emperors with a special devotion to Hercules, Caligula liked to be seen as a gladiator, imposing law and order upon wild beasts and criminals), nor strange to commune with Jupiter. That monotheism made it impossible for the Jews to accept the emperor as divine in this sense was beyond the comprehension of Caligula, as of so many other Romans. Recent excavations suggest that some anecdotes about Caligula's claims to divinity (eg. that Castor and Pollux were his 'doorkeepers') were based on his building activities on and around the Palatine.[34]

A number of the peculiar stories told about Caligula suggest that, more clearly than other emperors, he saw that the emperor's role symbolized the struggle of man against nature. Although unable to swim, he seems to have been particularly keen to impose his will upon the sea: according to Suetonius' grandfather, the astrologer Thrasyllus had once told Tiberius that Caligula had no more chance of being emperor than of riding a horse across the sea. To refute him, he built a bridge of boats from Baiae to Puteoli and rode across. Soon after his accession he braved the elements to sail to the island of Planasia, where his mother and brother had died in exile, in order to demonstrate his piety towards them; and control over the Ocean also featured in his military expeditions. In a successful emperor, such attempts to control nature were divine, but – like Xerxes' bridge over the Hellespont – they might also be the acts of a tyrant. It is not surprising that Caligula is reported to have suffered from nightmares in which he pitted himself against the Mediterranean Sea.

[34] Buildings and religion: Wiseman 1987 (E 140); Barrett 1989 (C 333) ch. 13.

Sexual licence was another characteristic of the typical tyrant. Stories of incest and homosexuality have to be understood as representing Caligula's tight political control over his family, and over others who might threaten him. We are told that he intervened to prevent a marriage between C. Calpurnius Piso (the man who was to lead the conspiracy of A.D. 65) and Livia Orestilla, presumably a relative of Livia's; he slept with her himself, to ensure that, if there were any children, it would not be clear that they were Piso's. Caligula took steps to control other Pisones, too. When Lucius Piso (consul in 27, and urban prefect under Tiberius) was proconsul of Africa in 39/40, he felt it necessary to remove the Third Legion from the proconsul's command (a decision which later emperors did not think it politic to rescind).

The threats represented by his sisters as well as by more distant relatives would be much less immediate if Caligula had a child of his own. In 38, he married Lollia Paulina, the granddaughter of Augustus' general (and Tiberius' enemy) the consul of 21 B.C. Paulina did not please Caligula, and she was divorced after a year (but survived to rival Agrippina for the hand of Claudius). His last wife was Milonia Caesonia, whose mother Vistilia was famous for marrying six husbands in succession; one of Caesonia's stepfathers, Cnaeus Domitius Corbulo (father of Nero's general), was given a suffect consulship in 39. Caesonia provided Caligula with a daughter, Iulia Drusilla; he was delighted, and his position *vis-à-vis* potential successors was greatly strengthened. Marcus Lepidus was no longer the heir-apparent, and could be dispensed with.

In the autumn of 39, Caligula claimed to have uncovered a major conspiracy to replace him with Lepidus; although the exact sequence of events is impossible to reconstruct, it is clear that he acted swiftly and decisively. He publicized the striking failure of the consuls to offer prayers on his behalf on his birthday on 31 August. Cnaeus Cornelius Lentulus Gaetulicus, consul in A.D. 26 and in command of the upper Rhine legions since 30, could be represented as constituting a military threat. Caligula gave orders for a major military force to be concentrated in Upper Germany, and marched north himself with the praetorians (he pretended that the object of the expedition was to levy Batavians for his personal bodyguard). Lentulus Gaetulicus' own legions were overawed by the display of imperial might, and he was executed; a considerable number of tribunes and centurions had to be retired.

Caligula had kept Lepidus, Agrippina and Livilla by his side during this expedition. Lepidus was now formally tried and executed; correspondence was produced incriminating both sisters, and Caligula sent to Rome three daggers with which he claimed they had intended to kill him. Agrippina and Livilla were condemned on the standard charge of adultery, and exiled. In a parody of the return of their grandfather Drusus' and father Germanicus' ashes to Rome, Caligula forced Agrippina to return bearing those of her 'lover' Lepidus. The future emperor Vespasian, who was praetor in that year, distinguished himself by his attacks on Agrippina in the Senate. The records of the Arval Brethren inform us that on 27 October 39, the *promagister* L. Salvius Otho sacrificed in thanksgiving for the unmasking of the conspiracy. The deaths of Calvisius Sabinus (the legate of Pannonia) and his wife at about the same time may have been connected with the conspiracy, pretended or real.[35]

Caligula's visit to the Rhine legions provided him with an opportunity to enhance his status by winning military glory. The first imperative was to regain the loyalty of the Rhine army. Gaetulicus' replacement was Lepidus' brother-in-law Servius Sulpicius Galba; his friendship with Caligula will have dated to the period when Caligula lived in Livia's household. Galba restored strict standards of discipline to the legions, and Caligula himself led a number of expeditions across the Rhine. They were not obviously less successful in reasserting Roman prestige in the eyes of the German tribes than his father Germanicus' had been in A.D. 14–16. It is only because of Caligula's own unpopularity that our ancient sources with one accord decry them as artificial and unreal, accusing Caligula of cowardice, and suggesting that he fabricated the fighting, and bought or kidnapped the captives in Gaul, where he spent the winter.

Accounts of Caligula's activities at Lyons during the winter emphasize his bad relations with the Senate, and his need for funds. The property of Gallic notables was confiscated, as well as senatorial estates in Italy (eg. those of Sextus Pompeius, cos. A.D. 14); he auctioned off the property of his exiled sisters, and even some of the effects of the imperial household. Such anecdotes illustrate the fiscal requirements of policies that were themselves likely to strengthen the regime. Coins advertise the abolition of the $\frac{1}{2}$ percent sales tax on slaves, which will have been welcome to wealthy Italians; the tax had already been reduced from 1 per cent by Tiberius, at the time when Germanicus had overseen the annexation of Cappodocia. To make up for the lost income, Caligula will have looked for another client kingdom to integrate into the empire. His choice fell on Mauretania, whose king, Caligula's cousin Ptolemy, was summoned to Lyons and executed (not, as has been suggested, because Caligula coveted his alleged position as high priest of the Isis cult).[36]

[35] Lepidus and Gaetulicus: Meise 1969 (C 375) ch. 5; Simpson 1980 (C 394); *Acta Arvalium, GCN* 9. For Vespasian's role, Jones 1984 (C 360).

[36] Ptolemy and Mauretania: Fishwick 1971 (E 732); Braund 1984 (C 254); Hoffman 1959 (C 275) (Isis). Coins advertising tax reduction ('RCC'): Sutherland 1987 (B 358) ch. 19. Victory over the Ocean: Suet. *Calig*. 46; Dio LIX.25.

But Caligula was also planning to follow in the footsteps of his ancestor Iulius Caesar by imposing Roman military control over Britain. The expulsion from his kingdom and flight to Gaul of Cunobelinus' son Adminius gave Rome an excuse to intervene. Two new legions (the Fifteenth and Twenty-second) seem to have been raised at this time; they were called *Primigeniae*, probably in honour of the emperor's first-born daughter. Their numbers suggest that they were intended to be twinned with two of the upper Rhine legions, the Fourteenth at Mainz and Twenty-first at Vindonissa, an indication of Caligula's caution regarding the loyalty of Gaetulicus' old army. Other preparations for the invasion included the construction of a lighthouse at Boulogne. Again, the ancient sources argue that Caligula was far too great a coward to have been serious about invading Britain; and anecdotes about the operation are selected with a view to suggesting that the whole affair was further proof of his madness. It is impossible to judge why the army never embarked. The story that Caligula intended to punish the legions by decimation suggests that there may have been a mutiny (he is said to have reminded them of the mutiny of their predecessors after Augustus' death, in which as a baby he had been taken away to Trier by Agrippina); alternatively, the British chieftains may have acceded to his demands without the need for an invasion. If there is any truth behind Suetonius' story that Caligula ordered his troops to collect seashells in the context of military operations either on the north German coast or against Britain, it may be that he meant these shells to be a symbol of his victory over the Ocean. (An unlikely alternative explanation has been that the *musculi* he ordered the troops to pack up were not sea-shells, but siege engines.)

Caligula returned to Italy in the summer of A.D. 40. The winter in Lyons had not been conducive to good relations with the Senate. Communications were a problem; when one of the consuls-elect died shortly before 1 January, there was not enough time for Caligula to be consulted about a replacement, and he was (very unreasonably) blamed for entering office without a colleague – perhaps the context of the story about his wishing to appoint the horse Incitatus to the consulship. There had been executions, such as that of the father of Tacitus' father-in-law Agricola. After the removal of Lepidus, any relative represented a threat, even his uncle Claudius. He was said to have thrown Claudius into the river Rhine when he arrived at the head of a senatorial delegation sent to congratulate him on the elimination of Lepidus and Gaetulicus.

Caligula remained outside Rome for a time, possibly simply to avoid the unhealthy summer months, rather than out of fear of conspiracies (although he is said to have remarked that he wished he could eliminate the entire Senate at a stroke). We should beware of taking Seneca's hostile remarks, or the later justifications for his murder, as evidence for widespread unpopularity. It is hardly surprising that Cassius Chaerea and the other disgruntled praetorian officers responsible for Caligula's death and the brutal killing of his wife and baby daughter on 24 January A.D. 41 should have justified their treason by claiming that it was tyrannicide. No doubt Chaerea was genuinely unhappy about Caligula's persecution of other members of Germanicus' family, but it also irked him that the emperor kept drawing attention to Chaerea's effeminate tone of voice.

IV. CLAUDIUS [37]

Most ancient sources treat Claudius as a fool who became emperor by accident. Already in Seneca's satire the *Apocolocyntosis*, written some months after Claudius' death, he is represented as vicious, stupid and fearful. It may not have been entirely Claudius' fault that he executed some two hundred equestrians and thirty-five senators, including many of his relatives, during a reign of just over thirteen years. But we should not be too keen to rehabilitate Claudius in the face of the judgment of antiquity. Nor should all Claudius' acts be ascribed to a grandiose and far-seeing overall 'policy', when many can be explained as particular responses to standard political threats. Claudius' 'policy' was above all that of any other Roman *princeps*: staying alive, controlling the succession, rewarding clients and winning glory – even though the form it took may have been influenced by traditions about the Claudii, and by his respect for Iulius Caesar.

The reported views of Augustus, of Claudius' grandmother Livia and his mother Antonia the Younger as to his unsuitability for public office should not be ignored. A public position was not something automatically inherited at Rome; it was something that each individual had to prove himself fit for. Neither Augustus nor Tiberius felt that Claudius was suitable for election to office, and he had remained an *eques*. Although he had been granted some honours by Tiberius, on the rare occasions when he appeared on the political scene it was only in a private capacity – for example, to accompany his brother Germanicus' ashes on their return from the East – or as the representative of the equestrian *ordo* at Augustus' funeral and to congratulate Tiberius on the overthrow of Sejanus. Tiberius had no intention of allowing Claudius to inherit the political support of his brother Germanicus. Like other Romans excluded from politics, Claudius turned to intellectual pursuits, and in particular to the study of history. He wrote about Carthage and the Etruscans (many of his associates, including his first wife Plautia

---

[37] Main literary sources: Tac. *Ann.* XI–XII, with Mehl 1974 (B 123); Dio LX; Suet. *Claud.*; Sen. *Apocol.* Assessments: Momigliano 1934 (C 377); Levick 1978 (C 367); Levick 1990 (C 372).

Urgulanilla, had an Etruscan background). The effect has been to make him particularly sympathetic to modern historians, who see a fellow-worker in Claudius. More crucially, the mask of pedantry enabled him to survive Tiberius' reign.

At his accession, Caligula brought his uncle fully into public life as part of his attempt to strengthen his position by enhancing the respect due to his relatives. From 1 July to 12 September A.D. 37 Claudius was Caligula's colleague during his first consulship. In 39 he married his third wife, Valeria Messallina; her father was Claudius' cousin Marcus Valerius Messalla Barbatus, son of the consul of 12 B.C. and of Augustus' niece Marcella the Younger, and her mother was Domitia Lepida. Although Octavia and Britannicus were not born until 40/1, the possibility that his uncle might produce children who, unlike Antonia (Claudius' daughter by Urgulanilla), had Augustus' blood in their veins, cannot have pleased Caligula.

When Caligula was unexpectedly assassinated, there was no precedent for the form which the transfer of power to a new *princeps* should take. Of course, death might come suddenly to political leaders then as now, and it should not surprise us that potential claimants had contingency plans ready. The speed with which some of them acted does not prove that they were involved in Chaerea's plot. Once it was clear that Caligula's baby daughter had been killed with him, the obvious person to claim to inherit the *domus Caesaris* was Marcus Vinicius, husband of the exiled Iulia Livilla (Caligula's other sister, Agrippina, was a widow). Where Vinicius erred was in turning to the Senate to confirm his position.[38]

The Senate was immediately summoned by the consul Quintus Pomponius Secundus: this need not indicate that he was privy to the plot. As a half-brother of Caesonia, he too had an interest in the succession. Later, after the Senate had failed to institute a Caesar of its own, it became politic for everyone, including the new emperor, to pretend that they had merely been acting in the public interest. The Senate debated the situation in the language of republicanism, and that language masked the ambitions of those involved. On the evening of the assassination, the hundred or so senators who had the courage to appear were in no mood to confirm Vinicius' claims. Instead, they celebrated the removal of a tyrant, and the consuls – for the first time since the establishment of the Principate – gave the urban cohorts their watchword for the following day. But the celebration of *libertas* did not exclude the search for a new *princeps*; the urban cohorts made it clear that that was what they wanted.

While the Senate debated, Claudius had taken control of the house-

---

[38] Accounts of the succession crisis: Joseph. *AJ* XIX.248–73 = *AN* 194; Timpe 1962 (C 403); Swan 1970 (C 395); Jung 1972 (C 361); Ritter 1972 (B 151).

hold of the Caesars. Tradition had it that after Caligula's death he was found hiding in the palace by a guardsman who acclaimed him as emperor, and taken to the praetorian camp where he was recognized as the legitimate head of the Caesars. In strict law, that may not have been so; but Roman law also recognized the principle of *possessio*. The Praetor's Edict protected the rights of the person who was in actual control of an estate until such time as the appropriate court (in the case of inheritances, the centumviral court) had passed judgment on the question of ownership in accordance with strict *ius Quiritium*. 'Whether (*possessio*) existed or not was regarded as a question of fact, but if it existed, it conferred rights'.[39] It was certainly a fact that Claudius now had *possessio*.

Claudius was not a member of the Julian household; but his uncle Tiberius and his brother Germanicus had been adopted into it, and they and his nephew Caligula had headed, or been expected to head, that household. After his acclamation as their new *imperator* by the praetorian guard, Claudius immediately adopted the name Caesar, to show that he had inherited that household; the name did not imply any fictitious posthumous adoption, nor was it pre-empting the bestowal of a title (like that of 'Augustus') by the Senate. Nor was Claudius arrogating any constitutional powers to himself by calling himself Caesar. It represented the fact that Claudius was now Caligula's successor as head of the *domus Caesaris*. In the aftermath of the assassination no will was sought out that would have to be adhered to, like that of Augustus, or set aside, like that of Tiberius.

When the Senate reconvened on the following day, it was too late to recognize the claims of Marcus Vinicius or any other candidate. The consul Pomponius allowed other names to be considered, including those of Annius Vinicianus (who supported his uncle Vinicius) and Decimus Valerius Asiaticus, who had been an early adviser of Caligula and was married to a sister of Lollia Paulina. There were a number of other consulars who were related to the Julian family through descent or by marriage; they too might want a say in who was to head the *domus Caesaris*, but most of them happened to be away from Rome as provincial governors in January 41, and January was not a good time for communicating with Spain or the Rhine or Danube, nor for travel thence to Rome. Servius Sulpicius Galba, who had given Caligula such excellent support in the aftermath of Gaetulicus' rebellion and was now legate of the upper Rhine army, Aulus Plautius in Pannonia, Camillus Scribonianus in Dalmatia, and Appius Iunius Silanus in Tarraconensis,

---

[39] *Possessio*: Buckland 1963 (F 646) 203. Legal recognition of *usucapio* of an estate was only granted after one year; but *possessio* itself was a matter of immediate fact. On the adoption of the deceased's name by an heir, Syme 1984 (D 72).

could not be consulted and could not intervene to affect the recognition of a new Caesar at Rome – even if their names may later have been mentioned as alternative candidates. In the end, the Senate summoned Claudius to discuss the situation. He politely pretended that the praetorians were keeping him against his will; but the consuls and other senators had to accept that the support of the praetorians for Claudius left them with no choice but to confirm his position.

Claudius' debt to the guard is reflected in his early coins. A gold *aureus* shows one of the first representations of a walled Roman camp with battlements, arched gateways, and a pair of columns supporting a pediment. A praetorian stands guard, and the inscription proclaims 'The Commander Received' [sc. into the guard's loyalty]. The other side of the special relationship between the new *imperator* and his soldiers is depicted by a bronze *as* with Claudius, in the civilian's toga, clasping hands with a soldier, and the inscription 'The Praetorians Received'. These issues were of course intended for the eyes of the guard, and were very probably the coins used to pay the unprecedented donative of 15,000 sesterces which Claudius had promised them at his elevation; we are told that he continued to give each soldier a payment of 100 sesterces annually throughout his reign.

Other coins celebrate decidedly non-military aspects of the image the new ruler wished to present of himself: there are representations of 'Augustan Liberty' holding a liberty-cap, and dedications 'To Augustan Peace' and 'Augustan Constancy'. A copper *quadrans*, listing the emperor's new honours (including his designation to a second consulship, i.e. the consulship of 42), may refer to a decision to return to the traditional metal-content of the coinage, debased by Caligula. Some of Caligula's coins were ceremonially defaced. Like some of the coin-issues by means of which Caligula at his accession had distanced himself from Tiberius, Claudius wanted to emphasize a return to legality, and to the precedents set by Augustus. A *sestertius* depicts the oak wreath awarded 'For Citizens Saved'. Claudius was also anxious to stress the links between his Claudian relations and the Julian family. Early coins show his father, Drusus; his mother Antonia (given the title Augusta); and his brother Germanicus, formally 'son of Tiberius Augustus and grandson of the Divine Augustus'. Livia, too, was honoured; and the dedication of an altar to 'Augustan Piety' in *c*. A.D. 43 symbolized the new emperor's claim to be close to Augustus.[40]

One way to show that he intended his reign to be an improvement on Caligula's was by recalling those who had been exiled (as Caligula himself had done at his accession). Those who returned included Agrippina and Iulia Livilla. The public honour Claudius bestowed upon

[40] Coins: *AN* 187–8, 194; *GCN* 81–6; Sutherland 1987 (B 358) chs. 30, 32.

his relatives did not mean that he could trust them. His fear of assassination was extreme (up to the last years of his reign, everyone who entered his presence was searched for weapons). Historians have expressed doubt about the extent to which Claudius' third wife Messallina was responsible for the executions of these early years of his reign. But many of those who threatened her threatened him too, and Claudius publicly thanked her for warning him against at least some of those he had put to death. Soon after her return, Iulia Livilla was exiled again and then executed. Agrippina fared better; her son Domitius Ahenobarbus returned to her care, and his property, confiscated by Caligula, was restored to him. Agrippina looked for the support of a new husband; her first choice was Livia's protégé, Galba, but Galba's mother-in-law pointed out to him that that would make his claim to the imperial office so strong that he could not expect to survive for long. (She also made a point of slapping Agrippina's face in public.) Instead, Agrippina married C. Sallustius Passienus Crispus, the adopted son of Augustus' closest associates (see above pp. 202). As a new member of the imperial family, and potential father of Caesarian children, Crispus had to be honoured with a second consulship in A.D. 44; but he died soon after – poisoned by Agrippina, according to Suetonius – so that Messallina allowed Agrippina to survive.[41]

Claudius and Messallina also looked for support through matrimonial alliances. In 42 Appius Iunius Silanus was recalled from the governorship of Tarraconensis to marry Messallina's mother Domitia Lepida, daughter of Augustus' niece the elder Antonia. Claudius' daughter by Aelia Paetina, Antonia, was married to Pompeius Magnus, son of Marcus Licinius Crassus Frugi (cos. A.D. 27); through his mother Scribonia, he was related to Augustus. Claudius' two-year-old daughter by Messallina, Octavia, was engaged to Augustus' great-great-grandson Lucius Iunius Torquatus Silanus (the youngest son of the consul of A.D. 19, proconsul of Africa under Caligula: not closely related to Appius Silanus), aged about sixteen. Silanus was identified as a suitable successor, sufficiently young to pose no immediate threat: he was made a *vigintivir* and *praefectus urbi feriarum Latinarum causa*. But the preference shown to Silanus naturally weakened the chances of others interested in the imperial office.

By and large Claudius was initially unsuccessful, or unlucky, in his attempts to build up a wide enough network of dependants to whom he had distributed *beneficia*. Supporters appointed to client kingships included Mithridates in Lesser Armenia, and Agrippa in Judaea (the latter's role in the events following Caligula's assassination is empha-

---

[41] Opposition: McAlindon 1956 (C 373), 1957 (C 374); Baldwin 1964 (C 330); Meise 1969 (C 375); Wiseman 1982 (B 198). Agrippina and Galba: Suet. *Galba*. 5.

sized by Josephus in his *Antiquities*); although Agrippa died in 44 after just three years, he was able to persuade Claudius to grant considerable *beneficia* to Jewish communities at Alexandria and elsewhere in the empire. As a reward for not challenging Claudius' *possessio* of the *domus Caesaris*, Marcus Vinicius was to be *consul ordinarius* for the second time in 45, and Valerius Asiaticus given a second consulship in 46.

Just under a year after his accession, on 12 January 42, it was felt that Claudius had distributed honours and offices to enough members of the political class to warrant accepting the title of *pater patriae*. (He also held a consulship, his second, for two months at the beginning of this year.) This merely masked his weakness. After Caligula's assassination, those powerful governors who happened not to be in Rome accepted Claudius' elevation as a *fait accompli*. But Claudius' political inexperience and lack of military *virtus* gave those who considered themselves more suitably qualified a temptation to act. Galba and Aulus Plautius remained loyal; Appius Silanus and Camillus Scribonianus did not. Appius Silanus may have judged that if Claudius were out of the way, he, as the husband of Octavia's grandmother Domitia Lepida, would be in a doubly strong position to gain recognition as Caesar. The weak point in his calculation was that there was no love lost between Messallina and her mother. Backed by the *libertus* Narcissus, Messallina informed Claudius of Silanus' ambitions, and Claudius tried and convicted Silanus, not in public but in his domestic court, the *consilium* of his *amici*.

The execution of Silanus was a sign of Claudius' insecurity as well as of his readiness to eliminate rivals. The legate of Dalmatia, Lucius Arruntius Furius Camillus Scribonianus (adopted son of Lucius Arruntius, one of those who, according to Tacitus, had been thought worthy of the Principate by Augustus), calculated that his chances of survival would be better if he made a bid for empire himself. Scribonianus commanded two legions, the Seventh and Eleventh, and his attempt was supported by a number of figures in Rome who had failed to respond positively to Claudius' acclamation in the previous year. They included Lucius Annius Vinicianus and the consul who had summoned the Senate, Quintus Pomponius Secundus. Our sources tell us that Claudius seriously discussed the advisability of surrendering his *imperium* to Scribonianus. Unfortunately for Scribonianus, he felt himself unable at this stage to declare himself emperor – either because he waited for confirmation from his supporters in the Senate, or because he was hoping for support from other provincial commanders such as Galba and Aulus Plautius. These commanders had no interest in forsaking Claudius for another emperor; and after a few days, the two Dalmatian legions abandoned Scribonianus. It was claimed that the legionary standards had become stuck in the ground as a sign of divine anger at their disloyalty. Scribonianus killed himself, and those of his supporters at Rome who did not were executed.

Claudius' third consulship in A.D. 43 was again a sign of weakness rather than strength. During these first years of his reign, he had to make every effort to ensure that he was popular with the Roman plebs – apart from staging games and spectacles, he initiated some major building operations, some of them directly raising the living standards of the Roman population. They included the draining of the Fucine lake, to provide much-needed agricultural land in the vicinity of the capital, a new aqueduct, and the construction of a safe harbour at Ostia. A riot early in his reign made it clear to Claudius that, since the time of Iulius Caesar, the supervision of the corn supply was one of the ruler's principal functions. Another was the supervision of the judicial system; particularly during his tenure of consular office. Claudius made himself visibly available in the law-courts. Even hostile sources (who dwell on his tendency to ignore the law in favour of so-called 'equity') had to admit that he was serious in his desire to be seen to be a hard-working judge.

In terms of the qualities required of a Roman *imperator*, Claudius' major weakness, like that of Caligula when he had come to power, was that he had no military experience. This explains his almost obsessive need to advertise any military success achieved during his reign; Claudius chose to accept twenty-seven imperatorial acclamations, more than any other emperor. Even in his first year, coins showed off a triumphal arch with trophies won by his father Drusus 'from the Germans'. Soon there were genuine military successes. In Mauretania, Suetonius Paulinus dealt successfully with a war against nomad tribes that had arisen out of Caligula's removal of King Ptolemy and imposition of direct Roman rule (see chapter 13*i* on Africa). Paulinus' successors completed the process of pacification; it gave Claudius the opportunity to honour Marcus Crassus Frugi, both a central figure of the old aristocracy and the father-in-law of Antonia. Crassus was now awarded triumphal *ornamenta* for finishing off the war effectively won by the *novus homo* Suetonius Paulinus.

Claudius reserved for himself the glory of conquering Britain. Ever since the time of Iulius Caesar, Britain, as an island in the Ocean, had had a symbolic importance for Romans: its conquest would indicate that not just the whole world, but even lands beyond the edge of the world, were subject to the dominion of the Roman people. The occupation of Britain would have the additional benefit of removing several legions from within striking distance of Rome: Caligula's new legions had raised the number in each of the German armies to five, and that made their commanders too powerful.

Claudius felt that he could trust the Pannonian governor, Aulus

Plautius, to undertake the actual military operation. Son of an officer of Claudius' father Drusus and brother Germanicus, Plautius had remained loyal during Scribonianus' rebellion, and he was a cousin of Claudius' first wife (although he had divorced Urgulanilla, Claudius is said to have remained on good terms with her). The other person Claudius trusted was Lucius Vitellius, the consul of 34, son of a mere *eques* but with two consular brothers. Loyal supporters of Germanicus, Vitellius and his brothers had returned to prominence during Tiberius' last years because of the support of Caligula's grandmother (and Claudius' mother) Antonia. Vitellius held a second consulship in 43, and Claudius entrusted the capital to his care for the duration of the expedition.

There were few others he trusted not to plot in his absence: a large number of senators had to accompany him. It was even said that Claudius put off the voyage to Britain by a few days because Galba claimed that he was too ill to travel. Galba was one consular Claudius could not afford to leave behind. Among others in the party were both Valerius Asiaticus and Marcus Vinicius. The Britons themselves presented considerably fewer problems (see chapter 13e), and the resultant triumph enabled Claudius to distribute the *ornamenta triumphalia* to all those consulars he brought with him, thus putting them under a stronger obligation to be loyal. For much of the rest of the reign, Claudius ensured that no one would forget the symbolic success of carrying the frontiers of the empire beyond the Ocean; coins advertised trophies won 'from the Britons'. An inscription dating to c. A.D. 51/2 and probably originating from his triumphal arch alludes to 'the surrender of eleven British kings without loss', and asserts that 'he was the first to subject to the rule of the Roman people barbarian tribes beyond the Ocean'. During his fourth consulship in A.D. 49, Claudius extended the *pomerium* of the city to demonstrate his success in extending the empire.[42]

But the integration of Mauretania, south-east Britain, and also Lycia-Pamphylia during these years did not imply a 'policy' of general expansion, in contrast to that initiated by Tiberius. Military adventures can be seen as a function of a weak emperor's need to buttress his *gloria*. There could be no question of allowing other commanders such military *gloria*. The imperial legate in Lower Germany, Cn. Domitius Corbulo (half-brother of Caligula's wife Caesonia), took action to suppress raids into Gaul by a Chaucian chieftain, Gannascus, in 47; Claudius had to restrain him from proceeding with operations along the Frisian coast.[43]

While the administrative measures of these years can be seen primarily

---

[42] Britain: Barrett 1980 (C 332); Murison 1985 (C 379); Boatwright 1986 (C 33) (*pomerium*). Arch: *GCN* 43. The representation of 'Bretannia' at Aphrodisias: *JRS* 1987, plate xiv; Levick 1990 (C 372) plate 20.   [43] Corbulo: Syme 1970 (C 397).

as responses to Claudius' political weakness, the form they took suggests that Claudius was keen to represent himself as following in the footsteps of the Claudii of old, and – like Caligula – of Iulius Caesar. This lay behind the policy of extending Roman citizenship to the provinces, and looking after the interests of the army. Serving soldiers were granted the legal *privilegia maritorum*. Claudius was also anxious to retain the support of the Roman plebs. When he released some of the quaestors from their archaic obligations as prefects of Ostia and 'Gaul' (possibly Senonian Gaul, the region south of Rimini), it was not so much as part of a 'policy of centralization', but rather – so Suetonius tells us – so that young men interested in a political career could pay more attention to providing the plebs with games. As far as the propertied classes were concerned, an emperor's chief function was to ensure that the law courts functioned swiftly and effectively. Service as 'jurors' ('lay judges' might be a better translation) was irksome, but essential for the peaceful ordering of citizen society; Claudius reduced the age at which equestrians were required to present themselves for such service from twenty-five to twenty-four. More courts required more presidents, and one of the reasons for the transfer in A.D.44 of responsibility for the *aerarium Saturni* from two of the praetors to a pair of titular quaestors, selected by the emperor himself for a term of three years, will have been to make these praetors available for court service. Certainly there is nothing sinister in the fact that the two new quaestors were the emperor's personal appointees: by this stage no magistrate was elected to office without the implicit support of the *princeps*, and an emperor who did not personally select the men who were to look after the state treasury would have been curiously negligent of his responsibilities. We need not ascribe any conscious policy of centralization to Claudius; centralization was implicit in the patronage system of the Principate.

The important role that ex-slaves were said to have played in Claudius' household is more interesting, and should not be dismissed entirely as hostile propaganda. Claudius had had little experience of politics, even during the reign of Caligula. He depended for advice on *amici* of his family like Aulus Plautius and Lucius Vitellius, and on freedmen such as Narcissus, the *ab epistulis* (secretary for correspondence), Pallas, the *a rationibus* (keeper of accounts), Callistus, the *a libellis* (petitions), and Polybius, the *a studiis* (perhaps a speech-writer). But it does not follow that Claudius was systematically creating departments of state, or using his own dependants instead of freeborn citizens as part of a conscious 'policy' of rationalizing or controlling everything that was going on. During the Julio-Claudian period, men of wealth and standing were not yet as prepared as they later were to serve the emperor in a subordinate capacity. Freedmen were not only obedient, but also expendable; it might be politic for a weak emperor to blame unpopular measures on his ex-slaves – or his wives. (For the imperial court, see chapter 7.)

One area in which Claudius was keen to demonstrate the 'democratic' tradition he had inherited both from the Claudii and from Iulius Caesar was the distribution of corn to the urban population. Responsibility was transferred from the *aerarium* to the fiscus; legal privileges were granted to importers of grain; there were changes in the system of distribution – to bring an end to the crush which had taken place once a month, eligible citizens were given tickets telling them on which day of the month to collect their allocation. The fact that it was the emperor, not the Roman state, who ensured that people did not starve, was symbolized by the fact that distributions were now undertaken by an imperial procurator (the *de Minucia*), though there is no positive evidence that the senatorial *praefecti frumenti dandi* were formally abolished; the post had in any case largely been a sinecure. The personal role of the emperor and his family in looking after their dependent people by ensuring the proper functioning of the corn supply is shown by its use to publicize the succession. In 45, Octavia's betrothed, Lucius Silanus, represented Claudius at the distribution of largesse.

Coins and inscriptions confirm the emperor's personal interest in providing his people with 'Augustan grain' and fresh water. Apart from constructing the Aqua Claudia, Claudius instituted a second gang of slaves to look after Rome's aqueducts. He took equally seriously his patronal responsibilities to protect the people from fire and flood damage. An inscription shows that the canal he had dug in the lower reaches of the Tiber as part of the works associated with the construction of new harbour facilities at Ostia was not only intended to assist navigation, but also advertised as having the result that 'he freed the city from the danger of flooding'.[44]

Claudius was consul yet again in 47. Together with Vitellius, he also held the first formal census for over thirty years. This again was a way of honouring his supporters, and seeking the support of potential opponents. A large number of new senators owed their position to Claudius; and many families which had played a political role for two or three generations were raised to patrician status. Of course, we should not exclude completely a genuine feeling for past tradition as one of Claudius' motives in wanting to hold the ancient office of censor, and ensuring that there were patricians to carry on archaic religious rituals.

---

[44] Corn: Momigliano 1934 (C 377); Meiggs 1973 (E 84); Chandler 1978 (C 338); Rickman 1980 (E 109). CERES AUGUSTA: *GCN* 312(a) = *AN* 815. Frontin. *Aq.* 106; 'urbem inundationis periculo liberavit', *ILS* 207 = *GCN* 312(b) = *AN* 815. On Pallas, Oost 1958 (C 383); Sutherland 1987 (B 358) ch. 34.

That Claudius had genuine antiquarian interests is clear from the speech in which he defended his decision to allow Gallic aristocrats who were Roman citizens to stand for political office and join the Senate. The speech is summarized by Tacitus, and fragments survive from a copy set up at Lyons.[45] When the census was completed in 48, the consul Lucius Vipstanus Poplicola duly suggested that Claudius should be granted the title *pater senatus*; that was rejected – it would have defined the relationship of dependence of all senators on the emperor too clearly for comfort.

In the same year, he arranged a series of magnificent spectacles associated with the ceremony of the *ludi saeculares*, the date of which he had himself re-calculated so as to coincide with the eighth centenary of the foundation of Rome. They included a performance of the 'Troy game'; it was noted that when Britannicus, aged six, and Claudius' grand-nephew, Agrippina's son the nine-year-old Domitius Ahenobarbus, led the two groups, it was Domitius, as a descendant of Germanicus, who won most applause. But notwithstanding his descent, Domitius was still too young to be considered by Claudius a potential transitional ruler to fill the gap until Britannicus was old enough to succeed. One suitable candidate for this caretaker role was Antonia's husband Cnaeus Pompeius Magnus. The likeliest immediate successor to Claudius was still Lucius Silanus, who had been elected *praetor peregrinus* in this year (ten years or so before the normal age). The prominence of the Silani in these years can also be deduced from the fact that Lucius' brother Marcus Iunius Silanus had been *consul ordinarius* for the entire twelve months of the year 46.

The year 48 also saw the last major threat to Claudius' rule, an attempt by his wife Messallina to replace him. Responsibility for the removal of a number of potential rivals both inside and outside the imperial household is ascribed to her by our sources: they include Germanicus' daughter Iulia Livilla and C. Appius Iunius Silanus in 42; Tiberius' granddaughter Iulia (wife or widow of Rubellius Blandus) in 43; powerful senators such as Catonius Iustus in 43; Marcus Vinicius in 46, and Valerius Asiaticus in 47. Also in 47, the husband of Claudius' daughter Antonia, Cnaeus Pompeius Magnus, was executed, together with the parents through whom he derived descent from Pompey and Crassus. Antonia was re-assigned to Faustus Sulla, a son of Domitia Lepida: as Messallina's half-brother, he was no threat to her. In at least some of these cases, the blame may be assigned to Messallina. She had a claim to Julian blood in her own right, and was building up a power base for herself and her two children. But her plans threatened not just Claudius' daughter Antonia, but also many of the servants of the *domus*

45 *ILS* 212 = *GCN* 369 = *AN* 570; cf. Griffin 1982 (B 237).

Caesaris. The freedmen Narcissus and Mnester organized the opposition to her; she was accused of planning – or perhaps actually carrying out – a divorce, followed by a remarriage to the patrician Gaius Silius, who would presumably rule Rome as her consort until Britannicus was old enough to take over. Claudius was convinced of the truth of these allegations, and Narcissus had Messallina executed.[46]

Although Messallina's plot was suppressed, it again underlined the weakness of Claudius' rule. Despite his promise to the praetorians never to have anything to do with women, another matrimonial alliance was essential to put an end to speculation about the succession. There were several possible candidates. Lollia Paulina, who had been married to Caligula, was supported by Callistus, who had served that emperor. Antonia's mother Aelia Paetina had been married to Claudius before, and was descended from an ancient republican family. Agrippina was the most direct descendant of Augustus. Her candidature was strongly opposed by the freedman Narcissus, who saw that it would be the end of Britannicus' chances of succeeding. Agrippina was selected, thanks to the support of Antonius Pallas, who had been the trusted procurator of Claudius' and Germanicus' mother Antonia. Vitellius was given the task of asking the Senate to set aside the legal objections to a marriage between uncle and niece, and the wedding was celebrated on 1 January 49.

The rise of Agrippina implied the fall of the man who had been nearest to being Claudius' successor during Britannicus' minority, Lucius Iunius Silanus. For several years, he had been engaged to Claudius' daughter Octavia, now aged ten. Again it was the loyal Vitellius who arranged what was necessary: he accused Silanus of incest with his sister Iunia Calvina, the wife of his own son Lucius. Four days before Claudius' wedding, Silanus was forced to give up the praetorship to which he had been appointed and was expelled from the Senate. His only option was to kill himself. The new dynastic relationships were demonstrated publicly during Claudius' fifth and last consulship in A.D. 50: on 25 February he adopted Agrippina's son Lucius Domitius Ahenobarbus as Nero Claudius Caesar. Agrippina herself was given the title of Augusta, and her birthplace Cologne honoured with the title *Claudia Ara Agrippinensis*. After Nero came of age in A.D. 51, the Arval Brethren prayed for him in the same terms as for Claudius himself; he was appointed *princeps iuventutis*; and Cassius Dio mentions an edict in which Claudius entrusted the *cura* of the empire to Nero. For the next ten years, those men against whom Agrippina bore a grudge – such as Galba and Vespasian – disappeared from public life.

Claudius' marriage to Agrippina greatly strengthened his position, and the last years of his reign were marred by far fewer executions and

---

[46] Messallina: Meise 1969 (C 375) ch. 6; Ehrhardt 1978 (C 343).

plots than the first. The need to win military prestige was no longer so great, though much was made of the capture of the British king Caratacus, who was displayed at Rome. In the East, on the other hand, there were difficulties which continued at great financial expense into the next reign; the Parthian king Vologases I succeeded in imposing his brother Tiridates as king of Armenia. There continued to be food riots in the capital, but these were not now a serious threat.

The situation was stable because for the time being the succession was as clear as the imperial system could ever make it. Agrippina managed to have her own nominee Sextus Afranius Burrus appointed to command the praetorian cohorts; Burrus came from Narbonensis, where the Domitii Ahenobarbi had exercised patronage for generations. But Britannicus too had his supporters, including his grandmother, Domitia Lepida (also Nero's paternal aunt), and the *ab epistulis* Narcissus. Nero's position was strengthened by his marriage in 53 to Claudius' daughter Octavia (who formally had to be adopted into another *domus* to marry her father's adoptive son), and his appearance before the Senate on a number of occasions. Agrippina succeeded in having Domitia Lepida condemned for failing to keep the herdsmen on her great ranching estates in the south of Italy under proper control.

But Britannicus would be fourteen on 12 February 55, and old enough to be introduced to public life; there were rumours that Claudius said that he wished to be succeeded by a 'real' Caesar. That would have been fitting for one who had emulated Julius Caesar in being the patron of the people and of the army, effecting the spread of citizenship in the provinces, and making Britain part of the empire. Suetonius reports him as telling Britannicus to 'grow up quickly, so that he [Claudius] could explain all his actions'.[47] On 13 October 54, Claudius suddenly died after eating mushrooms. The suspicion that Agrippina poisoned her husband is shared by all ancient sources (only Josephus calls it a 'rumour'). His death was most opportune for Agrippina and her son, and the fact that Narcissus happened to be away from the court for a short time seems too convenient to have been fortuitous.

V. NERO[48]

At the moment of Claudius' death, there was no question of any other candidate for the imperial office but Nero; he was his predecessor's adopted son and the husband of his predecessor's daughter (herself descended from Augustus' sister); he had been designated to hold a

[47] 'Crescent, rationemque a se omnium factorum acciperet': Suet. *Claud.* 43.
[48] Main sources: Tac. *Ann.* XIII–XVI; Suet. *Nero.*; Dio LXI–LXIII. Biographers are attracted to Nero: cf. Wankenne 1984 (C 408). Assessments: Warmington 1969 (C 409); Griffin 1984 (C 352); Cizek 1972 (C 340) and 1982 (C 341); V. Rudich, *Political Dissidence under Nero* (London, 1993).

consulship when he reached the age of twenty (for A.D. 58), and he had been granted proconsular powers in Italy *extra urbem*. In A.D. 52 he had been appointed to the symbolic magistracy of *praefectus urbi feriarum Latinarum causa*. Had Claudius died even a few months later, he might have made a public wish to leave the empire to his natural-born son Britannicus; but the removal of Britannicus' grandmother Domitia Lepida, and the temporary absence of Narcissus, left Agrippina supreme in the palace, and the transfer of power was as straightforward as it had been in A.D. 14 or 37. The news of Claudius' death was kept secret for several hours, and then Burrus accompanied Nero to the camp of the praetorian guard where he was enthusiastically acclaimed. The promise of a donative of 15,000 sesterces to each soldier will have helped. Although Tacitus pretends that some soldiers asked where Britannicus was, Britannicus could not have shared the imperial office. He was still a child, as Tiberius Gemellus had been at Caligula's accession.

Nero went on to a meeting of the Senate, where he was recognized with the full imperial powers; he turned down, for the time being, the title *pater patriae*, since it seemed inappropriate to a youth of sixteen. It was not considered necessary, or sensible, for Claudius' will to be read and either approved, or set aside (Tacitus perversely suggests that had the will been read, Britannicus' plight might have received some sympathy precisely because he was not named as Claudius' successor).

Nero's speech at Claudius' funeral, as well as his speech to the Senate accepting the imperial powers and outlining his approach to the office that had been bestowed upon him, were both composed for him by his rhetoric teacher Seneca. Like Caligula and Claudius at their accessions, Nero promised a new start, and a return to the principles of Augustus. There would be no more secret trials within the emperor's *cubiculum*, and the Senate would be respected. That respect was made manifest by the appearance of the letters 'EX S. C.' on *aurei* and denarii between A.D. 54 and 64, to show that the use of gold and silver from the *aerarium* had been authorized by the Senate.

Seneca's treatise *De Clementia*, composed in A.D. 55, gives us some idea of how this adviser of Nero's thought that a Roman emperor should exercise power. That Seneca makes much of both the absoluteness, and the arbitrariness, of imperial power, does not indicate a belief that Roman republican ideals should give way to those of hellenistic (let alone so-called 'oriental') kingship. Rather, it simply makes explicit the fact that since the Battle of Actium there was only one man in the Roman world who was ultimately responsible for any decision affecting public life, and many decisions affecting the private lives both of members of his own household and of others who wished to participate in the political process. Seneca pointed out to Nero that while the gods' gift to him of uncontrolled power and unrivalled wealth was glorious indeed, it also implied the responsibility to behave in accordance with *virtus*; and clemency – essentially, restraint in the justified application of the emperor's power to punish those who had offended him – was a major imperial virtue.[49]

The success of Seneca and Burrus in persuading contemporaries that they were guiding the young emperor along the path of virtue has had a considerable effect on the historical tradition. Our sources agree that Nero's reign began well, and that it was only in the last few years that Nero alienated the elite to the extent of provoking conspiracy and ultimately open rebellion. The propaganda levelled against him by the rebels in A.D. 68 made much of his personality and cultural interests, in particular his philhellenism and his un-Roman desire to appear publicly as a performer. Opponents in the 60s had to explain why these character-traits had not provoked hostility from the start; and since antiquity did not allow much scope for the concept of character development, it was argued that Nero directed his self-indulgence towards other ends during the years when Seneca and Burrus were in a position to advise him. Burrus died and Seneca retired in 62; while they are characterized in a generally favourable way in the historical tradition, Burrus' successor as prefect of the praetorian guard, Ofonius Tigellinus, is presented as a wicked contrast to Burrus, and even (unconvincingly) as Seneca's enemy. Partly at least this was so that Nero's last years could be painted even blacker.

One consequence appears to be the development of a myth of the *quinquennium Neronis*; the idea that there was a period of five years during Nero's reign when the empire was well governed, and the relationship between Senate and *princeps* was as harmonious as it could ever be. Historians in Late Antiquity who found references to such a *quinquennium* in their sources were puzzled (since Nero ended up as a typical tyrant figure). They assumed that since Nero could not have exhibited such 'virtue' in his relations with the Senate (or with his own family), such praise must either refer to his public building programme, or to the traditional field in which a Roman displays his *virtus*, military conquests. Nero's building programmes were in fact remarkable. Although the reconstruction of Rome after the great fire of 64 resulted in considerable opposition, both because of its cost and because of the amount of land in the city which Nero reserved for his reconstructed palace (including the Golden House), even hostile writers had to accept that some of Nero's

---

[49] Seneca and Agrippina: Griffin 1976 (B 71). Coins: *GCN* 107 = *AN* 240; Sutherland 1987 (B 358) chs. 35–6. Seneca and Nero: Leach 1989 (B 106).

buildings were in accordance with the best Roman traditions of public benefaction: 'What was worse than Nero? What is better than Nero's Baths?'[50]

The idea of Nero's *quinquennium* is unlikely to have been invented in order to explain the excellence of Nero's buildings, or the real (but marginal) military successes associated with Corbulo and other commanders. It was perhaps rather an attempt to explain why so many senators who later reviled Nero as a monster were prepared to support him for so many years. 'Five years' from 54 take us up to A.D. 59, the year in which Nero killed his mother, and one senator who paraded his belief in *libertas*, Thrasea Paetus, walked out of the Senate; Paetus was later hailed as a Stoic martyr. Whether or not such Stoic propaganda was the source of the concept of a *quinquennium Neronis*, the idea itself shows there was unease about the fact that Nero had been a popular emperor until the last years of his reign.

It would be naive to believe that Nero's rule was perfect so long as he was under the control of Seneca and Burrus – and not only because Cassius Dio tells us how rich Seneca managed to become during his years as imperial adviser, to the extent that he was at least partly to blame for the exasperation of the Britons which led to Boudica's rebellion in A.D. 60. Political conflict did not cease because the emperor was being advised by a Stoic. Nero may have been the obvious candidate to succeed Claudius; but should he make any false move, there were a number of men who had survived Claudius' reign who might provide a focus of opposition – Domitia Lepida's grandson Britannicus, of course, but also her son (by a different marriage from that which produced Messallina), Faustus Cornelius Sulla Felix, the husband of Claudius' daughter Antonia. And further candidates of Julian ancestry were available in the person of Rubellius Plautus (Tiberius' great-grandson), and the surviving brothers and sisters of Lucius Iunius Silanus, who were grandchildren of Augustus' granddaughter Iulia. Nero's position needed strengthening by fair means, and foul. Fair means included claims to military prestige; in A.D. 55, the administration made much of an imperial salutation for a temporary success in Armenia achieved by Domitius Corbulo. To buttress his *gloria*, Nero was awarded a statue in the temple of Mars Ultor and an ovation.

Nero's legitimacy as emperor also needed strengthening in dynastic terms. Immediately after Claudius' funeral, the Senate had voted the late emperor divine honours; although the unpopularity of Tiberius and Caligula at the time of their deaths had prevented them from being

---

50 Quinquennium: Aur. Vic. *De Caes*. v.2–4. Cf. Murray 1965 (C 380); Hind 1971 (C 355); Levick 1983 (C 368). Nero's baths: Mart. VII.34. The character of Tigellinus: Roper 1979 (C 389).

similarly acclaimed, some female members of the *domus Caesaris* had been deified (Livia, Antonia, Drusilla), and Nero and his advisers had little choice but to do this for Claudius. The problem was that while the new emperor could now describe himself as *divi f.* (and did so on his coinage for the next year or so), Britannicus was equally a *divi f.*, and Sulla the son-in-law of a *divus*. While they remained on the scene, they would be a constant threat. Just as the rift between Domitia Lepida and Messallina contributed to the latter's fall, so a rift between Nero and Agrippina might lead her to drop her son in favour of any one of the other descendants of Augustus who were her cousins. The immediate problem was Britannicus; Agrippina, after all, was formally Britannicus' mother as well as Nero's.

The death of Britannicus early in 55, whether or not Seneca and Burrus were personally responsible, certainly strengthened their position – and Nero's – against Agrippina. So did the removal of Agrippina's ally Pallas from his post as *a rationibus*; he went on condition that no one should ask questions about the finances of the *domus Caesaris* under his stewardship. Although the removal of Pallas seems to have been directed against him personally – his brother Felix was allowed to remain procurator of Judaea until A.D. 60 – it was interpreted as an attack on Agrippina; Domitia Lepida and Iunia Silana (a sister of Caligula's first wife Iunia Claudilla) accused her of plotting to replace her son with Rubellius Plautus. His father-in-law Antistius Vetus was Nero's colleague as consul in this year; he went on to become legate of Upper Germany, but was replaced after a year. Although the charge was not believed, Agrippina's weakness as an emperor's mother, compared to her power as an emperor's wife, is demonstrated by the disappearance of her portrait from the coinage after 55.

During these years, Seneca and Burrus seem to have used their influence to appoint associates to positions of honour and power. The brother of Seneca's wife, Pompeius Paulinus from Arles, commanded the army of Lower Germany from 56 to 58; he was succeeded by Lucius Duvius Avitus, who came from Burrus' home town, Vasio, also in Narbonese Gaul. (Nero's supporters from this region had been inherited from his paternal ancestors, the Domitii Ahenobarbi, rather than from the Julio-Claudians.) Avitus had been consul in 56. Another provincial who may well have been associated with them, Lucius Pedanius Secundus from Barcelona, had been consul in 43 and was appointed *praefectus urbi* in 56. Secundus' murder at the hands of his own slaves in A.D. 61 was a major scandal, and provoked the veteran consular and famous jurist C. Cassius Longinus (consul in A.D. 30) to propose strong measures to control slaves. In accordance with the strict interpretation of the existing law, about 400 of Secundus' slaves (present in his palace when he was killed) were executed, in spite of demonstrations by the urban plebs, many of whom were themselves ex-slaves.

It has been argued that Longinus' interpretation of the law should be seen as evidence of a new direction in imperial policy, no longer under the influence of freedmen as it had been under Claudius. This raises the question whether the events of Nero's reign should be ascribed to the 'policies' of the emperor and his advisers rather than to his individual personality and temperament. During his first consulship, Nero realized that he vastly enjoyed being a public figure and at the centre of attention. He was delighted to accept the title of *pater patriae* when the Senate offered it to him a second time in 56, and he took repeated consulships (the second in 57, and the third in 58), although a proposal put forward by the Senate in 58, that he be *consul perpetuus* (something the Senate clearly thought he would enjoy) was turned down as being without precedent. The young man's desire to be seen and heard led him to intervene in senatorial debates, sometimes without proper briefing. On one occasion he suggested, apparently on his own initiative, that all customs dues (*portoria*) throughout the empire ought to be abolished, since they caused much resentment against unscrupulous tax-farmers. Having committed himself to this astonishing proposal, he could only be persuaded not to implement his promise with the utmost difficulty. The incident is no evidence for any hypothetical imperial 'policy' towards the provinces, or towards trade (there was a time when scholars anachronistically suggested that it proved that Nero or his advisers favoured free market economics); but it does throw a great deal of light on Nero's desire to make spectacular public utterances. Examples of imperial beneficence, for instance settling veterans on Italian land, should not be confused with an economic or agricultural 'policy'. In 57, Nero founded formal veteran settlements at Capua and Nuceria, and in 60, Puteoli was raised to the status of a colony as *Colonia Claudia Neronensis*; that may have been less to provide for veterans than as a response to internal political difficulties which had led to major disturbances in the colony two years previously, necessitating the intervention of troops.

The desire to appear in public was not restricted to the political forum. Like other good emperors, Nero took seriously his duty to provide the Roman people with games. Unfortunately, he had an uncontrollable desire to be seen by the public as a performer himself, both on the stage and at the races. At first, Nero could be persuaded only to appear himself in contests held in the relative privacy of the imperial *domus* (for example, in the imperial hippodrome in the Vatican valley). The Juvenalia, held to celebrate Nero's achieving adulthood in A.D. 59, were still held in private, but senators and equestrians were expected to take part. In the quinquennial games which Nero held on Greek lines in A.D. 60 and 65, such inhibitions were laid aside; Nero thought that, like a Greek aristocrat, he would win fame and glory rather than opprobrium by performing in person on the lyre and in the hippodrome. In a Greek city, like Naples, he felt he was appreciated for his own personal qualities as a performer, rather than just for being emperor (though even here, he did not formally compete in public until A.D. 64).

Nero's personal tastes certainly affected the political scene when it came to his matrimonial affairs. Our sources suggest that his love for Poppaea Sabina (granddaughter of Tiberius' legate of Moesia) led to a complete rift with his mother. Later rumours suggested that Nero's relationship with Poppaea had existed several years before he divorced Octavia in order to marry her in 62. It was said that the emperor asked his friend Marcus Salvius Otho to marry Poppaea so that Nero could visit her secretly. Certainly there was a good political reason why Nero was unable to repudiate Octavia immediately: if he did so, then his claim to the loyalty of Claudius' supporters would be weakened in comparison with that of Antonia's husband Sulla Felix. This was seen by Agrippina, who is said to have advised her son against divorcing Octavia on the grounds that he would have to return her dowry – the empire. It is not inconceivable that the great crime for which Nero was to go down in history, the murder of his mother in A.D. 59, was the result of a personal conflict about whether or nor Octavia could be divorced; the fact that Seneca and Burrus seem not to have been involved in the initial plot to shipwreck a pleasure-boat on which Agrippina was returning home from dinner with her son suggests that this may not have been planned as an act of state. It may be that the original intention was not to kill Agrippina, but to frighten her so that she would not in future interfere with her son's wishes.

But in any case, once the shipwreck had been arranged by one of Nero's freedmen, Anicetus (who had been Nero's *paedagogus*), and Agrippina survived, Nero panicked; Agrippina threatened to publicize the incident, and that would have led to enormous unpopularity and perhaps Nero's replacement by another candidate who had Agrippina's support. The only answer now was a cover-up, and that meant the elimination of Agrippina. Nero consulted Seneca and Burrus, who apparently knew nothing of the plot. Burrus pointed out that the praetorian guard could not be expected to condone the killing of a member of the family they were sworn to protect. In the end they decided to claim that Agrippina had been detected conspiring to replace Nero – not an unlikely story – and she was executed.

Agrippina's killing may have brought an end to the *quinquennium Neronis*, but it made little difference to Nero's popularity. While Thrasea

Paetus walked out of the Senate in disgust, other senators accepted the explanation given by Nero and Seneca. But in future Nero needed the legitimacy conferred by his marriage to Octavia more than ever; we should not be surprised that there was a three-year hiatus between Agrippina's death and Nero's divorce of Octavia. Before that could happen, Nero needed to remove Sulla Felix, and also Rubellius Plautus (who seems not to have had the slightest ambition to become emperor). Sulla had been required to withdraw to Marseilles in 58. A comet in A.D. 60 led to rumours that a new *princeps* was at hand; Nero utilized the occasion to require Rubellius Plautus to go into exile in Asia. In the same year Servius Sulpicius Galba was sent to Hispania Tarraconensis as imperial legate; the fact that Nero left him there for the rest of his reign suggests that this too, was intended as a mechanism for removing a potential rival, though one who was now perhaps too old to require execution.

The same year also saw continuing success by Corbulo in the campaign to maintain Armenia as part of the Roman sphere of influence. After the installation of a pro-Roman king, Tigranes V, Corbulo was transferred to the governorship of Syria. Tigranes made the mistake of invading the Parthian dependent state of Adiabene in the following year, which not surprisingly resulted in a Parthian military response. It seems that Corbulo had to remove Tigranes from his throne, and in the year after that (62) an attempt by the new legate of Cappadocia, Caesennius Paetus, to reimpose Roman control resulted in the humiliation of his army by the Parthians at Rhandeia. In A.D. 63, Corbulo was given an unusual grant of *imperium maius* over the eastern provinces, with an additional legion from the Danube army. Both Romans and Parthians saw that a compromise was to their mutual advantage (both were becoming aware of the danger posed by recent migrations by the Alani from central Asia), and Corbulo negotiated an agreement whereby Armenia was to be ruled by the Parthian candidate Tiridates – who would be able to maintain order in the kingdom – but Rome's right to treat Armenia as part of its *imperium* was recognized in that he was to be formally granted his diadem by Nero at Rome as a gift of the Roman people. (Tiridates' visit took place in 66.) Although these military operations brought long-term peace to the eastern frontier, and glory to Nero, they were expensive.

So was the rebellion in Britain, brought about – at least in part – by the calling-in of debts of 40 million sesterces by the philosophical Seneca's procurators. A commission of three consulars was appointed to investigate the tax-collecting system in 62. Part of the results of this investigation is revealed in an inscribed dossier found at Ephesus, containing the accumulated regulations regarding the farming of the *portoria* of

Asia. The *leges* governing such tax-collection had the dual aim of restraining extortion by collectors and ensuring that the public treasury received its due. How far they commanded the respect of collectors is another matter. It is only too probable that the emperor and Senate were more concerned to secure revenue, whose chief destination was army pay, than to see that publicans acted more fairly towards provincials. The emphasis on avoiding abuses in tax-collection which can be found in a document issued in A.D. 68 on Galba's behalf by the prefect of Egypt, Tiberius Iulius Alexander, reflects the discontent of provincials throughout the empire at the exactions of Nero's tax-collectors.[51]

Nero's reign saw a considerable number of trials of ex-governors for extortion. Both extortion by provincial governors, and accusations lodged against them by their opponents after their term of office had come to an end, were constant factors in Roman political life, under the Principate as under the Republic. But concern that its subjects should be justly treated should not be denied out of hand. It is even possible that Stoic theory may have played a part: Thrasea Paetus was particularly keen to oversee provincial matters, and on one famous occasion drew the Senate's attention to the unacceptable influence of the leading man in Crete, Claudius Timarchus. In 57, Thrasea successfully prosecuted the son-in-law of Tigellinus, an associate of Seneca's who was to become Burrus' successor as praetorian prefect. But in general such trials reflect rivalry between senators, rather than a 'policy' on the part of the government.[52]

Some sources blame Nero for the death of Burrus in A.D. 62, suggesting that Nero (now aged twenty-four) wished to rid himself of the restraining influence of his advisers. Seneca retired in this year, too: but that does not mean that their 'party' lost influence, or was replaced by another supposedly centred on Tigellinus. Tigellinus owed his rise to Seneca, and the picture of him as an enemy of Seneca and Burrus is an attempt by those who loyally served Nero to draw a clear but artificial distinction between Nero's good 'early' years and his wicked later years. The deaths of Britannicus and Agrippina, the exile of Sulla and Rubellius Plautus, and the uprising in Britain, all occurred while Seneca and Burrus were Nero's ministers. Seneca's retirement from public life at the age of sixty-five is not unexpected.

Tacitus' account makes much of the reintroduction of trials for *maiestas* in 62. Tacitus wants us to believe that such trials were a sign of a systematic policy on the part of an emperor to destroy opposition; that may have been the case under Domitian. But we have seen that under

---

[51] Ephesus dossier: Engelmann and Knibbe 1986 (B 228). Egypt: edict of Tiberius Iulius Alexander, MW 328 = *GCN* 391 = *AN* 600; cf. Chalon 1964 (E 909), and ch. 14*a* below.
[52] Timarchus: Tac. *Ann.* xv.20

Tiberius, *maiestas*-accusations flourished as a result of too little control of affairs by the emperor, and particularly his absence from Rome. Like charges of extortion, these accusations arose from conflicts between senators, and the opportunities they provided for able *novi homines* to acquire wealth, glory and the emperor's friendship. Perhaps Seneca's retirement made it easier for such men to exploit Nero's inexperience and gullibility. Earlier in his reign, he had rejected *maiestas*-accusations on the grounds that nobody could possibly have reason to hate him. The first such trial that Tacitus reports was of Antistius Sosianus, accused of composing epigrams insulting the emperor. A senatorial debate took place, in which Thrasea Paetus objected to the consul designate's proposal that the death penalty be imposed. The consuls were unhappy to accept his milder proposal of exile, and referred the matter to Nero; Tacitus suggests that Nero was angry that the Senate had been lenient, but there is no reason to suspect that Nero was lying when he said that he would have preferred the milder punishment himself. Most of those accused of treason (when they did not commit suicide first) were exiled, not executed.

In general, those who suffered before A.D. 64 suffered because of their descent from the family of Augustus. Sulla Felix and Rubellius Plautus, exiled in 58 and 60, were both executed in 62; this made Nero feel secure enough to divorce Octavia (alleging barrenness) and exile her to Campania in order to marry Poppaea, which he did twelve days later. Her husband Otho had been sent to govern Lusitania shortly after Agrippina's death in 59. Public demonstrations in Octavia's favour by the urban plebs, who had perhaps not forgotten the benefits Claudius had bestowed upon it, made Nero realize that he had been wrong to discount her influence; he claimed that she was involved in a plot, and had her executed on 9 June. Although Poppaea gave birth to a daughter in January 63, the baby died after a few months. Her deification as Claudia Augusta was no consolation for the fact that Nero still had no direct heir. He was now frightened of anyone who might have a claim to be emperor. In 64, Decimus Iunius Silanus Torquatus, great-great-grandson of Augustus through the younger Iulia, had to commit suicide; the only child of the consul of A.D. 19 who had not been disgraced was now Iunia Lepida, wife of Gaius Cassius Longinus.

Nero's mistakes had hitherto affected mainly those whom he feared as rivals. But on the night of 18–19 July 64 there occurred a chance event which resulted in widespread dissatisfaction with Nero both in the city of Rome and throughout the empire. The fire of Rome and the subsequent programme of reconstruction were immensely costly, and contributed directly to Nero's loss of popularity among the wealthy throughout Italy and in certain other provinces. Later rumours ascribing responsibility for the fire to Nero himself, anecdotes about the pleasure he took in playing the lyre while Rome burnt, and the revulsion of writers normally hostile to the Christians at his attempt to mark them out as the incendiaries, illustrate the extent to which an emperor was seen as personally responsible for the disasters as well as the benefits experienced by those whom he ruled. In fact, Nero did what he could to prevent the fire from spreading by creating fire-breaks (only to be accused of pulling down buildings in areas he coveted for extensions to his own palace); and like the emperors before him, he assisted those made homeless and personally supervised the rebuilding programme.

But the reconstruction of large areas of the city was immensely expensive, and put additional strains on the finances of the *domus Caesaris* and of the empire as a whole. Nero's designs for a new palace were grandiose, and involved the wholesale expropriation of areas of Rome that had been the traditional habitation of the senatorial elite. Nero refused permission for the great families to rebuild their town houses on sites that he required for his *domus transitoria*. Here was a case of direct and unresolvable conflict of interest between an emperor and his senators.

Not only senators suffered. We are told that the free distribution of grain to the urban population had to be suspended for a time, and that some troops were not paid. Nero was now so desperate for additional sources of funding that – like a typical tyrant – he is said to have told magistrates to ensure that the maximum number of cases resulted in conviction, and confiscations. We are told that he confiscated 'half the province of Africa' (effectively the fertile Bagradas valley in northern Tunisia), executing six landowners to do so. Temple treasures were melted down; the need for precious metals resulted in considerable hostility in provinces both West and East, and contributed directly to the rebellions both of Vindex and of the Jews. In May 66, the procurator of Judaea, Gessius Florus, arrived in Jerusalem claiming that the Jews owed the imperial *fiscus* arrears of tax to the extent of 40 talents of gold. When the money was not forthcoming, he removed 17 talents from the Temple treasury; and it was this act which sparked off violent opposition to the Romans to an extent that the Jewish elite, including client kings, were unable to control. An attempt by Cestius Gallus, the governor of Syria, to suppress the rebellion with military might in November 66 failed (the reasons for his withdrawal were inexplicable to contemporaries as they are to us), and Nero had to embark on a regular war to restore Roman control over Judaea.

These fiscal problems were exacerbated by the great fire at Rome, but as Boudica's rebellion shows, they had already existed before. Throughout Nero's reign, the precious metal content of the coinage had been steadily declining. By A.D. 64, there had been a major reform of the currency: the number of *aurei* to the pound of gold was increased from 40 or 42 to 45, the number of denarii to the pound of silver from 84 to 96. The fact that Nero's new coins were beautifully designed could not disguise the fact that he was short of money.[53]

Nero's removal of the descendants of Augustus meant that the option to replace him was extended to others whose connexion with the Caesars was far more distant. Nero's unpopularity was exploited by a group of people who selected as their candidate C. Calpurnius Piso, the man whose marriage to Livia Orestilla had been barred by Caligula (see above, p.226); Claudius had recalled him from exile and gave him a consulship in 41. The members of the conspiracy were said to have included Faenius Rufus, co-prefect of the guard, who was afraid of the influence of Tigellinus, with three of the sixteen praetorian tribunes. The consul designate, Plautius Lateranus, was also involved, and many others were accused. To give legitimacy to the cause, Claudius' daughter Antonia was to be taken to the praetorian camp after Nero had been killed in the circus. There was nothing 'republican' about the plot.

The effect of the conspiracy was that Nero now became afraid of many who were not related to him; and he reacted by eliminating an extraordinary number of suspects. Seneca was one of those required to end their lives. Donatives were given to the praetorian guard, and other gifts to those Nero thought he could continue to trust: triumphal insignia to Tigellinus, Petronius Turpilianus, and the later emperor Cocceius Nerva. Nymphidius Sabinus, grandson of Caligula's freedman Callistus, was given *insignia consularia*, and appointed praetorian prefect in association with Tigellinus. Nero may have had doubts as to whether Tigellinus was as efficient a soldier as he had been a horse-breeder.

The death of Poppaea Sabina in A.D. 65 was a political as well as a personal disaster for Nero: she had not provided him with an heir.[54] There were rumours of further plots, and executions. C. Cassius Longinus, husband of Iunia Lepida, was forbidden from attending meetings of the Senate; soon after Nero asked the Senate to exile him and his wife's nephew Lucius Iunius Silanus. Silanus, son of the Marcus reputedly poisoned by Agrippina in 54, was a descendant of Augustus; although the Pisonian conspirators had ignored his prior claim to the position of Caesar, Nero felt he had to execute him after a trial for incest. Cassius himself was able to return from exile in Sardinia under Galba. Another casualty of a distant relationship with the imperial family was

---

[53] Problems in the provinces: confiscations in Africa: Pliny, *HN* XVIII.7.35. For Judaea, see ch. 14*d*. Bullion shortage: Sutherland 1987 (B 358) ch. 40.

[54] Nero responsible for Poppaea's abortion: Ameling 1986 (C 329).

Antistius Vetus, Rubellius Plautius' father-in-law, and once a protégé of
Agrippina.

Nero's execution of those he feared continued into 66. Ostorius
Scapula, son of an early governor of Britain, had consulted astrologers
about how much longer Nero was likely to survive. P. Anteius, an ex-
consul, was accused on the same charge; both killed themselves. The list
of casualties included Seneca's two brothers, Annaeus Mela (father of
Lucan, who had already killed himself on Nero's orders), and Gallio
(who appears in the Acts of the Apostles as governor of Achaea);
C. Petronius, Tigellinus' rival as Nero's boon companion; the ex-
praetorian prefect Rufrius Crispinus; Anicius Cerealis, who had been
consul in 65; and the two noted Stoics, Thrasea Paetus and Barea
Soranus. Stoicism may have given some of these the vocabulary and
slogans to articulate their opposition to the way Nero was behaving, but
those Roman families that now turned against Nero did not do so as a
'group' or 'party', nor, primarily, because of any philosophical beliefs
they may have held about 'ideal kingship', let alone 'republicanism'.

To strengthen his own dynastic position, Nero proposed to marry
Claudius' daughter Antonia; but she had no wish to oblige. Instead,
Nero married Statilia Messallina, the widow of another of his victims,
Vestinus Atticus. She counted amongst her ancestors Augustus' gener-
als Statilius Taurus and Valerius Messalla Corvinus.

Nero also made every effort to re-establish his military prestige after
65. He made the most of the solution to the Armenian problem which
had been achieved by Corbulo, and arranged some spectacular festivals
on the occasion of King Tiridates' visit to Rome in 66 to receive his
diadem from Nero's own hands. New issues of coins stressed 'Augustan
Victory', the Altar of Peace, and the fact that 'he shut the temple of Janus
after peace had been achieved by land and sea'. Nero honoured generals
like Vespasian and Suetonius Paulinus (who was granted a second
consulship), perhaps to counter any threat from the *virtus* demonstrated
by Corbulo. And he planned to gain military prestige himself by leading
a major expedition in the East during these years; it was a period when
both the Romans (on the lower Danube) and the Parthians felt that they
were coming under increasing pressure from tribes originating further
east (the legate of Moesia between A.D. 60 and 67, Tiberius Plautius
Silvanus, had already been involved in fighting). The good relations
between Nero (and later Vespasian) and the Parthians suggest that in the
context of the solution to the Armenian conflict, the two states had come
to an agreement about the need for military co-operation. Nero
advertised an expedition against the 'Caspian Gates' at the eastern end of
the Caucasus, and astrologers predicted that he would be enthroned in

glory at Jerusalem. In preparation for the campaign, the Fourteenth
Legion was withdrawn from Britain; it had distinguished itself in the
repression of Boudica, and was granted the title *Martia Victrix*.
Turpilianus (one man Nero trusted) was put in charge of raising a new
legion in Italy. The annexation of Pontus as a province in A.D. 64 may
also have been connected with Nero's eastern plans. The coins struck
during his last years reveal an increasing interest in military matters.[55]

But Nero's prime concern apparently continued to be the glory he
could achieve as a public performer. Only the Greeks, he was heard to
say, appreciated real virtue. He may originally have wanted to visit
Greece in A.D. 65, to be able to compete at the regular Olympic games. In
the event, certain quadrennial games had to be rescheduled in order to
allow him to participate, and carry off the prizes. It is clear that his visit
made him genuinely popular in Greece. At Corinth, he dramatically re-
enacted the 'liberation' of Greece from direct Roman administration, as
played out by Flamininus in 196 B.C.[56]

During Nero's journey to Greece with his entourage, a further
conspiracy was uncovered at Beneventum (details are sparse, and it is not
clear whether Nero was present when the conspiracy was brought to
light). The leading figure was Annius Vinicianus, who was executed.
Nor is it clear what this man's relationship was to the Annius Vinicianus
who was involved in Camillus Scribonianus' rebellion against Claudius:
his brother may have been the Annius Pollio implicated in the Pisonian
conspiracy in the previous year. What is known is that he was Corbulo's
principal supporter. He had been *legatus* of the Fifth Legion in Corbulo's
Armenian campaign of *c*. A.D. 58, and was the husband of one of
Corbulo's two daughters (the other was later to become Domitian's
wife). In the previous year, Annius had been sent by Corbulo to
accompany Tiridates on his journey to Rome; Cassius Dio says that this
was as much to put a hostage of his good faith into Nero's hands as
anything else. Tiridates had commented to Nero 'What a good slave he
had in Corbulo'. The conspiracy at Beneventum – whether real or
imagined – meant that Nero knew that he could now no longer rely on
Corbulo's support. The implication was clear, and Corbulo was summoned to meet Nero in Greece, where he was ordered to kill himself. A
little later (and presumably in connexion with the same conspiracy) the
legates of the upper and lower Rhine armies were also summoned to
Nero in Greece, and forced to suicide. They were the brothers Publius
Sulpicius Scribonius Proculus and Scribonius Rufus, sons of a senator

[55] Nero as *imperator*: *ILS* 233 (Luna) = *GCN* 149 = *AN* 287. PACE P. R. TERRA
MARIQUE PARTA IANUM CLUSIT: Sutherland 1987 (B 358) ch. 39.
[56] Liberation of Greece: *ILS* 8794 = *GCN* 64 = *AN* 127.

executed (in the very Senate-house, according to our sources) by Caligula in A.D. 40.

On his arrival in Greece Nero heard of the failure of Cestius Gallus, governor of Syria, to restore Roman control over Jerusalem in November 66. Gallus seems to have died soon after, and it was imperative for someone to be appointed quickly to take command in the full-scale war which needed to be fought for control over Judaea. In February 67 Nero appointed two men to replace Gallus, Mucianus as legate of Syria, and Vespasian to take command of the war itself; it is not surprising that the administrative problems involved in separating what had been a single provincial administration into two different commands should have caused friction between the two generals, and we do not have to suppose that there was any deep ill-feeling between the two. Their disagreements did not prevent Vespasian from pursuing the pacification of Galilee with general success during the years A.D. 67 and 68, as described in ch. 14*b* of this volume. By the time of Nero's death, when Vespasian ceased major operations in Palestine, there was little left for the Roman army to do apart from the recovery (and destruction) of Jerusalem itself and of a number of other forts whose reduction was more a matter of demonstrating Rome's might than of removing a serious threat.

By the winter of A.D. 67/8, it had become clear to Helius and the other members of the household who were looking after affairs in the capital that Nero's artistic victories in Greece had weakened, not strengthened, his position with the Roman elite. In January, Helius went to Greece in person (in spite of the dangerous winter weather) to persuade Nero that a return to Rome was imperative. As he travelled back to Rome via Naples, Nero's first concern was to be honoured as a Greek Olympic victor by driving his chariot through specially constructed gaps in the walls of the cities he passed on his journey to Rome via Naples. He showed much less concern when he heard that Gaius Iulius Vindex, legate of Gallia Lugdunensis, had thrown off his allegiance – news which reached him at Naples on the anniversary of his mother's murder.

CHAPTER 6

FROM NERO TO VESPASIAN

T. E. J. WIEDEMANN

I. A.D. 68

In January 68, Nero had been persuaded by his freedman Helius to break off his successful and popular tour of Greece and return to Italy immediately. The fact that Helius braved the winter storms to cross the Adriatic confirms that he was deeply concerned about the possibility not just of a conspiracy among members of the Senate at Rome, but of a rising by one or more provincial governors with their armies. The evidence for this was a series of letters calling for Nero's overthrow circulated to other governors by C. Iulius Vindex, probably the legate of Gallia Lugdunensis. Some of the recipients passed the letters they received from Vindex on to Rome via local imperial procurators. But those who were administering the government on Nero's behalf cannot have been certain which governors if any were still to be trusted.

Imperial procurators in Tarraconensis, for instance, will have realized that the legate, Servius Sulpicius Galba, was taking no action to punish those who were circulating verses hostile to Nero. No one could tell whether Galba might not be similarly tolerant of those – perhaps the same people – who were plotting armed disloyalty.

The only direct evidence we have for assessing Vindex's reasons for rebelling, and his objectives, are the anti-Neronian writings he circulated, and the inscriptions on the coins he minted to pay his followers. Suetonius tells us that Vindex referred to Nero as 'Ahenobarbus', emphasizing that he had not been born a member of the *domus Caesaris*, and condemned him for his philhellenism: he was a charioteer and lyre-player with a weak voice. The coinage issues confirm that Vindex sought to represent himself as asserting traditional Roman values, protecting the Roman community against a tyrant. Legends on coins refer to the 'Salvation of the Human Race', showing the oak wreath bestowed on a Roman soldier for saving a fellow-citizen's life, together with the letters SPQR. There is an *aureus* with Mars the avenging war-god, and a pair of military standards described as belonging to the Roman people. There are denarii depicting 'Rome restored (to freedom)', and Hercules and Jupiter as liberators. Very similar coins were minted by Galba in Spain after he had thrown off his allegiance to Nero. The Spanish denarii refer to the 'Freedom' and to the 'Life-force of the Roman People', with images of Mars the avenger and a liberty-cap. Perhaps the most interesting issue shows personifications of Spain and Gaul with a Victory between them, and the legend 'Harmony of the Spanish and Gallic Provinces'; the reverse represents the 'Victory of the Roman People' driving in a two-horse chariot. The similarity between Vindex's issues and those of Galba indicates collusion between the two legates after they had withdrawn support from Nero, but it cannot prove that Galba was actively involved in Vindex's conspiracy from the beginning. Nor does the fact that both legates minted coins with inscriptions asserting republican virtues and referring to the 'Roman People' mean that Vindex or Galba rebelled against Nero in order to re-activate a form of republican constitution. That was not what 'The Liberty of the Roman People' meant to Vindex, whose ancestors had not even been citizens at the time of the Republic. He will have wanted to replace a failed *princeps* by a better one, and will have been well aware that he himself had no chance of attaining that position. On the other hand that does not mean that an assertion of loyalty to the *SPQR* was simply a cover for treason against the legitimate emperor; for there was a sense in which the *SPQR* were sovereign. They could not of course *make* one man more or less powerful than another; but they could *recognize* which man, and which group of supporters, had the most power and authority. What Vindex recognized was the right of the Senate and people to decide who it was who was actually in control – hoping, of course, that it would not be Nero, but someone else who had a claim to inherit the property and powers of the Caesars. An obvious candidate was Galba in Spain, whose name had already been mentioned as a claimant in A.D. 41.[1]

Vindex was not just a legate of Caesar; he was also a powerful man in Gaul in his own right. We are told that his ancestors had been 'kings' amongst the Aquitanians (ethnically, Basques, although the root *vent-is Celtic). We should not be surprised that Vindex made use of his local connexions; and we hear of Basque fighters volunteering to join Galba. Rivalry between different Gallic tribes, as well as between Gauls and

---

[1] The narrative sources for A.D. 68 are unsatisfactory: we cannot even be certain that Vindex's province was Lugdunensis, Suet. *Ner.* 40–50; Plut. *Galba*; and Dio LXII(LXIII).22–LXIII.3. On the numismatic evidence, see Sutherland 1987 (B 358) chs. 41–6; Zehnacker 1987 (B 364). For Vindex's coin issues, see GCN 70 (cf. MW 27): SALVS GENERIS HVMANI; SPQR; MARS VLTOR; SIGNA POPVLI ROMANI; HERCVLES ADSERTOR; ROMA RESTITVTA; IVPPITER LIBERATOR. For Galba's coins, see GCN 72 (cf. MW 25–6): LIBERTAS P.R.; GENIO P.R.; CONCORDIA HISPANIARVM ET GALLIARVM; VICTORIA P.R.

For discussions of the end of Nero's reign, Griffin 1984 (C 352); Reece 1969 (C 387); Warmington 1969 (C 409) ch. 13. The 'native revolt' interpretation of Vindex's uprising can still be found; Dyson 1971 (A 25). Galba's supporters are discussed in Syme 1982 (C 400). There is a readable biography of Galba in French; Sancery 1983 (C 390).

communities of Italian settler origin with their traditional loyalty to the Ahenobarbi, will have played a role in determining who joined and who opposed Vindex. But there is no basis for the theory, popular earlier in this century, that Vindex's revolt was essentially a 'native' uprising against Roman rule. Tacitus follows the official Flavian interpretation of events in coupling Vindex with Civilis as though both were primarily native chieftains seeking to set up their own separate (but Romanized) states in north-west Europe. Like Civilis, Vindex will have exploited what opposition there was to Roman rule, aggravated by Nero's fiscal requirements; but it would be anachronistic to see him as a nationalist freedom-fighter rather than as a Roman senator reacting against Nero's 'tyranny'.

While the numismatic evidence demonstrates that those who rose against Nero agreed in recognizing the ultimate authority of the 'Roman Senate and People', the literary sources suggest that it was not clear from the start that Vindex would win the support of Galba, or of anyone else. Although Galba kept back evidence of Vindex's intentions from Nero's procurators, he was sceptical of Vindex's chances of success. It was Titus Vinius Rufinus, the commander of the Sixth Legion (currently the only legion stationed in Spain), who pointed out that if Nero's opponents did not all rally round Vindex now, the frightened and angry emperor would subsequently find it easy to deal with them one by one.

Galba was acclaimed as 'Caesar' by his troops at the regular gubernatorial assizes held at New Carthage on 2 or 3 April. He immediately rejected the imperial title, which soldiers had no right to bestow, but called himself 'Legate of the Roman Senate and People'. There was some opposition: the proconsul of Baetica, Obultronius Sabinus, and his legate, Cornelius Marcellus, had to be executed. Apart from Titus Vinius, Galba was sure of the support of the quaestor Caecina Alienus, who took over the government of Baetica, and in particular the legate of Lusitania, Marcus Salvius Otho. Between them, the three governors controlled most of the empire's resources of precious metals. Otho had for many years been an associate of the young Nero. Almost nine years before, Nero had sent him to Lusitania as governor in order to facilitate his own access to Otho's wife Poppaea. Poppaea was now dead; Otho had nothing to lose from Nero's overthrow, and much to gain. Galba would be seventy in December, and had no son to succeed him in the imperial office, while Otho was thirty-seven, and available as Galba's supporter and successor.

Nero had heard of Vindex's rebellion at Naples. He was not unduly concerned at news of unrest in Gaul, but Galba would have some chance of winning recognition as Caesar; his defection changed the picture completely. It confirmed that no governors could be trusted any longer.

Petronius Turpilianus, who had proved so loyal in the suppression of Piso's conspiracy, was sent to northern Italy to assemble an army, to include the Fourteenth Legion and a new one raised from the marines at Misenum. As a deterrent to others, Galba's estates in Italy were confiscated; Galba retaliated by auctioning off the property of the *domus Caesaris* in Spain, using the proceeds to raise a second legion from Roman citizens in Spain, the Seventh *Galbiana*. Its legionary eagle was formally presented on 10 June. Galba appointed as its commander a man from Tolosa, Antonius Primus; he had been expelled from the Senate in A.D. 61 for helping to forge a will, probably before reaching the praetorship, and exiled to Marseilles. As one of Nero's exiles – and almost certainly an acquaintance of Vindex – he had immediately given his support to Galba.

Primus, Otho, Vinius and Alienus had made it clear that they were deserting Nero in favour of Galba. Others who played an important part in Nero's overthrow did not make their intentions so clear, either to contemporaries or to us. At some point in A.D. 68, the legate of the Third Legion in north Africa, Clodius Macer, threw off the authority of the government in Rome, deposed the proconsul of Africa, and raised an additional legion, which he called *I Macriana Liberatrix*. A denarius, probably from Carthage, describes him not as emperor but simply as 'Propraetor of Africa' (it also carries the letters S[*enatus*] C[*onsulto*]). Galba had to use force to suppress Macer. We are told that members of Nero's household went to Macer in Africa and urged him to resist Galba; that may have been before or after Nero's death and Galba's recognition by the Senate in June. But Rome experienced a considerable shortfall of grain well before Nero's death; and that suggests that Macer had rejected Nero's authority, and prevented corn-ships from leaving Carthage for Italy, soon after he heard of Vindex's rebellion. Macer may have thought that by starving Rome, he could persuade the Senate to recognize that it was he, not Galba, who had the power to be Nero's successor.[2]

The actions of the legate commanding the upper Rhine army, Verginius Rufus, are even more difficult to interpret. We must assume that Rufus, like his colleagues, had been approached by Vindex. When Vindex offered Galba the support of Gaul, he claimed to have 100,000 soldiers to put at his disposal; since Vindex's own provincial levies only came to 20,000 men, this can only mean that he thought that some at least of the Rhine legions, and their commanders, would support his coup. On the other hand, it is also possible that Rufus stayed loyal to Nero. Tacitus says explicitly that the Rhine legions stood by Nero and the Caesars longer than other armies did.

Rufus mobilized his legions and marched south west through the

[2] Macer coins: Sutherland 1987 (B 358) ch. 42; *GCN* 73; cf. MW 24.

Franche Comté in the direction of central Gaul. When he heard of Rufus' march, Vindex was attempting unsuccessfully to reduce Lyons, which remained loyal to Nero out of gratitude for recent favours; he broke off the siege, marched towards Rufus, and met him at Vesontio, probably towards the end of May. There followed a battle in which Vindex's levies were defeated by the Rhine legions, superior in numbers, weapons and training; the only option left to Vindex was suicide. Soon (but not necessarily immediately) after the battle, Rufus was acclaimed emperor; he rejected the offer (or several such offers). Many years later, the epitaph on his tomb stated that 'after Vindex's defeat, he laid claim to the imperial power not on his own behalf but on that of the fatherland'.

Since the 1950s, the consensus amongst scholars – following the account given by Cassius Dio – has been that the Battle of Vesontio was a mistake. Vindex and Rufus were co-conspirators who had arranged to combine their forces and then to march on Italy together in support of Galba. Unfortunately, when Vindex's largely Gaulish levies met the legionaries from the Rhine, the resentment which the two groups felt for one another resulted in unexpected violence which the respective commanders could not contain. Similar uncontrolled violence by Roman troops during the campaigns of the following year suggests that this is not impossible. On this interpretation, the Rhine legions may have hated the Gauls and their upstart leader, but that does not mean that they were loyal to Nero; indeed, having flexed their muscles at Vesontio, they offered to put their own commander in Nero's place.

If Vindex was indeed certain of Rufus' support for himself and Galba, it is curious that he should have marched north to meet Rufus at Vesontio instead of waiting for his army at Lyons or Vienne. It is more likely that Vindex feared that Rufus and the Rhine army would stand by Nero. As for Rufus, he may well have destroyed Vindex on Nero's behalf; but very soon after the battle news reached Gaul that Nero had lost his nerve and killed himself. It was now essential for Rufus to hide the fact that he and his soldiers had supported Nero and destroyed Galba's allies, and it was perhaps only then that the Rhine legions acclaimed Rufus as an imperial candidate – not as an alternative to Nero, but as an alternative to Galba, who would not (and did not) look kindly upon what they had done to Vindex.[3]

Rufus was certainly not acting in association with Galba; Galba later separated him from his army in order to give him the 'honour' of

---

[3] On the difficulties of evaluating the tradition about Vesontio, see Brunt 1959 (C 334); Daly 1975 (C 342); Levick 1985 (C 370). Cassius Dio's account is at LXII(LXIII).24. Rufus' epitaph (Pliny, *Ep.* VI.10.4; cf. II.1):

> Hic situs est Rufus, pulso qui Vindice quondam
> imperium adseruit non sibi sed patriae.

accompanying him on his journey to Rome. The immediate effect of the news of Rufus' destruction of Vindex was to make Galba withdraw to his base at Clunia, where he is said to have contemplated suicide himself. It was later asserted that he erroneously thought that Rufus had betrayed him; he may rather have feared that the Rhine legions would impose their own candidate, or that their victory would allow Nero to re-establish his authority.

Rufus' victory at Vesontio turned out to be irrelevant to the final issue, since early in June Nero had lost his nerve and effectively abandoned the administration of affairs. We do not know enough about the exact chronology of events that year to be able to say whether he had heard of Vindex's defeat, or of the Rhine army's attempt to acclaim Rufus. He may have suspected the loyalty of Turpilianus' army in northern Italy. A plan to flee to Egypt led Nymphidius Sabinus, who in Tigellinus' continued illness commanded the praetorian guard, to promise them a donative of 30,000 sesterces each if they broke their oath of loyalty to Nero, on the grounds that their emperor had already abandoned them. The Senate's role was to confirm that Nero no longer had the authority to govern, and to decide who in fact had that authority. On 9 June (or possibly 11) it declared Nero an enemy of the Roman people, recognized Galba as Caesar, acclaimed him as Augustus, and voted him imperial powers. Nero, realizing that the only support he had left was that of certain members of his household staff (and, perhaps, of the Roman plebs), committed suicide; his last words – 'what a creative artist I have been' – show how much more interested he was in his public image than in governing. Galba's freedman Icelus was released from custody and travelled to Clunia in a mere seven days to inform the new emperor of the events in the capital.

Each new emperor of the Julio-Claudian dynasty had faced considerable but quite different problems in establishing himself. Galba had to face most of them together. At Tiberius' accession, there had been no previous transfer of power from one emperor to another; but Tiberius, Caligula and Nero had been the legitimate heirs of their predecessors. Galba's links with the Julio-Claudians were so tenuous as to be worthless in terms of loyalty. He made what he could of these links: an official document from Egypt calls him 'Lucius Livius Galba', and Livia's head appears on his coins.[4] But like Claudius, Galba was an 'outsider' taking over *possessio* of the *domus Caesaris* after the death of its previous *paterfamilias*, and in the absence of direct heirs. As in A.D. 41, there were others who put forward their own claims and who either had to be eliminated (like Clodius Macer in Africa), or whose support had to

---

[4] Galba is called 'Livius' in the Edict of Tiberius Iulius Alexander: MW 328 = *AN* 600 (see above, p. 249). DIVA AVGVSTA coin: MW 75.

be won, at least until they could be made safe, like Verginius Rufus. Galba had to ensure that all these groups would come to be as dependent upon him as they had been on earlier Caesars; under the circumstances, we should not be too surprised at his lack of success.

The nature of the Principate naturally gave any new emperor the advantage of having patronage to bestow, and being able to remove from positions of authority men upon whose loyalty he had no claims, to replace them with others who would be *ipso facto* in the new emperor's debt. While Verginius Rufus was beholden to no one, his successor Hordeonius Flaccus was indebted for his office to Galba. At the start of a new reign, individuals competed to win the favour of a man who brought few supporters with him from Spain. Thus although the legions on the lower Rhine, under the command of Fonteius Capito, had not been involved in the events at Vesontio, individual officers were keen to show exceptional loyalty to Galba. At Bonn, the legionary commander Fabius Valens (who claimed to have been a supporter of Rufus, and therefore, perhaps, an opponent of Nero) was quick to administer the oath of loyalty to Galba. Later on in the year he again tried to demonstrate his loyalty by executing his commander, Fonteius Capito, on the grounds that he was plotting against Galba. Valens will have assumed that he deserved a reward for his efforts, perhaps in the shape of the Rhine army command. Galba did not reward him, and instead appointed Aulus Vitellius to command the army on the lower Rhine in December. It was Otho who had to pay the price for Galba's ingratitude.

With the exception of Africa under Macer – whom Galba soon destroyed, possibly after a naval campaign – there was now no province which failed to recognize the new emperor. But not all those who held military power owed their authority to Galba. Galba's authority might be seen as stemming from the decision by the praetorian prefect Nymphidius Sabinus to abandon Nero. It was Sabinus who was in effective control of Rome. He allowed sections of the urban mob, those who thought that they had suffered under Nero, to indulge in attacks of physical violence on some of Nero's freedmen. He also removed the invalid Ofonius Tigellinus from his position as co-commander of the guard, claiming that Tigellinus had been particularly involved in all the evil aspects of Nero's administration (a myth which those who had loyally served Nero for many years were happy to accept). The removal of Tigellinus concentrated power in Sabinus' hands; and Sabinus soon came to think of himself as potentially more than a kingmaker. To justify a bid for control of the imperial household, rumours were circulated that he was in fact an illegitimate son of Caligula, whose freedman his grandfather had been.

Galba's insistence that, since he was a member of a republican family that could be traced back for several centuries, his authority stemmed from his own *domus* as well as, and as much as, that of the Caesars, is not likely to have endeared him to those who belonged to the imperial household. Like other emperors, Galba depended on the help of trusted freedmen – but his own freedmen, Asiaticus and Icelus (to whom he granted equestrian privileges), were naturally a threat to those who had served the Julio-Claudians. Otho was later to win considerable success by representing himself as Nero's successor as head of that *domus*. Anecdotes were told of how Galba's idea of distributing largesse was to give people tiny amounts of money, but stress that they came from his private purse, and not that of the Caesars. He had at first rejected the title of 'Caesar' altogether; although he accepted it from the senatorial delegation which met him at Narbo on his journey from Spain to Rome, the senators noted that they were entertained off Galba's family dinner-service, and not off that of the Caesars which had been specially sent out to him. Titus Vinius had to make it clear to Galba that this snobbery would not help him to gain legitimacy.

Galba's arrival in Rome would mean changes in the distribution of power there; he was bringing his own supporters with him, Icelus and Asiaticus to help him in the *domus*, and Titus Vinius and Otho in the government. These men were bound to replace not just the leading administrators within the *domus*, but also public officials appointed by Nero – for instance, the *praefectus urbi*, Flavius Sabinus. Rumours that Galba might appoint the commander of his legionary guard, Cornelius Laco, to the praetorian prefectship, implied that Nymphidius Sabinus would either have to accept a much less prominent role than that which as 'Benefactor of the Senate and People' he had been playing since Nero's death, or seize power before Galba and his supporters reached Rome. In addition, Macer's interruption of corn supplies from Africa was one of the factors that undermined Galba's popularity at Rome. We do not have enough evidence to be entirely certain whether Nymphidius Sabinus did in fact plan a conspiracy, or whether he and his friends were 'framed' either by those at Rome who wished to curry Galba's favour, or those accompanying Galba on his journey who had no wish to tolerate potential rivals. We are told that one night in late summer, Sabinus attempted to enter the praetorian camp; his way was blocked by one of the tribunes, Antonius Honoratus, who had him killed. It was claimed that Sabinus held in his hands a speech, composed by the senator Cingonius Varro, appealing for the support of the troops.

Whatever the threat Sabinus may have represented, Galba's reaction was harsh. He ordered the execution of Varro, and took the opportunity to kill other friends of Sabinus and of Nero, such as the exiled king Mithridates of Pontus (who had said some unpleasant things about

Galba's appearance). Petronius Turpilianus was ordered to commit suicide. These deaths did not bode well for those who hoped that *clementia* would be one of Galba's imperial virtues. As Galba's entourage approached Rome, the marines whom Nero had constituted into a regular legion during his last months appealed to be allowed the same privileges as the new Seventh Legion which was accompanying him from Spain. Galba rejected their pleas; several of them lost their lives in the violence that followed.

Galba was rapidly losing much of the goodwill with which he had set out. It was not just his parsimonious personal regime which led to resentment. He realized that Nero had been unpopular during his last years because of the need to raise funds in the provinces in order to pay for new buildings and spectacles in the capital. Galba's solution was to cut expenditure. He even went so far as to set up a commission of thirty senators to try to get back money which Nero had bestowed on his favourites. Needless to say they claimed to be able to recover only one tenth of what Nero had disbursed.

There were other aspects of Galba's administration that undermined support for him. On Nero's death, those exiled by the tyrant during the last few years returned to Rome, and some opened legal proceedings against those who had accused them; a praetor-elect, Helvidius Priscus, was particularly keen to begin a vendetta against all those who had supported Nero. When Galba arrived, he made it clear that the past should best be forgotten. As expected, he, or Icelus, arranged for the execution of some of the principal freedmen of the *domus Caesaris*: Helius, Polyclitus, Petinus and Patrobius. On the other hand many (including Helvidius Priscus) took it amiss that Vinius, a notorious womanizer, saved Tigellinus because he was interested in his widowed daughter. We are left with the impression that Galba was not displeased by rumours hostile to Vinius: Vinius' role as Galba's closest adviser – symbolized by his designation to the consulship for A.D. 69 as the emperor's colleague – gave him more power than was safe.

Historians once thought that one of Galba's strengths as an imperial candidate had been that he had no obvious successor. In fact there was a grand-nephew, Publius Dolabella, and the Caesars' personal bodyguard of German soldiers assumed that he would be Galba's heir. This displeased Galba: the history of earlier emperors had indicated that when the succession was clear, those who wished to prosper transferred their loyalty from the setting to the rising sun. A plurality of potential successors could be as much to an emperor's advantage as a source of instability for the empire (see above, ch.5 n.4). The fact that Galba should have thought that the adoption of a son and successor would be a solution to his present difficulties therefore requires explanation. Even more surprising is the identity of the man he adopted: Lucius Calpurnius

Piso Frugi Licinianus. This Piso was the youngest son of the consul of
A.D. 27, destroyed by Messallina in A.D. 47. Although he had been exiled
under Nero as a member of a family who seem consistently to have
represented a threat to the Julio-Claudians, Piso had no political
ambitions (we do not even know whether he had ever been a senator).
The choice of Piso was not made because Galba needed the support of
Piso's relatives. Galba claimed that he was choosing Piso on entirely
personal grounds; many years before, as a private citizen, he had decided
to make Piso his own heir, and now that Galba had become a Caesar, he
asserted that there was no reason to take any other factors into account
(in fact Piso was a brother of the Cn. Pompeius Magnus who married
Claudius' daughter Antonia and related to the Julians through Seribo-
nia: see Stemma III, p. 992). But if Galba's decision was determined by
private factors, why did he pass over his own nephew, Dolabella?

One explanation for the adoption of as unspectacular a successor as
Piso may be that there already was an obvious successor: Otho. Otho
was associated with Nero's 'good', early years; he was popular with the
praetorians, and had considerable support within the *domus Caesaris*. His
influence may be detected in the fact that Galba appointed, or retained,
Poppaea's brother Scipio Asiaticus as suffect consul for the last months
of 68. Otho also had the support of Titus Vinius. He had undertaken to
marry Vinius' daughter if Vinius persuaded Galba to adopt him. Thus
Vinius would ultimately, if all went well, end up as the grandfather of
Otho's son and successor. The moment Otho was formally recognized as
the emperor's successor, Galba's own role would have been played out.

II A.D. 69–70

Our knowledge of the calendar year 69 is much better than of 68, since
Tacitus' description of the events of this 'long' year in his *Histories*
happens to survive. Tacitus' account naturally has its limitations. It
depends upon pro-Flavian traditions and was written with hindsight,
with the problems of the reigns of Nerva and Trajan in mind. It also
suffers from the limitations of ancient historiography as a literary form –
in particular, its overemphasis on warfare. Certainly Roman armies won
and lost two great battles in A.D. 69; but the success or failure of
candidates for the imperial office depended on whether they could win
the loyalty of very much wider groups of people than merely the
particular soldiers who fought on the battlefields of northern Italy.[5]

By replacing Verginius Rufus with Hordeonius Flaccus, Galba had

[5] The events of A.D. 69 are covered by Tacitus in books I–III of the *Histories*: Heubner 1963–82 (B
84); Wellesley 1972 (B 193); Chilver 1979 (B 27). We also have Plutarch's *Galba* and *Otho*, Suetonius,
Dio LXIII and LXIV, and a summary by Josephus (*BJ* IV.10f).
   The readable modern narrative accounts by Wellesley 1975 (C 412) and Greenhalgh 1975 (C 351)
put more stress on the military action than on analysis of the political manoeuvring.

removed a potential rival for the imperial office, and Titus Vinius a personal enemy; they had not won the allegiance of the three legions of the upper Rhine army. The appointment of one of his earliest supporters, Caecina Alienus, as legate of the two legions encamped at Mainz is an indication of Galba's anxieties about them. It is not particularly surprising that on 1 January A.D. 69, Hordeonius Flaccus was unable to persuade the legions at Mainz to take the annual military oath to Galba; as in the previous year, an oath of loyalty to the 'Roman Senate and People' cloaked treason to the emperor. Such disrespect would only become a serious threat if the troops found an alternative candidate for the imperial office, more willing to risk civil war than Rufus had been. Flaccus was old and lame, and not a potential emperor.

Just a month or so previously, however, the lower Rhine army had received Aulus Vitellius as its commander in place of the executed Fonteius Capito. Vitellius, born on 7 September A.D. 12, and *consul ordinarius* in A.D. 48, was an illustrious figure; his father had been Claudius' foremost supporter (see above, p. 236), and he himself had been trusted by Tiberius, Caligula, Claudius and Nero. The suggestion that Vitellius should be offered the imperial office apparently came from Caecina Alienus. Our sources ascribe his readiness to abandon Galba to his fear of an impending prosecution for corruption committed as governor of Baetica; such a prosecution may cover a desire on the part of Vinius and Otho, Galba's two other early supporters, to have him out of the way. The revolt had been carefully prepared, possibly even before Vitellius' appointment. On the same evening the news from Mainz was brought to Vitellius in Cologne, presumably via Bonn. The legate of the legion stationed at Bonn was Fabius Valens, the man who had engineered Capito's execution. Valens was disappointed that Galba had insufficiently rewarded him for having removed Capito. He took the lead in persuading Vitellius to risk a bid for the imperial office, despite the dangers – quite apart from the military question, Vitellius' wife and children were in Rome. Although Vitellius had no reason to be dissatisfied with Galba, he had nothing to hope for from the coming regime of Titus Vinius and his prospective son-in-law Otho. When Valens appeared at the legate's palace at Cologne (the remains of which can still be seen underneath the present town hall) and saluted Vitellius as his *imperator*, Vitellius was prepared to accept. The legions further downriver at Neuss and Xanten joined Valens on the same day, and on the following day the upper Rhine army at Mainz took the oath to him as well.[6]

Galba's procurator for Belgic Gaul, Pompeius Propinquus, had immediately informed the government of the trouble at Mainz on 1

---

[6] Vitellius' proclamation: Murison 1979 (C 378).

January. Galba may well have thought that the animosity of Verginius Rufus' old army was directed not so much against himself, as against Vinius and Otho; 1 January was the day when Galba and Vinius entered upon their joint consulship, and many had assumed (Plutarch tells us) that on that day Otho would be publicly acclaimed as Galba's adoptive son and successor. Even if he had known that the Rhine armies had already gone so far as to proclaim a rival emperor, Galba will still have thought that his chances of regaining the loyalty of these armies would be improved if he showed that there was an alternative to Vinius and Otho. If he rejected making his nephew Publius Cornelius Dolabella his heir, then it was because he was too fond of him to force him into the position of being a foil to Otho. But Piso mattered less; Galba was willing to put his life at risk. On 10 January he announced his decision to his *consilium* of *amici*, and then presented Piso to the praetorians and to the Senate as the new Lucius Sulpicius Galba Caesar.

The adoption of Piso was not so much a matter of indicating who was to be the next emperor, as indicating who was not: Otho. Otho moved swiftly to recover the prize that had as good as been his. Vinius had let him down in the imperial *consilium*; Otho had no need of his support now, and Vinius seems not to have been aware of Otho's plans. Galba had alienated the *domus Caesaris* by executing its freedmen and replacing them with his own; he had alienated certain praetorian tribunes as a result of the coup ascribed to Nymphidius Sabinus, and the rank and file by refusing to pay out the donative of 30,000 sesterces per man promised them by Sabinus in June. (Strictly speaking, a donative had hitherto been a legacy paid out of a deceased Caesar's will as a reward for past loyalty, and Galba had no need to make such a payment on Nero's behalf. But the insulting quip that 'he levied his soldiers, and did not buy them' will have done his popularity little good.) Otho, perhaps with Vinius' backing, had no difficulty in finding supporters amongst the praetorians, the *vigiles* and the urban cohorts. Early in January Galba himself was frightened enough of the extent of that support to retire several tribunes. They and their friends were easily persuaded to back Otho's coup.

On the advice of his astrologer, Otho finally chose 15 January for his enterprise. He accompanied Galba to a public sacrifice at the temple of Apollo on the Palatine; at the appropriate moment his freedman Onomastus gave the agreed message – that 'the building surveyors are waiting for you at home' – and Otho slipped away to be saluted as emperor by just twenty-three soldiers of the bodyguard. When this small group of supporters reached the praetorian camp, there was no opposition from the officers. Galba's associates – including Vinius, apparently still unaware of Otho's plans – sent to the other troops present in Rome for military support, but without success. A false rumour that Otho had been killed by guards loyal to himself induced Galba to leave the palace in order to give thanks to the gods on the Capitol. As he and his entourage crossed the Forum, it became clear that their hopes were in vain. A small number of praetorians – considerably fewer than those who subsequently claimed the credit – attacked the party. Galba was killed in the Forum by a soldier from one of the Rhine legions. Piso died outside the temple of Vesta, where he had taken refuge. Titus Vinius failed to persuade the man who killed him that he was actually involved in Otho's conspiracy.

The Senate formally recognized Otho as the man who controlled the imperial household and the empire at a meeting held on the same evening. Otho was the first emperor to have seized power as a result of open bloodshed (Claudius had executed his predecessor's assassins). He also soon realized that he was faced with the candidature of a rival emperor on the Rhine. There was an exchange of correspondence with the usurper, and Otho suggested that Vitellius take Vinius' place as his prospective father-in-law. A senatorial embassy was sent to persuade Vitellius to abandon his claim, but it soon became clear that he was not a free agent, and that the Rhine armies would not countenance a peaceful resolution to the conflict.

Nevertheless Otho's regime was popular. He already had the support of the praetorians, and of their officers. For all that he had virtually been Galba's expected successor, he publicly dissociated himself from that unpopular emperor, and instead emphasized his association with Nero: Galba's freedman Icelus and his appointee as praetorian prefect, Cornelius Laco, were both executed. Statues of Nero and Poppaea were restored, and the emperor was acclaimed by the urban plebs as 'Nero Otho'. Any negative features of Nero's last years (when Otho was in Spain) were blamed on the unfortunate Tigellinus, whom Otho now executed. The disappearance of Vinius was a bonus; not only could unpopular decisions taken by Galba be ascribed to him, but Otho was freed from his promise to marry Vinius' daughter. Instead, he proposed to strengthen his claim to be the legitimate *paterfamilias* of the imperial household by marrying Nero's widow, Statilia Messallina. By representing himself as Nero's successor, and copying his liberality, Otho won the support of the urban population; and he did his best to win supporters among the Senate, not just by inviting senators to dinner at the palace (much to their discomfort when on one occasion the praetorians suspected them of plotting against their emperor), but also by appointing several additional suffect consuls, including Verginius Rufus. Marius Celsus, designated to a suffect consulship for the second half of the year by Galba, was confirmed in it by Otho. Otho himself was formally elected consul, together with his elder brother, Lucius, on 26 January.

Vespasian's elder brother, Flavius Sabinus, was re-appointed to the urban prefecture he had held under Nero.

Like other emperors, Otho made the most of news of military success. The defeat of a Sarmatian raiding party by the legate of Moesia, M. Aponius Saturninus, in February not only gave Otho some of the military prestige which he had hitherto lacked, but also enabled him to tie both the governor and one of his legionary legates, Aurelius Fulvus (grandfather of the emperor Antoninus Pius), to him by bestowing military honours. The governor of Pannonia, L. Tampius Flavianus, was honoured by being given Galba's place among the Arval Brethren; although related to Vitellius, he was to remain loyal to Otho. In any case, most provincial governors had no qualms about recognizing Galba's murderer. Even the governor of Tarraconensis, Cluvius Rufus, at first recognized Otho as emperor. So did the eastern armies: Antioch in Syria minted coins with his image and title. The gold coins issued in Otho's name and proclaiming 'peace throughout the world' were perhaps optimistic, but not absurdly so.[7] Only the German and British legions refused to take the oath. (The situation in Britain was confused; the governor Trebellius Maximus seems to have lost control, and fled to Vitellius; but the legionary legates also provided Vitellius with *vexillationes* of 8,000 men.)

Otho's coup was irrelevant to the plans of Vitellius, Valens and Caecina. Their rebellion had been as much against Galba's intimates as against Galba himself. For Vitellius to be a legitimate emperor – and he made no claim to be *Augustus* until he had won the approval of the Senate and people – those who ruled in Rome had to be removed, and the Rhine legions had the power to do this. The historical narrative of the year 69 gives the impression that it was the support of the armies that gave legitimacy to a candidate for imperial office; but that was not the whole story. Otho's failure shows that an emperor had to have control over his armies; but Vitellius' failure shows that military power alone was not enough to maintain control over the empire. While Caecina and Valens prepared to march on Italy with the greater part of the upper and lower Rhine armies, Vitellius proved to be markedly unsuccessful in winning support outside the western provinces. More particularly, there is little evidence that he was ever accepted by the client kings, freedmen and procurators of the *domus Caesaris*.

The two Rhine armies had probably not heard of Otho's accession when they set off to cross into Italy as soon as the Alpine passes were clear of snow, Caecina through Switzerland and across the Great St Bernard, Valens through central Gaul and then across the Mont

<hr/>

[7] Otho's coin issues: PAX ORBIS TERRARVM, MW 32; Otho recognized at Antioch, MW 77. For Sabinus: Wallace 1987 (C 407).

Genèvre. Later historians following pro-Flavian sources give a highly coloured account of the havoc the two armies caused along their route. In January, the Twenty-first Legion, based at Vindonissa, was involved in a regular battle against the *civitas* of the Helvetii, who had apparently arrested one of Vitellius' messengers on his way to the Danube to seek support from L. Tampius Flavianus. The Helvetians surrendered to Caecina when he arrived before their capital of Aventicum in early February. Tacitus' account of the progress of Valens' army through Gaul is similarly coloured by anti-Vitellian propaganda, and stresses the violence of the troops against the Gallic population – particularly the destruction of Vienne, for having supported Vindex – and against each other. And if we are to believe our sources, when Vitellius left the Rhineland in March with a third army, he did nothing but feast for the whole length of his journey.

Otho acted immediately and, as far as one can judge, rationally. It was not to be expected that an army would be able to cross the Alps until March or April (he could not predict the unusually early spring that year). Loyal legions from the Balkans could be marshalled in northern Italy well before Vitellius' main armies arrived, so long as the area was kept under the government's control. In winter, the only weak point on Italy's north-western border was the Via Domitia, the coastal road between the Ligurian Alps and the sea. A number of units commanded by officers who had backed Otho's coup (but who quarrelled amongst themselves) reached this sector by early February. The government was assisted by its command of the sea; when the governor of Corsica, Decimus Picarius, came out prematurely on Vitellius' side, he was soon killed. The legate of the Maritime Alps, Marius Maturus, also joined Vitellius before Valens' army was near enough to protect his province from the Othonians (among those who lost their lives at the hands of plundering Othonian soldiers was Agricola's mother). A cavalry force (including a unit of Treverans under Iulius Classicus, the later rebel leader) was sent south, but failed to dislodge Otho's troops.

The success of Otho's soldiers in Liguria prevented a quick dash by Valens' cavalry towards Rome along the Etrurian coast. What Otho cannot have foreseen was that Caecina would be able to take advantage of an early warm spell to cross the Great St Bernard with a force of about 18,000 troops, and establish himself in north-western Italy by the beginning of March. He advanced as far as Cremona without encountering significant opposition.

The fact that a rebel army had been allowed to enter Italy before the arrival of the loyal legions from the Danube was to mean that Otho had already lost. Nevertheless the officers he had sent to hold northern Italy managed to inflict a series of reverses on Caecina. A force based at

Verona under Annius Gallus, largely made up of three praetorian cohorts, and one based at Placentia under Vestricius Spurinna, consisting of Nero's *legio I Adiutrix* and two praetorian cohorts, forced Caecina back to Cremona. On 14 March Otho himself left Rome with all available forces (and with all those senators whom he could not trust; they were billeted in Mutina (Modena) for the duration of the campaign, where he could keep an eye on them). His troops (perhaps 15,000 men) were still outnumbered by Caecina. Early in April, Caecina, having heard that Valens' army had now also reached Italy, decided to try to deal with the Othonians before his colleague and competitor could assist, and share the glory. An attempt to lure the imperial army, under the command of Suetonius Paulinus and Marius Celsus, into an ambush at a place called Ad Castores about twelve Roman miles east of Cremona on the Via Postumia, resulted in another defeat for Caecina.

With Valens' arrival at Cremona, the advantage held by the Vitellian forces was, for the moment, overwhelming. But the emperor was already beginning to receive the reinforcements he had summoned from Pannonia; it would be another month before the Moesian legions were there in strength, but the main force of one of the Pannonian legions (the Twelfth) reached the Othonians a few days after Ad Castores, and the two others (the Seventh *Galbiana* and the Fourteenth) had already crossed into Italy. From a purely military perspective, it would have been in Otho's interest to put off a battle for a couple of weeks; that was what Suetonius Paulinus, Marius Celsus and Annius Gallus are reported as having proposed to the emperor's *consilium*. But the ultimate decision was the emperor's, and it had to be taken on political as well as military grounds. Because of their numerical superiority, the Vitellians had the option of detaching part of their army to cross the Po and march on the capital. Otho had no other troops between the Apennines and Rome. All Vitellius' supporters had to be prevented from moving south, and the only way to do that was to fight a battle immediately.

The battle, known as the 'First Battle of Cremona' or 'Bedriacum', took place on 14 April. The imperial army had the advantage of surprise, and gained some initial successes; but they were tired out by a 20-kilometre march to the battlefield, and the terrain – thick with vineyards and watercourses – was not to the advantage of the attackers. The Vitellians' greater military experience, as well as their numerical superiority, decided the battle. Needless to say, the emperor's troops believed that they had been betrayed by some, or most, of their officers. Suetonius Paulinus immediately decamped to beg pardon from Vitellius at Lyons. On the day after the battle, Marius Celsus, Salvius Titianus and the other officers surrendered on behalf of their troops.

Otho had awaited the outcome of the battle at Brixellum, 20 km away

on the south bank of the Po. He had the option of holding off the
Vitellian army for a few more days, in the hope that the two other
Pannonian legions would reach him, and that they would fight for him.
That was unlikely: their colleagues in the Twelfth Legion were part of
the army that had been defeated, and the emperor had to assume that the
war was over. After making those arrangements that antiquity expected
of a good monarch to protect his supporters from the vengeance of
Vitellius – including kind words for his nephew, Salvius Cocceianus,
whose relationship to Otho was not to prove fatal until the reign of
Domitian – he killed himself on the morning of 16 April. He was not able
to foresee that his death only freed Rome from the horrors of further
bloodshed for some months; it was applauded as a brave act, then and
later.

After the battle, Caecina and Valens both returned to Vitellius at
Lyons. There the usurper received and pardoned a number of Otho's
officers, and heard that the Senate had bestowed imperial powers on him
on 19 April. Vitellius accepted the grant of *imperium*, but did not see
himself as a 'Caesar', and for the time being even rejected the title
'Augustus'. A formal senatorial delegation met him at Pavia in mid-May.
Vitellius spent some time in northern Italy visiting the battlefield at
Cremona and attending gladiatorial games celebrating the establishment
of the new order given by Caecina at Cremona and Valens at Bologna.
In June, Vitellius and his considerable army – perhaps 60,000 soldiers –
entered Rome, to the great inconvenience of its residents.

Despite the military victory of his armies and his formal recognition
by the Senate, Vitellius' position was weaker than any emperor's had
been on his accession. He had ensured that the legions which had
remained loyal to the government of Otho were dispersed as widely as
possible: the Fourteenth was returned to Britain, Nero's First *Adiutrix*
was sent to Spain, the Seventh, Eleventh and Twelfth were sent back to
Pannonia, Dalmatia and Moesia, and the Thirteenth was kept in
northern Italy in the insulting position of helping build the amphitheatres required for Valens' and Caecina's shows. These legions were
not reconciled to the usurper. They would be ready to support any
candidate who presented himself instead of Vitellius. Suetonius states
that he was told, presumably by his father (who took part in these
events), that some soldiers of the Seventh *Claudia* were already canvassing Vespasian's candidacy. A more likely candidate would have been
Galba's nephew Cornelius Dolabella, who unwisely returned to Rome
after Otho's death in a vain attempt to rally Vitellius' opponents. He was
arrested and executed by the urban prefect, Vespasian's brother Flavius
Sabinus.

Vitellius' coins show his awareness of the deep split between those
soldiers who supported and those who opposed him. A Spanish *as*

proclaims the 'Unity of the Armies' (in the plural). A denarius that may have been minted for the Rhine armies before Vitellius was recognized by the Senate asserts that both the armies (obverse) and the praetorians (reverse) were loyal; both sides of the coin show a ceremonial pair of hands, clasped in friendship. The praetorians had loyally supported their emperor, and Vitellius thought it wise to discharge considerable numbers (those who were provided with plots of land in the Maritime Alps and near Aquileia were swift to join the Flavian cause in the autumn) and replace them with soldiers from the Rhine legions. He tried to advertise the support of other armies, e.g. with coins celebrating Vespasian's subjugation of Judaea.

Vitellius not only failed to reconcile the troops who had opposed him, but also failed to win popularity in other quarters. Coins advertising the imperial corn supply show that he was aware of the need for support from the plebs; and on the day after his arrival at Rome, he accepted the title 'Augustus' in response to popular demand (early coins describe him as 'Germanicus', with the *praenomen* 'imperator'). He accepted the title 'perpetual consul' which had been rejected by Nero. But he failed, or refused, to recognize the importance of being head of the *domus Caesaris*, and did not call himself 'Caesar' until the very last days of his reign. Instead, he emphasized the security which his new dynasty provided by the existence of a son and a daughter. His children appear on gold coins from Rome; the daughter was betrothed to Decimus Valerius Asiaticus, who as legate of Gallia Belgica had been an early supporter of Vitellius. Although only of praetorian rank, he was the son of the Asiaticus who had been mentioned as an imperial candidate in A.D. 41, and forced to commit suicide by Messallina in 47. The alliance with Asiaticus was perhaps both an attempt to reconcile those communities in Gaul that had backed Vindex, such as Asiaticus' *origo* Vienne, and to win the support of those families that had been associated with Vitellius' father during the early years of Claudius. Other *aurei* struck by Vitellius at Rome represent the censor. Another of his father's associates, Vespasian's elder brother Flavius Sabinus (cos. suff. *c.* 45), was confirmed in the position of *praefectus urbi* restored to him by Otho. His son was assigned a consulship. But neither Asiaticus nor Sabinus were able to give Vitellius much support when the army commanders appointed during Nero's reign came up with an alternative. Even Vitellius' own mother was sceptical of Vitellius' chances of establishing a new dynasty: she is reported to have said that the son she gave birth to was called Aulus, not Germanicus.[8]

[8] Vitellius' coin issues: IMP. GERMANICVS, Sutherland 1987 (B 358) chs. 47–9; CONSENSVS EXERCITVVM S.C.; FIDES EXERCITVVM/ PRAETORIANORVM; ANNONA AVG. S.C., MW 36–9; LIBERI IMP. GERM. AVG., MW 80; L. VITELLIVS COS III CENSOR, MW 82 (we may note that Josephus pretends to know nothing of these children: BJ IV.10.3(596)). *Consul perpetuus*; ILS 242 = MW 81.

Foremost amongst the provincial commanders was C. Licinius Mucianus, legate of Syria. Mucianus preferred literature to soldiering, and did not propose to put forward his own candidature. Although we do not have enough information about his family to know how 'aristocratic' he was, his own career – governor of Lycia and Pamphylia in 57; consul towards the end of Nero's reign – gave him the authority to recommend a name to the Roman establishment. And those officers whose careers had been advanced by Corbulo before his execution in A.D. 66 now looked to him to protect their interests against their fellow-officers in the Rhine legions, who were being given swift promotion by Vitellius. Vespasian, like Mucianus, had loyally served Nero in his last years; he had had much military experience, and distinction; and he also had two adult sons, ensuring that there would be someone to succeed him. Between them the two legates commanded six legions, enough at least to challenge the rebellious Rhine armies. Vespasian was prepared to take the initiative. Despite initial disagreements of the kind only to be expected when Syria and its army had been divided between the two of them by Nero in the spring of 67, Mucianus was prepared to back him.

Vespasian's son Titus was instrumental in arranging Mucianus' support for his father. At the end of 68, he had left Palestine for Rome to submit himself as a candidate for the quaestorship; Galba had been his father's superior at Strasbourg in A.D. 41–3, when Titus had been a child, and Titus was certain that he would favour him. But at Corinth he heard both of Galba's assassination, and of Vitellius' proclamation, and decided to return to Palestine. Oracles and omens along the way confirmed him in the view that Vitellius should be resisted. When news of Otho's defeat reached them, Mucianus and Vespasian were in no doubt about their responsibility to restore legitimate government. They informed governors, imperial procurators and legionary legates throughout the empire of their intentions, and won the support of the network of client kings in the eastern Mediterranean. Minor military operations against the Jewish rebels in Palestine in June had left Vespasian in control of most of the province except Jerusalem and three other strongholds; most of the Judaean army was free for operations elsewhere.

By the time Vespasian was publicly proclaimed emperor, the Danube armies were already throwing off their allegiance to Vitellius. The process by which they were persuaded to support Vespasian rather than a more legitimate Galban successor is unclear. Personal animosities between officers played their part; in Moesia, discipline collapsed when the governor, Marcus Aponius Saturninus, tried to kill the legate of the Seventh *Claudia*, alleging treason. Another Moesian legion, the Third *Gallica*, had recently been transferred from Syria. As soon as it heard that

the other Syrian legions were supporting Vespasian, it too expressed its
support for his candidature. Its legate, Titus Aurelius Fulvus from
Nîmes, rose high in Vespasian's service. He was to be honoured with a
first consulship *c.* 70; he was to be consul again as the emperor
Domitian's colleague in 85, and his grandson Antoninus Pius was
himself to hold the imperial office. By contrast, no rewards accrued to
Antonius Primus, still in command of Galba's Seventh Legion, and loyal
to his and Otho's memory. His legion, and the other Pannonian legion,
the Thirteenth, that had been forced to assist Caecina and Valens' victory
games in Cremona and Bologna, declared for the Flavians, but only
because that allowed them to re-open hostilities against Vitellius. They
accused the governor of Pannonia, M. Tampius Flavianus, of loyalty to
Vitellius – he was a distant relative, but as we have seen had been
honoured by Otho. Flavianus initially abandoned his office, but returned
at the request of the procurator Cornelius Fuscus. Fuscus had been
appointed to the post by Galba; he was to be another important
supporter of the new dynasty.[9]

The first official formally to proclaim Vespasian was in fact the prefect
of Egypt, Tiberius Iulius Alexander. Son of Alexander 'the Alabarch', a
procurator of the younger Antonia, he was the nephew of the Jewish
philosopher Philo, and his deceased brother had been the son-in-law of
King Iulius (commonly but incorrectly 'Herod') Agrippa I. Not surprisingly, he had done well during the early years of Claudius; from A.D. 46
to 48 he was procuratorial governor of Judaea. After some quiet years
probably to be explained by the primacy of Agrippina (when Vespasian,
too, had been in disgrace) his experience and connexions throughout the
eastern Mediterranean made him a suitable choice as an officer on
Corbulo's staff in 63 (probably *praefectus castrorum*, in charge of the
commissariat). In 66 he was appointed prefect of Egypt. The prefect of
Egypt was the only Roman provincial governor who was not shadowed
by an imperial procurator; this made it easier for him to declare his
support for a new emperor. The acclamation of Vespasian at Alexandria
on 1 July (two days before Vespasian's own army followed suit at
Caesarea) was enthusiastically received; Alexandria had only restricted
corporate rights as a city, and will have hoped that support for a
successful pretender would be rewarded by the privileges appropriate
for the second greatest city in the Mediterranean world. Vespasian was
to disappoint any such expectations; he had no wish to represent himself
as beholden to the Greek East.[10]

[9] For Vespasian's supporters, see Townend 1961 (C 404); Nicols 1978 (C 381); Gallivan 1981 (C
347); Jones 1984 (C 360); Wallace 1987 (C 407). See also following note.
[10] Tiberius Iulius Alexander: Turner 1954 (C 405); Burr 1955 (C 336); Sullivan 1985 (E 1224)
300–5. Vespasian's acclamation at Alexandria: MW 41 = *CPJ* II, 418a. Mucianus: Syme 1977 (C 399).

In mid-July, Vespasian and Mucianus held a conference at Berytus (Beirut) to plan their campaign. Agrippa, and representatives of other eastern clients of the Julio-Claudians such as Antiochus of Commagene, also attended. The Judaean countryside had been pacified; the glory of conquering the centre of the rebellion, Jerusalem, could safely be left to Titus, supported by Alexander as his *praefectus castrorum*. Titus needed an experienced counsellor, and it was perhaps politic to prevent Alexander from becoming too popular in his home town. Mucianus would proceed to the Balkans with an army consisting of one full legion and 13,000 men in *vexillationes* from seven others. Ships were organized for the crossing of the Bosphorus, and later events suggest that the Flavians approached the prefects of both Italian fleets with a view to winning their support for ferrying Mucianus' army from Dyrrhachium to Brundisium. Whether the intention was to invade Italy from the south or the north (or both), Vespasian cannot have expected any major military operations in Italy before the spring of the next year. In the mean time, it would be made clear to Vitellius and his supporters that no one could be emperor with the support of the Rhine legions alone. The supplies of corn from Egypt, upon which Rome depended, were cut off. Vespasian himself was to await the outcome of events at Alexandria.

What the plan decided upon at Berytus actually was cannot be known because by the time Mucianus reached the Balkans two months later, he found that the Danubian legions had already begun their own war against Vitellius under the command of Antonius Primus. To do that they had left the Danube frontier almost unprotected against the continuing Sarmatian pressure, and Mucianus was forced to turn north to repulse a serious invasion. Leaving his army behind, he hurried on after the Danube legions, to reach Italy in December. His haste suggests that Primus' advance into Italy at the beginning of September was by no means in accordance with the plans drawn up at Berytus. Tacitus says that Primus ignored Vespasian's written instructions to hold back at Aquileia. Vespasian and Mucianus were not pleased at Primus' victories, and he had to spend the rest of his days in peaceful retirement in his home town of Tolosa. On reaching northern Italy, Primus had shown where his loyalty lay: at Padua, he called for the busts of Galba to be restored. It is also remarkable that no coins bearing Vespasianic legends can be assigned to his army; serious objections have been raised to the view that a series of coins bearing Galba's portrait and referring to him as P[ater] P[atriae] were issued posthumously, perhaps at Lyons, but if such coins were indeed struck after Galba's death, it would be tempting to associate them with the pay given to Primus' soldiers.[11]

From Vitellius' point of view, the immediate effect of Primus' action

11 On the so-called 'posthumous' coins of Galba, see Kraay 1956 (B 332).

was to cut Italy off from any further reinforcements from the British and Rhine armies. It also made it clear to some of Vitellius' own supporters that there was now no chance that he would be accepted as a legitimate emperor. In September, Caecina and Valens entered upon the suffect consulship which was their reward for their victory. In response to Primus' invasion, Caecina took the entire army north (the praetorians, including the best of the soldiers who had come from the Rhine, were left behind; so was Valens, who was ill). He left it at Bologna, and then went to Ravenna to discuss with the prefect of the Adriatic fleet, Sextus Caecilius Bassus, the best way of solving the crisis without bloodshed. (Bassus was disappointed with Vitellius because he had hoped for promotion to praetorian prefect.) Bassus had already been in touch with an imperial freedman, Hormus, acting for Vespasian.

While military and civilian officers were trying to avoid bloodshed, that was exactly what the armies were looking for. Primus' legions, stationed at Verona, rioted against the two provincial governors, and both Tampius Flavianus and Aponius Saturninus were expelled from the camp. Meanwhile at Bologna, Caecina tried to remove Vitellius' portraits, but could make no headway in persuading his legions to accept Vespasian as emperor. He fled to Bassus, who had brought his sailors over to the Flavians without difficulty. Two legionary tribunes, Fabius Fabullus and Cassius Longus, took over command of the Vitellian army until Valens was to arrive.

Primus saw that he should force a battle now, before Valens could restore the Vitellians' morale. He advanced on the strongly pro-Vitellian city of Cremona, forcing the Vitellians to try to reach it first. Battle was joined to the east of the city in the late afternoon of 24 October, and lasted through the night; ancient sources give the expected vivid accounts of the horrors of this 'Second Battle of Cremona'. There were said to be 50,000 dead, and worse than the actual battle was the destruction of Cremona by the victorious Flavians which followed; the fire, started by the Thirteenth Legion in revenge for the insulting way it had been forced to help build an amphitheatre for Valens' games after the first battle, was said to have lasted for four days.

Caecina's defection showed that Vitellius could no longer trust some of his own officers. The praetorian prefect, Publius Sabinus, had to be replaced before the major part of what remained of the Vitellian army, fourteen praetorian cohorts, moved north along the Via Flaminia in support of Valens, who no longer had an army. Meanwhile Cornelius Fuscus had occupied Rimini on behalf of the Flavians, and the Vitellian army fell back, ultimately taking up a position at Narnia, about 100 km north of Rome. Valens himself travelled through northern Italy to Gallia Narbonensis, hoping to raise another army on the Rhine; but Valerius

Paulinus, the procurator – who, like many of the imperial procurators of whom we know, gave immediate support to Vespasian's bid for the empire – arrested him and sent him to Primus, who had him executed.

Late in November, a centurion of the fleet at Misenum was instrumental in effecting the fleet's transfer of loyalty to Vespasian. But here Vitellius had some success: he sent his brother Lucius to Campania with a few praetorian cohorts, and on 18 December – during the Saturnalia – Lucius' troops managed to recapture Terracina from the marines. But Lucius' actions came too late to save his brother: the cohorts at Narnia had surrendered one or two days before.

Vitellius' failure to bring about a swift end to the civil war after the second battle of Cremona has been unfavourably compared to Otho's suicide after the first. His indecision may be explained as due to uncertainty as to the extent to which Primus and his army were actually acting in support of Vespasian. Throughout the autumn, Vespasian's brother, the urban prefect Flavius Sabinus, had been available as a mediator; Vitellius seems to have been guaranteed his life, and the opportunity to retire to Campania. But Sabinus, too, was unclear about whether Primus would accept his authority (Vespasian's twenty-year-old younger son Domitian was not prepared to leave Rome in the company of Primus' messengers). Only when Mucianus himself had reached northern Italy could Sabinus and Vitellius act publicly. But the soldiers from the Rhine legions whom Vitellius had promoted to his praetorian guard had too much to lose to accept his abdication. When a formal *contio* was held in the Forum on 18 December to announce the surrender of Vitellius' *imperium*, those present shouted their opposition. An attempt to hand his dagger over to the consul, Caecilius Simplex, as a sign that he was resigning the imperial office, was rejected. Vitellius had to return to the palace while Sabinus (who, as *praefectus urbi*, was commander of the urban cohorts) and Domitian retired to the Capitol, assuming that they would be safe there until Vitellius regained control of his supporters.

While these negotiations had been in progress, Primus was in no hurry to rescue Vespasian's relatives in Rome. Independent action was taken by a cavalry unit commanded by Petillius Cerialis, described as a close relative of Vespasian; he was almost certainly the husband of Vespasian's daughter Domitilla (now deceased). Cerialis' attempt to break through the Vitellian defences on the northern outskirts of Rome was repulsed, and in revenge Vitellius' soldiers turned against Sabinus. It appears that some of the Flavian supporters set fire to buildings on the slope of the Capitol in order to protect themselves: the fire spread and engulfed the principal temple of Rome. Several Flavian supporters were killed. Sabinus himself was captured and brought before Vitellius, whose attempts to save his life failed. Domitian escaped in the garb of a priest of Isis, together with his cousin, Sabinus' son T. Flavius Clemens (consul in A.D. 95 as Domitian's colleague).[12]

When he heard of Cerialis' failure to enter Rome and of the destruction of the Capitol, Antonius Primus could no longer hold back his army. He may also have calculated that the death of Sabinus would enable him to present a candidate of his own choice to the Senate. Tacitus suggests that in the first days or weeks after the occupation of Rome, he tried and failed to persuade Licinius Crassus Scribonianus to become his own puppet emperor. As brother of the Piso adopted by Galba, and the Cn. Pompeius Magnus married to Claudius' daughter Antonia, Crassus had a stronger connexion with the household of Caesar than Vespasian. Primus entered the city on 20 December (possibly 21), and encountered considerable resistance. Vitellius attempted to flee the city – he may have heard of his brother's successes in Campania – but his praetorians would not let him go. He was discovered hiding in the deserted palace, dragged through the Forum by a mob of soldiers and civilians, and put to death.

Mucianus succeeded in reaching Rome within a few days of Primus, and acted swiftly to isolate him. Even before his arrival, Mucianus had sent written instructions to the Senate to ensure that it was Vespasian who was duly recognized as Caesar and Augustus, and that the people passed a law voting him all the legal powers that earlier emperors had had (one of the two bronze tablets bearing the text of this *lex de Imperio Vespasiani* still exists, and grammatical peculiarities suggest – the haste with which Mucianus drafted it).[13] It is not surprising that individual senators started to ask questions about just who it was who represented the new emperor. In January 70, with Domitian's consent, the Senate passed a decree honouring Galba and Piso; only later was it realized that this did not accord at all with the wishes of Mucianus and Vespasian. Domitian's re-appearance as Caesar provided a point of reference. He was duly elected as urban praetor, but with the unprecedented *imperium* of a consul. Mucianus arranged for rewards for those who had been a party to Vespasian's own plans. He himself was nominated to a second suffect consulship in A.D. 70, together with Petillius Cerialis; the client-kings who had supported Vespasian were honoured; and the freedman Hormus, instrumental in negotiations regarding the fleet, was granted equestrian status. But Antonius Primus, the man who had actually defeated Vitellius, was eased out of power and never again played a political role. For Vespasian's security, Mucianus arranged for the

---

[12] On the fighting in Italy and Rome in A.D. 69, see Tac. *Hist.* III; Suet. *Dom.* 1.2f. For the destruction of the Capitol, Murison 1979 (C 378); Wellesley 1981 (C 413). On Domitian's role, Waters 1964 (C 410) is still sensible.

[13] The *lex de imperio*: *ILS* 244 = MW 1 = *AN* 293; cf. Brunt 1977 (C 335).

execution of those who might attract the support of Galban partisans as candidates for the imperial office: C. Piso Galerianus (son of the conspirator of A.D. 65), and his father-in-law Lucius Piso (cos. 57), current proconsul of Africa. Lucius was a brother-in-law of Galba's heir and of Licinius Crassus Scribonianus; both were therefore related to Augustus' first wife Scribonia. Piso was killed by Valerius Festus, legate of the Third Legion and a relative of Vitellius who needed to prove his loyalty to the new regime.

Mucianus' next problem was to defuse the rivalry between Vespasian's two sons. Titus had won military glory as his father's legate in Judaea (he was to remain there for the prestige of destroying Jerusalem that summer). Domitian suspected that he would have little chance of surviving for long if his brother ever came to the throne. One option open to him was to win military glory himself by leading the Flavian legions north to deal with the remaining Vitellian units in Gaul, Britain and the Rhineland. Mucianus had already sent Petillius Cerialis to the Rhineland, and allowed Domitian to follow (thus removing him from Rome); later tradition had it that Domitian personally received the surrender of the Lingones, but he seems to have been prevented from seeing any fighting. Instead of seeking to rival the military glories of his brother Titus and brother-in-law Cerialis, Domitian dedicated himself to writing poetry, including epics recording the fighting on the Capitol and his achievements in Gaul.

The failure of the Rhine legions to accept Vespasian after Vitellius' death proved a major embarrassment to the Flavians, and to pro-Flavian historians. The events of A.D. 69/70 in the Rhineland had to be re-written in such a way as to avoid giving the impression that Vespasian had been supported by Batavians and (some) Gauls, while the citizen legions and (other) Gauls continued to constitute a 'Vitellian' force. In consequence, Tacitus' *Histories* describe the rebellion against Vitellius led by the Batavian leader Civilis as though it was an uprising by provincials against Roman rule. But Tacitus also has to admit that when the rebellion began, it was welcome to the Flavians: he says that at first it was only in secret that the rebel leaders expressed anti-Roman views. If Civilis was a traitor, he was a traitor to Vitellius. In the autumn of 69, at the behest of Antonius Primus, he took the oath to Vespasian and besieged a Vitellian legion at Vetera (Xanten). Tacitus misleadingly suggests that by the beginning of 70, the legions too had taken the oath of loyalty to Vespasian. In fact, the legate of Upper Germany, Hordeonius Flaccus (who had supported Civilis' action) was killed by his troops when he tried to administer the oath, and Vitellius' portrait restored. A pro-Vitellian legate, Dillius Vocula, came to the help of the soldiers at Vetera; when the legionaries tried to evacuate the camp there and march south in March 70, they were massacred by Civilis' Batavians (Tacitus emphasizes the presence of Germanic warriors from across the Rhine among Civilis' soldiers).

The leaders of a number of Gallic tribes also remained loyal to the Vitellian cause. With the Flavians recognized at Rome and the arrival of Cerialis and Domitian in Gaul in the spring of 70, their resistance could be re-interpreted as a tribal uprising. But these men were as little Gallic nationalists as Vindex had been. Iulius Classicus had led the Vitellian advance as far as the Maritime Alps in early 69; the other leaders, Iulius Tutor and Iulius Sabinus, were 'Romans' to such an extent that Dillius Vocula's legions accepted their command after the disastrous retreat from Vetera. In the absence of any senator who might be put up as the Vitellians' candidate for the imperial office, Iulius Sabinus made a bid by claiming that his grandfather had been an illegitimate son of none other than Iulius Caesar himself. The 'Gallic Empire' (*Imperium Galliarum*) which they called for was not an empire controlled by the Gauls, but a Roman empire in Gaul, a compromise which could be supported both by legionaries who wished to remain loyal to Vitellius and by Civilis' Batavians and other Gallic tribes who had fought them.

It was the absence of a plausible leader that gave the legionaries no alternative but to accept Vespasian. Their last hope was to persuade Cerialis himself to take up their cause; he passed their offer to make him emperor back to Domitian. The Flavians took what measures they could to win the loyalty of these supporters of Vitellius. Four of the Rhine legions had to be disbanded (*I, IV Macedonica, XV Primigenia, XVI*), and replaced by new ones, whose titles proclaimed their association with the new dynasty (*IV and XVI Flavia*). The loyalties of the British legions during this period are even more difficult to reconstruct (see ch. 13e). Cerialis took over command of the British army, perhaps to balance his brother-in-law Titus' command in the East. The military activities of the next three years, involving the subjugation of Brigantia and the founding of a new legionary base at York, gave the legions stationed in Britain an opportunity to prove their loyalty to the Flavians. In Britain, as in the Rhineland, the legionaries' conditions were improved by the construction of more permanent, stone camps, such as the one at Caerleon. The story of their war against Civilis was re-written to make it seem that they had always been loyal to Rome, fighting German barbarians and Celtic and Batavian traitors. Unlike Galba, Otho or Vitellius, the Flavians managed to win the support even of those who had fought against them. The coinage broadcast not just military victory over Judaea and the security represented by the new emperor's two sons, but the 'Revival of Rome', Peace, Liberty, and concord between emperor and Senate. As censors (A.D. 72–4), Vespasian and Titus freed the Roman people from the moral stain, and from some of the memories, of civil strife. The account of Vespasian's reign as the recognized successor of the Julio-Claudians is to be found in another volume. Mucianus enjoyed a third consulship in A.D. 72, and then spent his retirement writing books.[14]

[14] Civilis: Urban 1985 (C 406). Classicus' coins include the legends ADSERTOR LIBERTATIS, LEGION XV PRIM and CONCORDIA: FIDES may be an appeal for continued loyalty to the Vitellian cause. Cf. Zehnacker 1987 (B 364). Tacitus' admission that the rebels were only 'separatists' in secret: *Hist.* III.14. Brigantia: Birley 1973 (E 529), Hanson and Campbell 1986 (E 544). Vespasian's coin issues: ROMA RESVRGENS, PAX P. ROMANI, LIBERTAS RESTITVTA, AETERNITAS P.R., CONCORDIA SENATVI – MW 42–6; 90; 254.

CHAPTER 7

THE IMPERIAL COURT

ANDREW WALLACE-HADRILL

I. INTRODUCTION

If the powers of Augustus and his successors were monarchical, the most important arena where those powers were exercised was the court. Both as an institution and as a word, the court was alien to the Republic. *Aula*, a direct derivative of the Greek *aule*, the standard term in the hellenistic world for the courts of oriental and Greek kings, is almost unknown to republican literature (including Livy); but rapidly establishes itself under the early Empire (notably in the writings of Seneca under Nero) to refer both to the physical location of imperial power and to the type of power, the personnel, and the perilous way of life that were associated with it.[1] New though the phenomenon was to the Romans, they were well aware that what they now experienced was an old feature of monarchical societies. 'Reflect,' observed the emperor Marcus Aurelius in his *Meditations*, 'how all the life today is a repetition of the past . . . the whole court circle of Hadrian for example, or the court of Antoninus, or the courts of Philip, Alexander and Croesus. The performance is always the same; it is only the actors who change.'[2]

The historical and biographical sources recognize the role of the Julio-Claudian court. Stories told about Vespasian's early career encapsulate assumptions about how court life worked. His success under Claudius was ascribed to the influence of the freedman Narcissus; he also had a mistress, Caenis, among the imperial freedwomen. His son, Titus, was brought up at court (*in aula*) with Britannicus. The fall of Narcissus and the rise of Agrippina meant his political eclipse. Nevertheless, he remained in the court circle, and was taken by Nero to Greece among the *comites*. But his unconcealed lack of enthusiasm for singing brought him into bad odour, and he was banned not only from the inner circle (*contubernium*) but even from the general audience (*publica salutatio*). He

---

[1] See *TLL* 1.1457–8, s.v. *aula* II.3.c. Cic. *Fam.* xv.4.6 (of the court of Ariobarzanes) is apparently the only republican occurrence. Similarly used of foreign courts by Augustan and later writers, e.g. Virg. 11.504, Val. Max. vii.1.2; of court life in contexts applicable to Rome first in Seneca *Ira* 11.33.2, *Tranq.* vi.2; of Nero's court, [Seneca] *Octavia* 285 etc.; then regularly of the imperial court in Martial, Statius, Tacitus, Suetonius and later.

[2] *Med.* 10.27. On the views of Marcus, Brunt 1974 (b 19).

learnt of his disgrace from one of the freedmen who controlled admissions (*ex officio admissionis*), whose treatment of him was so acrimonious that he was scarcely rescued by the intervention of other courtiers.[3] We meet here a string of assumptions that run through the historical accounts of the Julio-Claudian and later periods: the fragility of political success and its dependence on imperial favour; the role of freedmen and members of the imperial family as mediators of favour; the emergence of subordinate personnel who help to define access to and exclusion from the court; and the intertwining of political and social life at court, and the consequent importance of imperial tastes.

The work of the last generation of historians has represented a large step towards a better understanding of the early imperial court. Several major studies have extended our detailed knowledge of the freedmen personnel,[4] the equestrian *amici principis*,[5] and of links among the senatorial elite.[6] Above all, study of contacts between emperors and their subjects, the decision-making process and the distribution of resources and patronage, show us the network of imperial personnel in operation and reveal something of the structures within which they operate.[7]

But in spite of these advances, the court remains partly veiled from our sight. Historiographically it leads a sort of twilight existence. This is true both of the ancient sources and modern scholarship. The difficulties that obstruct the historian were articulated by Cassius Dio: monarchical rule involved a retreat of political life and the decision-making process from open places (the Senate and Forum) into privacy. Dubious official announcements and hearsay represent the only access to what was going on.[8] Tacitus reacts to this problem by the tactic of irony.[9] Rather than focus on the court on the basis of suspect information, he directs his attention to public places in the style of his republican predecessors: he thereby underlines not merely the political impotence of the Senate, but the impotence of the historian, who can only approach the true locus of power indirectly. The majority of our direct information about the workings of the Julio-Claudian court is anecdotal: this is true not only of the biographies of Suetonius, but of the numerous reminiscences of contemporaries, Seneca in his philosophical dialogues, the elder Pliny in his *Natural Histories*, or the *Discourses* of the ex-slave philosopher Epictetus preserved by Arrian. The tendency to anecdote is not a

[3] Slightly differing versions in: Suet. *Vesp.* 3–4 and 14; *Tit.* 2; Tac. *Ann.* XVI.5; Dio LXXI.11; cf. Gascou 1984 (B 59) 323–6.

[4] Chantraine 1967 (D 9); Weaver 1972 (D 22); Boulvert 1970 (D 6) and 1974 (D 7).

[5] Pflaum 1960–1 (D 59); cf. Brunt 1983 (D 26).

[6] Syme's prosopographical work is informed by tacit understanding of the nature of the imperial court; for a rare statement, Syme 1939 (A 93) 385.

[7] Millar 1977 (A 59) is basic; also Crook 1955 (D 10) and Saller 1982 (F 59).

[8] Dio LIII.19.   [9] Syme 1958 (B 176) 206 and *passim*; cf. Ginsburg 1981 (B 61).

personal weakness of our sources, but a structural consequence of the retreat of politics behind closed doors.[10]

Modern historians have reacted to the problem differently. Suspicious of anecdote, and disinclined to see history as made by feminine schemes and palace plots,[11] we have moved away from study of the Principate as a political system to study of administrative systems and hierarchies. The temptation has not always been resisted to substitute modern bureaucratic structures for the unfamiliar structures of a court society.[12] The world of kings and courts is one of which the present age has lost sight, and it requires an effort of historical imagination to take its structures seriously.[13] In consequence, this chapter represents a sketch not only of what we have learnt, but of what we stand in danger of forgetting.[14] In discussing the nascent court of the Julio-Claudian period, it will be necessary to generalize more broadly about the function of the court in the structure of imperial power.

II. ACCESS AND RITUAL: COURT SOCIETY

The court and its membership had no 'official' definition, for this was a social not a legal institution, private in its composition though public in its importance. The contrast with the Senate is significant: membership of that body was a legal status, only open to certain social categories, age groups, and one sex, and Augustus at an early stage took measures further to define eligibility and to formalize procedures and conduct of business.[15] The court remained in its nature undefined: membership was constituted by proximity to the emperor, and only social ritual could distinguish degrees of proximity. At the negative extreme, the renouncement of *amicitia* was a formal token of imperial displeasure and expulsion from court; but the *amicitia* enjoyed by those who had not fallen from grace was fluid and imprecise (a point obscured by attempts to catalogue the *amici principis*, as if they were officials with a rank).[16] Many had access to the *aula*; far fewer were admitted to the private chamber, the *cubiculum principis*.[17] Nor did the court have any official or public function. Events of public importance took place on the Palatine from Augustus on, such as the reception of embassies, councils of state and trials, but they did so

[10] For criticism of use of anecdotes, see Saller 1980 (B 156).

[11] So explicitly Momigliano 1934 (C 377) xiii.

[12] Cf. the strictures of Brunt 1975 (E 906), Burton 1977 (D 8), Saller 1982 (F 59) 79ff.

[13] See (for a later period) the fundamental analysis of N. Elias, *The Court Society* (English trans. by E. Jephcott of *Die höfische Gesellschaft*, 1969) (Oxford, 1983).

[14] Friedländer 1922 (A 30) I. 33–103 remains the best discussion of the court as social phenomenon; see also Turcan 1987 (D 20).   [15] Talbert 1984 (D 77) 10ff, 137f etc.

[16] On the *amici*, Crook 1955 (D 10) 21–30; Millar 1977 (A 59) 110–22; Demougin 1988 (D 37) 743–51; on *renuntiatio amicitiae*, Rogers 1959 (D 19).   [17] Tamm 1963 (F 590) 113ff.

not as 'court' events, but in virtue of the personal obligations of the emperor. By tradition, any public figure at Rome was liable to use his house for occasions of a quasi-public nature.[18] This lack of definition only added to the power of the court: one of the secrets of power, the *arcana imperii*, was to be untramelled by rules.

Nor was its location fixed: *aula* represents an abstraction, not a description of a particular place. Under the late Empire the court was to be peripatetic, like the courts of many medieval monarchs; at all periods the court (but not necessarily all courtiers) moved with the emperor.[19] This does not mean that the imperial presence transformed all contexts into the court, as when the emperor attended the Senate or the games: these were public venues, in contrast to the private and domestic venues of the court, even the praetorian tent on campaign.[20] But despite the string of properties across Italy already developed by Augustus, and the fondness of the Julio-Claudians for the Bay of Naples, and specifically Capri, it is notable that in practice the court was from the start firmly centred on the city of Rome, and particularly the Palatine Hill.[21] This too has its echo in language. *Palatium* acquires the sense of 'palace' by the end of the first century A.D. (the metaphorical usage goes back to Ovid), and as Cassius Dio later pointed out, it was the facts of life rather than any decree that turned *palatium* into the name for any imperial residence, no matter where its location.[22] The rapid absorption of the show houses of the republican nobility on the Palatine, already far advanced by the end of Augustus' reign, neatly symbolizes the absorption of their social power.[23] Augustus and his successors manipulated this symbolism with care: the rich ritual and 'historical' associations of the hill of Romulus were exploited, and the potential of the site to overlook and dominate the public activity of the Forum and the mass meetings of the Circus Maximus was underlined by the choice of where to build.

Suetonius' emphasis on the modesty of Augustus' residence may create a false impression, engendered by the desire of a later age to idealize the simplicity of the past.[24] Contemporary reactions in the poets, explicit in Propertius and Ovid, veiled in Virgil, register the overwhelming impression made by the novel complex of private house and public temple (Actian Apollo), portico (adorned with Danaids) and libraries.[25] The tantalizing fragments that have emerged from recent archaeological

[18] Vitr. *De Arch.* VI.5.2; cf. Millar 1977 (A 59) 18ff.   [19] Millar 1977 (A 59) 28–57.

[20] Veyne 1976 (F 71) 682–5 perversely identifies the whole city of Rome as court.

[21] Millar 1977 (A 59) 15–28.

[22] Ov. *Met.* 175, Dio LIII.16.4–6; cf. *RE* XVIII 3 (1949) 10–15 s.v. *Palatium*.

[23] Wiseman 1987 (F 81).

[24] Suet. *Aug.* 72. Sources are collected in Lugli 1962 (E 82) 154–61.

[25] Esp. Prop. II.31; Ov. *Fast.* IV.951–4; *Tr.* III.1.31–48; *Pont.* II.8.17; Virg. *Aen.* VII.170ff, cf. Wiseman 1987 (F 81).

exploration give concrete documentation of the interweaving of public and private in the area of the temple of Apollo, approached from within Augustus' house by a series of ramps, which is more reminiscent of a hellenistic royal palace than a traditional Roman house.[26] This feature, dating back to 28 B.C., was extended in the course of the reign: in 12 B.C. the public cult of Vesta, symbolic hearthplace of the city, was incorporated within the private house of Augustus as *pontifex maximus*, and in A.D. 3 after a major fire and rebuilding of the palace on public subscription, the whole residence was declared public property. Thus the architectural ambivalence of public and private embodies from the first the essential ambiguity of the court as an institution, a private household with a central role in public life, the *domus* of a citizen and simultaneously the *praetorium*, the headquarters of a commander protected by the praetorian guard.[27]

The Augustan development lacked unity; it was rather a string of separate households absorbed piecemeal, and this was still true of the palace as Josephus describes it at the time of Gaius' murder.[28] Nero's vast building activities, both before and after the great fire, imposed coherence for the first time, and eliminated the final traces of independent houses of the aristocracy on the Palatine, such as the house of the orator Crassus with its famous lotus trees, finally owned by Claudius' courtier Caecina Largus.[29] Even without taking into account Nero's extension of his Golden House onto the Esquiline, we may be struck, as were contemporaries, by the staggering extent of the palatial complex.[30] Covering some 10 hectares, it exceeded the palace of Attalus at Pergamum by a factor of 30, though indeed if the palaces of Alexandria or Antioch were preserved, they might have approached somewhat closer to the Roman scale. This vast development implies human activity on a corresponding scale. The so-called Aula Regia of Domitian's palace was preceded by an earlier and not much less impressive auditorium. A small indicator is provided by the lavatories which constitute one of the few fragments of Nero's rebuilding on the Palatine: with a capacity of over forty, they exceed the public lavatories attached to the *fora* of towns like Ostia or Corinth, and approach the level of a major modern railway station. The palace should be seen as a major concourse of human activity.[31]

Rome was where the early emperors held court for serious business: Italian villas and the Bay of Naples, even in the case of Tiberius' last

---

[26] See Carettoni 1983 (F 316); Zanker 1983 (F 630); Coarelli 1981 (F 332) 129–34.
[27] Millar 1977 (A 59) 61–6; Turcan 1987 (D 20) 76ff.   [28] Joseph. *AJ* XIX.1.117.
[29] Asc. *Scaur.* 27c; Pliny, *HN* XVII.5.
[30] On the Domus Aurea and its extent, see Griffin 1984 (C 352) 134–42; further Frézouls 1987 (D 11).   [31] Giuliani 1982 (F 387) 246–54 on structures beneath Domitian's palace.

years, represented an escape from the pressure of people into relative
otium.[32] The choice of location had implications for the development of
Rome as an imperial city and as the monumental showpiece of the
empire. Many factors, not least tradition, may have dictated this choice;
but one factor of paramount importance was the question of accessibility. The emperor needed to be readily accessible to a very considerable
number of individuals. The prime function of a court is to provide and
control physical access to the ruler; the courtiers are those who
simultaneously have achieved some degree of regular access for themselves and are capable of mediating it to others. It is therefore the
structures and rituals through which access to the ruler is mediated
which give a court its distinctive character. Who could get at the
emperor, and on what conditions?

The composition and rituals of the imperial court were evolved from
patterns current among the Roman upper classes at large.[33] Three
groups can be broadly distinguished: family, servile household, and
friends. The first two represent the 'insiders', the *domus* or *familia
Caesaris*. Wives and children play a central role in court life. Other
relatives were more loosely attached: Roman social custom did not
favour the extended family, and many members of the imperial family
kept separate households. The exceptionally diffuse family network built
up by Augustus explains the physical structure of the palace in his day as
a nexus of partially separate houses: even Tiberius in the last decade of
his adoptive father's reign kept separate household in the Domus
Tiberiana, while Gaius' father Germanicus had his own house in the
reign of Tiberius.

Freedmen too, following Roman social custom, might be more or less
loosely attached to their imperial patron's house: they might reside
within the palace to perform daily services, but they might keep separate
households of their own. Augustus used the houses of freedmen on the
Palatine or elsewhere to escape from visitors or to watch the games,
while the independent houses of Claudius' great freedmen like Posides
and Callistus were among the wonders of the city.[34] What distinguishes
both family and freedmen as 'insiders' is their relationship to the
emperor, not their residential location. Fortune, whether through birth,
marriage or the slave market, had placed them in a permanent proximity
to the ruler to which no outsider had access. The imperial household,
unlike that of the medieval or early modern king, opened no avenues to
the talent and ambition of the subject: the element of sheer chance behind

---

[32] D'Arms 1970 (E 30) 73–115.
[33] For imperial ceremonial, Friedländer 1922 (A 30) I. 90–103; Alföldi 1934 (D 1); for republican
practice, Kroll 1933 (A 54) II. 59–81.   [34] Suet. *Aug.* 45 and 72; Pliny, *HN* xxxvI.60.

the making of a potent freedman was epitomized by Epictetus in the
figure of Felicio, the cobbler slave who by an exchange of hands emerged
as an imperial functionary, to the confusion of his old master.[35] To start
with, the *domus Caesaris* was many households as well as many houses:
different members of the imperial family kept their own establishments,
and Antonius Pallas, the most famous of Claudius' freedmen, began his
career as a slave in the confidential service of Claudius' mother
Antonia.[36]

The court is not simply the ruler's household, but the household
operating as an interface with the society over which he rules. The
distribution of power in monarchical society is likely to correspond to
the distribution of access to the ruler. In the hellenistic kingdoms there
was marked conflict between the status systems of the court and of the
cities. The royal *philoi* drew their status from proximity to the king; and
the grades of court hierarchy depended not on functional differentiation
but on closeness to the royal person – so in the Ptolemaic court the
descent is from relatives (*syngeneis*), to those honoured as if relatives, to
the bodyguard (in the sense of royal pages), to first friends, to friends.
The kings paid no attention to the ascriptive status systems of the cities;
consequently out of the court circle the royal friends were derided as
unworthy climbers, 'flatterers' or 'parasites'.[37] Correspondingly the
hellenistic courts developed rituals and ceremonials which opened a
sharp gulf between the king and the norms of Greek or Macedonian
society: pomposity of dress and setting (elaborately canopied thrones);
rituals like *proskynesis* which, whatever its significance and appropriate-
ness in Persian society, had in the context of Greco-Macedonian society a
profoundly distancing effect; and ceremonial language drawing on that
of cult.

The similarity has often been remarked between these hellenistic *philoi*
and the *amici Caesaris*, particularly in view of the apparent (but ill-
attested) distinctions introduced of a *cohors primae admissionis* (group of
the first admission), *secundae admissionis* and so on.[38] Doubtless there was
hellenistic influence on Roman social ritual, of which the Romans
themselves were aware, just as the differentiation of the freedman
secretariat is probably developed on a hellenistic model. But this
obscures the fundamental gulf between the imperial court and any
hellenistic analogue. For by and large the early Caesars paid elaborate
attention to the status hierarchy of Roman society, dovetailed the

[35] Epictetus, *Diss.* 1.19.16–23.   [36] Weaver 1972 (D 22) 90–2, 212–23.
[37] For hellenistic court hierarchy, Corradi 1929 (A 18), Mooren 1977 (D 16); for analysis of status
dissonance, Herman 1980–1 (D 12).
[38] Friedländer 1922 (A 30) I. 76f; Bang 1921 (D 5); Crook 1955 (D 10) 21–30.

privileges of their *amicitia* with the demands of ascriptive status, avoided rituals that set them apart from the aristocracy, and controlled the tendency of the court to generate a gulf between itself and society.[39]

The social rituals which channelled access, notably the morning *salutatio* and the afternoon *cena*, were those normal among the nobility of the late Republic and early Empire. Repeated descriptions of the bustle of the early morning *salutatio* at the great houses of Rome by Seneca and the satirists only underline its similarity to the imperial routine: the emperor was distinguishable in the scale but not the style of his admissions.[40] If he graded his friends into *admissiones*, so too did others; Seneca, our only informant on this, attributes the introduction of the custom to Gaius Gracchus and Livius Drusus.[41] Assuming that Vespasian followed the pattern of his predecessors, secretaries and officials were interviewed and their *breviaria* read before the admission of friends to the bedroom, followed by a general salutation. Vespasian may have started earlier in the day than some, but the daybooks of officials in Egypt show similar patterns of business.[42] Nor is there much trace at this stage of the evolution of distinctive imperial dress or pomp. The emperor wore the toga at his levee; if Caligula wore floral tunics, it was regarded as an aberration, and failed to establish a new ceremonial.[43]

Other institutions taken directly from the republican nobility include the appointment of *comites* (companions), duly rewarded with a *salarium*, to form a *cohors amicorum*, and to join the *contubernium* (mess) of the emperor on tour or campaign, and the summoning of *amici* to form a *consilium* to advise on specific issues.[44] Naturally, the 'friends' and 'advisers' of the emperor played a role in public affairs and wielded an influence which far outran any republican precedent, and the *amici principis* were busy men, and regarded by others with awe and even fear.[45] But it is an error to represent the imperial *consilium* as an established organ of government with a defined membership. Its informality was essential.[46] In building on republican precedent in all these varieties of *amicitia*, the Caesars not only established themselves as

---

[39] Wallace-Hadrill 1982 (D 21).

[40] Friedländer 1922 (A 30) 1.90ff. (imperial receptions), 240ff (aristocratic receptions); Saller 1982 (F 59) 128f; Turcan 1987 (D 20) 132ff.   [41] Seneca *Ben.* VI.34.2; *contra*, Alföldi 1934 (D 1) 28.

[42] Suet. *Vesp.* 21; Millar 1977 (A 59) 209f; cf. Pliny, *Ep.* III.5.9 with Sherwin-White *ad loc.*; cf. Wilcken 1912 (B 389) no. 41 for the *commentarii* of a local *strategos* in Egypt, the fullest of the handful of such documents to survive.

[43] Suet. *Calig.* 52. Alföldi 1935 (D 2) lays too much emphasis on exceptions.

[44] Crook 1955 (D 10) 4–7, 22–4; Millar 1977 (A 59) 110–18; Amarelli 1983 (D 4); Turcan 1987 (D 20) 143ff.

[45] Busy: e.g. Sen. *Ben.* 1.27.2, Pliny, *Ep.* III.5.7, Epictetus, *Diss.* 1.10.9. Held in awe: Tac. *Dial.* VIII.3; Pliny, *Ep.* 1.18.3.

[46] Crook 1955 (D 10) 104 and *passim*. Augustus may have planned something more formal: p. 331 (below).

respectors of the *mores maiorum*, but integrated the behaviour of the court into the patterns of behaviour current in the aristocratic society around them.

Perhaps the most striking feature of the anecdotal descriptions of imperial admissions and receptions is the predominance of senators and members of the upper stratum of the equestrian order. There was evidently widespread attendance at salutations by members of the senatorial order (including their wives and children); not until A.D. 12 in the infirmity of old age did Augustus ask the Senate to be excused his normal practice of greeting them all at his home.[47] As a rule they enjoyed precedence. Senators were greeted with a kiss – a hellenistic custom indeed, but one already current among the elite in Cicero's day.[48] Nero is said to have denied the kiss to all senators on his return from Greece: this was a powerful mark of imperial displeasure, not an attempt to reverse the assumption that senators were entitled to this mark of intimacy.[49] A vivid reflection of the social ties which interconnected the upper orders and linked them to the emperor is the elder Pliny's report of the outbreak of a facial disease in Tiberius' reign.[50] Pliny remarks on the way this epidemic was restricted in its incidence both geographically to Rome and socially to the upper orders (*proceres*): the disease was spread by kissing, and its extent and restriction reflected the exchange of kisses at the salutation. Tiberius, who appears to have been affected himself, put a temporary ban on the custom. The kiss was not reduced to a symbol of obeisance. Seneca vigorously protests at Gaius' gesture in proffering his foot to a consular to kiss: with its overtones of oriental court ritual, this was precisely the kind of gesture that did not establish itself as the Roman norm.[51]

Accounts of imperial dinners repeatedly feature senators and equites.[52] Even if Gaius was tickled by the macabre thought that he could execute both consuls at will, they were reclining next to him in the positions of honour when the thought arose.[53] Conversely there is a dearth of anecdotes illustrating the entertainment of the socially humble, or complaining of their access to the imperial table. Augustus is said only once to have admitted a freedman (not his own) to his table.[54] His successors were not necessarily so strict; but there is no sign of imperial freedmen jostling for places with the *proceres*. The prime access of freedmen to the emperors was not on formal occasions, but informal and backstairs. Helico owed his influence with Gaius to his access to him at

[47] Dio LVI.26.2–3.   [48] Cic. *Att.* XVI.5.2; Kroll 1933 (A 54) II.59ff.

[49] Suet. *Ner.* 37.   [50] Pliny, *HN* XXVI.3; cf. Val. Max. XI.6.17; Suet. *Tib.* 34.4; 68.2.

[51] Alföldi 1934 (D 1), 40ff; Sen. *Ben.* II.12.1; cf. Epictetus, *Diss.* IV.1.17.

[52] Friedländer 1922 (A 30) I. 98–103: Turcan 1987 (D 20) 237ff; cf. D'Arms 1984 (F 23).

[53] Suet. *Calig.* 32.

[54] Suet. *Aug.* 74; but cf. Macrob. *Sat.* II.4.28 for the entertainment of a slave dealer.

intimate moments, 'when he was playing ball, taking exercise, at his bath and at his breakfast, and retiring at night'.[55] But as far as social life was concerned, the early emperors behaved as members of their own social class, greeting, entertaining, and on occasion reciprocating offices by accepting hospitality and attending functions.[56]

Senators and *equites* were by no means the sole members of the court circle. One notable group which regularly met in the court of Augustus and his successors was that of Greek intellectuals and men of learning – the philosopher Areius at Augustus' court, the grammarian Seleucus or the astrologer Thrasyllus at Tiberius', the doctor Xenophon at Claudius', the musician Terpnus at Nero's. The majority of these are attested as living at court, sharing the *contubernium principis*.[57] Here again, emperors were not setting themselves apart from, but assimilating themselves to, the habits of the republican and early imperial nobility. When the historian Timagenes forfeited the *amicitia* of Augustus, he went to live with Asinius Pollio.[58] In supporting such intellectuals, emperors were not promoting a group otherwise neglected by society, but providing themselves and their friends with cultural stimulus of the type the Roman upper class had come to expect. On the other hand, because the resources and importance of the imperial house so far outran those of any aristocratic house, the effect was to introduce a new pattern of effectively 'public' patronage of the arts in place of the strictly private patronage of the Republic.[59]

Because integrated into the social and cultural life of the Roman upper class, the court not only served to reflect existing norms but dictated the tone of society.[60] The emperor was seen as a model eagerly imitated by others. The hothouse atmosphere of the court helped to disseminate tastes and fashions as well as facial disorders. Fashions in hairstyles or the decoration of houses throughout the empire closely and rapidly respond to models set by the court in Rome, and art history points to the deep penetration of the lives of Romans by the stylistic and moral values of the imperial circle.[61]

The role of the court in shaping fashion was aided by its use as a place for the upbringing of the children of favoured courtiers (as well as the children of foreign and barbarian kings). In hellenistic courts, the pages or *basilikoi paides* were a formal institution, enjoying especial prestige, and kings took into their innermost circle the *syntrophoi* with whom they

---

[55] Philo, *Leg.* 175, cf. Millar 1977 (A 59) 74.

[56] Millar 1977 (A 59) 112; Wallace-Hadrill 1982 (D 21) 40.

[57] Friedländer 1922 (A 30) I. 86–8; Millar 1977 (A 59) 83ff; Turcan 1987 (D 20) 208ff.

[58] Sen. *Ira* III.23.4–8.   [59] Rawson 1985 (A 79) 100ff, 319.

[60] Wallace-Hadrill 1983 (B 190) 177ff; Friedländer 1922 (A 30) I. 33–5.

[61] Zanker 1988 (F 633) ch. 7 on the court circle as model for taste. On the parallel role of courts in the evolution of European culture, see Elias, *Court Society*, esp 258ff.

themselves had been brought up. At Rome there is no trace of royal pages as a formal rank, but the children of the distinguished certainly frequented the court, received schooling there (under Augustus at the hands of the grammarian Verrius Flaccus), attended dinners (explicitly attested under Claudius), and enjoyed the attentions of emperors and their wives.[62]

Looking back from the complacent respectability of the Flavian and Antonine eras, our historical sources regard the *mores* of the Julio-Claudian court with a mixture of shock and astonishment. Profligacy of sexual morals, grossness and wanton pursuit of the exotic in eating, above all lavish waste in the construction and decoration of houses combine with sophistication of taste in literature and an (unRoman) delight in music. In all this, the imperial court continues in a direct line the 'hellenizing' tendencies of the aristocratic houses of the late Republic. Such social and cultural trends could not be manipulated by the emperors at will: the attempts of Augustus and even Tiberius to impose restraint, whether by legislation or by example, proved futile. In fact they (probably unwittingly) promoted the trends they professed to oppose. For by suppressing the traditional channels by which prestige was generated and made visible under the Republic, through glory in war and demonstrations of popular favour,[63] they redirected the competitive energies of the elite into the social displays upon which success in a court society depended.

This display contained the seeds of its own destruction. Their very magnificence, as Tacitus observes, was the ruin of the great houses, and Nero, who outstripped all competition with the sumptuousness of his Golden House and the wasteful dinners when guests were drenched in perfume from the ceiling, was surely aware of the political advantages of ruining his rivals financially with the aid of his unique access to the wealth of empire.[64] But Nero in turn was ruined by employment of this technique, both financially and, more damagingly, morally. The acceleration in extravagance of his reign produced a revulsion of taste within the court circle itself, among men from municipal and provincial backgrounds who perceived the implications of the way of life into which they found themselves sucked.[65] The tone of the Flavian court, for which the elder Pliny acts as spokesman, was palpably different.

Just as the court had a decisive impact on the culture and morality of Roman society at large, it is likely to have played a central role in the formation of opinion. It is frequently stated that the outlook of our

[62] Suet. *Gram.* 17 (Verrius Flaccus); Suet. *Claud.* 32, cf. Tac. *Ann.* XIII.16. Friedländer 1922 (A 30) 1.85f.   [63] Eck 1984 (D 39).

[64] Tac. *Ann.* III.55. Cf. Elias, *Court Society*, esp. 183ff on the use of the technique by Louis XIV.

[65] Tac. *Ann.* XVI.5; cf. Warmington 1969 (C 409) 169f.

sources is 'senatorial'. In some ways this is undeniable. Republican historiography had been dominated by senators, and imperial historians were conscious inheritors of the republican tradition. Respect for the upper classes in general and for the Senate in particular is one of the criteria on which emperors are most consistently praised or condemned. Social contacts within the relatively small group of senators could have been close, and doubtless many of them saw eye to eye on many issues. But what cannot be demonstrated is that such a 'senatorial' viewpoint is at variance with an alternative viewpoint, and that things looked rather differently from the perspective of the Palace.

It is notable that two of our major sources for the Julio-Claudian period, the elder Pliny and Suetonius, were men of equestrian rank who held posts in the service of the emperor. Their judgments of individual emperors and their underlying ideals do not appear to differ significantly from those of the senatorial Tacitus; on the other hand, both can be taken to reflect the views of the courts at which they served, Pliny in his loyalty to the Flavians and their puritanical morality, Suetonius in his implicit acceptance of the ideals of the 'golden age' of Trajan and Hadrian.[66] Other non-senatorial sources follow the same pattern. Josephus' blackening of Gaius, though in line with senatorial opinion, was determined by his own Jewish sensibilities, and was evidently quite acceptable to his Flavian patrons. Epictetus' reminiscences of court life are based on his experience as slave of Epaphroditus; though his master was close to Nero, he fully shares the 'senatorial' view of Nero as a tyrant.[67]

Without suggesting that the court always had a homogeneous point of view (there could be deep internal conflicts, as under Nero), it is not hard to imagine that it may have acted as a focus for discussion, gossip, and eventual opinion formation. Gossip it generated in abundance, and courtiers at all levels might be the source of anecdotes, from Augustus' attendant Julius Marathus who could describe his physique, and the *interiores aulici* who had theories about Gaius' Baiae bridge, to reminiscences by consulars about what had been said at the imperial table.[68] Imperial freedmen were a source of valuable information to contemporaries: leaking of inside information, or to use their own expression, the 'sale of smoke', became a familiar abuse in the Antonine court, but already we are told that Augustus broke the legs of a secretary for selling the contents of a letter.[69]

Behind trivial gossip lies concealed the serious purpose of the

[66] Wallace-Hadrill 1983 (B 190) 99ff; Gascou 1984 (B 59) 711ff; Lambrecht 1984 (B 103).
[67] Rajak 1983 (B 147) 185f on Josephus; Millar 1965 (D 14) on Epictetus.
[68] Suet. *Aug.* 79 and 94.3; *Calig.* 19.3; *Tib.* 61.6.
[69] Suet. *Aug.* 67; Friedländer 1922 (A 30) I. 47 on the sale of smoke; cf. Mart. IV.5.7.

exchange of observations and impressions by those in the imperial entourage. Court life, as Saint Simon appreciated, is a watching game. It could be vital to second-guess the imperial mind, to see who was rising in favour and who falling, and what changes were in the wind, for on such observations, as Sejanus' faction discovered to their cost, fortune and even life depended. Tacitus' description of the dinner at which Britannicus was poisoned suggests something of the sense of urgency of the game, and of the simultaneous need to see into the minds of others while concealing one's own: 'those sitting nearby were thrown into confusion; the imprudent fled, but those with deeper understanding remained rooted to the spot and watched Nero'.[70]

Assessments of individual emperors and their characters are surprisingly constant in the different sources, and it was once the fashion of source-criticism to posit a single source from whose initial assessment of an emperor all successive accounts derived. This perhaps underestimates the potential of the social circles around the court, the *convivia et circuli* of whose part in shaping public opinion Tiberius was aware,[71] to evolve a stereotype of the character of the ruler. In his lifetime assessments will have been fluid; but after his death, the court of the succeeding ruler could impose a definitive stamp. The image of Claudius as a fool was one Nero deliberately encouraged, both by his own chance remarks, and by the publication of the *Apocolocyntosis* by his closest adviser; Nero was surely drawing on and encouraging court gossip here, and there is no need to lay the blame for the image of Claudius solely on the malice of senators outraged by the power of the secretariat.[72]

In social terms, then, the Julio-Claudian emperors, whatever the political strains they may have experienced with the Senate, and however much power they may have allowed to their freedmen, drew their friends and companions from the upper class, afforded them easy access, failed to elaborate rituals that set themselves apart, and were bonded to them by the integrating force of common culture. Rather than regarding the court as an institution apart, we might think of it as the centre of a sort of solar system. Numerous houses of the rich and powerful in the city of Rome acted as lesser courts, centres of influence round which social activity clustered, to which visitors and clients thronged in the morning, and where sophisticated entertainment was provided later in the day. The palace was both similar to them and yet outshone them, the centre round which they themselves revolved, and from which ultimately they derived their own radiance.

[70] Tac. *Ann.* XIII.16. See Elias, *Court Society*, 104ff on observation at court.
[71] Tac. *Ann.* III.54.1.
[72] Griffin 1976 (B 71) 129f on the context of the *Apocolocyntosis*.

III PATRONAGE, POWER AND GOVERNMENT

The social rituals of a court may act as a façade to screen the realities of power. The endlessly elaborate etiquette and ceremonial of the French court of the seventeenth and eighteenth centuries partly served to mask the diversion of power from the old nobility by substituting the façade of social precedence for the realities of control.[73] The 'civility' for which 'good' emperors are praised by the sources has also been seen as a charade designed to screen the unpalatable truth of imperial power. The disjunction between appearance and reality has been greatly exaggerated. For while emperors undoubtedly used the court to control and limit the power of the upper classes, they also used it to strengthen their own power by embedding it within the existing social structure. The relationship of emperor and upper classes is thus complex and ambivalent.[74]

What drew men to court was more than social life. The court was the font of power and favour – and so the scene of anxieties and humiliations. Men love or hate Caesar, according to Epictetus, only because of his power to confer and take away advantages, wealth, military rank, praetorships or consulships.[75] The court inspires fear, not just of bodyguards and chamberlains and the like, but because of anxiety to secure the benefits Caesar distributes, governorships, procuratorships, praetorships, consulships, money; the courtiers behave like children fighting in their scramble to gather the scattered figs and nuts.[76] The lure of court is irresistible: the returning exile who swore to live in peace could not resist the invitation to court, and found himself praetorian prefect.[77] Yet was success worth the humiliations involved? The rising early, the running around, the kissing hands, rotting at others' doors, speaking and acting like a slave, sending gifts?[78]

From the first, emperors derived power from their ability to distribute resources. Claudius had shown, according to Seneca, how much more effectively imperial power was secured by favours (*beneficia*) than by arms.[79] The range of *beneficia* was enormous: status and legal privileges (citizenship, equestrian and senatorial rank, privileges like the *ius trium liberorum* etc.), magistracies, posts in the army and administration, financial benefits (fiscal concessions and immunities, subventions after disaster, grants to enhance status, and numberless liberalities to favourites and courtiers) and judgment (from resolution of disputes to cases of life and death). Documents and anecdotes evoke a vivid picture of the pressure of petitions and requests from individuals and communities

---

[73] So Elias, *Court Society*, 78ff.   [74] Wallace-Hadrill 1982 (D 21).
[75] Epictetus, *Diss.* IV.1.60; cf. Millar 1965 (D 14).   [76] *Diss.* IV.7.   [77] *Diss.* I.10.
[78] *Diss.* IV.10.   [79] Sen. *Cons. ad Polyb.* 12.3.

across the empire on the person of the emperor, and the personal nature of his involvement.[80] Yet though he and not any subordinate bureaucracy was the source of the benefits, inevitably the requests were mediated through others. Hence the patronage of the emperor is the centre of a complex web, in which the courtiers act as brokers as well as beneficiaries.[81]

The network emerged rapidly. One aspect is the swift evolution of a ramifying secretariat of slaves and freedmen. Over 4,000 inscriptions, mostly sepulchral, attest the sheer scale of the imperial secretariat over the course of the Empire.[82] The shape of imperial business dictated the division and organization of labour, and it is significant that the lines along which it divided were not areas of government but the channels of communication between subject and ruler. The letters, petitions, embassies and legal hearings which brought contact with the emperor generated the Palatine 'offices' of *ab epistulis, a libellis, a legationibus* and *a cognitionibus*, and alongside these record-keeping (*a memoria*) and above all supervision of the vast imperial wealth, ambivalent in its status between the public and the private (*a rationibus*), account for the main activities of the secretariat.[83] Such divisions may go back at an informal level to Augustus,[84] but it is notoriously under Claudius that the formal titulature that became standard is first seen in the literary sources in the naming of Polybius, Narcissus and Pallas as *a studiis, ab epistulis* and *a rationibus* respectively, and on the testimony of one who himself held two of these posts.[85] At once, such titles acquired an imperial ring: the charge against the two Torquati Silani under Nero of nursing imperial ambitions in calling their secretaries *ab epistulis, a libellis* and *a rationibus* shows how for all its origins in the bloated servile households of the aristocracy, the imperial household had grown into something of quite another order.[86]

In some respects, the *familia Caesaris* betrays characteristic features of bureaucratic government. We can detect the emergence of bureaux with their own hierarchy of subordinate posts, from slave *tabellarii*, through junior freedmen *adiutores, tabularii* and *a commentariis*, to the senior grade of *proximus* immediately below the head, himself known simply by the name of his *officium* (e.g. *ab epistulis*). The grades seem clearly distinguishable in terms of age-range (senior officials were normally old men), even if a set salary structure must be regarded as hypothetical.[87] The personnel could be regarded as 'officials' embarked on a quasi-public career

---

[80] Millar 1977 (A 59) *passim* and 1967 (D 15).   [81] Saller 1982 (F 59) 41ff.

[82] Weaver 1972 (D 22) 8.   [83] Millar 1977 (A 59) 203ff.   [84] Boulvert 1970 (D 6) 53ff.

[85] Suet. *Claud.* 28; cf. Wallace-Hadrill 1983 (B 190) 73ff.

[86] Tac. *Ann.* XV.35 and XVI.8.

[87] Weaver 1972 (D 22) 227ff; Boulvert 1974 (D 7) 127ff on grades is too schematic, cf. Burton 1977 (D 8).

partially analogous to the *cursus honorum*: this much is implicit in Statius' panegyrical account of the career of the father of Claudius Etruscus, whose promotions through a series of posts brought him progressive honour,[88] and also in those epitaphs which imitate senators and equestrians in listing posts in ascending or descending sequence.

But in analysing the functions and powers of the *familia Caesaris*, it is misleading to assimilate it to a modern bureaucracy. Much more fruitful analogies lie in the royaĺ households of medieval and Renaissance Europe. One essential feature of the household is that it serves the person of the ruler in all his activities, private or public, small or large. Private functions of the ruler (the bedchamber, the table, the stables etc.) are hard to separate from the public and administrative. Just as the medieval English court generated numerous – and to us faintly ludicrous – subdivisions in the private sphere, of spicery, napery, ewery, and apothecary, of garçons of the sumpterhorse or valets of the garbage,[89] or as the court of Francis I of France gloried in its sixty categories of household officials, down to furriers, spit-turners, tapestry-makers and laundresses,[90] so the imperial court displays a dizzy proliferation of minutely defined functions, such as the many divisions of the wardrobe (*a veste privata, forensi, castrensi, munda, alba triumphali, matutina venatoria, regia et Graecula* etc.) or of the buttery (*a crystallinis, a cyatho, a lagona, a potione* etc.).[91] The fact that a freedman might advance like Ti. Claudius Aug. lib. Bucolas from taster (*praegustator*) and butler (*tricliniarchus*) to *procurator aquarum*, with care for the aqueducts of Rome, and *procurator castrensis*, steward of the Palace,[92] certainly affected contemporary perceptions of imperial freedmen, and should at least make us pause before categorizing them as 'civil servants'. Separation of *domus* and *respublica* was an empty promise.[93]

The range of posts within and without the Palace reflected the diversity of its activities, from distribution of resources and judgment to feasting and entertainment. Certainly the appointment of equestrians to the major secretarial posts which Vitellius initiated shows their development under the Julio-Claudians to a conspicuous role in public life; yet equestrians had been employed before this in the imperial household in less 'political' functions, like Pompeius Macer as *a bibliothecis* under Augustus, let alone Tiberius' shocking appointment of an equestrian to charge of his 'pleasures' (*a voluptatibus*), a post regarded by a later

[88] Stat. *Silv.* III.3.63f, cf. Weaver 1972 (D 22) 284ff.

[89] C. Given-Wilson, *The Royal Household and the King's Affinity. Service, Politics and Finance in England 1360–1413* (New Haven–London, 1986), 58f.

[90] R.J. Knecht, *European Studies Review* 8 (1978) 2.

[91] Hirschfeld 1912 (D 13) 307ff; Duff 1958 (F 28) 143ff; Turcan 1987 (D 20) 51ff.

[92] *CIL* XI 3612, XV 7279 = *ILS* 1567, 8679, 7280.

[93] Tac. *Ann.* XIII.4; Pavis d'Escurac 1987 (D 18).

freedman as a splendid promotion.[94] It does not help to draw a hard and fast line between private and public functions. The role of the important post *a studiis* is notably obscure, but may have ranged from advice on imperial speeches to grammatical commentary on private reading of literature.[95]

In trying to understand the power of the imperial freedman, then, it is not enough to say that the early emperors turned their household into a new arm of government (though this is clearly the case). The power of the freedman derived from his proximity to the emperor and his consequent ability to influence specific aspects of resource-distribution. The word even of a court-jester might cost a man his life.[96] Claudius' prepotent freedmen, who included Posides the eunuch and Harpocras as well as the 'heads of bureaux', owed their power to their master's combination of an insatiable appetite to bestow favours and judgment with an inability to control the detail of so many transactions. The mistresses of emperors, as of many later kings, were in an ideal position to extract favours, as Vespasian's Caenis, with her long experience of the court, well understood.[97] That the elite resented the wealth and influence which flowed from such brokerage is not surprising, not because the use of political position to amass *gratia* was new to Roman society, but precisely because the exercise of patronage was how the elite traditionally defined its own standing. Imperial freedmen established no monopoly in this respect, and the fact that the court became the focus of elite patronage too underlay the tension.

The reign of Augustus was one of transition from the pluralist patronage system of the Republic, whereby the nobility competed with each other to maximize their following and thus their influence with the *populus Romanus*, to the imperial pattern under which the emperor monopolized the support of the *populus*, and the elite looked to him for favours, which they in their turn distributed to others.[98] The number of benefits within the imperial gift multiplied throughout the Julio-Claudian period: the number of posts in the imperial service rose, and rights and privileges like the *ius trium liberorum* or even leave of absence from the Senate were quietly absorbed by successive emperors by steps we can mostly no longer trace. But the core of imperial patronage, round which all else accrued, was there from the start: the wealth that flowed from victory in civil war, and the control over appointments in the army and 'imperial' provinces.

From the first, then, the elite looked to the emperor for favours, and

---

[94] Suet. *Tib.* 42.2; *CIL* VI 8619 (Ianuarius Aug. lib.), 'ad splendidam voluptatum statio[nem promotus]'.   [95] Millar 1977 (A 59) 205; Wallace-Hadrill 1983 (B 190) 83–6.
[96] Suet. *Tib.* 61.6.   [97] Suet. *Vesp.* 3 and 21; Dio LXVI.14.
[98] Saller 1982 (F 59) 73ff; Wallace-Hadrill 1989 (F 75) 78ff.

their attendance at court was motivated by pursuit of favours. The court thus played a vital role in consolidating imperial power within the context of imperial society.[99] First, it enabled the ruler to control the elite. In order to pursue power it was necessary to come to Rome and enter the intrigue of the court. That firmly established Rome as the arena of political conflict and discouraged the emergence of alternative regional power bases. The 'big men' of the empire were under the immediate eye of the emperor. He could manipulate their ambition by playing them off against each other, using his control of the distribution of resources to keep them on tenterhooks, withholding favours and elevating new favourites if the influence of old favourites threatened to become entrenched. Secondly, he could through the elite exercise a progressively wider control throughout the empire. The elite, senatorial and equestrian, was drawn from the municipalities of Italy and, in this period, increasingly the western provinces. Those at court acted as brokers for their contacts at home, securing benefits for them and drawing further compatriots into the circle of power at Rome – a marked example of this process is the rise of Spaniards in various posts in the administration during the Corduban Seneca's period of influence with Nero.[100]

Within the broad circle of the hopeful and ambitious who attended the court, there was an inner circle of *amici* upon whom emperors called for advice in a variety of circumstances: to assist in giving judgment, whether in public imperial *cognitiones*, or in the more sinister trials *intra cubiculum*, and to handle a whole range of questions from the trivial and routine to matters of high state. Perhaps there were times when not even the *amici* could predict the gravity of the questions to be considered: Juvenal's picture of an imperial council debating the preparation of a fish may be satire, but Nero is said to have called the *primores* to his house in the Vindex crisis only to spend the day, after brief political consultation, discussing types of musical organ.[101] Augustus' innovation of a standing committee of senators with regular meetings and a defined and rotating membership which prepared business for the Senate was not continued by his successors; thereafter such business was dealt with on the same informal and *ad hoc* basis as other matters. There was no such thing, as the classic study of the subject has emphasized, as the *consilium principis*.[102] Lack of definition, in membership and function, only increased the discretionary powers of the ruler: this too was among the *arcana imperii*. Even so, some were called for consultation more regularly, and on more

[99] Cf. Elias, *Court Society*, 146ff.   [100] Griffin 1976 (B 71), 81–96.
[101] Juv. *Sat.* 4; Suet. *Ner.* 41.2, better than Dio LXIII.26.4.
[102] Crook 1955 (D 10) 8–20; 104ff.

sensitive issues, than others, and these could be seen as *the* friends of Caesar.

The accessibility of the emperor to the elite thus worked to their mutual advantage. Individual members of the elite had access to power and influence; the emperor was able to reduce the elite to dependence on himself. That does not mean that the court operated smoothly and without tension. On the contrary, it was a battleground – much more so than the Senate, where the only real battles were trials. In the Julio-Claudian period the battle was particularly bloody, for while the system was still emergent, major tensions were unresolved. The sharpness of the conflict is reflected in the bitterness of the accounts given by the sources, for instance the power of the praetorian prefect Sejanus under Tiberius, or that of the freedmen Pallas and Narcissus under Claudius. Two areas of tension are apparent: that within the senatorial-equestrian elite, and that between the elite and members of the inner imperial household, especially the freedmen officials.

Because of the obvious contrast between the monarchical nature of the court and the republican nature of the Senate, it is tempting to envisage a permanent tension between senators as a group and non-senators, whether *equites* or imperial freedmen, as an opposed group, a temptation strengthened by the old theory of a legal separation of powers between emperor and Senate. This is to understate the complexity of the conflict.[103] It is true that Augustus' creation of the great equestrian prefectures, and the power attained by the chief freedmen secretaries under Gaius, Claudius and Nero, created a new disjunction between power and status, which resulted in strange inversions of social precedence, as when the equestrian prefects followed the consuls, but preceded the other magistrates, in swearing the oath of allegiance to Tiberius, or Claudius' freedman Polybius walked in public between the two consuls.[104] A divorce between status and power meant that the emperor was less trammelled by social constraints in distributing power, and could neutralize those by whom he felt threatened by palming them off with marks of high status that carried little power.[105] It is not unlikely that even Augustus saw the advantages of such a strategy and played it deliberately.

But it is wrong to represent the senators as a coherent group, either socially or politically. They were as much creatures of the court as the imperial freedmen. Patronage cut across status barriers: senators enlisted the support of *equites* and freedmen, but conversely equestrian and

---

[103] See Millar 1977 (A 59) 275ff; Brunt 1983 (D 26); Demougin 1988 (D 37).

[104] Tac. *Ann.* 1.7; Suet. *Claud.* 28; cf. Tac. *Ann.* XVI.17 on the 'praepostera ambitio' of Annaeus Mela.   [105] Hopkins 1983 (A 46) 176ff.

freedmen posts might be owed to the brokerage of senators. Alliances like that between Vespasian and Narcissus worked to the advantage of both parties. Within the Senate distinctions may be drawn: not perhaps between men in the 'imperial service' and others, since imperial patronage also affected posts that were not direct imperial appointments, but between a 'grand set' of those swiftly promoted in status who enjoyed little power, and a 'power set' of those who rose more slowly but were entrusted with greater responsibility.[106] But even this distinction may understate the influence wielded at court by members of the grand set, who having risen rapidly thanks to good connexions may well have continued to exercise their connexions to the benefit of others. The lines of division of the elite at court were not between the social ranks of senator, *eques* and freedman, which were united by multiple ties of family, friendship and interest, but between groups of mixed status: the fissures were vertical not horizontal.

The heyday of the power of freedmen coincides with a period of intrigue and influence among the female members of the imperial household. Wives and freedmen have it in common that they are 'insiders' and therefore stand apart from the 'outsider' elite. In no sense were freedmen in competition with members of the elite: they were not eligible for army rank nor senatorial positions (even if they could be awarded military and senatorial decorations); they did not function as *amici*, and there is no sign that they were invited to attend the *consilium* – it is with high irony that Tacitus depicts Claudius *in consilio* when consulting his freedmen.[107] Nor, as we have seen, do they appear to have shared in the social life of the court. Unlike elite brokers of patronage, they were not themselves competitors. Their competition was with each other (Pallas' award of the insignia of the praetorship reflects competition not with senators but with his fellow-freedman Narcissus, previously decorated with the quaestorship); in exactly the same way the imperial women competed for influence with each other, excluded by their sex from the men's world of offices. The influence of freedmen should therefore be seen in the context of the pattern of court intrigue in which the women were simultaneously involved. Their power came from the conflict of competing groups.

The women of the Julio-Claudian household were openly involved in the operation of patronage. We hear casually of Livia's role in promoting Galba and the grandfather of the emperor Otho.[108] An inscription shows her openly acknowledged by Augustus for her role in securing privileges

106 Hopkins 1983 (A 46) 171; Elias, *Court Society*, 169ff.
107 Tac. *Ann.* XII.1; cf. Crook 1955 (D 10) 42.
108 Suet. *Galba* 5; *Oth.* 1; cf. Purcell 1986 (F 50).

for the island of Samos.[109] Networks of friendship extended from the palace among the women of the Roman elite. Seneca (who owed the start of his career to his aunt Helvia, and its furtherance to Agrippina) takes for granted that Marcia, as an intimate of Livia, used her influence to secure a priesthood for her own son.[110] Messallina abused her position not by exercising but by selling patronage: together with Claudius' freedmen, she sold the citizenship so liberally that it was said to be had in exchange for glass beads, and not only the citizenship, nor even military commands and provincial governorships, but everything in general.[111] Her presence at the trial *intra cubiculum* of Valerius Asiaticus was something altogether more sinister.[112]

Female involvement in patronage was not simply a side product of the system. From Augustus to Nero the imperial court is characterized by sharp intrigue that periodically surfaces in the eruption of major conflicts between competing groups; in almost all these conflicts, the women play a central role. The court of Louis XIV was analysed by participants as split between cabals that clustered round various members of the royal family; any distinctions of political or religious principle that could be detected between the cabals were of secondary significance.[113] A similar analysis seems to apply to the Julio-Claudian court. The power groupings are heterogeneous in composition: female members of the *domus Caesaris* and their children, leading freedmen, senators and *equites*. Lucius Vitellius, that epitome of a courtier, thrice consul and censor, was said to have carried around Messallina's slipper and kissed it from time to time, and to have kept the images of Narcissus and Pallas among his *lares*.[114]

The aim of a cabal is to maximize its own influence in the distribution of resources. Naturally groupings tend to form around potential candidates for the succession: there are already hints of rival groups round Octavia and her son Marcellus on one side, Agrippa, Livia and her sons on the other early in Augustus' reign,[115] clear signs of rival groups round Julia, Livia and their respective sons later,[116] and under Tiberius explicit feuding between the supporters of Agrippina and those of Sejanus, adulterously linked to Livilla.[117] It should not be assumed that such cabals formed with explicit designs on the throne: the mere existence of a potential successor is enough to constitute a catalyst for intrigue, and much of the policy of intermarriage and interadoption,

[109] Reynolds 1982 (B 270) no. 13 line 5, cf. Suet. *Aug.* 40.   [110] Sen. *Cons. ad Marciam* 24.3.

[111] Dio LX.17.5–8.   [112] Tac. *Ann.* XI.2.

[113] See E. Le Roy Ladurie 'Versailles observed: the court of Louis XIV in 1709' (in *The Mind and Method of the Historian.* Trans. S. and B. Reynolds. Brighton, 1981) for analysis of cabals.

[114] Suet. *Vit.* 2.   [115] Syme 1939 (A 93) 340–2.

[116] Syme 1984 (A 94) III. 912–36.   [117] Levick 1976 (C 366) 148ff.

particularly as practised by Augustus, must have been designed (how-ever ineffectively) to frustrate the formation of rival cabals. The marriage of Tiberius to Iulia, for instance, though it did little to clarify the line of succession to power, must have aimed to obviate precisely the sort of tensions and rivalries that erupted with such unfortunate consequences.

A characteristic of conflict between rival groupings is that they come to a head in accusations of adultery – against the two Iulias, Livilla and Sejanus, the sisters of Gaius, Messallina, and Nero's betrothed Octavia. The charge of adultery is often regarded as a sham to disguise political realities; indeed the strings of 'accomplices' of the adultery of the Iulias indicate that no ordinary adultery is involved.[118] But we should not underestimate the threat posed to stability within the court by adulterous liaisons (nor overestimate the innocence of the accused). Since marriage was used as an official instrument of dynastic policy, to mark succession and to unify potentially divergent groups, adultery represented the inverse, the dark underside of intrigue and group formation out of the emperor's control. Sejanus' adultery was seen as a vital step in his rise to influence and his establishment of a stranglehold over the network of patronage. Of course, some accusations of adultery were false, and could be cooked up by rival interests to discredit the accused (Livia must be suspect on this count). But, as with accusations of magic, which was the inverse of the divine protection behind imperial power, the charge reflected a threat to imperial power which the participants felt to be real.

Finally, we should not exaggerate the rigidity of such cabals. Their membership was unstable and fluid. Loyalties and friendships could evaporate in a moment (it was the misfortune of Sejanus' supporters that they had no warning of his fall). Courtiers watched carefully to see whose stock was rising with the emperor, whose falling. 'Nothing in human affairs is so unstable and fluid as the reputation of power': Agrippina's crowded threshold was deserted in an instant when the whisper circulated of her son Nero's displeasure.[119] Epictetus compares court life to the lot of a traveller who attaches himself to the convoy of a passing official for protection from bandits; the friendship of Caesar is an equally undependable method of progress, hard to pick up, easy to be lost, and limited by the life chances of the Caesar himself.[120] The point applies similarly to friendship with Caesar's friends. Moreover, the groupings were fissile, potentially divided into further groupings. Messallina was overthrown by a combination of her old supporters, Narcissus and Vitellius; during the crisis, Narcissus did not feel sure even of Vitellius and had him excluded from the imperial litter.[121] Though supported in the overthrow by Pallas, Narcissus was ruined by the combination of

---

[118] Tac. *Ann.* III.24; cf. Syme 1984 (A 94) III.924f.   [119] Tac. *Ann.* XIII.19.
[120] Epictetus, *Diss.* IV.1.91–8.   [121] Tac. *Ann.* XI.33.

Pallas and Agrippina, having unwisely shown too much interest in
Britannicus. Agrippina was abandoned by her protégés Seneca and
Burrus. Such cases serve as warning against any attempt to detect long-
term political groupings and alliances.

With new patterns of politics, the court generated new styles of life
peculiar to itself. Even survival, let alone success, was fraught with
dangers. Seneca reports the reply of the old courtier asked with
amazement how he had reached old age at court: 'by accepting insults
and expressing gratitude for them'.[122] Flattery and the concealment of
true feelings were a structural necessity. Seneca goes on to tell the tale of
the distinguished *eques* Pastor who, on the very day that his son was
executed by Gaius, was bidden to make merry at the imperial table.
There was a reason for the courtier's bizarre compliance with the
invitation – he had a second son. A degree of self-abasement and
hypocrisy seemed necessary even under the best-intentioned emperors:
Tiberius complained of the servility of his senators, but failed to stop it.
In this respect, the Senate acted as an extension of court life; the *adulatio*
of which Tacitus complains, the incessant manufacture of honorific
decrees and inflated language, came from men with an eye to promotion
or merely survival at court.

Hypocrisy and flattery stood in direct antithesis to the *libertas* of frank
expression and independent opinion on which the republican nobility
prided itself.[123] It was not however mere traditionalist sentiment which
made men under the Principate hanker for the old *libertas*. The new court
life was highly unstable, and placed gross psychological strains on the
courtier, who hardly knew whom to trust and whom to back from one
moment to another. The agony felt by the friends of the disgraced
Sejanus, eloquently voiced by M. Terentius, struck a chord with every
anxious courtier: 'It is not ours to reason whom you choose to elevate
above others and on what grounds; the gods have given you the final say;
it is left to us to take pride in loyalty.'[124] But such *obsequium* was no
defence for those who backed a loser.

In this context of instability and psychological strain, philosophy had
an important role to play. Stoicism, with its stress on the value of single-
minded pursuit of public duty and virtues irrespective of the dangers,
offered a vital antidote to the hypocrisy of court life.[125] It is no
coincidence that Stoicism flourished, in martyrs like Thrasea Paetus,
when the excesses of Nero's court were at their peak. The philosophy of
both Seneca and Epictetus emerges from men with a court background

---

[122] Sen. *Ira* II.33.2.   [123] Wirszubski 1950 (A 107) 124ff; Brunt 1988 (A 11) 281ff.
[124] Tac. *Ann.* VI.8.
[125] On Stoicism and politics, Brunt 1975 (F 107); on Nero's court, Griffin 1976 (B 71);
Warmington 1969 (C 409) 142–54.

and offers explicit reaction against court morality. In the long run the
Stoics carried their point, and the tone did change. Yet a century later,
the Stoic emperor Marcus still needs his philosophy as antidote to court
life, its vain pomp and superficiality, its transitory quarrels and ambitions, and the sheer irritation of working with the pettiness of his
courtiers.[126]

IV. CONCLUSION

The court, as social and political institution, lies at the heart of the new
regime established by Augustus and his heirs. It also encapsulates the
paradoxes of that regime, and the way it transformed the structures of
the old city-state to create those of the new monarchy. The household of
a private citizen, based on the forms and practices of the households of
the republican nobility, became the centre of the state; the focus of
political activity shifted irrevocably from a plurality of households to a
single one, sprawling monstrously over the symbolical heart of Rome. In
drawing to itself the threads of patronage, the court brought the
transactions of political dealing under imperial surveillance.

The similarities to the royal courts of the East were only too apparent
to participants. Court life brought servility in the place of the freedom of
a society of citizen equals. The tone of public discourse changed, from
bold self-advertisement and uninhibited attack on rivals, to self-conceal-
ment and lip-service to the source of power. And yet the transition from
city-state to monarchy was a hesitant and gradual one, and the reuse of
old forms was essential. The Julio-Claudian court preserved the social
hierarchy of the Republic, while yet seeming to undermine it and subject
senators to slaves. The early emperors needed to exercise power with,
not against, the traditional ruling class. They used republican forms to
establish their own dominance while appearing to respect their fellow-
citizens. The rituals of court allowed them at one level to use the
republican status hierarchy to legitimate their own position, while at
another playing off the aristocracy against new men promoted from the
provinces and against *liberti*, ignoble but potent. The accessibility of the
emperor to the upper classes and his 'civil' treatment of them as 'equals'
was an essential part of the strategy of power, and it makes the imperial
court fundamentally different from the court of any hellenistic ruler.

Between Augustus and Nero the patterns of court life were developing, and still far from fixed. But there is an unmistakable movement
towards formalization and institutionalization. The differentiation of the
secretariat and the evolution of its internal hierarchy is one tangible

[126] Cf. Brunt 1974 (B 19).

example of this. It is also right to emphasize the element of continuity.[127] When we ask what made possible the stability of the government evolved by Augustus, which despite its extraordinary lack of legal definition and its reliance on Augustus' own charismatic personality, nevertheless managed to survive the eccentricities of four members of his own house and a return to civil war, to become the system without which peace was unthinkable, the answer must lie partly in the imperial court. Despite notable instances of the fall of political favourites, like Sejanus or Seneca, there was an underlying continuity of personnel. The Flavians were served by many with long experience of power in the Julio-Claudian court. The anonymous father of Claudius Etruscus, who served as freedman of every Caesar from Tiberius to Domitian to die in his ninetieth year excited Statius' admiration by surviving so many changes of yoke and so many stormy seas.[128] But though few could rival him in longevity, imperial slaves and freedmen, originally personal to Augustus, came to transfer automatically to the new regime, giving rise to a stability of staff.

The same continuity can be observed at higher social levels. It is striking what long and intimate links each of Nero's successors display with the Julio-Claudian court. Galba started as a favourite of Livia, and served successive emperors, being especially favoured by Claudius who admitted him to his *cohors amicorum*.[129] Otho was grandson of another of Livia's protégés and son of one so admired by Claudius as to be honoured with a statue on the Palatine; his own intimacy with Nero was notorious.[130] Vitellius, grandson of an Augustan procurator, and son of that most adept of Claudian courtiers, also had an uncle whose links with Sejanus cost him his life; while he himself followed the tastes of each Caesar with remarkable pliability, a sexual favourite under Tiberius, a charioteer under Gaius, a dicer under Claudius, a musician under Nero.[131] Vespasian, as we have seen, met both favour and disgrace at court, while his son Titus was intimate enough with Britannicus to have risked sharing his fate. Even in Nerva, at the end of the century, we find a sexagenarian, whose loyalty to Nero had earned him a statue on the Palatine, and a member of a family whose three generations of loyalty to the dynasty stretched back to the treaty of Brundisium in 39 B.C.[132] If others were as well served biographically as were emperors, such family histories of continuous service would be multiplied.

Good friends, Trajan is supposed to have said, compensated for

[127] Crook 1955 (D 10) 29, 115ff etc.
[128] Stat. *Silv.* III.3.83f, 'tu totiens mutata ducum iuga rite tulisti|integer, inque omni felix tua cumba profundo'; Weaver 1972 (D 22) 284f.
[129] Suet. *Galba* 5 and 7.   [130] Suet. *Oth.* 1.   [131] Suet. *Vit.* 2–4.
[132] Crook 1955 (D 10) 159f; for the consulate of Nerva's father, *AE* 1979, 100.

Domitian's bad rule.[133] But emperors inevitably took over their predecessors' friends and servants, good or bad, since these made themselves indispensable. Vested interests were at stake. Augustus and his successors needed a court in order to rule; but if imperial rule came under question, the court needed its emperor. Thus, despite its conflicts and distasteful features, the court was a system of power which tended to its own perpetuation.

[133] SHA *Alex. Sev.* 65.5; cf. Tac. *Hist.* IV.7.3, 'nullum maius boni imperii instrumentum quam bonos amicos esse.'

CHAPTER 8

THE IMPERIAL FINANCES

D. W. RATHBONE

The economic resources at the disposal of the emperors from Augustus to Vitellius and the uses which they made of them are most clearly explained against the background of the state expenditure of the Roman empire.[1]

The empire required an army, and under Augustus a standing army was developed, of which the size and terms of service of the legionary component remained broadly stable throughout this period, although the nature of the auxiliary component took much longer to crystallize.[2] Annual pay for a legionary was 900 sesterces, while cavalrymen, higher ranks and the praetorian guard received considerably more. There were stoppages against this pay for replacement equipment and clothing and almost certainly for food. On discharge a surviving legionary in theory received a bounty of 12,000 sesterces – equivalent to over twelve years' basic pay, and so a third of a surviving veteran's total remuneration – but he may often have been given a plot of land in a frontier zone instead or in part payment. The conversion of auxiliary forces, traditionally supplied *ad hoc* by allied states, into regular units of the Roman army and the standardization of their terms of service and remuneration were slow processes which lasted into the Flavian era. The rate of pay for auxiliary troops remains frustratingly uncertain (footsoldiers may have received a half or five-sixths or some intermediate fraction of the basic legionary rate), as does the date of its standardization (perhaps under Claudius, but perhaps not until the Flavians). There is no evidence that auxiliaries in this period regularly received either cash or land on discharge. Instead, from Claudius on, Roman citizenship was used as a cheap reward, along with the limited tax immunities which were probably granted to all veterans. Pay for all soldiers was sometimes supplemented by bonuses given by emperors on political occasions (booty was another possible extra, though hardly state expenditure). Other military expenditure included materials for defences, camps, all kinds of equipment, transport and riding animals, and supplies. There were also the fleets to maintain.

---

[1] General treatments: Frank 1940 (D 128) v. chs. I–II; Neesen 1980 (D 151); Lo Cascio 1986 (D 145); Noè 1987 (D 152). [2] See below, ch. 11.

The total annual cost of the imperial armed forces cannot be computed with accuracy because of the mass of variable and unknown factors. Most modern estimates of the average annual wage bill before Domitian's pay-rise would put it, if we include discharge bounties, at 400 million sesterces, at least.[3] Even if not fallacious, such estimates are misleading. Because of the system of deductions at source from pay, much of the theoretical wage bill was probably never paid in cash. On the other hand, the total bill will have increased steadily as the number of auxiliary units grew and their remuneration was regularized. Actual cash expenditure also swelled when campaigns were mounted, probably mainly to mobilize extra supplies – the slave *dispensator* for Nero's Armenian manoeuvres allegedly managed to siphon off 13 million sesterces with which to buy his freedom.[4] In general terms, however, military expenditure was kept artificially low insofar as conscription, rather than the payment of attractive salaries, was used regularly to fill auxiliary units and sometimes to fill legions.

The empire required administration, mostly in the spheres of finance and law and order. Salaried officials were few – the senatorial governors and legates and the slowly growing number of equestrian procurators – but their salaries were substantial, perhaps totalling over 50 million sesterces per annum, and presumably were paid in cash; revenues were also skimmed off by the increasingly numerous and permanent clerical staff in their offices.[5] However, many of the costs of administration were hidden. The emperor, senators and town councillors throughout the empire were meant to perform public functions at their own private expense, an obligation which helped to justify and to reinforce their economic dominance.[6] As subordinates they would also use their own dependants – which was initially the position of the *familia Caesaris*, the imperial slaves and freedmen, although it came to live at least partly off state revenues. The central government and its representatives also employed seconded soldiers in civil police and administrative roles. When transport, labour or supplies of any kind were required in the public interest both central and local governments and their individual representatives could commandeer virtually at will from the subject population. The prime examples of this are the *cursus publicus* and the uniquely well-documented local corvée obligations in Egypt.[7]

The empire had no economic or social programmes, but it still incurred massive expenditure on public buildings and roads, on the rituals of civic life such as sacrifices, games and banquets, on rewards to

---

[3] Hopkins 1980 (D 133) 124–5; MacMullen 1984 (D 146).
[4] Pliny, *HN* VII.129.   [5] Frank 1940 (D 128) v.6.   [6] Veyne 1976 (A 98).
[7] Pflaum 1940 (D 153); Jones 1974 (D 137) 169 n. 96, 180; Mitchell 1976 (B 255); Lewis 1982 (E 945).

artists, athletes and educators, on minting coinage, and on ensuring a
reasonably regular supply of staple foodstuffs to its urban populations, in
short on producing and maintaining what we recognize as Roman
civilization. In the provinces and Italy this expenditure normally fell on
the local aristocracy, who were mostly, in this period, not unwilling to
bear it in return for the prestige and power which it conferred. In Rome
itself, though senatorial commissions to supervise public buildings and
facilities had been instituted by Augustus, who had also revived the
priestly colleges, a *de facto* ban on aristocratic initiatives had been
imposed to reduce the risk of challenges to imperial munificence.[8]
Senators could still, on defined occasions, give games, but all main
public buildings and facilities, the major festivals and the grain supply
became the responsibility of the emperor. From Augustus on, emperors
haphazardly extended their operations in this line to the towns of Italy
and the provinces, using tactics which included, for example, paying for
buildings through their relatives, and diverting or remitting imperial
taxes to local councils to aid municipal projects.[9]

Beyond this state munificence which was arguably necessary there was
the *ad hoc* liberality expected of all rich and prominent men in the empire,
and most expected of the richest and most prominent of all, the
emperor.[10] Friendship with the emperor and his trust were demonstrated
in a courtier's receipt of estates and other gifts in cash and kind.
Individual deeds had to be rewarded appropriately, whether a huge sum
to an important freedman or a few coins to a street poet. An emperor
could remit some of the taxes due from a city purely as a mark of his
favour; a Nero could remit those of a whole province. In an ego-
boosting display of superiority as well as of generosity the emperor
could throw to the Roman crowd tokens for mystery prizes including
cash and all kinds of objects. The range of imperial giving cannot be
described exhaustively, nor was it meant to be: 'there is nothing that
might not be hoped for from my magnanimity', said Nero.[11] Since such
'spontaneous' giving was an integral part of the role of emperor as, on a
smaller scale, it was of local magistrates, it must be counted as an area of
state expenditure.

The cost of all this munificence, both necessary and spontaneous, is
impossible to compute. More important is its size in relation to military
expenditure. Under Claudius, for example, the draining of the Fucine
lake over eleven years is said to have employed 30,000 men (though
perhaps 30,000 was the aggregate total of man-days), and the estimated
costs of the new port at Ostia were expected to kill off his enthusiasm for
the project. There were other imperial building projects in Rome, lavish

[8] Eck 1984 (D 39).   [9] Bourne 1946 (D 115); Corbier 1985 (D 124); Mitchell 1987 (D 150).
[10] Kloft 1970 (D 138).   [11] *GCN* 64 (lines 10–11).

shows and several handouts. The freedmen Pallas and Narcissus between them allegedly accumulated a sum equal to one and a half years' military budget.[12] It is likely that Claudius spent in and around Rome – and necessarily in actual coin – as much each year as the army in theory cost him, and in practice much military expenditure was notional since it was covered by supplies in kind. If we allow also for civil expenditure outside Rome and its environs, it is likely that the army, even if it was the single largest regular item in the imperial budget, in this period accounted on average for less than half of all imperial spending. The claims in later Roman writers that the reason for taxation was the need to pay for the armies which guaranteed peace have a propagandist whiff about them.

To meet this varied expenditure the state had a correspondingly varied range of assets and incomes. As heir to the ideology of the Greek city-state, the Roman government did not subject its own citizens, wherever they resided, to regular direct taxation on the person, and did not tax its own 'citizen land' (i.e. that held *iure Quiritium*), which meant mainland Italy and also the territories of Roman overseas colonies and of provincial cities which enjoyed the *ius Italicum*.[13] As an imperial power Rome levied direct taxes or rents on the rest of its subject lands and populations. It is dubious whether any coherent legal justification for this fiscal exploitation was elaborated under the Principate; instead pragmatism ruled.[14] Where sophisticated pre-Roman fiscal systems existed, mainly in the old hellenistic kingdoms, they tended to be adapted and maintained, and more generally there flourished a defensive ideology of fiscal minimalism (no new taxes, no increases to old ones). But, starting in Egypt, Augustus introduced an annual poll-tax in cash, Roman-style census arrangements gradually spread through the eastern provinces, and Roman fiscality – and, with it, monetization – was brusquely introduced to the northern and central European provinces.[15] Although the new regular provincial poll-tax allowed Augustus and his successors to dispense with the irregular hellenistic capitation taxes which republican governors had continued to levy on occasion and to discontinue the revived triumviral levying of *tributum* in Italy, all Rome's subjects and even her own citizens remained liable to random summary exploitation such as confiscation of land for colonies or veteran settlement (not always to punish disloyalty), requisition of housing, animals and supplies for the use of the military and the administration, and conscription into the army.[16]

In the early Principate different direct taxes, assessed on different bases

---

[12] Thornton 1989 (F 594) chs. V–VI; Frank 1940 (D 128) v. 42, 57; Noè 1987 (D 152) 49–51.

[13] Neesen 1980 (D 151) esp. 19–22.   [14] Neesen 1980 (D 151) 22 n. 4.

[15] Brunt 1981 (D 118); Rathbone 1993 (E 962).   [16] See n. 7 above; also Brunt 1974 (D 171).

and according to different rates, continued to be levied from province to province. Republican modes of thinking and terms persisted: the fiscal value of a province was estimated as an annual cash sum, the word *vectigalia* could still be used of all fiscal revenues, direct and indirect, from a province, and *stipendium* of the totality of direct taxes from a senatorial province. But a new categorization was developing: *vectigalia* often now denoted only indirect taxes, and *tributum* was used of regular direct taxes (not, as in the Republic, of emergency cash levies), conceptually subdivided into those assessed on land (*tributum soli*) and those assessed on persons (*tributum capitis*). This was not a programmatic scheme for standardizing direct taxation – indeed some scholars deny that capitation taxes were levied in all provinces – but these terminological changes reflect some attempt to simplify and improve the overall administration of taxation and the loss by provincial governors of independence in fiscal matters in favour of the central imperial government.[17]

The collection of direct taxes was now mostly devolved to the theoretically autonomous cities and tribes of the empire, each of which was meant to produce a fixed annual sum of direct tax assessed in cash terms. The elimination of tithes and of their collection by Roman *publicani* in the Greek-speaking provinces seems to have been mainly the work of A. Gabinius and Iulius Caesar. Both the tithe and *publicani* persisted in Sicily, but neither Augustus nor his successors introduced *publicani* to collect direct taxes in newly created provinces.[18] The total of direct taxes due from each community was computed by multiplying the taxable base – quantity of land and (probably) number of people – by the relevant rates. In some cases this will have followed on a Roman census; in others, presumably, it was simply what the city claimed was the traditional figure, while for many tribes it must have been an arbitrary guess. The city council (or tribal leaders) were obliged to make up any shortfall in the aggregate sum due, but probably more often made a nice profit, whether through extortion or because the actual taxable base had grown since the original assessment. The job of the local Roman financial official, the quaestor in a public province or the procurator in an imperial province, must have been mainly to ensure that the total due was paid on time, in full and (to introduce a further complication) in acceptable proportions of cash and kind.

Although the total tax dues of provinces and communities were usually expressed in terms of a lump cash sum, direct taxes on land were often assessed and collected in kind, mainly wheat, rather than cash. (Peasants presumably often paid local collectors in kind, and the collectors sold the produce and made the payments to the government in

[17] Neesen 1980 (D 151) 25–9, 117–20.
[18] Brunt 1990 (D 119); Jones 1974 (D 137) 164–8, 180–3; Cimma 1981 (D 121).

cash, but this is a different matter.) The early evidence from Egypt and Britain for *adaeratio*, the commutation of wheat-dues for a cash payment at a fixed official exchange rate, and the more widely attested government purchases of grain (implying that, relative to needs, too much tax had in practice been paid as cash rather than in kind), suggest that from the start the Roman government could be flexible about the medium of payment.[19] The existence of an official exchange rate permitted the calculation and recording of taxes in cash terms whatever the proportion actually paid each year in kind. No figure can be put on the average annual empire-wide ratio between direct taxes collected in cash and in kind, but probably more came in kind under the early Principate than is conventionally assumed.

Many indirect taxes, called *vectigalia*, were also levied in the Roman empire.[20] The main category of these were customs-dues (*portoria*) which were usually exacted at ports, on the imperial frontiers, at the boundaries between provinces or groups of provinces, and sometimes at internal boundaries within provinces. The rate on the eastern frontier was apparently 25 per cent of the value of all goods; known inter-provincial rates range from 2 per cent to 5 per cent. In Italy the imperial government drew revenue from a 1 per cent auction tax (*centesima rerum venalium*), a 4 per cent (originally 2 per cent) tax on sales of slaves, and the tolls at the gates of Rome; it was also the recipient of the 5 per cent inheritance tax (*vicesima hereditatum*) which applied throughout the empire to Roman citizens of a certain wealth and without closely related heirs, and of a 5 per cent tax on the value of slaves manumitted by Roman citizens. In the cities of the empire other indirect taxes were imposed by and benefited the local authorities.

The collection of imperial indirect taxes continued in the early Principate as in the Republic to be farmed out to *publicani*. The old censorial task of fixing the contracts and supervising their execution must have passed to new imperial financial officials – in Italy this was certainly one function of the prefects of the state treasury.[21] In theory the state conceded some profit margin to the contractors, but in practice the system avoided extra bureaucracy and stabilized receipts. The relative value to the imperial government of indirect as against direct taxes is impossible to assess, but they were probably crucial to the imperial finances. Being indirect they were politically easier to increase or invent than direct taxes, and in fact all the new taxes imposed in the early

[19] Tac *Agr.* xix.4; Neesen 1980 (D 151) 104–16; Brunt 1981 (D 188) 161–2; Rathbone 1989 (E 960) 173–4.

[20] General: de Laet 1949 (D 140); Neesen 1980 (D 151) 136–41; see n. 18 above. Cases of Asia and Egypt: Engelmann and Knibbe 1989 (B 229); Sijpesteijn 1987 (E 965); Wallace 1938 (E 979).

[21] Dio LX.10.3; Corbier 1974 (D 122); Millar 1964 (D 149); see nn. 18 and 20 above.

Principate were indirect. Other advantages were that they produced a fairly immediate cash revenue, which in several cases was actually paid over in Rome, and that Roman citizens, perhaps with the exception of veterans, were not exempt. Indeed, if we except the landholdings of Roman citizens in territories not exempt from *tributum soli*, indirect taxes were almost the only regular means of exploiting private Roman wealth open to the imperial government.

The state also had fixed assets consisting principally of land, urban properties and mines. In theory all *ager publicus* which had not been granted away into private ownership still belonged to the Roman state and bore a rent. It is unfortunately unclear how much remained, and whether and how rents from it were collected, but it is known that the government still farmed out to *publicani* the collection of fees, called *scripturae*, for the use of public grazing lands in Italy, Cyrene and perhaps elsewhere too. Many cities in their own right also owned and leased out estates, not just in their own territories, and this category of public ownership was constantly being increased by bequests from private individuals. As regards other fixed assets of the state, public buildings should perhaps be counted rather as financial liabilities. Temples, however, contained treasures which could be 'borrowed' in times of emergency, and warehouses, the shop areas in porticoes and other functional buildings could be leased out by the civic authorities.

The possessions of the emperor himself, his *patrimonium*, must also be counted as state assets.[22] The emperor was not just another member of the empire-wide wealthy elite who discharged public functions and funded public projects out of their own private resources. Much imperial property may have been acquired through private transactions such as inheritance, personal gifting or purchase, and emperors made wills as if they were private persons. However the imperial *patrimonium* passed from emperor to emperor as part of the office rather than through normal inheritance, as is patent in the cases of the emperors from Otho to Vespasian but was perhaps first recognized on Gaius' accession, whereas no consul, for example, inherited his predecessor's personal fortune.[23] Furthermore, the *patrimonium* gradually established its claim to a number of 'public' sources of income, and although it was in theory managed separately from the state finances, its personnel, both equestrian procurators and imperial freedmen and slaves, soon became an integral part of the state bureaucracy.

The basis of the *patrimonium* was the family estates, urban properties, slaves and other possessions of the Iulii, Octavii and Claudii. Under Tiberius the *patrimonium* in Italy was still modest, according to Tacitus –

[22] Millar 1977 (A 59) ch. IV and Apps. 1–3; Rogers 1947 (D 154); Crawford 1976 (D 125); Parássoglou 1978 (E 956); Rathbone 1993 (E 962). [23] Bellen 1974 (D 112).

that is by senatorial standards; the comment implies significant growth by the end of the century. Emperors were also from the beginning massive landowners in the provinces. Augustus' acquisition of substantial estates in Egypt (known locally as *ousiai*) is a prime example; another is Nero's confiscation of 'half' of Africa.[24] The *patrimonium* grew in ways unparalleled by any private estate because the emperor's position opened unique avenues for increasing his possessions. Like any Roman noble, he expected and received legacies from relatives and friends, but under an acquisitive emperor the category of 'friends' could embrace almost all the Italian nobility and some prominent provincials, especially client kings. In the first century the *patrimonium* gradually usurped from the *aerarium* the right to *bona vacantia* and *caduca* and *bona damnatorum* (that is property with no known owner, usually because the former owner had died intestate and without kin, property whose testamentary disposition was legally invalid and property of condemned criminals). Since in Egypt these had all fallen to the fiscus since annexation, this was clearly a royal prerogative adopted from hellenistic practice. The *patrimonium* was also the beneficiary of booty (*manubiae*) from imperial campaigns, and of the gold crowns sometimes spontaneously offered by communities to mark victories. The emperor's landed properties, like those of any noble, contained sub-enterprises such as transhumant flocks, clay pits and potteries, tanneries and textile processing facilities, urban craftshops and so on. Under Augustus and Tiberius almost all mines not already run by the state came into the hands of the *patrimonium*, and often if not normally were put under military supervision, and new mines, like those in Britain, followed suit. Some quarries too became imperial properties.[25] In Rome itself the emperors had warehouses where they stored everything from produce of their own estates to exotic gifts from foreign embassies. There was also the palace, enlarged successively by each Julio-Claudian emperor, together with the imperial gardens; though the site and buildings were hardly saleable, the rich furniture and furnishings represented a significant reserve of wealth. The contribution of the *patrimonium* to the imperial finances cannot be quantified, but its political importance is clear: it enabled emperors to claim that they subsidized rather than exploited the state revenues.

These, in outline, were the resources available to the imperial government to meet its expenditure. The last topic which must be added before the management of the imperial finances can be discussed is the imperial coinage and its production.[26] The coinage of Rome as stabilized

---

[24] Tac. *Ann.* IV.6; Pliny, *HN* XVIII.35.
[25] Domergue 1990 (E 216); Dodge 1992 (D 127) ch. 5.
[26] Burnett, Amandry and Pipollès 1992 (B 312); Sutherland 1984 (B 357); Crawford 1985 (B 320) ch. 17; Walker 1976 (B 361).

by Augustus in or by 19 B.C. was trimetallic, consisting of almost pure gold and silver coins and a range of what is for convenience termed 'bronze' (or *aes*) coinage, though some pieces were almost pure copper while others were orichalcum, an alloy of copper and zinc. In the system established by Augustus the main coins in circulation and their official relationships of value were as follows: the gold *aureus*, the silver denarius of which there were 25 to the *aureus*, the copper *as* of which there were sixteen to the denarius, and various fractions of the *as*; the normal unit of account, however, remained the *sestertius*, equivalent to four *asses*, though the actual (orichalcum) coin was rare. As regards weight, forty or forty-two *aurei* were struck from one Roman pound of gold, and eighty-four denarii from one pound of silver. These standards held until Nero's reform of A.D. 64. He retained the relative face values of the Augustan system but struck forty-five *aurei* and ninety-six denarii respectively to the pound. The silver content of the denarius was also reduced to an average of 93.5 per cent. Although Nero's attempt to introduce a wholly orichalcum 'bronze' coinage was a rapid failure, his system in its essentials lasted until Commodus.

The various denominations in the Augustan-Neronian system were minted in varying quantities, often discontinuously, from two main and some minor mints. The mint at Lyons (Lugdunum) produced almost all the imperial gold and silver coinage from 15 B.C. onwards until Nero (or possibly Gaius) transferred production to the mint at Rome. From 23 or 19 B.C. the Roman mint produced most of the imperial 'bronze' coinage, but in most reigns there were sporadic and sometimes heavy regional issues of imperial type from provincial mints. Output of mainstream imperial coin was supplemented by the issue of silver tetradrachms, didrachms and drachmas by the mints of a number of Greek cities, notably Ephesus, Pergamum, Caesarea (in Cappadocia) and (Syrian) Antioch. These and other city-mints also produced sporadic issues, occasionally quite large, of bronze fractions. Egypt had its own internal coinage based on the Alexandrian tetradrachm. In the west local mints had always been rare. Most were in Spain, they produced only bronze coin, and those which survived Tiberius were shut down by Gaius. The broad pattern of supply of coinage in the period as a whole is thus that the mints at Rome and Lyons produced gold coins for the whole empire and silver and bronze for all the western provinces; western silver coins also reached the East but were outnumbered by the regional productions there, and the eastern provinces were almost wholly dependent on very locally produced bronze coinage.

Minting was essentially controlled by the emperor. Most of the bullion used must have come from sources under imperial control – an early example is the exaction of bullion in Gaul by Augustus' freedman *procurator* Licinus, presumably to prime the new mint at Lyons.[27] Supervision of the state mints, at Rome at least, was again entrusted to young senatorial *tresviri monetales*, whose full title (*aere argento auro flando feriundo*) implies oversight of the production of all coins. Briefly under Augustus they were allowed to choose the types for some issues, but that was the extent of their independence. The letters 'S.C.' (*senatus consulto*) which appeared on Augustus' new bronze coinage, and on some provincial and some Neronian imperial issues, do not, it is now generally agreed, indicate any continuing senatorial control of minting, but advertise that this was the official Roman coinage, perhaps originally with reference to a senatorial vote of approval for the new weight standards of the Augustan system.[28] In the provinces many 'local' coinages, such as the cistophoric tetradrachms of the province of Asia (which bore Latin legends), were in effect 'imperial' coinages. The mint at Alexandria was under direct imperial control, and under Tiberius the silver-weight of its tetradrachms was adjusted to match that of the denarius; around the same time Palmyra and the Jewish rulers were made to bring their silver coinages into line. The closing of all the local mints in Spain must indicate imperial intervention, and it is noticeable that many sporadic eastern issues coincided with military operations in the area.[29] The emperor could control minting when and wherever he wanted; that he sometimes allowed local initiative is not evidence for a real division of authority. The emperor thus was in theory able to regulate in broad terms the quantity and type of coinage in circulation; the questions of whether and why he did or did not lead into the wider issue of the management of the imperial finances in general.

Detailed quantification of coin production in the early Empire must await systematic study of the number of dies used for each issue, although even this will leave considerable uncertainty about the scale of issues.[30] Compared to earlier and later eras the surviving gold and silver coinage of this period is relatively rare; significant quantities of the heavier republican denarii continued to find their way into hoards through to the end of the first century A.D. Augustus had to mint extensively to establish his new system of bronze coinage, but there was a drastic fall in production later: Tiberius and Gaius, for example, closed the western provincial mints, and no imperial bronze was struck in the first ten years of Nero's reign. There is no evidence for regular recall and re-minting of old coins (which would have been very expensive). Old coins collected by the state were simply re-issued. The main sources of metal for minting new coins were bullion acquired through taxation or

[27] Dio LIV.21.
[28] Wallace-Hadrill 1986 (B 362); Kraft 1962 (B 334); Griffin 1984 (C 352) 57–9, 120–5.
[29] Crawford 1985 (B 320) 271; Howgego 1982 (D 134).   [30] Howgego 1992 (D 135).

confiscation and above all the mines which had rapidly fallen under imperial control. It is therefore very likely that the overall stock of coinage in the early Empire was constantly if gradually increasing.

The rationale underlying this pattern of minting is a controversial topic.[31] It is likely that the imperial government recognized some political responsibility, incurred through its near monopoly of minting, to maintain in circulation an adequate supply of the full range of denominations. The rare but heavy issues of small denominations, however, must be taken as one-off responses to particularly noticeable shortages and thus as indicators of a lack of any forward planning. The famous 'crisis of liquidity' at Rome in A.D. 33 tells the same story for the higher denominations.[32] Clearly there can have been no government statistics for the volume of coinage in circulation, for any lump of gold or silver, including coins of the Roman Republic and of the hellenistic kings, could be used for exchange, while imperial gold and silver coins could be hoarded or melted down as bullion. These considerations undercut modern theories that changes in the rate of output and in the weight and purity of the imperial coinage represent attempts to keep it in tune with the changing market values of the uncoined metals; it is more plausible that the 'bronze' was a largely token coinage from the start, and that the denarius was deliberately overvalued in relation to the *aureus* so that it had a token premium against gold which discouraged private melting down of silver coins. Indeed it is very difficult to construct any satisfactory economic explanation for Nero's 'devaluation' of the silver and gold coinage, the only major monetary adjustment in this period. The common view that it was a device to stretch imperial funds is unsatisfactory, partly because earlier heavier coins were not all driven out of circulation, and mainly because it ignores the simultaneous attempt to introduce an all-orichalcum *aes* coinage.[33] Nero was probably trying to reform the whole monetary system for a mixture of administrative and aesthetic reasons. Normally, however, emperors seem to have thought little about minting, which was ordered primarily in response to specific immediate needs. As long as the mines, supplemented by booty and confiscations of bullion from individuals, continued to produce sufficient new metal for minting, there will have been no obvious need to worry about questions of policy.

State income and expenditure in cash in the Roman empire is best visualized not as a massive annual ebb and flow of coin between the provinces and Rome, but as a series of provincial whirlpools, some of them spilling over into others and all being sporadically topped up from the imperial mints at Rome and elsewhere. The whole system functioned

[31] For example Crawford 1970 (D 126); Lo Cascio 1981 (D 144); Howgego 1992 (D 135).
[32] Rodewald 1976 (B 348) ch. 1.   [33] Bolin 1958 (D 113) ch. 4; Lo Cascio 1980 (D 143).

largely under its own momentum with little direct intervention from the central government. It seems that, following republican practice, each province had a 'fiscus' (literally 'basket', sc. for holding coins), a sort of branch office of the main state treasury (*aerarium*). The chief task of each fiscus was to receive and record the lump sums of direct and indirect taxes due from the local communities and tax-farmers. It also had to pay out for expenses in that province: the salaries of the governor and his subordinates, any imperially funded building projects, and the cash costs of the garrison if there was one.

In republican Rome the central state treasury, to which all state revenues were in theory due and from which expenditure was made – though in practice many transactions were handled entirely by the provincial fisci – was the *aerarium*, located in the temple of Saturn. This treasury continued to exist in the Principate, now called the *aerarium Saturni* to distinguish it from the *aerarium militare*, the separate 'military treasury' established by Augustus in A.D. 6 with the new and limited function of paying the discharge bounties due to veterans out of the revenues earmarked for them.[34] In addition to these public treasuries formally constituted under senatorial supervisors, there existed the originally private administrative organization of the emperor's *patrimonium* or fiscus (as it was sometimes known), staffed by imperial slaves and freedmen, which swiftly came to assume the leading role in the administration of the state finances as a whole; hence the trend for fiscus to supplant *aerarium* as the general term for the fiscal and financial centre of the Roman state.

Admittedly the nature and origins of this imperial fiscus have been keenly disputed.[35] A common view is that a new imperial treasury called the fiscus, separate from the *patrimonium*, was set up parallel to the *aerarium Saturni*, probably by Claudius and perhaps together with the creation of an 'accounts department' (*a rationibus*) of the imperial *familia* headed by Pallas. Another suggestion is that this fiscus was a sub-unit of the *aerarium* which, on the analogy of provincial fisci, handled the finances of the emperor's composite *provincia*. The evidence, however, tells against any neat division between 'imperial' and 'senatorial' finances and their control. Under Augustus the *aerarium Saturni* was credited with the revenues of the new imperial province of Egypt, as was the *aerarium militare* in A.D. 17 with those of Cappadocia; the *aerarium Saturni* administered the financing of the *vigiles*, the new imperial fire-brigade, and continued to do so into the third century, and the *aerarium militare* functioned independently into the same period.[36] In the summary

34 Corbier 1974 (D 122); Corbier 1977 (D 123); Millar 1964 (D 149).
35 Millar 1963 (D 148); Brunt 1966 (D 116); Jones 1950 (D 136); Rathbone 1993 (E 962).
36 Vell. Pat. II.39.2; Tac. *Ann.* II.42 (cf. 1.78); Dio LV.26.5.

account of the finances of the empire which Augustus left on his death, along with his private will, he listed the cash in the *aerarium*, the cash in the provincial fisci and the sums due from the tax-farmers.[37] Clearly no new imperial treasury was officially recognized under Augustus, and there is no good evidence for one under his Julio-Claudian successors. The emperors were able to control state finances without diverting revenues into a new separate treasury.

The *aerarium Saturni* had no real financial independence. Although it was supervised by senatorial officials, the changes from praetors selected by lot to quaestors and then to ex-praetors chosen by the emperor are one sign of subordination to imperial control.[38] The duties of these officials, as under the Republic, and of the senatorial prefects of the *aerarium militare*, were restricted to technical functions such as administering the tax-farming contracts, investigating accusations of tax avoidance and prosecuting defaulters; because this often meant dealing with upper-class Italians, it was politic to employ officials of senatorial status.[39] It is, furthermore, unclear what revenues and expenditure continued in practice to be accounted for – let alone actually received or disbursed – by the *aerarium Saturni*. When Augustus, for example, drew up his summary of the state finances, a large percentage of the sums involved will have been in the fisci of imperial provinces under the control of imperial freedmen or equestrian officials, and any cash he held in Rome was presumably accounted for as being 'in' these fisci or as 'due' to the *aerarium*. These sums, as well as not passing through the *aerarium*, had apparently not been reported to its officials, for Augustus referred the Senate for details to the members of his *familia* who kept the accounts. These imperial clerks, technically the financial administrators (*a rationibus*) of the *patrimonium*, were thus not invented by Claudius, even if he was responsible for giving them a more formal 'departmental' organization. This may have encouraged people to think in terms of an imperial treasury based on the administration of the *patrimonium*, and hence called the fiscus, and in practice the role of the *aerarium Saturni* may increasingly have been confined to receiving the fiscal surpluses from public provinces and revenues raised in Italy and to administering public expenditure in Rome and Italy which was nominally under senatorial control such as that on aqueducts and temple maintenance and rituals.

In some respects Augustus had behaved in the tradition of late republican commanders, notably Pompey. There had not, therefore, been any formal division of responsibility, and in theory the *aerarium Saturni* remained the state treasury. In practice, however, the emperors controlled all financial policy. After Augustus only Gaius ever again

---

[37] Suet. *Aug.* 101.4.   [38] Millar 1964 (D 149) 34.
[39] For example, the case of Claudius: Suet. *Claud.* 9.2.

offered any account of the imperial revenues and expenditure to the Senate. Instead of the emperor's agents reporting to the *aerarium*, we must suppose that its prefects had to make their records available to the imperial accountants who drew up overall statements of the state finances for the restricted benefit of the emperor and his advisers. The question of administration is really a red herring: Augustus and his successors controlled the state finances by monopolizing the decision-making on financial matters. More precisely state finances were depoliticized by the death of republican politics – it was no longer open to ambitious individuals to propose controversial expenditure (wars, buildings, doles) or fiscal changes. Now a standing army received automatic payment in cash and kind, the Roman populace had a permanent grain supply laid on by the emperor, the provinces had a system of regular taxation which for over two hundred years underwent only minor adjustments.

The stability of Roman taxation at a level which, if it hurt individual peasants, was low for each community as a whole is often used to help explain the acceptance and support of Roman rule by the upper classes of the provinces.[40] But the proposition should perhaps be reversed: the Romans were so dependent on this local co-operation that to avoid the risk of disaffection they rarely dared to increase provincial taxation, and its level constrained rather than was determined by imperial expenditure. In the Julio-Claudian period expenditure on the army must have increased gradually as auxiliary forces were turned into regular units. Total state revenues, however, will also have increased as new areas were converted into provinces subject to direct Roman taxation. The evidence suggests that, outside Egypt, censuses were not regular and neutral operations but occasional deliberate attempts to increase the tribute assessments of individual provinces; if so, it would appear that as Gaul developed economically, its tribute was increased.[41] Similar increases probably occurred in other relatively new and underdeveloped provinces as, for instance, in Moesia under Nero through the settlement of Transdanubians.[42] In the Principate, however, only Vespasian is credited – and dubiously so – with widespread increases of tribute, examples of imperial caution about the general level of provincial taxation are numerous, and individual communities could petition for reductions in their tribute assessment and doubtless frequently did so, sometimes with success.

It is difficult to estimate the size and nature of the public profit made from the provinces by imperial Rome. The situation can be pictured as an outer ring of coin-hungry fisci of frontier provinces with large

---

[40] Jones 1974 (D 137); MacMullen 1987 (D 147).
[41] Cf. Brunt 1981 (D 118), modified in 1990 (A 12) 533.   [42] *GCN* 228.

garrisons which kept solvent by drawing on the cash surplus of the fisci of interior civilian provinces.[43] How much or little cash surplus this left to be shipped to Rome is unknowable; against it must also be set all the newly minted coinage injected into the provincial system. But the profits of imperialism did not come only in cash. Direct taxes, although assessed and accounted for in cash terms, were partly collected in kind. Thus, for instance, insofar as soldiers received supplies in place of cash remuneration, the fisci of frontier provinces need not always have been seriously short of coin; on the other hand civilian provinces may have produced surpluses in kind rather than cash. More importantly, the one provincial revenue which is certainly known to have been shipped to Rome is the annonal wheat.

While the revenues which could be drawn in cash from the provinces were limited, emperors were under constant pressure to spend munificently, especially in Rome. Tiberius was exceptional in his accumulation of a large cash reserve, and Gaius' immediate spending of it was almost inevitable. Such savings undermined the justification for taxation, a mentality which was in part the legacy of the republican system of *ad hoc* financial arrangements, but in part derived from the emperor's monopolization of the control of the state finances. While emperors were happy to take the credit for beneficial expenditure, they also had to face personal criticism for the level of taxation, and preferred to spend rather than save. There could normally be no centralized reserves of wealth at all comparable to those, for instance, of the Achaemenid kings. It is also clear why for emperors who wished or were obliged to fund major new projects such as wars or building schemes and whose needs were normally for ready cash, the income from indirect taxes, particularly those raised in Italy, and that from the *patrimonium* had a special importance. In effect needy emperors turned to the Senate (and other rich nobles), whether it was Augustus instituting the 5 per cent inheritance tax or the villain of later senatorial rhetoric, the emperor who killed and confiscated to raise cash. The imperial wealth was enormous but, through a combination of political weakness, difficulties of communications and transport and incomplete monetization, much of it could not be mobilized effectively by the central government. Although the period from Augustus to Nero saw an overall rise in expenditure which was at least matched by an overall increase in revenues, the lack of central reserves was a weakness embedded in the system from its inception and one which was to cause problems for the rest of the Principate.

[43] Hopkins 1980 (D 133).

CHAPTER 9

THE SENATE AND SENATORIAL
AND EQUESTRIAN POSTS

RICHARD J. A. TALBERT

I. THE SENATE[1]

There can be no question that the 20s B.C. and the half century which followed were a time of unparalleled change for the Senate and its members. Augustus was its principal instigator. Once peace had been secured after the long civil wars, the 'restoration of the Republic' was one of his foremost aims. By definition that touched closely the central institutions of the Republic, the Senate among them. The size and quality of senatorial membership engaged his attention first. In size it had expanded to 1,000 or more, partly because of numerous adlections by Iulius Caesar as dictator, partly because following his death others successfully used influence and bribery to gain admission by the same means. Moreover, by raising the total of quaestorships from twenty to forty, Caesar had doubled the number of new members each year, since tenure of this junior magistracy in practice offered life membership of the Senate. As early as 29 B.C. Octavian (as he then was) used a review of the senatorial roll to exclude 190 members on one ground or another. It was

---

[1] Since contemporary testimony is largely lost along with the Lex Iulia of 9 B.C. which governed procedure, the main sources of knowledge for the Senate during the Julio-Claudian period are the later historical writers Tacitus, Suetonius and Cassius Dio – in particular Tacitus, who certainly drew upon the detailed record of senatorial proceedings (*acta senatus*) for his *Annals*, although to what extent and by what means remain matters of considerable dispute (Talbert 1984 (D 77) ch. 9; Brunt 1984 (A 10)). Inscriptions and papyri make a growing contribution. An impression of the nature and scope of senatorial legislative activity can be formed by drawing together material from legal writers and elsewhere (Talbert 1984 (D 77) ch. 15 sect. 5). Seneca's vivid sketch of the heavenly senate in session on Olympus, presided over by Jupiter (*Apocol.* 8–11), parodies its Roman counterpart of which he was himself a member, and offers a rare piece of contemporary insight. If it is accepted that Diocletian's Curia in Rome (built near the end of the third century and still standing today in a restored state) is in effect a reconstruction of the Curia Iulia, then it is possible to observe closely the meeting-place where most of the Senate's sessions were held: see further A. Bartoli, *Curia Senatus, lo scavo e il restauro* (Rome, 1963).

Inscriptions are the main source for knowledge of senatorial and equestrian administrators and their work. Significant in this connexion from Augustus' reign onwards is the growing frequency with which records listing all the offices a man had held were no longer inscribed just posthumously, but during his lifetime too (Millar and Segal 1984 (C 176) ch. 5).

Modern discussion: Talbert 1984 (D 77) offers a starting-point on most aspects; for senators and their careers, see also Hopkins 1983 (A 46) ch. 3. Much relevant documentary material is assembled in *FIRA* I.

probably also during the 20s that he reduced the number of quaestorships to the old figure of twenty. Either then, or during the 'teens B.C., he took the consequential step of reducing the lower office holders (mostly aspirants to the Senate, not yet members) from *vigintisexviri* (twenty-six) to *vigintiviri* (twenty).

A Senate of about 800 still seemed too large. When Augustus returned to the task of reducing it further by another review of the roll in 18 B.C.,[2] his preference is said to have been for a body of just 300: the simultaneous removal of as many as 500 members would thus be required. Unless he was displaying an astonishing lack of foresight, a more profound reappraisal of the role of the Senate would have been called for next, since all the existing functions assigned to the corporate body and its members could barely have been carried out by such a reduced group. In the event, however, Augustus abandoned any drastic aims of this type, and enrolled about 600 members by a peculiar method which combined co-option and the drawing of lots. Thereby the Senate returned to the approximate size which the dictator Sulla had made it. Up to the end of the Julio-Claudian period there are known to have been at least two more revisions of the roll during Augustus' reign (around 13–11 B.C. and in A.D. 4), and a third carried out by the emperor Claudius and L. Vitellius as censors in A.D. 47/8. But in none of these instances does there appear to have been further significant alteration to the size of the membership. Rather, the regular number remained about 600, though it should be understood that this figure was always just a notional optimum, never a fixed maximum or fixed total. The normal method of entry continued to be through the twenty annual vacancies in the quaestorship. On present evidence at least, the alternative of 'adlection', or direct elevation of a non-member to a grade of membership within the Senate (at the emperor's instigation), was only used very sparingly indeed during the Julio-Claudian period.[3]

The quality of senatorial membership concerned Augustus, as well as its size. As his conduct of the reviews in 29 and 18 B.C. demonstrated, he was determined to rid the Senate of members who were immoral, irresponsible, or lacking means. His purpose was to create a body which should be an outstanding elite of princes – high-minded, statesmanlike, wealthy. He waited until 18 B.C. to translate this ideal into reality. From that time all members had to be worth at least one million sesterces rather than just showing the modest equestrian census of 400,000, which was all that had previously been required.[4] He appreciated the strain which would result, and over the years did help both worthy existing members who could not show the increased amount, and many prospective

[2] Dio LIV.13–15.   [3] Demougin 1982 (D 36) 81–2.
[4] Nicolet 1976 (D 53); Millar and Segal 1984 (C 176) ch. 4.

entrants. Among Augustus' Julio-Claudian successors similar assistance is known to have been given by Tiberius (albeit sometimes in rather grudging fashion) and by Nero.

Also from 18 B.C. in all likelihood, the old custom was abandoned whereby every prospective entrant wore the distinctive badge of the senator – the broad stripe (*latus clavus*) on the tunic – even before he had ever gained the lowest senatorial magistracy and actually joined the corporate body as quaestor.[5] In future this was to be the exclusive privilege of those senators' sons who chose to follow in their fathers' footsteps. Other young men seeking to become the first members of their family to enter the Senate could certainly pursue this quest, as ever, but they could not wear the coveted *latus clavus* until they became quaestors.

This particular way of marking out senators' sons and encouraging them to emulate their fathers was one of Augustus' many experiments which did not endure. The restriction had evidently come to be disregarded by the 30s A.D. at the very latest. Instead the practice developed whereby all equestrian aspirants to a senatorial career were obliged to gain the emperor's permission to wear the *latus clavus*. How selective successive emperors were in their consideration of such applications is completely unknown. None the less it is clear that Augustus' experiment formed part of a wider effort to exalt not just senators themselves, but also members of their families, whom he actually defined for the first time ever as a separate, superior 'senatorial class'.

The class first appears formally in Augustus' marriage legislation of 18 B.C., and of course it did endure. Membership belonged to senators and their descendants to the third generation, plus wives. Once a distinct class had been formed on this pattern, it was natural for a haphazard growth of privileges and restrictions to become attached to it. Among privileges, special front seats at shows and a certain precedence at elections were introduced early; limited exemption from particular local obligations may also have been granted.[6] Among restrictions, a series of bans on marriage with the lowest classes, prostitution, and appearances in shows or on stage, were all intended to maintain the dignity of the highest class in society.[7]

Regardless of how they gained the *latus clavus*, all those intending to pursue a senatorial career had to undertake the *cursus honorum* as reformed by Augustus.[8] Tenure of one of the twenty minor offices in the vigintivirate bestowed annually by the emperor was now made a

---

[5] Chastagnol 1975 (D 33); Saller 1982 (F 59) 51 n. 58; Talbert 1984 (D 77) 513.
[6] Millar 1983 (D 101) 88–90.   [7] Levick 1983 (C 369) 97–115.
[8] Morris 1964 and 1965 (D 51).

compulsory prerequisite. Either before or afterwards a limited period of service in a legion as *tribunus militum* was recommended, though it was never compulsory and was often omitted by those of aristocratic background. Entry to the Senate itself was gained by election to one of the twenty annual quaestorships, for which a candidate had now to have reached his twenty-fifth year (previously the qualifying age had been thirty). Thereafter, notionally with minimum intervals of just over one year between each magistracy, plebeians had first to hold one of the six aedileships or ten tribunates (patricians were excused this stage); next all competed for the praetorship, which could not be held before a candidate's thirtieth year (previously thirty-nine or forty). The degree of rivalry sharpened at this vital stage, depending upon the number of praetorships, which it was the significant prerogative of the emperor to fix from year to year. Augustus at first permitted as few as ten praetors each year, and even by the end of his reign seldom more than twelve. As a result, at this date an average first-generation senator could take pride in having climbed even this high. Augustus' Julio-Claudian successors became somewhat more generous (not least because the range of duties assigned to senators of this rank was extended), so that by the end of the period the total of praetorships seems to have been fluctuating between fourteen and eighteen. None the less the risk of rejection was still a real one.

Beyond the praetorship a minority of favoured senators could sooner or later proceed on to the highest magistracy, the consulship. Both the number of consulships each year, and the choice of holders, in effect quickly came to be a choice for the emperor alone to make. Initially there was no more than one pair of holders for the entire year on the traditional republican pattern. But from 5 B.C. these two 'ordinary' consuls, who retained the prestige of opening the year, were regularly replaced by one or two further pairs of 'suffect' consuls at variable intervals, with the result that up to six men were permitted to attain this distinction within a single year. Thereby competition for it became less intense, and there were more members eligible to occupy posts reserved for senators of this standing. Certain highly distinguished men might be privileged to enjoy the supreme honour of a second, and even a third, consulship.

In time Augustus formed the opinion that it was not just the membership of the Senate which required his attention, but also the workings of the corporate body. His revival of fines for non-attendance in 17 B.C. is an early sign of his impatience with members who failed to match up to his ideals. Though in theory a presiding magistrate had always had authority to fine absentees, not since the second century B.C. perhaps had it been normal practice to do so, with the result that this clumsy measure by Augustus merely served to give offence. Only in 11

B.C. did he act further, when he formally abolished the quorum of 400 which was still required for any measure passed to be valid. In all likelihood it dated back to Caesar's dictatorship, but must have been a dead letter ever since the reduction of the membership to 600 in 18 B.C.

The abolition at least cleared the way for positive reform in the shape of the comprehensive *lex Iulia de senatu habendo* (9 B.C.), which was intended to regulate every aspect of the Senate's workings. The principal purpose of the law was seemingly to improve levels of attendance, which had for some time been giving Augustus cause for concern. To this end fines were increased, but they proved as ineffective as ever, and were quietly dropped, never to be revived. Quorums (a modest 200 is the only one known)[9] were introduced for every kind of business: in themselves they were no novelty, but never before had they been laid down so comprehensively. Even more important was the innovation of fixed days for meetings, the Kalends and the Ides of each month, so that members would know to set these aside for attendance. As some alleviation, for the four stated meetings of the holiday months, September and October, the law did permit no more than a quorum chosen by lot to be present, while the likelihood is that perhaps two stated meetings were normally cancelled around our Eastertime, when traditionally there had been a recess (*res prolatae* or *discessus senatus*). However at all seasons special meetings in addition to the stated ones could be called, if necessary at very short notice. It was equally in connexion with regulating attendance that the law made two further provisions. First, it required a list of all senators' names to be displayed publicly and updated each year. Second, it introduced a 'retirement age' for senators. Previously the formal position had been that every member was obliged to keep up his attendance for life. Augustus appreciated that it would be neither practical nor sensible to insist upon this, and thus had the law stipulate that members were no longer required to come beyond the age of sixty or sixty-five (it is not known which). All the same, they were still welcome to come voluntarily, and many did.

Beyond all this the Lex Iulia codified senatorial procedure. That really did represent a new departure, since previously the proceedings seem to have been governed almost exclusively by custom, rather than by written statute. So it was probably now for the first time that features like the order in which opinions were to be asked for, or the manner in which a vote was to be taken, were actually written down. Such codification no doubt appealed to Augustus' sense of order. Even so it is striking that he does not appear to have exploited the opportunity to change procedure much. In practice meetings seem to have been generally conducted in just the same way after 9 B.C. as before. There is no foundation to the

[9] *FIRA* 1 68 col. V lines 106–7.

modern claim[10] that the law in some way curtailed the ancient right of a member, when called upon for his opinion (*sententia*), to speak first without time limit on whatever subject he chose (*egredi relationem*). This right was retained and was still exploited.

Of course what neither the Lex Iulia nor any other law ever codified was the position of the emperor in the Senate. His presence was a major new feature to which the corporate body had to adjust from the 20s B.C. All emperors were patrician senators and must have headed the list of members during their reigns, though Augustus alone of the Julio-Claudians took the title *princeps senatus* (from 28 B.C.). In his case, too, formal difficulties were few before 23 B.C., since he was always consul and frequently out of Rome. Thereafter, however, the need was felt to offer him the guaranteed opportunity of bringing forward one item at any stage of any meeting – what has been dubbed somewhat inaccurately the *ius primae relationis* – as well as authority to summon the Senate as often as he pleased (in theory he could already do this by virtue of his *tribunicia potestas*). In 19 B.C. he was granted the right to sit on the president's tribunal at meetings, in between the two consuls. At some stage, too, as early as Augustus' reign, there was recognition (not necessarily formal perhaps) of a unique right of the emperor to have business put forward by letter rather than in person. All these privileges must have been conferred upon subsequent emperors on their accession.

At least up until A.D. 8, when old age compelled him to reduce his activities, Augustus showed the Senate respect by attending not just as president, but also as a private member. The one meeting which we know him to have missed deliberately was the occasion in 2 B.C. when the discovery of his daughter Iulia's scandalous behaviour had to be made public: in his shame he could not face the Senate in person, but sent a letter instead. Unfortunately the source-material is lacking which would allow us to build up a picture of his participation and performance at meetings in the way that can be done for Tiberius through Tacitus' *Annals*. In general, however, it is clear that he did take an active enough part in debate, although two major difficulties in this connexion quickly made themselves felt.

The first was the nature of members' reaction to the superior position of the emperor, which might take the form of respect, or fear, or resentment, according to different individuals' viewpoints. These feelings sprang from a variety of causes: the knowledge that in practice nothing which the emperor requested or openly supported could be refused; the recognition that every senator's advancement depended in large measure upon his approval; and the realization that control of many key spheres of government had effectively become his alone. Even

[10] Mommsen 1888 (A 65) III.2. 940.

many of the Senate's meeting-places were now powerful symbols of the imperial regime – the Curia Iulia, begun by Iulius Caesar, dedicated by Octavian in 29 B.C., and thereafter adorned with a growing number of monuments and dedications in honour of the emperor and his family; the temple of Apollo on the Palatine, close by the emperor's residence; and from 2 B.C. the temple of Mars Ultor in front of which was sited a great statue of Augustus victorious in a chariot. Under such circumstances, and in such surroundings, members came to feel, more or less willingly, that it was pointless any longer to take an active, critical, independent part in sessions, when the result seemed a foregone conclusion, and no more than officially selected extracts from the detailed record of proceedings – *acta senatus*, instituted by Iulius Caesar in 59 B.C. – were now permitted to be made public. In addition certain matters of the highest importance were never even referred to the Senate at all. It is hardly surprising that the only two known instances of open senatorial disagreement with Augustus were cases where he perhaps expected opposition to be voiced anyway – a request to have not one colleague, but two, whenever he held the consulship, and an offer after his illness in 23 B.C. to read out his will. Perhaps more characteristic were the meetings under Augustus' presidency where frustration at members' reluctance to formulate independent opinions led him to call names at random rather than in the customary order of seniority.

Despite Augustus' efforts to counter the trend, this understandable reluctance was to persist indefinitely. Tiberius' impatience with it as emperor prompted his allegedly regular exclamation on leaving sessions 'O homines ad servitutem paratos', 'O men ready to be slaves!'.[11] It must be reflected again by the otherwise unknown Titius Rufus whose claim that 'the Senate thought one way and voted another'[12] led to his indictment in A.D. 39; and there is no doubt that it was a principal target of the consular Thrasea Paetus, who consciously risked Nero's disapproval by his outspoken encouragement of greater independence on the part of fellow members in the late 50s and early 60s. The most vehement attack on such senatorial reluctance, however, is made in the speech of an unidentified senator (in all likelihood the emperor Claudius) preserved on a papyrus fragment:

If these proposals meet with your approval, Conscript Fathers, say so plainly at once, in your own considered words. But if you disapprove, find another solution, yet do so in this temple, or, if you perhaps want a more generous interval in which to think, take it, provided you remember that, whatever the place you should be summoned to, you must give us your own opinion. For

---

[11] Tac. *Ann.* III.65.   [12] Dio LIX.18.5.

Conscript Fathers, it is most unbecoming to the dignity of this order here that just one consul designate should deliver a *sententia*, and even this drawn word for word from the *relatio* of the consuls, while others utter the single word *adsentior*, and then when they depart say 'Well, we spoke'.[13]

Even where the emperor took care not to express a view, his relatives (who generally pursued senatorial careers) might still be regarded as speaking for him. Thus in A.D. 13, when alternatives to the 5 per cent inheritance tax were under discussion, Augustus specifically forbade Germanicus and Drusus to make any suggestion, for fear that it would be regarded as his, and adopted without more ado.

The second main difficulty which acted as a curb on the freedom and vigour of senatorial proceedings in Augustus' reign was his introduction some time between 27 and 18 B.C. of a *consilium* to consider items of business in advance of their being laid before the full corporate body (distinct from the *consilium principis*, for which see p. 290). It must be acknowledged that this committee was intended to have no more than such a preparatory function. Yet for all Augustus' efforts to uphold that aim, members in the full Senate would hardly have been human if they still did not suspect that they could exercise only the most limited influence after the 'real' debate had already occurred in the committee, and the 'real' decisions had been taken there. Under such conditions few members were going to have the appetite for a wide-ranging, frank discussion in the full Senate. Their worst fears can only have been confirmed in A.D. 13 when Augustus (now in extreme old age) had the membership of the *consilium* reformed and its decisions granted authority equal to that of the full Senate.

In a pithy summary Tacitus later wrote of Augustus 'drawing to himself the functions of the Senate, the magistrates and the laws'.[14] There is a large measure of truth in the allegation: even though not only Augustus but also all his successors studiously derived their formal authority from the Senate, it did still have to adjust itself to a curtailed prerogative. Of course many traditional functions remained. The Senate legislated actively, and its resolutions came to be recognized as law without the need for confirmation by a popular assembly. Honours were bestowed in greater quantity and variety than ever. The Senate's authority in matters of religion was still accepted as supreme, and it continued to be approached by embassies, albeit in reduced numbers. On the other hand the emperor in large measure reserved to himself matters relating to the army and foreign affairs; public finance; and the administrative oversight of a large group of existing provinces, together with that of all new ones. In consequence the Senate lost for ever the major

---

[13] *FIRA* I 44 col. III lines 10–22.   [14] *Ann.* 1.2.

prerogative (already challenged formidably in the late Republic) of determining the disposition of the state's military forces year by year and the extent of the territory to which it laid claim. The creation of supervisors for roads, aqueducts, the distribution and supply of corn, and for other concerns (treated further below), in practice represented further encroachment upon its formerly exclusive authority.

However, despite the fact that the republican Senate had seldom shown more than the most desultory concern for such matters, Augustus was still scrupulous in arranging not just for the new officials to be appointed by the Senate, but also for their activities to be authorized by it. He likewise constantly informed and consulted the Senate about military, provincial, diplomatic and financial affairs, in addition to inviting its approval of significant changes or unusual expedients in these spheres.[15] In many instances it may be that this was not merely tact or caution, but rather that he was genuinely seeking to hear a range of proposals, to test opinion and to mould his reaction to it, as well as ensuring reasonable acquiescence in whatever might finally be decided. More than anyone Augustus knew how vital it was that he should not lose touch with upper-class opinion or seriously alienate it. Yet however open to advice he might appear, it always remained awkward for members to be confident of his purpose, or to judge the point at which they might be considered to have overstepped the mark in risking a frank statement of views. In this dilemma the majority preferred to take no risk at all, and the Senate as a deliberative body suffered.

Altogether Augustus' impact upon the Senate proved a mixed one. He showed it the greatest respect. While reducing the size of the membership, he raised its moral and social standing, he promoted regular attendance by a variety of means, and codified (though hardly altered) procedure. But for all his assiduous consultation of the Senate, and his avowed encouragement of frankly expressed opinions, it was impossible for members to ignore his overriding supremacy in the state and his effective usurpation of certain major senatorial prerogatives. The senatorial *consilium*, especially after the strengthening of its authority in A.D. 13, acted as a further discouragement to the corporate body.

Tiberius' impact was equally mixed. Up to a point in the case of the Senate, as elsewhere, he merely continued Augustus' approach. While this is by no means an unfair assessment, it perhaps fails to give due weight to our sources' emphatic claim that the widest possible range of issues, public and private, great and small, was brought before the Senate by Tiberius, at least in the earlier part of the reign. Discreet warnings against such openness from Augustus' confidant, the *eques* C. Sallustius

---

[15] Brunt 1984 (D 27); *FIRA* I 99 lines 1–7.

Crispus, were ignored. Moreover the Senate could feel that it enjoyed greater freedom to handle all this business, following the radical step taken by Tiberius on his accession: he was not content merely to reduce Augustus' senatorial *consilium* to its status prior to A.D. 13, but actually abolished it altogether. As a result the primacy of the full Senate was quite unexpectedly reasserted.

The Senate received a further boost during the early weeks of Tiberius' reign when elections to magistracies were transferred to it from the popular assemblies (though the latter continued to meet for the purpose of ratifying the choice of candidates). To what extent this development was an idea of Augustus rather than of Tiberius is obscure: but on present evidence there is no sign that the former ever wanted to do more than give the upper classes a prominent role in assembly elections, while at the least there can be no question that the timing of the change must have been decided by Tiberius.[16] The Senate, of course, gained no formal power from it. Neither was there any relaxation of the existing constraints imposed upon both candidates and voters by the emperor's interest. For the consulship he continued to support as many candidates as there were vacancies. For all other magistracies, however, his candidates would usually comprise no more than a proportion of the vacancies, so that there was genuine, fierce competition for the remaining places. Thus the transfer still gratified members, and did offer the corporate body a regular, active function to which much significance was attached.[17] The details of how far in advance magistrates were elected thus in the Julio-Claudian period, and at what times of year, remain almost a blank: in all probability no set pattern emerged until a later date. An attempt by Gaius to return the elections to popular assemblies was frustrated by senators and soon abandoned.

Even more welcome to members was the trend which Tiberius more or less consciously encouraged whereby the Senate should exercise a regular jurisdiction as a high court.[18] It had never done this during the Republic nor during the reign of Augustus. Rather, in his scheme of things this function was to be fulfilled by the jury-courts (*quaestiones*), which he overhauled and added to, and in which he gave senators an established place; in addition, from 4 B.C. certain charges of extortion (*repetundae*) might be heard by small panels of senators. Only for needs and cases beyond the normal routine did Augustus occasionally turn to the full Senate – in particular cases where his own prestige and interest were closely involved, or where the complexity or novelty of the issues were beyond the competence of a *quaestio*. In the earlier part of Tiberius' reign such formerly occasional referral became so frequent as to

16 Brunt 1961 (c 47); 1984 (d 27) 429.   17 Talbert 1984 (d 77) 202–4 and 341–5.
18 Bleicken 1962 (d 248); Garnsey 1970 (f 35); Talbert 1984 (d 77) ch. 16.

constitute regular jurisdiction, while many more *repetundae* cases were considered to require a hearing before the full Senate rather than mere reference to a small panel. The trial of Cn. Calpurnius Piso in A.D. 20 for the murder of Germanicus may have been a turning-point. According to Tacitus,[19] Tiberius himself openly acknowledged that it was exceptional to bring the case before the Senate rather than a *quaestio*. Yet from the 20s there remains no doubt that the senatorial court was well established, and the likelihood is that the *quaestiones* for treason (*maiestas*) and extortion (*repetundae*) became practically defunct in consequence.

Established senatorial procedure required little adaptation to accommodate judicial hearings, especially as the Senate had long been accustomed to entertaining pleas and applications, and adjudicating disputes. It is unlikely that its regular jurisdiction was ever sanctioned formally by law: none was necessary if the development enjoyed the emperor's support. While in theory the Senate as a supreme legislative body claimed the right (unlike a *quaestio*) to hear any charge and to fix any penalty, certain conventions quickly developed. The Senate became the principal court chosen to take cases of *maiestas* and *repetundae* in the Julio-Claudian period. Otherwise it normally confined itself to cases where individuals of high rank were involved; where the issue was particularly serious or scandalous; or where an affair attracted a special degree of public attention. Thus, for example, the Senate was a natural choice of court to hear adultery cases where persons of high rank were implicated, and where there might be associated charges, not to mention delicate political overtones. It was equally well fitted to investigate the collapse of an unsafe amphitheatre at Fidenae in 27 which caused catastrophic loss of life among the spectators: this resulted in the banishment of the builder, a freedman, and the drafting of regulations to prevent the recurrence of such a disaster.

The further convention seems to have developed that the emperor remained aloof from *repetundae* trials, according the Senate complete freedom to decide these as it pleased – a detachment which represented no special sacrifice on his part. It could only be otherwise with cases of *maiestas*, however. These were often brought to the emperor in the first instance and only referred to the Senate on his initiative. Since by definition they did touch his own safety and interest, he considered it important to make his views known and to have them adopted by whatever means might prove necessary. As a result the Senate was seldom left free to decide such cases, and bitterly resented the inevitable imperial interference, especially when the defendants were from the senatorial class. It became a major tragedy of Tiberius' reign that he did

---

[19] *Ann.* III.12.

less and less to control the bringing of *maiestas* charges. Moreover in any politically sensitive case he was above all concerned to see his own wishes met, rather than to encourage senatorial independence.

No less harmful was his withdrawal to Capri in 26, which turned out to be permanent. Up till that time his attendance – at debates and trials, as president and private member, even on election days – had been outstandingly conscientious. He had participated actively in proceedings too – suffering insults, being drawn into embarrassing exchanges, and even on occasion finding himself outvoted. Taken together with his other measures this behaviour understandably increased the Senate's confidence in the nature and value of its role, so that the effect of the emperor's isolation from the corporate body after 26 was all the more damaging.

Gaius' declaration[20] at his accession that he would never write to the Senate (and thus by implication would always attend in person) did indicate a fleeting initial reaction against Tiberius' behaviour during the previous eleven years. But it was left to Claudius to make a serious effort in this regard. While perhaps never as assiduous as Tiberius had been, he did none the less regularly attend meetings and trials, both as president and private member, and was an eager participant, bringing much business before the corporate body. He seems also to have been exceptionally severe in insisting upon good attendance by others. The ban on unauthorized private travel beyond Italy (and after 49 Sicily and Narbonese Gaul) by senators was stringently enforced. Nero's personality and lack of experience led him to attend the Senate much less than Claudius, in particular towards the end of the reign when he became more and more estranged from it. But strikingly Vitellius' background and training led him to revert to the example of Augustus, Tiberius and Claudius. Tacitus[21] notes that during his brief reign in 69 he made a point of attending the Senate even when the items on the agenda were only trivial.

Of all the emperors between 37 and 69 it was Claudius who made the most lasting impact upon the Senate by widening its membership. It is true that he stressed to the Senate itself the desire of both Augustus and Tiberius 'that there should be in this *curia* all the flower of the colonies and municipalities everywhere, namely good men and rich'.[22] Yet in making such a claim he appears to be over-generous. Even though Iulius Caesar had introduced a few provincials, both Augustus and Tiberius – whatever may have been their ideal – in practice seem to have continued this trend no more than cautiously. Despite the favour regularly shown

[20] Dio LIX.3.1.   [21] *Hist.* II.91.   [22] *FIRA* I 43 col. II lines 2–4.

by emperors to respectful senators of distinguished ancestry, many old families soon ceased to be represented for a variety of reasons.[23] As a result there was room for a steady influx of *novi homines*, or first generation senators, who at this date were still mainly Italian. There was evidently no shortage of aspirants except for a limited period during the 'teens B.C. New patricians were created by both Augustus and Claudius. But it was only because of further initiative by the latter that provincials became in any way a notable element in the membership of the Senate. Even then, the great majority of these newcomers originated from the West of the empire: by contrast, not until after the Julio-Claudian period did more than a handful of easterners have qualifications and contacts which encouraged them to put themselves forward.[24]

Hostile emperors like Gaius and Nero inflicted no more than short-term damage upon the Senate as a corporate body. For by the latter part of Tiberius' reign reform of its membership and workings was complete, while its functions had been satisfyingly enough redefined within the new constraints which the Principate imposed. In the spheres of legislation and jurisdiction the Senate remained notably busy. Meetings might last the entire day from sunrise to sunset; even so, many were required beyond the minimum of two each month prescribed by the Lex Iulia. Such miscellaneous attendance and voting figures as survive range from respectable to high[25] and are all the more remarkable in view of the considerable proportion of members who would always have to be out of Rome on official business or had reached the 'retirement age'. Debate was often sharp, and participation in it by no means confined just to the two highest grades, *consulares* and *praetorii*, who were consulted first. Great pride was taken in senatorial membership, and there was evidently never difficulty in attracting fresh aspirants, or in inspiring loyalty to the institution on the part of those who were elected. Moreover, even though the Senate may no longer have exercised much formal power, its members individually and collectively still exerted a decisive influence upon all the empire's affairs. While in one sense the well-being of the Senate, like everything else, remained painfully dependent upon the emperor's pleasure, in another the attitude of Augustus and Tiberius during their long reigns set a standard which senatorial opinion could ever afterwards demand that each of their successors maintain. These values were strongly advocated by senators and to a significant extent observed by responsible emperors, very much to the benefit of the corporate body and its prestige. Thus, as Tacitus[26] has Otho emphasize in the most high-flown surviving statement of the Senate's significance

---

[23] Hopkins 1983 (A 46), ch. 3.   [24] Halfmann 1979 (D 44).
[25] Talbert 1984 (D 77) ch. 4 sect. 2; González 1984 (B 234) 76.   [26] *Hist.* 1. 84.

for Romans, it was the institution which continued to be seen as the permanent embodiment of the ancient *respublica*.

II. SENATORIAL AND EQUESTRIAN POSTS

No *princeps*, however active, could run the empire single-handed. Moreover the administrative functions fulfilled by the annual magistrates elected at Rome were deliberately curtailed in scope. It is true that they continued to preside over a variety of courts there, and that quaestors acted as financial officers in the ten or so senatorial provinces. In addition three magistrates in office acted as mint supervisors, while between 23 B.C. and A.D. 56 there were others who administered the state treasury in Rome. But that was about all. For everything else the emperor had to seek assistance, principally from the upper classes. Here the role of senators was an outstanding one. The individuals invited to advise the emperor in his private *consilium* would be drawn largely from their ranks. Their formerly exclusive privilege to govern provinces and command legions was barely infringed either during the Julio-Claudian period or long afterwards. These were two functions of vital importance which alone by A.D. 68 called for the services of over fifty members at any one time, nearly all of them *consulares* or *praetorii* (men who had been consul or praetor respectively); further senators would accompany governors as legates.

The proconsuls of the senatorial provinces were still chosen according to the traditional method of the lot to serve for just a one year term, which would normally be expected to begin between our Easter and mid-summer. The arrangements for drawing lots, and the timing, are mostly obscure. Appointment as proconsul of Africa or Asia came to be offered to the senior *consulares* who had not held either post already. In this instance, therefore, once the two men eligible and willing to accept appointment had been identified, the drawing of lots was confined to deciding which province each would take. It may be that a broadly similar procedure was followed in the case of other proconsulships too, all reserved for *praetorii* (although tenure of more than one such post was permitted). Since there were as many as eight posts to be assigned thus, the lot could operate very much at random, and it does seem to have been left to do so. Such instances of individual manipulation as have been suspected appear exceptional; the same applies to extended terms of office.[27]

Apart from these ten or so proconsulships, all governors and all legionary commanders were appointed by the emperor to serve for as long as he required. The same in effect applied to most of the new

[27] Talbert 1984 (D 77) ch. 10 sect. 3 and App. 8.

Table 1 *New senatorial posts within Rome and Italy*

Title	Function	Number and rank	Date	Remarks
PRAEFECTUS AERARII SATURNI[28]	Management of state treasury	2 *praetorii*	29 to 23 B.C. and from A.D. 56	Function carried out between 23 B.C. and A.D. 56 by praetors and quaestors in office
PRAEFECTUS FRUMENTI DANDI[29]	Distribution of corn dole at Rome	4 *praetorii*, notionally chosen by lot	2 from 22 B.C., 2 more added in 18 B.C.	
CURATOR VIARUM[30]	Management of roads in Italy (though precise scope of functions remains obscure)	Board of uncertain composition	From 20 B.C.	Regular assignment of one or more named main roads to an individual senatorial *curator* almost certainly postdates the Julio-Claudian period
CURATOR AQUARUM[31]	Management of aqueducts of Rome	3 notionally chosen by lot, comprising 1 *consularis*, 1 *praetorius*, 1 senator of lesser rank	From 11 B.C.	Board was granted legal authority to maintain the responsibility exercised informally by Agrippa for just over twenty years prior to his death in 12 B.C.
PRAEFECTUS AERARII MILITARIS[32]	Management of military treasury	3 *praetorii*	From A.D. 6	
PRAEFECTUS URBI[33]	Oversight of law and order in Rome, and command of the three urban cohorts (formerly under the direct control of Augustus)	1 senior *consularis*	Archaic office permanently re-instituted in new form from A.D. 13	

CURATOR AEDIUM SACRARUM ET OPERUM LOCORUMQUE PUBLICORUM[34]	Management of sacred buildings and public works and places	2 (normally *consulares*)	Instituted by either Augustus or Tiberius
CURATOR LOCORUM PUBLICORUM IUDICANDORUM[35]	Supervision of judicial business in connexion with state property	5, headed by a *consularis*	Only attested under Tiberius
CURATOR TABULARUM PUBLICARUM[36]	Management of public records	3	Attested at most from late in Augustus' reign to that of Nero
CURATOR RIPARUM ET ALVEI TIBERIS[37]	Maintenance of the banks and bed of River Tiber (in particular to reduce danger of flooding)	5, notionally chosen by lot and headed by a *consularis*	Almost certainly from A.D. 15
AB ACTIS SENATUS[38]	Keeper of the record of senatorial proceedings	1 of unknown rank	Only attested once, in A.D. 29	Regular tenure (by a *quaestorius*) is only attested after the Julio-Claudian period

Notes:
28 Corbier 1974 (D 122) 476–8.
29 Pflaum 1963 (D 108) 234–7.
30 Eck 1979 (E 38) ch. 3.
31 Frontin. *Aq.* 99ff; Ashby 1935 (F 257).
32 Corbier 1974 (D 122) 570–1.
33 Vitucci 1956 (E 136); review by Cadoux 1959 (D 29); *AE* 1972, 174.
34 Gordon 1952 (C 350) 283–4.
35 *ILS* 942, 5939–41; *CIL* VI 37037.
36 M. Hammond 1938 (D 45).
37 Le Gall 1953 (E 73) 137–45.
38 Talbert 1984 (D 77) 310–12.

senatorial posts within Rome and Italy established on a permanent basis by Augustus and Tiberius, albeit with the Senate's approval. Although these posts (set out in Table 1) without doubt represent a haphazard growth, rather than a planned series, none the less all were equally intended to improve public services and thereby strengthen the emperor's own position. At the same time the creation of one or more posts with a particular responsibility did not deter him from still taking personal initiatives in the same sphere from time to time.

Not only did adjustment and experiment continue, as Table 1 shows. Senators might also be called upon at any time to assist in tackling some short-term crisis or difficulty. But all the same it can be seen that the substantial group of new senatorial administrative posts within Rome and Italy was largely organized by early in Tiberius' reign. To some extent the same may be true of the new posts throughout the empire to which *equites* were appointed, although the ancient sources' lack of interest in tracing the development of the equestrian service usually makes it impossible to claim with confidence when a particular post was instituted.[39]

Already during the late Republic certain officerships in the army were normally held by *equites* (a small number of whom would advance to pursue senatorial careers). Augustus increased the opportunities for military service of this type, so that in time there developed the pattern whereby most legionary tribunates and all auxiliary prefectures were reserved for *equites*; some prefects of fleets were also equestrian (the others being freedmen). A limited proportion of all these officers were ex-centurions who had gained equestrian status through working their way up to the primipilate; but the majority were *equites* by birth, newly recruited into the army and likely to serve there for some years. It seems to have been understood that such military service would be required of any *eques* who aspired to a civil appointment in the emperor's service.

Like any republican magnate Augustus needed procurators to manage estates which he could not see to himself and to represent him in the courts. He generally asked *equites* to fulfil this function, and from the beginning of his reign he must have had such representatives in most, if not all, provinces. In senatorial provinces (where a quaestor was stationed) the procurator's function was technically confined to the administration of the emperor's private property. Even during the reign of Augustus, however, procurators in imperial provinces took on a wider role, handling public money and commanding troops; some were actually put in charge of a region or even an entire province, answerable either to the nearest army commander, or to the emperor direct. Most

[39] Hirschfeld 1912 (D 13); Stein 1927 (D 66); Pflaum 1950 (D 56); 1960–1; 1982 (D 59); 1974 (D 58). Many of Pflaum's dates for the creation of new posts should be viewed with caution.

notable among the latter was the prefect of Egypt, who was regarded as the senior equestrian official during the Julio-Claudian period, and whose immediate subordinates (even the commanders of the two legions stationed outside Alexandria) were all *equites*.[40] Some enlargement of the procurator's role inevitably developed in senatorial provinces too, and it must have been as a reflection of this general expansion that Claudius gave all his procurators jurisdiction in fiscal cases.[41] Indeed by his day there was even one *eques* who believed that in occupying posts normally given to members of his class he could achieve the same degree of wealth and influence as a *consularis*.[42]

In Rome Augustus handed direct command of the praetorian cohorts to a pair of equestrian prefects from 2 B.C. A few years later crises in two spheres prompted him to tackle their persistent problems much more decisively than hitherto. First, after a serious fire in A.D. 6 he took the step of appointing an equestrian *praefectus vigilum* who commanded a force of 7,000 freedmen to combat fires. Though ostensibly experimental,[43] this innovation soon became a permanent feature. Second, a severe shortage in the same year led him to appoint a pair of *consulares* to supervise the corn supply in two successive years; then at some date between A.D. 7 and his death in 14 he put the task in the hands of an equestrian *praefectus annonae*, whose office was permanent.[44] There is reason to believe that an equestrian prefecture of vehicles in Italy may also date from Augustus' reign,[45] while it was certainly from early in the Julio-Claudian period that equestrian assistants (*adiutores*) of various grades came to be attached to many of the senatorial and equestrian administrative officers mentioned above.

It should be stressed that the growth of all these equestrian posts was as much an unco-ordinated response to immediate problems as in the case of the senatorial appointments already outlined. There was no equestrian 'civil service' whose members were guaranteed permanent employment within a planned career structure which encouraged them to develop a particular expertise.[46] Augustus' general reasons for turning to the equestrian order for the assistance which he sought seem easy enough to conjecture. On the negative side, it might not have been diplomatic to appoint senators to some of the posts concerned, even had there been sufficient members of their class; there may have also been instances where senators' competence was doubted. On the positive side, while *equites* ranked below senators (and could thus accept orders more readily), they had always been inextricably linked with them; a

---

[40] Brunt 1975 (E 906).   [41] Brunt 1966 (D 87); Alföldy 1981 (D 23).
[42] Tac. *Ann.* XVI.17.   [43] Dio LV.26.4–5.
[44] Pavis d'Escurac 1976 (D 55); Rickman 1980 (E 109).   [45] Eck 1979 (E 38) 88–94.
[46] Brunt 1983 (D 26).

favoured few were even numbered among the emperor's closest advisers. In addition as a group *equites*, like senators, were wealthy, educated, and conservative in outlook. Many had experience of public life as jurors, contractors and municipal magistrates, as well as through army service. In general they were an obvious recourse for the emperor in his search for administrative assistance.

All the same it is less easy to be sure why he specifically chose members of the equestrian class to occupy particular posts. In Rome for example, the prefectures of the fire brigade and of the corn supply (both spheres formerly of general concern to senatorial magistrates) could seemingly just as well have been senatorial appointments. Among provinces it is impossible to find convincing general characteristics which distinguish the diverse areas entrusted to *equites* from those continuing to be governed by senators. Even in the case of Egypt the claims of later ancient writers,[47] that the country was too turbulent and altogether represented too great a security risk to be safely assigned to a senator, hardly ring true, all the more so in view of the alarm created by the first prefect, the *eques* Cornelius Gallus. As to the choice of *equites* to fill procuratorships, the modern contention that the background of the class enabled its members to draw upon unique expertise in the areas of finance, trade and manufacture may seem an unsatisfactory oversimplification, which overlooks the fact that most *equites* were no more than owners of large estates, and that the type of expertise attributed to the class is not hereditary. Any assumptions that equestrian officials would generally prove more honest in their conduct than senators, as well as displaying greater loyalty to the emperor, are equally misplaced. It is worth recalling in this connexion the point made above that equestrian *adiutores* came to be attached to both senatorial and equestrian administrative officers. While their appointment may have been intended in part to provide a check on malpractices, it is equally likely that the burden of work carried by their superiors did genuinely call for some assistance.

It may be more satisfactory to admit that Augustus' motives for choosing to employ *equites* in the way that he did can no longer be identified with any certainty for the most part. At the least, however, his concern must have been to ensure that each individual responsibility was tackled in the most effective manner at the time, rather than that assignment of posts to members of different classes should conform to some general system or theory. Later, Augustus' successors in all likelihood just continued to appoint to most posts men of the same class as the retiring holders, partly out of respect for established practice, and partly because no pressing cause to overturn existing arrangements was apparent. Exceptionally, towards the end of the Julio-Claudian period

---

[47] Tac. *Ann.* 11.59; *Hist.* 1.11; Dio LI.7.1.

pressure did develop on a number of grounds for *equites* to be appointed to senior positions in the emperor's secretariat, which hitherto had normally been given to freedmen. Although the shift itself only occurred later, it does at least serve to highlight in conclusion the extent to which the ambition of *equites* had grown within the relatively short span since their first employment by Augustus. It confirms, too, their willingness to serve the emperor and their full appreciation by this date of his boundless prerogative as patron and ruler.

CHAPTER 10

PROVINCIAL ADMINISTRATION
AND TAXATION

ALAN K. BOWMAN

I. ROME, THE EMPEROR AND THE PROVINCES

The reorganization of provincial government which began with Augustus' so-called first settlement in January 27 B.C. gave to the imperial administration in the provinces a fundamental structure which it was to retain for more than three centuries. Its basis can only be fully appreciated in the light of the developments of the late republican period.[1] In the East the Roman organization of Greece and Asia had taken advantage of the urban legacy of hellenization and set the pattern of which the far-reaching arrangements of Pompey's eastern settlement were a logical extension. Here, the ubiquitous phenomenon of organization through the hellenized *poleis*, based on specific and definable relationships between the city and the ruling power, was to find its clearest expression, whilst the military and fiscal interests of Rome knitted diverse communities into a loose provincial structure. In the West, Spain, Africa and Narbonensis required a longer period of development and acclimatization to Roman rule, accelerating noticeably only in the last three or four decades of the first century B.C. and drawing in their wake the newly acquired regions of Gallia Comata. If East and West differed in pace of 'Romanization' and in many a significant detail, the broad objectives did not: the need to encourage or create civilized and self-sufficient communities (whether based on *polis* or *civitas*) governed by their indigenous aristocracies; the need to ensure Rome's military security and the protection of her imperial interests in the broad sense, the cost of which would be met (at the least) by the revenue which Rome could draw from the province enjoying her protection; finally, as a natural corollary, the need to support and promote the interests of Romans in the provinces, senators and *equites* at the top of the social and

---

[1] See *CAH* ix², ch. 15. The evidence for provincial administration under Augustus and the Julio-Claudians is mainly inscriptional, supplemented by scattered references in the literary sources. No attempt is here made to provide exhaustive documentation. Care is needed in using the more abundant documentary and literary sources for the period from the Flavians to the Severi which are likely to reflect a more highly developed provincial administration than that which existed between 43 B.C. and A.D. 69. Some later items of evidence are cited in what follows, but only those which seem unlikely to be seriously anachronistic.

economic scale, then *negotiatores*, veteran colonists and increasing numbers of assimilated provincial Roman citizens. For all this the visible and effective support system lay in the military establishment, the institutions of provincial and civic government, the power of Rome's currency, the increasing dominance of her economic interests, and the gradual spread of Roman law.[2]

The patterns of provincial government established in the late Republic certainly survived the triumviral period, although it is difficult to see whether the political and military disturbances entailed any long-term disruption on more than a local scale. From the point of view of Roman magistrates and officers serving in the provinces, the arrangements enunciated in the Lex Titia of 27 November 43 B.C. and emended after Philippi offered the triumvirs the opportunity to exercise patronage and appoint supporters to provincial governorships and legateships; the more general implication was the evolution of 'spheres of influence' which gave them access to the military and financial resources provided by the provinces in their areas.[3] But it would be mistaken to deduce from this that either the constitutional power or the influence of a triumvir was limited by any 'iron curtain'. Antony might write to the *koinon* of Asia on the subject of privileges enjoyed by athletes and artists, but Octavian was also able to maintain his close relationship with Aphrodisias-Plarasa in Caria, to bestow personal privileges on the naval captain (*nauarchos*) Seleucus of Rhosus and to issue an edict on veteran privileges whose beneficiaries were not confined to one part of the empire.[4] But the solicitude of a triumvir for Rome's subjects was not universal even in his own area; some communities suffered from neglect or from inability to enlist effective aid and support, as is suggested by the evidence for internal faction and belated reparation for damage caused in the Asian cities of Aphrodisias and Mylasa during the invasion by Labienus and the Parthians.[5]

The enduring administrative arrangements made at the beginning of 27 B.C. will certainly have owed something to the experience of the previous fifteen years, even though it was politic to suppress any overt appeal to triumviral precedents. The assignation to Augustus of a large *provincia*, with leave to govern it through senatorial legates appointed for terms determined by the *princeps*, might rather have recalled the Spanish

---

[2] Calculation of the revenue to be derived in return for protection is explicit in Strabo IV.5.3 (200C), reflecting that Britain would need a legion plus cavalry forces to ensure collection of tribute and the expenditure on troops would equal the revenue. On the spread of currency and economic interests in general see Crawford 1985 (B 320) ch. 17.

[3] App. *BCiv.* IV.2.7, Dio XLVI.55.3–56.1.

[4] Antony to the *koinon*, *RDGE* 57; Seleucus, *RDGE* 58; veterans, *FIRA* 1 56; Aphrodisias, Reynolds 1982 (B 270) nos. 6, 10, 12.

[5] Reynolds 1982 (B 270) nos. 7, 11, 12; Mylasa, *RDGE* 59, 60.

governorship of Pompey the Great in 55 B.C. As defined in the first instance, Augustus' province was to include Spain (though Baetica was soon removed), Gaul, Syria, Cilicia, Cyprus and Egypt (governed, since 30 B.C. by an equestrian *praefectus* personally appointed by the *princeps*).[6] Within a few years Cyprus and Narbonensis were to be returned to the control of proconsuls, selected by the traditional lot for annual governorships and by the end of Augustus' reign Illyricum, now reorganized to form the provinces of Pannonia and Dalmatia, was in the emperor's hands.[7]

New provinces, by their very nature, demanded assignation to the emperor. Distinctions of rank existed within the categories of governors of 'imperial' and 'public' provinces, the major military imperial provinces being entrusted to men of consular status, the lesser to praetorians, the Senate appointing ex-consuls only to Africa and Asia, ex-praetors to the remainder. For those imperial provinces normally entrusted to *equites*, the prefecture of Egypt was perhaps the prototype; others were governed by men whose positions evolved from military *praefecturae* or civil procuratorships, becoming assimilated under the general title of procurator in the reign of Claudius. These governorships were in no constitutional sense reserved for men of equestrian rank – a freedman could be appointed deputy-prefect of Egypt and there is no evidence that Pallas' brother, Antonius Felix, was elevated to equestrian rank to hold the prefecture of Judaea.[8]

It is essential to emphasize that under Augustus and his successors practice remained flexible. It allowed provinces to be governed in groups, a province to be transferred from the control of a proconsul to that of a senatorial *legatus Augusti* or an equestrian governor (or, occasionally, vice versa), to place public and imperial provinces under a combined governorship, to allow a province to be 'upgraded' from equestrian control to that of a legate or from a praetorian to a consular legate, to recognize, in adjacent provinces, although perhaps only in special circumstances, the superior status of the *legatus Augusti* of the one to the equestrian *praefectus* of the other.[9] There are obvious differences between the categories of governors in length of tenure and method of

---

[6] Dio LIII.12; Baetica was transferred to the Senate probably soon after 27 B.C., see Mackie 1983 (E 753) 353–4.   [7] Dio LIII.12.7, LIV.4.1, Thomasson 1975 (D 110) I 87ff.

[8] Strab XVII.3.24–5 (839–40C); Egypt, Tac. *Ann.* XII.60.3, Dio LVIII.19.6, Philo, *In Flacc.* 1.2; Felix, Tac. *Ann.* XII.54. The use of the term 'senatorial' to refer to provinces governed by proconsuls is here deliberately avoided, in favour of the word 'public' which more accurately reflects Strabo's assertion (*loc.cit.*) that these were the provinces of the people.

[9] Illyricum, divided into Pannonia and Dalmatia, was transferred from proconsuls to legates, as was Macedonia (see above, n. 7); Sardinia was governed by proconsuls, then *praefecti*, then proconsuls again in the Julio-Claudian period; Lycia-Pamphylia was transferred from legate to proconsul in the second century (Thomasson 1975 (D 110) I. 275ff); Moesia combined with Macedonia and Achaea, Tac. *Ann.*I.80.1, Dio LVIII.25.4; Thrace, Noricum and Raetia were at first

appointment. Legates and procurators, appointed directly by the *princeps*, normally enjoyed a tenure of several years; proconsuls were appointed by lot and served for one year, although there are isolated examples of prolongation and of appointment without the lot (*extra sortem*). Beyond that, powers and responsibilities tended to become increasingly assimilated (this had been the purpose and effect of the law regularizing the position of the equestrian prefect of Egypt[10]) and proconsular independence of the emperor is all too easily exaggerated.

The evolution of this 'system' shows that the implications were far-reaching, although not in any sense which imposes a misleading division of the empire into two halves or two separate methods of government. Augustus could have claimed, if he were ever asked, to be entitled to act in his own and in the public provinces in virtue of his consular *imperium* until 23 B.C.; a consular decree of Augustus and Agrippa was certainly applicable in the province of Asia not long after 27 B.C. Thereafter he might claim to act by virtue of the lifetime grant of *imperium proconsulare maius*. But the renewal of the grant of the *provincia* in 18 B.C. (and at five- and ten-year intervals thereafter until the practice lapsed after A.D. 14) seems to show that at first the *imperium* was in principle separable from the territories assigned to him.[11] That these were all regarded, at least in the beginning, as provinces of the *senatus populusque Romanus* seems evident if we accept Velleius' implication that Egypt's tribute was properly the revenue of the *aerarium*, Tiberius' censure of his legates for not sending reports on their provinces to the Senate, or the fact that the operation of the emperor's Special Account (*Idios Logos*) in Egypt could be affected by regulations made by the Senate.[12] On the other hand, there is abundant evidence to show that, in fact, business from both public and imperial provinces tended to gravitate towards the emperor as the most clearly identifiable and effective source of power. The first of Augustus' Cyrene edicts can just as naturally be taken to show this as any implied exercise of *imperium maius*, since it clearly shows the Cyreneans taking the initiative by consulting the *princeps*, and it is noteworthy that Tiberius, by contrast, thought it appropriate in similar circumstances not to handle the business himself or in conjunction with the Senate, but to allow the Senate an illusion of its traditional functions (*imaginem antiquitatis*) by remitting to it embassies from cities in proconsular provinces.[13]

---

governed by procurators, then transferred to legates in the second century; for the relationship between the prefect of Judaea and the legate of Syria see Joseph., *AJ* XVIII.88–9, XX.132, *BJ* II.244 and Schürer 1973 (E 1207) I. 360–1. For the status of the provinces in A.D. 69 see Table 2.

[10] Extended tenure of legateships: Tac. *Ann*.I.80; proconsul appointed *extra sortem*: *GCN* 237; Egypt: Tac. *Ann*.XII.60.3, Ulpian, *Dig* 1.17.

[11] *RDGE* 61 (Cyme). Dio LIII.16.2–3.   [12] Vell.Pat. II.39.2, Suet. *Tib*.32, *BGU* 1210, *praef*.

[13] *EJ*² 311.1–40, Tac. *Ann*. III.60.3.

Growth in the emperor's influence and control may also be illustrated by observing his relations with governors. In 22 B.C. public embarrassment was caused by Augustus' role in the misbehaviour of the proconsul Primus in Macedonia, brought to book for waging war on the Thracian Odrysae outside his province.[14] Obscure though the details of the affair are, it is evident that Augustus' advice to Primus carried so much authority that it might have helped him avoid conviction for treason (*maiestas*); what was potentially embarrassing to Augustus was the alleged intermediary role of his nephew Marcellus. But later the emperor's control of governors could easily be exercised overtly. He could intervene, when convenient, in the sortition of senatorial governorships; Augustus' explicit refusal to criticize a proconsul of Crete and Cyrene for despatching a provincial to Rome suggests that he could easily have done so had he thought it appropriate; in the reign of Claudius, an inscription yields explicit evidence that the emperor might furnish senatorial proconsuls, as well his own legates, with imperial instructions (*mandata*) and this may well have been the case under Augustus. It is worth noting, conversely, that the prolongation of legateships by Tiberius looks from its context as if it may well have been discussed in, or at least reported to, the Senate.[15]

The gradual establishment of patterns of control was as much a process of trial, adaptation and evolution as design. The flexibility is most obvious in the emergence and definition of new provinces during the early Principate but it is no less significant in those acquired earlier. An established province could be defined as a specific geographical area: sometimes its boundaries were clearly delineated by natural features, but often there was no clear border, and then the province would be defined as comprising the communities in it and their dependent *territoria*. A new province could be delimited (confirming or modifying the area originally assigned to a military legate with *imperium*) and given a gubernatorial structure, a military establishment, developing communication routes and a tax assessment. Various features (none of them universal) might further emphasize the unity of a province: the existence of a charter (*lex provinciae*), defining the basis of taxation, the military establishment and, in broad terms, the nature of local government; the governor's provincial edict setting forth his intentions in administration; the encouragement or creation of a *koinon* or *concilium*, a federal representative assembly for the communities of the province, with a particularly important role in the organization of imperial cult.

On the other hand, the picture is far from uniform within the provinces, except for certain broad features of the military establish-

---

[14] Dio LIV.3.1–4; for the uncertainty over the date see above, p. 84.
[15] EJ² 311.40–55, Tac. *Ann*.1.80.

ment. In many provinces, even those of long standing, the degree of military control was incomplete in less civilized regions; there could be no blanket of administrative organization and hence the role of the towns and cities was crucial. The provincial superstructure did not cut across or invalidate other pre-existing or developing institutions and relationships; rather, 'Romanization' went beyond simple intrusions like the building of arteries of communication or the introduction of the Roman currency and encouraged the persistence or development of certain kinds of institutions, fostering and moulding the relationship between Rome and individual community, between disparate elements within the provincial communities. Thus, established city-foundations in the eastern provinces might have their subjection to Rome tempered by a treaty written in the language of 'freedom' or of 'friendship and alliance', their aristocracies encouraged to undertake the burdens of civic government in return for the prospect of prestige and social advancement.[16] Even in the less urbanized province of Egypt, the district capitals (*metropoleis* of the nomes) assumed some of the features of the Greek *poleis* – magistrates and a 'Greek' gymnasial class.[17] Local laws (*nomoi*) would be allowed to subsist in many places, survivals of pre-existing laws, religious and judicial institutions like the Athenian council of the Areopagus or the Jewish Sanhedrin. Where 'freedom' was maintained, the lives of the citizens might largely be conducted according to local law, but the civic magnates could easily be made to see that the 'independence' of the community was at the disposal of the ruling power.[18] Even a city like Palmyra, on the fringe of the empire in the early Principate, had accepted Germanicus' instructions on the details of payment of local taxes in cash; if there was a precise moment at which it became integrated into the province of Syria, it is not clear when that was.[19] An example of firmer and more overt extension of control can be seen in the west with Corbulo systematically imposing 'senatus, magistratus, leges' on the borders of Gallia Belgica in A.D. 47.[20]

Roman control did not end at provincial boundaries. As important as the patterns of control within provinces, from the point of view of the consistent desire to create the conditions for further annexation of territory, are the tentacles which reached out beyond the frontiers, signs of a presence designed to impress Roman power upon tribes and client kings. The methods used outside provinces hardly differed from those used inside and must surely have emphasized the insignificance, in important respects, of the frontier between 'Roman' and 'non-Roman'

---

[16] *RDGE* 26, Reynolds 1982 (B 270) no. 8.   [17] See below, p. 696.   [18] Tac. *Ann*.III.60.6.
[19] *CIS* II.3.3913.181–6 (Greek text), Matthews 1984 (E 1037) (translation); on Palmyra's status see J.C. Mann in M.M. Roxan, *Roman Military Diplomas 1978–84* (*ICS* 1985), 217–19.
[20] Tac. *Ann*.XI.19.2–3.

territory. In Germany, for instance, occupation of military sites in sensitive areas beyond the frontiers is probable for a few years after the defeat of Quinctilius Varus and the loss of three legions in A.D. 9, and again in A.D. 47, but it is only part of the story. Neighbouring tribes supplied soldiers; Segimundus, the son of a Cheruscan chief, was appointed priest of the imperial cult at Ara Ubiorum, though still domiciled on the east bank of the Rhine, and Arminius' nephew Italicus was educated at Rome in the reign of Claudius; c. A.D. 2/3 the governor Aelius Catus, perhaps legate of Moesia and proconsul of Macedonia, transplanted 50,000 Getae into Thrace, Aelius Plautius Silvanus settled more than 100,000 transdanubians in Moesia in the reign of Nero; in Juba's Mauretania there were twelve Roman veteran *coloniae*, founded between 33 and 25 B.C. and attached to Baetica for administrative purposes; in 4 B.C. auxiliary units of Gauls were operating in Herod's Judaean kingdom.[21]

For provinces and their towns, villages and individual subjects, as for client kings and tribal chieftains, the embodiment of Roman power and authority was in practice inescapably and increasingly identifiable as the emperor. It is important to emphasize that he was far more than a mere figurehead, for his administrative role was always an active one. His position as a magistrate could be invoked (if it were ever necessary) to justify the issuance of edicts and *epistulae* addressed to specific provinces and communities within them, and imperial pronouncements in these forms soon hardened into a central feature of the development of a body of administrative law for the provinces. Pronouncements of a general nature which illustrate the emperor's role as an executive on a broad front are relatively few: the Augustan measure establishing a new procedure for extortion cases is in the form of a *senatus consultum* but the imperial edict which prefaces it makes the emperor's central role clear; imperial edicts guaranteeing the privileges of the Jews or of veterans, or regulating the system of *vehiculatio* (requisitioned transport) are not limited by civic or provincial boundaries and retain validity beyond the lifetime of an individual emperor until they are explicitly modified or superseded or occasionally, if in danger of being overlooked, reiterated.[22]

It is not difficult to see how groups of communities and individual communities and persons naturally perceived the emperor as the prime

---

[21] German forts: Schönberger 1969 (E 591) 151, Tac. *Ann*.XI.19.7; soldiers: Tac. *Ann*.I.56.1; Segimundus: Tac. *Ann*.I.57.2; Aelius Catus: Strab. VII.3.10 (303C) (for the conjectured date see Syme 1971 (E 702), 40–72, at 53–5, J.H. Oliver, *GRBS* 6 (1965), 51–5); Silvanus *GCN* 228; colonies in Mauretania: Pliny, *HN* V.2, 5, 20–1, cf. Mackie 1983 (E 753); Gauls: Joseph. *BJ* 1.397.

[22] Extortion: EJ² 311.72–141; Jews: Joseph. *AJ* XIX.286.91; veterans: *FIRA* 1 56; *vehiculatio*: Mitchell 1976 (B 255) (= *AE* 1976, 653), cf. *GCN* 375, 382.

focus of power and tended to direct embassies and requests to him, normally, though not always, through the filter of the governor, as the most natural source of effective action and patronage. This impression will have been further reinforced by the evident interests of the emperor and his property (*patrimonium*) in many provinces and areas. Imperial reaction by verbal decision or rescript thus also became a central feature of the growing corpus of law and regulation. How much of the actual decision-making was done by the emperor in person (as opposed to the palatine bureaucracy), how much was action and how much reaction does not alter the significance of the role. As the volume of business naturally increased, provincial officials multiplied; a matter brought to an emperor's attention by an embassy might be referred back to a provincial governor for investigation, as happened at Cnidus under Augustus.[23] A significant illustration of the occasional need to define responsibility is Claudius' explicit pronouncement of A.D. 53, amplified in a *senatus consultum*, that the decisions (*res iudicatae*) of his procurators were to be regarded as having validity equal to his own. Under Tiberius a procurator of Asia who had overstepped the mark was castigated by the emperor but neither of these acts can have entirely prevented abuse of their powers by officials.[24]

II. STRUCTURE

The functioning of the administrative system in the provinces depended upon a superstructure of military and civil officials, appointed to their positions by the central government and directly responsible to it. The relatively small corps of senators and *equites* who occupied the higher posts were normally not natives of the provinces in which they served, although there are sufficient exceptions, especially later in the Julio-Claudian period, to assure us that this was not an inflexible rule.[25] The infrastructure consisted of the elements of local government in the provincial communities – towns and villages – with varying degrees of autonomy. In this section these two elements will be examined in detail and some final observations will be made on the nature of the relationship between them.

Governors of all ranks, legates, proconsuls and prefects or procurators, exercised the full range of administrative, military and judicial powers within their provinces which their *imperium* implied; if a proconsul or a procurator had only a handful of auxiliary troops in his province, his authority over them was no weaker than that of the legate

[23] *RDGE* 67.   [24] Tac. *Ann.* XII.60.1–2, IV.15.3.
[25] Vindex, governor of Lugdunensis in A.D. 68 an Aquitanian, Dio LXIII.22.1(2); Ti. Iulius Alexander, Tac. *Hist.*I.11, cf. *PIR*² I 139.

of Syria over his four legions and auxiliary troops. The governor's responsibility for maintaining the *quies provinciae* was paramount and Ulpian's description of his duties as they were in the early third century indicates a breadth of authority which must be valid for the early imperial period.[26] Needless to say, the governor's freedom to act was subject to the will of the emperor, as it was to that of his delegated agent, be it Agrippa, Gaius Caesar, Germanicus or Corbulo, with overriding powers. The events surrounding the death of Germanicus in the East in A.D. 19 and his difficult relationship with Piso, the legate of Syria, illustrate the tensions which might arise; as they similarly might if an imperial procurator, as personal agent of the *princeps*, encroached on a governor's prerogatives, as is shown by the quarrel in Britain in A.D. 62 between the governor Suetonius Paulinus and the procurator Julius Classicianus which Nero attempted to solve by despatching the imperial freedman Polyclitus.[27] At the other end of the spectrum, a governor's powers were, in theory, limited by the privileges of particular communities or individuals; often they no doubt chose to observe them, in practice they could certainly be overridden.

There was a variety of officials in direct subordination to the provincial governor. As far as the routine work of the governor's *officium* was concerned, there is very little evidence for the early imperial period but an inscription of the second century shows that his staff consisted of a retinue of lictors, messengers (*viatores*), slaves and soldiers (*beneficiarii consulares* seconded from their units); in the first century it might perhaps have been smaller but similar in character.[28] At a higher level legates and proconsuls would have civil and (where there were legions) military *legati*; military tribunes, commanders of auxiliary units and centurions would also play an important role in civil as well as military administration. Proconsular governors had quaestors who performed their traditional role in public finance, whilst the financial interests of the imperial property (*patrimonium*) were tended by a *procurator provinciae* (normally an *eques*, sometimes a freedman) with subordinate equestrian or freedmen procurators assigned to specific estates or sources of revenue. Their degree of independence from the governor cannot always be precisely measured and the issue was gradually more obfuscated by the increasingly public nature of the fiscus and the fact that in imperial provinces the *procurator provinciae* had, from the first, assumed the traditional duties of the quaestor in the sphere of public finance. Only in Egypt can it be clearly seen that the equestrian officials of procuratorial status acted directly as 'departmental heads' for the governor but the same may be true, and increasingly so as time

---

[26] *Dig.* 1.16.4.3, 1.18.3, XLVIII.18.1.20.   [27] Tac. *Ann.*II.57, XIV.38–9.
[28] J.H. Oliver, *AJP* 87 (1966), 75–80, P.R.C. Weaver, *AJP* 87 (1966) 457–8.

passed, in other imperial provinces too.[29] From these officials the governor was relatively free to select those who would assist him in their own areas of expertise by sitting on his advisory council (*consilium*), but he was not restricted to co-opting a quaestor, legate, procurator or military officer; he might also summon a client king, a local magnate, a city magistrate or an expert in local laws and institutions.

The evidence for subdivision of provinces into regional administrative units is patchy and sporadic and it is impossible to imagine anything like a general pattern. In newly acquired or less Romanized areas special arrangements might be appropriate. In the Alpine regions in the early imperial period we find military *praefecti* assigned to groups of *civitates* in a region; as the regions became more organized and subjugated these *praefecturae* were integrated into the more regular gubernatorial pattern.[30] The requirements which dictated such an arrangement were doubtless analogous to those which later produced centurions in charge of regions (*centuriones regionarii*) in Britain, for example, and they serve to emphasize that in many if not all 'frontier' provinces the organization of the military establishment was inseparably linked to the development of the embryonic civil administrative structure.[31] In some provinces the evidence shows the survival of traditional regional units – the three (or four) *epistrategiae* and their constituent nome divisions in Egypt, the *strategiae* in Thrace (gradually phased out from the late Julio-Claudian period), toparchies in Syria and Judaea. In some places groups of cities were agglomerated into administrative units (the Syrian Decapolis, for example), in others *pagi* were created perhaps mainly with a view to facilitating the organization of taxation.[32] The officials in charge of such divisions will have formed an important bridge between the civic authorities and the officials with province-wide responsibility, theoretically without prejudice to whatever degree of autonomy in internal government obtained in the individual communities. Finally, it should be added that, in effect, another type of regional unit was created by the growth of large imperial estates, often embracing numbers of small communities within their boundaries and assigned to the administration of an imperial procurator. The efficient functioning of this relatively small central bureaucratic superstructure (perhaps not more than 300 officials in all) depended upon an infrastructure of effective local administration in the towns and villages of the provinces. In this respect there are bound to be striking differences from province to province and region to region, particularly noticeable in broad terms between East and West; in much of the East Rome acquired provinces which retained

[29] Below, pp. 682–4.   [30] EJ[2] 243, 244.   [31] *Tab Vindol* 22 (= II 250).

[32] Egypt, below, p. 682; Thrace, below, p. 567–8; the Decapolis, *IGRR* I 824, cf. Isaac 1981 (D 93); Pflaum 1970 (E 755).

their Greek or hellenistic legacy of *poleis* whilst many of the western provinces required a greater degree of direct initiative in the organization of communities or tribal units into *civitates*, a process in which the military presence played a vitally stimulating social, economic and technical role. If a general pattern can be extrapolated from this diversity, it should probably be defined in terms of the aim of Roman imperial government to perpetuate or create a system of civic government which depended upon the primacy of the urban centre in its region and the supremacy, within that urban centre, of the wealthy aristocracy. Urbanization, thus defined, was the essence of social and political control and this process of development is one of the most important features of provincial history in the first century A.D. There was the foundation of *coloniae* in both the East and the West. The *poleis* of the East could be encouraged to better their status and their corporate privileges. In Gaul (and, to a lesser extent, in North Africa, Spain and Sardinia), existing urban centres were developed as *civitates*; some of the native *oppida* were developed, others were replaced by new *civitates* which, sooner or later, could aspire to the status of a *colonia* or *municipium*.

The structure of government in the provincial *poleis* and *civitates* depended heavily upon the oligarchical institutions of councils and magistrates, based upon qualifications of wealth and birth and vested with the executive power to govern their communities internally and to represent them in their dealings with the central authority. The more broadly based assemblies, whose composition was carefully defined so as to distinguish citizens from non-native residents (*incolae*), constituted a more democratic element but it was one with a restricted role, exercised under the direction of the local Senate and the curial class.[33] In some cities specific groups were permitted their own communal laws and institutions, so long as they did not infringe the laws of the city as a whole.[34] Of more general importance are other sorts of civic institutions whose functions fitted into the administrative pattern and whose officials exercised power and influence and gained status and prestige: local courts, temple foundations, *gerousiai* (councils of elders), *collegia* (guilds) and associations of all kinds. The curial classes may well have played an important part in these institutions as executives or patrons but many of them were, for others below that level, catalysts of social and political upward mobility in a pattern which systematically linked privilege and obligation and gave the ruling aristocracies the responsibility for apportioning the burdens of local government among both themselves and the lower status groups of the citizen body. The best illustration of this as a general feature of the system comes in the form of

[33] MW 454, cap.LIII, cf. Mackie 1983 (E 231) ch. III.
[34] The best known is the Jewish community of Alexandria, see *CPJ* I, p. 7, below, ch. 14*d*.

the ubiquitous public services (called liturgies in the East and *munera* in the West) which distributed the necessary burdens of local administration (including such functions as tax-collection for the central government) amongst the populace according to property qualification. The highly developed and organized liturgical system of the later Empire cannot safely be retrojected to the earlier period nor can it be assumed that it developed *pari passu* in different areas. But the vestigial and scattered evidence for the early imperial period makes it clear that the roots are to be sought here, at a time when it was probably still meaningful to make a clear distinction between such public services (whether prestigious and theoretically voluntary or, to an increasing extent, menial and compulsory) and the elective magisterial offices (*honores* or *archai*).[35]

Although the cities normally enjoyed a primal position in relation to the villages of their *territorium*, it is important to emphasize that this only rarely seems to have involved direct administration of villages from the civic centre. Some Alpine tribal villages were governed from their neighbouring *municipia* and in Africa magistrates of Carthage were involved in the administration of villages whose population included Roman citizens. But even there, other native settlements probably had their own magistrates and in Spain a *vicus* may be found acting independently of its *civitas*.[36] In western Asia Minor and Syria village political life was vigorous, involving village assemblies, sometimes councils of elders (*gerousiai*), and boards of magistrates; in Cappadocia, which had been little affected by Hellenism and consequently boasted few cities, it was the villages which were at first the centres of organization and of economic and religious life; internal village administration in Egypt did not depend on the nome-capitals, though it was perhaps subject to a greater degree of supervision by government officials than was the case elsewhere. In Gallia Belgica, where some 150 *vici* are known, periods of growth have been identified immediately after the conquest and in the middle of the first century A.D., involving both pre-Roman *oppida* and new foundations appearing close to the main roads. Here the grouping of villages in *pagi* and the development of the major *vici* as cult-centres emphasizes the variation in size and the general tendency of groups to form their own central-place hierarchies.[37] An important role as a centre of market, commerce and manufacture together with the existence of a wealthy landowning (and hence magisterial) elite will have been the basis for claims to city-status which

[35] EJ² 311.55–62, FIRA I 56, I 21, cap.XCII.

[36] Anauni and Tridentum, GCN 368.21–36; Carthaginian magistrates, ILS 1945, CIL VIII.26274; Spanish *vicus*, AE 1953, 267; compare Hierapolis sending peace-keeping officials to villages in OGIS 527 (date uncertain).   [37] Wightman 1985 (E 520) 91–6.

larger villages made with increasing frequency in the second and third centuries.

This sketch of the governmental system as consisting of a central bureaucratic structure and the local administrative institutions ignores one feature which deserves mention in this context – the existence of leagues of cities and provincial federate assemblies (*koina* or *concilia*). The former were never very widespread and where they did exist were probably a concession to local traditions (as in Greece, where limited rights of coinage were enjoyed) or a pre-existing and convenient instrument of organization in a new province like Lycia-Pamphylia. The provincial assemblies, of which only the Asian and the Gallic (serving the Three Gauls) are known in any detail during this period, played an important role in emperor-cult and might be the medium for transmission of measures affecting the province as a whole or for expressing the common grievances of the provincial cities at the imperial court, but neither they nor the leagues had a role of any vital administrative importance, nor did they occupy a regular role as intermediary between the cities and the central government; it is, however, worth noting one interesting instance from the reign of Tiberius of the Thessalian League attempting, by vote of the constituent members, to resolve an inter-city dispute which was remitted to it by the provincial governor.[38] A more important feature is the fact that they allowed concentration of the city aristocracies in a broader and more prestigious context, reinforcing their standing and control in their individual cities.

Effective links between the central and the local administrative structures, nevertheless, did exist. As far as function was concerned, the main feature is the way in which the provincial authorities of the central government exercised a supervisory or controlling interest over the local, sometimes under the pressure of requests from the communities themselves. This is illustrated in more detail in the following section, but it is worth noting here first, that even if such intervention frequently went beyond what the central government would have chosen to do of its own accord, this possibility was always inherent in the relationship between Rome and the provincial community and second, that the inability of the communities to exercise their autonomy satisfactorily foreshadows the situation in the later Empire when the higher echelons of the local administration were effectively incorporated in the central bureaucracy; in the early Empire it might occasionally be expedient to send a person who already enjoyed influence at the imperial court back to his native city to regulate its affairs, as happened to Athenodorus of Tarsus under Augustus.[39] Intervention by central government and the use of local people was greatly facilitated by the opportunity for local magnates or their descendants to enter imperial service, perhaps availing themselves of the patronage of provincial governors or other powerful contacts; in doing so, they thus effectively withdrew from direct participation in local government, and deprived the communities, in the long run, of the use of their administrative capability and the resources upon which it was based. This may be seen as an inevitable consequence of the opening up of the equestrian status to the wealthier provincials. Antecedent to this might be the opportunity for a local magistrate, such as Lampo of Alexandria, to assist the provincial governor in his court or to sit on his *consilium*. A local dynastic family, like the Euryclids of Sparta, which gained citizenship under Augustus, could boast a member of equestrian procuratorial status by the reign of Claudius.[40]

III. FUNCTION

In contrast to the relative formality of the bureaucratic structure, an attempt to describe how provincial administration worked in practice must take account of the flexibility which the structure permitted and observe the patterns and relationships which developed in the early imperial period. A useful analysis of the working of provincial government can be presented in terms of the role of the various elements in the structure – emperor, Senate, the provincial governor and his subordinates, communities, institutions and individuals – the relationships between them and the factors which limited or determined the scope and nature of their action. Their functions can be illustrated by examples which show what kind of action they were free to take in what kind of situation and how different kinds of situations affected the complex of their interrelationships.

Here it is perhaps best to begin at the bottom of the structure and discuss the villages first. In general, they seem to have enjoyed a considerable degree of autonomy in communal affairs (though this doubtless varied from region to region), electing boards of magistrates from amongst the local landholders to manage village funds, gifts and bequests, the administration of markets, temples, public buildings and common property. The democratic element in local government survived quite vigorously in the form of village assemblies which discussed substantive matters as well as making corporate dedications and honorary decrees.[41] Detailed evidence for village affairs can be found only in

---

[40] Lampo, Philo, *In Flacc.* 131–4; Euryclids, Bowersock 1961 (E 817) 117–18.

[41] *IGRR* IV 1304 (Hierocaesarea), honours for a priest who dedicated an altar from his own resources to Rome, Augustus and the *demos*; *OGIS* 488, an assembly held by the *gerousia* discusses division of communal property.

Egypt but we should not underrate the significance of what we know of a village like Tebtunis in the Fayum (an area particularly affected by large-scale settlement of Greeks in the Ptolemaic period) where, for instance, documents of the reign of Claudius show the administration of the village record office which kept detailed account of contractual transactions between villagers and the activity of the local guild of salt-merchants in organizing members' rights to ply their trade in and around Tebtunis.[42] Here government officials played a significant supervisory role as a matter of course and, as in other provinces, the links with larger towns in the region may normally have been quite tenuous except in so far as the towns functioned as the nuclei of their regions for the purposes of taxation. Even where there were significant links with the towns a degree of tolerated independence and autonomy was not precluded but the lack of clearly defined status and privileges will have meant that small communities were more readily subject to interference and control by a provincial governor and his subordinates.[43]

The more abundant evidence from the provincial towns and cities naturally affords a more detailed picture. The status of the urban communities varied a good deal and the privileged cities were, at least in the early period, relatively few; of the 399 towns enumerated by Pliny the Elder in the three Spanish provinces, for instance, 291 were merely *civitates stipendiariae* (tribute-paying communities).[44] The more favoured communities might enjoy freedom and immunity from taxation, or freedom established by charter, *senatus consultum*, imperial edicts or letters; but the gradual emergence of general patterns did not preclude the existence of rights and concessions specific to a single community.[45] In the West the early pattern of peregrine and citizen communities defies simple classification but it is clear that, in general, elevation of status meant achievement of the status of *colonia* or of *municipium* with the Latin right, which could be confirmed by charter and which normally conferred Roman citizenship on the magistrates and their families. Native towns such as those of Spain or Africa might prepare themselves for higher status by imitating Roman institutions in their patterns of magistracies and local civil law. In consequence even in the Republic an issue in a peregrine Spanish community could be described in Roman legal language; in early imperial Africa a local magistrate marked the elevation of his town to municipal status merely by a change of title,

---

[42] *PMich* 237–42, 245.   [43] See above, n. 36.

[44] *HN* III.7, 18, 4, 117. The lists are generally agreed to be based on sources of the Augustan period.

[45] *Ius Italicum: Dig.* 50.15.1; *senatus consulta* etc.: Reynolds 1982 (B 270) nos. 8, 9, 13; rights of asylum for the temple of Zeus at Panamara: *RDGE* 30; income from indirect taxes given by Augustus to the Saborenses, requests for additions to be addressed to the proconsul of Baetica: MW 461.

from *sufes* to *duovir*.[46] Sometimes the process operated in reverse, for the imperial authority could diminish or revoke the privileges of a specific community or group of communities. Even when this was not done on a permanent basis, there was always the potential for a ruling by an emperor or governor which could override the rights of the community for some specific reason.[47]

Differences between the old-established *poleis* of the East and the developing *civitates* of the western provinces and the wide range of status enjoyed by the different communities does not make it impossible to identify the general features of their role in provincial government. In both East and West the privileged communities exercised their local autonomy and met their obligations to the imperial government through the institutions of councils and magistrates recruited from the propertied classes. Their role is adumbrated by Plutarch in a frequently cited passage which must primarily reflect the experience of the Greek East under Roman domination: the civic magistrate is also a subject, controlled by proconsuls, and should not take great pride in his crown of office, for the proconsul's boots are just above his head; he must avoid stirring the common people to ambition and unrest and he must always have a friend among the powerful, for the Romans are always very keen to promote the political interests of their friends.[48] In the East, as one might expect, the propertied families which provided these magnates and dynasts were frequently old-established ones which had been powerful when the *poleis* were city-states rather than merely provincial towns. An old aristocracy could absorb influential new elements (such as Italian immigrants), a less hellenized one could adapt to the pattern. In the West, aristocratic tribal patterns might be suitably modified to encourage the development of a pro-Roman upper class, as they seem to have been in the Three Gauls (though not so effectively as completely to suppress anti-Roman feeling).[49] Free birth and sufficient wealth were the technical prerequisites of curial status; freedmen with only the latter qualification were normally debarred from office, but freedmen's sons were entitled to enter the curial order and by the second century they were to make their mark in local politics in increasing numbers.[50]

---

[46] Roman citizenship: Lex Irnitana, cap.21 (González 1986 (B 235)), cf. Sherwin-White 1973 (A 87) ch. 14; the *tabula Contrebiensis*: Richardson, 1983 (B 271) 33–41; the first *duovir* at Volubilis: *GCN* 407b.

[47] Note the precision with which Pliny and Trajan describe the position *vis-à-vis* the request of Amisus, a *civitas libera et foederata*, to be allowed to have a benefit society: 'ut tu . . . dispiceres quid et quatenus aut permittendum aut prohibendum putares' (*Ep.* X.92), 'possumus quo minus habeant non impedire' (*Ep.* X.93); compare *Ep.* IV.22, Trajan's *consilium* upholding the right of a magistrate of Vienne to abolish games endowed in a will.   [48] Plutarch, *Praecepta rei publicae gerendae* 17, 18.

[49] The Syrian prince Dexandros, first high-priest of imperial cult: Rey-Coquais 1973 (B 269) 42ff (=*AE* 1976, 678); Gaul: Drinkwater 1978 (E 323), cf. the revolt of Florus and Sacrovir, Tac. *Ann.*III.40–6.   [50] The Lex Visellia of A.D. 24, *CJ* IX.21.

City government was thus essentially oligarchic. From the beginning of the second century, as the attractions of civic office faded, effective power was concentrated in the hands of an ever-smaller group which, by the later Empire, became institutionalized and appears in the legal texts as the *principales* (leading decurions). Many towns, however, retained democratic citizen assemblies which could theoretically exercise electoral powers and pass resolutions; by the end of the first century A.D. the electoral function had become less meaningful, as co-option to councils and appointment of magistrates by those councils became more common, but it is noteworthy that voting procedures in popular assemblies still find a place in the municipal charters of the Flavian period; popular decrees may never have been concerned with much more than the formal or honorific, but their survival in the inscriptional evidence from the Greek East is none the less significant of the fact that the assembly (*demos*) remained a formal element in the communal structure.[51]

Autonomy in internal administration conducted through the bouleutic or curial class allowed economy in the number and function of government administrators. The areas in which self-government was theoretically exercised add up to an impressive list. The regulation and organization of the councils and magistrates and other communal institutions such as *gerousiai*, trade- and cult-associations and gymnasia; performance of public services through a system of *munera* or liturgies; regulation of food supply and market facilities; general control of communal finances, including the exploitation of particular resources, management of property owned by the community, imposition of some tolls or local taxes; management of temples and cults (including some degree of control in emperor-cult once permission for its establishment had been granted) with attendant festivals and games; exercise of such specific legal powers as were permitted to individual institutions or officials (perhaps less severely limited than is commonly believed); the maintenance of public order and the supervision of prisons; sometimes rights to local coinage; organization of building projects in the town, frequently accomplished through the munificence of the local elite.

The ways in which the autonomy of communities in internal government were restricted and limited were nevertheless effective and significant. It was subject to general regulations applicable to a province as a whole, such as those embedded in a *lex provinciae* (which could be modified by imperial or senatorial authority) or those promulgated by individual governors; or to general enactments which affected the status

---

[51] Elections at Malaca, MW 454, caps.55–9; the *demos*, many examples including EJ² 114 (Alabanda), 318 (Cos), *RDGE* 26, col.d (Mytilene), 60 (Mylasa), *AJ* 68, cf. J.H. Oliver, *GRBS* 6 (1965) 143–56 (Histria), *GCN* 371 (Thasos).

and privileges of particular groups in the empire such as Jews or veteran soldiers.[52] Not dissimilar was the effect of the spread of Roman citizenship through personal grants to individuals, military service and the institutions of municipal government. The citizenship extended privileges to individuals and groups which could override or curtail the hold which their community's laws and institutions had upon them. We may note the complaints made in A.D. 63 to a prefect of Egypt by a mixed group of veterans that their citizen rights were being ignored; and conversely a striking instance from the Augustan period at Chios which makes it clear that Roman citizens resident there were subject to local laws.[53] An important indication of the general need to limit the scope for using Roman status to avoid local obligations occurs in the third Augustan edict from Cyrene which forbids Cyreneans with Roman citizenship to evade liturgical service in Cyrene; general recognition of this principle meant that provincial towns could continue to benefit from what was, in effect, a form of local taxation.[54] But, on the whole, the upward mobility of the local elite into citizen and sometimes ultimately equestrian or senatorial status made that elite more remote from the needs and the control of the cities, which could only retain their hold by encouraging ties of patronage.

Explicit interference in city autonomy by government officials tended to become more frequent in the course of time, partly because the nature of the ruling classes in the cities was always potentially factious; when the community itself did not have the means or the power to resolve internal difficulties which resulted, it would be likely to resort to an appeal to the central authority. The invitation to intervention was bound to weaken the confidence of the Roman government in the ability of the communities to govern themselves peacefully and efficiently, and ultimately to lead to erosion of their independence.

The phenomena which most frequently demanded the attention of central government were the inability to resolve internal conflicts, the reaction of communities to attempts to erode their privileges, and disputes between communities. Internal conflict evidently underlies the fourth of Augustus' Cyrene edicts, which attempts to deal with the problem of the bias of Romans against Greeks in juries dealing with non-capital cases, or the criminal accusation brought by a Cnidian embassy in 6 B.C. to Augustus and referred by him to the proconsul of Asia.[55] Attacks on communal privilege are illustrated in an inscription which records the fixing of boundaries for the town of Histria and the area of

[52] Augustan emendation of the Lex Pompeia: Pliny, *Ep.* x.79; governors' regulations: Lex Irnitana, cap.85 (González 1986 (B 235)); Jews and veterans: above, n. 22.

[53] Egyptian veterans, *GCN* 297; Chios, EJ² 317 (for a possible precedent from the republican period see J. and L. Robert, *Claros I, Les décrets hellénistiques* (Paris, 1989) p. 64, lines 43–4).

[54] EJ² 311.55–62.   [55] EJ² 311.62–71.

operation for a contractor of customs dues by decision of the governor
of Lower Moesia, Laberius Maximus, in A.D. 100. Earlier letters of three
legates of the Julio-Claudian period are quoted, repeatedly asserting the
rights of the town to revenues from fish-pickling and pine-forests in its
area. One cannot but conclude from the frequency with which these
rights were upheld that they were constantly under threat, presumably
from contractors collecting taxes for the imperial government, as the
letter of Laberius Maximus implies.[56] As for disputes between communities, reference has already been made to the case referred to the
Thessalian League by a governor in the reign of Tiberius. Greater detail
is to be found in a decree of A.D. 69, issued by the proconsul of Sardinia,
Helvius Agrippa, dealing with a dispute between the Patulcenses and
Galillenses over territorial boundaries. These had originally been established by an adjudication of a republican proconsul, recently reiterated
by an equestrian governor in A.D. 66/7, apparently acting in accordance
with the advice of the emperor Nero. It was this situation which the
Patulcenses wished to have upheld, but the Galillenses had been
encroaching on their property and had informed Agrippa's predecessor
that they could produce a document (presumably the original judgment)
from the imperial archives in Rome which would support their case and,
by implication, invalidate whatever local documentation the governors
were using. However, after two adjournments they had failed to produce
it and Agrippa's decree ordered them to vacate the disputed territory.[57]

Internal self-government was not the only important aspect of the role
of the cities. They also functioned as guarantors of the fulfilment of
obligations imposed upon them by the central government. The overall
assessment of the burden of direct personal and property taxes on a
province was imposed *en bloc*, but individual liabilities were determined
on the basis of the provincial census. It was the civic authorities who
were responsible for providing their portion of the tribute, and they
were free to determine, at least in the cases of those taxes which were not
assessed at a fixed rate, the liability of individuals, as is shown by an
inscription from Messene which gives details of the division, and
honours the magistrate who organized it.[58] Much of the work of
collecting these taxes was devolved upon the towns who appointed local
collectors and if they failed to meet their quota the responsibility for
making up the deficit fell on the community. Collection of indirect taxes
through farming remained common and the administration of some
contracts was in the hands of the civic authorities. The same practice
obtained with regard to impositions for military purposes – requisitions

---

[56] AJ 68, cf. J.H. Oliver, *GRBS* 6 (1965) 143–56.
[57] Thessalian League, EJ² 321; Sardinia, *GCN* 392.
[58] *IG* 5.1.1432f with A. Wilhelm, *JÖAI* 17 (1914) 1–120; for the dating to A.D. 35–44 (not
universally accepted) see A. Giovannini, *Rome et la circulation monétaire en Grèce* (Basel, 1978) 115–22.

of supplies, the provision of transport and billeting facilities – according to a schedule which divided the burden imposed on the province between its constituent communities.[59]

It is not difficult to see how the interests of the central government weighed heavily on the independence of the cities in these areas, where close monitoring and liaison with provincial officials were essential. The inscription from Messene, mentioned above, states that the apportionment of the tax burden by the magistrate was carried out in the presence of the praetorian legate.[60] Evidence of tax-payers failing to meet their obligations could lead provincial officials into direct intervention, either on their own initiative or at the request of the local authorities. These same officials, or sometimes the civic authorities themselves, might take opportunities to exact taxes and services above the quota, and complaints about such abuses might, on occasion, attract the attention of the provincial governor or even of the emperor; it was abuses of this kind, *inter alia*, which prompted the benevolent edict issued by the prefect of Egypt, Tiberius Iulius Alexander, in A.D. 68.[61]

The areas in which the central government exercised direct administration were very broad. The responsibilities for the military establishment, for financial affairs and for the administration of justice were interlocking and any implied division may be misleading unless it is borne in mind that, apart from the strictly military command and use of troops, a matter falling most obviously into one of these categories might also involve elements relevant to the others. The powers of officials subordinate to the governor tended to be defined by their function; a legate with judicial responsibility (*legatus iuridicus*) could handle cases involving property or financial matters, a military officer or a financial procurator would naturally deal with questions involving legal issues and the competence to do so was conferred by their administrative function. Even in matters of criminal jurisdiction, except for clearly defined and limited powers like the right to impose the death penalty (*ius gladii*), officials enjoyed great latitude and discretion, especially in dealing with non-citizens. There were occasional attempts to define the powers of governors or procurators in a specific way (and it is probably significant that these were more frequent in the second and third centuries) but more often limits and restrictions were imposed by the limits of their administrative role and the need to observe the prerogatives of other officials and the rights of communities and individuals with whom they were dealing.[62]

Organization of the functions and upkeep of the military establish-

---

[59] Mitchell 1976 (B 255), cf. *GCN* 375, 382.   [60] *IG* V.1.1432.6, 10–11.

[61] *GCN* 391.10–15, 26–9, 46.

[62] Rights of procurators and *lex* for the prefect of Egypt, Tac. *Ann.*XII.60.1–3; later evidence, Ulpian in *Mos. et Rom. leg. coll.* 14.3.1–2 (*FIRA* II, pp. 577–8), *CJ* III.26.1–4 (A.D. 197–233).

ment in a province involved a variety of tasks, normally the responsibility of the military legates, the junior officers (tribunes and *praefecti*) and the centurions. Groups of soldiers or units needed to be moved around for garrison, guard or escort duties. Numbers had to be maintained by recruitment, either in the legionary recruiting grounds or, in the case of auxiliaries, in the local area or the home province of the unit. The administration of soldiers' pay and military supplies may seem to be largely internal to the army but it must be borne in mind that these, like the organization of requisitioned transport and billeting, had wider repercussions for the province as a whole in terms of the circulation of currency and the availability, collection and movement of commodities. Some of its functions brought the army into closer contact with the civilian populace – road-building, policing, supervision of mines and quarries and of other specific establishments such as mints, factories or markets, assisting in carrying out the provincial census and transporting the *annona*; it is also likely that military personnel supervised the assignment of land to discharged veterans and performed an important escort role in frontier provinces when large numbers of inhabitants were moved and resettled. More crucially and not infrequently, the army was called upon to perform its peace-keeping role when civil disturbance or banditry threatened the *quies provinciae*.[63]

The administration of provincial finances was complex. Proconsuls had quaestors with responsibility for public finances, but in the imperial provinces this task fell on the equestrian or freedman procurators and their staffs and the regional provincial officials. The conduct of the provincial census was fundamental to the taxation system and to the general management of the controls applied to the population by fiscal means. The census, which may well have occurred at fixed intervals in all provinces although it is only sparsely attested, was probably the regular responsibility of the governor and his staff. Records of property ownership and personal status must have necessitated periodic large-scale revision, and there are likely to have been arrangements which allowed for running amendments. It was also of vital importance to maintain effective liaison with provincial communities and with the collectors and transporters of direct and indirect taxes. In some provinces management of the leasing of public land to state tenants and the collection of rents was also in the hands of provincial officials but it is impossible to make anything like a general estimate of the amount of land which fell into this category.[64]

---

[63] Civil functions: *RMR* 51; census: *ILS* 2683; transport of *annona*: O. Guéraud, *JJP* 4 (1950) 107–15; resettlement: above, n. 21; peace-keeping: Joseph. *BJ* 11.266–9, EJ[2] 227, *Dig.* 1.18.3.

[64] Evidence for the provincial census collected by Brunt 1981 (D 118); public land in Egypt, Rowlandson 1996 (E 963).

In all provinces the procuratorial officials were responsible for supervision of the interests of the imperial property (*patrimonium*), ever growing and playing an increasingly important role in the public economy.[65] Management of imperial agricultural estates is the most obvious feature but by no means the only one, since the *patrimonium* also gradually acquired widespread ownership of mines, quarries and various kinds of manufacturing establishments.[66] It exercised a more general financial control through regulation of the money supply and exchange; in this sphere above all, perhaps, the blurring of the distinction between public and patrimonial interests needs stressing, for the coinage was the emperor's, the mines were owned by the *patrimonium*, but the organization of the volume and use of money in the provinces affected all areas of the administration.[67]

The very wide interests of the fiscus in Egypt are early attested in the Code of Regulations of the Special Account (*Gnomon of the Idios Logos*), whose operations affected the status of individuals and groups (Egyptians, Greeks, Romans, metropolites, freedmen and women, priests and soldiers), and matters relevant to property, inheritance and confiscation. It is possible that it provided the precedent for the similar extension of the role of the fiscus more generally which features prominently in later legal sources.[68] The ramifications of its activity at a modest level of society are illustrated in detail by a group of papyri from the village of Socnopaiou Nesos in the Fayum concerning a dispute between two villagers named Nestnephis and Satabous.[69] In A.D. 12 Nestnephis assaulted Satabous and stole a mortar from his mill. Satabous sent letters of protest to the chief official of the nome (the *strategos*), his assistant, a centurion named Lucretius and the prefect of Egypt, informing them of this attack. Whether the matter was investigated we do not know, but in A.D. 14/15 Nestnephis sent a statement to the royal scribe of the nome accusing Satabous of having added, in that year, some vacant land (*adespotos*), which was technically the property of the *Idios Logos*, to a house which he had purchased in A.D. 11. The official in charge of the *Idios Logos*, Seppius Rufus, placed the matter on the prefect's assize list and the disputants were summoned to appear in Alexandria. In fact, Satabous did not appear and the investigation, largely conducted through correspondence, extended into the next year. The upshot was that Satabous was compelled to pay the sum of 3,500 drachmas to the *Idios Logos* for the land. This affair also illustrates the wide scope and variety of 'legal business' and emphasizes the impossibility of isolating it

[65] The much debated question of the relationship between *patrimonium* and fiscus is here avoided, cf. Millar 1963 (D 148), Brunt 1966 (D 116) and above, ch. 8.

[66] Evidence for agricultural estates and other imperial properties collected by Crawford 1976 (D 125), Millar 1977 (A 59) 175–89.   [67] See above, ch. 8.

[68] *BGU* 1210, cf. *POxy* 3014.   [69] Documents listed by Swarney 1970 (E 972) 41–2.

from other areas of administration. Provincial governors, legates and some procurators had jurisdictional powers in both criminal and civil matters. Governors and their legates, usually acting with the advice of a *consilium*, would deal with hordes of cases, petitions and disputes during their assize tours. The assize circuit (*conventus*) is central to the judicial administration of the provinces since it provided the only opportunity for dealing with business outside the provincial capital. Even so, it was far from comprehensive and, from the point of view of the provincial subject, the elements of time and space might be decisive: for almost everyone outside the capital and for almost all the time, the governor was not to hand. Naturally, the governor would not expect to deal with all judicial matters himself. Some cases could be directly delegated by provincial officials to appointed judges or jury-courts; subordinate officials in the hierarchy are also to be found performing judicial functions in matters arising within their administrative competence whilst civic authorities and institutions were permitted to retain defined and limited jurisdictional powers. For each governor, his province generated a mass of criminal charges, major or minor disputes between central government and an individual community or subject, between one community or one individual and another. Cases of murder, criminal assault, public violence or treason (*maiestas*) would naturally attract the attention of the governor, who possessed the power of capital jurisdiction, or even the emperor. Disputes between communities over property or rights to revenue, between individuals over contracts, property, inheritance, public liability or questions affecting the status of particular persons or groups might also do so, especially if the parties concerned were persistent, but many such matters were doubtless settled by officials lower down the hierarchy.

In matters dealt with at the highest level, procedure was relatively clear-cut. The first and second Augustan edicts from Cyrene present a fairly straightforward picture of the emperor responding to a provincial embassy and regulating the composition of jury-courts which heard cases delegated by the governor, and dealing with an individual sent from the province, perhaps under suspicion of *maiestas*.[70] Further down the hierarchy there was a great deal more uncertainty and confusion, as is sharply illustrated by the experiences of St Paul at Jerusalem. There, it was a tribune who arrested Paul during riots, but then allowed him to address the Jews; after further unrest he ordered Paul to be examined by scourging but on discovering that he was a Roman citizen he detained him, released him the following day to appear before the priests and the Sanhedrin but fearing another riot after his address, took him back to the barracks. After discovering a plot against Paul's life, the tribune wrote to

[70] EJ² 311.1–55.

the governor Felix and sent Paul under armed escort to Caesarea. The
trial before Felix was inconclusive and Paul was held in detention. Two
years later the Jews again initiated a prosecution before Festus, the
successor of Felix. On this occasion Paul produced his famous appeal to
Caesar and Festus, after consulting his advisers, felt compelled to allow
it. But a few days later Festus took the opportunity to discuss the matter
with the client king Herod Agrippa II, the upshot of which was a second
hearing for Paul before Festus and Agrippa. After Paul's defence Festus
and Agrippa conferred and concluded that Paul had done nothing to
merit death or imprisonment and Agrippa remarked that he could have
been discharged if he had not appealed to the emperor.[71] Earlier episodes
in Greece emphasize the blurring of the lines of demarcation between the
jurisdiction of the civic authorities and that of the provincial officials. At
Philippi Paul and Silas had been brought before the local magistrates in
the market-place by the owners of a slave girl and were ordered to be
stripped, beaten and thrown into jail. Later, however, alarmed by the
discovery that they were Roman citizens and therefore entitled not to be
punished in this way, the magistrates ordered their release. At Corinth it
was the Jews who had taken Paul before the proconsul's court but
Gallio, who happened to be on the spot, considered it a matter of internal
Jewish Law, refused to judge the case and disregarded the beating of the
synagogue leader.[72]

The incoherence of the system, if it can be called such, has recently
been described in terms to which the evidence of the Acts of the Apostles
gives point: 'The process might involve individuals of the same or
differing status, Roman or non-citizen, local communities or officials,
Roman officials or any combination. No matter, either, that all manner of
processes jostle each other: in trial by jury in the provinces or at Rome on
charges established by statute; inquiries into conduct alleged by
informers to be criminal; civil cases brought by litigants; arbitration
between communities and decisions administrative rather than legal;
police action ...'[73] From the government's point of view it had two
outstanding virtues: it was very flexible and economical with the time
and energies of the officials available and, by and large, it worked.

IV. CONCLUSION

From one point of view, the provincial administration can be analysed in
terms of the complex of coexisting relationships between the different
elements, the emperor, the provincial governor and his subordinate
officials, the province, the provincial communities as a group, the
individual community and finally the individual subject. There is a

[71] *AA* 21.31–26.32.   [72] *AA* 16.16–40, 18.12–17.   [73] Levick 1985 (D 98) 46.

temptation to argue (especially on the basis of the more abundant evidence for specific detail from the Roman East) that policy-making was not part of the dynamics of this complex of relationships, that the empire was governed, in effect, by a series of *ad hoc* decisions, the formation of which was significantly influenced by precedent. This is clearly a valid characterization of one aspect of provincial administration and it is true that observable change was rarely comprehensive and sharp, rather a series of gradual modifications. One noticeable feature is the flexibility of administrative practice and this emphasizes the importance of reaction to specific stimuli which might or might not harden into patterns and rules by the discriminating application of precedent; discrimination occurs when a decision has to be made as to whether a matter is to be dealt with in the same way as some previous, similar case or whether some new solution is to be devised. This might be described as, in essence, a system of rule by case-law with an infinite capacity for fine tuning according to the particular circumstances. Relevant circumstances might include the nature of the province, features surviving from the pre-Roman era, the status of the community, institution or individual, the positions and powers of the officials involved. Roman provincial government was not a matter of deciding, a priori, how administration was to be conducted and fitting any situation into a preordained procedure. Rather, it worked because of its capacity to grasp the essential point of any issue, to deal with it according to the means available and certain general notions governing the relationship between the imperial power and its subjects and, once dealt with, absorb it into a developing mosaic of flexible patterns and institutions.

It is notoriously difficult to extract from the items of evidence which illustrate specific cases and different relationships in action any coherent notion of an emperor forming or implementing a 'policy of provincial administration'; even less do we have programmatic statements which explicitly set out any such broad view, except in terms of general benevolence or intention to rectify known abuses. If consistent themes and policies are to be observed in the Julio-Claudian period and credited to the vision of particular emperors, they have to be drawn from disparate individual items of evidence, unevenly spread in time and space, or from observable trends: the spread of Roman citizenship, particularly in the reigns of Augustus and Claudius; the encouragement of urban communities and their aristocracies (especially in the West, where it was intimately linked to the spread of citizenship through the spread of colonial and municipal status); growth of communication systems; integration of the economic structures of town and country; the fostering of trading links within the structure of a relatively coherent

Table 2 *Provinces and governors at the end of the Julio-Claudian period*

Province	Title	Rank	Remarks
SICILIA	Proconsul	Ex-praetor	
SARDINIA	Proconsul	Ex-praetor	Governed by *praefecti/ procuratores* earlier in the Julio-Claudian period and again under the Flavians, cf. ch. 13*b*
HISPANIA TARRACONENSIS	Leg.Aug.p.p.	Ex-consul	
BAETICA	Proconsul	Ex-praetor	
LUSITANIA	Leg.Aug.p.p.	Ex-praetor	
NARBONENSIS	Proconsul	Ex-praetor	
AQUITANIA	Leg.Aug.p.p.	Ex-praetor	
LUGDUNENSIS	Leg.Aug.p.p.	Ex-praetor	
BELGICA	Leg.Aug.p.p.	Ex-praetor	
GERMANIA SUPERIOR	Leg.Aug.p.p.	Ex-consul	Until the reign of Domitian, these were military commands rather than provincial governorships, cf. ch. 13*f*
GERMANIA INFERIOR	Leg.Aug.p.p.	Ex-consul	
ALPES MARITIMAE	Procurator	*Eques*	
ALPES COTTIAE	Procurator	*Eques*	
ALPES POENINAE	Procurator	*Eques*	
BRITANNIA	Leg.Aug.p.p.	Ex-consul	
RAETIA	Procurator	*Eques*	Coupled with Alpes Poeninae until A.D. 47
NORICUM	Procurator	*Eques*	
DALMATIA	Leg.Aug.p.p.	Ex-consul	
MOESIA	Leg.Aug.p.p.	Ex-consul	Cf. ch. 13*b*
THRACE	Procurator	*Eques*	
MACEDONIA	Proconsul	Ex-praetor	
ACHAEA	Proconsul	Ex-praetor	
ASIA	Proconsul	Ex-consul	
BITHYNIA-PONTUS	Proconsul	Ex-praetor	
GALATIA	Leg.Aug.p.p.	Ex-praetor	
CAPPADOCIA	Leg.Aug.p.p.	Ex-praetor	During Nero's Parthian War governors were ex-consuls. At the beginning of the Flavian period the governor was an ex-praetor but the post was later upgraded again.
LYCIA-PAMPHYLIA	Leg.Aug.p.p.	Ex-praetor	
CYPRUS	Proconsul	Ex-praetor	
SYRIA	Leg.Aug.p.p.	Ex-consul	Included Cilicia Campestris from *c.* 44 B.C. – *c.* A.D. 72
JUDAEA	Procurator	*Eques*	Governed by an equestrian procurator until the outbreak of the First Jewish War (A.D. 66). During the war the command was held by Vespasian as consular legate. Thereafter it was normally governed by a Leg.Aug.p.p.

Table 2   (*cont.*)

Province	Title	Rank	Remarks
AEGYPTUS	Praefectus	*Eques*	
CRETE-CYRENE	Proconsul	Ex-praetor	
AFRICA	Proconsul	Ex-consul	
NUMIDIA	Leg.Aug.p.p.	Ex-praetor	Cf. ch. 13*i*
MAURETANIA CAESARIENSIS	Procurator	*Eques*	Coupled in A.D. 68/9 and again (under a Leg.Aug.p.p.) in
MAURETANIA TINGITANA	Procurator	*Eques*	A.D. 75

fiscal and taxation system in which (it has been argued[74]) the volume of currency was adjusted in a rational manner; a military establishment which infused new urban, social and economic structures into new provinces and a frame of mind which always aimed to ensure the security and peaceful development of territory in possession whilst keeping open the options for further expansion.

[74] Lo Cascio 1981 (D 144).

CHAPTER 11

THE ARMY AND THE NAVY

LAWRENCE KEPPIE

I. THE ARMY OF THE LATE REPUBLIC

By the middle of the first century B.C. the Roman army had developed over centuries of all but continuous warfare into a professionally minded force. At least fifteen legions (a total of about 60,000–70,000 men) were maintained in being each year, their manpower drawn from all Italy south of the Po. Military service was the duty of every Roman citizen aged between seventeen and forty-five. Those who enlisted were usually held for at least six years of continuous service, after which they could look for discharge. In law they remained liable for call-out as *evocati* to a maximum of sixteen years (twenty years in a crisis).[1] Some men were happy to remain in the army well beyond the six-year minimum and constituted a core of professionals for whom soldiering had become a lifetime's occupation; but conscription was employed throughout the late Republic, and it should not be imagined that the legionaries were always predominantly volunteers. Until the later second century, cavalry was formed from the *equites* (as the name implies), who might be expected to serve three years, with a maximum of ten. Thereafter Rome looked to her allies, in Italy and beyond, to make up the deficiency. (In theory the *equites* remained liable for service, but were not called upon.)

At first, military service had been viewed as an essential public duty: only men with substantial property were permitted (or could afford) to serve. However, the property-requirement was gradually reduced, and from the time of Marius no more is heard of it. No pay was at first considered necessary, but from the early fourth century a payment (*stipendium*) was introduced to cover out-of-pocket expenses; in Polybius' day (*c.* 160 B.C.) the *stipendium* stood at one third of a denarius per day, an annual rate of 120 denarii.[2] Soldiers looked to supplement it with booty. The *stipendium* was 'doubled' by Caesar, probably about 49 B.C.,

---

[1] Knowledge of the length of service rests on Polybius (VI.19.2), but the text is corrupt. The manuscripts give ten years in the cavalry and six in the infantry as the normal service requirement. The latter figure is generally emended to sixteen, given that it should be *more* than that required for the cavalry (cf. Tab. Heracleensis, *ILS* 6085. 90). Sixteen years were established as the service norm by Augustus in 13 B.C. (Dio LIV.25.5, and below, p. 377).   [2] Polyb. VI.39.12.

to 225 denarii.[3] Out of this sum the soldier had to pay towards his food, clothing and weaponry.[4] Soldiers were armed with an oval shield (*scutum*),[5] one or more throwing javelins (*pila*), a short sword of Spanish origin (*gladius*), a dagger (*pugio*), and a bronze helmet. They wore shirts of chain-mail over a leather tunic, and leather sandals.

The individual legion was a body of some 4,000–5,000 men divided into ten cohorts; in battle these could be arranged in three lines, but other dispositions are known. Each cohort was made up of six centuries, each commanded by a centurion. The centurions were soldiers of many years' experience, normally promoted from the ranks. The legions were given numerals on formation, and might remain in service for several years; but there was no permanent 'army list'.

The legions of a province came under the direct control of the proconsul or propraetor who was its governor. The legions raised each year were distributed according to current needs; some provinces had no legions at all, and might lie exposed to unexpected attack. The legion had no individual commander, but day-to-day responsibility lay with the military tribunes, six to each legion, who held command by rotation in pairs. This lack of a single permanent commanding officer in the legion had not seemed very important when armies were small and under the direct eye of the proconsul or propraetor, but as armies grew in size and the geographical extent of provinces and areas of military operations increased, some delegation of responsibility became essential. From the later third century legates were appointed, to act as assistants to the magistrate. These legates were senators, varying in age and military experience, to whom some part of the military or juridical duties could be delegated. Legates were placed in command of one or more legions, but had no long-term link within any particular unit.

No rewards were envisaged at the end of the individual's military service; men returned home to their families, to take up the threads of civilian life. Only in exceptional circumstances might they be specifically rewarded for their years of service, with a cash donative at the time of a triumph, or with a land grant on discharge, should their commander make a special effort to obtain it.

The legions had always been supported in battle by contingents drawn from their allies. Up till 90 B.C. these consisted mainly of detachments from the towns of Italy, grouped together to form *alae sociorum*. In addition infantry and cavalry had been, and continued after 90 B.C. to be, raised in the provinces and from allied kingdoms, often those in the

---

[3] Suet. *Iul.* 26.3.   [4] Polyb. VI.39.15; cf. Tac. *Ann.* 1.17.
[5] Different from the more familiar rectangular shield of the Principate (below, p. 379); illustrated at Keppie 1984 (D 202) 112–13, pl. 3.

immediate area of the war zone; each group served under its own chieftains and aristocracy, with Roman *praefecti* in overall control. Some regiments, including bodies of Cretan archers and Numidian cavalry, seem to have been kept in Roman service on a more permanent basis, and served throughout the Mediterranean.

Just as the size of the army fluctuated according to the needs of the moment, so also did the navy. Only a few ships were maintained in permanent commission in Italian ports or in dock, to be supplemented by the summoning of squadrons from allied states in the Aegean and eastern Mediterranean. A governor might appoint one of his legates to command such fleets; the ships' captains offered him professional advice. The lack of a navy adequate to keep sea lanes open was particularly evident in the 70s B.C. when pirate squadrons from bases in Cilicia operated openly and with success in the Mediterranean.

II. THE ARMY IN THE CIVIL WARS, 49–30 B.C.

The onset of civil war in 49 B.C. between Caesar and the legitimate forces of the Republic brought a swift military build-up. The legions then serving under Caesar in Gaul, numbered in a set sequence from V to XIV, formed the basis of his army thereafter. In the months following the invasion of Italy and during his consulship in 48, Caesar formed many more legions, probably numbered I–IV (the numerals tradition-ally reserved each year for the consuls to use) and from XV to about XXXIII. After Pompey's defeat three or four more were formed out of the latter's soldiers, so that by 47 B.C. the number of legions in service stood at a minimum of about 36–8; all but a few had been raised or reconstituted under Caesar's direct command. With the ending of effective resistance, Caesar's longest serving legions (composed of men who had been with him in Gaul and who had over the years agitated several times, and with good cause, for release) were discharged and settled in colonies in Italy and southern Gaul. New legions were raised to replace them. Caesar evidently intended a tight grip over Roman territory, some of it newly won. Sixteen of the legions, drawn largely from the garrisons of Macedonia and Syria, were to participate in the planned Parthian campaign.

But fate decreed otherwise. Caesar's assassination was ill-received by the serving legionaries and by the discharged veterans, most of whom had by now received the promised allotments and were settling to a new life. In the months following Caesar's death several of the protagonists, jostling for position and power, drew to their side groups of Caesar's veterans; many, perhaps all, of the recently disbanded legions were

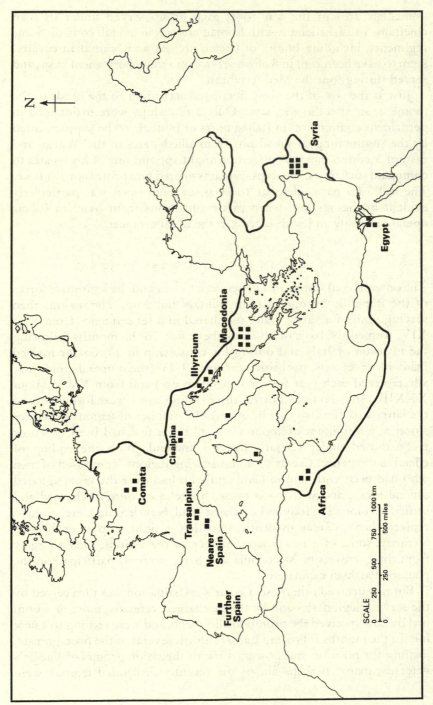

Fig. 2. Distribution of legions, 44 B.C. (After Keppie.)

reconstituted. Much emphasis was placed on their glorious antecedents; they formed the backbone of the triumviral army for the Philippi campaign and played a significant role in the victory.

After Philippi Caesar's veterans, together with time-served men of the extensive levies of 49–48 B.C., who had now fulfilled the six-year service norm, some 40,000 men in all, were released and given land in Italy. Many of the towns selected (e.g. Capua, Ariminum, Bononia)[6] lay at important road junctions, controlling access to Rome. Eleven legions were formed now from those who had not yet served the six-year minimum; many bore the old numerals and titles of formations which had been prominent in the service of Caesar and subsequently the triumvirs, and had fought at Philippi. Those legions, with their battle-honours, titles and emblems, had become household names and were important as visible supporters of the triumvirs, the natural successors of the dead and deified Caesar. After the sea battle at Actium, in which the legions had played little part, a week of negotiation ensured that Antony's soldiers received adequate rewards for their long years of service: land in the provinces, but probably not in Italy itself. Some of the most senior of the Antonian legions were accepted intact into Octavian's army. Octavian could pose as reuniting the old Caesarian army under himself as the dictator's intended heir. His own legions received land in Italy, in twenty-eight colonies.[7] The legions which emerged from the civil wars were to remain in permanent commission throughout the following three centuries or more, unless disgraced or destroyed in battle.

Bodies of native infantry and cavalry serving with the legions on campaign in the civil wars of the later first century B.C. are repeatedly mentioned in the literary sources. They were numbered in thousands, and formed an important adjunct to the armies of each protagonist. Bodies of slingers, foot-archers, horse-archers and even elephants are reported. Caesar's wide-ranging campaigns carried Gallic, German and Spanish troops to the furthest corners of the empire; 10,000 Spanish and Gallic cavalry participated in Antony's Armenian campaign.[8] Octavian continued to recruit auxiliaries from the western provinces under his control. In the East Pompey, the Liberators and later Antony were able to draw on the armies of client kings in Thrace, Asia Minor, Syria, Judaea and Egypt, summoned to service by virtue of treaty obligations or *force majeure*. They often served (as during the Republic) under their tribal chief, or a member of his family, or local nobility. Contingents of

---

[6] App. *BCiv* iv.3.
[7] *RG* 28.2. For a decree of Octavian conferring practical benefits on veterans in a provincial context, *CIL* xvi, p. 145, no. 10 = EJ[2] 302.   [8] Plut. *Ant.* 37.3.

varying strength are reported, and it is uncertain whether they were yet organized into regiments of standard size.

Seapower and the ability to transport troops overseas became important in the civil wars. Substantial fleets, gathered by Pompey, and later by the Liberators, Sextus Pompeius and Antony from the allied states of the Aegean and the eastern Mediterranean, made a formidable force. Octavian had much less opportunity to gain access to warships from these traditional sources, and was forced to build up his own navy almost from scratch. After initial setbacks through inexperience and ill-luck, this new fleet was to prove superior in the end, at Mylae, Naulochus and Actium.[9] In the mid-30s, in preparation for an offensive against Sextus Pompeius, Agrippa saw to the construction of a major harbour and stores complex at Lake Avernus on the Bay of Naples; it was given the name Portus Iulius in honour of Octavian. Foundations of some of its quayside buildings have been located below the shallow waters of the bay.[10]

Squadrons of ships with legionaries on board acting as marines cruised in the Mediterranean; some civil-war legions even adopted the title *Classica*, an epithet which must reflect their service at sea.[11] At Actium we know that Antony embarked 20,000 legionaries (i.e. four legions) for the battle, and Octavian placed eight legions on his ships (including legion XI, some of whose veterans adopted a surname *Actiacus* in later years, in proud commemoration of their role), together with five praetorian cohorts.[12]

III. THE ARMY AND NAVY OF AUGUSTUS

1. The Legions

By the middle of Augustus' reign the number of legions in service stood at twenty-eight. Almost all had seen service in the civil wars. They were numbered from I to XXII, with some numerals duplicated, the result of the acceptance into an already complete sequence of Antonian legions after Actium. The highest number in the sequence is XXII, a legion surnamed *Deiotariana* to commemorate King Deiotarus of Galatia, an ally of Pompey and later Caesar in the civil wars, who had raised local troops on the Roman model. The legion seems likely to have gained its numeral by 25 B.C. at the latest, when the kingdom of Galatia was

---

[9] For a Cilician navarch who served Octavian and was suitably rewarded, see P. Roussel, *Syria* 15 (1934) 33–74; *CIL* XVI, p. 145, no. 11 = EJ 301.

[10] Strab. V.4.5 (244C); Vell. Pat. II.79.2; Virg. *G.* II.161; Suet. *Aug.* 16.1; G. Schmiedt (ed.), *Atlante aereofotografico delle sedi umane in Italia; parte II, le sedi antiche scomparse* (Firenze, 1970) tav. cxxxvi.   [11] *ILS* 2231, 2232.

[12] Plut. *Ant.* 64; Oros. VI.19.8; L. J. F. Keppie, *CR* 85(1971) 329–30.

incorporated into the empire. The Augustan sequence of legions had thus reached its final form by that date, and older theories about the gradual increase in forces throughout the reign, and especially at the time of the Pannonian revolt and the Varian disaster, can be set aside.

The legions were disposed in the frontier provinces of the empire, mostly in those provinces controlled by Augustus himself through his legates. As new provinces were added under Augustus, the legions moved forward to aid in the conquest. The precise areas of service of many legions are unknown in the Augustan period; much movement of forces can be assumed as provinces were pacified or extended. For a time Egypt had three legions; by A.D. 23 the garrison was reduced to two.[13] Spain in the 20s B.C. had upwards of seven legions; by about A.D. 14 the garrison had been cut to three.[14] The loss of three legions (numbered XVII, XVIII and XIX) on the Rhine frontier in A.D. 9 with Varus led to substantial westward transfers to fill the gap.[15] In all, twenty-five legions were in service at the close of the reign. The total had not been increased to match the enlargement of the areas to be controlled, or to make good the losses of A.D. 9: the financial burden was simply too great.

Throughout the late Republic the length of service required of a man joining the legions had been a minimum of six years. But the civil wars witnessed a lengthening of the period spent with the standards. Sometimes, it is clear, men were willing to remain under arms, but others certainly were not, and made their feelings clear whenever the opportunity arose. In 16–14 B.C. Augustus and Agrippa oversaw a substantial programme of colonization and land-settlement in the provinces, very probably to cater for men who had enlisted in the aftermath of Actium. On his return to Rome in 13 Augustus ordained that army service in the legions should in future be for a fixed term of sixteen years (which had in any case been the republican maximum, though not the norm), and that those who survived would obtain a cash reward, in place of the land allotments which had become common in recent decades, especially during the civil wars. Cassius Dio's report[16] indicates that the soldiers would still have preferred land, but it was no longer politically acceptable to establish colonies in Italy itself, with the attendant ill-feeling and disruption. The sixteen years of service were to be followed by a further four years in reserve. (This too had a republican precedent, as men could be asked to serve a maximum of twenty years in times of special danger.)[17] In A.D. 5 the service requirement was further increased, to a minimum of twenty years, plus five in reserve. There is no record of the amount of gratuity fixed in 13 B.C., but Dio's account of the new regulations implies that in A.D. 5 it was *increased* to 3,000 denarii.[18]

---

[13] Strab. XVII.1.12 (797–8c); Tac. *Ann.* IV.5. Speidel 1982 (E 969).   [14] Jones 1976 (E 226).
[15] Syme 1933 (D 238).   [16] LIV.25.5.   [17] Polyb. VI.19.4.   [18] Dio LV.23.1.

Centurions were paid at much higher rates, and could become wealthy men. To deal with the problem of financing the army, Augustus in A.D. 5 began by proposing that public funds be allocated annually for military pay and rewards.[19] This proposal came to nothing, and in the following year he took the initiative in establishing an *aerarium militare* (military treasury); Augustus himself provided pump-priming funds, and introduced a 5 per cent tax on inheritances, none too popular with the citizenry, which, together with the proceeds from an evidently pre-existing 1 per cent tax on auctions, went to maintaining its cash reserves.[20] The purpose of the *aerarium militare* was to dispense cash gratuities to time-served veterans.[21] Whether the *aerarium* also provided funds to *pay* serving soldiers – as might seem natural and as both Dio and Suetonius seem to indicate – is not clear;[22] but the soldiers themselves thought of both their pay and their gratuities as coming direct from the emperor. By fixing cash rewards and regulating the length of service to be completed before receiving them, Augustus swept away the uncertainties of past generations. Yet he and his successors did not always live up to their responsibilities.[23] Soldiers were forbidden, probably by Augustus, to marry during service, and any marriages already existing were dissolved on enlistment.[24] Voluntary enlistment was preferred, but conscription was employed as the occasion demanded, notably in A.D. 6 after the outbreak of the Pannonian revolt, and in A.D. 9 after the Varus disaster.[25]

During Augustus' reign changes were introduced in the command structure of the legions, which took account of the fact that they had become permanent, self-perpetuating formations. Legates, usually ex-praetors, but sometimes ex-quaestors, ex-aediles and ex-plebeian tribunes, began to be appointed by Augustus directly to command a specific legion and held office, with the title *legatus legionis* (legionary legate), for a period of several years. An equestrian officer with the title *praefectus castrorum* (prefect of the camp) was appointed to supervise the running of each legion's permanent base-camp. The military tribunes remained, but in the hierarchy of command ranked below the *praefectus castrorum*, except that one of their number who held senatorial status necessarily outranked the *praefectus*, and nominally at least was second-in-command below the legate. In Egypt, from which senators were excluded, command of a legion fell to the *praefectus castrorum*. So far as can be determined, the internal organization of the legion remained unchanged, except that a small body of cavalry (the *equites legionis*) was

[19] Dio LV.24.9.

[20] Dio LV.24.9; Suet. *Aug.* 49.2; cf. Tac. *Ann.* 1.78, 11.42; Suet. *Calig.* 16; Dio LIX.9.6.

[21] *RG* 17.   [22] Corbier 1977 (D 123).

[23] Below, p. 379; cf. also Suet. *Tib.* 48, *Calig*, 44, *Ner.* 32.1.

[24] Dio LX.24.3; Campbell 1978 (D 172).   [25] Suet. *Aug.* 24.1; Tac. *Ann.* 1.16ff.

added to its complement, seemingly for escort and scouting duties.[26] The size of the legion, at full strength, was probably about 5,000–5,200 men.

Some alterations in equipment can be detected from the archaeological and sculptural record: the oval shield gave way to a curving rectangular or near-rectangular shield, and the shirt of chain mail to a cuirass of articulated iron strips (the *lorica segmentata*). The new shape of shield and sophisticated body-armour afforded greater protection to the individual soldier. Whether the changes were imposed from Rome, or came about more gradually is not yet clear. Later it seems that there might be a substantial variation in equipment between provincial armies. Archaeological evidence has also identified some of the army's temporary and permanent installations of this time, especially along and beyond the Rhine.[27] In other provinces little is known, though for Spain mention can be made of the recently identified legionary fortress at Rosinos de Vidriales south of Astorga, which seems likely to have been built before the end of Augustus' reign.[28]

Augustus had introduced fundamental changes, which were not universally popular. In A.D. 14, when his death was announced to the legions on the Rhine and in Pannonia, the legionaries saw a chance to voice their grievances: long service (well beyond the limits set down by Augustus), low rates of pay, harshness and corruption of the centurions, and a prospect for the survivors of settlement on poor upland soils far from home.[29] The legionaries asked to be released at the end of sixteen years (the old republican maximum) and to have their *praemia militiae* (rewards of military service) in cash, paid immediately upon release. Concessions extorted from Germanicus were rescinded in A.D. 15.[30]

2. Auxiliary forces

The task of maintaining the integrity of the empire did not fall on the legions alone; it was shared between Rome and her subject peoples. With the close of the civil wars, many of the regiments formed from tribal groups and allied kingdoms were disbanded or went home, but others, whose lifespan had been lengthened out by the civil wars and had acquired a permanence akin to the legions, seem likely to have been retained to act in support of the legions in the wars of Augustus' reign.[31] Such forces were normally supplemented, in time of active war, by substantial bodies of troops drawn from client states and tribes in close proximity to the theatre of operations; there was at this time no clear dividing line between the two categories. These *auxilia* (or *auxiliares*)

[26] Breeze 1969 (D 166).   [27] See below, pp. 524–8.   [28] Le Roux 1982 (E 228) 105.
[29] Tac. *Ann.* 1.17ff, 78; Wilkes 1963 (C 414).   [30] Tac. *Ann.* 1.78.
[31] Saddington 1982 (D 227).

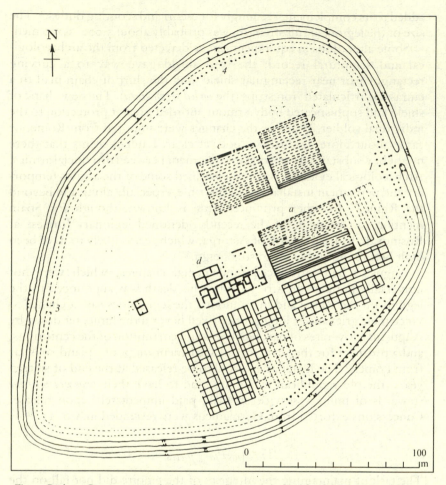

Fig. 3. Rödgen, Germany: ground-plan of Augustan supply base. (After Schönberger and Simon.)
A growing number of installations have been identified east of the Rhine, which can be related to the
various campaigns between 13 B.C. and A.D. 16. The supply base at Rödgen had an area of 3.3
hectares (8 acres). Within a rampart and double ditch were a number of timber-framed buildings:
three granaries (a–c), a headquarters or commandant's house (d), and barracks (e). There were 4
gates (1–4); the chief entrance lay on the east side.

were formed (now, if not earlier) into *cohortes* (cohorts) of infantry and
alae (wings) of cavalry. There were also some regiments which combined
infantry and cavalry; these were termed *cohortes equitatae*. Most regiments
were about 500 men strong.

   The auxiliaries of the early Empire were usually drawn from the non-
citizen populations of newly won provinces of the empire, often those
under the emperor's direct control. Regiments attested under Augustus

or his immediate successors were drawn from Gaul, Spain, the Rhineland and the Alpine territories, Dalmatia, the Danube lands and Thrace,
north Africa and the East. Recruitment (initially, it must be supposed,
under treaty obligations), served to draw off the young tribesmen and
harness their vigour in the empire's defence.[32] Often, regiments were
stationed in, or close to, their area of origin, and local deployment was
taken for granted. The *cohortes* and *alae* were normally named after the
tribe from which they were recruited (e.g. *cohors VI Nerviorum* from the
Nervii of Gallia Belgica), or the name of the city-state of origin in the
more urbanized East (e.g. *ala I Hamiorum*, from the town of Hama in
Syria). A few regiments, mainly *alae* of cavalry, were named in honour of
distinguished Romans (for example, *ala Agrippiana*, probably from
Agrippa), or sometimes after their founder or first prefect (for example,
the *ala Scaevae*, from Caesar's stalwart centurion, *ala Atectorigiana*, after a
Gaul Atectorix, and *ala Indiana*, from Iulius Indus). Recruitment from
the homeland was kept up; very probably this was part of the treaty
obligation. Auxiliary regiments were equipped according to local
custom and tradition, with the weapons they knew well. Those regiments stationed along a major frontier such as the Rhine lay in close
proximity to the legionary encampments.

Tacitus, in a valuable comment, notes the strength of auxiliary forces
in A.D. 23 as about the same as the legions, i.e. some 150,000 men.[33] It was
not, he felt, worthwhile giving the numbers in each province, as these
did not remain constant; indeed the total in service fluctuated according
to the needs of the moment. Few regiments in service under Augustus
can be identified by name from the epigraphic evidence, and the listing of
provincial garrisons hardly becomes possible before the Flavian period.
Conditions of service at this time are not well attested: whether or not
auxiliary regiments supplied under treaty obligations always received
pay from Augustus is uncertain. There may have been no standard
length of service – some auxiliaries are known to have served over thirty
years. It is unlikely that any gratuity was automatically payable on
completion of service, but individuals might be rewarded, with citizenship, privileges and cash bounties.[34]

Legions and auxiliaries operated in tandem on campaign: Varus in
Germany in A.D. 9 marched with six cohorts of infantry and three *alae* of
cavalry, in addition to his three legions. Tiberius at Sirmium in A.D. 7
mustered ten legions, more than seventy cohorts, and ten *alae*.[35] In any
garrison cohorts of infantry were normally in the majority.

Regiments of *auxilia* were commanded by prefects, with the title
praefectus cohortis (of infantry) or *praefectus equitum* (of an *ala* of cavalry).

[32] Dio LIV.22.5.   [33] Tac. *Ann.* IV.5.   [34] *ILS* 2531.   [35] Vell. Pat. II.117.1, II.113.1.

Often the prefects were tribal nobles, though the closeness of the link with their tribe is sometimes obscured by the Roman names they bore as a result of an individual grant of citizenship. Arminius, later to spearhead the successful resistance to Roman domination east of the Rhine, had gained Roman citizenship and equestrian status in return for his military exploits, probably as a *praefectus*, in the wars of Augustus' reign.[36] Where Roman officers were appointed as prefects, these were often centurions of substantial military experience, especially *primipilares* (former chief centurions of a legion), or men of equestrian rank, often former tribunes in a legion. For a time Augustus appointed sons of senators in pairs to command *alae*, seemingly as an alternative to the legionary tribunate.[37] There was as yet no set sequence or hierarchy in the grading of such appointments.

Excessive reliance on the military potential of recently subjected peoples entailed some risk. Loyalty to the communities from which they had been raised might prove stronger than to Rome. The Pannonian revolt in A.D. 6 was fuelled by an unwise concentration of Dalmatian auxiliaries for the campaign against Maroboduus, when the auxiliaries saw a chance to throw off the Roman yoke.[38]

Regiments were formed on the Roman model in the territories of client kings, especially in the East. Herod used Roman officers to command his forces, which included Gauls and Germans.[39] Maroboduus, on the fringe of the Roman world, based the organization and training of his own forces on the successful Roman exemplar.[40] Rather later, during the reign of Tiberius, cohorts nominally serving a client king in Thrace mutinied on the rumour that they were to be posted away from their homeland, and their ethnic homogeneity diluted; fierce fighting ensued before they admitted defeat.[41]

A few auxiliary cohorts were raised among Roman citizens. Under the Empire there are records of at least six *cohortes ingenuorum civium Romanorum* ('cohorts of freeborn Roman citizens') and a large number (at least thirty-two) *cohortes voluntariorum civium Romanorum* ('cohorts of Roman citizen volunteers'). Almost certainly the creation of these regiments belongs during the crises of A.D. 6–9. The literary sources are unanimous in emphasizing the difficulties faced by Augustus in raising extra forces to meet these emergencies.[42] A *dilectus ingenuorum* ('levy of free men') was held at Rome itself in A.D. 9;[43] in part this supplied recruits

---

[36] Vell. Pat. 11.118.
[37] Suet. *Aug.* 38.2. For examples, see *ILS* 911 = EJ[2] 195 = H. Devijver, *Prosopographia Militiarum Equestrium quae fuerunt ab Augusto ad Gallienum* (Leuven, 1977) (hereafter *PME*), N.15; *ILS* 912 = *PME* A 162; *CIL* VI 3516 = *PME* C 257.   [38] Dio LV.29.1; cf. Tac. *Ann.* III.41–2.
[39] Joseph. *BJ* 1.20(397), 1.27(535), 1.33(672), 11.3(52), 11.5(74).
[40] Vell. Pat. 11.109.1.   [41] Tac. *Ann.* IV.46.
[42] Dio LV.31, LVI.23; Vell. Pat. 11.111; Pliny, *HN* VII.149; Suet. *Aug.* 25.2.
[43] *AE* 1973, 501 = EJ[2] 368; Tac. *Ann.* 1.16, 31; Brunt 1974 (B 214).

for the legions, but it may also have produced the *cohortes ingenuorum*, from men unfit or unsuitable for the legions. The *cohortes voluntariorum c.R.* seem likely to have been formed out of freed slaves summoned to service by Augustus; the epithet *voluntariorum* highlights a willingness to serve not shared by other elements of society.[44] A few other citizen cohorts seem also to have been raised early in Augustus' reign in Italy and beyond. The commanders of these citizen cohorts were styled tribunes. Their intermediate status, between legionaries and auxiliaries, was emphasized in Augustus' will in A.D. 14: they received the same donative as legionaries.[45] Later it seems that they were treated as auxiliaries and drew their manpower from non-citizens.

3. The navy

The value of retaining a substantial fleet in permanent commission had been amply demonstrated during the civil wars. Two major bases were established by Octavian in the years immediately following Actium: one was placed at Cape Misenum, at the western end of the Bay of Naples (replacing Portus Iulius, which was abandoned, despite the considerable efforts expended on its construction). The other base was at Ravenna, near the head of the Adriatic.[46] From 31 B.C. (or even earlier) a squadron was maintained at Forum Iulii (Fréjus) on the south coast of Gaul where substantial storage and administrative buildings have been postulated; but the base there soon ceased to have a major role.[47] From later evidence it seems that ships based at Misenum patrolled the western Mediterranean and the coastline of Africa and Egypt, while those at Ravenna had a more restricted role in the Adriatic and the Aegean. Both major fleets had out-stations on Corsica and Sardinia, at Ostia and at Rome itself.

The combined strength of the two major fleets can be estimated only roughly, at about 15,000–20,000 men, perhaps manning some 75–100 ships. Their crews formed a useful source of trained manpower within Italy. From epigraphic sources and sculptured reliefs it can be seen that the ships were mainly triremes, with a few quadriremes, together with some light vessels, known as liburnians. The ships were individually named, after rivers, gods, goddesses, and personifications, male and female. Individual ships were commanded by trierarchs, squadrons by navarchs, and each of the major fleets by a *praefectus classis*. The strong tradition of seamanship in the Greek East and the lack of matching Roman expertise is reflected in the Greek names given to the ships, the

---

[44] Dio LV.31.1, LVI.23.3; Vell. Pat. II.111.1; Suet. *Aug.* 25.2. Note especially Macrob. *Sat.* 1.11.32. See also Kraft 1951 (E 672) 87ff.   [45] Tac. *Ann.* 1.8.   [46] Pliny, *HN* III.119.

[47] Strab. IV.1.9 (184c); Tac. *Ann.* IV.5, *Hist.* III.43; Cf. *ILS* 2688 = *PME* A 201 for a *praefectus classis* there under Tiberius. Tac. *Hist.* III.43 implies that the port retained some importance in A.D. 69.

titles of officers and skilled personnel; under Augustus trierarchs and navarchs were often recruited from maritime city-states of the East. The fleet-prefects at this time were usually ex-legionary tribunes or ex-chief centurions. The crews were drawn from non-citizen provincials, together with some freedmen; slaves, briefly employed in the civil wars of the late Republic when manpower was scarce, were not used. Sentencing criminals to the galleys was not a punishment employed in Roman times. The crews were organized on a military model, with oarsmen and marines forming a *centuria*, under the command of a (non-citizen) centurion. The fleets kept the Mediterranean safe for merchant shipping; very little is heard about piracy.

4. The praetorian guard and other troops at Rome

In the Republic a magistrate on campaign in his province regularly formed a small bodyguard from the troops at his disposal. It was given the name *cohors praetoria* ('commander's cohort'). Caesar never formed such a battalion, though he once flattered the soldiers of legion X by claiming that they fulfilled this role.[48] In the civil wars several commanders are known to have had praetorian cohorts. After Philippi 8,000 time-served veterans who rejected the proffered land-allotments were retained by Octavian and Antony to serve as praetorians.[49] At Actium we know that Octavian had five cohorts present, of uncertain size; rather earlier there is a report that Antony had three cohorts.[50]

After Actium, Octavian continued to employ *cohortes praetoriae* which became a permanent 'household division'; they were attached to the military headquarters (*praetorium*) which he maintained as a proconsul. In A.D. 23 nine cohorts were in being.[51] At first, for political reasons, Augustus based only three of the cohorts at Rome itself, and had them billeted about the city in small groups, to avoid the overt appearance of armed force.[52] Initially the cohorts were responsible directly to Augustus himself, but in 2 B.C. he appointed two equestrians as *praefecti praetorio*, i.e. prefects of the *praetorium*.[53] These were men of administrative ability rather than military expertise. Normally, throughout the Julio-Claudian period, there continued to be two prefects, but on occasion a single individual held sole command (Aelius Seianus, 14–31; Sutorius Macro, 31–8; Afranius Burrus, 51–62). The role of the cohorts was to support the emperor's position in Rome, and accompany him on his travels. They served too as ceremonial troops on state occasions.

During the civil wars the manpower of praetorian cohorts had been drawn from time-served veterans, or men of long experience, heavy with

---

[48] Caes. *BGall.* 1.42. [49] App. *BCiv.* v.3. [50] Oros. VI.19.8; Plut. *Ant.* 39, 53.
[51] Tac. *Ann.* IV.5. [52] Suet. *Aug.* 49, *Tib.* 37.1; Tac. *Ann.* IV.2. [53] Dio LV.10.10.

honour and medals.[54] They were thus an elite force made up of specially chosen individuals. However under Augustus (and later) the praetorians were recruited directly from civilian life, in Italy itself; at first recruits were drawn chiefly from Latium, Etruria and Umbria, and from the old colonies of the Republic.[55] In 13 B.C. service in the praetorian cohorts was fixed at twelve years, later increased in A.D. 5 to sixteen years.[56] Pay was set at well above the legionary rate; by A.D. 14 it had risen to 750 denarii per year.[57] The legionaries far away in the frontier provinces of the empire soon became jealous of the privileged position and higher pay of the praetorians.[58]

The nine cohorts of the guard (if we may use this term, which has no Latin equivalent) were each commanded by a tribune; most tribunes had already been *primus pilus* (chief centurion) in a legion. The size of each cohort under Augustus is not reported, but it most probably consisted of 480 men on the legionary model, divided into centuries of eighty men. The praetorians were armed as legionaries, but interestingly they retained into the Empire some of the equipment used by soldiers of the late Republic. The ceremonial uniforms of Britain's Guards Brigade may be compared. On duty in Rome the praetorians carried weapons, but wore civilian dress.[59] Each cohort had a small cavalry component.

To match the three praetorian cohorts stationed at Rome itself, three *cohortes urbanae* were formed, soon to be placed under the supervision of a senatorial *praefectus urbi*. These urban cohorts served as a police force for the city. A fourth cohort was soon formed, and stationed at Lugdunum, presumably to protect the imperial mint there.[60] The cohorts, which were commanded by tribunes (ex-chief centurions), were probably 480 men strong. Soldiers of the urban cohorts at Rome (numbered X–XII, in continuation of the praetorian series) had to serve for twenty years.

In A.D. 6, seven *cohortes vigilum* (of uncertain initial size) were formed as a fire-watch for the fourteen *regiones* into which Augustus had divided the city, under an equestrian *praefectus vigilum*.[61] The establishment of this permanent force replaced earlier haphazard attempts to protect the city from all too frequent conflagrations; the *vigiles* may also have acted as a night-time police force, but they were not armed as soldiers. Members of the cohorts were freedmen; from later evidence it may be inferred that after six years (which may have been the service norm), they obtained full citizenship. The *cohortes vigilum* were officered by tribunes who had been chief centurions of a legion.

For his personal protection Augustus established a small body of

---

[54] App. *BCiv.* III. 45, 67–9, V.3, 95; Plut. *Ant.* 53.   [55] Tac. *Ann.* IV.5.
[56] Dio LIV.25.6, LV.23.1.   [57] Dio LIII.11.5; Tac. *Ann.* I.8.
[58] Tac. *Ann.* I.17; *Hist.* II.67, 92–4.   [59] Tac. *Ann.* XVI.27, *Hist.* I.38.
[60] Tac. *Ann.* III.41.   [61] Dio LV.26.4; Strab. V.3.7 (234–5C); Suet. *Aug.* 25.2.

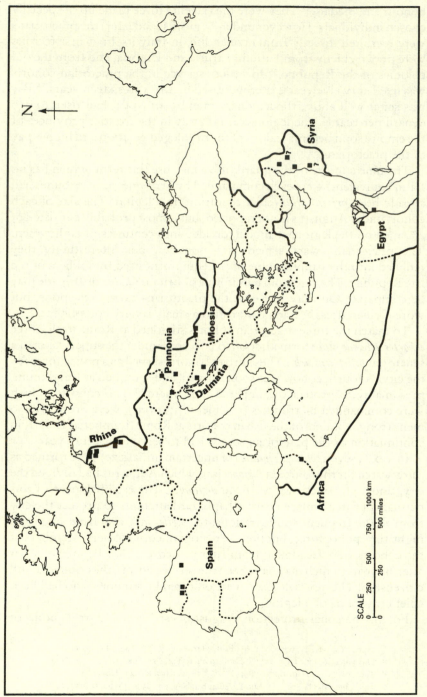

Fig. 4. Distribution of legions, A.D. 14. (After Keppie.)

mounted bodyguards, the *Germani corporis custodes*, recruited from Rhineland tribes, principally Batavians.[62] This force, the successor to bodyguards recruited during the civil wars of the late Republic, remained in being until disbanded by Galba.

IV. ARMY AND NAVY UNDER THE JULIO-CLAUDIANS

When expansionist policies were abandoned late in Augustus' reign, the empire settled to a generation of peaceful development. The army was stationed largely along the outer limits of the empire, and was principally engaged in the consolidation of Roman control. As time passed, large concentrations of military forces, assembled at strategic points along the frontiers in preparation for further advance, gave way to a more even distribution. Temporary encampments gradually took on a more permanent air. The role of the army became increasingly defensive, greater attention being paid to preserving the integrity of those areas controlled by Rome against attack from without. This attitude was to lead, from the later first century onwards, to the physical construction of frontier lines which in some areas constituted a clear demarcation line between land under full Roman control and the tribes beyond.

The distribution of the legions at the death of Augustus can be fairly well defined, though the location of individual legions within a province may remain somewhat uncertain.[63] The army of a province could consist of up to four legions (Syria and the two German 'districts' each had four), along with auxiliaries in perhaps a roughly equal number. Some provinces, less threatened by external foes, had a garrison consisting of auxiliary *cohortes* and *alae*, but no legions. The epigraphic evidence, which increases enormously in volume as the century progresses, allows a picture to be built up of dispositions and transfers of legions and auxiliaries, as imperial policies (or external pressures) changed. A careful balance was evidently maintained between the total strength of forces on the Rhine, on the Danube and in the East. The needs of a major campaign for additional troops in a particular area were met by the temporary, sometimes permanent, transfers of legions and auxiliary troops. For example, legion IX Hispana was sent from the Danube to Africa for four years in the middle of Tiberius' reign; in the course of Corbulo's campaigns in the East, three legions were transferred in succession from the Balkans to augment his forces.[64] Thus pressure on one frontier of the empire was often met by weakening the defences at another. Soon, however, the practice developed of putting together *vexillationes* (detachments) from the increasingly static garrisons to form

---

[62] Bellen 1981 (D 160); Speidel 1984 (D 236).
[63] Tac. *Ann.* IV.3 gives the disposition of the Roman army in A.D. 23.
[64] Tac. *Ann.* III.9, IV.23, XIII.35, XV.6, 25.

Table 3 *The legions of the early Empire*

Legion	Station in A.D. 14	Station in A.D. 70
I Germanica	Lower Germany	(disbanded A.D. 70)
I Adiutrix	(formed A.D. 68)	Upper Germany
II Adiutrix	(formed A.D. 69)	Britain
I Italica	(formed A.D. 66)	Moesia
II Augusta	Upper Germany	Britain
III Augusta	Africa	Africa
III Cyrenaica	Egypt	Egypt
III Gallica	Syria	Syria
IV Macedonica	Spain	(disbanded A.D. 70)
IV Scythica	Moesia	Syria
IV Flavia	(formed A.D. 69–70)	Dalmatia
V Alaudae	Lower Germany	(?disbanded A.D. 70)
V Macedonica	Moesia	Moesia
VI Ferrata	Syria	Syria
VI Victrix	Spain	Lower Germany
VII Claudia	Dalmatia	Moesia
VII Gemina	(formed A.D. 68)	Tarraconensis
VIII Augusta	Pannonia	Upper Germany
IX Hispana	Pannonia	Britain
X Fretensis	Syria	Judaea
X Gemina	Spain	Lower Germany
XI Claudia	Dalmatia	Upper Germany
XII Fulminata	Syria	Cappadocia?[65]
XIII Gemina	Upper Germany	Pannonia
XIV Gemina	Upper Germany	Upper Germany
XI Apollinaris	Pannonia	Pannonia
XV Primigenia	(formed A.D. 39–42)	(disbanded A.D. 70)
XVI Gallica	Upper Germany	(disbanded A.D. 70)
XVI Flavia	(formed A.D. 69–70)	Syria[66]
XVII	(lost with Varus, A.D. 9)	
XVIII	(lost with Varus, A.D. 9)	
XIX	(lost with Varus, A.D. 9)	
XX Valeria	Lower Germany	Britain
XXI Rapax	Lower Germany	Lower Germany
XXII Deiotariana	Egypt	Egypt
XXII Primigenia	(formed A.D. 39–42)	Lower Germany

	A.D. 14	A.D. 70
Total in service:	25	28 or 29

task-forces, to be sent to another province; this avoided leaving a long stretch of the frontier devoid of its garrison.[67] Major campaigns could still lead to the creation of new legions, which were normally raised in Italy itself: under Caligula or Claudius two new legions, XV and XXII Primigenia (First-Born) were formed, to release seasoned troops for the projected invasion of Britain; in A.D. 66 Nero formed a new legion, I Italica (Italian), for his planned expedition to the Caucasus.[68] Otherwise

[65] *AE* 1983, 927; D. van Berchem, *MH* 40 (1983) 185–96.   [66] *Ibid.*
[67] Saxer 1967 (D 228).   [68] Ritterling 1925 (D 223) 1758, 1797, 1407; Suet. *Ner.* 19.

the number of legions in service remained constant, until the particular requirements of the civil war after Nero's death led to the formation of new legions and its aftermath to the disbandment of several long-established entities (see Table 3).

The legions of the Republic had been composed of Italians, the traditional manpower source, though during the civil wars all the protagonists from Caesar onwards succeeded in augmenting their forces by forming 'legions' from the non-citizen populations of their provinces and by training and arming them in the Roman manner. Though Octavian sent home non-Romans found serving in Antony's legions, he was prepared soon to accept XXII Deiotariana into his permanent army, and later in his reign he had recourse to non-Roman sources to fill out the ranks, especially in the East.[69] Italians who had been prepared to serve in the civil wars for a fairly short term proved unwilling to spend a span of twenty-five years or more, much of their adult life, in a frontier province far from home. Greater emphasis was placed on seeking recruits in the provinces, where (it seems clear) men were eager and willing to serve, and saw in legionary service a route to social advancement.[70] Some of these men would be citizens, sons of Italian families long resident there, or of colonists of the Caesarian and Augustan periods, but it is suspected that increasingly non-citizens were enlisted, and given citizenship and Roman names on enlistment. By the close of the Julio-Claudian age it is likely that less than half of all legionaries throughout the empire had been born in Italy; in the East the proportion was probably very small indeed.

The realization that the empire had all but reached its manageable limits deprived the army of its traditional role. Long decades of relative peace could easily sap morale, as Corbulo discovered in Syria early in Nero's reign.[71] Energetic commanders occupied the troops' energies with route marches and manoeuvres; the troops were much involved with the internal security of the provinces in which they were stationed. The army also formed a useful reserve of disciplined manpower, to be drafted in to undertake construction and labouring work, a role the soldiers deeply detested.[72] The very presence of the army had a substantial impact on the developing economies of the provinces; the soldiers had to be fed and clothed, and had money to spend. At the close of their military service (which between 40 per cent and 50 per cent might be likely to survive), most legionaries received a gratuity in cash, but some were settled (as of old) with land grants in colonies, in or near the provinces where they had served, and constituted bulwarks of loyalty to the system which they had once served. Under Claudius

---

[69] ILS 2483 = EJ² 261.   [70] Tac. Ann. IV.4.   [71] Tac. Ann. XIII.35.
[72] Plut. Mar. 15; Tac. Ann. 1.20, XI.20, XIII.53; Suet. Aug. 18.

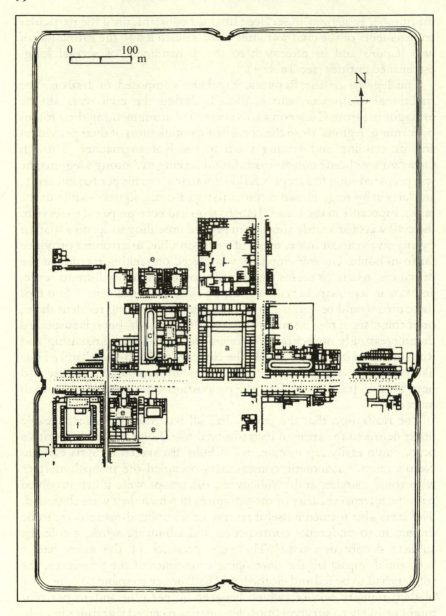

Fig. 5. Vetera (Xanten), Germany: ground-plan of a double legionary fortress, Neronian date.
(After Bogaers and Rüger.) By the end of Augustus' reign the chief control points along the west
bank of the Rhine had been established. Little is known of the fortress built at Xanten at that time, or
about Tiberian or Claudian successors. The Neronian fortress was 56 hectares (138 acres) in size.
Note: stone-built headquarters (a), two houses for legates (b, c), workshops (d), tribunes' houses (e)
and hospital (f). Tacitus vividly describes the siege of Vetera by rebels in A.D. 69, after which the
fortress was resited in a more commanding position.

veterans of the legions stationed in Britain, then newly added to the empire, were settled at Colchester (Camulodunum), those of the Rhine legions at Cologne and those of Syria at Akko (Ptolemais). An attempt by Nero to resume colonization in Italy itself met with little success.[73]

While legionary organization and service conditions under the early Empire were more or less fixed by the time of the death of Augustus, the auxiliary forces and the fleet took longer to reach their permanent form. An important stage in the integration of auxiliaries into the armed forces of the empire belongs under Claudius, who regularized the system of rewards for honourable service: citizenship after twenty-five years of that service (which might continue longer), and the regularization of any marriage contracted during service, so that children already born obtained citizenship, as well as any born to the same couple in the future. These grants were recorded on pocket-sized, folding bronze tablets called diplomas, presented to the soldier as documentary proof of his privileges.[74] These grants were seen as an important inducement to enlistment and made a useful contribution to the spread of citizenship in the provinces, which was seen as allied to loyal service to the emperor. Regiments continued to be formed, mainly in newly acquired territories such as Britain. When a client kingdom was absorbed, its army might be taken over into the Roman service.[75] By the death of Nero the total number of auxiliaries under arms, or available for service, was probably near 200,000. We still cannot name all the *cohortes* and *alae* in existence, or pinpoint where they served.

As the legions began to be spaced out along the frontiers of the empire, so too we find a more piecemeal distribution of auxiliary regiments placed singly or in pairs. The earliest recognizable ground-plans of forts, at such sites as Valkenburg, Hofheim and Oberstimm, belong under Claudius. It was perhaps about this time (if not earlier) that fixed rates of pay were established for auxiliaries. For the Flavian era, the figures of $\frac{3}{4}$ or $\frac{5}{6}$ of the legionary's pay have been proposed, but these seem over-generous for the Julio-Claudian age.[76]

Furthermore, Claudius regulated the sequence of commands held in auxiliary units and defined more precisely who should hold them. He ordained that command of auxiliary regiments should be given solely to equestrians (to the exclusion of *primipilares*), and that the posts should be held in a set order: the prefecture of a cohort followed by the prefecture of an *ala*, followed by the tribunate of a legion.[77] Thus he rated the post in a citizen legion more highly than independent command over a body of

[73] Tac. *Ann.* XIII.31, XIV.27; Suet. *Ner.* 9.

[74] *CIL.* XVI, *passim*; M.M. Roxan, *Roman Military Diplomas, 1954–77* (London 1978); *eadem, Roman Military Diplomas, 1978–84*, (London, 1985).   [75] E.g. Tac. *Hist.* III.47.

[76] Speidel 1973 (D 233).   [77] Suet. *Claud.* 25.1.

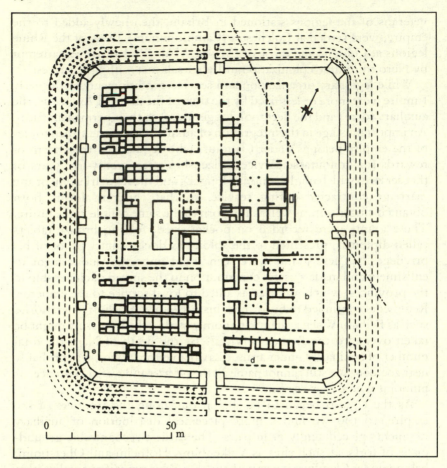

Fig. 6. Valkenburg, Holland: fort-plan, *c.* A.D. 40. (After Glasbergen.) The earliest recognizable examples of forts built for individual auxiliary regiments belong at this time. Valkenburg, a fort of 1.5 hectares (3.7 acres), was probably built for a *cohors quingenaria equitata.* Within a rampart and triple ditch were a timber-built headquarters (a), commandant's house (b), long barracks, for cavalry? (c) hospital (d), and barracks (e).

non-citizen auxiliaries. Some examples of this sequence can be documented within Claudius' reign,[78] but it did not become universal: by Nero's death (or at least in the aftermath of the civil war of A.D. 68–69) it had become normal for the tribunate of the legion to be held between the two prefectures rather than after both. Centurions were excluded from these commands, but a set sequence of tribunates in the cohorts at Rome became the preserve of the *primipilares*: a tribunate in a cohort of *vigiles* would be followed by that of an urban cohort and finally that of a cohort

[78] *CIL* II 4239 = *PME* P 96; (?) *CIL* V 4058 = *PME* C 25; *ILS* 2681 = *GCN* 280 = *PME* V 137; *AE* 1966, 124 = *PME* D 33; Devijver 1970 (D 178).

of the praetorians. These avenues of promotion could lead in due course to the higher posts in the equestrian civil service as procurators. The prefectures of the fleets at Misenum and Ravenna were seen as having a place in the same developing hierarchy; military expertise was not considered a prerogative for these two posts, which were mainly administrative, and sometimes an imperial freedman, having the special trust of the emperor, held one of the fleet prefectures.

It may also have been Claudius who fixed the length of service for fleet personnel at twenty-six years, with citizenship and regularization of marriage on discharge, though the earliest secure evidence on the duration of service belongs under Vespasian.[79] Small locally based naval squadrons came gradually into being, some perhaps already under Augustus, to police the Rhine, English Channel, the Danube, the Black Sea, Egypt, Syria and the coasts of north Africa.

In Rome itself the early years of Tiberius saw the concentration of the nine praetorian cohorts and the three Rome-based urban cohorts in a fortress built on high ground in the north-eastern outskirts of the city, beyond the old Servian Wall. It was named the *castra praetoria*. By A.D. 23 its construction was probably complete.[80] Limited excavation – the interior is again a military enclave – has yielded a partial ground-plan of its barrack accommodation.[81] This concentration of the cohorts can be ascribed to the initiative of Aelius Seianus, sole praetorian prefect in A.D. 14–31; one almost inevitable consequence was an increase in the influence of the prefect himself on political events in the city. The number of praetorian cohorts was increased from nine to twelve before the death of Claudius, and perhaps much earlier.[82]

V. THE ROMAN ARMY IN A.D. 70

Two detailed accounts survive of the Roman army in action in the last years of the Julio-Claudian era. Firstly, Josephus provides an appreciation of the Roman army of the eastern provinces, supported by auxiliaries and levies from the adjacent client kingdoms, engaged in traditional warfare against rebellious subjects, the Jews, and a full account of the reduction of successive military strongholds between A.D. 66 and 73; archaeological evidence of siege-camps round Masada and at other sites offers dramatic confirmation of the historical record. The second account is from the hand of Tacitus, the surviving portion of whose *Histories* constitutes an almost day-by-day account of the military events of A.D. 69, when Roman armies from the northern and eastern provinces mobilized to fight one another. Here the expertise built up

[79] *CIL* XVI 1, 12–17; Mann 1972 (D 214).   [80] Tac. *Ann.* IV.2; Suet. *Tib.* 37.1; Dio LVII.9.7.
[81] Nash 1968 (E 87) 221ff.   [82] *AE* 1978, 286; C. Letta, *Athenaeum* 56 (1978) 3–19.

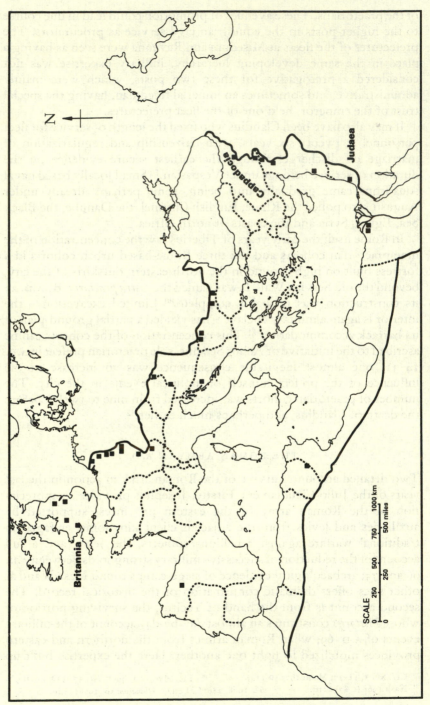

Fig. 7. Distribution of legions, A.D. 23.

over a hundred years was turned against other legionaries, with similar tactics and weaponry deployed on both sides.

To the Roman public, the army of A.D. 69–70 probably seemed little different from its counterpart in the days of Julius Caesar. The legionaries wore familiar equipment and marched behind the silver (or sometimes gold) *aquila*, their legions bearing names and titles which reflected their origins and the exploits of earlier days. But in reality much had changed: what had been an army of Italians was now increasingly made up of provincials owing no particular allegiance to, or common bond with, the Senate or the people of the *urbs Roma*; rather they were loyal to the emperor who paid them and whose benevolent rule had brought great advantage to their homelands. Rome was a city they were pledged to defend, but which they would mostly never visit. Increasingly they began to identify their interests with those of the provinces in which they were stationed. Only the praetorian and urban cohorts continued to be recruited principally in Italy, so providing an outlet for the military aspirations of young men for whom the legions with their long service in distant provinces held little appeal. The emperor, if he was wise, took pains to maintain a meaningful bond with the army, by donatives and special coin issues honouring the troops; Nero's lack of real interest in military affairs was a significant factor in his downfall. In the spring of A.D. 69 the invading army of Vitellius appeared to the citizens of northern Italy to consist of barbarous foreigners.[83] At the Second Battle of Cremona, a crucial turning-point came at daybreak on 25 October when soldiers of legion III Gallica (which had been based in Syria since Actium a hundred years before) turned to salute the rising sun in oriental fashion, a gesture which wrongly suggested to the weary Vitellians that Flavian reinforcements had reached the battlefield. By A.D. 69 the ranks of III Gallica, like other legions long stationed in the East, contained a very high proportion of men born in the eastern provinces.[84] The spectacle of legions swearing loyalty to a Gallic empire, and a veteran colony (Cologne, founded A.D. 50) making an easy transition to the party of Civilis, becomes a little more comprehensible, when localized recruitment over several generations is considered.[85] In the summer of 69 a rumour circulating in Syria, that Vitellius proposed to reward his Rhine legions by transferring them *en bloc* to Syria and, in turn, sending the Syrian garrisons to the cold northern frontiers, was guaranteed to galvanize the eastern legions to fight on Vespasian's behalf.[86]

A blurring of the traditional distinctions between branches of the army can be observed. Physical and mental attributes would soon become more important in determining whether a man became a

---

[83] Tac. *Hist*. II.21.   [84] Tac. *Hist*. III.24. Cf. Joseph. *BJ* IV.38, with VI.54, 81.
[85] Tac. *Hist*. IV.54ff, 63ff.   [86] Tac. *Hist*. II.80.

legionary or an auxiliary than his cultural or ethnic antecedents. In the crisis of A.D. 68–9 the manpower of the major fleets was utilized to form two new legions, I and II Adiutrix ('Supportive'), which became a permanent part of the imperial army. Galba formed a new legion in Spain, at the time of his bid for power. Many legions were given fresh postings after the civil war of A.D. 69–70, with those legionary bases nearest Italy in the secure hands of Flavian legions.

Until A.D. 69–70 many auxiliary regiments had retained close contacts with their tribe or area of origin, sometimes being stationed at no great distance. It was only after the events of A.D. 69–70, when several Gallic and Rhineland units deserted *en masse* to Civilis, and ties to Rome were found to be more fragile than imagined, that local links were for a time decisively broken. Many regiments were posted to far-off provinces, and their ethnic homogeneity was destroyed. The practice of employing tribal nobility to command their own tribesmen was discontinued. Yet as the decades passed, the auxiliaries like the legions began to draw their manpower increasingly from the province in which they were stationed, so developing new loyalties. Now if not earlier a fairly standard uniform was evolved: mail shirt or scale-armour, sword and throwing spears for the infantry, long slashing sword and heavier spears for the cavalry; yet some regiments retained their traditional equipment, among them the oriental archer-cohorts with their long flowing robes, conical helmets and curving bows. In the aftermath of the civil war, larger-sized *cohortes* and *alae*, up to 1,000 men strong (entitled *milliariae*) were formed, perhaps on a model already serving in the East. The gradual integration of auxiliary formations into the armed forces of the empire is marked too by the beginnings of adoption of Roman nomenclature and the more widespread use of tombstones, which commemorated the deceased auxiliary in Roman fashion, with a suitable Latin text.

The Roman army of the later first century A.D. could still look on occasion to forward movement (for example in Britain and Germany), but for the most part it was settling to a static role of frontier defence. The era of rapid advance and easy victories was over.

CHAPTER 12

THE ADMINISTRATION OF JUSTICE

H. GALSTERER

I

The following chapter is concerned with the application of law, not with law and justice itself. We shall have to deal with the different courts and officers of law, with judges and procedure, with actions and punishment; the development of law from the late Republic to early Empire, its pre-classical shape and the birth of Roman legal science are described in chapter 21 of this volume.[1]

The limits of time given for this volume are irrelevant insofar as law and administration of justice are concerned. Caesar was killed before he could start on any reform programme he may have planned,[2] and the civil wars which began after his death postponed any serious reform until peace was restored by the new *princeps*. The end of the period dealt with in this volume is even less of a rupture in the field of justice. So it is best to begin with the situation as it had developed in the wake of Sulla's reforms, treat rather briefly some reforms under Augustus and his successors, and end with the state of affairs in the second half of the first century A.D.

There will be many 'probablys' and similar expressions in the following pages, too many perhaps in view of the fact that the period between Cicero and Tacitus is one of the best known in ancient history. But it is a lopsided picture we get, overstressing Rome and the upper classes. Legal literature on the other side is transmitted to us mostly in the pruned state passed down by Justinian's lawyers, who eliminated or altered many subjects no longer valid in the sixth century. This concerns municipal jurisdiction especially. But other fields too are less well known than one would like to think.

---

[1] The best introduction 'to get a feeling' of how Roman law worked in practice, is probably still to read over large parts of the *Digest*, the collection of legal literature made by Justinian, of which there is a good new English translation. Of modern works Crook 1967 (F 21) esp. ch. 3, and Garnsey 1970 (F 35) are outstanding in their endeavour to combine legal and social history, and are eminently readable too. The same may be said of chs. 13 and 14 of *CAH* IX², by D. Cloud and J. Crook.

[2] Suet. *Iul.* 44.2; Isid. *Etym.* 5.1.5 and Polay 1965 (D 274).

II

It is best to start with the city of Rome, as the administration of justice there is best known, and with civil jurisdiction.[3] In the final years of the Republic the main law officers of the *populus Romanus* were still the two senior praetors, the *praetor urbanus* responsible – in principle – for jurisdiction among Roman citizens, and the *praetor peregrinus* for jurisdiction among foreigners and between foreigners and Roman citizens. The six other praetors were, from the time of Sulla, presidents of the different courts of criminal law.

The consuls, whose *imperium* contained jurisdictional rights as well as that of the praetors, usually did not meddle in the administration of justice, even if they could quash acts of the praetors.[4] More important was the jurisdiction of the aediles: as superintendants of the urban markets, and thus responsible for standards of trade and quality, they helped to shape Roman commercial law to a considerable degree.

The procedure at the praetors' and the aediles' court was what is called the formulary system, at least for most cases (cf. Crook *CAH* ix², ch. 14). Roman jurisdiction was from the beginning bipartite – the praetor (or aedile) examining the case in the presence of both parties, as to whether it was admissible according to the law, and then transferring the factual decision to a private judge.

Now the praetor could, and progressively did, accept cases not foreseen by the written laws or slightly different from the situation presupposed in these laws. If he did so, the case no longer depended upon civil law (*ius civile*) in strict interpretation, but upon the *imperium* of the magistrate. He drew up the *formula*, a kind of scenario for the case to be decided by the judge. In its simplest form the *formula* ran as follows:

Let Titius be *iudex*. If it appears that N.N. ought to pay 10,000 sesterces to A.A., let the *iudex* condemn N.N. to pay 10,000 sesterces to A.A. If it does not so appear, let the *iudex* absolve him.[5]

Formulae which successfully met new economic or social needs were taken over by successive praetors, who gave notice in their proclamation of intentions (*edictum*), published at the beginning of their term, that they would grant this or that *formula*.

A civil suit began *in iure*, in the presence of one of the two praetors.

[3] 'City of Rome' being defined since Sulla at the latest by 'in urbe Roma propiusve mille passus', as e.g. in the *lex Cornelia de sicariis* (*Mosaicorum et Romanorum Legum Collatio* 1.3.1).

[4] Val. Max. vii.7.6 on a case of 77 b.c.

[5] N.N., standing for Numerius Negidius, the man who denies, and A.A., i.e. Aulus Agerius, the plaintiff, are stock blanks, as well as 'Titius' for the judge. For introductions to the formulary system cf. Jolowicz and Nicholas 1972 (f 660) 199–232 and Kunkel 1973 (f 667) 91–8; also below, ch. 21, pp. 959–60.

The plaintiff and the defendant, or their representatives, had to be present. Normally they had made an appointment, a *vadimonium*, with him: 'for 3 December next at Rome in the Forum of Augustus before the tribunal of the urban praetor at the second hour', as it is stated in one of the new documents from Murecine near Pompeii.[6] A money penalty in the *vadimonium* was meant to make both parties appear, and if your adversary neither gave sureties nor appeared on the stated day, the praetor could take him for *indefensus* and eventually grant you entry into his property. How far this system worked against recalcitrant defendants or between parties of very different social standing is uncertain.

If both were present, the praetor in discussion with the parties and their counsel and with the help of *iuris periti* he had upon his *consilium* shaped the *formula* according to the needs of the case – or he might refuse to accept the case, if he thought the claim not justiciable. The *formula* would rarely be so simple as stated above. There might be clauses, replications and many other specifications in it. An example of a *formula* to recover possession of property, the so-called *actio Publiciana*, runs like this: 'Let Titius be *iudex*. If A.A. has purchased that slave Stichus in good faith, on whom there is suit, and he has been transferred to him, and he has possessed him for a year, then if this slave ought to be his by the *ius Quiritium*, and this slave is not N.N.'s by the *ius Quiritium*, or if N.N. did not sell and transfer that slave on whom there is suit to A.A., and if in this matter no duress has been involved, *iudex*, if that slave at your award be not returned to A.A., do you condemn N.N. to A.A. of so much of his property as that slave may be worth; if it does not appear, dismiss.'[7]

There was ample opportunity given to the parties to state their points, and there was probably much discussion in this stage already, when questions of law were deliberated, but in the end it was the praetor who decided – he was never a simple referee between parties' claims.

With the naming of the *iudex* and the giving of the *formula* the transaction before the praetor, the part *in iure*, ended and the hearing before the judge, *apud iudicem*, might begin. For a long time all judges were taken from among the senators, the *album iudicum* being identical with the *album senatorum*. C. Gracchus first took the judges for his extortion court from among the knights. There is no need to recall the battles fought over the nomination of judges, mostly in the *quaestio repetundarum* (extortion court); they ended for good with the compromise reached by the Lex Aurelia of 70 B.C. From then on the panel from which judges were taken was composed of socially different *decuriae*: the first one composed of senators, the second from knights and the third one from a somewhat mysterious category, the so-called *tribuni*

---

[6] *TabPomp* XIV. The translation is by Crook 1967 (F 21) 75.
[7] Schiller 1978 (F 689) 439f with commentary.

aerarii.[8] These *tribuni* were removed by Caesar and reinstituted by Antony. Augustus created a fourth *decuria* of judges *ex inferiore censu*[9] and Caligula a fifth one, which ranked as third because composed of *equites*. These *decuriae* had in the early Empire a thousand or more members each,[10] Roman citizens from Rome, Italy and (probably from the time of Caligula) from the provinces, between thirty (twenty-five under Augustus) and sixty years old. One of the *decuriae* was granted leave each year, the members of the other four divisions had to serve at Rome if they were not enjoying a *vacatio* as imperial or municipal magistrates, because of military duty, or for other *excusationes*. That even important officials like the curators of streets, curators of aqueducts, and prefects of the corn supply were delegated three months each year to serve as judges shows the importance of this organization.[11]

The *album iudicum* supplied judges to the criminal courts and to the centumviral court, but most of them worked as single judges (*iudex unus*), or in boards of summary judges (*recuperatores*) in civil cases. The system whereby judges were allotted to cases was rather complicated and need not be discussed here in detail;[12] but it may easily be imagined that a procedure working well when all – parties, judges and magistrats – were living in or near Rome, rapidly got into difficulties when parties and judges were summoned to Rome from the whole empire, from the shores of the Black Sea to those of the Atlantic.

The parties could in principle agree upon any fit person to act as judge,[13] but most cases seem to have gone to these *iudices ex V decuriis*, so that quite naturally the judicature became somewhat oriented to the upper class. Suetonius, Aulus Gellius and Pliny the Younger are only some of the known judges, and the latter wrote to a friend that he acted as a judge almost more often than as counsel.[14]

It was up to the judge to find out the facts in the law suit, to find out whether Numerius Negidius really owed the 10,000 sesterces to Aulus Agerius or what the circumstances were in the sale, if there was any, of the slave Stichus. As an additional difficulty the judge in most lawsuits had not only to condemn or acquit, but also to assess the value of something to be given or to be done, and (to complicate things still further) there were no acknowledged rules of relevance to restrain the

---

[8] As Augustus decreed a minimal census of 200,000 sesterces for members of his new, the fourth decuria, and *tribuni aerarii* were evidently located between them and the knights, a census of 300,000 sesterces does not seem improbable; but cf. D. Cloud, *CAH* IX² 509 for arguments that *tribuni aerarii* had a census qualification of 400,000 sesterces like *equites*.   [9] Suet. *Aug.* 32.3.

[10] Pliny, *HN* 33.30.   [11] *Senatusconsulta de aquaeductibus* (*FIRA* I² 276–7) cap. 100.

[12] Behrens 1970 (D 245) with Galsterer 1973 (D 255). Readers should be warned however that Behrens' interpretation is not accepted by all, cf. W. Eder, *Gnomon* 46 (1974) 583–9.

[13] Excluded were slaves, women, the mentally ill and those persons who had been convicted of certain delicts, cf. Kaser 1966 (F 661) 140, and below, n. 20.

[14] Gell. *NA* xiv.2; Pliny, *Ep.* 1.20.12, vi.2.7.

parties and their counsel from burying the evidence as much as possible under heaps of irrelevant statements – some of Cicero's speeches (e.g. the *pro Balbo*) are very good examples of this technique. The judge, on the other hand, was in a strong position because he was not restricted by too many rules, and if he really didn't find his way out, he could as a last resort declare that he did not understand the case, *sibi non liquere*, and decline judgment. Aulus Gellius did just that in the second century when, in his very first case as a judge, he was presented with a man of splendid reputation ('vir bonus notaeque et expertae fidei') suing a rather disreputable character ('homo non bonae rei vitaque turpi et sordida') for a debt without presenting a scrap of evidence. Gellius gave up the case in the end, but only because he thought himself too young and of too little social standing to decide, as he evidently wanted to do, in favour of the 'good' man.[15] Incidentally, 'good' and 'bad' in this case are coupled with 'rich' and 'in straitened circumstances', a correlation which upper-class judges might easily take for normal.

After judgment, the duty of the *iudex* was at an end, unless the plaintiff had other suits running which he was entitled to present to the same judge immediately afterwards. It was now up to the winner either, if he had been the accused, to sue his adversary *de calumnia*, or, if he had been plaintiff, to get the defendant to do the thing the lawsuit was about. As there were nothing like bailiffs, court police or other enforcement officials, he had to bring another action against a recalcitrant defendant, this time the *actio iudicati*. At first sight it seems rather strange that the praetor did not grant immediately an executory title to the winning side, and there has been some speculation whether this second lawsuit served as a kind of procedure of appeal.[16] More probably the second suit was introduced because with this title in hand the plaintiff now could wield the whole force of the law, up to selling his adversary's property.

III

So far civil jurisdiction in the city of Rome. Criminal justice had not much altered since the days of Sulla, at least before Augustus.[17] The main organs of this justice were the courts of law erected by statute and dealing each with specific crimes, with extortion (*repetundae*), embezzlement (*peculatus*), improper canvassing (*ambitus*) and so on. There were also courts for less political crimes, as for instance against murderers and poisoners (*de sicariis et veneficis*), but on the whole it is political misdemeanour which was tried in these standing jury-courts (*quaestiones*

---

[15] Gell. *NA* XIV.2.2-11.   [16] Cf. the discussion in Kaser 1966 (F 661) 298-9.

[17] The *iudicium domesticum*, the justice of the *paterfamilias*, probably still was active and took over a number of cases which might otherwise have gone to the courts (cf. Cloud, *CAH* IX[2] 499-500).

perpetuae). Judges were taken from the *album iudicum*; probably there was a panel of names for each court from which the jury was taken by lot and by alternate elimination of names.[18] The actual number of judges was often not very large, so that the allegations of venality throughout the history of the courts are probably not too farfetched. Presidents of the courts were – from Sulla on – praetors and other, junior magistrates.

Procedure in the *quaestiones* was by *nominis delatio*, accusation before the president of the relevant jury by a citizen (normally) who was either concerned himself in the case or was prompted by the reward – informers and accusers, the notorious *delatores* and *indices*, were as ineradicable a defect in this system of 'popular accusation', as were the sycophants in Athens.[19] If there was more than one prospective accuser (and there might be rumour of collusion by one of them with the accused, *praevaricatio*), there was a first hearing of magistrate and jury (*divinatio*) to find out who should be the main accuser. This and the following steps can best be seen from the Verrines, Cicero's speeches in the extortion trial of Gaius Verres. After formal accusation and the constitution of the jury came the presentation of the evidence, of testimony and witnesses. All this had to be organized by the prosecution – there was little help from the state here too and no police, even if witnesses could be subpoenaed to appear at Rome. After the final speeches of prosecution and defence the jury voted by ballot. If the *reus* was absolved, he was free to sue his accuser for libel (*calumnia*). If condemned, his civic existence was at stake, because condemnation brought at least loss of *fama*,[20] and in most courts the capital penalty was the measure provided for in the law, even if culprits usually were not hindered if they prevented it by going into exile.

Beside this upper-class justice of the *quaestiones* and – possibly, if it had survived till now – process before the people, there existed at least from the second century B.C. a summary jurisdiction of the *IIIviri capitales*, who normally looked after jails and the executions of *confessi*. Their office was the first step in the hierarchy of magistracies; it's incumbents were under twenty-five and had no *imperium* whatsoever, so it was doubted whether they were entitled to sentence people to death. But as their clientele was composed probably of 'thieves and evil slaves' ('fures et

[18] The procedure is best known from the Gracchan *lex repetundarum*; cf. A. Lintott, *Judicial Reform and Land Reform in the Roman Republic* (Cambridge, 1992), 116–22.

[19] During the Republic rewards had been mostly political, i.e. promotion in civic status. Pecuniary awards seem to be first introduced by the Lex Pedia against the murderers of Caesar and became usual (consisting in a quota of the condemned's fortune) in the Empire, especially in *maiestas* trials.

[20] *Infamia* was the consequence of condemnation in some civil and all criminal trials. There exist several, slightly different lists of infaming actions, in Gai. *Inst.* 4.182; *D* 3.2.1; Tab.Heracl. 108–25; and now in ch. 84 of the Lex Irnitana.

servi nequam'), that is, the scum of the metropolis, this lack of competence may not have mattered too much. It is not very probable either that all minor delinquents were given a process before the *quaestio*.[21] As the *IIIviri* had a *consilium* of experienced counsellors to compensate for their lack of experience, on the whole one should probably accept this capital jurisdiction.

IV

Jurisdiction in Italy in the last century B.C. was shaped mainly by the consequences of the Social War, when all communities up to the Rubicon became citizen towns. Few will subscribe today to Rudolph's theory that the Italian municipalities received their own jurisdiction only by a law of Caesar instituting municipal jurisdiction.[22] Latin colonies and cities of *socii* retained their own jurisdiction after 89 B.C., which only had to be adapted somehow to the Roman system – in the same manner probably as had been the case with old citizen towns (*municipia* and *coloniae*) before the Social War.

There were still – down to Augustus – *praefecti iure dicundo* in some towns, who were delegates of the Roman praetor (*urbanus?*) and responsible for local jurisdiction. But we need not spend much time on the thorny question about their duties and competences, as by the second half of the first century B.C. probably all towns in Italy had gained their own administrative structures and with that their own jurisdiction. Where *praefecti iure dicundo* are now mentioned in inscriptions, they are delegates of municipal magistrates, when the local law officers the *IIviri* or *IIIIviri iure dicundo* were away or when this office was given to a prominent Roman politician or even to the emperor.

Differences in jurisdictional competence between colonies and *municipia*, which may have existed in the Republic, had disappeared by the beginning of the Principate; laws dealing with municipal jurisdiction like the so-called Lex Rubria treat all towns on an equal footing. But there existed now, and we do not know from what date, upper limits of jurisdictional competence for municipal law-courts. The Lex Rubria of 41 B.C., adjusting municipal jurisdiction in the former Gallia Cisalpina to that of Italy after the abolishment of the province, seems to fix this limit at a value of not more than 15,000 sesterces and for several categories of cases involving *infamia* to not more than 10,000 sesterces but limits probably differed not only in the provinces but also in Italy according to

[21] Jones 1972 (D 264) (but cf. the critical reviews of Behrens 1973 (D 246) and Brunt 1974 (D 251)); Crook 1967 (F 21) 69 and Brunt 1964 (D 250) are sceptical about this capital jurisdiction; Cloud in *CAH* IX² 501 accepts it as far as slaves, perhaps even working-class citizens were concerned.

[22] For the arguments against a general *lex Iulia municipalis* cf. Galsterer 1987 (D 92).

the status and the importance of cities (cf. below, p. 410). As the right or the obligation to have one's case tried at Rome (*revocatio Romam*) became more and more diffused, especially among the local elites, municipal jurisdiction even in this way tended to be restricted to petty cases.

In criminal law it seems as if at the beginning of our period municipal juries existed and still enjoyed far-reaching competence. It is difficult to avoid the impression from Cicero's speech for Cluentius that there were local *quaestiones* for capital cases like murder and poisoning,[23] and as the competence of the Sullan *quaestio de sicariis* was restricted to Rome and her near surroundings such *quaestiones* were necessary to deal without too much delay with local crime.[24] Whether their sentences were appealable at Rome is not known.

Procedure in the Italian towns probably followed Roman practice, i.e. formulary process with the chief magistrates in the role of the praetors at Rome. They too had been called praetor from the beginning, so it seems, because their main duty was in jurisdiction, and when later this title seemed too grandiloquent for small town magistrates, now they were simply named *IIviri iure dicundo* or *IIIIviri iure dicundo*. Judges in the municipalities were taken from a roll (*album*) which was mostly identical with the *album decurionum*, the list of members of the council. There may have been local variations however: at Narbo an inscription was set up in honour of Augustus because he had added plebeian courts to those of the councillors (*iudicia plebis decurionibus coniunxit*); at Irni too there were judges of inferior census, but evidently with the same competence as those taken from among the *decuriones*.[25]

V

Finally jurisdiction in the provinces, originally areas under the supervision of magistrates or pro-magistrates with *imperium*. As they were few and their provinces generally large, there could be no idea of intense administration. In civil jurisdiction they were concerned mostly with the affairs of Roman citizens living in the province and with those of Italian *socii*, insofar as those had not the right of *revocatio Romam*, to have their case heard at Rome.

The governor used formulary jurisdiction as did the praetor at Rome. The recently published inscription of Contrebia shows the governor of Hither Spain giving in 87 B.C. a *formula* to two communities of the Ebro valley litigating about water rights; it is very complex and shows

[23] Cf.Cic. Clu. 176 for capital proceedings initiated by municipal magistrates against Cluentius. These are probably the *iudicia publica* mentioned in Tab.Heracl. 119 (*FIRA* I[2] p. 149).
[24] *Mosaicorum et Romanorum Legum Collatio* 1.3.1, cf. Cloud in *CAH* IX[2] 522 n. 157 for the *lex Iulia de vi*.   [25] Narbo: *CIL* XII 4333 of A.D. 11, *pace* Dessau *ILS* 112 ad locum; lex Irnit. 86.

complete mastery of the technique. In the *nominatio* the Senate of a third community is named to be judge in the case.[26] This lawsuit is between peregrine communities, but if he had to give judgment to Romans, the governor gave single judges and *recuperatores* from a provincial *album*. On the other hand the governor was in no way forced to use the formulary process. With peregrine provincials mostly (not always, as we have just seen), but also with Romans he could, instead of naming a judge and instructing him in a *formula* what to do, inquire himself – in the presence of his *consilium* – into facts and legal circumstances. This jurisdiction, based entirely upon his *imperium*, was called *cognitio*; it played a certain role already in the doings of Verres in Sicily, but became really important, and then dominant, only with the Principate.[27]

Jurisdiction in the provinces had one further peculiarity too, in that the governor did not reside all the time in one city where people had to go if in need of him but, following a certain calendar, he toured the main cities of his province where people from the surrounding areas could come to bring actions before him and to transact other legal business.[28] From the 'coming together' of plaintiffs, defendants, witnesses, judges and business people of all sorts this meeting was called *conventus*, but the word soon acquired a geographic sense, meaning the circuit. So we know from the provincial lists given by the Elder Pliny the composition of the four circuits of Baetica, the seven circuits of Tarraconensis etc., and this partition into circuits soon served other purposes too, as was shown some years ago by new evidence for Asia Minor.[29]

VI

The introduction of one-man rule affected the different branches of the administration of justice in different ways. The mainstay of civil jurisdiction remained the two praetors' courts at Rome. The number of praetors was augmented by Caesar to between ten and sixteen and remained the same number under Augustus. Later they oscillated between twelve and eighteen, with twelve more or less the norm.[30] Some of them were presidents of the *quaestiones perpetuae*, some others had special competences in civil jurisdiction, like the *praetor hastarius* who (in the place of the old *Xviri stlitibus iudicandis*) now became responsible for the centumviral court, or the two (from Titus one) *praetores fideicommis-*

---

[26] Richardson 1983 (B 271) and Birks, Rodger and Richardson 1984 (D 247).

[27] Cf. Cic. *Verr.* II.2.70ff and Augustus' fourth edict for Cyrene (*FIRA* I² 409).

[28] Sometimes the governor would call together (*evocare*) the inhabitants of more than one *conventus*, as did Cicero in his province of Cilicia (*Att.* v.21.9, vi.2.4).

[29] Habicht published an inscription from Ephesus giving a register of towns in Asia Minor by *dioiceseis/conventus* (*JRS* 65 (1975) 64–91); Burton deals with the assize organization in a more general way (*JRS* 65 (1975) 92–106). [30] Dio LVI.25.4.

sarii whom Claudius set over the *fidei commissa* (informal requests from the testator to heirs) newly actionable since Augustus. But the increasing number of praetors was due not so much to the requirements of jurisdiction as to political exigencies and the need for ex-praetors to fill administrative posts. The importance of the praetors diminished as imperial jurisdiction grew; development of law became impossible for the praetor because the *edictum*, which was taken over almost unaltered from one praetor to the next for a long time, was now almost standardized;[31] and the famous jurists of the Severi tended to be not praetors, but *praefecti praetorio* on the emperor's staff. Jurisdiction of the aediles was taken over by various officials in the emperor's service, the lion's share going to the governor of Rome (*praefectus urbi*), the chief of the watch (*praefectus vigilum*) and the prefect of the corn supply (*praefectus annonae*). These imperial officers might on any occasion be members of the *consilium* of the *princeps* too, which by and by became the most important body for the development of law.[32]

But the republican courts were still functioning and were reorganized by Augustus in a couple of very detailed laws, the *leges Iuliae iudiciorum privatorum et publicorum* of 17 B.C. From what we can see the whole field of procedure and organization was touched: abolition of *legis actiones*, times of hearing and recess, obligations of judges, adjournments and so on. The *leges Iuliae* together with *senatusconsulta* giving specifications and updatings remained fundamental for several centuries.

The old jurisdiction by praetor and private judges was hemmed in now in two ways. One we will deal with later, the now regular use of the juridical competences of the consuls, acting with the Senate as their jury and functioning mostly as a peers' court for delinquent senators. More important and ever more increasing was the role of the emperor. Using the *tribunicia potestas* which gave the emperor *ius auxilii* against judgments based on *imperium* – this *ius auxilii* was reshaped in 30 B.C. as a prerogative to *appellatum iudicare* – and the permanent consular and proconsular *imperium* which allowed him *cognitio* in his own right, and his predominant *auctoritas*, the emperor very soon became the most important institution in law: even if not all cases went to his court, the idea that a citizen might appeal to him as a last resort extended, till it reached even the last and least of the provincials.

Augustus, as we are told, was a most diligent judge who sat until the end of the day, very lenient according to Suetonius or, if we believe Cassius Dio, most severe.[33] Another emperor of outstanding zeal in jurisdiction was Claudius, but of him too people doubted whether he did

---

[31] For the arguments about the codification of the *edictum perpetuum* under Hadrian cf. Guarino 1980 (D 261).   [32] Cf. Crook 1955 (D 10).   [33] Suet. *Aug.* 33; Dio LV.7.2.

not do so only to have an outlet for his natural cruelty.[34] Of one of his reforms in jurisdiction we have first-rate evidence, a papyrus giving parts of what is probably a speech by Claudius in the Senate on the minimum age of *iudices ex albo* and on the repression of *delatores*.[35] 'Let us stop the lawless tyranny of the accusers' at least sounds good, even if the consequences were not nearly so impressive.

VII

The administration of justice continued to develop with the Principate. In civil jurisdiction at Rome the *praetor urbanus* and the *praetor peregrinus* worked as in the Republic, but of the old separation of their fields of competences, *provinciae*, next to nothing is left. These two praetors still made use of the *formulae*, as the *praetor hastarius*, the new president of the *iudicium centumvirale*, used the still older *legis actio sacramento*. The new 'special' praetors appearing since Augustus all made use of *cognitio*, i.e. they were not bound by the limitations in procedure and timing characteristic of the old *ordo iudiciorum*. Some quasi-judicial functions in civil law were given to the consuls too, probably to make good the loss of political influence of the former chief magistrates. At the end of Augustus' reign Ovid already regards jurisdiction as one of the main occupations of consuls, and Suetonius distinguishes carefully between Claudius' jurisdiction as consul and as a *privatus*.[36] But most of the job fell to the emperor himself. He took up some cases in the first instance, cases probably where decisions based on *cognitio* would serve as *exempla* and where the ordinary law did not suffice. Later on, the emperors delegated part of their jurisdictional tasks to officials in their service, so that the *praefectus urbi*, the *praefectus annonae*, the *praefectus vigilum* and occasionally even the *praefectus praetorio* might wield civil jurisdiction in the first instance, based of course on the *imperium* of the emperor. It seems rather doubtful if there were any precise delimitations of their prerogatives, so that – as in criminal justice – plaintiffs might have the possibility of choice among different courts.

The emperor's main activity lay of course in the field of appeals. Regular appeal from the sentences of ordinary judges or courts had not existed in the Republic: *provocatio* had always been a political measure directed against acts of *imperium*, and it was apparently with judgments in *cognitio* cases, that is, based on *imperium*, that appeals started under Augustus; it may have seemed logical to allow appeal from lower to

[34] Sen. *Apocol.* 12.2, cf. Garzetti 1974 (A 35) 137f, 600f.
[35] The causes for retaining the attribution to Claudius, as against Millar 1977 (A 59) 350 n. 59, in Talbert 1984 (D 77) 499f.   [36] Ov. *Pont.* iv.5.17, iv.9.43; Suet. *Claud.* 14.

higher and from delegated to original *imperium*. From the beginning it was more than *provocatio*. In 30 B.C., after the capture of Alexandria, Octavian was given – together with the tribunician *ius auxilii* – the right to ἔκκλητον δικάζειν i.e. *appellatum iudicare*, and the *calculus Minervae* in all courts, wherewith votes of the jury might be rescinded.[37] Later on, when in possession of the *imperium consulare*, he received appeals from praetors and proconsuls in virtue of his *imperium maius*. Already in the first years of the Principate the number of appeals had grown to such dimensions that Augustus had to delegate appeals, those of *urbani litigatores* to the *praetor urbanus* and those coming from the provinces to selected consulares.[38] Nero enacted that all appeals from Italy and the public provinces should go to the Senate – as the consuls' *consilium* – and that the same caution-money should be paid for appeals to the Senate as to the emperor.[39] This policy failed blatantly: litigants preferred to go to the emperor's court, whether they came from Italy, from public or from imperial provinces.

VIII

The co-existence of different courts became much more problematic in the field of criminal justice. When Cn. Piso in A.D. 20 was accused of (among other crimes) poisoning Germanicus, the *delator* brought his accusation before the consuls, but the friends of Germanicus claimed that the emperor himself should inquire into the case. This even Piso accepted, 'studia populi et patrum metuens'.[40] So, along with the Senate and the emperor, the Roman people, i.e. the appropriate *quaestio de sicariis et veneficis*, was competent in this case. The decision which court to choose lay with the accusers who – at least in *maiestas* cases – for evident reasons will have preferred to go to the emperor's court.

As the *quaestiones* dealt mostly with political crimes connected with the upper strata of society, they were the first to go. Augustus and the following *principes*, in virtue of *tribunicia potestas* and of *consulare imperium*, could and did exercise criminal jurisdiction, and so did the consuls with the Senate.[41] This body was not a peers' court proper but since the first century the senators felt that they should be tried by no one

---

[37] Dio LI.19.7 and Lintott 1972 (D 271) 263–7.   [38] Suet. *Aug.* 33.3.

[39] Tac. *Ann.* XIII.4; Suet. *Ner.* 17. Though slightly different, Suetonius means probably the same proclamation of Nero as Tacitus.

[40] Tac. *Ann.* III.10.2; Dio LVII.18.10 (according to Dio, Piso was brought before the Senate) and Jones 1960 (A 47) 87.

[41] Jones 1960 (A 47) 90f suggested that it was the *lex Iulia de iudiciis privatis* which reintroduced the criminal jurisdiction of the consuls. In view of the decidedly political implications of many such cases it is not very probable that such senatorial jurisdiction was permitted by Augustus before the final settlement of power in Rome. The trials of 23 B.C. still took place *apud iudices* and before the

below them in social standing, at least in cases of *maiestas* and *repetundae*.[42] Emperors agreed with that in theory but most of them were more hesitant to apply this principle to cases of treason in the face of a potentially hostile Senate. Emperor and Senate divided between them now most of the trials which in former times had gone to the jury-courts. So almost all the *quaestiones* seem simply to have passed away by the end of the first century A.D., with the one possible exception of the Augustan *quaestio de adulteriis*, which seems to have been in existence till the third century A.D.[43]

As courts multiplied, so did fines and penalties. In the Republic, with the exception of some rather archaic punishments, like burying alive the Vestal Virgin who was found guilty of unchastity, or the drowning of parricides in a sack, together with snakes and other animals, there were either pecuniary fines or capital punishment, execution or voluntary exile, which involved *deminutio capitis* too, loss of citizenship. In the *quaestiones* system the appropriate penalty was laid down in the law instituting the *quaestio*.[44] Not so in the jurisdiction based on *cognitio*, either the emperor's or the Senate's. Even crimes for which there was a statutory penalty if brought before the jury-court, might in *cognitio* be punished in a quite different manner. In *cognitio* there also developed the system of penalties one tends to connect with imperial jurisdiction after reading Tacitus: the different ways of disposing of real or suspected opponents by *deportatio* or *relegatio*, commitment to forced labour or to gladiatorial troops, 'public-fair execution' (*Volksfesthinrichtung*). Here belonged also the increasing differentiation between *honestiores* and *humiliores* in criminal law.[45] Prison, by the way, was not a penalty, nor was torture: both were used only in the period before judgment, as custody for defendants or to enforce confessions.

The emperor besides giving judgement in the first instance and functioning as judge of appeal from all his delegates (and more and more Roman officials came to be in public and in their own opinion the emperor's delegates!) became the heir of the *populus Romanus* too, in that he now was the addressee of *provocatio*, which for all practical purposes became identical now with appeal.[46] 'Provoco ad Caesarem' was the

---

praetor. It is only in the later years of Augustus, that we hear of the Senate acting as a court, as a possibility from Ovid in A.D. 8 and, with concrete cases, in A.D. 12 and 13, cf. Talbert 1984 (D 77) 460–87. Already in 4 B.C. Augustus had, in the fifth edict of Cyrene, given the Senate jurisdictional competences in less important, i.e. non-capital, cases of *repetundae*, cf. *FIRA* I² 410–14.

[42] Cf. Talbert 1984 (D 77) 470f.

[43] Paul in his commentary on the *lex Iulia de adulteriis* still cited the *libellus* (indictment) to be presented to the praetor who was president of this *quaestio* (*Dig.* 48.2.3 *pr.*).

[44] The younger Pliny's opinion 'licere senatui, sicut licet, et mitigare leges et intendere' (IV.9.17) was still at the beginning of the second century opposed by other senators, cf. also II.11.2ff and B. Levick, *Hist.* 28 (1979) 358–79.   [45] Cf. P. Garnsey, *Natural Law Forum* 13 (1968) 141–62.

[46] Tac. *Ann.* XII.60 and Garnsey 1966 (D 257).

password now of the Roman citizen, whose immunity from torture and from execution on the spot was even guaranteed by the Augustan law on *vis publica*. Καίσαρα ἐπικαλοῦμαι, 'I appeal unto Caesar', said Paul, and Festus, after discussion with his council, stopped all further proceedings: 'You appealed unto Caesar, you shall go up to Caesar.'[47]

IX

In Italy jurisdiction in the *municipia* and *coloniae* went on as before. As in political supervision it was consuls and Senate who were responsible for Italia between the Alps and the Straits of Messina, so jurisdiction in cases exceeding the value allowed to municipal courts went to the praetors at Rome. According to the late republican Lex Rubria the limit of value apparently was 15,000 sesterces in 'normal' civil suits and 10,000 in trials which might bring *infamia*, at least in the cities of former Cisalpine Gaul. There is no distinction between towns according to size, status or anything else. On the other hand the new Lex Irnitana has shown that in Spain Latin *municipia* had different limits of value: 500 sesterces at Irni and 1,000 at Malaca.[48] This is in the provinces, in Flavian times and with Latins, but it shows at least that there was differentiation, and so we probably had better think of a gradation of cities according to import-ance, political and economic weight and so forth, in Italy too. One of the new tablets from Pompeii strongly suggests that local jurisdiction there might deal with cases worth well over 20,000 sesterces.[49] The *IIviri* of Milan are called *manumittendi potestate* in some inscriptions, and the same may be true of those of Herculaneum, while as a rule emancipation of slaves was permitted only to holders of *imperium*.[50] The procedure to be followed in the municipal courts was the formulary process. In the so-called Florentine fragment of a muncipal law *cognitio* seems to be forbidden to colonial magistrates, but we know neither the field wherein magistrates are not permitted to *cognoscere* nor whether this was a rule for all towns or only for some.[51]

Criminal justice in Italian towns probably declined even earlier than civil jurisdiction. It used to be maintained that capital jurisdiction had never been given to the *municipia* and *coloniae*, but if there were municipal

---

[47] Acts 25:12.

[48] The relevant chapter is 69, which in the Lex Malacitana gives 1,000 sesterces as the upper level, in the otherwise identical Lex Irnitana 500 sesterces.

[49] Cf. G. Purpura, *Tabulae Pompeianae 13 e 34: due documenti relativi al prestitio marittimo, Atti 17. Congr. Intern. di Papirol.* (Napoli, 1984) 1245–66.

[50] *AE* 1947, 47, cf. Kaser 1966 (F 661) 129, 134. Manumission at Herculaneum was inferred by V. Arangio-Ruiz, *Studi Epigrafici e Papirologici* (Napoli, 1974) 568–70 from one of the tablets of the Justa-dossier, probably rightly. Maybe it is not by chance that Milan and Herculaneum were colonies. In the late Republic magistrates of Italian and provincial towns might still have *imperium*, as is shown by Lex Ursonensis 125, 128 and Lex Rubria 20.

[51] C. W. Bruns, Foutes Iuis Romani Autiqui[7] (Tübingen 1909) 158 nr. 33.

quaestiones they may have had considerable competences, at least against defendants from lower social strata. This situation may still be the background to the contract of lease (*lex locationis*) of a local funeral, killing and torturing enterprise operating in the first century A.D. in Puteoli. Its clientele probably was composed not only of slaves but of free persons as well.[52] But in the course of the first two centuries A.D. all criminal jurisdiction in Italy was taken over by the emperor's delegates, the city prefect for the territory up to 100 miles from Rome and the praetorian prefects for the land farther away; for Ulpian the municipal magistrates were not even allowed to sentence slaves to death – only 'moderate punishment is not to be denied to them'.[53]

X

In the provinces the jurisdictional duties of the governor became more and more important as the waging of wars became the exception.[54] After 27 B.C. the distinction between public and imperial provinces was relevant for jurisdiction because *proconsules* had an *imperium* of their own, while the *legati Augusti* participated in the emperor's *imperium*. Therefore the proconsuls could appoint *legati* of their own to help them in jurisdiction, but the governors of the imperial provinces could not, having themselves a delegated *imperium*.[55] So the emperor had himself to send officials for jurisdiction, *iuridici*, into provinces where he thought it appropriate, for example to Hispania Tarraconensis. The prefect of Egypt did possess an *imperium ad similitudinem proconsulis*, *imperium* like that of a proconsul, but that was given to him by law under Augustus.[56] On the other hand the emperor, by his *imperium proconsulare maius*, could give instructions to proconsuls too, and he issued *mandata* to them as to his own delegates, so in reality the difference between public and imperial provinces was less than might be expected.[57]

The governor could, as before, use *iurisdictio* giving a *formula* based on his edict and naming *iudices* from a provincial *album*. The *edicta, formulae, stipulationes* etc. published by the governor are made compulsory for municipal magistrates in the Lex Irnitana. Even in new provinces like Arabia with little or no Romanization, strictly Roman forms of litigation

[52] *AE* 1971, 88f and Agennius Urbicus (in Corp.Agrim. p. 47 Th.), implying that all cities had *loca noxiorum poenis destinata*. The view given in the text is that of Kunkel, *PW* 24 (1963) 779–83 as against F. de Martino, *Labeo* 21 (1975) 211–14.   [53] *Dig.* 2.1.12.

[54] Cf. Garnsey and Saller 1987 (A 34) 34–40.

[55] Another question concerns the *ius gladii* given to some or to all governors, cf. Jones 1960 (A 47) 58–65.

[56] *Dig.* 1.17 for the *praefectus Aegypti*. The position of *iuridicus Hispaniae Citerioris* was a creation of Augustus too.

[57] Cf. Burton 1976 (D 89). The inscription from Cos (*AE* 1974, 629) is relevant too for people trying to evade municipal jurisdiction.

were introduced, as has been shown lately by models for an *actio tutelae* found in the archive of one Babatha, dating from the first quarter of the second century A.D.[58] On the other hand the governor could try cases by *cognitio* and give judgment himself or by a judge delegated by himself (*iudex pedaneus*). In criminal justice the double procedure holds good too, at least in the first century. The first edict of Cyrene sets up for capital cases a mixed panel of judges from Greeks and Roman citizens living in Cyrene and having a census of more than 7,500 denarii, but it becomes evident from the fourth edict that the governor could just as well conduct the inquiry and render decision himself.[59] Decisions of proconsuls wielding their own *imperium* and those of provincial jury-courts in theory might be final, without appeal, but in reality *provocatio* or *appellatio* were attempted wherever possible.

Municipal jurisdiction in the provinces was different, depending on whether a city had Roman or Latin rights or was simply non-Roman, *civitas peregrina*, and among the latter there was a small, privileged group, the *civitates liberae et foederatae*, which were in theory free from Roman intervention. But already in the first century A.D. theory and reality were quite different. In 6 B.C. a case of killing by throwing a filled chamberpot out of the window was transferred from the jurisdiction of the free city of Cnidus to that of Augustus, who ordered the proconsul of Asia to investigate.[60] In the second century differences such as this had largely disappeared.

XI

According to Velleius Paterculus, the loyal historian of Augustus and Tiberius, after the end of the civil wars laws, juries and Senate regained their former authority: 'restituta vis legibus, iudiciis auctoritas, senatui maiestas'.[61] So it might seem, and senators would be happier and certainly fared better if they believed in this phraseology. Tacitus knew otherwise: the emperor slowly began to arrogate to himself the functions of Senate, magistrates and laws, without meeting opposition.[62] As in politics, so in the administration of justice the old institutions first operated next to imperial jurisdiction and then slowly withered away, first in the provinces, then in Italy and finally in Rome, first in criminal justice, then in civil jurisdiction. Senators in the capital might, in the

---

[58] This is not the place to discuss the many problems connected with this archive, still not entirely published, which contains documents in Aramaic, Greek and Latin; cf. Wolff 1980 (D 278) and Bowersock 1983 (E 990) 76–9.   [59] Cf. the fourth Edict of Cyrene, *FIRA* I² 409.

[60] *FIRA* III 185; this was not, to be sure, a straightforward case, but mixed up with local intrigue, cf. the commentary of Millar 1977 (A 59) 443.   [61] II.89.3.

[62] *Ann.* I.2.1 'insurgere paulatim, munia senatus magistratuum legum in se trahere nullo adversante'.

period comprised in this volume, still sometimes try to live under the illusion of the old *respublica*. But in addition to *cognitio extra ordinem*, there now existed regular appeal in private law cases as in criminal justice, and a supervision which, if not always and everywhere efficient, was at least decidedly better than anything the Republic had known. In the view of the large majority of the population, the new trends in the administration of justice were undoubtedly 'progress'.

CHAPTER 13a

ITALY AND ROME FROM
SULLA TO AUGUSTUS

M. H. CRAWFORD

I. EXTENT OF ROMANIZATION

The enfranchisement of peninsular Italy in and immediately after 90 B.C., and of Transpadane Gaul in 49 B.C., was the culmination of a process which had begun in the fifth century B.C.[1] Similarly, the Romanization of Italy and the 'Italianization' of Rome, although both proceeded at an accelerated pace in the generations which followed the Social War, were phenomena whose roots lay deep in the past. In offering an interpretation of the essential features of the changing relationship between Rome and Italy from Sulla to Augustus, one must perforce take for granted much of their earlier history.[2]

A few words, however, by way of introduction. Within both the insurgent and the loyalist areas in 91 B.C., there were substantial variations in the extent of Romanization. Thus, of the Samnites and the Marsi, who both rebelled, the former still spoke their own language and used their own alphabet, the latter wrote and spoke Latin. The linguistic diversity of rebel Italy is indeed perfectly reflected in its bilingual coinage. The Samnites moreover remained directly acquainted with Greek cultural models down to the outbreak of war, for the Marsi these had probably long been mediated through Rome.[3] Similarly, of the Etruscans, whose part in the rebellion lay somewhere on a scale between the minimal and the non-existent, the southern peoples had largely ceased to speak Etruscan or to function as autonomous centres of artistic production in the third century B.C., the northern cities remained Etruscan in their language and in their art.[4]

A similarly variegated picture emerges if one looks at other areas of activity. Traditional forms of agriculture survived in some parts of Italy

---

[1] I should like, with the customary disclaimer, to offer my warmest thanks to Dr A.K. Bowman, Professor P.A. Brunt, Dr T.J. Cornell, Miss A.C. Dionisotti, Professor E. Gabba, the late Professor A. Gara, Mr Ph. Moreau, Dr J.A. North, for their comments on earlier drafts of this chapter. I should also have liked it if my thanks had been able to cross the Styx to Martin Frederiksen, without whose fertility in ideas and generosity with them this chapter would have been a much poorer thing.

[2] I have tried to lay out its essential features in Crawford 1986 (E 27).

[3] See Crawford 1981 (E 26).   [4] Torelli 1976 (E 130).

in the second century B.C., against a general background of the spread of
plantations and also of pastoralism oriented towards the market;[5] by way
of contrast, the whole of peninsular Italy had come to use the same
coinage and the same system of reckoning within a generation or so after
the end of the Second Punic War.[6] The coinage which the insurgents
struck in 91–89 B.C. was a coinage of denarii, with one issue of *aurei*. It is
also worth drawing attention in this context to the Lex Osca Tabulae
Bantinae, an inscription on bronze which conserves part of the charter of
the Lucanian community of Bantia, to be dated just before the Social
War.[7] It is in the Oscan language, but the Latin script; its institutions are
largely borrowed from those of the nearby Latin colony of Venusia, but
the text still struggles to create a vocabulary in Oscan to describe them.

Romanized and non-Romanized, insurgent and loyalist, all had a
common citizenship from (let us say) 86 B.C. Attempts had been made in
the immediate aftermath of the Social War to limit the distribution of the
new citizens either to a small minority of the existing Roman tribes or to
a small number of specially created additional tribes; and Sulla had tried
to deprive some Italian communities of full Roman citizenship. But once
these manoeuvres had failed, the whole of Italy south of the Po, perhaps
with the exception of some parts of Liguria, formed in theory a single
political unit centred on Rome. Even if they remained subject to the
jurisdiction of the governor of Gallia Cisalpina, the citizens of the former
Latin colony of Placentia were fully entitled to vote in elections at Rome.
Entitlement and practice, however, need not coincide and it would be
rash to suppose that the orientation of men's political consciousness
necessarily changed very much or very fast. One small piece of evidence
suggests that it did begin to change. Unknown on inscriptions outside
Roman territory and of extreme rarity outside Rome itself before the
Social War, consular dating formulae begin to turn up in all parts of Italy
with some regularity (see Appendix I, p. 979).

Let us consider first, then, the problem of political structures. Censors
were elected for 86 B.C., but they evidently did no more than nibble at the
problem of compiling a list of all those who were now Roman citizens.
No further census was held for sixteen years; for Sulla certainly took
steps to ensure that the Republic could function without censors,
whether or not he intended or directed that the census should disappear
and whether or not he hoped or wished that the vast mass of new citizens
should not be registered.[8] Even the censors of 70 B.C., in the context of
an abandonment of some of the more conspicuously objectionable
features of the Sullan settlement, failed to register more than a propor-

---

[5] Lepore 1981 (E 75).   [6] See Crawford 1985 (B 320).
[7] *Roman Statutes* 1995 (F 684) no. 13.   [8] Wiseman 1969 (E 137).

Map 3. Italy.

tion of those whom they could in theory have registered. No further census was completed before that of Augustus in 28 B.C. But this was not the only problem. The sheer size and dispersion of the citizen body now made plain what had long been the case, namely that no assembly at Rome could be regarded as reflecting the views of the citizen body as a whole; no longer could even the Roman system of group voting be regarded as achieving this end, despite the fact that if a few people from Arpinum travelled to Rome to vote, they could in some sense be seen as the representatives of their section of the *tribus Cornelia*. And in fact within a very few years of the failed census of 70–69 B.C. there emerged a new way in which the aristocracies, at least, of the towns of Italy could make their views known – decrees passed by their councils and transmitted to the Senate at Rome, as for instance in the course of the Catilinarian crisis of 63 B.C., evoked by Cicero in his defence of Flaccus in 59 B.C.:

Let the *laudationes* of great *municipia* and colonies serve to defend him, let the lavish and accurate *laudatiᵥ* of the Senate and people of Rome also serve. To think of that night which almost consigned this city to everlasting darkness . . .[9]

Of course, in the age of Cicero, the *domi nobiles* who passed these decrees also attempted at the same time, to a greater extent than ever before, to make their way in politics or society at Rome, emulating the office-holders of the imperial Republic or, like Catullus, sleeping with their wives, sisters and daughters.[10] Now, as earlier, contact of whatever kind between Rome and Italy was to a large extent mediated through personal relationships between members of the Roman and Italian aristocracies and was never insulated from the political life of either. The extension of Roman citizenship and any accompanying acculturation always involved a very delicate balance between the transformation and the conservation of existing political and economic structures.[11]

A sense of the tensions emerges in the passage in which Velleius Paterculus singles out for praise the help given to Rome in the Social War by his ancestor Minatius Magius of Aeclanum, who was himself the descendant of a man of Capua loyal to Rome in the Second Punic War; Velleius was well aware that the Italian cause was just, but that loyalty to

---

[9] Cic. *Flac.* 101–2; compare *Sest.* 9–11; Gabba 1986 (E 49).

[10] Syme 1938 (D 68); Syme 1939 (A 93) 90–4; Wiseman 1971 (D 81), documents at length and for all periods down to Augustus the incorporation of Italians in the Roman governing class; see also Nicolet 1966 (D 52) I. 387–422; Cébeillac Gervasoni 1978 (E 14); the papers in *Epigrafia e ordine senatorio* 1982 (D 42); David 1983 (E 32); D'Arms 1984 (E 31); for the jurists, see Frier 1985 (F 652) 253–4; for cultural links, see Wiseman 1983 (E 138); Dumont 1983 (E 36); Wiseman 1985 (E 139); Rawson 1985 (A 79).

[11] See the fine remarks of Gabba 1984 (E 48) 214–17; for two case studies see Castrén 1983 (E 13); Sensi 1983 (E 120).

Rome was an overriding obligation, that Rome granted after the outbreak of war what she had denied in time of peace (II.16.1–2):

The most important leaders of the Italici, however, were Popaedius Silo, Herius Asinius, Insteius Cato, C. Pontidius, Pontius Telesinus, Marius Egnatius, Papius Mutilus. Nor will I from modesty subtract a particle of glory from my own family, while continuing to tell the truth; for tribute must be paid to the memory of Minatius Magius of Aeclanum, my *atavus*, the grandson of Decius Magius, a leading Capuan and a most outstanding and loyal man; his loyalty to Rome in this war was such that with a legion which he had raised among the Hirpini he captured Herculaneum along with T. Didius, and Pompeii along with L. Sulla, and seized Compsa . . .

The poignancy of the juxtaposition, Minatius Magius beside the insurgent leaders, speaks for itself. We should also pause for a moment to stand before the Arringatore, a splendid bronze statue of an orator in full flood, now in the Museo Archaeologico di Firenze; belonging to the early Julio-Claudian period, he represents perfectly these men who stood between their two worlds, with the *toga* and *calcei* of a magistrate of Perugia, the *anulus* and *angustus clavus* of a Roman *eques*.[12]

But it is more than doubtful whether such men pursued their careers in the context of any kind of systematic policy in favour of administrative centralization or social conformity. It is true that there are a few coin-types which seem to advertise the *popularis* themes of *libertas* or the union of Italy and Rome;[13] but the ideology of a modern nation state seems to be wholly absent from the Roman world and perhaps too much emphasis has been put on the pressures making for the decline of local patriotism in the Italy of the late Republic.[14] We need to remember that, even within the Roman elite, the age of Cicero was a period of exuberant diversity and experimentation with new social and cultural models.[15] And the enfranchisement of Italy actually removed one powerful reason for the privileging of Roman models, namely the need to emphasize the difference in status between, say, a Latin colony with all its rights and privileges, such as Aesernia, and a neighbouring Samnite village. On the other hand, another factor may have been relevant. Just as in the third century B.C. the final stages of the extension of Roman control over Italy coincided with and were influenced by the beginning of Roman expansion overseas, so the period with which we are concerned

---

[12] Demougin 1988 (D 37) 781; M. Cristofani 1986–7 (F 338).

[13] Crawford 1974 (B 319) I nos. 391 (C. Egnatius Cn.f. Cn.n. Maxsumus), 392 (L. Farsuleius Mensor), 403 (Kalenus, Cordus).

[14] E.g., Galsterer 1976 (E 52) 13–14; for the ideology of a modern nation state, see e.g., E. Weber, *Peasants into Frenchmen. The Modernization of Rural France, 1870–1914* (London, 1979); for the absence of an Italian consciousness in the early Empire, see Gabba 1978 (E 45).

[15] Beard and Crawford 1985 (A 3) ch. 2.

witnessed the beginning of large-scale grants of citizenship in the provinces, massive colonization overseas and the emergence of Rome not simply as a world power, but also as a world state. It is in this context significant that the possibility of holding Roman citizenship along with that of a foreign state emerges for the first time in the age of Caesar.[16] Contrasts between Italian communities formerly of different statuses will perhaps have seemed secondary to the need to create and conserve a sense of Italian identity against the background of a rapidly changing outside world. It is worth noting that when Augustus seized power in Rome and served as a focus of loyalty to Italy and the empire alike, the privileged status of Italy was carefully preserved.

Against this background, Cicero captures for us towards the end of his life both the awareness that much had changed in Italy in the previous generation and a sense of the constraints on change (*De Legibus* II.1.2–2.5):

'... this is my and my brother's real country (*germana patria*)' ... 'But' replied Atticus 'what was it that you said just now, that this place – for I take it that you mean Arpinum – is your real country. For surely you do not have two countries; rather Rome is the country of us all. Unless perhaps the country of Cato was not Rome, but Tusculum.' 'But I do think that he and everyone from a *municipium* has two countries, one by descent, one by citizenship.'[17]

The central problem, then, is to try and understand just how far, and why, the different local cultures of Italy, in the sense of shared and transmitted practices and values within particular regions, survived into and beyond the age of Augustus.

One point must first be made, namely that the tenacity of Greek culture in some cities of the south cannot be taken as typical. Its survival was helped by two factors, the existence outside Italy of thousands of cities of Greek language and culture, contact with which reinforced Greek culture and institutions in Italy, and the value attached by the Roman elite to Greek culture, which served to nurture those centres of Greek civilization which lay close at hand.[18] This factor had probably already begun to operate before the Social War. And the Greek cities of Italy were largely exempt from the convulsions which we shall shortly see to have played a major part in the Romanization of Italy in general. It is in this context that we should understand the hesitation of Neapolis

[16] See Rawson 1985 (E 107); Pais 1918 (E 88) I antedates the process where Rome and a foreign state are concerned, as opposed to Rome and a *municipium*. Brunt 1982 (F 644) seems to me in the end right to argue, against Braunert 1966 (E 9), and Galsterer 1976 (E 52) 162–4, that in purely legal terms there was no case against Balbus.

[17] See Hammond 1951 (E 54); also de Ruggiero 1921 (F 686); Bonjour 1975 (E 7). Gely 1974 (E 53) romanticizes.   [18] D'Arms 1970 (E 30).

and Heraclea before accepting Roman citizenship when they were offered it in 90 B.C.; the survival of local issues of coinage at Heraclea, Velia and indeed Paestum;[19] and the persistence of the Greek language and of Greek institutions in general, at Neapolis, Velia, Rhegium, Tarentum, Canusium.[20] It is curious that the two Latin municipal charters of the republican period which we possess come from the Greek city of Tarentum and from a shrine in the territory of Heraclea; Heraclea drifted quietly out of existence in the age of Augustus; but Tarentum continued as a recognizably Greek city in the early Empire. And the separateness of the south in the age of Augustus is reflected in the fact that Strabo discusses Bruttium, Lucania and Magna Graecia in the context of a Greek tradition which contrasted the archaic and classical periods with the hellenistic and Roman, but saw the whole as the single history of a separate area.[21] Even so, and despite the disappearance of much evidence – C.T. Ramage, an intrepid Scot who walked the length and breadth of Magna Graecia just after the Bourbon restoration, saw a Greek inscription of the second century A.D., now lost, recording an agonistic festival at Scolacium – there is no good reason to suppose that any part of Italy remained recognizably Greek beyond the middle of the third century A.D.[22]

Of local practices, and of men's attachment to them, Cicero preserves a couple of rare glimpses. The first is no more than a casual reference to the occasion, 'cum eius in nuptiis more Larinatium multitudo hominum pranderet', 'when at his marriage according to the custom of the people of Larinum a large number of people were dining together' (*Clu.* 166). But the second relates to the slave *ministri*, attendants, of Mars at Larinum, where 'repente Oppianicus eos omnis liberos esse civisque Romanos coepit defendere', 'suddenly Oppianicus began to claim that they were all free and Roman citizens'; so attached were the people of Larinum to their customs that they persuaded A. Cluentius Habitus to be their advocate and take their case to Rome (*Clu.* 43–4). A further glimpse

---

[19] Crawford 1985 (B 320), 71–2; for isolated survivals of non-Roman units of reckoning, weights and measures, see *ibid.*, 14–16, 177–8; there is a full description, based on autopsy, of the *mensa ponderaria* at Pompeii in Conway 1897 (E 23) I, App. I. The stone is cut according to the Oscan foot. When the *mensa ponderaria* was converted to the Roman system, the five original holes were enlarged and four new ones cut (Prosdocimi 1978 (E 100) 1072–3); but the *sextarius* remained Oscan, while the ratios with the other measures of capacity became Roman.

[20] A provisional statement in Crawford 1978 (F 20) 195 n. 12; note a statue of a Greek in a toga at Velia, de Franciscis 1970 (E 40); and see Sartori 1976 (E 118); Keuls 1976 (E 67); Lepore 1983 (E 76); see Appendix II, p. 981. It will not do to talk in the same breath of Tarentum and the rest of Italy as does Torelli 1984 (E 132) 42–3.   [21] Prontera 1988 (E 99).

[22] *The Nooks and Byways of Italy. Wanderings in Search of Its Ancient Remains and modern Superstitions* (Liverpool, 1868) 133; there is no reason to believe that the Pettorano fragment of the Prices Edict of Diocletian is of Carrara marble or that it was ever displayed in a Greek-speaking part of Italy; Guarducci (1985 (B 238)) has now revealed that the sample shown to her experts was diminutive; and visual identifications of diminutive fragments are worthless.

comes from a letter of the emperor Marcus Aurelius to Fronto in the middle of the second century A.D., recording how a native of Anagnia knew and cared enough to explain to him, when he visited the city, that a religious formula inscribed in Latin above a gate of the city used a technical term of Hernican origin (Fronto, 66–7 Naber = 60 van den Hout).

The survival of such practices was no doubt favoured by the extent to which the communities of Italy not only administered their own cities, but also performed tasks which other societies assign to central structures. The main lines for the government of Italy were presumably laid down in the immediate aftermath of the Social War, in order to cope with the incorporation of half the communities of Italy into the Roman citizen body. But it is also important to remember that the age of Cicero was in addition a period which saw the normalization of the government of communities which had long been Roman. Capua, deprived of the right to govern itself in 211 B.C., became a colony in 59–58 B.C. A constitution was given to Cingulum by T. Labienus on the eve of the outbreak of war in 49 B.C. The constitution of Arpinum was revised in 46 B.C., with the support of Cicero, by his son and his nephew and a colleague. The same period saw the progressive elimination, by promotion to municipal status or by incorporation in another *municipium*, of the *praefecturae, fora* and *conciliabula* which had served as provisional communities for groups of Roman citizens in the course of the conquest and settlement of Italy. Normalization may also be observed in a different context. The *pagi* of the Frentani, Carricini, Marrucini, Paeligni and Vestini, the *vici* of the Vestini, Marsi, Aequiculi and Sabini, both were accommodated into the structure of Roman Italy in the generation after the Social War, but were eliminated thereafter, probably by Caesar. Naturally, there was never one single measure which regulated all the affairs of every single *municipium*. But there are some minimal elements which must have figured in the Lex Iulia granting citizenship in 90 B.C. or in a subsequent statute; and there are many institutions which are common to many of the new *municipia* of the period.

It is perhaps not very important to decide whether these were imposed by measures passed at Rome or introduced by the men who provided the new communities with their charters, drawing on the shared experience of centuries of giving constitutions to communities in Italy or overseas. The Lex Iulia itself must have imposed the rule that a community must vote to accept the Roman citizenship; it may also have laid down the obligation that the new *municipia* must be constituted by an appropriate person or persons.[23] Their supreme magistrates seem normally to have

[23] For particularly interesting cases of *constitutio*, see Harvey 1973 (E 57); Gabba 1983 (E 47); for this paragraph as a whole, see Crawford, forthcoming (E 29).

been *IIIIviri*, probably flanked by *praefecti iure dicundo*, prefects in charge of jurisdiction, as replacements when necessary; the institution of the *interrex* was perhaps also transmitted to the government of the *municipia* at this point.[24] Such aspects of municipal government were perhaps directly imposed by statute, rather than emerging from the consensus of the men who constituted the new *municipia*. And at some point a general statute was certainly passed that governed the co-optation of decurions in *municipia*.[25] The arrangements for local censuses recorded in the Tabula Heracleensis almost certainly go back to the period immediately after the Social War;[26] and the recurrence in the late Republic and early Empire of the phrase 'coloni (*or* municipes), incolae, hospites, adventores', 'citizens of the colony (or of the *municipium*), resident outsiders, guests, visitors', suggests very strongly that this was an official definition of the population of an Italian community.[27] There are in addition references already in the late Republic to formal rules governing expenditure by local magistrates on games or buildings.[28] Municipal charters probably also included rules for the location of *ustrina*, crematoria, and cemeteries.

Surviving fragments of charters alas often pose more problems than they solve. The only straightforward text is the Lex Tarentina, the preserved part of which makes it clear that the text relates solely to Tarentum; it contains the remains of chapters dealing with the improper handling of *pequnia publica*, *sacra*, *religiosa*; the security given by the first *IIIIviri* and aediles of the *municipium* and by candidates for election; the property qualification for decurions; the demolition of buildings; *viae*, *fossae*, *cloacae*; and departure from the *municipium*.[29] By way of contrast, the fragments of statutes from Falerio seem to be concerned with the regulation of jurisdiction, but in more than one community;[30] the fragment from Ateste certainly regulates jurisdiction in any subordinate community without restriction of locality.[31] In some ways, our best evidence comes from the substantial portion which has been preserved of the charter for the Caesarian colony of Urso in Spain, where the text relates once again solely to Urso.[32] The range of material is similar to that

---

[24] *ILLRP* 555 (Beneventum); 627 (Narbo); *ILS* 6285 (Formiae); 6279 (Fundi); *ILS* 6975 (Nemausus); *CIL* IV 54, also 13, 50, 53, 56, 70 (for C. Popidius at Pompeii. The import even of these texts is not wholly clear; and 48, 3822 and 9827 are manifestly irrelevant; Castrén 1975 (E 12) 51 is misleading); González, *Actas I Cong. And. Est. Clas.* (Jaén, 1982), 223 = *AE* 1982, 511 (Siarum); see also *Roman Statutes* 1995 (F 684) no. 25, ch. 130 (Urso).

[25] See the Lex Irnitana, González 1986 (B 235), ch. 31, where 'quod ante h(anc) l(egem) rogatam iure more eiius municipi fuerunt' is clearly the result of imperfect adaptation of a chapter of a general statute; the charters of the Flavian *municipia* of Baetica can hardly have been individually passed through an assembly at Rome.　　　[26] *Roman Statutes* 1995 (F 684) no. 24, lines 142–58.

[27] Paci 1989 (B 260) 125–33; the phrase is echoed by Cicero, *Leg. Agr.* II. 94: 'nos autem hinc Roma [to Capua] qui veneramus, iam non hospites, sed peregrini atque advenae nominabamur'.

[28] *ILLRP* 648 (Pompeii); compare 675 (Telesia).　　　[29] *Roman Statutes* (F 684), no. 15.

[30] *Ibid.* nos. 17, 18.　　　[31] *Ibid.* no. 16.　　　[32] *Ibid.* no. 25.

in the Lex Tarentina, though, since much more is preserved, there are many aspects which are not represented at Tarentum; but two of the chapters at Tarentum reappear at Urso, as also in the charters issued by the Flavian emperors to the new Latin *municipia* of Baetica, those dealing with the demolition of buildings and with *viae, fossae, cloacae*.[33] Inferences about earlier charters on the basis of the Flavian charters, however, would be very dangerous; it is clear that they are much better organized and much more economically drafted than the Tarentum or Urso charters and it may be that they are more comprehensive. The two remaining texts are both entirely *sui generis*.[34] The Tabula Heracleensis comes from a sanctuary near the borders of the territories of Heraclea and Metapontum; it appears to contain excerpts from a Roman statute dealing with roads and public space in the city and from another (or from others) dealing with qualifications for decurions and magistrates, censuses in the towns of Roman Italy, constitution of *municipia*. What we have of the text of the Lex de Gallia Cisalpina comes from Veleia, in the Apennines near Parma, and seems to be a statute which transmitted to Cisalpine Gaul after it became part of Italy in 42–41 B.C. many, perhaps all, of the substantive rules of the Roman *ius civile*; the single surviving tablet bears the number IIII and goes from the middle of Ch. XIX to the middle of Ch. XXIII, dealing with *operis novi nuntiatio, damnum infectum, pecunia certa credita*, any other debt, the *actio familiae erciscundae*, all at a very high level of technicality and complexity.[35]

The communities of Italy did not possess capital jurisdiction after the Social War;[36] but it is striking that they preserved some military and police functions, not only in the late Republic, but even beyond. Archaeological evidence reveals substantial wall-building in the late Republic, for instance at Spoletium and Ferentinum, not surprising in the disturbed circumstances of the period and carefully to be distinguished from the symbolic walls with which Augustan foundations like Saepinum or Augusta Bagiennorum were equipped.[37] And an inscription from Praeneste refers to the building of *vigiliae*, guard posts, two inscriptions, from Brundisium and Formiae, to the building of an *armamentarium*, arms depot;[38] while Cicero refers to the Larinates who have come to Rome to defend his client who would otherwise have been

---

[33] González 1986 (B 235) chs. 62 and 82.   [34] *Roman Statutes* 1995 (F 684), nos. 24 and 26.

[35] For what may be inferred about developments in municipal charters in the Caesarian and Augustan ages, see M.H. Crawford (n. 23).

[36] M.H. Crawford (n. 23).

[37] Spoletium: *CIL* XI 4809, not in *ILLRP* or *CIL* I², fasc. 4, but see Gaggiotti *et al.* 1980 (E 50) 107; Ferentinum: *CIL* X 5837 = *ILLRP* 584.

[38] Praeneste: *ILLRP* 653; Brundisium: *ILLRP* 558; Formiae: A. Colombini, *Athenaeum* 1966, 137; for local military exercise grounds, see Devijver and van Wonterghem 1981–2 (E 35).

available to defend their city (*Clu.* 195). And at some point in the troubled history of the late Republic, Ostia was perhaps rescued from attack not by a Roman magistrate, but by C. Cartilius Poplicola, *IIvir* of Ostia.[39]

It is then not surprising that these largely autonomous local administrations of late republican Italy should have invested heavily in building programmes in general, to create an urban centre where none existed before, to provide for the administration of the newly constituted community, simply as an expression of civic pride.[40]

And naturally enough also, the existence of local administration in the late Republic and in the imperial age was reflected in the inscription of lists of local magistrates and priests and in the erection of *elogia* of local worthies, past and present. But such practices are as much evidence of the influence of Roman models as they are of local particularism. As evidence of the survival of a local culture, in the sense in which we have defined it, they leave much to be desired. In particular, the Elogia Tarquiniensia and the Fasti of the *haruspices* reflect the fact that the senatorial families of Etruria were competing in the political life of Rome; for they transfer to Tarquinii practices characteristic of the urban aristocracy.[41] Against the background of this general pattern, little weight should be attached to the occasional use of a local era for dating purposes, conspicuously at Patavium, where a handful of inscriptions are dated by an era beginning in 173 B.C.; Rome had intervened to resolve internal strife in 174 B.C. (Livy, XLI.27.3–4) and the magistrates of the following year no doubt regarded themselves as the first of a refounded community.[42]

II. SURVIVAL OF LOCAL CULTURES

The following discussion, then, of the survival of local cultures concentrates on what seem to be four important identifying features of any ancient culture with a claim to be individual and distinctive: language, religion, family structures, disposal of the dead. We shall of course never know in detail in what ways the behaviour and mentality of the peasants of Etruria or Samnium changed during the century which

---

[39] Zevi 1976 (E 142) 56–60. For the overly zealous police of Saepinum in the second century A.D., see now Lo Cascio 1985–90 (E 79); Brunt 1990 (A 12), 427–8.　　[40] Gabba 1972 (E 44).

[41] Fasti: *IItal* XIII 2, no. 6 (Venusia); *CIL* x 1233 (Nola); 5405, with Solin 1988 (B 285) 90–1 (Interamna); *AE* 1905, 192 (Teanum). Lists of *pontifices*: *CIL* IX 3254 (Sutri); Elogia Tarquiniensia: Torelli 1975 (B 291); Cornell 1976 (E 24); Cornell 1978 (E 25); Gabba 1979 (E 46), arguing rightly that the erection of the Elogia Tarquiniensia is to be explained in the context of the antiquarianism of Rome of the second century A.D., rather than in that of the local culture of Tarquinii.

[42] Harris 1977 (E 56); Linderski 1983 (E 78) (the resolution of the letter N); there are isolated examples of the same phenomenon at Feltria, also at Interamna Nahars, Bovillae and Puteoli (*ILLRP* 518); compare also Cato, *Orig.* fr. 49 P = II. 16 Chassignet, on Ameria.

saw the collapse of the Republic and the establishment of the Empire. But the four themes discussed have the merit that the evidence for them carries us to a level far below that of the inner core of the elite. And, in principle, the catalysts which were at work should have affected all levels of society in largely equal measure.

1. Language

The only two indigenous non-Latin languages of Italy for which there is any significant evidence later than the Social War are Etruscan and Oscan, though little of the evidence for the latter comes from Samnium, because of the ravages of Sulla.[43] Furthermore, the process of transition seems to have been extremely rapid; there is only one Oscan bilingual inscription; and even in the case of Etruria, where the phenomenon is on a somewhat larger scale, it is actually quite restricted.[44] As for late texts in Etruscan, apart from a gem from Tarquinii, which may have migrated after being inscribed, and a stone from Pesaro, which certainly did so, the thirty or so texts, mostly of the very end of the second and the first half of the first century B.C., all come from the region of Clusium, Arretium, Perusia and Volaterrae, mainly from Clusium. No local language can be shown to have lasted in public use much into the first century A.D.; only Etruscan survived in some form for a time, a preserve of scholars and antiquarians. It is in this context significant that the family of Urgula-nilla, wife of Claudius, emperor and Etruscologist, was quite untypical in the extent to which it consciously kept itself Etruscan.[45]

We simply do not know to what extent Rome willed the disappear-ance, at any rate at an official level, of languages other than Latin. If we could hold that the Lex Osca Tabulae Bantinae fell after the Social War, we should have an indication that Latin was not prescribed for municipal charters. But it is almost certainly earlier (see above); and the municipal charter of the indubitably Greek city of Tarentum was promulgated in Latin, probably sometime in the 80s or 70s B.C. In any case, it is unlikely that in Italy after 90 B.C. Rome recognized any language other than Latin for her own purposes; and certain institutions, such as ethnic con-tingents in the Roman army, which will have helped to preserve local languages before the Social War, disappeared at or soon after the same date.[46] The literary language of late republican and early imperial Italy

---

[43] See in general de Simone 1980 (E 121); Coleman 1986 (E 22). The best account of the disappearance of Etruscan is still that of Harris 1971 (E 55) 172–84; note also 1975 (E 64); Michelsen 1975 (B 254): Etruscan letters in texts inscribed in Latin are of extreme rarity. For the disappearance of Oscan at Pompeii, see Castren 1975 (E 12), 44–6. See Appendix III, p. 983.

[44] Poccetti 1988 (E 97): the single Umbrian bilingual seems earlier than the Social War.

[45] Heurgon 1953 (E 59); Briquel 1990 (E 10).

[46] Ilari 1974 (D 196); the ethnic contingents in the army of Spartacus perpetuate earlier Roman practice.

is remarkably uniform, despite the diversity of origin of those who wrote it.

2. Religion

The evidence suggests a similar change in the orientation of religious practice. First, calendars, whose centrality to Roman (as well as Greek) religion needs no emphasis. We know from a variety of antiquarian sources that in early times a number of Italian communities, even some close to Rome, had calendars substantially different from each other and from that of Rome (Varro, *Antiquitates rerum divinarum*, fr. 262 Cardauns):

... but in the town of Lavinium one whole month was assigned to Liber ...

and (Solinus 1.34 (so also August. *De civ. D.* xv.12); see also Appendix IV, p. 985):

... for before Augustus Caesar they reckoned the year in different ways, since in Egypt it contained four months ... in Italy at Lavinium thirteen, where the year was of 374 days ...

We know also that communities could and did change their calendars.[47] And they seem on the whole to have changed them systematically in the direction of abandoning local peculiarities. Thus, a local calendar is last attested epigraphically in Etruria at Ferentis in 67 B.C., that of Furfo in 58 B.C.[48] The next stage was the massive diffusion in Italy under and after Augustus of copies of the Julian calendar.[49]

The Romanization of the religious map of Italy had indeed long been under way. It had been the *pontifices* who had seen to the preservation of the cults of communities which had become *municipia* (Festus 146 L). And it seems clear that the best interpretation of the pattern of Roman reactions to prodigies outside Rome is to suppose that it was always up to the Senate to decide which to notice; and that it gradually took notice of more and more on territory that was not Roman.[50] The culmination of this process is the position under the Empire; for shrines in Italy now belong to the *populus Romanus* (Tac. *Ann.* III.71):

[47] To the texts cited above, add Suet. *Aug.* 59; Galsterer 1976 (E 52) 128–9, does not give sufficient weight to the phenomenon.

[48] *ILLRP* 589 (Ferentis), to be read with Emiliozzi 1983 (E 39) (the name of the month is uncertain, but is in any case not Chosfer); Degrassi 1961–2 (B 225); *ILLRP* 508, to be read with Laffi 1978 (E 69).

[49] *IItal* XIII 2, nos. 5, 6, 7, 8, 9, 15, 16, 17, 21, 22, 24, 25, 37, 39; the *elogia* of Roman type from Arretium and Pompeii form part of the same phenomenon.

[50] McBain 1982 (F 177), with the review by Beard 1983 (F 90).

It has been established ... that all ceremonies and temples and images of the gods in Italian towns are under the control and power of Rome.

and (Frontinus, 56 L):

(... sacred groves in Italy), whose territory indubitably belongs to the Roman people, even if they are within the boundaries of colonies and *municipia* ...

The position described by Tacitus and Frontinus was no doubt the result of the enfranchisement of Italy; but it had been prepared by a long process of growing Roman involvement in the religion of Italy.

Evidence for change in religious practice is also provided by the pattern of votive offerings in the rural shrines of Italy, small and large alike. Here the evidence is now sufficient in bulk to show that the frequentation of rural shrines in Italy is a phenomenon which largely comes to an end at the turn of the eras (for some examples see Appendix V, p. 987).

Naturally, this is not to be regarded simply as a consequence of a process of Romanization, not least because it also affected shrines situated in areas which had long been *ager Romanus*, Roman territory. In part, we are presumably witnessing the consequence of the process of urbanization which affected much of Italy, albeit on a scale not to be exaggerated, in the first century B.C. and the first century A.D.[51] It was this process which helped to put an end to the independence of the *pagi*, which had flourished as a form of local administration in the territory of the Frentani, Carricini, Marrucini, Paeligni and Vestini between the Social War and Caesar, electing magistrates, raising money, passing decrees, erecting buildings.[52] Corroboration for such a view may be found in the fact that those rural shrines which survived tended to do so because their organization was incorporated into the administrative structure of a nearby city: such is the case of the sanctuary of Hercules Curinus and Sulmo or of that of Rossano di Vaglia and Potentia; the result was similar for the sanctuary at Lacus Clitumni, given by Augustus not to a neighbouring town, but to Hispellum.

None the less, a shift of population and power from country to town is neither the only nor perhaps the principal factor at work. Rather, as we shall see, the social transformation of Italy in the last generation of the Republic and the age of revolution was responsible. Rural shrines were necessarily dependent on supporting social structures; and it was precisely these that were destroyed, in Roman and Italian territory alike, but with far more devastating consequences in the latter.

It is in the sphere of religion, moreover, that we are confronted with

---

[51] E. Gabba (n. 40).   [52] Frederiksen 1976 (E 42).

specific evidence for the adoption in Italy of Roman models. One of the most important recent discoveries relevant to the religion of the late Republic has been the excavation of the *auguraculum* of Bantia: a platform from which an augur observed the flights of the birds and a series of inscribed *cippi* indicating the significance of the birds which appeared above them. It now appears that a first phase of the structure, in which the Oscan names of the deities recorded on the *cippi* were used, is to be dated to the nineties. At a later stage, at least one text was replaced with a Roman name of the deity concerned.[53] Consonant with this evidence is Cicero's remark on augury by birds, as practised in Phrygia, Pisidia, Cilicia and Arabia (*De Div.* 1.92): 'we have heard that this also used to be practised in Umbria'.[54]

3. Family structures

To turn to the third theme, we are told by Aulus Gellius that the enfranchisement of all Latin communities after the Social War meant the disappearance there of actionable *sponsalia*, legally enforceable engagements to marry;[55] and the Tabula Siarensis, a copy of part of the measures honouring Germanicus after his death, now provides dramatic confirmation that some rules for *sponsalia* were indeed different for Romans and Latins.[56] We may also suppose that after the Social War the serf population of Etruria, insofar as it still existed, became free. Otherwise, we are lamentably ignorant of the private law of the different Italian communities, even in the case of Larinum, for which we have the information in the *pro Cluentio*;[57] and it is not at all clear that the statement of Cato, 'If an Arpinate dies, the *sacra* do not follow his heir' (*Orig.* fr. 61 P = 11.31 Chassignet), even refers to the law of persons in Arpinum,[58] rather than to the sacred law. But it is probably legitimate to suppose that a faint reflection of original diversity is to be found in patterns of nomenclature different from the Roman.

To take three examples, a traditional Etruscan practice was to give the mother's name; this practice of metronymy is still attested on some bilingual inscriptions or texts in Latin only of the late Republic and then dies out.[59] Oscan practice was to give the father's *praenomen* in the

---

[53] M. Torelli, *RAL* 8, 24, 1969, 9–48, 'Contributi al Supplemento del *CIL* IX', at 39–48; Torelli 1983 (E 131); 1984 (E 133); a *cippus* from Frigento, published by C. Grella, *Economia Irpina* 1976, 1, pl. 9, is alas probably a mere boundary stone, not a *cippus* from a similar *auguraculum, contra* (n. 3), 156.

[54] See also Rawson 1978 (E 106), citing Philodemus on Stoicism in 'what was once Etruria' (not to be taken as a way of referring to Rome).

[55] Gell. *NA* IV.4.1–4; for the probable position at Rome, see Watson 1967 (F 700) 11–18: the arguments from Plautus are not very safe.   [56] *Roman Statutes* 1995 (F 684) no. 37.

[57] Moreau 1983 (E 85) 117–18.

[58] As held by Humbert 1978 (E 61) 305 n. 71a, whom I originally followed (n. 3), 155.

[59] *ILLRP* 790 (Montepulciano), 570, 904 (Clusium), 638, 814 (Perusia).

genitive, after the *cognomen*, but without the equivalent of 'f(ilius)'; again, the practice is still attested on a few Latin inscriptions and then disappears.[60] In this case, it is particularly striking that the Romanization of Oscan nomenclature, which occurred in Italy after the Social War, took place among Oscan speakers on Delos before the Social War.[61] Notoriously, the experiences and interaction of Romans and Italians as men of business abroad was a major factor in the assimilation of the two. Umbrian practice was to give the father's *praenomen* in the genitive, between the *praenomen* and the *cognomen*; a group of funerary inscriptions from Tuder, of a single family, illustrates the process of transition (Vetter 232): the male of the first generation adopts Umbrian practice, as well as still writing from right to left; his daughter and her husband write from left to right; their son adopts Roman practice, though his language is still Umbrian, even if written from left to right.

On one level, the explanation of the changes we have just been considering is to hand. With the enfranchisement of Italy, the Roman civil law was the only system which a magistrate could apply; and when a man was listed in the Roman census, he was naturally obliged to use the Roman system of nomenclature. But we have already seen that the first complete census of Italy was that of Augustus in 28 B.C. and there is in any case no a priori reason to suppose that a man would describe himself in the same way to a Roman censor (whether via a local magistrate or not) and on his own tomb; and one should not overestimate the effectiveness of enfranchisement in spreading the Roman civil law.[62] Rather, much deeper convulsions in Italian society are to be invoked, as we shall see.

4. Disposal of the dead

Here, if anywhere, we should expect conservatism of practice. Yet it is precisely here that the late first century B.C. and the early first century A.D. see the disappearance of dozens of local styles of funerary monument and the abandonment of cemeteries with centuries of use behind them.

The phenomenon was originally identified by M.W. Frederiksen, publishing a group of funerary monuments characteristic of Capua and the immediate vicinity, which cease to be produced with the coming of

---

[60] *ILLRP* 286 (Trasacco of the Marsi), 483 (Ager Falernus), 1254 (Forum Novum in Sabina); Vetter 195 (Lucania); see in general Lejeune 1976 (E 74), for the loss of the rich variety of Oscan *praenomina*, the emergence of standard abbreviations for the *praenomina* that survived, the adoption of the abbreviation 'f(ilius)' and the appearance of *cognomina*.   [61] Poccetti 1984 (E 96).

[62] Domitian's letter to Irni shows for a later period how difficult the process was; Mourgues 1987 (B 257) is not persuasive.

the Principate.[63] A few kilometres away, the area between Pompeii and Nuceria Alfaterna had a quite different type of monument, equally characteristic of the locality and equally doomed to disappear. In Latium, a type of monument characteristic of the Volsci has a similar chronology. North of Rome, the great Etruscan cemeteries go out of use in the age of Augustus or shortly afterwards (for documentation of some examples see Appendix VI, p. 987). In one particular case, we can link the abandonment of a family tomb with Romanization in its most complete form: the tomb of the Salvii at Ferentis was abandoned in 23 B.C. as the family transferred to Rome.[64] We shall see in a moment what came after.

It is time to return to Cicero. 'Hinc enim', he observed of Arpinum, 'orti stirpe antiquissima sumus, hic sacra, hic genus, hic maiorum multa vestigia', referring surely to the cults, the long family history, the tombs of his ancestors.[65] His characterization of what was to him distinctive of Arpinum coincides precisely with those aspects of local culture, omitting language, in which traditional local practices were abandoned during the late Republic and the early Empire.

The evidence of material culture, when not embedded in religious or funerary practice, naturally needs to be handled with caution. Yet surely, in the light of what we have seen so far, it is legitimate to point also to the uniformity of building styles in early imperial Italy as further evidence of cultural assimilation.[66] Further striking evidence of integration is provided by an altogether humbler artefact, the red-gloss table-ware that graced the tables of the middle classes of Augustan Italy. Whereas the black-gloss table-ware of the Republic had been produced in dozens of kilns the length and breadth of Italy, the age of revolution witnessed concentration of production at a relatively small number of centres, of which the best known is that of Arretium. Diffused from these centres throughout Italy, the pottery in question is clear evidence of a considerable degree of economic integration and the counterpart of the process of cultural assimilation discussed above.[67]

It seems likely then that Augustan (and early imperial) Italy was more homogeneous than at any time before or since. Her unity was expressed

---

[63] Frederiksen 1959 (E 41) = (in part) Frederikson 1984 (E 43) 285–318, 281–4.

[64] Degrassi 1961–2 (B 225).

[65] See *Leg.* II.1.2–2.5, with n. 17 above; compare *Off.* I. 54–5, 'magnum est enim eadem habere monumenta maiorum, iisdem uti sacris, sepulcra habere communia'; the passage has nothing to do with the institution of a common tomb for a single family, *contra* de Visscher 1963 (E 135) 129–30.

[66] Bejor 1979 (F 269) 126; Rossignani 1990 (E 115); Italy is hardly present in the great exhibition catalogue *Kaiser Augustus und die verlorene Republik* 1988 (F 443).

[67] A similar pattern on a smaller scale is also evinced by the red-gloss table-ware produced at Puteoli, Pucci 1981 (E 101) 107–10; and in the pottery style discussed by Lavizzari Pedrazzini 1987 (E 72). See also M. Torelli (n. 20), at 34–6, for the spread throughout Italy between 50 B.C. and the turn of the eras of the 'villa system', whatever precisely that may have been.

in the creation by Augustus of a single system of administrative regions, seven in peninsular Italy and four in the Po valley, whose boundaries regularly cut across earlier ethnic and cultural boundaries, placing Ligurian Luna in Etruria, Campanian or Samnite Caudium in Apulia, Latin Tibur in Samnium.[68]

This relative unity of Augustan Italy, however, remains to be explained. In part the answer must lie in the nature of military service in the years after the Social War.[69] The legions consisted of men from all over Italy, probably without wives or families until after their period of service, removed from their homes, insofar as they had them, for long periods, further mixed by the drafting of reinforcements to existing legions, all with Latin as their only common language. We have already seen that the use of ethnic contingents came to an end with the Social War. The unity of Augustan Italy was surely in part forged on the battlefields of the late Republic.

Yet that is not all. The late Republic and the age of revolution are periods when on a quite unparalleled scale men were removed from their homes not simply for long periods, but for ever, and resettled as individuals or in colonies at the other end of Italy.[70] The process begins with Sulla, accelerates with the *lex agraria* of Caesar in 59 B.C. and reaches massive proportions in the triumviral period and the early years of Augustus. It is this mixing process which explains the origins of the culture of Augustan Italy.[71]

Nor were soldiers the only people affected. Generally speaking, we have no idea of what happened to those who were dispossessed to make way for the veterans settled after 42 B.C. For it is a mistake to suppose that the *Eclogues* have any value as evidence for the biography of an individual known as Virgil; there remains naturally a faint possibility that one or two of the dispossessed were poets who commended themselves to the imperial authorities. But there seem to have been some refugees from Mantua who were settled near Bononia;[72] others from Cremona turned up in Concordia in the age of revolution.[73] There must have been thousands who found somewhere new in Italy to live, even allowing for those who died or emigrated.

Archaeological evidence allows us a glimpse of men who clung to

---

[68] Thomsen 1947 (E 127); Nicolet 1988 (A 69) 221–3; for Italy under the Empire, see Eck 1979 (E 38).

[69] Smith 1958 (D 232); Harmand 1967 (D 193); Keppie 1983 (E 65).

[70] Vittinghoff 1952 (C 239); Keppie 1983 (E 65); for Schneider 1977 (D 231), see the review by Keppie 1981 (D 201), rightly dismissive; for some recent new evidence, see Tagliaferri 1986 (E 125); Solin 1988 (B 285) 99–101.

[71] Note that in the eyes of Aulus Gellius intermarriage with other groups by men of the Marsi led to the loss of their magic powers, *NA* XVI.11.1.   [72] Susini 1976 (E 124).

[73] Panciera 1985 (E 91).

some of their ancestral traditions in their new homes. Within the general uniformity of the grave monuments of early imperial Italy, stelae or altars, there are for instance traces in Gallia Cisalpina of the funerary practices of the central Apennines; or of those of Rome in Umbria or Sabinum (for some examples see Appendix VII, p. 989). It is also important to remember that the convulsions just described must have affected equally the elites of the communities of Italy; in large numbers, their members joined the armies of the late Republic, to serve as junior officers. It is these men who, survivors of and enriched by the murderous battles of the civil wars, diffused in central Italy the habit, limited to the early Julio-Claudian period, of erecting lavish monumental graves decorated with 'fregi d'armi', friezes portraying weapons and armour.[74] They also no doubt played a large part in the diffusion of grave monuments with Doric friezes;[75] it should come as no surprise to observe that such monuments are unknown in Magna Graecia, but it is interesting that they are equally unknown in much of Etruria. *Relatively* little veteran settlement – only Luca and Pisa are certainly later than Caesar – and a certain Etruscan cultural cohesiveness will explain the pattern.[76] Someone who may stand as a symbol of the age, geographically and socially mobile, a pillar of a new society, is P. Otacilius Arranes, the son of a Spanish horseman enfranchised by Cn. Pompeius Strabo at Asculum, who ended up as a municipal magistrate at Casinum.[77]

With these convulsions in mind, let us return to problems of family structure and religious practice. The total abandonment at Ateste, at the turn of the eras, of traditional Venetic practice over nomenclature, at the same time as traditional funerary customs, was not simply the result of enfranchisement and the passage of time. Rather it must have been largely the result of the brutal injection into the community of the veterans of the Fifth and Eleventh Legions, along with some others, after the Battle of Actium. We should be surprised, not that there was some change, but that the worship of the Venetic Dea Raetia continued at all.[78]

As far as religious practice is concerned, we should surely, in considering the abandonment of rural sanctuaries which had attracted worshippers for centuries, attach great importance to the way in which the period between Sulla and the reign of Augustus saw Italian

---

[74] For the phenomenon in general, see the articles in *Studi Miscellanei* 10, 1963–4; Torelli 1976 (E 130) 101, for a case at Falerii Novi linked to colonization.

[75] Torelli 1969 (E 129): one of the monuments at Beneventum is again that of a veteran; see now also Sena Chiesa 1986 (E 119) (at least from the area of Mediolanum).

[76] L. Keppie (n. 69) supersedes the speculations of Ciampoltrini 1981 (E 16).

[77] *CIL* I² 3107.

[78] Crawford 1989 (E 28), correcting (n. 3), 160; for the gravestones of the imperial period, see Bermond Montanari 1959 (E 3).

community after Italian community lose its own young men for ever, rich and poor like, often to suffer in addition the enforced settlement of total strangers.[79] This is the process which created the relative unity of Augustan Italy. We have for the Roman world no documents comparable to those available to the modern historian. But it is not hard to project back into the Roman world the situation of the villages of France in our own century:[80]

The war of 1914–18 was different. As Father Garneret described it for the Franche-Comté, it was 'the bloody break that struck our villages such a blow: 20 dead for 300 inhabitants and all the customs shattered'.

[79] Compare Coarelli 1981 (E 18) 242–4, for the disappearance between Republic and Empire of a group of families installed there earlier in the republican period.

[80] Weber, *Peasants into Frenchmen* (above, n. 14) 476.

SICILY, SARDINIA AND CORSICA

R. J. A. WILSON

Shortly before his death in 44 B.C. Iulius Caesar granted Latin rights (*Latinitas*) to all free-born Sicilians. Cicero, to whom we owe this information, clearly did not approve of the grant, still less of Antony's conversion of it into full citizenship in March or April 44, on the dubious pretext that such had been Caesar's intention;[1] for, despite being a Roman province for close on two hundred years ('the first to teach our ancestors what a fine thing it is to rule over foreign nations', as Cicero put it),[2] Sicily remained at the time of the late Republic a fundamentally Greek island. Italians had of course been involved there as landowners or *negotiatores* in considerable numbers from at least the second century B.C., forming themselves in 'conventus civium Romanorum' outside the administrative jurisdiction of the Sicilian towns. Very few Sicilians had been granted Roman citizenship, the evidence of Cicero yielding only some fourteen names, and of two possible *novi homines* in the Senate who came from Sicily neither are likely to have been Sicilian Greeks by birth.[3] Latin in the province was still a foreign language spoken and understood by a tiny minority: Cicero has to remind his audience that the Syracusans call their *curia* the *bouleuterion*, expound in detail the Greek calendar system still in use throughout Sicily, and explain Sicilian usage of Greek words in the documents read out in court.[4] Latin inscriptions of republican date are rare (and in any case set up either by Italian immigrants or by the provincial administration),[5] and the city constitutions were still those of the hellenistic Greek world, with decrees issued by 'the council and the people' (ἡ βουλὴ καὶ ὁ δῆμος), and with magistrates bearing such titles as *prostates*, *strategos* and *agoranomos*. It was, therefore, on a considerably un-Romanized Sicily that Caesar decided to confer the *ius Latii* in 44 B.C.

The Sicilian communities duly celebrated their new status in a number of coins and inscriptions recording *duoviri* or the title *municipium*;

---

[1] Cic. *Att.* XIV.12.1.   [2] Cic. II *Verr.* 2.1.2.

[3] Wiseman 1971 (D 81) 22–3, 190; Sherwin-White 1973 (A 87) 306–7. Cf. also Fraschetti 1981 (E 159).   [4] Cic. II *Verr.* 2.21.50; 2.52.129; 5.57.148.

[5] E.g. *ILS* 864; *AE* 1963, 131; Manganaro 1972 (E 169) 453.

significantly, with the exception of the occasional coin legend, the language used was still Greek (δύο ἄνδρες, τὸ μουνικίπιον).[6] The documents belong to the period between 44 and 36, for the Sicilians retained their privileges throughout this period: the Senate's decision late in 44 or early in 43 to rescind all Antony's *acta* was ignored, for late in 43 the island was seized by Sextus Pompeius, and for the next seven years she lay outside the direct political and military control of Rome.

How disastrous this period and its aftermath were for Sicily is uncertain, but although the surviving sources, which depict Sextus Pompeius as a ruthless freebooter determined to exploit the island to further his own ends, are undoubtedly biased, it is hard to paint a rosy picture of life in Sicily under Sextus Pompeius.[7] The sudden blockade of the corn supply to Italy from 43 until the Misenum accord with Octavian in 39,[8] with the resultant slump in demand and, presumably, in income, together with the enlistment of Sicilian farmers in Sextus Pompeius' legions, can hardly have been good news for Sicilian agriculture; nor can the cities, for all their tacit acceptance of Pompeian control (with the notable exceptions of Messana and Centuripae) have fared much better, pressed to supply money and men for Sextus Pompeius' army and fleet. Yet more upheaval was caused by the arrival of thousands of fugitive slaves and the victims of triumviral proscriptions and confiscations in Italy, who found a haven in Pompeius' Sicily. When the final showdown came in 36 it was a bitter encounter, causing further devastation. Lepidus landed in the west and stormed several cities, although Lilybaeum, protected by her newly strengthened defences, resisted him; he then marched across Sicily to meet up with Octavian, who had narrowly escaped with his life when Sextus Pompeius surprised him at sea off Tauromenium.[9] Octavian's final crushing victory came off Naulochus, and culminated in the capitulation of Pompeius' land forces; in its aftermath Messana was looted and burned. In the autumn of 36 Octavian at last found himself master of Sicily, but of a province in disarray.

Octavian was in no mood to be forgiving. A massive indemnity of

---

[6] Coins: Grant 1946 (B 322) 190–2, 195; Burnett 1992 (B 311). Inscriptions: H. Willers, *RhM* 60 (1905) 321–60; G. Manganaro, *Cronache di Archeologia e Storia d'Arte* 3 (1964) 53–68 (Tauromenium); *IG* XIV 367 (Haluntium); *IG* XIV 954 and *AE* 1966, 168 *bis* (Agrigentum). See also Wilson 1990 (E 197) 357 notes 25–6. I take *AE* 1966, 165 (= 1990, 437), referring to an ἀποικία at Centuripae, to belong to 44 B.C. immediately after Caesar's grant and before Antony's conversion of it to full citizenship (Wilson 1990 (E 197) 41–2); if so Caesar planned *coloniae Latinae* in Sicily along the lines of those established in Narbonensis *c.* 45 B.C.

[7] *Pace* Stone 1983 (E 188). For this period in detail, Hadas 1930 (C 108) 71–150; Tarn 1934 (E 189); Goldsberry 1982 (E 161) 489–97; Roddaz 1984 (C 200) 117–38.

[8] Cessation of corn exports: App. *BCiv.* IV.84–6, cf. Dio XLVIII.17.4–19; their resumption: App. *BCiv.* V.56, 67–74; Dio XLVIII.36.1.

[9] Lepidus: App. *BCiv.* V.98.408. Lilybaeum defences: *ILS* 8891. Later stages: App. *BCiv.* V.105; 109; 110–12.

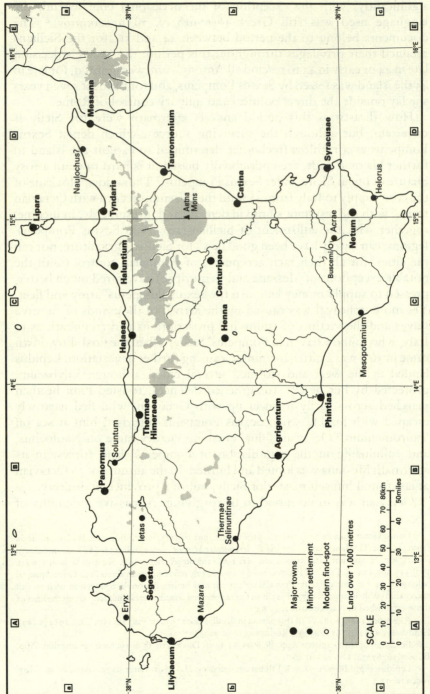

Map 4. Sicily.

Major towns ●
Minor settlement ●
Modern find-spot ○

Land over 1,000 metres

SCALE

0 10 20 30 40 50 60 70 80km
0   10   20   30   40   50miles

Messana
Tauromenium
Naulochus?
Tyndaris
Syracusae
Catina
Lipara
Haluntium
Aetna Mons
Helorus
Centuripae
Acrae
Buscemi
Netum
Halaesa
Henna
Mesopotamium
Thermae Himeraeae
Phintias
Panormus
Soluntum
Agrigentum
Ietas
Thermae Selinuntinae
Segesta
Eryx
Mazara
Lilybaeum

1,600 talents was levied on cities which had actively supported Sextus Pompeius, and his leading supporters were rounded up and executed. Land was confiscated and some given as a reward for loyal service, such as Agrippa's Sicilian holdings managed by Horace's friend Iccius; the remainder formed the nucleus of what was later to become the huge imperial estates in the island. The unfortunate inhabitants of Tauromenium, who had championed Pompeius' cause and vigorously supported him in the fighting of 36, were summarily deported.[10] But Octavian's feelings towards the Sicilians were expressed in most telling fashion by his decision to strip the Sicilians of the Latin right (*ius Latii*) granted them by Caesar. Octavian himself soon left the island, and the initial steps to restore order to a chaotic province were entrusted to his lieutenants. The Sicilians were left to count the costs of being on the losing side in a bitter struggle, and to begin the slow and painful road to recovery.

No ancient testimony specifically tells us that Sicily lost the Latin right in 36, but it is implicit in the changes that were made fifteen years later in 21 B.C., when Augustus (as he now was) returned to Sicily (which in the reorganization of 27 had become one of the provinces of the Roman people, governed by a proconsul) at the beginning of a provincial tour. Whether these changes involved the abolition of the tithe system (*decumana*), which had operated throughout the Republic, and its replacement by a fixed levy (*stipendium*), possibly but not certainly to be paid henceforth in cash rather than in corn (as is sometimes argued), is far from certain: the evidence for a change at this period is slight, and the quota system certainly operated in other provinces during the early Empire.[11] Six veteran colonies were founded, at Syracusae (Syracuse), Catina (Catania), Tauromenium (Taormina), Tyndaris, Thermae Himeraeae (Termini Imerese) and Panormus (Palermo), perhaps all in 21 B.C., although Dio only specifies that Syracuse 'and the others' were settled in that year.[12] Pliny also adds that Messana and Lipara were 'oppida civium Romanorum', a term of uncertain significance, and that Segesta, Netum (Noto) and Centuripae were 'Latinae condicionis', i.e. possessing the Latin right. All other communities were listed as stipendiary and so non-privileged. Since Pliny's source for the status of these communities was

[10] Indemnity: App. *BCiv.* v.129. Execution of Pompeians: Dio XLIX.12.4. Iccius: Hor. *Epist.* 1.12.1. Tauromenium: Diod. XVI.7.1 (presumably only the leading men if no *colonia* was founded there until 21: see n. 12).

[11] Cf. P. Garnsey in Garnsey, Hopkins and Whittaker 1983 (D 130) 120–1, and P.A. Brunt, *JRS* 71 (1981) 162 (on lack of evidence for change); *contra*, Rickman 1980 (E 109) 60, 64–5.

[12] Dio LIV.7.1. Foundation dates at Panormus and Tauromenium are uncertain: for the latter, modern scholarly opinion is equally divided between 36 and 21 B.C. (Diod. XVI.7.1 and App. *BCiv.* v.129 appear to be contradictory). Panormus is an Augustan *colonia* in Strab. VI.2.5 (272C) and *CIL* x 7279 but not designated as such by Pliny (*HN* III.90), probably in error. For the case that both were also founded in 21 B.C., Wilson 1990 (E 197) 33–4 (Tauromenium) and 37 (Panormus).

almost certainly based on an Augustan census, the unavoidable conclusion is that the wholesale grant of Latin rights had been revoked, presumably in 36,[13] and only later, in the settlement of 21, was it restored to certain chosen communities. Four further cities (Halaesa, Haluntium, Lilybaeum and Agrigentum) are known from coins and inscriptions to have gained municipal status before A.D. 14,[14] presumably at a date later than that of Pliny's source.

The availability of Sicilian land confiscated from supporters of Sextus Pompeius and the island's proximity to Italy made her an obvious and no doubt popular choice for veteran settlement, and the influx of settlers further swelled the Italian element of the population, an element already proportionately larger than in any comparable area of the Greek-speaking world. The foundation of *coloniae* may indeed have been consciously intended to act as a spur to the further Romanization of Sicily, and the decree allowing senators to travel to the province without specific permission from the emperor[15] can be interpreted as further evidence of an attitude which regarded Sicily almost as an additional *regio* of Italy. The fact that other communities sought and won municipal status later in Augustus' reign suggests that the *ius Latii* was something the Sicilians reckoned as worth having. Certainly it was only from Augustan times onwards that the cultural Romanization of Sicily began in earnest. Latin had come to stay. It was adopted almost universally on official inscriptions and coin issues; and it now came into widespread use for the first time in private dedications such as tombstones.

The *coloniae* also acted as a spur to economic growth. Strabo reckoned that the arrival of colonists always acted as a springboard for prosperity,[16] and in 21 B.C. Sicily was certainly ripe for redevelopment, for it was no part of Augustus' long-term policy to let the province languish in a permanent state of economic decay. An active building programme may well have been a tangible sign of economic stimulation, and Strabo specifically says that Augustus restored Syracusae and Catina as well as Centuripae, without giving details.[17] Nevertheless the list of public buildings of probable Augustan or Julio-Claudian date in the Sicilian *coloniae* is not inconsiderable: it includes, for example, at Syracusae, the

---

[13] Not all scholars agree. Beloch 1886 (A 4) 327 emended Pliny's text (*HN* III.91) to imply that all the communities were *Latinae condicionis*, but that Centuripae, Netum and Segesta were tax free (*immunes*), the rest stipendiary. Scramuzza 1937 (E 187) 343–7, Manganaro 1980 (E 170) 452, and Clemente 1980 (E 154) 466–7 have followed Beloch, but tampering with Pliny's text is unwarranted (Wilson 1990 (E 197) 36–7).

[14] *CIL* x 7463 (Haluntium), 7458 (Halaesa). Coins: Grant 1946 (B 322) 195–7; Burnett 1992 (B 311). Full references in Wilson 1990 (E 197) 42.

[15] Probably Augustan, certainly pre-Claudian: Tac. *Ann.* XII.23.1 (A.D. 46), cf. Dio LII.42.6 (29 B.C.).

[16] Cf. Strab. VIII.7.5 (386–8c) (on Patras) and VI.1.6 (257–9c) (on Reggio); cf. also *RG* 28.1; Suet. *Aug.* 46.　　[17] Strab. VI.2.4 (269–72c).

amphitheatre, a monumental arch, the piazza and surrounding porticoes laid out on the west side of the Altar of Hieron, alterations in the theatre, and a repair of the walls (under Caligula), as well as waterworks and a possible bath-house (the last under Claudius); reorganization of the forum at Tauromenium and possibly the aqueduct and extensive rebuilding of the theatre there; possibly the aqueduct and a version of the theatre at Catina; and the aqueduct and major buildings in the forum at Thermae Himeraeae. All this, together with the evidence of domestic rebuilding at Tyndaris around the middle of the first century and the suggestion of continued intensive occupation of the excavated residential quarter at the heart of Agrigentum, indicates economic vitality rather than stagnation in the early Empire, and points to a relatively rapid recovery and revitalization of these urban centres after the uncertain period of the 40s and 30s.[18]

The choice of places for colonial settlement is also significant. Most possessed excellent harbours and extensive fertile *territoria*; all were on the north and east coasts where they were well situated to take maximum advantage of exports to the Italian mainland. By contrast no inland town was selected for colonial settlement, Augustan advisers correctly assessing that long-term chances of survival were not good. Many may well have been in an advanced state of decay, such as Morgantina which finally petered out in the Tiberian period. Others, such as Ietas (Monte Iato), were beginning to decline around the same time; by the middle of the first century, for example, the theatre there, last altered under Augustus, had ceased to function, a fine peristyle house had collapsed never to be rebuilt, the *bouleuterion* was walled up and disused, and rubbish was gathering in the *agora*. Helorus and Soluntum at least, possibly Acrae, and no doubt many others, were also in decline in the early Empire. Even those inland towns that were favoured in the Augustan settlement with municipal status did not enjoy long-term prosperity: Halaesa, for example, where the hellenistic city centre was never rebuilt under the Empire, went into decline, and the same is possibly true at Segesta (where, however, less excavation has been carried out).[19] The famous sanctuary of Venus at Eryx in Segesta's *territorium* had fallen into disrepair by A.D. 25, and although its restoration was completed by Claudius the cult never regained the popularity it enjoyed under the Republic.[20] Centuripae alone of the inland towns granted Latin rights by Augustus can be shown to be still thriving at the time of the middle Empire, a prosperity no doubt won from the famed fertility of her surrounding territory.

[18] Wilson 1988 (E 196); 1990 (E 197) with full discussion of the evidence.
[19] Wilson 1985 (E 194); 1990 (E 197) 143–59.
[20] Tac. *Ann.* IV.43; Suet. *Claud.* 25.5.

Little was done, therefore, by either Augustus or his successors, to foster urbanization in the interior of Sicily. The decay of the old hill-towns is hardly surprising, for life on a lofty and often waterless mountain top (Ietas, for example, is 852m high) was neither comfortable nor convenient, and made no sense once security ceased to be a factor in determining the location of nucleated settlement. Urban decay in the interior, however, did not represent depopulation in real terms, for it is likely to have been matched by a corresponding growth in the prosperity and importance of the sprawling agricultural settlements and market centres, which had began to be established in the well-watered valleys and along the trunk roads from the end of the third century B.C. onwards. Sicily under the Empire was dotted with such settlements, the fully fledged towns being far apart and mainly on or near the coast. This was a land fully geared to maximum agricultural production. Africa and Egypt were now more important producers and exporters in terms of quantity, but that grain continued to be produced in Sicily on a huge scale in the early Empire is not in doubt.[21] Local and imperial coinage advertises the symbol of Sicily (a Medusa head with *triskeles*) with wheat ears attached, and the potential political importance of the Sicilian corn supply, highlighted by Sextus Pompeius' manoeuvrings, was further echoed by the pretender in Afria, Clodius Macer, in 68, who also featured the symbol of Sicily with wheat-ears on his coin issues; similarly Sicily takes her place beside Africa, Egypt and Spain on a mosaic of the middle of the first century at Ostia symbolizing grain (and, in the case of Spain, oil) producers.[22] Sicilian wine was also famous. Mamertine from the north east was the most respected, 'the rival of the best Italian wine' according to Strabo, and widely exported, to Rome, Africa and else-where. Tauromenium wine, which was sometimes passed off for Mamertine, is known at Pompeii, and *vinum Mesopotamium* from the south coast is attested at Carthage (in 21 B.C.) as well as at Pompeii and as far north as Vindonissa in Switzerland.[23] Animal husbandry, especially sheep, also made an important contribution to the agricultural economy, wool being mentioned as a Sicilian export commodity by Strabo. Among other exports were timber, especially from Mount Etna, black basalt corn-mills from the same region, found in Italy and Africa as well

[21] Gabba's case for a considerable reduction in Sicilian grain production is not persuasive (Gabba 1986 (E 160) 79–80).

[22] Coins: Sutherland and Kraay 1975 (B 359) no. 1088 (Panormus); *RIC* I² (1984), 195 (Macer). Mosaic: G. Becatti, *Scavi di Ostia* IV, Rome, 1961, no. 68.

[23] Mamertine: Strab. VI.2.3 (268–9c), cf. Pliny, *HN* XIV.66 and 97; Vitr. *De Arch*. VIII.3.12; Mart. XIII.117; Athenaeus, 1.27d; Dioscorides, V.6.11. Africa: *CIL* VIII 22640.60. Tauromenium wine: Pliny, *HN* XIV.66. Mesopotamian: *CIL* IV 2602–3 (Pompeii); M.H. Callender, *Roman Amphorae* (Oxford, 1965) 37 (Vindonissa); *AE* 1893, 111 (Carthage). Other Sicilian vintages: Gal. X, 834–5; Strab. VI.2.3 (268–9c), 6.7; XIII.4.11 (628c); Pliny, *HN* XIV.35 and 80; Poll. *Onom*. VI.16; Ath. 1.31b; Ael. *VH* XII.31. On Sicilian wine production in general, Wilson 1990 (E 197) 22–3, 191–2 and 263–4.

as all over Sicily, and sulphur from the Agrigentum hinterland, the Roman world's only major supplier.[24]

About the pattern of land use and the farming economy we are largely ignorant, in the absence of detailed archaeological investigation. That Sicily continued to be an island where large estates were commonplace is not in doubt: its fertility, its relative accessibility from Rome, and the concession which enabled senators to travel there without special permission, all combined to make the province an attractive area for land investment. The interest of Italian *privati* in Sicilian land, and the scale of it (even allowing for literary hyperbole) is indicated by Ovid's quip that Sextus Pompeius (the senator of the first century A.D.) could claim Sicily as his, so extensive were his properties there, and by the fictional Trimalchio's joke that a holding in Sicilian land would allow him to travel to Africa via Sicily without leaving his own estates.[25] The sweeping generalizations of ancient commentators must, however, be treated with reserve. A famous passage of Strabo, for example, describing how the whole of northern and western Sicily except Agrigentum and Lilybaeum were 'deserted' – 'the rest, as well as most of the interior, has come into the possession of shepherds'[26] – has been taken as an indication of a depressed rural Sicily with huge *latifundia* dominated by slave labour encompassing vast tracts of countryside. Yet there is increasing evidence from western and south-western Sicily for a well-populated countryside dotted with farms, villas and villages in early imperial times,[27] and the true pattern of land-use, here as elsewhere, is likely to have been complex, with a variety of different-sized holdings in any one area. Archaeology, of course, cannot tell us about the ownership of such holdings, nor distinguish between tenant farmer and owner-occupier, so that even a string of smallholdings might in theory be under single rather than multiple ownership; but Strabo's picture of a depopulated rural Sicily is likely to be grossly exaggerated. Ranching alone was in any case not a profitable way of using extensive tracts of land, and even on large estates mixed farming was no doubt widely practised. More archaeological documentation, however, is needed.

In the countryside the Romanizing influence detectable at the towns in the early Empire hardly made itself felt. Buildings were still erected in traditional Greek fashion, with mud-brick walls on stone foundations.[28] The Sicilian Greek calendar remained in use, as indicated by an inscription of A.D. 35 from the rustic sanctuary of Anna and the Nymphs

---

[24] Wool: Strab. VI.2.3 (268–9C); 2.7 (224–5C). Timber: Strab. VI.2.8 (273–4C); cf. Diod. XIV.42.4, and G. Manganaro, *Cronache di Archeologia e Storia d'Arte* 3 (1964) 43–4, col. II, lines 25–6, 51–2 (export of wood from Tauromenium). Basalt: Strab. VI.2.3 (268–9C). Sulphur: E. De Miro, *Kokalos* 28–29 (1982–3) 320–5; Wilson 1990 (E 197) 238–9.   [25] Ov. *Pont* IV.15.15; Petron. *Sat.* 48.
[26] Strab. VI.2.6 (272–3C).   [27] Bejor 1975 (E 147); Bejor 1983 (E 148) 365–72.
[28] Wilson 1985 (E 195).

at Buscemi in south-east Sicily;[29] and Greek remained the spoken language, Latin inscriptions being rare. In the far west Punic influence may have lingered on, as Apuleius in the second century described the Sicilians as *trilingues*, the third language presumably being Punic; but there are no neo-Punic inscriptions as there are in Sardinia and north Africa at this period, and even in a Carthaginian foundation such as Lilybaeum Greek was already deep-rooted by the time of the late Republic (even if, as Cicero implies, it was not of the purest strain).[30] Greek and Latin bilingualism was widespread in the towns, but even there Greek roots died hard. Before the end of the second century, for example, an honorific inscription was set up, in Greek, by the 'council and people of the glorious city of the Tauromenitans', showing that by then a *colonia* could set up an official dedication in Greek using terminology which ignored the existence of a Roman charter.[31] For all its proximity to Italy, for all the influx of veteran colonists under Augustus, for all the interest of Italians in land speculation there, Sicily retained a pronounced Greek flavour down to the end of antiquity.

Sardinia and Corsica were culturally very distinct from Sicily. Greek influence in both islands was negligible, but in Sardinia there was a considerable legacy of Carthaginian culture in the principal cities of the west coast, which had started life as Phoenician foundations. Both islands received a generally bad press from Roman writers. Corsica (Latin Cyrnus) was a wild land, its inhabitants wilder than animals claimed Strabo; much more rugged than Sardinia, its only decent plains are near the east coast. Although Diodorus mentions Corsican honey, milk and meat, her sole significant asset was timber, Corsican pine and box being especially prized.[32] Sardinia was far more fertile, though less so (and more mountainous) than Sicily, and was likewise a major corn supplier of Italy at the time of the late Republic; herein lay her sole political importance.[33] Yet her inhabitants were not to be trusted, banditry was rife, and the climate notoriously unhealthy. Strabo in particular paints a gloomy picture of a land 'plague-ridden in summer, especially in the most fertile regions, which are continually laid waste by mountain peoples'.[34]

[29] *Notizie degli Scavi* 1920, 327–9.   [30] Apul. *Met*. XI.5; Cic. *Div. Caec*. 12.39.
[31] *IG* XIV 1091.
[32] Inhabitants: Strab. V.2.7 (224–5c), contrast Diod. V.14.1. Produce: *ibid*. and V.13.4–5; cf. also Livy, XL.34.12; XLII.7.2 and Pliny, *HN* XVI.71 (honey). Box: Pliny, *ibid*. Pine: Theophr. *Hist.Pl*. V.8.1. Corsican red mullet was also highly rated: Juv. V.92.
[33] Cic. *De Imp. Cn. Pomp*. 12.34: 'tria frumentaria subsidia reipublicae', the third being Africa. Sardinian fertility: Polyb. 1.79.6; Varro, *Rust*. II Introd. 3; Strab. V.2.7 (224–5c); Luc. III.65; Val. Max. VII.6.1 ('Siciliamque et Sardiniam, benignissimas urbis nostrae nutrices').
[34] Strab. V.2.7 (224–5c), cf. Livy, XXIII.34.11, Pompon. II.123; Paus. X.17.11; Tac. *Ann*. II.85.4. Sardinian malaria: Brown 1984 (E 153) 225–30. Untrustworthiness: Festus, *Gloss.Lat*. 428L ('Sardi venales'), cf. Cic. *Scaur*. 38ff. Banditry: Varro, *Rust*. 1.16.2.

The importance of Sardinian grain to Italy is highlighted by the events of 40–38 B.C. The cutting off of the Sicilian supply since 43 was bad enough, but when both Corsica and Sardinia were occupied in Sextus Pompeius' name in 40 by his lieutenant Menas[35] and Sardinian corn also blockaded, the starvation of Rome loomed, a political weapon that could not be ignored. Hence the Misenum accord of 39 with Octavian, by which Sextus Pompeius' control of the three islands was duly recognized, and Sicilian and Sardinian grain shipments to Rome resumed. Early the next year, however, on the defection of Menas, Sardinia and Corsica passed firmly under Octavian's control.[36]

In the provincial reorganization of 27 B.C. Sardinia and Corsica were reckoned peaceful enough to be made, like Sicily, a province of the Roman people, administered as a single unit under a proconsular governor. It proved a miscalculation. In A.D. 6 we hear of serious restlessness among the peoples of the Sardinian interior and of piracy in the Tyrrhenian sea.[37] Troops were sent to the island, and both Sardinia and Corsica passed to the emperor's control; the organization of the islands as two separate provinces, each probably administered by an equestrian *praefectus*, almost certainly dates from now.[38] Despite military rule trouble in Sardinia rumbled on. There was no concerted military push to tame the province once and for all, and Strabo even suggests that the malarial climate was a major factor in the failure to pursue a policy of total conquest. The sending of 4,000 Jewish dissidents to Sardinia in A.D. 19, as raw recruits to help quell the still rebellious interior, with a clear hint that they were expendable in case of disease, suggests continuing problems in establishing a firm military stranglehold.[39] To Rome this was the hostile territory of *Barbaria*, and although its collective peoples (*civitates Barbariae*) are recorded as paying homage on an inscription of either Augustan or Tiberian date,[40] a military garrison of auxiliary units was needed to keep a watchful eye on the interior for much of the first century.

By 67 Nero thought Sardinia quiet enough to be handed back to

---

[35] So all sources (and apparently *CIL* x 8034) except Appian, who calls him Menodorus: see *BCiv.* v.56 with Gabba 1970 (B 55) *ad loc.*

[36] App. *BCiv.* IV.2; V.56, 67, 72, 78–80; Dio XLVIII.28.4; 30.7–31.2; 36.1–6; 45.4–9; Plut. *Ant.* 32.

[37] Dio LIII.12.4 (27 B.C.); LV.28.1–2 (A.D. 6), cf. Livy, XL.34.13.

[38] *Praefectus Corsicae*: *CIL* XII 2455 (Julio-Claudian); *praefectus Sardiniae*: *EE* VIII 744 (A.D. 46); *AE* 1893, 47. I take T. Pompeius Proculus on an Augustan milestone (*ILS* 105) to be governor; he appears as *pro legato* (*sc. praefectus?*), perhaps in acknowledgment of legionaries in his command (so Meloni 1958 (E 174) 11–17). Others, however (J. Šašel, *Chiron* 10 (1974) 467–72; Thomasson 1972 (E 190)), take *pro legato* and *praefectus Corsicae* to be subordinates of a single governor of Sardinia-Corsica, the split in administration not occurring until 67. Cf. also *RE* XXII 2 (1954) 1291–2.

[39] Strab. v.2.7 (224–5C). A.D. 19: Tac. *Ann* 11.85.4 (with Goodyear *ad loc.*), cf. Suet. *Tib.* 36 and Dio LVII.18.5a.

[40] *AE* 1921, 86 = Sotgiu 1961 (B 286) no. 188; not necessarily post-19, *pace* Meloni 1958 (E 174) 15–17.

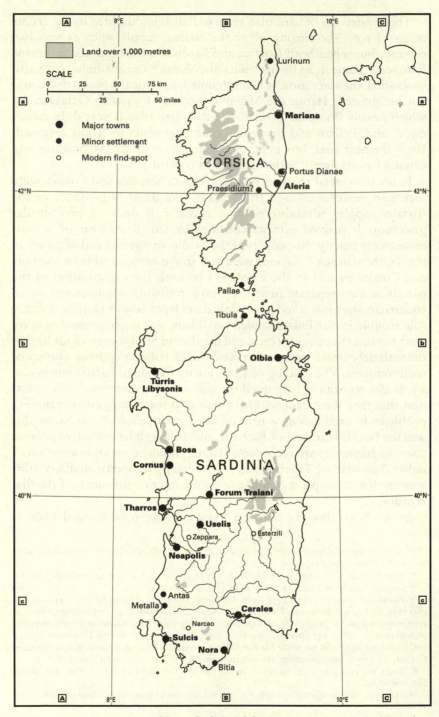

Map 5. Sardinia and Corsica.

senatorial control, the province being given to the Senate as a consolation prize when the cities of Achaea were granted freedom and immunity from taxation.[41] Corsica, however, remained separately administered, since the Decimus Pinarius, *procurator Corsicae*, who tried unsuccessfully to win that island over to Vitellius' cause during the upheavals of 69 (he was murdered in his bath for his efforts), was clearly the governor, the title *praefectus* having by A.D. 56 given way to that of procurator, as elsewhere.[42] Once again the inclusion of Sardinia among the provinces of the Roman people proved premature. A revealing insight into one aspect of the continuing unrest is provided by a bronze tablet of A.D. 69 from Esterzili in central Sardinia, which documents not only the long-standing problem of mountain tribes (here the Galillenses) trespassing on richer plains further south (in this case those of the Patulcenses Campani, presumably descendants of Italian immigrants whose boundaries, the document tells us, had been fixed by Metellus some 180 years before), but also the failure of successive proconsuls of Sardinia to grasp the nettle and resolve the problem in decisive fashion; and the references in the inscription to 'rebellion' (*seditio*) and to occupation by force (*quos per vim occupaverunt*) suggest that the recent trouble was not minor but a sudden and violent uprising.[43] By 73 Vespasian had lost patience. The troops returned, and the province came under imperial control once more, the governor being now styled a *procurator et praefectus* (a title which combined old- and new-style designations). Corsica remained separate, under a procuratorial governor.[44]

With both islands so unsettled it is hardly surprising that the progress of Romanization was slow. Corsica in particular remained largely undeveloped throughout antiquity, and we can sympathize with Seneca's gloom about what he saw as a dismal place of exile.[45] *Coloniae* had been founded at Mariana by Marius and at Aléria by Sulla, but there was no later attempt to foster urbanization, and Pliny mentions only these two settlements by name in his account of the island. At Mariana excavations have revealed only late Roman structures, apart from some first- and second-century burials, but at Aléria more extensive work has uncovered the *forum* and several adjacent houses.[46] The *forum* with its

---

[41] Paus. VII.17.3; Suet. *Ner.* 24.

[42] Tac. *Hist.* II.16 (with Chilver *ad loc*). The title had changed before 56: Vipsanius Laenas, the procurator of Sardinia condemned for extortion in that year (Tac. *Ann.* XIII.30.1), was clearly the governor.

[43] *Pace* Rowland 1985 (E 185) 110 and Dyson 1985 (E 157) 258. The inscription is *ILS* 5947.

[44] Sardinia: *CIL* X 8023–4 (A.D. 74). Corsica: *CIL* X 8038 (A.D. 72).

[45] Sen. *Dial.* XII.6.5; 7.8–10. Sardinia, too, was used to exiles: Anicetus, C. Cassius Longinus and Crispinus were banished there by Nero (Tac. *Ann.* XIV.62.6, XVI.9.2 and 17.2).

[46] Pliny, *HN* III.80; Moracchini-Mazel 1971 (E 177) and 1974 (E 178) (Mariana); for Aléria, Jéhasse and Jéhasse 1982 (E 166), but I have not followed their chronology, which is too high. On the dating of double-precinct *fora*, Todd 1985 (F 595) 64.

surrounding porticoes is of the double-enclosure type with a Capitolium
in the centre and a temple of Rome and Augustus at the east end; in its
developed form such a layout is hardly likely to be pre-Flavian, but
reticulate masonry in a monumental arch and in shops on the forum's
north side may indicate an earlier (Augustan or Julio-Claudian) phase of
building. The amphitheatre, a modest structure on a tiny scale for a
provincial capital (its long axis measures only 29.60m), reflects the
undeveloped nature of Roman urbanization in Corsica.[47] The interior of
the island remained largely untamed. There was a permanent garrison at
Praesidium, and piracy was suppressed by a detachment of the Misenum
fleet in the lagoon at Portus Dianae, just north of Aléria. In the
mountains Ptolemy lists fourteen *oppida*, but these are unlikely to have
been developed cities of classical Mediterranean type: excavation on Cap
Corse at Castellu de Luri, surely Ptolemy's Lurinum in the territory of
the Vanacini, has revealed stout stone fortifications and simple rectangular structures within them, recalling the type of Gaulish *oppidum* well
known from examples such as Ambrussum and Les Castels de Nages
near Nîmes.[48] Occupation at Castellu de Luri, which started in the third
century B.C., continued throughout the first century A.D. Yet for all the
apparent lack of sophistication in at least one of their *oppida*, the
Vanacini, who had received unspecified *beneficia* from Augustus, possessed the trappings of the imperial cult with *sacerdotes Augusti* (Lasemo
son of Leucanus, and Eunus son of Tomasus, men clearly lacking the
Roman citizenship): this we know from a rescript of A.D. 72 addressed by
Vespasian to the 'magistrates and senators' of the Vanacini, concerning a
border squabble with their neighbour, Mariana, to the south.[49]

Sardinia in time became more developed. Many of the cities on the
western seaboard retained a distinctly Punic flavour down to the late
Republic, with neo-Punic inscriptions and *suffetes* as magistrates. The
first Roman *colonia* was Turris Libysonis (Porto Torres), founded for
proletarians, probably *c.* 42–40 B.C., on a virgin site in north-west
Sardinia, and by Augustus' time Carales (Cagliari) possessed municipal
rank: so at least implies Pliny, who was drawing on an Augustan source,
but Uselis too must have had municipal rights early on, as 'Iulia Augusta'
were among her titles when she was promoted to colonial status by the
middle of the second century.[50] When Carales became a *municipium* is not
known for certain, but it is just possible that it may have been shortly
before 44 B.C., for she had remained loyal to Caesar when the rest of
Sardinia embraced the Pompeian cause, and her magistrates were

[47] *Gallia* 34 (1976) 503–5; 36 (1978) 463; 40 (1982) 430–3.
[48] Ptolemy (*Geog.* III.2) and Corsica: Jéhasse 1976 (E 164). Luri: *Gallia* 34 (1976) 507; 36 (1978)
468. Ambrussum: Fiches 1982 (E 351), 1986 (E 353). Castels: Py (E 466) 1978.
[49] *CIL* x 8038.   [50] Pliny, *HN* III.85; cf. Brunt 1971 (A 9) 597, 605.

quattuorviri, not the *duoviri* customary in Augustan municipia.[51] In any case Augustus showed little interest in fostering urban development in Sardinia; unlike Sicily the island was passed over as a candidate for veteran settlement.[52] Slowly Latin rights were extended to other communities, including Nora, Sulcis and Cornus, probably before the end of the first century A.D.; interestingly their constitutions were modelled on that of Carales and so had *quattuorviri* rather than *duoviri*.[53] But there is scant evidence, epigraphic or archaeological, for major public building programmes in either Augustan or Julio-Claudian Sardinia,[54] and it was only in the second century that the towns of the province began to display more tangible signs of material prosperity, constructing aqueducts, bath-buildings and the like. During the first century, however, the communications network was upgraded and improved, especially the main north–south artery between Turris Libysonis and Carales; milestones document activity in A.D. 13/14, 46, 67/8, 69 and 74.[55]

Sardinia's economic importance lay of course, as already noted, in grain. Always less productive than Sicily, she too declined in importance as a wheat exporter when Africa and Egypt took over in the early Empire as central Italy's most important suppliers; but as in Sicily there is no hint of a decline in Sardinian agriculture, or any suggestion that cereal production-levels did not remain high. About the details of the agricultural economy of the early Empire we are ignorant, as in Sicily, in the absence of excavated villas of the right date or of reliable field-survey evidence; the notion of ubiquitous *latifundia*, often repeated by modern commentators, is doubtless as over-simplistic for Sardinia as it is for Sicily. Metals too were not ignored. The mining district of the Iglesiente, centred at Metalla ('Mines'), produced lead, iron and copper; a stamped lead ingot documents Augustan production.[56]

Away from the coastal regions and the main towns, Romanization made little impact under Augustus or the Julio-Claudians. Sard

---

[51] Meloni 1975 (E 175) 209. *Quattuorviri*: ILS 1402, 6763; CIL x 7600, 7605.

[52] It is omitted in the list in *RG* 28.

[53] Sotgiu 1961 (B 286) no. 45 (Nora); Sotgiu 1961 (B 286) no. 3, ILS 6764, and CIL x 7519 (Sulcis). For Cornus, Meloni 1975 (E 175) 242. Carales, if it remained provincial capital, was doubtless later made a *colonia* (cf. *AE* 1982, 423); Olbia is a likely candidate for at least municipal rank. On the rarity of *quattuorviri* in provincial *municipia* under the Empire, A. Degrassi, *Scritti vari di antichità* I (1962) 150ff, IV (1971) 79.

[54] Exceptions include *ambulationes* at Carales before A.D. 6 (CIL x 7581), a Neronian temple of Ceres at Olbia (Sotgiu 1961 (B 286) no. 309), and probably the theatre at Nora (on its date Wilson 1980–1 (E 193) 222, n. 7). The Porto Torres baths are not late first century B.C., *pace* Maetzke 1966 (E 168) 162, as the axial type is not pre-Neronian in Rome; a brick-built provincial example on an imposing scale such as this is hardly pre-100 (cf. Boninu, Le Glay and Mastino 1984 (E 151) 13–18). On the cities in general, Tronchetti 1984 (E 191). [55] Meloni 1975 (E 175) 268 with references.

[56] Grain: Rickman 1980 (E 109) 106–7; Rowland 1984 (E 183). Countryside in general: Rowland 1984 (E 184). Mines: Meloni 1975 (E 175) 157–61. Iron: Dio XLII.56.3 (46 B.C.). Ingot: CIL x 8073.1.

remained the everyday language of the mountainous interior, and although it was something for the dedicators of a building near Zeppara to have erected in A.D. 62 a tablet inscribed in Latin, their names (Mislius, Benets, Bacoru, Sabdaga) are wholly un-Roman.[57] A significant proportion of the nuraghic village settlements continued to be inhabited down into imperial times. Religion, not surprisingly, remained conservative, and Punic cults in particular continued to flourish, often with the thinnest of Roman veneers. The cult centre at Antas of the deity Latinized as Sardus Pater (formerly worshipped as Sid Baby) enjoyed a long and faithful following throughout the Republic and early Empire, but it was only in the early third century that his temple took on recognizably Roman form (tetrastyle and prostyle, raised on a podium) in the Ionic order; while shrines elsewhere, including Mulciberus (Vulcan) at Nora, Tanit disguised as Demeter-Ceres at Tharros and Narcao, and Bes-Eshmun at Bitia, all show survival well into the imperial period.[58] The *municipia*, of course, adopted the outward form of a Roman constitution, but elsewhere both Punic language and Punic nomenclature continued in use. Striking confirmation of this is provided by a second-century A.D. neo-Punic inscription from Bitia, which demonstrates that in a non-chartered community in Sardinia the old Punic administrative system of local government remained intact well into imperial times, with *suffetes* as chief magistrates.[59]

---

[57] *AE* 1907, 119 = Sotgiu 1961 (B 286) no. 177.
[58] Acquaro *et al.* 1969 (E 143) (Antas); Meloni 1975 (E 175) 231, 325 and 338.
[59] Guzzo Amadasi 1967 (E 162) 133–6.

CHAPTER 13c

SPAIN

G. ALFÖLDY

I. CONQUEST, PROVINCIAL ADMINISTRATION
AND MILITARY ORGANIZATION

The Iberian peninsula, the first overseas country in which Roman rule
had been established (in 218 B.C.), became one of the most important
areas of the empire at the beginning of the imperial period.[1] This was due
above all to the fact that the wars of conquest gave it an increasingly
important military and political role. At the end of the Republic and
during the triumviral period, when nearly two centuries of almost
constant warfare had passed, and Roman civilization had struck root
particularly along the eastern coast and in the south of the peninsula,
north-western Spain, with its hardly accessible mountainous regions,
still resisted Roman rule. From 39 B.C., there was a single proconsul with
consular rank for both Hispanic provinces, Hispania Citerior and
Hispania Ulterior (the 'consular era' of Hispania Citerior was later
reckoned from 38 B.C.); he held the army command and was responsible
for the civil administration under the mandate of Octavian/Augustus.
Until the time of the last proconsul, Sextus Appuleius in 28/27 B.C., these
governors were constantly occupied with war – in the Fasti Triumphales
six triumphs are recorded for proconsuls of this period. But it was the
first *princeps* who completed the task of subduing the rest of the
peninsula, with the aim of seizing the chance to demonstrate his care for
his *provincia*, to win laurels, and at the same time to be absent from Rome

* This chapter was written in 1987 and revised in 1988. In 1991 the author requested some
supplements and changes. It was unfortunately not possible to include these and the editors bear the
responsibility for the fact that this does not reflect the current state of research. It can be noted, at
least, that two parts of *CIL* II² were published in 1995: *CIL* II²/14, part 1 (southern part of the
Conventus Tarraconensis) and II²/7 (Conventus Cordubensis), edited by A. Alföldy, A. U. Stylow *et
al.* For local mints see Burnett *et al.* 1992 (B 312). For the history and archaeology of the Iberian
peninsula, see particularly L. A. Churchin, *Roman Spain. Conquest and Assimilation* (London–New
York, 1991), W. Trillmich *et al.*, *Hispania antiqua. Denkmäler der Römerzeit* (Mainz am Rhein, 1993).

[1] The literary sources for Roman Spain are edited by A. Schulten *et al.*, *Fontes Hispaniae Antiquae*
I–IX (Barcelona, 1922–47). The number of Roman inscriptions known from the Iberian peninsula
has increased during the last hundred years from some 6,000, published in volume II of the *Corpus
Inscriptionum Latinarum* by E. Hübner, to some 20,000. These include important new documents,
such as the Tabula Siarensis, a new version of the Tabula Hebana (*AE* 1984, 508, see, above all,

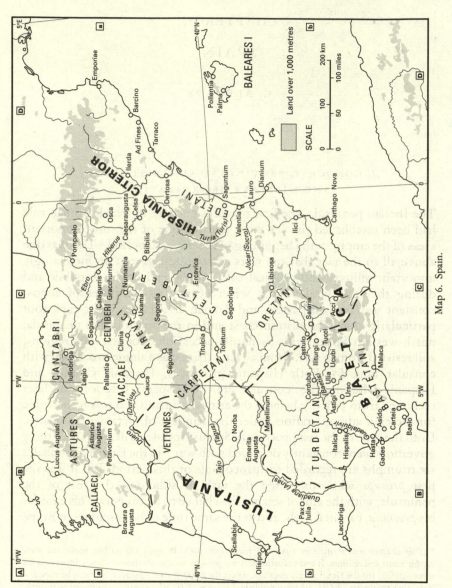

Map 6. Spain.

W.D. Lebek, *ZPE* 66 (1986) 31–48) and the Lex Irnitana (cf. below with no. 20). The edition of a new Corpus containing all inscriptions (*CIL* ɪɪ²) is being prepared under the direction of G. Alföldy, M. Mayer and A.U. Stylow. For local mints, the standard work is presently A. Vives y Escudero, *La moneda hispánica*, ɪ–ɪv, (Madrid, 1924–6) repr. (in two vols.) Madrid, 1980. The abundant archaeological sources, considerably augmented by intensified excavation throughout Spain and Portugal during the last two decades, are too numerous to survey here. For the archaeological and historical topography, cf. Tovar 1974–6 (ᴇ 243), Keay 1988 (ᴇ 227). A new synthesis of the history of Roman Spain (somewhat antiquarian in concept and not free of error) is provided by J.M. Blázquez *et al.* 1982 (ᴇ 210).

where his presence, after the provisional settlement of the new regime, might raise political problems.

In the spring or the summer of 27 B.C. Augustus went to Gaul and thence to Spain. At Tarraco (Tarragona), the new capital of Hispania Citerior, which had replaced the republican capital of Carthago Nova (Cartagena), he entered his eighth and ninth consulships on 1 January 26 and 25 B.C., respectively, and received embassies. Tarraco was thus for a short period the scene of political decisions of the highest importance and thus the centre of power. The attention of the Roman world turned to Spain, where in 26 B.C. the *princeps* personally led the campaign against the Cantabri in the mountains between Burgos and Santander. During the second campaign in 25 B.C., in Asturia and Callaecia, west of Cantabria, he lay ill at Tarraco. In the last months of 25 B.C., after he had left Spain for Rome, his legates completed the conquest, subduing the last insurrections. Resistance was definitively broken by Agrippa in 19 B.C.

The successful wars which made it necessary to concentrate six or more legions and numerous auxiliary units here, and, above all the presence of Augustus for two years and the administrative work which brought him there again for a period between 16 and 13 B.C., clearly emphasized the importance of Spain in the Roman empire. It is symptomatic of its importance that during the early Principate a large number of Spanish communities enjoyed the patronage of leading senators at Rome and even of members of the imperial family.[2] In continuation of a republican tradition, social and political contact with Spain was a highly esteemed source of prestige and influence.

Augustus established in the Iberian peninsula, as elsewhere, a system of provincial administration which was to undergo only a few modifications during the following three centuries.[3] From 27 B.C., the representatives of the *princeps* in the governance of Spain and particularly in command of the armies were the *legati Augusti pro praetore*, one in Hispania Citerior and another in Hispania Ulterior. The first legates were Gaius Antistius Vetus (27–25/24 B.C.) in the former and Publius Carisius (27–c. 22 B.C.) in the latter province. Definitive form was given to the new system about 13 B.C., but not by any single reform. Not only were provincial boundaries changed, but Hispania Ulterior was divided into two provinces, and Roman Spain consisted, for the next three centuries and more, of the *Hispaniae tres*, that is, of the provinces of Baetica, Lusitania and Hispania Citerior.

The province of Baetica, formerly a part of Hispania Ulterior and also known as Hispania Ulterior Baetica until the early second century,

---

[2] Cf. M. Koch, *Chiron* 9 (1979) 205–14, on M. Agrippa.
[3] See Albertini 1923 (E 198) 25–42; Alföldy 1969 (E 201) above all 285–96.

comprised Andalusia, minus the eastern part of the region which
belonged to Hispania Citerior. While both other provinces remained
under imperial control, Baetica, with Corduba (Córdoba) as its capital,
was a public province. The governor was a proconsul with the rank of a
senior ex-praetor, appointed to his office annually by the procedure of
sortitio by the Senate. In carrying out his administrative tasks he was
supported by the *legatus pro praetore*, who was a junior ex-praetor or
younger senator chosen by the proconsul, and by the *quaestor* responsible
for dealing with the taxes paid by the provincial communities. Lusitania,
that is Portugal minus the northern sector of the country, but including
the Spanish Estremadura and the region of Salamanca in the western part
of Castilla la Vieja, had Emerita Augusta (Mérida) as its capital, and was
under the control of a *legatus Augusti pro praetore*, a senior ex-praetor. The
recently occupied region of *Asturia et Callaecia* (including northern
Portugal), hitherto a part of Hispania Ulterior, was separated from the
demilitarized Lusitania and joined to Hispania Citerior, which remained
the only province in the Iberian peninsula which had a legionary
garrison. This province, the largest one in the empire, comprised the
eastern coast of Spain down to Almeria, the eastern sector of Andalusia
and most of the interior of Spain together with the northern and north-
western areas of the peninsula. The governor of this highly important
province, residing at Tarraco, was a senior ex-consul, normally distinguished both by birth and by a successful public career: at any rate,
unlike the governors of Baetica and Lusitania, he was a person from the
top stratum of the aristocracy of the imperial period. In the dispensation
of justice he was supported by a praetorian senator (who, in the first
century A.D., was called *legatus Augusti*, later also *iuridicus*). The governor
also had under him as office-holders of senatorial rank the legates of the
legions of his province. In the later years of Augustus and at the
beginning of the reign of Tiberius, as we can deduce from Strabo's
account of the administrative system in Spain and from an inscription,[4]
two of the three legions, certainly brigaded together in one fortress, were
subordinated to a single legate.

A further new element of the provincial administration was the
subdivision of the provinces into *conventus iuridici* for the purpose of
jurisdiction, as well as for the administration of the imperial cult. In
Hispania Citerior there were seven *conventus*, those of Tarraco, Carthago
Nova, Caesaraugusta (Zaragoza), Clunia (Peñalba de Castro), Asturica
Augusta (Astorga), Lucus Augusti (Lugo) and Bracara Augusta (Braga);
in Baetica, four – Corduba, Astigi (Ecija), Hispalis (Sevilla) and Gades
(Cádiz); in Lusitania, three – Emerita Augusta, Pax Iulia (Beja) and

---

[4] Strab. III.4.20 (166c); *CIL* IX 4133 = *ILS* 2644. On Strabo's account of Spain, cf. J.M. Blázquez,
Hispania Antiqua 1 (1971) 11–94.

Scallabis (Santarém). While some scholars assign the establishment of these *conventus* to Vespasian, the system described certainly goes back to Augustus at least in an earlier form and is attested by a *tabula patronatus* from the year A.D. 1.[5] Lack of evidence is not necessarily a sign of lack of organization. Whereas imperial procurators for the financial administration of Hispania Citerior and of Lusitania, who would hold the rank of a *ducenarius* under the system as it was later consolidated, are already attested in the reign of Augustus, the first known procurator of Baetica (who, it is true, was responsible only for the imperial revenues from this senatorial province, not for the taxes of the communities) belongs to the reign of Vespasian; but this does not mean that the foundation of this post may not go back to an earlier period, the reign of Augustus being the most obvious possibility.

According to Strabo, the main task of the procurators in Spain was to supply the army.[6] At the beginning of the Principate Spain was one of the most important military areas of the empire. In the wars of the conquest of north-western Spain at least six legions participated, namely the *legiones I, II* (*Augusta*), *IV* (*Macedonica*), *V* (*Alaudae*), *VI* (*Victrix*) and *X* (*Gemina*), all clearly attested by epigraphic and numismatic sources. Thus, for example, we know that veterans were settled at Emerita Augusta, in 25 B.C., from the *legiones V* and *X*; at Caesaraugusta, probably between 16 and 13 B.C., from the *legiones IV, VI* and *X*; and at Acci (Guadix), clearly at the beginning of the Principate, from the *legiones I* and *II*. But there is some evidence which allows us to conclude that in the early years of the Augustan Principate *legio IX* (*Hispana*) and *legio XX* (*Valeria Victrix*) also formed part of the Spanish armies.

After the conquest had been completed, Augustus decided to leave three legions to hold the Iberian peninsula, concentrating them in the reorganized Hispania Citerior. The disposition of these legions, which from the reign of Tiberius lay in a bow-shaped formation in the north-western part of the high plain of Castilla la Vieja, facing the Cantabrian and Asturian mountains, clearly demonstrates that the main task of the army in the early Principate was to control the recently subjected areas. *Legio IV Macedonica* was stationed in the Pisuerga valley, which allows entry into the Cantabrian Cordillera from the direction of Palencia to the south; a long series of boundary-stones (*termini Augustales*) found in this area shows the boundaries between the *prata leg(ionis) IIII* on the one side and the *ager* of the towns of Iuliobriga (Retortillo) in the north and Segisamo (Sasamón) in the south, respectively. *Legio VI Victrix* and *legio X Gemina*, whose first common fortress has not been identified, lay in

[5] M.D. Dopico Caínzos, *Gerión* 4 (1986) 265–83; cf. *AE* 1984, 553.

[6] Strab. III.4.20 (167c). On the Roman army in Spain, see now, above all, Le Roux 1982 (E 228), cf. Alföldy 1987 (D 159) 482–513.

Asturia; later *VI Victrix* may have had its headquarters at Legio (León),
which was the fortress of the *legio VII Gemina* from the reign of
Vespasian until late antiquity, while *X Gemina* can be located at
Petavonium (Rosinos de Vidriales). In the same area the bulk of the
auxilia of the *exercitus Hispanicus* also seems to have been stationed,
including *cohors IV Gallorum* in a fort on the road between Asturica
Augusta and Petavonium, near La Bañeza, where we know of a series of
the *termini pratorum coh(ortis) IIII Gall(lorum)*, erected under Claudius.[7]

The concentration in north-western Spain of all these troops, particularly of the legions recruited in Italy and, in increasing measure, from the
inhabitants of Spanish *coloniae* and *municipia* as well, prevented armed
resistance on a large scale, although there was still some fighting under
Nero against smaller gangs of highland robbers who disrupted the
country.[8] This concentration also contributed considerably to the
Romanization of the tribes thus controlled. In approximately the third
generation after the conquest of north-eastern Spain, a reduction of the
military forces could begin. In 39, or at the latest in 43, *legio IV
Macedonica* left Spain for the Rhine frontier; in 63 *legio X Gemina* was
ordered to the Pannonian frontier. Only *legio VI Victrix* remained in
Spain, together with some auxiliary units. The number of the *auxilia* was
of course also reduced after the reign of Augustus along with that of the
legions.[9]

One of the tasks of the army was to engage in the construction of
public works, primarily a road system. During his second stay in Spain,
between 16 and 13 B.C., Augustus initiated the systematic establishment
of a road network. The Via Augusta, which led from the Coll de Perthus
in the Pyrenees along the eastern coast of Spain to Tarraco and Valentia
(Valencia), and from here through the south of the peninsula, passing
Corduba, to Gades, was constructed at least partially under Augustus,
and was marked by milestones in the following years, in Baetica, for
example, in 2 B.C. This road which, according to Strabo, was of cardinal
importance, was still called *via militaris* in Domitian's time, as were some
other main roads of the empire.[10] The road network in north-eastern
Spain was certainly constructed with the participation of the army. The
building-stones of the Roman bridge at Ad Fines (Martorell), near
Barcino (Barcelona), built probably between 16 and 13 B.C., show the
abbreviated names of the legions IV, VI and X, as do the milestones in

[7] Cf. Le Roux 1982 (E 228) 107–18, with the list of the inscriptions attesting the *prata* (pasture-lands) of *legio IV Macedonica* and *cohors IV Gallorum*.

[8] *CIL* XI 395 = *ILS* 2648: [*p(rimo) p(ilo)*] *leg(ionis) VI victr(icis), donis donáto ob res prosper(e) gest(as) contra Astures* (*c.* A.D. 60 or some years before). [9] Cf. Le Roux 1982 (E 228) 85–93.

[10] Strab. III.4.9 (160c); P. Sillières, *REA* 83 (1981) 255–71. On the Via Augusta which was, unlike its predecessor, the republican Via Domitia, more a system of roads than a single road, cf. F. Pallí Aguilera, *La via Augusta en Cataluña*, Bellaterra, 1985.

the region of Caesaraugusta, set up in 9 and 5 B.C. respectively.[11] Several
other roads, known from the *Itineraria*, milestones and archaeological
discoveries, demonstrate clearly that the network of the *viae publicae*
extended through the whole peninsula. There were, for example, two
principal diagonal roads from the north west to the south east and from
the south west to the north east which intersected exactly in the
geographical centre of the peninsula, at Titulcia (in the area of the
present Titulcia, formerly Bayona de Tajuña, south of Madrid). In the
west, the main Roman road was that from Asturica Augusta to Emerita
Augusta and from here to Hispalis, the so-called Camino de la Plata,
where the earliest milestone belongs to the reign of Augustus.[12]

II. URBANIZATION

Conquest, pacification, reorganization of the provincial government and
the road network were only a part of the Augustan achievement in
Hispania. Because of its enormous impact on the political system, social
order, economy and cultural development, urbanization, that is, the
foundation of *coloniae* and the grant of municipal status to native
communities, was one of the most effective elements in the policy of the
first *princeps* towards Spain. Although urban life had a long tradition in
the Iberian peninsula, with the existence of Phoenician and Greek
colonies and the urban development of some native settlements, Roman
urbanization did not reach a high level there until the last decades of the
Republic. Until the 40s of the first century B.C., if we exclude communities whose status is still debated, we have evidence of only some towns
which either certainly or probably possessed the Latin right, such as
Carteia (Cortijo El Rocadillo near Gibraltar, later a *municipium*) or
Valentia, and for some towns such as Tarraco and Carthago Nova, which
seem to have had the status of a *conventus civium Romanorum*.[13] The
changes which occurred after the last years of Caesar and above all
during the reign of Augustus, may be illustrated by the list of towns
given by Pliny the Elder, who relied mainly on a source from the middle
period of the Augustan Principate (before 12 B.C.). Besides a large
number of communities without a privileged status, Pliny enumerates in

[11] G. Fabre, M. Mayer and I. Rodà, *Inscriptions romaines de Catalogne* 1, *Barcelone (sauf Barcino)*
(Paris, 1984) no. 1; C. Castillo, J. Gómez-Pantoja and M.D. Mauleón, *Inscripciones romanas del Museo
de Navarra* (Pamplona, 1981) no. 1; *ibid.* no. 2 = G. Fatás and M.A. Martín Bueno, *Epigrafía romana de
Zaragoza y su provincia* (Zaragoza, 1977) no. 11; *ibid.* no. 19 cf. *AE* 1984, 583–5. On the road system in
Roman Hispania, cf. Roldán Hervás 1975 (E 236).
[12] J.M. Roldán Hervás, *Iter ab Emerita Asturicam. El Camino de la Plata* (Salamanca, 1971) 51 no.
25.
[13] On urbanization in Roman Spain, see, above all, Galsterer 1971 (E 221); Wiegels 1985 (E 245);
Alföldy 1987 (E 205).

Baetica nine *coloniae*, ten *municipia civium Romanorum* and twenty-seven towns with the 'old' Latin right (by which he means Latin status granted before the general extension of the *ius Latii* in Spain by Vespasian); in Hispania Citerior (together with the Balearic Islands) twelve *coloniae*, fifteen *municipia civium Romanorum* and twenty communities which were apparently without exception *Latini veteres*, and in Lusitania five *coloniae*, one *municipium civium Romanorum* and three communities with the 'old' Latin status.[14] These numbers, however, do not at all represent the full extent of urbanization in Spain before the end of the Augustan Principate (not to mention the number of privileged towns from the Flavian period). Several towns received their urban charter in the last decades of the reign of Augustus, and are thus not registered in Pliny's lists, which are earlier in origin. Thus, for example, the inhabitants of Segobriga (near to Saelices, 100 km south east of Madrid), one of the most important centres of the Celtiberi, were according to Pliny *stipendiarii*, that is, they formed a peregrine community; from epigraphical documentation, however, we can deduce that Segobriga had already obtained the status of a *municipium*, administered by *IIIIviri* and aediles, by A.D. 12/14.[15]

Unfortunately, our sources, in particular Pliny's lists of cities, the inscriptions and the local coinage of several towns, do not allow us to establish an exact list of the *coloniae* and *municipia* founded by Augustus. The evidence is not clear enough. The communities whose citizens are enrolled in the *Galeria tribus* belong, it is true, to an earlier phase of urbanization than the towns with the *Quirina tribus*, founded by the Flavian emperors; but although the citizens of most towns which received their privileged status from Augustus were inscribed in the *Galeria tribus*, this tribal affiliation certainly does not always indicate an Augustan grant of urban autonomy, and by the same token at least some of the Augustan colonies did not have their citizens enrolled in this tribe. Nevertheless, the general trends and the enormous importance of the Augustan policy of urbanization in Spain are clear. First of all in Baetica, in the eastern parts of Hispania Citerior and in the southern half of Lusitania, the first *princeps* founded several Roman colonies and granted the status of a *municipium* with either Roman or Latin rights to numerous native communities. As is indicated by the case of Segobriga, but also, for example, by that of Ercavica (Castro de Santaver near to Cañaverue-las, north of Segobriga) or Valeria (now Valeria, formerly Valera de Arriba, east of Segobriga), municipalization also began in the interior of the peninsula in the early Principate.

---

[14] Pliny, *HN* III.7, III.18, III.77–8, IV.117.

[15] *CIL* II 3103–4 (aed., A.D. 12/14); *CIL* II 381* (certainly authentic, *aed. IIIIvir*). Cf. Alföldy 1987 (E 205) 77–80.

Of the nine *coloniae* of Baetica attested by Pliny (in his lists he actually mentions ten *coloniae*, but one of them, Munda, must have been completely destroyed in 45 B.C.), some received their status either directly from Caesar or – like Urso (Osuna) – immediately after the death of the dictator, but on his instructions. Under either Caesar or his heir Itucci (near to Baena) and Ucubi (Espejo), were founded. Augustus founded the colonies of Astigi (Ecija) and Tucci (Martos) and changed the status of Corduba and Asido (Medina Sidonia) into that of a Roman *colonia*. Of the five colonies of Lusitania, only Emerita Augusta is certainly an Augustan foundation; Metellinum (Medellin), Norba (Cáceres), Pax Iulia and Scallabis were founded either under Caesar or during the period before 27 B.C. Among the colonies of Hispania Citerior, Carthago Nova seems to be a Caesarian *colonia* and Celsa (Velilla del Ebro) was a *colonia* of Lepidus (founded perhaps in 48/47 B.C.). Either in the last years of Caesar or in the subsequent period before 27 B.C. the new capital, whose full name was Colonia Iulia Urbs Triumphalis Tarraco, and Acci (Guadix) were founded. Colonies of Augustus founded after 27 B.C. were Barcino (Barcelona), Caesaraugusta, Ilici (Elche), Libisosa (Lezuza) and probably also Salaria (near to Ubeda).[16]

Considerably less clear is the number of the Augustan *municipia*. The earliest Spanish *municipia* with a certainly attested date are Caesarian foundations, such as Asido and Gades. Unfortunately, for only a few of the Spanish cities with this status can an Augustan origin be suggested with a sufficient basis of evidence, like the Municipium Augusta Bilbilis, for example, the native town of Martial. But there is no doubt that several of the Spanish *municipia* which received their privileged status before the death of the first *princeps* were Augustan foundations, as were a large number of other towns with the *Galeria tribus* which can be considered as *municipia*.[17]

The extent of this urbanizing programme in Spain at the end of the Republic and under Augustus can be contrasted with the fact that the Julio-Claudian emperors did not consider it necessary to extend colonial and municipal status to other communities of the Iberian peninsula on a large scale. One of the few *municipia*, or indeed the only *municipium* (unless it was simply a city with elevated status), founded during the period from Tiberius to Nero may have been Baelo (Bolonia) on the Atlantic coast of Baetica, attested as *municipium Claudium*.[18] Clunia, which was a *municipium* from the time of Augustus or Tiberius, obviously obtained the rank of a *colonia* from Galba, who was in this town when he received the news of his proclamation as emperor by the

---

[16] A list of the *coloniae* in Spain: Brunt 1971 (A 9) 590–3.
[17] Cf. Alföldy 1987 (E 205) 53–4 and 104–5; cf. also the lists and maps in Wiegels 1985 (E 245) 164–8. [18] *AE* 1971, 172; cf. Wiegels 1985 (E 245) 20–2.

Senate of Rome. It was the Flavian dynasty which took over the task of completing the urbanization of the peninsula.

III. ECONOMY AND SOCIETY

The numerous municipal foundations at the end of the Republic and under Augustus changed the situation in Spain fundamentally. The juridical status of several communities was elevated. Apart from the existence of communities of Roman citizens in the older and the newly founded colonies, a high number of peregrine communities of the native population now received autonomous status. In contrast with their former status, which had allowed the local authorities self-government only to a limited extent, they achieved the status of *municipia* and with that, on the basis of a specifically defined relationship with the provincial governor or other Roman officials, the right of administering their own affairs through proper magistrates elected by the assembly of the citizens, and through the decisions of the local *ordo decurionum*. This privilege was granted on the basis either of the Roman citizenship or at least of the *ius Latii*, which enabled rich fellow-citizens to obtain the *civitas Romana* by holding municipal *honores*.[19] The communal organization of the cities with the *ius Latii* was regulated according to principles for the constitutions of Latin *municipia* laid down in town charters which may go back to a general Augustan law for the *municipia* of the provinces, as has been deduced from the Flavian Lex Irnitana, the recently discovered town charter for the *municipium* of Irni in Baetica.[20] The towns experienced considerable economic growth from the Principate of Augustus onwards. The urban *territoria* comprised the best areas for agriculture as, for example, in the valley of the river Baetis (Guadalquivir), which was, according to Strabo, full of farms improved with groves and gardens of various plants.[21] The towns became centres of industry and trade. The same author praises the export of corn, wine and oil from Baetica, emphasizing the importance of the Spanish trade for Italy and Rome; he also mentions several other products of the country, among them fish-sauces (*garum*), which are also clearly attested by archaeological evidence. He also emphasizes the wealth of the Iberian peninsula in minerals, noting that no other country furnishes gold, silver, copper and iron in the same quantity and quality as Spain. That mining was another of the sources of wealth in the towns, is clear from Strabo's remark that

[19] On municipal institutions in Roman Spain, cf. Alföldy 1987 (E 205) 27–9 (with further bibliography).

[20] See on this A. d'Ors, *Anuario de Historia del Derecho Español* 54 (1984) 535–73; *id.*, *Lex Flavia Municipalis* (Rome, 1986); González 1986 (B 235).

[21] For what follows see Strab. III.2.3–10 (142–8c).

the silver mines in the neighbourhood of Carthago Nova, and also in other places, had passed from state into private ownership.

The degree to which the owners of mines and other economic resources could enrich themselves during the early Empire, can be demonstrated by the example of Sextus Marius, probably from Corduba, who was, according to Tacitus,[22] the richest man of his time in Spain. After he had been put to death in A.D. 33, his enormous wealth, consisting particularly of gold-mines and other mines, was taken into the imperial *patrimonium* and was given a procuratorial administration, which still existed in the Flavian period. Not only was the road-station Mariana (now Nuestra Señora de Mairena) in the eastern Sierra Morena named after him, but so too was the whole Sierra Morena, a name derived, it seems, from the ancient name of the mountain range, Mons Marianus.

At the same time, it was due above all to the new local elites that towns received magnificent public buildings. Some of these were gifts from emperors and from members of the imperial family, such as the marvellous theatre at Emerita Augusta, given by Agrippa, or the amphitheatre of the same colony, a donation by Augustus; but public buildings were normally paid for by local magistrates or by other rich citizens; in the reign of Augustus, for example, the *forum* of Saguntum (Sagunto), was paid for from a legacy from one Cnaeus Baebius Geminus, a member of the most prestigious family of that *municipium*.[23]

The accumulation of wealth entailed changes in the social structure. A local elite developed in each town, comprising the rich land-holders in the *territorium*, who were frequently also engaged in industry, trade and mining. This elite furnished the magistrates and constituted the *ordo decurionum* of the cities. In Roman colonies, which normally had a population of lower origin but at the same time offered highly favourable conditions for making money by trade, and in the provincial capitals where there were also good opportunities for social advancement through service in the imperial administration, these elites constituted, as at Tarraco and Barcino, the uppermost group of a society which allowed social mobility on a relatively large scale and generally admitted into the political elite the sons of rich freedmen and immigrants. In at least some *municipia* such as Saguntum, however, the upper class, composed of a small group of old leading families, carefully guarded its privileges, building a 'closed' society, closing its ranks to people of humble origin and to newcomers, and holding in dependence the lower population both of town and countryside through the institutions of slavery and *clientela*. That social differentiation deepened can be deduced

---

[22] Tac. *Ann.* VI.19.
[23] F. Beltrán Lloris, *Epigrafía latina de Saguntum y su territorium* (Valencia, 1980) no. 64.

not only from the official distinction of *ordo* and plebs in the population of the towns, but also from the spread of slavery in the towns and their neighbourhoods. Above all, slaves were frequently manumitted in the urban centres but in the countryside, in particular on the estates of the interior, manumission seems to have been rarely practised.[24]

The most emphatic sign of social differentiation in the context of the Roman social order was that the richest and most distinguished members of the urban elites could enter the equestrian and the senatorial orders. It may be symptomatic of the general level of Romanization in Spain and of its importance in the Roman empire, that the first Roman senator of non-Italian origin, Quintus Varius Severus, *tribunus plebis* in 90 B.C., from Sucro near Valencia, was a Spaniard, as was the first consul born outside Italy, Lucius Cornelius Balbus the Elder, from Gades, consul in 40 B.C.; and later, the first emperor with a *patria* outside the Italian peninsula, Trajan, was from Spain. Apart from the Cornelii Balbi at Gades, at the end of the Republic and under the early Principate, there were already some senatorial families in the towns of Baetica, such as the family of the Aelii at Italica who were the ancestors of Hadrian, and the Annaei, the family of Seneca, at Corduba. In the imperial period this province provided an extremely high number of senators for Rome. The social background for the ascent of such families may be revealed by the statement of Strabo that under Augustus there were no fewer than 500 knights at Gades, a figure matched only at Patavium (Padova) in northern Italy.[25] One or two generations later, about the middle of the first century A.D., we also find the first senators from the cities of the eastern coast of Hispania Citerior, such as the Pedanii from Barcino, Raecius Taurus from Tarraco and Marcus Aelius Gracilis from Dertosa (Tortosa). To the same generation as the two latter belongs Quintus Iulius Cordus, a praetorian senator under Nero, who seems to have come from Lusitania and who may have been the first of the few senators from this province.[26]

The evolution of urban life, particularly the rise of the upper classes of the urban society, also created the conditions for cultural development. Over and above the spread of literacy, several towns offered good opportunities for education and stimulated intellectual ambitions – especially in Baetica with its high concentration of urban centres. As in northern Italy and southern Gaul, the elites of the urban society in

[24] Slavery in Roman Spain: See now V.M. Smirin, in: E.M. Štaerman *et al.*, *Die Sklaverei in den westlichen Provinzen des römischen Reiches im 1.-3. Jahrhundert* (Stuttgart, 1987) 38–12; cf. G. Alföldy, *ZPE* 67 (1987) 249–62.	[25] Strab. III.5.3 (169c) and v.1.7 (213c).

[26] On Roman senators from Spain, including the persons mentioned here and below, see, above all, Le Roux 1982 (E 229) (Hispania Citerior); Castillo García 1982 (E 214) (Baetica); Etienne 1982 (E 218) (Lusitania).

Baetica produced under Augustus and the Julio-Claudian emperors not only an increasing number of new equestrian and senatorial families, but also, from exactly the same social environment, men at the peak of contemporary intellectual life. The family of the Annaei from Corduba, with Seneca the Elder, the *rhetor* and historian of equestrian rank under Augustus, Seneca the Younger, who was not only one of the richest but also one of the most erudite senators in the reigns of Claudius and Nero, and Marcus Annaeus Lucanus, the poet and the nephew of the philosopher, furnishes the best example of intellectual interest and capacity in an ambitious leading family of this kind, which had risen from the provincial upper class of the capital of Baetica. But there were also other men of letters from this province, like the *rhetor* and senator Iunius Gallio, probably from Corduba, who adopted one of the brothers of Seneca the Younger, Pomponius Mela the geographer, from Tingentera near Algeciras, and Lucius Iunius Moderatus Columella, the author of the *Res Rusticae*, a knight from Gades.[27]

IV. THE IMPACT OF ROMANIZATION

The political, economic, social and cultural development of Spain in the period between the collapse of the Republic and the end of the Julio-Claudian dynasty was enormous. The Iberian peninsula, once a field of continuous resistance to Rome, became, in spite of its geographical situation on the periphery of the Mediterranean world, an area of central importance in the Roman empire. But it would be wrong to believe that all the changes which took place in the period covered in this volume produced a uniform picture in the Iberian peninsula by the end of the period. On the whole, it may be less important that some older trading centres of the Mediterranean coast did not participate in the general boom: Emporiae (Empuries), for example, an amalgamation of Greek colony, native settlement and Roman town, was not able to compete with the flourishing harbour cities of younger foundations, such as the colonies of Tarraco or Barcino.[28] There was an immense contrast between the intensively urbanized regions of Baetica, the eastern parts of Hispania Citerior and southern Lusitania on the one hand, and the backward areas in the interior and in the north west on the other. In the latter areas, where less favourable geographical conditions and, above

---

[27] On the rise and importance of these 'colonial elites' from Roman Spain, cf. R. Syme, *Colonial Elites. Rome, Spain and the Americas* (Oxford, 1958) 1–23.

[28] On Emporiae, cf. now J. Aquilué *et al.*, *El fòrum romà d'Empúries (excavacions de l'any 1982). Una aproximació arqueològica al procés històric de la romanització al nord-est de la Península Ibèrica* (Barcelona, 1984).

all, a very different historical background presented a framework for further development of a kind quite different from that in the south and in the east, Roman influence was by no means as deep as it was in the regions early Romanized. Literary, epigraphical and archaeological evidence here shows a continuity not only of the native population, but also of its social order and culture.[29]

Indigenous nomenclature and local cults were preserved in the interior and particularly in north-western Spain not only during the early Empire, but also later. The social framework was provided by the *gentilitates*, that is, the native clan organizations (which were replaced in Callaecia by the alliance of the inhabitants of *castella*, native settlements with a proper organization). The Roman administration was based, before municipalization, on the existence of communities which consisted of several clans and were called either *gens*, *civitas* or *populus*. They had their own authorities, that is, a local senate and office-holders called *magistratus* or *magistri* and, as they were frequently the counterpart of a more important settlement and its territory, they were often the nuclei of an urban development.[30] Originally, these communities were parts of larger tribes, which had a rather loose organization, loose enough even to allow armed conflicts between single population groups. As this tribal system was not suitable for the purposes of the Roman administration, it was not in Rome's interest to maintain the tribal units. While the *conventus* of Asturica Augusta, Lucus Augusti and Bracara Augusta corresponded to the tribal organization of the Astures and Callaeci (the latter were divided into two *conventus*), in other parts of Spain the tribes did not retain their own organizations. On the contrary, the population group of the Celtiberi, for example, in central Spain were not only divided into several *populi*, such as the Segobrigenses, but at the same time the *populi* from Segobriga to Clunia were distributed among the three *conventus* of Carthago Nova, Caesaraugusta and Clunia.[31]

In spite of the survival of native traditions, the impact of Romanization was also evident in these backward areas in the Julio-Claudian age. Apart from the construction of roads and the consequences of contacts with the Roman population of the peninsula through trade, administration and military control, the main method of Romanization was, as elsewhere, to make at least the upper classes of the native population see that their interests coincided with those of Rome. At the beginning of the imperial period, the recruitment of the youth of native tribes into the numerous auxiliary units raised from the population of the backward

---

[29] Cf. especially the development in the north-western part of the Iberian peninsula; on this Tranoy 1981 (E 244) esp. 261–384.
[30] On clan organization, see now González Rodríguez 1986 (E 225); on local magistrates and senates cf. now esp. Alföldy 1987 (E 205) 50–1.   [31] Alföldy 1987 (E 205) 110–11.

areas, was also a safety measure; it contributed, moreover, for the first time to educating people in the Latin language and Roman *mores*.[32] The extension of the Roman citizenship created new privileged groups in the population. But peregrine chiefs of the native communities also became representatives of the political interests of Rome. The foundation of the first *municipia* in the interior opened a channel of deeper Romanization similar to that in the south and the east. And there was one institution which bound together local aristocracies from all parts of the country: imperial cult, organized not only in the *coloniae* and in the *municipia*, but also for the whole population of larger areas, on the level of the *conventus*, and even of the provinces as a whole (in Baetica, the provincial cult seems to have been institutionalized first under Vespasian). The provincial cult was established in the form of an annual meeting of the *concilium provinciae*, comprised of representatives of communities with different statuses, under the presidency of the *flamen provinciae*, and it became a very important factor in the integration of local elites with different social backgrounds into a new, homogeneous 'provincial' aristocracy. How interested Spanish elites were in this cult which, at the same time, contributed to their own prestige, may be illustrated by the fact that the construction of the famous temple of Augustus at Tarraco, begun in A.D. 15 and setting an *exemplum* for other provinces, had been approved at the request of the *Hispani*.[33]

On the whole, a century after the establishment of the Principate at Rome and after the conquest of north-western Spain by the first *princeps*, the southern and eastern areas of the Iberian peninsula were fully integrated into the political, economic, social and cultural system of Rome, while the backward regions of the interior and of the north west were well on their way to overcoming the retardation caused by geographical and historical factors. By the end of the Julio-Claudian period Spain was in a certain sense mature enough to become the centre of political power, not as a result of the presence of a *princeps* from Rome, as under Augustus, but by virtue of its own efforts. The revolt against Nero by Servius Sulpicius Galba in A.D. 68, who had been governor of Hispania Citerior for ten years, and his proclamation as emperor by the Senate at Rome, revealed, according to Tacitus, the secret of the imperial power: that it was possible to create an emperor outside Rome.[34] That Spain could be the country where this truth was demonstrated for the first time was a consequence of its development from the end of the Republic onwards.

[32] On the recruitment of Spaniards for the Roman army, see, above all, Roldán Hervás 1974 (E 235) esp. 233–86; cf. Le Roux 1982 (E 228) 284–90.
[33] Tac. *Ann.* 1.78. Imperial cult in Spain: cf. Etienne 1958 (E 217); cf. now also Fishwick 1987 (F 137) esp. 150–8, and 219–39.   [34] Tac. *Hist.* 1.4.

GAUL

C. GOUDINEAU

I. INTRODUCTION

Caesar's conquest of Gaul fundamentally shifted the balance of the Roman world, up until then based on the Mediterranean, with the single exception of the Black Sea. The 'new territories' represented a vast addition to the empire, comprising some 30 per cent of its land area apart from Italy. Exposed to central Europe, and especially to the German barbarians and other groups, amongst them the Cimbri and Teutones, who had already left their mark on Roman history, they stretched to the northern oceans, and to Britain, which Caesar had abandoned, after suffering his only failure. The occupation of the new provinces demanded, in the short term, that the Alps and the Pyrenees be subjugated and that control be established over the Rhine and the Danube. The Gallic Wars had utterly and irreversibly transformed the geopolitics of the ancient world. Conversely, the history of Gaul reflected its new environment, and the new strategic geography formed by the German frontier and the proximity of Britain, with all the attendant social and economic repercussions.[1]

---

[1] Despite the enormous amount written about Gaul, the bibliography of the subject is limited, most of all because no one has been brave or foolish enough to revise and update Camille Jullian's great *Histoire de la Gaule*, which was published in eight volumes between 1907 and 1926. Similarly, the basic guide to the archaeology is still Albert Grenier's *Manuel d'Archéologie gallo-romaine*, also comprising eight volumes, the first of which appeared in 1931 and the last in 1960. Both works are in many respects out of date, but the high reputation they rightly possess has prevented anyone from trying to produce anything similar, particularly as any modern version would have to be multi-disciplinary and thus a collaborative venture which might be difficult to organize. Duval 1971 (E 332) contains an exhaustive bibliography covering all areas of research in Roman Gaul. There have been a few general accounts, but on the whole scholars have devoted their energies to compiling a series of specialist *corpora*, catalogues of literary references, of inscriptions, of mosaics, of sculpture, of coins and, most recently begun, of wall-paintings. No syntheses, however, have emerged from these *corpora*. Two kinds of studies which have proved popular over the last twenty or thirty years are investigations focused on a particular town or alternatively a given *civitas*, often taking the form of a local gazetteer or inventory. But little has been written on the countryside, let alone the economy as a whole. Another complicating factor is that the area known to the Romans as Gaul is today divided up among Switzerland, Luxembourg, Belgium, Germany and France. Each nation has its own distinctive working methods and traditions, and, quite rightly, the image of Gaul in each country reflects its place in the national heritage. In France, the universities have traditionally accorded a special place to the study of the classical world. As a result, attention has been focused on

But it is impossible to understand ancient texts or decisions, such as those that created the administrative structure or the road system, if we continue to base our analyses on present-day cartography. It is important to remember that as late as Pliny, and perhaps as late as Ptolemy, geographical knowledge remained extremely approximate. Book IV of Strabo's *Geography*, devoted to Gaul and completed about A.D. 18, illustrates the point. The information is more or less reliable for southern Gaul: the descriptions of the relief and of the rivers, the distances (sometimes given in Roman miles), the territories occupied by different peoples and cities are all presented with a high degree of accuracy, for the period. But for the remainder of Gaul the account is staggering: following Caesar,[2] all the coastlines (including those on the shores of the Atlantic) are described as facing the north and the Pyrenees as running north–south, parallel to the Rhine and also to the courses of the Garonne, the Loire and the Seine. The coast of Great Britain lies

epigraphy, law, cities, monuments and art history at the expense of research into regional analysis, stratigraphic sequences, rural studies and everyday life. The economy has been studied only through the medium of pottery, the importance of which has consequently been greatly exaggerated, and more recently other categories of small finds, including glass and metalwork. It has proved much more difficult to win acceptance for subjects such as landscape archaeology, research into field systems, pollen analysis, environmental archaeology and the study of human and animal bones. Fieldwork in France has for a long time been conducted on a piecemeal basis. In some areas that continues to be the case, but in recent years the demands of rescue excavation have led to some very large-scale projects in some of the more important Roman towns and also some programmes of rural survey in advance of motorway construction or the extension of the high speed rail network. Before these developments, the majority of excavations had been in small urban centres, albeit ones of some historical interest, such as Glanum and Alésia. Rescue archaeology has changed all that, but the conditions under which it has to be undertaken mean that much of the enormous new database it has generated remains unpublished.

Texts: Duval 1971 (E 332) Lerat 1977 (E 415). Inscriptions: the basic material is to be found in *CIL* XII and XIII (for supplements to the latter see ch. 13*f*, n. 1) and *ILTG*. The most important recent collections are *ILGN* and *RIG*; note also R. Marichal, *Les graffites de la Graufesenque, Gallia* suppl. 47 (1988). Mosaics: see the *Recueil général des mosaïques de la Gaule*, appearing regularly in Suppl. X of the journal *Gallia*. Painting: Barbet 1974 (E 267), the first volume of a *Recueil général des peintures murales de la Gaule*. Coinage: *Corpus des trésors monétaires de la France* (1982–).

The *Carte archéologique de la Gaule*, published by the Académie des Inscriptions et Belles-Lettres was originally compiled in 1930, and began to be revised in 1988. Each volume analyses discoveries covering the period from the Iron Age to the eighth century A.D. Since 1988, the sections covering the following *départements* have appeared: Allier, Creuse, Finistère, Indre-et-Loire, Loire-et-Cher, Loire, Loiret, Lozère, Maine-et-Loire and Manche.

Surveys of work on Gaul continue to appear in *REA*. Note also *Résumés d'archéologie suisse* (from 1981) and, for archaeological discoveries, a new series in the journal *Gallia*, entitled *Gallia-Informations*. The Centre National d'Archéologie urbaine de Tours publishes a *Bibliographie d'archéologie urbaine*; two fascicles have appeared, for 1975–85 and 1986–7 (Tours, 1989). There are numerous museum guides and catalogues with bibliographies. Note particularly the collection of the Ministère de culture français, *Guides archéologiques de la France* (from 1984: 1. Vaison-la-Romaine, 2. Saint-Romain-en-Gal, 4. Alésia, 5. Alba, 7. Les Bolards, 8. Narbonne, 12. Autun, 13. Bibracte) and the *Guides archéologiques de la Suisse*. There are noteworthy catalogues or guides for Lyons (rue des Farges), Autun, Trier, Neuss, Geneva and other cities but, unfortunately, many of these are not to be found in libraries.

2 Caes. *BGall*. IV.20.1.

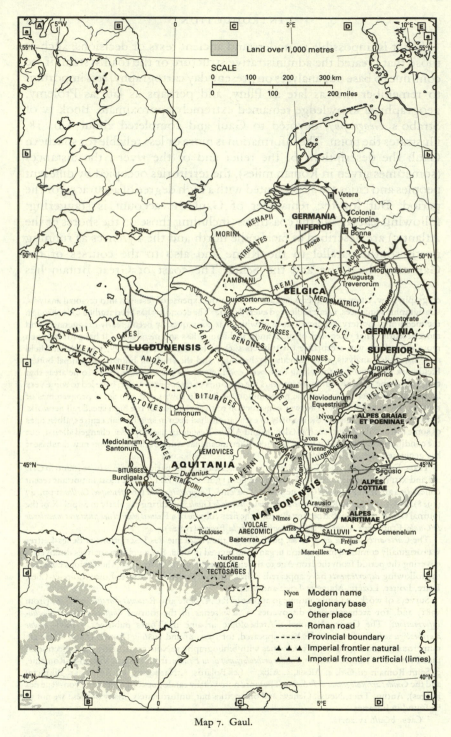

Map 7. Gaul.

The map shows only Roman sites within the Gallic, German and Alpine provinces and not those in Spain or Britain.

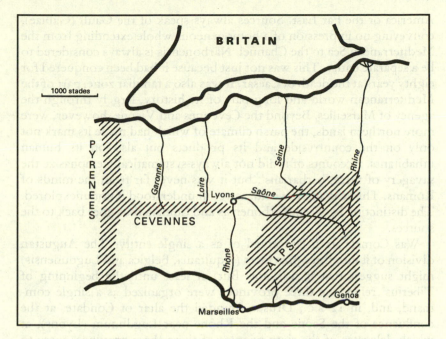

Fig. 8. The geography of Gaul according to Strabo.

opposite that of Gaul, from the mouth of the Rhine as far as the Pyrenees, and the channel between Britain and Gaul is said to be 320 stades (some 50 km) in width. All the distances are wrong, some of them by a huge margin.

Finally, our sources are both poor and uneven in coverage. Literary sources provide a certain amount of information for the period 43 B.C. – A.D. 69, but it mostly relates to the German Wars or to just a few episodes, which, as a result, tend to be accorded disproportionate importance. From then on, the silence of the texts is almost unbroken for a century and a half. Epigraphic evidence is distributed very unevenly: inscriptions are common in Narbonensis in the Julio-Claudian period, but rare in the Tres Galliae, and mostly later than the first century A.D.

1. Gaul or the Gallic provinces?

In what follows, I shall treat Narbonensis (formerly Transalpina) separately from the Tres Galliae (formerly Comata). This distinction contrasts with that of traditional histories that present Gaul as a unity. Is there any point in it?

From the Augustan period, neither texts nor inscriptions ever use the term Gallia except in a purely geographical sense, as we might say South

America or the Far East. Sources always speak of the Gauls (Galliae), conveying no impression of a homogeneous whole extending from the Mediterranean Sea to the Channel. Narbonensis is always considered to be a separate entity. This was not just because it had been conquered for eighty years at the death of Caesar. It was also a familiar zone, part of the Mediterranean world and long part of its history, largely through the agency of Marseilles. Beyond the Cevennes and Vienne, however, were more northern lands, the harsh climate of which had made its mark not only on the countryside and its products but also on its human inhabitants. Accounts of it did not always systematically emphasize the savagery of these 'barbarians', but it was never far from the minds of Romans. This was a new world, as yet ill understood if not unexplored. The distinction between Narbonensis and Comata thus goes back to the sources.

Was Comata itself conceived of as a single entity? The Augustan division of it into three provinces (Aquitania, Belgica and Lugdunensis) might suggest that it was not. But, at least until the beginning of Tiberius' reign, the three provinces were organized as a single command, and, in 12 B.C., Drusus founded the altar of Condate, at the confluence of the Saône and the Rhône near Lugdunum (Lyons), at which delegates of the sixty peoples of these three provinces were to assemble for the next three centuries.[3] Each year on the 1 August, the representatives of the elites of Saintes and Chartres, Langres and Périgueux met to celebrate the imperial cult. There they competed, to be sure, in the election of the chief priest (the *sacerdos*) and his assistants, elections which brought glory to the *civitates* of the successful candidates, but they were above all united in defence of their common interests. One occasion when this happened was in A.D. 48, in the reign of Claudius, when the issue was winning permission for the Roman citizens of non-Mediterranean Gaul to become magistrates at Rome. In fact, Claudius himself, when defending the legitimacy of this request to the Roman Senate, used the term Gallia Comata.[4] Besides, the official dedications made at the Confluence, in so far as epigraphic discoveries can tell us, were made in the name of the Tres Provinciae Galliae, which should be translated not as 'the three provinces of Gaul' but as 'the three Gallic provinces'. Does this make Gaul a unity?

In fact, administration should be distinguished from psychology. Gauls never represented themselves, in all the honorific and funerary inscriptions they set up, either as Gauls or as members of a given province, but rather as belonging to the *civitas* of the Remi, the Pictones, the Redones or the Aedui. One inscription shows that the emperor

---

[3] For a different view on the date of the dedication of the altar see above p. 98.
[4] *CIL* XIII 1668.

Claudius allowed the Silvanectes to establish their own *civitas* separate from that of the Lingones.[5] Tacitus writes that in the course of the events of A.D. 68–9, the states of non-Mediterranean Gaul could not agree on a common policy because long-standing quarrels and rivalries continued to divide them: 'who was to lead the war? . . . Some based their claim on treaties [i.e.: their status as *foederati*], others on their wealth and manpower, yet others on the antiquity of their origins – the debates were furious.[6] Although arising from other matters, the hostility between Lyons and Vienne expressed the strength of *civic* patriotism.[7] The coinage struck in Galba's reign bearing the legend TRES GALLIAE emanates from imperial propaganda in a period of crisis, asserting the unity found, or believed to have been found, at the altar of Condate.

There was no Gaul then, except in the sense of the conceptual geography of the ancients. The Three Gauls constituted administrative divisions, loosely based on a faulty ethnography which did not itself correspond to any more ancient population. The divisions we see, even if they may have exercised some slight influence on the emergence of a new identity, were as artificial, *mutatis mutandis*, as those colonial boundaries imposed on Africa in the nineteenth century. All the same, the imperial cult and the annual ceremonies held at Condate played some unifying role, in a political sense rather than an administrative or psychological one.

2. *Caesar: his death and his legacy*

Did Caesar's death in 44 B.C. mark a turning-point? The question is not as naive as it appears. There is no doubt that it influenced the course of events, even if we do not know the dictator's plans. One clear example may be cited. Towards the end of 45 B.C., just a few months before he was assassinated, Caesar had sent Tiberius Nero, the father of the future emperor, to 'found colonies in Gaul, among them Narbonne and Arles'.[8] In the case of Narbo Martius, founded in 118 B.C., this amounted to a re-foundation for the benefit of veterans of the Tenth Legion (Decumanorum), while at Arles it was a new foundation for veterans of the Sixth (Sextanorum).

Suetonius' expression 'among them' (*in queis*) suggests that other colonies were founded. Why are they not mentioned? One possibility is that these were not Roman colonies, like Narbonne and Arles, but Latin colonies, which, from the first century A.D., would not have the right to be titled *coloniae*. I shall return to these foundations below, but for the moment I would like to set this passage in relation to Dio's famous account of the foundation of Lugdunum (Lyons).[9] In 43 B.C. the Senate

[5] *ILTG* 357.   [6] Tac. *Hist.* IV.69.   [7] Tac. *Hist.* I.65.   [8] Suet. *Tib.* 4.   [9] Dio XLVI.50.

ordered Lepidus, the governor of Transalpina, and Plancus, who was in charge of Gallia Comata, 'to found a city for those who had previously (*pote*) been ejected from Narbonensian Vienne by the Allobroges and who had established themselves at the confluence of the Rhône and the Arar [the Saône]'. This was the occasion of the foundation of Lugdunum.

What does this text mean? Had colonists been installed at Vienne and then ejected by the Allobroges? If so, when? The most likely occasion is as follows: Tiberius Nero founded a Latin colony at Vienne in 45 B.C., then, on the death of Caesar, the Allobroges drove out the colonists, who took refuge among the Segusiaves at the confluence of the Saône and the Rhône. The expulsion was a serious matter, which the Senate took steps to rectify, but it was unable to force the Allobroges, (whose military power made a considerable difference in time of civil war) to implement Caesar's decision. As the result of a compromise, a colony was founded at Lyons. What is important in this context is the indirect evidence of violent disturbances following the death of Caesar. They were short-lived, but Rome's representatives were only able to retain control of the situation thanks to the personal links that the dictator had fostered, and which were taken up by his lieutenants, Plancus and the triumvir Antony, and then by his adopted son Octavian. Even more importantly, Iulius Caesar's direct descendants continued to rule the world for more than a century. Continuing loyalties, *clientelae*, campaigns on the Rhine, in which many members of the imperial family took part, imperial visits and the occasional chance imperial birth in Gaul all combined to outweigh and neutralize the effects of that 'anti-Gallic' hostility which had been so strongly felt in Italy, ever since the sack of Rome, and which was still strong among the senatorial class as late as the reign of Claudius.[10] A direct, personal relationship with the emperors is notice-able on several occasions up until the reign of Nero. It was a two-way relationship: after a period of agitation, the Gallic provinces, or rather their elites, remained faithful to the descendants of Caesar, who in turn kept faith with the Gauls.

The nature of the evidence and the issues that arise from it lead me to make two preliminary observations. First, it is pointless to make Romanization the main theme of this account. The Gallic provinces *are* Roman. In so far as an account of them contributes to our understanding of the Roman world, it is to qualify and emphasize its heterogeneous character, and perhaps its composite nature. What is the point in trying to assess the Gallic provinces against a standard of 'Romanity' that cannot itself be characterized? Far better to attempt, if it is possible, to study the transformations, their rhythm and the processes at work

---

[10] Tac. *Ann.* XI.23–4.

behind them. Second, rather than treat in turn two periods with very unequal evidence in *CAH* x and xi, I have decided to reserve discussion of the complex questions of long-term developments, for example in agriculture, the economy and religion, for *CAH* xi, except in so far as the period now under consideration played an important role in them.

I. GALLIA NARBONENSIS

Despite one ambiguous reference of Cicero,[11] it seems that the term Narbonensis is Augustan in origin. Its first occurrence is in the *cursus* of Cn.Pullius Pollio, proconsul of *provincia Narbonensis* around 18–16 B.C.[12] The term doubtless became official in 27 B.C., when Augustus held a *conventus* at Narbonne and 'made a census of the Gauls and organized their civic and political status'.[13] The limits of the province were more or less the same as those of the former province of Transalpina.

Some adjustments were probably made in 13 B.C., in the case of Convenae, for example, after the completion of campaigns of pacification in the Pyrenees. Similarly, other changes followed the conquest of the Alps, marked by the Tropaeum Alpium at La Turbie which was set up while Augustus held tribunician power for the seventeenth time, that is between 1 July 7 B.C. and 30 June 6 B.C. Three new Alpine districts were set up (Alpes Maritimae, Alpes Cottiae and Alpes Graiae) which were not part of the Gallic provinces and so will not be treated here, but as a consequence it was necessary to establish boundaries between those areas belonging to the new districts, those of Narbonensis and perhaps those attached to Italy. The state of Antibes, previously part of Italy,[14] was incorporated in Narbonensis at this point while Cemenelum, in the immediate vicinity of Massilia's old trading post Nikaia, became the capital of the new district of Alpes Maritimae.

The Tropaeum of La Turbie, contrary to what is commonly written, did not mark the frontier between Italy and Transalpina, or Narbonensis. It was set up at the most western point reached by the campaigns of conquest of the Alps 'a mari supero ad inferum', that is from the Adriatic to the Ligurian coast of the Mediterranean.[15] Set up on the Via Iulia Apta that ran from Italy into Narbonensis, it marked the conquest of the mountains and the freeing of that road from banditry. It was probably conceived as the twin of the trophy set up by Pompey at the Pyrenees, also on the road linking Spain and Italy. It is almost certainly that trophy which has recently been found on the col de Panissars, straddling the present day frontier between France and Spain. It symbolizes the permanent control established from then on over communications

---

[11] *Fam* x.25. [12] *CIL* xi 7553. [13] Dio LIII.22. [14] Strab. IV.1.9 (184c).
[15] Pliny, *HN* III.136.

between Italy and the western provinces. From this point on, Narbonensis, like Tarraconensis and Baetica, was completely integrated into the Roman world, to the extent that no historical event worthy of mention is recorded until the Neronian crisis.

A comparison of two key texts provides a convenient starting-point for an analysis of the province. If we are to believe Cicero's *pro Fonteio* written around 70 B.C., the province of Transalpina was populated by wild and untamed tribes in the midst of which civilized values were upheld by the Roman administration, Italian farmers and traders, the colonists of Narbonne (since 118 B.C.) and Rome's faithful ally Marseilles. Pliny, writing *c*. A.D. 70, described Narbonensis as *the* province *par excellence*, 'Italia verius quam provincia'.[16] The contrast between the two passages is striking, even if we are dealing with the biased account of an advocate defending a governor accused of misappropriation of public funds and other irregularities in the first text, and in the second with a phrase that is so brief it can only be a simplification. The two authors are similar in many respects, both Romans, both engaged in public life but also educated and scholarly writers, but their opinions of the province are completely different. What had changed? The province itself or the opinion of the ruling classes of Rome? The answer is that both had changed, and the problem is to take account of this interaction, not to ignore it.

The two texts are separated by 140 years, about six generations, which is a short space of time, in pre-modern conditions, for such a fundamental transformation. Pliny emphasizes the scale of the change, as he felt it, in another passage when he describes the marvellous silverware of Pompeius Paulinus, the son of a Roman *eques* from Arelate (Arles) but then goes on to remark that Paulinus' paternal grandparents had dressed in animal skins.[17] Similar expressions can be found in other authors. A topos existed, then, according to which Narbonensis had been suddenly and dramatically civilized. Our task is to use our scanty sources to assess the basis of this claim.

1. Juridical integration

The importance of the preceding period makes it necessary briefly to summarize developments. We know little of the stages by which the province was originally set up, although we may presume that Pompey played an important role in the years between 78 and 75 B.C., but it is clear that several states had been granted individual civic statuses by various Roman politicians, among them C. Valerius Flaccus, Pompey and, of course, Caesar. Despite Cicero's rhetoric, examples of litigation,

[16] Pliny, *HN* III.31.   [17] Pliny, *HN* XXXIII.50.

such as the charges made against Fonteius, show that a 'pro-Roman' elite had emerged. In the course of the Gallic War, Caesar included on his staff several of the sons of southern *principes*, some of whom had been his guests in Rome. He congratulated himself on the loyalty of the *provincia*: but the implication is that it did not go without saying.

The growing integration of *auxiliarii* into the army had affected broader social classes, including the inhabitants of rural areas and villages which had been largely unaffected by commerce or the influence of the Roman administration. Through their experience of military service, and the wealth and knowledge of Latin they acquired through it, these men contributed to a transformation of indigenous *mentalités*. Caesar's destruction in 49–48 B.C. of what may be termed 'Massiliot imperialism' – an imperialism that was all the more harsh as it was not accompanied by any political integration – was an important factor. We do not know the precise point at which the Latin right was granted to the communities which Pliny described as *oppida latina*,[18] but it makes most sense to attribute the change to Caesar. The important thing is that in a period of at most fifteen years, that is between 58 and 44 B.C., the whole of southern Gaul was granted Latin status. We know of no group which was excepted from this measure.

No attempt at colonization had been made since the founding of Narbo Martius, despite the hypotheses that have been advanced, on no evidence, for foundations at Vienne and Valence. Caesar began a new colonial programme with the refoundation of Narbonne, the foundation of Arles and the Latin colonies, the abortive foundation at Vienne described above, the colony at Nyon in Switzerland and others as well, probably one at Nîmes and certainly one at Valence.

It is against this background that the activities of Caesar's successors must be seen. Octavian renewed the colonizing programme by founding in his turn Roman colonies at Béziers, Orange and Fréjus, although the dates of these foundations are controversial. Most importantly, several imperial decisions promoted the integration of the elites of Narbonensis. The province was 'returned to the Roman people' around 22 B.C.,[19] that is to say the emperor handed over its administration to the Senate, and it no longer played any strategic or military role. Augustus and Tiberius together decided in A.D. 14, just before the former's death, to grant the right to stand for election to magistracies in Rome to *all* the Roman citizens of the province, both those who had gained citizenship through an individual grant and those who had obtained it by holding a civic magistracy in a Latin community, in other words anywhere in the province. This allowed them to aspire to membership of the senatorial classes, a privilege which had hitherto been reserved for the citizens of

[18] Pliny, *HN* III.31–7.   [19] Dio LIII.12.

Roman colonies. Another symbolic, but important, decision in A.D. 49 allowed Roman senators to move without permission not only to Italy and Sicily but also to Narbonensis.

It is worth assessing the extent of this juridical integration, too often obscured by a litany of famous names. The names are always the same: knights like Pompeius Paulinus, who served as prefect of the *annona* in Claudius' reign; L. Vestinus, a prefect of Egypt; and Burrus who was Nero's tutor, served as praetorian prefect and was awarded consular *ornamenta*, and senators like Valerius Asiaticus from Vienne, who held two consulships, on the second occasion, in A.D. 46, as Claudius' colleague. But alongside these famous names, statistical analysis shows that Narbonensis was ahead of all other provinces from the end of the republican era, and remained in first place to the end of the first century A.D. Both in terms of the number of equestrians and senators it produced and in the brilliance of their careers, it surpassed every other part of the Roman world, except for peninsular Italy. It is particularly striking that it outdid the Spanish, African and Eastern provinces, most of which had been created before Narbonensis, and many of which also had numbers of Roman colonies. To understand the reasons for this success, it is necessary to leave aside the broader picture and examine the component parts of the province, the *civitates*.

2. The organization of territory

The emperor Augustus' main concern during his stay at Narbonne in 27 B.C.[20] was, according to Dio,[21] the organization of the areas conquered by Caesar, in other words non-Mediterranean Gaul. As for Narbonensis, he must simply have put the final touches to the organization already set up by Caesar, with a few adjustments, in particular the colonial foundations of the triumviral period. The *formula provinciae* listed five Roman colonies (Narbonne, Arles, Fréjus, Béziers and Orange), two allied states (Marseilles and the Vocontii) and about seventy-five *oppida latina*, that is to say seventy-five communities granted the Latin right, enjoying some limited administrative autonomy and with at least junior magistrates – aediles, quaestors or the equivalent – of their own.

Although this *formula* was not replaced with a new one, there were some later modifications which Pliny records. Two communities, Vienne and Valence, were granted full Roman status at an uncertain date. But most importantly, forty-three *oppida latina* lost their autonomy and were integrated into neighbouring communities. We do not know which communities this affected, except in one case: Pliny notes that twenty-four of them were attached to Nîmes, and Strabo confirms this,

---

[20] Livy, *Per.* 134.   [21] Dio LIII.22.

adding that 'they paid it tribute',[22] which suggests that Rome gave Nîmes the privilege of collecting taxes for its own benefit. That measure must date to the Augustan period, perhaps during Augustus' visit in 16–13 B.C. No later date can account for the agreement between Pliny and Strabo.

The number of Latin communities with their own legal identity was thus drastically reduced, by nearly 60 per cent. On the other hand, some of the *oppida*, which retained their Latin status, kept at least their junior magistracies which provided a means of gaining Roman citizenship, and were incorporated into much larger states by some unknown mechanism. Although it is always difficult to be certain of the exact number of *civitates* or of their precise boundaries, it seems that Narbonensis was made up of around twenty-two.

The replacement of a large number of tiny communities by a small number of unified states was a feature of the Augustan period. These developments demonstrate the emperor's desire to promote urbanism, to concentrate the elites in the larger centres and perhaps to limit the channels by which individuals might automatically become entitled to Roman citizenship. The case of Nîmes is the most striking: even if the city was already the capital of the Volcae Arecomici and even if federal magistrates already were based there, Nîmes had only been one among twenty-five Arecomican communities. Augustus attached the twenty-four others to it, politically and fiscally, paid for its circuit wall,[23] and established or authorized the mint which produced the famous 'crocodile' series of *asses*. The monuments of this city are among the most splendid in the Roman West. There were limits to this policy of centralization, limits imposed by tradition and geography. Alongside the vast territories of the Tectosages with their capital at Toulouse, of the Arecomici centred on Nîmes, of the Vocontii of Vaison and of the Allobroges of Vienne, there were also smaller *civitates* among them the Roman colonial foundations of Béziers and Orange.

Tradition also exercised an influence at the institutional level. The new *civitates* did not immediately adopt Italian administrative forms and the principle of collegiality only replaced the idea of a single magistrate by slow stages. The title of praetor was replaced first by *praetores IIviri* and *IIIIviri* and then by *duoviri* in the Roman colonies and *quattuorviri* in the Latin states, except among the Vocontii, who continued to be ruled by *praetores* up until the third century. Similarly, individuals with unusual titles, which seem to have military connotations or which possibly refer to police duties, are attested at Nîmes (*praefectus vigilum et armorum*), Nyon (*praefectus arcendis latrociniis*) and among the Vocontii (*praefectus praesidiorum et privatorum*).

22 Strab. IV.I.12 (186–7c).   23 *CIL* XII 3151.

The record of personal promotions in legal status, elevations to the senatorial and equestrian orders, shows that the majority did not come from Roman colonies, but from Vienne and Nîmes. Together with Narbonne, these cities are also those which have left the largest numbers of inscriptions. Strabo's source Posidonius, writing at the beginning of the last century B.C., mentioned those two centres, and them alone, as 'capitals' of great peoples, the Allobroges and the Arecomici respectively.[24] The *pro Fonteio*, written about 70 B.C., also mentions those two alone. Narbonne, on the other hand, is not mentioned by Posidonius either as a colony nor as the capital of the province, but simply as the 'the port of all Celtica'.[25] Despite the fact that the colony of Fréjus provided the empire with famous men like Agricola's grandfathers and his father Iulius Graecinus, it seems clear that veteran colonists and their descendants, even those of Narbonne, were less successful than the sons of the great cities of Vienne and Nîmes, at least in the early period.

How can this be explained? One factor might be the participation of the Allobroges and the Arecomici in the military expeditions of the last century B.C. Perhaps the ability of their *principes* to mobilize thousands of armed followers[26] might have encouraged *imperatores* or governors to take care to secure their support. Maybe personal ties were established between them and prominent figures at Rome. Possibly the basis of their power derived as much from the lands they controlled, as from the manpower they could raise. All these factors probably played some part. But most importantly, Augustus' arrangements did not just take the existing inequalities in power into account wherever possible, but actually entrenched them.

3. An economic transformation?

Ever since the conquest, Italians had been accumulating land in Narbonensis. Cicero's *pro Quinctio* documents the process at the beginning of the last century B.C., and shortly afterwards the presence of farmers and ranchers in the province provides the background to the *pro Fonteio*. Narbonne had been founded in 118 B.C. as an exercise in agricultural colonization, for the benefit of Italian civilians. Marseilles had, in the meantime, come to possess extensive territory partly through her own efforts,[27] partly by force[28] and then through benefits bestowed on the city by Rome. Caesar states that Pompey had, on behalf of the Roman state, given Marseilles land in the territories of the Volcae Arecomici and the Helvii to the west of the Rhône.[29]

---

[24] Strab. IV.1.11 and 12 (185–7c). [25] Strab. IV.1.12 (186–7c).

[26] Cic. *Fam.* x.21 and xi.11. [27] Strab. III.4.17 (164–5c). [28] Strab. IV.1.5 (179–81c).

[29] Caes. *BCiv* 1.35.

Although no text mentions it, mining seems to have been important from the first conquest of Transalpine Gaul. Dressel 1 amphorae have been found beside mine shafts and galleries at Corbières, at la Montagne Noire, in the valley of the Tarn and in the Pyrenees. Silver and copper, rather than gold, were probably extracted at these sites. The oldest mausoleum known on French soil portrays a mounted warrior of the first half of the last century B.C., who must have presided over the silver mines at Argenton in the Alps. The place-name Argenton is itself significant.

But land was the real objective of the Caesarian colonizations of Narbonne, where the territory was surveyed and redivided, and of Arles. Did the same apply to the Latin colonies, which I argued above were probably set up at Vienne, Nîmes and Valence? Recent studies of land divisions, based largely on finds from Orange, tend to support this hypothesis. The explanation for the foundations at Arles and at Nîmes is found in the fact that after the siege of Marseilles in 49–48 B.C., all the Phocaean city's lands were confiscated, apart from its immediate territory, the Lérin Isles and the city of Nice. As usual, this confiscated territory was distributed as gifts to individuals and communities, but more importantly it enabled Caesar to settle veterans and auxiliaries at a period when the need for land for this purpose was particularly acute.

Between 40 and 28 B.C., Octavian settled veterans of the Seventh Legion at Béziers, of the Second at Orange and of the Eighth at Fréjus. If we are to believe Dio, he also gave colonists land in Gaul between 16–14 B.C., after he had taken the title Augustus.[30] The only way of accounting for this is to suppose that he added new contingents to colonies he had already founded: he himself says that he compensated cities that had suffered from this fresh influx.[31]

The main difficulties arise not so much from interpreting the social impact of this colonization as from assessing its economic effects. The notion that the arrival of so many new families invigorated agriculture in the south has now given way to a highly sceptical view that sees little, if any, development in this area. A more balanced perspective seems preferable.

For many years, the land divisions of Narbonensis have been the object of considerable research. These studies have necessarily advanced mainly through the development of new methods of analysis. But the first results, based on the Rhône valley and the Languedoc, seem to indicate that patterns of land division aligned on different orientations were laid out contemporaneously in adjoining areas, rather than being superimposed on each other on a variety of occasions. So one set of divisions would be laid out on one orientation, perhaps to fit in with the

---

[30] Dio LIV.23.   [31] RG 16.

relief or else aligned along a road or some other direction. But it would be abutted by a second set of divisions, which would continue the cadastre but following some other orientation, which in its turn was determined by a different constraint or convenience, only to be met in turn by some other division ... and so on. The first cadastration might divide up the best lands, those easiest to farm, the second might apportion the second best fields and so on.

Cadastre B of the well-known marble tablets from Orange, marks out the best lands, those assigned to the veteran colonists; the lands let out by the colony; and finally the lands 'returned to the Tricastini' (*Tricastinis reddita*), left, that is, for the indigenous inhabitants. This last category consisted mostly of land located in the least promising areas for cultivation, so they would have needed to be improved. The land let out was not marvellous either, but there are good vines there today. Finally, archaeological discoveries continue to appear in areas abandoned at the end of the Roman period. Colonization thus probably constituted a powerful impulse towards the opening up and reclaiming of new land.

Romanization also promoted the development of bigger and more diversified landholdings. Archaeology, and particularly aerial photography, makes it possible to identify the cultivated lands, usually based around a villa, but not the property divisions. But epigraphic evidence reveals nobles who were honoured in more than one *civitas*, suggesting that they probably owned large estates. The growth of larger and larger landholdings explains how it was possible to introduce crops that required substantial capital investment but which offered no immediate return, such as olive trees, cultivated for oil, and vines. Apart from in the area controlled by Marseilles, where similar processes had long been underway, the Augustan period saw the beginning of these developments, but a major expansion occurred in the middle of the first century and under the Flavians.

But the major problem is to assess the significance of these changes for the transformation of the economy as a whole, and in particular the importance of changes in commerce.

Earlier interpretations were based largely on the evidence of pottery. The Augustan layers of every excavated site produce large numbers of sherds of *terra sigillata*, a red-gloss ware often stamped with Latin names, and sometimes decorated with classicizing motifs. This pottery, sometimes termed 'samian ware' in Britain, was first produced in Arezzo (Arretium) and then at Pisa and Pozzuoli (Puteoli). Sherds of Arretine are usually found along with other north Italian fine-wares, especially the type known as Aco goblets. But around A.D. 10–20, these wares were replaced by others made in Gaul. The products of Montans, near Toulouse, and of La Graufesenque, near Millau, were widely distributed to the Roman camps on the frontier, to Spain, to Britain and even to Italy. This phenomenon was interpreted as an economic boom in southern Gaul, at the expense of Italian products.

That view has been abandoned for two reasons. First, it was realized that pottery, always being a cheap commodity, could hardly indicate the workings of a global economy. Second, recent research has shown that Italian potters actually moved workshops and equipment (moulds for decorated wares) to Gaul around 20–10 B.C. and set up branches at Vienne, at Lyons, to which I shall return below, and probably at Narbonne and other centres. In other words, Italian producers made determined efforts to decentralize production. The only possible explanation is in terms of a reorganization of the global trade in Italian produce. Why then did their workshops so quickly stop production, in favour of those of Montans and La Graufesenque?

The evidence of amphorae is even more difficult to interpret. Up until about 30 B.C., wine, mostly Italian, was transported in amphorae of the type known as Dressel ¯. A large number of shipwrecks loaded with these containers have been located and huge numbers of amphorae, sometimes hundreds of thousands, have been found in excavations of settlements, of mines and of what might be termed market-*oppida*, that is central places from which goods were redistributed. One site near Toulouse has produced enormous quantities. Dressel 1 amphorae were replaced around 30–20 B.C. by amphorae of a different shape and capacity termed Dressel 2–4. Both the number of wrecked ships which transported them along the southern coast of Gaul and the number of finds in excavations on land show a dramatic drop in the number of amphorae. Far fewer Dressel 2–4 amphorae, in other words, arrived in Gaul than Dressel 1 containers. Why? It may be that Italian wine was transported in new kinds of containers, such as *dolia* or barrels. Some wrecks are now known in which *dolia*, huge pottery vessels, made up the major part of the cargo, implying that the wine would be decanted into other containers later on. Barrels, on the other hand, leave no archaeological trace. It has also been recently discovered that some kilns in Gaul produced not only the local styles of amphorae (called Gauloise amphorae) but also imitations of Italian and Spanish vessels. We do not know whether these were produced to carry trans-shipped Italian and Spanish wines or local vintages.

So the thirty or forty years following the imposition of the *pax Augusta* saw a number of separate developments. Archaeology can only shed light on some aspects of the picture and the result often seems contradictory and disorganized. But a very tentative synthesis can be built up from this evidence.

Most importantly, agricultural practice did not undergo any sudden transformation. It takes time to improve soils and introduce new crops like vines and olives. The changes do not, in any case, become important until the middle of the first century and even then were not dramatic in scale: Narbonensis never became a major wine- or oil-producing region, far from it.

Trade, on the other hand, was transformed. The best explanation proposed for the dramatic fall in the number of Italian amphorae is a sociological one. The Augustan reorganization had put an end to the Celtic tradition of great banquets given by the chiefs, who were encouraged to engage in euergetistical benefactions instead of making gifts of food and drink. All the same a great deal of traffic passed through Narbonensis, some following the Rhône valley to Vienne and Lyons, other goods going via Narbonne to Toulouse and Bordeaux. A number of different trade routes were created. The pottery producers of Montans were linked to Toulouse and so, no doubt, to the Atlantic seaways, while La Graufesenque was more closely tied to Languedoc, where its products were distributed along with other commodities.

The most astonishing discovery of recent years has been made at Vienne. The city straddled the Rhône and recent excavations there have uncovered warehouses (*horrea*) covering an area that is enormous compared with that of others known from the Roman world. The surface area, excluding any additional storeys, is 50,000 square metres, more than double the size of those at Ostia. The structures date from the reign of Tiberius or Claudius. Even making allowance for the chance of excavation (and we know Ostia well), the capacity of this amount of storage space is phenomenal. How should these finds be interpreted? Were the goods stored in these warehouses intended for the Gaulish interior, for Britain or Switzerland or for the garrisons on the *limes*? Or were they destined for the Mediterranean, and in particular for Rome? If so they could be stores for the *annona*. The two hypotheses are equally plausible, nor are they mutually incompatible.

Archaeological evidence privileges commerce above all, and we must be aware of this source of bias. All the same, there can be no doubt that some towns in Narbonensis were important centres of redistribution in the first century A.D. and that trade intensified both with Comata and with the Mediterranean world. But much more important to the *civitas*, were relations between a city and its own rural hinterland, and it was this relationship which played a formative role in the development of the province.

4. Urbanization

Unlike many of the areas conquered by Rome, southern Gaul had a long tradition of nucleated settlement, which had been accentuated over the previous two hundred years. Settlements were medium sized, on average about 3 hectares in area, with populations in the hundreds or less commonly the thousands, consisting of the peasant cultivators of nearby fields together with some artisans and members of the elite. Some principles of urban organization are suggested by the ramparts, town planning and main streets revealed by the recent excavation of sites such as Entremont, Nages, Lattes, Ambrussum and Ensérune. The public buildings are mysterious in nature, consisting of porticoes decorated with sculpted reliefs. Domestic structures consist of a mixture of one- or two-room houses and some larger buildings arranged around little courtyards, sometimes with a second storey. Some settlements, under the influence of Marseilles and her outposts, may already have developed 'proto-urban' features. Impressive circuit walls and towers that dominated the landscape as did that of Nîmes, built in the second half of the third century and later transformed into the famous Tour Magne, may have been symbols of this new urban pride.

Urban archaeology has recently contributed to the debate by demonstrating examples of settlement continuity, that may be set against the picture of great Roman foundations *ex nihilo* proposed in standard theories. It is true that no major pre-Augustan levels have yet been found on the sites of the Roman towns of Fréjus and Orange, but they have been found in the vicinity and in the case of most towns, pre-Roman levels are attested on the same site. Excavations have recently demonstrated this for Béziers, Nîmes and Arles. Other sites conform, in general terms, to the picture Strabo paints of Vienne:[32] the site was transformed from a simple village (at least by the standards of a Mediterranean observer) into the city inhabited by the Allobrogian elite.

In fact, the Augustan reorganization replaced medium-sized centres based on limited territories with much larger urban sites. This was both a result of the processes of colonization and *attributio* described above and also one of its objectives. The *oppida* (the fortified villages) seem to have been abandoned fairly rapidly, although some traces of subsequent occupation are occasionally discovered and some new villages were sited at the base of the abandoned hilltop sites. But cities like Narbonne, Arles and Vienne grew very fast. Vienne is a case in point. Recent excavation has shown that in Saint-Romain-en-Gal and Sainte-Colombe, the districts located on the right bank of the Rhône comprising residential areas, artisans' workshops and large-scale public works, occupation began not in the late first century A.D., as had previously been thought, but at the end of the last century B.C.

Some towns did develop more slowly, it is true. The original town plan laid out for Fréjus covered about 50 hectares, and it took time to fill in the area north of its *decumanus*. Large areas of Vaison-la-Romaine were

32 Strab. IV.I.II (185–6C).

never built on in antiquity. The *forum* of Aix-en-Provence was not built until the end of the first century A.D. But the scale of all these towns is quite different to anything that had gone before. The original area planned for towns like Arles and Fréjus was at least 50 hectares in extent, while in the case of towns like Nîmes, Orange and Vienne it could exceed 200 hectares. Whether or not the town was enclosed by a rampart, its extent is defined by the locations of the cemeteries that surrounded it. Marseilles, the largest pre-Roman city in the area, had never covered more than 50 hectares, while its outposts like Olbia, Antibes and Agde were less than 5 hectares in area. Clearest indication of all is the unprecedented scale of the public works involved: sharp reliefs were terraced and land prone to subsidence was banked up and drained.

The urbanization of the south was not just a product of the institutional linkages created between social mobility, the rise of local elites and urban lifestyles. Those links would not have been enough on their own, and an important part was played by encouragement of all sorts, for example of the kind that Tacitus describes being given in Britain.[33] The lead might be given by prominent Romans like Agrippa, but the most important example was set by the emperors, either through the gifts they gave from their own resources to sponsor large public works or else through incentives, the details of which are unclear, but may have included tax exemptions. So, for example, an inscription on the Augustan gate at Nîmes tells us that the emperor himself had provided the city with walls and gates (*muros portasque*).[34]

The early date at which huge monumental programmes were begun in honour of the imperial cult and in particular of Augustus, has only just become clear. The most striking example is Nîmes, where the hillside of Mont-Cavalier provided the setting for an *Augusteum*, comprising a complex of sanctuaries, temples, theatres and gardens, grouped around a spring and marked out by the Tour Magne. The *forum*, in the town below, was aligned on the same axis and formed a counterweight to the sanctuary, including as its most impressive monument the Maison Carrée, a temple to Gaius and Lucius Caesar, the Leaders of the Youth. It would also be possible to reconstruct in the heart of towns like Vienne, Arles and Glanum, huge *fora* where the public space was surrounded by temples, the porticoes of which rested on cryptoporticoes, by basilicas, by administrative buildings and so on. Theatres, too, are often early in date.

The power of the imperial cult had sociological, monumental and financial implications. The city constituted the fullest expression of a well-ordered and magnificent universe, the safety of which was guaranteed by the *princeps*. It seems symbolic, in this respect, that a marble copy

<hr />

[33] Tac. *Agricola* XXI.   [34] *CIL* XII 3151.

of the *clipeus virtutis*, awarded by the Senate to Augustus in 27 B.C., was discovered in the cryptoporticus of Arles. The *forum* of Arles is certainly one of the oldest in Gaul. Along with the other monuments of the city, like the theatre and the arch near the Rhône, and the sculptures found there, it conjures up teams of highly skilled Italian craftsmen working to make the city into a showpiece of the architectural and artistic Romanization of Narbonensis.

The fact that theatres were built so early on, often located, as at Arles and Orange, in the immediate environs of the *forum*, and the triumphal arches built in the reigns of Augustus and Tiberius, all show the pre-eminent role played by the town in symbolizing membership of the civilized world. The iconography depicts barbarians in chains: there is no point in trying to identify the barbarians as they are purely generic. But there are also elements of classical symbolism, emphasizing the transition from barbarism to civilization, from chaos to order.

Can we go so far as to say that the cities of Narbonensis were so many perfectly ordered little universes? It is difficult to be sure since no Roman town in southern Gaul was 'fossilized' and preserved from the ravages of history. Every town has been transformed on numerous occasions since, in the course of the medieval and modern periods. But it does seem that the southern towns only conformed to a limited extent, to regular orthogonal grid plans. In some cases the reason was pre-Augustan settlement, in others it derived from features of the terrain: that was the case at Vienne, squeezed between the Rhône and the valley slopes, while at Nîmes a number of different street plans had been laid out since the Iron Age. Vaison-la-Romain, on the other hand, had a completely unconstrained development.

Besides, with the passage of time, many towns underwent predictable changes. At Arles, part of the circuit wall was demolished when the amphitheatre was built, and at Fréjus, houses spilled over onto the streets and a section of the walls went out of use to make way for the entry of an aqueduct. Quite often the construction of new buildings, bathhouses in particular, disrupted a neighbourhood, and the construction of the warehouses of Vienne required a huge terrace to be built on the banks of the Rhône.

The towns must have presented bewildering contrasts. The ruling classes directed their attention to public areas, which probably absorbed most of the resources in terms of architectural specialists, prestigious materials and imported techniques, like *opus caementicium*. Meanwhile, other parts of the town continued to use methods of construction inherited from the pre-Roman period: adobe, dry stone walls and walls held together with clay. So at Nîmes, immediately next to the sanctuary of the spring, a residential quarter was built almost identical to the kind of structures found at contemporary *oppida* in the area. At the same time, in towns like Vaison and Vienne, huge houses were being built in foreign styles around courtyards or gardens, but constructed, sometimes only roughly, out of dry stone walls or wooden panelling. At the Roman colony of Fréjus, the Augustan and Tiberian houses, perhaps those built for the colonists, were modest structures, consisting of three rooms built in front of a courtyard. But throughout Narbonensis, the motifs of mosaics and wall paintings diffused rapidly. The Second Pompeian Style appeared briefly at Glanum, but it was the Third Style which captured the Rhône valley, transmitting Roman fashions around 15 B.C. Just as in the case of the economy, then, cultural dynamics, tensions and differences appear which cannot easily be reduced to the application of a single model.

The urbanization of southern France may have been slower and less uniform than it has often been presented, but all the same it represented an irreversible transformation in this period. Secondary urban centres did develop, often arising from pre-Augustan centres. Some, like Glanum or Die, developed around sanctuaries while others like Ugernum (modern Beaucaire) grew up at road junctions or at a major crossing. Yet others developed within huge *civitates*, the capitals of which were not central enough to serve all their territory: this was the case with Grenoble, Annecy and Geneva in the *civitas* of the Allobroges, and with the Vocontian towns of Gap and Sisteron. But almost all the major southern cities, from Toulouse to Antibes, originated as Augustan capitals. Some, notably Narbonne, Arles, Vienne and probably Orange, already possessed an impressive monumental complement, including *fora*, temples, theatres, amphitheatres and sometimes circuit walls, at the beginning of the first century A.D. The urbanism of other centres was a little sparser and towns like Vaison, Fréjus and Aix had to wait until the Flavian period for many of their monuments. But the basic pattern went back to the reign of Augustus.

The beginnings of urbanization thus provoked a major shift. Inspired by the emperor or elite members, the rapid expansion of some cities attracted town-planners, architects, wall-painters and sculptors, each with their team of specialists and a local workforce. In so far as they stayed in the cities, they attracted in their turn trade and service industries. The monuments were not just architecture: they provided the framework for a new kind of society and a new way of life.

But it is important not to draw a false distinction between town and country, since all the evidence suggests that the relationship between the two was an intimate one. Some towns, like Béziers, were surrounded by rings of *villae*; nobles are attested living on suburban estates, as the Domitii did on their lands outside Aix-en-Provence; and town magistrates and *seviri Augustales*, priests of the imperial cult usually recruited from among rich ex-slaves, made dedications in the countryside. The new lifestyle was one in which the urban elites divided their time between town and country. Perhaps that is the clearest indication of the diffusion of Italian manners.

5. A new culture?

Even though Rome had conquered the *provincia* in 124–123 B.C., the Latin language has left no trace, not even in official documents, from before the time of Caesar.[35] In fact, it is not until the Augustan period that Celtic inscriptions in Greek letters (Gallo-Greek inscriptions) were replaced by Latin epigraphy. Even in Narbonne, founded in 118 B.C., it is remarkable that the two oldest inscriptions (*CIL* XII 4338 and 4389) only go back to the end of the last century B.C.

All the same, Latin seems to have spread rapidly from the Augustan period on. It does not seem so surprising in high society, where it promoted the rise of famous orators like Domitius Afer from Nîmes and Votenius Montanus from Narbonne, of poets like Varro Atacinus and of historians like Trogus Pompeius. The elite played an important role in the development of epigraphy as well, but the phenomenon makes no sense unless inscriptions could be understood by a reasonable proportion of the population. Probably, like Trimalchio's friends,[36] the urban population could read inscriptions (*litterae lapidariae*), just as they could recognize signatures or trademarks on pottery vessels. If not, it would have made no sense for a counterfeiter at La Graufesenque to mark his vases *verum vas arretinum*, that is 'genuine Arretine ware'. Furthermore, Latin graffiti begin to appear scratched on plates and dishes with a stylus, from the reign of Augustus. Often they just comprise two or three letters, standing for the owner's name, but sometimes there are also phrases written in longhand. One example from Vaison reads *Flacci Nemo Attlerit*, or 'I belong to Flaccus. Let no-one lay a hand on me'. The handwriting on the famous tallies of kiln firings at La Graufesenque from around 40 A.D., is identical to handwriting known from Pompeii. Inscriptions set up by nobles in the depth of the countryside, like the one at Saint-Vincent-de-Gaujac in the Gard, show the extent to which Latin had spread even at an early date. The spread of the language and of a basic written culture, encouraged by the influence of administrative decisions and public performances, was a major change. As for the Gaulish language, it no longer appears except as an element in the names of people and places, or else in very rare graffiti on potsherds.

[35] *ILS* 884. An inscription from Valence that probably refers to a L. Nonius Asprenas.
[36] Petron. *Sat.* 58.

It is well known that changes in burial customs are an important component in acculturation processes, so it is particularly interesting to see the speed with which Roman practices were adopted. Cremation had, to be sure, been common throughout Transalpina for a long time, but up until the Augustan period, each particular style of tomb and each variety of burial rites was restricted to a relatively narrow area, such as the lower Rhône valley. Besides, the fact that so few burials are known – less than 200 from Narbonne to Nice from the last two centuries B.C. – suggests that human remains were disposed of informally, in some unknown manner. But from the time of Augustus, cemeteries appear on the outskirts of towns, along the roads, with tombs organized and ordered in a hierarchy of mausolea, groups of chambers and individual graves, marked by headstones and scattered within a wide area, which from A.D. 50 was usually enclosed. At the same time the great mausolea came to serve as landmarks, while the smaller graveyards fitted neatly into the centuriated landscape, as they did at Augusta Tricastinorum, Saint-Paul-Trois-Chateaux. Some regional variations remained but major changes were attested by the grave goods, by the design of the tombs and by the presence of *ustrina*. The sculptural decoration of tombs so strongly recalls Italian models, that some have even suggested that as early as the last century B.C., teams of sculptors toured Gaul, offering the nobility sepulchres worthy of their status. Tombs like the mausoleum of the Iulii at Glanum would represent the most prestigious of their creations. But irrefutable evidence of Italian influence is perhaps better provided by more common examples, the fragments of small monuments from Narbonne, Fréjus and Arles, and by the first Latin epitaphs.

Finally, the imperial cult. There is no evidence for its official inauguration in the province comparable to the evidence available from the East, or, in the West, from Tarraco. But some inscriptions from Nîmes suggest that from 25 B.C. it existed as part of the sanctuary of the Spring, the monumentalization of which began between 20 and 10 B.C. Two temples were dedicated to Rome and Augustus at Glanum around the same date, while the Maison Carrée at Nîmes, the temple of Augustus at Vienne, the portraits of Augustus, his relatives and his successors all combine to give the impression that cult appeared early and was performed with enthusiasm, at least in the more dynamic cities.

Narbonne, in particular, contributes notably to the record of the imperial cult. Around 25 B.C. a private individual dedicated an altar to the *Pax Augusti*, two other inscriptions show a very early example of the worship of the *Lares Augsti*,[37] and then there is the famous altar recording the eternal vow to the *numen* of Augustus made in A.D. 11 by

[37] See above, n. 34.

the *plebs Narbonensium*, those citizens who did not belong to the municipal *ordo*, setting up an altar in the *forum* and a ceremony enacted five times a year.

The institutions set up as part of the imperial cult, like the flaminate and, from Tiberius, the *severi Augustales*, who are very prominent in Narbonne and in Nîmes, played an important role in promoting social cohesion. The cult provided the occasion for numbers of lavish acts of euergetism and for ceremonies which united the population of each state and encouraged it to engage in rivalry with its neighbours. The importance of the *civitas* cults of the emperor confirms the view that a provincial cult organization was not set up until much later, under Vespasian.

The new political framework had been rapidly put in place: by the reign of Tiberius, at the latest, collegiate magistracies of the Roman type were installed in every *civitas* except in the allied city of the Vocontii. All Roman citizens in the province were granted the right to stand for magistracies in Rome in A.D. 14. Public monuments, Italian-style houses and an army of statues had begun to invade the squares, the roads and the cemeteries. Thousands upon thousands of families, mostly from Italy, had settled in the course of several colonizations. The urban centres, the *civitas* capitals, had supplanted the old *oppida* and traditional feasts had been replaced by Roman style public euergetism. The countryside had been redivided, many of the fields had been redistributed and even the crops growing in them were gradually changing. There can be no doubt that the changes wrought were unprecedented in scale. It is possible to qualify the picture a little, by pointing out instances of settlement continuity or the survival of some traditional technique, or by showing that these transformations are less marked in the mountainous regions lying behind the great plains of the Mediterranean littoral and the Rhône valley. But the extent of the transmutation cannot be denied. Pliny's phrase, *Italia verius quam provincia*, continues to be confirmed by more and more illustrations. No surprises there: after all, he knew more about it than we do.

III TRES GALLIAE [38]

Gallia Comata, which had been organized as a single province since Caesar, was divided into three by Augustus, probably in 27 B.C. Several passages of Strabo show that this was the period at which the Loire and the Pyrenees were fixed as Aquitania's final boundaries.[39] The same did

---

[38] In memory of Edith Wightman.   [39] Strab. IV.1.1 (176–7c); IV.3.1 (191–2c); IV.4.3 (196–7c).

not apply to Belgica or Lugdunensis, which ran east–west in parallel. Belgica included all the peoples bordering the Channel and the North Sea, while Lugdunensis grouped together those who lived 'in the central plains' as far south as the courses of the Loire and the upper Rhône. One boundary that survived from this initial organization was the distinction between the military districts of Germania Inferior and Germania Superior, which corresponded to the boundary between Belgica and Lugdunensis. At some point, perhaps at the beginning of Tiberius' reign, the system was reorganized and Belgica was allocated the north east of Gaul, and Lugdunensis acquired the remainder.

These changes show how the provincial organization was, to begin with, fairly arbitrary and based on very rudimentary geographical knowledge. The aim was simply to create three provinces of roughly the same size. The adaptions made to the initial plan show the importance assumed by the Rhine frontier and problems with the Germans after 27 B.C. So much, at any rate, for those theories that saw these divisions as designed in part to separate the three most powerful peoples of the late Iron Age, the Arverni, the Sequani and the Aedui, into different provinces. Nor is it certain that Reims, which Strabo cites as capital of Belgica,[40] retained this position after the reorganization. Lyons was capital of Lugdunensis, but we are not even sure of the identity of the provincial capitals of Belgica and Aquitania. The latter may have been ruled from Saintes, then Poitiers and perhaps, later on, from Bordeaux. Nor is the number of *civitates* any more certain, since the texts disagree, varying between sixty and sixty-four, and the situation in southern Aquitania is hedged with difficulties. Most of our sources do say that these *civitates* occupied the territories of late Iron Age groups. The exceptions to this general rule are the Bituriges Vivisci, who may have split off from the Bituriges Cubi who lived around Bourges, ancient Avaricum, and migrated to the mouth of the Garonne in the second half of the last century B.C.; the Tricasses of the region of Troyes (Augustobona) who may have been divided from the Senones by Augustus and finally the Silvanectes, whom Claudius separated from the Suessiones.[41]

Three balanced provinces, then, each containing powerful peoples with strong traditions and fertile lands. It might be expected, then, that they would undergo parallel developments, especially since the unbelievable wealth of Gaul was one of the recurrent clichés of both literature and official discourse at Rome.[42] But the image presented to us by archaeological evidence stresses sharp differences between them.

[40] Strab. IV.3.5 (194c).   [41] See above, n. 5.

[42] e.g. Dio LIX.22; Tac. *Ann.* XI.23; *Hist.* I.51 and IV.74; Suet. *Ner.* 40.

1. The impact of events

It is only possible to guess at a few of the consequences of the Gallic War and of Caesar's policy. Tens of thousands were killed or taken prisoner and reduced to slavery, and many chieftains and their relatives saw their wealth diminished or even confiscated in order to enrich those who had supported Caesar within their own tribes or abroad. Seeing as the city of Massilia[43] and individual Allobroges[44] had been given land and the revenues (*vectigalia*) of lands in the interior, how much more did the new Iulii of Gallia Comata stand to gain in the way of responsibilities, honours, up to and including membership of the Senate of Rome, and riches of all kinds. This redistribution of power and wealth explains the strong personal bonds established between the new Gallic chiefs and the dictator, and their willingness to join him when he summoned them *nominatim* on the outbreak of the civil war.[45] His more general policies, after all, had been moderate: the tribute imposed had been a light one, the integrity of tribal territories had been respected and no colonies had been imposed, except for Noviodunum among the Helvetii.

Caesar's death had given rise to fears in Rome of a *tumultus Gallicus*.[46] It never happened, but in the following months Cicero's letters show first L. Munatius Plancus, the governor of Gallia Comata, and then Decimus Brutus trying to win over the *principes Galliae*, although with what promised incentives we do not know. After those events, our sources only contain short references to disturbances. Unrest in 39–38 B.C.[47] was the reason for Agrippa's mission to Gaul, where we know he defeated the Aquitani[48] but also had to cross the Rhine.[49] Was this a general uprising or just local outbreaks of unrest? Most likely the only regions affected were the Pyrenees, where M. Valerius Messala also campaigned shortly after 30 B.C.,[50] and the north east, where the names of the Morini, the Suebi and the Treveri are recorded. Reports of triumphs *ex Gallis* or *ex Gallia* do not imply victories over all the peoples of Gaul. Augustus finally put a stop to the disturbances endemic among the Aquitani when he campaigned in the Pyrenees in 13 B.C. Sorting out the troubles on the Rhine was to necessitate rather more effort.

The problems in the north east and the south west explain the planning and construction of the road system described by Strabo[51] and attributed to Agrippa. The intention was to construct two lines of communications starting from Lyons, one leading to the Rhineland and

---

[43] Caes. *BCiv.* 1.35.   [44] Caes. *BCiv.* III.59.
[45] *BCiv.* 1.39: 'ex omnibus civitatibus nobilissimo et fortissimo quoque evocato'.
[46] Cic. *Att.* XIV.1.   [47] App. *BCiv.* V.75.318.   [48] App. *BCiv.* V.92.386.
[49] Dio XLVIII.49.   [50] Tib. 1.7.11.   [51] Strab. IV.6.11 (208c).

the north and the other going to Aquitaine, in the old, pre-Augustan sense of the area south of the Garonne. The plan for these two strategic routes, designed for troops coming from Italy, must have been fixed at a fairly early date, perhaps during Agrippa's first term in Gaul between 40 and 37 B.C. They required engineering works, in particular bridges, and must have absorbed considerable time, resources and manpower, perhaps encouraging the growth of some towns in the process.

One of the most important Roman actions in Gaul before the reign of Augustus was the foundation of Lyons (cf. above, p. 469–70). The founder, L. Munatius Plancus, established Raurica in the same year, which was to become Augusta Rauricorum, modern Augst in Switzerland. But if Augst had been a strategic colony, which is far from certain, it soon fell behind Lyons, which in only a few years acquired a key role, as the linchpin of the Agrippan road system, then as capital of Lugdunensis, the location of a mint and of the federal sanctuary of the Three Gauls.

The main events of Augustus' reign, except for those in Aquitaine, centred on the Germanies and the eastern frontier, where the troops were concentrated. Does this imply that the rest of the country was completely pacified? In the absence of any literary documentation, various scholars have argued that the distribution of Arretine ware or concentrations of Gallic coinage struck in this period indicate the presence of Roman troops. But the theory is completely untenable. Several military installations have been found, at Aulnay in Saintonge, at Mirebeau near Dijon and at Arlaines and other sites on an axis linking Reims, Soissons and Amiens. But the chronology of these sites is unclear, perhaps Tiberian or even much later. All the evidence suggests that the *pax Augusta* reigned in the Three Gauls, despite the censuses carried out in 27 and 12 B.C. and then in A.D. 14 and despite the (probably exaggerated) administrative abuses of characters like C. Iulius Licinus around 16 B.C.[52] The theory based on the excavation of Stradonitz in Bohemia, that numbers of Gauls went into voluntary exile in 12 B.C. to follow Maroboduus,[53] whose kingdom collapsed in A.D. 19, probably exaggerates the significance of the finds.

The major historical event recorded in the first century A.D. is the revolt of A.D. 21, described by Tacitus[54] and, in a few lines, by Velleius Paterculus.[55] Tacitus' account is very romantic in flavour. Two descendants of the most noble families of the Gauls gather together a motley crew of criminals and debtors in secret meetings. The Andecavi of Angers and the Turones of Tours are the first to rise up but are easily crushed. Iulius Florus with the Treviri, and Iulius Sacrovir with the Aedui, armed as best they can, are defeated in their turn, again without any difficulty. Both Velleius and Tacitus point out that 'the Roman

[52] Dio LIV.19.6.   [53] Vell. Pat. II.129.   [54] *Ann.* III.40–47.   [55] Vell. Pat. II.129.

people heard that they had won before they heard they were at war'. But while Velleius tells the story in praise of Tiberius, Tacitus makes it the basis of complaints, that the Senate of Rome had been kept in ignorance and that the revolt had been caused by the heavy burden of taxation, by usury and by the high-handed behaviour of the governors.

The significance of this episode has been over-estimated by historians of Gaul. Quite apart from the tendency to invoke it to explain archaeological destruction layers, for example burnt layers in the east, all sorts of sociological inferences have been drawn from these incidents. Either it represents the last revolt of the *equites*, the elite created by the Gallic War whose place was then taken by a new ruling class of artisans and merchants, or else, on the contrary, it represents an attempt to seize power from those *equites* whose sons were taken hostage by Iulius Sacrovir when he found them in the schools of Autun. But these interpretations are unacceptable: Tacitus himself relates the activities in A.D. 69 of Gallic aristocrats who remain as obsessed as ever by privilege and status.[56]

In fact, the story of Florus and Sacrovir clearly shows just how difficult these two nobles found it to stir up support among their peers. With the help of the hostages captured from Autun, they were just able to secure their neutrality, but the Gallic ruling classes were thoroughly implicated in Roman structures and only a tiny minority took up arms.

The reign of Claudius was marked by renewed activity on the Rhine frontier. Two projects seem to have been important, first the cutting of a canal between the old Rhine and the Meuse and second, in A.D. 50, the foundation of Cologne, the colonia Claudia Ara Agrippinensium. The conquest and colonization of the south of Britain must have stimulated trade between Britain and Gaul, especially with the west. Claudius' energy and influence were felt in every sphere. New roads were built, towns expanded and secondary urban sites were set up including Martigny in Switzerland (Forum Claudii) and Aime in the Tarentaise. Euergetistical construction of civic monuments was actively encouraged. The emperor's relationship with the Gallic elite is expounded in the speech he made to the Senate[57] proposing that Gauls who were Roman citizens should be allowed access to the Senate and to stand for magistracies in Rome. Opposition was bitter, and in the first instance only the Aedui, Rome's oldest allies, were allowed to enjoy this dispensation. The anecdote shows how differently the Three Gauls were regarded, in senatorial circles, from Narbonensis, the inhabitants of which had possessed this right from A.D. 14.

Apart from a reference to a census,[58] only a few anecdotes survive

---

[56] Tac. *Hist.* IV.68–9 cf. above, p. 000.   [57] Tac. *Ann.* XI.24; *CIL* XIII 1668.
[58] Tac. *Ann.* XIV.46.2.

about Gaul in Nero's reign. A statue of Mercury was built among the Arverni and there was a fire in Lyons in A.D. 65.

Some general observations emerge from this brief survey. For most of the period, the major events centred on the north east where tens of thousands of troops were stationed, an equivalent population, in ancient terms, to that of a number of cities. The troops acted as a huge economic magnet but also a political magnet in so far as emperors and members of the imperial household visited the area frequently. The other region affected by military activities at this period was Aquitaine, in the narrow sense of the area south of the Garonne. Agrippa's road system, decided on very early but constructed over a long period of time, accorded importance to both the north east and the south west. Finally, regardless of misinterpretations of the events of A.D. 21, the strong links established by Caesar between the 'Julian' aristocracies and the imperial power showed no signs of weakening.

2. Innovation and inertia

Attempts to assess the impact of the conquest and of the imposition of new structures on Gaul run up against a major problem. On none of the sites that were to develop into Gallo-Roman towns, are there any archaeological levels datable to the period between the end of the Gallic Wars and about 20 B.C., or even later. The most striking examples are the three colonies founded by Caesar and Plancus. At Nyon, the colonia Iulia Equestris, nothing has been found dating from before 15 B.C., at Augst, Augusta Raurica, the earliest levels date from the end of the reign of Augustus and at Lyons the first traces apart from defensive ditches, perhaps those of Plancus' camp, date from between 30 and 20 B.C. Dendrochronology has dated the first encampment at Petrisberg in Trier to 30 B.C., but there is no contemporary material. The few exceptions are often ambiguous. There have been a few sporadic finds at Reims, where two ditched and banked enclosures have been found, remains of settlement are known from Metz, thousands of Gallic coins have been found at Langres and the excavations of 'ma Maison' at Saintes in the south west, have produced some sherds of 40–30 B.C.

Should we conclude that the first towns took their time to appear? In fact, the argument *ex silentio* should be distrusted for two reasons. The first reason is that urban archaeology is a relatively recent innovation in France. The second is that, when it comes to these early periods, the stratigraphic frame of reference depends on finds from Roman military camps, and the earliest camps to have been excavated date from after 19 B.C. Neuss is dated after 19 B.C., Dangstetten from 15 to 9 B.C., Rödgen between 12 and 9 B.C., Oberaden between 11 and 9 B.C., Haltern from 7

B.C. to A.D. 9 and so on. The result is that archaeologists are often unable to date material that is after 50 B.C. but before 20 B.C., especially if the material does not consist of imported pottery. It is quite likely, then, that research will advance rapidly in this area, but for the moment it is only possible to stress the slowness of developments.

The birth of urbanism can only be traced from the Augustan period, and then only from the end of his reign, since almost every town site produces sherds of Arretine ware and then of early Gaulish *terra sigillata*. It is important to distinguish several categories among these sites. For a start we must set to one side the cases of Lyons and of Autun. Lyons grew enormously from 20 B.C. onwards. Although it was doubtless unfortified, the hilltop of Fourvière was covered with settlement, a theatre was built there with stone imported from quarries in the south, in particular from Glanum, and there was probably a *forum* too. Craft workshops developed on and around the hilltop, and branches of the great pottery manufacturers of Arezzo, Pisa and the north of Italy, were set up there to supply the Roman military camps. From the Augustan period they even imitated amphorae of Dressel 2–4 type and several other varieties. Lyons became a distribution centre for Mediterranean products including wine, olive oil and fish preserves *en route* to Switzerland, the Moselle valley and the Rhineland, not to mention central and western Gaul. After the federal sanctuary was set up at Condate in 12 B.C., euergetism increased and more and more monuments were built, like the amphitheatre, given by aristocrats from Saintes in A.D. 19. Lyons became a political, religious and economic metropolis adorned with a striking array of monuments. The first houses were built of wooden panels, had several rooms, floors made 'en terrazzo' and wall-paintings inspired directly by Roman fashions.

The case of Autun is rather different. The late Iron Age capital of the Aedui had been Bibracte, mentioned several times by Caesar who had stayed there. It was located on the summit of Mont Beuvray, some 20 km from Autun. Excavations in the nineteenth century, which have recently been resumed, uncovered public zones, a wide variety of private housing, including some huge houses of Roman design, and artisan quarters, all surrounded with a massive rampart. The whole town was moved to Autun, and the population transfer must have been fairly rapid as the finds from Bibracte hardly go beyond the turn of the millennium. The name Augustodunum expresses Augustus' desire to bestow his personal favour on Rome's oldest allies. Plenty of other evidence shows his favour in action: Autun was surrounded by the only circuit wall built in the Three Gauls in this period, crowned with towers and adorned with four ornamental gates, enclosing an area of some 200 hectares. Autun was also the home of the famous 'universities' for young aristocrats from

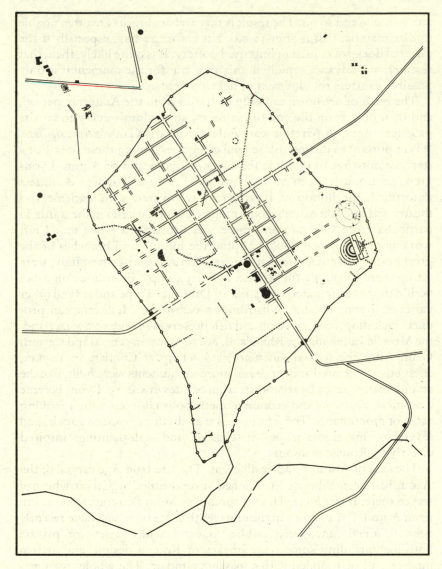

Fig. 9. Autun: town-plan.

all over Gaul, and of the school for gladiators. Built from scratch with a
regular orthogonal street plan from the first, Autun was *the* showpiece
city. The city drew its livelihood from the elite who lived within its walls,
but drew their wealth from the land. Craftsmen were attracted by the
city's position at a natural crossroads, and Autun probably had great
religious prestige, as the sacred quarter based around the temple of Janus
shows. But the town never really took much part in the great commercial

movements which were the lifeblood of Mâcon and Chalon. The early prominence of the city derived from a desire for an urban lifestyle, based on the integration of the elite and on practical assistance from the Roman authorities, perhaps in the form of tax exemptions or gifts.

Other towns in Gaul had very different experiences. In Switzerland, orthogonal grids were laid out at the very start, and filled in little by little by buildings constructed of wood and earth. Spaces were reserved for public use, but monuments were rare: Augst was partly enclosed by a circuit wall and had a theatre and Nyon had a building of basilica-type. It is possible that the colonial status of Augst and Nyon exerted an influence on other centres like Avenches.

The road network must also have played a part. For some time now, excavations in the towns on the main route to the south west have been revealing Augustan layers and Augustan street grids. These are towns like Limoges and Clermont-Ferrand, the Roman names of which alone suggest an early origin.[59] Recent discoveries at Feurs, Roman Forum Segusiavorum, support this picture, revealing an Augustan street plan, a *forum* dated to around A.D. 10–20 and an inscription attesting a wooden theatre.[60] So although the unrest in Aquitaine had been settled fairly early on, the route to the south west continued to promote urbanism.

The same applied in the north east and the east. Langres, Metz, Trier and Amiens all grew up at key points on the road system. So too did less important centres like Bavai, or nearby sites like Paris. When the road junctions were also on navigable rivers, towns developed even earlier and became even more important. For example, Amiens had a town grid based on the *pes drusianus*, and its wattle and daub buildings covered an area of 40 hectares. Trier, Metz and Reims were probably broadly similar. Craft activity is well attested but no sign of public monuments.

Almost everywhere else is it difficult to reconstruct the earliest stages of town life. The best known of the towns of the south west is Saintes, Mediolanum Santonum. The town is famous for the family of Iulii descended from the Gaul Epotsoviridus, whose great-grandson C. Iulius Rufus built the amphitheatre of the Three Gauls at Condate, and in A.D. 18 or 19 put up the arch of Germanicus in his own city. But the Augustan town itself is haphazardly laid out, with tiny winding streets and both houses and workshops built of wattle and daub and only 20 to 30 square metres in size.

At Bordeaux, the late Iron Age 'emporium' covered an area of at most

[59] A number of Gallic towns had names beginning in Augusto-, for example, Autun, Clermont, Limoges, Troyes, Bayeux and Senlis; in Caesaro-, for example, Tours and Beauvais; or in Iulio-, for example, Lillebonne and Angers. In other cases the element Augusta was followed by the name of the people, as in the cases of Trier, Saint-Quentin, Soissons and Auch. The names might have been granted as a favour at any point during the Julio-Claudian period.

[60] *CIL* XIII 1642. A civic benefactor, of the reign of Claudius, announces that he has rebuilt in stone a wooden theatre.

5 or 6 hectares on a promontory surrounded by soft ground on the banks of the Garonne. The Roman conquest had no impact on the site until the beginning of the Christian era. At the end of Augustus' reign and the beginning of Tiberius' the city expanded outwards to cover some 12 to 15 hectares, and the first traces of regular town-planning and Roman building techniques appeared, but the main period of expansion did not start until the middle of the first century. Much the same sort of sequence could be described for a number of towns, from Poitiers and Périgueux to Avenches and Trier. As for Brittany, Normandy and the Loire valley, all that can be said is that the remains are very slight.

To put it another way, perhaps we should imagine many of the *civitas* capitals of the Three Gauls as sparsely populated centres, only roughly planned out, with a few clusters of public buildings, maybe wooden ones at that, a little trade going on, a few craftsmen and houses built in much the same way as in the late Iron Age.

Epigraphy and architectural elements can be used to elaborate the picture a little, although there again the evidence concentrates in Switzerland, in the north east and in the south west. At Langres, a text refers to a temple of Augustus vowed by Drusus in 9 B.C. The Princes of the Youth received epigraphic or monumental honours in Lyons, Sens, Trier and Reims, where there was a cenotaph. In 4 B.C. Bavai, Bagacum, acclaimed the *adventus* of Tiberius. The columns and capitals found at Saintes and Périgueux follow Roman models from the end of the last century B.C., and in Switzerland sculpture was made and imported from the reign of Augustus. It is worth bearing in mind that many buildings, including basilicas, theatres and amphitheatres, may well have been built in wood, on the lines of those we know of from the military camps, and so would have left no trace. All the same, with the odd exception, the Three Gauls had not produced a thick crop of towns in the Augustan period. The contrast with the situation in Narbonensis is striking.

The forty years between the accession of Tiberius and the death of Claudius corresponded, in most of the towns discussed above, to a period of growth and monumentalization. The street plans were systematized and in many places, especially in Switzerland, masonry began to be used. The first trunk roads were built, like that linking Saintes, Poitiers and possibly Paris. Amphitheatres were built at Saintes, perhaps at Senlis as well, and in Périgueux, where it took the family of the Auli Pompeii, whose first member was called Dumnotus, three generations to complete the task. Public baths were constructed, aqueducts were built as at Bordeaux, and houses were bigger and decorated with wall-paintings based on the Pompeian Third Style. At Lyons, excavations at the site of le Verbe Incarné show that the plateau of la Sarra was levelled to allow the building of a temple, surrounded with porticoes resting on cryptoporticoes, and dedicated to the imperial family. Also at Lyons, a monumental fountain, supplied with water by a new aqueduct, was dedicated to Claudius and a major programme of reclamation made the tongue of land between the Rhône and the Saône habitable and suitable for a trading district.

New towns appeared and others expanded to become real urban centres most of all as a result of greatly improved communications, affecting many regions but especially the west. Claudius' reign witnessed large scale road building projects, especially in the Loire valley, but also supplementing road networks in the north, the centre, Brittany, Normandy and elsewhere. The conquest of Britain stimulated development all along the Atlantic strip. This was also the period of the great expansion of Poitiers and Bordeaux, as well as of the growth of Tours, Bourges, Angers, Rennes as well as of many other centres which would not all become quite so successful.

Why was it that urbanization was such a slow and often such a limited process in the Three Gauls? The Celtic *oppida* do not seem to have been intensively occupied for very long after the conquest, in fact one of the most recent contributions of archaeological research to the debate has been to show the early origins of many of the secondary urban centres which comprised the closely packed network of sites usually termed *vici*. Some originated when populations moved down from hilltop sites to the neighbouring plains, others developed from indigenous sites of similar scale which were rarely located on hilltops, despite the famous example of Alésia, but many seem to have been created *ex nihilo*. Apart from those sites that developed around places of pilgrimage, these *vici* tended to be located on routes, whether terrestrial or riverine, that had been important ever since the Neolithic period, in other words astride those communications channels that had organized local life from time immemorial. Almost everywhere in the Three Gauls these small centres have produced evidence of craft working, often at quite a sophisticated level, including bronze and iron working, carpentry, weaving and pottery production. The small towns had a commercial role, then, sometimes directed towards a military camp, as in the case of the *canabae* of Mirebeau or Strasbourg or Baden in Switzerland, but more often serving a local catchment area. Early on some of these *vici* were planned and acquired some public buildings. Vidy, Lousonna, had a street plan from 20–10 B.C. and a building with a basilical plan was constructed there round A.D. 30–40; Alésia and Mâlain were planned under Augustus and organized properly under Claudius, Alésia acquiring streets, porticoes with façades, masonry buildings, temples and a square. Some of these towns were more dynamic than the cities that were the capitals of their *civitates*: Orléans, for example, grew much faster than Chartres. The

first land divisions discovered by aerial photography show that Three
Gauls did not exhibit the same strong links between cities and their
suburban and rural *villae* as characterized Narbonensis. Town and *villa*
relations were much more typically centred on the *vici*.

Does this mean that, in general, apart from those regions affected by
colonization and perhaps by proximity to Narbonensis, the Gallic
landscape was structured not so much by the new constraints introduced
by Roman rule, but by longer term factors? We need to know more about
these long-term structures before that hypothesis can be assessed and the
notion of 'tribal survivals' should be shunned. But it does seem likely
that the influence of the local territories predominated over the impact of
the Roman *civitates*.

3. Unifying factors

The Latin right had been granted to all communities in Narbonensis in
the Caesarian period, and although some juridical complexities had been
introduced by granting some *civitates* treaties or Roman citizenship as
privileges, a general principle had been established. In the Three Gauls,
on the other hand, the principle was one of diversity. We can reconstruct
from various sources, and in particular from Pliny, the list of states with
treaties. It comprises the Helvetii, the Carnutes, the Remi, the Aedui and
the Lingones. But it is much less clear which cities were free, (*liberae*) and
which exempt from taxation (*immunes*), and the epigraphic evidence does
not always agree with the literary sources.[61] Strabo states that Rome had
granted the Latin right to some Aquitanian peoples, 'in particular the
Ausci and the Convenae'.[62] This may have been on the occasion of the
Pyrenean campaigns or possibly it was because the Convenae had once
been included in Gallia Transalpina. Other civitates were granted the
Latin right,[63] but we do not know when it became widespread. Any
period from the reign of Claudius to the Flavians is possible, but there is
no means of deciding for sure.

An almost complete absence of epigraphy makes it very difficult to
trace the development of governmental institutions within the *civitates*
with any confidence. A *vergobret* (magistrate) is mentioned on the coinage
of the Lexovii, whose capital was Lisieux in Normandy, and an
inscription from Saintes reads 'C. Iulius Marinus, son of C. Iulius
Ricoveringus, of the Voltinian tribe, first [*flamen*] of Augustus, curator
of Roman citizens, quaestor, *vergo[bret]*'.[64] The early date of this

---

[61] For example the *civitas* of the Turones is referred to as *libera* by *CIL* XIII 3076 and 3077.
[62] Strab. IV.2.2 (190–1C).
[63] At least the allied states were awarded this, to judge from Tac. *Ann.* XI.23.
[64] *CIL* XIII 1048 and 1074.

inscription fits in with a graffito found at Saint-Marcel, Indre, ancient Argentomagus, which reads 'the *vergobret* has performed the sacrifice (*vercobretos readdas*)' and which dates to around A.D. 20–30. The Gallic office of *vergobret* may have corresponded to the post of praetor, known from Claudian Bordeaux.[65] But the name of the office, whether indigenous or Romanized, is much less significant than the fact that it refers to an individual, rather than a collegiate, magistracy. The data are so rare that no firm conclusions can be drawn from them. All the same Saintes and Bordeaux were among the most urbanized states of the Three Gauls. The pride with which the powerful recalled their ancestors is also very striking. Also from Saintes was C. Iulius Rufus who proclaimed his descent from C. Iulius Otuaneunus, the son of C. Iulius Gedomo, the son of Epotsoviridus.[66] The impression created by the sources, then, is that, outside the colonies, late Iron Age institutions survived under the cover of vague Roman terminology, and that the great families of the Julian aristocracy preserved their superordinate power *vis-à-vis* their fellow citizens.

As we have already seen, Roman citizens from the Three Gauls did not have the right, before the reign of Claudius, to stand for the magistracies in Rome. But they could gain entry to the senatorial order by imperial favour. It is surprising that only three senators are known before A.D. 70, all of them from Aquitaine. The small number of *equites* is also surprising: we know of only twenty or so examples in the first century A.D., from the Three Gauls and the Germanies together, only a quarter as many as are known from Narbonensis. It is as if the greatest ambition of these magnates was to be elected to the priesthood at the federal sanctuary at Condate, so winning the highest honour in the Three Gauls for themselves and their states.

It is difficult to define the exact role played by the federal sanctuary, and the ceremonies that took place there each year, beginning on 1 August, the date of the fall of Alexandria and the festival of the *Genius Augusti*. The events included the worship of the emperor and of Rome, competitions, and the opportunity for 'political' representation, through the medium of the *concilium*, the provincial assembly. All the same, the theory that Celtic traditions had been incorporated into the festival cannot be rejected out of hand. Occasional accounts of the site suggest that a sacred grove and a crowd of statues stood alongside the altar and the amphitheatre, and the organization of the *concilium* is also peculiar to Gaul, the chief official being a *sacerdos*, rather than a *flamen*, the other officers being a *iudex*, an *allectus arcae Galliarum* and an *inquisitor Galliarum*. The gathering was not an exact copy of the famous Druidical meetings mentioned by Caesar, but it may have been some sort of

---

[65] *CIL* XIII 590, 596–600.   [66] *CIL* XIII 1036.

transmutation of them. The place was different, as were the forms of the meeting, but important business was transacted there and it was the occasion for equals to recognize each others' paramount prestige. The creation of the Ara Ubiorum for the Germans living west of the Rhine, and of a *conventus* at Saint-Bertrand-de-Comminges (Lugdunum Convenarum) for Aquitanians south of Garonne, also at an early date, showed the Romans' willingness and perhaps their need, to perpetuate traditional annual festivities. Unfortunately there are too few inscriptions from either the Confluence or the Gallic states to say for certain where the *sacerdotes* came from, although we know that the first, elected in 12 B.C., was the Aeduan Iulius Vercondaridubnus, and that in the early first century his successors included the Cadurcan M. Lucterius Sencianus, probably a descendant of the chief Lucterus who had fought against Caesar between 52 and 51 B.C., and also C. Iulius Rufus from Saintes. The assembly of the Three Gauls offered Augustus a gold neck-ring, a torque, that weighed 100 pounds, and it was also the assembly, rather than the city of Lyons, who welcomed Caligula, who established a contest in Greek and Latin rhetoric there.[67] The *concilium* demanded of the elite that they demonstrated their loyalty to the emperor and their acceptance of Latin culture and that they indulged in extravagant euergetism, but most of all it was the premier stage on which aristocrats paraded their wealth, their prestige and their rivalries. The return of a new *sacerdos* to his home state must have been the occasion for triumphal honours, and more than one wanted to reproduce, on a smaller scale, the entertainments he had given, and over which he had just presided.

It is necessary to return, once more, to the scarcity of inscriptions. The usual explanation given is that it represents resistance to the Latin language, although it may be more a sign of psychological difficulties surrounding the use of writing, perhaps deriving from the circumstance that in the late Iron Age the Druids had monopolized writing and it had therefore never been publicly displayed. On the other hand, Gauls made a major contribution to the Roman army. Before A.D. 68 they provided twenty-eight cavalry divisions and seventy-six cohorts, that is to say about 65 per cent of the auxiliary strength of the western provinces. Many also served as legionaries: 25 per cent of the inscriptions found in Gaul, including Narbonensis, from the reigns of Claudius and Nero, are those of legionaries. The return of substantial numbers of men who had served for years in the Roman army must have had all sorts of consequences for both the language and more generally the 'civilization' of the Three Gauls.

Assimilation had begun, albeit slowly, not only among the elite but also among other groups lower down the social scale. The process is

---

[67] Sue. *Calig.* 20.

often described as being accompanied by extensive economic and commercial integration, but this is unlikely to have been the case. Recent numismatic studies have shown a shortage of coin that seems to have grown progressively more severe until the Flavian period. Local coinages were accepted at least until the end of the last century B.C., and after that forgeries multiplied and the countermarks designed to authorize money as official were themselves being forged under Claudius and Nero. The implications are that central government was not concerned to create an integrated monetary system, nor any real kind of economic organization. As a result *laissez-faire* predominated, allowing the frontier regions, where soldiers were paid in cash, to exercise a powerful attractive force, and permitting the development of profitable barter with neighbouring 'barbarians', the basis of the economy of ports like Bordeaux and perhaps Rézé near Nantes, and of the great centres of distribution, above all Lyons. Apart from in some cities with special advantages, then, commerce was not a major force in creating a new mix of Gauls and Italians. The activities of the elite and the army were much more important.

Mortuary studies show that cremation was widely used, but also reveal a number of local peculiarities. Around Lyons, Briord and Roanne inhumation was none the less important, and it is virtually the only rite used in some cemeteries along the Seine between Paris and Rouen, and especially in Paris itself. By contrast, the inhumations found in the centre-west of France, in Poitou and Saintonge, are those of 'high status' women, buried either in stone sarcophagi or in huge wooden coffins. These tombs are very rich in grave-goods. In the same way, the isolated tombs of the Berry, that date to the period between Augustus and Claudius, contain either inhumations or cremations but also very rich assemblages of amphorae, ceramic table services, tools, weapons and bronze objects including wine pourers, bowls, plates and *simpula*. The same applies to the territory of the Treviri, while in present-day Belgium, *tumuli* have been recorded. The aristocracy had evidently not unanimously adopted Roman customs, and alongside those nobles who had mausolea built for them at a very early date, like the example from Faverolles in the *civitas* of the Lingones, there were others who preferred to preserve older traditions.

I will not deal with religion here except briefly to summarize the argument I will develop at greater length in *CAH* xi. The slender evidence we have suggests two main lines of inquiry. First, although the literary evidence tends to focus on the banning and then the suppression of Druidism, recent excavations are turning up more and more temples with concentric plans, temples of the type called *fana*, constructed on the sites of pre-Roman shrines. Second, Romanized religious monuments like the Boatmen's Pillar put up by the Parisii at Lutecia, juxtapose not only indigenous deities and Roman gods, but also tend to include some reference to the emperor. The epithet *Augustus* appears very frequently on religious inscriptions, either applied to the god, or associated with him. This is the clearest indication that the Roman emperor descended from Caesar was seen in the Three Gauls as a charismatic leader, who safeguarded peace and unity but also protected the autonomy of those peoples, even the smallest communities, who worshipped him alongside their own local gods in order to make him more truly their own.

Compared with other areas incorporated into the Roman empire, the Tres Galliae stick out like a sore thumb. The Gauls were marked out as different by their climate, by memories of ancient Gallic invasions and of Caesar's war, by their closeness to the Germans, and by their image as barbarians, possessed of great riches, but indulging in human sacrifice. Archaeology makes clear just how much rhetoric there was in Claudius' speech to the Senate, better preserved in *CIL* XIII 1668 than in Tacitus' rendition. Compared to Narbonensis, so quickly assimilated, the Tres Galliae seem like a world still resting on Iron Age foundations. Cities were slow to establish themselves, the aristocracies were reluctant to go beyond their territorial power bases, and the locality exercised a determining influence over all spheres of life. But the yeast was already at work. Gaul now opened onto the outside world, first the Germanies and then Britain, Gauls were serving in the Roman army, and civilization, spreading contagiously, was transforming public buildings and private houses alike. The worship of the emperor was more and more closely bound up with the power of the leaders of the state, and of its gods. Claudius, whom Suetonius called 'the Gallic emperor' predicted the future more accurately than he described the present.

CHAPTER 13e

BRITAIN 43 B.C. TO A.D. 69

JOHN WACHER

I. PRE-CONQUEST PERIOD

Rome's first formal contact with Britain came with the expeditions of Iulius Caesar in 55 and 54 B.C.[1] By then, most of the major late Iron Age migrations from Gaul to Britain had already occurred, although within Britain much political and cultural movement was still to take place. Caesar named only six tribes, among which were the Trinovantes and Cenimagni (Iceni?), with four more unnamed in Kent, and with the implication of a nameless eleventh, probably the Catuvellauni, ruled by the leader of the British opposition, Cassivellaunus. Other tribes which were to play a part in the period between Caesar and Claudius and immediately thereafter were the Brigantes, Corieltavi, Cornovii, Dumnonii, Atrebates and Dobunni in present-day England and the Silures and Ordovices in Wales. The Atrebates arrived in Britain after the Caesarian episodes, brought over by their king Commius, who, at first an ally of Caesar, later unwisely joined the unsuccessful rebellion of Vercingetorix in Gaul; the Dobunni are usually considered to be an offshoot of the Atrebates.[2] The Catuvellauni gradually emerged as the most powerful tribe in south-east England, occupying an area roughly equivalent to the kingdom of Cassivellaunus. In addition, the four tribes which inhabited Kent eventually merged to form the single tribe of the Cantiaci. Apart from the tribes mentioned by Caesar and some other literary sources, most of our knowledge of their existence and geographical positions is gained from detailed study of the coinage which they minted.[3]

Caesar's expeditions, even if they bore no long term success, nevertheless made Rome more aware of Britain's existence. This is partly to be seen in the greatly increased volume of trade between the island and the Roman empire, now expanded to the Channel. The trade is mentioned by Strabo[4] and attested archaeologically in the numerous goods found especially on sites in the area north of the lower Thames. Politically and

---

[1] Caes. *BGall.* v. [2] Allen 1961 (B 304) 75–149.
[3] Allen 1958 (B 305) 97–308. It must be admitted, however that some modern authorities view this list of coin distributions with suspicion, e.g. Collis 1971 (B 317) 71–84.
[4] Strab. IV.5.1–4 (199–201C)

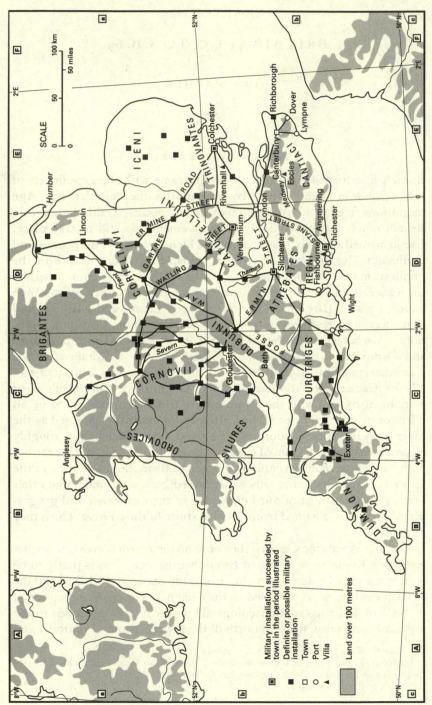

Map 8. Britain as far north as the Humber.

militarily, Caesar left unfinished business in Britain, and Augustus three times, in 34, 28 and 27 B.C., planned expeditions; all were called off because of needs elsewhere. Deprived of military conquest, Augustus aimed at the maintenance of a balance of power between the major tribes, at first befriending Tincommius, son of Commius of the Atrebates, so as to balance the waxing strength of the Catuvellauni. But this diplomacy did not prevent the latter from invading and occupying the territory of the Trinovantes, an act which was contrary to the terms of the old Caesarian treaty. It appears to have been quite deliberately timed, *c.* A.D. 10, when Augustus was more than preoccupied with the aftermath of the Varian disaster in Germany, and it came about through the actions of a man who was to become the most powerful ruler in Britain before the Claudian invasion: Cunobelin. Suetonius gave him the title *Britannorum Rex*, and he was probably a direct descendant of the great Cassivellaunus.[5]

An alternative theory on his origin sees him, however, as a Trinovantian monarch who had gained ascendancy over the Catuvellauni; certainly his capital was at Camulodunum near modern Colchester, in Trinovantian territory.[6] This view strains the information which we have beyond logical bounds. The Catuvellauni and not the Trinovantes were, by implication in Dio's account of the Claudian invasion,[7] the prime enemy of Rome. By implication also Cunobelin had been their king. It is extremely unlikely that he would have abandoned his own tribe's name in favour of that of an enemy, whether conquered or not.

Despite the apparently anti-Roman bias of some of Cunobelin's early actions, he seems to have given a temporary stability to the tribal affairs of Britain. In Rome's eyes all was well so long as his deeds were balanced by the friendly presence, south of the Thames, of its allies the Atrebates. Unfortunately, following the death of Commius and the accession of his son, Tincommius, the kingdom was rent by fraternal squabbles, Tincommius being ousted by Eppillus, and he in turn by Verica. In each case, Augustus recognized the successful claimant, despite the appeal of Tincommius for help towards reinstatement; both Eppillus and Verica seem to have been acknowledged as client kings.

Cunobelin was not averse to allowing even more flourishing trade to grow between his kingdom and the empire, since, with its extension to the sea, he now controlled the lucrative trade routes from the Rhineland and elsewhere. His anti-Roman attitude also seems to have abated sufficiently for him to send embassies to Rome, and he may have been among the British rulers who set up offerings on the Capitol.[8] But with the death of Augustus and the succession of Tiberius, he resumed in the

[5] Suet. *Calig.* 44.   [6] Rodwell 1976 (E 553) 265–77.   [7] Dio LX.19–22.
[8] Strab. IV.5.3 (200–1C).

next fifteen or so years the expansion of his kingdom, adding the rest of Kent and penetrating into the middle and upper Thames valley. Pressure was also applied to the Atrebatic kingdom for the first time and it would appear that its centre at Calleva now became part of the Catuvellaunian domain. Tiberius apparently did not react to this provocation, although it is unlikely that it was carried out without protest to Rome.

Tiberius died in A.D. 37 to be succeeded by Gaius. By then Cunobelin must have been sinking into old age and he was perhaps losing his grip on tribal affairs, a factor which was aggravated by the growth to manhood of his sons. The apparent philo-Roman outlook of one of them, Adminius, may well have led to his expulsion and flight to Gaius to support his reinstatement. Gaius was then in Germany and was persuaded by Adminius that Britain could easily be conquered. Gaius assembled an army at Boulogne in A.D. 40, but a mutiny prevented it from sailing; Gaius thereupon called off the enterprise. But the expulsion of Adminius showed that all was not well among the Catuvellauni, a situation which was made worse by the death of Cunobelin and the division of the kingdom between two other sons Caratacus and Togodumnus.

Ambitious, hot-headed and possibly resentful of Roman influence in Britain, they set out on a policy of unlimited aggression which led, not only to the partial, or even total, absorption of the Dobunni, but also to the overrunning of the Atrebates, forcing their king, Verica, to flee to Rome for help, and finally to the total alienation of Rome. Verica was a client king and Roman ally, so that his expulsion could be interpreted as an insult to Rome, which, if left unavenged, would have called into question a whole area of foreign policy at a time when Rome very much relied on client rulers to maintain peace on or near the frontiers. The situation was, moreover, exacerbated by a demand for Verica's extradition and, when this was refused, by aggressive action being taken against Roman merchants in Britain and possibly even against the coast of Gaul. Verica's expulsion, therefore, served as the political vindication for the direct intervention of Rome in Britain in A.D. 43.

II. THE INVASION AND ITS AFTERMATH

Numerous reasons, apart from that advanced above, have been put forward to explain Rome's decision to invade Britain at this precise juncture. Among them can be listed the military ambition of Claudius, now emperor after Gaius' assassination; the prospect of mineral and other wealth; a surplus of legions on the German frontier after Gaius had created two more to back his abortive invasion attempt; the final suppression of druidism, which had been outlawed in Gaul, no doubt causing many adherents to seek refuge across the Channel. There was also the question of military strategy; if Britain were not invaded, the coast of Gaul would require protection from a hostile force controlling the other side of the Channel. To protect it would mean raising the strength of the army to dangerous levels in the western mainland of the empire and no extra territory would be gained to provide its food. If the same army were placed in Britain it would be safely isolated, with fresh sources of food and other supplies. Whatever the reasons, Claudius decided to invade. A force composed of four legions and auxiliaries, altogether amounting to some 40,000 men, under the command of Aulus Plautius, until then governor of Pannonia, was assembled at Boulogne. That part of the Annals of Tacitus which included the account of the invasion is lost, and for literary evidence we have to rely on the later account of Cassius Dio,[9] which is neither exhaustive nor entirely clear in its descriptions. The evidence of archaeology helps a little, but is again restricted, pointing definitely to only one landfall at Richborough.[10] Yet Dio stresses that the force was divided into three sections; consequently three possibilities can be envisaged. The whole force could have landed at Richborough in three consecutive waves; but it must be admitted that the fortified beachhead there is not nearly large enough to contain so many men, while no other encampment has yet been found nearby. Secondly, it has been argued that whilst one division landed at Richborough, the other two landed at Dover and Lympne respectively; it should be noted, however, that there is no evidence at all from either site of an early Roman presence. Thirdly, it has been ingeniously argued that one division at least was directed to a landing in the neighbourhood of Chichester, in order to carry out the very necessary reinstatement of Verica as soon as possible in his kingdom.[11] The balance of probability would seem to favour the first hypothesis.

The landing was apparently unopposed. After some slight skirmishing inland, in which Togodumnus was probably killed, the first major action against the Britons was at the crossing of the river Medway, where the Roman army was victorious; it then advanced to the Thames. At this stage Caratacus is said to have fled to Wales. After a pause to allow Claudius to arrive on the scene, the advance was resumed and the emperor was able to enter the Catuvellaunian capital in triumph. There then ensued further campaigns which carried the Roman advance to a position marked roughly by a line drawn from the Humber to the Severn, where for a time it ceased. It has been claimed that it was always the intention of Rome to conquer the whole of Britain.[12] If that was so, it is very difficult to explain why, having reached the line established by *c.*

[9] See n. 7.   [10] Cunliffe 1968 (E 533) 232–4.   [11] Hawkes 1961 (E 545) (see n. 2) 62–7.
[12] e.g. Mann 1974 (C 286) 529–31.

A.D. 47, another twenty-three years elapsed before the major advance into Wales and the north was resumed. The army lacked neither the manpower nor the capability to advance immediately.

It seems more likely, therefore, that the original intention was only to seek a pragmatic solution to the Catuvellaunian problem by conquest and occupation; the line at which the advance stopped did just that. That it also raised a new set of military problems, which in time required their own solutions, cannot have been entirely foreseen in A.D. 43.

The limit of the advance was marked by the construction of a road, the Fosse Way, for lateral communication from Lincoln to Exeter and by the siting of forts and fortresses along it, to the front and to the rear of it, forming a broad military zone to protect the newly conquered territory. Most of the forts were occupied by auxiliary regiments but some at least contained battle groups consisting of detachments of *legiones II Augusta*, *XIV Gemina*, and *IX Hispana* brigaded with cavalry. The whereabouts of the headquarters fortresses of these legions in the years immediately after the invasion is imperfectly known and still the subject of some speculation. *Legio XX Valeria* appears to have been left in reserve at Colchester until just before the foundation of the *colonia* in A.D. 49, after which it too was moved forward to the frontier.

But not all remained peaceful, even after the primary objective had been reached. Caratacus stirred up his new Welsh allies to attack the province in A.D. 47 just as Ostorius Scapula was taking over the governorship from Aulus Plautius. A campaign against Caratacus was preceded by the disarming of tribes within the new province, an act which itself caused trouble and led to a minor revolt among the allied Iceni. Once started, the campaign against the Welsh tribes was interrupted by disturbances among the northern Brigantes, whose queen Cartimandua professed a pro-Roman outlook. Indeed Caratacus, after his defeat in Wales, fled in vain to Cartimandua for protection, only to be handed over to Rome.[13] There followed some years of almost continuous but confused and ill-recorded fighting in Wales and occasionally in Brigantia, the only permanent result of which was the advance of the frontier zone to the Welsh Marches, probably executed by Ostorius. Then in A.D. 60, a much more serious threat faced the province, which nearly resulted in its loss through the rebellion of Boudica, queen of the Iceni, together with the neighbouring Trinovantes.[14]

Much has been written about the causes of the rebellion. It is generally accepted that among them were the forcible reduction of the Iceni, following the death of the Roman client king, Prasutagus, and the refusal of Rome to recognize his queen or daughters as successors. The

[13] Tac. *Ann.* XII.36; see also Hanson and Campbell 1986 (E 544) 73–90.
[14] Tac. *Ann.* XIV.29–39.

reduction was carried out in a heavy-handed and arrogant way by the provincial procurator, Catus Decianus, which led to the flogging of Boudica and the rape of her daughters. A contributory cause was the requisitioning of Trinovantian land, including their principal religious site, for the *territorium* of the new *colonia* at Colchester; another was the probable expense of maintaining the newly introduced imperial cult. It has also been suggested that a rebellion, just at that time, was intended to act as a diversion and to distract the governor, Suetonius Paullinus, from his campaign against the headquarters of druidism on the island of Anglesey;[15] if so, it failed. Be that as it may, in A.D. 60, while Suetonius was campaigning in north Wales with most of the British garrison, the rebellion exploded; Colchester, London and Verulamium were sacked and burnt, and excavations at each site have produced eloquent evidence for the fires. The small force deployed by the procurator in defence of the *colonia* was useless, as were the resident veterans. *Legio IX*, advancing against the rebels from Longthorpe, suffered many casualties and had to withdraw in disorder. Suetonius, apprised of the rebellion, hastened from Wales in advance of his main army, and reached London before the rebels, but realized that there was little that could be done to save the town. He fell back to join his advancing army and finally brought the rebels to battle, probably somewhere along the middle section of Watling Street. The rebels were routed and the province saved. The resulting punitive campaign in East Anglia, together with the battle casualties, must have seriously impoverished the Iceni and Trinovantes for at least a generation, leading to a much slower rate of Romanization in later years.

In the ensuing decade, attempts were made to restore the province. A new and more enlightened procurator, Iulius Classicianus, replaced Catus Decianus, who had fled to Gaul at the outbreak of the revolt, while a succession of milder governors ended hostilities and helped to placate the natives. So successful were these measures that the province was deemed sufficiently safe for *legio XIV* to be withdrawn in 66. Unfortunately, the peace was shattered by the Roman army itself, disillusioned with the resulting period of inactivity. A mutiny led by a legionary commander, Roscius Coelius, forced the governor, Trebellius Maximus, to flee the province in 69. But by then affairs of greater moment gripped the whole empire. Nero had committed suicide in 68 and the power struggle which ensued left its mark on Britain. Its new governor, Vettius Bolanus, was a supporter of Vitellius, who was eventually defeated by Vespasian. Moreover, *legio XIV* which had supported Otho also returned to Britain for a short time, while the remaining legions had supported Vitellius. Vespasian therefore inherited a province of doubt-

[15] Webster 1978 (E 564).

ful loyalty and it was not until the early 70s that he was able to take remedial action.

III. ORGANIZATION OF THE PROVINCE

Once the midland frontier zone had been created, much of the south east seems to have been demilitarized, and by A.D. 49, with the dispatch of *legio* XX from Colchester to Gloucester, the way was open for the development of the newly constituted province. It embraced two client kingdoms: the resurrected sometime kingdom of Verica, now renamed as the *civitas* of the Regni, with a new king, Cogidubnus, in west Sussex and Hampshire, and the Iceni in East Anglia.[16] These two kingdoms enabled Rome to make economies in manpower, although they were very different in character and dependability. According to Tacitus, Cogidubnus proved a staunch ally to Rome and led his kingdom steadily towards peaceful Romanization until his death, probably in the Flavian period.[17] Indeed for a short time during the Year of the Four Emperors (A.D. 69) he may have helped to hold the province against a mutinous army and an unreliable governor on behalf of Vespasian. The idea that he was given the status of an imperial legate has now been undermined by a re-reading of the damaged inscription from Chichester[18] which records his name and titles. Certainly, whether legate or not, something significant was happening in his kingdom at that time, for some of what are probably the earliest urban defences in Britain are to be found there. The Iceni appear to have been less ready to accept the benefits of the conquest, and, on being forcibly disarmed by Ostorius Scapula, staged a minor revolt, which was quickly put down; but it was a presage of more serious things to come.

In the remaining area of the south east, through which the Roman army had passed rapidly, it is possible to detect the establishment of three *civitates*: units of local administration, formed from the Iron Age tribal territories embraced by the Cantiaci, the Catuvellauni and the Trinovantes.[19] The latter first appear in history in Caesar's account of Britain, in a somewhat paradoxical way. Although he refers to them as the most powerful tribe in Britain, they are at the same time also depicted as seeking his protection and assistance to repel attacks by their western neighbour, the tribe of Cassivellaunus. There is no further mention of them, not even at the conquest, until they again appear, embroiled in the Boudican rebellion; consequently, it must be assumed that they had re-emerged under Rome as an independent unit of local government after

---

[16] Wacher 1995 (E 560) 242. It has, however, been argued that the Iceni lay outside the province, see Wacher 1981 (E 561) 136.   [17] Tac. *Agr.* XIV.   [18] *RIB* 91. See Bogaers 1979 (B 211) 243–54.   [19] Frere 1961 (E 535). Wacher 1995 (E 560) 23, 189–241.

years of Catuvellaunian domination. But it was their territory that was
chosen by the Roman administration for the foundation of the first city
in Britain, to act as an example of urbanization to the inhabitants of the
new province: an act that was to have far-reaching consequences.

IV. URBANIZATION AND COMMUNICATIONS

The foundation of the *colonia* at Colchester, on the site of the recently
evacuated legionary fortress, in A.D. 49, is mentioned by Tacitus as a
deliberate act of policy, whereby a reserve of legionary veterans was
maintained in the south east in the absence of any worthwhile regular
garrison.[20] It was also intended to act as a model of urbanization for the
native Britons, and *incolae* – native inhabitants – were included in the
population from the first. The earliest houses of the veterans have been
shown by excavations to owe much to the legionary structures that had
preceded them, although there were significant changes in layout; yet
some of the streets of the fortress were perpetuated.[21] The position of the
forum is still not known with certainty although several sites have been
proposed; Tacitus mentions a *curia*. He also refers to a theatre which has
now been identified by excavation, but he stresses that there were no
fortifications at the time of the Boudican rebellion, which implies that
the legionary defences had been dismantled.[22] Astride the main road to
London on the western boundary, a triumphal arch was constructed,
presumably to commemorate the foundation of the *colonia* and to honour
its founder, Claudius. His memory, though, was more than adequately
recognized in the construction of the principal building connected with
the new city. This was the great temple of Claudius, which was also to be
the centre of the imperial cult in Britain.[23] All that remains now is the
podium, lying beneath the Norman castle; originally, it stood within a
great colonnaded courtyard with an entrance to the south. It is often
argued that Colchester was also intended to be the provincial administrative capital, a function that was later to fall on London. It should be
stressed, however, that there is no evidence to support this suggestion,
and in the extremely fluid state of the new province, it is more likely that
the 'capital' would tend to be where the governor was; there is nothing
to link him specifically with Colchester.

Some other urban centres had their beginnings in the years immediately after the invasion. Canterbury, a recognized Iron Age site, early
became the capital of the *civitas Cantiacorum*, although many of the
features originally attributed to its foundation are now thought to be
somewhat later, and the main development did not occur until the turn

---

[20] Tac. *Ann.* XII.32.   [21] Crummy 1982 (E 532) 125–34.   [22] Tac. *Ann.* XIV.32.
[23] Sen. *Apocol.* 8.3; see also Fishwick 1972 (E 534) 164–81.

of the first and second centuries. But the final street plan may owe some of its irregularities to the lines of earlier streets and existing buildings.[24] London was recognized by Tacitus as a flourishing trading centre even before the Boudican rebellion;[25] houses and shops of the first town, burnt in the rebellion, have been uncovered over a wide area, but little is known of any public buildings. There are indications of an embryonic street system in the area north of the Thames bridge, the possible northern abutment of which has been identified in excavations in Pudding Lane.[26] There is also evidence to show that at least some provincial administrative functions were centred on London, possibly even before the Boudican rebellion, and certainly after it. The procurator, Iulius Classicianus, died in office and was buried at London; his ornate, altar-style tombstone was found reused in the later town wall on Tower Hill.[27]

Verulamium, like Canterbury, was also founded on the site of a major Iron Age centre, the probable sometime *oppidum* of Tasciovanus. It almost certainly served as the administrative centre for the Catuvellauni from its beginning. Arguments, however, still continue over whether, and if so when, municipal status was conferred. The most recent view holds that it was granted under Claudius and at about the same time as the foundation of colonial Colchester.[28] But the evidence is not decisive and relies to a large extent on the interpretation of a passage of Tacitus.[29] Excavations have identified a rudimentary street system of Claudian date, and a number of buildings, mostly, as at both London and Colchester, constructed with timber frames and wattle-and-daub walls, and so consumed in the Boudican fire. One block in *Insula XIV* has been identified as a range of shops, possibly built as a speculative venture by a Catuvellaunian noble and rented out to his retainers or managed by slaves.[30] The *forum* and *basilica* are dated by the dedicatory inscription to A.D. 79,[31] although earlier structures may still lie undiscovered beneath them. The town was encompassed, probably in the Claudian period, by a bank and a ditch; when the town later expanded beyond them this line was commemorated by two triumphal arches set astride the London–Chester road.[32]

Two other embryonic urban settlements may be considered as belonging to this period and both lie within the likely kingdom of Cogidubnus. The site of the town at Chichester, in the kingdom's heartlands, had an early military presence, but it is not known precisely

---

[24] Bennett 1984 (E 528) 47–56.   [25] Tac. *Ann.* XIV.33.   [26] Milne 1982 (E 549) 271–6.
[27] *RIB* 12.   [28] Frere 1983 (E 536) II. 26–8.
[29] Tac. *Ann.* XIV.33. But see also J.E. Bogaers, 'Review of Wacher 1966 (E 559), *JRS* 57 (1967) 233–4.   [30] Frere 1972 (E 536) I *passim*.
[31] Frere 1983 (E 536) II 69–72.   [32] Frere 1983 (E 536) II 33–54.

how long it lasted. Yet, alongside the military base, or after it, there is evidence for a major public building dedicated during Nero's Principate.[33] Probably slightly later, the Cogidubnus inscription[34] displays advancing Romanization, not only in the existence of a temple to the purely classical cult of Neptune and Minerva, but also to social organization in the *collegium fabrorum*, or guild of craftsmen. Also, very likely situated in Cogidubnus' kingdom, the Iron Age *oppidum* at Silchester has produced elements of early urbanized development which included a bathhouse and amphitheatre[35] of Neronian date, and a slightly later, but still Neronian, timber building on the site of the later *forum* and *basilica*.[36] This building has been variously interpreted as a market square, a residence for Cogidubnus or military *principia*. But the two phases of fortification on different alignments which were thought to belong in the same context, have now been shown to be of pre-Roman origin.[37]

Communications rapidly came to play a crucial part in the development of the new province. Roads, such as Watling Street, Ermine Street, Stane Street and the Fosse Way, were primarily constructed for military reasons, but, once in existence, would have been used by all.[38] They linked a series of burgeoning ports such as Richborough, Dover, Fishbourne, Colchester and London, which provided havens for the increasing number of merchants wishing to exploit the new markets. No doubt the major rivers were likewise pressed into service; it is worth noting that water transport was much cheaper.[39] It should also be remembered that the main roads, even with their straight alignments, metalled surfaces and good drainage, probably degenerated into a series of muddy potholes in winter, possibly making road transport in Britain, apart from pedestrians and pack animals, a seasonal affair which was confined mainly to the summer. The upkeep of the road system, together with its ancillary structures such as bridges, devolved upon the local magistrates of the town or *civitas* through whose area they passed.

V. RURAL SETTLEMENT

The Romanization of the countryside was generally a slower process, and there is little change to be observed in most farmsteads and agricultural communities until much later, their owners continuing to live in the traditional Iron Age manner, even though they began to use new agricultural and domestic equipment and utensils. The first villas, which are the best measure of the rate of adoption of Roman ways, were to be found, as might be expected, not far from the new towns,

[33] *RIB* 92.   [34] *RIB* 91.   [35] Fulford 1989 (E 541).   [36] Fulford 1985 (E 540).
[37] Fulford 1984 (E 539).   [38] Margary 1973 (E 547).   [39] Duncan-Jones 1974 (A 24) 366–9.

Verulamium, Colchester and London, and in the kingdom of Cogidubnus. It has, indeed, been claimed that in these rural areas the pace of
Romanization outstripped that in the new towns, with better quality
housing appearing in the countryside at an earlier date.[40] It may be,
though, that these first ventures into Romanized country life were not
the work of native Britons, but of migrants from Gaul or further afield,
eager to invest in the new province. Such villas as Eccles (Kent), or
Angmering (Sussex), both probably of late Neronian or early Flavian
date, would seem to fit best into this category, but the early foundation at
Rivenhall (Essex) is held to have been built by a rich native landowner.[41]
The stimulus given by the Roman occupation to increased agricultural
production was at first twofold: the demands of the tax-collector and the
food requirements of the army. Whenever or wherever troops have been
stationed in foreign or occupied territory, they have always created a
demand and have become a source of accessible wealth for the local
populations; the Roman army in Britain was no different. It is unlikely
that British farmers could have immediately supplied all the food needed
by the army. Total requisition would probably not have been a workable
policy for an army of permanent occupation, since it would have left the
producers to starve. Nevertheless, it must be reckoned that, within a
reasonable time, production would have been stimulated sufficiently to
meet most needs. This could only have been done by increasing the areas
of arable land, the clearance of which would have helped in supplying the
sudden demand for the huge quantities of timber required for constructing the many new military and urban buildings. Once production had
begun to expand, it must have occurred to many British farmers that
there were profits to be made by increasing it still further, in order to
supply other markets offered by the new towns. This, or something like
it, will have been the economic base on which, in time, the villa system
grew.

VI. TRADE AND INDUSTRY

Improved communications undoubtedly helped to expand trade connexions. But the introduction of Roman currency into the province,
primarily to pay the army, will have created a pool of low-value coins for
small, everyday transactions, thus performing a function which the
mostly high-value coinage of the Iron Age had failed to do. Trade in
Britain, and between Britain and the rest of the empire, increased rapidly,
much of it at first probably connected with supplies under army
contracts. Large quantities of samian pottery came mainly from factories

[40] Walthew 1975 (E 563) 189–205.   [41] Rodwell and Rodwell 1973 (E 554) 115–27.

in southern Gaul, and other fine wares from places like Lyons;[42] *mortaria*, kitchen mixing bowls, also came in quantity. At first, British potteries only supplied coarse wares, many still of Iron Age, wheel-made, traditional types. Gradually, however, new forms began to infiltrate, and within a decade or two, several centres were in full production, supplying both military and civilian markets. Other imports included glassware from the eastern Mediterranean and metalwork from Gaul and Italy. But Britain slowly built up its own industries, which, apart from the manufacture of pottery, were usually situated in the towns. A bronze-smith's workshop existed at Verulamium before the Boudican rebellion, where goods would have been both manufactured and sold on the premises.[43] Unfortunately, the evidence for industries and trade connected with organic materials such as wood, leather or cloth, does not often survive. But there is evidence for the exploitation and export of minerals such as Wealden iron and more notably the lead/silver ores in the Mendips worked possibly as early as A.D. 49 by a detachment of *legio II*.[44] It is interesting that the pattern of trade between Britain and other parts of the empire in some ways resembled that of modern trade between developed and undeveloped countries, the former exporting manufactured goods and the latter raw materials. Strabo listed corn, cattle, hides, slaves, gold, silver, iron and hunting dogs as British exports in the time of Augustus; ivory ornaments, amber, glass and other manufactured trinkets came in return, although wine and oil might well be added to the list.[45]

VII. RELIGION

The new province was already well served by its native cults, which tended to be localized; yet there is evidence from the Roman period for the existence of tribal deities, such as Brigantia,[46] and for sites which had more far-reaching significance, such as Bath with its deity, Sulis, presiding over the hot springs.[47] In most instances, Celt and Roman possessed a common basic level of superstition.[48] Consequently, the introduction of classical cults would have struck an immediate response; Celtic and Roman deities often shared similar areas of supernatural influence, so that Minerva could be identified both with Sulis at Bath and Brigantia in the north. But totally foreign to British religious practice was the introduction of the imperial cult, with its physical centre at Colchester. This provided a common element in the empire which had

[42] Greene 1978 (E 542).   [43] Frere 1972 (E 536) 1. 18.
[44] But see reservations expressed by Whittick 1982 (E 566) 113–24.   [45] Strab. IV.5.3 (200–1C).
[46] *RIB* 2091.   [47] *RIB* 141–50.   [48] Wacher 1978 (E 562) 217–26.

an enormous diversity of religious practice and at the same time incorporated expressions of loyalty to the imperial household. It required an expensive commitment on the part of the leading inhabitants of the province – the size and magnificence of the temple of Claudius attracted unfavourable comment even in Rome. Yet the concept had worked well in Gaul, with its great centre at Lyons, and there was no reason to believe that it would not work in Britain; that it was to become one of the causes and focal points of the Boudican rebellion could not have been foreseen.

The account given above suggests that the process usually described as Romanization in Britain was very uneven in place, time and depth. Although the Romans encouraged *aemulatio* in their provinces and often provided models of behaviour or structure, little pressure was applied to force the change. The rate, therefore, at which any individual or community adopted the new ways was largely a matter of personal inclination. Provided that existing ways of life and behaviour were acceptable to the Roman administration, and taxes were paid, no change was demanded. Naturally, therefore, the fastest rate of Romanization is to be detected in those areas of Britain which had been affected by the most recent migrations from Gaul, whose people had already been in closer contact with Roman culture. Practical, less often financial, help might be provided for Romanizing communities, as in the founding of new towns; but in the end, the main burden of the cost had to be paid by those same communities or its individual members. This, in itself, imposed the limit to the progress of Romanization. Strictly, the Roman civil administration was not concerned with the welfare of society, except insofar as a well-ordered province made tax collection easier. Nor could it do much more to help, even given the best of intentions. It was probably no more than a few hundred strong, consisting mainly of military personnel seconded for these duties, and simply did not have the manpower to influence every individual member of the estimated 2 to 3 million population of the province. Consequently, it could only function properly through delegation of responsibilities to the native people; the degree of delegation could vary greatly from place to place depending on the natives' fitness to accept it. Hence, also, the towns, villas and other structures of Roman Britain ultimately exhibit many variations in size, planning and degree of sophistication, mainly conditioned by the presence or absence of financial restraints, or will.

CHAPTER 13f

GERMANY

C. RÜGER

I. INTRODUCTION

After 50 B.C. when Caesar left Gaul, Gaul's eastern and northern border lay on the Rhine.[1] The aim of securing the Roman north west against migratory movements and wild attacks from north and east by means of a border line that could be precisely marked out was achieved. In the upper Danube region of central Europe, to be sure, the policy was limited to gaining control over the alpine passes through which for almost 300 years uncontrollable attacks on Rome's alpine approaches, indeed attacks on the city itself, had been launched.

Caesar's conquest of Gaul had an effect on the migratory movements which had obviously been taking place for centuries in the north-west part of the European continent. Caesar would not countenance the continued crossing to the left bank of the Rhine by Germans. But Germani Cisrhenani were already present on the left bank of the river. According to Caesar's own definition the latter included the Eburones in the area between the Rhine and Maas and the Caerosi, Paemani, Segni and Condrusi who inhabited the Eifel and the Ardennes. But the epithet Germani might never have meant more to him than 'stern warriors'. Geographically one must include the Texuandri to the west of the Dutch and Belgian river Maas. Although the amount of Celtic in their languages seems easier to isolate and define than the Germanic, which was still at its earliest stage of development, we can identify some characteristics of primitive Germanic character, like the doubling of

---

[1] The main literary sources for Germany in this period are Cassius Dio (Books LIV–LVI), Velleius Paterculus (II, 60–132) and Tacitus (*Ann.* II, XI.16–19, XII.27–8, XIII.55–6; *Hist.* IV.12–37, 54–79, V.14–26 (Civilis and the Batavian Revolt)), Strab. IV.3ff (190Cff) and 289–329C Book VII). Tacitus' *Germania*, although written at the end of the first century A.D., contains a great deal of relevant and important information. The literary sources are collected by Capelle 1937 (E 572) and Klinghoffer 1955 (E 582). The inscriptions are collected in *CIL* XIII; for later additions see R. Finke, *BRGK* 17 (1927) 31–105, 201–14; H. Nesselhauf, *ibid.* 27 (1937), 66–13, H. Lieb, H. Nesselhauf, *ibid.*, 40 (1959) 129–216, U. Schillinger-Hafele, *ibid.* 58 (1977) 473–561. For coins see the volumes of *Die Fundmünzen der römischen Zeit in Deutschland.* There is a huge amount of archaeological evidence, much of which may be found in the periodicals *Germania, Bonner Jahrbücher* and *BRGK.* There are useful surveys by Schönberger 1969 (E 591) and Raepsaet-Charlier 1975 (E 587). See also ch. 13d, no. 1.

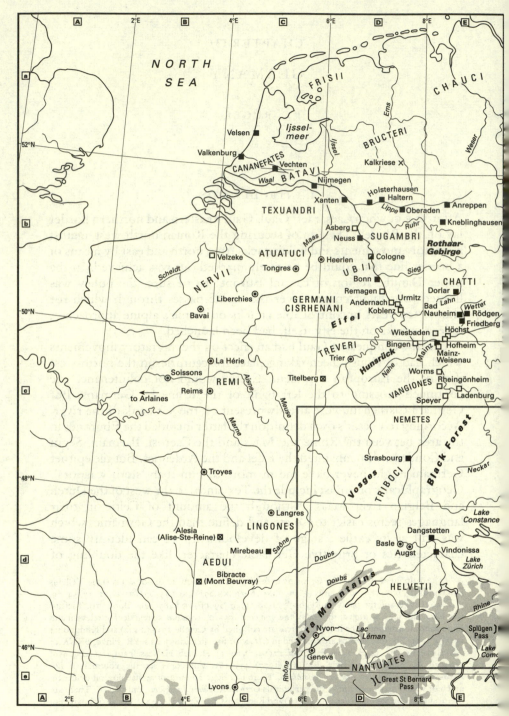

Map 9. Germany.

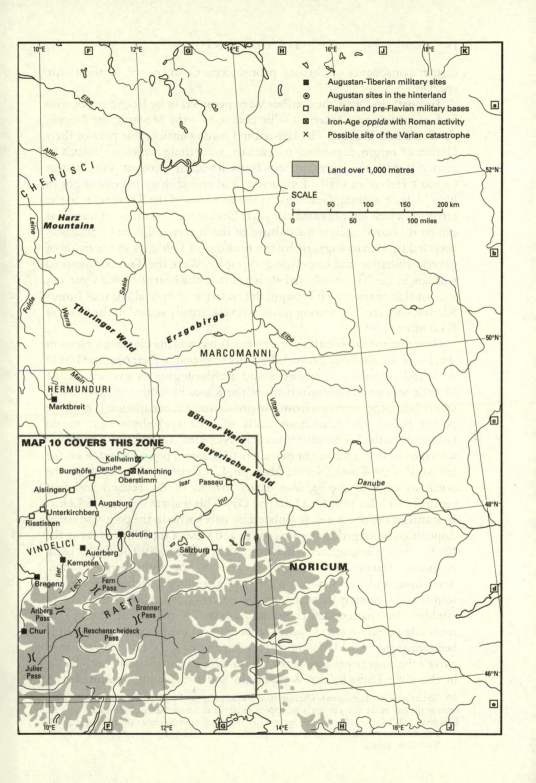

■	Augustan-Tiberian military sites
⊙	Augustan sites in the hinterland
□	Flavian and pre-Flavian military bases
⊠	Iron-Age *oppida* with Roman activity
×	Possible site of the Varian catastrophe

Land over 1,000 metres

SCALE

0   50   100   150   200 km

0   50   100 miles

CHERUSCI

Harz Mountains

Thüringer Wald

Erzgebirge

MARCOMANNI

HERMUNDURI

Marktbreit

Böhmer Wald

Bayerischer Wald

MAP 10 COVERS THIS ZONE

Kelheim
Burghöfe   Manching
Oberstimm
Aislingen
Augsburg
Unterkirchberg
Risstissen
Gauting
VINDELICI
Auerberg
Kempten
Bregenz
Fern Pass
Arlberg Pass
Brenner Pass
Chur
Reschenscheideck Pass
Julier Pass
RAETI

Passau
Isar
Inn
Danube
Salzburg
NORICUM

certain consonants or throaty pronunciations unknown to the Celtic speaker.[2]

To north and west these tribes were hemmed in by Belgic tribes who had, according to Caesar, a Gallic character – the Menapii, the Nervii, the Remi and Treveri. The last-named made considerable play of their Germanic origin, according to Tacitus, something which is difficult to reconcile with the 'Germani qui trans Rhenum incolunt' involved in Caesar's Helvetian affair.[3] Linguistics and archaeology have brought to light little or nothing Germanic in the territory of the Treveri, or in the territory which later became the Agri Decumates – nothing at least that can be measured against the culture of the Weser and Elbe Germans as revealed by archaeology, or by the findings of Celticists in the fields of genetic affiliation and linguistic geography. Were the Treveri involved perhaps in the 'Germanic' tribal thrust into the heart of Gaul after 113 B.C., or that of 109 which brought defeat to the ex-consul, Marcus Iunius Silanus, or were they among those who eventually settled in the heart of Gaul after 115?[4]

How ancient can tribal traditions be? What was the Germanic element that made the Tacitean Treveri allegedly so proud of their origins? It is to be found according to linguists and archaeologists as sparsely in the Moselle area as on the right bank of the Rhine in south-west Germany, where language survivals from the pre-Germanic occupation (i.e. in the period before the Alamannic raids of A.D. 233) show next to no Germanic traits. That is also true of the Nemetes, Triboci and Vangiones who moved under Caesar or in the post-Caesarian period to settle on the left bank of the Rhine. Nervii, Menapii, Eburones and Treveri mark the northern edge of the *oppidum*-based *civitates* of the second and first centuries B.C. (La Tène C to La Tène D1). This is always viewed as Celtic. By contrast the north was populated by tribes who in the post-Caesarian disposition belonged to the area south and west of the Rhine as far as the North Sea: Cananefates, Batavi, Suebi (Sugambri/Ciberni), Ubii, Nemetes, Triboci and Vangiones, and on the right bank Tacitus' 'levissimus quisque Gallorum' in the abandoned Helvetian area of south-west Germany, later the *agri Decumates*.[5] It is not possible, as yet, to establish the pattern of these migrations. A successful attempt to reconcile literary sources with archaeological evidence has so far only been made in the field of coinage. As Tacitus says, the Batavians formed part of the large tribal unit of the Chatti whose centre was on both banks of the river Lahn in the Westerwald and the Taunus mountains. A

---

[2] The names of soldiers (such as Chrauttius) at Vindolanda, garrisoned by Tungrian and Batavian units at the end of the first century A.D., appear to be the earliest evidence of this kind, see A.K. Bowman, J.D. Thomas, J.N. Adams, *Britannia* 21 (1990) 33–52; Weisgerber 1968 (E 599) 143–68.

[3] Tac. *Germ* XXVIII, Caes. *BGall.* 1.22–9, esp. 28.4.   [4] Livy, *Epit.* 63, App. *BCiv.* 1.29.

[5] Tac. *Germ.* XXIX.4.

Chattan dependency has proven to be obvious for the Batavian coinage in La Tène D2.[6] We can say nothing, however, about other material remnants of a migration which occurred a generation after Caesar, although one might expect these people to have had the ability and experience to produce pottery and to have brought with them the techniques of production which would leave their mark, for at least a generation or two, in the type of ware and the shapes of the vessels.

The settlement of these tribes in the north west of Caesar's Gaul took place with or without Rome's approval and supervision. The literary sources for the period between Caesar's departure and the arrival of troops on the Rhine under Augustus (16 B.C.) make repeated comments, particularly with reference to the time between M. Agrippa's two periods of activity in this region (39/8 and 19/18 B.C.), which lead to the conclusion that there was a deliberate policy of settling right-bank Germans on the left bank of the Rhine. And many a commander on the Rhine claimed prestige at Rome for a victory 'de Germanis' or for outstanding feats of military engineering such as the digging of canals or the re-routing of waterways. Of course the post-Caesarian forces in Gaul were distributed according to plans which were in no way directed to give them a function protective of the Rhine zone, as is shown by both the literary and the archaeological evidence for the deployment of winter garrisons throughout the interior of Gaul. Tiberius and Claudius provided for that for the first time between A.D. 17 and 47. Moreover, a miserable defeat, like that of the general Lollius in 17/16 B.C. ('maioris infamiae quam detrimenti', 'involving more ignominy than actual damage'),[7] demonstrated the tactical deployment of the post-Caesarian army as a striking force. That left the Germans on the right bank enough time to settle down, even without Rome's blessing, in the devastated land formerly belonging to the Eburones and the Menapii who had been pushed to the Channel coast.

The north-west European lowlands reveal that cultural movements spread from south to north, doubtless for the whole of post-Neolithic prehistory and particularly during the Hallstatt and La Tène periods (800–50 B.C.). The most northerly evidence for large-scale tribal organization and aristocratic tradition can be traced in Treveran territory. The war coalition of the Eburones fell apart again immediately after their defeat by Caesar. The name of the Eburones is no longer found in the Roman period. Their heartland on both sides of the Maas is for the well-informed elder Pliny a diffuse tribal area, 'pluribus nominibus'.[8] The impoverished isolation of the north, which until the third century B.C.

---

[6] Tac. *Hist.* IV.12. Batavian coinage: N. Roymans, W. van der Sanden, *Berichten van de Rijksdienst voor het Oudheidkundig Bodemonderzoek* 30 (1980) 173–254.   [7] Suet. *Aug.* 23.1.

[8] Pliny, *HN* IV.106.

enjoyed an 'epilithic culture', using old-fashioned stone tools and implements, can only be explained in terms of lack of local metal resources and the lack of economic opportunities for obtaining metal by exchange. It was very difficult in the first millennium B.C. for the new technology to gain a foothold in the poor diluvial geology of north-west Europe. In the rich south of the area, as in central Gaul, we come across names of local aristocrats whom we can recognize as the *clientelae* of those families who in the second and first centuries B.C. played a part in Roman campaigning in Gaul: Domitii, Cornelii, Valerii, Vibii, Calpurnii. In this Romanized *clientela* we often find the title *amicus populi Romani*.

In the north such pre-Caesarian involvement with Rome as an important instrument of Romanization is missing. There are no lowland finds of early first-century amphorae of type Dressel 1A in the continental north west.[9] Diplomatic contact with the German king Ariovistus went as far as the exchange of exotic royal gifts in hellenistic style.[10] Caesar did not change the system, but with frontier security in mind emphasized the difference between cis- and trans-rhenane people. Here there arises a curious dichotomy between archaeology and linguistics on the one hand and ancient (and also modern) historiography on the other. To judge by the canons of typology and language the north–south divide follows an east–west line north of the Eifel and Ardennes, while historians place it east and west of a north–south line along the Rhine. This division takes the form of a cross – it is, quite literally, a crux. All the models advanced to account for the popular groupings and process of ethnogenesis in the north-west quarter of this crucial field, such as the idea of an independent north-west block that differs from the Germanic and Celtic and represents a genuine third force, have so far proved unsatisfactory, despite all the efforts of historians and archaeologists.

The establishment of Roman rule in north Gaul can be seen archaeologically at central places like the great Treveran *oppidum* of the Titelberg in Luxembourg. Here we have names of money-coining Treveran chieftains who are dated by the numismatists to between the arrival of Caesar in Gaul and the crushing of a Treveran revolt in 29 B.C. They produced the so-called second Treveran group of coins (the first belongs to pre-Caesarian times).[11] Vocarant[ ] and Lucotius appear as pre-Caesarian chieftains' names, while Pottina and Arda occur under Caesar. None of these personalities crop up in Caesarian literary records. There seem to be no later coin legends belonging to Treveran chieftains. Then there appear the issues of Aulus Hirtius, probably of 45 B.C. In this year, in which he became pro-praetor of Gaul and received the title *imperator*, his minting perhaps reflects the triumphal elephant-ride of Cn. Domitius

---

9 Roymans 1987 (E 588).   10 Caes. *BGall.* 1.44, Pliny, *HN* 11.170.
11 See Heinen 1985 (E 580) 27–30.

Ahenobarbus (cos. 122 B.C.), after his victory over the Allobroges in 121 B.C., which saw the end of tactical deployment of elephants on the European continent. The final type in the Treveran coin series was issued by the freedman Germanus, mint-master of an aristocrat Indutil-lus in about 10 B.C., and thereafter it was perhaps minted in the new Treveran capital of Augusta Treverorum.[12] Interestingly, a Roman garrison was posted on the Titelberg from 29 B.C. until the Augustan offensive of 16 B.C., without causing the abandonment of the surround-ing *oppidum*. This garrison must have needed the large quantity of small change which was found there and which had to a large extent been minted there, too. For the first time now, Roman imported goods appear in the north west of continental Europe. The merchants who followed Caesar's army must have left behind Mediterranean amphora types and Campanian ware along with types of this period. So far they have been found neither on the Rhine nor in the whole region attributed to the northern tribes. The few Campanian-style black sherds and the wine and *garum* amphorae were found at hill-sites belonging to the post-Caesarian period. That sets the north-western area of Gaul clearly apart from the south. Here exports from the coast of Campania have left their traces on the Ligurian coast and the Côte d'Azur, then up the Rhône and Saône and so on to the Rhine bend, where typically the goods are not carried down the Rhine, but north-eastwards right across the later Raetia to the Danube. It seems that there was a trade route in wine from the Mediterranean before the great upheavals in our area which took place between La Tène B and La Tène C in the Eifel-Ardennes region. These upheavals may perhaps lie behind the tribal tradition of the Treveri about their Germanic origin. Be that as it may, these Mediterranean imports have nothing to do with Romanization. The few black sherds of Campanian ware and the wine and *garum* amphorae of the north west turn up at places which must be the result of post-Caesarian military logistics and associated trade, such as we see on the Titelberg in Luxembourg and perhaps on the Petrisberg at Trier.

A number of other matters bear on the question of Romanization. It is useful and valid to adduce Roman nomenclature in the north west as an indicator of Romanization. It can be emphasized that we know many Iulii, Tiberii and Claudii in our area of interest. The list of the north-west Gallic nobility from the Ubii, Treveri, Batavi and Cananefates caught up in the revolt of A.D. 69/70 is full of these names. Their families will scarcely all have received Roman citizenship in Caesar's time – perhaps not even the majority did so. It seems that the Romanization of Gaul after the second triumvirate will have followed the same course as it did in the East, where *clientelae* were formed in the triumviral period through

<hr>

[12] See Heinen 1985 (E 580) 29–30, 38–9.

the Aemilii and Antonii. Obviously in Octavian's territory and during the interregnum the same process took place in the name of the Iulii as a reaction to his adoption. One must not underestimate the vivid memory of Caesar expressed in myths about him in eastern Gaul and the Rhineland. The temple of Mars at Cologne for example possessed a sword of Caesar's, a precious relic steeped in omens:[13] in the frontier lands of eastern Gaul there was a noble whose pedigree reflected descent from a liaison of Iulius Caesar with his maternal ancestor.[14] As early as the time of Agrippa's presence and under the later governors of both Germanies, bridge building over the Rhine – and much else besides – must have had its origins, at least to some extent, in emulation of Caesar (*aemulatio Caesaris*). The tendency of modern historiography to assign fixed dates to everything, and to offer other explanations for the Rhine bridges should not obscure the fact that Iulius Caesar's image was still a living force on the Rhine throughout the first century A.D.

Agrippa, the most intelligent and promising of Augustus' generals, did not see himself in a leading role. Both his periods of activity in this region, that of 39/38 B.C. and that of 19/18 B.C., served less to give him a high profile in Gaul than to reinforce the position of Octavian/ Augustus. The most important date for the establishment of the ideology of the new Caesar was the erection at Lugdunum of the Pan-Gallic altar, the Ara Galliarum, traditionally dated to 12 B.C., the year of Agrippa's death.[15] There followed, probably in the first decade A.D. the foundation of an Ara Ubiorum along the same lines as the ideological centre of the cult of Rome which had already been provided for the Gauls at the confluence of the Saône with the Rhône at Lyons. But the Ara Ubiorum was not brought into being until a firm basis had been laid for the occupation of the land between the Rhine and the Elbe, a development designed to protect Gaul and to create a new province north of the Alps which bordered Caesar's old conquests.

II. ROMAN GERMANY, 16 B.C.–A.D. 17

Agrippa's recall from his second period of activity in Gaul and the elaborate celebration of the extraordinary Secular Games marks the end of a phase in the military activity between the Mediterranean coast and the Euphrates and north-west Spain. With the achievement of pacification, the *princeps* Augustus was able for the first time to turn his attention to *aemulatio Caesaris* and to conquest through a *bellum externum*. In Caesarian fashion he attempted this feat in north-west Europe with a large-scale movement which was to make the land between the Danube bend at Vienna and the mouth of the Weser into imperial territory.

[13] Suet. *Vit.* 8.   [14] Tac. *Hist.* IV.55.   [15] For a different view, see above, ch. 2, p. 98.

The period between 16 B.C. and the defeat of Varus in A.D. 9, or rather to the final abandonment of the policy of conquest east of the Rhine in A.D. 17, is characterized by a long-term strategy of pincer manoeuvres. On the Rhine and on the North Sea coast, on Lake Constance and on the Hochrhein, on the Lech and Danube, these depended on amphibious tactics. The precondition was the collection of military and geographical intelligence from a base on the Rhine; the compilation of such information could well have been started by Agrippa, given his geographical interests, in 39/8 or 19/18 B.C. Likewise the alpine passes from the south and on the east flank of the zone of occupation were secured by the annexation of the kingdom of Noricum.

It is an attractive hypothesis that Camp A at Novaesium/Neuss, so far the only camp dated to between 16 and 12 B.C., was built principally for this intelligence-gathering operation. The construction of all other fortresses and forts seems to have taken place after 12 B.C. and may be supposed to have followed the establishment of the reconnaissance camp at Novaesium/Neuss c. 16 B.C. This camp lies at the end of an important road that links the continental north west with the Mediterranean, the Rhine with the Rhône. It leads from Marseilles, up the Rhône via Lugudunum/Lyons to Andematunnum/Langres and Divodurum/Metz, then down the Moselle to Augusta Treverorum/Trier and through the Eifel-Ardennes range via Beda Vicus/Bitburg, then down the river Erft to Novaesium/Neuss. After about 5 B.C. a branch road was built which later became more important – the road from Belgica Vicus/Billig to Ara Ubiorum/Cologne.[16]

The troops were transferred from the interior of Gaul to their operational base camps on the Rhine. The most important role in the scheme was played by the sites which lay opposite the mouths of the tributaries which flowed into the Rhine north or east of Cologne: Mogontiacum/Mainz opposite the mouth of the Main, Novaesium/Neuss opposite the Ruhr, Vetera/Xanten opposite the Lippe, Noviomagus/Nijmegen opposite the Yssel, perhaps also a site opposite the mouth of the Neckar, another in the area of Basle and certainly Fectio/Vechten as a base for amphibious operations towards the North Sea.

The major events of the period between 16 B.C. and A.D. 17 on the Rhine are in the mainstream of imperial history: here we are mainly concerned with the important stages in the Romanization of this area. Four lines of penetration from the Rhine have been identified. The first is the line from Nijmegen via Vechten along the Frisian and Chaucan coast to the mouth of the Weser; the second is the line from Xanten up the Lippe towards Cheruscan territory and the Weser; the third a line from Mainz northwards through the Wetterau towards the middle Lahn, Fuld

16 For bibliography see Raepsaet-Charlier 1975 (E 587) 92–3.

and Werra towards the Weser and Elbe. A fourth line of penetration appears to have had its base of operation south of Mainz in the territory of the Vangiones and to strike west–east into the territory of the Marcomanni, touching at a tangent the two southward bends of the river Main; the evidential support for the existence of this line is, however, still poor. In addition, there is another line of penetration leading from the Basle area by way of Dangstetten and Hüfingen to the north east and the Danube.

The result of the offensives along these routes was the conquest of the area by Drusus and Tiberius in the period up to 8 B.C. when the protection of Gaul seems to have been secured by a German buffer zone. Between 6 B.C. and A.D. 1 Domitius Ahenobarbus as commander-in-chief would have used the operational routes out from Mainz to reach the Elbe. Perhaps the recently found traces of a Roman camp in the vicinity of Würzburg are evidence for his activities in the settlement of the Hermunduri in southern Thuringia and north Franconia.[17]

Various enterprises were launched at this time by Roman commanders using the pressure of annexation, as well as the practice of securing the allegiance of the nobility through attachment to the army. This is the period when chieftains' sons like Arminius obtained officer rank in the Roman army and Roman citizenship for themselves, and when Ahenobarbus became involved in the internal affairs of the Cherusci by attempting to reintroduce political refugees.[18]

The disturbances which broke out in A.D. 1, described by the eyewitness Velleius Paterculus as an 'immensum bellum', demanded renewal of the measures taken in the previous generation.[19] Tiberius took energetic action. An amphibious army and fleet operation on the old pattern took place again up to the Elbe. While the land between Rhine and Elbe had, on the face of it, been restored to dependency on Rome, a new threat in the guise of the Marcomannic Empire of King Maroboduus arose on Tiberius' eastern flank. The combined troops of Germania, Raetia and Illyricum were mobilized against him. Once more the line of advance from Mainz through Chattan territory, up the Main towards the Saale and Elbe was used as the western offensive route against Maroboduus. The identity and location of the easternmost fortress belonging to those forward thrusts seems now to be confirmed by the recent discovery of a military base at Marktbreit on the river Main, 25 km east of Würzburg.[20]

In or before A.D. 7 P. Quinctilius Varus took over the command of the

[17] Cüppers 1990 (E 574) 83, Abb. 39.
[18] Arminius: Vell. Pat. II.118.2, Ahenobarbus, Dio LV.10a.2–3.
[19] Vell. Pat. II.104.2.   [20] Cüppers 1990 (E 574) 83, Abb. 39.

army in Germania. Varus was married to a daughter of Agrippa and Claudia Marcella senior, and so belonged to the immediate circle of Augustus and Agrippa.[21] After Augustus' eastern journey of 21 B.C. he came to the *princeps'* attention and enjoyed his personal patronage. Velleius Paterculus describes him as more of an administrator than a general[22] and the organization of supply routes and an infrastructure for the imposition of tribute was clearly now thought necessary. In A.D. 9, however, Arminius, a Roman *eques* and aristocratic leader of the Cherusci, succeeded in uniting the disaffected circles of the nobility between Rhine and Elbe to such effect that he was able to achieve the catastrophic defeat of the Roman forces in the Teutoburg Forest in which three legions, three *alae* and six cohorts, over 20,000 men all told, were lost.

The result was an immediate abandonment of the strong points built between 8/7 B.C. and A.D. 9 along the lines of communication. Nevertheless, the bridgehead on the right bank of the Rhine opposite Mainz was held, as also, perhaps, was a bridgehead on the right bank opposite Vetera.

On the right bank of the Rhine the influence of the Elbe Germans was now strengthened. The latter took over the area round Bad Neuheim and Wiesbaden, with its important salt reserves, as their administrative centre. It had previously been occupied by the Ubii who had now migrated to the left bank of the Rhine. This immigrant element of the Chatti, the Mattiaci, is also described by Tacitus as German,[23] but all the traces of their language which we can recognize are Celtic. They have this in common with the Nemetes and the Triboci, tribal units with Celtic names, who likewise crossed to the left bank of the Rhine; in this area only the Vangiones are linguistically Germanic. Of the Elbe Germans, contingents of the great tribal coalition of the Suebi settled on the upper Rhine on the right hand side of the river. Perhaps they were sections of tribes from Maroboduus' realm who migrated under Roman pressure to the vicinity of the Rhine.

The earliest Romanizing tendencies revealed by the historical sources concern only the high Germanic nobility of the area between the Rhine and the Elbe. Thus, members of the right-bank aristocracy served as priests at the Ara Ubiorum. The Romans, probably consciously, made the decision not to erect another provincial altar on the Lugdunum pattern between Rhine and Elbe; indeed, the altar founded among the Ubii in the last decade B.C. remained the ideological cult-centre for the newly conquered territories. When Gaius and Lucius Caesar the grandsons and adopted sons of the emperor died, institutionalized commem-

---

[21] *PKöln* 1.10.   [22] Vell. Pat. 11.117.2–4.   [23] Tac. *Germ.* XXIX.

oration of them in cult form (perhaps at dynastic altars, inscriptions from which have been found in several north Gallic cities) served to reinforce the presence and impact of Rome in the newly conquered territory.

III. THE PERIOD OF THE ESTABLISHMENT OF THE MILITARY ZONE (A.D. 14–90)

The overall command of Germanicus over the armies of both Upper and Lower Germany came to an end in A.D. 16. The separation of the two armies (*exercitus superior, exercitus inferior*) of the Rhine, had taken place in A.D. 14, as Tacitus states.[24] It took Tiberius three years after the death of Augustus to pacify the troops of Lower Germany, to repair the unavoidable political damage on the right bank of the Rhine through carefully targeted campaigns, and to recall the troops to the bases on the left bank of the Rhine which had been used for the offensive towards the Elbe. Thereafter there was an *exercitus Germanicus superior* and an *exercitus Germanicus inferior* with respective command centres in Mogontiacum/ Mainz and Ara Ubiorum/Cologne. Since the Caesarian period, Rome had been in no doubt that the people living on the left bank of the Rhine included Germans. The terminology and the mixed military and civil character of Rome's administration through provincial legates (*legati Augusti pro praetore*) allowed the institutionalization not only of the two German armies but also of two *provinciae*, a term which in its strictest traditional sense denotes a military command. It was a brilliant stroke of political propaganda to disguise the abandonment of the land between the Elbe and the Rhine. 'Germania' existed despite the abandonment and in the following sixty years the region was developed into two regular provinces on the left bank of the Rhine, which were really only pocket-handkerchief-sized military zones along the eastern boundary of the Tres Galliae. Successful attempts at consolidation under Vespasian and his sons, however, eventually made it possible to design a new positive programme that led in about A.D. 85 to the foundation of the two official provinces, Germania Superior with its capital at Mainz and Germania Inferior with its capital at Cologne.

The Gallo–German nobility on both sides of the Rhine, whose allegiance Rome as the occupying power sought to secure through individual grants of citizenship and absorption into the ranks of the *equites*, was a pillar of Romanization. But Romanization was unstable, as the crisis provoked by Arminius between A.D. 5 and 9 demonstrated. That remained manifestly the case until the Batavian revolt. Within the major tribes on the eastern border who had remained strong, conflict between the pro-Roman and the tribally conservative forces was

[24] Tac. *Ann.* 1.31.

constantly breaking out, as it did in A.D. 21 with the revolt of the
Treveran and Aeduan nobles, Iulius Florus and Iulius Sacrovir; the pro-
Roman element among the Treveri was led by Iulius Indus.[25] As always,
the Treveran affair ended in victory for the occupying power and its
supporters. The losers were penalized by loss of land on the Rhine
between Bingen and Koblenz, a loss which affected the whole of the
Treveran *civitas*. There may have been other, similar episodes, less well
attested. Tacitus mentions a Chattan war which should be placed in the
mountains of Westerwald and Taunus and is confirmed by the recent
discovery of a bridge across the Rhine which can be dated by dendrochronology to A.D. 42.[26] It may have been incidents of this kind in
Friesland which lay behind the taking of hostages from the Frisii, after
the defeat of L. Apronius, and their settlement in A.D. 47 by Corbulo.[27]

The second category of obviously reliable allies of the Roman
occupation were the native east-Gaulish long distance traders, often
identical with the shipowners on the Gallic and German inland waterways. We meet them in shippers' guilds on Lake Geneva, on the Seine, in
the warehouses of Lyons and as wealthy, self-confident riverine carriers
on the Rhine. Here they present themselves, sometimes proudly, on the
monuments as non-citizens, like the *nauta*, Blussus, in Mainz.[28] They
maintain local burial rites and even on their tomb inscriptions they retain
the individual dialect characteristic of their Gallo-Germanic region – the
millstone exporters at Nickenich in the volcanic zone of the Eifel
provide a good example of this phenomenon. These traders transport
and import Mediterranean goods, above all wine and other Italian and
Spanish commodities like *garum*, through Gaul to Britain. On a tribal
basis they form club-like groups of *consistentes* with the army and in the
mercantile centres on the Rhine – the merchants' clubs of Remi and
Lingones, for example, associated with the military base at Vetera.[29] As
merchants with good Gallic names they turn up even in Pompeii.
Others, like the prosperous non-citizen (*peregrinus*) from Nickenich are
connected to the army because it needed their merchandise, in this case
the military quernstones which, like the helmets of the unit, were the
property of the legionary *centuriae*.[30]

Parallel to the assimilation of the nobility through a deliberate policy
of granting citizenship, and through favours shown by the military to
local *negotiatores* and *mercatores*, barge-owners and long-distance traders,
a deliberate effort was made to urbanize important native settlements,

---

[25] Tac. *Ann.* III.40–7.
[26] Chattan War: Tac. *Ann.* XII.27–8. Dendrochronology of bridge: B. Schmidt, *BJ* 181 (1981)
301–11.   [27] Tac. *Ann.* XI.19.   [28] *CIL* XIII 2.7067.
[29] Citizen *consistentes* in civilian village and linked by trade to the army: *CIL* XII 11806 and C.
Rüger, *ZPE* 43 (1981) 332–5.
[30] J.L. Weisgerber 1969 (E 600) 87–102 = *Germania* 17 (1933) 14–104.

first under Augustus and then more intensively under Claudius. Vespasian slowed down the process in the left-bank area of the frontier zone and concentrated on the Agri Decumates, but Trajan and Hadrian again forced the pace.

North of Lyons in the direction of the Rhine two colonial settlements came to prominence, Iulia Equestris (Nyon) and Augusta Raurica (Augst) both in northern Switzerland. In their cases the government seems to have been more generous with its grant of colonial rights than it was to Lugdunum/Lyons itself, which was first raised to colonial status under Claudius. Equestris and Raurica must therefore be seen as genuine military *coloniae* of veterans, while Lugdunum as a Roman provincial town was planned principally for the Gauls themselves as a centre for administration, and was to become a centre of coin production and of the cult of Rome and the emperor.[31]

The development in the north seems to have run along similar lines. Trier was founded by the emperor as Augusta Treverorum in the second decade B.C., but not at first raised to the status of *colonia*. In the north there was the altar to Rome at the Oppidum Ubiorum/Cologne. The creation of more *coloniae* and *municipia* in the Roman north west remained a slow process compared with other marginal parts of the empire such as Mauretania. Instead, the development of a *civitas* system was promoted as appropriate in a hinterland with few urban centres. In this way aspirations to legal grants of chartered status might be satisfied in due course – an obviously deliberate policy on the part of the imperial authority. The urbanization process continued in the Lower German military zone and in Gallia Belgica, proceeding from south to north, while in the Upper German military zone west of the Rhine there was no significant progress at all. In the Agri Decumates not one single settlement, even later on, was raised to the rank of *colonia*: the town with the highest legal status was the *municipium* of Arae Flaviae/Rottweil.

Under Claudius Trier perhaps and Cologne certainly were raised to the status of *coloniae*. At Trier one might well imagine that Claudius, in keeping with his policy in other provinces, would simply raise the local settlement to the rank of *colonia* and make Roman citizens of its peregrine inhabitants, drawn from the upper echelons of the Treveri; Colonia Claudia Ara Agrippinensium/Cologne, on the other hand, was made up of veteran colonists. That does not mean of course that a few Ubian notables were not to be found amongst the new citizens. There will certainly have been such instances – perhaps even nobles from the right bank of the Rhine as well. Without them, the institutional Romanization of the region would not have proceeded as quickly as it did in the period that followed. But the new *colonia* at Cologne, founded in A.D. 50, lay on

[31] Dio XLVI.50, cf. ch. 13*d*, pp. 469–70.

the Rhine between the legionary garrisons. There was consequently a strong enough veteran presence nearby for it to have been taken into consideration. Many of the first generation of Cologne's new citizens, Mediterranean by origin, certainly migrated to the south again. Perhaps there were later additions to the citizen body of Cologne under the Flavians and Trajan. Perhaps the 'domino' effect which we have seen under Claudius was behind the capital of the Cugerni or Ciberni at Xanten (?Cibernodunum) obtaining the status of a *municipium*. At any rate, under Trajan it was given colonial status as the Colonia Ulpia Traiana, perhaps in 98, but certainly by 104. At the same time the administrative centre of the Batavians became an Ulpian *municipium*. The last act of municipalization falls in the reign of Hadrian or Pius. Roman chartered town status was extended to the territory of the Cananefates where a *municipium Aelium* (Municipium Aelium Cananefatium) was created near the coast.

The elite core of the Roman army, the Rhine legions, remained completely Mediterranean, while the east Gaulish-Rhenish nobility could only aspire to Roman citizenship through serving in the higher ranks of the auxiliaries. If, in Caesar's case, fear of the adversary was still a factor, it soon ceased to be. Even the catastrophic defeat in the Teutoburg Forest (A.D. 9) did not re-awaken the old Cimbric terror of the Germans. The decision against conquest as far as the Elbe was clearly taken on fully rational grounds; *aemulatio Caesaris* was confined to spectacular engineering achievements, like the copying of his exploits in bridging the Rhine. The latter became a kind of fashion among the commanding officers of the Upper and Lower German armies in the first half of the first century, undertaken on the part of the Rhine which Caesar had twice crossed in a remarkably short time. It is conceivable that every legate of Germania who strove for another posting and had military ambitions bridged the Rhine in Caesarian fashion as the pinnacle of his career in Germany.

The official view of the German opposition across the Rhine, particularly in the northern sector, was the logical reverse of that attitude: there was no broad defence in depth in the hinterland. The left bank which had been the old springboard for the conquest of Germania served everywhere as a defensive line against a possible German attack. To deploy the troops 'per ripam Rheni', as it was probably expressed, without the tactical support of the legionary reserves on the lines of penetration to the south into the heart of Gaul, meant (assuming, as we surely must, a realistic evaluation by the Roman military planners) that for the Roman army the German opposition on the right bank of the Rhine represented a negligible factor: land and adversary were simply not worth the trouble of occupation, and any hostile movements close by could be easily reconnoitred from bases on the Rhine itself. Accordingly no legionary garrisons were required in Besançon or Trier, in Tongeren or Bavay; the only exception was the legionary deployment on the upper Rhine, a shifting pattern between Vindonissa/Windisch on the Aare, Argentorate/Strasbourg and Mirebeau, an earlier posting of the Strasbourg garrison south-westward toward Langres. All that seemed necessary was to hold auxiliary garrisons in north-east Gaul to extinguish possible local uprisings in the Gallic hinterland of the frontier. This tactical deployment came to an end in the 80s. In general the idea of maintaining in reserve a striking force drawn from the legionary garrisons away from the frontier was kept for the more serious opposition in Britain, Syria and north Africa.

The result of the Tiberio-Claudian arrangement along a river frontier stretching over 1,000km from Basle to Valkenburg (with offshoots on the right bank for military advances in Upper Germany) would have been a handicap if the enemy had been really strong. Not just in A.D. 69/70, but in 260 and 274 too, the frontier line was successfully penetrated; the attacks were driven home deep into the heart of the Gallic provinces and, in 274, right through to Spain. This frontier system was not designed against a powerful enemy.

The situation among the tribes on and in the vicinity of the left bank of the Rhine, even under Nero, remained one of considerable variety, so increasing Romanization is hard to recognize among those ranked below the aristocracy whose members had been given grants of Roman citizenship. Cananefates and Batavi were at first treated as *foederati* who could independently raise their own troops, so neither tribe was subject to Roman *dilectus* (levy), but both enjoyed the status of *socii* (allies). Their capital was Batavodurum. In accordance with the principle that grants of chartered town status spread northwards along the Rhine, the town will have received the name of Ulpia Noviomagus (perhaps in 104) and the right to hold a periodic market (*ius nundinarum*) in the second half of the second century. Together with the capital of the Cananefates it will have been raised to the rank of *municipium*. The Batavian units kept their national character however and at least during the period under consideration here (Augustus to Vespasian) they were in no sense the melting-pot from which a new Roman citizenry arose.

The Frisians in the north had co-operated with the Romans from the beginning. In the 20s there was a visible tightening of the Roman administrative grip on this area, but even under Tiberius interest in the area relaxed. In A.D. 47 Cn. Domitius Corbulo again attempted to bring about the formal subjection of the Frisian area. Though achieving some success, this development was no longer in accord with the imperial policy of Claudius, and the emperor ordered all military garrisons back to the left bank of the Rhine.[32] A chain of forts which is now attested in the archaeological record was built along the Oude Rijn in Holland and the Niederrhein in Germany. It can be recognized as a Lower German *limes* on the left bank of the river, and represents a defensive measure to protect Lower Germany in that it simultaneously excluded the right-bank tribes from the empire and left them to fragment at the hands of their own quarrelling aristocratic factions. The Bructeri were the particular object of repeated successful Roman intervention until almost the end of the first century, up to the time of Nerva's governors of Lower Germany. This did not, however, prevent free passage to the left bank of the Rhine by unarmed right-bank Germans on a short-term basis.[33]

North of the Lahn the Mattiaci (who like the Batavians are obviously of Chattan origin) and the pro-Roman Germanic population of the Wetterau appear on the scene as early as Germanicus' time. There are archaeological indications of settlement by Mattiaci round Wiesbaden in a *civitas Mattiacorum* in the years following A.D. 16.[34] Further south and directly adjacent are the *civitates* of the Triboci who transferred under Augustus to the left bank of the Rhine, and of the Nemetes and Vangiones who were integrated into the empire in the reign of Claudius at the latest. Their old homes beyond the frontier on the right bank of the Rhine appear to have been taken over by Elbe Germanic groups whose names we do not know.

The Upper Rhine in contrast to the Lower Rhine clearly represents a single settlement zone which has its western border in the Vosges and its eastern on the Black Forest ridge. As a result, from Augustus' day the Rhine was not conceived as a frontier, but was constantly being crossed by troops and controlled civilians. That continued to be true until the definitive establishment of Roman government in the Agri Decumates, that is the area between the Rhine and the Upper German *limes*. Here, groups of settlers filtered in, but they were evidently not politically organized; Tacitus, amongst others, assures us of that.[35]

The frontier situation in the two German provinces was characterized by and large by an effective Roman border control and good trading contacts with the Germans on the right bank of the Rhine. At the same time there was an absence of any strong Roman pressure for a thoroughgoing Romanization. The framework of native society in the Germanies was comparatively strong. The impact of Romanization on them, however, was very weak: in default of that, control was maintained by the iron grip of a large concentration of Roman forces along the whole riverbank. After the death of Nero both German military zones were the stage for a three-year drama, an internal upheaval which

---

[32] Tac. *Ann.* XI.19.   [33] Tac. *Ann.* XIII.56.2.   [34] Baatz and Herrmann 1982 (E 569) 53.
[35] Tac. *Hist.* IV.32, 37, 67.

was supported by right-bank interests and is known by the name of the Batavian revolt.

The revolt demonstrates the surprising talents of the native leaders among the nobility of the left-bank tribes, from the Cananefates to the Lingones. They looked to their own special interests and those of their respective followers, often with great adroitness, and so far as the Batavian ringleader Iulius Civilis is concerned, perhaps also with some political success. This shows that either Rome did not succeed in suppressing, or the military leadership on the Rhine did not choose to suppress, or neutralize, the political gifts and instincts of the rich Rhenish nobility. There can be no question but that the interests of the left-bank tribal nobility lay in the maintenance of imperial unity, though Tacitus felt able to declare the revolt to be a 'bellum externum' in view of the particular form of the treaty arrangement between Rome and the Batavians.[36] So it may be seen that Romanization was making good progress among the aristocracy, at least after the reigns of Claudius and Nero. The strong Mediterranean element in the culture of the military rested like a thick blanket over every archaeologically tangible expression of the indigenous substratum. In the course of the second century, however, the army took on a strongly Gallic character and this period affords us our first uninterrupted view of a Germanic and Gallo-Roman civil population.

[36] Tac. *Hist.* IV.22.

CHAPTER 13*g*

RAETIA

H. WOLFF

At first glance it is an astonishing fact that Rome did not conquer the Alpine region and the southern German foothills of the Alps before 15 B.C., although she had already seized power over northern Italy more than 200 years before. This was, however, perfectly in accord with the Roman conception of security and foreign policy: principally it required reaction to military threats, which could manifest themselves either in hostile attacks on Rome or on her allies and would thus provoke a military crisis, or simply in the form of a mere display of power by an alien nation, that is one which only potentially jeopardized Roman security interests. As a rule, Rome did not take the initiative in attempting to obtain possession of specific areas as a consequence of internal policy decisions, although exceptions occur with increasing frequency during the late Republic. As a matter of fact, there was no important power in the region of the Alps and their northern foothills on which Roman foreign policy might focus. Apart from raids by small bands, which could radiate from the prehistoric tribal world at any time and in any place, the Alpine tribes had never threatened northern Italy.

The peoples of the Alps were dissipated into a multitude of smaller tribes or valley dwellers, who were in fact partly interconnected by linguistic and cultural bonds, although not by significant socio-political ties. No larger tribal agglomerations (such as a single tribal unit of all Raetians) had developed and there had been no bigger settlements of an urban type except in the Vindelician area north of the Alps. These tribes had learned literacy from the Italians, especially the Etruscans, and they used it for dedicatory, burial and building inscriptions. But this literacy was apparently not accompanied by the development of a system of administration.

Rome had at least conquered some of the valleys to the south of the Alps during the first century B.C. Particularly noteworthy is the growth of Tridentum, a *municipium Iulium*, which underwent significant development under Caesar or Augustus at the latest; the latter had an important building erected here, possibly in 23 B.C. Between the Lex Pompeia of the years 89–87 B.C. and Augustus, even the Anauni, Sinduni and

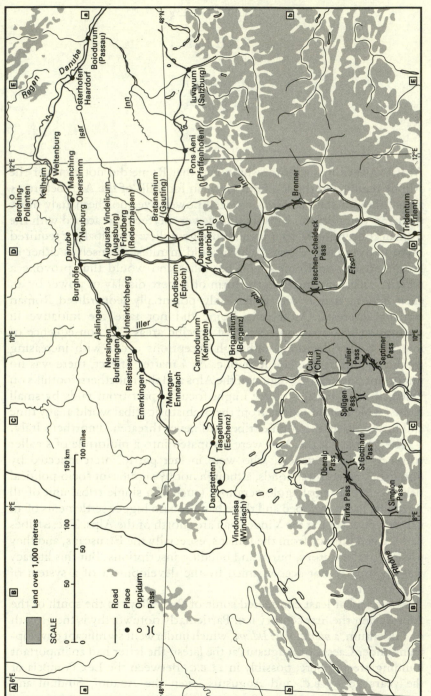

Map 10. Raetia.

Tulliassi, who lived in the western side-valleys of the Adige (Etsch), had been attached to the 'town' by *adtributio*.[1] Noricum, which comprised the tribal units of the eastern Tyrol (Osttirol), Carinthia (Kärnten) and Styria (Steiermark), had never been hostile to Italian traders and had usually maintained a peaceful attitude towards Rome. On the other hand, the tribes of the Alpine foothills, for the most part probably Celtic, suffered severely from raids by German warriors from Suebian Thuringia, Brandenburg and Saxony. The *oppida* of Manching, Kehlheim and Passau as well as the open settlement of Berching-Pollanten (situated north of Ingolstadt) had, according to the recently established chronology, undoubtedly been destroyed by those bands in about 50–40 B.C.

In 15 B.C. Rome's interests in the central Alps and the Alpine foothills were only indirect. This was a consequence of the change in policy concerning Germany east of the Rhine – a redefinition which had primarily been caused by the defeat of M. Lollius: in order to deny the Germans the possibility of escaping southwards to Italy when attacked, Rome had to control the central Alps and their foothills. In contrast, the attacks of the 'Kammunioi' (Camunni) and the 'Vennioi' on the one hand and of some Noricans and Pannonians further in the east on the other (countered by P. Silius Nerva as proconsul of Illyria in 16 B.C. and avenged with the subjugation of the three Alpine peoples)[2] had probably played only a peripheral role of specious justification for the campaign of 15 B.C.; this gave Tiberius and Drusus, the two stepsons of Augustus, the opportunity of winning military glory cheaply and easily.

I. 'RAETIA' BEFORE CLAUDIUS

The military details of the campaign of conquest in 15 B.C. are fiercely disputed in scholarly literature and cannot at present be conclusively elucidated with the evidence available. The principal difficulty is that the order of the defeated tribes as listed in the only detailed source, the inscription of the Tropaeum Alpium at La Turbie (near Monaco),[3] cannot be definitively interpreted, because in too many cases the precise location of the tribal unit is unknown. From the evidence of Cassius Dio, Horace and other authors[4] it is nevertheless possible to reconstruct at least some essential features of the Roman action, which, because of the geographical conditions in the Alps, must have consisted of several independent and well-co-ordinated operations. Drusus and the main body of his forces attacked advancing from the Adige valley, where he

[1] Iulia Tridentum in *AE* 1984, 707; building: *ILS* 86; on the Anauni-edict (*ILS* 206) cf. Th. Mommsen, *Gesammelte Schriften* 4 (Berlin, 1906) 291–311; E. Frézouls, *Ktema* 6 (1981) 239–52, esp. 243. [2] Dio LIV. 20.1–2. [3] Pliny, *HN* III.136f; *CIL* v 7817 = EJ² 40.

[4] Dio LIV.22; Hor. *Carm.* IV.4; IV.14; Strab. IV. 6.8 (206C); VII.1.5 (292C); Vell. Pat. II.95.1f.

fought the first major battle up-river from Trento. From there he moved forward into the valley of the Inn, certainly using the Reschenscheideck as well as the Brenner Pass. Possibly one of his subordinate commanders penetrated into the Alpine Rhine valley over the Splügen Pass or the Maloja-Julier from Lake Como. A little later, Tiberius advanced by an unknown route, on which he had to face Raetians of the interior Alpine region, towards other hostile tribes, against whom he is assumed to have fought at Lake Constance and elsewhere. In a day's march from Lake Constance he is supposed to have reached the headwaters of the Danube (whatever is meant by this). On 1 August, the anniversary of the capture of Alexandria,[5] the two brothers defeated the remaining enemies in a major battle. These might have been the Vindelicians and other tribes of the Alpine foothills, of whom, if we may believe Strabo,[6] the Rukantioi (Runicates?) and the Kotuantioi (Cosuanetes?) belonged to the Raetian language-group. Of the tribes of adjacent Noricum, the Ambisontes were subdued by Drusus, possibly in the Salzach valley. Thus, in the course of a single summer's campaign Roman arms reached their target, and the two stepsons were able to bring the laurel of victory to Augustus in Gaul – giving Horace sufficient reason to praise the three of them to the skies. After that war we know of no anti-Roman revolts. The Alpine peoples wisely bowed to the superior power of Rome.

The most important political result of the campaign was the establishment of Rome's military presence in the northern Alpine foothills. For a few years – at most from about 15/14 B.C. to 8 B.C. – the greater part of a legion, probably the Nineteenth which later perished with Varus in the Teutoburg Forest (Wiehengebirge), was moved, together with auxiliary troops, to Dangstetten on the northern bank of the upper Rhine (opposite Tenedo/Zurzach). Further, a line of communication running along the Limmat, the Zürichsee and the Walensee to the Alpine Rhine valley was secured with several watch-towers. After the death of Drusus Dangstetten was abandoned and at the same time – an important weapons site (Oberhausen, now part of the city of Augsburg) was founded at the confluence of the Wertach and the Lech. It existed until about A.D. 9 (or perhaps even A.D. 14–17) and should perhaps be explained in connexion with the recently discovered legionary fortress of Marktbreit-upon-Main. The Alpine foothills and the southern German region in general, however, were apparently not an important base for the attempted pacification of free Germany. The insignificant amount of military precaution in evidence seems more likely to have been intended for flank defence, a role which was assigned to the Upper German army. Surprisingly, the eastern part of the Bavarian Alpine foothills, especially the region where the river Inn flows out into the diluvial hilly country,

---

[5] Hor. *Carm.* iv.14.34ff; Vell. Pat. ii.95.2.   [6] iv.6.8 (206C).

remained unnoticed (just as the northern part of Noricum received no attention in the Augustan period): for unknown reasons, the Suebi and other German bands seem even in the Caesarean and Augustan periods to have been more attracted by the region now called Suebia.

As regards the imposition of an administration, the organization of newly annexed areas proceeded slowly and hesitantly during the first two generations after the conquest. In this respect Raetia can again be compared to Noricum: for the period of legionary occupation, we have evidence for a *legatus pro [pr(aetore) i]n Vindol(icis)* together with his subordinate native prefect of the *cohors Trumplinorum*.[7] From the reign of Augustus (before A.D. 2) we probably have evidence of a former equestrian officer as *procurator Caesaris Augusti in Vindalicis et Raetis et in valle Poenina per annos IIII* ('procurator of Caesar Augustus in Vindelicia and Raetia and the Poenine Valley for four years').[8] To approximately the same social rank belonged a former *primipilus* of the lower German *legio XXI Rapax*, who discharged his duties in the central region of the Alps early in the reign of Tiberius as *pra[ef(ectus)] Raetis Vindolicis valli[s P]oeninae et levis armatur(ae)* ('prefect of the Raetians and the Vindelicians and the Poenine Valley and the light-armed auxiliaries').[9] Thus the central Alpine region apparently had no provincial governor before Claudius and still seems not fully to have been a province at that time: with the exception of the receipt of tribute,[10] which the tribes paid peaceably from 15/14 B.C., and the military supervision of light auxiliary troops including the native militia (*levis armatura*),[11] no obviously major administrative tasks or positions were created. So the title of the Roman representative might have alternated between *procurator* and *praefectus*, probably depending on the individual officer's previous career. We certainly should not expect that the later area of the province of Raetia at this time possessed clearly drawn borders with the German military command, with the external tribes and with what was to become the province of Noricum. Only on the border with Italy do we have to take into account a definitive territorial delimitation, because in this region the territories attached to the *coloniae* and *municipia* by *adtributio* must have been clearly defined; but even here the Claudian edict on the Anauni counsels caution.[12] The large federated *civitas* of the Helvetii, the small tribes of their former entourage (the Latobriges, Rauraci and Tulingi) and the two colonies of their former areas, certainly belonged to the administration of Gaul, whereas the Norican tribes in some way remained in their own *regnum*. Before the comprehensive organization of

---

[7] *CIL* v 4910 = *ILS* 847 = EJ² 241.   [8] *ILS* 9007 = EJ² 224.

[9] *CIL* IX 3044 = *ILS* 2689 = EJ² 244.   [10] Strab. IV.6.9 (206C).

[11] If the *castellum Ircavium* was situated in the area of the province of Raetia as it was later defined, *CIL* XIII 1041 = *ILS* 2531 would attest such a unit of militia, the *gaesati DC Raeti*.

[12] *ILS* 206 = GCN 368.

the western Alps, therefore, the most sensible solution was to join the Valais (*vallis Poenina*) to the central Alpine region.

For military reasons the central Alpine region urgently needed roads. Drusus had already marked out the later Via Claudia Augusta from the Po to the Danube. This might similarly have been the case for the roads over the Splügen or Julier Passes. Even the road leading from Bregenz through Kempten, Epfach and Gauting and finally to Iuvavum/Salzburg, belongs to those early years. Whatever the details, according to Strabo at any rate,[13] Augustus was responsible for fundamental improvements to the Alpine roads and the passes.

Continuity of occupation by the pre-Roman population cannot be demonstrated in the archaeological record. But Cassius Dio[14] specifically tells us that the conquered area was highly populous and that Rome for that reason recruited most of the young men into auxiliary formations and posted them out of the region, leaving only sufficient manpower for agricultural work. Amongst other tasks they fought under Germanicus against the Germans. In contrast, Rome seems to have shown great restraint in reforming the civil institutions of the tribal units. Nor did she attempt to promote the legal or socio-cultural Romanization of the Raetians and the Celts. There is no foundation of colonies, and even the construction of urban centres for the established tribes progressed only slowly. Not until the second decade after the conquest do archaeological discoveries attest the beginnings of urban settlements. As far as we can see, these were not developments of pre-Roman settlements, and the artefacts which have come to light give the impression of the presence of Roman manual workers and traders, who seem newly to have immigrated from the Mediterranean. These settlements are mostly situated on the northern side of the Alps: Chur (Curia), Bregenz (Brigantium), Kempten (Cambodunum), Auerberg (probably Damasia), Epfach (Abodiacum), Augsburg (Augusta Vindelicum) and Gauting (Bratananium). Brigantium, Cambodunum and Damasia had, according to Strabo,[15] been the *poleis* of the Brigantii, Estiones and the Licates. But Cambodunum alone seems to have been planned in the Roman manner, whereas the thriving 'town' on the Auerberg, lasting only one generation, had actually been situated, astonishingly, at the altitude of 1,000m. The contribution of the military seems to have been small: only in Bregenz and in Rederzhausen near Augsburg have fortresses of the Tiberian period been found, whereas the other sites have yielded military equipment merely in the form of scattered finds; here, however, we have to allow for the possibility that these were merely locations for the manufacture or repair of military implements. If that were so, the central Alpine foothills and the mountains would hardly have been controlled at

---

[13] IV.6.6 (204C).   [14] LIV.22.5.   [15] IV.6.8 (206C).

all during the reign of Tiberius by Roman occupying forces – the closest military force was the legion which was stationed in the fortress of Vindonissa/Windisch after A.D. 16/17. Nor do we know of any new settlements in the Augustan–Tiberian period in the Inn valley, the upper Adige valley, the eastern part of the later province of Raetia, or along the Danube. In the early imperial period the centre of Raetia lay in Suebia.

From the economic and fiscal point of view, what was to be the province of Raetia was not enticing – apart from a certain strategic importance for the German campaigns this area was apparently of no genuine worth to Rome.

II. THE CLAUDIAN PROVINCE

It was probably Claudius who abandoned Rome's reservations with regard to the Alpine region, assuming that we refuse to credit Caligula (who is supposed to have planned to build a city high up in the mountains)[16] with such a degree of practicality and astuteness. One reason for the change in Roman attitudes may have been the more advanced state of development in Upper Germany and Pannonia, which gave an increased importance to the communication lines on and along the Danube. By now a massive dislocation of auxiliary units along the Danube had taken place and it was probably more logical to place the Raetian units under their own provincial governor. An attempt to improve the organization of the administrative machinery fits our general impression of the emperor Claudius and his interests.

Claudius sent an equestrian procurator to Raetia and Vindelicia. Because the troops which this official had under his command at this early stage included Roman citizens (at that time at least the *cohors I civium Romanorum ingenuorum*), the first known praesidial procurator (*procur(ator) Augustor(um)*) held the additional title of *pro leg(ato) provinciai Raitiai et Vindelic(iai) et vallis Poenin(ai)*.[17] He had his residence presumably in Kempten, not yet in Augsburg which at that time was only slowly developing into a 'town'. Under Claudius the Valais (*vallis Poenina*) probably remained separate from 'Raetia et Vindelicia' and was united with the Alpes Graiae as another procuratorial province. It was at this time, at the very latest, that the border was defined. In the north it followed the Danube, in the east the Inn, before turning to the south, soon after entering the Alps, and then making a final bend to the west, south of the Puster valley. The southern border with Italy ran for the most part along the heights of the Alpine watershed, but it included in Raetia the upper Isarco and Adige valleys up to Klausen and Merano, as well as the Tessine up to Bellinzona. The western border with Gallia Belgica and Upper Germany ran from St Gotthard to Mt Todi and Mt

---

[16] Suet. *Calig.* 21. [17] *CIL* v 3936 = *ILS* 1348.

Glärnisch, passing between Zürichsee and Walensee to the north, then crossing the Rhine west of Tasgetium (Eschenz) and finally reaching the Danube east of Tuttlingen.[18]

The fortifications along the Danube were possibly first created at the end of the 30s A.D., even before the formal establishment of the province; in that case, the legion stationed at Vindonissa was probably in charge of this construction, because the line of fortresses had the function of safeguarding its right flank. The fortress of Aislingen together with the two small fortresses of Nersingen and Burlafingen are the earliest camps on the Danube so far known, dating back to late Tiberian times. Not very much later, in about A.D. 40, or between 40 and 50, the entire chain of fortresses from Emerkingen to Oberstimm (perhaps even as far as Weltenburg) was built. But again we have no evidence of camps in the interior Alpine region, which suggests that Roman rule was not threatened by internal unrest. Together with the camps, in whose surroundings soon civilian settlements (*vici*) developed, the roads which had earlier been delineated were upgraded and strengthened. This, in fact is attested only for the Via Claudia Augusta[19] in 46, but, because a corresponding need existed, it is reasonable to hypothesise the same development for the other south–north and west–east connexions, as far as and along the Danube.

The most important issue for our understanding of the civil administration is the question of how long the tribal units (*civitates*), which survived from pre-Roman times, continued in existence. This seems to be of fundamental importance, because there was no Roman 'town' in the province except the later, Hadrianic *municipium Aelium Augusta Vindelicum* and, apart from the *civitas Curia* and the *civitates* which are assumed to have existed around Brigantium and Cambodunum, no other local towns of peregrine status are attested; Curia, Brigantium and Cambodunum at least (as well as Augusta, later on) developed an urban character of a kind during the first century. To judge from the stated *origines* of soldiers, the Runicates, the Catenates and recently the Licates, seem to be attested as regional administrative bodies for the second half of the first century A.D. or even the second century A.D.[20] Further the Breones, whom Strabo claims to have been Illyrians, are still attested as a political unit in the sixth century.[21] This justifies the belief that a comparatively large number of pre-Roman *civitates* continued to exist as

---

[18] Many of the precise details of the route are open to dispute. Since its course had to be traced in a variety of sources covering the entire Roman period (some as late as the sixth century A.D.), it is impossible, except in the case of the frontier with the external tribes, to specify precisely what changes in the position of the borders may have occurred from time to time.

[19] *CIL* v 8002–3 (cf. *ILS* 208).

[20] Licates: *RMD* 119; *AE* 1988, 905. Runicates: *AE* 1940, 114. Catenates: *AE* 1935, 103.

[21] Cf. Heuberger 1932 (E 621) 149–67. Strab. IV.6.8 (206C).

local units and to deal with the local administration of their own citizenry even as late as the middle Empire.[22] Most of them obviously did not develop urban centres and perhaps for that reason have left no inscriptions. It is consequently impossible to locate all of these tribes accurately; we may only argue with some degree of probability that those of the Licates who were not absorbed by the *municipium Augusta Vindelicum* had settled on the upper Lech not far away from the Alps. With the end of the settlement on the Auerberg *c.* A.D. 40, Abodiacum (Epfach) may eventually have gained the position of capital of the Licates. The remainder of the tribes of the Alpine foothills listed on the Tropaeum Alpium or mentioned by Strabo and Ptolemy probably lived near the principal chain of the Alps, thus possibly leaving the northern part of Lower Bavaria to a large extent unpopulated during the early first century A.D.

The Illyrian customs stations (*publicum portorium Illyrici*) in Passau (Boiodurum) and Pfaffenhofen (Pons Aeni) were certainly established in the reign of Claudius. Further detailed information for early Raetian economic and social history is not available, however, because the native population which certainly existed and which had mainly been an agricultural one, scarcely appears in our sources. In the attested settlements, which were about to take on some characteristics of urban centres, craft and trade certainly predominated. We hear but little of an upper stratum; especially noteworthy is the family of Claudius Paternus Clementianus from the vicinity of Epfach, whose parents received the Roman citizenship from Claudius (or possibly Nero) and who himself rose to procuratorships under Trajan or Hadrian.[23] For whatever reasons, we again have no evidence from the Alpine region and eastern Raetia for this social stratum.

Similarly we know scarcely anything of the political history of the province. In A.D. 14 the Suebi are supposed to have threatened the Alpine foothills and veterans of the rebellious German army were therefore sent against them.[24] In the year 69 the province was inevitably dragged into the struggles for power between Otho, Vitellius and Vespasian. The decision of the Raetian troops in favour of Vitellius and the Norican troops in favour of Otho and Vespasian was connected with the respective commitment of the German and Pannonian armies: until long into the second century the orientation of Raetia was to the West. For that reason in 69 the Raetian troops, including the local militia of the province, were instructed to attack the rebellious Helvetians[25] and were probably then removed to Italy. Later the Raetian and Norican troops found themselves facing each other across the Inn, though without

---

[22] For another possible solution see Wolff 1986 (E 643) 166f.
[23] Pflaum 1960 (D 59) 150 *bis* (61).   [24] Tac. *Ann.* 1.44.4.   [25] Tac. *Hist.* 1.67.2; 68.1–2.

coming to blows.[26] And after Vespasian's victory, when the Norican troops were moved to be deployed in the area of the Batavian revolt,[27] they may have destroyed the hostile Raetian camps as well as Augsburg, Kempten and Bregenz. At least, that is one conclusion which scholars have drawn from the existence of destruction levels at these sites. The reality may have been much more complicated but such uncertainty is characteristic of the politically marginal situation of this province, of which the historiographic tradition tells us hardly anything, except incidentally.

[26] Tac. *Hist.* III.5.2. [27] Tac. *Hist.* IV.70.2.

CHAPTER 13*h*

THE DANUBIAN AND BALKAN PROVINCES

J. J. WILKES

I. THE ADVANCE TO THE DANUBE AND BEYOND, 43 B.C.–A.D. 6

'Magnum est stare in Danubii ripa' proclaimed the Younger Pliny to the emperor Trajan. An approach to the river, either dilated in the plains or surging awesomely in one of its several gorges, rarely fails to stir the imagination. The river Danube figures in some of Europe's oldest myths, some from remote prehistory, such as the tale of the returning Argonauts sailing upstream from the Black Sea to the Adriatic. Throughout history conquerors and their armies have exulted at gaining the river, though perhaps none more emphatically than the emperor Augustus who boasted in his *Res Gestae* of the advance, achieved by his stepson and legate Tiberius Nero, of the boundaries of Illyricum to the bank of the Danube. Not until the middle course of the Danube had been secured could Rome hold and exploit the overland route between Italy and her eastern territories.[1] That remains today the principal land route

[1] Greek and Latin authors and inscriptions on stone are the principal sources for the Danube lands in the Julio-Claudian era. For the narrative of conquest Appian's lengthy description of the campaigns of 35–33 B.C., *Ill.* XIV–XXVIII, is based directly on a memoir composed by Octavian. Velleius Paterculus' account, II.110–16, of the Pannonian uprising of A.D. 6–9 drew on his experiences as an officer on the staff of Tiberius for a part of that period, although his promised full-scale account of the conquest of Dalmatians and Pannonians (II.96.3) was, it appears, never completed. Save for a full description of the Danube campaigns of Licinius Crassus in 29–28 B.C., LI.23.2–27, the *Roman History* of Cassius Dio furnishes little more than occasional summaries, often with the events of several years compressed into a few sentences, for example under 16 B.C., LIV.20.1–3. The *Lives* of Suetonius, the *Epitome* of Livy's *History*, along with the works of later compilers such as Florus, Rufius Festus and Orosius, can furnish significant detail although, in the case of the latter, are just as likely to import confusion. For some periods the written record is seriously deficient, above all for the years 9 B.C. to A.D. 4, where some folios are missing from the MS of Cassius Dio while Velleius was not disposed to discuss military activities when his hero Tiberius was off the scene. From the accession of Tiberius the *Annals* of Tacitus provide valuable accounts of affairs in Thrace and among the Suebic Germans north of Pannonia, while the *Histories* record the Sarmatian attacks on Moesia during A.D. 69. Finally two contemporary writers also contribute to the record, albeit in a rather different manner. From his bleak exile in Tomis the poet Ovid furnishes a picture of life close to the lower Danube. The geographer Strabo provides valuable accounts of the indigenous population of the area, their history, habits and economy, in the course of which are many valuable references to recent Roman campaigns.

The evidence from inscriptions increases towards the end of the period. There is little for the wars of Augustus, save for passages in the *Res Gestae* and a few texts relating to the activities of his legates, for example *ILS* 918 and 8956. By the period of Claudius the numbers of military epitaphs in

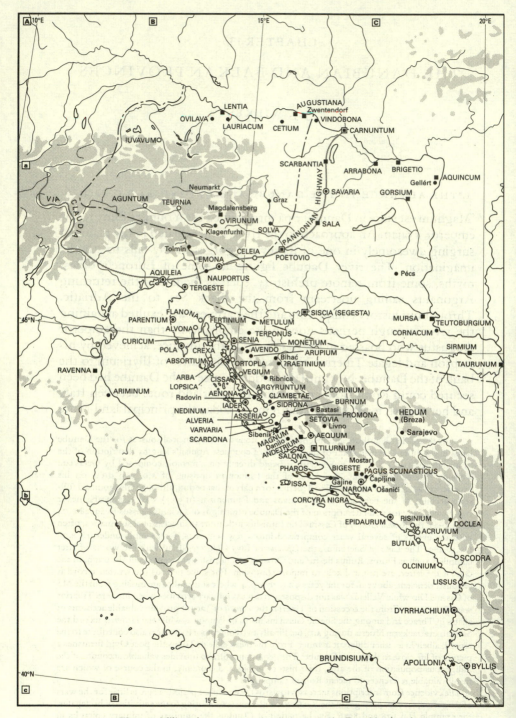

Map 11. Military bases, cities and settlements in the Danubian provinces.

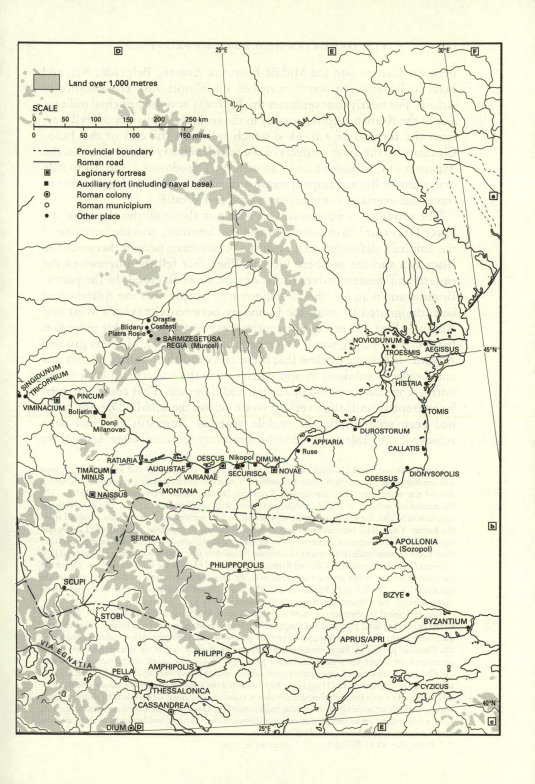

Oraştie
Blidaru · Costeşti
Piatra Rosie
· SARMIZEGETUSA
REGIA (Muncel)

NOVIODUNUM
TROESMIS AEGISSUS

SINGIDUNUM
TRICORNIUM

PINCUM

VIMINACIUM
Boljetin

Donji
Milanovac

HISTRIA

TOMIS

RATIARIA
OESCUS Nikopol DIMUM
TIMACUM   AUGUSTAE   SECURISCA   Ruse
MINUS   VARIANAE   NOVAE
NAISSUS   MONTANA

APPIARIA

DUROSTORUM

CALLATIS

ODESSUS

DIONYSOPOLIS

SERDICA

APOLLONIA
(Sozopol)

PHILIPPOPOLIS

SCUPI

BIZYE

STOBI

BYZANTIUM

VIA EGNATIA

APRUS/APRI

PELLA
PHILIPPI
AMPHIPOLIS

THESSALONICA

CASSANDREA

CYZICUS

DIUM

between Europe and the Middle East, via Zagreb, Belgrade, Niš, and Sofia to Istanbul, or south from Niš via Skopje and Thessalonica to Athens. For nearly four centuries this highway was the principal military axis of the Roman empire, notably in the recurrent episodes of civil war, from the turmoil of A.D. 68–9 which followed the end of the Julio-Claudians to the great conflicts of the fourth century which troubled the dynasties of Constantine and Valentinian. Theodosius I, the last to rule over a united Roman empire, was in A.D. 394 the last reigning emperor to travel the overland route between East and West.[2]

The province of Pannonia, and within it above all the region of the lower Drava and Sava around Mursa and Sirmium, was the keystone of the empire's defensive arch against the northern peoples between the Black Sea and the northern Ocean. When that fell the interests of the eastern and western halves of the empire soon diverged. In the pact at Brundisium in 40 B.C. the Illyrian town of Scodra near the Adriatic had been designated to mark the boundary between Octavian's West and Antony's East.[3] In reality the frontier was the near impassable mountain barrier of the north–south watershed through Bosnia, Montenegro and Albania. It became evident that these areas and their sturdy inhabitants could only be subdued by approaches from the encircling plains to the north, from the direction of Zagreb and Belgrade. That could not even be attempted until the overland route across the middle Danube basin had been secured. By the middle years of Augustus this had been achieved, a notable success for the new army recruited after Actium. Its

Noricum, Pannonia and Dalmatia, are sufficient to indicate the identities and locations of legions and auxiliary units, while the military production of stamped bricks and tiles appears to commence around the same time. The inscriptions from the Danube lands were first assembled by Th. Mommsen for volume III of *CIL*, published in 1873 with supplements in 1902. This is now being supplemented and, for some provinces, superseded, by new collections. Inscriptions recorded from the former Yugoslavia between 1902 and 1970 are collected in the three volumes of *ILIug*, while those from Moesia Superior are currently being entirely republished (*IMS*). It is to be regretted that most of the modern collections tend to be defined by modern frontiers, for example Hungary (*RIU*), Bulgaria (*IGBulg*), Greece (*ILGR*) and Romania (*IDR* and *ISM*). In the matter of coin evidence the presence of Roman issues among the hoards from the Danube lands is now well documented, as are the local Celtic, Dacian and Thracian issues. The function and significance of the latter have been much debated; for a recent discussion see Crawford 1985 (B 320) 219–39.

Archaeological investigations, most undertaken since the Second World War, have furnished evidence for the plans, principal buildings and adjoining cemeteries of several Roman cities, though many important discoveries have yet to be fully recorded and published. Many military sites along the Danube have also been examined, although the earliest levels of occupation are rarely penetrated. In recent years there has been a great deal of valuable work on the classification and distribution of important Roman pottery, including amphorae and *terra sigillata* table-ware, notably in the former Yugoslavia and Hungary, which has aided the location of garrisons and settlements of this period. As a rule the archaeological evidence consists of imports or products of Roman origin which owe little or nothing to indigenous traditions of the Danube lands. For many areas this seems to be a true reflection of the state of relations between the invaders, soldiers and settlers, and the native peoples throughout the Julio-Claudian era.

[2] Pliny, *Pan.* 18.1; *RG* 30.1.   [3] App. *BCiv.* v.65.

strategic value was to be amply demonstrated when it held firm, though only just, during the rebellion of Pannonia in A.D. 6–9. While the deeds of Drusus, Germanicus and Arminius stirred the imagination of poets and panegyricists the truth was that in the reckoning Germany beyond the Rhine was expendable and was finally discarded in A.D. 15/16. Not so Illyricum and the Danube.

The Balkans witnessed the death-agony of the Roman Republic in the aftermath of Caesar's murder. The Senate granted command in Illyricum, Macedonia and Achaea, to Brutus, who delegated his authority to Q. Hortensius Hortalus, proconsul in Macedonia. Caesar's former lieutenant P. Vatinius ended his operations against the Delmatae around Narona and returned to Rome, where he celebrated an Illyrian triumph on 31 July 42 B.C. The republicans found allies among Illyrians and Thracians, although a rash attempt to march from northern Italy to Macedonia by Decimus Brutus met its inevitable end among the Iapodes. The pact at Brundisium in September 40 B.C. left Illyricum under Octavian and Macedonia under Antony. The latter ordered attacks on the Illyrian Parthini, the allies of Brutus, and the Dardani, a perpetual menace to Macedonia. For victories over the Parthini a triumph was awarded to Asinius Pollio but neither the commander nor the outcome of Antony's *Bellum Dardanicum* happen to be on record and may indeed have been suppressed by his rival.[4]

In the domain of Octavian the expansion of Dacia under Burebista had reawakened in Italy the old fear of invasion from the north east. It was no accident that the reported schemes of Philip V of Macedon to direct the ferocious Bastarnae overland against Italy figured prominently in the history of Livy, a native of Patavium. Burebista was now dead and his realm divided between four or five rulers, most no more than shadows in the historical record, Comoiscus, Coson, Cotiso and Dicomes, the first three ruling in south-west Dacia, the last in the south east. The triumvir's belated victory over Sextus Pompeius at Naulochus on 3 September 36 B.C. was acclaimed far away among Roman settlers in Illyricum[5] but it was not to be long before that region became the scene of Roman campaigning. Caesar's heir devoted two full seasons of operations against peoples beyond the Adriatic (see p. 172), though for reasons largely unconnected with affairs in that quarter. In 35 B.C. a march

---

[4] Ancient sources relating to Roman commanders are collected in *MRR* vol. II (down to 30 B.C.), in *PIR²* which has currently reached the letter O and also in the *Laterculi Praesidum* compiled by Thomasson 1975–84 (D 110). The siege equipment captured from D. Brutus in 43 B.C., Dio XLVI.53.2, was used eight years later by the Iapodes against Octavian, App. *Ill.* XVIII. Before his operations against the Parthini, Asinius Pollio may have attacked the Delmatae and seized Salona, but the sources are late and confused. Some have rejected the story, e.g. Syme 1979 (A 94) I 18–30, while others have accepted it, Bosworth 1972 (C 34) 464–8. Antony's attack on the Dardani is noted in App. *BCiv.* v.75.   [5] *CIL* III 14265: 'Sicilia recepta'.

through the Iapodes and Pannonians left a garrison of twenty-five cohorts at Siscia. There was some talk of an advance against the Dacians, and this may have been the occasion of a reported contact with Cotiso, which provoked Antony's subsequent alliance with Dicomes. In the next year the Delmatae were attacked and some hard fighting in the valleys and forests behind Salona won a capitulation and return of the standards captured from Caesar's luckless general A. Gabinius at Synodion in 48 B.C., though not before a winter blockade in 34/3 B.C. maintained by one of Caesar's leading field commanders. The register of surrendered peoples suggests that the entire coast and hinterland between Istria and Macedonia were now in Roman hands, though no advance had yet been made against the Pannonian peoples across the mountains, in the valleys of Bosnia, the Drava and the Sava.

For nearly twenty years following victory over the Delmatae, which furnished Octavian with the first instalment of his triple triumph on 13 August 29 B.C., almost nothing is reported of events in the Danube lands. The exception is Dio's unusually full record of the campaigns in 29 and 28 B.C. by M. Crassus, proconsul in Macedonia with an army of four legions. The first season saw victory over the Bastarnae near the Danube at the river Ciabrus (Cibrica), in which the proconsul killed King Deldo in personal combat. A triumph was decreed, though the title *imperator* was denied. Moreover, there are grounds for suspecting that Crassus' true achievement was a victory over the Dacians but that the record was later distorted to avoid embarrassing Octavian. The next year saw action in the northern Dobrudja which led to the recapture of Roman standards seized by the Bastarnae more than thirty years before from C. Antonius, Cicero's disreputable colleague in the consulship of 63 B.C. Back in Rome Crassus triumphed 'over Thrace and the Getae' on 4 July 27 B.C. but there was no display of recaptured standards, and a claim for the immensely prestigious *spolia opima* for his killing of the king was denied on a constitutional technicality.[6]

During this period the troubled affairs of the kingdom of Thrace drew Roman armies more than once into the area, a recurring pattern being conflict between the Odrysae of the more settled east and the powerful Bessi of the mountainous west. Though the Sapaean Rhoemetalces (I) may have gained sole power in Thrace for his desertion of Antony before Actium, he was to prove an effective ruler, whose long and prosperous reign is reflected in a silver coinage minted to the standard of Roman

[6] Dio LI. 23.2–27; cf. *PIR*[2] L 186, with Mócsy 1966 (C 289) 511. The Dacian prisoners who fought with Germans in the arena at Rome a few days after Octavian's triumph, Dio LI.22.6–9, may have been supplied by Crassus' victory over the army of Cotiso, Hor. *Carm.* III.8. On the affair of the *spolia opima* see Syme 1939 (A 93) 308–9.

denarii.[7] The affair of M. Primus, the governor of Macedonia accused of making war against the Odrysae, reported by Cassius Dio under 22 B.C., remains no less obscure in its Balkan context than it is in politics at Rome. We are on firmer ground with the activities of the consular M. Lollius, whose intervention on behalf of Rhoemetalces, perhaps in 19/18 B.C., may have been the occasion for the transfer of the Macedonian army to the new command of 'Thrace and Macedonia'. Lollius' successor may have been L. Tarius Rufus, the consul of 16 B.C., who fought with the Sarmatians, the first reported collision with these Iranian horsemen.[8] The Balkan command may also have been entrusted to Tiberius following his Alpine campaign in 15 B.C., for operations which brought the Scordisci around Sirmium into a Roman alliance that was to prove crucial in the subsequent conquest of the Pannonians. It is possible that the engagement of the Balkan armies in the far north west caused the task of crushing a major uprising by the Thracian Bessi to be assigned to L. Piso with an army from the East. The bloody Thracian war lasted three years, probably 12–10 B.C., during which the Romans recovered from defeat to gain a victory which rewarded the commander with triumphal honours.

Illyricum, not among the territories assigned to Caesar Augustus in 27 B.C., will presumably have been administered by proconsuls, though none happens to be recorded. Dio's summary of recent events under 16 B.C. refers to the operations of P. Silius Nerva against peoples of the eastern Alps, in the course of which his legates repelled an attack on Istria by Noricans and Pannonians. The province of Silius was not, it seems, Illyricum but rather Transpadana which included Istria and Liburnia. In the same passage Dio refers to an uprising in Dalmatia that was soon dealt with, presumably by a proconsul. The overland connexion between Italy and the Balkans was achieved by Tiberius in the *Bellum Pannonicum* (see p. 175–6) when, building on the achievements of M. Vinicius and M. Agrippa in 14–13 B.C., he overcame the Breuci of the Sava valley with help from the Scordisci in 12 B.C. Four more seasons of warfare, under Tiberius in 11–9 B.C. and Sextus Appuleius in 8 B.C., completed the conquest south of the Drava and advanced the boundary of Illyricum to the Danube. The defeated Pannonians were disarmed and the young men of military age deported to the slave markets of Italy. A triumph was voted to the general but only the honour was permitted. Thus, according to a contemporary, was ended a 'rebellion of the

---

[7] On the identities and relationships of the rulers of Thrace, see Sullivan 1979 (E 698). The numbering of rulers follows that in the entries of U. Kahrstedt in *RE*, IA, 255–7, 1003–4.

[8] Dio LIV.20.3. The reading of an inscription recording construction of a bridge over the Strymon at Amphipolis, *AE* 1936, 18 = *ILGR* 230, is not sufficiently clear to determine whether Tarius Rufus was proconsul or legate.

Dalmatians' that had lasted for more than 220 years, reckoning, that is, from Rome's first Illyrian war in 229 B.C.[9]

The conquest of Pannonia, along with the takeover of Noricum which evidently followed the operations of Silius (see above), brought control of the Drava and Sava valleys that enabled the Romans to dictate the fortunes of most peoples in the middle Danube basin. How that power was exploited is not reported, since the historical record for the middle years of Augustus is seriously deficient, though the Dacians come again into prominence. Late in 10 B.C. a raid across the frozen Danube had frustrated an intention to close the temple of Janus, and the Roman response may have been the operations of Cornelius Lentulus, perhaps successor to Piso in the Balkan command, against Dacians, the same group who surrendered to Crassus in 29 B.C., and their Sarmatian mercenaries. Lentulus' successor may have been the unknown general (though likely to have been M. Vinicius) whose activities beyond the lower Danube involved the Bastarnae and contacts, not necessarily hostile, with lesser peoples to the west of Dacia.[10] The scale and direction of these operations suggest considerable confidence on the part of the Romans towards their new Danubian conquests, which is also reflected in the appointment *c.* 1 B.C. of the *princeps'* eldest grandson to command 'the legions on the Ister', where 'he fought no war, not because no war broke out, but because he was learning to rule in peace and security'.[11] Though the Dacians were to prove troublesome again in A.D. 6, Augustus felt entitled to claim a major victory over them, first by the defeat of an invasion with heavy casualties, then by a counter-offensive which brought a surrender. According to Strabo, the Dacians were on the point of submitting but still held out in the hope of help from the Germans.[12] In this quarter Domitius Ahenobarbus, in the course of a march from the Danube to the Elbe in this period, settled the friendly Hermunduri on the west of the formidable Marcomanni, who themselves had recently migrated to Bohemia, where they appeared to threaten the Roman hold on the upper Danube.[13]

What is reported of the activities of Roman commanders in the Balkans implies a control of the lower Danube that may, from time to

---

[9] Dio LIV.20.3. Most have assumed the province of Silius to have been Illyricum, though nothing connects him with that region while a dedication honouring him as proconsul was erected at Aenona in Liburnia, *ILS* 899. The end of the Dalmatian 'rebellion' is noted by Vell. Pat. II.90.1.

[10] Most have accepted the identification of the [. . . . ..] CIVS on the Tusculum elogium, *ILS* 8965, with the consul of 19 B.C. Most have also taken the general's province to have been Illyricum, e.g Syme 1971 (E 702) 26–39, though the surviving text does not record that and the peoples involved point to a command on the lower Danube.   [11] Dio LV.10.17 (under 1 B.C.).

[12] *RG* 30.2, with Suet. *Aug.* 21 and Strab. VII.3.11, 13 (303–4C).

[13] Dio LV.10a.2–3 (under A.D. 1).

time, may have been extended through use of the fleet to the Black Sea. At Callatis, a Greek city of that region which had been a Roman ally for more than half a century, the praetorian legate P. Vinicius, under whom the historian Velleius Paterculus served as tribune, is named on an honorific inscription.[14] Both the Romans and their allies will have been aware of the movements of new peoples, caused by turmoil in remote Asia, westwards across the Pontic steppes and into the plains beyond the lower Danube. There had already been conflict with Sarmatians, steadily roaming westwards, on at least two occasions. Some peoples pressed up hard against Roman territory were evidently begging admission, to which a response could be postponed, though not indefinitely. Late under Augustus Strabo records that Sex. Aelius Catus allowed 50,000 Getae to cross the river and settle in Roman territory.[15]

In the mean time the later years of Augustus' Principate were marred by misfortunes, none worse than the rebellion of the Pannonians.

II. REBELLION IN ILLYRICUM AND THE ANNEXATION OF THRACE (A.D. 6–69)

When the warriors of the Daesitiates and other Pannonians had assembled in A.D. 6 for the expedition against Maroboduus they were minded instead to turn their arms against the Romans (p. 176–8). Led by Bato of the Daesitiates and Bato of the Breuci they attacked Roman settlements, the colonies on the Adriatic and even penetrated to Macedonia. Sirmium near the mouth of the Sava, the key to the middle Danube, was saved by the Balkan army and the Thracian cavalry under Rhoemetalces, while in the west the army of Illyricum held fast at Siscia. There in the following year the two armies were briefly united and were directed in concert by Tiberius until the Pannonians surrendered at the river Bathinus (Bosna?) on 3 August A.D. 8. In the next season the Pannonians between the Sava and the Adriatic, including the Daesitiates and Pirustae, were attacked until the surrender of Bato at Andetrium (Muć), near Salona in the territory of the Delmatae, brought the terrible war finally to an end. Tiberius, back in Rome at the beginning of A.D. 10, was soon called to the Rhine by the disaster of Varus and the Illyrian triumph was postponed until 23 October A.D. 12. The celebration of victory, marked by salutations as *imperator*, triumphal honours for the army commanders, and the erection of triumphal arches in Illyricum, cannot have concealed the real cost of 'the most serious of all foreign wars since the Punic', when 'ever so many legions were maintained but

[14] The Callatis treaty, *ILLRP* 516, is generally assigned to 72/1 B.C. For Vinicius at Callatis see *AE* 1960, 378 with Syme 1971 (E 702) 68–9, and 1979 (A 94) II 533.   [15] Strab. VII.3.10 (303C).

very little booty taken'.[16] Less than two years after his triumph Tiberius was again in Illyricum, though he had barely arrived when news of Augustus' final illness drew him back to Italy.

For long after the Pannonian revolt the provinces of Pannonia and Dalmatia, formed by a division of Illyricum probably in A.D. 9, were placed in the charge of senior consulars. The fighting had caused the loyalty of the legions to be strained until, on hearing news of the death of Augustus (19 August A.D. 14), the army of Pannonia mutinied. The legions demanded better and more speedy reward for what they had endured in the recent wars. Even the appearance on the scene of Drusus, the son of Tiberius, did not bring an end to the disorder until a lunar eclipse in the early hours of 27 September, followed by a break in the weather, undermined the morale of the rebels and impaired their mobility. Drusus on his return to Rome was praised for his resolute conduct, though, observes Tacitus, the concessions made by Germanicus to the mutineers on the Rhine were extended to the army of Pannonia.[17]

Three years later the attention of Romans in Illyricum, in which the direction of affairs had been assigned to Drusus, was diverted to turmoil among the Suebic Germans, where the long supremacy of Maroboduus among the Marcomanni was coming to an end. Challenged first by the great Arminius in A.D. 17 he was expelled the following year by his kinsman Catualda and accepted an exile at Ravenna where he lived on for eighteen years. The followers of Maroboduus and also of Catualda, who was himself speedily removed by the Hermunduri and consigned by the Romans to an exile at Forum Iulii in Gaul, were settled beyond the Danube between the rivers Marus (March) and Cusus (perhaps the Váh) in southern Slovakia. Here they became subjects of Vannius, whose thirty-year reign over the Suebic Quadi gave the Romans a generation of peace in this quarter. It may have been around this time that the Romans permitted the Sarmatian Jazyges to occupy the plains between Pannonia and Dacia, though their presence is not recorded until A.D. 50, in the service of Vannius (see below). On 28 May A.D. 20 Drusus celebrated the award of an ovation granted in the previous summer for the reception of Maroboduus and other achievements. Only a renewal of strife among the Thracians now disturbed the *pax romana* in the Danube lands.[18]

16 Suet. *Tib.* 16; Dio LVI.16.4. The victory of Tiberius is the likely subject of the 'Gemma Augustea' now in Vienna, Bianchi Bandinelli 1970 (F 275) 195. Among the defeated peoples represented in the recently excavated Sebasteion at Aphrodisias were the Pannonian Andizetes and Pirustae. Other Danubians include the Bessi, Dacians, Dardanians and Iapodes; see Smith 1987 (F 580) 96.   17 Tac. *Ann.* 1.16–30.
18 Tac. *Ann.* 11.44–6; 53; 62–3; 111.2; 19; 56. The presence of Drusus is commemorated in the dedication of an exercise ground on the Dalmatian island Issa (Vis) in A.D. 20, *ILIug* 257. Mócsy 1977 (E 678) 439, cites the victory over Sarmatians credited to Tiberius in A.D. 7 by the Eusebius-Hieronymus Chronicle (p. 170 Helm) as a possible context for the settlement of the Jazyges.

The role of Roman forces in the region of the Danube delta, beyond the presumed formal limits of Roman territory, is described in the *Tristia* and the *Letters from Pontus* from Ovid's nine-year exile (A.D. 9–17) at Tomis. Life was hard and the barbarians were always close at hand. A poem of A.D. 16 thanks the emperor's legate Flaccus for gaining the loyalty of the Moesians and keeping out the Getae. In A.D. 12 the latter had seized the fortress at Aegis(s)us (Tulcea) and raided as far as Tomis. A Thracian column came to the scene, and a Roman expedition came down river to recover the fortress. The conduct of the chief centurion (Iulius) Vestalis, an Alpine prince and perhaps a descendant of King Donnus, is singled out for praise. Another poem describes a similar episode involving the fortress at Troesmis (Igliţa), recaptured by the legate Flaccus after a fight.[19] Further south in Thrace a division of the kingdom following the death of Rhoemetalces (I) around A.D. 12 brought a renewal of strife. After the death of Augustus, Cotys (VIII), the son of the late king who had been awarded the more favoured east, was threatened by his uncle Rhescuporis (III) in control of the rougher and more backward west. In A.D. 18 Tiberius sent a warning but when Cotys was seized and killed his uncle was brought to Rome and accused before the Senate by Antonia Tryphaena, widow of Cotys and a descendant of Mithridates and Antony. Rhescuporis was exiled to Alexandria, where he was later killed 'in an attempt to escape, genuine or not'. The kingdom was assigned to his son Rhoemetalces (II) and the children of the murdered Cotys, for whom the ex-praetor Trebellenus Rufus acted as regent. In connexion with the same affair it is reported that a leading Roman from Macedonia was charged with a treasonable association with Rhescuporis and that his island banishment was stipulated as having to be 'inaccessible from Macedonia or Thrace'. The Romans intervened again in A.D. 21, when Rhoemetalces was besieged in Philippopolis, and then in A.D. 26 to put down a rebellion in the Haemus mountains provoked by conscription to the Roman army. For his services in this campaign, which earned triumphal honours for the Roman commander, the king may have been rewarded with Roman citizenship and the title *rex*. His reign was evidently over when Caligula confirmed Rhoemetalces (III), son of Cotys (VIII) and Antonia Tryphaena, in the realm of his father. His close association and distant kinship with the emperor was advertised on dedications at Cyzicus, across the Hellespont from Thrace, where the family had resided since the death of Cotys in A.D. 19.[20]

In A.D. 44 the unified Balkan command of Moesia, Macedonia and

[19] Ov. *Pont.* I.8, IV.7. On Vestalis see *PIR*[2] J 621.

[20] Tac. *Ann.* II.64–7 (fall of Rhescuporis), III.38–9 (A.D. 21), IV.47–51 (A.D. 26). *IGRR* 4, 145–6 and 147 (Cyzicus), on which see Sullivan 1979 (E 698) 200–4.

Achaea, formed at the beginning of Tiberius' reign, was broken up. The latter two were returned to the charge of proconsuls appointed by the Senate, while Moesia was formally constituted a province under a consular legate.[21] The new arrangement was evidently bound up with the annexation of Thrace following the murder of Rhoemetalces (III). The takeover, which met with a degree of resistance requiring the presence of the legions, was directed by A. Didius Gallus, first governor of Moesia. His activities also embraced the Crimea, where the kingdom of the Bosporus had long-standing connexions with Thrace. In his first year Claudius had revoked Caligula's award of the Bosporus to Polemo of Pontus, son of Antonia Tryphaena, and confirmed the authority of Mithridates, stepson of Gepaepyris the widow of King Aspurgus (died c. A.D. 37/8). The new king's over-assertive policies brought his replacement by his half-brother Cotys whose coins commence in A.D. 46/5 (342 of the local era), when he was installed by an expedition under Didius Gallus. The attempt by Mithridates to recover his kingdom was defeated by a Roman prefect in charge of some auxiliary cohorts stationed in the Bosporus, aided by the Sarmatian Aorsi, who roamed the plains between the Tanais (Don) and the Caspian. The deposed king was consigned to an exile in Italy until executed by Galba on suspicion of plotting. Though the army of Moesia took part, it seems that the Roman interest in this quarter was directed from Pontus in Asia Minor rather than from the lower Danube.[22]

The affairs of Pannonia and Dalmatia after A.D. 9 present a notable contrast to those of Moesia and Thrace. The hold on the Danube was now secure and there is no record of trouble among the Pannonians. During the Principate of Tiberius their governors were senior consulars, retained in office for exceptional terms. The tenure of the Balkan command by C. Poppaeus Sabinus was ended only by his death after twenty-three years, and his successor Memmius Regulus remained for a decade. L. Munatius Plancus held Pannonia for seventeen years, while Dalmatia knew only two governors, P. Cornelius Dolabella until A.D. 20 and L. Volusius Saturninus. The extent of Roman confidence towards the area is indicated by the transfer of a legion from Pannonia to Africa for the campaign against Tacfarinas in A.D. 20–4, and by the permanent removal, without replacement, of the same legion IX Hispana for the expedition to Britain in A.D. 43. An attempted rebellion by the governor of Dalmatia in A.D. 42 ended after five days when the legions returned to their allegiance and a grateful Claudius rewarded them (VII and XI) with

---

[21] Suet. *Claud.* 25; Dio LX.24.

[22] Tac. *Ann.* XII.15–21; cf. Gajdukević 1971 (E 664) 338. The war was named *Bellum Mithridaticum*, *ILS* 9197 (Tarracina).

the titles 'loyal and faithful' (*Claudia pia fidelis*).[23] Otherwise the only event of note in the area was the fall of Vannius, whose long reign among the Suebi beyond the Danube (see above) came to an end with civil war. In A.D. 50 the Romans refused aid to the dissidents but offered Vannius a refuge, while the Roman governor was ordered to secure the Danube bank with legions and auxiliaries 'to provide help for the defeated and to overawe the victors'. After the royal cavalry of the Sarmatian Jazyges had provoked a disastrous fight with the Lugii, the king was rescued by a Roman fleet, and his followers were settled in Pannonia. The kingdom was divided between his nephews Sido and Italicus – 'once popular when winning power they were even more strongly detested after they had gained it'.[24] The Romans paid close attention to dynastic struggles among their German neighbours for they realized that once matters had been resolved there was a prospect of peace and stability for a generation.

The middle and later years of Nero saw a storm gathering on the lower Danube. An unusually full record of the activities of a governor of Moesia from around this time tells how 'he brought across, with the object of keeping up the payment of tribute, more than 100,000 of Transdanubian peoples, along with wives and families, chiefs or kings'. 'He nipped in the bud a growing threat from among the Sarmatians, even though he had sent the greater part of his army for the expedition into Armenia.' 'Kings hitherto unknown or hostile to the Roman people he brought to the river bank to pay solemn respect to the Roman standards. To the kings of the Bastarnae and Roxolani he restored their sons and to the king of the Dacians his brothers, whom he had either captured or rescued from enemies; from other rulers he received hostages. By these measures he strengthened and extended the security of the province.' He was busy also in the Crimea: 'he pushed back the kings of the Scythians from a blockade of Chersonesus (near Sevastopol), which lies beyond the river Borysthenes (Dniepr). Finally, 'he was the first to obtain from the province a large quantity of wheat for the grain supply of the Roman people'. For these achievements Ti. Plautius Silvanus Aelianus was not awarded triumphal honours until years later under Vespasian, though it came then with marks of special favour. Moreover, by that time disasters suffered by the Romans on the lower Danube will likely have served to cast a more favourable light on what appear to have been largely diplomatic comings and goings.[25]

The reported schemes of Nero's later years in the direction of the

---

[23] By L. Arruntius Camillus Scribonianus, Suet. *Claud.* 13.2; Dio LX.15.1–2. For the legionary titles see Wilkes 1969 (E 706) 96.   [24] Tac. *Ann.* XII.29–30.

[25] *ILS* 986 (Tibur). On these events see Pippidi 1962 (E 685) 106–132, revised and reprinted in Pippidi 1967 (E 686) 287–348.

Black Sea, involving annexation of Bosporus and Pontus and the raising of a new legion for an expedition to the Caucasus, may have been in part a response to an increasing threat from the Sarmatians and other Iranians. Rebellion within the empire brought them to an end and when the Sarmatians attacked the Roman world was on the point of being engulfed by civil war. In the winter A.D. 67/8 the Roxolani had cut to pieces two auxiliary cohorts and in the following winter they crossed the river for a raid on Moesia. A sudden thaw put the Sarmatian horsemen at a disadvantage when attacked by a legion and its auxiliaries, and a victory had been reported to Rome by 1 March A.D. 69, for which the emperor Otho made generous awards to all concerned.[26] A second attack later that year found the province almost devoid of troops, and even the legionary bases were in danger until the timely appearance of Mucianus and the eastern legions on their march to Italy. Legion VI Ferrata was diverted to deal with the invaders, who were Sarmatians rather than Dacians, since it was for victory over the former that triumphal honours were later awarded to Mucianus.[27] During the following winter, with Moesia evidently still disorganized after the civil war, the Sarmatians came again, killed the governor and ransacked the province from end to end. A new governor could do no more than chase off a few stragglers.[28] Now there began a comprehensive reorganization of the defences of Moesia which marks the beginning of a new era in the history of the Roman Danube.

III. THE DANUBE PEOPLES

Within little more than a generation a large tract of the Danube lands, extending across the north of the Balkan peninsula, had been added to the Roman empire. Control of the river Danube, achieved first through the conquest of the Pannonians and extended through the annexation of Thrace, gave to Rome the means of encircling and securing the mountain ranges, some rising to over 2,500m, and the dense forests that covered most of the Balkans. In the east the lower basin of the Danube is defined by a semicircular chain of mountains formed by the southern Carpathians and the Stara Planina, through which the river forces its way out of the Hungarian plain, once a great inland sea. In the west the undulating plain of Pannonia, to the west of the Danube, is bounded on the south by the rivers Drava and Sava. Further south the Dinaric watershed and several ranges run mainly from north west to south east, parallel with the Adriatic coast, and continue south through Montene-

---

[26] Tac. *Hist*. 1.79. The victory was acknowledged on that day with sacrifice on the Capitol by the Arval Brethren, MW p. 13.   [27] Tac. *Hist*. III.46 cf. IV.4.

[28] Tac. *Hist*. III.46.3; Joseph. *BJ* VII.4.3.

gro and Albania and the Pindus range of Greece. The south east is dominated by the mass of the Rhodope mountains that extend across the central Balkans, throwing out spurs towards the Black Sea and the Aegean. Most of this area and its peoples could only be approached and controlled from the direction of the Danube via its major tributaries.

Europe's greatest river flows more than 2,800km from the Black Forest to the Black Sea. Since Roman times the Danube has rarely served as a political frontier, save for that between Bulgaria and Romania in modern times. That has rather been the role of several major tributaries, while the great river has been more the highway for movement across Europe. In the upper and lower basins, bounded by Alps, Carpathians and the Balkan mountains, the south bank tends to be higher, sometimes with cliffs where ranges of low hills meet the river. The north bank is generally lower, marshy and hard to approach, save when ice covers both marshes and river between January and March. Below Belgrade passage between the upper and lower basins is obstructed by a succession of gorges for nearly 130km, formed by the southward continuation of the Carpathians. Fast currents, rocks and whirlpools combine to form such a barrier that in antiquity the upper and lower courses of the Danube were treated virtually as separate rivers. The lower gorge (Donja Klisura), where the river narrows to 150m in the Kazan defile, is more difficult than the upper (Gornja Klisura). A distance of 5km downstream from the gorge comes the great barrier of the Iron Gate (Prigrada), where a wall of rock across the bed of the river blocks any form of passage. Here a stretch of 5km, where the river boils through shoals and cataracts, was eventually bypassed with a canal in the year of Trajan's first invasion of Dacia,[29] a precedent imitated by Austro-Hungarian engineers at the end of the last century. The decision to hold to the river after A.D. 9 was to make permanent an occupation of the great plains along the upper and middle Danube. Later, when the river had become a fortified line of defence, it was in the lowlands of Pannonia and Moesia that the empire was vulnerable to sudden invasion, especially when the river was bridged with ice.

The indigenous peoples of the Danube lands at the time of the Roman conquest fall into four groups, whose languages all belonged to the Indo-European family.[30] These were Celts in the north west, Illyrians in the west, and Dacians and Thracians in the east, respectively north and south of the Danube. The brief comments regarding their social organization and material culture to be found in the ancient sources can be supplemented by epigraphic and archaeological discoveries. Inscriptions of the Roman period have been the basis for the study of personal names, family structures and other groupings. The Thracians were

[29] Šašel 1973 (E 692).   [30] Polomé 1982 (E 687).

Map 12. Geography and native peoples of the Danubian provinces.

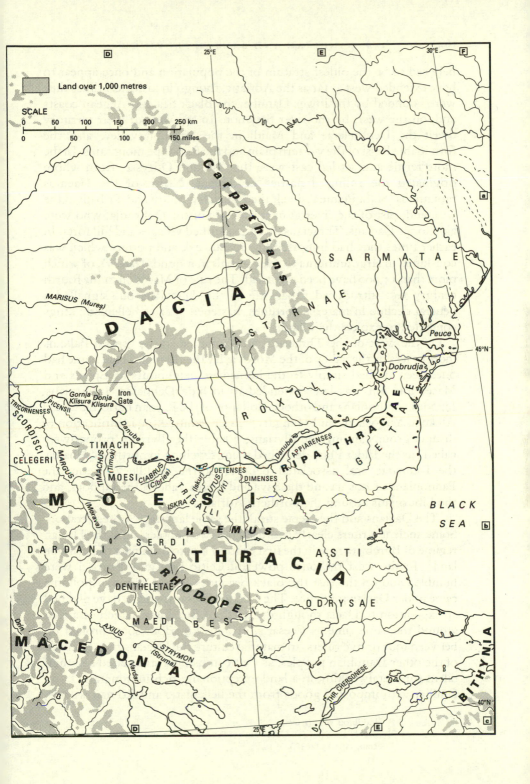

SCALE
Land over 1,000 metres

0 50 100 150 200 250 km
0   50   100   150 miles

CARPATHIANS

SARMATAE

DACIA

BASTARNAE

MARISUS (Mureş)

ROXOLANI

Peuce

Dobrudja

45°N

TRICORNENSES
PICENSII
SCORDISCI
CELEGERI
MARGUS (Morava)
TIMACHI
TIMACHUS (Timok)
MOESI
CIABRUS (Cibrica)
Gornja Klisura
Donja Klisura
Iron Gate
Danube

Danube

OETENSES
DIMENSES

APPIARENSES

RIPA THRACIAE

G E T A E

BLACK SEA

ISKRA (Iskut)
UTUS (Vit)
TRIBALLI

M O E S I A

HAEMUS

DARDANI

SERDI

THRACIA

ASTI

RHODOPE

DENTHELETAE

ODRYSAE

MAEDI
BESSI

AXIUS (Vardar)

M A C E D O N I A

Drin.

STRYMON (Struma)

CHR. CHERSONESE

BITHYNIA

40°N

believed to be the oldest stratum of the population and once appear to
have extended west as far as the Adriatic, though in historical times they
were bounded by the lower Danube, the Black Sea and Aegean coasts
and, on the west, by the river Strymon. In the west of their territory
dwelt the Dentheletae and Maidi in the Strymon valley, also the
formidable Bessi of the western plain and the Rhodope mountains. In the
more fertile and settled east were the Asti and Odrysae, from whom
originated the ruling dynasties of Thrace. North of the Haemus
mountains (Stara Planina) dwelt the associated Moesi and Triballi in the
west and, east of the river Utus, the Getae of the Dobrudja, who were
akin to the Dacians. Thracians dwelt in fortified villages and hill forts. In
earlier times they had imported fine metalwork and pottery which was
consigned in large amounts to their burials in mounds (*tumuli*), of which
more than 15,000 have been recorded. The rule of Macedon in the fourth
century B.C. introduced urban life to the Thracians but signalled a
general decline in material fortunes, hastened later as hellenistic kings
competed to exploit their lands.[31]

On the west of the Thracians, and bounded in the central Balkans
more or less by the valley of the Morova, lay the Illyrians. That name had
once been applied simply to the immediate neighbours of Epirus and
Macedonia but was later extended to include Delmatae, Liburnians,
Iapodes, Pannonians and others. Epitaphs of the Roman period found in
Albania, Yugoslavia and Hungary, have permitted the identification of
distinct groups among the Illyrians, notably the Illyrians 'properly so-
called', as the Elder Pliny described them, dwelling in northern Albania,
the Delmatae and associated peoples of the middle Adriatic, the
Pannonians of Bosnia and the Sava and Drava valleys, the Iapodes, and
the Liburnians around the northern Adriatic.[32]

'The Dacians and the Getae speak the same language' notes Strabo.[33]
Some ancient writers clearly confused the two peoples, until the Dacian
regime of Burebista rose in the first century B.C. to dominate the Danube
lands. In the west the once powerful Celtic Boii and Taurisci were
humbled and on the east the Black Sea cities from Olbia to Apollonia
came under Dacian influence. The dictator Caesar is said to have planned
an expedition to Dacia though the death of Burebista, which occurred
around the same time as Caesar's, saw his kingdom soon broken up
between four or five rulers. In material culture the Dacians moved ahead
of the other Danubian peoples, as Celtic influences stimulated a natural
talent for metalworking in a land exceptionally rich in minerals. Long
familiar with imported goods from the hellenistic and Roman worlds,

[31] Hoddinott 1981 (E 670).
[32] Alföldy 1964 (E 647); Garašanin 1982 (E 665) 586–7 and 598–610.
[33] Strab. VII.3.13 (305C).

jewellery, pottery, wine and oil, their commerce with the latter may also have involved slave-trading on a large scale, for which large quantities of Roman coins reached the area around the middle of the first century B.C.[34]

Celtic peoples had moved into the middle Danube basin during the fourth century B.C. They were soon in conflict with Illyrians and early in the third century they reached the southern Balkans, on one famous occasion (279 B.C.) all but destroying the kingdom of Macedon. Later they dispersed, some bands moving to Asia, others returning north to settlements near the Danube.[35] Survivals of the Celtic migrations included the Scordisci around the lower Sava, who were prominent in the middle Balkans during the late second and early first centuries B.C. Settlements of Celts are suggested by place names apparently of Celtic origin on the lower Danube, such as Ratiaria, Durostorum and Noviodunum. Celts remained dominant along the middle Danube, in Noricum and in Pannonia, where remnants of the Boii and the Eravisci are found separated by the Illyrian Azali, the latter perhaps transported there during the *Bellum Pannonicum* of 14–9 B.C. Generally Celtic influence was widespread in the western Balkans, notably in weapons and other metalwork. The nature of their influence is indicated by Strabo's comment on the Iapodes: 'their armour is Celtic, they are tattooed like the rest of the Illyrians and Thracians'.[36]

Not a great deal is known of the economy, social organization and material culture of the majority of the Danube peoples, although it is now possible, in some measure, to put forward the necessary corrective to unflattering stereotypes in the ancient sources, 'ignorance' of agriculture and viticulture, 'intemperance' in drinking and sexual behaviour and 'uncivilized conduct' among themselves and towards foreigners. In several areas more is now known of the layout and general character of settlements. In the south, among the Illyrians, Greek influence is evident in the fortified settlements of the Illyrian kingdom, at Lissus, Scodra and elsewhere.[37] The centre of the Illyrian Daorsi at Ošaniči near Stolac possessed walls and towers reminiscent of Greek work.[38] Along the Adriatic coast from Istria southwards are found the remains of many fortified hill-settlements, the so-called *castellieri* of Istria and *gradina* of Dalmatia. Among the Delmatae the settlement of the Riditae at Danilo near Šibenik is noteworthy for the many Latin inscriptions containing native names, many apparently from the period before a *municipium* was instituted under the Flavians.[39] Many settlements of this type lasted well

[34] Crişan 1978 (E 656); Crawford 1985 (B 320) 227–35.   [35] Papazoglu 1978 (E 681) 272–8.
[36] Strab. VII.5.4 (314–15C); Dion. Hal. *fr.* 16, calls them a Celtic people.
[37] *Iliria II: La Ville Illyrienne* (Tirana, 1972) 239–68 (Lissus).   [38] Marić 1977 (E 673).
[39] Alföldy 1968 (E 650) 1213–14.

into the Roman period, dominated by native families whose members often describe themselves as *princeps castelli*, 'chief of the fortress'.[40]

Among the Iapodes, some of the hill-settlements in the northern Lika attacked by the Romans in 35 B.C. have been identified, notably Monetium, Avendo and Arupium, and excavated; further east, in the Una valley around Bihać, some large cemeteries, most of cremations, have been explored. Their grave goods include traditional types of pottery, weapons, brooches and jewellery dating from early Iron Age to Roman times. Unique to the area are the dozen or so stone cremation chests, suggesting some Etruscan or Italic influence, with an incised decoration of warriors, horsemen, funeral processions and dances, in a style that shows little classical influence, although some are clearly of Roman date since they bear also Latin epitaphs.[41] The influence of seaborne contacts with other peoples is evident in the material culture of the Liburnians, notably in the extensive cemeteries excavated around Zadar and Nin. The Liburnian settlement at Radovine had stone houses built to a regular plan, imported Greek and hellenistic pottery and dry-stone, later mortared defences, and remained inhabited throughout the Roman era.[42] Several of the larger Liburnian hill-settlements were transformed into Roman towns when city institutions were introduced in the Julio-Claudian period.

The warrior-led Celts in the Danube lands are identified with the spread of fortified settlements (*oppida*) and by cemeteries which contain metal weapons, helmets, armour and ornaments often of remarkable quality. At Tolmin in Slovenia have been discovered the dressed stone footings of pre-Roman houses.[43] At the summit of the Magdalensberg in Carinthia was an *oppidum*, built *c.* 100 B.C., with a stone-faced double rampart (*murus duplex*).[44] The *oppidum* of the Eravisci in Pannonia was on the Gellért hill overlooking the Danube at Budapest and continued to be occupied well into Roman times, as the settlement spread down the slopes towards the river. From here were circulated, possibly down to Augustan times, the Eraviscan 'denarii' that imitated Roman republican issues.[45] In Dacia recent excavations have revealed much of the history and character of the citadels in the Oraştie mountains of south-west Transylvania where the regimes of both Burebista and Decebalus were centred. The earliest of these appears to have been Costeşti, which occupies a hill (561m) commanding the exit of the river Apa northwards from the mountains. The earliest phases of other citadels, Blidarul, Vîrful lui Hulpe, Piatra Roşie, Banita and Capilna, may also be dated

[40] For example, *ILIug* 1852–3.   [41] Stipčević 1977 (E 696) 207–14.
[42] Batović 1968 (E 653) 1973 (E 654).   [43] Svoljšak 1976 (E 699).
[44] Piccottini and Vetters 1981 (E 684) 10–17.
[45] Mócsy 1974 (E 677) 56; this dating is judged to be too late by Crawford 1985 (B 320) 236 n. 59.

before the end of the first century B.C., if not to the period of Burebista. At the centre lay the great complex of the Gradiştea Muncel, consisting of a large fortress and the major shrine, which has been identified as the Dacian capital Sarmizegetusa. Most of what has been found there is dated to the era of Decebalus, *c.* A.D. 80 to 105, but the place was already a major shrine in the time of Burebista, where sanctuaries consisted of rows of timber columns set on circular bases of andesite to represent groves for the hanging of offerings to the gods.[46]

IV. PROVINCES AND ARMIES

By early in the reign of Claudius the Danube lands had been organized into five provinces. The core consisted of the three great commands of Pannonia, Dalmatia and Moesia, each in the charge of a consular legate and with armies totalling seven legions along with their equivalent auxiliaries.[47] In the north west and south east lay the smaller provinces of Noricum and Thracia, once ruled by native dynasties but now in the charge of procuratorial governors.

Noricum lay astride the Tauern Alps of Lower Austria, between the upper Drava and the Danube, and was bounded on the west by the river Inn.[48] Though narrow gorges make travel difficult in several places, some broad valleys are inviting for settlement, notably the Drau (Drava) and the Zollfeld around Klagenfuhrt, the Mur around Graz and, north of the watershed, the Traun around Wels. The main route into Noricum from Italy crossed the Saifnitz saddle (812m) into Carinthia and continued north to the Danube via Neumarkt, Ovilava (Wels) and Lauriacum. A branch from the road heading for the Brenner Pass entered Noricum from the west via the Eisacktal and the Pustertal, while that from the south crossed the Karavanken by the Loibl (Lubelj) Pass. Routes along the Mur and Drava valleys led to the main Pannonian Highway at Poetovio (Ptuj) on the Drava. Though a seasonal route crossed the High Tauern via the Hochtor (2,500m) the principal crossing was via the Katschberg (*In Alpe*, 1,740m), Radstadt and Lueg Passes, between Teurnia and Iuvavum (Salzburg). North of the mountains the

---

[46] Daicoviciu 1972 (E 658) 127–99.

[47] The date of the division of Illyricum into Pannonia and Dalmatia remains a problem and has most recently been considered by Fitz 1988 (E 663) (suggesting A.D. 19/20). A belief that a division of Illyricum, either in A.D. 8 or 9, produced two provinces known for a period as Illyricum Superius (Dalmatia) and Inferius (Pannonia) is now to be abandoned since it rests on a doubtful MS record of the full text of the now fragmentary *CIL* III 1741 (Epidaurum) as a dedication to the early Tiberian legate Cornelius Dolabella by the 'civitates superioris provinciae Hillyrici'. See Novak 1966 (E 680). The earliest record of Dalmatia is a monument, probably of Claudian date, erected at Rome, *AE* 1913, 194, but Illyricum, evidently denoting Pannonia still appears in official documents as late as A.D. 60, *CIL* XVI 4.

[48] Alföldy 1974 (E 652) 7–13.

main west to east road led from Iuvavum, Ovilava, Lauriacum and Cetium to Vindobona (Vienna) across the border in Pannonia.

The boundary between Noricum and Pannonia down the east side of the Alps left in Pannonia territory that had once been reckoned part of Noricum, including most of the Pannonian Highway (part of the 'Amber Road' of prehistoric times) between Aquileia and the Danube via Emona, Celeia, Poetovio, Savaria and Carnuntum. The boundary between Pannonia and Dalmatia along the south edge of the Sava valley probably went back to a strategic division of command in Illyricum following the Pannonian surrender in the late summer of A.D. 8.[49] The long course of the Danube through the Hungarian plains marked the northern and eastern limits of Pannonia, between Vindobona and Singidunum (Belgrade) where Moesia began at the mouth of the Sava. In terrain, climate and material culture there were differences between Pannonia north and south of the Drava. The former was largely a continuation of the Great Hungarian plain, with some more favoured areas near Lake Balaton, in the Bakony hills nearer the Danube bend and around Pécs in the south east. In the south the overland routes between Italy and the Balkans branched off the Pannonian Highway at Emona and Poetovio to follow the broad and fertile valleys of the Sava and Drava. Further north the two principal routes across northern Pannonia led from Poetovio to Aquincum (Budapest) via Balaton, and from Savaria along the Arabo (Raab) to Arrabona (Győr). There was at this period no road along the Danube bank in Noricum or Pannonia.

The greater part of the southern boundary of Moesia followed the northern foothills of the Haemus.[50] Though a towpath was constructed at least through the upper part of the Danube gorge by the Moesian legions under Tiberius,[51] there is no evidence at this time for a unified route along the Danube between Ratiaria (Archar) and Aegyssus at the apex of the delta. The most direct approach from the south to the centre of the province, that is 'Moesia et Triballia' around Ratiaria and Oescus, followed the Strymon (Struma) valley to Serdica and the Iskur valley to Oescus. A longer and more difficult route followed the Axius (Vardar) and Margus (Morava), via Scupi and Naissus, and then the Timacus (Timok) to the Danube near Ratiaria.

Though an 'unarmed province' before the end of the first century A.D. Dalmatia embraced a great tract of forests and mountains which had seen hard fighting during the Augustan conquest.[52] In the south the waterless and bare limestone karst of the hinterland makes a contrast with the coast and islands, almost everywhere green with Mediterranean vegetation.

---

[49] Mócsy 1974 (E 677) 33–4. A more southerly line for the Pannonian-Dalmatian boundary has been suggested by Dušanić 1977 (E 661) 64–6.   [50] Gerov 1979 (E 668).
[51] *ILIug* 57 and 60 (A.D. 33/4).   [52] Wilkes 1969 (E 706) xxi–xxvii.

From the Julian Alps in the north to the valley of the Drin in the south routes to the interior are uniformly difficult. Beyond the watershed of the Dinaric ranges the Bosnian rivers flow north to the Sava, from east to west the Glina, Colapis (Kulpa), Una, Sana, Vrbas, Bosna and Drina. Hardly a single trace of Roman influence can be observed in this area during the Julio-Claudian period, though Roman forces crossed and re-crossed it as military roads were driven across the land.

Most of what may be termed provincial administration in the Danube lands under the Julio-Claudians was intended to secure military ends, the conquest, pacification and exploitation of native peoples, and the security and support of the occupying armies. Until 27 B.C. Illyricum and Macedonia (which also included Achaea) were administered by procon-suls chosen from ex-praetors or ex-consuls. After that date Macedonia, which included Epirus and Thessaly, and Achaea were constituted separate provinces, each under a proconsul of praetorian rank, residing normally at Thessalonica and Corinth respectively. Illyricum, also proconsular, may not have extended north of the river Titus (Krka), leaving Liburnia still grouped along with Istria and Transpadana. Even when later part of Dalmatia, Liburnia retained its separate organization for the imperial cult.[53]

As for the arrangements in Thrace, Macedonia and Moesia, the view here accepted is that after more than one Thracian crisis a new Balkan command was constituted with the legions of Macedonia, perhaps by M. Lollius in *c*. 19/18 B.C. (see above, p. 551), and perhaps titled 'Thracia Macedoniaque'. It may be presumed, though there is no proof, that Macedonia was subsequently restored to administration by proconsuls, though no longer with undefined military responsibilities. In A.D. 15 Macedonia and Achaea, having suffered many burdens during the recent wars, were added to the emperor's Balkan command, which by now may have been known as 'Moesia' or 'Moesia et Treballia' to assist recovery from the effects of those wars. This arrangement continued until A.D. 44 when Moesia was constituted a separate province and Macedonia and Achaea were returned to their proconsuls.[54] Newly annexed Thrace was placed in the charge of a procurator, a form of administration evidently favoured by Claudius for former client kingdoms. The Roman governor resided on the coast at Perinthus, rather than inland at the former capital Bizye, but the royal system of administration by districts was retained. The Thracian Chersonese (Gallipoli), an imperial possession since 12

---

[53] *CIL* III 2810 (Scardona): 'sacer(dos) ad aram Lib[burn(iae)]'; cf. III 2802 with 9877 (later lost and republished, *AE* 1938, 68), a dedication to Nero, son of Germanicus (d. A.D. 31). The provincial cult for Dalmatia was centred first at Epidaurum, *CIL* III 1741, then later at Doclea, *CIL* III 12695 cf. p. 2253.

[54] Vell. Pat. II.101.3; Tac. *Ann.*I.80; Dio LV.29.3; *ILS* 1349. It is to be noted that the sources for the history of Moesia before Claudian times are incomplete and tend to be anachronistic.

B.C., retained its separate administration, while Byzantium was included in the Asian province Bithynia. Not long after the annexation of Thrace that city appealed successfully for a remission of taxes in recognition of its contribution to the Roman war effort. A similar regime was introduced for Noricum, with a procuratorial administration based at the new city of Virunum in the Zollfeld.[55]

In several areas military conquest was, in typical Roman fashion, followed up by driving new roads though areas of mountain and forest. The Via Claudia Augusta across the eastern Alps via the Resia Pass was completed under Claudius,[56] and roads across the Alps in Noricum may have been built around the same time. In Dalmatia at least five major roads, radiating in all directions across the province from Salona, had been completed by A.D. 20.[57] In Pannonia the road across the Julian Alps from Aquileia to Emona was under construction in A.D. 14.[58] In Moesia a towpath through the upper gorge of the Danube was complete by A.D. 33/4, and was repaired under Claudius and doubtless on several other occasions given the conditions on the river when the thaw comes and the ice breaks.[59] In Thrace the early procurators were occupied with building police posts on the main roads across the Haemus to the Moesian legions on the Danube.[60] The organized construction of defensive walls for Roman colonies also indicates the essentially military character of these new foundations (see below).

Only among the enfranchised communities of southern Liburnia is there evidence for administration of a more civilian character. Under the governor Cornelius Dolabella a survey of the region was completed (*forma Dolabelliana*), that defined boundaries and rights in such matters as water supply. It seems that many disputes soon arose which required the governor's attention. The implementation of his judgment on the ground was normally assigned to a senior centurion who would see to the placing of boundary markers in the right places.[61]

Since the victory over Mithridates of Pontus the Greek cities along the Thracian coast of the Black Sea had come steadily under Roman influence and one, Callatis, is known to have entered a formal alliance. For centuries the cities of the Dobrudja had, under the leadership of Histria, exploited the resources of the delta and had managed a profitable commerce with the peoples of the interior. The five cities along the coast

---

55 *AE* 1957, 23, in which a procurator is honoured by 33 *strategiae*. Tac. *Ann.* XII.62–3 (appeal of Byzantium in A.D. 53).   56 *ILS* 208.

57 *CIL* III 3198–201, 10156–9, and Wilkes 1969 (E 706) 452–5 (readings based on Alföldy 1964 (E 648) 247). The road beyond Burnum to the Sava valley was completed in A.D. 47, *CIL* III 13329ff. On 'viae militares' in the Danube lands see J. Šašel, *Studien zu den Militärgrenzen Roms II* (Köln, 1977) 235–44.   58 Tac. *Ann.* I.20.

59 *ILIug* 56, 55 and 58. One of the two Tiberian texts is illustrated by Swoboda 1939 (E 701) pl. V.

60 *ILS* 231 and p. CLXX (*CIL* III 6123 cf. p. 1059 = 14207³⁴), *AE* 1912, 193, recording work in A.D. 61 under the procurator T. Iulius Ustus.   61 Wilkes 1969 (E 706) 456–9 and 1974 (E 707).

south of the delta, Histria, Tomis, Callatis, Dionysopolis and Odessus, formed together the Pentapolis of the 'Left Pontus'. Down to the Principate of Nero a common coinage had been produced for local circulation, and the Pentapolis was incorporated into the province of Moesia. An assembly for religious ceremony and matters of common interest met at Tomis under a pontarch. This city had taken over from Histria as the principal port of the region and since the time of Augustus a flotilla had been stationed there under a 'prefect of the sea-coast'.[62] They were the local agents of Roman authority and acted as intermediaries between the cities and higher authority. For the exiled Ovid at Tomis the freezing of the river between January and March brought the danger of attack, but the poet also describes the peaceful transit in winter by the lumbering carts of the Jazyges and other Sarmatians over the newly bridged river. When Getae threatened, the cities of the Dobrudja looked to Rome for protection although, as we have already seen, this tended to arrive after the damage had been done. Ovid's advertised feeling that his safety depended on the Roman general and his legions was no doubt heartfelt, and his private shrine to the imperial family was likely, in part at least, a compensation for his feeling of insecurity. Further north in Histria the erection or repair of a temple to Augustus in his own lifetime testifies to the increasing ties between Rome and this region before it was formally incorporated in the province of Moesia.[63]

Some indication of how these cities fared after the imposition of direct rule under Claudius is furnished by a document, inscribed in at least two copies, that defined the territories and economic privileges of Histria early under Trajan, to which was appended a dossier of letters addressed to the city from earlier governors. When Roman taxes were imposed along the lower Danube the Thracian Bank (*Ripa Thraciae*) was organized as a separate district within the taxation province of Illyricum. Evidently the zealous agents of this bureau had challenged the traditional privileges claimed by Histria in the delta, which included gathering pinewood and fishing in the Peuce mouth. On appeal it seems that the city's claims were upheld on more than one occasion by the governor, before whom they had been supported by the local Roman prefects. Under Nero one governor made the comment that the principal revenue of Histria was derived from pickled fish, suggesting that another matter at issue may have been salt extraction, normally an imperial monopoly, traditionally carried on at several places along the coast.[64]

On the matter of military deployment, that is apart from the presence of armies on expeditions, little is known until the army reforms of

---

[62] Danoff 1938 (E 659) (Pentapolis), and Vulpe and Barnea 1968 (E 704) 66. The walls of Odessus (Varna) were repaired under Tiberius, *IGBulg* I² 57.   [63] *ISM* I no. 146.

[64] *ISM* I nos. 67 and 68.

Augustus which resulted in the standing provincial armies of legions and *auxilia*. Aquileia is likely to have been the base for the legions until they were moved to camps in Pannonia, probably in or after the *Bellum Pannonicum* of 14-9 B.C. The legions in Macedonia, at least four in Crassus' army of 29–28 B.C., may already have been stationed in Dardania, perhaps at Scupi and Naissus, before the imperial command in the Balkans was instituted. Then one legion may have been moved up to the river, V Macedonica at Oescus. In the south of Illyricum the legionary bases known later at Burnum and Tilurium may have been established following the extension of the new imperial Illyricum to the Adriatic, perhaps in 11 B.C. After A.D. 9 the seven Danube legions were deployed as follows: in Pannonia VIII Augusta (Poetovio), IX Hispana (?Siscia) and XV Apollinaris (?Emona); in Dalmatia VII, formerly titled Macedonica, (Tilurium) and XI (Burnum); in 'Moesia et Triballia' V Macedonica (Oescus) and in Dardania IV Scythica (?Naissus).[65] So far excavation has contributed little to our knowledge of legionary deployment in this period. Emona has not yielded any certain trace of the supposed base of XV Apollinaris that preceded the foundation of the colony in A.D. 14/15. Nor have Carnuntum or Burnum furnished evidence for occupation before the end of Tiberius' reign, though epitaphs indicate the presence of XV Apollinaris at the former and of XX at Burnum before it was replaced there in A.D. 9. In addition, numerous epitaphs of serving soldiers, datable to the period before A.D. 42 because they lack the titles *Claudia pia fidelis* (see above), testify that they were based at Burnum and Tilurium, though not necessarily in camps on the site of later fortresses, under Tiberius and Gaius. On the south bank of the Drava at Poetovio quantities of Augustan pottery from the buildings of the canabae relate to the presence of VIII Augusta. Among the large haul of Roman military equipment dredged from the river at Siscia was a helmet that belonged to a soldier of IX Hispana. In the Balkans the first dated record of IV Scythica and V Macedonia are the inscriptions on the rock-face of the upper Danube gorge dated to A.D. 33/4 noted above. From the find of an early epitaph, it has been suggested that Oescus was the base of the latter unit from the middle years of Augustus. Where the other was based is quite uncertain: Ratiaria on the Danube is a possibility but a more likely place is Naissus, the strategic crossroads of Dardania. The fact that no material evidence for an early occupation has been found at Naissus seems to count against this, though recent evidence cited above from Illyricum makes that inference less certain.[66]

[65] The evidence is summarized in Wilkes 1969 (E 706) 92–5, and Mócsy 1974 (E 677) 42–4.
[66] Emona: Šašel 1968 (E 691) 562–3. Carnuntum: Kandler, in Stiglitz, Kandler and Jobst 1977 (E 695); cf. Zabehlicky-Scheffenegger and Kandler 1979 (E 710) 13. Tilurium: Wilkes,1969 (E 706) 97. Poetovio: Klemenc and Saria 1936 (E 671) 56; cf. Curk 1976 (E 657) 64. Siscia: Šašel 1974 (E 693) 734. Oescus: Gerov 1967 (E 667) 87–90. Naissus: P. Petrović, *IMS* IV (1979) 30–1.

Later alterations in legionary deployment were caused by events elsewhere in the empire. Legion IX Hispana departed finally for Britain in A.D. 43 and was not replaced at Siscia, leaving the garrison of Pannonia with two legions. When VIII Augusta moved to the lower Danube in A.D. 44/5 its place at Poetovio was taken by XIII Gemina, transferred from the upper Rhine. With VIII Augusta possibly at Novae on the Danube below Oescus the army of Moesia now comprised three legions. Late under Claudius IV Scythica was moved to the East and its place taken by VII Claudia, perhaps first stationed at Scupi, then later on Viminacium on the Danube above the gorge, and the army of Dalmatia was now reduced to a single legion. In A.D. 62 a crisis in Armenia saw two legions withdrawn from the Danube, XV Apollinaris from Carnuntum, its place being taken by X Gemina from Spain, and V Macedonica, which was not replaced at Oescus, leaving Moesia temporarily with two legions until, late under Nero, III Gallica arrived for its brief sojourn on the lower Danube.

Though perhaps yet to be fully organized with permanent bases, Roman fleets on the Danube and its tributaries played a major role in military operations and their logistics. The attack on Siscia (Segesta) in 35 B.C. (see p. 550) was effected with ships provided by the allies, but Roman fleets participated in expeditions against the Dacians under Augustus and also, slightly later, in the incidents on the lower Danube described by Ovid. The west coast of the Black Sea was also patrolled by a Roman flotilla stationed at Tomis. Under Claudius the Roman fleet patrolling the Danube was on hand to rescue Vannius from his kingdom, and the reported activities of Plautius Silvanus Aelianus on the lower Danube under Nero (see above) would not have been possible without a fleet in control of the river, not to mention the excursion to the Crimea. The Pannonian and Moesian fleets, later based at Taurunum and Noviodunum – in each case the last harbour proceeding downstream – will have functioned quite separately as long as there was no through passage at the Danube gorge and the Iron Gate. In the Black Sea the Pontus fleet was based on the coast of Asia Minor, and for the Adriatic Ravenna on the coast of Italy remained the principal naval base, with stations elsewhere, including one at Salona.[67]

Most of the auxiliary units in Dalmatia were placed in the territory of the Delmatae. Several were in or close to coastal colonies, with two cavalry *alae*, one of which was a regiment of Parthian refugees, and two infantry cohorts at Salona, with cohorts also at Iader, Narona and Epidaurum. The latter are also found at the legionary bases, two at Burnum and one at Tilurium, with an *ala* at the latter perhaps being a part replacement under Claudius for the departed VII Claudia. The four cohorts named on early epitaphs at the camp of Bigeste near Narona are

[67] Starr 1960 (D 237) 23 and 125–41.

unlikely to have been in garrison there simultaneously. Other stations along the road linking the legionary bases Burnum and Tilurium were Promona (a cohort), Magnum (*ala*) and Andetrium (cohort). In the case of some units, for example a cohort of Syrian archers (*cohors II Cyrrhestarum*), no base can be identified since serving members are found in several places. In Pannonia a larger number of cavalry units was deployed along the main roads leading to the Danube, notably on the Pannonian Highway at Sala (Zalalövo), Savaria, Scarbantia and Carnuntum. Roman pottery indicates a military base at Mursa on the Drava, similar to that known to have existed at Sirmium. By Claudius, if not earlier, some cavalry units had been placed near the Danube termini of other roads in the north and east of Pannonia, at Arrabona, Brigetio, Aquincum, Gorsium, Mursa and Teutoburgium (Dalj). Under Augustus the military presence in Noricum included a detachment from the Pannonian VIII Augusta at Magdalensberg and perhaps there was another at Celeia (Celje) which, although within Noricum, lay on the Pannonian Highway. Around the end of Augustus' reign a locally recruited auxiliary unit (*cohors Montanorum prima*) had replaced the legionaries at Magdalensberg. By the time of Claudius the *auxilia* in Noricum, which in A.D. 69 comprised an *ala* and eight cohorts, had been moved up to the Danube bank, to bases at Lentia (Linz) and Lauriacum in the west, and Augustiana (Traismauer) and Zwentendorf in the east.[68]

In Moesia auxiliary units may have preceded the legions in their later bases at Singidunum (Belgrade) and Viminacium. Signs of early occupation have been reported in the forts of the Danube gorge at Boljetin and Donji Milanovac. On the lower Danube some early epitaphs, though no precise dating is possible, indicate cavalry units at Augustae (Hurlec), Securisca, Variana, Utus, Oescus and Nikopol. Infantry units were stationed on main roads in the interior, at Timacum Minus (Ravna) in the Timacus (Timok) valley, at Naissus and possibly already at Montana (Mihailovgrad), the later station of the *cohors Claudia Sugambrorum veterana*, a unit that was already serving in Thrace under Tiberius. Finally the cavalry veteran buried at Tomis may have been serving in the newly occupied Dobrudja under Claudius or Nero.[69] Julio-Claudian military deployment in the Danube lands saw the legions mainly held in the rear before Claudius, with cavalry regiments pushed out as far as the Danube crossings and infantry cohorts patrolling the intervening roads. Under Claudius and Nero a gradual move towards the river is discernible but the date when several of the later known legionary bases were first occupied, for example Carnuntum, Viminacium and Novae, remains

---

[68] Dalmatia: Alföldy 1987 (D 159) 239–97. Pannonia, Mócsy 1974 (E 677) 48–51. Noricum: Alföldy 1974 (E 652) 65.

[69] J.J. Wilkes in Hartley and Wacher 1983 (C 274) 266–7.

uncertain. Before the Flavian period there was no Roman frontier, at least in any military sense, along the Danube.

V. ROMAN COLONIZATION AND THE ORGANIZATION OF THE NATIVE PEOPLES

Long before the time of Caesar, Roman merchants and settlers had reached Macedonia and Illyricum but the formal institution of Roman colonies in both areas began only in the aftermath of civil war between Caesar and Pompey. Colonies were established following the decisive battles at Pharsalus in 48 B.C., Philippi in 42 B.C. and Actium in 31 B.C. Subsequently, new colonies of Roman citizens were rarely instituted and then only for legionary veterans from the same or adjacent provinces.[70] Foundation dates of the early colonies remain uncertain, especially of those in Achaea and Macedonia where the evidence often consists of a few locally minted coins. Several colonies were evidently refounded with an infusion of new settlers along with the conferring of new titles. No overall strategic scheme is evident in the places chosen for new settlements, though major harbours and overland routes were doubtless a consideration. Caesar's foundation at Corinth (Laus Iulia Corinthiensis) was more a commercial enterprise than a settled colony and later dominated the rest of Achaea. Patrae (colonia Aroe Augusta), a veteran settlement from legions X Fretensis and XII Fulminata and strengthened by deportations from southern Aetolia, was the main port for traffic with Italy. In spite of more than one attempt at settlement, a colony at nearby Dyme was later absorbed by Patrae. The new city of Nicopolis on the Gulf of Ambracia, founded to commemorate the victory at Actium, was not a colony but rather a concentration of several existing settlements to form a new city. Further north, Caesar's new settlers may have contributed to the later prosperity of Buthrotum (Butrint) on the coast opposite Corcyra and in the same area the Augustan foundation at Byllis (Gradisht) overlooking the river Aous also flourished.

The five colonies in Macedonia originated in reparations following civil war.[71] Cassandrea on the Pallene isthmus of Chalcidice and Dium on the Thermaic Gulf were first settled on the orders of Brutus, Philippi with veterans by Antony after the battle. After Actium Octavian permitted Antonians dispossessed in Italy to settle at Dyrrhachium, Philippi and other places. The titles Iulia Augusta suggest that these may have included Cassandrea, Pella and Dium, in addition to Philippi. Dyrrhachium, formerly the Corinthian colony Epidamnus, lay at the

[70] Vittinghoff 1952 (C 239) 85–7 and 124–9; Brunt 1971 (A 9) 597–9.
[71] Papazoglu 1979 (E 682) 357–61.

western terminus of the Via Egnatia and, like Philippi, Dium and Cassandrea, possessed a large territory. The exceptional privilege of 'Italian status' (*ius Italicum*), carrying immunity from taxation, reported for the colonies Dyrrhachium, Cassandrea, Philippi and Dium was evidently a recompense to refugees from Italy and was extended also to those settled in the later *municipium* at Stobi in Paeonia. Among other communities, Thessalonica, residence of the proconsul, enjoyed the status of 'free city' (*civitas libera*) probably from 42 B.C., while the 'freedom' of Amphipolis may go back to the institution of the province. Elsewhere, nothing is recorded of the 'free people of Scotussa' or of privileges conferred on Amantia near the border of Epirus and Illyria. Existing federations (*koina*) of the native peoples were retained to give an impression of an autonomy that persisted for centuries.

Along the Adriatic coast of Illyricum the few Greek colonies, Issa, Pharos, and Corcyra Nigra being the principal settlements, had been threatened by the growth of Roman settlement. By the time Pliny wrote of 'several Greek cities and powerful communities of fading memory' the early Roman settlements (*conventus civium Romanorum*) had grown into flourishing cities enjoying the status of *colonia*.[72] The colonia Martia Iulia at Salona, and the coloniae Iuliae at Narona and Epidaurum were likely creations of Caesar to strengthen and reward Roman settlers of that area for conspicuous loyalty in the civil war. In the pre-colonial period at Narona there is a record of the civic organization of the *conventus*, a college of two *magistri* and two quaestors, one of each being a freedman.[73] The new colonies possessed large territories, that of Salona including not only settlements on the mainland that had once belonged to Issa but also the island Pharos (Hvar), which was administered as a prefecture. Uncertainty persists over the status of several smaller Roman settlements on the Dalmatian coast described by Pliny as 'towns of Roman citizens' ('oppida civium Romanorum'), Risinium (Risan), Acruvium (Kotor), Butua (Budva), Olcinium (Ulcinj), Scodra (Shkodër) and Lissus (Lezha). Risinium had the epithet Iulium and Scodra is called *colonia* on a later inscription but most likely they were irregular settlements later constituted as *municipia*.

In Liburnia the colony at Iader boasted of Augustus as its creator (*parens coloniae*) and the donor of its defences.[74] The occasion was probably following Agrippa's seizure of the Liburnian navy in 35 B.C. The same event may be the occasion for the foundation of a colony at the Liburnian port of Senia (Senj), and in Istria at Pola (colonia Iulia Pola Pollentia Herculanea) and Parentium (Poreč), while the slightly earlier foundation at Tergeste (Trieste) received the benefit of walls following a

---

[72] Pliny, *HN* III.144. Wilkes 1969 (E 706) 192–261.
[73] *CIL* III 1820, Wilkes 1969 (E 706) pl. 28.   [74] *CIL* III 2907, Wilkes 1969 (E 706) pl. 24.

destructive raid by the Iapodes. The Italian status enjoyed by several Liburnian communities may have been conferred in recompense following their inclusion in the province of Illyricum in 11 B.C., following a period when Liburnia had been administered along with north-east Italy. Those with *ius Italicum* are Alvona (Alutae) and Flanona (Flanates) on the west of Istria, Lopsica (Lopsi) south of Senia, and Varvaria (Varvarini) near the border with the Delmatae of Illyricum. A similar reason may explain the exemption from tribute (*immunitas*) of Curicum (Curictae) and Fertinium (Fertinates) on the island Curictae (Krk) and Asseria (Asseriates) in the south near Iader. The presence of enfranchized native Iulii suggest that several of these places were organized as *municipia* under Augustus and it seems certain that most had acquired that status by the end of the Julio-Claudian period: Alvona, Flanona, Lopsica, Ortopla, Vegium and Argyruntum along the coast; in the gulf of Flanona (Kvarner), Fertinium and Curicum on Curictae, Crexa and Absortium on Apsorus (Osor), Arba (Rab) and Cissa (Pag). On the mainland behind Iader lay Nedinum, Corinium, Asseria, Alveria and Varvaria, and, less certain, Clambetae, Sidrona, Ansium and Pasinum (the last two not located).[75]

The postponed discharges of veterans from the armies of Illyricum caused by the wars of Augustus' later years are reflected in the high totals of years of service (*stipendia*) among veterans settled near Burnum and at Pagus Scunasticus in the territory of Narona.[76] In Dalmatia many veterans moved to the coastal colonies nearby. The mutiny of A.D. 14 in Pannonia was set off in part by the unappealing prospect of settling at the newly organized colony of Emona, whose defences were being completed in A.D. 14/15.[77] New colonies to accommodate Danubian veterans were instituted under Claudius. Savaria lay on the Pannonian Highway a few km south of a major settlement of the Celtic Boii, Aequum in Dalmatia near the vacated legionary base at Tilurium, and Aprus or Apri in Thrace near the Sea of Marmara. Legionary veterans were evidently the dominant group in these places, from VIII Augusta and XV Apollinaris in Savaria (though here civilians may have been among the original settlers), VII and XI Claudia at Aequum and VIII Augusta at Aprus. Well-placed smaller settlements also attracted veterans, evidently with official encouragement. In Pannonia along the road north of Savaria, the mixed veteran and civilian settlement Scarbantia boasted the title Iulia though it was not formally instituted as a *municipium* until the Flavian period.[78] The settlement of veterans by Claudius at a village in

[75] Wilkes 1969 (E 706) 107–15. [76] Alföldy 1987 (D 159) 298–312.

[77] Šašel 1968 (E 691) 564–5.

[78] Mócsy 1974 (E 677) 74 (Scarbantia), 76–9 (Savaria). Pliny, *HN* IV.47–8; *ILS* 2718; cf. Velkov 1977 (E 703) 122 (colonia Claudia Aprensis). Veterans were also settled at strategic places on the main highways of Thrace, Gerov 1961 (E 666).

the territory of Salona may have preceded the foundation at Aequum and have been a special provision for members of V Macedonica after service on the bleak wastes of the lower Danube.[79]

In Celtic Noricum five of that province's eight *municipia* were instituted under Claudius.[80] The establishment of Virunum in the Zollfeld brought an end to the commercial settlement on the Magdalensberg, though other factors, including the imposition of an imperial monopoly on the Norican iron workings, may have contributed to the demise of what seems to have been a centre of unbridled free enterprise. Virunum remained the seat of the provincial administration for more than a century and was the leading city in the province. Other *municipia* were Teurnia and Aguntum in the upper valley of the Drau/Drava, the former on a steep-sided hill above the river that ensured its survival in later centuries. Celeia in the south east had been a Celtic oppidum on the main highway between Emona and Poetovio. Iuvavum (Salzburg) lay north of the Tauern, where the Salzach emerges from its gorge. Though three new *municipia* were created in Noricum after the Julio-Claudian era, Flavian Solva in the Mur valley and Hadrianic Cetium and Ovilava near the Danube, the Claudian urbanization of Noricum marks the first external assimilation to Roman ways of the bulk of the native peoples in a Danubian province.

The third book of the Elder Pliny's *Natural History* includes lists of native communities (*civitates peregrinae*) of the Danube provinces which in part appear to be based on official lists drawn up following the Roman conquest. The lists of peoples in Ptolemy's *Geography*, which although compiled in the second century A.D. uses earlier information, differ at several points. Both accounts nevertheless furnish a reasonably comprehensive account of the native peoples as organized, divided or amalgamated following the formal imposition of Roman rule.[81]

In Illyricum an earlier scheme of administration had included a judicial district (*conventus*) based on Narona that included as many as eighty-six separate communities. Later the peoples of Dalmatia were grouped into three such districts, based on Scardona, Salona and Narona. The first was the smallest and contained the Iapodes and fourteen *civitates* of the Liburnia, evidently some smaller inland groups of whom Pliny deems only the Lacinienses, Stulpini, Burnistae (the native inhabitants of Burnum), and Olbonenses worth naming. To the lists of communities in the districts of Salona and Narona are added numerical totals of *decuriae* as an indication of their strength, and which may have been a unit of the Roman census roughly equivalent to existing native groups. Some of the peoples named are known from earlier times

[79] Pliny, *HN* III.141; *CIL* III 8753 (2028); cf. *AE* 1984, 228.
[80] Alföldy 1974 (E 652) 91–6.   [81] Mócsy 1974 (E 677) 53–4; Wilkes 1969 (E 706) 482–6.

and can be located with reasonable precision, while others were new Roman groupings of several smaller communities, some of whom are also named by Pliny.

The Delmatae, with 342 *decuriae*, belonged to the Salona *conventus* and were the largest people in the province that was named after them. Their territory extended along the Adriatic between the rivers Titus (Krka) and Narenta (Neretva) and extended inland across the watershed to include the high plains around Livno, Glamoč and Duvno. Deprived of much of the coast through Roman settlements, they had, for ease of communication, virtually the entire garrison of the province based within their territory and even when a legion was transferred its place was taken by a colony of veterans. There are indications that after A.D. 9 some of the Delmatae were transported to new settlements in the interior. The Ditiones (239 *decuriae*) lay north west of the Delmatae and occupied the forests and valleys of western Bosnia around the river Unac. Their territory was the initial terminus of one of the military roads constructed following the conquest, 'to the foot of mons Ulcirus of the Ditiones' (see above). North of these were the Pannonian Maezaei (269) in the Sana and Vrbas valleys, against whom Germanicus had led an expedition in A.D. 7. The Sardeates (52), possibly to be connected with the place Sarnade or Sarute on the main road between the Sava and the Adriatic, perhaps dwelt around Jajce in the Pliva valley, while the Deuri (25), the Derrioi of Ptolemy and perhaps the Derbanoi of Appian, dwelt around Bugojno in the upper valley of the Vrbas.

The thirteen communities of the Narona *conventus* represent a major reorganization of the earlier eighty-nine. They include the (V)ardaei, 'once ravagers of Italy but now reduced to a mere 20 *decuriae*', and the D(a)uersi (17), or Daorsi, who also figure in the warfare of the second century B.C. The Deraemestae (30) were a new formation from several smaller peoples in the hinterland of Epidaurum, including the Ozuaei, Partheni, Hemasini, Arthitae and Armistae. The peoples who had formed the core of the old Illyrian kingdom of the third to second centuries B.C., the Labeatae, Endirudini, Sasaei, Grabaei, the Illyrii 'properly so-called', Taulantii and Pyraei (the former Pleraei) were grouped to form the Docleatae based at Doclea, later a Flavian *municipium*, at the confluence of the rivers Zeta and Morača. Many of these communities were the inhabitants of a single settlement, for example Enderon (near Nikšić) of the Endirudini or Kinna (on the east of Lake Scodra) of the Kinambroi, who figure in the list of those who surrendered to Octavian in 33 B.C. The much diminished Daesitiates (103), who had begun the uprising in A.D. 6, inhabited central Bosnia around Sarajevo and the river Bosna. Their fortress (*castellum*) of Hedum, perhaps in the east of their territory near Breza, was the terminus of another of the military roads driven across the province after the conquest (see above). The Narensii (102) were evidently another new formation of peoples and from their name were centred on the river Naron or Narenta, perhaps the middle and upper course and including the plain around Mostar. Since they are listed among those peoples who submitted in 33 B.C. the Melcumani (24) are not likely to have lived any great distance from the coast. It has been suggested that they may have been inland of the Deraemestae, in the plains around Gačko and Nevesinje in eastern Hercegovina.

East and south of the Daesitiates, among the mountains around the upper Drina, Piva, Tara, and Lim valleys, dwelt the formidable Pirustae, 'almost unconquerable on account of the position of their strongholds in the mountains, their warlike temper and, above all, the narrow defiles in which they lived'.[82] Though named by Ptolemy they do not appear in the list of Pliny and, for reasons of security, had evidently been broken up into the hitherto unknown Siculotae (24) and Cerauni (24). The former may have included Delmatae transferred from the coast and perhaps occupied the area of Pljevlja in what is now northern Montenegro. Perhaps also once part of the Pirustae, though Ptolemy lists them separately as the Skirtones, were the more numerous Scirtari (72) who dwelt close to Macedonia, probably in northern Albania around the middle Drin. Also part of the Pirustae may have been the Glintidiones. As they are recorded also to have surrendered in 33 B.C. they were evidently more accessible than the rest and could have occupied the region of Foča in the upper Drina valley. The possible record, dating to the second century A.D., of a *princeps* at Skelani seems to locate the Dindari (33) in the middle Drina valley. Celtic names on epitaphs in that area suggest that they, like the Celegeri just across the border in Moesia, were really a group of the powerful Celtic Scordisci, whose northern communities survived as a *civitas* with their original name across the border in Pannonia.[83] Like the Pirustae it may have been deliberate policy to break them down into smaller groups and, in the case of the Scordisci, to divide them between three different Roman provinces.

Nothing on relative strength or *conventus* organization appears in Pliny's list of Pannonian *civitates*, which corresponds closely with the account of Ptolemy. As in Dalmatia several new formations appear, some named after rivers or places, while along the Danube in the north the Romans appear to have wrought major changes through the movement of whole communities on either bank of the river. The following communities can be located, downstream along the three

[82] Vell. Pat. II.115.4.

[83] Alföldy 1964 (E 646). The reconstruction has been rejected, on various grounds, by Papazoglu 1978 (E 681) 371–8.

major rivers: along the Danube the Boii, Azali, Eravisci, Hercuniates, Andizetes, Cornacates, Amantini and Scordisci; along the Drava the Serretes, Serapilli, Iasi, Andizetes and, between Serapilli and Boii, the Arabiates; along the Sava, the Catari, Latobici, Varciani, Colapiani, Osseriates, Breuci, Amantini and Scordisci. The Belgitae named by Pliny cannot be placed. A later addition was the *civitas* of the Cotini, perhaps in the low-lying ground south of Lake Balaton. Some of the above were well-known peoples before the conquest, notably the Boii, Breuci, Andizetes, Amantini, Scordisci and Latobici. Others are named from single places, the Cornacates from Cornacum (Šotin on the Danube above Belgrade), the Varciani from Varceia (attested but not located) and the Osseriates from a place somewhere on the middle Sava. Colapiani and Arabiates are named from the rivers Colapis (Kulpa) and Arabo (Raba), while perhaps the Hercuniates recalled in some way the Hercynia Silva, the great German forest beyond the Danube. Breuci and Amantini, prominent during the rebellion in A.D. 6–8, are likely to have been broken up into several *civitates*. Possibly the Cornacates belonged to the latter, while the Osseriates, Colapiani and Varciani were all created from the powerful Breuci. Similarly the Arabiates and Hercuniates in the west perhaps belonged to the Boii. The Illyrian Azali may also have been detached from the Breuci and transported north to a new home on the Danube between the Celtic Boii and Eravisci, possibly after the *Bellum Pannonicum* of 14–19 B.C. Beyond the river such changes were matched by the eastward migration of the Suebic Marcomanni and, somewhat later, the move of the Sarmatian Jazyges into the plain between Pannonia and Dacia (see above).

The identification and location of native communities in Moesia is hindered by an almost total lack of inscriptions earlier than the Flavian period. It can be assumed that Roman occupation and organization of Moesia was attended by less drastic measures towards the native population than had been the case in Illyricum. Pliny's list of peoples derives from the period before Moesia was extended to the Black Sea following the annexation of Thrace under Claudius and comprises Dardani, Celegeri, Triballi, Timachi, Moesi, Thraces and Scythiae 'adjacent to the Black Sea'.[84] Since the arrangement is geographical rather than alphabetical it may not be the official register of *civitates*, and seems to identify individual communities only as far east as the Triballi. Among these the Celegeri in the north west may, it has been suggested above, have belonged to the Celtic Scordisci, while the Timachi are the inhabitants of the Timacus (Timok) valley. The account of Ptolemy, which corresponds with Pliny's only in respect of the Moesi and Triballi, described arrangements following the Claudian reorganization. The

[84] Pliny, *HN* III.149, Ptol. *Geog.* III.9.2; Mócsy 1974 (E 677) 67–9.

Tricornenses of Tricornium (Ritopek) replaced the Celegeri, the Picensii of Pincum (Gradište) at the mouth of the Pincus (Pek) the Timachi, but the Dardani in the south and the *civitas* of the Moesi (around Ratiaria) continued as before. New *civitates* on the lower Danube were the Oetenses of Utus, at the river Utus (Vit), the Dimenses of Dimum (Baline), the Obulenses (who cannot be located), the Appiarenses of Appiaria (Ryahovo) and the Peucini named from the island Peuce (Chilia) in the Danube delta. Conditions were far from stable along the lower Danube under Claudius and Nero, and there is some evidence for a short-lived *civitas* of Dacians in the area, probably the result of deportations from across the river.[85]

Like that of Moesia the organization of Noricum as a Roman province appears to date from Claudius but a much earlier record of the native peoples under Roman rule are the dedications set up at the Magdalensberg in 10/9 B.C. to the three ladies of Augustus' family, Livia and the two Iulias.[86] The eight peoples involved were the Norici, Ambilini, Ambidr(avi), Uperaci, Saevates, Laianci, Ambisont(es) and Elveti. Ptolemy's list of the Norican peoples is broadly similar but adds the name of the Alauni. The Norici occupied the heartland of the old kingdom around Magdalensberg, perhaps the ancient capital Noreia, in Carinthia and part of upper Styria. The Ambilini, whose name suggests that they lived on both sides of a river, have been placed in the Gail valley, and may be linked with a place Ilouna somewhere in south-west Noricum. The Ambidravi were obviously along the Drau/Drava, and the Uperaci perhaps on their east in the direction of Pannonia, where they may be connected with a place named Upellae somewhere north of Celeia. A place named Sebatum appears to locate the Saevates in the Pustertal. These at first were grouped in a single *civitas* along with the Laianci, who may then have been their neighbours on the west in the area of Lienz, where the *municipium* Aguntum was later created. The Ambisontes, who appear also among the list of defeated Alpine peoples on Augustus' monument near Monaco (La Turbie), occupied the long valley of the Isonta or Ivarus (Salzach). Beyond them the Alauni dwelt around Salzburg and the Chiemsee, where dedications were erected to the local deities Alaunae, Alounae and Alona. The Elveti were doubtless somehow connected with the Helvetii far to the west, and may originate from the Helvetian Tigurini who entered Noricum in the second century B.C. From their place in the order of the peoples on the Magdalensberg dedications they were neighbours of the Ambisontes and possibly dwelt on the upper Mur or lower Salzach. These nine *civitates* will not have been the full total of Norican peoples since they cover only the

---

[85] Mócsy 1970 (E 676) 29 n. 32, citing *CIL* XVI 13, a military diploma issued to a 'Dacus' on 9 February A.D. 71.   [86] Šašel 1967 (E 690); Alföldy 1974 (E 652) 67.

south and west of the province. A suggestion that the total may have been thirteen, to match the number of niches in the 'meeting-hall' at Magdalensberg has been received with some scepticism.

The *civitates peregrinae* of the Danube provinces, perhaps totalling more than eighty by the period of Claudius, remained under military control for at least a generation. Some peoples not directly involved in the fighting under Augustus were administered through *ad hoc* commands, such as a prefecture of Iapydia and Liburnia during the war against Bato in A.D. 9. Local leaders fought on the Roman side, such as the leading citizen of Aenona in Liburnia awarded a 'greater torque' by Tiberius for service in the 'Dalmatian war' of the same year.[87] With legions and *auxilia* now in more or less permanent bases the decades of relative inactivity under Tiberius and his successors furnish some evidence of how the military administration of the native peoples was organized. Under Claudius or Nero the chief centurion of XIII Gemina at Poetovio is found in charge of the neighbouring Colapiani. The Boii and Azali in northern Pannonia were under the commander of the auxiliary regiment at Arrabona, who was also charged with responsibility for that section of the Danube bank. The Pannonian Maezaei and Daesitiates in northern Dalmatia were administered by the chief centurion of the XI Claudia at Burnum. The first recorded procuratorial governor of Noricum had earlier in his career administered the '*civitates* of Moesia and Triballia', either after or along with the post of chief centurion of V Macedonica at Oescus, indicating the pre-Claudian administration of what later became the *provincia* Moesia.[88] The communities of the Dardani may, in like fashion, have been the charge of senior officers of the other legion in the Balkans, IV Scythica at Scupi or Naissus. Among some of the peoples in Dalmatia there are signs that native chiefs may have been entrusted with power not long after the conquest, perhaps even avoiding altogether the unpleasantness of a military administration, for example among the Iapodes, some of the Delmatae and the Docleatae.[89] That stage may have been a preliminary to the later creation of cities, though in some cases long after the Julio-Claudian era. All the recorded titles of rank, such as *princeps*, or social and family organization, *gens, cognatio, centuria, decurio* and *decuria*, are of Roman origin, though the structures they denoted already had a long history and were to persist in some areas throughout the Roman era.[90]

All valid indicators combine to testify that Romanization, that much

---

[87] *ILS* 2673 and 3320 (probably from Aenona, *VAHD* 52 (1939–45), 55 fig. 1).

[88] *ILS* 9199 (Colapiani); 2737 (Boii and Azali); *CIL* IX 2564 (Maezaei and Daesitiates); *ILS* 1349 (Moesia et Treballia).

[89] *CIL* III 14325–8; 15064–5 ('principes' and 'praepositi' of the Iapodes at a shrine of Bindus Neptunus near Bihać in western Bosnia); III 2776 ('princeps' of Delmatae with Claudian citizenship); *ILIug* 185 ('princeps' of the 'civitas Docleatium'). [90] Wilkes 1969 (E 706) 185–90.

observed process of material and cultural diffusion during the early
Principate, made little or no headway among the Illyrians in the Julio-
Claudian era.[91] The same holds good for most of the Thracians,
notwithstanding their contacts with the Greek and hellenistic world, and
perhaps also for many of the Celtic peoples in the north west, where their
early adoption of what has been called the 'epigraphic habit' may have
led to an overestimation of Roman influence as a whole.

It is a fact that around the middle of the first century B.C. hellenistic
and Roman coins were entering the Danube lands in some quantities,
while several local groups among Thracians, Dacians, Illyrians and Celts
were producing their own coins to imitative standards. On the other
hand, it seems reasonable to accept the view that neither imports nor
local issues appear in sufficient quantities and nor do they exhibit a range
of denomination to indicate that there was a genuine economy based on a
circulating coinage. The many coins of Dyrrhachium and Apollonia that
appear in the area from *c*. 100 B.C. onwards may, as has been recently
suggested, relate to a slave trade, perhaps to meet the demands of a
Roman slave-based pastoral economy which had existed in the south-
west Balkans since the defeat of Macedon in 167 B.C. Similarly, the many
Roman denarii which appear in Dacia around the middle of the first
century B.C. may also derive from a traffic in slaves, in this case
Burebista's Dacia acting as a much-needed procurement agency after
Pompey's suppression of Mediterranean piracy in 67 B.C. Moreover,
when Burebista's powerful Dacia had gone and Rome had advanced to
the Danube, the amounts of Roman silver found beyond the river
suggests that supplies of slaves had then to be sought from beyond the
river. Roman coins came first to Illyricum with the armies and their
followers. Hoards are found along the Pannonian Highway, at Emona,
Celeia and Poetovio, and in the area of Mursa and Sirmium on the lower
Drava and Sava, all undoubted military centres in the time of Augustus.
A similar origin is likely for hoards found among the Delmatae, at
Bastasi and Livno, and among the Iapodes at Ribnica in the Lika, though
a more authentic economy is indicated by coin hoards from the more
settled areas near the coast, Zadar and Kruševo in Liburnia, Čapljina and
Narona in the Narenta valley and on the island Pharos at Hvar and
Gajine.[92]

Italy's commerce with the north east was based on Aquileia and the
road from there across Pannonia to the Danube. Across the Julian Alps a
Roman trading settlement (*vicus*) had already existed at Nauportus
(Vrhnika) in the late Republic, where once the native Celts had

---

[91] Note, however, Velleius' comment on the widespread knowledge and use of Latin among the
Pannonians, II.110.5; discussed by A. Mócsy in Hartley and Wacher 1983 (C 274) 235–7.
[92] Mirnik 1981 (B 345); Crawford 1985 (B 320) 235–7.

maintained their own customs station.[93] In addition to the traffic in slaves, cattle, hides and amber from the Baltic, Aquileia was also the focus for the wholesale import of finished metal products from Noricum. By around 50 B.C. a terrace (920m) below the summit (1058m) of the Magdalensberg was the site of a flourishing Roman emporium. Its prosperity is perhaps best signified by the lifesize bronze of the Celtic god Mars Latobius, dedicated by merchants from Aquileia, including one of the well-known Barbii family. Iron, copper, lead, zinc and brass (an alloy of copper and zinc) were all traded in quantities of finished utensils. Some of the timber-framed houses of Roman merchants exhibit a high standard of interior decoration. On the walls of some of the cellars, which were filled with debris c. 35 B.C., each with its own shrine of Mercury in a niche, were scratched inventories of finished wares; of iron or steel, rings (*anuli*), axes (*secures*), anvils (*incudes*), and hooks (*unci*); of brass or copper, jars (*cafi*), cups (*cumbae*), plates (*disci*), goblets (*scifi*) and jugs (*urcei*). After the annexation of Noricum Magdalensberg became the centre of a Roman administration and parts of the emporium were levelled to make space for a complex of official buildings. On some of the walls were scratched informal greetings to the emperors Augustus and Tiberius, whose features appear in caricature, along with notices of sacrifice, in addition to the more formal dedicatory plaques set up in 10/9 B.C. to ladies of the Augustan house by eight peoples of Noricum. Close to these buildings a classical temple, 30m by 18m and still unfinished when the settlement was abandoned, had perhaps been intended for a newly instituted cult of *Roma et Augustus*.[94]

Far from being precursors to Roman political and economic domination, the Roman settlements in Illyricum of the late Republic had little or no impact on the native peoples. Some *latifundia* may have existed around the lower Neretva on lands seized from the Delmatae but elsewhere the coastal settlements rather seem to have turned their backs on the interior, as has often happened in Dalmatian history. When the proconsul P. Vatinius responded to an inquiry by Cicero, addressed to his predecessor, regarding a runaway slave last seen at Narona, the proconsul's headquarters, the report that the fugitive had last been heard of among the Ardiaei implied that that was really the end of the matter, though Vatinius promised to do his best to find him if he was still within the province.[95] Veteran and civilian settlements in Achaea and Macedonia in the period up to Actium contributed little to urban development in those areas, save for the major centres of Patrae, Corinth, Nicopolis and Philippi. In Illyricum colonies around this time were also a mix of civilian and military settlement but with barely any trace of a native

[93] Tac. *Ann.* 1.20; Pliny, *HN* III.128; *ILLRP* 33–4 ('magistri' of *vicus*); Šašel 1966 (E 689).
[94] Piccottini 1977 (E 683) and for the graffiti, Egger 1961 (E 662).   [95] Cic. *Fam.* v.9.

component. By contrast the Julio-Claudian urbanization of Liburnia and Noricum owed little to Roman settlement, civil or military.

In the matter of town-planning and civic architecture the early Roman cities were far from uniform. Narona (Vid) retained the character of an emporium on a hill enclosed by pre-Roman walls but containing some fine buildings and monuments, many erected by prosperous freedmen. Here the landowning class, if it figured at all in the life of the city, chose to reside in the elegant and well-appointed residences known to have existed in the surrounding country during the first century A.D. At Salona a new *forum* was planned within a street-grid at the centre of the old *conventus*, though in the grandeur of its architecture it cannot compare with the impressive double-precinct *forum* and Capitolium at Iader, which occupied a large block, 180m by 130m, at the centre of the city's street-grid. At nearby Aenona the Capitolium stood within a new *forum*, in which were placed several larger than lifesize statues of the Julio-Claudians carved in Carrara marble. The symmetrically planned defences and street grid of Emona, 524m by 435m, recall those of Augustan foundations at Augusta Praetoria (Aosta) or Augusta Taurinorum (Turin). The later veteran colonies at Aequum and Savaria were also planned cities, as was the *municipium* Virunum in Noricum, though the latter lacked defensive walls. Not all Roman cities were on new and level sites: the Claudian *municipia* in Liburnia saw native hill-settlements physically transformed into Roman cities, for example Asseria and Varvaria, with a regular *forum* and other public works inserted within the defended precinct. The territory of several colonies in Illyricum is known to have been surveyed and divided by roads and paths into grids of square *centuriae*. The systems so far known, at Salona, Iader, Narona, Epidaurum, Pola and Savaria, had *centuriae* measuring 20 by 20 *actus* (*c.* 710m by 710m) giving an area of *c.* 124 acres (*c.* 51 ha), the prevailing standard of the early Principate.[96]

Though some vestiges of hellenistic traditions survived in the Adriatic cities, the Roman cities in the Danube lands as a whole exhibit a wholly Roman and Italian character. Throughout the Julio-Claudian era bricks and roof-tiles produced in large factories around Aquileia, at least one of which (the Pansiana) was imperially owned, were shipped down the Adriatic, although the army began to make its own bricks and tiles locally under Claudius.[97] The Danube armies stimulated local produc-

[96] Zaninović 1977 (E 711) 791–3, and 1980 (E 712) (Narona); Clairmont 1975 (E 655) 38–82 (Salona); Suić 1976 (E 697) 150–3 (Iader and Aenona), 138 fig. 74 (Asseria), 88–104 (centuriation); Šašel 1968 (E 691) 549–55 (Emona); Mócsy 1974 (E 677) 74–89 (Emona and Savaria), 78–9 (centuriation); Wilkes 1969 (E 706) 359 fig. 15 and 369 (Aequum), 366–7 (Asseria); Alföldy 1974 (E 652) 87–9 (Virunum). Bradford 1957 (A 7) 175–93 (centuriation).
[97] Wilkes 1969 (E 706) 499–502; Matijašić 1987 (E 674) 495–531.

tion of ornate tombstones, especially in the fine limestone of the Dalmatian coast. Some early legionary monuments in Dalmatia are in the style of the 'door-stone', a type originating in Asia Minor favoured by recruits of eastern origin, notably in legion VII. The most popular form, both among soldiers and in the cities, incorporated the 'window-portraits' of the metropolitan Roman fashion within an architectural frame of pediment and columns in relief on a standing tombstone, with the framed panel for the epitaph below. A similar version became popular in Noricum and Pannonia, where Celtic and Roman funeral images appear in combination. Roman epitaphs are found on the Liburnian circular tombstones, a native tradition which remained popular in the new *municipia* of the Julio-Claudian era. It is a relief sculpture in Dalmatian limestone which provides perhaps the most authentic image of Rome in the Danube lands at this time, a monument at Tilurium which depicts the trophy (*tropaeum*) or Roman victory with two native Illyrians chained to its base, awaiting a fate that was all too certain.[98]

Before the conquest was completed Thracians, Illyrians and Celts were being recruited for service in the Roman *auxilia*, both as cavalry and infantry. Several units appear bearing the names of such peoples as Breuci, Delmatae and Pannonii. The many Dalmatians who served in the imperial fleets at Ravenna and Misenum came it seems as much from the inland peoples as from the seafarers along the Adriatic.[99] No consequence of this recruitment is discernible before the end of the Julio-Claudian period in respect of the spread of Roman ways and habits. Doubtless there were some, their origins concealed, who rose from these lands to high positions in the Roman hierarchy.[100] No Roman governor praises the Danubians for their eager embrace of Roman *mores*: indeed the contrary was for long to prevail.

Conquest and retention of the Danube lands was, in the military sphere, the distinguishing achievement of Augustus' Principate. A harsh, underdeveloped and for long intractable part of Europe brought no profit and much loss. Yet completion of the task was essential for a strategy which deployed the new standing armies around the borders and far from the centre of affairs where their presence nearly always posed a threat to order. The Via Egnatia no longer saw the passage of armies to fight civil wars, and only the fall of a dynasty drew the legions back to the heart of the empire from their remote bases along the Danube.

[98] Illustrations in Wilkes 1969 (E 706).

[99] Kraft 1951 (E 672); Starr 1960 (D 237) 75.

[100] Certainly Liburnia had links with some leading senators in the first century. The consul of 16 B.C. L. Tarius Rufus may be of Liburnian origin, and the distinguished jurist of the Flavian era L. Iavolenus Priscus had Liburnian family connexions. See Alföldy 1968 (E 651) 100–16.

CHAPTER 13*i*

ROMAN AFRICA: AUGUSTUS TO VESPASIAN

C. R. WHITTAKER

I. BEFORE AUGUSTUS

If the province of Africa under the Roman Republic was not quite a land without a history, as Mommsen described it, it was certainly not central to Roman interests. The administration from the Punic town of Utica was rudimentary, largely a matter of supervising the local communities and contracting out the taxes. Nor is there much evidence of a military garrison apart from the small contingent with the governor. This did not, of course, prevent Roman and Italian immigrants from coming, whether as settlers on the land or as businessmen and tax-farmers. But the impression we get is that the numbers were not great, even in the coastal towns, where Roman enclaves formed.[1] The official foundation of the colony of Carthage in 122 B.C. had been a disaster that had left stranded we do not know how many on its territory. Conservative Roman sentiment had resented the expense of the province and had feared to send out colonists. Evidence of Romans and Italians being settled by Marius is so thin that it is unwise to guess too much about their numbers, although some immigrants probably did arrive.

The only exception to this was the Gaetulian veterans of Marius, settled beyond the far borders of the province, who proved a valuable aid to Iulius Caesar in his campaigns in Africa in 46 B.C., and who were to be an important element in the new Augustan dispensation.[2] During the civil wars between Pompey and Caesar a fair number of Romans took refuge in Africa. But even so, the Pompeians were hard put to it to raise 12,000 men and, even after reinforcements of 10,000 from Cyrene, they almost certainly had to include native Africans, slaves and freedmen to raise a force of 40,000.

If immigration was relatively light, economic interest in the Roman province of Africa and the adjacent territories of the Mauretanias was considerable – in particular because of the fertile land, the corn and (probably) the slaves. By Cicero's day Africa was regarded as a 'bulwark' of Rome's food supply. Beyond the provincial borders Libyan cities like Vaga (mod. Beja) and Cirta (mod. Constantine) were teeming with

---

[1] Cf. Caes. *BAfr.* 97.2.   [2] Caes. *BAfr.* 35.4.

Italian *negotiatores* in the second century B.C. Archaeological sites in modern western Morocco are reported to contain the relics of as many Italian republican amphorae as those in southern France.[3] Sales of land in the African province are recorded in the Agrarian Law of 111 B.C. to have taken place on several occasions, probably to absentee owners in Rome. There may have been further sales thereafter. All this interest was to have its influence on Augustan policy.

Precisely what Iulius Caesar intended or achieved during the brief period of his dictatorship between 46 and 44 B.C. is not always clear. Massive indemnities were laid upon the coastal cities of Byzacium (south-eastern Tunisia) and Tripolitania, the latter being required to pay an annual tax of 1 million litres of oil, which probably continued until the third century A.D. The adjacent territory of Numidia was organized into a second province named Africa Nova, which Caesar announced would pay 8,000 tonnes of corn in tax, to the acclaim of the Roman people. New settlers came, too, not only to the province of Nova, with its curious annex around Cirta, but also to other places in the old province. Many were veterans of the civil war, hastily demobilized to avoid trouble. But many were surely some of those 80,000 inhabitants of the city of Rome whom Caesar sent abroad. Africa's land and food continued to excite Roman interest.[4]

Here we run into intractable problems of identifying and dating the colonial foundations which absorbed many of these settlers. While there can be little doubt about Caesar's intentions to reorganize the African province, there is no way of proving whether the final act of foundation was Caesar's or his heir's. The best evidence we have of Caesar's work is an inscription from the *colonia* of Curubis (mod. Korba) on Cape Bon, recording an urban magistrate in 45 B.C. But in a sense it hardly matters. Both Caesar and Octavian acted under similar pressures and it seems perfectly possible that what was *de facto* begun by Caesar was formally completed by Augustus. Those who perceive grandiose hellenistic schemes in the settlements[5] perhaps forget the simple logic of what took place. Civil wars left confiscated land available for allocation to the victors. Veterans and the Roman poor could reanimate and control some of the most productive territory known in its day.

The foundation of the colony of Carthage illustrates perfectly the difficulty we have in separating Caesar and Augustus. By the end of Augustus' rule Carthage had become the administrative capital of the united provinces of Africa Vetus and Nova and a city of some size and

---

[3] Cic. *Leg. Man.* 34; cf. shipping at Utica, Caes. *BCiv.* 11.25.6. For amphorae, A. Hesnard in Lancel 1985 (E 748) 49–59.

[4] Dio XLIII.14.1; Suet. *Iul.* 42.1. The best discussion of Caesarian settlements is Teutsch 1962 (E 765).   [5] See Broughton 1971 (E 721), against Kornemann, who put forward this view.

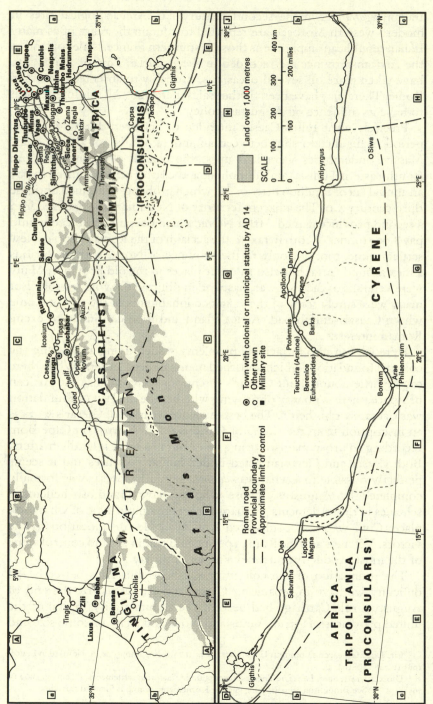

Map 13. Africa.

splendour. The territory or *pertica* of Carthage stretched at least as far as Thugga (mod. Dougga), 100km down the Bagradas valley,[6] incorporating a whole series of communities of both Roman settlers and natives. But who was the founder of Roman Carthage? Most now agree that, although Caesar may have drawn up plans, the actual, physical foundation was probably not his, if only because the *pertica* of Carthage extended into lands which formed part of Caesar's province of Africa Nova – surely an impossibility until after his death, when the two provinces became one.

But when after 44 B.C. this happened is impossible to be sure. An enigmatic statement by the Christian theologian, Tertullian, two centuries later, claimed that it was 'after the violent abuse of Lepidus and after long delays by Caesar, when Statilius Taurus set up the walls and Sentius Saturninus pronounced the religious rites'. The most plausible date is perhaps 36 or 35 B.C., when Cassius Dio records that Octavian sent out Statilius Taurus as his agent to win over 'both the Africas'. The old provinces were evidently not yet united and were 'in need of a settlement'. Taurus accomplished both, at a time when Octavian's army was racked with mutinous troops demanding their rewards and just after the two governors of Vetus and Nova had been fighting each other. The grant of municipal status to Utica in 36 B.C., presumably after adjustment of its boundaries, adds some corroboration that this was the period of reorganization for the whole territory.[7]

The most cogent objection to such a date is that the prestigious cult of the Cereres fertility gods in Carthage, for which we have a lot of inscriptional evidence in later periods, adopted a system of dating its priesthoods which probably went back to before 35 B.C., although the evidence is not entirely consistent. It is not, however, compellingly self-evident that the start of the cult, which had had a long Libyan history before this, and the foundation of the Roman colony were linked.[8] Nor is it difficult to accept the evidence that the final colonial charter and 'freedom' of the city waited until 29 or 28 B.C., since delays between the award of status and the adoption of a charter are not unknown elsewhere.[9]

---

[6] *NTH* 510.

[7] Tertull. *De Pall.* 1; Dio XLIX.14.6, 34.1. Utica–Dio XLIX.16.1. M. Le Glay in Lancel 1985 (E 748) 235–48 is the most recent to put the view contradicted here.

[8] Février 1975 (E 731), *contra*, the view of Fishwick and Shaw 1978 (E 733). Gascou 1987 (E 740) has radically undermined the accepted dates of inscriptions and favours 44 B.C. as year 1 of the Cereres priesthood.

[9] Dio LII.43.1. A sensible summary of the evidence is in Van Nerom 1969 (E 754).

II. AFRICA AND THE CIVIL WARS, 44–31 B.C.

The civil wars which broke out after the death of Iulius Caesar in 44 B.C. inevitably sucked in not only the two provinces of Africa Nova and Vetus but also the allied kings of the Maghreb who depended on the favours of Roman politicians but were not above profiting from their rivalries.[10] The Libyan prince Arabion, for instance, returned to central Mauretania in 44 B.C. and, encouraged by the sons of Pompey in Spain, killed Caesar's old ally Sittius, who had been settled with his mixed bag of followers at Cirta. Having arrived at an accord with the remaining Sittiani, he brought them over in support of the senatorial governor of Vetus, Q. Cornificius, against the Caesarian governor of Nova, T. Sextius – only to switch support completely in favour of Sextius against Cornificius as the luck of Caesar's murderers ran out in 42 B.C. He subsequently resisted Octavian's nominee, Fango, but was executed by Sextius (by now a supporter of Antony) on the suspicion of his too great ambition, which caused his supporters to change sides yet again in support of Fango. Sextius finally drove the whole lot out of the African provinces.

Further west in Morocco a similar power struggle was being played out between King Bogud, who supported Antony against Bocchus when the latter gave his support to the revolt of Tingis (mod. Tangiers) against Bogud. For his opportunistic action Octavian rewarded Bocchus with Bogud's kingdom plus the rest of western Mauretania from Tingis to Cirta. This large territory Bocchus ruled until his death in 33 B.C.

The events of the civil war are confusing and confused. After Brundisium the two African provinces were allotted to Lepidus in 40 B.C. as his share of the triumviral dispositions and he built up an enormous army there of sixteen legions for the invasion of Sicily in 36 B.C. against the Pompeians. This massive army group certainly included many native recruits and must have denuded Africa of its defences. After the disappearance of Lepidus, Octavian – as we saw – realized the pressing need to restore order and sent one of his iron men, Statilius Taurus, in 36 B.C. to do the job. The archives record three triumphs *ex Africa* between 34 and 28 B.C., which we may assume to have been won for border wars to secure the newly formed province of Africa Proconsularis and its colonists.

But the wars were also partly the consequence of the death of Bocchus in 33 B.C., who had controlled the Mauretanias as Octavian's nominee. Dio claims that Octavian actually annexed this vast territory, and this has been taken as explanation of the anomalous fact that later, after a new puppet ruler, Juba II, had been installed in 25 B.C., we find a number of

[10] The complex narrative is mainly in App. *BCiv.* IV.53ff; supplemented by Dio XLVIII.21–23.

Roman veteran colonies existing within the native kingdom. On balance it seems unlikely that Octavian went this far. There is no allusion to Mauretania as a province in the account of the settlement of 27 B.C.; nor to the name of any governor. Whereas the fact that some new colonies were founded in western Mauretania, probably in 33 B.C., is no proof of Octavian's intention, since we know that later, after 25 B.C., the Mauretanian colonies were administered from Spain, which shows that such an arrangement was not an institutional impossibility.[11] To install Juba as ruler in 33 B.C., after he had been raised at Rome in Octavian's own household, would have provoked a violent reaction among the Mauri (as indeed happened later) just at a point when the civil war was at its most critical. But so too would annexation. Octavian simply shelved a decision until 25 B.C., when, after his expedition to Spain, he saw the pressing need for action. Juba, as we shall see, was an important agent of what Augustus intended for the whole of the African settlement.

III. AUGUSTAN EXPANSION

Very little is known of the details of the Augustan expansion. We have to be content with names on triumphal lists plus a few names in the literary sources, some of them inadequate for positive identification. Wars are recorded in 21 B.C., 19 B.C., c. 15 B.C., c. A.D. 3 and A.D. 6. The end result was a permanent winter camp for the army at Ammaedara (mod. Haidra), at the source of the river Bagradas (mod. Medjerda) on the high plains of Tunisia, and a road completed by A.D. 14 dropping down from the uplands via Capsa (mod. Gafsa) to Tacape (mod. Gabes) on the Tunisian coast.[12]

Much speculation has gone into just how far beyond this line the Roman armies advanced, fuelled by an intriguing report full of mysterious place-names from the Elder Pliny concerning a desert campaign against the southern Garamantes by L. Cornelius Balbus, who triumphed in 19 B.C.[13] There are also some briefer references to a victory over the Gaetulians, after they had rebelled against Juba, won by Cossus Cornelius Lentulus in A.D. 6. Between these two dates we also learn of a victory gained by a certain Quirinius over the Marmaridae and Gara-

---

[11] Dio XLIX.43.7, LIII.12.4–6; Pliny, *HN* v.2. Gsell 1930 (E 741) 223, Gascou 1982 (E 738) 144 and Mackie 1983 (E 753) accept the brief provincial period of Mauretania from 33 to 25 B.C., perhaps governed from Spain; but the main argument, that Octavian would not have handed over Mauretania because of the propaganda war against Antony, is not persuasive, given the difficulties of annexing a huge, wild territory just when preparing for civil war in 33 B.C. For the colonies, see Mackie 1983 (E 753).

[12] *CIL* VIII 10018; EJ² 290; *ILAFr* 654 – *Asprenas ... pr.cos ... viam ex castris hibernis Tacapes muniendam curavit. legio III Augusta* (*Tacapes* is an indeclinable variation of *Tacape* – here 'to Tacape').

[13] Pliny, *HN* v.35–8; Flor. II.31; Dio LV.28.3–4. Pliny's names are analysed by Daniels 1970 (E 725) 13–16 and Desanges 1957 (E 727).

mantes (see ch. 13*j*, p. 635–6) and of triumphal *ornamenta* being granted to L. Passienus Rufus. But wild theories about Balbus' penetration to the Niger Bend via the Tasili and Hoggar Mountains can really not be credited, given the terrible problems encountered by far better equipped French expeditions to the Sahara in the nineteenth century, and we must settle for the more sober judgment that what we are witnessing is the reaction of Libyan tribes to Roman imperialism over the whole of the southern pre-desert.

The appointment of Juba II in 25 B.C. over a huge territory that extended not only to the Mauretanias (roughly central Algeria to Morocco) but also in theory along the whole Gaetulian or Numidian borders of the Roman province as far as Cyrenaica, provoked a chronic and violent response from the various 'nomadic' peoples, as Strabo calls them.[14] Some of these peoples in loosely confederated groups tradition-ally migrated up onto the plains of Constantine and to the Tunisian Dorsal, recognizing no artificial frontiers. An inscription recording disturbances, which was set up by a Roman settler about A.D. 3 near the colony of Assuras (mod. Zanfur) in the rich Tunisian corn-lands, perhaps reflects the problem this caused. At all events, Cossus is said to have 'held back the Musulami and Gaetuli in their widespread wander-ing to a restricted territory and forced them through fear to keep away from Roman frontiers'.[15]

References to the Marmaridae, who are normally associated with Cyrenaica, and to the Garamantes of the Fezzan in modern Libya show how far eastwards these African borderlands extended – so much so that there have been hypotheses that Tripolitania was temporarily detached from the province of Africa to that of Cyrene and that there was a joint strategy conducted by the two governors. If so, it was brief and little of permanence was achieved, since the archaeology of the Fezzan and Libyan Valleys reveals no Roman contact with the hinterland before the Flavian period.[16] But we can be sure that Juba's kingdom was regarded as an integral part of the defences of Africa and it was his inability to handle such a large remit that drew the Romans southwards.

The southern tribes saw Juba for what he was, a Roman agent, and they did not in any case recognize the authority of super-kings. It is not hard to see what they were fighting for. The Musulami, one of the principal names mentioned in the campaigns, controlled a region near Ammaedara, and it was here that the legion's headquarters was finally

---

[14] Strab. XVII.3.7 (828C); cf. VI.4.2 (286–8C). 'Nomades' in Greek can also mean Numidian. For Juba's kingdom, see Desanges 1964 (E 728).

[15] *CIL* VIII 16456; Oros. *Adv. Pag.* VI.21.18; Flor. II.3.

[16] The UNESCO Libyan Valleys Survey has been reported in successive volumes of *Libyan Studies* since 1979. It was Gsell 1930 (E 741) who first suggested Tripolitania may have been temporarily attached to Cyrenaica.

established. The road running from the base to the Gulf of Gabes constituted a check to the traditional, seasonal movements northwards of the Gaetulian Libyans from the oases and Chotts (salt marshes) of south-eastern Tunisia. Further east, Tripolitania needed protection from the Garamantes of the Fezzan and the Nasamones of the Syrtic Gulf and both must have seen the road that was completed soon after Augustus' reign along the eastern Jebel Nefoussa as a threat to their independence.[17] Whether Augustus really had in mind a grand design or was merely reacting to protect the provincials is discussed later. It is clear that he did not solve the problem.

IV. TIBERIUS AND TACFARINAS

Armed resistance after the initial conquest was fairly typical of the process of pacification in most western provinces, the revolt of Sacrovir and Florus in Gaul, Boudica's rebellion in Britain, the attempt of Civilis in Germany being obvious examples. A variety of reasons for this resentment against Roman rule is given in our sources; hatred of arrogant or corrupt officials, dislike of military recruiting officers. Often, no doubt, it was sheer opportunism when Rome seemed to be otherwise engaged. But above all it was the imposition of Roman taxation on land which caused the greatest anger.[18]

The revolt of Tacfarinas must be seen within the context of the Roman advances, which brought with them steady appropriation of land, the imposition of an ordered tax system and obligations to provide recruits. Although little is known about the tax arrangements, an undated dedication by forty-four *civitates* of Africa to a tribune of the III Augustan legion who had conducted the census, shows the hand taken by the military in the operation.[19] Tacfarinas, a chief of the Numidian Musulami, had served in the Roman auxiliaries, no doubt as part of an ethnic unit. So we can see all the elements of imperialism which absorbed the southern Gaetulians into the Roman administration.

The cadastration of southern Tunisia for tax purposes, completed in A.D. 29/30, was probably begun as soon as Ammaedara became the legionary headquarters, since the *decumanus maximus*, the base line of orientation for the cadaster, was probably fixed on the conical peak of Jebel bou el Hanĕche just north of the camp.[20] The various 'Gaetulian' tribes – the name is used by the Romans loosely to mean southerners – such as the Musulami, the Cinithii, the Nybgenii and the Tacapitani,

[17] EJ[2] 291 is a milestone recording the road.
[18] Dyson 1975 (C 266). For causes in general, see Dio LXVII.4.6; Tac. *Ann.* III.40; *Hist* IV.14; *Agr.* XXXI. [19] *CIL* III 338. Tacfarinas' land demands, Tac. *Ann.* III.73.
[20] Trousset 1978 (E 768) 141.

therefore, found their seasonal movements controlled by the frontier roads and fortifications. Equally provocative, they were probably expected to acknowledge the Roman puppet Juba as their overlord, which gave them common cause for resistance with the western Mauri. Juba's silver coins recording victories in A.D. 16 – a year before the date of Roman intervention – perhaps show that Juba had been trying to deal with the troublesome tribes already.[21]

It is hard to believe that the war between Tacfarinas and Rome, which eventually developed in A.D. 17 and lasted until A.D. 24 was a serious threat to Roman power in Africa. Velleius Paterculus, a contemporary, barely mentions it and, apart from brief references in later epitomators, it is only really Tacitus who gives the episode any prominence, because he was obsessed with the story of the emperor Tiberius, in whose reign the events occurred. He had little interest in the geography of the war and none in its causes. Various place-names are mentioned in the fighting – Thubuscum, Thala, Auzia, Cirta, Lepcis and the river Pagyda; various tribes like the Cinithii and Garamantes are said to have been involved.[22] But how much we can reconstruct out of this is very uncertain. Auzea, if the same as the later town of that name (mod. Sour El Ghozlane) south east of Algiers, lies 1,600 km west of Lepcis Magna. Thubuscum may be later Thubursicum Numidarum (mod. Khamissa) in east Algeria, or Thubursicum Bure (mod. Teboursouk) in Tunisia or one of half a dozen other like-sounding names. The basic fact, however, remains; the war was wide-ranging and it both implicated the Garamantes in the east and extended deep into Algeria in the west.

The fighting, which began with an attack on Thala near Ammaedara, extended to other 'cities'. This probably means that there was a series of hit-and-run raids or *razzia*, typical of mounted nomadic people, deep into the African province. The Gaetulians eluded Roman reprisals by retreating into the 'desert', until the arrival of Iunius Blaesus, uncle of Sejanus, as the new governor in A.D. 18. His tactics, like those of his successor, P. Dolabella in A.D. 23–4, were to isolate Tacfarinas from his base by what was called 'blockhouse' strategy in the Boer War – the location of permanent *castella* and fortifications at 'suitable places', most plausibly at points like Kasserine, Sbeitla and Thelepte to control the passes up on to the Tunisian Dorsal, where later Roman towns developed.

The IX legion (or detachments of it) was posted from Pannonia,[23]

[21] Desanges 1964 (E 728).

[22] Tac. *Ann.* II.52; III.20–1, 32, 73–4; IV.13, 23–6; Vell. Pat. II.125. Places discussed by Syme 1951 (E 764).

[23] Tac. *Ann.* III.74 and EJ² 210 show the commander, P. Cornelius Lentulus Scipio, came with the legion.

partly to protect Lepcis Magna from the threat of the Garamantes and partly, it would seem, to keep the Libyan peasants in check in the old province, since they erupted when the legion was withdrawn about A.D. 22. Blaesus' settlement, for which he was awarded triumphal honours that year, further deteriorated when Juba's son, Ptolemy, succeeded his father in A.D. 23 and alienated many of his Mauri troops. Despite this, Dolabella, an experienced commander on the Danube, finally trapped Tacfarinas at Auzia in Mauretania in A.D. 24, killing him and executing several of his Musulami leaders. Soon after this a Roman military prefect was set up over the *nationes Gaetulicae*. The end of the Musulami also brought the Garamantes to Rome to beg for peace, for which they had probably to pay by the loss of some of the territory that we now find being allotted to Lepcis Magna.[24]

From now until the end of Tiberius' rule we hear of no more African resistance, although we may suspect there were continual troubles caused by the cadastration that was carried out by the army over a great breadth of land in south-eastern Tunisia. Judging by the existing, numbered marker stones, it extended over at least 27,000 square km, as far as the Chott el Fedjaj. Although this cadastration divided the land into large blocks for the purpose of tax, there is occasional evidence of centuriation into smaller units and probable allotment of land. By A.D. 29/30 the main work of survey had been finished and the marker stones, of which we have twenty surviving examples, were set up by the governor C. Vibius Marsus. Dolabella, who was almost certainly the initiator of the survey, for which he had recently had experience in Dalmatia, was not much honoured in Rome but he was remembered in Lepcis.[25]

The Tacfarinas episode is less important for the threat that it posed than for the information it provides about the character of African society and frontier relations in this period. Several features need explanation: the width of native territorial alliances, yet the feebleness of the resistance; the close relationship between the desert and the sown and the effect on this of Roman intervention. The use of general terms like *tota Gaetulia* or Numidia by ancient and modern historians gives a misleading impression of African unity, which did not exist. Modern comparative evidence from semi-nomadic peoples of the southern Tunisian and Algerian marches suggests that 'tribes' are themselves highly unstable alliances of both sedentary and mobile fractions whose unity depends on success in raiding warfare and economic reciprocity. Rights of movement, rights of grazing and rights of exchange, which can

[24] Aur. Vict. 4.2; *ILS* 2721; *IRT* 331; EJ[2] 218a (dated A.D. 35/6).
[25] Land markers – *CIL* VIII 22786 (cf. EJ[2] 264), 22789; *ILTun* 71, 73, 74. Lepcis monument – *AE* 1961, 107–8. See Trousset 1978 (E 768).

take place over quite wide distances, are more important than complete ownership of the land and territorial demarcation.

Tacfarinas was a Numidian or Gaetulian member of the Musulami 'tribe', who, having proved his leadership in war, established far-ranging but fragile alliances with other Mauri, Gaetulian and Garamantes groups, based on resentment of Roman rule. His own Musulami apparently maintained specific links with people on the Tunisian and Algerian uplands, as well as operating from winter bases in the regions of the southern oases and Chotts. We are told that peasants of central Tunisia supported him, and Tacitus says that he traded for the corn that grew there. His request for a land concession for his people could mean that he wished to become sedentary; but it could just as well mean a demand for free access to historic grazing grounds. We know from Massinissa's dispute with the Punic Carthaginians that access to the 'Great Plains' of central Tunisia, the fertile uplands where the main production of wheat took place, was regarded by Libyan nomads in those days as their historic right.[26]

Almost certainly Roman property rights and boundaries were concepts unknown in customary practice for southern groups like the Tacapitani or Nybgenii who had had little or no contact with either Punic or Roman republican powers. The Roman term for 'marking out' (*limitare*) the land by boundary stones of the cadaster was a word that came to be used of a frontier and carried with it even at this stage the implication of 'limiting' and controlling the movements of the southern tribal groups.[27] If Tacfarinas had used the routes south of the Aures Mountains to reach the plain of Constantine, as seems probable, then the need to control such routes must have been evident already to the Romans.

V. GAIUS TO NERO

The emperor Gaius has been credited with two important changes in north Africa: the separation of the army under its *legatus* from the province of Africa; and the ending of the independent status of Mauretania. Neither is strictly correct. Each stemmed from a single cause. Tacitus and Dio record the first event briefly and with contradictory information,[28] but they broadly agree that fear of senior senators in command of an army stimulated Gaius in A.D. 37 into separating the legion, not from the province but from the direct command and

---

[26] Note the Numidians at Masculula not far from Simitthu (cf. n. 29 below), EJ² 111. Tacfarinas' corn – Tac. *Ann.* IV.13. Massinissa's claims – App. *Pun.* 68.

[27] *leg(io) III Aug(usta) leimitavit*; e.g. EJ² 264.

[28] Tac. *Hist.* IV.48; Dio LIX.20.7. Bénabou 1972 (E 714).

patronage of the governor, by placing an imperial legate in charge. The army remained active within the province.[29] Such a form of split command was not unparalleled nor even remarkable, and proconsular governors continued from time to time to take the military command. It is, however, geographically correct that soon after this, in the Flavian period, the army's base moved into the ill-defined region of Numidia south and west of Ammaedara, first to Theveste (mod. Tebessa) and then to Lambaesis (mod. Lambèse).

The annexation of Mauretania, the huge territory extending from Algeria west of the Ampsaga (mod. Oued el Kabir) to the Atlantic, was the decision of Gaius' successor, Claudius, following the war which broke out after Gaius had executed Ptolemy in A.D. 40. Exactly why Gaius did this is a matter for debate, since Tacitus, Suetonius and Dio, our main sources for the episode, had no love either for Gaius or for a native king and they let their prejudices show.[30] Suetonius gives us a childish story about how Ptolemy upstaged the emperor at a public spectacle in Lyons by appearing adorned in a purple cloak. Dio more realistically says there were fears that Ptolemy was becoming too wealthy. Tacitus portrays Ptolemy as a weak, unpopular fop, dominated by his freedmen.

The danger of the large kingdom of Mauretania to Rome always lay in a ruler who might become too independent to control. Ptolemy's striking of gold coins, very much an imperial prerogative, suggests his assertion of emancipation, just at the time when Gaius had been badly shaken by a plot of distinguished senators on the northern frontier, one of whose leaders was Cornelius Lentulus Cossus 'Gaetulicus', son of Juba's ally in A.D. 6 and therefore heir to his father's political friends. Ptolemy himself, no doubt fearing Roman penetration further and further into Numidia and Mauretania, became a willing target for conspiratorial plans. He was, after all, Antony's grandson and cousin to the emperor. It was no coincidence that Gaul was the place to which Ptolemy was summoned in A.D. 39, since Gaius had gone there to deal with the northern crisis. The bravado of the appearance confirmed that he must go. With him went the last of the great Libyan kings.

If Ptolemy had been as unpopular as Tacitus described him, his death would hardly have provoked a violent reaction in western Mauretania, much less a rebellion conducted by one of his 'freedmen', Aedemon. One suspects that Aedemon was in reality a vassal, one of the Mauri princes at court, and that many Mauri chiefs saw in Ptolemy a symbol of their

---

[29] E.g. EJ² 260 – a soldier who served nineteen years in an outpost at Simitthu in the north west of the province over this period; Tac. *Hist.* IV.50 – the legate at Hadrumetum.

[30] Suet. *Calig.* 35; Dio LIX.25; Tac. *Ann.* IV.23. Faur 1973 (E 730) in preference to Fishwick 1971 (E 732).

freedom. In later years Roman governors thought it politic to honour the name of Juba II and Ptolemy with commemorative statues and one Roman pretender in A.D. 69 even took the name of Juba to win local favour.[31] From archaeological evidence it would appear that the rebellion concentrated on violent attacks on towns of western Mauretania, centres like Tamuda, Lixus and Kouass where Romans were no doubt trading. At Volubilis, an important centre which may have had special treaty status, Roman citizenship had already been extensively granted to local families, as we know from two famous inscriptions commemorating M. Valerius Severus, son of Bostar, who raised a troop of irregular horse and was subsequently able to petition for privileges, including 'Roman citizenship' (meaning, probably, municipal status) for the town.[32]

The Roman campaign was a long and arduous affair, requiring supplies from Spain. The main details come from the Elder Pliny, a contemporary, supplemented by Cassius Dio.[33] It is clear, however, that Dio is correct against Pliny to date the war from A.D. 40 before Claudius' accession. In A.D. 41–2 the theatre extended down the Moulouya gap to the Middle Atlas and into the desert; but by 44 the campaign was over and the whole territory was annexed as two Roman provinces, Mauretania Caesariensis and Mauretania Tingitana, administered respectively from Caesarea (mod. Cherchel) and Tingis (mod. Tangiers).

The war against Aedemon may have been the spark to set off the Musulami once again, since we know that the future emperor Galba was appointed governor of Africa *extra ordinem* for two years in about A.D. 45 to deal with unrest in Numidia, a task that also took him into Juba's former territory of eastern Algeria.[34] But, as before, we should resist the temptation to think in terms of unified, African nationalist, resistance movements and see these as endemic but discrete outbreaks.

One way of checking such outbreaks was by extending Romanization through colonial foundations of Roman veterans and individual grants of citizenship, for which Claudius was celebrated.[35] Tingis was refounded, Lixus was raised to colonial status and probably, though not necessarily, reinforced. A new veteran settlement was located at Oppidum Novum to protect Caesarea inland, while Tipasa and Rusucurru on the coast were granted municipal status with Latin rights. Caesarea itself

---

[31] *AE* 1966, 595; Tac. *Hist.* ii.58–9.

[32] *praef(ectus) auxilior(um) adversus Aedemonem oppressum bello* – *GCN* 407. Whether municipal status is implied by the grant of *civitas romana* is controversial; for this and for possible federated status of Volubilis, Gascou 1982 (E 738) 148–9.

[33] Romanelli 1959 (E 760) 260; cf. Dio lx.24.5. Dio lx.8–9; Pliny, *HN* v.11–15.

[34] Aur. Vict. 4.2; Suet. *Galba* 7–8; cf. Tac. *Hist.* 1.49; Dio lx.9.6; Plut. *Galba* 3; *AE* 1966, 595. The history of 'national consciousness' and 'permanent insurrection' in Roman Africa is discussed by Benseddik 1982 (E 716) 145–62.   [35] Gascou 1982 (E 738) 145–58, Mackie 1983 (E 753).

was given colonial status, though again this does not imply new settlers. Volubilis, as we saw, did well out of its loyalty.

Why the two Mauretanias were administered by equestrian procuratorial governors is not easy to say, particularly since senatorial legates were appointed from time to time (e.g. in A.D. 75 and 144) and procurators occasionally held command over a united territory *pro legato*. Was it simply because no legion was stationed in the provinces? Was it because Claudius saw himself as in some sense the heir of Ptolemy (on the analogy of Egypt)? Or was it because the territory was too wild to regard as a settled province (like the Alpine territories)? It is certainly true that the provinces were never much developed, their southern frontiers were hard to define and communications between the two were tenuous.[36]

Nero's contribution to the history of Africa lay, as far as we know, in a single action – the confiscation of a large amount of property in central Tunisia. With colourful exaggeration the Elder Pliny says that six owners had possessed half Africa before their execution by Nero. Some relics of this brutal change may be conserved on inscriptions of the second century A.D. from the middle Bagradas valley, where an estate named *saltus Neronianus* is recorded in the vicinity of other estates bearing the names of old Roman families, *saltus Lamianus*, *saltus Blandianus*, *saltus Domitianus*.[37] There is no reason to suppose these imperial confiscations were linked to some policy by Nero to increase the supply of grain to the citizens of Rome, as some have argued (see below, p. 616).

Cruel execution of Africans, perhaps on behalf of Nero, was a reputation gained by Nero's last legionary legate in A.D. 68, L. Clodius Macer. Once the secret was out that an emperor could be created outside Rome, he developed imperial ambitions of his own having apparently already taken over as governor. In the rivalries which developed on Nero's death he tried to manipulate the grain supply to Rome for his own advantage, urged on by one of Nero's court friends.[38] But he was assassinated on Galba's orders and, after Galba himself fell, the province became a prey to the rival supporters of Vitellius and Vespasian. Oddly enough three of the contenders, Galba, Vitellius and Vespasian, had served in the province, the last being the least popular. But, thanks to the independent power of the legionary commander of Africa, Valerius Festus, who favoured Vespasian, the proconsul, L. Calpurnius Piso, was killed – an act for which Festus received his due reward.[39] It was said that

36 See the discussions by J. Marion and M. Euzennat in *Bull. Arch. Maroc.* 4 (1960) 442–7, 525–7.
37 Pliny, *HN* xviii.35. *NTH* 463 and 464 are translated and discussed by Kehoe 1988 (E 746); Carcopino 1906 (E 723). The best text is Flach 1978 (E 734).
38 Plut. *Galba* 6; cf. Tac. *Hist.* 1.11. Suet. *Galba* 11; Tac. *Hist.* 1.73. J. Burian, *Klio* 38 (1960) 167–73 implausibly considers that Macer made common cause with senatorial sympathizers.
39 Tac. *Hist.* iv.38, 48–50; MW 266 (showing military decorations and career under the Flavians).

Piso, like Macer before him, had been tampering with the corn supply for Rome.

In Mauretania Galba during his brief rule had given the governor of Caesariensis, Lucceius Albinus, command also over Tingitana – perhaps to counter the influence of Macer. Having gathered a large force of 12,000 auxiliaries together, Albinus declared his independence after Galba's fall and prepared to invade Spain. Assassination, however, by friends of Vitellius ended his claim.

By the time the civil wars were over Roman rule in Africa was in need of reorganization. Rival sides had offered too many tax concessions. Cities in Africa had used the wars to pursue their own vendettas, like Oea which had called in the Garamantes against Lepcis. The tension between the legionary legate and the proconsular governor had to be resolved. And we may guess that the Mauri and Numidian tribes of the interior had not remained inactive, making it a necessity to increase the security of the frontiers. Above all, the importance of protecting and encouraging the production of African grain and, increasingly now, oil was underlined. That was all work for the new Flavian administration.

VI. THE ADMINISTRATION AND ORGANIZATION
OF THE PROVINCE

Whatever Caesar intended, there is little trace of his actual achievement. The province of Nova was, of course, his creation, running probably from the old *fossa regia* – the republican boundaries taken over from the Numidian kings – westwards. But whether he incorporated the enclave of Sittiani around Cirta is unclear. Octavian immediately saw the undesirability of having two provinces of Africa, particularly if he wanted the new colony of Carthage to include the Gaetulian veteran settlements beyond the *fossa regia*. There is just a hint in Dio that Augustus began by giving Juba II the territory of Nova which had formerly been ruled by his father, Juba I.[40] But given the importance of the corn of Africa, the idea seems implausible.

The single province of Africa Proconsularis was therefore formed in 35 B.C., as argued earlier, to incorporate all the former territories, including that around Cirta. The only legion we know to have been permanently stationed in the province was the III Augusta, not in fact recorded until A.D. 14, but obviously present earlier and stationed perhaps first at Carthage before moving to Ammaedara. There was almost certainly also a fair number of auxiliaries recruited locally, a normal obligation laid upon native communities in this period. But how many outside or local auxiliary units there were at this stage one can only

[40] Dio LI.15.6, LIII.26.2.

guess. At Ammaedara we have a pre-Flavian stela recording a *cohors XV Voluntariorum*, without doubt Roman citizen irregulars; the *ala Siliana* is also recorded as serving in Africa.[41] Both were probably recruited locally.

The problem of the relationship of the provincial governor to the army and the relationship of both province and army to Augustus himself is perhaps something that concerns us more than it did Augustus. Although Africa became technically a public province in the settlement of 27 B.C., the emperor's grip was always firmly on the army, where he could – and sometimes did – nominate the legionary legate, despite the theoretical right of the governor to appoint his own legates. Furthermore, the emperor could always manipulate appointments of governors when there was occasion for important military campaigns. Tiberius had no difficulty in 'persuading' the Senate of the wisdom of appointing Iunius Blaesus to the post for the campaign in A.D. 18.[42] Galba was appointed *extra sortem* when the need arose under Claudius. So the arrangement remained basically *ad hoc*, even after Gaius ended the anomaly of a legionary commander who was subordinate to the governor, while selected by the emperor.

It is impossible to talk about precise boundaries under Augustus when the territory was in the process of being defined. Some fifty years after Augustus' death the Elder Pliny preserved in his description of the Maghreb coast two undated and different lists of the colonies and towns, which have been thought to have had their origin in the early *formulae provinciae*.[43] But this seems unlikely. Part of the lists must go back to Iulius Caesar, since there is a reference to the two separate provinces of Vetus and Nova. Other parts are updated to include colonies founded by Augustus or Claudius. Many of the towns are not listed in any strict juridical or tax category but only vaguely in non-technical language as *oppida*. To reconstruct the Augustan settlement from this is a more or less hopeless task. But Pliny's list does provide some clues.

For the taxes of the province we have only the guidance of the few inscriptions already mentioned recording the new land cadaster in the south. In the northern part of the province there are quite extensive signs of cadastration and centuriation along the lines of the republican orientation, which may have been the work of Augustan governors in distributing lots to new settlers, since the cadaster extends well beyond the *fossa regia*. Between the two cadasters is a third major orientation and

---

[41] Legion – EJ²290 (A.D. 14); *CIL* VIII 22786; auxiliaries – *CIL* VIII 23252, 23255, 25646; *AE* 1972, 969; Tac. *Hist.* 1.70. It is impossible to calculate the numbers in this early period; But see Cagnat 1913 (E 722) 107–10, 140ff; Holder 1980 (D 195) 289, 330.

[42] Blaesus – Tac. *Ann.* III.32, 35. The relationship between the governor and the legate is laid out in Dio LIII.14.7 and Tac. *Hist.* IV.48 and discussed by Bénabou 1972 (E 714).

[43] Pliny, *NH* v.1–30. Discussed by Teutsch 1962 (E 765), Brunt 1971 (A 9) App. 13.

a few smaller ones in the coastal regions of Byzacium which could be the work of early emperors.[44]

But cadasters do not tell us much about how the tax was collected or assessed. Most probably in the Julio-Claudian period, at least, there was a continuation of the republican system, since some of the evidence suggests that the taxation units and the agents of the pre-imperial period persisted. In other words, the mixed system established by the Agrarian Law of 111 B.C. was maintained, whereby a fixed sum (*stipendium*) was imposed on native communities or those with movable property and a tithe (*decuma*) on Roman purchasers of former public land. This was in addition to the pasture tax on animals. In the absence of other evidence we must assume that new Roman settlers were treated like those already there, unless they were veterans. The latter were granted tax immunities by Augustus for their own lifetime and that of their children, according to a papyrus copy of his edict in 31 B.C. But it is possible that the Gaetulian veterans of Iulius Caesar had been given some form of tribute immunity for their heirs in perpetuity.[45]

If this is correct, taxes would have been farmed out from the quaestor's office to publican entrepreneurs, who bid for the contracts based upon block assessments of the native *civitates stipendiariae*. It is unfortunate that the only real evidence of such an arrangement – a dedication by the *mancupes* of the *stipendiarii* to the quaestor – cannot be dated, although it is probably Augustan. The *civitates*, however, do not seem, as later, to be independent tax communities but more like villages grouped together into rural districts, as they had been under Punic Carthage. In fact, we have Roman inscriptions referring to these old Punic land divisions – called in Latin *pagi*. One such records the sixty-four *civitates* of the *pagus* of Tuscus and Gunzuzus, recalling Appian's description of the Punic 'land of Tusca' with its fifty towns. We also have an inscription dating from soon after the refounding of Roman Carthage mentioning an administrative district of eighty-three *castella* under a law officer of Carthage, M. Caelius Phileros, who was responsible for allocating their taxes quinquennially.[46]

As Roman rule extended southwards, the military districts were

---

[44] Chevallier 1958 (E 724) and *Atlas des centuriations romaines de Tunisie* (Paris, 1954). Dilke 1971 (A 21) 151–8.

[45] Republican taxes are discussed in *CAH* ix² 585–9. Augustan edict on veterans – EJ² 302. Gaetulians – discussed below, p. 608.

[46] *mancupes* – EJ² 191. *civitates stipendiariae* etc., – *AE* 1963, 96; App. *Pun.* 68; cf. *ILS* 9482 recording *pagi Muxsi, Gususi et Zeugei*. EJ² 355 refers to *civitates stipendiariae* in a *pagus* which seems to be called *Gurzenses* and it contains the names of three places, one of which is Uzita known by Julius Caesar as an *oppidum* near Hadrumetum (*BAfr.* 41) while Gurza was a *civitas* later in the same locality. *CIL* VIII 23599 records a prefect of sixty-two *civitates* at Mactar in a later period. All are discussed by Picard 1966 (E 758). Phileros – EJ² 330; he had served the governor T. Sextius *c.* 43–40 B.C.

possibly regionalized in the same way, since an inscription commemorates the census of forty-three *civitates* taken by a tribune of the III legion (p. 593). We also know of the existence of an imperial procurator in the 'plain of Byzacium' under Augustus, perhaps a military supply officer or an agent of imperial estates. None of this, however, is much to go on.

VII. CITIES AND COLONIES[47]

It is a banality that the Roman empire was fundamentally no more than a collection of city-states, around which the emperor provided a protecting frontier that was paid for by their taxes. The city or *civitas*, therefore, was the administrative unit upon which the empire depended. The problem for the Romans in Africa, different from other western provinces, was not to persuade scattered, rural communities to collectivize into city units, as in northern Gaul and Britain, so much as to find a formula that would organize the scores of small, independent villages and hill-top forts that already existed into manageable communities. Despite the Carthaginian coastal cities and a few native centres (like Thugga), one hundred years of Roman republican rule had done little to advance this process.

What changed all that was the civil wars and the Principate. The wars created a desperate need to demobilize and provided the land on which to settle veterans. Augustus possessed the will to order such events and the self-interest to know that his political survival depended on satisfying this need and on supplying the volatile population of Rome with regular food. Colonies, communities and corn were the informing principles of Roman imperialism in Africa.

Colonies first. Apart from Carthage, Iulius Caesar and Augustus between them founded some twenty-six to twenty-eight colonies the length of the Maghreb. They cannot all be assigned with certainty to the Caesarian and Augustan periods – some may have been founded just after Augustus' death.[48] Their names and those about which there is greater certainty than others, are marked on Map 13. Some of these settlements obviously had a defensive, military purpose that was usual when veterans were kept together in their original army units. Soldiers of the thirteenth legion were established at Thuburbo Minus (mod. Teboura) and at Uthina (mod. Oudna) as buttresses for Carthage, controlling the southern and western plains of the Medjerda and Miliana rivers. In the same way the colonies at Zuchabar (mod. Miliana) and Aquae (mod. Righa Hammam) protected Caesarea, Juba's capital, from

[47] The evidence is now well collected by Gascou 1972 (E 735) and 1982 (E 738).
[48] The complex difficulties are discussed by Teutsch 1962 (E 765). See also Brunt 1971 (A 9) App.

inland raids in Mauretania. The colonies along the Algerian and
Moroccan coast were useful ports of communication, just as the colonies
along the coast of eastern Tunisia and Cape Bon controlled the former
Punic ports. In former Africa Nova, the Punic town of Sicca Veneria is
the only colony to commemorate Augustus as *conditor*;[49] all the other
colonies of Thuburnica, Simitthu and Assuras may have started life as
military or veteran satellites of Sicca. Ammaedara, the legionary base by
A.D. 14, became a colony under Flavian rule.

After the annexation of the Mauretanias, Claudius continued the
policy of colonial foundation (p. 598), although in many cases it was
more a matter of raising the status of towns rather than actually sending
out new settlers. This is testimony to the Romanization and unofficial
immigration during the rule of Juba and Ptolemy. Oppidum Novum,
which now became a colony of veterans, may have started life as a
garrison of Roman auxiliaries to help Juba, since we hear of a *curator* of a
fort there.[50]

At Iol Caesarea (mod. Cherchel) Juba, in imitation of other hellenistic
rulers, deliberately constructed a show-piece city, laid out on an
orthogonal plan, with a number of monumental buildings.[51] Most
important were the temples, including a temple of Augustus, of which a
colossal statue of the emperor survives, showing the deliberate political
intention of bringing urban Roman culture to the Mauri, as well as
organizing the resources of the countryside. The grant of colonial status
did not necessarily involve any new settlement but Italian craftsmen may
have come to produce pottery in the city. The many Roman names
inscribed in the city, almost certainly from the period of Juba, include
some who were probably Italian *negotiatores*.

As to the numbers of Roman settlers in each colony, best estimates
suggest a figure of about 300 to 500 adult males, giving a total for the
Augustan colonies of some 8,000–13,000 families. This is not counting
Carthage or Cirta, which are discussed below. But a colony's territory
was not only occupied by Roman settlers from Italy. The land cadaster
from Arausio in Narbonensis and the manuals of Roman surveyors show
that native inhabitants remained. Some of the elites were given citizenship and formed joint communities, as happened at the veteran colony of
Emerita in Spain.[52] Native wives of veterans were granted citizenship,
too, quite apart from the fact that many of Caesar's and Augustus'
veterans had themselves been local native recruits for the emergency of
the civil wars in both the legions and as Gaetulian auxiliaries.[53]

[49] *CIL* VIII 27568.　　　[50] *AE* 1926, 23.

[51] Gsell 1930 (E 741) 206–84. Recent work is in Leveau 1984 (E 752) and Benseddik, Potter
forthcoming (E 717).

[52] Brunt 1971 (A 9) 246–61; Romanelli 1959 (E 760) 207. *Grom. agrimens.* 155. 6–8 (Lachmann);
Strab. III.2.15 (151C).

[53] Grants to Octavian's veterans included citizenship *ipsis, parentibus liberisque eorum et uxoribus* –
EJ² 302; and probably the right to join in a colony or remain in a native community; cf. *FIRA* I 55.

So we must not overestimate the cultural impact of the new foundations. Colonial status, Roman citizenship and often large plots of land – a third of a century, 16 hectares was the least an Augustan veteran could expect – created a privileged minority, loyal to the settlement and anxious to prove their Romanness. But they were men who were often linked culturally to the local population by language, religion and custom. We see how commonly the name of Iulius was taken by new citizens in a colony like Sicca Veneria – overall about 20 per cent of recorded names. At another colony, Simitthu, the name Iulius Numidicus (which occurs twice) speaks for itself.[54] The oldest inscriptions record religious homage from the Algerian colony of Rusguniae to the Mauretanian king, Ptolemy in A.D. 29 and to the African god, Saturn; but the latter is honoured in his Romanized form and the prominent families who make the dedications also betray their new Roman status by their names.[55]

Carthage was quite different from the military colonies on the coast. Appian, describing its foundation, says that he had 'found out that Augustus gathered together some 3,000 Roman colonists and the rest from those dwelling around (*perioikoi*) in the region'. The easiest interpretation of this statement is that Roman immigrants plus Romans already in the territory came to a total of 3,000, to which were added native peregrines. There were certainly some veterans of Caesar included but the unusually large proportion of freedmen recorded in civil and religious offices in the early colony suggests that many of the immigrants came from the city of Rome. Among country folk, Virgil tells us, there was no great enthusiasm to go to 'thirsty' Africa.[56]

Archaeology gives us some idea of what the early colony of Carthage was like.[57] The most interesting feature is that, despite the earlier, different Gracchan cadastration, the city was refounded on the old Punic orientation and made much use of Punic foundations, building material and cisterns that had lain unused or in ruins since 146 B.C. The Punic citadel on the Byrsa was the central point for the centuriation of the town and the hill itself began the first stage of its transformation as the monumental focus for the city. Little remains of the Augustan city but there are signs that a start was made on the dramatic levelling of the citadel summit and infilling on top of Hannibal's city on the south side. It was on this site that a huge new *forum* centre was to be created in the

[54] Thompson and Ferguson 1969 (E 767) 132–81; modified by Lassère 1977 (E 749) 152–3.
[55] EJ² 163; *CIL* VIII 9257. Leschi 1957 (E 751) 389–93; Salama 1955 (E 761).
[56] App. *Pun.* 136; Strab. XVII.3.15 (832–3c); Plut. *Caes.* 57; Virg. *Ecl.* 1.64.
[57] For a summary and interpretation of the results of the UNESCO project at Carthage, see Hurst 1985 (E 745). Saumagne 1962 (E 762) discovered the centuriation. The latest information and bibliography on Carthage is published regularly in the bulletin of the Institut National d'Archéologie et d'Art de Tunis, *CEDAC (Centre d'Etudes et de documentation archéologique de la conservation de Carthage)*. Before the UNESCO project it was a common view that Virgil's description of Dido's city was an accurate guide to the Augustan colony.

second century. Near here, appropriately, an altar to the *gens Augusta* was put up on private ground by one of the first generation of settlers.

The monumental preparation of the Byrsa, however, contrasts with the tentative and poor buildings of the shore and harbours. Mud brick and unpaved streets suggest that the early colony was quite a humble affair which grew only gradually. Some of the Punic ruins were not rebuilt for two generations and the early Roman cemeteries were inside what was later part of the city street grid. Virgil's romantic portrait of colonists constructing Dido's first city – the great citadel, the paved streets, the gates and the theatre – which was probably written to celebrate the Augustan colony, did not exactly resemble the reality.

The difficult feature of the foundation for us to understand is how the rural settlements within the territory or *pertica* of Carthage, which stretched at least 100km down the Bagradas valley, were organized. A series of inscriptions in the earlier imperial period record communities of Roman citizens, confusingly called *pagi* but nothing like the other *pagi* districts of native communities (p. 602). These were single enclaves, many of them bunched together just beyond the old *fossa regia* boundary of Africa Vetera in the fertile middle Bagradas and Siliana valleys at places like Thugga, Uchi Maius and Thibaris.[58] They were part of Carthage, containing citizens and later even magistrates of the colony, administered by a 'prefect of justice' from the city. But at the same time they were quartered on top of native settlements.

Some of these *pagi*, like Uchi Maius and Thibaris, but not all, are recorded by the Elder Pliny as *oppida civium Romanorum*. The inscription noted earlier of M. Caelius Phileros,[59] who had been a freedman attendant of the governor before 40 B.C. and had then joined the new colony to become aedile, prefect of justice and officer for taxes in charge of 'eighty-three *castella*' (native sites), is matched by another inscription from Uchi Maius, damaged but probably of Phileros, too, recording his arbitration between the *coloni* and the local Uchitani. Not only were the gentile names Marius and Iulius common in these communities but several explicitly honoured Marius when they later acquired a municipal charter.

Pagi are recorded within the old province, too.[60] Two of them, Saturnuca and Medeli, are not far from the colony of Uthina in the Miliana plain; both have inscriptions stating they were veteran settlements; and one claims Augustus as benefactor. A similar settlement was at Hippo Diarrytus (mod. Bizerta) and two others were near Thabraca. Apart from these *pagi*, other types of Roman communities appear on

---

[58] Evidence given by Pflaum 1970 (E 755); most recently discussed by Gascou 1980 (E 737).
[59] EJ² 330; *CIL* VIII 26274.   [60] *ILAFr* 301; *CIL* VIII 885; 25423.

inscriptions:[61] 'Roman citizens who are in business (*negotiantur*) at Thinissut' on Cape Bon; 'Roman citizens who are living at (*morantur*) Suo' in the Bagradas plain; 'a community' (*conventus*) of Romans and Numidians who live at Masculula, west of Sicca Veneria.

Finally, there is the puzzling relationship between Carthage and a number of sites on the Tunisian coast which eventually became colonies bearing the title of 'Iulia' in their names. The inscription of Phileros, examined earlier, records his career not only as a magistrate at Carthage but also twice as chief magistrate (*duovir*) of Clupea (mod. Kelibia) on Cape Bon. Clupea is listed by Pliny as a 'free *oppidum*' but it became a Julian colony. That is also the case at Curubis, Neapolis and Carpi (not 'free' in the last case), two of which also had magistrates, freedmen again, who held office at Carthage.

As far as we can tell, Cirta also, was given a very large territory, administered by prefects and subdivided into *pagi* and other communities where Roman citizens lived attached to the main colony. Augustus is known to have taken over the former Sittiani veterans and to have supplemented them with further colonists in 26 B.C. That, as far as we can judge, was also the origin of the special relationship of *contributio* recorded in the second century A.D., by which three of these sub-communities had rights of interchanging magistracies with Cirta when they later became colonies.[62]

There is some suggestion that this was the earliest form of organization at Sicca Veneria, too – the only one of Augustus' colonies in Africa Nova to figure in Pliny's list, antedating the colonies of Thuburnica, Simitthu and Assuras. Two of these later colonies are called *oppida civium Romanorum* by Pliny, so may have begun as *pagi* just as we have records of *pagi* and other types of small Roman communities near Sicca. The fact that some of these *pagi* appear to have been on sites that also contained *castella* may mean that an elaborate system of Roman settlements (*pagi*) was constructed to supervise native hill-forts. At Cirta, however, the *castella* were part of the *pagus* and look like fortified points of security for the early colonists.[63] Despite this confusion, however, both Cirta and Sicca look surprisingly like Carthage.

So what can be made of these scraps of information? There is no need to read into Carthage's foundation some sort of new, super-hellenistic model city, since contemporary Augustan colonies with similar extensive territorial *pertica* are known in France (Arausio) and Spain (Emerita)

---

[61] EJ² 106; *ILTun* 682; EJ² 111.

[62] *ILAlg* II(1) 36; *AE* 1955, 202; *ILAlg* II(1) 3596.

[63] The latter is argued by Gascou 1983 (E 739), against Beschaouch 1981 (E 719). The Phileros inscription above (*CIL* VIII 26274) shows him demarcating land of the *castellum* at Uchi between the native Uchitani and the *coloni*, where there was a Roman *pagus*. This suggests that a *castellum* can be either peregrine, Roman or both.

– the latter also administered by prefects. *Pagi* as subdivisions of a city's territory were also perfectly normal. But it is difficult to resist the conclusion that at Carthage, in addition to the new, veteran settlers, most or all of the *pagi* beyond the *fossa regia* were not new settlements at all but villages of Gaetulian auxiliaries who had been rewarded with land and perhaps citizenship by Marius and Iulius Caesar and whose families were now incorporated as citizens of the new colony. Perhaps the same was the case with the Sittiani at Cirta. As for the coastal Julian colonies, they may have kept some sort of special relationship with Carthage after they became colonies in their own right.

In addition to colonies and the *oppida civium Romanorum* (probably *pagi*), Pliny lists other categories of communities within the African province – about which it is difficult to say anything of their organization or physical appearance. There are a number of *oppida libera*, some simple *oppida* and *civitates*, one *oppidum stipendiarium*, one *oppidum Latinum* and finally Utica, the former provincial capital, which, Pliny said, had Roman citizenship – presumably as a recognized *municipium Romanum*. In other words, apart from Utica and the single town with Latin rights, all the rest were what would be juridically classified as peregrine (native) *civitates*, towns with their own territories which were self-governing and recognized within the *formulae provinciae*. We have the record of two of them, Thysdrus (mod. El Djem) and Hadrumetum (mod. Sousse) in a land dispute about the middle of the first century A.D. Some of them, former royal strongholds of the kings of Numidia, such as Zama Regia, Hippo Regius, Bulla Regia, were probably the creations of Caesar in his new province of Africa Nova. Others along the Tunisian and Tripolitanian coast had a long Punic and republican history of urbanization.[64]

We can only guess whether Pliny's list was complete or what exactly the differences were between his categories. Lepcis Magna, for instance, the rich Punic centre of olive oil export, was only called an *oppidum*, while its rival Oea was called a *civitas*. Was Lepcis disgraced for opposing Caesar? If so, it was rehabilitated by Augustus, since it had the right of a 'free town' to strike its own coins and there began to appear a number of spectacular, public Roman-styled buildings as early as 8 B.C. But for Thugga, which had been a royal capital of Massinissa and where a *pagus* of Roman citizens was installed, Pliny gives no evidence of *civitas* status, which is not recorded before Claudius. Yet Thugga almost certainly was recognized before that, since we hear of the Thuggenses commemorating a governor in A.D. 3. The same is probably true of Musti nearby.[65]

[64] For Pliny's list, see n. 43; Utica – Dio XLIX.16.1; Thysdrus – *Grom. agrimens.* 57.3 (Lachmann); Caesar – *BAfr.* 77.1, 97.1.

[65] Building at Lepcis – e.g. EJ² 105b (9–8 B.C.). Thugga – *ILS* 6797, *CIL* VIII 26580. Poinssot 1958 (E 759), Beschaouch 1968 (E 718) 151.

Puzzlingly, on some early inscriptions we find small villages being called *civitates* when they were clearly not recognized communities.[66] So the confusion is considerable.

Many of these small village communities were strongly Punicized and continued with their own Punic magistrate, called *sufet* (pl. *sufetim*), long into the Empire without any evidence, in some cases, that they were ever recognized as independent cities by the Julio-Claudian emperors. There was a number of them just west of, and possibly including, the later colony of Thuburbo Maius, in the rich Miliana valley 50 km south of Carthage. The interesting suggestion has been made that these were the original inhabitants of Carthage, exiled when the city was destroyed in 146 B.C. If so, they were appropriately incorporated once again into the great *pertica* of Carthage, though only as peregrines. Another group of communities, many of them near the *sufet* villages, possessed governing councils called in later periods *undecimprimi* which may also have had Punic origins.[67] We may guess that life in these villages or small towns was much as it had been when Punic Carthage collapsed over one hundred years earlier.

We must not forget the southern territories of Tunisia, the land brought under Roman control by Augustus and Tiberius south east of the legionary base of Ammaedara. Pliny describes some of the communities as 'not so much *civitates* as *nationes*'. In other words, tribes like the Musulami, Capsitani and Cinithii, were recognized but not as urban units, despite the fact that some of the leading families among groups like the Cinithii had been strongly Punicized and quickly accepted Roman urban structures, too. But until their centres of Gigthis (mod. Bou Grara), Tacape (mod. Gabes) etc. were given recognized status, they were probably put under the control of a military prefect. One such person, C. Flavius Macer, prefect of the Musulami in the later first century or early second century may himself have been a native leader, who became an officer of the auxiliaries and was given citizenship by the Flavian emperors.[68]

It is thought, too, that many of the later towns on the edge of the Tunisian dorsal, places like Cilma (mod. Djilma), Sufetula (mod. Sbeitla), Cillium (mod. Kasserine) and Thelepte, became Romanized through soldiers or veteran stationed there to control the routes in this period. That was certainly true of Thala, the former Numidian strong-hold near Ammaedara, according to Tacitus, and perhaps of the oasis

[66] *CIL* III 338.

[67] Discussion of Punic *sufet* towns by C. Poinssot, *Karthago* 10 (1959–60) 93–131. The Punic origin of *undecimprimi* is discussed by B.D. Shaw, *Museum Africum* 2 (1973) 1–10 – but this is controversial.

[68] Macer – *IL Alg* I 285, *NTH* 260; cf. Pflaum *CP* no. 98. Gigthis had long been a Punic port and centre – N. Ferchiou in Picard 1984 (E 758A) 65–74.

centre of the Capsitani at Capsa (mod. Gafsa), which had also been Punicized.[69]

Further west in Mauretania, in addition to the colonies, Claudius granted a limited number of municipal rights and recognized a few communities as *civitates*, mainly places along the coast which had a Punic background. Tipasa, for instance, became a Latin town, Rusucurru (mod. Dellys) became a Roman town. Volubilis was rewarded for its loyalty by getting Roman municipal status and Tucca (mod. Zucca) on the border of the African province became a *civitas*. But not very much seems to have been done to develop the interior before the Flavian emperors.

VIII. ROMANIZATION AND RESISTANCE

Two conclusions follow from these administrative arrangements for the provinces of north Africa. First, since the number of new Italian immigrants was relatively small, their impact was less dramatic than has sometimes been supposed. Secondly, the local African elites, including those who were incorporated in the colonies, many of whom had long been Punicized, were those most readily integrated into the urban system. Both these conclusions contribute to our understanding of the process of Romanization.

The precise juridical status of a community made little difference to the realities of life in the small *castella* and *vici* of the countryside, which continued to be administered by their own *principes*, *magistri* and *seniores* and which still thought of themselves in terms of their own sub-groups (*domus* and *familiae*) and tribal alliances (*gentes*). In many parts of Africa these categories persisted until the late Empire. Pomponius Mela, a geographer in the middle of the first century A.D., wrote of African society as made up of nomadic wanderers and the rural masses (*vulgus*), still living in their huts (*mapalia*) under their own leaders. We have a good collection of Libyan funerary inscriptions from a region of eastern Algeria around Hippo Regius (mod. Annaba), which date in some cases from the Roman period, since they are bilingual. They show that, even in the case of a man with as Romanized a name as C. Iulius Gaetulus, who looks like a veteran, he was also a chief of the Misiciri group and lived in a traditional, Libyan-speaking community.[70]

Many of these Libyans simply continued to be peasants working on the lands of their former chiefs. Iulius Caesar had allowed his friend, C.

---

[69] Cillium – *CIL* VIII 211–16; Thala – Tac. *Ann.* III.21. Broughton 1968 (E 720) 95; Gascou 1972 (E 735) 39.

[70] Mela, 1.42. Julius Gaetulus – R. Chabot, *Recueils des inscriptions libyques*, no. 146. See Whittaker 1978 (E 770) esp. 341–4.

Iulius Massinissa, to keep land that probably belonged to his royal ancestor. In the *pagus* of Abuzza, near Sicca Veneria, an inscription commemorates a woman, Maria Plancina, who is called 'foremost of all Numidian women, descended from a royal family', whose daughter married a large landowner, Licinius Fortunatus. Around Sicca especially we have a number of inscriptions of later periods showing that *castella* under their own *seniores* continued to function.[71] So, one wonders what difference the peasants working on these lands would have noticed when the owners adopted their Roman names. The continuity of dependent relations between the rich and poor Libyans must explain why there is so little evidence of Roman-style imported slavery on the land.

On the other hand the history of two former Numidian royal towns, Bulla Regia and Thugga, shows how quickly native towns adopted Roman styles of building and culture.[72] Bulla, recognized as a 'free town' in the Augustan province, contained many Romanized families bearing the name of Iulius, including some of the most prominent, that go back to the earliest period. Fairly soon we see the Roman reticulated technique being used for a public building in the centre, showing how urbanization was fostered by Roman rule.

Thugga, which had probably been Massinissa's capital in the second century B.C. and had long ago acquired administrative institutions, much influenced by Punic culture, plus a number of monumental buildings, was now increased by a Roman *pagus*. The enclave adjoined the old native town and a Roman type of town centre with *forum* and market began to be laid out in this early period. But the rapid Romanization of the *civitas* was partly due to the domination of two prominent Numidian families, the Gabinii and the Iulii, who had probably been given citizenship by Caesar or Augustus and prided themselves on it. An inscription dating from A.D. 48 records the dedication by the patron of the *pagus*, a citizen of Carthage, of a temple which had been paid for by the local magistrate, Iulius Venustus, husband of Gabinia Felicula; Venustus had served as *flamen* of the Roman imperial cult, like his father, Faustus Thinoba, before him – for which both had been given the honorary Punic title of *sufet*.[73]

The double communities of *pagi* and *civitates*, therefore, speeded up the Romanization of the African elites. The exact constitutional relationship between the two groups became complex as time went on, since Roman citizens of the native town sometimes married Romans of the *pagus* and acquired land there. On some inscriptions the words *utraque*

---

[71] Massinissa – Vitr. *De Arch.* VIII.3.24–5; Maria Plancina – *ILTun* 1633; *CIL* VIII 16159. See Broughton 1968 (E 720) 187 for *castella* inscriptions of Sicca.

[72] Bulla – Thebert 1973 (E 766); Thugga – Poinssot 1958 (E 759).

[73] *ILS* 6797; referred to again below.

pars civitatis or *uterque ordo* give the impression that the two formed a single civic community, even though the *pagus* continued to exist as a territorial offshoot of Carthage.[74] The reason why the two did not coalesce is clear. Holding land in the *pagus* was a jealously guarded privilege, which carried with it the economic advantage of tax immunity granted to the original members. On an inscription of the second century A.D. a man significantly called Marius Faustinus (a Marian veteran family?) at Thugga proudly calls himself 'defender of the immunity of the *pertica* of the Carthaginians' after a mission to have this immunity confirmed. Apparently, unlike later, Augustus or Caesar had granted these settlers (perhaps limited to descendants of the Gaetulian veterans) tax freedom for their heirs in perpetuity.[75] If this interpretation is correct, such a valuable asset would have widened the economic gap between Roman colonists and most natives.

The social and political benefits of the Augustan system for the elite had already become apparent in the Julio-Claudian period. Under Tiberius a citizen of Musti, L. Iulius Crassus, reached equestrian status and under Vespasian the first known African consuls, Q. Aurelius Pactumeius Fronto of Cirta and his brother Clemens, were created.[76] All may have been Italian *émigrés*, but Iulius Crassus looks like an enfranchised Libyan. The patronage of high Roman officials, such as the governor, was a valuable asset that encouraged native elites to imitate Roman institutions, as we see when the people of Thugga commemorated their 'friendship' with the governor in A.D. 3.

Lower down the scale, too, the patronage of Roman officials must have encouraged Romanization. As early as 12 B.C. we have an inscription set up by 'the senate and people of the *civitates stipendiariae* in the *pagus* (of) the Gurzenses' to record their formal *clientela* links with the ex-proconsul, P. Sulpicius Quirinius. One cannot miss the obvious attempt of these villagers who lived in the region of Hadrumetum on the Tunisian coast to prove their Romanness by their high-sounding institution and it contrasts starkly with the names of the men commissioned to set up the inscription, and with the native *oppida* from which they came, Ammilcar of Cynsyne, Boncar of Aethogursa, and Muthunbal of Uzita. A similar inscription records a former officer of the III Augustan legion living at Brixia (mod. Breschia) in north Italy, who had *hospitium* relations with four tiny African communities in the Miliana valley.[77]

The service of Africans in the auxiliaries, whether in ethnic units like

[74] Thugga – *CIL* VIII 26591, 26615; Thignica – *CIL* VIII 15212.

[75] *NTH* 510; for veterans, see n. 53.

[76] Iulius Crassus – *CIL* VIII 15519 and 26475; *ILTun* 1393. Cirtan senators – MW 298; *ILAlg* II (1) 642.

[77] Two of the inscriptions are recorded in EJ² 354–5; for the set, see *CIL* V 4919–22.

the *cohors Musulamiorum* that were recruited quite early on, or in mixed units, was another way in which Roman ideas were transmitted. In A.D. 69 'a large number' of Mauri were serving in the twenty-four units of Albinus, although we have no details.[78] Gaetulians and their influence within the *pagi* have been mentioned several times. But the revolt of Tacfarinas, who had served in the Roman war should warn us not to exaggerate the effect of such indoctrination.

The fact is that the pre-Roman culture of Africa, including the strong Punic and hellenistic elements, inevitably remained embedded in the make-up of the new provincial society, not just at the level of the poor but of the rich, too. The Thugga inscription noted above records a man who was priest of divine Augustus but also honorary *sufet*. At Volubilis in Morocco, the local dignitary, M. Valerius, son of Bostar, had probably become a Roman citizen, as were many others in the town, before it was incorporated into a province; as such, he held the office of *sufet* originally and became the first *duovir* and *flamen* when the town became a *municipium* (see p. 598). At Lepcis Magna, which had been an important Punic port, an inscription was put in Latin to commemorate the market built by Annobal Tapapius Rufus, son of Himilcho, one of the leading families of the town. He also held the office of *sufet* and added to the Latin inscription another one in Neo-Punic.

The emperor-cult, as we can see from these examples, was a vehicle by which local aristocracies demonstrated their Romanness and should not be regarded as insincere flattery or impositions by the state authorities. At Carthage, for instance, the altar of the *gens Augusta* was explicitly on private land. Elsewhere the dedications look like isolated enclaves of Roman citizens asserting their identity in predominantly Libyan towns – at places like Thinissut, Thysdrus or Vaga. Soon *civitates* themselves took the initiative, as at Mactar, to set up a temple as part of their civic cult. At Lepcis Magna the imperial cult went together with the monumental transformation of the Punic town into a Roman city; statues of the imperial family were set up in the temple of the new *forum* and the rich elite who paid for the great new theatre and markets – men with names like Iddibal Tapapius, son of Mago – were also those who took on the priesthoods of the cult.[79]

There has been much debate about the survival and continuity of African and Punic political organizations within the Roman provincial towns.[80] Apart from the *sufet* magistrates, who are found in every part of north Africa where Phoenician settlers had preceded the Romans, the

[78] Tac. *Hist.* 11.58–9. cf. Benseddik 1982 (E 716).
[79] Early imperial cult inscriptions – *ILAfr* 306; EJ² 106; some may be only honouring Augustus – 14392, 22844; city cult – *IRT* 273; EJ² 105b; *IRT* 321–3. See Smadja 1978 (E 763).
[80] Gascou 1976 (E 736), against Kotula 1968 (E 747). See also above, n. 67.

Thugga inscription above also refers to a decree voted by 'all the gates' (*omnium portarum sententiis*) of the town. Whether this organization was the same as the Punic *mizrah* – brotherhood with religious affiliations – which persisted into Roman times at Mactar and Althiburos on the Tunisian high plain, or whether it was an exclusively Libyan council meeting hardly matters since pre-Roman African life was already a cultural fusion.

Similarly, the popularity of Afro-Punic cults in Roman Africa shows how a new amalgam of provincial culture was emerging.[81] The pre-Roman cult of the Cereres corn gods became one of the most prestigious in Roman Carthage, its priesthoods dating back to beyond the formal foundation of the colony itself. The cult of the earth goddess Tellus, which was probably practised near the altar of the *gens Augusta* on the Byrsa, where her statue was found, was elsewhere assimilated with the local African divinity Gilva. The Libyan bull-god Gurzil (compare the name Gurzenses, above) was used as a motif on a Roman lamp in first-century Carthage. And we have already seen how the Saturn cult, a Romano-African version of the important Afro-Punic cult of Ba'al, was popular with the earliest Romanized African elites in the colony of Rusguniae. Above all, the Punic moon-goddess Tanit never ceased to be venerated in Roman Carthage in her Romanized form as Dea Caelestis. The child sacrifice associated with this cult was carried out 'openly', according to the African, Christian writer Tertullian, until 'the proconsulship of Tiberius' – presumably he meant the emperor Tiberius – and it is clear that thereafter it continued clandestinely.

Whether examples like this represent a form of passive resistance to Rome or the steady progress of Romanization is to some extent a matter of semantics.[82] Advocates of the 'resistance' model regard Romanization like a layer of paint which was easily stripped off later when Roman rule deteriorated to reveal the true Africa lurking below the surface. Modern studies of acculturation, however, demonstrate not only how compatibility varies enormously according to the social class and the isolation of individuals, but how even in indigenous resistance movements (cargo cults and the like) the language is not so much that of the old culture surviving beneath a veneer as that of a new vocabulary which emerges from the fusion of two civilizations, preserving elements of both. Romanization and resistance were two sides of the same coin.

In the Julio-Claudian period there was still an active, physical resistance among the southern, semi-nomadic populations and the *montagnards* of central Algeria and Morocco which spilled over from time

---

[81] Le Glay 1966 (E 750), esp. 62–80; Picard 1954 (E 757) 21–27. The evidence is summarized by Bénabou 1976 (E 715).

[82] 'Resistance' is the theme of Bénabou 1976 (E 715).

to time even into the heart of the old province. We may assume that some Libyan leaders bitterly resented Roman rule because of its interference in their own power and that many Libyan poor were virtually untouched by it. This continued in remoter communities until the last days of Roman rule. But the success of Roman provincial rule lay in its capacity to capture the allegiance of the African elites by its *laissez-faire* attitude to administration and local autonomy, while providing financial and social rewards to those who were prepared to participate in the system. Urban government under Roman rule was by and for the rich, reinforcing social inequalities and leaving social relations with the rural poor much as they had always been.

IX. THE ECONOMY

It is not easy to judge how much the economy – and especially rural production – changed during this period. Presumably the trends already in motion under the Republic continued. Not surprisingly most of the information from the late Punic and republican periods relates to the production of grain, which is also the subject of dominant interest in the early Empire. The extraordinary productivity of the soil of Africa, and notably that of Byzacium – the south-eastern coastal region of Proconsularis – was a byword in Rome. But the notion, derived from the Elder Pliny, that Africa was *entirely* dedicated to the crops of Ceres is a misreading of the text and explicitly contradicted by the many references we have to oil, wine and garden produce.[83] Archaeology is increasingly confirming the importance of oil production and its continuity with the Punic tradition, particularly in the region of Tripolitania and, probably, of Byzacium. This also fits the evidence of the Punic period, when the hinterland of Carthage and Cape Bon were noted for mixed farming, and from where, we may suppose, Mago derived the experience for his famous treaty on estate management which enjoyed such respect in Rome in the first century A.D.[84]

The popularity of Mago's treatise suggests the influence of Punic farming methods on early Roman settlers. And that in turn indicates the principal development of this period – the growth of large estates and villas of the sort encountered by Iulius Caesar on the Byzacium coast. Sale of land under the Republic, plus the allocation or sale of confiscated land after the civil wars, must have accelerated the process which led the Elder Pliny to report that before Nero's confiscations half Africa was

[83] Productivity – e.g. Varro, *Rust.* 1.14.2, Pliny, *HN* XVIII.94–5, Columella, *Rust.* I.pr.24. Ceres – 'Cereri totum id natura concessit, oleum ac vinum non invidit tantum', Pliny, *HN* xv.8, but *tantum* means 'almost'; *contra*, Columella, *Rust.* XI.2.80, Plut. *Caes.* 55.

[84] Archaeology, van der Werff 1977/8 (E 769), Aranegui and Hesnard forthcoming (E 713). Mago – Heurgon 1976 (E 744).

owned by six landlords. Whatever the exaggeration, it was to Africa that imperial writers regularly turned to illustrate a land of large estates. Petronius imagined Trimalchio and his guest as owners of vast properties in Numidia and Africa, while Seneca moralizes about the thousands of tenant *coloni* working for single landlords in Africa.[85] The emperor himself, of course, was one such estate owner. It was an imperial procurator who brought to Augustus and to Nero prolific ears of corn to demonstrate the fertility of the soil; and the first slave-bailiff of an imperial estate is recorded in the region of Calama (mod. Guelma) in Nero's reign.[86]

Many of these property owners were, like the emperor, absentees and it is not evident how their estates were organized in terms of labour or produce. Petronius talks of an army of slaves and Seneca of tenant farmers. The latter were certainly more common in later periods and there are a priori reasons, given earlier, for thinking this was always the more usual type of farm worker. But in neither case is there any real reason to believe that the growth of large estates radically altered – let alone ruined, as Pliny says – African farming methods or productivity. What it did was to change the social balance, by concentrating wealth in the hands of a minority and by providing them with the means to pay for the growing number of expensive, public buildings in towns such as Thugga, Lepcis Magna or Carthage, which have been noted already. That is, of course, when the profits did not leave Africa to pay for the expenses of the aristocracy and emperor in Rome. By expanding southwards and westwards the Roman–African economy was reaching a point where it was about to become a major supplier of the empire as well as of Rome.

X. ROMAN IMPERIALISM

The Roman conquest of the Maghreb in the first century A.D. began as the by-product of civil war and ended up with the acquisition of new territories as African chiefs and princes were swept up in the turmoil. Octavian's defeat of Antony led directly to the southern 'Gaetulian' problem, drawing Roman arms as far as the pre-desert. The allied Mauretanian kingdoms of the west were an unstable solution to this involvement which eventually broke down under Claudius and led to the annexation of two more provinces.

The question is, did the Roman emperors have a coherent policy of imperialism that went deeper than this kind of reflex reaction to

---

[85] Caes. *BAfr.* 40, 65. Confiscations – e.g. Caes. *BAfr.* 97. Pliny, *HN* xviii.35. Petron. *Sat.* 48,117. Sen. *Ep. ad. Lucil.* 114.26.

[86] Pliny, *HN* xviii.95; *ILAlg* i 324.

emergencies? Even in the republican period, when Africa was relatively neglected, we can see that the territory was regarded as a source of private wealth in land and of public food and oil. The climax was Caesar's public announcement of the acquisition for the Roman people of 8,000 tonnes of grain and 1 million litres of oil from the new province he had acquired, 'in order to impress the people with the size of his victory'.[87]

That tradition of public patronage was continued by Augustus who boasted in 23 B.C., for instance, that he had made a grant of one year's ration of corn to 1 million Romans, as well as claiming to have saved the city on various occasions from corn shortages. The emperor was fully aware of the 'fear and danger' which could lead to city riots if supplies broke down. In A.D. 51 the emperor Claudius came uncomfortably close to being lynched when it was correctly rumoured that the warehouses of Rome were almost empty.[88]

Given this background of propaganda and need, it would have been surprising if the corn of Africa had not figured somewhere when emperors pondered the prudence of military campaigns, even if our sources do not specifically link it to southern conquest. Can it be only chance that the raids of Tacfarinas deep into the African province and the consequent wars between A.D. 19–24 coincided with a sharp rise in the price of corn in A.D. 19, which remained high until about A.D. 23 or 24? Tacitus himself was in no doubt about Rome's dependence on Africa (and Egypt) for her livelihood nor about the strategic importance of African grain in the civil wars.[89] All Rome knew the value of Africa.

The central importance of African and Egyptian corn in supplying Rome is confirmed by two much discussed ancient texts. The first, referring to Nero's reign, states that Africa maintained the people of Rome for eight months of the year and Egypt for four; the second that Egypt in Augustus' rule provided 20,000,000 *modii* (about 130,000 tonnes) of grain for Rome. Unfortunately, there is no basis here for a simple mathematical calculation, since a regular annual import of about 40 million *modii* of grain would have far exceeded any calculable consumption rate of Rome's population, even if this were the only source of supply.[90] Nor does the need to increase the *annona* supply or imperial largesse provide a plausible reason for Nero's confiscations of senatorial estates in Africa, since it falsely assumes that productivity

---

[87] Plut. *Caes.* 55; Haywood 1959 (E 743) 21.

[88] Augustus, *RG* 5, 15.1; Dio LV.26.1 – 27.3. Tac. *Ann.* XII.43; cf. Sen. *De Brev. Vit.* 18. Claudius – Suet. *Claud.* 18.2.

[89] Tac. *Ann.* II.87, IV.6, XII.43; *Hist.* I.73, III.48, IV.38.

[90] Joseph. *BJ* II.383; [Aur. Vict.] *Epit. de Caes.* 1.6; Haywood 1959 (E 743) 43; Picard 1956 (E 756); Lassère 1977 (E 749) 296. Garnsey 1983 (D 130) 118–19.

increased when property passed under imperial management or that free corn distributions dramatically increased under Nero at the expense of the market.

What is clear, however, is that African corn was always a vital imperial asset, a weapon of control in the emperor's hands and a commodity for which there was a chronic need in Italy. The unreliability and wild fluctuation of grain yields in the pre-industrial Mediterranean are well known. 'Poverty and uncertainty of the morrow', says Braudel, were endemic pressures in the Mediterranean world that underlay 'certain, almost instinctive forms of imperialism'.[91] Augustus' and Tiberius' push to the southern pre-desert more than doubled the arable area of Roman Africa. Claudius' annexation of Mauretania added to the source of *frumenta fiscalia* that could be and was sometimes used, while protecting the western flank of the old province. These may not have been the articulated motives but they were surely powerful and instinctive ones.

[91] F. Braudel, *The Mediterranean and the Mediterranean world in the age of Philip II* (London, 1972) 224–5.

CHAPTER 13*j*

CYRENE

JOYCE REYNOLDS AND J. A. LLOYD

I. INTRODUCTION

Modern Cyrenaica, in the Roman period variously named Cyrenae (from its chief city), the Cyrenaea, the parts around Cyrene, Libya around Cyrene, was bequeathed to Rome in default of an heir by its king Ptolemy Physcon in 155 B.C., and inherited by her on the death of his son, Ptolemy Apion, in 96 B.C.[1] Rome freed the Greek cities (we are not told whether or not she also gave them immunity from taxation); she probably accepted ownership of the royal property at once (the estates

---

[1] The literary evidence for the history of Roman Cyrenaica is limited and often terse and obscure. Archaeological discoveries, including coins and inscriptions add important new information, but it is often fragmentary and insecurely dated. A particular problem arises from the many inscriptions which were dated by reference to an eponymous priest of Apollo, for whose year of office we have no other evidence, or to an era which is not specified. The present writers have conjectured that after 96 B.C. the cities used an era dating from the Roman declaration of their liberty. It would be understandable if they started another era in 75/4 or in 67 (the latter has recently been proposed, although not quite proved, for Berenice). It is certain that Cyrene, and almost certain that Teuchira, took Actium as a new starting-point and likely (as is assumed here) that the other cities did the same. Even at Cyrene, moreover, many inscriptions of the Principate are dated in a year which is patently not Actian and is sometimes explicitly stated to be the regnal year of a named emperor. Unfortunately the texts often fail to specify the emperor whose regnal year they were using, thus making the precise chronology and sequence of events obscure to us. In general, see J. Reynolds, in Gadullah 1968 (E 780A) and on Berenicean practice, Bowsky 1987 (E 776). The main items of ancient evidence are the following:

Inscriptions *CIG* III 5129–362; *CIL* III 6–11; *SEG* IX; items s.v. Cyrenaica in *SEG* XIII, XVIII, XX, XXVI–XXVII and *AE* 1946, 1950, 1961–2, 1967–69/70, 1973, 1974, 1976–8, 1980–3, 1985, 1987, 1989; Smith and Porcher 1864 (E 804A) App. IV; D.M. Robinson, *AJA* 17 (1913) 157–200; de Visscher 1940 (B 293); G. Oliverio, *QAL* 4 (1961) 3–54; G. Pugliese-Caratelli, D. Morelli, *ASAA* 39–40 (1961–2) 217–375; G. Giambuzzi, *QAL* 6 (1972) 43–104; Lüderitz 1983 (B 250); and *corpora* published in the excavation reports on Apollonia (E 785), Berenice (E 793), Cyrene (E 775, E 780, E 795, E 798, E 805, E 807, E 809) and Ptolemais (E 789, E 799).

Coins Robinson 1927 (B 347A); Chapman 1968 (B 316A); Buttrey 1983 (B 315), *id.* 1987 (B 315A); some recent coin discoveries are published in the excavation reports listed above.

Literary sources are very scattered; all important ones are collected in the footnotes to Thrige 1940 (E 807A) and some are given in the footnotes below.

Current archaeological discoveries are reported mainly in three journals which specialize in Libyan archaeology, *Libya Antiqua* (= *LA*, published Tripoli), *Libyan Studies* (= *LS* published London), *Quaderni di Archeologia della Libia* (= *QAL*, published Rome); note also *Africa Romana* (= *AR*, published Sassari). *Mises au point* may be found from time to time in these journals, and are occasionally published separately, notably Stucchi 1967 (E 805A), Gadullah 1968 (E 780A), Barker, Lloyd and Reynolds 1985 (E 775A), Stucchi 1990 (E 806A).

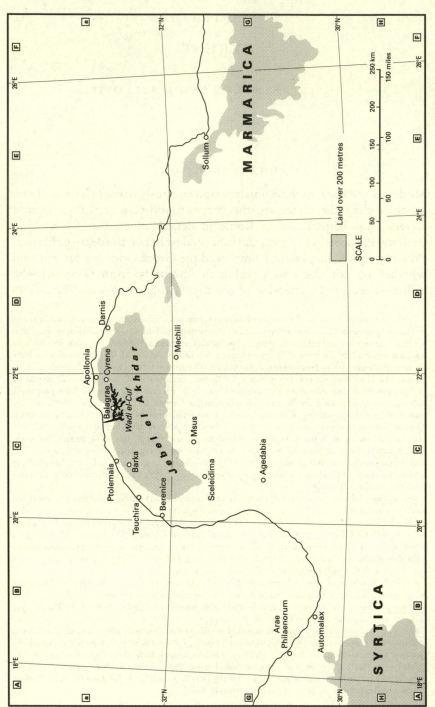

Map 14. Cyrene

are first unequivocally attested in her possession in 63 B.C.). The Libyans of the region were perhaps regarded as dependants of the cities.[2]

By 75/4 B.C. it was clear that this attempt to exercise suzerainty at no cost had failed. To the literary evidence for Cyrenaican instability in the intervening years inscriptions have recently added vivid detail; there were dissensions and tyrannies within the cities, and sometimes, apparently, between them, attacks probably from Libyan raiders and certainly from pirates, famines, sieges, lootings.[3] In this context a continuous Roman presence may well have seemed preferable to freedom, bringing a hope of peace and revived prosperity to the local population as well as to the Roman *negotiatores* attested at Cyrene and probably present in all the cities. A senatorial decision to send a quaestor to Cyrenaica is reported of 75 or 74; the first indication of serious administrative activity is of 67, when a cluster of inscriptions records action by Cn. Cornelius Lentulus Marcellinus, a legate of Pompey in the Pirate War. Eutropius in fact dated the annexation in 67 rather than 75/4, and it may have been locally regarded as the first effective year of the new dispensation. We know very little, however, of what was involved in that. Although commonly stated, it is not certain that Cyrenaica was governed with Crete at this stage, nor that governors were invariably of quaestorian standing (although that may seem more likely than not). What we know consists of the names of several quaestors who served there, of references to *negotiatores* and to *publicani* there, and to the presence of Cyrenaican *silphium* in the Roman treasury (some of which, however, was deposited before annexation). The *publicani* were doubtless managing the royal estates and may also have collected tax, but there is no evidence; the *silphium*, a plant which produced a gum-resin used as a condiment and for medicinal purposes, may have come as rent in kind from the estates, or as tax in kind, but we do not know that either.[4]

If there had been hopes that annexation would revive prosperity, they were soon disappointed, for within a very few years Cyrenaica felt the impact of the Roman civil wars. Pompey took Cyrenaican corn to feed the troops he mustered against Caesar; after Pharsalus Pompeian refugees collected there – eventually, it is said, 10,000 of them – under Cato, who forced the reluctant to accept them and, indubitably, to provide supplies for them. It is not surprising that depression is written very clearly in the archaeological evidence for the middle of the first century B.C. recently discovered at Sidi Khrebish, Benghazi, a suburb of ancient Berenice.[5]

[2] *SEG* IX.7; Livy, *Per.* 70; Tac. *Ann.* XIV.18; Cic. *Leg. Agr.* 1.19.51.

[3] Plut. *Luc.* 2.2–4, [Plut.] *Mor.* 255E–257E; Joseph. *AJ* XIV.7.114; *SEG* XXVI.1817, XXVIII.1540.

[4] Sall. *H.* II.fr.43; App. *BCiv.* I.111, Eutrop. VI.11; for inscriptions, *JRS* 52 (1962) 97–103. Cic. *Planc.* 26.63; Pliny, *HN* XIX.15.30.

[5] Caes. *BCiv.* 3.5; Luc. IX.39f, 294f; Plut. *Cat. Min.* 56; Strab. XVII.3.20 (836–7c). Lloyd 1977–85 (E 793).

II. THE COUNTRY

The eastern and western limits of Cyrenaica were indicated by Ptolemy I as the Great Catabathmos, a steep pass near the modern Egyptian town of Sollum, and Automalax, a fort on the Syrtican coast probably at modern Bu Sceefa, a little east of the traditional eastern limit of Carthaginian influence at Arae Philaenorum.[6] These were approximately the limits of the Roman province too in 44 B.C.

How far Ptolemaic and Roman suzerainty penetrated the interior is less clear. The forts established by the Tiberian period (see below) in the Syrtican approaches to the Cyrenaican plateau are clues to the location of the frontier zone there. Very recently Libyan archaeologists have found classical material in the desert south of Mechili, including part of a stone set up in A.D. 53/4 to mark the boundary of an estate inherited by the Roman people from Ptolemy Apion; if it belongs where it was found it indicates that Ptolemaic as well as Roman control was much deeper than has been supposed.[7]

The sub-Saharan climate and poor soils of the western and eastern Cyrenaican littorals render them for the most part unsuited to settled cultivation. However, certain areas favoured by underground water, and sometimes also by anchorage facilities, were developed in antiquity as road-stations and minor ports. Systematic survey in the Tripolitanian Syrtica suggests that the intensity of early Roman agrarian activity associated with them (no doubt accompanied by pasturage) has been seriously underestimated; the productivity of the Marmaric region, close to the Great Catabathmos, in the late second century A.D. is illustrated by a cadastral papyrus which records a highly organized landscape given over to cereals, vines, figs and olives. Terracing, water collection and storage systems and irrigation contributed to effective husbandry in these marginal areas. A kinder environment in antiquity has not yet been proven.[8]

The chief cultivable area, and so the zone of the classical cities, small towns and villages, lies in the northern part of Jebel el Akhdar or Green Mountain and its coastal plain. The Jebel is a limestone plateau, cuestaform, which stretches *c.* 250km as the crow flies from Berenice (Benghazi) in the west to Darnis (Derna) in the east and slopes down to the Sahara in the south. Where it juts northwards into the sea (in the direction of the Peloponnese) it has distinctly Mediterranean qualities in its relief, climate, soils and vegetation. The coastal plain is usually

---

[6] *SEG* IX.1 (now thought to date to 322/1 B.C.).

[7] Fadel Ali and Reynolds, *AR* 11 (1994).

[8] Reddé 1988 (E 860); *P. Vat. Gr.* 11 (E. Catani in Barker, Lloyd and Reynolds 1985 (E 775A) with references).

narrow and sometimes interrupted where the mountain reaches the sea; except, therefore, where it broadens at its western end behind Teuchira (Tocra) and Berenice, it offers little room for cities and no possibility of a continuous coast road (the narrowness is accentuated by a rise in the sea level since the classical period but not, apparently, on a scale significant enough to change the essential facts).

The mountain rises steeply on the north, by two main escarpments from sea level to an upper plateau which reaches 500m over much of its length and nearly 900m at Sidi Mohamed el-Hamri a little south of Cyrene. The lower plateau, narrow at its eastern end, broadens towards the west where it accommodates the one extensive fertile plain in the country, controlled by the Greek city of Barka and its hellenistic successor Ptolemais-Barka. Outside this plain the landscape is frequently undulating, with soil often collected in comparatively small depressions and fields surrounded by rocky outcrops. Arable land is, however, quite extensive in the area of Cyrene. In general the soils of the north Jebel are deeper, heavier and more water-retentive than those of the coastal plain, although there are some stretches of thinner soil which are only useful for pasturage. They are also better watered. Rainfall, concentrated in the winter months, may be up to 650mm annually on the high ground; whereas in the coastal plain at Benghazi it is 250–300mm, which is close to the minimum for dry farming; the rate is variable, however, even on the mountain and there is everywhere danger of periodic drought. Moreover, much of the rainfall permeates the limestone and runs underground. It gushes out at points along the edge of the escarpments (as, very notably, at Cyrene); but permanent fresh surface water is rare. There was heavy dependence, therefore, on wells and cisterns, both in the cities and in the countryside; and some construction of aqueducts for cities is attested, at least in the Roman period. There are also a number of water-courses (wadis) which are dry for much of the time but fill briefly on occasions of winter flooding. They commonly run east–west in their early stages but later turn north to reach the coastal plain where they have often deposited good soil which attracted settlements. When broad enough, their beds were cultivated in their upper reaches, although it was necessary to build series of retaining walls across them, to limit the removal of soil by flood water. On their south–north sections, however, they have often cut deep ravines into the limestone, thus providing passes through which movement between the coast and the several levels of the Jebel is comparatively easy, despite the precipitous character of the escarpments. On the upper plateau too they might provide convenient routes for movement between the settled areas and the interior. Naturally, settlements often occur on their banks and at their exits at the sea end.

The most spectacular of the wadis, the Wadi Kuf, to the south and west of Cyrene, runs for much of its length in a deep gorge which sharply divides the territory of Cyrene in the east from that of Barka or Ptolemais-Barka to the west. Since it was not bridged until the twentieth century it had a marked effect on the settlement patterns and the system of communications. No doubt some ancient tracks crossed it at much the same point as the modern bridge-builders have chosen, but it seems very likely that the main ancient road from Cyrene westwards turned north to follow the east bank of the wadi which it crossed near the sea, where it becomes broad and shallow;[9] and, since the mountain interrupts the coastal plain to the west very soon thereafter, the road then turned south again to run approximately parallel to the west bank for some distance before resuming a westward direction. An alternative, but probably minor, route by-passed the eastern end of the wadi by running south from Cyrene through what seems to have been Libyan tribal territory, before turning westwards. Both detours, of course, attracted settlements along their lines and in their proximity.

On the gentle southern slopes of the Jebel the soil is decreasingly rich and the rainfall steadily diminishing as the desert is approached. The main value of this steppe area lay in its production of the wild plant *silphium* and the pasturage of its scrub. Sedentary occupation was hardly possible beyond the 32nd parallel except in the occasional isolated oasis. Both steppe and desert were certainly in the domain of Libyan tribes.

Ancient accounts of the country are schematic and principally concerned with the Cyrene area but they show some appreciation of the configuration and its effects. Herodotus identifies three belts of land, which he says were harvested in succession: the coastal plain, a middle region of hills and the highest country behind. Strabo and Pliny describe a zone extending for about 15 Roman miles south of the coast in which trees could be grown, then a band of similar depth, devoted largely to cereal production. Diodorus notes that the land around Cyrene (which falls within the first zone) grew many crops (wheat, olives, vines and wild trees) and possessed rivers (by which he probably meant the springs which gush out along the edge of the escarpments). Beyond, Pliny describes an area 30 miles deep and 250 miles across, in which the only crop was the *silphium* plant. Diodorus makes no mention of *silphium* but his uncultivated and featureless zone, located south of Cyrene, lacking springs and surrounded by desert, is to be equated with the steppe country in which the plant flourished.[10]

9 Laronde 1987 (E 790) 263f.
10 Hdt. IV.196; Strab. XVII.3.23 (838–9c); Pliny, *HN* V.5.33; Diod. III.50.1.

III. THE POPULATION, ITS DISTRIBUTION, ORGANIZATION AND INTERNAL RELATIONSHIPS

The ancient sources encourage belief that the Cyrenaicans were all Greeks or Greco-Romans; but the indigenous Libyan population was large and a significant element in regional history. Equally they tend to suggest that all Libyans were nomadic shepherds, little touched by civilization and usually at odds with the Greeks; but the realities were certainly much more complex.

Greeks, mostly Dorians, had come to Cyrenaica in a series of groups beginning in the seventh century B.C. Settling within the cultivable zone they had established, by the hellenistic period, four cities and an unknown number of villages. The hellenistic kings, who ruled Cyrenaica either as a dependency of or an appendix to Egypt, introduced additional settlers; certainly a number of hellenized Jews and perhaps also others of Macedonian, Thracian or Anatolian origin, to judge from the names associable with these peoples that appear in the later inscriptions. The evidence for the hellenistic settlers is clear in the cities, much weaker in the country; that some of them did settle in the country is certain, but it is rash to attempt an estimate of their numbers. There may have been yet more immigrants in the first century B.C., if it is right to deduce from an inscription at Ptolemais that in 67/6 B.C. Pompey authorized settlement of former pirates there. Moreover, there were certainly Italian *negotiatores* at Cyrene by 67 B.C. and some indication that some men and women, predominantly South Italian in origin, and/or their slave and freedmen employees, may have been established in Cyrenaica more or less permanently.[11]

The indigenous Libyans, depicted by Herodotus as tribally organized, lived both in the cultivable zone and in the steppe to the south, no doubt moving between the two as the need for pasture and tillage required; but the tradition suggests that where geography favoured it some of them developed villages or even agglomerations of dwellings which might resemble towns; and this receives a little support from the discoveries of such Libyan 'townships' recently made in the interior of Tripolitania (no surveys on the same scale have yet been made in the Cyrenaican hinterland).[12] Those living in the relevant areas are said to have helped the first Greek settlers; and although later Cyrenaican history is punctuated by Libyan wars, it is probable that peaceful interchange, intermarriage and cultural influence in both directions were regular. Herodotus

---

[11] *JRS* 52 (1962) 99–101, and other inscriptions especially at Ptolemais and Teuchira.
[12] Hdt. IV.158f; G. Barker and G.D.B. Jones, *LS* 15 (1984) 1–44.

already reports it, and the process certainly continued after his time. It was furthered by the trade in *silphium*, collected by the Libyans but marketed by way of the cities (see below); no doubt also by trade in animals and animal products, of which a trace may be visible in a large enclosure outside the south sector of the hellenistic/Roman city wall of Cyrene, now attractively interpreted as a caravanserai for herdsmen who brought animals from the steppe to the city market.[13] Ptolemy I thought it necessary to rule that the sons of Greek fathers and Libyan mothers were citizens; and it accords with this that already in the hellenistic period portrait sculptures of citizens may show Libyan facial types; no doubt the Libyan names transliterated into Greek which appear in civic inscriptions often indicate men from families of mixed blood (but recent analysis of Greek naming patterns suggests that Libyan names in elite families of Cyrene and Barka may sometimes reflect relations of *xenia* between these families and Libyan tribal chiefs).[14] Evidence for Libyan cultural influence on Greek cults is particularly clear, but it was certainly much more extensive than that.

The *ochloi* apparently resident in the cities, and mentioned in an inscription of the first century B.C. from Teuchira, can hardly be other than Libyans. They were, presumably, detribalized and at least partly hellenized, but not absorbed into the citizen body. Similar groups are likely to have existed in all cities and perhaps in the villages too.[15]

At the same time in the first century B.C. many Libyans apparently continued to live very much in their traditional way, even when they had accepted something from the incoming culture. That is doubtless true even within the more highly developed areas of the cultivable zone – traces of them there can be seen, for instance, (from as late as the Roman period) in the upper occupation strata of the cave called the Haua Fteah on the coast near Apollonia;[16] more would certainly be found by systematic survey. Such people were often, no doubt, engaged in agriculture, some as dependent labour on land owned by Greeks, others, more probably, on land communally owned by their own tribes whose main locations were in the steppes but who would bring flocks and herds northward for grazing after the harvest. This system of transhumance was probably practised in ancient Cyrenaica on much the same pattern as was observed in the middle of the twentieth century. For the tribal groups in the steppe there is little useful evidence. Plutarch shows a tribal chieftain in the area south of Cyrene in *c*. 87/6 B.C., in touch with aristocrats of the city and clearly able to communicate with them, in fact

[13] M. Luni, *QAL* 10 (1979) 49f.   [14] G. Herman, *CQ* 40 (1990) 349–63.
[15] *SEG* ix.1, xxvi 1817.
[16] C.B.M. McBurney, *The Haua Fteah (Cyrenaica)*, Cambridge, 1967.

called in to help in the overthrow of a tyranny. Diodorus Siculus, in a passage which may in part have derived from a knowledgeable hellenistic source, wrote of four Libyan tribes in the region of Cyrenaica and of three Libyan life-styles. There were, he said, peaceable farmers and peaceable nomads (presumably transhumants whose seasonal movements were on fixed routes), both groups obedient to their chiefs, but a third group consisted of robbers living off the loot of their raids, and sometimes able to coerce the peaceable into joining them. Greeks, it is implied, were aware that many Libyans were acceptable neighbours and that the seriously disturbing element came from further afield.[17] It has become common recently to interpret much of Cyrenaican history as a series of cycles in which Greek expansion of sedentary agriculture threatened Libyan transhumance patterns and led to war, after which an imposed peace opened the way for renewed Greek expansion of sedentary agriculture. Events did sometimes occur in this sequence, but Diodorus' account suggests that it is not the key to all Greek–Libyan clashes. The Libyans were in touch via overland routes with kindred to the south, the east and the west; Libyan raids on Greek lands were certainly sometimes the result of social, political or climatic change outside Cyrenaica.

Some further information can be gleaned from the story of the plant *silphium*, which grew in a belt of land south of the Greek cities (see above). There is good reason to suppose that it was in normal supply at least as late as 50 B.C., but by the reign of Nero the plant was a rarity; it is generally said to have died out, but is probably a plant found in 1990 still growing in one part of the ancient *silphium* belt. Strabo explains that barbarian invaders had deliberately destroyed it as an expression of their hostility; his evidence accords with that of Diodorus, for it must mean that tribesmen from a distance were damaging the resources of the peaceful Libyan pastoralists who harvested it. Pliny, on the other hand, blames Roman *publicani* with a contract for the *pascua* (presumably the grazing tax collected for use of *ager publicus populi Romani* as pasture land) who had, he said, found it profitable to encourage grazing on a scale that prevented the plant's survival. We cannot at present make a satisfactory assessment of the two explanations; but they are not wholly incompatible. Serious damage to the plants may well have occurred in the Marmaric War of the reign of Augustus (see below); after that there would be little or no *silphium* to harvest for a time and the only profit to be made would come from the grazing tax. For present purposes however, what matters is Strabo's belief in an interruption of the

---

[17] Plut. *Mor.* 257A–C, Diod. III.49, with F. Chamoux, *QAL* 12 (1987) 57–65.

activities of one group of Libyan pastoralists in normally peaceable relations with Greeks by another from further afield.[18]

In the early second century B.C. there had been four Greek cities, Cyrene, Ptolemais (originally the port of Barka, but becoming its centre of government in the third century B.C.), Teuchira (called Arsinoe in the hellenistic period, but reverting to its original, Libyan, name under the Romans) and Berenice (the name given to the new harbour site to which the citizens of Euhesperides had moved in *c.* 246 B.C.). Between the early second century and 67 B.C. a fifth, Apollonia, was created through promotion of Cyrene's main port; and since hellenistic royal creations were normally given dynastic names it is possible that this was due to Roman intervention. Whatever its date the creation must have been disadvantageous to Cyrene, although perhaps less so than it might seem; it is clear in fact that a good deal of land near Apollonia had already been taken from Cyrenaeans into the possession of the king; and after 75/4 it seems likely that harbour dues there would all be collected for the benefit of Rome. Apollonia and Cyrene were in dispute in 67, but there is no evidence for tensions between them later. Apollonia soon became so much part of the Cyrenaican scene that the whole region acquired the name of Pentapolis, land of the five cities (first attested in the usage of the Elder Pliny).[19]

The cities, especially Cyrene, Barca and Teuchira, were sited with a view to exploitation of particularly extensive fertile areas. There were many other fertile and well-watered areas beyond their immediate environs to tempt exploitation, but not of a size to support a city. The settlers were also interested in coastal sites with a view to harbours, for connexions with Greece, for export and import and for the convenience of coastwise shipping by which movement eastwards and westwards was easier than by overland routes (see above). If good harbours are scarce on this coast, quite modest facilities would meet the needs of much ancient shipping; but in the coastal strip even modest harbourage rarely coincides with a sufficient hinterland to support a city. Both in the interior, therefore, and on the coast, there were far more villages than cities; in consequence, most city territories were unusually large. Some villages became substantial places, as road-stations where tracks crossed, for instance, and/or as collecting places for goods to be transmitted between the interior and the coast; but very few ever achieved the status of cities, even in late antiquity when this became easier to do.

There is little information about the government of these Greek communities either before or after they came under Roman rule. A copy of a constitution established for Cyrene in 322/1 B.C. survives, but we do not know how much, if anything of significance, remained of it by 96,

---

[18] Strab. XVII.3.20 (836–7c); Pliny, *HN* XIX.15.3.   [19] *SEG* XX 709; Pliny, *HN* V.5.31.

much less 44 B.C. A decree of the first century B.C. at Teuchira shows that the number of voting citizens there at that time was very small; and that is likely to have been the pattern in all the cities. The Libyan residents in them presumably had no civic rights. Of their other inhabitants the group of Roman *negotiatores* at Cyrene clearly formed a self-governing community separate from, but within the city, and a community of Jews at Berenice was similarly privileged, as no doubt were the Jews in all the cities; at Berenice they called themselves a *politeuma* and conducted their own affairs, non-religious as well as religious, through quasi-civic institutions. That gave them an autonomy which might very easily lead to clashes with the civic authorities.[20]

Within the city territories many of the Greek villages were too distant from their city centres to allow of day-to-day administration from them. Most, therefore, must have had institutions not unlike those of the Jewish *politeuma* at Berenice for handling their own affairs; the model was presumably that indicated by the one village decree so far found, which shows something very like a civic organization with localized euergetism and local initiatives in the matter of public building and corn supply, probably in the early first century B.C. Strabo called the Cyrenaican villages πολίχνια, and about a century later Ptolemy the Geographer listed a number of them under the heading of πόλεις; they must have seemed rather more than ordinary villages to both. The precise character of their relation to the cities cannot be defined. The only real evidence is that in the territory of Cyrene a number of them used the Cyrenaean dating system by Cyrene's eponymous priest of Apollo; and that in two villages Cyrene's priests of Apollo are known to have taken some responsibility for other cults; in both cases these were cults which were attracting foreign visitors, but we cannot tell whether this had anything to do with the matter or not.[21]

In addition to the Greek villages we must envisage also a number of areas within city territories but not part of them. So 'king's land', which became *ager publicus populi Romani*, is known to have existed within the territories of all (see below) and in principle was surely outside civic authority. It is probable that there were villages on some of these estates; their inhabitants, in some cases perhaps Libyans, in others probably Jews or other hellenistic immigrants, were surely outside the citizen bodies; they were probably provided with the institutions of a *politeuma* or something similar. Finally there will have been pockets of Libyan tribal land also outside the civic system, none of which can now be precisely pinpointed.

The relationship of the Greek cities one to another is also unclear.

---

[20] *SEG* IX 1, XXVI 1817, XX 715, XVI 931, XVII 823.
[21] *SEG* IX 354; Strab. XVII.3.21 (837c), Ptol. *Geog.* IV.4.7; *SEG* IX 349 for an example.

Cyrene claimed to be the *metropolis* of all the others; Strabo called them her περιπόλια. Taken with the ancient use of Cyrene's name for the whole region this has led some to think that they were her dependencies; but that is not consistent with what we know of the independent civic life of Berenice and Teuchira in the first century B.C. Under the Principate, perhaps already in the time of Augustus, there seems to have been a *koinon* or common council of cities, meeting in Cyrene (see below); it may well have existed earlier and might account better for the language used than dependency.[22] As for relations with the Libyans, one might conjecture that an eminent Cyrenean, honoured shortly after the death of Ptolemy Apion for services to Cyrene, the other cities and the tribes of the territories, had negotiated between the cities and the tribes relationships that had formerly depended on agreements between the kings and the tribes.[23]

It is a natural supposition that all the peoples and types of community described above were comprehended within the four categories, which Strabo is said to have distinguished in 'Cyrenaea' – citizens, farmers, *perioeci* and Jews. There are, however, obscurities in his formula. Citizens should be the Greeks of the villages as well as of the cities; the farmers might well be dependent labourers, presumably Libyan, on Greek-owned land, but could also, perhaps, be the term for immigrants other than Jews who worked the royal land and sedentary Libyans on Libyan tribal land within city territories; *perioeci* are even more problematic – possibly, but far from certainly, Libyan tribesmen in the steppe.[24]

IV. FROM THE DEATH OF CAESAR TO THE CLOSE OF THE MARMARIC WAR (C. A.D. 6/7)

In summer of 44 B.C. Cyrenaica was assigned to C. Cassius, as Crete was to M. Brutus. There is no sign that Cassius ever went near this province. After Philippi it naturally became part of Antony's command and was probably used by him, along with Crete, in the first place as a naval base. There is a series of coins, some minted in Roman denominations, and with parallel issues for Crete and for Cyrenaica, which have often been connected with this; but on present evidence few can be dated precisely enough for the connexion to be certain. By the 'Donations of Alexandria' Antony cancelled the Roman annexation of Cyrenaica and gave it as a kingdom to a Cleopatra, either Cleopatra herself or Cleopatra Selene; the discovery at Cyrene of a coin of 31 B.C. from an issue which features both Antony and Cleopatra herself has been taken to suggest that the whole issue should be attributed to Cyrene, with the implication that the new queen was Cleopatra herself. There is no indication that anything

---

[22] Strab. XVII.3.21 (837c).   [23] *SEG* XX 729.   [24] Strabo *ap.* Joseph. *AJ* XIV.7.114.

was done to reconstitute a royal administration however. Antony garrisoned Cyrenaica with four Roman legions under L. Pinarius Scarpus (coins have survived from several of the issues that he made to pay his men); and the cities must have borne the burden of providing supplies for them. After Actium, Scarpus was quick to change allegiance, refused Antony a landing and, in due course, handed over Cyrenaica and its garrison to Cornelius Gallus as Octavian's representative; surprisingly he had time to issue coins carrying the name of Octavian before he left. The recovery of Cyrenaica for Rome – mentioned in the *Res Gestae* – was undoubtedly celebrated in Octavian's triumph. But what he recovered was an area in poor shape; the excavation at Sidi Khrebish shows unchecked decay throughout the third quarter of the century.[25]

Octavian/Augustus introduced a new order, which was recognized in Cyrene by the use of a provincial era starting in 31 B.C. At any rate from 27 B.C. Cyrenaica was administered together with Crete, governed by a proconsul of praetorian status. He and the quaestor appointed with him, normally held office for one year, and divided their time between the two parts of the province. The provincial Fasti are full of gaps and uncertainties, so that it would be rash to generalize from them about the kind of men who served in the province and the kind of careers to which they proceeded, at any rate for the reign of Augustus, and indeed, for most of the first century A.D.

The provincial capital was at Cyrene; but it is likely that the governor also held assizes at Ptolemais where there are, as at Cyrene, a number of official inscriptions in Latin. These official texts include prayer formulae of the type used by the Arval Brethren at Rome on 3 January each year and certainly prove that Latin rituals (concerned with the preservation of the current emperor and his family) were conducted in the *agorae* of each of these cities. There are also from each a few soldiers' tombstones, some probably of the first century A.D., perhaps for men who served as the governors' guards.[26]

Whatever had been the case earlier, the cities had now lost their freedom and the province was certainly taxed. Collection of *portoria* on goods passing in and out of provincial harbours and frontier stations would normally be let to *publicani*. Given the large areas occupied by Libyans as well as the complex character of most city territories, it would be understandable if Augustus thought it best to use *publicani* also for collection of the land tax rather than to entrust it to the cities; but as *publicani* must also have managed the *ager publicus* it is not always possible

[25] App. *BCiv.* III.1.8 with Cic. *Phil.* II.38.97, XI.12, 27. For coins Buttrey 1983 (B 315); Plut. *Ant.* 54.4, 69.2; Dio XLIX.32.4–5, LI.5.6; *RG* 27. Sidi Khrebish: Lloyd 1977–85 (E 793).

[26] *PBSR* 30 (1962) 33–6.

to distinguish contractors for tax collection from contractors for the public estates in our sparse evidence. A very recently discovered inscription, probably of the Julio-Claudian period, records a dedication to Ceres Augusta in a major precinct of Demeter and Kore at Cyrene, by a *promagister publici Cyrenen(sis)*, who, on the face of it, was the representative in Cyrene of a company of *publicani* collecting tax. Given his connexion with Ceres, this was probably the land tax, which may well have been collected in kind, and so mainly in cereals. It is a reasonable conjecture that the contract for collection of all Roman taxes in Cyrenaica was let to one company (hence the *publicum Cyrenense* in contrast to, for example, the *quattuor publica Africae*), since the profits from each individual tax were perhaps insufficient to tempt bidders. Possibly the contract for management of the *ager publicus* was let along with that for taxation.[27]

No imperial estates are at present attested in Cyrenaica in the first or second centuries A.D.; certainly no procurator is attested there before the early third century A.D. and there are no adequate grounds for accepting the view that the procurators of Crete also operated in Cyrenaica. One inscription of uncertain date at Ptolemais shows that there were, at some stage, members of the imperial household there; but at present we have no information at all about their function.[28]

The arrangements of Augustus provided, in the long term, for a reasonably stable and prosperous Cyrenaica; in the short term, new problems arose, recovery was certainly interrupted and the period of the reign cannot be regarded as an unqualified success. That is best illustrated at Sidi Khrebish where the district remained in a dilapidated and deserted state throughout it, although the one small temple there was receiving votives, and a channel aqueduct was constructed across it to carry water to a point beyond it, showing that developments were taking place nearer to the city centre. Of those we have a little positive evidence in two inscriptions erected by the Jewish community of Berenice; they seem to show an active group, possessing a meeting house that is grandly called an amphitheatre, which one of the members could afford to redecorate at his own expense; nevertheless, and despite the inclusion of a few Roman citizens in the community, its financial competence seems to have been modest overall, since the stelae carrying the inscriptions are small.[29]

There is more evidence from the centres of the other cities, and although comparatively little of it can be firmly dated in the first three-quarters of the reign it seems to justify belief that normality was

---

[27] *SEG* IX 8, XXVII 1159, Pliny, *HN* XIX.15.3, Fadel Ali and Reynolds, *LS* 25 (1994) 214–17.

[28] *CIG* III 5194.

[29] *SEG* XVI 931, XVII 823. JR does not accept the view that this was a civic amphitheatre in which the Jews had a right to display their inscriptions and an obligation to contribute to maintenance.

returning. At Cyrene that is demonstrated by a stela of *c*. 16–15 B.C. containing the end of a civic decree which conferred the annual priesthood of the cult of Augustus on Barkaeus son of Theuchrestos (we know that he held it in 17/16) and others relating to the will in which he bequeathed one estate to Apollo and Artemis for the use of their priests and another to Hermes and Herakles for provision of oil in the civic gymnasium. Prized amenities of city life were available to citizens, then, and at least one rich citizen showed his patriotism in the traditional way by benefactions. Civic administration was proceeding as it should. In addition, imperial cult had been quickly established and integrated into the local system of honours (and, no doubt, liturgies); in fact we know from other inscriptions that at this period the name of the priest of Augustus was being used, along with that of the priest of Apollo, to date civic documents.[30]

Nevertheless the dated inscriptions on public works suggest that an extensive programme of repair and new building was still needed in the last decade of the reign and was, in part at least, undertaken by Roman officials; that should perhaps be related to a series of problems that can be detected earlier.

The first of these problems to appear in the record concerns the Jewish communities. At a comparatively early date in the reign they complained that the cities were preventing the dispatch of the money that they offered annually to Jerusalem and harming them in other ways; Augustus responded with a letter to the governor confirming both their right to dispatch the money and their *isoteleia*, which perhaps meant their immunity from the metic tax paid to the cities by resident aliens. By the time of Agrippa's command in the East (17/16–13 B.C.) this decision was being ignored; in Cyrene at least, and probably in the other cities too, informers were accusing the Jews of failure to pay civic taxes due from them and the civic authorities were therefore preventing dispatch of the sacred money again. After hearing a Jewish embassy Agrippa wrote to the city of Cyrene, with a reference to the other cities also, reaffirming the rulings of Augustus. That the provocative factor was clearly financial suggests that the cities were conscious that their means were limited. Nothing more is heard of the matter. By A.D. 3–4, moreover, a few Jewish names appear in a list of ephebes at Cyrene and among the graffiti on monuments in the gymnasium; while in A.D. 60–1 one of the Cyrenaean magistrates called νομοφύλακες had a Jewish name. It would appear that some kind of accommodation had been reached between Greeks and Jews, perhaps in order to secure Jewish financial contributions to civic life, as happened in Asia Minor in the Severan period.[31]

---

[30] *SEG* IX 4, and some unpublished texts.
[31] Joseph. *AJ* XVI.160.9f, 165f; *SEG* XX 737.8, 740.2–3, 741a.34, 47, 48, 57, 741c.13; *D* 50.2.3.3.

When the cities of Cyrenaica, probably acting jointly, sent ambassadors to Augustus in 7–6 B.C., there were quite other problems to put to him, mainly concerned with the administration of justice in criminal cases, but involving also the relations of Greeks with Roman citizens and, to some extent, of Greeks with Greeks. The fact that the embassy was sent is, in itself, evidence for some enterprise in the cities (and perhaps for co-operation among them in a *koinon*). The facts that necessitated it provide unusually sharp insights into the continuing defects of Roman provincial government, as well as into the specific difficulties of this province.[32]

The first striking point is that Roman citizens resident in Cyrenaica (most of whom were probably immigrants, judging by their nomenclature) had been successfully ganging up against Greeks, to procure sentences, including death sentences, on innocent men. They were aided by an obviously unsatisfactory system of jury-courts in which prosecution, witnesses and jurors might all be drawn from a very small group of resident Romans. The second edict may add a further insight if, behind its obscurely allusive formulae, we may see a plot by the three Roman citizens it names to involve Greeks in charges of disloyalty to Augustus.

A second point is the implication in Augustus' provisional proposals for reform of the jury system that Greeks could not always trust other Greeks to give them justice; he thought it wise to offer them the option of all-Roman juries in the courts for which he proposed that there should normally be mixed juries, and, in those for which he proposed all-Greek juries, advised that no juryman should be drawn from the same city as anyone directly involved in the case. It must be admitted that it is not certain that this was based on anything in the recent Cyrenaican record rather than on wider experience of Greek feuding, but it is not unlikely, given Cyrene's earlier reputation for violent *staseis*.

Thirdly, there are now clear indications of financial weakness in the province. The panel from which the Roman jurymen were drawn consisted of 215 names, all that could be found to meet a minimum property qualification as low as 2,500 denarii; Augustus proposed a minimum property qualification of 7,500 denarii for Greek as well as Roman jurymen and was conscious that there might be difficulty in finding enough men who could meet it. We should not, of course, suppose that there were no rich men in Cyrenaica, but must accept that there was no substantial number of reasonably well-off men even among the resident Roman citizens. A similar implication underlies Augustus' decision that a Cyrenaean Greek who received Roman citizenship must continue to fulfil his local obligations unless specifically given exemption from them at the time of his enfranchisement (and then only in respect of property that he owned at that time).

It is hard to believe that there can have been any perceived threat of attack from outside at the time when the embassy went to Augustus; and it is still hard when two years later the province received its copy of the fifth edict (setting out a new procedure for certain types of extortion and addressed to all provinces, not specifically to Cyrenaica), for Cyrene then decided, in an apparently carefree mood, to have all five documents inscribed on a marble stela for erection in the *agora*. It is reasonable then to take 5/4 B.C. as the *terminus post quem* for the next major problem, the raids, on a scale justifying use of the word war, made by the Libyan tribe of Marmaridae (who were located both in the area between Cyrenaica and Egypt and in the Syrtica, between Cyrenaica and Tripolitania). An inscription at Cyrene celebrated the conclusion of this war for the city in A.D. 3, attributing it to the merits of Pausanias, eponymous priest of Apollo in that year. To what happened in between these two dates there is an almost certain reference, without context, in an extract from Dio, Book LV, apparently of A.D. 1. Raids, we are told, had gone unchecked by others and by soldiers coming from Egypt, until a praetorian tribune was brought in, when control was established but only after a long period when no senator was sent to govern the cities. A number of Cyrenaican inscriptions can also be associated with these events, most usefully two decrees from Cyrene. The first of these honours Alexandros son of Aiglanor who himself fought in them, killing many of the enemy and taking prisoners. It may well be that when the raids began there were no Roman troops in the province because the cities were expected to deal with that kind of trouble by local militias – using ephebes and *neoi* (young men just past their ephebic training years), the practice described in the early first century B.C. in a decree at Berenice. If so the system proved inadequate and troops had to be summoned, but they too were, at first, unsuccessful. The second decree details the activities of Phaos son of Kleandros who undertook a dangerous embassy in winter storms during the war and brought back most timely help; the language would accord with a journey to Rome to persuade Augustus to send Dio's praetorian tribune, presumably accompanied by new military forces. The decrees may, of course, exaggerate the weight of responsibility which fell onto the cities at the onset of trouble; but it is certain that Augustus' arrangements had failed to provide for the defence of Cyrenaica. A small gobbet of literary evidence, from Florus, adds that, at an unstated date, Augustus entrusted a war against the Marmaridae and Garamantes to P. Sulpicius Quirinius, a senator whose career is full of problems. Florus' evidence might refer to a governorship of Crete and Cyrene held by him in *c.* 15 B.C. soon after his praetorship; but Florus seems to suggest that he was associated with the campaign of Cossus Cornelius Lentulus, proconsul of Africa, against the Gaetuli in the Syrtica in A.D. 5–6. By then Quirinius was a rather senior man to hold such an appointment unless, perhaps, we suppose that he was given responsibility not simply for finishing the desert campaign, but for constructing a defence system for Cyrenaica in the Syrtica. It would appear that there was no such system when the Marmaridae began their raids; but a line of forts had been built by the reign of Tiberius, the earliest evidence being perhaps of A.D. 15 and certainly of A.D. 21. There is, unfortunately, nothing at present which firmly links these forts to Quirinius, but the chronology may be thought to favour it.[33]

The Syrtican forts provided a screen behind which the province could develop in security from desert raiders and their establishment marks a new phase in the history of Cyrenaica. The screen consisted of a series of strongpoints intended to protect the western and south-western approaches to Cyrenaica, each placed beside a major watering-point for the effective oversight of the populations using it and providing bases for patrols who moved further afield. The garrisons were drawn from auxiliary units of the Roman army and in some cases have left informative graffiti on fort walls and at local shrines. At Sceleidima and Msus (ancient names unknown) there were mounted as well as infantry soldiers, some of the men spoke Latin and several, to judge from their names, were recruited in Spain or Gaul. At Agedabia (ancient Corniclanum) a number of men came from Syria, chosen no doubt because of their desert experience. At the same time, and along with the graffiti of men who were certainly regular auxiliary soldiers of the Roman army, there are also graffiti of men whose names are drawn from a recognizably Cyrenaican repertoire, and in their mixture of Greek, Libyan and Latin, recall the ephebic graffiti of Teuchira and Ptolemais. Their interpretation is uncertain. They might indicate one episode of military recruiting in Cyrenaica (such as is attested during the Julio-Claudian period), but since they very rarely include any reference to military status, they may be the work of ephebes or *neoi* from the cities, doing tours of duty alongside, or in substitution for, Roman soldiers.

V. A.D. 4–70

After the Marmaric War reconstruction in the cities was taken in hand quickly. At Cyrene a series of inscriptions of the last decade of Augustus' reign and the early years of Tiberius' shows Roman officials concerned with repairs to public buildings in the *agora* and its neighbourhood, in

[33] *SEG* IX 63; DIO. LV.10a; *ASAA* 39–40 (1960–1) 321, no.8; *OGIS* 767; Flor. II.31; Desanges 1969 (E 778); *SEG* IX 773–95; J. Reynolds, *AR* 5 (1988) 167–72.

the sanctuary of Apollo, in the temple of Zeus, and perhaps on the defensive walls of the acropolis (but that may have been earlier). In some cases the credit is attributed to a commander of a cohort, suggesting that it began before normal proconsular government was resumed, although it certainly carried on after that for some years.[34] The involvement of Roman officials in building, for which they presumably made funds available, could perhaps be compared with the help that Rome was beginning to give to provincials suffering from natural disasters; although there is no clear evidence that these repairs were necessitated by direct enemy action (failure to maintain the soft local building stone might be sufficient explanation). The inscriptions on the buildings are more often in Latin than might have been expected, which may reflect the presence of Latin speakers, not only soldiers but also the resident Roman *negotiatores* who have left at least one Julio-Claudian record (not precisely dated), apparently from a building which they themselves erected.[35] But it would be mistaken to ignore the part which the Greek citizens were playing too. Fragments of a series of inscribed civic decrees give glimpses of the city's government in operation.[36] The texts of several of these stress the public spirit of the honorands, making it clear that during the Marmaric War men had given very generously indeed in personal effort as well as in money, and continued to do so. Minor monuments show that there were candidates enough for the expensive priesthood of Apollo, and that the ephebic organization was active. Among dedications, the city's large marble altar for the cult of Gaius and Lucius Caesar in the *agora* is a notable – and surely costly – demonstration of the point.[37] Moreover, by the middle of the first century A.D. the lists of Cyrene's priests of Apollo begin to show men with Roman citizenship (usually with the names Tiberius Claudius, implying enfranchisements under the emperors Claudius and Nero); that should mean that the public services of these men were of some note.[38] It is possible also that one man from Cyrene entered the Senate at Rome, Antonius Flamma, the proconsul of Crete and Cyrene who was prosecuted and exiled in A.D. 70 for extortion in Cyrenaica. Several men with the names M. Antonius Flamma appear as priests of Apollo and as sponsors of public works at Cyrene in the middle of the first century A.D. and the grandson of one of them (by his daughter) was certainly a Roman senator in the time of the emperor Trajan. It is tempting, therefore, to identify the earliest of the Antonii Flammae of Cyrene with the proconsul; but since it is inherently unlikely that a Greek from this province would have obtained entry to

---

[34] *AE* 1927, 140, 1968, 536–8, probably also 532–4, 539, 540; G. Oliverio, *Africa Italiana* 3 (1930) 198f; L. Gasperini, *QAL* 6 (1971) 3–22; and some unpublished inscriptions.
[35] For instance L. Gasperini in Stucchi 1967 (E 805A) 175, no. 38.
[36] See the inscription cited in n. 28.   [37] Unpublished.   [38] E.g. *SEG* IX 183, 184.

the Senate at so early a date, his family should probably be seen as one of Italian immigrants which accepted Cyrenaean citizenship and probably married into the local aristocracy. If the proconsul was from Cyrene (whether a true Greek or not) we should know at least one really rich man in the province. His prosecution might be held to show feuding within the elite class at Cyrene which, perhaps, expressed itself in support of different Roman factions in the months of civil war after the fall of Nero.[39]

At Cyrene then recovery is clear. What little we know of Apollonia at this time suggests a similar series of developments there. For Ptolemais and Teuchira there is a different type of evidence. At present building inscriptions, civic decrees and dedications are rare in these cities, but there are plentiful ephebic graffiti and funerary inscriptions throughout the first century A.D.;[40] that seems to show that there were quite sizeable citizen populations able to afford ephebic training for their sons and a literate, if often modest, memorial for themselves. For Berenice the evidence is different again. Aside from a few statues of Tiberian date which may have come from the city centre or nearby, it consists in what is shown by the excavation of Sidi Khrebish. At approximately the middle of the first century A.D. the whole desolate area was levelled, new paved streets were laid and new houses were built. These had ground plans and external façades like those of their hellenistic predecessors but more substantial foundations and some more elaborate features such as peristyle courtyards, underground cisterns and a little architectural decoration. At the least, they seem to imply that the population of Berenice was growing again and needed more living-space. A Jewish inscription of Neronian date from the city has been used independently of this evidence to argue for an increase in the size of the *politeuma* population, since the number of its officials is greater than in the earlier inscriptions; it certainly shows reconstruction of the synagogue funded by its members, through subscriptions that were quite numerous although in no case large.[41]

In the villages too there appears to have been an increase in the number of funerary inscriptions erected, most of them quite modest, some very much so, but nevertheless evidence that more of the rural people valued a literate funerary record than before, and perhaps indicating an increased rural population. At any rate a military levy was held in Cyrenaica in the fifties suggesting that there was no perceived manpower shortage at that time.[42]

Evidence for Roman official activity is now limited. We know that

---

[39] Reynolds 1982 (E 802).
[40] *SEG* IX 361–726 (in need of revision). There are also some unpublished texts.
[41] *SEG* XVII 823.   [42] Tac. *Ann.* XIV.18.1.

once in the reign of Tiberius the routine was broken and the tenure of a governor prolonged for three years – but perhaps for reasons connected with the fall of Sejanus rather than with Cyrenaica. Four times we hear that Roman officials provoked Cyrenaeans to prosecute them at Rome, usually for extortion. Only for two Roman initiatives, both due to Claudius, can anything more be said, one concerned with roads, the other with *ager publicus*.[43]

It is generally held that there was already a good system of communications in Cyrenaica before the Romans came, linking villages and cities, interior and coast, quite adequately. Its tracks may often be recognized as shallow cuttings in rock-surfaces, perhaps also showing deep wheel-ruts, and sometimes lined by rock-cut sarcophagi and other tombs; there is no sign that any other method of road construction ever superseded it. Neither construction of such tracks nor their repair (a simple process of cutting away a damaged surface) are datable. So although we might expect the Romans to have paid attention to the system quite early, even to have extended it in connexion with the Marmaric War, there would be no indication of that unless their work included the erection of milestones. On present evidence the earliest milestones in Cyrenaica are those erected in the name of Claudius, on the Cyrene–Apollonia road, the crucial link between Cyrene and the outside world, and on the Cyrene–Balagrae road which led from the city towards some of her most fertile territory, from there on towards the cities of Ptolemais-Barka, Teuchira and Berenice and beyond them to the Syrtican forts.[44] We cannot be sure how much to put to Claudius' credit and especially whether he was responsible for the very important development which involved rerouting the road from Cyrene to Apollonia on a new line which was less steep and less subject to winter flooding than its predecessor. Nor do we know his reasons for action on the Cyrenaican roads; but he may well have been strongly influenced by his concern for the corn supply of the city of Rome, which should have given him an interest in Cyrenaican cereal production and in the movement of the grain from the interior to the coast.

An interest in cereal production may also have been a factor, along with straightforward fiscal considerations, in his decision to appoint a praetorian senator, L. Acilius Strabo, as his legate with a commission to recover *ager publicus* in Cyrenaica which had been occupied by squatters.[45] Acilius Strabo appears to have spent a good deal of time dealing with a number of small estates in the cultivable zone and apparently with some land in the *silphium* belt (see above). The series of stelae that he erected after reclamation of land begins in Claudius' reign, when he was

---

[43] *InscrCret* IV 272 (*ILS* 158); Tac. *Ann.* III.38.1, XIV.18.1, *Hist.* IV.45.2.
[44] Goodchild 1950 (E 781).   [45] J. Reynolds, *LA* 8 (1971) 47–51.

at work in country districts east and south of Cyrene; it carries on after
Nero's accession and while some of his Neronian stelae are in country
districts, a number stand in close proximity to Cyrene and Apollonia.
That apparently brought him up against articulate and powerful men in
the city elites so that in A.D. 59 he was prosecuted for misconduct. Nero,
who heard the case, acquitted him, but nevertheless allowed the
squatters to remain in possession, although the survival of many of
Strabo's stelae could mean that some of his reclamations were retained.

   In the circumstances it would not be surprising if some Cyrenaicans
regarded the fall of Nero with regret. Their attitudes and fortunes during
the course of the year of the four emperors are not recorded but it is fair
to wonder how enthusiastic they felt about the accession of Vespasian,
who had once been a quaestor in the province. If they did have doubts
they were, in a sense, justified for one of his early acts was to resume the
reclamation of *ager publicus*.

CHAPTER 14*a*

GREECE (INCLUDING CRETE AND CYPRUS) AND ASIA MINOR FROM 43 B.C. TO A.D. 69

B. M. LEVICK

I. GEOGRAPHY AND DEVELOPMENT

The area to be dealt with here was in some senses a unity, in others, less important, diverse and falling into three regions, mainland Greece and the islands, western Asia Minor, and the Anatolian plateau.[1] What unified it was geography – common subjection to Mediterranean geology and climatic conditions and the seasonal aridity that governs Mediterranean agriculture; language – it was all predominantly Greek-speaking; history – the entire area had come under the sway of Alexander the Great and then that of Rome; and devotion to common political ideals, those of the city-state (*polis*). Within these categories came also the variety. In Asia Minor the thin border of arable soil that fronts the limestone mountains of mainland Greece, the 'bare bones' of Attica, as Plato calls them,[2] was being enriched and extended by accretions brought down by the rivers; to such an extent that cities such as Priene, built like most Greek cities for communication by sea, had already found themselves stranded inland; even Miletus and Ephesus were to lose their position on the coast in the end. Inland and to the east, as the mountains rise into the Anatolian plateau and then into the Taurus range, with its

---

[1] The most important literary sources are the *Geography* of Strabo, Books VIII–X (332–489C) (Greece) and XII–XIV (490–685C) (Asia Minor), the Acts of the Apostles, Pausanias' *Guide to Greece*, and Pliny's *Natural History*, especially Books III–VI; historical material is supplied by Cassius Dio's *Roman History* Books XLVII–LXIII, Appian's *Civil Wars* Book V, and Tacitus' *Annals*. A prime contribution has been made by archaeology (e.g. *Forschungen in Ephesos veröffentlicht vom Österr. archäolog. Inst. in Wien* 1–9 (Vienna, 1906–81); *Altertümer von Pergamon* 1–15.i (Berlin, 1911–86); *Corinth: Results of Excavations of the American School of Classical Studies at Athens* 1–17 (Cambridge, MA, 1932–85); for recent work see the *Archaeological Reports* published by the Society for the Promotion of Hellenic Studies and the British School at Athens); and inscriptions, of which the main collections are to be found in *CIL* III, *IG, IGRR, SEG*, and *SIG³, TAM* and the *Inschriften griech. Städte aus Kleinasien (Kommission f. d. arch. Erforschung Kleinasiens bei d. Österr. Akad. d. Wiss., Inst. f. Altertumsk. d.Univ. Köln)*, 1-   (Bonn, 1972–   ); J. and L. Robert, *Bulletin épigraphique* in *REG* 51–97 (1937–84), is indispensable. Coins are hardly less important, and B.V. Head's *Historia Numorum* is the most succinct guide to them; the main publications are W.H. Waddington, E. Babelon, and Th. Reinach, *Recueil général des monnaies grecques d'Asie Mineure* (Paris, 1904–1912, vol. 1, edn 2 1925), *BMC* and *SNG* (notably *SNG von Aulock*), and *RPC*, and Burnett *et al.* 1992 (B 312).

I am much indebted to Dr S. Alcock (Reading) for many helpful comments and suggestions, and especially for directing my attention to a number of useful books and articles.

[2] Pl. *Criti.* 111b.

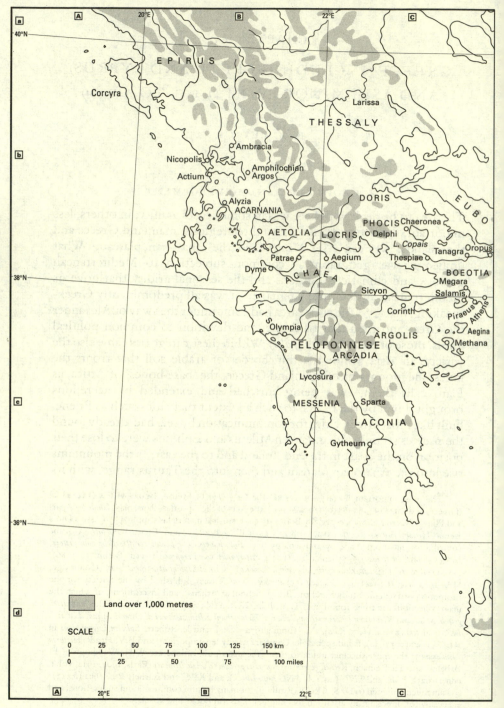

Map 15. Greece and the Aegean.

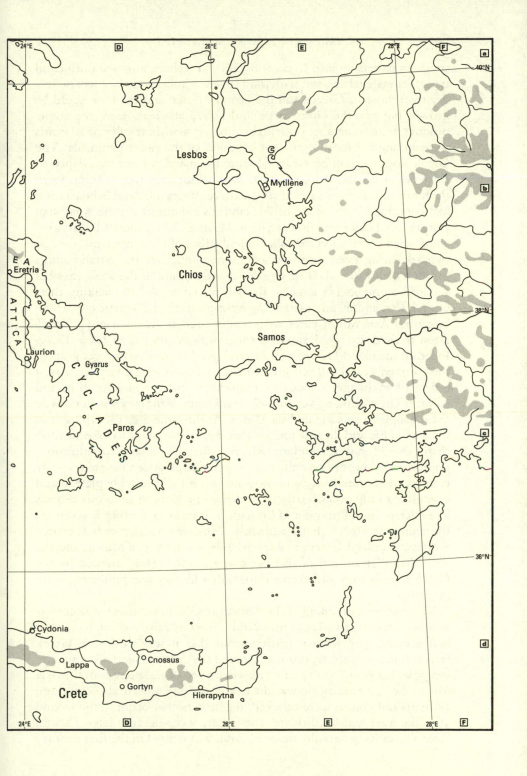

40°N

Lesbos

Mytilene

Chios

38°N

Samos

E A
Eretria

ATTICA

Laurion

Gyarus

C Y C L A D E S

Paros

36°N

Cydonia

Lappa   Cnossus

Crete   Gortyn

Hierapytna

24°E

26°E

28°E

southern extension into Lycia and Cilicia Tracheia, a more continental type of climate takes over, with long severe winters and summers no less dry than those of Greece and the islands. Grain and the vine could be grown, but not the olive; cattle and above all sheep were the staple product, with minerals a potential source of wealth; textiles of all kinds were among the most important products of the entire peninsula. The Greek language had been carried from the mainland and the islands to the west, north and south coasts of Asia Minor by waves of colonists in the tenth and then the seventh and sixth centuries B.C., and hellenization had continued in the wake of Alexander's conquests. In the Anatolian plateau its advance was slow; Lydian, Mysian, Celtic, above all Phrygian and Lycian survived in the villages and tribes of the hinterland, the last two appearing even on inscribed monuments; but the Attalid kings promoted and consolidated Greek art and culture in the west, in what was to become in 133 B.C. the Roman province of Asia, making their capital, Pergamum, an outstanding example of the hellenistic city. Even in central Asia Minor cities with names such as Apamea and Antioch attest the activity of Alexander's successors as creators of *poleis*. Developed in mainland Greece as a natural product of divisive geography, they proved a means of self-government, a source of military security, a centre of exchange, a focus of religion, a fosterer of education and culture. The wealth, power and self-confidence of the city-dwellers made them people to emulate in Asia Minor. At the same time the strength of the way of life and the institutions that were giving way to urbanization there should not be underrated. A tribal or village organization, reinforced by a common cult, suited sparse populations isolated in hilly country or scattered over a homogeneous and inhospitable plateau and assembling only occasionally to exchange produce at religious centres like Hierapolis in Phrygia and Comana in Pontus or at other markets on the main routes through the peninsula. The differences between the three regions, mainland Greece and the islands, western Asia Minor, and the Anatolian plateau, remained clear and are only lightly masked by the Greek terminology and nomenclature that literacy and public life were imposing.

The manner and timing of the Roman acquisition of these regions was another important variable: mainland Greece fell first, in 146 B.C., after half a century of Roman protestations that it was to ensure Greek freedom that Roman troops had crossed the Adriatic, and after a bitter struggle that ended with many cities deprived of their freedom. In Asia Minor the first acquisition was the bequest of 133, the Attalid kingdom; Bithynia and Pontus were annexed, the first another bequest, the second after the wars with Mithridates the Great, seven decades later. Central Anatolia, as its geography made natural, was treated in the first century as a military problem under the name of Provincia Cilicia: a base for action against pirate strongholds in the mountains and a means of safeguarding the route from western Asia Minor to Syria. The islands of Crete and Cyprus were allowed to survive for longer outside direct control, Cyprus until P. Clodius Pulcher passed a bill for its annexation in 58 B.C., Crete in part at least until the end of the Republic.

The Romans were heirs of Alexander and his successors, and benefited from the urbanization achieved under them. In Greece proper there was little more to be done in that direction: it was more a question of preserving the *poleis* without which control of the empire, for a ruling power whose resources were stretched to the utmost, would be close to impossible in the absence of any alternative organization. Greece was in economic decline in relation to Asia Minor, with its superior fertility and resources. The lot of Roman governors of Asia was easy, and tempting to the unscrupulous. Even in spite of their greed, urbanization and prosperity would have prevailed, if this area and Bithynia-Pontus had been left in peace. Instead, Greece and western Asia Minor were involved in foreign wars, directly between 88 and 84, indirectly from 74 to 63, and disastrously caught up in civil struggles from 49 to 31 B.C.

II. THE TRIUMVIRAL PERIOD[3]

The Greek East suffered more in the thirteen years of intermittent civil war that followed Caesar's death than in the swift campaigns that made him supreme. In Asia Minor devastation of the countryside, destruction of cities and their inhabitants, the imposition of fines and exceptional levies came successively at the hands of three parties. First the republicans: late in 43 Brutus forced Lycia to contribute to his war chest, stormed Xanthus, and, together with Cassius, robbed Rhodes (in spite of a plea from Cassius' old teacher Archelaus), Tarsus, and other cities. Client kings also suffered. Ariobarzanes II Eusebes Philoromaios of Cappadocia was executed, Deiotarus of Galatia brought to join the Liberators and send cavalry to Philippi under his secretary Amyntas. Even after the triumvirs' victories at Philippi and Naulochus, Sex. Pompeius' raiding of 35 damaged the area round the Propontis. A second factor was the Parthian invasion under Q. Labienus, 40–38: they advanced along the highway from Syria to Asia and, in spite of resistance from the brigand chief Cleon of Gordiucome, plundered the cities of Caria, notably Mylasa and Aphrodisias, where sanctuaries and private property alike were looted. Finally, Antony: on his arrival in Asia Minor in 40 his first demand was the same ten years' worth of taxes that had been produced for Brutus and Cassius. After Philippi there was the

<hr>

3 For these events, see App. *BCiv.* 1.57ff; Dio XLVIII.26–34; XLVII.24–41; XLIX.19–33.

disbandment of thirty legions to be paid for, and in 39–38 and 36–34 campaigns against the Parthians to be financed. The period ended with Antony's mobilization of the East against Octavian, when even the sacred grove of Asclepius on Cos was cut down to supply timber for ships. The damage armies could do was limited and business carried on; but the effects of uncertainty on the availability of credit, cash loans and all long-term enterprise must be taken into account.

By the Treaty of Brundisium (40 B.C.) Greece from Scodra southwards was under the control of Antony (although in 39 the Peloponnese was abortively assigned to Sex. Pompeius), and so was the whole of Anatolia. Antony exercised patronage in the area, but so did Octavian, granting citizenship to individuals such as Seleucus of Rhosus,[4] who continued as his protégés, and extending the privileges of cities. Through a well-placed intermediary who became the city's favourite son, Octavian's freedman C. Iulius Zoilus, 'Caesarian' Aphrodisias secured a decree of the Senate and a law of the People guaranteeing freedom, immunity from taxation, and enhanced asylum rights; an attempt was also to be made to recover looted property.[5]

The area under discussion falls into three regions. Rulers confronted with the problem of controlling each would be guided by political, military and economic factors. Mainland Greece, Crete and the Cyclades in political terms were well able to govern themselves; economically the mainland at least was an area in decline and depopulation, unlikely to make much contribution to the cost of running it and very unlikely to present any threat to security. Next, western Asia Minor and the adjacent islands: the provinces of Asia and Bithynia were long habituated to obedience as the subjects of Lydian, Persian and hellenistic monarchs; they, like the more remote southern coast, Pamphylia and Cilicia Pedias, had enormous economic possibilities: two-thirds of the cities coining in Asia Minor under Augustus and Tiberius were in the province of Asia. Third, the Anatolian plateau, politically and economically underdeveloped, in spite of Pompey's city foundations in Pontus, was daunting and as yet unprofitable. The three regions were accordingly handled differently both by Antony and by his successors in power, the emperors.

It was for sound political, economic and military reasons, then, that only Asia, Bithynia and Cilicia Pedias were governed as Roman provinces between 42 and 31 B.C. The rest of Asia Minor was subject to skilfully chosen client princes[6] (Lycia was an autonomous federation of

---

[4] EJ[2] 301.   [5] Reynolds 1982 (B 270) 7–12.

[6] For the vicissitudes of dependent rulers, see Magie 1950 (E 853) 427–515; Bowersock 1965 (C 39) 42–61; Jones 1971 (D 96) 110–214; Sullivan 1978 (E 878) 732–98; 1980 (E 879) 913–30; 1980 (E 880); stemmata at Sullivan 1980 (E 879) 928 and 1980 (E 880) 1136; Braund 1984 (C 254) for individuals. For Strabo's insight into the value of client kingdoms, that their rulers, unlike Roman governors, were always on the spot and armed, see XIV.5.5–9 (671C).

twenty-three cities[7]). They, not Rome, had the burden of defending and administering it and the duty of supporting their patrons, who could give, take, or trim their kingdoms as he chose. On Deiotarus' death in 40 his son Castor received Galatia and the interior of Paphlagonia; Deiotarus' share of Pontus, the coastal area, went to Darius, son of Caesar's enemy Pharnaces and grandson of Mithridates the Great; Amyntas received northern Pisidia, and Polemon I, son of Zeno of Laodicea, who had resisted Labienus, took Lycaonia, Iconium and the adjacent parts of Cilicia Tracheia; Pedias, like Cyprus, passed into Cleopatra's hands, Olba, west of Pedias, was ruled by the priestly house of the Teucrids and the kingdom of the Amanus in the east was left under its hereditary ruler Tarcondimotus.

Antony rewarded success. On Castor's death in 37, Galatia, Lycaonia and the Pamphylian coast were added to Amyntas' domain; Castor's son Deiotarus Philadelphus received Paphlagonia. Polemon, having to surrender Lycaonia to Amyntas and his possessions in Tracheia to Cleopatra, was given in return Pontus beyond the Iris river, with Phazemonitis, Armenia Minor and Colchis; while Archelaus, son of the hereditary priest-ruler of Comana, acquired Cappadocia on the departure or death of its king, Ariobarzanes' brother Ariarathes X. Cleopatra was also given part of Crete, although Antony claimed to have found a Caesarian decree freeing it.[8] The remaining cities were left to govern themselves and their territories.

III. THE AUGUSTAN RESTORATION[9]

Octavian's estimate of the eastern regions that came under his sway after Actium and the decisions he took about their future government were based in part on autopsy, as he passed through Asia Minor in 30 B.C. and wintered on Samos, while his further journey to Italy was broken at Corinth. Under the considered arrangements established in 27 only minor adjustments were made to the overall system devised by Antony, with two areas now brought under direct Roman control: Crete (only Lappa and Cydonia keeping their freedom) and Cyprus, which had no privileged cities.

There were further distinctions to be made: were any of the provincial areas to have Augustus as their governor, with his legate acting on the spot, or were they to be left to other senators selected on seniority and by the lot? Which of these latter, the 'public' provinces, were to have ex-consuls as their governors? The answers were determined by past tradition, present and especially military needs, and the *princeps'* own

---

[7] Strab. XIV.3.3–9 (665cf).   [8] Dio XLIX.32.4f; Cic. *Phil.* II.97, with Sanders 1982 (E 871) 5.
[9] See especially Strab. VIII–XVII (332–840C), and Dio LI–LVI.

security. All the areas were entrusted to governors selected by seniority and the lot except Cyprus. That was a place where a governor might see action, unruly perhaps after its second takeover by Rome; but the trouble it could cause was minor and in 23 or 22 it was returned to the lot, an unpromising assignment for its proconsuls; the copper-mines were to be handed over on lease to a client monarch, Herod of Judaea.[10] Even Macedonia was normally to be a public province, although *legati Augusti* are also found there.[11] Greece was detached from Macedonia in 27 and became the separate senatorial province of Achaea, including Aetolia, Acarnania, part of Epirus, and the Cyclades, probably with Corinth as the main seat of government. In spite of cultural and economic ties with Athens, the islands and Asia Minor, Crete was united with Cyrene as another province for proconsuls of praetorian status. Not Cnossus, which had had land worth 12,000 sesterces a year assigned to Capua in compensation for territory lost to veterans in 36 and which now itself became a colony,[12] but pro-Roman Gortyn, in the south of the island and more convenient for commuting governors, was the administrative centre. In our second region, western Asia Minor, Bithynia likewise and the parts of Pontus that still belonged to the province were assigned to another proconsul of praetorian status, but wealthy Asia was declared consular and in 27 became one of the two plum posts that the Senate could offer ex-consuls, the other being Africa, which had a legion but fewer amenities. The Lycian federation, whose prudent administration was admired by Strabo,[13] had earned and retained nominal autonomy. The federation employed a sophisticated system of proportional representation on its administrative bodies, the electoral assembly and council.

How much was meant by the freedom accorded to leagues like the Lycian and that of the free Laconians (Eleutherolacones), to whole islands like Corcyra, to individual cities like Delphi, Athens and Nicopolis (some, like Mytilene,[14] were in possession of treaties too), is a question. Theoretically enclaves exempt from the governor's jurisdiction, they still had to reckon with the emperor. Augustus intervened in Athens and Sparta, where down to about 2 B.C. he had relied on a partisan, C. Iulius Eurycles, son of a privateer, to guide the state in his own and Rome's interests; he actually deprived Thessaly and Cyzicus of freedom altogether. Cyzicus lost its freedom for five years for executing Romans, though a proconsul of Asia declared Romans subject to local

---

[10] Dio LIV.4.1; Joseph. *AJ* XIV.128.

[11] Tarius Rufus, cos. 16 B.C.: EJ² 268; L. Piso, cos. 15 B.C.: EJ² 199 with R. Syme, *Akten des VI. Intern. Kong. für gr. und lat. Epigr. München 1972, Vestigia* XVII (Munich, 1973) 595f. Cf. ch. 10, n. 9, ch. 13*h*, p. 567.

[12] Dio XLIX.14.5; for date and interpretation, see Rigsby 1976 (E 867) 322–30.

[13] Strab. XIV.3.2 (664C).   [14] EJ² 307.

law on Chios. Other free cities learnt the lesson: in 6 B.C. Cnidus recognized the *princeps'* jurisdiction in a local homicide case.[15] The governors of unarmed provinces spent much time on jurisdiction, going on circuit round the assize centres (although no circuit is attested in Crete); in Asia the task was alleviated by having the *conventus* centres on the coast or on the highway that led from Ephesus over the plateau to Cilicia.

Considering the third region, Octavian no more than Antony took it to be ready for direct Roman rule. Already during the tour of 30–29 he had made it clear that the dispositions of 36 would not necessarily be changed, although there had to be adjustments and it took a decade to achieve stability. Loyalty to Rome and himself brought rewards, but loyalty to Antony was not an unforgivable offence; indeed, it promised well, if it could be transferred to the new master. Amyntas of Galatia, like Deiotarus Philadelphus of Paphlagonia and Cleon of Gordiucome, who was promoted to the priesthood of Comana Pontica, secured confirmation by changing sides before Actium, and received part of Cilicia Tracheia. But Archelaus of Cappadocia was not displaced and, despite internal efforts to unseat him, retained his underdeveloped but lucrative and strategically important kingdom until A.D. 17, taking over in Tracheia after Amyntas' death. Polemon I of Pontus lost Armenia Minor to Artavasdes, a displaced claimant to the Parthian throne, but was to remain the chief support of Rome in the north of Asia Minor. He kept the southern shore of the Black Sea (an area that had been strengthened with settlements official and unofficial at Heraclea Pontica – a Caesarian venture that had not survived – and Sinope, which became Colonia Iulia Felix in 47), Colchis, and the mines behind Pharnacea. Polemon was less successful in his charge of keeping the Bosporan kingdom on the northern side of the sea under Roman control, and perished there in 8 B.C. He was succeeded in his Anatolian possessions by his widow, Pythodoris of Tralles (she died in A.D. 7–8). In one of the marriages that created for Augustus a nexus of dynastic families and a supply of potential client rulers who were born to the job, Roman citizens, and educated at Rome, Pythodoris' daughter Antonia Tryphaena was given to King Cotys of Thrace – whose sons were also to become rulers in Asia Minor; she herself went on to marry Archelaus of Cappadocia.

Only in minor principalities did Octavian assert a conqueror's rights. At Heraclea Pontica, where Antony's nominee Adiatorix had massacred Caesar's colonists, there had to be a change, but the tyrant's elder son Dyteutes was given a compensating position, the priesthood left vacant through the untimely death of Cleon. Nicias the tyrant of Cos had to pay for his patron's depredations; at 'free' Tarsus the Antonian dynast and

---

[15] Dio LIV.7.6, 23.7 (Cyzicus); EJ[2] 317 (Chios); 312 (Cnidus).

poet Beithys was replaced by Augustus' old tutor Athenodorus; and the kingdom of Hierapolis Castabala was kept from its natural heir, the son of the late Tarcondimotus Philantonius, until 20 B.C. The same year saw Augustus achieving a stable settlement of Commagene, probably at his third attempt. The regime of the new ruler and his son Antiochus III survived until A.D. 17, like that of Archelaus and Tarcondimotus Philopator. Archelaus' kingdom was enlarged in 20 B.C. by the addition of Armenia Minor on the death of its ruler, and the Teucrids of Olba, the Cilician city devoted to Zeus, now resumed the priestly and secular power that their forbear, Aba the protégé of Antony, had lost.

The core of the system was the Galatian kingdom, for its size, and because the main route from Asia to Syria passed through it. Not far to the south of that route was the untamed mountain area of Pisidia, which disjoined the plateau from Pamphylia. Amyntas lost his life carrying out the duties of his position. The Homanadenses of Pisidia captured and killed him, and by the end of 25 B.C. Augustus had created a third province in the peninsula, Galatia, of which only a part was inhabited by the Gallic tribes of the Tectosages and Tolistobogii (west of the Halys) and Trocmi (east of the river). The unwieldy kingdom was incorporated wholesale, with the exception of central Tracheia. Galatia like all newly acquired provinces was under the charge of Augustus, who sent a legate to deal with his new responsibility. M. Lollius had not yet held the consulship, but some later governors under Augustus were to be of consular rank and until A.D. 6 the province probably had a garrison of one legion (VII Macedonica) or even two.[16]

The particularly dangerous area of Pisidia was put under guard in 25 B.C. by the foundation of six veteran colonies, the chief being Pisidian Antioch. In 6 B.C. a road was constructed, the Via Sebaste, to link them, and probably within the next two or three years (rather than beforehand) the forty-four *castella* of the Homanadenses were captured by the distinguished governor of Galatia P. Sulpicius Quirinius, and the tribe broken up. It was not a complete pacification of southern Asia Minor: a rising was put down in A.D. 6 but Quirinius had done the main work and it was not necessary to put the province under another consular governor, as far as is known, until Cn. Domitius Corbulo took command under Nero.[17]

When in 6 B.C. Deiotarus Philadelphus or his heir died, not only eastern Paphlagonia but Phazemonitis was joined to it. With the accession three years later of the region south of Phazemonitis and east of Galatia (including the city of Sebastopolis) another district hitherto

---

[16] Dio LIII.26.3 seemingly implying that Pamphylia was assigned to a governor of its own; but see Syme 1937 (E 882) 227–31, Garrison: Mitchell 1976 (E 854).

[17] Quirinius: Levick 1967 (E 851) 24–41; 203–14; A.D. 6: Dio LV.28.3.

under a dynast came into the province, making it the same size as Asia and twice that of Bithynia. The following year Amasia too passed from dynastic control into the province of Pontus, but eastern Pontus remained under the widow of Polemon I.

These were acute administrative decisions, taken some in the first months after the victory at Actium, others in response to sudden crises, others again after mature reflection. As the responsibility of one man and his advisers they may be considered as part of a policy, that of the gradual advance of direct Roman rule, when that was safe and profitable. But these decisions did not themselves solve the political, social and economic problems that Octavian inherited from the period of the revolution. Overall it is true to say that Roman rule was not popular in the Greek-speaking provinces and many communities (Athens is a single but the most distinguished example) had three times committed themselves to the losing side in civil war. Economic problems stemmed in part from these wars and, in Greece especially, from the Actium campaign – Plutarch's great-grandfather used to tell how the entire male citizen population of Chaeronea was carrying grain down to the sea under the whips of Antony's agents when the news of the battle arrived and 'saved the city'[18] – but also from longer term causes. If they could be relieved, political problems might also diminish, but there was an irreducible dissonance between the realistic, power-orientated Roman view of the empire and the idea of Greek *poleis* as to their position in the world. In a work that can be dated nearly as late as a century after Augustus' death Plutarch had to warn his Greek readers to forget what their ancestors had achieved as sovereign peoples in the Persian Wars of the fifth century B.C.[19] The regime of Augustus did not succeed in putting an end to anti-Roman feeling and prophecies that foretold the end of Roman rule, but here again, although loyalty was rewarded (Hybreas, the *rhetor* of Mylasa who had resisted Labienus, won Roman citizenship and a high priesthood of Augustus, and the descendants of Zeno of Laodicea have been seen benefiting from his staunchness), Augustus did his best for reconciliation, and his first acts included distributing grain to the cities and remitting their debts.[20]

Greece and Asia Minor were to continue to receive personal attention from the *princeps* and his family. In 23 B.C. Agrippa was in the East, able to take authoritative decisions, while Augustus himself returned in 21, carrying out an inspection of Asia Minor and spending the winters of 21–20 on Aegina and 20–19 on Samos. The East fell once again to Agrippa's care between 18 and 13 and this time he saw more of it than the

18 Plut. *Ant.* 68.4.
19 Plut. *Praec. reip. ger.* 17 (*Mor.* 814C), dated by C.P. Jones, *JRS* 56 (1966) 72.
20 Dio Chrys. xxxi.66.

island of Lesbos. But for a last-minute refusal it would have been in Tiberius' charge from 6 to 1 B.C. (he already knew Asia Minor from his mission to Armenia in 20 B.C.). As it was, Gaius Caesar was there from 1 B.C. until his death in A.D. 4. Thirteen years later came another Caesar with *imperium maius*, Germanicus.

Whether close at hand or in Rome or the western provinces, Augustus and his successors were accessible to embassies (for the cities in their own estimation were conducting diplomacy) bearing letters and oral requests, as they were also to private individuals. Strabo tells how in 29 B.C. the tiny fishing community of Gyarus went to make representations to their new ruler about its tax burdens.[21] Before he had been established as *princeps* for more than a period of months Augustus had been approached in Spain by parties from all three regions with which we are concerned: the Thessalian League and Archelaus were engaged in litigation, as was Tralles, a city of Asia which had also suffered earthquake damage, along with Thyatira, Chios, and Laodicea. A personal friend, the *eques* Vedius Pollio, was sent to supervise the restoration of the cities of Asia.[22]

Besides pleas for help and tax remission, questions of status and privilege were frequently the subject of embassies, as they had been (and were to remain) of concern to Aphrodisias: freedom, immunity, grant of a treaty, asylum rights; even, when communities of humbler status were involved, the right to become a *polis* at all and to possess the institutions of a city, above all a city council. Petitions of this last kind must have been heard with sympathy: the emperors inherited from the hellenistic monarchs a wish to be immortalized as founders and restorers of cities. In the time of Augustus himself many towns came to be called Caesarea, like Tralles, or -caesarea, like Hierocaesarea, in Lydia, once Hiera Kome (the sacred village), Sebastopolis, Sebaste, or -sebaste. Not all belong to areas under direct rule: they were creations of, or were renamed by, client rulers, like Caesarea Mazaca, capital of Cappadocia, Kayseri to this day, or Caesarea Anazarbus, refounded in 9 B.C. probably by Tarcondimotus Philopator.

Greece in particular needed help. It had not suffered as parts of Asia Minor had done, but its natural resources were more meagre and the wealth that comes from empire had eluded Athens and Sparta three centuries previously. The prospect before it was one of economic competition with regions such as Italy and Spain which were better able to produce the same crops and manufactures. Strabo on Arcadia, Messenia and Laconia repeats a story of depopulation already told in general terms by earlier writers; he says that except for Tanagra and

---

[21] Strab. x.5.1 (485C).
[22] Suet. *Tib.* 6; Strab. XII. (579C); Agathias, II.17; Sutherland and Kraay 1975 (B 359) 1363.

Thespiae the cities of Boeotia (which had suffered heavily from Sulla and where the flooding of Lake Copais had played its part: a warning not to expect uniform conditions even over a single province) had become little more than villages or (in the case of Oropus and two other cities) fallen into ruin. Arcadia, Aetolia and Acarnania are given over to ranching like Thessaly, and the copper-mines of Euboea had given out like the silver of Laurion. Looking back a century and a half later Pausanias wrote that the fortunes of Greece reached their nadir between the fall of Corinth and the reign of Nero.[23]

It is not surprising, then, that Roman intervention bordered on the invasive. A special effort had been made at Caesar's instance to restore Corinth by colonizing what remained of the city destroyed in 146 B.C. with civilian settlers from Rome under the name Laus Iulia Corinthiensium. The colonists, including freedmen as they did, were not well thought of, but by 7–3 B.C. Corinth was once more in charge of the biennial Isthmian games, as well as celebrating quadrennial Caesareia; and the colonists were to become thoroughly assimilated.[24] Another colony was founded on the Gulf at Dyme at about the same time, reinforcing Pompey's settlement of ex-pirates there. But nearly three decades later a new colony at Patrae acquired territory across the water and incorporated villages close to it, so that Dyme was completely eclipsed. Patrae was to be the centre of the manufacture and export of flax.[25]

But Augustus' personal creation in Greece was an entirely new city, Nicopolis, which he established near the site of the battle of Actium through a synoecism of surrounding peoples: Ambracia, Amphilochian Argos and Alyzia became dependencies. It was an artificial entity in an undeveloped area, and must have uprooted some of the country population, but the festival it celebrated brought visitors to its two harbours, business and revenue; it began to grow rapidly, a precocious harbinger of the Greco–Roman culture of the second century.[26]

New and redeveloped cities could not usurp Athens' artistic and intellectual primacy. That depended on her past, as current archaism in art, architecture and epigraphy showed. A mecca for students, tourists and devotees of religion, she also exported works of art and derived a

---

[23] Strab. VIII.7.5–8.3 (388C); IX.2.16–18 (406C); X.1.8–10 (447C); cf. Polyb. XXXVI.17.5. Wallace 1979 (E 886) 173–8, confirms; Dr S. Alcock draws attention to Bintliff and Snodgrass 1985 (E 816); see also Baladié 1980 (E 812) 313f. But Dr Alcock rightly warns against taking what may be a literary *topos*, a moralizing tone, or disregard for contemporary Greeks too much on trust: she draws attention (e.g.) to N.K. Petrochilos, *Roman Attitudes to the Greeks* (Athens, 1974) 63–7; Pausanias: VII.17.1, with Baladié 1980 (E 812) 323.

[24] Strab. VIII.6.20 (378C); (381C); hellenization: [Dio Chrys.] XXXVII. 26.

[25] Strab. VIII.7.5 (387C).

[26] Strab. VII.7.6–7 (325C); N. Purcell, 'The Nicopolitan synoecism and Roman urban policy', *Proceedings of the First international Symposium on Nicopolis* (1984).

notorious income, the more valuable now that her silver-mines were exhausted, from selling her citizenship: 'Ten sacks of charcoal imported and you too will be a citizen; if you bring a pig as well you're Triptolemus himself', wrote Automedon.[27]

Connexions with Athens, as well as with other Greek cities, were sought after by rulers within the Roman sphere of influence and by literary men. Antony had shown respect for Athens in spite of her support for Pompey and the Liberators. He and Octavia had been hailed as Theoi Euergetae and the aristocrats he had put in power in 38 B.C. were grateful for that and for his return of Aegina and other islands, with the revenue they brought.

Augustus' treatment of Athens was paternalistic. He showed his displeasure with her by residing at Aegina for part of a winter (22–21) and by freeing that island, and Eretria, from paying tribute to Athens. He also forbade the citizenship sales. The Athenians made up for the loss of revenue by granting foreigners the right to have statues erected in the city, but the statues were not always freshly carved for the individual honorand. For exceptional benefactions there were choicer honours: C. Iulius Nicanor of Hierapolis in Syria, a poet who restored the island of Salamis to Athens at his own expense, earned the titles of New Homer and New Themistocles. Embarrassing or invidious, they were later expunged.[28]

In spite of periods of estrangement, Athens benefited from Augustus' generosity. *Tesserae* found in the city[29] reveal that she had been included in the grain distributions of 31 and Augustus' reign saw the reinstitution of Athens' embassy to Delphi, on a more modest scale than before, as the Dodecas. There was also considerable building activity, the restoration of sanctuaries in Attica, perhaps also in the Piraeus. In the city itself Augustus personally, on appeal from an embassy led by Eucles of Marathon, had by 20 B.C. accepted responsibility for the completion of the Roman market; in the old Agora Agrippa built his Odeion, moving the temple of Ares from outside the city into juxtaposition with the new building, and a new set of baths was constructed outside the old Agora. The overall conception and detail of the complex alike showed the influence of Roman ideas, in particular echoing the Forum Augusti and the temple of Mars Ultor; the buildings left little room for the vigorous public activity of the past.[30]

Augustus was not insensitive to Athenian susceptibilities. He was

[27] Dio LIV.7.2f, with G.W. Bowersock, *CQ* NS 14 (1964) 124f; *Anth. Pal.* XI.319.

[28] Dio Chrys. XXXI.1.6; *IG* II² 3786–9, etc., with Jones 1978 (E 1020) 226–8, reaffirming an Augustan date.   [29] See Rostovtzeff 1903 (E 870).

[30] Shear 1981 (E 873) 361; Thompson 1987 (F 593) 4–9, for imperial political interpretation of the reconstruction of Ares, see Bowersock 1984 (C 40) 173.

initiated at Eleusis in 31 and about four years later the city is found beginning to issue a coinage that does not bear his head on the obverses. This 'autonomous' coinage continued until the reign of Gallienus; the privilege was enjoyed also by Corcyra, Delphi, Sparta and Corinth. In return Athens did not stint honours to Augustus and his family. A round Ionic temple on the Acropolis which may have been influenced by the temple of Vesta at Rome, though its order is modelled on the Classical Erechtheum, belongs to the decade immediately following his accession to sole power; Augustus is Theos on a dedication made at Delphi, a decree of the Council of Six Hundred resolved in 27–26 to celebrate his birthday (a day already associated with the restoration of freedom), and the ephebes held a festival called the Augustan Contest. The moving of the temple of Ares may be connected with the imperial cult, for in A.D. 2 Gaius Caesar, then in the East, was honoured under that name.[31]

Eucles was a member of the oligarchy that emerged in Augustan Athens. He succeeded his father as supervisor of the construction of the Roman market, held the positions of *archon* and *strategos* and five times acted as priest of Apollo in the Dodecas. The stability of the oligarchy is suggested by the fact that the same three men held the leading positions in that embassy on all five occasions of its dispatch under Augustus.

Discontent remained in Greece. In A.D. 6, according to Cassius Dio, it was prevalent in cities throughout the Roman world. At a date unknown, (Cassius) Petreius, son of a loyal Caesarian, was burned alive in Thessaly, and the district lost its freedom.[32] In the Peloponnese even Eurycles had to be exiled in about 2 B.C.: he certainly involved himself in eastern Mediterranean politics, visiting both Archelaus of Cappadocia and Herod of Judaea, perhaps also in imperial court intrigue, and it was claimed that he had disturbed the cities of Achaea.[33] At Athens the swivelling round of Athena's statue to face west and her spitting blood, which heralded a visit from Augustus (probably that of 21), were no good signs, and unrest is attested in A.D. 13, presumably on the part of the less well-off members of society; it was fatal to its leaders. Athens did not enjoy good repute under the Empire. When the whole province joined Macedonia two years later in complaining, not only about taxes, but about the cost of maintaining the proconsuls in their state, it must have been the upper classes who took the lead. The two episodes, which ended in the transfer of Achaea and Macedonia to the jurisdiction of the governor of Moesia, were connected, though it was probably not the

[31] Delphi: J. Bousquet, *BCH* 85 (1961) 88–90; birthday: *IG* II/III² 1071; ephebes: 1069; *CIA* III 444.   [32] Dio LV.28.2; see Bowersock 1965 (E 818) 280–2.

[33] Strab. VIII.5.5–6 (366C), with Bowersock 1961 (E 817) and 1984 (C 40).

unrest that induced Senate and emperor to make the transfer.[34] Economic problems affecting all classes were probably only mitigated with the establishment of peace in 30 B.C. They may be illustrated from an inscription of A.D. 1–2, which shows Lycosura in Arcadia unable to attract competitors for its games in an Olympic year, and in debt to the provincial fiscus because of crop failure.[35]

As Roman armies advanced north and east in the Balkans, necessitating the creation of a new province, Moesia, Greece fell further behind the market constituted by legions and auxiliaries and became ever more a backwater. One of her most important exports, marble, which came from Euboea, Attica, Laconia and Paros, was in any case in the hands of the state; imperial marks begin in A.D. 17. Athens became more prosperous under Augustus, but her ceramics were giving way even at home to Arretine ware and her cheap lamps could hold only the domestic market.

That the provinces were able to appeal in concert shows that the leagues of the classical and hellenistic periods, created to deal with problems and powers too great for individual cities, still had a role to play in the absence of a provincial *koinon* such as we shall find in Asia and Bithynia. The Achaean League, though much smaller that its earlier namesake, which had been dissolved after the catastrophe of 146 B.C., and representing only twelve towns in south-east Thessaly and on the north coast of the Peloponnese, including Elis and Sicyon, must have acted with the Panhellenic League of Free Laconians (Eleutherolacones), containing twenty-four cities whose freedom from Spartan rule had been granted, or more probably confirmed, by Augustus. In Thessaly another league survived, centring on Larissa, its council representing towns in proportion to their size and exercising considerable authority in local affairs; and under Augustus the constitution of the Delphic Amphictiony had Athens, Delphi and the emperor's own Nicopolis sending delegates to each session (respectively one, two and ten), while the remaining members were represented in rotation (Macedonia and Thessaly by two each).[36] Nicopolis' dominance did not survive: by Pausanias' own time it was on a par with Macedonia and Thessaly with six votes. Other districts had minor leagues that survived: those of the Phocians, Boeotians, Magnetes and Arcadians. Crete too,

[34] Blood: Dio LIV.7.3, with Bowersock 1964 (C 38) 120f. Discontent at the end of Augustus' reign: Eus.-Jer. 170 Helm (146f Schoene), with Graindor 1927 (E 832) 41–3. Transfer requested: Tac. *Ann.* 1.76.4, with *IG* v (2), 268, for implied dissatisfaction with earlier proconsuls. For the view that the unrest led to the transfer, see G.W. Bowersock, *Entretiens Hardt* 33 (Geneva, 1987) 292. Athens' ill repute: Dio Chrys.XLVIII.13.

[35] Smallwood 1967 (B 284) 404, with A.J. Gossage, *ABSA* 49 (1954) 51–6 (I owe these references to the kindness of Dr Lintott).   [36] Paus. x.8.3, with Daux 1975 (E 823) 352.

land of a hundred cities in Homer's time,[37] had a *koinon*, of twenty cities only as a result of amalgamation and the absorption of one by another.

But it was the province-wide organization of western Asia Minor that scored the first and paradigm diplomatic success of the new age by establishing a firm relationship with the ruler when he was in the area in 29 B.C.[38] Octavian on Samos received delegations from both Asia and Bithynia, the first representing an organization of long standing, the peoples and tribes in Asia and those individuals judged friends of the Roman People, or in short the *koinon* of the Greeks. Already known from the nineties B.C., when they were doing honour to the proconsul Mucius Scaevola, they had a fully-fledged council by 48 at the latest and were addressed by Antony in a letter giving permission to the Association of Victorious Athletes to commemorate its privileges on a bronze tablet.[39]

Octavian accepted the temples offered by these embassies on condition that Rome too received cult. Roman citizens in the provinces were to devote themselves to Rome and the Deified Iulius at Ephesus and Nicaea; the more modern Pergamum and Nicomedia were chosen for Octavian's temples. Partial acceptance of the honours showed the cities of Asia Minor that Octavian was well disposed, though not theirs outright. Prominent individuals benefited from the cult through the opportunities for self-advertisement that management offered them, and the city populations of Pergamum and Nicomedia and other large cities through the festivals laid on and the crowds that they attracted. Similar provincial *koina* came into existence as the benefits were perceived or as new provinces such as Galatia were created.

Homage to proconsuls of Asia did not long continue: the last known to have received it was C. Marcius Censorinus who died in office in A.D. 2. They were not even accorded the honorific titles of Saviour and Founder, which likewise became a prerogative of the *princeps*, the last to bear them again being Censorinus. Similarly, outstanding local dignitaries ceased to be offered cult; the last known was Artemidorus of Cnidus. The divine honours which had been accorded to Theophanes of Mytilene, Pompey's secretary and biographer, contributed to the downfall of his descendants in A.D. 33.[40]

For his part Octavian's first concern in the years after his victory must have been the restoration of prosperity, and so taxability. Recovery was promoted by the resumption at Ephesus and Pergamum between 28 and 18 of the issuing of coins, the *cistophori*, tetradrachms last struck by Antony in 39 B.C. The quantities now issued were not to be approached

---

[37] Hom. *Il.* 11.649.   [38] Dio LI.20.6–8.   [39] Reynolds 1982 (B 270) 5; EJ² 300.
[40] *Anc. Greek Inscr. in the British Mus.* 787, with Price 1984 (F 199) 48 (Artemidorus); Tac. *Ann.* VI.18.3–5 (Theophanes' posterity).

again until Hadrian's time. Octavian was also attentive to the plaints of
cities which he knew to have suffered as a result of the Parthian invasion,
and his ready aid after the earthquake of 27 was again available to Cyprus
when it was striken in 15 B.C., after which Paphos took the *princeps*' name
and adopted a new calendar, and to Cos.[41] Not everyone gained: on his
visit of 21–20 Augustus did indeed make gifts of money to some
communities of Asia and Bithynia, but he imposed additional burdens
on others.[42]

Imperial attentions were more easily secured if a community possessed such an advocate at court as Tralles did when it sought help after
the earthquake of 27;[43] Chaeremon may have been brother-in-law to
Polemon I and he was certainly a member of a notable pro-Roman,
although also previously pro-Pompeian and pro-Antonian, family. The
practice, valuable to both sides, of granting favoured individuals and
families privileged access to the ruling authority, was to continue. More
generally, it was to ancestral connexions that Ilium owed the rebuilding
of its temple to Athena.[44] Not surprisingly cities made every effort to
bring themselves to the *princeps*' attention through embassies and
patrons known to him, as they had to that of earlier statesmen and
dynasts. By 9 B.C. Augustus' benefactions were such that the proconsul
Fabius Maximus could tell the *koinon* that they would never be surpassed,
and it agreed to make the *princeps*' birthday the start of the new year in
Asia.[45]

Homage from individual cities also went along with the benefactions,
acknowledging or encouraging them. Some cities combined it with
reconstruction: Ephesus had its upper square modified to incorporate
imperial temples and a *stoa basilike*;[46] others, notably those of Lydia,
adopted the year of the Battle of Actium as their new era. Twenty years
after the institution of the provincial cult ten Roman assize centres had
their own temples, and together thirty-four cities in the whole of Asia
Minor are known to have celebrated Augustus' cult, including even such
remote places as Gangra. In eleven of them, including Mylasa, he shared
it with that of Rome, his cult an addition to hers. Here too prominent
individuals benefited, as on Chios, where the descendants of the founder
participated in the ceremonial.[47]

Although the cult was the creation of organized communities, notably
of *poleis*, and some uniformity may have resulted from guidance offered
by governors, it was not confined to provinces or acquired only on
provincialization. Lycian Xanthus had a temple of 'Caesar', Myra and

---

[41] EJ² 303 of 31 B.C.; Dio LIV.23.7 (Cyprus); Eus.-Jer. 168 Helm (144f Schoene) (5 B.C.), with
S.M. Sherwin-White, *Ancient Cos* (Hypomnemata 51), (Göttingen, 1978) 148.
[42] Dio LIV.7.5.   [43] Agathias, II.17.   [44] *IGRR* IV 202.   [45] EJ² 98.
[46] See Price 1984 (F 199) 140.   [47] *IGRR* IV 947, with Price 1984 (F 199) 62.

Tlos called Augustus Benefactor and Saviour (or Founder) of the whole universe.[48] Indeed, the foundation of a festival in the *princeps'* honour played its part in maintaining inter-city connexions and diplomacy. Mytilene announced the establishment of games in honour of Augustus, and copies of the decree were to be set up in Pergamum, Actium, Brundisium, Tarraco, Massilia, Antioch and elsewhere.[49]

In Asia Minor as in Greece Augustus encouraged the development of city life, more by way of innovation here than in restoration; even in the province of Asia it was lacking in remoter, inland districts. The synoecism of Sebaste in Phrygia, attested in a verse inscription, may be paralleled at Caesarea Trocetta in Lydia.[50] This is not to be compared with Nicopolis. The *princeps* merely acceded to the wish of leading inhabitants of a district for organization and status as *poleis*. A more gradual development was one by which an existing capital of the *koinon* of a number of villages became a city within a territory: in Mysia the Abbaeitae crystallized into the cities of Julia Ancyra, Synaus and Tiberiopolis. The people who were coining under the name of 'Cilbiani about Nicaea' in Nero's reign became the 'Nicaeans Cilbiani' or 'in the Cilbian region' only under Septimius Severus.[51] Changes of name could easily be made and did not necessarily involve changes of substance, physical or in organization: so at Caesarea Anazarbus in Cilicia Pedias, and Caesarea, later Germanice, in Bithynia, inhabited by former serfs of the Mygdonian tribe; Iuliopolis, the former Gordiucome, never amounted to much. What the *princeps* contributed is uncertain; what he spurred others on to do may have been almost as important.

Augustan intervention in Asia and Bithynia by official settlement and colonization was not conspicuous; the colony of Alexandria Troas was exceptional. But there were independent immigrants. After the Sullan settlement the numbers grew again, and in Cicero's province of Cilicia a generation later they were already numerous enough to be subject to a levy. There was also substantial immigration into mainland Greece, notably in the Peloponnese where they acquired landed property on a large scale and formed a persistent element in their communities. Romans formed a relatively wealthy stratum in the cities in which they settled, but they do not seem to have held aloof from their neighbours: Roman citizens collaborated with natives in the restoration of Messene; L. Vaccius Labeo of Cyme, who endowed the gymnasium under Augustus,[52] is only one of many such Roman benefactors. Intermarriage between Romans and local aristocrats was soon to produce candidates

[48] *IGRR* III 482 (Xanthus); 546 (Tlos) 719 (Myra).   [49] *IGRR* IV 39.
[50] *IGRR* IV 682.   [51] See Jones 1971 (D 96) 78.
[52] Immigration: Wilson 1966 (A 106) 127–51; effect on Strabo: Baladié 1980 (E 812) 195; Messene: *Bull. ép*, 1966, 200; Labeo: *IGRR* IV 1302; land-owning: *IG* V I. 1432.

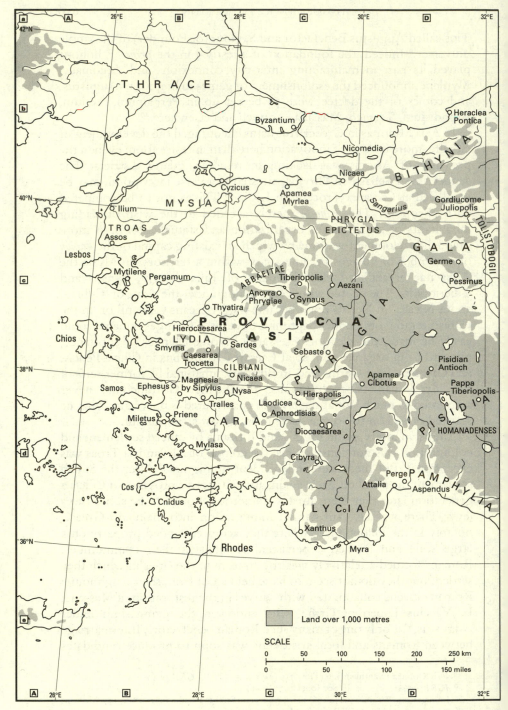

Map 16. Asia Minor.

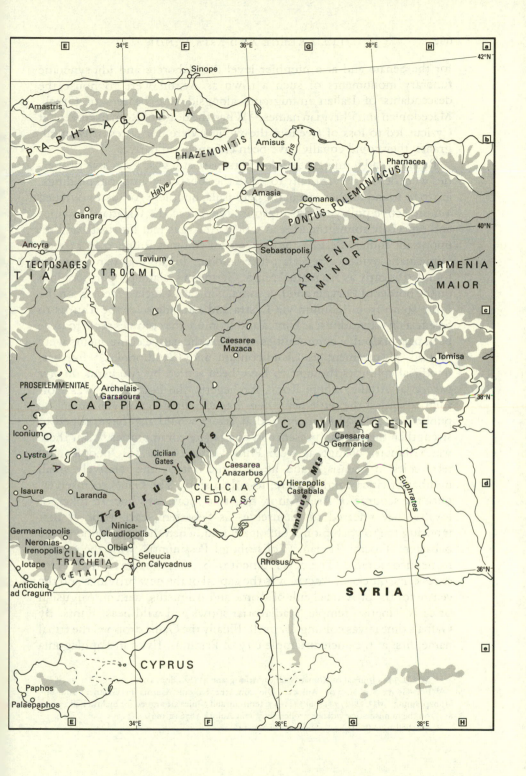

for the Senate and at a humbler level the elaborate and idiosyncratic funerary monuments of such a town as Aezani were to house the descendants of Italian immigrants alongside the bearers of Greek, Macedonian and Phrygian names.[53] When the death of Roman citizens at Cyzicus led to loss of freedom the victims were not necessarily immigrants: they could equally have been enfranchised natives.

Business and immigrant landowners, part of whose extensive properties were destined eventually to go to the substantial imperial holdings, are to be found further east in the peninsula, but there Augustus pursued a more active policy of urbanization, notably in the Galatian province and especially round the area in which Amyntas met his death and on important routes. Besides the six veteran colonies founded in 25 B.C., numismatic evidence reveals other colonies in the Galatian province founded as early as Augustus' reign: Germe in Galatia proper, Iconium on the border of Phrygia and Lycaonia, Ninica in Cilicia Tracheia, on the route south from Iconium via Lystra and Laranda over the Taurus to Seleucia on Calycadnus; at Ninica and Iconium the colonies seem to have been part of double communities of which the native components were to find advancement as Claudiconium and Claudiopolis.[54] Further, unofficial colonists thought to have been settled by Augustus on *ager publicus* at Attalia, where Roma Archegetis, the Foundress, was worshipped (unless the settlement there was a spontaneous development on public land sold off to them) and at Isaura would also have helped to strengthen the Roman presence in composite communities.[55] But there was voluntary change as well: Pliny writes of the 195 'peoples and tetrarchies in Galatia,[56] and he is borne out by the relatively small number of cities coining there, less than sixty. The Gauls themselves, once the scourge of Asia Minor, began to move into line. In token of loyalty they referred to themselves as Sebasteni, each tribe at first ignoring the township on which it centred. Then they are found as the Sebasteni Trocmi Taviani (Tolistobogii Pessinuntii) with the town's name incorporated. The development of Sebaste Ancyra of the Tectosages came quickest: Ancyra was the capital of the new province and the centre for the provincial cult of Rome and Augustus, with an Augustan or early Tiberian temple, gladiatorial shows and wild beast hunts. By Galba's time it was coining for itself. Finally the Gauls dropped the tribal name, first at the ancient temple city of Pessinus. Even in Paphlagonia

---

[53] *MAMA* ix (Journal of Roman Studies Monograph 4) (London, 1988) 1xf.

[54] For Germe see H. von Aulock, 'Die römische Kolonie Germa in Galatien und ihre Münzprägung', *MDAI (I)* 18 (1968) 221–37. Iconium and Ninica are argued for by Mitchell 1979 (E 857), on the numismatic evidence proffered by von Aulock 1976 (B 306).

[55] Mitchell 1978 (E 855).   [56] Pliny, *HN* v.146.

early urbanization is attested by the name of Caesarea of the Proseilemmenitae.[57]

IV. CONSOLIDATION UNDER THE JULIO-CLAUDIANS

The stable conditions created by Augustus required his successors to be maintenance engineers in the provinces, adjusting his scheme rather than making radical alterations, and his immediate successor Tiberius firmly professed close adherence to Augustan precedent. But the accession of a new emperor, even one well known in the East as Tiberius was (he enjoyed divine honours at Nysa by 1 B.C.) and for ten years the designated heir, a period in which he was being courted even by relatively unimportant cities such as Aezani, inevitably caused a stir. The new man could have new friends and favourites; relationships have to be developed or entered into. So in the Peloponnese, where the Claudii had hereditary influence, the League of Free Laconians in 15 passed a sacred law establishing ceremonies in honour of Augustus, Tiberius, Livia, Germanicus and Drusus, as well as for T. Quinctius Flamininus and the two local dynasts Eurycles, now posthumously rehabilitated, and his son Laco, who may have been particular partisans of Tiberius; Laco continued in favour for another nineteen years. At Paphos on Cyprus the people were quick to take an oath of loyalty to Tiberius and his blood line. From the beginning of the next reign there survives another oath taken at Assos in the Troad, in which play is made with Gaius' childhood visit to the city nearly twenty years previously. At Cyzicus Gaius accepted the local magistracy, the hipparchy, and was designated the 'New Sun'. These were prudent measures: Gaius had his own ideas about his position in the empire, different again from Tiberius'.[58]

Ironically, in view of his publicly proclaimed adherence to the Augustan blueprint, it was Tiberius who in the earliest years of his reign made significant changes in two of the regions with which we are concerned. The answer that Tiberius and the Senate returned to the request from Macedonia and Achaea for transfer to imperial rule was favourable but unflattering. Instead, economy was served: the two provinces were to have no governor of their own, but were attached to the province of Moesia. (Already in A.D. 6, when the proconsul died in office, his province had been divided between his quaestor and his legate.)[59] But the change brought into the open the fact that Macedonia

[57] Jones 1971 (D 96) 119 and for Caesarea 168.

[58] EJ² 316 (Nysa); 319 (Aezani); 102, with Bowersock 1961 (E 817) (Gytheum); 105*, with Mitford 1960 (E 858) 75–9 (Palaepaphos); GCN 33 (Assos); 401 (Cyzicus).

[59] Dio LV.27.6 (A.D. 6); Tac. Ann. 1. 80.1.

and Achaea were backwaters removed from the scene of action nearer the Danube.

The unification was followed by the amalgamation of the two main leagues. The enlarged *koinon* (called variously Panachaean, Hellenic and Panhellenic) went back at least to the end of Tiberius' reign and consisted of representatives of Achaea proper, which itself incorporated a *koinon* of the Argolis under Augustus or Tiberius, Boeotia, Locris, Phocis, Doris and Euboea;[60] a number of cities and lesser leagues, such as the Eleutherolacones and Thessalians, were not included. The Greek *koina* were not as alert as the organizations of Asia and Bithynia – areas that had been directly controlled by monarchs since the time of the Persian Empire – to the value of offering cult, but they eventually did so, electing a high priest as well as a political leader; the earliest signs are Neronian at latest, the official C. Iulius Spartiaticus, a descendant of Eurycles and, like all the high priests, a Roman citizen.[61]

The new arrangements lasted until 44, when Claudius returned Achaea to the jurisdiction of ex-praetors selected by lot.[62] So it remained until Nero, claiming to be the only emperor who was a philhellene, conferred freedom on Greece on 28 November, probably 67 rather than 66, during his performing tour of the province.[63] It was a reiteration (not the first) of Flamininus' declaration of a quarter of a millennium previously, but the Greeks appreciated the gesture of recognition and the abolition of taxes that went with it. Even in Plutarch's view, that of an upper-class intellectual in full sympathy with senatorial opinion, freeing those who were 'noblest and dearest to the gods' earned Nero reincarnation as a singing frog rather than as a viper.[64]

Nero's cultural philhellenism was genuine and strong. It too was appreciated. The tour he made (the four great festivals, Pythian, Olympic, Isthmian and Nemean, were rescheduled so that he might compete in all) was the first personal visit from a member of the imperial family since that of Germanicus and Agrippina, when Germanicus had a commission similar to those previously held by Agrippa, abortively by Tiberius, and by Gaius Caesar. The respect that Germanicus showed at Athens in 18, when he visited it after Nicopolis, was set off by the brutal assertion of Roman supremacy by his coadjutor Cn. Piso.[65] Tiberius himself was a cultured philhellene and Athens' benefactor before his adoption, although Livia apparently attracted more attention than the emperor. Surprisingly enough Claudius won more dedications than Nero, more than any emperor between Augustus and Hadrian. A whole

[60] *GCN* 361, with Kahrstedt 1950 (E 846) 70f.   [61] *GCN* 264.
[62] Suet. *Claud.* 25; Dio LX.24.1.
[63] *GCN* 64. For 67 as the year see Griffin 1984 (C 352) 280, n. 127.   [64] [Plut.] *Mor.* 567F.
[65] Tac. *Ann.* 11.55.1.

series honours him as Saviour and Benefactor: probably he paid for stairs leading to the Propylaea, not only adorning the Acropolis but providing work for quarrymen and craftsmen.[66] Nero contributed a new *skene* for the Theatre of Dionysus, which was dedicated to Dionysus Eleutherius and to the emperor, whose priest and high priests were reserved front row seats.[67] But Nero could not free Athens along with the rest of Greece: freedom was a privilege she already enjoyed.

The reign of Tiberius, like the last decade of Augustus' Principate, had to be one of retrenchment in Italy and perhaps elsewhere. Areas self-sufficient and exporting would suffer less. Asia and Bithynia came into that category, as building activity during the reign suggests; Crete too. Parts of Achaea already in decline did not: at the end of the reign, Boeotia claimed not to be able to afford an envoy to congratulate Gaius on his accession.[68] Some insight into the collection of taxes – and into the difficulties that some cities encountered in meeting their obligations – is given by inscriptions from Messene and Lycosura.[69] And Achaea's capital, artistic and financial, was diminished when Nero's agents began to scour the provinces for works of art in a systematic effort quite different from the haphazard acquisitiveness of Verres or Antony. The centres of Greece and Asia known to have suffered were Athens, Delphi, Olympia, Thespiae and Pergamum. At Athens the imperial agent C. Carrinas Secundus was made eponymous *archon*, as if to blunt his zeal.[70] There was a certain irony in Nero's regret, expressed when he freed Greece, that he could not do it at a time when she was at her peak – though his generous act sprang from good will, not mere pity.

A recurrent, even chronic problem was shortage of grain, which had to be countered at any cost. Even in Asia Minor, where grain was a staple product, a severe winter could cause difficulties, especially in cities distant from the sea, where importing supplies would be particularly expensive. Aspendus in Pamphylia is not far from the sea, but vetch is said to have been on sale in place of grain there on one occasion under Tiberius. One of the titles accumulated by Agrippina on her travels with Germanicus was that of Divine Harvest-bringer, Aeolis, at Mytilene, like her daughter and namesake who took a place in the imperial pantheon on Cos as Demeter Harvest-bringer and was shown on city coinages with corn ears and poppies – similarly too on a panel from the Sebasteion at Aphrodisias. The divinities would hardly allow their votaries to go hungry.[71]

---

[66] *IG* II² 3269, 3271f, 3274. See Shear 1981 (E 873) 367, n. 52. [67] *IG* II² 5034.
[68] *GCN* 361. [69] *IG* V 1.1432; 2.516.
[70] *IG* II/III² 4188, with Graindor 1931 (E 833) 14f.
[71] Aspendus: Philostr. *VA* 1.15; Mytilene: *ILS* 8788, *IG* XII 2.258, with L. Robert, *REG* 72 (1960) 286ff. Cos: A. Maiuri, *Nuova silloge epigr.* (Florence, 1952) 468; coins: *BMC Lydia* 146, nos. 53–5 (Magnesia by Sipylus); Aphrodisias: *JRS* 77 (1987) Pl. VIII.

Greece was more accessible by sea than the interior of Anatolia, but there were still questions of procurement and distribution, and of the cost of the operations. Athens had been importing corn since the time of Pisistratus; there was no imperial revenue to pay for it under the Principate. A special treasury for the reception of grain was created there in the reign of Augustus, significantly perhaps under the supervision of no less an official than a hoplite general. Under Claudius the *curator annonae* appears at Corinth, and on one occasion there was a famine in Greece that took a *modius* of grain to a price of six didrachms, about eight times the normal price at Rome.[72]

The other natural calamity to which both Greece and Asia Minor are subject is earthquakes. The Roman government did its best to help wherever they struck. One night in A.D. 17 twelve distinguished communities of the Hermus basin in Asia fell victim. Sardes suffered worst and was granted five years' remission of all taxes as well as a gift of 10 million sesterces from the emperor; Magnesia by Sipylus was held to have suffered next worst and was compensated accordingly, while the rest were relieved of tribute for five years and a commissioner was sent to inspect the damage and help restore it. Six years later it was Aegium, centre of the Achaean League, and Cibyra, an assize centre of Asia, that were devastated and granted three years' remission of tribute on the initiative of the emperor.[73]

This generosity, and his pitiless attitude towards officials who enriched themselves at the expense of provincials – a proceeding that the people of Asia must have come to regard as almost as inevitable as natural calamities – won Tiberius popularity; on both fronts he was following the example of Augustus. The coming of the Principate did not destroy the hereditary connexions that families such as the Messallae, Galbae and Pisones had with the East and their natural claim to serve there, any more than it eliminated the expectations of some senators that they could reimburse themselves for the cost of attaining office in the course of their pro-magistracies and even make a profit. The wealth of Asia was a particular temptation, especially when the fortunes of Italian senators were in decline. Fierce competition for the province is attested in the twenties and thirties, made fiercer by Tiberius' proneness to prolonging even strictly annual terms of office: P. Petronius held Asia for about six years, *c.* 29–35; a C. Galba, excluded in 36, killed himself.[74]

Envoys even from Achaea had complained about their governors even under Augustus, but the series of known prosecutions for

[72] Treasury: *IG* II/III² 3504; general: Philostr. *VS* 526; Corinth: A.B. West, *Corinth* VIII, 2: *the Latin Inscr.* (Cambridge, MA, 1931) 83 n.; 86 n. (references to famines); price of grain during a famine: Eus.-Jer. 181 Helm (A.D. 49).   [73] Tac. *Ann.* II.47 (A.D. 17); IV.13.1 (23).

[74] Vogel-Weidemann 1982 (E 885) 274–80 (Petronius); Tac. *Ann.* VI.40.3 (Galba).

misconduct in Asia begins with a particularly outrageous case, that of Valerius Messalla Volesus, who during his proconsulship of about 10–11 had not only enriched himself but done so with open brutality, stalking amongst the corpses of 300 men he had executed and preening himself on a right royal deed. The case of Granius Marcellus, the proconsul of Bithynia prosecuted in A.D. 15, was unsensational, but Tiberius' handing over of his procurator in Asia, Lucilius Capito, for trial in the Senate in 23 made history and, like the relentless handling of C. Silanus on the precedent of Volesus the year before, won the emperor high opinions in Asia.[75]

These were the first attested prosecutions conducted at the instance of the *koinon* of Asia, which lost no time in securing permission to erect a temple to Tiberius, his mother and, Tiberius insisted, the Senate. It was not until three years later that Smyrna, which had celebrated the cult of Rome since 195 B.C., was selected from eleven contestants as the site. When it came to Gaius, Miletus was successful;[76] but by no means all emperors were honoured in this way: both Claudius and, more surprisingly, Nero were omitted. But a city of the first rank such as Ephesus might become 'warden' (*neocorus*) of no fewer than three imperial temples as well as that of its own patron deity. By at least eleven cities too Tiberius was honoured with cult, becoming 'the greatest of the gods' at Cyzicus.[77] After him emperors tended to be objects of cult from the *koinon en bloc*, but within this limitation cities went on doing what they could to attract favourable attention by demonstrating loyalty.[78] Their efforts were not always well judged: what was a community in Lydia doing with a public area commemorating Gaius' German campaign, and why should Amisus in Pontus be honouring Nero, Poppaea and Tiberius Claudius Britannicus on the same monument?[79] It was a different matter when a sophisticated *polis* with long-standing connexions with Rome, such as Aphrodisias, embarked on the construction of a Sebasteion with a processional way between porticoes leading to a raised temple and of proficient sculptures adorning the complex.[80]

The *princeps* himself was a powerful neighbour to many cities and individual landowners as he acquired estates, mines and quarries by purchase, inheritance, or confiscation, or controlling them in virtue of his role as governor. Patchy at first, especially the relatively isolated quarries, his estates in Asia Minor were to form large tracts of territory in the second century. Lucilius Capito's encroachments on the prerogatives

[75] Sen. *Ira* II.5.5 (Volesus); Tac. *Ann.* 1.74 (Marcellus); IV.15 (Capito); III.66–8 (Silanus).
[76] Tac. *Ann.* IV.55; Gaius' temple: Dio LXIX.28.1.   [77] *SEG* IV 707.
[78] See Price 1984 (F 199) 58.
[79] *GCN* 34 (Kula); 112 (Nero, Poppaea – unless Agrippina is to be read – Britannicus).
[80] See Smith 1987 (F 580).

of a governor illustrate the growing importance of officials charged with administering the imperial property and the recognition they were being accorded. Under a governor of less than the highest seniority or calibre, such as the proconsul of Bithynia, the procurator's responsibilities and his prestige might eclipse those of the pro-magistrate. East–West communications and increasing wealth made Bithynia more important than it had seemed under Augustus: the *princeps* would not leave it all in the hands of the proconsul. Iunius Cilo, procurator at the end of Claudius' reign, managed imperial business there and escorted a deposed monarch to Rome in 49, winning consular decorations. His subjects brought charges of extortion against him but he was acquitted and apparently prorogued. The services of Publius Celer, procurator of Asia when the Principate changed hands in 54, were political, the murder of a potential rival of Nero; it was they that saved him from accusations levelled against him by the provincials, at least long enough for him to die a natural death. By contrast a determined citizen of Cibyra, which under Claudius was temporarily detached from Asia and assigned to Lycia, was able to have an oppressive procurator removed from his duties of collecting grain from the city.[81]

Political considerations were also important in the trials of senators charged with misconduct. Only the most strenuous efforts secured the conviction of Nero's man Cossutianus Capito in 57 for misconduct in Cilicia; the valuable prosecutor Eprius Marcellus, charged with *repetundae* in the same year, was acquitted, secured the exile of some of those who had accused him on behalf of the Lycian *koinon*,[82] and lived to return to Anatolia under Vespasian for a three-year term as governor of Asia.

When Germanicus travelled the coasts of Greece and Asia Minor in 18, he worked to restore places exhausted by internal disputes and mismanagement on the part of their own magistrates.[83] Having paid to secure the positions they held, members of the ruling class in the cities sought to recoup their expenditure. This was a failing that Aristotle remarked in timocracies such as the Romans favoured, and the venality of Greeks was already commonplace for Polybius and Cicero.[84] A Claudian proconsul of Asia, Paullus Fabius Persicus, issued a long and elaborate edict curtailing (he hoped) inefficiency, waste and dishonesty in the administration of the temple funds established by Vedius Pollio for the cult of Artemis at Ephesus.[85] One trick was to lend young slaves to the temple, where their upkeep would be paid; another to anticipate temple revenue and speculate with it.

Paullus was a friend of Claudius and knew what was expected of a

[81] Tac. *Ann.* xii.21; Dio lx.53.5 (Cilo); Tac. *Ann.* xiii.1.3; 33.1f (Celer); *GCN* 408 (Cibyra).
[82] Tac. *Ann.* xiii.33.3f. | [83] Tac. *Ann.* ii.54.2.
[84] Arist. *Pol.* ii.1273b; *Pol.* vi.56.13; Cic. *Att.* vi.2.5.   [85] *GCN* 380.

governor. Others became involved with local malefactors, giving them protection and an opportunity for blackmail. Those who did not co-operate could be threatened with the prospect of being passed over when it came to votes of thanks for their administration. Augustus had already in A.D. 12 forbidden such votes to be passed within six months of a governor's departure (perhaps in the wake of the Volesus Messalla case). The abuse came to light most blatantly in Neronian Crete, where the leader of the *koinon*, Claudius Timarchus, boasted that it depended on him whether governors were given votes of thanks. The dispatch of embassies to express such thanks before the Senate was now banned altogether – for a time.[86]

In Crete it seems that the *koinon* had acquired a particular ascendancy in relation to the individual cities, whose coinages ended under Gaius and were superseded by that of the *koinon* (in Cyprus too the currency became federal). In spite of the failings of city and *koinon* officials, which could not be cured and were to develop further (the history of Crete under the Julio-Claudians has been called a recital of earthquakes and trials for extortion; encroachment of magnates on city land is another failing detectable there),[87] the Romans had no alternative. *Koina* were a prime means of conveying instructions to the leading men of a province, of focusing their loyalty and satisfying their ambition. Private clubs were banned from the time of Caesar and Augustus onwards, as attracting the lower classes in the cities and otherwise likely to turn into radical political groups; exceptions were allowed only for those exclusively religious and social in character, and they had to be licensed. Associa-tions of boys (ephebes), young men (*neoi*), and elders (*gerousiae*), which were integral parts of the city, and professional associations of men of respectable standing were a different matter. In 41 the Guild of Hymnodoi of Asia – choruses who performed at the celebration of the imperial cult – had occasion to honour Claudius and the privileges of stage artists (the World-wide Guild of Crowned Victors in the Sacred Contests of Dionysus and their Fellow-competitors) had already been granted by Augustus before Claudius guaranteed them in 43 and 48–9. Athletes too, as Antony's letter to the *koinon* shows, had long been recognized as a group with legitimate interests and the Itinerant Athletic Association was careful to inform Claudius in 47 of the successful festival held in his honour by the kings of Commagene and Pontus.[88]

As to the success of the provinces of western Asia Minor as a whole, the Romans can have felt no misgivings. They continued to encourage

[86] Tac. *Ann.* xv.20–2; for Augustus, see Dio LVI.25.6.

[87] See Sanders 1982 (E 871) 132; encroachment: *GCN* 385; 388.

[88] *GCN* 372 (*hymnodi*); 373 (a) and (b) (Dionysiac artists); EJ² 300 (Antony's letter); *GCN* 374 (the Claudian festival).

communities who aspired to *polis* status. Besides restoring damaged cities Tiberius allowed two to take his name: one Tiberiopolis was in Phrygia Epictetus, the other (Pappa) in the Galatian province, on the borders of Phrygia and Pisidia: within the greater cities both Aphrodisias and Pisidian Antioch had squares named after him.

But it was in eastern Asia Minor, in the third of the regions with which we are concerned, that Tiberius made his most important changes in the Augustan political map. Germanicus' mission to the East in 17–19 had two main positive purposes: to deal with the Parthians and to establish a new Roman client on the throne of Armenia Maior. But the visit came at a time of change for long-standing client states: the deaths of Antiochus III of Commagene, of Philopator in the kingdom of the Amanus, and, at Rome where the *princeps* had summoned him to stand trial before the Senate (he had faced charges from his subjects on an earlier occasion), that of the aged Archelaus of Cappadocia.[89]

Tiberius made a clean sweep of the client kingdoms. The 85,000km[2] of Cappadocia, with its eleven eastern-style 'satrapies' – *strategiae* in Greek – – and its few cities concentrated in the most westerly of them, required direct rule. After the preliminary arrangements had been made by a legate of Germanicus, Q. Veranius, the new province was entrusted to an equestrian prefect. To make Roman rule more acceptable, taxes were reduced, but even so Tiberius was able to halve the 1 per cent inheritance duty on Roman citizens. Commagene was taken over by Q. Servaeus, another legate, and, like the kingdom of the Amanus, incorporated in the province of Syria. Only Pythodoris, until her death,[90] Archelaus' son in part of Cilicia Tracheia, and the Teucrids of Olba were left in place, and Olba came to be overshadowed by a new foundation of uncertain date, Diocaesarea. As far as Cilicia was concerned, it was a wise decision: the younger Archelaus' subjects, the Citae, were still giving trouble in 36, when they refused a census and all its implications, and in 52.[91] But some of Tiberius' arrangements were reversed by Gaius, a true great-grandson of Antony who had been brought up at court with eastern royalties. In 38 he returned Commagene to Antiochus (IV), with the addition of eastern Cilicia, and Pontus to Polemo (II) who also acquired the Teucrid kingdom when the dynasty died out in 41. Antiochus kept his kingdom, with one interruption, until 72, Polemo his until 64, when it was annexed as Pontus Polemoniacus. Gaius assigned Armenia Minor to another friend and grandson of Pythodoris, Cotys. Whatever his motives, it is usually agreed that the territories he assigned to clients were well suited to that form of government; how potently his actions were felt in the Greek East, is attested by a decree of Cyzicus: 'Since the new Helios Gaius Caesar Augustus Germanicus wished also to illuminate with his

---

[89] See Tac. *Ann.* 11.42; 56.   [90] Sullivan 1980 (E 879) 921.   [91] Tac. *Ann.* VI.41; XII.55.

own rays the kingdoms that are the bodyguard of the empire ... even
though the kings, however hard they think, are unable to find appropriate ways of repaying the benefactions conferred on them to show their
gratitude to so great a god, he has restored the sons of Cotys (VIII of
Thrace), Rhoemetalces (III of Thrace), Polemon and Cotys, who were
brought up with him and were his companions, to the kingdoms that
were due to them from their forefathers and ancestors. Reaping the
abundance of his immortal grace, they are greater than their predecessors
in this respect, that they inherited from their fathers, while these men, as
a result of the grace of Gaius Caesar, have become kings to share in the
government of these great gods.' Small wonder to find Tryphaena,
mother of the kings, in the same document celebrating the cult of
Drusilla the New Aphrodite, and Polemon jointly celebrating the games
with Antiochus IV.[92]

But Gaius' donations went against the trend. In 43 direct Roman rule
spread to the south-west corner of Asia Minor when mountainous Lycia,
with its thirty-six cities – the earlier number considerably advanced since
the assessment of Strabo – was annexed, Rhodes also losing its freedom
in the following year. Claudius' pretext was disorder in the cities and the
killing of Roman citizens, but he allowed an appeal from Rhodes, backed
by the young Nero, in 53.[93] As far as Lycia's external independence went
the change was a nominal one; cult had been offered since 188 B.C. to
Roma Thea Epiphanes and to powerful Romans such as Agrippa;
Tiberius' cult survived until the third century alongside the federal cult
of the Augusti.[94] But the federated cities now had to pay tribute and the
first praetorian legate, Q. Veranius, doing for Claudius what his father
had done for Germanicus in Cappadocia, seems to have met resistance.[95]
To loyal subjects Veranius was able to offer the reward of citizenship,
and the new province settled down with Pamphylia, the district joined to
it under the new arrangement, its upper class crystallizing into a nobility
of Lyciarchs and (at least from Vespasian onwards) high priests, who
often served as secretaries of the League, with *archiphylax* and *hierophylax*
to guarantee order and collect the tribute. If we are to trust Suetonius,
Lycia regained its freedom some time before Vespasian's reorganization
of the eastern provinces, either from Nero, after the freeing of Achaea, or
under Galba; but epigraphic evidence suggests that Lycia had a governor who survived from Nero to Vespasian.[96]

[92] Dio LIX.8.2; LX.8.1 (Antiochus). Braund (C 254) 42, on LX.8.2 (Polemo); Suet. *Ner.* 18, with
Magie 1950 (E 853) 1417 n. 62 (annexation of Pontus Polemoniacus). *GCN* 401, with Price 1984 (F
199) 244f (restoration of the three monarchs).

[93] Dio LX.17.3; 24.4; Tac. *Ann.* XII.58.2. Pliny, *HN* V.101 (number of Lycian cities).

[94] Rome: *SEG* XVIII 570; Agrippa: *IGRR* III 719; Tiberius: 474; high priests: 487.

[95] *GCN* 231(c).

[96] Suet. *Vesp.* 8.4, but see W. Eck, *Senatoren von Vespasian bis Hadrian* (Vestigia 13) (Munich,
1970) 4.

It was under Nero that the main structural change in eastern Asia Minor came. Made in 54 for military purposes, it provided Cn. Domitius Corbulo with freedom of action against the Parthians and a wider recruiting ground amongst the warlike Gauls, and it became the model for Vespasian's permanent scheme. Cappadocia and Galatia were united under the consular legate Corbulo, and his routine work in remoter areas was performed by a separate legate.[97] The strategic importance of eastern Asia Minor was being realized; if its wealth was also increasing, that was a process that would be speeded up under the Flavians.

The client monarchs prepared for their own supersession by following the tradition of their kind and founding cities. M. Antonius Polemon of Olba may be the founder of Claudiopolis on the Calycadnus; Antiochus IV founded Germanicopolis, Antiochia ad Cragum, Iotape and Neronias, later the city on the main road to Caesarea from the west that Archelaus made from the typical 'village-town' or 'fortlet' Garsaoura, administrative centre of the *strategia* named after it; it became a colony under Claudius. Urban development is suggested elsewhere in the south-eastern sector of Asia Minor by the appearance of city names compounded, as before, with those of the emperors, but how substantial any accompanying changes may have been is not clear. Certainly the reigns of Claudius and Nero saw road construction and repair in Anatolia: in Asia (the road from Smyrna to Ephesus and Tralles in A.D. 51), Pamphylia (under the imperial procurator in 50), Bithynia (the Apamea–Nicaea route in 57–8) and Paphlagonia (*c.* A.D. 45 near Amastris).[98]

V. CONCLUSION: FIRST FRUITS

The century between Octavian's accession to sole power and the death of Nero was one of almost unbroken peace in the areas under discussion, a condition ideal for political and economic development for regions capable of it. Western Asia Minor was in the van, in part because of its proximity to the new Danubian provinces of Moesia and Pannonia, in part as encasing the routes that led from Ephesus and Byzantium through the Cilician Gates into Syria or by more northerly branches to the Euphrates crossing at Tomisa. From this last factor, proximity to main lines of communication, central and eastern Asia Minor also benefited, especially communities that lay on the highways, such as Ancyra, Iconium and Caesarea Mazaca.

From the Roman point of view increased prosperity meant an increase in the amount of tax that the regions would yield and, almost equally

[97] *GCN* 244.
[98] Asia: *CIL* III 476, 720; Pamphylia: *GCN* 347; Bithynia: *CIL* III 346; Paphlagonia: *ILS* 5883.

important, their contribution to manpower at all levels. It is significant that in spite of the obstacles in the way of easterners (language difficulties, prejudice against new men) a beginning was made during this century in recruiting men to the imperial service which culminates, in the Neronian period, in the admission of a considerable number of easterners into the Senate.

Grants of citizenship were the prerequisite, and the rate of progress varied from city to city and province to province. From actual or, at a pinch, potential citizens, legionaries might be recruited, but even non-citizen areas could contribute soldiers to the auxiliary forces. For these the places of origin are significant: no units bear names that show them originally levied in Achaea, Bithynia, or Asia. Levying a troop of horse or auxiliary infantry from freshly provincialized territory would be removing potentially dangerous manpower from its home area, and some units at least (notably *numeri* and those with specialized weaponry) continued to be drawn from their original recruiting grounds even after they had moved; this was not a motive that would apply in the two western regions, Greece and the proconsular provinces of Asia Minor. But mountainous Crete provided a cohort, Galatia apparently an *ala* (*VII Phrygum*), and Cyprus four cohorts.[99]

Achaea equally fails to turn up any legionaries in this period, an indication of impoverishment: recruiting officers perhaps did not think it worth visiting. Asia and Bithynia have seven to show, eastern Asia Minor eight times as many (with the three Gallic capitals contributing over half), and Roman colonies such as Troas, Antioch towards Pisidia, and Ninica seven. Potential fighting quality and a stake in the land were desiderata fulfilled above all by men from military colonies and apparently by the Gauls.[100]

At a higher social level the picture changes. Equestrian procurators had to satisfy a census requirement (400,000 sesterces) and high qualities of character were expected.[101] These were conditions not different in kind from those applied to legionaries, but for equestrian posts patronage and recommendation played a vital part and men from out of the way places did not stand a good chance. Pompeius Macer of Mytilene, procurator of Asia and librarian at Rome already in the time of Augustus, came of a family that had been close to the Roman dynasts since the middle of the first century B.C. C. Iulius Spartiaticus, son of the disgraced Laco and grandson of Eurycles, became a procurator of Claudius and Agrippina; not surprisingly he claims to be 'first of the

[99] For auxiliaries, see Cheesman 1914 (D 174); for consistent recruitment from provinces or tribes after which units were named as something exceptional, see also, *e.g.*, Mócsy 1974 (E 677) 154.
[100] For legionary recruitment, see Forni 1953 (D 188), and 1974 (D 189); for Galatia, see Mitchell, 1976 (E 854). [101] For equestrian recruitment, see above all Pflaum 1960–1 (D 59).

Achaeans'. From Asia too came the later Julio-Claudian prefects of Egypt Cn. Vergilius Capito and Ti. Claudius Balbillus, and C. Stertinius Xenophon, military tribune and *ad responsa graeca*, from Lycia M. Arruntius Aquila, the procurator whose name appears on Pamphylian milestones of 50. Balbillus came from a family close to Tiberius. Stertinius was son of a tutor to the imperial house and the famous physician of Claudius Caesar at whose request his native Cos was granted perpetual immunity from tribute in 53. Amastris provided another procurator, C. Iulius Aquila, who had been in charge of detachments in the Bosporan kingdom with Cotys in 49 and had performed distinguished service there, receiving praetorian insignia; it may be that the Augustan prefect of Egypt of the same name was his father. Pisidian Antioch has already figured as a source of legionary recruits. At the equestrian level it offers the Neronian *iuridicus* in Egypt and procurator of Cappadocia and Cilicia Iulius Proculus, who was connected by marriage with a family from another place of Roman settlement, Attalia in Pamphylia.[102]

The same criteria apply to senators as to knights, only the financial requirements and the barriers of prejudice were higher and more effective.[103] Q. Pompeius Macer, son of the procurator, is not surprisingly the first known; he rose to the praetorship in A.D. 15. But Italian descent (from veteran or civilian settler) is important, and that is why M. Calpurnius Rufus of Attalia, whose mother held the priesthood of Livia and Rome, is the next known entering under Tiberius and serving as legate in Lycia-Pamphylia, his province of origin. T. Iunius Montanus, who reached the suffect consulship in 81, the first easterner to rise so high, represents the military colony proper, that of Alexandria Troas. Rufus would soon be followed by M. Plancius Varus from neighbouring Perge, a Neronian entrant. L. Servenius Cornutus belongs to Acmonia, but has a comparable ancestry in the Italians there, although his mother was descended from client dynasts, making her a representative of a group that was to come into great prominence in the Flavian period. Cornutus was quaestor in Cyprus under Nero and early in Vespasian's reign also served in his own province as legate to the proconsul. Another man who must have entered the Senate under Nero is the unknown citizen of Miletus who boasted of being the first senator from his city and the fifth from Asia.[104] These men are harbingers of a swarm, versed as they were in the administration of cities and eager for metropolitan

---

[102] Suet. *Iul.* 56.7 (Macer); *GCN* 264 (Laco); 127 (Capito); 261 (Balbillus); 262 and Tac. *Ann.* XII.61.2 (Xenophon); *GCN* 347 (Arruntius Aquila); Tac. *Ann.* XII.21 and *GCN* 349 (Iulius Aquila); 267 (Proclus).   [103] For senators from the East see Halfmann 1979 (D 44) and 1982 (E 836).

[104] Halfmann 1982 (E 836) nos. 1 (Macer), 2 (Rufus), 6 (Montanus), 8 (Plancius Varus), 5 (Servenius); 12 (unknown from Miletus).

political life,[105] familiar with Greek language and ways, and loyal subjects of Rome and the *princeps*. The absence of any representative of Achaea is due to the want of wealth and influence there outside the (still possibly suspect) family of the descendants of Eurycles; those of his rival Brasidas did not attain even the citizenship until the reign of Claudius.[106] The lands east of Asia lacked connexions and culture, and still in some areas the city life that made these things possible. Uninterrupted peace would bring them more firmly into the fold of hellenism and carry the cities of the west to unparalleled levels of prosperity and brilliance.

[105] Plut. *De tranq. anim.* 10 (*Mor.* 470C).
[106] Plut. *Apophth. Aug.* 14 (*Mor.* 207F), with *PIR*² C 818.

CHAPTER 14b

EGYPT[1]

ALAN K. BOWMAN

I. THE ROMAN CONQUEST

'Aegyptum imperio populi Romani adieci.'[2] Augustus' stark factual statement, published almost half a century after the event it records, spotlights the final act of the drama of Rome's absorption of the hellenistic kingdoms. In August of 30 B.C., some ten months after the Battle of Actium, Octavian had pursued Cleopatra and Mark Antony to Egypt; both had perished by their own hand in the city founded by Alexander the Great. The conqueror perhaps flirted with the notion of formally inaugurating his 'dominion' (*kratesis*) from the date of the capture of Alexandria but he finally settled on the first day of the new Egyptian year (1 Thoth = 29 August), bridging the gap with a nominal eighteen-day 'reign' of the children of Antony and Cleopatra. Octavian was in Egypt for the first and last time. He saw and touched the corpse of Alexander the Great, causing a piece of the nose to fall off; but he scorned to view the remains of the Ptolemies, remarking that he wished to see a king, not corpses, and he affected insensitivity to local religious susceptibilities by his attitude to the venerated Apis bull, observing that he was accustomed to worship gods, not cattle.[3] Egypt was now under the sway of a non-resident monarch; as a Roman province the country was effectively depoliticized and a good proportion of its resources was

---

[1] Recent general surveys of material relevant to the early Roman period may be found in Bowman 1976 (B 367) and 1990 (E 901), Geraci 1983 (E 924) and Lewis 1983 (E 946) and Montevecchi 1988 (E 952). Still immensely valuable are Mitteis and Wilcken 1911–12 (B 379) and (especially for taxation) Wilcken 1899 (B 388). For a good selection of private and public documentary texts see the Loeb *Select Papyri* I–II, ed. A.S. Hunt, C.C. Edgar (1932–4). The spread of evidence for Roman Egypt is uneven, the first century A.D. being much less well documented than the subsequent two centuries. This chapter therefore necessarily draws upon second-century evidence, whilst trying to avoid giving the impression that what is known to be true for that period must therefore also be true for the earlier era. This is also partly intended to compensate for the fact that Volume XI of *CAH* (2nd edition) will not contain a separate treatment of Egypt.

The most frequently cited publications of papyri are included in the List of Abbreviations (p. 1006). Others will be found in E.G. Turner, *Greek Papyri, an Introduction* (2nd edn, Oxford, 1980) 154–79 and J.F. Oates, R.S. Bagnall, W.H. Willis, K.A. Worp, *Checklist of Editions of Greek Papyri and Ostraka* (4th edn, Atlanta, 1992).   [2] *RG* 27.   [3] Dio LI.16.5.

henceforth oriented towards the consuming nucleus of the empire, Rome itself.

The governmental system whose foundations were reshaped in the Augustan period was to last, in its essential features, for more than 300 years. During that period there were certainly important modifications of detail but it was not until the late third century that Egypt saw fundamental change. The effective division of the empire into East and West and the foundation of Constantinople were events which knitted Egypt more uniformly into the structure of the eastern empire and gave it again an important political role in what was in many ways a more natural context. Hence it is legitimate to suggest that a treatment of Egypt under Augustus and the Julio-Claudians might, with due attention to changes and developments between the accession of Vespasian and the death of Commodus, stand as valid for the 'high' imperial period. Its history in the difficult years of the third century can then form a suitable prelude to a discussion of the important changes under Diocletian and Constantine which shaped its role in the Byzantine Empire.

The transformation of a nominally independent kingdom into a Roman province may have been the act of a moment but Egypt had long been prepared for the coming of Rome. Her history in the dozen years before Actium shows a powerful and intelligent client monarch attempting to use the capacity of a Roman military dynast to aggrandize a friend and ally of the Senate and People of Rome. The story of the political struggle is told elsewhere.[4] As for the internal state of the country in the triumviral period, there are only scraps of evidence. The latest of the Ptolemaic royal decrees to have survived, issued in the names of Cleopatra and Caesarion in 42/41 B.C., offers protection to Alexandrians who owned land in the delta against depredations of Crown officials which will have been exacerbated by the need to purchase Roman goodwill.[5] The fabled wealth of the Ptolemies (Auletes' annual revenue was still 12,500 talents according to Cicero[6]) had been plundered to good purpose in recent years.

It is difficult to be sure that Cleopatra's reign as a whole was marked by declining prosperity. Some have postulated an upturn after the departure of Caesar and the recovery of Cyprus.[7] In any event, Cleopatra found popularity with her Egyptian subjects. She spoke the Egyptian language, she personally attended the installation of the sacred Buchis bull at Hermonthis, she continued the tradition, albeit perhaps sparingly, of temple building and embellishment (construction is attested at

---

[4] Above, ch. 1.   [5] *COrdPtol* 75–6.   [6] Quoted by Strab. XVII.1.13 (798C).
[7] Maehler 1983 (E 948).

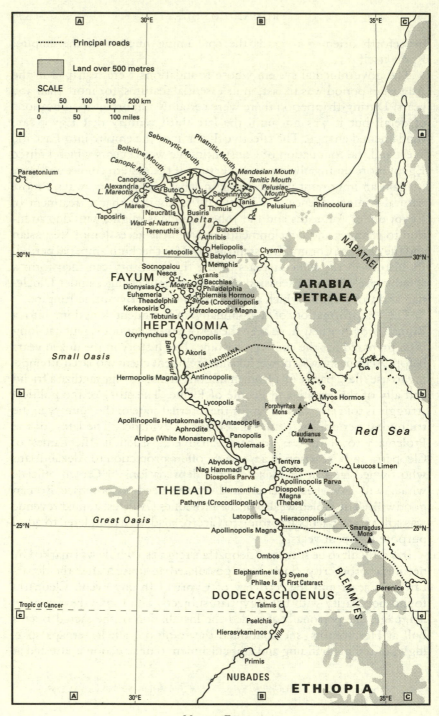

Map 17. Egypt.

Athribis, Coptos, Hermonthis and Tentyra).[8] By 36/35 B.C. she had
added a new element to the royal titulature, 'Philopatris'. Her Roman
consort might receive a Greek votive dedication and the appellation of
'god' (*theos*), but on the Egyptian temple reliefs Cleopatra's consort is her
son Ptolemy XVI Caesarion.[9] Antony may have made little impression
in Egypt outside Alexandria.

Obviously, Cleopatra's contribution to Antony's war effort was of
paramount importance; the Ptolemaic army and navy were still considerable; the latter, or what was left of it after Actium, went to provide the
nucleus of the Alexandrian arm of the Roman imperial fleet. Signs of the
Roman military presence are noticeable in 55 B.C. after the intrusion of
the *Gabiniani*, and with Caesar's installation of troops in the aftermath of
the Alexandrian War.[10] The Greek translation of *cohors* occurs in a
papyrus of the period from Heracleopolis; a Roman *praefectus* named C.
Iulius Papius makes a dedication in the temple of Isis at Philae in the
twentieth year of Cleopatra's reign.[11] After Actium greater care was
taken at a higher level. Senators and illustrious *equites* were forbidden
entry to Egypt without permission of the *princeps*. One of the few people
put to death in the aftermath of the royal suicide had been a Roman
senator named Q. Ovinius who had disgraced his senatorial stripe by
undertaking supervision of the Queen's textile factories and perhaps
provided an admonitory example of the economic power-base available
in Egypt.[12]

II. BUREAUCRACY AND ADMINISTRATION

From the first, care was taken in the establishment of the status and
administration of a province which yielded almost as much revenue as
did the Gallic provinces added to the empire by Augustus' adoptive
father and twelve times as much as the province of Judaea was to
provide.[13] The emperor immediately took on the role of a Pharaoh and
the familiar cartouches were to appear on temple reliefs until the reign of
Decius (A.D. 249–51); the lamplighters of Oxyrhynchus duly adapted
their customary oath of office and swore by Caesar, 'god, son of a god'
(*theon ek theou*) in 30/29 B.C.[14] But Egypt was to be anomalous in being
governed by an equestrian *praefectus* appointed by and directly responsible to the *princeps* (though a freedman could also hold the office as did
one Hiberus for a brief period in A.D. 32, replacing the deceased Vitrasius

[8] *CAH* IX², ch. 8c; Porter and Moss 1937, 1939 (E 958) V 31, 33, 128, 133, 151–7, VI 79.
[9] *BGU* 2376; *OGIS* 195; Porter and Moss 1972, 1939 (E 958) II² 714, VI 79.
[10] On the *Gabiniani* see *CAH* IX², ch. 8c.
[11] *BGU* 1763, 1806; *IPhil* I 63; *WChr* 462 (= *FIRA* I 56).
[12] Tac. *Ann.* II.59; Oros. VI.19.20.   [13] Vell. Pat. II.39; Joseph. *BJ* II.386.
[14] Porter and Moss 1939 (E 958) VI 114; *POxy* 1453.

Pollio).[15] The first prefect was the poet Cornelius Gallus who had led
Octavian's army into Egypt from the west in the war against Antony and
Cleopatra. His first responsibility, to ensure internal security, was met by
prompt reduction of rebellious towns in the region of Coptos in the
Thebaid but he boasted, perhaps too vaingloriously, of that and of his
feat in carrying Roman arms further south than they had hitherto gone.[16]
Within a couple of years he was removed from office, banned from
entering the *princeps*' provinces and finally driven to suicide.

For the first decade of Roman rule, we have more evidence for the
preoccupation with military security than for the development of the
civil administration. The history of Egypt in the decade after Actium
well illustrates the major features of the Augustan frontier strategy.
Cornelius Gallus' inauspicious foray to the south of the First Cataract
was perhaps the first attempt to test the viability of further annexation of
territory. In the Arabian expedition of his successor, Aelius Gallus, the
security of the Indian trade routes will certainly have been an important
consideration, but that need not have been the primary motivation for
expansion. In effect, with the Nabataean kingdom to the east left
independent until A.D. 106, the trading links maintained with India
through the ports of the Red Sea coast and the developing road network
of the eastern desert functioned perfectly satisfactorily.[17] The expeditions of the next prefect, P. Petronius,[18] to the south between 25/4 and 22
B.C. brought a short-lived Roman occupation of the region beyond the
Dodecaschoenus and a Roman garrison to Primis (Qasr Ibrim), a site
which has yielded the earliest Latin literary manuscript, fragments of
elegiacs, most probably by Cornelius Gallus.[19] Augustus soon decided,
however, to remit tribute, perhaps calculating that the cost of occupation was not justified, and within a few years the formal limit of the
province had been set at Hierasykaminos, some 80km to the south of the
First Cataract. But the impact of the Roman presence further south, in an
area accessible to Rome and to Meroe, was still by no means negligible
and served as a reminder of the latent interest and power of Rome. In the
southernmost part of the province the most obvious signs of Roman
dominion are the great temples, largely constructed in the Augustan
period, at Dendur and at Kalabsha (Talmis) where there seem to be two
distinct temples of the Augustan period on a site which also shows signs
of building in the late Ptolemaic period.[20]

Military sensitivity and the importance of the grain supply help to

---

[15] Dio LVIII.19.6; Philo, *In Flacc.* 1.2.   [16] *IPhil* II 128; see above, ch. 4.
[17] See below, pp. 732–6.   [18] For the *praenomen* see Bagnall 1985 (E 889).
[19] Anderson, Parsons and Nisbet 1979 (B 4).
[20] Strab. XVII.1.54 (820–1C); Porter and Moss 1951 (E 958) VII 10–20, 27–33; de Meulenaere, *CE*
36 (1961) 98–105; for an exploratory expedition to East Africa in the Neronian period see Pliny, *HN*
VI.184.

explain the direct imperial appointment of the prefect and are perhaps sufficient to account for Tacitus' insistence that the *princeps* controlled Egypt especially closely.[21] The Senate was thus effectively excluded from any direct responsibility, although even regulations for the administration of the emperor's Special Account (*Idios Logos*) might still be modified or affected by senatorial acts.[22] One factor of obvious importance is that the conquest brought a great deal of land into imperial possession (the *patrimonium*). There is evidence under Augustus for possession of estates (whether through purchase or gift) by the emperor's relatives and friends (Livia, Antonia the Younger, Germanicus, Maecenas), though none for direct personal ownership by Augustus. Later emperors did, however, own estates and continued to bestow them on friends and favourites such as Seneca, Narcissus, Pallas, Doryphorus; these latter properties would naturally revert, whether *de iure* or merely *de facto* is unclear, to the *patrimonium* on the death of the individual.[23] The presence of imperial property, if nothing else, emphasizes that it is very misleading to characterize the whole province as in some sense the 'personal property' of the emperor. But Egypt was nevertheless a province with important differences.

The office of prefect of Egypt was to develop, as might have been foreseen, into one of immense latent power, as Tiberius Iulius Alexander was to demonstrate in A.D. 69 with his support of Vespasian's bid for the imperial throne; Avidius Cassius, the son of a former prefect, was to claim the support of Egypt and its prefect in his unsuccessful attempt at usurpation in A.D. 175.[24] The authority of the prefecture was spelled out in a law, presumably enacted in or very soon after 30 B.C., which gave the incumbent's acts and decrees the same validity as those of any Roman magistrate.[25] The list of prefects appointed by Augustus and the Julio-Claudian emperors shows some illustrious (and notorious) names: C. Turranius, Seius Strabo, father of Sejanus, Avillius Flaccus, Sutorius Macro. Prefects held office for three years, on average, and in the absence of any specialist Egyptian training relied on their general knowledge of the principles of military and civil administration and law, backed up by readily available local expertise, to cope with the diverse and intricate bureaucratic demands of the job.[26] Promotion from Egypt to the praetorian prefecture is regularly attested in the period A.D. 70–235. Tiberius Iulius Alexander, nephew of Philo and member of a prominent Alexandrian Jewish family, is important as the earliest example of an official who held an equestrian post in Egypt (that of *epistrategos*) and

[21] *Ann.* II.59, *Hist.* I.11.   [22] *BGU* 1210 *praef.*
[23] Parássoglou 1978 (E 956) App. II, 69–83.
[24] Joseph. *BJ* IV.616ff; *SB* 10295 cf. Bowman 1970 (E 899), with Sijpesteijn, *ZPE* 8 (1971) 186–92.
[25] Tac. *Ann.* XII.60; *D.* 1.17.   [26] Philo, *In Flacc.* 3, cf. Brunt 1975 (E 906).

advanced to the prefecture, proceeding later in all probability to the
praetorian command; Caecina Tuscus and Claudius Balbillus both held
equestrian posts slightly later than Alexander and reached the prefecture
earlier. Before them, three examples are known of men who proceeded
from the praetorian prefecture to Egypt, namely Seius Strabo, Sutorius
Macro and Lusius Geta, all perhaps in circumstances of political
sensitivity.[27]

Like any Roman provincial governor the prefect exercised control,
subject only to the emperor's overriding power, over all aspects of the
administration of his province. Innovatory regulations could be introduced either by the application of imperial pronouncements or *senatus
consulta*, or by prefectural edicts. The degree of independence which a
prefect enjoyed was presumably a matter of fine tuning and sensitivity to
the limits of his emperor's tolerance, indifference or ignorance. The
transgressions of Cornelius Gallus were not administrative but military
and political. Tiberius, however, castigated a prefect for stripping the
provincials rather than shearing them. By contrast, Tiberius Iulius
Alexander showed the required sensitivity to the need to link a general
statement of benevolence to the inauguration of a new reign.[28]

The functioning of the administration depended upon a complex
bureaucratic structure which certainly owed a great deal to Ptolemaic
precedents, although it should be firmly emphasized that the changes
introduced by the Romans were at least as important as the continuities.
In direct subordination to the prefect stood a variety of officials of
equestrian rank: one in charge of the emperor's Special Account, the
iuridicus supervising the judicial administration, various procurators
with specific responsibilities, the higher-ranking military officers. We
cannot be sure quite how clearly defined the roles of the civil officials
were in the early years. Much of the evidence is from the second century
and it suggests that status and function tended to become more clearly
defined in the course of time. In the Flavian period the estates account
(*ousiakos logos*) was created to supervise patrimonial properties; at least
two new officials were probably instituted in Hadrian's reign – the
dioiketes, a financial officer with responsibility for the land economy, and
the high-priest (*archiereus*) of Alexandria and all Egypt, in charge of
religious institutions. Slightly different in character, although also of
equestrian procuratorial status, were the *epistrategoi*, three or four in
number, assigned to territorial divisions comprising groups of districts
called nomes (one in the Thebaid, one in the Arsinoite Nome and the
Heptanomia, one or two in the delta).[29] The evidence shows that the
epistrategoi, rather than being miniature prefects in their regions, had

---

[27] For this view see Hanson 1982 (E 930).
[28] Dio LVII.10.5; Chalon 1964 (E 909) lines 3–10.   [29] Thomas 1982 (E 973) II ch. 3.

specific and limited functions (relating most importantly to the liturgical system and the judicial administration); again, much of the evidence comes from the second century, by which time the office might have developed wider powers than it had earlier enjoyed. An important general feature of this innovation was that it constituted an injection of paid officials of high rank virtually all of whom, at least in the early years, will have been outsiders who might be expected to perform their duties with a greater degree of impartiality than natives. This is one feature which emphasizes the fundamental division between officials at this level and the native administrators occupying positions at the nome level or below.

It is difficult to provide a tidy description of the upper levels of the administrative structure by which the Roman government organized the affairs of Egypt, largely, no doubt, because the activities of officials at the procuratorial levels, even in the later period, were less apt to be compartmentalized than in modern government. Obviously the authority of the prefect was supreme within the province in all areas. The administrative activities of the head of the Special Account entailed judicial functions in matters affecting the account he administered; how independent his judicial role was depends on the strictness with which the matter of prefectural delegation is viewed. Equestrian military officers are found performing non-military functions – acting in judicial capacities and conducting admission (*epikrisis*) procedures for Roman citizens (many of whom will have been veterans).[30]

A more detailed consideration of the administration of the emperor's Special Account, a Ptolemaic survival whose character was radically altered under Roman rule, provides a good example of the complexities and developments in the system. Under the Ptolemies this account had managed land which fell into Crown possession but under the Romans it seems to have supervised only ownerless property (*adespota*) and land 'in deduction' (*ge en hypologoi*) which was to be sold off; supervision of imperial land and estates belonging to the fiscus (*ousiai tamiakai*) was, at least in the later period, separately administered. But it was given new responsibilities such as supervision of the sale of temple offices and the admission to Egyptian priesthoods (*eiskritikon*). Our best single piece of evidence for its sphere and mode of operation comes in the form of a copy of its *Gnomon* (Code of Regulations); this gives us the form in which it existed in the Antonine period but it is explicitly tralatician and goes back to the reign of Augustus.[31] In the *Gnomon* we see the account exercising wide-ranging powers which affected escheatable and owner-less property (*bona caduca* and *bona vacantia*), matters of status, testamen-

30 BGU 258; FIRA III 171; MChr 84–5; for a list of *epikrisis* documents (all post-A.D. 103) see Nelson 1979 (E 953) 40–2.   31 BGU 1210 *praef.*

tation, manumission, the activities of priests, the rights of soldiers to own land and so on; its administrative functions are thus intimately bound up with legal powers. Whether it possessed the latter from the first or whether they are a gradual later accretion is difficult to see; but a fragment of the *Gnomon* which is thought to date to the middle of the first century suggests that, despite variations in detail, the text was relatively stable.[32] This would tend to emphasize the public nature of those interests of the fiscus which it dealt with in the earlier period and the Special Account may, indeed, have provided a model for the establishment and growth of the public role of the fiscus elsewhere.

Beneath this administrative superstructure, the traditional nome divisions, which numbered between forty and fifty in the Roman period, remained the basic territorial units for administrative purposes. In the second century natives drawn from the Greco-Egyptian populace were appointed to paid posts in these districts. They did not normally serve in their native nomes nor were they permitted to acquire unproductive or auctioned land in the nomes where they did serve. But in the first century there is evidence to suggest that they were recruited from Alexandrians with Roman citizenship and from the ranks of the magistrates in the nome-capitals (*metropoleis*).[33] The most important of these nome officials were the *strategoi* and the royal scribes (*basilikoi grammateis*), and the former, in particular, had a crucial role (much greater than that of the officials with the corresponding title in the Ptolemaic period) in the system of tax-collection with direct responsibility to the prefect; they are, in many respects, the key to understanding the way in which the Roman government ensured the co-operation or compliance of the local authorities in the towns and villages. A eulogizing inscription of the reign of Tiberius describes the virtues of a *strategos* in dispensing justice without corruption in accordance with the will of the prefect, managing the upkeep of the dykes and the irrigation system, and farming out public positions.[34]

Although there were also officials whose functions were exercised in regional divisions of the nome (toparchies), it is the officials of the towns and villages who form the keystone of administration at its most basic level. The role which the metropoleis developed as administrative centres for their nomes had always been inherent in the Ptolemaic system but the evidence suggests that it was much enhanced under the Romans. The villages in the nome tended to form their own hierarchical groupings but they were oriented towards the metropoleis as the main administrative centres of operations which directly served central government interests, principally record-keeping, taxation and the administration of justice. In this respect there is some analogy with the

---

[32] *POxy* 3014.   [33] *BGU* 1210, section 70.   [34] *SEG* VIII 527 (A.D. 22/3).

development of *poleis* or *civitates* with their dependent *territoria* in other provinces. It is also very important to note that the Romans did make innovations in introducing magisterial offices (*archai*) in the metropoleis (gymnasiarchs, *exegetai*, *kosmetai*) which were the means of affording a degree of self-government in internal administration – public buildings, games, markets and so on.[35] This is completely different from anything in the Ptolemaic period and allows comparison, to some degree, with the character of local administration in other Roman provinces. It is true, however, that in the first two centuries of Roman rule the metropoleis conspicuously lacked the distinguishing feature of the autonomous *polis* or *civitas* elsewhere, namely a council (*boule*). The absence of a corporate organ of administration meant that there was no *locus* of communal responsibility and that the nome officials had, in effect, to supervise and organize the local authorities in the performance of their obligations to the government. As for the villages, their boards of *presbyteroi* (elders) enjoyed enlarged authority under Roman rule, but less independence than their metropolitan counterparts and their appointment was probably made or vetted by the village scribe (*komogrammateus*).[36] Their main functions lay in the areas of supervision of leases of land on behalf of the community, collection of taxes and provision of guards (*phylakes*).

Government supervision of these local authorities was particularly noticeable in the area of appointment to liturgical services, the nature and scale of which was to become so radically different from anything that had existed in the Ptolemaic period as to make it, in effect, another Roman innovation of the utmost importance. There is no doubt that the range and complexity of the liturgical system developed greatly in the course of the second century but its origins must certainly be put in the Julio-Claudian period.[37] In due course distinctions became apparent between the various types of liturgies, all of which were dependent upon the property qualification (*poros*) of the individual: administrative tasks performed by metropolitans of the gymnasial class, by other metropolitans and by relatively well-off villagers, then, at the lowest level, tasks performed by poorer individuals as liturgies requiring personal service (*leitourgiai somatikai*). These liturgists performed a wide variety of tasks, some internal to the functioning of the town or village, others in areas of

[35] Despite Tac. *Hist.* 1.11, 'ignaram magistratuum', which must be taken as a general comment on the lack of municipal institutions. For holders of *archai* in the Julio-Claudian period see, for example, *POxy* 246, *WChr* 176 (*kosmetai*), *PMert* 62, *SB* 9109, *PLond* 1166 (gymnasiarchs); note that corporate responsibilities of the *koinon ton archonton* (corporation of magistrates) are not attested until the late second century (the term occurs in *WChr* 34, of A.D. 201 and it may be inferred that this is the body whose proceedings are recorded in *PRyl* 77, of A.D. 192). See now Bowman and Rathbone 1992 (E 903).

[36] *PPhil* 1.11.37ff (A.D. 103–7); note the early evidence for an official called *hegoumenos tes komes* (headman of the village) in *PTeb* 401, 484.

[37] *PMich* 582; *SB* 9224; Hübner, *ZPE* 24 (1977) 43–53, cf. Thomas 1983 (E 974); *contra*, Lewis, *ZPE* 31 (1978) 141–2.

more direct interest to the central government such as tax-collection or the dyke-corvée. In the absence of local councils it was natural that the nome officials, the *strategoi* in particular, should play an important role in vetting the nomination of suitably qualified persons and supervising the performance of liturgists who performed tasks of direct interest to the government. For the first two centuries A.D. it is important to make a distinction, in principle, between these compulsory services and the voluntary metropolitan magistracies (*archai*), confined to 'Greeks' of the gymnasial class. This distinction was later to become meaningless as the magistracies became so burdensome as to be regarded in the same light as liturgies and to necessitate compulsion, even though they theoretically retained their prestige and exclusiveness.

Only a handful of communities stood outside this system – the so-called 'Greek cities'; three had existed in the Ptolemaic period, Alexandria, Naucratis and Ptolemais and a fourth, Antinoopolis, was to be added in the reign of Hadrian. As far as internal administration was concerned these were distinguished by having a greater degree of autonomy and independence from government officials. They were the only communities which possessed councils (though Alexandria is a famous exception) and their magistracies and civic institutions (such as tribes, demes and some local courts and protected laws) were much closer to the traditional institutions of the Greek *polis* than anything elsewhere in Egypt.[38] But the Roman introduction, early in the period, of *archai* in the metropoleis nevertheless seems to mark an important and deliberate, albeit gradual, attempt at development along these lines and, as such, it must be seen as the foundation of the Egyptian version of the type of civic or municipal government which the Romans encouraged or introduced in other provinces; and, as elsewhere, it has important repercussions on the physical development of the administrative centres.

In describing the details of the business handled by means of these bureaucratic structures, it is convenient to make a conventional division between the military, financial and judicial administration but it should be emphasized that there are in practice very few rigid lines of demarcation; the application of law and the administration of justice, in particular, pervades every area of bureaucratic activity in a way which modern notions of administration and jurisdiction tend to obfuscate.

1. Military organization

The introduction of a standing army marked a sharp break from Ptolemaic practice. The monarchs had relied upon soldier-cleruchs (Greek immigrants at first, latterly native Egyptians as well), supple-

[38] *WChr* 27; *SB* 9016, 7603; see Bowman and Rathbone 1992 (E 903); for Alexandria see below, pp. 700–1.

mented by the use of mercenaries.[39] In the reign of Augustus Egypt was garrisoned by a force of three Roman legions, nine auxiliary cohorts and three cavalry units (*alae*); there was also the *classis Alexandrina* whose strength cannot be gauged and the river-patrol which was separately organized. At first the legions were stationed at Alexandria, Babylon and Thebes; by A.D. 23, with increasing internal security they were reduced to two and stationed in the Roman camp at Nicopolis near Alexandria, sending detachments upriver as and when necessary. Three auxiliary cohorts (and perhaps one *ala*) had been based there from the first, with another three at Syene near the southern border. The other units cannot be securely located but will have been distributed in Middle and Upper Egypt, sending small detachments for service away from their permanent bases, to towns in the valley or to crucial strategic points in the deserts. The overall strength of the Egyptian garrison fluctuated somewhat in the course of time. The legionary establishment was maintained at two until the reign of Hadrian, then reduced to one; in A.D. 105 there were still three *alae* but only seven cohorts and in the middle of the second century four *alae* and twelve cohorts.

The command structure in the Egyptian units differed from the norm only in one important respect. Since senatorial legionary legates were excluded, the legions were commanded by the prefect of the camp (*praefectus castrorum*). One such has been identified as having held this post in the 60s and then to have pursued a career of distinction – namely Minicius Iustus, an old friend of Pliny the Younger, who rose to the primipilate (senior centurionate) and eventually married into a consular family; another, Aeternius Fronto, advanced to the prefecture of Egypt early in the Flavian period.[40] The officers of the early period will have predominantly hailed from Italy and the West. Rankers from Gaul and other western provinces are attested too, but recruitment for the ranks concentrated mainly on the eastern provinces outside Egypt. This will be one thing which distinguished them from the surrounding civilian populace but, even so, there is early evidence of a few native Egyptians in auxiliary units, a trend which certainly became more marked with the passage of time. A unique early example of an Egyptian legionary soldier in the middle of the first century is an Oxyrhynchite named Lucius Pompeius Niger, a veteran of *legio XXII Deiotariana*, whose father was called Syros, son of Apion.[41]

After the first decade of Roman rule when attempts to expand the

[39] That the disappearance of Ptolemaic military ranks was gradual is indicated by the existence of a thirty-seven-year-old *katoikos*, described as *tes y hipparchias ton hekontarouron*, in a document of A.D. 12/13, *PKöln* 227.4–6.

[40] Iustus, *RMR* 51 with Davies 1973 (E 913); Aeternius Fronto, *PIR* (2) L287 (*sic*).

[41] Gilliam 1986 (D 192) 335–40; Whitehorne 1988 (E 982).

province were abandoned, the role of the army in ensuring external security was effectively confined to keeping an eye on the Dodecaschoenus and the borders with Meroe, not entirely a sinecure in this period (and even less so in the later empire); a papyrus of the later first century appears to describe an engagement between Roman troops and combined forces of Ethiopians and Trogodytes who inhabited areas of the Red Sea coast to the south of Berenice.[42] Matters of internal security bulk larger in our evidence. Alexandria was always potentially volatile and trouble between Greeks and Jews in A.D. 66 necessitated action by the two legions and extra drafts of troops from Africa.[43] The much more serious Jewish revolt of A.D. 115–17 was by no means confined to Alexandria – there was exceptionally fierce fighting in the *chora* too and, once again troops had to be brought in from abroad (as well as a distinguished commander, Marcius Turbo); there is some surprising evidence, too, for the involvement of a civil official, Apollonius the *strategos* of Apollonopolis-Heptakomias, in military action near Memphis.[44]

Such disturbances interrupted the routine duties of the army only infrequently. Of surpassing importance is the evidence for its centrality in the economic and social development of the province. Supervision of the exploitation of the mines and quarries of the eastern desert was particularly important, as was the construction and guarding of the roads which brought goods from the ports of the Red Sea coast to Coptos; a well-known inscription of the reign of Tiberius records the activities of a working party from the Egyptian legions, cohorts and *alae* which constructed watering-stations (*hydreumata*) in the eastern desert and a camp at Coptos; ostraca of a later period provide more vivid personal evidence for the duties of individual soldiers in detachments assigned to such posts.[45] Greater general participation in the civilian life of the province is attested by first-century papyri which show that soldiers provided virtually the only form of effective policing, did duty in a jail, supplied guards for river-transport, supervisors for the mint, were assigned to the manufacture of papyrus or to the supervision of weights in a market.[46] All of this presupposes a high degree of integration in the life of the province and such links between civilians and the military will have been strengthened by the increase in local recruitment, the tendency for sons to follow fathers into service and the generally greater visibility and importance of veterans, highlighted in an incident of the Neronian period when veterans of legions, auxiliary cohorts and *alae* and the fleet petitioned the prefect about the fact that their privileged status was being ignored.[47] By contrast, illustration of

[42] Turner, *JRS* 40 (1950) 57–9.   [43] Joseph. *BJ* 11.487–93.   [44] *CPJ* 439.

[45] *ILS* 2483; *OFlorida, OWadiFawakhir* (= *CPL* 303–9, *SB* 9017).   [46] *RMR* 10, 51.

[47] *FIRA* III 171.

the price which the provincials paid for all this comes in the form of evidence for the burdens of billeting and requisitions which the military presence imposed on the civil population. Alleviation of these burdens was a preoccupation of Germanicus during his visit of A.D. 19 and an edict of the Claudian prefect Vergilius Capito inveighs against fraudulent requisitions and orders local officials to send accounts of such expenditures to an imperial freedman.[48]

2. Finance and taxation

Fundamental to an appraisal of the financial administration in Egypt is the nature of the monetary system and the organization of taxation. Whilst the Romans inherited from their Ptolemaic predecessors a province which was already extensively monetized and exploited through a wide variety of taxes and rents in cash and kind, fundamental changes were made under Augustus and the Julio-Claudians which determined the basic shape of the financial administration for the next three centuries.

For half a century after Actium the Alexandrian mint produced only bronze coinage, the notional value of the old tetradrachma being artificially supplemented to equate it to the new universal denarius standard. Minting of the silver tetradrachma was re-established by Tiberius in A.D. 19/20, though with a smaller percentage of silver than its Ptolemaic predecessor, and it remained the basic unit until A.D. 296 when the Alexandrian mint ceased to operate in isolation from the rest of the empire. The fixed equivalence of the tetradrachma to the denarius seems to have been established in the Julio-Claudian period, probably in the reign of Claudius, but the fact that it was more overvalued than the denarius had two important effects; first that the imperial government profited directly from this overvaluation and second that the Egyptian currency became 'closed', *de facto* if not *de iure*, because the purchasing power of the tetradrachma outside Egypt was bound to be weaker than that of the denarius. This isolation did not mean that Egypt was immune from the economic effects of a deteriorating currency but there was stability for over a century after the Neronian reform (see p. 252) and the ill-effects do not begin to be evident until the later part of the second century. There is now no reason to accept the once widely held view that coinage did not circulate extensively in the villages as well as the towns of the delta and the valley or that the government lacked any appreciation of the need to maintain and regulate the volume of currency available. It is, however, impossible to document either of these

[48] EJ² 320; H. Evelyn White, J.H. Oliver, *The Temple of Hibis in El-Khargeh Oasis* II (New York, 1938) 1–19.

phenomena in detail nor can we reconstruct the processes whereby the credits earned from overseas trade were internalized and contributed to payments of tribute made to Rome. There is some later evidence which implies that such operations were managed by Alexandrian financiers working under government contract.[49]

The extraordinary amount of evidence which the papyri provide for the details of the taxation system, in particular, means that Egypt is by far the best known of all provinces in this respect, even though there are many important features about which we are uninformed. The tribute which the Roman government drew from Egypt was extracted in the form of land-tax (*tributum soli*) and a wide variety of personal taxes (*tributum capitis*), as well as *ad valorem* impositions. Some of this tribute will have left the province in the form of cash and of the *annona* which fed the city of Rome, a great deal will have remained in the province to pay troops and other government costs (e.g. salaries for officials). The tax burden was divided among the nome-capitals and the villages in their nomes but, beneath this level, there must have been a complex series of mechanisms according to which the communities determined how they apportioned their liability among individuals and collected the revenues. One radical change brought by the Romans was the provincial census, established in the reign of Augustus; the earliest certain incidence is that of A.D. 19/20 but it seems very unlikely that this was the first.[50] The fourteen-year census cycle, with intermittent updating, required the submission of house-by-house returns (*kat' oikian apographai*) by individual heads of households and these provided the basis for determining liability to capitation taxes and to taxes on domestic property. Taxes paid on land were determined according to the records of the annually revised land survey. A second important feature is the system of direct collection of taxes. Local people were appointed to compulsory service as collectors (*praktores* or *sitologoi*), for example, and supervised by officials. Tax-farming on a large scale had probably never been common in Egypt (at least for land taxes), so it is unlikely that there was any significant change in this respect. But there is nevertheless considerable evidence throughout the period for the farming, occasionally under duress, of a variety of cash taxes in particular towns or small areas.

The great variety of taxes attested in the papyri can only be indicated in a summary form. Much of the revenue from the land was raised in grain, levied as tax on private property and as rent on imperially owned and public land; vineyards and garden-land were subject to cash assessments. A straight poll-tax was the basic personal imposition, imposed at different rates according to status and even varying from

[49] *PBad* 37.   [50] *POxy* 254, cf. *PMich* 578, Montevecchi 1988 (E 952) 177–8.

place to place and exempting Roman citizens, Alexandrians and women altogether. There were numerous small impositions (*merismoi*) – trade taxes, bath-tax, dyke-tax, for example – sometimes supplemented to compensate for defaulters; taxes on domestic property, on animals, charges on sales and transfers of property, on specified products (salt and oil); taxes paid by Roman citizens (manumission, inheritance); customs dues and tolls; requisitions for military purposes; taxes on temples. Finally, the great burden of compulsory public services imposed on all strata of the populace was also a form of taxation.

These general characteristics of the taxation system apply to the province as a whole but there is great variation in detail from place to place. Local and temporal variations in rates and methods of collection are bewildering but clearly attested. This makes it impossible to assess how great the burden of taxation was for individuals beyond the simple observation that the basic rates of tax on privately owned land during the Principate seem to have been quite low (little more than perhaps 10 per cent of yield). Assessments could, of course, be varied from year to year to take account of the level of the flood and consequent fertility or peculiar local conditions. Difficulties in collection are often apparent. During the reigns of Claudius and Nero substantial numbers of tax-payers from Philadelphia in the Fayum fled from their obligations. The edict of Tiberius Iulius Alexander of A.D. 68 presents a vivid picture of widespread abuses in the tax-system; impressment of people into tax-collection, the imposition of new and unauthorized levies and so on. Some have seen the edict as an attempt to cope with a general economic crisis in Egypt in the Neronian period but the evidence for universal difficulties is very slender. Abuses and complaints of the kind described in Alexander's edict are by no means confined to this era. The difficulties in tax-collection attested at Philadelphia are likely to be chronic and the situation was perhaps exacerbated during the forties by low fertility as a result of a run of unusual levels of inundation.[51]

3. Justice

The judicial competence of the prefect within the province was supreme, subject to the possibility of appeal to the emperor. The exercise of personal jurisdiction by the prefect was carried out by the introduction of an assize-circuit (*conventus*) organized in three districts of which the centres were Alexandria (western delta), Pelusium (eastern delta) and Memphis (Middle and Upper Egypt). A certain amount of choice and flexibility existed, however, and judicial sessions are known to have been

[51] Chalon 1964 (E 909), cf. *SB* 8900; Hanson 1988 (E 932)

held in other towns in the districts such as Arsinoe or Coptos and, after
A.D. 130, Antinoopolis.[52] In these sessions the prefect would deal with
cases, applications and petitions presented to him, assisted by his
advisers (*consiliarii*) who might include the *iuridicus*, the head of the *Idios
Logos*, military officers, local officials and lawyers (*nomikoi*) who were
familiar with the Egyptian institutions and laws.[53] One clear indication
that the use of the term 'jurisdiction' can be misleadingly restrictive is the
fact that the proper and full title by which this exercise was known was
dialogismos kai dikaiodosia (review of accounts and dispensation of
justice).[54] It is doubtful whether the prefect of Egypt was ever constrained or guided by the institution of a provincial edict (*edictum
provinciale*) and, certainly in the area of criminal cases which fell under
Roman law, he was able, as a second-century papyrus shows, to decide
what specific categories of cases he would handle personally.[55] Thus
described, the outlines of the superstructure are consonant with the way
in which we should expect a provincial governor to exercise his judicial
powers. It is, however, much more difficult definitively to identify and
describe the major features of the system at the lower levels because it
involves an analysis of the relationship between the 'Roman' officials
(down to and including the *epistrategos*) and the local (from the *strategos*
downwards) and their areas of competence and power and of that
between Roman criminal and private law strictly defined, on the one
hand, and Egyptian laws and institutions on the other.

The exercise of 'judicial' functions by officials lower down the
hierarchy is commonly described by modern scholars in terms of
'delegation' by the prefect. Thus, particular matters might be dealt with
by a procurator, an *epistrategos*, a *strategos* or even a centurion according
to, perhaps even sometimes outside, their particular area of administrative function. Or the prefect could appoint judges (*iudices*) to handle
particular cases. And, in principle, any matter might be thrown back into
the prefect's court if the issue at stake, the incompetence of a lower
official or the status of the persons involved necessitated it. Officials at
the nome or local level would necessarily handle matters within their
administrative role which might involve decisions which had to have
legal validity. Thus a prefect can state that his personal appearance in the
Thebaid is unnecessary because the local *strategoi* have dealt with the
business;[56] an *archidikastes* (chief judge), in charge of the operation of
civic courts in Alexandria, handles matters pertaining to the status or
ownership of land of Alexandrian citizens and, when these necessitate

[52] *PRyl* 74; *POxyHels* 19; *SB* 4416.27; *PRyl* 434.   [53] *FIRA* III 171; *POxy* 2757, 3015.
[54] *SB* 4416.28–9, cf. Philo, *In Flacc.* 133.
[55] N. Lewis, 'Un nouveau texte sur la juridiction du préfet d'Egypte', in *RHDFE* 1972, 5–12, cf.
ibid. 1973, 5–7.   [56] *PRyl* 74.

further investigation in the *chora*, he is able to require it from local officials.[57] It is perhaps better, however, not to represent this as a hierarchy of 'delegated jurisdiction', the competence of officials at each level of the hierarchy being strictly inferior to that of the level above. Rather there is a range of officials and institutions applying administrative and necessarily often legal decisions in accordance with the rules and laws appropriate to the matter in hand and the status of the persons involved; but it was in principle always possible for the persons involved to seek satisfaction from a higher authority. This is surely how the so-called 'judicial' functions of the *strategos*, the validity of Egyptian laws (*nomoi*), the independent local courts of the Greek cities, the legal privileges of the Jewish *politeuma* are to be explained and the explanation rests firmly on the notion that it is fundamentally misleading to draw a sharp dividing line between 'administration' and 'jurisdiction'.

There remains the difficult issue of the precise status of this heterogeneous mass of institutions *vis-à-vis* the Roman law. Here no certainty is possible, especially for the early period of Roman rule. But it seems likely that, in practice, Roman law will have been applied as a natural and appropriate privilege to those of the highest status in the province; others further down the social order might benefit according to the choice of those officials applying it. The continued existence and validity of peregrine laws and institutions is natural and convenient; Roman law and legal institutions are superimposed and become more pervasive as time goes on. These would not necessarily displace or invalidate local laws automatically; the latter would retain their applicability as 'the laws of the Egyptians' unless removed or modified for some specific reason and the notion that their status was merely that of 'customs' rather than 'law', *stricto sensu*, seems to be based on a rather austere view of what, in practice, constituted law.[58] The practical proposition is thus that we are dealing with a continuum of institutions, whose legal or judicial operations correspond roughly to the administrative pattern in the country and the range of social status and legal privilege in the various groups of the population.

III. ECONOMY AND SOCIETY

An attempt at a brief description of Egyptian economic and social institutions and practices under the early Roman Empire has to proceed from a somewhat conjectural base. The population of the province may have reached 7.5 million by the Flavian period, with Alexandria accounting for perhaps another half a million, though it has recently

---

[57] *BGU* 136; *PMilVogl* 229.
[58] For differing views see Brunt 1975 (E 906) 132–6 and Modrzejewski 1970 (E 951) esp. 331–4.

been argued that this estimate is far too high.[59] The ability of the agricultural base to feed this population can only be reckoned by approximation. Thus, *if* a figure of 9 million *arourai* (*c.* 2.5 million hectares) under cultivation is plausible; *if* the fertility of the land ensured an average ten-fold yield; *if* the subsistence requirement of the population in wheat equivalent were about 60 million artabs, that is about 3.3 billion litres (disregard of peripheral sources of food and other revenue-generating activities compensates for the fact that all land did not produce food of as high calorific value as wheat), the surplus would still be considerable.[60] It will be correspondingly greater if our estimate of the population is lower or if we regard as an overestimate the statement of a fourth-century source which suggests that Egypt shipped 20 million *modii* of grain a year to Rome – surely enough to pay for government expenditure in the province even without any guess at the volume of cash revenue raised from other economic activities.[61] However we may rationalize or dismiss these estimates, the fact is that Egypt was indisputably a very wealthy province.

Management of the agricultural base was the foundation of this wealth. A very significant feature of the Roman period is the great increase in private ownership of land, perhaps as much as 50 per cent in some areas, though proportions clearly varied greatly.[62] Private land, directly managed or farmed through lease and tenancy, stood cheek by jowl with public land, rented to public tenants (*demosioi georgoi*) and with imperial land farmed by tenants or sometimes let in larger parcels to chief lessees(*misthotai*); an individual farmer might cultivate land in more than one of these categories and the unit of cultivation was probably in general small rather than large: even the holdings of wealthy landowners often tended to be fragmented.[63] A holding of 5 or 6 *arourai* of land might be a reasonable estimate of what an average family would need for bare subsistence.[64]

Productivity depended on the annual inundation and management of the irrigation system was therefore crucial. Private owners shouldered the responsibility for this on their own land, whilst the public dykes and canals were maintained by the introduction of the regular dyke-corvée as a compulsory service for the peasantry. As well as the staple cereals, a great variety of fodder crops, legumes, vines, olives and other garden produce was grown. Much labour came in the form of tenants and their

---

[59] Joseph. *BJ* II.385–6; Diod. XVII.52.6; for a higher estimate of the Alexandrian population see Fraser 1972 (E 921) 90–1. Rathbone 1990 (E 961).   [60] Bowman 1990 (E 901) App. II.

[61] [Aur. Vict.] *Epit. de Caes.* 1.6, cf. Garnsey *et al.* 1983 (D 130) 119, Rathbone 1990 (E 961).

[62] *WChr* 341 (63 per cent private land at Naboo in Apollonopolis Heptakomias in the early second century); *PBouriant* 42 (29 per cent private land at Hiera Nesos in the Fayum in 167).

[63] *POxy* 2873 (Seneca); *POxy* 3047 (Calpurnia Heraclia).

[64] Bowman 1990 (E 901) App. II.

families but there is substantial evidence for wage-labour, some of which was surely provided by these same tenants; only a small proportion of the required labour was supplied by the limited number of slaves employed on the land.[65] This suggests a picture which is rather different from the traditional notion of a peasant society supporting itself by subsistence farming and the evidence of the papyri makes it clear that even modest landholders, who might produce little or no overall surplus in a year would have to trade off surpluses in some crops or commodities to make good deficits in others. Exchange of goods and agricultural produce was thus universal and warns us against an oversimplified economic model which relegates trade and commerce to a purely 'secondary' role in comparison with 'primary' agricultural activity. Transportation and commercial services were essential to move goods from village to town, or village to village and the widespread use of coin, even in villages, suggests that barter was by no means a dominant feature in economic transactions.[66]

In fact, in Egypt the relationship between town and countryside was very close indeed and any distinction between the agricultural economy on the one hand and trade, industry and commerce on the other is likely to be very misleading. The ubiquitous taxes on trades and the variety of goods and services available not only in the metropoleis but also in the larger villages of the Fayum like Tebtunis, Karanis and Philadelphia attest to a great range of small-scale activity in trade and manufacture with the concomitant existence of transport, banking and commercial services. These facilitated both the movement of goods to market centres accessible to the people who earned their livelihood from the land, and the payment and delivery of taxes. At the same time, however, there are manufacturing enterprises like linen-weaving and pottery-making which are much more intimately linked to the agricultural economy and these are often found in villages or even on sizeable individual estates. It is worth emphasizing that an agricultural economy of the kind described could not have existed at all without these services. The evidence from the Roman period may be misleading but it does suggest an increase in this kind of economic activity, as also in trade over greater distances, especially in the luxury items of the eastern trade which entered Egypt via the ports of the Red Sea coast to be routed thence across the desert to Coptos and downriver to Alexandria.[67] With the relaxation of the rigid state control imposed by the Ptolemaic monarchs

[65] PLond 131 verso (Johnson 1936 (E 940) no. 105) (A.D. 78/79).
[66] PMichTeb 121–8, 237–42 (reign of Claudius).
[67] Illustrated generally by the Periplous maris Erythraei (ed. W.H. Schoff, New York, 1912 and L. Casson, Baltimore, 1988); Pliny, HN VI.101 attests 50 million sesterces-worth of annual trade with India and Arabia; for exhaustive documentation see Raschke 1978 (C 298), Sidebotham 1986 (C 310).

in the form of so-called monopolies, there was certainly greater scope for private enterprise.

By contrast, it might plausibly be maintained that there was a greater degree of social control in the Roman period. The tendency to classify the population according to status, privilege and obligation becomes much more clearly marked, as the *Gnomon of the Idios Logos* shows.[68] In one important respect this was essential to the structure of government because it was intimately bound up with the spread of Roman law and the introduction of institutions like the provincial census, the metropolitan magistracies and the liturgical system. Whilst most of the Greco-Egyptian populace were designated simply as *Aigyptioi* (though not necessarily prevented from improving their status), the higher status of metropolites was reflected, for instance, in lower rates of poll-tax. Within the metropolis, the Romans created a higher order, the gymnasial class which was part of the development which saw the gymnasia become public instead of private institutions, and the creation of magisterial *archai*. This order was based on the drawing up of a list of such privileged metropolites in A.D. 4/5, henceforth to be perpetuated by admission procedures (*epikrisis*) which required prospective entrants to document their pedigree (though the degree of intermarriage between Greeks and Egyptians in the Ptolemaic period must have ensured that the 'purity' of this Greek class was to a considerable extent notional).

All the citizens of the 'Greek cities' enjoyed such status because of the very nature of their communities. Other Egyptians could obtain citizenship of Alexandria, which possessed an additional unique feature in being, for *Aigyptioi*, a necessary prerequisite to Roman citizenship (except for veteran soldiers); this presumably served to ensure a sufficient degree of 'hellenization'.[69] Thus there must have existed the possibility of qualification by residence and status and there is evidence, lower down the social scale, for a good deal of population movement between villages and towns which shows that people were by no means immutably tied to their *origo*. Nevertheless, the number of people who attained Roman citizenship was presumably quite small in the early period and perhaps predominantly composed of veteran soldiers, at least in the *chora* where their high status and relative wealth must have made them, as in many other provinces, an important element in the scenario of town and village life.

There were, of course, other status categories apart from these. The groups of Jews in the towns of the *chora* enjoyed religious privileges and

[68] *BGU* 1210.

[69] Pliny, *Ep.* x.6; on the difficult questions of Alexandrian status see Sherwin-White, *ad. loc.*, el-Abbadi 1962 (E 888) (not commanding universal agreement), Fraser 1972 (E 921) 91, 796.

the large and important Jewish community of Alexandria was organized in a separate *politeuma* with quasi-public institutions. There were freedmen, some indigenous, others perhaps immigrants who settled in Egypt after employment in the emperor's service, and attainment of the status of Roman freedman (not available to freed slaves of Greco-Egyptians) will have placed a person high in the social order. The slave class, from which they rose, was never very large in Egypt and in this respect there appears to have been little change by comparison with the Ptolemaic period. For what it is worth the evidence suggests that their presence was more marked in the domestic context than the agricultural. Women constituted the other main underprivileged sector of the population. The privileges which were extended to them in Roman law will have applied to only a few at first and they are not radically different from what may be observed elsewhere. One significant factor, which is both local and pre-Roman, is the effect of Egyptian or Greco-Egyptian inheritance practices which concentrated more property in the hands of women than elsewhere (perhaps about 30 per cent) but the effects of this should not be overestimated; women perhaps more commonly inherited domestic goods and movables if they had brothers and their participation in economic transactions in general has been seen as an indicator of economic hardship in the family or community.[70] More significant, perhaps, in this context is the closeness of family structure and the phenomenon of consanguineous marriage, a practice whose importance in preserving the integrity of family property must have outweighed any natural revulsion against it.

The Roman presence made relatively little impact on the cultural and religious patterns in the *chora*. Use of Latin is apparent in military documents and spread on a minor scale amongst veterans. Some legal documents required Latin, there are a few private letters and even the odd literary text.[71] But the major feature continues to be the interaction between native Egyptian and Greek cultural patterns. Literacy in Greek was perhaps quite widely pervasive (even though it will never have been possessed by more than a small percentage of the population as a whole), and Greek literary texts dominate the papyrological legacy with relatively little evidence of direct influence in either direction. But the use of hieroglyphic and demotic is still noticeable in the early period. The interaction between demotic and Greek can be seen in Greek translations of demotic literature made in the Roman period and the bilingual

[70] See Hobson 1983 (E 934), 1984 (E 935).

[71] *PMich* 467–72; *POxy* 3208; *PRyl* 608 with Rea, *CE* 43 (1968) 373–4; *FIRA* III 8; for a corpus of Latin non-literary papyri see *CPL*; for literary texts see Pack 1965 (E 955), 2917–52 and the useful citations in Anderson, Parsons and Nisbet 1979 (B 4) n. 43.

business texts, though now less numerous than in the Ptolemaic period, show that there was an important area of overlap within which both language groups could function.[72]

As for religion, the major distinction had always been that between Greek and Egyptian cult and this the Romans preserved. The native temples submitted to more stringent state control, losing economic power, but the innumerable Egyptian cults and the traditional caste-like character of the priestly and other temple offices survived well into the Christian period.[73] The Greek cults which proliferated under the Ptolemies also remained strong, especially in the villages of the Fayum, but they were, as is characteristic, much more closely linked to civic institutions than the Egyptian, their priests more analogous to local magistrates and drawn from the upper strata of the Greco-Egyptian populace. The difference is strikingly illustrated by the fact that civil administrators might participate in libations in a gymnasium or a *Caesareum*, or make sacrifices to the Greco-Egyptian river-god Neilos but could only be passive spectators at Egyptian rites or processions.[74]

Roman cults and temples of Roman divinities, notably Jupiter Capitolinus, did eventually make some perceptible mark, but hardly at all before the third century; a veteran soldier is even found celebrating the Saturnalia in about A.D. 100,[75] but these novelties surely did little to disrupt existing patterns. Some adaptation was required in a more general way. The Roman prefect would make sacrifices to the Nile, as the Pharaohs had done, and avoid sailing on the river when it was rising. The emperor had to be accommodated, as Pharaoh, in the traditional institutions, whether on a temple relief or a stela recording the installation of a sacred bull (and the emperor Titus (A.D. 79–81), indeed, did attend such a ceremony in person).[76] Above all, there was cult of the Roman emperor, visible at Alexandria in the great *Caesareum* (begun by Cleopatra for Antony) and the existence of a group of freedmen *Caesariani*, and in the acclamation of Germanicus or Vespasian as a god (the latter as son of Amon and Sarapis incarnate).[77] *Caesarea* were established in the towns of the delta and valley too, the emperor became a god and his name a natural element in the swearing of an oath. Outside those institutions which were specific to imperial cult, it is a matter of intrusion and supervenience as local Greek and (to a much lesser extent) Egyptian cults accommodated to the new order.

---

[72] E.g. *PLugd-bat* 19. 26–8; *OLeidDem*, *passim*; *ORom* 8 (cf. n. to line 7), 16, 25, 46–7; West, *JEA* 55 (1969) 161–83.

[73] Chaeremon, fr. 10 (ed. P.W. Van der Horst, *EPRO* 101, Leiden, 1984); *BGU* 1210, sections 71–96.   [74] *WChr* 41; *POxy* 1211.

[75] *BGU* 362; *PMilVogl* 233; *SB* 4282; *ChLA* 10, 11; *PFay* 119.

[76] Sen. *QNat.* 4a.2.7; Pliny, *HN* v.57; Suet. *Tit.* 5.3.   [77] *WChr* 112; *CPJ* 418a.

IV. ALEXANDRIA

The fact that official terminology marked out the great city of Alexandria as separate from the Egyptian *chora* indicates the justification for giving it special attention. The city certainly reached its apogee in the Roman period. Strabo, who visited it early in the reign of Augustus in the company of the prefect Aelius Gallus, pays resounding tribute to its physical splendours, makes special mention of the suburb of Nicopolis, added under the Romans, and notes the volume of waterborne trade, particularly that carried upriver to the towns of the delta and the valley. The *Alexandrian Oration* of Dio of Prusa, delivered early in the Flavian period, emphasizes its economic importance and pays less than flattering attention to the vibrancy of public entertainment and the volatility of the mob.[78] Since Alexandria remained the administrative capital under the Romans, that volatility could have an important impact. The prefect Petronius was almost stoned to death by the mob; Germanicus accepted extravagant acclamations in A.D. 19 but was concerned to control public demonstrations of his divinity; the Tiberian prefect Galerius took his wife to Egypt with him but she never set foot outside the official residence or admitted a provincial into it.[79] After Augustus, who alleged that after Actium he had only spared the city as a favour to his Alexandrian friend Areius, emperors (or pretenders) were liable to take some trouble to appear beneficent and conciliatory.[80]

The main motives for this were doubtless political but emperors cannot have been unaware of Alexandria's immense economic importance throughout the early imperial period. Its role in the shipment of Rome's corn supply was only one aspect of this. Its central importance for the papyrus industry, the manufacture of glassware, mosaics and works of art and the transport of grain is badly documented but cannot be doubted and emphasizes its contribution to the profitable exploitation of indigenous resources. Goods of Alexandrian manufacture found their way to all parts of the Roman world as well as to areas beyond the southern frontier of Egypt. The perfume and jewellery industries and the spice trade point to its significance as the main entrepôt of the Mediterranean littoral for the great volume of luxury goods imported from the East.

The cultural climate was to change somewhat by comparison with the Ptolemaic period for the days of open-handed royal patronage had long gone. But the Museum remained important, albeit swelled by an admixture of members distinguished for administrative rather than

---

[78] Strab. XVII.1.8–10 (793–5C); Dio Chrys. XXXII.36, 55, 59, 62.
[79] Strab. XVII.1.53 (819C); *POxy* 2435.1–28; EJ² 320; Sen. *Dial.* XII.19.6.
[80] Plut. *Ant.* 80; *POxy* 3022; *SB* 10295.

intellectual pursuits. The Royal Library and the 'daughter' library in the Serapeum survived too, the losses of books incurred in the Alexandrian War partly compensated by Antony's gift to Cleopatra of the collection of the royal library of Pergamum. In the Roman period the practitioners of literature were not to attain the same eminence as their predecessors of the Ptolemaic era. The literary pursuits were to yield pride of place to the philosophical for Alexandrian philosophy was greatly enriched by the influx of immigrants after the sack of Athens by Sulla. In the Julio-Claudian period the most distinguished philosopher was Philo, member of a prominent Jewish family and uncle of Tiberius Iulius Alexander; his works, along with those of the other Middle Platonists, point forward to the second century when the foundations of Christian theology and philosophy were to be laid in the interaction of Christian doctrine with the Platonic tradition, with gnosticism and with the legacy of Jewish thought.

At the same time, Alexandria retained her established pre-eminence in the traditional areas of scientific endeavour, among which the development and practice of medicine stands out. In the second century Galen of Pergamum studied there and Alexandria's reputation in this field was still paramount in Ammianus Marcellinus' day. The same is true of the applied scientific disciplines, particularly engineering. In the middle of the second century, the dominant figure was Claudius Ptolemaeus, whose writings reveal an astonishing range of expertise – in mathematics, astronomy, music, optics, geography and cartography. His *Almagest*, the most comprehensive ancient astronomical work, is heavily influenced by Aristotelian doctrines and attempts to account for the movements of the moon and planets within the concept of geocentric system. In his treatise on optics he describes extensive experimentation with the phenomena of reflection and refraction of light. In his geographical work he amassed a mine of invaluable physical and topographical information, as well as discussing the principles of cartography and projection.

In the early imperial period, however, the peaceful arts were overshadowed by uglier events. At the root of the disturbances were the issues arising from the state of Alexandria's civic institutions, the privileges and aspirations of the large and important Jewish community and the relations between the Greeks and the Jews. Alexandria had almost certainly possessed a council (*boule*) under the early Ptolemies; when this privilege was removed is a matter of dispute (the reign of Ptolemy VIII Euergetes Physcon and the Augustan period are the most likely candidates), but it was presumably intended to neutralize the political power of the citizen body. Certainly it did not have a *boule* in the early imperial period and the 'Boule Papyrus', probably to be dated to the reign of Augustus, shows Alexandrian ambassadors petitioning for its reinstatement on the grounds that it would safeguard imperial revenues and enable the local magistrates to ensure the purity of the Alexandrian citizen body by protecting it against infiltration by 'the uncultured and uneducated', probably a veiled reference to the Jews, or that part of the Jewish community which showed overt tendencies to hellenize. A reiterated request to Claudius, which provoked the famous 'Letter to the Alexandrians' shows that Augustus had not yielded; neither did Claudius and Alexandria was not to recover its *boule* until the reign of Septimius Severus when the privilege was considerably diluted by the fact that the metropoleis of the nomes received *boulai* as well.[81]

In the mean time, there had been serious trouble between Jews and Greeks in the late 30s and early 40s, vividly described, no doubt with some partiality, by Philo. The Greeks were organized in guilds and cult associations; attempts were made to put statues of the emperor in synagogues, Jewish houses were overrun and looted, victims were dragged out and burned, torn limb from limb in the market-place or scourged and executed in the theatre. Rival delegations went to Rome to plead their respective cases. Philo, who was himself a member of the Jewish embassy describes how his party pursued the deranged emperor Gaius from Rome to the Bay of Naples and waited for a hearing whilst the emperor enjoyed himself in his seaside villas.[82] Reports of the opposing case take a much stranger form than the *Legatio ad Gaium* – the so-called *Acts of the Alexandrian Martyrs*, semi-fictional accounts, based, in form at least, on genuine documentary reports of ambassadorial proceedings, which purport to give verbatim reports of the audience of the Alexandrian Greek notables before the emperor and their revilement of the Alexandrian Jews. There is certainly a factual foundation in these martyr-acts, as the names of the dramatis personae show, but it is perhaps of equal significance that the historical contexts in which they are set run down to the reign of Commodus and that in the later examples the anti-Jewish element is absent or subordinate to the expression of anti-Roman feeling. This, together with the fact that all the copies of such acts which have survived were written in the late second or early third centuries A.D., probably tells us more about Alexandrian nationalistic attitudes at that time than about the historical events.[83] But we cannot doubt that the unrest of the Jewish community was a significant factor, still felt a quarter of a century after Claudius' letter when they rebelled in sympathy with the outbreak of revolt in Judaea and even more so fifty years later in the great revolt of A.D. 116–17 which saw the virtual annihilation of the Jews in Alexandria and the *chora*.[84]

[81] *CPJ* 150, 153, cf. ch. 14*d*.   [82] Philo, *Leg.* 120–31, 184–5.
[83] Musurillo 1954 (B 381).   [84] Barnes 1989 (E 1087).

V. CONCLUSION

The Roman annexation of Egypt in 30 B.C. was an event of the greatest historical significance, marking as it did, the conclusion of the struggle for supremacy between Octavian and Antony and the elimination of the last of the powerful hellenistic kingdoms. Egypt's role as a province in Rome's empire was of immediate importance, largely because of the enormous wealth which it generated. This, together with the fact that it is uniquely well documented, has induced modern scholars to go too far in according it a special status and, in doing so, they have tended to emphasize the perseverance of the peculiar administrative and economic features of Ptolemaic Egypt, allowed by the characteristic *laissez-faire* attitude of the Roman government.

In fact, the opportunity to examine in some detail the process of creation of a Roman province provides a corrective to this view. The terminology of the Ptolemaic period survives in many areas, but there are fundamental changes of such importance that it is seriously misleading to posit a vague and general continuity from Ptolemaic to Roman Egypt. The institutions and structures of central and local government were radically altered. The creation of a 'Greek' magisterial class in the nome-capitals introduced a type of local civic government previously unknown. With it came the introduction of a new and wide-ranging liturgical system. These features, in turn, rest upon the creation of a wholly different kind of propertied class from that of the Ptolemaic period, one which is based largely on the Roman introduction of genuine and widespread private ownership of land (*ge idiotike*). With that we may link fundamental changes in the taxation system, to which the introduction of the Roman census was a necessary adjunct. The combined importance of census, property and social status will inevitably focus attention on that feature of Romanization which encapsulates all aspects of the Roman social and economic system, the spread of Roman law.

These changes can all clearly be traced to the Augustan period. Emphasis on their importance need not blind us to the continuities – in the character of the agricultural economy, in religion, in Egyptian culture. A balanced account will give due emphasis both to the continuities and the changes. During the Augustan era the role of Egypt in the empire for the next three centuries was determined. That role was again to change radically only with the coming of Christianity and in response to the very different political and economic conditions of the late third century.

CHAPTER 14*c*

SYRIA

DAVID KENNEDY

I. INTRODUCTION

1. Prologue

Pompey's annexation in 64 B.C. of what remained of Seleucid Syria after the fratricidal struggles of the preceding century, introduced into the Semitic Near East a Roman rule which was to endure for seven centuries. Moreover, as a development and extension of a long period of hellenistic rule, it represented the greater part of almost a millennium of Greco-Roman political dominance and cultural influence. Throughout this long period, however, underlying the Greco-Roman veneer, local indigenous language and culture retained their vitality, to be released in the seventh century by the renewed political dominance of a Semitic people. The point is neatly illustrated by the re-appearance under Islam of many place-names, for centuries overlain by official Greek or Roman ones, but which had apparently remained in oral use amongst the native population.[1]

Yet Roman rule did make an impact in many ways which helped determine the distinctive character of this part of the Near East for several centuries. The creation of conditions of peace and political stability, the unification of the region, the reconciliation of its population to Roman rule and the subsequent participation and influence of many Syrians – most strikingly the Emesene ruling family (below, p. 731) – in and on the developing government and civilization of the Roman Empire, are all the work of the first three centuries.

The history of Syria in the two and half centuries after Pompey's settlement is dominated by three major themes. First, the establishment and development of a Roman province, and the influence and conse-quences of its role as the major military province of the East. Second, the character and role of the client states, their evolution, then disappear-ance. And third, the gradual emergence and flowering under the influence of the *pax romana* of a prosperous, more unified culture,

[1] Beroea, once Harabu is again Halab; Epiphania, once Hamath is now Hama; and Philadelphia, once Rabbatamana is again Amman: cf. Jones 1971 (D 96) 231. Cf. Joseph. *AJ* 1.121, 138.

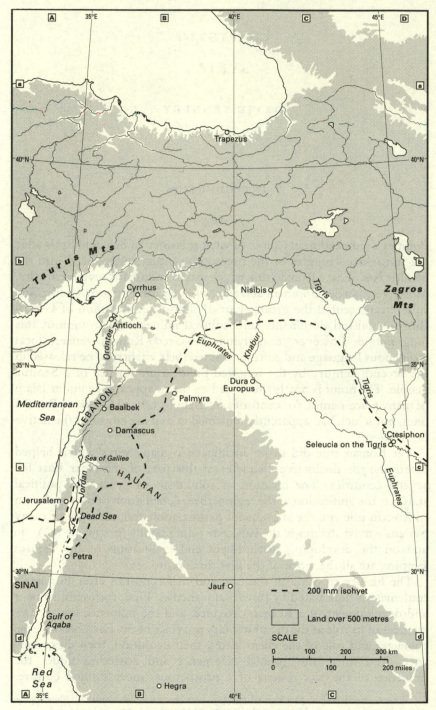

Map 18. Physical geography of the Near East.

essentially Semitic in character but with a Greco-Roman influence clear to some extent in each of its many facets.

None of this, however, occurred in a vacuum. Geography and previous historical development all played a part. Moreover, what may be said about any one of them is not just a matter of its relative importance in the Julio-Claudian or Flavian-Antonine period, but is constrained by the nature and distribution of the evidence.[2]

2. Physical and human geography

The geographical unit known in antiquity as Syria, was bounded on two sides by the Mediterranean and the Taurus Mountains; in the south and east there lay the Sinai and North Arabian and Syrian Deserts into whose fringes it merged; and finally, in the north east, though often limited politically by the bend of the Euphrates, north-western Mesopotamia as far as the river Khabur should be included. It is an immense area of some half million square kilometres (Map 18).

It is not possible to detect any fundamental changes in the appearance of the landscape or in the climate since Classical Antiquity. There have, however, been some notable alterations. Thus, deforestation – already far advanced in the pre-classical period – has been taken still further and erosion has destroyed once arable hill terraces; a wetter period in Late Antiquity washed soils away, creating in the lower reaches of water courses what is today called the Younger Fill, overlying ancient remains or making their current location hard to understand.[3]

---

[2] The foremost literary source for the period treated in this volume is Josephus (*Jewish War* and *Antiquities* (xiv onwards)), although his focus is primarily on Judaea and matters relating to Jewish communities in Syria. Tacitus and Cassius Dio have several long passages, though mainly concerned with military matters. Strabo (*Geog.* xvi (737–85c)) provides an important description of Syria and some commentary and the Elder Pliny has valuable – though at times anachronistic – information (*HN* v.13–22). Brief but useful references are also to be found in numerous other sources, most notably Appian, Caesar, Cicero, Malalas (see now the new English translation by Jeffreys *et al.* 1986 (B 92)), Nicolaus of Damascus, Philo, Plutarch (*Vitae*), Suetonius and Velleius Paterculus.

For *corpora* of Latin (several hundred) and Greek (several thousand) texts, the bedrock continues to be the relevant parts of *CIL* III and *IGRR* III. However, many of these as well as newer texts are to be found in the volumes of *IGLS* and *I Jord*. Many others are published in *AE*. Cf. the survey by van Rengen 1978 (B 268). Inscriptions in Semitic languages may be traced in the volumes of *CIS*; additionally, Palmyrene texts (some 1,000) are being collected in *Inventaire des Inscriptions de Palmyre*, and Nabataean (several thousand) and Safaitic (c. 15,000 published of an estimated 100,000) collections are also in progress.

For coins, Wruck 1931 (B 363) continues to be useful, as are the *Arabia, Syria, Palestine* and *Phoenicia* volumes of the *BMC*, to which may now be added volumes of *SNG*. Valuable recent corpora are those of Kindler 1983 (B 331), Meshorer 1975 (B 343), and Spijkerman 1978 (B 353).

Note also the publications of the American (*AAES*) and Princeton (*PAES*) expeditions to Syria and R.E. Brünnow and A. von Domaszewski, *Die Provincia Arabia* (Strassburg, 1904–9). The results of some major excavations are summarized and discussed in Ward-Perkins 1981 (F 615). Field surveys are of increasing importance, not least those of Saudi Arabia reported in the journal *Atlal*.

[3] Vita-Finzi 1969 (E 1068); Bintliff 1982 (E 989); Raikes 1985 (E. 1053).

The typical Mediterranean climate of the coastal belt – hot dry summers and mild wet winters, gives way to the harsher extremes of great heat and little rainfall in the deserts to the east and south. The land varies from the fertile plain of eastern Cilicia and the narrow coastal belt of the Levant, across the mountain ranges of the Amanus, Bargylus and Lebanon, which parallel the coast, to the broad belt of first pre-desert, then desert, which stretch beyond. In the west and north, rainfall, supplemented by snow-melt and rivers, is sufficient for dry farming. Some small rivers flow down from the coastal ranges but the major rivers of the region all rise beyond them. The Orontes flows through a broad fertile valley with major cities along its course, before passing through to the coast between Amanus and Bargylus; the Leontes, far less attractive to urban development, also eventually flowed west into the Mediterranean. The Jordan, however, runs south through the Sea of Galilee, dropping below sea level before flowing into the Dead Sea, the rift valley continuing as the broad waterless trough of the Wadi Araba then the Gulf of Aqaba.

The whole broadening curve of land from the Sinai north-eastwards to the mountains of Armenia, is desert, largely devoid of any perennial water source. The major exception is the valley of the Euphrates which, together with its tributaries on the north, the Balikh and Khabur, offered a ribbon of rich well-watered land on either bank. A major problem, however, was that after flowing south parallel with the coast opposite Antioch, the river turned first east then south east, away from the Mediterranean, to flow eventually into the Persian Gulf, leaving a huge unwatered expanse of land, on both sides, but principally that stretching off to the south. There, with the exception of Palmyra, the few springs could offer only modest settlement attractions.

There are rich agricultural lands in northern Syria, in the Hauran, in Galilee and in the land immediately east of the Jordan. Even the pre-desert and parts of the desert can be farmed, though there the principal determinant is the availability of water. In practice that means a reliable minimum annual 200mm of rainfall; when traced on the map, this isohyet helps to explain a great deal about the shape and development of the directly administered Roman province which emerged, and the location of client states.[4] The line, of course, has never been static and farming did not necessarily everywhere stop at it nor even reach it; land in this 'border' area has gone in and out of use with periodic climatic fluctuations, the level of political security and population pressures,

---

[4] Scholars are generally agreed that while there has been no significant change in climate since Classical Antiquity, there have probably been minor changes which could have disproportionately large impacts in marginal areas.

while, given suitable soil, rainfall could be and was 'harvested' in areas with far less than 200mm.[5]

Hill slopes, and poorly watered regions of steppe and desert provided attractive grazing for animals but these supported a less settled and thinner population. Settlement pattern was influenced too by the presence of natural resources other than soil and fresh water: thus the fisheries on the Mediterranean coast and Sea of Galilee, the timber of the Lebanon, and the salt and bitumen of the Dead Sea.[6] Trade too: Syria was sandwiched between the great centres of early civilization in Egypt and Anatolia-Mesopotamia; its own geography determined that the coast of the Levant, and routes across northern Mesopotamia, along the Euphrates, across the desert through such oases as Palmyra and Jauf, and up the eastern shore of the Red Sea, would all remain obvious lines of communication between Iran and the Mediterranean, Egypt and Anatolia.[7]

The population was overwhelmingly Semitic. Within this group, four major elements can be identified by the criteria of language and, in one case, religion. In the south west lay the Jews of Judaea and the semi-Judaized Arabs of Idumaea and Ituraea;[8] other Jewish communities, some extensive, were to be found in every city of Syria (below, p. 708 and 724). North of Judaea lay the Phoenicians, notably in the great coastal trading cities from Arados to Tyre. The Arabs were located on the eastern fringes of the province, the outcome of over two millennia of migration from the Arabian Peninsula into not just Syria but across Mesopotamia and as far as the Taurus and Zagros mountains. Between and to some extent intermingled with the others, lay the earlier Aramaic population. People of Greek stock were the major intrusive element – many by now of mixed blood – and largely to be found in the cities, especially those of North Syria.

Linguistically, Aramaic was dominant – the 'Syrian language', employed even in Judaea where Hebrew was used only for liturgical purposes. The peoples of Edessa, Palmyra and Arabia Petraea all had written versions of their spoken languages, Aramaic dialects which seem to have been a proto-Arabic. Likewise the Safaitic and Thamudic graffiti of the nomadic tribes of central and southern Syria are probably a primitive Arabic. As elsewhere in the East, Greek was common – though far from universal – amongst the urban populations.

[5] For more recent and better documented periods see Hütteroth and Abdulfattah 1977 (E 1013); Lewis 1987 (E 1034).

[6] Heichelheim 1938 (E 1012); cf. the handbooks of the Naval Intelligence Division, *Syria* (1943) and *Palestine and Transjordan* (1943).   [7] Teixidor 1984 (E 1066) 19–45.

[8] Both groups had probably become mixed with the pre-existing Aramaic population: Schürer 1973 (E 1207) I 562; Dussaud 1955 (E 1007); 163ff; in general, Millar 1987 (E 1039).

At no time do we know the size of the population. Locally we know that Apamea (and its territory) had 117,000 'citizens' (probably only males and females of tax-paying age) at the time of Aemilius Secundus' census in A.D. 6;[9] and Antioch, said by Strabo to be little smaller than Alexandria or Seleucia on the Tigris, probably had a population, in city and country, of several hundred thousand.[10] A rough guide to the size of some city populations may be drawn from Josephus' references to the size of their Jewish minorities, e.g. the 10,500 slaughtered in Damascus in A.D. 66.[11] Precise figures are given for the military contribution of various kings (cf. below, p. 730 and 732), e.g. 5,000 Commagenians sent to join Cestius Gallus in A.D. 66.[12] Likewise, we can estimate quite confidently the overall size of the Roman forces (40–50,000 in the Julio-Claudian period). From all of these one can roughly infer a probable population for Syria inclusive of the allied states in the first century A.D. of at least two or three million.[13]

II. ESTABLISHMENT AND DEVELOPMENT OF THE PROVINCE

1. Introduction

The terms of Pompey's settlement of the East had created a *provincia* of Syria the government of which embraced both a narrow territorial province and, in practice, supervision of the conduct of a number of allied rulers in the region (Map 19). The province was a modest part of geographical Syria: essentially those cities of the region to which a wide range of functions could be delegated under the Roman system of provincial administration. Thus, the 'Greek' cities of the Syrian Tetrapolis in the north[14] and of the Decapolis in the south,[15] and the city-states of the Phoenician coast.[16] Few were more than 100km from the coast. The allied rulers were widely spread, extending in an arc from the

---

[9] *ILS* 2683. The meaning of the term *homin. civium* is discussed by Cumont 1934 (E 996).

[10] Strab. XVI.2.5 (750C); the implications of various references to population at Antioch are discussed by Downey 1958 (E 1005).

[11] Joseph. *BJ* II.559–61; cf. 461–5 and 477–80 for the numbers massacred in other cities.

[12] Joseph. *BJ* II.500f. A crude estimate of population size may be drawn from the proportion of population in a pre-industrial society which could be supported as a professional army. The figure has been given as not more than 5 per cent, although the German Constitution of 1871 prescribed 1 per cent. For Commagene this would suggest a total population of between 100,000 and 500,000.

[13] Census figures for the French Mandated Territories of Syria and Lebanon in the 1930s gave a total of almost 4 million inclusive of nomads: Naval Intelligence Handbook, *Syria*, 191.

[14] Antioch, Apameia, Seleucia and Laodicea: Strab. XVI.2.4 (749C); cf. XVI.2.8–10 (752–3C).

[15] Canatha, Damascus, Dion, Gadara, Gerasa, Hippos, Pella, Philadelphia, Raphanaea and Scythopolis, are listed by the Elder Pliny (*HN* v.16); the additional names which seem to be provided by Ptolemy (*Georg.* v.15.22–3) should probably not be included: Schürer 1979 (E 1207) II 125–7.

[16] Principally Aradus, Tripolis, Byblus, Berytus, Sidon and Tyre: Strab. XVI.2.13–24 (754–8C).

Nabataean kingdom on the Red Sea to the Commagenian in the foothills of the central Taurus Mts. But because Rome failed to provide adequately for the security of eastern Anatolia, the Syrian governor also exercised some supervision over states there as distant as Iberia and Albania in the Caucasus.

Pompey's settlement brought a new regime but no lasting peace or stability during the succeeding generation. Within a decade, the disastrous campaign of Crassus (55–53 B.C.) had exposed the province to invasion by Parthia. The renewed civil wars which followed in 49 B.C. initiated a long period of insecurity, instability and exploitation for the province. The great civil war battles were fought far to the west, but their ripples were felt. For Syria that meant the rebellion of the Pompeian Caecilius Bassus (47–44 B.C.)[17] and the opportunism of various Arab phylarchs and Parthian mercenaries who had become involved;[18] Cassius' struggle with Dolabella for control of the province (44–42 B.C.);[19] the denuding of the province of its troops and the consequent military adventurism of at least one of Cassius' appointees;[20] Parthian occupation and subsequent campaigns to drive them out (40–39);[21] and the succession of campaigns of pacification – against the Jews, Commagene and Arados.[22] Above all, these years saw the systematic and unprincipled extraction by a succession of Romans of much of the movable wealth of the province, as advance taxation, 'gifts', indemnities and undisguised robbery. Thus Laodicea, devastated by the siege of Cassius and its subsequent sack (44–42), was then required to pay huge sums to his war chest;[23] the agents of Antony were killed at Arados which was then subjected to a two-year siege (40–38);[24] and the Nabataeans were fined for their sympathy for the invading Parthians.[25]

The final turmoil came with Antony's gifts to Cleopatra: all of Phoenicia except Tyre and Sidon, the kingdom of Chalcis, and parts of the kingdoms of Herod and the Nabataeans. Later, by the 'Donations of Alexandria', these regions, as well as the overlordship of all of the client kings of Syria, were transferred to their son, Ptolemy Philadelphus.[26]

The victory of Octavian opened the way for restoring stability and at least creating the conditions which would allow a naturally wealthy region to regain its prosperity. Antony's gifts were of course nullified,

---

[17] App. *BCiv.* III.77, IV.58f; Cic. *Fam.* XII.11f, 17ff; *Att.* XIV.9.3; Dio XLVII.26.3–27.5; Joseph. *AJ* XIV.268–72; *BJ* I.216f; Strab. XVI.2.10 (752C).   [18] Dio XLVII.27.3; Strab. XVI.2.10 (753C).

[19] App. *BCiv.* IV.60ff, 64, V.4; Dio XLVII.29.1–30.5; Strab. XVI.2.9 (752C).

[20] App. *BCiv.* IV.63; Joseph. *AJ* XIV.297f.

[21] Dio XLVIII.26.1f; XLIX.19.1–20.3; Joseph. *AJ* XIV.330–64; *BJ* I.248–70.

[22] Jews: Dio XLIX.22.3f; Joseph. *AJ* XIV.394–412; XIV.447; XIV.468–86; *BJ* I.290–302, 345–57. Arados: Dio XLVIII.41.6, XLIX.22.3. Commagene: Dio XLIX.20.4–22.2

[23] Dio XLVII.30.2–7; App. *BCiv.* IV.61f; Cic. *Fam.* XII.132.4.

[24] Eus. *Chron.* II.139.i (ed. Schoene); Dio XLVIII.24.3, 41.4–6, XLIX.22.3.

[25] Dio XLVIII.41.5.   [26] Dio XLIX.41; L.1.5; Plut. *Ant.* LIV.3–6.

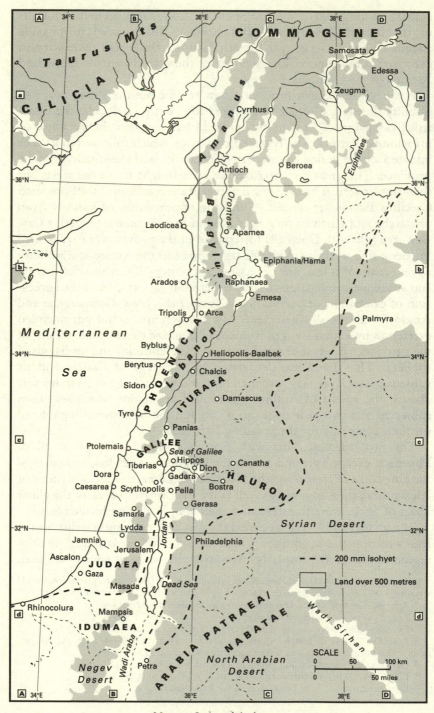

Map 19. Syria and Arabia.

but there was no change in the fundamental arrangements of the previous generation which provided for a modest province under direct government and a network of alliances with petty rulers in the rest of Syria. However, within that basic formula much important reform and re-organization was required; that was to be largely the contribution of Augustus.

Relative to the preceding century, the Julio-Claudian period was one of general peace. After Herod's death in, probably, 4 B.C.,[27] creation of the new province of Judaea removed a major segment of Syria from day to day supervision, though direct administration was soon extended to eastern Cilicia, Commagene and, intermittently, parts of Ituraea and the Hauran. Internally, although banditry seems to have been endemic in the Herodian or former Herodian realms at least, security and order had been enormously improved by the provision of a much enlarged and permanent army (below, p. 715). With the important exception of intervention in Judaea to calm passions or put down revolt, governors had little worry over internal insurrection. Even the campaign of Vitellius in 37 to punish the Nabataeans for their short 'war' with Herod Antipas, and Petronius' punitive expedition against the Jews, were halted by the deaths of Tiberius and Gaius respectively.

But the large army of Syria was a recognition too of the external threats – or opportunities – in the region. The expeditions of Aelius Gallus deep into the Arabian Peninsula in 26/5 B.C.,[28] and the obscure *expeditio Arabica* of Gaius Caesar in A.D. 1,[29] expanded direct Roman familiarity with remote regions in the south and emphasized their inclusion in her sphere of interest. The role of the governors of Syria in very high level international diplomacy and in immediate dealings with the Parthian Empire, cannot be underestimated. The defeat of Crassus and the subsequent invasions of Syria, had inflicted a blow on Roman prestige – and confidence – which were never to be expunged. However, bullying and diplomatic successes enormously improved the local perception of restored Roman power. The colourful pageantry of Gaius Caesar's meeting on the Euphrates with Phraates V in A.D. 1 described by Velleius Paterculus, was only the first of three such high level meetings in the period.[30] The province would have been scarcely less impressed by the passage of Parthian hostages and royal refugees, and by the periodic

[27] On the probable date of Herod's death see Schürer 1973 (E 1207) 1 326ff n. 165.

[28] Principally Strab. XVI.4.22f (780cf); cf. *RG* v.26; Pliny, *HN* VI.32.160f; Joseph. *AJ* XV.317; Dio LIII.29.3–8.

[29] Pliny, *HN* II.168; VI.141, 160, XII.55f, XXXII.10; *FGrH* III A 275, F 1–3. It has now been suggested that this expedition resulted in the annexation, temporarily, of the Nabataean kingdom: Bowersock 1983 (F 990) 54ff (cf. below, p. 732f).

[30] Vell. Pat. II. 10.1; Joseph. *AJ* XVIII.101–3 and Suet. *Vit.* 2 (Vitellius' meeting with Artabanus in 37); Joseph. *BJ* VII.105 (Titus' meeting with envoys of Vologases in 70); cf. Tac. *Ann.* 1.60 (Germanicus in 18).

introduction by Rome of claimants to the Arsacid throne. Despite the interventions in Armenia, the Parthian menace was controlled; there was no direct conflict with Parthian troops until the reign of Nero, and no threat to Syria's borders materialized until the time of Marcus Aurelius. The everyday management of relations with most of the nomad tribes was in the hands of various allied rulers (below, p. 715).

2. Government, administration and security

In 27 B.C. the status of Syria was enhanced and fixed. As the most vital and sensitive of the provinces assigned to Augustus in the East, it was endowed with the largest army. The legateship, invariably to be held henceforth by a person of consular standing, was the most powerful and prestigious in Rome's Asiatic provinces.

Syria's very importance demanded the careful selection as governor of men who were *politically* reliable. *Novi homines* like C. Sentius Saturninus, P. Sulpicius Quirinius (characterized by Syme as one of the 'safe men and time-servers'), or great aristocrats like P. Quinctilius Varus and, perhaps, L. Calpurnius Piso, probably selected because related, however tenuously, to the dynasty. Moreover, the power of any governor was qualified by the presence and character of the imperial procurator. Only two are known in the early Principate, but both appear as powerful and influential men, willing to demonstrate their independence of their superior. Indeed, in the case of Sentius Saturninus and the procurator Volumnius, they are paired several times by Josephus as 'governors' of Syria.[31]

There were other imperial appointees in the region. Quintus Servaeus was given charge of Commagene after its annexation in A.D. 18,[32] and that may have been a common practice with many newly annexed territories. The administration of some discrete regions of the province, distant from Antioch, may likewise have been delegated. Thus, the prefecture of the Decapolis found in the time of Domitian, may have had its origins in the early Principate,[33] and there is a suggestion that the *boule* and magistrates at Palmyra may have been largely directed in their actions by a Roman Resident.[34] Finally, there were the men who administered the imperial estates: Herennius Capito, the procurator of Jamnia,[35] must have had colleagues administering the other imperial properties in the region.

[31] e.g. Joseph. *AJ* XVI.344: *tous tes Surias hegemonas.* Syme 1974 (C 229) = (A 94) 915.
[32] Tac. *Ann.* II.56.5.
[33] *BCH* 4(1880): 506ff; the suggestion is made by Isaac 1981 (F 1016).
[34] Teixidor 1984 (E 1066) 63f.
[35] Joseph. *AJ* XVIII.158 (cf. Philo, *Leg.* 199–202; *AE* 1941, 105). The career is discussed by Pflaum 1960 (D 59) no. 9. The inscription describes him as procurator of the successive owners of the property: Livia, Tiberius and Gaius; under this last, according to Philo, he was also tax-collector for Judaea.

The remoteness of Syria which could delay decision-making in Rome by months, combined with an unwillingness to allow too great an initiative to its governors, helps explain the employment and role in the East of members of the imperial house and close associates. Agrippa (and Augustus himself) in the early years of the Principate overhauled the arrangements with client states (below, p. 728f). Later, first Varus then Gaius Caesar were sent at a time of rising tension and internal upheavals following the deaths of Herod and the Nabataean Obodas, and Germanicus was instrumental in supervising the annexation of Cappadocia and Commagene, dealing with Arabia Petraea, the closer assimilation if not annexation of Palmyra,[36] and for diplomatic exchanges with Parthia. His diplomatic contact with Mesene at the head of the Persian Gulf must be associated with stimulation of trade with the Far East; it cannot be coincidence that the first attested Palmyrene caravans are of 19 and 24.[37]

With the exception of Corbulo's appointment to the governorship (A.D. 60–3), the actual ability and experience as administrators or soldiers of most governors, was not of course a criterion in their selection. Some, probably most, were corrupt and venal: we are told this explicitly of Sentius Saturninus and Varus, though neither these nor any others are known to have been prosecuted for misgovernment.[38] Whether the procurators were more experienced and able we cannot tell. The better evidence for the prefects and procurators who governed Judaea does not encourage optimism.[39]

From the pages of Josephus we get a detailed picture of these men at work. The administration of justice and keeping the peace were high on the agenda of all governors. Some at least of the assize-centres outside Antioch can be inferred: Berytus, Tyre, Damascus, Lydda and Jerusalem; and we may suppose too Apamea, Laodicea, Tripolis and Sidon. The complaints of the Jews against their procurator Cumanus,[40] the intercession of Herod Agrippa I on behalf of the Jews of the city of Dora, persecuted by their Gentile neighbours,[41] and the boundary dispute between Damascus and Sidon,[42] all provide interesting glimpses of some of the preoccupations of the governor. Keeping the peace was, however, more than just a matter of arbitrating in such disputes. Turbulent cities like Antioch had to be policed,[43] religious festivals brought large

---

[36] The status of Palmyra vis-à-vis the Roman empire is much debated. See below, p. 720.

[37] Teixidor 1984 (E 1066) 49.

[38] Brunt 1961 (D 86); Cn. Piso was prosecuted for treason after attempting to regain control of the province by armed force (Tac. Ann. III.10f).   [39] Schürer 1973 (E 1207) I 381–98, 455–70.

[40] Joseph. BJ II.239; AJ xx.125–33.   [41] Joseph. AJ xix.300f.   [42] Joseph. AJ xviii.153.

[43] That Antioch and Apameia are conspicuously absent from the cities in which Jews were massacred in 66 (above, p. 708 and n. 11) may reflect the long-standing grip the army had on those places. Note the immediately calming effect on the mob at Ephesus when a magistrate reminds them of the consequences of provoking the intervention of the proconsul for their near-riotious behaviour (Acts 19:35–41).

numbers together in potentially unruly circumstances,[44] and banditry had to be controlled.

An aspect of the governor's activities which receives little attention in the ancient literature is that of relations with the cities. The intervention in the affairs of Dora (above) and the order to its leading men to hand over the offenders to a military officer is instructive; more useful is the series of references in the Tax Law at Palmyra revealing intervention in the internal economic affairs of that city not just by Germanicus, but by the governors Corbulo and Mucianus.[45]

Both governor and imperial procurator were resident at Antioch. The city was no longer a royal capital, but henceforth, because of the status and wide jurisdiction of the governor, it was effectively capital of the Asiatic East; in the Greek East as a whole, second only to Alexandria in size. Appropriately, Tiberius was to emphasize the status of the city by his contribution of that quintessential symbol of Roman sovereignty, a statue of the she-wolf and twins atop the new East Gate.[46] The city housed the provincial bureaucracy and at least the governor's guards. For much of the year, however, the governor was absent on tour and some of the paraphernalia of government will have been established in successive provincial cities.

More than for any other province, it was a major function of the Syrian governors to deal with and watch over the activities of kings and princes. The meetings and correspondence Herod had with governors of Syria cannot have been unusual except perhaps in their frequency. Relations were not always easy for any governor ... or king. M. Titius was at odds with Archelaus of Cappadocia until reconciled by Herod,[47] and Vibius Marsus earned the enmity of Herod Agrippa I for his interferences in that king's bolder activities.[48] The heart of the problem was, as Tacitus observed in another context,[49] that kings do not like to be treated like other men, and occasionally those in the East forgot the true nature of their position; conversely, a governor in office for only a few years at most needed to exercise considerable tact when dealing with men whose positions were 'permanent' and some of whom enjoyed very close relations with the emperor.

The governor disposed now of a large army. In place of the two legions of the late Republic and the wildly fluctuating numbers of the civil war

---

[44] The only such gatherings in which we know governors interested themselves, are those of the Jews, but there it is surely no coincidence that time and again they turn up in Jerusalem at the Passover, when, according to Josephus, huge numbers gathered (he claims 3 million) (Joseph. *BJ* II.280; cf. II.10; *AJ* XVII.213, 254, XX.106.   [45] Teixidor 1984 (E 1066) 102–3.

[46] Malalas, 235.3–6; Strong 1937 (E 1063).   [47] Joseph. *AJ* XVI.270.

[48] Joseph. *AJ* XIX.326f; *BJ* II.218f, V.152; *AJ* XIX.338–43.   [49] Tac. *Ann.* II.42.

period, Augustus allocated Syria four. We may roughly estimate the *auxilia* in the early Julio-Claudian period at about 20,000; by the time of Nero, risen to some 30,000. The armies of the client rulers could reach perhaps 15–20,000 (cf. below, p. 730; 732).

The Roman forces performed two principal functions: the maintenance of internal security and the confrontation of potential external threat. The very presence of a powerful army in Syria would have had a deterrent effect and in practice the Parthians never renewed their invasions of Syria of 51/50 B.C. and of 40–38. The major external wars involving the army of Syria were those fought out far away in Armenia by the generals of Augustus (Tiberius in 20 B.C. and Gaius Caesar in A.D. 2: see above ch. 4) and Nero, but Syrian troops were involved too, internally, in the Homonadensian War of *c.* 5/3 B.C. and in the suppression of the Cietae in western Cilicia in A.D. 36 and 52.[50] Internal security was a matter of policing the potentially turbulent city populations, suppressing banditry and controlling the nomads. The last of these does not appear as a problem for imperial governors after the interventions of the Arab sheikh Alchaudonius in the civil wars of the late Republic (see n. 18); most will now have been the direct responsibility of various allied kings and princes, as was certainly the case with the Herodian rulers in the Hauran at a later date.[51] Most action against bandits would likewise have been the responsibility of petty rulers; certainly most of that known to us concerns Judaea. Nevertheless, imperial troops were also involved in what was probably a common enough task in any province. The governor Varro himself suppressed widespread banditry in the Trachonitis *c.* 23 B.C. after Damascus complained of their depredations,[52] and later imperial troops were employed *c.* A.D. 6 against the Ituraeans on Mt Lebanon.[53] Although Antioch with its large population represented the greatest potential threat of urban unrest, in practice it was almost always Jerusalem which called for the involvement of Roman troops, just as it was Judaea as a whole in which time and again Roman troops intervened to restore order.[54] Imperial forces seldom had to intervene in allied states. In the early years of his reign, Herod had needed assistance to secure his kingdom (see n. 21) and troops would certainly have been involved in the annexation of client states. However, only once do we hear of troops intervening to coerce an allied ruler.[55]

[50] Tac. *Ann.* VI.41, XII.55.
[51] The evidence, largely epigraphic, is collected and discussed by Sartre 1982 (E 1056) 121–32, esp. 122f with texts referring to *strategoi Nomadon.*   [52] Joseph. *BJ* 1.399.   [53] *ILS* 2683.
[54] E.g. Varus in A.D. 6 (Joseph. *AJ* XVII.25f; *BJ* II.1); Petronius in 39/40 (Joseph. *AJ* XVIII.274); and Quadratus in 52 (Tac. *Ann.* XII.54).
[55] In 37 Vitellius was ordered by Tiberius to invade the Nabataean kingdom and send its king or his head to Rome. Tiberius' death gave him the pretext to halt the attack before it can have got much beyond the Jordan (Joseph. *AJ* XVIII.113f).

The legions were all in the north; only the occasional intervention in Judaea brought one south of the river Eleutherus to be stationed in Jerusalem. At various times, legions are located at Cyrrhus and Raphaneaea, and – we can infer or guess – Antioch, Apamea, Chalcis, Samosata and Zeugma as other bases for long or short periods.[56] The evidence is slight but the impression – derived partly from the evidence of their locations in the later first and in the second centuries – is of already in the Julio-Claudian period, a gradual movement of the legions eastwards to the Euphrates. The *auxilia* were more widely scattered. Like the legions, many seem to have been stationed in or near cities and towns; others were in strategic locations from the Euphrates bend (Tell el-Hajj) to Judaea (Masada).[57] Only with prior imperial permission could royal forces operate outside their own borders. Cavalry and archers are prominent amongst the auxiliary units, but it is not till the second century that a camel corps appears. A further, indirect, element of security was provided by the three veteran colonies at Berytus, Heliopolis and Ptolemais (cf. below p. 717).

Already in the late Republic, Rome had begun to recruit locally – not just the auxiliary Ituraean archers employed by Caesar and Antony, but even into the legions. With a limited pool of Roman citizens in the East as a whole, inevitably the practice continued under the Principate, relying on the hellenized population of the cities. Likewise the formation of locally recruited *alae* and *cohortes* was soon under way – albeit more slowly than elsewhere – with units from Cyrrhus, Apamea, Damascus, Antioch and Ituraea; some were drawn from the native Semitic population. The annexation of allied states led to the incorporation of royal armies from Commagene and Judaea. Although royal armies seem to have mimicked some at least of the ranks and organization of the Roman army (below, p. 717 and 732), their continued existence for so long prevented the direct Romanization of a large part of the military manpower of Syria, with consequences for the Romanization of parts of the region. Some of these units were dispatched for service in other provinces; some remained in Syria. For all the units in garrison in Syria from the outset local recruitment was probably the commonest method of replacement for most vacancies.[58]

---

[56] The evidence is collected and discussed by Keppie 1986 (D 203).

[57] Gracey 1981 (E 1010) chs. 1 and 4. In some cases at least, precise locations may have had much to do with the availability of supplies or the means of bringing in food and equipment for a large body of men.

[58] Positive evidence detailing the origins of legionaries (Forni 1953 (D 188); 1974 (D 189)) and auxiliaries (Holder 1980 (D 195) 109–39; esp. 121) serving in Syria, is slight. The supposition above is based on the likely implications of the known indications of Roman attitudes towards local recruitment in the region.

3. Urbanization and urban development

The numbers and locations of the cities of hellenistic Syria are well known (above, p. 708). Much less can be said of their condition at the outset of Roman rule. The capital, Antioch, was of course already a major city by any contemporary standard, embellished over two and a half centuries by the building activities of successive kings and, under the last of these, even by a palace and circus donated by a Roman magistrate, Q. Marcius Rex in 67 B.C.[59] Apamaea likewise had benefited from being the Seleucid military centre. In contrast to the irregular layout of the Phoenician and Jewish cities, these and the other hellenistic foundations had been laid out on a regular grid pattern which remained the basis of planning and development throughout the succeeding centuries. We may plausibly infer decline in the hellenistic cities during the final chaotic years of the Seleucid dynasty and the period of Armenian occupation (83–64 B.C.). The Roman civil wars and Parthian invasions took their toll: Apamaea, Laodicea, Arados, Tyre, Samosata and Jerusalem were all besieged at one time or another, and all cities suffered from the demands of successive dynasts seeking to fill their war chests. For the cities of Syria as for those of other provinces, Octavian's victory would have brought welcome relief.

The early Principate, especially the reign of Augustus, saw extensive urbanization in Syria, though little of it in the province itself. There were only three 'new' foundations, all of them veteran colonies, and all on the sites of existing urban settlements. Antony may have established a colony at Berytus,[60] but if so Augustus, through the agency of Agrippa in 15/14 B.C. re-established and expanded it.[61] Then, or soon after,[62] colonists were established at Heliopolis-Baalbek in the Beqaa valley. A major route opened eastwards over the mountains and this solid block of veterans of V Macedonica and VIII Augusta would have exerted a pacifying influence over the central region of the difficult Ituraean territory. More to the point, as a major 'Roman' city, strategically and attractively sited, Berytus rapidly became a mustering point for troops,

[59] Malalas, 225.7–11; cf. Humphrey 1986 (F 427) 456f.

[60] The Antonian origin may be inferred from a Berytan coin, undated but issued under Commodus (*BMCPhoenicia* 68f nos. 113–18), bearing the legend *sec(undo) Saec(ulo) col(oniae) Ber(ytensis)*. An Augustan *saeculum* of 110 years points to a date between 41 and 29 B.C. However, Commodus' 'grandfather' Antoninus Pius had celebrated the Roman *ludi saeculares* on the traditional calculation of a *saeculum* of 100 years which, if adopted by Commodus, would point rather to 21–9 B.C., i.e. perhaps to the induction of Agrippa. Lauffray 1978 (E 1033) 147 notes even Caesar as a possible original founder. [61] Strabo XVI (756C).

[62] The date of foundation of Heliopolis remains unresolved. Extreme views see it as the work either of Augustus contemporary with Berytus or as dependent on the latter until given independent status by Septimius Severus (preferred most recently by Millar 1990 (E 1040) 18f). The recently proposed case (Rey-Coquais 1978 (E 1054) 52f) for independence coming rather under Claudius is attractive.

an assize-centre, and a resort for visitors and client princes. Ptolemais, the former Akko, probably founded between A.D. 51 and 54, but developed under Nero was also a veteran settlement,[63] located so as to stabilize the increasingly restless areas of northern Judaea in the late Julio-Claudian period.

The peaceful conditions which allowed the recovery of the cities, were augmented by active imperial interest in urban development. Antioch had attention lavished on it from the outset. After the palace and circus attributed to Q. Marcius Rex in 67 B.C. (above, p. 717), Caesar, twenty years later, donated a Caesareum and amphitheatre, built or rebuilt a Pantheon and a theatre, and constructed an aqueduct. Augustus, Agrippa, Herod and Tiberius were the great benefactors, adding a new quarter, baths, temples, a theatre and a great colonnaded street, and Gaius and Claudius were active in restoration after earthquakes. Between them these men transformed much of the city, making it a worthy metropolis of the province. In doing so, all of them were conforming to an established tradition of aristocratic benefaction to cities; with Antioch, however, one sees, *par excellence*, the convergence of the more lavish expectations of the capital city of the Asiatic East and the enormous resources for such gifts available to the Roman emperors.[64]

Outside Antioch we have no explicit evidence of direct imperial civic building even if one may suppose such involvement in the new colonies at least. From literature, however, we do know of major public works elsewhere in Syria. Exedras, porticoes, temples, an *agora*, theatre, amphitheatre and baths were constructed at Berytus, all of this the work of Herod and his descendants, Agrippa I and II. The same Herodian rulers embellished several other Syrian cities: Laodicea, Tripolis, Byblus, Tyre, Sidon, Ptolemais, Ascalon, Damascus and, of course, Antioch (cf. below p. 725).[65] The appearance of these structures is largely unknown – only at Antioch and Berytus is there some physical evidence[66] - but we may turn for information to those of Herod's new works within his own kingdom, which have been investigated. The most interesting feature of Herod's work is his rapid employment of new Roman techniques and materials, here appearing rapidly and with more impact than in Greece or Asia Minor. Thus we find the extensive use of

---

[63] Foundation by Claudius is explicitly attested by Pliny (*HN* v.17.75) and that testimony and the likely date of between 52/3 and 54 proposed by Seyrig 1962 (B 350) 44f and now modified by Millar 1990 (E 1040) 24 n. 76, are to be preferred to the arguments of Kadman 1961 (B 329) 23 in favour of a Neronian foundation in Claudius' name. That it was a proper veteran colony is likely (Mann 1983 (D 215) 41); *contra*, Rey-Coquais 1978 (E 1054) 52f (cf. *PECS* s.v. 'Ptolemais') who regards it as a colony in name only on the basis of *D* 50.15.1.3.

[64] See now the important discussion of the ramifications of imperial building in Greece and Asia Minor by Mitchell 1987 (F 503). [65] Joseph. *BJ* 1.422–5; *AJ* xvi.148, xix.335ff.

[66] Antioch: Lassus 1972 (E 1032) 72; Berytus: Lauffray 1978 (E 1033) 148 and 157.

concrete and vaulting to permit elaborate engineering and landscaping works.[67]

The most extensive urbanization of the early Principate did not in fact take place in the province at all. The monarchs of the Herodian dynasty were all great founders of cities, several of which became major centres In due course, all of these were to become part of the provinces of Syria, Judaea or Arabia. Their importance for their founders, as for the Romans in turn, was in the creation of largely hellenized communities with a cultural, administrative and military role to play. Thus, Herod's highly hellenized city of Caesarea was not only firmly pro-Roman in the time of Jewish revolts (and rewarded with colonial status by Vespasian) but became the provincial capital of Judaea, a role which, together with the substantial military forces there, would have given it a more distinctly Greco-Roman character. Herod's cities thus began the process of replacing the old toparchies into which the four major regions of his kingdom had been divided for administrative purposes.[68] The urbanization of the Ituraean lands, involved a mixture of procedures. In the north, much of the territory was allocated to the veteran colonies of Berytus and Heliopolis, the rest attributed to Arca/Caesarea ad Libanum. In the south, territories were transferred to Herod and his descendants who introduced military colonies and cities in the western region,[69] and were probably behind the process elsewhere which was to lead to the appearance in the second century of large villages with extensive administrative functions.

One of the most interesting developments of the period concerns Palmyra and is clearly associated with Germanicus' visit to Syria – perhaps even to the remote town itself. There is a complete silence in the literary and epigraphic sources about Palmyra between Antony's abortive raid in 41 B.C. and the beginning of Tiberius' reign, when suddenly we get a spate of information.[70] Prior to this, the town – probably

---

[67] Thus, at Caesarea in the construction of the great artificial harbour and of the temple of Roma and Augustus on the neighbouring high ground; in the palace of Herodium; and of course the great 'landscaped villa in the contemporary Italian manner' at Jericho (Ward-Perkins 1981 (F 615) 312). Other client states too may have been active in promoting urban development in the cities of the province; without the testimony of Josephus our impression of Herod the Great's work would be very different. Recent fieldwork at Samosata has revealed that the kings of Commagene employed *opus reticulatum* extensively both in buildings on the citadel (the palace?) and in the facing for the lengthy town walls (Tirpan 1989 (E 1067)).　　[68] Jones 1931 (E 1018) 81–5.

[69] Discussion by Jones 1931 (E 1019) has not been superseded.

[70] *c.* A.D. 11–17 we find the governor Silanus active defining the western border of its territory with either Apameia or Emesa (Schlumberger 1939 (E 1058)); the earliest Latin inscriptions – statue dedications to Tiberius, Drusus and Germanicus by the commander of one of the Syrian legions – appear in 17 (*AE* 1933, 204), the earliest bilingual Palmyrene–Latin texts, soon after; the first usage in Greek of the name Palmyra appears *c.* 17–19; bronze coins of Tiberius were countermarked with a Palmyrene 'T' and Greek 'Π' (Howgego 1985 (B 325) nos. 683, 694); Germanicus is cited in the city's Tax Law as active in regulating internal tariffs; and he is named too on an inscription as instrumental in sending a Palmyrene, Alexandros, as an envoy to the Mesene at the head of the Persian Gulf (Cantineau 1931 (E 993) 139–41).

originally located mainly south of the wadi and just to its north[71] – began to develop on the north bank. The temple of Allat seems to have been taking shape at the end of the first century B.C., and that of Baalshamin was dedicated A.D. 11–23. The major development, however, was the dedication in 32 of the immense temple of Bel which dominated the city. It has so much influence in its decoration which is classical and was completed so rapidly that it is probable that it was financed by the Roman emperor and worked on by many craftsmen imported from the cities to the west.[72] As was probably the case with the temples of Allat and Baalshamin, most construction work would have been locally financed; this can be seen explicitly in the case of the temple of Zeus at Gerasa, paid for by private pledges.[73]

The commonest structures in the cities at all times were the houses of their inhabitants. Very little is known of town houses at any time; they are almost entirely unknown for this period, though the evidence from Hama would suggest that the forms of earlier periods continued to be influential for years to come.[74] Josephus provides us with an illuminating observation which sheds light on the appearance of the cities and towns of southern Syria. In the course of Cestius Gallus' invasion of Galilee in A.D. 66, he destroyed the large village of Chabulon but reluctantly because of the beauty of its houses, 'built in the style of those of Tyre, Sidon and Berytus'.[75] Earlier, Strabo had observed that the houses of Tyre (many of them on the 'island') were many stories high, higher even than those of Rome. On the other hand, the dye works at Tyre and some of its neighbours produced a distinctive and unpleasant smell.[76]

The governments of the cities were predominantly hellenistic in character, with a *boule*, archons, *agoranomoi*, *argyrotamiai*, *dekaprotoi* and gymnasiarchs. Colonies of course adopted Roman practice and we have references to the decurions and to *duoviri*, aediles and quaestors. At Palmyra, many of the magistrates bear traditional titles but, as noted earlier (above, p. 712), it has been suggested that the functions of these men were different and that Palmyra was in fact very closely supervised by Rome, the activities of its magistrates largely directed by the Syrian governor.[77]

The century of Roman peace which followed Actium saw, if not extensive urbanization in Syria, at least major urban development. The new colonies and the major Herodian foundations would have made a significant impact locally at least, Berytus, Ptolemais and Caesarea all

---

71 Van Berchem 1976 (E 987) 170.
72 Lyttleton 1974 (F 476) 93–6, 183–5; Colledge 1976 (E 994).
73 Welles in Kraeling 1938 (E 1031) 373–8. nos. 2–7.   74 Ploug 1985 (E 1051) *passim*.
75 *BJ* II.504.   76 Strab. XVI.2.23 (757C).   77 Teixidor 1984 (E 1066) 63.

rapidly developing as major cities. Elsewhere, by the end of the Julio-Claudian dynasty, many of the major cities of the province displayed the physical benefits of Roman benefactions whether directly from the emperor or through surrogates.

4. Economic development

The basis of the Syrian economy was farming. Not just agriculture to produce the fundamental corn harvest, but the cultivation of olives, vines, dates and figs, and the rearing of animals for food, wool and hides (as well as the tools and ornaments which were made from bones). Within the largely unchanging limitations imposed by rainfall and soils (above, p. 705–8), altered circumstances could provide scope for increased activity in marginal areas and for a changed balance between different crops as well as between tillage and stock raising. Little of such change can be demonstrated, though much may be inferred.

Security and stable conditions provided a suitable environment for the development of farming. Moreover, 'new' cities and urban growth opened up new or extended markets for agricultural surplus, to which had to be added the tens of thousands of unproductive soldiers who had to be fed. The probable extension of agriculture which resulted would in itself, by encouraging the settlement of potentially productive land, have further stimulated the economy and enhanced stability.[78]

There were, of course, some traditional agricultural regions which continued to produce surpluses. The inhabitants of Sidon and Tyre, for example, were dependent on Galilee, and it may have been from this same region that much of the non-'Grecian' oil required by the Jewish communities of all of Syria, was exported.[79] The movement of corn by land would at all times have been expensive except in very local terms. Herod, however, had imported huge amounts of corn from Egypt at the time of the famine in the 20s, supplying too, some of neighbouring Syria.[80]

New lands were opened up to agriculture. Thus Herod obliged the bandits of Trachonitis to turn to farming,[81] and the growth of the Nabataean towns of the Negev must be associated with the development of the water-harvesting structures and 'farms' still visible in the region.[82]

[78] The process can be documented for the nineteenth and early twentieth centuries. Well-armed soldiers in the towns and along roads, and at selected points in the semi-desert and desert, encouraged resettlement of abandoned land, turned semi-nomads into farmers, encouraged the growth of investment by the urban merchants and the Sultan, and provided not only new markets in towns and garrisons for food and hides, but even, during the Crimean War and the loss of Black Sea sources, a vigorous export market to Europe for Syrian grain (Lewis 1987 (E 1034)).

[79] Joseph. *Vit.* LXX; *BJ* II.591f; *AJ* XII.120. Cf. above, p. 720.   [80] Joseph. *AJ* XV.299–302.

[81] Joseph. *AJ* XVI.271–92; cf. Archelaus' irrigation of new land near Jericho: *BJ* XVII.340; cf. *BJ* XVIII.31; Pliny, *HN* XIII.44.   [82] Evenari *et al.* 1982 (E 1008) chs. VII–IX; cf. below, p. 732f.

In the late Republic, the great caravan trade up the Euphrates had been virtually halted by the predatory activities of Arab phylarchs. Peace and the probable settlement of semi-nomads of the region along the river and towards Beroea re-opened the routes,[83] and not only the growing populations in Syria itself, but access to a huge Mediterranean market stimulated activity. Aelius Gallus' expedition into south Arabia in 26/5 B.C. was certainly motivated by cupidity. Likewise, imperial interest in trade is probably behind the sudden concern for Palmyra (above, p. 714). On the other hand, the southern routes through Arabia Petraea, already in decline (below, p. 734), suffered a further blow as trade routes were polarized between those direct to Egypt and those from the head of the Persian Gulf.

Evidence from the Julio-Claudian period reveals a network of trading links within and beyond the province; more can be inferred. Thus timber from Lebanon for the sanctuary at Jerusalem,[84] metals for both work-shops and mints,[85] Italian pottery appears on Syrian sites, following presumably the same routes as Italian wine and oil; Syrian glass is found as distant as south Russia,[86] South Arabia and India, and Syrian wine was exported to India.[87] The needs of the army too would have stimulated trade within and between provinces: metals, hides, clothing, building materials and, of course, huge quantities of food. Further stimulus would have come from the market created in Antioch by a bureaucracy, those around the army camps with their bodies of regularly paid soldiers and, of course, from the demands of the labour forces on the new building projects. The most striking economic activity in the period – the one, certainly, for which we have some useful evidence – is in public construction. Whatever the source of the finance, this provided long-term employment opportunities: in the case of a massive structure like the temple of Jupiter at Damascus, such construction work was still highly labour intensive; 18,000 were threatened by unemployment when the Temple was completed in Jerusalem.[88]

None of this should be exaggerated. There is little doubt that trade in food and other commodities increased and created a greater interdependence between communities in Syria and beyond. The underlying reality, however, is that most economic activity remained local and of a subsistence character, and the overwhelming majority of the population

---

[83] Strab. XVI.1.27f (748Cf); 2.10 (752–3C); cf. Lewis 1987 (E 1034).

[84] Joseph. *BJ* v.36. These huge timbers for a specialist purpose would have been only one amongst many such items imported for the great building programmes of the client kings and the cities.

[85] Copper from the mines of Cyprus and, perhaps, the Wadi Araba; cf. in general Muhly 1973 (E 1044).   [86] Rostovtzeff 1957 (A 83) 69f.

[87] Raschke 1978 (C 298) 903f, n. 999; Sidebotham 1986 (C 310) 13–47. Some at least of the silk appearing in Rome in the period may have come through Syria (but cf. Miller 1969 (E 1042) 119f; 133–6).   [88] Joseph. *AJ* xx.219.

continued to live and work on the land.[89] Nor need we doubt that for most small farmers, 'pre-harvest famine' remained a continuing feature of life unchanged – and unchangeable – by Roman rule.[90]

An important basis for this revived and developing economic life after 30 B.C., was the Augustan stabilization of the imperial coinage and the regularization of minting at Antioch. There were, however problems and setbacks. The population of the region would plainly not have suffered uniformly under a non-progressive tax regime. Indeed, in A.D. 17 Tacitus[91] reports the financial exhaustion of the province from over-taxation; one of the reasons for the dispatch of Germanicus in that year. Just who was complaining – and how it was articulated – we are not told.

Natural disasters took their toll, though the extraordinary could expect imperial relief. A great famine and plague struck Judaea in the mid-20s B.C. and afflicted neighbouring regions. Another famine, portrayed by Luke as universal, is reported in c. A.D. 47/8.[92] An earthquake had struck Judaea in 30 B.C., a second in A.D. 37, and others in north and south respectively, in the period A.D. 41–54 and 48.

5. Society and culture

As part of the Mediterranean-wide Roman empire, the urban population of the great cities of northern Syria and the Levant became still more cosmopolitan both in racial mix and outlook than in the Seleucid period. Despite the considerable body of evidence for the very active involvement of Syrians in overseas trade, there is virtually none showing any interest by the aristocracy to enter imperial service. In contrast to Asia Minor, there is no certain senator before the Flavian period,[93] and the two, possibly three, 'Syrians' who appear as equestrian officers in the Julio-Claudian period are all probably from the veteran colonies of Berytus and Heliopolis.[94] Only a handful of the aristocracies of the cities appear prominently. Malalas reports on the wealthy Antiochene councillor, Sosibius, who accompanied Augustus to Rome in either 30 or 20 B.C., and left his wealth to the city for entertainments;[95] and now we have

---

[89] The only city for which we get anything approaching an insight into its internal economy at this period, is Palmyra through the Hadrianic Tax Law, elements of which are derived from a Julio-Claudian 'Old Law'. There one finds references to the importation of a wide range of produce from the Palmyrene territory, and extensive services in the city ranging from the selling of clothes to prostitution (Teixidor 1984 (E 1066) 69–90; Matthews 1984 (E 1037)).

[90] Clark and Haswell 1970 (A 17) 19.   [91] *Ann.* II.42.

[92] Gapp 1935 (C 349); cf. Gapp, 1934 (A 32) chs II and III, Garnsey 1988 (A 33).

[93] Bowersock 1982 (D 25) 652f.

[94] The best known of these, Q. Aemilius Secundus, who commanded regiments in Syria, campaigned against the Ituraeans, and conducted the famous census at Apameia for Quirinius in A.D. 6, is probably but not certainly from Berytus (Devijver 1986 (D 179) 183–9).

[95] Malalas, *Chron.* IX.20 (224).

the inscription reporting on the quondam tetrarch Dexandros, who remained at Apamea as the founder of one of the leading families, and served as first High Priest of the Imperial Cult for the province (below, p. 727).

An obstacle to assimilation of the city aristocracies of Syria outside the veteran colonies – as elsewhere in the Greek East – was of course the slowness with which Roman citizenship was extended in the province. The aristocracies of ancient and great cities such as Antioch, Apamea and Damascus would see little advantage in it for them. Significantly, it was from the descendants of now deposed allied rulers – who had often been granted Roman citizenship and had more direct contact with Rome and Romans – that many of the earliest Syrian senatorial families were drawn.

Roman citizenship *was* spreading. Many time-expired legionaries as well as enfranchised former auxiliaries stayed on as settlers, some in the new colonies. One might expect those cities closely associated with the military – especially the legions – to have had larger numbers of Roman citizens. That would be particularly true of Antioch, both as a military centre and seat of the provincial bureaucracy. Presumably too the Apostle Paul was not the only Roman citizen amongst the petty officials of Syria. Instructive of the process in the Syrian cities is an inscription of 60 from Tyre of C. Iulius Iucundus, *agoranomos* in charge of nominations for Roman citizenship, suggesting that at Tyre at least, such an office was necessary. Whatever the ethnic origin of Iucundus, his colleague, the *agoranomos* Nicolaus, son of Baledo, clearly a native, a Phoenician who has adopted a Greek name,[96] exemplifies an older and probably more widespread process at work in varying degrees across the province. An interesting exception is Dexandros (above, p. 727), whose rare Greek name may reflect a genuine 'Greek' background.[97]

With native Semites appearing amongst the aristocracy of the cities, it seems certain that most of the remainder of the population, whatever their names, were likewise part or wholly Semitic. The Jewish community in most cities was especially noticeable; some such communities were substantial – that at Antioch had its own *politeuma* and was allowed its own archon.[98] Conversely, Gentile 'Syrians' in large numbers had been implanted by the Herods in their new cities.

The influx of people from outside Syria would have been principally through the army. While the numbers are potentially large, in practice many soldiers, even in the legions, will have been recruited locally (above, p. 716). Outside recruitment to the legions seems to have drawn

[96] Mouterde 1944–6 (E 1043). Cf. Aristomachus, son of Zabdion at Gerasa (Kraeling 1938 (E 1031) 373f no. 2).   [97] Rey-Coquais 1973 (B 269) 51.

[98] Kraeling 1932 (E 1030); Meeks and Wilken, 1978 (F 185) 2–13. Joseph. *AJ* XVII.23–7.

on the neighbouring provinces rather than the West, and outsiders were rapidly assimilated, through contact and intermarriage, to the local communities. An unexpected element is the Parthian, Arsacid refugees and their retainers who were settled in Syria; and the Babylonian Jew Zamaris with his family and 500 archers who arrived *c* 9–6 B.C. to be initially settled at Daphne, is unlikely to have been unique if one may judge from the evidence of 'Parthian' regiments and mercenaries in the Roman army.[99]

Evidence for romanization – as opposed to the greater scope for hellenization – is limited and largely superficial: Italian names (not least 'Agrippa'), some citizenship, mainly in pockets, the local cultural influence of the three veteran colonies and the influence of the imperial cult in cities and around the camps. The army was indeed the principal source of Romanization through the imposition of an influential Roman institution with established and thoroughly Roman practices in administration, language and religion. But the 40-50,000 soldiers were scattered and increasingly locally recruited even in the Julio-Claudian period. Those in cities, like the Thracians of the *ala I Augusta Thracum* at Gerasa in the first century,[100] were more likely to be influenced by Syrian culture than the reverse. Conversely, Roman military practices made an impact on the armies of the allied rulers. Not surprisingly they sought to emulate the most efficient and effective army of the time (cf. below, p. 732).[101]

Opportunities for refined entertainment and relaxation were extended beyond that handful of cities in the north which had theatres in the hellenistic period. Theatres remained less common than in Asia Minor, but Herod and his family were responsible for their construction and for the provision of baths and gymnasia in several cities in their own realms and in the Syrian province. The notion that the Greek East had no taste for the barbarism of the Roman wild beast and gladiatorial fights must now be jettisoned. Although the positive evidence is slight and amphitheatres are uncommon, literature attests to both practices – at the time of Herod's dedication of his new city of Caesarea in 10 B.C. and by Titus after the destruction of Jerusalem 80 years later. It is clear that theatres were used instead of purpose-built amphitheatres.[102] Athletic and dramatic contests, often associated with religious festivals, were revived

[99] Applebaum 1989 (E 1075) ch. 4; Kennedy 1977 (E 1021).

[100] Kraeling 1938 (E 1031) 446f nos. 199–201.

[101] Cf. Braund 1984 (C 254); Gracey 1981 (E 1010). When Josephus set about organizing an army in 67, he adopted Roman practices and ranks (*BJ* II.577–82).

[102] Robert 1940 (F 57) 239–66. At Antioch, gladiatorial games went back to Antiochus IV Epiphanes who had developed his taste for them while at Rome: Livy, XLI.20. The amphitheatre discovered by aerial reconnaissance at Caesarea has received only a little attention but is presumably that of Herod (Holum *et al.* 1989 (E 1140) 85–6).

or established in various cities providing periodic attractions and entertainment: the councillor Sosibius (above, p. 723) established a quinquennial festival at Antioch extending over thirty days,[103] and Herod introduced them too into the cities of his realm, including Jerusalem.[104]

Religion played a large part in both politics and everyday life. Most detailed evidence belongs to a later period but the principal features for the current century are clear. Semitic religions had much in common with one another as indeed with those of their Mesopotamian neighbours with whom they had a shared cultural and political unity extending back to Persian times. A common feature was a Supreme God. By the Persian period the host of minor gods which had obscured the prominence of the supreme deity had moved into a more subordinate role. The 'Assemblies of Gods' which had characterized this earlier phase gave way to Angels, messengers of the Supreme God, who might have their own devotees. A consequence was a trend towards monotheism which facilitated the spread of Judaism and was to do so again for Christianity.

The character no less than the name of the Supreme God varied considerably between settled peoples and nomads, townsmen and farmers. The preoccupations of the citizens of Phoenician Tyre were far removed from those of the merchants of Palmyra or the nomads of Nabataea. Naturally, for most people, the fertility of the soil and the needs of agriculture were dominant; industry, trade, commerce or a nomadic life involved different priorities. Thus, Baalshamin, identified as a deity concerned with agriculture was popular around the Palmyrene oasis, and the Nabataean Supreme God, Dushara, perhaps equated with Mercury by the nomadic Nabataeans of the south, was assimilated to Dionysus amongst the farmers of the Hauran.

There is also a distinction to be made between the public religion of the towns and the popular religion of the masses. For the latter, their religion was probably very simple and their relationship with their god close: inscriptions often characterize traditional pagan gods as *epekoos* 'the One Who Listens', symbolizing the expectation amongst devotees that they would be listened to and taken care of. For the more sophisticated townsman, Semitic cults such as those of Azizos, Hadad, Melkart, Atargatis and Baalshamin, had come to be equated with Greek gods during the hellenistic period. The trend continued in the Roman period with shrines and dedications flourishing in the cities to gods from Apollo and Athene to Pan and Zeus, either in their own right or in a dual form with the local Supreme God. The Roman equivalents made little

---

[103] Malalas, *Chron.* IX.224; X.248; XII.284.
[104] Joseph. *AJ* XVI.137; *BJ* 1.415 (Caesarea); *AJ* XV.268 (Jerusalem).

impact outside the army camps and colonies. For the latter, the cult of Jupiter Optimus Maximus Heliopolitanus at Heliopolis-Baalbek, represents the most striking example. For the former, the official Roman cults which formed part of formal military festivals and worship were still vibrant in the early third century as the *Feriale Duranum*, the Dura Military Calendar, makes clear.[105]

The most significant Roman import was the introduction of the imperial cult in the time of Augustus (above, p. 724). Temples and priesthoods for Augustus, or Rome and Augustus, were established during his lifetime, as they were for his successors and for the *divi*. Significantly, the first High Priest of the imperial cult for the province as a whole was the Apamaean tetrarch Dexandros, a man who would have understood better than most the importance of the cult, and provided a striking model for others to emulate. Once again, Herod was at the forefront of this development with known temples built at Samaria and Panias and, in particular, at Caesarea Maritima.[106] Indeed, it has been plausibly suggested that wherever else temples of the imperial cult were established, they were an inevitable feature of those cities named for and dedicated to Caesar or Augustus/Sebastos. Of interest too in the realm of politics, was the establishment under imperial patronage, of the great temple of Jupiter at Baalbek, which became a focus of political loyalty for central Syria at least, as that at Seeia may have been for the Nabataean population of the Hauran.

The prominence of religion in everyday life is clear enough from the numerous temples and shrines, the altars and *baetyls* (rectangular stone pillars), theophoric elements in personal names and the inscriptions attesting to the gratitude of the common man for divine protection and aid. For many it would have provided a vital reassurance.[107] Influence is harder to gauge. At one extreme, the political role of the imperial cult, the newest cult in the region, is clear enough. At the other, Judaism, one of the oldest, through the Jewish diaspora of Syria and new converts, exerted a humanitarian influence on its neighbours, since it, uniquely, had a tradition of compassion for the destitute.[108]

A handful of Syrians are prominent in the field of scholarship. The numbers of philosophers, rhetoricians and orators is small by comparison with, for example, Alexandrians. Nicolaus of Damascus, the minister and historian of Herod the Great, is to be ranked alongside Strabo, Timagenes and Dionysius amongst the outstanding Greek writers of the Augustan period. Other notable figures are Tiberius'

[105] *PDura* 54.
[106] Holum *et al.* 1989 (E 1140) 88f; cf. 110f for an inscription of Pontius Pilate recording a Tiberieum.   [107] Sourdel 1952 (E 1061); Teixidor 1977 (F 227); 1979 (E 1065A).
[108] Hands 1968 (F 39) 77–88. See e.g. Joseph. *AJ* xx.219; Acts 11.27–301.

tutor, the rhetorician Theodorus of Gadara, and his fellow-townsman, the epicurean philosopher Philodemus, teacher of Calpurnius Piso and Virgil; from Tarsus and Cilician Seleucia, respectively, came Nestor and Athenaeus, tutors of Marcellus.[109] However, while these Syrians appeared in the imperial household, no Antiochene – in the absence of a precise role for Sosibius (above, p. 723) – is known to have held a position of prominence there in the way Alexandrians did, and neither the city nor the province held the attraction for eminent Roman hellenophiles which Greece, Asia Minor and Egypt did.[110]

III. CLIENT STATES

1. Character, role and development

Pompey's settlement of Syria had involved the recognition of a number of men as rulers over much of the region. Although they subsequently appeared prominently in support of the vanquished in three successive rounds of Roman civil war, they were still numerous in 30 B.C. Indeed, numbers may have increased: Antony had swept away the many tyrants set up by Cassius[111] to rule over newly created principalities, but then established other such states himself.[112] However, it is only in the 20s B.C. that we get an indication of just how numerous these states were. Alongside the kingdoms – Commagene, Judaea and Arabia Petraea, there were numerous minor dynasts and tetrarchs: more than a score in Syria Coele, and several more in the south.[113]

The usefulness of a network of allied rulers in and around the periphery of a province was not in doubt.[114] Rather, the task confronting the new *princeps* was to re-assess the balance between directly administered province and the area under the control of allied rulers, and to determine which to retain. The solution was to have fewer but larger states. The three major kingdoms were retained and two were resuscitated: the kings of eastern Cilicia and Emesa had been victims of the Actian campaign, but their families were now restored in 20 B.C. The year, of course, was that of Augustus' visit to Syria and it seems likely that the rest of the major re-organization attributable to his reign was also the outcome of this visit and/or of those of Agrippa in 23/1 and 16–13 B.C. during his period of authority in the East (23–13 B.C.). The arrangements cannot be followed in detail but they involved the removal

[109] Bowersock 1965 (C 39) ch. III. We might note too, apparently from Syrian Hierapolis, a great local benefactor at Athens, Julius Nicanor, hailed as the New Themistocles and New Homer (Jones 1978 (E 1020)).   [110] Bowersock 1965 (C 39) 73–84.   [111] Joseph. *BJ* 1.239; *AJ* XIV.297.
[112] App. *BCiv.* V.10; Dio XLIX.32.4f.   [113] Pliny, *HN* V.81f; 74.
[114] Caesar had recognized petty rulers on condition they defended the province (*BAfr.* 65.4).

of the plethora of tetrarchs. The case of Zenodorus indicates that their lands could simply be re-allocated: in 24/3 he had lost part of his Ituraean tetrarchy to Herod the Great, then in 20, after his death, Herod received the rest too.[115] On the other hand, the ending of the Apamaean tetrarchy[116] seems to have been purely administrative: the territory was annexed to the province, and the family of Dexandros with their 'royal honours' remained dominant in the local aristocracy for at least a century more. Other tetrarchies may have been subsumed in the restored kingdoms of Cilicia and Emesa (from which indeed they may have sprung). Important lacunae concern the nomad tribes and Palmyra: in particular, the Arab phylarchs in the north in the late Republic are heard of no more, and after Antony's raid in 41 B.C., Palmyra does not reappear in our evidence until c. A.D. 11–17 (above, p. 719f and n. 70).

The terms of Roman friendship, alliance and recognition for kings and princes – whether officially stated or not – varied considerably. There had always been limitations on the freedom of action of such rulers, but the defining of parameters was one of the achievements of Augustus' reign. The character of a ruler and the location and size of his kingdom all went to determine the extent of his freedom of action and behaviour. Inevitably it is from Josephus' account of Herod and his descendants that we learn most about the rulers of Syria, but from what may be gleaned both from the same author and other writers, it is clear that the same parameters of rights, obligations and behaviour applied. Equally inevitably, some rulers either did not recognize these or sought to break them.

Location of course was important. Commagene's capital, 260km from Antioch as the crow flies, would have given its ruler a measure of remoteness until the annexation of Cappadocia in A.D. 17 brought another province into existence in the north. The nearest Roman troops would have been about four days distant. Its dynasty felt akin to Parthia and just beyond their Euphrates border lay a dangerous example: Osrhoene, a powerful Parthian vassal, whose kings had been able to shake off Roman overlordship after the Battle of Carrhae. Rome was often uneasy about Commagene's reliability. It had colluded with the Parthian invasion of 40–38 B.C. which had led to Antony's abortive siege; strategic considerations almost certainly lay behind the decision in A.D. 17 to take direct control of the major crossings of the upper Euphrates by annexing Cappadocia and Commagene; and its final

---

[115] Joseph. *AJ* xv.344–9, 359–63, xvi.271; *BJ* 398–400.

[116] *AE* 1976, 677–8; Rey-Coquais 1973 (B 269). The Roman census at Apameia in A.D. 6 suggests the tetrarchy had ended by that time (*ILS* 2673) – perhaps precisely at that time. The sole auxiliary regiment named for Apameia, the *cohors I Apamenorum*, lacks an imperial title, which may point to formation before Claudius – again perhaps the result of taking over the tetrarchic army.

elimination in 72 was precisely on the grounds of alleged conspiracy with Parthia.[117]

Tarcondimotus' Cilician kingdom, though divided from the rest of Syria by the Amanus Mountains was hemmed in by the Taurus and the province of Cilicia and easily open to Roman influence and intervention. Emesa was close to the heart of the province.[118] Under Claudius, when the governor Vibius Marsus appeared at Tiberias and ordered the dispersal of Herod Agrippa I's guests including the kings of Commagene and Emesa, both complied rapidly, recognizing the nature of their position even if their host had believed Claudius' friendship and indebtedness had accorded him greater latitude.

Arabia Petraea is rather different. Unlike Commagene, there was no powerful neighbour beyond; on the other hand, the remoteness of Petra – some 700km from Antioch, hedged in by mountain and desert – with consequent difficulties either of controlling or bringing the region under direct administration, conferred a certain amount of immunity from day-to-day interference. But there were limits and warnings. Aretas IV had acceded without prior approval in 9 B.C., and in A.D. 37 made war on his neighbour Herod Antipas. Augustus had considered deposing the dynasty but was too preoccupied to pursue a radical solution; Tiberius actually despatched an army into Nabataean territory but Vitellius seized the pretext of Tiberius' death to withdraw his forces from Nabataea. Luck had saved Aretas on both occasions but the lessons would not have been lost: in 4 B.C. Nabataean troops were sent to aid Varus in his Judaean expedition[119] and in A.D. 18 Germanicus was fêted by Aretas.[120] Moreover, with the growth of Nabataean possessions in the Hauran, the kingdom was now rather more vulnerable.

The function of these client kings is largely a matter for conjecture from the totality of evidence for client rulers everywhere and in particular from the well-attested Herodian examples. The advantages to Rome of leaving the less urbanized and poorer parts of Syria under their traditional rulers, was obvious. Except in the cases of the Herods and the Nabataeans (below, p. 732) we are largely ignorant of the character of the individual royal armies. Both Commagene and Emesa contributed significant forces to Roman expeditionary armies: in 66 that was 5,000 and 4,000 troops respectively;[121] in 67 it amounted to 3,000 men from each, both offering especially useful archers and cavalry.[122] Moreover, the annexation of Commagene between A.D. 17 and 38 had resulted in the

---

[117] Joseph. *BJ* VII.219–22; cf. Kennedy 1983 (E 1023).

[118] By the end of Nero's reign at least, an entire legion was based only 45km away at Raphanaea (Joseph. *BJ* VII.18).   [119] Joseph. *AJ* XVII.287; *BJ* II.68; cf. below, n. 135.

[120] Tac. *Ann.* II.57.   [121] Joseph. *BJ* II.500f.   [122] Joseph. *BJ*. III.68; Tac. *Hist.* V.1.2.

absorption of some at least of the former royal army into the Roman *auxilia*.[123] Presumably, like the Herodian realms and Arabia Petraea, these substantial forces reflected not just the needs of personal security for the monarch, but troops to maintain order in the cities and to police the countryside as well as to secure the periphery of the directly administered province (cf. above, n. 114).

The king-lists provide a bare indication of politics and government. Interruptions at Commagene from 17 to 38 and again under Gaius, did not, however, prevent the family remaining deeply involved in Roman politics. Antiochus IV was one of the 'tyrant-masters' of Gaius and with him in Gaul in 39. A generation later, his son, Antiochus Epiphanes, fought with the Othonians at the First Battle of Bedriacum before joining Titus at Jerusalem. Interestingly, when Antiochus III died in A.D. 17 and the kingdom was annexed, it appears that the masses supported the continued monarchy and it was the aristocracy which petitioned for annexation.[124] Presumably the aristocracy saw political advantage to themselves if removed from the shadow of a monarch; indeed after final annexation, the ruling family was catapulted into senatorial politics. The 'masses' were largely Semitic and it is interesting to see their support for a ruling family which, as we know from its nomenclature and the character of the art preserved in the best-known monument, the great tumulus at Nemrud Dagh, was Iranian with a Greek influence. The kingdom itself was reputed to be wealthy – the wealthiest of them all; Strabo refers to rich valleys and upland pastures; Antiochus I had offered to buy off Ventidius Bassus with 1,000 talents (24 million sesterces); and later, Gaius reimbursed to Antiochus IV the 100 million sesterces said to be the accumulated revenue to Rome from twenty years.[125]

Less can be said of Emesa. Only four monarchs span the period from restoration in 20 B.C. to annexation probably not long after A.D. 72. The family lived on as hereditary priests of the local Syrian deity (Baal). Emesa, like the other allied kingdoms, had become enmeshed in a network of family alliances through royal marriages.[126] None, however, were to be as successful as the marriage, more than a century after the ending of the kingdom, of Iulia Domna to the future emperor Septimius Severus. The result was to be three Emesan empresses and their children ruling in Rome.

[123] As an *ala* and probably five *cohortes Commagenorum – c.* 3,000 men: Kennedy 1980 (E 1022) 91–7.
[124] Joseph. *AJ* XVIII.53; *contra*, Tac. *Ann.* II.42.5. Cf. the parallel situation in Judaea after Herod's death in 4 B.C.: Joseph. *AJ* XVII.299; 304–14; *BJ* II.80; 84–91.
[125] Tac. *Hist.* II.81; Suet. *Calig.* 14. 3.
[126] Sullivan, 1978 (E 1065); (E 1224); (E 878); (E 1064).

2. The Nabataean kingdom

In contrast to Commagene and Emesa, we know a great deal about the government, character and development of the Nabataean kingdom. Arabia Petraea – the heart of the kingdom – is unpromising terrain for human settlement. Composed in large part of rock and desert, lacking any substantial perennial water course and dependent on seasonal rains, it is no surprise that in the late fourth century,[127] its Arab population was nomadic, albeit already engaged in a lucrative commerce. Three centuries later Strabo knew them as a settled people living in houses. By then too, their realm included the Hedjaz, the Negev Desert and the fertile Hauran. In the first centuries B.C. and A.D. they developed a politically powerful and culturally vigorous and innovative society.

Nabataean monarchs enjoyed long reigns: only five between c. 58/7 B.C. and A.D. 106. On the other hand, it appears from Strabo that effective power lay with an appointed minister (epitropos).[128] The only named minister, Syllaeus, evidently wielded considerable power and influence; he proposed marriage for himself to Herod's daughter and evidently sought the kingship at Petra. It was Syllaeus too whom we twice find visiting Rome;[129] indeed, no Nabataean king is ever known to have visited Rome nor apparently did any ever receive either Roman citizenship or the marks of honour accorded their neighbours: toga picta, praetorian or consular ornaments.[130] Like Herod's kingdom, Arabia Petraea may have been divided into toparchies; certainly, regional administration was in the hands of strategoi (strg), who were probably local tribal chiefs recognized as royal governors.[131]

Security was provided by a standing army which was modelled to some extent on that of Rome. Thus, alongside the hellenistic chiliarch and hipparch one finds the centurion (qntryn').[132] Despite explicit statements as to their unwarlike character,[133] over two centuries the military record of Nabataean soldiers is good.[134] Moreover, they were called upon to assist Roman campaigns on at least four occasions[135] and ultimately the royal army was absorbed into the Roman auxilia as six cohortes Petraeaorum, some 4,500 men.

---

[127] Diod. II.48. 1f or XIX.94.2–5.   [128] XVI.4.21 (779C).

[129] Joseph. AJ XVI.224, 322; BJ 1.487 (marriage); Joseph. AJ XVI.295f (kingship); Joseph. AJ XVI.250 and 335–52 (9 and 6 B.C.); cf. Strab. XVI.4.25 (782–3C) (embassies).

[130] Cf. Braund 1984 (C 254) 39–53.   [131] Cf. Joseph. AJ XVIII.112.

[132] Jaussen and Savignac 1909 (E 1017) I 189f, no. 29; 154f no. 7; 120f no. 20; 202ff no. 38; 192f no. 44.; Periplus 19.   [133] E.g. Joseph. AJ XIV.31; Diod. II.54.3; Strab. XVI.4.23 (780–1C).

[134] See D. Graf, 'The Nabataean army and the Cohortes Ulpiae Petraeorum', in E. Dabrowa (ed.) The Roman and Byzantine Army in the East (Krakow, 1994) 265–311.

[135] Caesar at Alexandria (47 B.C.), Aelius Gallus (26/5 B.C.), Varus (6 B.C.) and for the Jewish Revolt (A.D. 68–70).

The sudden Nabataean appearance at Hegra, deep in the Hedjaz 500km south east of Petra, may have been inspired by Rome.[136] The new territory may in fact have been that ruled by a kinsman of the Nabataean king at the time of Aelius Gallus' campaign. There, in a region of Lihyanite and later Thamudic settlement, appeared a series of some seventy-nine monumental rock-cut tombs similar in design and quality to those at Petra. Unlike the latter, many bear dated inscriptions, often naming civil and military officers, a few citing distant origins, and ranging in date from A.D. 1 to 75. All of this points to a major development there, perhaps a military colony, but so far nothing more of the town has been unearthed than an apparent 'residential area'.[137] Now too we have evidence of settlement elsewhere in the region: ten similar tombs have come to light at al-Bad (Ptolemy's Madian) and another at al-Disa.[138] More exciting still are the numerous other small Nabataean sites in the Hedjaz identified especially in the coastal region around Aynunah (probably Leuke Kome – see below, p. 734).[139]

There is similar evidence from the other two major acquisitions. The Negev underwent a phase of development in the early Principate. The evidence suggests growing settlements at Mampsis and along the line of the Petra–Gaza road which continued through into the Roman period. In the north, Zenodorus had sold Auranitis to the Nabataeans in 30 B.C. for a modest 50 talents. The scanty physical evidence so far suggests intensification of occupation about the middle of the first century A.D. At Bostra there is growing evidence to suggest a substantial Nabataean settlement there. The 'Nabataean' arch is now confirmed as first century A.D., probably second half, and it would seem that the main thoroughfare leading to it may have been a contemporary *via sacra* joining the settlement at its west end to a religious enclave at the east.[140]

Of existing settlements, Petra was also being developed: some of the tombs date to this period, the theatre is early first century, and the *temenos* at least of the Qasr el-Bint temple is of the reign of Aretas IV (9 B.C.–A.D. 40). With the benefit of precisely dated examples at Hegra, many of the very striking monumental tombs of the city may be placed in the same period, and it is arguable that the Khazneh, the 'Treasury', too is of this same period.[141]

---

[136] What appears to be a foundation coin naming Hegra dates to between 9 B.C. and A.D. 18 (Meshorer 1975 (B 343) 53f) and the earliest of the dated inscriptions there is for A.D. 1, the same year in which the *expeditio Arabica* of Gaius Caesar brought him to the head of the Gulf of Aqaba.

[137] Winnett and Reed 1970 (E 1070) 178ff.

[138] Parr *et al.* 1971 (E 1048) 30–5 (al-Bad); Ingraham *et al.* 1981 (E 1014) 76 (al-Disa).

[139] Ingraham *et al.* 1981 (E 1014); cf. Dayton 1972 (E 997) 46; Bawden 1978 (E 986) 11; Parr *et al.* 1968/9 (E 1048); 1971 (E 1048).

[140] Peters 1983 (E 1050) 273–7; cf. Miller 1983 (E 1041); Dentzer 1984 (E 998); 1986 (E 999) 1.2, 406; Sartre 1985 (E 1057) 57–62. See now the evidence for Umm el-Jemal: De Vries 1986 (E 1003) 229ff.

[141] Schmidt-Colinet 1980 (E 1059) 217–33; cf. Wright 1962 (E 1071); McKenzie 1990 (E 1038).

All of these developments suggest expanding economic activity and a more cosmopolitan outlook. Certainly, so much construction at Petra – over 500 monumental tombs – and in other centres will not only have provided employment for the architects, masons, plasterers and other artisans attested in inscriptions, but have stimulated urbanization. The construction techniques and design show evidence of Alexandrian influence and some at least of the many foreigners at Petra,[142] may have been imported artisans and artists. The finished product, however, is both impressive and unique to the Nabataeans. Some of these foreigners will have been merchants selling as well as buying. The Nabataeans had already begun to produce their own highly distinctive fine painted pottery in the late Republic, but at several sites imported wares have turned up. The Nabataean potter's workshop at Avdat (first half of the first century A.D.), for example, seems to have sold alongside its own produce 'Herodian' lamps, Eastern and Italian *sigillata*.[143]

Financial support for such endeavours no longer rested so firmly on trade. By the beginning of the Christian era, much of the south Arabian trade had long been moved direct by sea to Egypt[144] with serious consequences for Nabataean commercial well-being. Caravans did still operate through Arabia Petraea. Strabo[145] refers to traders with loads of south Arabian aromatics travelling between Leuke Kome and Petra thence to Rhinocolura 'in such numbers of men and camels that they differ in no respect from an army', and in the time of Malichus II (A.D. 40–70),there are reports[146] of many but modest sized ships coming loaded from Arabia to Leuke Kome which had a centurion supervising the collection of a 25 per cent tax, and from which a road led to Petra. Leuke Kome has now been identified with Aynunah.[147] Nearby one finds a major roadstead at Khuraybah and a series of Nabataean and Roman sites in and around the springs and gardens of Aynunah itself, which has produced over one hundred rock-cut tombs and a major building with over 130 rooms, corridors, towers and courtyards.[148] Such activity required protection and it is probably no coincidence that most of the attested Nabataean garrisons and camps are in the Hedjaz, Hisma and Negev.

Trade links in the north, possibly reflecting a development of the Wadi Sirhan route from Jauf to counter the decline in Arabian traffic and also to exploit the developing Palmyrene monopoly of trade from the Gulf, are suggested by the presence of a Nabataean ethnarch at

---

[142] Strab. XVI.4.21 (779C).

[143] Negev 1974 (E 1045) 23–42. There were Nabataean merchants at Puteoli *c.* 30 B.C. (*CIS* II 1.2: 158).

[144] Strab. XVI.4.24 (781–2C). Dihle 1965 (E 1004) 25 suggests the transfer had begun in the late hellenistic period.   [145] XVI.4.23 (780–1C).   [146] *Periplus of the Erythraean Sea*, 19.

[147] Kirwan 1981 (E 1028) 1984 (E 1029).   [148] Ingraham *et al.* 1981 (E 1014) 63ff.

Damascus in the last years of Tiberius.[149] To this may be added the significant physical evidence from Decapolis cities, notably Philadelphia and Gerasa, for Nabataean communities there too.[150]

There was some industry in the kingdom apart from the ceramic. Copper was extracted from the mines in the Wadi Araba and in the Sinai[151] and those south of Petra, and asphalt had been exploited around the Dead Sea since the fourth century. Although no silver source is known in Arabia Petraea, both bronze and silver coinage appear throughout the two centuries before annexation,[152] and at least one Roman extorted an indemnity in silver from the Nabataeans in the late Republic.[153]

The foundation of the Nabataean economy continued to be sheep-and camel-raising as it had been in the early fourth century.[154] Now, however, they were much more involved in arable farming. Part of their realm offered good farming land, especially in the new lands of the Hauran; in the low rainfall of the Negev and Hedjaz the key lay in their skill in hydraulic engineering. No longer just the collection and storage in cisterns of water for their flocks, now too there was the beginning of 'water-harvesting'.[155]

The long reign of Aretas IV appears as a golden age of tranquillity and development in Arabia Petraea. Eighty per cent of known Nabataean coins belong to his reign.[156] Nor were they struck to pay extra troops. Quite the reverse; after assisting Varus in 4 B.C. there was no warfare again for forty years: in part the removal of a royal neighbour from Judaea itself and the marriage of Aretas' daughter to Herod Antipas, but largely the peace demanded by Rome between neighbours and an end of the raiding which was a feature of Nabataean life until the early Principate.[157]

The population of Petra at least is characterized in Strabo as a harmonious one: formal litigation was exclusively between foreigners or by foreigners against Nabataeans.[158] They appear as very materialistic, but with few slaves. Drinking parties were popular but drunkenness said to be limited; singing girls performed at their communal feasts. These last were probably religious. Temples included *triclinia*, funerary banquets formed part of the ceremonies at the famous rock tombs and they are attested also in the cemetery at Mampsis.[159]

---

[149] 2 Cor. 11.32; an official in charge of a Nabataean community is the more likely explanation rather than unlikely Nabataean rule.

[150] Graf 1986 (E 1011) 788–93; Gatier forthcoming (E 1009).

[151] 'Smith' is a common element in Sinaitic Nabataean names: Negev 1986 (E 1047) 10f.

[152] Meshorer 1975 (B 343) 00.

[153] Joseph. *AJ* XIV.81f; *BJ* 1.159 (Scaurus); cf. *AJ* XIV.103; *BJ* 1.178 (Gabinius).

[154] Joseph *AJ* XIX.94.4.   [155] Evenari *et al.* 1982 (E 1008) 95–178; Ingraham *et al.* 1981 (E 1014).

[156] Meshorer 1975 (B 343) 41.   [157] Strab. XVI.4.21 (779C).   [158] XVI.4.21 (779C).

[159] The meal included olives, dates, fowl and mutton (Negev 1986 (E 1047) 92).

The Nabataean religion involved worship both at sacred high places
and in temples (above, p. 726f). Their Supreme God, Dushara, 'the One
of Shara', the escarpment south of Petra, is widely commemorated.[160]
However, one of the earliest and grandest 'Nabataean' temples is that of
Baalshamin at Seeia in the Hauran.[161] There, a huge isolated sanctuary,
dedicated (probably by Herod the Great) between 33/2 and 2/1 B.C., was
constructed.

IV. CONCLUSION

On a July day in 69, Antioch witnessed an event which would have
astonished its inhabitants of a century before. The governor of the
province, Mucianus, made a speech to the populace in the theatre in
justification of Vespasian's proclamation as emperor and sought their
support for the civil war. Equally remarkable, he was able to gain the
sympathy of the populace by suggesting that the local garrisons were to
be transferred to Germany, and that they were to lose the troops they
were used to and with whom there had been a great deal of
intermarriage.[162]

Attitudes had changed and the reasons are not hard to find. Stable and
more efficient government had been introduced and the hand of Rome
was relatively light in its effect on local culture. Peace and security had
been firmly established. Even the recent wars of Corbulo had had little
direct effect on the province and there was no sympathy for the Jewish
rebels. A few cities had been founded and urban development given a
significant impetus. Trade had recovered and shrewd Syrian merchants
could fully exploit their safe access to Mediterranean markets. The
contrast with the last generation of Seleucid rule and of the last days of
the Republic was only too clear.

The shape of the province was not yet complete – that was to be the
work of the Flavians and, finally, Trajan, in removing the last of the petty
rulers. But the transition from the bitter, resentful, ravaged province of
the 40s B.C. to the stable rapidly integrating province of the second
century A.D. was well advanced.[163]

---

[160] Wenning, 1987 (E 1069).   [161] Dentzer and Dentzer 1981 (E 1002).   [162] Tac. *Hist.* 11.80.
[163] The text of this chapter was completed in 1987 and it has therefore not been possible to take
account of recent important work, in particular, F. Millar, *The Roman Near East* (Cambridge, Mass.,
1993); M. Sartre, *L'orient romain* (Paris, 1991).

CHAPTER 14d

JUDAEA

MARTIN GOODMAN

I. THE HERODS

The political history of Judaea in the period covered by this volume is particularly well attested through the preservation of the work of the Jewish historian Josephus, who wrote after A.D. 70 first a detailed account of the Judaean revolt against Rome from A.D. 66 to A.D. 73 or 74 and then an apologetic version for non-Jewish readers of Jewish history to the outbreak of that war.[1]

A priest from Jerusalem and a commander of the Jewish forces in Galilee during the war, Josephus was steeped in the traditions of his nation. He was an acute observer, but his evidence is tainted by the traumas of his own career. Captured by Roman forces in A.D. 67, he espoused the enemy cause with a wholeheartedness that won him the favour of the future emperor Vespasian and enabled him to spend the last part of his life, including his active years as a writer, in comfort, probably in Rome.

The bias in Josephus' narratives, particularly of the first century A.D., when Judaea fell under direct Roman rule, can be partly checked from other sources. Inscriptions provide less useful evidence than elsewhere in the Roman East, for the Judaean ruling class never picked up the epigraphic habit except in the medium of coinage, but the contribution of archaeology is large and growing. The Gospels and Acts of the Apostles add further evidence although, since they are theological documents, their accuracy cannot be taken for granted. But Josephus' narrative is best checked through his own inconsistencies: his detailed account often reveals information that his more sweeping generalizations and general tendentious approach tend to obfuscate.[2]

---

[1] The main sources for the reign of Herod are the parallel accounts in Joseph. *BJ* I.211–II.166 and *AJ* XIV.271–XVII end. In both narratives Josephus used but corrected Nicolaus of Damascus. In *AJ* he may have had additional material from Strabo, *Historiae* and possibly a biography of Herod by a certain Ptolemy. Cf., above all, Schalit 1969 (E 1206). For a basic introduction to the rabbinic sources used in this chapter, and the form of citation, see Stemberger 1992 (E 1215A).

[2] On approaches to Josephus, cf. Rajak 1983 (B 147) and works cited in Feldman 1986 (B 50). For the coins of Herod and his successors, cf. Meshorer 1982 (B 344). For recent excavations, see Avi-Yonah and Stern 1975–8 (E 1078); Avigad 1984 (E 1080).

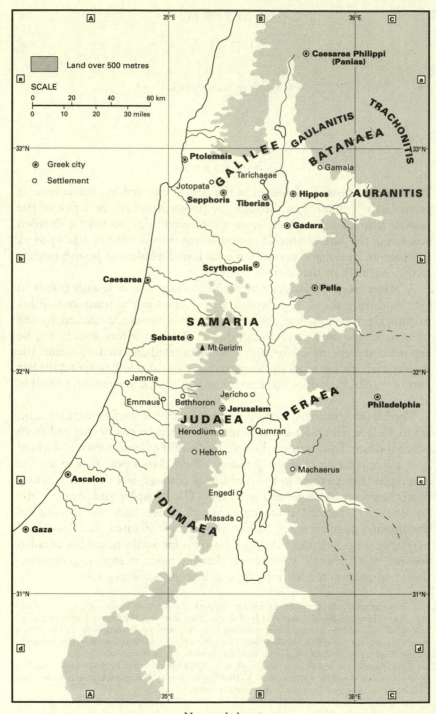

Map 20. Judaea.

Herod to some extent presented himself as a Jewish monarch, and for some Romans his family were seen as representative of Jewry.[3] But his rule over Judaea was inaugurated in 40 B.C. and preserved until *c.* 4 B.C. almost entirely at the behest of Rome.

Herod's story begins with the career of his father Antipater, who had taken advantage since the sixties B.C. of internal dissensions within the Hasmonaean dynasty to promote himself, trading on the obscurity of his own Idumaean lineage, which made him appear no danger to his Hasmonaean patron, Hyrcanus II; the Idumaeans had only been forcibly converted to Judaism in the 120s B.C. and could still be insulted as only half-Jews by some Judaeans.[4] At the same time he cultivated Roman officials in the East, for their influence had been decisive since 63 B.C. in the balance of power between the various Hasmonaean factions. In 44 B.C. Antipater's position thus relied on his friendship with Caesar, but by 43 B.C. he had rapidly won the confidence of Cassius and persuaded Hyrcanus to support the Liberators of Rome. His power was cut short only by his assassination in a court intrigue.

That it was Herod who inherited Antipater's position and not the latter's older son Phasael was due to Herod's demonstration of energy and competence in his father's lifetime. At the age of twenty-five in 48 B.C. he had already acted briefly as governor of Galilee on Caesar's behalf. When in 43 B.C. he proceeded to destroy his father's murderer and the latter's supporters with Cassius' approval, his role as Hyrcanus' chief adviser was certain.

Herod's further progression to the crown was brought about by the continuing chaos in the eastern Mediterranean before and after Philippi. The Liberators urgently needed funds and Herod dutifully raised considerable quantities, first in Galilee and later in Judaea and Syria. When some cities in Judaea refused to pay, he ruthlessly subjected them to slavery. Meanwhile his position in Hyrcanus' estimation was strengthened when he routed the king's nephew Antigonus.

Cassius' defeat at Philippi did not check Herod's rise: Antony, concerned not to lose a powerful friend of Rome, accepted the fiction that Hyrcanus and his side had supported the Liberators unwillingly and advanced Herod and Phasael to the position of tetrarchs; the precise relationship between the brothers and Hyrcanus, who was entitled ethnarch, is unclear.

This promotion of Antipater's sons was greeted with rioting by the Jews but enforced with bloodshed, only to be rendered nominal in 41/40 B.C. by the Parthian invasion of Palestine and the installation in Judaea of Antigonus; he was to be king over the Gentile population and High

---

[3] Cf. 'Herodis dies' at Pers. v.180, as a description of the sabbath in the middle of the first century A.D.   [4] Joseph. *AJ* XIV.403.

Priest of the Jews, who welcomed his accession and the legitimacy which he advertised on his coins. Phasael was killed or forced to commit suicide. Hyrcanus was sent to Parthia and, by mutilation of his ears, rendered incapable of holding the high priesthood. Herod in early 40 B.C. fled to Rome.

That flight, which implied that only in Rome did he have a hope for the future, proved opportune. The triumvirs, especially Antony, to whom the eastern provinces had been allotted, saw in Herod the surest way to return Judaea to Roman control. No adult male Hasmonaean was readily available for promotion as a puppet ruler. The installation of a new family as monarchs of a client state was new in Roman foreign policy; but Herod was known in Roman society, he was a competent soldier, his father had been Caesar's friend, as an associate of Hyrcanus he was assumed to understand Jewish society. Less tangible but no less important a factor was his luck: he was in Rome just after the treaty of Brundisium, the right place at the right time.

Herod was granted the throne of Judaea and Samaria by the triumvirs with the support of the Senate in autumn 40 B.C. He celebrated, incongruously, with a sacrifice to Jupiter Capitolinus and set sail for Syria to take possession of his kingdom.

For three years all his efforts were without avail since he lacked sufficient forces. Only in 38 did Antony send two legions under Sosius for an attack on Jerusalem. Despite an attempt to win popular support by celebrating his delayed marriage with the Hasmonaean Mariamme, Herod was faced by the implacable opposition of his putative subjects. The reduction of Jerusalem, probably in July 37 B.C. after a siege of more than seven months, was Sosius' victory, for which he was not slow to claim credit and a triumph; Herod prevented the sack of his new capital only with difficulty. Antony, once again breaking with precedent, had Antigonus, who begged for mercy, executed.

Herod's loyalty to Antony was as great as his enthusiasm for Cassius had once been, and he proved his worth to his new patron during the Parthian campaign.[5] Antony in turn protected Herod even when Cleopatra demanded Judaea for herself or her children; the triumvir allowed her to take in 36 B.C. only the territory of Jericho and the rich balsam groves of Engedi near the Dead Sea, which Herod then cleverly leased back, thereby retaining political control over his domain despite the financial cost. That cost was augmented by his forced agreement to guarantee the rent of territory that Cleopatra had taken from the Nabataean king Malchus.

This friendship with Antony made Herod's position precarious after Actium, but a campaign in Nabataea in 32–31 B.C., undertaken at the

[5] Joseph. *AJ* XIV.439–46.

instigation of Cleopatra, prevented his presence on Antony's side in the battle itself, and in spring 30 B.C. Octavian not only confirmed his rule but presented him with an enlarged kingdom which included both the territory taken by Cleopatra and the fertile coastal plain of Judaea. Herod was to reign without further serious threat until his death in *c.* 4 B.C., becoming so firm a friend of Augustus that his territory was enlarged first by the addition of Trachonitis, Batanaea and Auranitis in 24/23 B.C. and then by Ulatha and Panias in the north in 20 B.C.

The apparent peace of these years was only achieved by continuing repression of opposition to Herod's rule by his subjects. In 26 B.C. Costobar, the governor of Idumaea, who was justifiably suspected of treason, was put to death. Disaffection in the Trachonitis caused endemic banditry in these border lands but no political threat. The refusal of more than 6,000 Pharisees to take the oath of loyalty demanded from them in *c.* 8 B.C. caused Herod annoyance but was not dangerous. Only as Herod approached death did an uprising in Jerusalem gather momentum in objection to the erection of a golden eagle above the Temple; even then it was only on his demise that widespread revolt broke out.

More dangerous to Herod was the disaffection within his family which was a constant feature of his reign from the beginning. His marriage to Mariamme in 37 B.C. was intended to boost his own prestige, but as a Hasmonaean princess she carried the hopes of all Jews who resented the Idumaean intruder. Herod needed either to eradicate or to harness the power she represented. That he was in two minds can be shown from his treatment of her younger brother Aristobulus III, whom he installed, aged sixteen, as High Priest in *c.* 35 B.C., only to panic when he was acclaimed with too much enthusiasm by the pilgrim crowd in Jerusalem. Herod staged an 'accidental' drowning for Aristobulus in the swimming bath in his palace in Jericho. Similar ambivalence was shown towards his old patron Hyrcanus, whose release Herod contrived from Parthia in 36 B.C. only to have him executed in 30 B.C. for alleged conspiracy with the king of Nabataea.

Such treatment of her father and brother was not calculated to endear Herod to Mariamme. He suspected her, probably with some justification, of rebellious designs, particularly during his own absences from the country; concern at the political threat she represented was augmented by fierce sexual jealousy of possible marital infidelity with those to whom she was entrusted while he was away. In 29 B.C. she was put on trial and executed. Herod's personal sorrow was perhaps compensated by the diminution of open opposition to his rule for the next twenty years, but it is at least possible that the subtle calculations of the power-seeker had in this case been upset by the savage passions of the infatuated lover.

The bitter harvest of Mariamme's execution was reaped when her mother Alexandra attempted rebellion in 28 B.C. and was killed; the poison lingered also in Herod's relationship with her two elder sons, Aristobulus and Alexander, when they reached manhood. Herod had sent the young princes to Rome in 24/23 B.C. for an education in the house of a Pollio,[6] and when they returned to Jerusalem in *c*. 16 B.C. he made it clear that he wished them to succeed him. But such plans proved disingenuous. Herod's own sister Salome and his brother Pheroras, who had been since 20 B.C. tetrarch of Peraea, were unwilling to see their Idumaean family eclipsed by their half-Hasmonaean nephews. They persuaded Herod to recall his eldest son Antipater, whose mother was the Idumaean Doris; Antipater was accordingly also marked out for preferment by being sent to Rome in 13 B.C.

If Herod hoped in this way to control the ambitions of Mariamme's sons and the jealousy of his other relations, he was disappointed. Antipater began a concentrated intrigue to prove the treachery of the young princes to their father. The charges may even have been true, for Mariamme's sons had little reason to like Herod and by virtue of their Hasmonaean ancestry could expect some popular support. But the truth hardly mattered. Herod accused his sons before Augustus in *c*. 13 B.C. They were acquitted then and given a future share in the kingdom with Antipater, but Alexander at least was suspected of continued plots, perhaps with Herod's brother Pheroras. After further accusations, in *c*. 7 B.C. the young men were tried before a partially Roman court at Berytus and condemned. Herod had them rapidly executed before disaffection spread. Their main accuser Antipater, after brief glory as heir apparent in Rome in 5 B.C., was in turn accused of conniving with Pheroras against Herod; Pheroras died of natural causes before execution, but Antipater was put to death a few days before his father expired in *c*. 4 B.C., as much for contriving his brothers' downfall as for his own ambitions.

Such turmoil within the dynasty left the line of succession hardly clear when Herod died. Herod had in a final will left his kingdom to Archelaus, the offspring of a Samaritan wife Malthace. Archelaus' younger full brother Antipas was left Galilee and Peraea, while Philip, son of a woman from Jerusalem called Cleopatra, was to rule the north-eastern wild country of Gaulanitis, Trachonitis, Batanaea and Panias. These provisions overrode an earlier will which, for reasons now unclear, had left everything to Antipas, and in disappointment he went to Rome to persuade Augustus to uphold his father's earlier intention.

The fraternal struggle took place before Augustus' *consilium* in Rome rather than in Judaea. The choice would be made by the *princeps* alone. None of the three men had been groomed as successor by Herod, since

---

[6] Probably Asinius Pollio, but Vedius Pollio is also possible, cf. Syme 1961 (D 69).

the three dead sons had been preferred for that role, though all of them had received part of their education in Rome.

In Judaea, immediate unrest, reviving the cause of the religious enthusiasts put to death for taking down the eagle from the Temple (see above, p. 741), was partially defused first by Archelaus' promise to accede to demands for lower taxes and the removal of Herod's favourites from high positions and then by bloodshed, but more serious disturbances erupted when Archelaus had set off for Rome accompanied by his rivals and by a delegation of Jews who had been encouraged by the legate of Syria to request that Judaea be incorporated within his province and the troublesome Herods deposed.

The causes of these more serious agitations in the absence of the Herodian princes were probably varied.[7] In Galilee a certain Judas, son of a bandit named Ezekias who had opposed Herod in the forties B.C. (above, p. 739), sought power; he was perhaps a remnant of a powerful Hasmonaean family, in which case his aim will have been independence from both Herodian and Roman control.[8] In Peraea a certain Simon, a former slave of Herod, proclaimed himself king. In the Judaean countryside a former shepherd called Athronges, with his four brothers, also sought royal power.

It is not likely that these two latter rebellions were serious political attacks on the Herodian dynasty. The humble origins of the rebel leaders may perhaps be significant in assessing their motivation. It is possible that Athronges, with his four brothers, deliberately evoked the spirit of the Maccabees. Both he and Simon may have claimed religious sanction for national rebellion, but there is no direct evidence for this in the scanty report in Josephus.[9]

Meanwhile in Jerusalem itself riots were sparked off by the behaviour of the procurator Sabinus, who had been sent into Judaea from Syria by Augustus to control the country while the will was being debated: a pilgrim crowd during the feast of Pentecost attacked him for reasons not known, and Sabinus retaliated by taking 400 talents from the Temple, thereby exacerbating the hostility. Quite different in intention and political significance was the revolt in Idumaea by some of Herod's veteran soldiers, for this mutiny was led by some of Herod's own relatives; their names are not known, but the weakness of Archelaus' position was emphasized by such disaffection even in the heartland of his family's traditional support.[10]

Suppression of all these disturbances was carried out with efficient

---

[7] For events after Herod's death, see Joseph. *AJ* XVII.206–323; *BJ* II.1–100; Nicolaus of Damascus, *FGrH* 90 F 136(8)–(11).

[8] See discussion of the role of this Judas in Freyne 1980 (E 1115) 214–17.

[9] For the link to the Maccabees, see Farmer 1958 (E 1113).   [10] *BJ* II.55–78.

ruthlessness by Varus, the legate of Syria, with two legions. Herod's final will was upheld by Augustus: Archelaus was confirmed as ruler in Judaea but with the title of ethnarch rather than king and the cities of Gaza, Gadara and Hippos removed from his territory; Antipas received Galilee, and Philip was granted his domain east of the Galilean lake. Both these latter had only the title of tetrarch, but they both enjoyed independence from their brother's sway.

On his return from Rome Archelaus found his land pacified but his subjects deeply hostile; a legion was left in Jerusalem to prevent further violent outbreaks. Josephus' account of Archelaus' rule is very skimpy; it seems that the history written by Nicolaus of Damascus, Herod's court historian, on which Josephus relied for the narrative of Herod's own rule, now came to an end. At any rate, in A.D. 6 Archelaus was deposed by Augustus and banished to Vienne in southern Gaul, and Judaea was taken under direct Roman control.[11]

Archelaus' brothers fared somewhat better. Philip remained for most of his rule ensconced peacefully in his somewhat remote territory, administering it, according to Josephus, with conscientious moderation until his undramatic death while still tetrarch in *c.* A.D. 33. Antipas ruled for some years in greater style in Galilee, but in *c.* A.D. 34 his marriage to his elder brother's wife Herodias brought him the enmity of the neighbouring Arab king, Aretas IV of Nabataea, whose daughter, Antipas' first wife, was slighted by the incestuous relationship. Enmity led to war in A.D. 36, and both kings suffered censure by Tiberius. When, at Herodias' insistence, Antipas in A.D. 39 requested the title of king from Gaius, he was deposed and sent into exile in Lugdunum; Herodias accompanied him.

The beneficiary of Antipas' misfortune was his nephew and Herodias' brother, Herod Agrippa I.[12] Agrippa's career, which had fluctuated from extreme misfortune to the heights of power, was nearing its peak when, probably in A.D. 40, he added Antipas' ethnarchy in Galilee to the territory which he had already inherited from Philip in A.D. 37. Agrippa's success exemplifies the Herodian technique in the pursuit of political power. The son of Aristobulus, who was executed by Herod in *c.* 7 B.C., he grew up close to the imperial court in Rome, but without official position or private income he ran up enormous debts and returned at some time after A.D. 23 in despair to Palestine. Rescued briefly by his brother-in-law Antipas, he made his way eventually in spring A.D. 36 to Italy, where his charm enabled him to join the emperor on Capri and to win the friendship of Gaius. Imprisoned by Tiberius for referring too

[11] Sources for Archelaus' rule are Joseph. *AJ* XVII.339–55; *BJ* II.111–17.

[12] For the career of Agrippa I, see Joseph. *AJ* XVIII.143–239, XIX.274–359; *BJ* II.178–82, 206–22; Acts 12; *m.Bikk.*3: 4; *m.Sot.* 7: 8. See Schwartz 1987 (E 1209).

openly to his wish to see Gaius succeed to the Principate, he was released with honour when that event came about in spring A.D. 37 and was granted by the new emperor both the territory once governed by Philip and the tetrarchy of Abila in the Lebanon, with the title of king.

Skill at court intrigue and the friendship of a Roman prince had thus elevated Agrippa, and the same factors were to enlarge him still further. While Gaius was alive Agrippa preferred to rule his subjects through deputies, and frequently returned to Rome where real power lay. It was a wise decision: in a dramatic episode described in detail by Josephus (see above, p. 230), Agrippa played a central role in the elevation of Claudius to the Principate in A.D. 41 after the assassination of Gaius, and Claudius showed his gratitude by granting him the entire kingdom once ruled by Herod.

Agrippa now went to Jerusalem to enjoy the benefits of his intrigue. Popular with the people partly because of his Hasmonaean links through his grandmother, he ruled in a style sufficiently magnificent to arouse a suspicion in the mind of Marsus, the legate of Syria, that, by convoking in Tiberias a meeting of five other petty kings allied to Rome, he might be plotting rebellion. The charge was implausible, for Agrippa would have gained nothing and lost much by independence, but his painful death 'eaten up by worms' put an end to speculation.[13]

No other member of the dynasty of Herod was to achieve such power in Judaea. Some of Herod's less prominent descendants were granted territories, but these were in obscure parts of the eastern empire and little connected with Judaea:[14] Agrippa's own children were still young on his death in A.D. 44.[15] Their later considerable influence on Judaean society was achieved more through their prestige among Jews derived from their father than from the grant of power by Rome. Thus Agrippa II, who was in Rome in A.D. 44, was given in A.D. 49 the kingdom of Chalcis in the Lebanon that his uncle Herod had enjoyed from A.D. 41 to 48, and then in A.D. 53, in exchange for Chalcis, a larger territory including both the tetrarchy once ruled by Philip and other land east of the Sea of Galilee. Furthermore, some time after A.D. 54, Nero added to this kingdom parts of Galilee itself near the lake and a small area in the northern Peraea. But his political importance rested less on these territories, which merely brought him revenue, than on his role in Jerusalem, where he was granted the right, previously held by his father and uncle, to control the administration of the Temple. Not that even this control was entirely secure, for despite strenuous efforts he was

---

[13] Descriptions of Agrippa's death are given in *AJ* XIX.343–52; Acts 12:19–23.
[14] See Jones 1938 (E 1152) 259–61.
[15] For the careers of Agrippa's children see Joseph. *AJ* XVIII–XX; *BJ* II–VII; Suet. *Tit.* 7; Tac. *Hist.* II.2.81; Dio LXVI.15.3–5, 18.1.

unable to prevent the priests building a wall in the late fifties A.D. to block the view from his palace into the interior of the Temple.[16]

Agrippa II's sisters, who had no formal powers at all, wielded hardly less influence. Drusilla married the Roman governor of Judaea, Antonius (or Claudius) Felix. Berenice achieved notoriety as paramour of the future emperor Titus.

Throughout this long and complex history over more than a hundred years, Roman favour to Herod and his descendants was remarkably constant and public. Their power depended upon Rome, which guaranteed their fidelity, while on the whole they showed fair competence in the administration of areas which, though not of major consequence in the immediate context of the empire's defence, were not themselves easy to hold in subjection. Each Herodian ruler was judged by his efficiency; at any rate, when they were grossly incompetent at keeping the peace, they were easily enough deposed, as Archelaus and Antipas discovered.

Jewish support for the Herods was, not surprisingly, much less enthusiastic, particularly when their regime was contrasted unfavourably to the Hasmonaeans they had supplanted. The myth of the Hasmonaeans as national liberators remained potent even in the first century A.D.[17] Herod and his successors could only survive through a complete break with this past. All the male members of the Hasmonaean dynasty were dead by 30 B.C.; the women were married to Herod's own close relatives. It is probable that the supporters and friends who had formed the courts of the last Hasmonaeans were ruthlessly eliminated: forty-five of Antigonus' associates were killed. It is unlikely to be chance that no family whose original prominence can be traced to before Herod can be discerned in the detailed prosopography of Judaea in the first century A.D.[18]

In their place Herod promoted his own men. His court was largely composed of Gentiles who could be guaranteed not to seek influence except through his patronage; thus, most of his closest advisers, his generals and the tutors of his children were not Jewish. Exempted from this rule were only two categories of Jews. His own family was trusted by Herod to a remarkable extent, as in the nomination of his brother Pheroras as tetrarch of Peraea in 20 B.C.; in his case, such trust proved misplaced (see above, p. 742). The second category comprised the occupants of those positions in Judaean society which by their nature could only be filled by Jews.

Most important of these was the high priesthood, which had since the Persian period marked out its holder as a secular as well as religious leader. When the attempt to install Aristobulus III foundered (see above,

---

[16] Joseph. *AJ* xx.189–94.   [17] Cf. Farmer 1956 (E 1112).
[18] Cf. the discussion in Stern 1976 (E 1218) II.561–630.

p. 741), Herod filled the post with Jews from Babylonia and Alexandria whose unsullied priestly birth could not be disputed but whose influence in Judaea was probably negligible. Only the family of Boethus, an Alexandrian who held the office from *c.* 25–4 B.C. was permitted some secular advancement. The clothes of the High Priest, which had once enshrined oracular powers and still apparently bestowed exceptional prestige on the wearer, were kept in Herod's possession further to limit the pontiffs' power. Most dramatically of all, Herod inaugurated a custom derived from pagan cults of shortening the tenure of the office.

Thus was opposition effectively silenced. Herod's sister's husbands proved some danger: both Joseph, executed in 34 B.C., and Costobar, executed in *c.* 26 B.C., had been married to Salome, and their ambition was suspect because of this proximity to the royal house. Few other Idumaean friends were allowed to join the circle of power; of these, only Salome's third husband Alexas is known to have retained his family's influence. The power of the ancient theocracy was broken. Any change in institutions of government was probably less significant than this removal of key personnel and their replacement with Herod's own supporters.[19]

Such measures did not still the abiding hatred of Herod within the wider Judaean population. Many Jews had been killed or enslaved in 37 B.C. when Sosius seized Jerusalem on his behalf. Herod's origins, not just as an Idumaean but as the son of a non-Jewish mother who is not known to have converted, were held against him, especially since it is possible that for some Jews, in this period as later, Jewish citizenship was held to be passed down through the female line.[20] His interference in the prestige of the high priesthood was resented, as was his insistence that his unwilling subjects should forswear themselves by taking an oath to him in 17 B.C. and probably again in *c.* 8 B.C.

It is also probable but not certain that the populace was heavily taxed to pay for Herod's grandiose expenditure and the huge reserves which he accumulated.[21] Herod may have enjoyed a considerable income from hereditary estates in Idumaea, from confiscated land in Judaea, both royal and private, and from letting out grazing land to the Nabataeans. The right to collect taxes for Rome and to farm half the revenue of the Cyprus copper-mines will have added considerably to his revenues. His expenses will have been less if, as is probable but not certain, he did not pay tribute to Rome after Actium. It is thus possible that the tax burden

[19] On the administration under Herod, see Schalit 1969 (E 1206) 183–223.

[20] There is much debate over the date when the inheritance of citizenship through the female rather than male line was generally accepted by Jews. See Cohen 1985 (E 1101).

[21] On the weight of Herod's taxes, and the continuing debate about the imposition of *Roman* taxes on the client kingdom, see Schalit 1969 (E 1206) 262–98; Gabba 1990 (E 1117).

on Judaea was not excessive: emergency measures in famine conditions in 25, 20 and 14 B.C. have no implications for the weight of normal exactions. Perhaps his Jewish subjects objected to paying taxes of any kind to a king whose legitimacy they questioned. Later Jewish literature in antiquity depicted Herod as a monster.[22]

Herod had few weapons with which to ward off such hostility. Apart from attempting to smother disaffection at an early stage by the use of a secret police, his most blatant reaction was the building of fortresses within the country for his own protection. The massive construction of surviving parts of his palaces in Jerusalem, Masada and Herodium bears witness to the importance of such defences.[23] It is probable that these fortresses, like the military colonies planted mostly on the eastern edges of his territory, were intended as much to control the subject population as to fend off external foes. In Jerusalem a highly trained mercenary force composed mainly of Gentiles and largely recruited from the Greek cities in and near Palestine kept the peace; the Jews included in their number were mostly Idumaeans and Babylonians, though it is not known whether the omission of Judaeans was through their reluctance or Herod's insistence.[24]

But Herod also took steps to woo his Jewish subjects. At least while in Jerusalem he adhered to the main tenets of Judaism. His decision not to advertise his own portrait on his coins was in deference to the biblical prohibition on graven images. His avoidance of pork was the subject of a famous joke ascribed to Augustus: 'I would rather be Herod's pig than his son.'[25] Above all he spent lavishly on the embellishment of Jerusalem and its Temple, creating a monument to the glory of his people as well as himself. The building was tactfully left under the supervision of the priests – except for the eagle, whose erection over the Temple door at Herod's command provoked violent opposition (see above, p. 741).

The extent of Herod's commitment to such 'double book-keeping' – presenting himself as Jewish to Jews, Greek to Gentiles – should not be exaggerated; such an attitude was in fact more characteristic of his grandson Agrippa I than of Herod himself.[26] Herod did not hesitate to use hellenistic titles on his coins or to welcome many Greek-educated Gentiles to his Judaean court. Nevertheless he undoubtedly tried hard to promote his Jewish credentials, even claiming rather ludicrously that he was really descended from a line of Babylonian Jews.[27] He prevented the marriage of the Nabataean Syllaeus to his sister Salome when the former

[22] *b. Baba Bathra* 3b–4a; *b. Taanith* 23a; *Lev. Rab.* 35:8; *Num. Rab.* 14:20.
[23] See especially Yadin 1966 (E 1235) 40–156.
[24] On Jewish levies in Herod's army, see Schalit 1969 (E 1206) 167–83.
[25] Macrob. *Sat.* 11.4.11, based on the play of the Greek words υἱός and ὗς.
[26] For analysis of Herod's rule in these terms, see Baumann 1983 (E 1091) 264.
[27] Joseph. *AJ* xiv.9 (= Jacoby, *FGrH* 90 A F96).

refused to convert to Judaism, and he liked to present himself as the protector of all Jews under Roman rule, wherever they might live.

Such bids for popularity seem to have failed to change Herod's image at least in Judaea. Much of the credit for rebuilding the Temple was destroyed by the riots against the erection of the eagle above it. Josephus writes that at Herod's death the 'notables of the kingdom' had been shut up in the hippodrome in Jericho under threat of execution; Herod is said to have planned their demise to coincide with his to prevent unseemly joy when he died.

Neither Archelaus nor Antipas achieved any more popularity than their father. Philip, who did not rule over many Jews and, unlike his brothers, did not use 'Herod' as a dynastic name, avoided evoking such resentment, but the first Herodian to be accepted by at least part of the Judaean populace as more or less a genuinely Jewish king was Agrippa I. It is significant that Agrippa managed this not least by avoiding in Judaea any public connexion with his grandfather, preferring to be known as Agrippa rather than Herod; in his favour was his Hasmonaean grandmother Mariamme. Both he and his son won some further support by their championing of the Jewish cause at Rome when disturbances broke out in Alexandria and Judaea under Roman governors,[28] but neither ever won a really enthusiastic following in Jerusalem.

The Herods compensated for this uneasy relationship with their Jewish subjects by seeking support elsewhere. They preserved excellent relations with the gentile population of the Greek cities in and around Palestine, increasing their number by various foundations, of which the most important was the great port of Caesarea. Herod and his descendants gave huge gifts to numerous Syrian cities, partly just to emphasize the Hellenic culture of the Jewish dynasty. Herod made grand donations also to cities and shrines in mainland Greece and Asia Minor. In Judaea itself, however, the Greeks were kept under firm control as part of the Herodian realm.

More important for the Herods themselves was their self-conception as the most glorious of the petty dynasties which ruled the Near East in the early Empire in friendly alliance with Rome and under her watchful eye. Influence on this plane was encouraged by intermarriage between Herod's relatives and the families of other client kings from areas as far afield as Nabataea, Emesa, Cilicia, Cappadocia and Africa.[29] Relations with these dynasties were only strained when proximity encouraged Herodian dreams of expansion; such dreams help to explain the

[28] For Agrippa I and II in Rome, cf. Joseph. *AJ* XVIII.289–301; XIX.279, 288; XX.135. For Agrippa II's patronage of Josephus see Joseph. *Vit.* 362, 364–7; *Ap.* 1.51. For the rabbinic view, see *m.Bikk,* 3: 4; *m. Sotah* 7: 8.

[29] For these relations, see Sullivan 1978 (E 1064).

occasional hostility shown towards the Nabataeans, particularly in the wars of 9 B.C. and A.D. 36.[30]

Good relations with the emperor were of overriding importance to all the Herods. Cities were named in the emperor's honour; Herod entitled himself on official inscriptions 'Friend of the Emperor' and 'Friend of the Romans'; in about 8 B.C. he added to the oath of allegiance the name of the emperor; in the non-Jewish cities he established the imperial cult with great enthusiasm soon after Actium; in Jerusalem he began the practice of a daily sacrifice in the Temple for the well-being of the emperor and, less in accordance with Jewish custom, quadrennial games in the emperor's honour. Both Herod and his successors paid frequent visits to the imperial court in Rome.

The Herods thus functioned as much on the international as on the purely Judaean stage, intriguing for power in Rome as in Jerusalem. In neither city were they entirely accepted. Their Judaism, strikingly superficial though it seemed to Jews, distinguished them from the Roman senators and emperors in whose company they were found: the prospect that Berenice might marry the future emperor Titus caused outrage among the latter's associates.[31] Not until the second century A.D., when all their territorial rights had disappeared along with the vestiges of their Judaism, did the descendants of Herod win full acceptance in Roman society.[32]

II. ROMAN ADMINISTRATION[33]

Direct Roman rule over Judaea began in A.D. 6 on the deposition of Archelaus. There was probably no deeper cause than that announced in public: Augustus' personal dissatisfaction with the ethnarch's immoderate and brutal behaviour towards his subjects.[34] Other explanations, however, have been proposed and may be correct: Rome benefited financially by the transfer of royal property such as the Engedi balsam groves to the imperial fiscus; the tribute raised by Rome despite provincial hostility was not small; the Judaean hill country had been held by the Parthians from 40 to 37 B.C. and was of some, albeit slight, strategic importance for the defence of the eastern Roman frontier; in

---

[30] On this uneasy coexistence, see Bowersock 1983 (E 990) esp. pp. 50–3, 65–7.

[31] Suet. *Tit.* 7; Dio LXVI.15.3–4; 18.1. See Crook 1951 (E 1106).

[32] See Sullivan 1978 (E 1064) 935–8 on C. Claudius Severus and other consular descendants of the eastern client kings; Smallwood 1976 (E 1212) 551, on C. Iulius Severus.

[33] The history of Judaea from A.D. 6 to A.D. 70 is found in Joseph. *BJ* II.117–VII end; *AJ* XVIII–XX; *Vit.*; Philo, *Leg.* The emphasis in the three narratives by Josephus varies in accordance with their different purposes, but they can usually be reconciled.

[34] Joseph. *AJ* XVII.342–3; *BJ* II.111–13; Dio LV.27.6; cf. Smallwood 1976 (E 1212) 117.

general, Augustus seems to have assumed that the imposition of direct rule in the place of client kings was desirable when appropriate.

Whatever the cause, direct rule proved to be Rome's more or less permanent solution to the squabbles of Herod's descendants over Judaea. Apart from the brief period (A.D. 41–4) when Agrippa I reigned (see above, p. 745), the same kind of Roman administration remained in force until A.D. 66, when a great rebellion led first to the establishment of an independent Jewish state and then to the fall of that state in an orgy of violence.

The decline towards catastrophe was gradual and probably intermittent but the signs were evident from the beginning. Despite the unpopularity of the deposed Archelaus, the first months under a Roman governor already witnessed considerable unrest. The immediate cause of discontent was the imposition of a provincial census under the supervision of the governor of Syria, P. Sulpicius Quirinius. It is not clear whether the complaint was aimed at higher taxation or the notion of being registered or the unpalatability of so blatant a sign of foreign domination. The trouble was soon stilled, for the moment.

Despite this early evidence that the administration of Judaea would not be easy, neither Augustus nor his successors seem to have taken great pains in the selection of suitable governors. All those chosen were of equestrian or lesser ranks; the province was too small to insult a senator with its rule, especially since no legions were stationed there. The title *praefectus* on an inscription set up by Pilate, governor *c*. A.D. 26 to 36, shows the earliest governors to have exercised military authority;[35] the term *procurator* used after Claudius, and by Josephus in discussing also the earlier governors, reflects a change in terminology rather than function. All governors owed their position to the direct patronage of the emperor, to whom they also reported. All retained the military *ius gladii*.

Nothing is recorded of the origins of the governors before A.D. 41, and none is known to have progressed further in his career; a salutary reminder of the insignificance of Judaea in Roman terms and also, perhaps, of Josephus' ignorance of events which preceded his own recollection. Of the later procurators, the historian records more detail of only three, whose appointment he evidently considered exceptional. The emperor Claudius appointed in *c*. A.D. 46 the apostate Jew Tiberius Iulius Alexander, who came from a leading Jewish family from Alexandria; Claudius evidently hoped to assuage the Jews' disappointment at their loss of autonomy on the death of Agrippa I in A.D. 44, but, though the success of this policy can no longer be judged since Iulius Alexander

---

[35] Frova 1961 (B 232); cf. Weber 1971 (B 296).

was probably still a powerful figure in Rome when Josephus wrote, it is
unlikely that the Jews were very enthusiastic at the prospect of rule by a
public apostate.[36] Less well intentioned and probably more disastrous
was the appointment in *c.* A.D. 52 of the freedman Felix, brother of the
influential Pallas; both Tacitus and Josephus express disgust at his
elevation.[37] Worst of all was the last procurator Gessius Florus (A.D. 64–
6) whose origins from Clazomenae inclined him fatally to sympathize
with the Greeks of the province against the Jews; he owed his position to
his wife's friendship with Poppaea. Of the other procurators, ten or
eleven in number, little more than the name is known.

The extent to which the unrest engendered by the census in A.D. 6 was
continued in the years immediately following has been much debated.
Tacitus records a complaint in A.D. 17 against the weight of Roman
taxation but not the principle of its imposition; for the rest he asserts that
'under Tiberius all was quiet'.[38] The disturbances surrounding the
crucifixion of Jesus are thus passed over by the Roman senator without
mention. Other disorders in the time of Pilate were also treated by the
Roman authorities as of less significance than with hindsight they
deserve: Josephus records how Pilate provoked a mass demonstration
against his introduction of legionary standards into Jerusalem and later
caused a storm of protest, quelled only with bloodshed, by sacrilegiously
using money taken from the Temple to build an aqueduct for the city;[39]
another incident, mentioned by Philo alone, when Pilate was compelled
to withdraw from Jerusalem shields bearing the emperor's name,
perhaps because the reference therein to the divine Augustus was seen as
idolatrous, may be identical with the episode involving the standards.[40]
Tiberius, ensconced on Capri, ignored such trivialities. Pilate lost his
office only after an even more appalling crime in which a crowd of
Samaritans was slaughtered in an eager search for the treasure said to be
hidden on their holy mountain of Gerizim.

These symptoms of unrest were entirely overshadowed for later
historians by the sudden, unexpected and climactic events of A.D. 40.[41] A
complaint sent through the procurator of the city to the new emperor
Gaius in late A.D. 39 by the Gentile inhabitants of Jamnia, to the effect
that their Jewish neighbours had refused to allow them to set up altars
for his worship, elicited the response that a statue with the emperor's
effigy must be set up in the Temple in Jerusalem. The effect was
pandemonium: of the two detailed surviving accounts, that of the
contemporary Philo is preferable to Josephus', but the very fact that the

---

[36] Burr 1955 (C 336).   [37] Tac. *Ann.* XII.54; *Hist.* v.9.3; cf. Joseph. *AJ* xx.182.
[38] Tac. *Ann.* II.42.5; *Hist.* v.9.2.   [39] Joseph. *BJ* II.169–77; *AJ* xVIII.55–62.
[40] Philo, *Leg.* 38 (299–306).
[41] Joseph. *AJ* xVIII.261–309; Philo, *Leg.* 188, 207–333; Tac. *Hist.* v.9.

story of these events was treated almost as a dramatic myth by those, like Josephus, who were children at the time is highly significant. Agrippa I in Rome tried to dissuade his old friend, in Judaea the populace refused to harvest (or, depending on the precise chronology, perhaps to sow) their crops; Publius Petronius, the governor of Syria, to whom the task of installing the statue had fallen, baulked at the consequences of so grave an assault on the Jewish cult and prevaricated. Josephus and Philo state that the people were prepared to die to prevent Gaius' sacrilege, and Tacitus adds that they were close to rebellion. According to Josephus, Gaius repented his intention, at least temporarily, after Agrippa's intervention; but Philo states more plausibly that only the emperor's death in A.D. 41 forestalled calamity – and brought a remarkable change in fortune with the advent of a glamorous Jewish king, Agrippa I, only for this renaissance to be in turn abruptly terminated by his demise (see above, p. 745).

The unhappy events of A.D. 44–66 need to be seen against this background of the arbitrary imposition and removal of persecution, the raising and dashing of hopes. A border conflict in A.D. 44 between the Jewish inhabitants of Peraea and the citizens of Philadelphia was easily crushed and agitation against the new procurator Cuspius Fadus (A.D. 44–c. 46) for failing to return the high priestly garments to the Jews was mostly confined to the ruling class, but the band urged by a messianic prophet named Theudas to retire into the desert was apparently reckoned more dangerous and suppressed by the execution of Theudas himself. A period of comparative peace under Tiberius Iulius Alexander (c. A.D. 46–8) was followed by riots in Jerusalem under Ventidius Cumanus (A.D. 48–c. 52) when one soldier displayed himself indecently near the Temple and another burnt a copy of the Jewish Law during retaliatory action against a Judaean village whose authorities had failed to apprehend some brigands who had stolen goods from an imperial slave. More serious intercommunal fighting was to lead to Cumanus' exile: when a Galilean pilgrim was attacked by Samaritans while he was on the way to Jerusalem, a mob which rushed north from the festival celebrations caused such bloodshed before the procurator could control the combatants that the legate of Syria sent all parties, including Cumanus, to Rome, where they were duly punished.

Felix (c. A.D. 52–c. 60), who had probably already been sent to Samaria to control the populace and help with the trial of Cumanus, proved no better as the new governor. Brigandage in the countryside was matched by urban terrorism in Jerusalem. Members of the ruling class began to use gangs on the streets of the city. An Egyptian Jew led a large group fired with eschatological hopes to Jerusalem from the Jordan, and they were only dispersed by the attack of Roman cohorts.

The followers of other visionaries suffered a similar fate under Porcius Festus (c. A.D. 60–2), and both banditry in the Judaean hills and violence in Jerusalem were further stimulated by the venality or incompetence of his successor Albinus (A.D. 62–4). But 'the patience of the Jews lasted until the procurator Gessius Florus' (A.D. 64–6),[42] when their willingness to accept Roman rule was finally put into question not by any of the preceding unrest but the quite separate issue of the rights of the Jews of Caesarea.

The Jews claimed Caesarea as their city because it had been founded by Herod; the Greeks, more plausibly given the prominence of pagan temples in the city from the start, claimed it as theirs. The intermittent dispute was decided by Nero in c. A.D. 60 in favour of the Greeks, but the Jews did not drop the issue, and in spring A.D. 66 intercommunal rioting broke out more seriously than ever before. Florus, bribed by the Jews to intervene, accepted the money but did nothing despite the increasingly unhappy effects of the disorders on the Caesarean Jews. Such venality aroused even more resentment when Florus compounded the Jews' hostility by taking 17 talents from the Temple treasury; in this case the action probably had more justification since the province had fallen behind in tribute payments, but this did not diminish horror at the sacrilege.

The antagonism thus aroused towards the procurator led quite rapidly to the outbreak of rebellion in the early summer of A.D. 66. Some youths lampooned Florus' meanness; the governor marched to Jerusalem to demand their surrender; the authorities refused to surrender the guilty; Florus let his troops loose on the city as punishment, arraigning before his tribunal even the richest Jerusalemites – Josephus claims that some were *equites* – and crucifying some of them.[43]

Despite the efforts of some of the Jerusalem ruling class it proved impossible to restore order under the procurator's aegis. Florus attempted a public demonstration of the Jews' submission by ordering them to greet two cohorts sent to Jerusalem as reinforcements, but the soldiers' arrogance caused so much offence that rioting and further bloodshed were the only outcome. The governor's withdrawal to Caesarea eased tension slightly and both Agrippa II and Berenice tried hard to prevent further escalation of disaffection, but in vain: in May/ June A.D. 66 some young priests, led by the captain of the Temple Eleazar son of Ananias, proclaimed defiance of Rome by halting the sacrifices regularly offered up on behalf of the Roman emperor.

The theological justification for this action, that it was not right to accept offerings from a Gentile, was exceptionally tenuous since this had

[42] Tac. *Hist.* v.10.1.
[43] Joseph. *BJ* 11.301–8; for analysis of this episode, cf. Goodman 1985 (E 1129).

been the custom for centuries, and the ruling class of Jerusalem split on the issue, the cautious advocating the restoration of the sacrifices perhaps more on prudential than theological grounds. Fighting between the different factions reached an intensity not known in the gang warfare of previous years, and within a few days the viciousness increased still further when brigands under a certain Menahem son of Judas attached themselves to Eleazar's faction: Eleazar's father and uncle, the leaders of the main faction trying to avoid war with Rome, were killed, and the troops which had been sent by Agrippa to help quell the disturbances were either brought onto the rebels' side or expelled from the city; a small contingent of Roman auxiliaries hoped similarly to escape with their lives but were treacherously murdered by Eleazar's followers.[44]

Now that rebellion was irrevocable Jews in many of the cities around Judaea rose against their Gentile neighbours, who in turn took advantage of Rome's blessing to plunder and kill the Jews. As in 4 B.C., A.D. 6 and A.D. 40 the task of restoring Roman control was entrusted to the legate of Syria, and in Antioch Cestius Gallus gradually collected a large force which included the Twelfth Legion (Fulminata), other legionaries, and troops provided by allied kings including Agrippa.

It took until September for this force to reach Ptolemais. Cestius with little opposition secured Galilee, presumably to protect his rear, and ravaged some villages and small towns in the Judaean coastal plain, perhaps in the hope that exemplary massacres would terrify the Jerusalem rebels into submission. Josephus gives no details about events in Jerusalem over the summer months, perhaps out of embarrassment at the participation in rebellion of his own class, whom he later wished to exculpate from responsibility for the revolt, but the Jews were clearly not unprepared by October, when they confronted Cestius as his forces emerged from the Bethhoron Pass and despoiled him of much baggage even before he reached Jerusalem.

Cestius was impressed and daunted by the strength of this opposition. He rapidly captured the northern suburbs but after a few days decided that the city could not be taken that year; his main concern was perhaps his lack of supplies and the problems of transporting reinforcements through hostile hill territory. At any rate, he retreated to the coast in incompetent disorder, losing many men and much equipment in the Bethoron defile.

Whether or not the Jewish rebels had organized themselves coherently before Cestius' attack, they did so now. Josephus himself was chosen as general of the rebel forces in Galilee, and Ananus son of Ananus, who had briefly held the high priesthood in A.D. 62, was

---

44 Joseph. *BJ* II.437, 449–56. For some of Agrippa's troops joining the rebels, cf. *BJ* II.430, 520.

appointed joint commander-in-chief. On the Roman side Nero entrusted the war in February A.D. 67 to Titus Flavius Vespasianus, with the rank of *legatus*, three legions (two from Syrian Antioch, one from Egypt), auxiliary cohorts, cavalry and contingents from the client kingdoms.

By June A.D. 67 Vespasian was in Galilee where Josephus, lacking proper troops and weapons, was reduced to defending hill-top fortresses. According to Josephus' detailed report the Galileans seem to have been less enthusiastic for revolt than their reputation as the most warlike of men would suggest;[45] Vespasian's aim may have been less to secure his flank than to instil terror in Jerusalem by the ruthless treatment of the rebels, but if so the determined defence of Gamala after mass executions in Tarichaeae proved that such tactics might backfire.[46]

Josephus himself had been captured in Jotapata before the fall of Galilee after a siege of forty-seven days and, at any rate according to the story as told later, had rapidly won Vespasian's attention and leniency by prophesying his elevation to the Principate.[47] The historian's place in command of Galilee was taken by his arch-rival John son of Levi of Gischala; but John too proved ineffective against siege and escaped to Jerusalem, where he joined Ananus and his associates in late summer A.D. 67.

Meanwhile in the capital city the populace was not happy at the incompetence of the leadership which had permitted the loss of Galilee, and dissatisfaction spread further when Vespasian began in spring A.D. 68 systematically to encircle the capital. Opposition to Ananus was fuelled particularly by the peasants who, deprived of their homes, flooded into the city, finding leaders among a group of well-born priests who described themselves as Zealots, by which name they seem to have claimed a special zeal for the Temple cult.[48] These priests accused Ananus' faction of a lack of enthusiasm for the war. The charge of treachery was probably not justified since Cestius' failure had shown that the rebels' strength lay in the strong walls of Jerusalem, but it was rendered plausible by the fact that many of Ananus' associates, including by now Josephus, had joined the Roman side. At any rate the Zealots established themselves in opposition to Ananus' government, barricading themselves inside the Temple. When they were joined in spring A.D. 68 first by the opportunist John of Gischala and then by a force of Idumaeans, they proved sufficiently powerful to wrest control of the whole city from Ananus, who was soon put to death.

---

[45] Joseph. *BJ* III.41–2.

[46] The siege of Gamala is described at Joseph. *BJ* IV.11–53, 62–83. For the harsh treatment of prisoners at Tarichaeae, see *BJ* III.536–41.

[47] Suet. *Vesp.* 5; Dio LXVI.1.4; Joseph. *BJ* III.399–407.

[48] Cf. Joseph. *BJ* IV.160–1, where these rebels are said to have claimed that they were 'zealous in the cause of virtue'.

Josephus claims in his account of the war that from this moment the Judaean state declined rapidly into savage civil war.[49] His assertion has often been believed but perhaps unwisely, for he himself had by now joined the Roman side, and at the time of writing he wished to distance himself and his friends from the defenders of Jerusalem whose intransigence had caused the destruction of the Temple. Against this picture of social and political disintegration is the evidence from Josephus' own narrative both of the continued presence in Jerusalem of some of the ruling class and of the continuation of the public courts and the municipal burial of paupers;[50] furthermore, the issue of a fine silver coinage and some bronze change by the Jerusalem authorities still in the fourth year of the war, i.e. until the last months of the siege in A.D. 70, suggests a quite stable state.[51]

The efflorescence of this independent Jewish state from spring A.D. 68 to A.D. 70 was facilitated very largely by factors external to Judaea. In June A.D. 68 Vespasian suddenly halted the subjugation of the countryside because Nero's death had ended his mandate as imperial legate for the war. The renewed campaign in May/June A.D. 69 had just recovered the territory subdued the previous year and completed the encirclement of Jerusalem when in July Vespasian was proclaimed emperor and Roman operations against the Jews again ceased.

With the enemy thus distracted the Judaean leaders indulged in internecine struggle for control of the state. During A.D. 68 some of those ousted from power by John and the Zealots left Jerusalem to join an increasingly powerful figure in the countryside, Simon son of Gioras. This Simon had led troops against the rearguard of Cestius Gallus in autumn A.D. 66 but had been ousted from all influence by the deep hostility of Ananus son of Ananus; only after Ananus' death in early A.D. 68 did he take further part in the war. By spring A.D. 69 he had occupied Hebron and was powerful enough to take Jerusalem with the help of the Idumaean forces who had become disenchanted with John and the Zealots. His regime retained control of all the city except the Temple until Roman forces finally arrived outside the walls.

Vespasian, now *princeps*, appointed his son Titus to prosecute the war, and the new commander reached Jerusalem in March A.D. 70 with the aid of an extra legion. Within the city the Zealots held the inner Temple, John of Gischala its outer precincts and Simon the rest of the city, but within a few days of Titus' arrival they united against him. Titus' circumvallation, intended to cut off supplies to the defenders, was completed in a few weeks, but the city was captured not by famine but by

[49] Joseph. *BJ* IV.318, 355–6, 365.
[50] Joseph. *BJ* IV.334–44; V.568; VI.113. This point is argued more fully in Goodman 1987 (E 1130) 176–97.   [51] Kadman 1960 (B 328) 78.

a direct assault in which Titus demonstrated unusual disregard for casualties among his own soldiers.

The reasons for Titus' zeal in the prosecution of the siege again lay outside Judaea: he and his father needed a rapid victory to serve as a propaganda base for the new Flavian dynasty. By May the outer (third) wall was in Roman hands. In June the Antonia fortress fell and siege was laid to the Temple; the daily sacrifices ceased and famine began. On 10 Ab (August) A.D. 70 the Temple was destroyed, probably, despite Josephus' denial, on Titus' express order.[52]

Pockets of resistance in the upper city were slowly mopped up during September. The Herodian fortresses held out longer; Masada, the last stronghold, fell only in A.D. 73 or 74 with the suicide of the defenders: the surviving ramp confirms Josephus' account of the efforts of the Romans to secure complete pacification.[53] Judaea was put under a praetorian legate with a legion permanently stationed at Jerusalem. A veteran colony was established at Emmaus.

The Temple was not rebuilt and its treasures were carried in triumph to Rome, as the reliefs on the Arch of Titus record. Of the rebel leaders Simon was executed on the Capitol, and the others were either imprisoned or enslaved. No attempt was made to reconstitute Judaean society: the province's desolation was deliberately stressed by Flavianic propaganda, especially on imperial coins.[54] Only the religion of the Jews survived, and that too underwent great adaptation as the significance of the Temple's destruction was gradually interpreted during the late first and second centuries A.D. and a new understanding forged of the relation of God to his people. (See *CAH* xi[2]).

Such disasters and so much bloodshed must be accounted evidence of a failure in Roman provincial administration. The causes of such failure were undoubtedly complex; nor can Josephus, the main guide to the facts, be accounted of much use in the ascriptions of blame in which his prejudices are blatant. Nonetheless some causes specific to Judaea can profitably be pointed out.

Both Josephus and Tacitus accused the procurators of Judaea of incompetence and deliberate wickedness,[55] and a charge of at least tactlessness in the handling of Jewish religious susceptibilities is hard to refute. On the other hand failure to comprehend the intricate regulations of Judaism was particularly venial in the light of the variety of religious attitudes and authorities in Judaea in this period (see below, p. 762).

On the Jewish side Josephus attempted to shift all blame onto rebels

[52] Joseph. *BJ* vi.254–66; *contra*, Sulp. Severus, *Chron.* ii.30.6–7. For arguments supporting Josephus' defence of Titus, see Rajak 1983 (b 147) 206–11.

[53] Joseph. *BJ* vii.252, 275, 304–406; Yadin 1966 (e 1235).

[54] *BMCRE* ii nos. 115–18.   [55] Cf. Joseph. *AJ* xx.253–8; Tac. *Hist.* v.10.1.

from the poorer classes, attempting to portray the rich as loyal subjects of Rome despite the involvement of many of them in the war. According to his account the nation was destabilized by bandits in the countryside and urban terrorists in Jerusalem, and the war was a direct result of their wicked acts.[56]

These terrorists, described as *sicarii* or dagger-men because they used short daggers hidden beneath their cloaks before escaping in the pilgrim crowds, first appeared in Jerusalem in the early fifties A.D. when they murdered the ex-High Priest Jonathan son of Ananus. At whose instigation they operated was unclear to Josephus, who makes two different suggestions in his two accounts of this assassination;[57] such uncertainty was a natural corollary of their underhand methods. It is often assumed that all their terrorism was dedicated to the overthrow of Roman rule and of the rich whose power derived from Rome: not only did Josephus explicitly blame the *sicarii* in one passage for the outbreak of the war,[58] but two of their leaders in A.D. 66 and in A.D. 73 were descendants of the founder of the anarchist Fourth Philosophy, Judas the Galilean (see below, p. 761). Against such a view, however, is Josephus' claim that the *sicarii* fought on behalf of Roman governors when paid sufficiently well.[59] These thugs were perhaps available to all for hire: hence their use in A.D. 62 to kidnap the secretary of the future instigator of the revolt, Eleazar son of Ananias, in order to blackmail Eleazar's father.[60] In the war itself the *sicarii* were strikingly quiescent: Menahem son of Judas seized Masada from its Roman garrison at the very start, but, arriving in Jerusalem possibly only after revolt was already in train,[61] he was killed with the dispersal of his followers within days; for the rest of the war, the *sicarii* seem to have lived in isolation on Masada, profiting from the opportunities for brigandage in the disorder of the countryside, refusing even to help Simon son of Gioras in his successful bid for supreme power in the capital.

Other factors are less stressed by Josephus. The riots and massacres in cities of mixed Jewish and gentile occupation near Palestine in A.D. 66 were symptomatic of an intermittent hatred whose origins probably went back to the Hasmonaean period. Most of the auxiliary forces used against the Jews were volunteers from these cities. Their antagonism was fuelled and reinforced by the cultural divide which hindered intermarriage and all except the most superficial social contact. Within Judaea the widening of class divisions, for which there is much evidence

---

[56] Cf. Bilde 1979 (E 1094).   [57] Joseph. *BJ* II.254–7; *AJ* xx.162–6.
[58] Joseph. *BJ* VII.253–8, 262.   [59] Joseph. *AJ* xx.163, 255.   [60] Joseph. *AJ* xx.208–10.
[61] Some take ἐπάνεισιν at Joseph. *BJ* II.434 to indicate that Menahem had been present in Jerusalem earlier in the revolt. This passage contains a doublet of *BJ* II.408 about the seizure of Masada, which suggests that Josephus, who was hidden in the Temple throughout those exciting times (*Vit.* 21), was confused about their chronology.

(see below, p. 769), embittered the poor, especially since biblical law through the (now disregarded) institution of the Jubilee prohibited the accumulation of landed wealth over generations;[62] but although the rich in normal times sided with Rome and class hostility could thus be expressed by rebellion, in A.D. 66–70 many of the wealthy also joined in the revolt.

This transfer of allegiance by the ruling class was itself a cause as well as a consequence of the outbreak of war. The ruling class was expected to help the governor in the suppression of disorder in the province, and when they proved incapable of doing so, the procurators tended to treat them as if they were themselves implicated: in *c*. A.D. 52 the High Priest and some of his predecessors were held responsible by Cumanus for the attack on Samaritans by a Jewish crowd which, according to Josephus, they tried in vain to check (see above, p. 753).[63] This suspicion reached a peak with the crucifixion of upper-class Jews by Florus in Jerusalem in A.D. 66.[64] It was fuelled by the resort to violence by some of the ruling class in the pursuit of power on their own behalf: by A.D. 63–4 there were constant clashes on the streets of Jerusalem between rival gangs hurling stones and insults, led by incumbent and past High Priests as well as by other members of the ruling class, including relatives of Herod named Saul and Costobar.[65] These rivalries, which resorted on occasion also to kidnap, were not directly aimed against Rome, but they fatally weakened the ability of Judaean leaders to stand up to unsympathetic procurators.

The struggle within Jewish society continued inside the independent Jewish state of A.D. 66 to 70. With the raising of the stakes, the methods used by the factions became closer to outright warfare; their rivalries struck even the outside observer Tacitus.[66] It is possible that these factions represented different ideologies, sects, classes or areas of origin, but since both John of Gischala and Simon son of Gioras included Jews of all classes and origin among their followers and Josephus' vituperative rhetoric about the disreputable origins of his opponents is hardly to be trusted, reconstructions of such parties by modern historians are necessarily speculative. It should be noted that the slogans on the coins issued by the different factions when in control of Jerusalem do not differ materially. It is possible that the struggle of the faction leaders was solely for power, while their supporters were mercenaries, often former bandits, culled from the dispossessed peasantry; in the opposition to Rome all the factions united in an appeal to the nationalist sentiments of the general population.

There is only little evidence for the common assertion that the prime causes both of the rebellion and of this civil strife were explicit religious

---

[62] Lev. 25:9–10.   [63] Joseph. *BJ* II.243; *AJ* xx.131.   [64] Joseph. *BJ* II.308.
[65] Joseph. *AJ* xx.213–14.   [66] Tac. *Hist.* v.12.3–4.

beliefs. Josephus, Tacitus and Suetonius all mention widespread belief in an oracle that a man from Judaea would become ruler of the world. Josephus states that the initiation by the rebel leader Judas the Galilean in A.D. 6 of the new ('Fourth') philosophy, according to which Jews should obey no ruler except God, was responsible for the war;[67] but this may refer to divine displeasure at alleged unauthorized religious innovation as much as to the arousal of anti-Roman sentiment by this anarchist doctrine, and the explicit connexion made by Josephus between the Fourth Philosophy and the *sicarii* may be based on little more than the familial descent of their leaders from Judas.[68] Most Jews probably saw no religious impediment to living in peace under Roman rule as they had under Persians and Greeks: despite the desecration of the Temple by Pompey and in 4 B.C. by the procurator Sabinus, and despite Gaius' crazy schemes in A.D. 40, there was no reason in A.D. 66 for Jews to believe that their religion was under threat by a suzerain which had long tolerated their cult.

Nonetheless it is striking that most disturbances which required forcible suppression were sparked off by religious issues and that many occurred at the pilgrim festivals where the religious atmosphere was highly charged. One reason may be the lack of a clear all-embracing orthodoxy in first-century Judaism (see below, p. 762): behaviour which to some Jews, including perhaps the governor's advisers, seemed permissible, was anathema to others. More pervasive was the general hostility to the Romans simply because they were Gentile: in a society where holiness was achieved through separation from impurity and non-Jews were believed to be in a vague sense a source of pollution (see below, p. 765), the liberation of the land from foreign rule might well seem desirable. But it must be stressed that the legends on the coins issued by the rebels to put forward their public message bear no such overt religious meaning, although the objects illustrated were evidently designed to emphasize the centrality of the Temple worship; they proclaim the freedom of Jerusalem and Israel.[69]

III. JEWISH RELIGION AND SOCIETY

1. Judaea [70]

Much of the evidence for Judaean society derives from sources which are only dubiously reliable since they were written for theological rather

---

[67] Joseph. *BJ* II.118–19; *AJ* XVIII.24–4.   [68] Joseph. *BJ* VII.253–9.

[69] Kadman 1960 (B 328).

[70] The main sources, apart from the gospels, the Acts of the Apostles and the rabbinic texts, are Joseph. *Ap.*; the Dead Sea scrolls written and preserved by the sectarian community in Qumran (translation in Vermes 1987 (E 1231)); and the apocrypha and pseudepigrapha preserved by the

than historical purposes and were composed either much later than the
first century A.D. (the rabbinic texts, i.e. Mishnah, Tosefta, Talmuds and
midrashim) or outside Palestine (most, and possibly all, of the New
Testament material). The apocrypha and pseudepigrapha, which survive
entirely through the Christian tradition and mostly in Greek or translations from the Greek, can rarely be demonstrated with certainty to be
Jewish or to originate from Judaea. The contemporary writings of
Josephus, particularly *contra Apionem*, are correspondingly important,
but even here the author may have provided a distorted picture in order
to please his intended Greek audience. Much light has been shed by
excavation of settlements at Qumran and the parallel site at En el-
Ghuweir and by the Dead Sea scrolls found in the caves above the former
site; lest the sectarian and therefore non-typical nature of this contemporary evidence be overplayed, recent discoveries in the Upper City of
Jerusalem close to the Temple area and elsewhere in Judaea have
confirmed that some at least of the religious and cultural preoccupations
of the people at Qumran were widely shared.[71]

(a) Religion No single all-embracing set of systematic religious dogmas
enjoyed universal assent in first-century Judaea any more than elsewhere
in the Roman world in this period. A great variety of belief and practice
was tolerated within the accepted confines of Judaism. Apostasy was
possible only by deliberate denial of all ancestral customs. The diversity
of acceptable doctrine is most clearly observed in the development in the
hellenistic period of distinct sects: the Pharisees, Sadducees and Essenes,
whose origins and tenets have been discussed in *CAH* ix[2], 299–309,
were all also full members of the wider Jewish religious community.

Most Jews did not belong to any sect or (in Josephus' terminology)
philosophy, for worship was a matter not of belief but of practice. None
the less a central core of dogmas most of which were common to all Jews
can be defined. Prime among these is devotion to monotheism and to the
Jewish law enshrined in the Pentateuch, the Torah. The exact requirements of the Torah were much discussed, to the extent that interpretation of the text became in itself an important mode of worship,

Christian Church along with but outside the canonical books of the Old Testament (translations in
Charles 1913 (B 25); a much larger but not fully reliable collection in Charlesworth 1983–5 (B 26); a
smaller selection in Sparks 1984 (E 1214)). Of the rabbinic texts, the Mishnah and Tosefta, both
edited in the early to middle third century A.D., deserve more respect as evidence for Judaism in the
first century A.D. than the Palestinian Talmud (compiled *c.* A.D. 400) or the Babylonian Talmud
(compiled *c.* A.D. 500). The compilations of biblical commentaries (*midrashim*) are hard to date, but
some of the material at least in *Mechilta*, *Sifra* and *Sifre* is likely to have originated in the second
century A.D. or before. For the rabbinic sources, see Stemberger 1992 (E 1215A); more briefly,
Schürer 1973 (E 1207) I 68–118.

[71] On the excavations at Qumran, see de Vaux 1973 (E 1229); on En el-Ghuweir, see Bar-Adon
1977 (E 1085); on discoveries in Jerusalem, Avigad 1984 (E 1080).

divergence on the correct exegetic method constituting one of the defining characteristics of the various sects. The whole adult male community was required to meet at least once a week in synagogues to hear and learn about the Torah; this was the main and perhaps the sole function of synagogues in Palestine in this period, for the scarcity of clearly identified buildings from the first century A.D. or before suggests that, unlike in the diaspora (see below, p. 777), Judaean synagogues in this period were not yet treated as sacred places.[72] Understanding of the Torah was expedited by translation into the vernacular and by detailed interpretation of the implications as well as the plain meaning of the text.

Most Jews also acknowledged the paramount importance of the Temple in Jerusalem, where a highly professional hereditary priesthood administered the minutely organized sacrificial service with scrupulous ceremonial. Twenty-four groups of priests served in turn. Public and private offerings were made in a state of exceptional purity; the ordinary people meanwhile stood outside in the courtyard, while the Levites, a clearly defined caste of less prestigious Temple servants, sang psalms. The architecture of the sanctuary enhanced its function as the centre of purity: the grand colonnade built by Herod surrounded a great court-yard into which all were permitted to enter; that courtyard enclosed entirely a smaller court (the Court of the Women), through which it was necessary to pass to reach the Court of the Israelites; enclosed by the latter court lay the Court of the Priests, who alone could enter the sanctuary itself; beyond the reach of all except the High Priest on the Day of Atonement lay the Holy of Holies, the purest place of all. While the sacrifices continued divine approval would ensure rain, harvests and prosperity; their cessation in A.D. 70 was seen at the time as calamitous[73] and led to the development in coming centuries of more than one novel and distinctive Jewish theology (see *CAH* xi²).

Of those few Jews known to have dissented from the high value placed by their fellows on worship in the Jerusalem Temple, the adherents of the Dead Sea sect are striking. Whatever the original reason for their treatment of the priests in Jerusalem as sinners whose sacrifices were invalid (see *CAH* ix², 301–4), it was reinforced by their adoption of a lunisolar calendar different from the lunar calendar used by most Jews, which ensured that, in their eyes, the priests celebrated the festivals on the wrong days. Any such calendaric infringement was seriously regarded by all Jews: pagans regarded Jews as fanatical in the devotion to their Sabbath rest which even occasionally (though probably never normally) led them to die rather than fight on the sacred day, and

---

[72] Buildings dating before A.D. 70 have been identified as synagogues at Masada, Herodium and Gamala, although none of these identifications is beyond dispute. Cf. Levine 1981 (E 1168).

[73] Joseph. *BJ* VI.94.

festivals, on which no travel or work was allowed, were treated with only slightly less rigour. Indeed the observance of one festival, the Day of Atonement, on which Jews fasted in repentance for sins, was considered as even more important than the Sabbath.

The significance attributed to the Torah and the Temple and the strict observance of personal restrictions on the Sabbath and festivals were characteristics of Judaism inherited from Persian and early-hellenistic times when the last books of the Hebrew bible were still being composed. Less pervasive but, perhaps because of their novelty, well attested in the sources are the new elements introduced in the last centuries B.C. and in the Roman period.

One such new development was the evolution of distinct theologies by the three major sects, the Pharisees, Sadducees and Essenes; all three have been discussed in detail in CAH IX². So far as is known, neither of the two latter groups underwent any great shift in ideology, membership or political significance during the period covered by the present volume; the identity of the Essenes with the sectarians who produced the Dead Sea scrolls, and of the latter with the inhabitants of the settlement at Qumran, is likely but not certain.

Much more evidence survives about the Pharisees in the first century A.D. The authors of the gospels, particularly that of Matthew, depicted the Pharisees as opponents of Jesus and subjected them to a fierce polemic. Josephus showed a particular interest in them, claiming to be of their number, as did St Paul.[74] The rabbis of the second century A.D. saw some of the Pharisees as their spiritual forbears: thus the family of Hillel, a Babylonian Jew who came to Jerusalem under Herod and founded a dynasty of teachers including Paul's instructor Gamaliel, are described by Josephus and the New Testament as Pharisees but by Judah the Patriarch, Hillel's long-distant descendant who compiled the Mishnah in c. A.D. 200, as rabbinic sages.

The different pictures of the Pharisees in these sources cannot be satisfactorily reconciled. The teachings specifically attributed by later rabbis to named authorities who taught before A.D. 70 concern to a large extent the intricate laws governing physical purity and the tithing of foodstuffs, and it has been argued that such matters constituted the prime or sole interests of first-century Pharisees; but it is also possible that such concerns were confined to a small group within the Pharisaic movement – the later rabbis described those individuals particularly zealous about such matters as *haverim* ('fellows'). As to the other characteristic teachings of the Pharisees, of which the existence can reasonably be postulated, it is impossible to be certain how many of the ethical and

---

[74] Joseph. *Vit.* 12; Phil. 3:5.

religious ideas presupposed by the rabbis after A.D. 70 should be attributed to the Pharisees before that date.

Most of the leading Torah scholars of this period mentioned in later rabbinic writings were probably Pharisees. According to the rabbis, two distinct schools ('Houses') emerged in the first century A.D., one constituted of the followers of Hillel, the other of Shammai; both these teachers lived in the time of Herod. Later tradition depicted the controversies between the Houses as fierce, but the issues mentioned as under dispute are mostly quite trivial and presuppose wide areas of agreement.

The extent of the wider influence of the Pharisees in the first century is also uncertain. The rabbis assumed that their forbears, like themselves, were the natural leaders of the nation, and Josephus, in describing the Pharisees of the Hasmonaean period, attributed to them great authority over the masses. But the Pharisees are not ascribed a prominent role as a group in Josephus' detailed narrative of the politics of Judaea in the first century A.D.; if they had acted as a political faction in the Hasmonaean state, it would appear that they had lost this role in the Herodian period or soon after. In any case, the number of Pharisees was probably never great – the only figure mentioned by an ancient writer is the 'more than 6,000' who, according to Josephus, refused to take an oath in support of Herod. Their influence in religious matters spread beyond their immediate circle, partly because in their interpretation of the Torah they often took account of popular customs.[75]

A more widespread development than the emergence of distinct philosophies was a concern by Jews for physical purity in a general sense. Both purity as a metaphor for holiness and pollution standing for sin are frequently found in the language of the Hebrew bible, but such usage gained added significance in the post-biblical period as a symbol of the separation of Jews from Gentiles. This tendency was expressed in an interest in what entered the body as sustenance and in bodily excretions, going well beyond the biblical definitions of the limited sources of uncleanness which debarred priests from the sanctuary. Not only were Jews renowned among outsiders for scrupulous observance of the dietary prohibitions listed in Leviticus but,[76] probably in late hellenistic times, they also adopted further taboos which lacked any obvious biblical base, including the avoidance of Gentile milk, bread, wine and olive oil. Later rabbinic tradition, aware of the anti-Gentile tendency in

---

[75] Joseph. *BJ* II.162–3; *AJ* XIII.171–3,288,294,297–8, XVII.41, XVIII.12–17; *Vit.* 2, 191. On the rabbinic texts, see Neusner 1971 (E 1184). On the extent of the Pharisees' influence, see Neusner, *Politics to Piety* (Leiden, 1971) and the summary of the arguments in Goodblatt 1989 (E 1123).

[76] Jews' avoidance of pork was particularly notorious, cf. Joseph. *Ap.* II.137; Plut. *Quaest. conv.* IV.4–6.2.

these customs, ascribed them, probably wrongly, to the eighteen anti-
Roman decrees said to have been agreed by the Houses of Hillel and
Shammai at the start of the Great Revolt.[77] Finds of ritual baths in a
number of early-Roman Palestinian sites suggest that total immersion
was a widespread practice, at least among those believed most susceptible to pollution such as menstruating women.

The symbolism of purity was elaborated in the idiosyncratic theologies of the Dead Sea sect, for whom the consumption of meals in purity
was a central rite, and of the *haverim*. John the Baptist proclaimed
forgiveness of sins through the waters of the Jordan. The importance of
seeking to preserve physical purity may have been strengthened,
psychologically if not theologically, by the notion, according to the
gospels deeply embedded in Jewish society, that sickness often derived
from contamination by external demons whose expulsion from the body
could bring a return to health.

The avoidance of pollution occasionally led to asceticism which had
its roots in the conduct of some of the biblical prophets. The austere
surroundings of the Qumran sect were probably believed to be intrinsi-
cally desirable. The ascetic Bannus whom Josephus claims to have joined
in the Judaean desert was admired for his avoidance of everything
beyond necessities.[78] John the Baptist won fame by refusing to use
manufactured food or clothes; it is not clear whether his denial of
comfort or achievement of purity was perceived as more praiseworthy.
Nonetheless asceticism was not widespread in contrast to the early
Christian church. For most Jews fasts were restricted to times of such
emergencies as drought.[79]

There were at least three other significant theological innovations in
the religion of first-century A.D. Judaean Jews, but neither the extent nor
the depth of their influence can be determined with certainty. Some Jews
began to believe in a life after death; some lived in confident expectation
of the Messiah; some tried to adopt Greek philosophical explanations of
the world while retaining loyalty to the Torah.

Belief in a life after death was certainly a novelty in the hellenistic
period, for no Jewish text before the Book of Daniel (12:2), which was
redacted to its final form in the second century B.C., unambiguously
refers to such a notion. Since in the first century A.D. the issue was still
fiercely debated by the Pharisees and Sadducees and extant texts are
unclear when, how and with what accoutrements this after-life would
take place, this hope was perhaps not an important element in religious
consciousness. Mourning practices continued to assume the unalloyed
grief of the deceased's relatives. The introduction of secondary burial in

[77] *m.A.Z.* 2: 3, 6; cf. on the ban on use of gentile oil, Joseph. *BJ* II.591–2; *AJ* XII.120.
[78] Joseph. *Vit.* 11.   [79] Cf. the tractate *Taanith* ('Fasts') in the Mishnah.

stone ossuaries after the flesh had rotted is more likely to reflect a desire for purity than the after-life; the practice was confined in the Jerusalem area and parts of the Judaean countryside to the late first century B.C. and the first century A.D.[80]

The importance of messianic beliefs in first century A.D. Judaea may have been exaggerated by the Christian tradition through which most of the literary texts of the period survive but some Jews at least expected that a Messiah (however defined) would eventually appear, accompanied by a radical reorganization and judgment of the world.[81] There was no agreement about the nature of the new world: the messianic age depicted in the Dead Sea scrolls differs markedly from that in other texts and no group developed any precise doctrine on the subject. It is impossible to know how many Jews would accept all of this composite picture which can be created only by amalgamation of a number of texts but it is likely that many would subscribe to at least part of it: a final ordeal and confusion would lead to Elijah, who would come as precursor to the Messiah; this latter would be assaulted by Gentile powers but, proving victorious, would renew Jerusalem, gathering the dispersed to enjoy the kingdom of glory in the holy land; in a new heaven and earth the dead would be resurrected to face the last judgment and assignation either to bliss or to damnation for eternity. The role of Israel was always seen as central but the new age was frequently taken to have universal application.

The precise nature of the Messiah himself was also a matter for speculation. The concept as expressed in the Hebrew bible involved a king of the line of David, but at Qumran a second Messiah of priestly stock was envisaged; the notion of a suffering Messiah was in this period uncommon and perhaps unknown outside the early Christian community. The practical consequence of such messianic beliefs was often political quietism since it might be felt impious to force the divine timetable; it is thus debated whether such doctrines were a major element in any of the disturbances preceding the revolt of A.D. 66.

The extent to which further changes in the theology of Judaean Jews were occasioned by adaptation of hellenistic religious ideas cannot be clearly determined since many intertestamental texts which now survive only in Greek cannot be certainly assigned either to Judaea or to the diaspora (see above, p. 762). Folk memories of the events preceding the Maccabean revolt (see *CAH* VIII[2], 346–50) may have made conscious

---

[80] On ossuary burial see Hachlili and Killebrew 1983 (E 1132); Rahmani 1986 (E 1192). On the debate over life after death, cf. Acts 23:6–8.

[81] Discussions of messianism in Klausner 1956 (E 1158); Schürer 1979 (E 1207) II 488–554; Neusner, Green and Frerichs 1987 (E 1185).

borrowing rare, but such Greek notions as the immortality of the soul divorced from the body were held for instance even by the Essenes.[82]

(b) Society No rigid division can readily be drawn between Judaean religion and Judaean society, for religion invaded all aspects of life. Thus the most important factor in the development of, and growth of tensions within, Judaean society in the first centuries B.C. and A.D. was the economic role of the Jerusalem Temple. The hills of Judaea, as of Samaria and Galilee, were only moderately fertile: vines and olives flourished but the grain grown in the valleys sufficed only for a moderate population. The much greater productivity of the coastal plain was enjoyed by the inhabitants, mostly non-Jewish, of the coastal cities, while the luxuriant fruit crops of the Jordan rift valley, especially by the Lake of Tiberias, rarely benefited the Jews in Judaea. The balsam groves of En Gedi, the richest natural resource of all, were first a royal and then an imperial monopoly.

The agrarian economy of Judaea thus could not by itself support a city of the size and magnificence of Jerusalem, which Pliny the Elder described as 'by far the most illustrious of the cities of the Orient'.[83] Nor could agricultural wealth alone have paid for the multifarious imports and impressive expenditure of the rich inhabitants of Jerusalem whose houses have been revealed by recent excavations. The Judaean economy was fuelled by a constant influx of wealth brought to the Temple both by Jews and by others from all over the Mediterranean and the Near East. This wealth percolated into society through the spending power of the priests, the provision of employment in the beautification of the sanctuary, and the influx of pilgrims who required service industries for their comfort. The splendour thus acquired by Jerusalem was all the more remarkable in contrast to the rustic poverty of its hinterland.

The evidence for such poverty is extensive. The prevalence of the debt burden which afflicted the poor is clear from the attempt by the rebels in A.D. 66 to persuade debtors to join them by burning the debt archives in Jerusalem;[84] apart from the natural effect on small farmers of bad harvests, an important cause was probably investment by the rich of surplus wealth in loans when there was insufficient land to purchase: a legal innovation, the *prosbul*, enabled the poor anxious for loans to waive the right to the cancellation of debts every seven years which was enshrined in Deuteronomy,[85] while the offer of land as security made such loans attractive to the prosperous. Problems were further exacer-

---

[82] Joseph. *AJ* XVIII.18; *BJ* II.154. The extent of hellenization in religious ideas is emphasized by Hengel 1974 (E 1135) and 1989 (E 1137); contrast Millar 1978 (E 1177).

[83] Pliny, *HN* v.14. For the excavations, see Avigad 1984 (E 1080). See the discussion in Goodman 1987 (E 1130) 51–75.   [84] Joseph. *BJ* II.427.

[85] Deut. 15:1–2. On the *prosbul*, see *m. Shebi.* 10: 6, 9. On the whole debt problem, see Goodman 1982 (E 1127).

bated by overpopulation, of which a main cause must have been the common unwillingness of Jews on religious grounds to practise contraception, abortion or infanticide. Surplus children were more likely to survive in Jewish society than other rural economies because Jewish concepts of charity required the rich to provide food and shelter up to a (very low) minimum standard to all who seemed to be in need.

Conflict between rich and poor took different forms in the town and in the countryside; since before A.D. 66 the rich were often identified with the Roman suzerain, class and political motives were sometimes mingled in the struggle. According to Josephus rural violence became endemic in the late fifties A.D.[86] Bandits found refuge on the hill-tops and in artificial caves; many such caves have been discovered, though some may have been dug out of the limestone only during the Bar Kochba revolt in A.D. 132–5.[87] Such places of concealment sufficed for the brigands to escape the attention of the small forces of the Roman governor; the awareness of their presence by the local peasant population may have been of less concern since their attitude seems sometimes to have been sympathetic or at least not hostile.[88]

In Jerusalem the poor formed an urban proletariat of a size rarely found in this period outside the city of Rome. They were attracted by hopes of charity or of employment either on such public works as the building of the Temple or on private projects for the richer families of the city. Their numbers and volatility are evident from the account by Josephus of the consternation of the city's leaders when, on the completion of the Temple in c. A.D. 64, 18,000 were left unemployed without the support of a regular wage.[89]

Resentment at economic disparities was not apparently channelled into direct class warfare partly because social identification of individuals in terms of their property ownership, which was natural in Greek and Roman society, was less obvious among Jews, for whom the possession of wealth, though considered only in a few marginal religious groups such as the Essenes as positively undesirable, was rarely seen as in itself a criterion for status: the rich in Judaea, apart from the Herods, did not practise evergetism.[90]

Jewish society in fact lacked the clear social hierarchy which marked contemporary Rome; it is probably a mistake to treat the religious sects as important social groupings or to identify their interests with those of particular economic classes. There was probably general agreement

---

[86] Joseph. *BJ* II.264; *AJ* xx.172.

[87] Kloner 1983 (E 1159); Kloner and Tepper 1987 (E 1160).

[88] On complicity of locals with brigands, see Joseph. *BJ* II.253; *AJ* xx.121; cf. Horsley 1979 (E 1141).   [89] Joseph. *AJ* xx.219.

[90] Class warfare is emphasized by Kreissig 1970 (E 1166). On the different criteria for status in Jewish compared to Greek or Roman society, see Goodman 1987 (E 1130) 109–33.

about the low social and religious status of Gentiles and slaves. There was consensus too among men about the position of women, who were generally excluded from positions of influence, although royal princesses were excepted from this rule and the introduction of the *ketubah* (marriage contract), which guaranteed rights and money to wives on divorce or widowhood, gave richer women some freedom in the control of property. The extensive financial dealings of a rich widow called Babatha have been revealed by the chance survival of her private documents in the cave in the Judaean desert where she perished during the revolt of A.D. 132–5.[91] But for the adult male Jewish population the variety of overlapping and competing statuses and the lack of a definitive authority able to mediate between them contributed not a little to the dissolution of the social order.

High priority was given to genealogy, even though most Jews, apart from priests, were probably unable to trace their ancestry more than five generations. Men used their patronymics after their own name. Dynasties preserving family pre-eminence can be found among the Pharisees and the *sicarii* as well as the royal houses. Lack of longstanding Jewish origins was held against the Idumaeans (see above, p. 739) despite the religious injunction to treat proselytes as full members of the community in all matters except marriage into priestly families. Josephus boasted of his Hasmonaean ancestors,[92] Saul and Costobar of their link to Herod (see above, p. 760).

Such claims were made only for the sake of prestige and not as a statement of social ties. Extended families based on shared ancestry do not seem to have played an important social role in Judaea in this period. Endogamy, which was still highly praised in the Book of Tobit, which was written probably in the third century B.C., is almost unknown in the first century A.D. outside the Herodian family. The characteristic tombs of the rich in this period, comprising central chambers surrounded by *loculi* for individual coffins or ossuaries, were designed to house nuclear rather than extended families.[93]

Among the most highly regarded origins was that of priests. Only those whose fathers were priests could serve in the Temple and receive tithes from other Jews. Intermarriage with proselytes or divorcees was forbidden for fear of throwing doubt on the paternity of the offspring. In their zeal to protect the purity of their lineage the priests kept their own archives which stretched back far into the Hasmonaean period and perhaps beyond. Of exceptionally high status were those whose ancestors had as High Priests acted as the religious and (except under the

[91] Lewis, Yadin and Greenfield 1989 (B 375); see in general the tractate *Ketuboth* in the Mishnah; cf. Epstein 1942 (E 1111); Archer 1983 (E 1076) and 1990 (E 1077).
[92] Joseph. *Vit.* 2.   [93] Tobit 6:12; Hachlili and Killebrew 1983 (E 1132).

Herods) secular leaders of the nation; in the first century A.D. these families were known collectively as the High Priests.[94]

But even such status from birth could in this period be undercut or nullified by an alternative route to status through learning. The centrality of the Torah in Judaism led directly to the prestige and popular influence of the scholars who interpreted it. Such scholars, the 'scribes' of the gospels, might come from a range of social backgrounds and were never a hereditary caste like the priests. Nor were they a unified professional group, for methods of interpretation differed drastically from one scholar to another: for instance a scholar in the Pharisee tradition would take account of popular custom but a Sadducaic scholar would not (see *CAH* IX[2], 304–8).

Some Torah interpreters gained further authority from the accident of birth since some at least were priests, though not all priests were scholars; others perhaps increased their influence by ostentatious personal piety in the synagogue and streets.[95] Less common were charismatic teachers who did not aim to interpret Torah. Their rarity gave particular power to such figures as Honi the Circle-Drawer, whose prayers could end droughts, and Hanina son of Dosa, whose cures were famed. Stories about both men survive much embroidered in late rabbinic texts; the picture painted there of Honi is confirmed by Josephus' stories of the same man, whom he names Onias.[96]

The career of Hanina son of Dosa seems to have been confined to Galilee, and the regionalism of many of these religious leaders, and indeed of local loyalties in general, militated further against national acceptance of any single man or group. In constitutional terms (in the eyes of both Jews and Romans) the national leader should have been the High Priest of the day, but his authority was weakened in this period first by the policy initiated by Herod of usually permitting each incumbent only a short term (see above, p. 747) and second by the selection of what was probably a quite new priestly family, that of Ananus, by the procurators after A.D. 6: Ananus and his five sons, who all held the post, dominated the high priesthood until A.D. 66.[97]

Lack of confidence in the High Priest prejudiced also the prestige of the council over which he presided, the Sanhedrin. Later rabbinic stories that the Sanhedrin was an appeal court composed entirely of Torah

[94] This interpretation is doubted by Jeremias 1969 (E 1151) 175–81, but remains the most plausible explanation of the evidence, cf. Schürer 1979 (E 1207) II 232–6.

[95] Cf. Matt. 6:2, 5, 16; 23:5–7. For the claim that the priests as a group regulated religious behaviour, see Joseph. *Ap.* II.187, 194.

[96] Joseph. *AJ* XIV.22–5. On the rabbinic traditions, see Vermes 1973 (F 231).

[97] On the family of Ananus, cf. Stern 1976 (E 1218). The identification, proposed by Stern, of Σεθί at Joseph. *AJ* XVIII.26 with Σεέ at *AJ* XVII.341 would link Ananus to a High Priest appointed briefly by Archelaus.

scholars are probably not trustworthy: inventions of the late second century A.D. and after may have been retrojected to the period before A.D. 70; the evidence of Josephus and the New Testament, although itself not perfect, is to be preferred.[98] The precise composition of the council is not certain, except that some members of the high-priestly families and both Pharisees and Sadducees could be included. It seems probable that the Sanhedrin sometimes acted also as the *boule* for tribute collection since a few references to *bouleutai* are found;[99] in such cases all members will at Rome's insistence have been rich. It is possible that the High Priest had the power to convene whichever advisers he thought most appropriate for a particular case to act as his *consilium*. According to some opponents of Herod quoted by Josephus, it was forbidden to put anyone to death unless he had first been condemned by a Sanhedrin of some sort.[100]

The lack of clearly accepted authority in first-century Palestine, and the resulting social confusion, were exacerbated by Roman failure to recognize any of the competing local criteria for status. Roman insistence on wealth as the prime requisite for the governing class promoted to power men who sometimes lacked the local respect which might have enabled them to control popular disaffection.

(c) Culture Except in the religious sphere in the Maccabean period, Judaean Jews did not deliberately reject the hellenistic culture dominant in much of the Near East, but nor did they in general unconsciously assimilate to surrounding peoples. Instead they tended to adapt Greek and Roman customs to serve a Jewish purpose.

This process is clearly seen in the art and architecture of first-century Judaea. The decoration of houses excavated in Jerusalem uses Greek motifs even to the extent of plaster painted in imitation of marble columns, but both mosaics and murals are with few exceptions aniconic. Many tomb markers in the city's vicinity have Greco-Roman façades although the tomb layout is derived from near-eastern custom. Herod's stoa around the Temple did not interfere with the Semitic plan of the inner sanctuary. Theatres, amphitheatres and hippodromes were built by the Herods at Jerusalem and Jericho; there was (probably) a theatre alone at Sepphoris; Tiberias had a stadium and Tarichaeae a hippodrome; but the cultural activities in these places brought prestige to the dynasty only outside Judaea, for such activities were, according to Josephus, alien to Jewish custom.[101]

---

[98] For a conservative approach towards the rabbinic evidence, postulating the existence of two Sanhedrins, see Mantel 1961 (E 1175); cf. the more sceptical remarks in Sanders 1985 (F 212) 312–17.

[99] Joseph. *BJ* 11.405.

[100] Joseph. *AJ* xiv.167; cf. Joseph. *AJ* xx.200, 202. For the term συνέδριον used to mean *consilium*, see Joseph. *BJ* 11.25.

[101] Joseph. *AJ* xv.268. On buildings in Jerusalem, see Avigad 1984 (E 1080).

Less certain is the extent to which the Greek language was adopted by Judaean Jews; it was the normal tongue of at least the upper-class Gentiles of the cities in the vicinity of Palestine. Some Greek religious texts were found at Qumran, though the great majority are in Semitic tongues. The letters and legal documents of the early second century A.D. discovered in the Judaean Desert are apparently trilingual in Greek, Hebrew and Aramaic.[102] It is probable that the rural poor knew less Greek than the urban rich and that no Judaean spoke good Greek – hence, perhaps, the tribune's surprise that St Paul spoke Ἑλληνιστί.[103]

A major hindrance to any deeper hellenization of Judaea was the Jewish educational curriculum in which, as Josephus boasted, the Torah took the place of Greek literature and rhetorical ability was not highly prized.[104] Judaean literature itself was probably little affected by Greek literary genres, but both the Greek histories of Josephus and of Justus of Tiberias and the uncertain provenance of many extant Jewish Greek writings make this unsure; on the other hand, the common assumption that texts originally composed in a Semitic language were written in Palestine is also not entirely warranted since there was a large Jewish diaspora in Mesopotamia.

At any rate, it is striking that all surviving Hebrew and Aramaic texts are religious documents which show a passionate concern for ancestral customs and bible interpretation and only slight influence by Greek culture in, for instance, vocabulary. Semitic national annals were no longer written after the fall of the Hasmonaean dynasty but, following biblical models, religious poetry, such as the *Psalms of Solomon* and the Qumran hymns, and wisdom literature were still popular. Characteristic of the first century A.D. were pseudepigraphic apocalyptic prophecies such as the *Assumption of Moses* and the *Fourth Book of Ezra*: the pseudonymity gave necessary authority to the message in a confused society, while the prophecy imparted comfort in present sorrows, encouraging sincere repentance by stress on the certainty of eventual judgment. Equally characteristic of Judaean literature from the hellenistic to late-Roman period was *midrash*, the re-telling of familiar scriptural stories to reinforce their impact by reflecting the contemporary world in such works as the *Book of Jubilees* and the *Genesis Apocryphon* from Qumran; such rewriting often concentrated on the careers of individual biblical figures, sometimes in the guise of their testaments. Particularly characteristic of the Dead Sea sect was the *pesher*, an exposition in which the meaning of a biblical text treated as prophetic is determined by the historical event or personality which the author is thought to have predicted. It is not clear whether the interest found at Qumran in the

---

[102] Benoît, Milik and De Vaux 1960 (E 1093); Avigad *et al.* 1962 (E 1081); Lewis, Yadin and Greenfield 1989 (B 375). [103] Acts 21:37. [104] Joseph. *Ap.* 11.204; *AJ* xx.264.

elaboration of codes of conduct such as are also found in later rabbinic Judaism was shared by other Jews in the first century A.D.[105]

Perhaps the most fundamental cultural change through Greek influence was in the area of law, where the Pharisees seem sometimes to have elevated popular custom to sacred status. The rabbinic texts of the early third century A.D. reveal the incorporation of many hellenistic legal customs into Jewish law and the Judaean Desert documents of the early second century (see above, n. 102) confirm that this was law in practice in property sales, leases, marriage and divorce. Of most social and economic significance were the laws governing tenancies of land and the enhanced rights of women protected by marriage contracts.

2. The diaspora[106]

The great spread of the Jewish diaspora was largely a phenomenon of the late-hellenistic and Roman periods. There are good a priori reasons to suppose that such Jews living outside Palestine may have developed differently from their compatriots in Judaea in various ways.

Exceptional weight in the reconstruction of the history of diaspora Jews is necessarily accorded to the voluminous writings of Philo of Alexandria. A pious Jew from one of the leading families in the city in the first century A.D., Philo was highly educated in Greek literature and Platonic philosophy. In his theological works he tried systematically to interpret the bible as an esoteric allegory of Greek moral philosophy; he claimed this exercise to be a necessary corollary to, rather than substitute for, the literal interpretation of scripture. His high social status and the peculiar political problems of Alexandrian Jews led him also to write historical works on the vicissitudes they suffered in his own day.

Caution is however necessary in extrapolating from Philo's evidence to the rest of the Jewish diaspora. Other Jewish Greek writers are known to have existed, but, of non-Christian Jewish authors, only Philo's theology was sufficiently congenial to the early Church to be extensively preserved; by the third century A.D. most of the rest of this literature was known to Clement of Alexandria and later patristic authors only in very fragmentary selective quotations from earlier, often

---

[105] On these texts, see Schürer 1986 (E 1207) III.1, 177–469, 1987 (E 1207) III.2, 746–808, with bibliographies of editions and secondary discussions. Translations of Qumran material in Vermes 1987 (E 1231), and of the other material in Charlesworth 1983–5 (B 26).

[106] The main evidence for Jewish society in the diaspora in the hellenistic and Roman periods comes from the writings of Philo. Also important are Joseph. *AJ*, especially Book XIV; Acts of the Apostles; remarks by a variety of non-Jewish Greek and Latin authors (cf. the comprehensive collection by Stern 1974–84 (B 168)); a good number of inscriptions set up by Jews cf. Frey 1952–75 (B 230); papyri produced by or about Jews in Egypt (cf. *CPJ*); and excavations both of synagogues at Dura Europus, Sardis and Ostia and of catacombs in the city of Rome. For material on the diaspora in general, see Schürer 1986 (E 1207) III.1, 1–176, with bibliographies.

non-Jewish, compilations, particularly that by Alexander Polyhistor.[107]
It is therefore likely that Philo's theology was not typical of Greek-
speaking Jews and it is certain that the politics of Alexandria were
specific to that city. No less untypical of Greek Jews was that other
prolific Jewish writer, St Paul. Generalizations about the diaspora can
thus only be tentatively proposed.

(a) Religion The customary designation of the religion of Jews in the
Mediterranean diaspora as hellenistic Judaism is one such potentially
misleading generalization: of none of the ideas in any surviving text can
the popularity be estimated beyond the author's immediate circle. In
favour of a wide acceptance of Philo's theology is only the favourable
reception accorded to St Paul in his own fusion of Jewish with Greek
thought. But many of those attracted by Paul's teaching were not Jews at
all but Gentile and some space must be preserved for Paul's own
originality (see below, p. 851–63).

According to the often disparaging remarks of non-Jewish writers in
antiquity, the religious practices of diaspora Jews were similar to those
in Judaea: circumcision, the Sabbath and food taboos were all seen by
these authors as sometimes amusing, sometimes obscene, but always
characteristic of Jews. The theft by the proconsul of Asia Lucius
Valerius Flaccus in 62–61 B.C. of a huge sum collected by Asia Minor
Jews for the Jerusalem Temple[108] demonstrates the respect for the
sanctuary of those who contributed. Many diaspora Jews visited the
holy city on pilgrimage at least occasionally, although the Temple's
overwhelming religious importance in Judaea seems to have been
diminished somewhat by distance: at Leontopolis, near Memphis in
Egypt, indeed, the temple founded in the middle of the second century
B.C. by the Oniads (see *CAH* ix², 299) was only finally closed in A.D. 73,
though it had apparently never attracted many adherents outside its
immediate vicinity.

Most of the new religious trends found among Jews in Palestine in
this period are also attested in the diaspora. The extension of purity
taboos to Gentile olive oil was also practised at Antioch in Syria;
messianic hopes are probably implicit in Philo; expectation of life after
death at least for a disembodied soul is quite often expressed; the sect of
the Therapeutae in Egypt made, like the Essenes, a virtue of asceticism.
But besides this a more distinctive feature of the diaspora Jews at least of
the Mediterranean coastlands was a more thoroughgoing hellenization
in the expression of their religion than was normal in Palestine; Jews like
St Paul naturally spoke and read good Greek.

[107] Such texts are discussed in Schürer 1986 (E 1207) III.1, 509–66, 617–700.
[108] Cic. *Flac.* 28.66–9.

Thus Greek genres were employed by a number of hellenistic Jewish writers. The Wisdom of Solomon is a protreptic or encomium. The Fourth Book of Maccabees is a diatribe. The philosophy of Aristobulus employs an eclectic variety of Stoic and other Greek teachings.[109] The extraordinary play about the Exodus written by a certain Ezekiel provides precious evidence for the composition of tragedy in the hellenistic period. Significantly some forger now unknown tried to pass off pious Jewish verses under the guise of such archaic and classical Greek poets as Orpheus and Phocylides, probably with the intention of impressing his fellow Jews as much as Gentiles.

For probably most Jews in the hellenistic diaspora the Septuagint was the standard text of the bible. This translation, which had come about gradually in the third and second centuries B.C. in Alexandria, was nearly always used rather than the original Hebrew in surviving Jewish writings in Greek. For Philo the Septuagint bore divine authority. It was only in the second century A.D. that Aquila and Theodotion tried to revise it in line with the Hebrew, although the survival of Theodotionic readings in the New Testament and probably in the Greek scroll of the Minor Prophets found at Qumran suggests that Theodotion had available an earlier text from before A.D. 70 which represented either a predecessor's efforts at revising the Septuagint or a Greek version of the bible quite separate from the main Septuagint tradition.

Reliance on this Greek version of the sacred Torah had in itself some effect on theological development as Greek terms which corresponded to only one meaning of a Hebrew word were equated to the whole range of its meanings, creating thereby a range of 'septuagintalisms' which made Jewish religious Greek nearly incomprehensible to outsiders while simultaneously importing the extraneous overtones of the Greek word (e.g. δόξα, εἰρήνη, δικαιοσύνη) into new contexts.

This power of language to stimulate new concepts may be illustrated by the presence of terminology reminiscent of the mysteries in some hellenistic Jewish writings including, though not prominently, the Septuagint: it has been argued, mostly because of mystery terminology in the works of Philo and St Paul and (rather fancifully interpreted) the iconography of some late-Roman Jewish artefacts, that a Jewish mystery cult existed in the hellenistic diaspora.[110] But there is no direct evidence for this, and it is striking that many of the contemporary traditions incorporated in the classic midrashic fashion in the interpretation of the Hebrew text by the Septuagint translators preserve teachings otherwise

---

[109] The fragments of Aristobulus are preserved in part in Clement of Alexandria and in Eusebius, *Hist. Eccl.*, and most extensively in Eus. *Praep. Evang.* VII.22.16–18; VIII.10; XIII.12.

[110] Goodenough 1953–68 (E 1126).

known only in later semitic midrashic compilations rather than comprising specifically hellenistic versions of the text.

(b) Society By the first century A.D. Jews were found not only in Egypt and the parts of Syria closest to Palestine (the largest diaspora communities) but also in large numbers in Asia Minor, Greece, Cyrene, Cyprus and Rome. There was some settlement on the coast of the Black Sea and in some areas of southern Italy but no Jews are known from the western Mediterranean until the late-Roman period. Emigration from Judaea to the diaspora had begun in earnest in hellenistic times for reasons discussed in *CAH* IX², 275, 297. There were further surges after the suppression of revolts in A.D. 70 and A.D. 135 – many such *émigrés* must have been exported as slaves – but the essential configuration of diaspora communities had already been set by the period covered by this volume.

Jewish communities were found in the countryside in Syria and Egypt but were largely an urban phenomenon. In foreign cities they were self-regulating either *de facto* through voluntary social isolation or by special permission of the city authorities as at Alexandria in the time of Augustus. Their magistrates, whose titles ranged from ethnarch (in Alexandria) to *archisynagogos* or *presbuteroi*, imposed communal law with the ultimate sanction of exclusion from the community: deviants such as St Paul[111] preferred to submit to their own court's jurisdiction even at the risk of corporal punishment rather than face such social death. The law imposed was presumably based upon the Torah, but by what principles it was interpreted is unknown: the view that Philo's theoretical elaboration of legal minutiae reflects the law in practice among Jews in Egypt is not tenable.[112]

The physical foci of these communities were the synagogues, of which each settlement would have at least one and the larger communities several scattered around the localities. Because the sanctity of the Temple site loomed less large outside Judaea these synagogues became more than just meeting-places: they were places of sanctity – Josephus even describes one as a ἱερόν.[113] Thus the first-century B.C. synagogue at Delos, identified by inscriptions to 'the most high god', was an impressive structure; nothing is known about the earliest Jewish buildings which underlie the extant fine third- and fourth-century synagogues at Dura Europus, Ostia and Sardis, but literary references to the magnificence of synagogues in the first century A.D. elsewhere in the diaspora are quite common.[114] The primary function of such edifices

---

[111] 2 Cor. 11:24.   [112] Goodenough 1929 (E 1124).   [113] Joseph. *BJ* VII.44–5.
[114] Philo, *Leg.* 20 (132); Joseph. *BJ* VII.44–5; *t.Sukk.* 4: 6. On synagogue buildings, see Shanks 1979 (E 1210).

was, as in Judaea, the stipulated reading of the Torah, but around this role accreted a regular liturgy which probably included the public recital of blessings and other prayers,[115] and, at least by the fourth century A.D., the chanting of psalms.[116]

The need to live close to a synagogue was one cause of the tendency of Jews to cluster in particular quarters in each city, but this trait reflects also the general attitude that separation from the non-Jewish world was in itself desirable and pious; in confirmation of this attitude but not its motive, to the pagan Tacitus it appeared that Jews 'stayed apart in their meals and their beds' out of 'a certain hatred of the human race'.[117] Jews abstained from the meals which might have formed social bonds, provoking particular resentment by not participating in the public feasts which constituted an important element in civic paganism (see below, p. 845). Explicit evidence for intermarriage is scanty, but this may reflect not the rarity of such liaisons but a reluctance to advertise them. Such unions took place with Jewish approval only after the conversion of the Gentile partner and this was possibly a factor in the decision of some proselytes to become Jewish (see below, p. 851). In other cases the Jewish partner may have chosen to abandon Judaism, but it is impossible to judge the frequency of such apostasy.

Hostility between the Jews and their neighbours was by no means constant, but the massacres perpetrated or threatened by each side in the Syrian cities in A.D. 66 must reflect sentiments which had originated before violence was precipitated by the events of that year in Judaea. It is likely that when antagonism flared up, it was provoked by local issues which can no longer be discovered. Thus at Alexandria in Egypt, the only place where the detailed history of Jewish–Gentile relations is recorded, many of the stresses which led to bloodshed were specific to the city.

The Jews of Alexandria, who had prospered exceptionally under the late Ptolemies through direct royal patronage, were relegated by Augustus to the status of the native Egyptians because of the *princeps'* policy of entrusting power to Greeks in the eastern part of his domain. Such treatment was particularly irksome to the highly hellenized Jewish elite. The writings of the philosopher Philo show that some such Jews felt themselves to be fully part of the wider culture of their time while retaining their distinctive Jewish identity. The Jews' struggle to be rid of subjection to the ignominious *laographia* or poll-tax, and their demand for *isopoliteia* (which may have meant either the right to participate in the city's government or treatment of their own *politeuma* as of equal

[115] Hengel 1971 (E 1134); Justin Martyr, *Dial. c. Trypho* 16, 117.
[116] Fasola 1976 (E 1114).   [117] Tac. *Hist.* v.5.1–2.

standing to, and independent of, the city administration)[118] are thoroughly documented not only by Philo, who was himself a leading figure on the Jewish side, but also by Josephus and by papyrus fragments of writings belonging to a curious genre known to modern scholars as the *Acts of the Pagan Martyrs*.[119] The conflict in Alexandria reached a peak under Gaius, partly because of the excessive partiality shown near the end of Tiberius' reign towards the Greeks and against the Jews by the prefect of Egypt A. Avillius Flaccus.

Such local disputes only exceptionally brought diaspora Jews into conflict with the Roman government, which in general protected Jewish interests in line with the highly sympathetic declarations made in their favour – probably for immediate political advantage – by Iulius Caesar, Antony and Augustus.[120] In the city of Rome itself, however, Jews were expelled by Tiberius and either ejected or forbidden to congregate by Claudius, in the former case as punishment for a fraud practised on a Roman matron, in the latter case because of rioting which had probably been confined within the Jewish community.[121] The Jews of Rome were a large group mostly descended from prisoners brought to the capital as slaves by Pompey in 63 B.C. and Sosius in 37 B.C. Their numbers had expanded under Augustus when many of these immigrants won their freedom: thus synagogues were named after Augustus and Agrippa.[122] But they remained confined to the poorest class among the plebs and became notorious as beggars. The expulsions reflect Tiberius' concern to uphold Augustus' propaganda of the restoration of old Roman cults – adherents of Isis were also driven out – while Claudius was perhaps only intent on the preservation of order in the crowded metropolis. At any rate Jews returned rapidly after each expulsion and probably few ever in fact went beyond the suburbs. By late antiquity the catacombs reveal a large Jewish population.

The diaspora communities apparently made no move to participate in the anti-Roman uprising of A.D. 66 to 70 except in the immediate vicinity of Palestine and briefly in Alexandria, but this loyalty to Rome was severely strained both by Titus' destruction of the Temple and by the imposition on *all* Jews in the empire after A.D. 70 of the *fiscus Iudaicus*, the annual payment to Jupiter Capitolinus by both male and female Jews of the regular offerings previously sent to Jerusalem by adult male Jews alone. In A.D. 116 the Jews of Cyprus, with those of Egypt and Cyrene,

[118] This latter interpretation is argued in full by Kasher 1985 (E 1154).

[119] Musurillo 1954 (B 381). The Philo treatises are *In Flaccum* and *Legatio ad Gaium*.

[120] Joseph. *AJ* XIV.185–267, 301–23, XVI.160–78; cf. Rajak 1984 (E 1194).

[121] On banishments under Tiberius, see Tac. *Ann.* II.85; Suet. *Tib.* 36; Joseph. *AJ* XIII.84; for action against Jews by Claudius, see Dio LX.6; Acts 18:2; Suet. *Claud.* 25.

[122] *CIJ* I² nos. 284, 365.

rose in bloody revolt as much against their Greek neighbours as the Roman government. Totally crushed after two years, the Jewish communities of Egypt and Cyrene disappear from the historical record for centuries, while the death penalty was decreed for any Jew who set foot on Cyprus.[123]

But the world around these diaspora Jews was not always so antagonistic. The separateness of the Jews in itself proved attractive to some pagans, for Gentiles were enticed to become proselytes in the diaspora far more than in Judaea and there is little evidence that this resulted from deliberate Jewish missionary activity. Such conversion had dramatic consequences for the proselyte, who was cut off from family and friends by voluntary self-exclusion from their meals and worship. The number who took this step is variously estimated at a huge or minimal figure; epigraphic evidence for proselytes of the first century A.D. is rare, and Josephus is informative only about the famous conversion of the royal family of Adiabene.[124]

Better testimony to amicable relations between Jews and Gentiles in some cities is the role of Gentiles who accreted to the synagogues in a great variety of ways without joining the Jewish community. Such people were perhaps attracted by the theology of Judaism or wished to placate the Jewish along with other powerful deities; this latter motive presumably lay behind the offerings made by many non-Jews to the Jerusalem Temple. Such 'god-fearers' (*theon phoboumenoi* or *seboumenoi*) are assumed by the Acts of the Apostles and Josephus; a list of *theosebeis* distinguished both from Jews and from full proselytes shows that a formal group attached to a Jewish community was clearly identified by this name in late-Roman Aphrodisias, but the precise status in Jewish eyes of such sympathetic Gentiles was perhaps less well defined by Jews in earlier periods.[125]

IV. CONCLUSION

The impression that Jewish history in this period was different in kind from that of other provincials is probably exaggerated by the religious orientation of much of the surviving evidence, but since that impression was shared by contemporary Gentiles and not least by Roman administrators it must be accounted a major factor in the peculiar and frequently unhappy fortunes of the Jews within the Roman empire. In the attempt

---

[123] Dio. LXVIII.32.1–3; cf. Pucci 1981 (E 1190); Barnes 1989 (E 1087). See *CAH* XI[2].

[124] Joseph. *AJ* XX.17–96. On god-fearers and proselytes, see Schürer 1986 (E 1207) III.1, 150–76; McKnight 1991 (E 1174).

[125] Acts 10:2, 22; 13:16, 26, 43, 50; 16:14; 17:4, 17; 18:7; Joseph. *AJ* XIV.110. On the Aphrodisias inscription, see Reynolds and Tannenbaum 1987 (E 1198). On changing attitudes towards 'godfearers', see Cohen 1989 (E 1103); Goodman 1989 (D 132).

of the Roman elite during the late Republic and early Empire to define the correct place of religion within the state, Judaism was generally excluded from the body of respectable cults and designated a *superstitio*. Since Jews' social and political relations were almost always expressed by them in terms of their religion, all Jews who did not apostatize were treated as outsiders in the Roman world. Such wilful hostility towards, rather than simple ignorance about, the native culture of a subject people was not typical of Roman provincial administration. It resulted in the two great Judaean revolts of A.D. 66–70 and 132–5, and in the no less sanguinary conflict in the diaspora in A.D. 116–17.

CHAPTER 15

ROME AND ITS DEVELOPMENT UNDER AUGUSTUS AND HIS SUCCESSORS[1]

NICHOLAS PURCELL

Augustus' own summary of the impact of his rule on the city of Rome was the boast, often quoted, almost proverbial 'urbem... marmoream se relinquere, quam latericiam accepisset', that the city he had taken charge of in brick he passed on in marble (Suet. *Aug.* 28.3, cf. Dio LVI.30). The philosophically inclined Cassius Dio took him metaphorically and referred the contrast to the might of Rome's power (LVI.30.4); the aim of this survey likewise is to proceed from the physical aspect of the city and the messages which it proclaimed on into the changes in the behaviour of its ordinary inhabitants which were promoted by the arrival and development of the Principate. The double interpretation of the first *princeps*' remark does suggest after all that changes of this kind were in fact perceived as a unitary achievement, and that the achievement was considered important. This account hopes to show why it was thought important, and why it is impossible to partition off the architectural and physical history of the city from the social and economic history of its populace.[2]

The enormous brick ruins of the monuments of Augustus' heirs which characterize the centre of Rome today make Augustus' words sound paradoxical to the modern visitor: they need some explanation and interpretation.

The 'brick' in question, to begin with, is not the kiln-fired, almost indestructible product of later Roman architecture: it is the traditional sundried mud brick of Italian domestic architecture, and also, probably, refers to the terracotta decorations which had so characterized the sacred architecture of Italy from the seventh century B.C. For Augustus was thinking primarily of the city as defined by its public architecture, and above all by its religious buildings. It was here that his own personal

---

[1] I am grateful to the editors for their opinions on this piece. It takes for granted the account of the demography, composition and economic activities of the urban plebs which will be found in *CAH* IX[2], ch. 17 and is designed to introduce the much more problematic world of the urban populace in the middle Empire which is discussed in *CAH* XI[2]. I have naturally not attempted to cover every facet of the architectural and social history of Rome between 44 B.C. and A.D. 70.

[2] Zanker 1988 (F 633) now has pride of place among studies of this subject, but there is a good deal of further work required.

initiatives had done most to effect a change, and it is important that his *mot* refers not to a sweeping alteration just of substandard old-fashioned cheap building materials in general architecture, but a revolution which replaced style, content and form in some of Rome's – traditional Rome's – most venerable and significant monuments.[3] It is also important to notice that in this phrase we have testimony to Augustus' taking a general view of the visual face of the city of Rome, and forming a clear idea of how he thought it best that that face should be changed.

Our knowledge of the fabric of the city in the last century and a half of the Republic is scanty: this is an ignorance which must be recognized before a limited picture can be evolved. It will not do to retroject too casually the better documented conditions of the middle Empire. An improved organizational structure, the revolution in architectural technology, changing social conditions combined with the perennial opportunities of the fires and floods to produce a very different urban atmosphere in the Flavian and subsequent periods. What can we say of the earlier city?

Rome's site provides all the raw materials for a city. Strabo, enthusing about the 'concurrence of advantages which surpasses all the beneficence of nature' (v.3.7 (234–5C)) makes a point of setting the supply of brick stone and wood beside the resources of local agriculture as the explanation of the city's survival. The Alban volcanoes are the real source of this endowment. Only a few kilometres down the Appian Way from the city gate lies the furthest-reaching lava flow, providing the indestructibly hard *silex*, 'selce' with which Roman roads were paved; still more important, across the site of Rome and along the Anio to the north east of the city where they were easily accessible to waterborne transport, the easily worked tufas of the Alban volcanoes are found: they outcrop on all the scarps of the Seven Hills, which were far more precipitous in the Republic than can easily be imagined today. The scarps themselves provided opportunities for myriad semi-troglodytic dwellings, extended outwards, one on another in a muddled jumble, with the cut rock and with the dried mud-brick of the Tiber's alluvial clays, bound and roofed likewise with the products of the thickets of the valley-floors – wattle of the giant reed, *harundo donax*, willow withies, saplings, boughs and even substantial timber. For domestic housing in the early years no formal planning or allocation of lots in the Greek style was possible or necessary; the city inevitably grew by accretion, woven and built like a modern shanty town out of the substance of the locality itself. Unlike a shanty town or the warrens of a medieval Levantine city – and the warrenlike nature of republican Rome was a commonplace in the first century B.C. (Cic. *Leg. Agr.* II.96, cf. Livy, v.55.2–5) – from the first, the

[3] Zanker 1988 (F 633) esp. chs. 3–4; Gros 1976 (F 397) 15–52.

habitations of Rome had a strong vertical component, created by the slopes of the hills and the winding defiles of the valleys between them. As archaeology begins to unravel the less monumental parts of the urban fabric, the organic growth of the tangled clusters of rooms out from the naked tufa (as well as into it in many cases) in layer after layer ascending from the winding streets of the valley bottoms, is being revealed in case after case.[4] Naturally the bulkiest, most elaborate of these structures are the ones of imperial fired brick like those which extend the Palatine towards the Forum and the Velabrum; but the principle is much older. These stacked cellular accretions, extending the hillside into the air, are what the Romans first called *insulae*; the name is clearly as old as the middle Republic, but we should not imagine the free standing block-by-block island lots of Ostia at that period. The tendency to make the casual accretions on the hillsides more regular, to give them more architectural form and legal definition, to build freestanding equivalents of the level ground of hill-top or valley floor, started in the Republic – the legislation on party-walls and the like recorded by Vitruvius (II.8.16–17) shows that – but we have no way of knowing how far it had progressed by the Augustan period. We need not doubt, however, that Pliny's description of Rome as *urbs pensilis* 'suspended city' was true from a very early date.[5] Equally part of the population lived informally in the crevices of the towering buildings, sleeping rough in *tabernae* or huddled in the vaults beneath the seating of the theatres, circuses and amphitheatres, right to the end of Antiquity (Amm. Marc. 14.6.25).

An architecture appropriate to a 'hanging city' had emerged in west central Italy by the third century B.C. It is difficult to be sure where it was developed – Rome is not the only city-site with complex and varied relief to contend with, and some of our early examples are Campanian. The architecture comprised the use of strong concrete and squared stone, the arch and – at first on a limited scale – the barrel vault, to extend hillsides at will with platforms, terraces, ramps and stairways. The purpose was a monumental urbanism like that of the hellenistic East, seen at its acme in the acropolis of Pergamum; its finest example in Italy is the sanctuary of Fortuna Primigenia at Praeneste (Palestrina). At Rome this was the

---

[4] For the temporary nature of these buildings and their vulnerability to redevelopment, Phillips 1973 (F 524). The vocabulary of *maeniana, tabulatio, contignationes* is expressive; Festus, s.v. *adtibernium*; Pliny, *HN* XVI.36 on use of shingles, making a connexion of thought with the vanished timber of the site of Rome; for good and bad practice in *insula*-building, Vit. *De Arch.* II.8.18–20. On collapses, Strab. v (234–5C) XIV.5.4 (670C), and Dio XXXIX.61 (dissolving of unbaked brick by floodwater). For the piling up of tall buildings, Sen. *Controv.* II.1.11–12; Sen. *Ep.* 90–7; Amm. Marc. 27.9.8. On *insulae* in general, Boethius 1960 (F 290) 129–85. For the materials, note also the passage of Ovid quoted on p. 803.

[5] Pliny's description covers both the *opera pensilia* of substructions and platforms, and the sewers which lay beneath the city to serve as storm drains: cf. Strab. v.3.8 (235C); Soranus, II.xx (XL).44 (113). These were a standard ingredient in the praises of the city.

architecture of the great projects of the 'building censors' of the age after the Hannibalic War, and in the late Republic was deployed for the sculpting of the Forum face of the Capitol by Lutatius Catulus, with the monumental public complex (the so-called Tabularium) which still survives; and for private enterprises like the suburban estates of the hills north of the city. Here it is important to stress one negative point: although Claudius and Nero, Trajan and Septimius Severus, continued the approach with the improved materials available to them, creating hills where there had been empty space, Augustus and his fellow builders largely ignored this traditional approach to urbanism for most of their ascendancy. Indeed it can be argued that through the laws on building, controlling the heights of the *insulae* and regulating such matters as party-walls, which were enforced at this period, Augustus actually explicitly discouraged the tendency towards an *urbs pensilis*. It must be remembered that the development of kiln-fired brick during the next century made it much safer to develop the traditional tall architecture; it was that progress that made possible the 'New Rome' of Nero after the Great Fire, with regular blocks of very tall *insulae* and regular wide streets between them, and the later elaboration of this architecture in complexes like the Markets of Trajan or the northern substructures of the Palatine. It is hard to imagine a public building more alien to Augustan Rome than the former.[6]

In order to understand the preferences of the age we must return to the ideological background to Augustus' dealing with the city of Rome. Building had been a prominent part of the self-presentation of the Roman elite since time immemorial, and Augustus needed to excel at all the activities which conferred *auctoritas*; so he could not but display his power in this way, could not refrain from adding his *monumenta* to the accumulated record of the great men of the past which could be read in the architecture of Rome. It would have been absurd, too, to pass up the opportunities of subtle communication of political and ideological messages which architecture provided. Caesar had planned and started projects which were very much in the vein which we have discussed, grandiose and elaborate reworkings of the physical and structural landscape of the city – the new course of the Tiber, the Capitol sculpted with a great theatre, the opening out of the Forum and Saepta with great colonnaded enclosures.[7] The style of thought as of architecture was hellenistic and regal; the glitter and the power were the point, the people

[6] On this architectural tradition see Gros 1978 (F 398); Gros 1976 (F 397) ch. 2 for the weaknesses in Augustan design.

[7] Caesar's plans: see esp. Suet. *Iul.* 44; Cic. *Att.* IV.16.8; *RG* 20.3. It is noteworthy that Augustus saw his own work as to some extent the realization of Caesar's plans, with the extension of his Forum and the completion of the Basilica Julia; but as in the world of ceremonial and self-celebration his work had a different and often more cautious nuance.

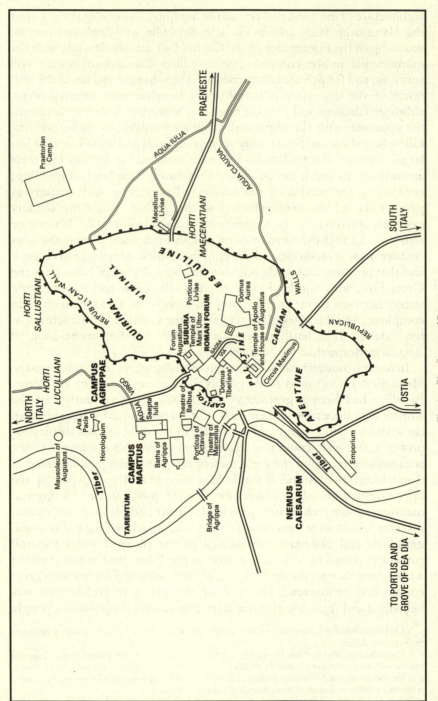

Fig. 10. Sketch map of Rome.

the audience: at close quarters, since the buildings were designed as the stage for the activities in which the elite encouraged them. Alexandria and Pergamum were the inspiration. The great theatre and *porticus* complex of Pompey in the Campus Martius was a statement in the same language, and it may well be that this nuance should be read in much of the new architecture of the hundred years before Augustus. The conquerors and exploiters of the East, the people of the Italian peninsula, brought home to their communities the ambitious architectural airs of those they had conquered.[8] Strabo expresses the mood well (v.3.8 (235–6C)); the Romans of old had more serious things on their mind, but Pompey, Caesar, Augustus, his sons, friends, wife and sister (the list, thus, is Strabo's) have added beauty, filling the city with their offerings. The word used is *anathemata*, notable for its religious flavour.

The party of Octavian had been compelled to adopt this type of benefaction during the politically complex years between Philippi and the restoration of the *res publica*. With Antony in Alexandria, the capital of hellenistic culture, it was essential for his rivals to make some statement about their attitude to the East, and it was not at first obvious that this would be the rejection espoused in the months before Actium by 'tota Italia'. These were the years when the people of the capital were at their most dangerous; more numerous than at any previous time, they were easily swollen by the arrivals of all the displaced of the times of trouble, and at no point in the years after the Gracchi had they so much identified political strength with brute force and had so clear a prospectus of aims as they had acquired in the years which stretched from Catiline through the struggle of Clodius and Milo to the ascendancy of Caesar. So the affairs of the city were a pressing objective for Octavian and his party, and for their opponents likewise.

The mood was religious. Sulla and Pompey had not omitted the temples of Rome from their building programmes; Cicero contributed to the reconstruction of the temple of Tellus. But the sophisticated religious policy of Caesar and chaos of the times combined to produce a competition among some of the *principes viri* for which there is no recent precedent in what is, after all, a well-documented period. Munatius Plancus' restoration of the temple of Saturn (42 B.C.), the massive retaining-wall of the sanctuary of Juno Lucina built by Q. Pedius, Domitius Ahenobarbus' temple of Neptune (between 42 and 38), Domitius Calvinus' lavish reconstruction of the Regia (36), C. Sosius' restoration of the temple of Apollo near the Circus Flaminius and Marcius Philippus' of that of Hercules Musarum in 29 B.C.; these make a varied and impressive list. This is the background against which we must

[8] Gros 1976 (F 397) 235–42; Zanker 1976 (E 141) *passim* for the hellenistic architecture of Italy, cf. Gros 1978 (F 398); Zanker 1988 (F 633) 33–77.

see the vows of Octavian himself, the temple to Divus Iulius voted in 42
B.C. and that of Mars Ultor, first conceived in that year also; the temple of
Apollo Palatinus, dedicated in 28 B.C., as well as the more mundane
reconstruction work on the temple of Jupiter Feretrius in 31 B.C., which
began the great record of his temple maintenance that was to last the
whole of his rule. The keynote of much of this building was eastern
magnificence. Pedius' work seems to have been in the tradition of the
great substructure architecture of the late Republic. Sosius' temple is a
splendid display of Hellenism, from its own elegant floral marble-work
to the re-used Greek pediment sculptures, now recently re-discovered,
which graced its façade. Likewise Ahenobarbus displayed an enormous
sculptural *tour de force* by Scopas in his temple (Pliny, *HN* xxxvi.26);
Calvinus' Regia was another very costly display-piece (*HN* xxxvi.48;
Dio xlviii.42), some of the sculpture in which he very cannily managed
to borrow from Octavian: it included two of the caryatids which had
held up the tent of Alexander the Great. The triumphal mood is
prominent, and the recently discovered fragment of an elegy by Gallus
referring to the enrichment of Rome's temples by the conquests of a
'Caesar' well fits the mood of the moment whether it refers to Julius or,
as is perhaps preferable, Octavian.[9]

The religious fervour is striking, and, as we shall see, left its mark on
the character of the Augustan Principate. But not all the *monumenta* of the
period were sacred: we may cite the dedication of the ambitious
reconstruction of the Basilica Paulli in 34 and the rebuilding of the Villa
Publica by Fonteius Capito. These were more than matched by Octavian
and Agrippa: the former restored the Porticus Octavia and – with great
display of modesty – the complex of Pompey's buildings nearby. A key
moment was the aedilate of Agrippa in 33 B.C., a freak itself for an ex-
consul, in which he devoted himself to works which were at once
popularis, in that they could be seen as utilitarian benefactions, and potent
demonstrations of power, power over Nature, power to alter the
landscape. The reworking of the world beneath the hanging city was
carried out with great display, Agrippa inverting nature by going along
the duct of the restored Cloaca Maxima in a cart. The aqueduct-system
was overhauled, and a whole new aqueduct, the Aqua Iulia, added to the
system and the Aqua Virgo perhaps planned.[10] We hear an echo of the
great triumphal inscriptions of the dynasts, with their enumerations of
conquered cities, in what seems to be a quotation from Agrippa's own *res*

---

[9] Gros 1976 (F 397) 207, the temple of Divus Iulius as 'une sorte de manifeste architectural'.
Apollo Sosianus: La Rocca 1980–1 (F 459). Apollo Palatinus: Lefèvre 1989 (F 466). On the
Corinthian order, Wilson-Jones 1989 (F 622); Gros 1976 (F 397) 197–234. Zanker on building, 1988
(F 633) 42–31. Gallus fragment: Anderson, Parsons, and Nisbet 1979 (B 4).
[10] Shipley 1931 (F 571) with Boethius 1934 (E 6); Roddaz 1984 (C 200) 145–57.

gestae: 'he made 700 cisterns, and 500 fountainheads besides, and 130 water-towers, very many of them lavish in ornamentation; and on those works he set 300 bronze or marble statues, and 400 marble columns – and all this in the space of one year. He added, in commemoration of his aedilate, games which were held for 59 days, and 170 occasions to use bath houses, without charge' (Pliny, *HN* xxxvi.121; Peter *HRR* ii p. 64).

So even before Actium the victorious party was in the ascendant, already beating the other *triumphatores* at the game that was being so earnestly played with the city's architecture. After the victory the style remained; restraint, whether of means or modesty, was over. The dedications of the temples of Divus Iulius (29) and of Apollo Palatinus announced the triumphant outcome of the epoch; and on the Campus Martius rose a complex of monuments which outdid Alexandria and Antony forever in their regal oriental splendour. The first is the trophy itself, the obelisk dedicated to Alexandria's god, the Sun, to commemor-ate the city's subjection in the centre of the gigantic sundial which was the work of the citizens' scientific genius. The second, immediately adjacent, is the artificial mountain on the Tiber's bank, dominating the approaches to Rome by road and river, in a man-made nature of gardens, which was to be Augustus' resting-place and memorial, the Mausoleum. The third, likewise, has a significance which is overtly dynastic and monarchic: the Pantheon of Agrippa, in which images of Augustus and Agrippa enjoyed a divine context in a building whose siting and design seems to have been designed to recall the apotheosis of the city's first Founder, Romulus. The Greekness of the nearby artificial lake and of the hot baths which adjoined it was obvious; the luxury was almost more than Egyptian.[11]

But the mood did not last, or Rome might have been transformed by A.D. 14 into the most remarkable instance of all that was most grandiose in hellenistic taste. It was after the buoyant mood of the early twenties, restored peace, sole power, family harmony, that the style of Augustan planning for the monuments of Rome changes. The 'Crisis in Party and State' of 23–19 may be the main explanation. Just as the most careful symbiosis of the *novus status* with old constitutional forms begins at this moment, so the type of building and of architecture becomes more 'democratic' and less Asiatic in its florid extravagance. Some of the themes of the earlier phase are developed – the popular utilitarianism, the religious atmosphere, the beautification of the city with public suburban benefactions, which we shall investigate. But the magnificence of the monarchic *princeps*, the hubristic luxury and the grandiloquence of style, these disappear. Contrast the archaizing polychrome alien glories

[11] Buchner 1982 (F 306) the sundial; on the Pantheon, Coarelli 1983 (F 333).

of the complex of Apollo Palatinus with the sober mix of Athenian and old Roman in the temple of Mars Ultor, which formed the centre-piece of the greatest project of the later part of Augustus' rule, the Forum Augustum.[12]

Augustus continued to enjoy the best of both worlds. His own house on the Palatine could with justice be regarded as modest by the standards of the day, and it was not until the reign of Nero that a great purpose-built palace complex dominated the Palatine (the platform, like that of an enormous villa, whose substructions remain beneath the Farnese Gardens, and which supported the pavilions and peristyles of the complex misleadingly known today as Domus Tiberiana). But it was not wholly a private house; Augustus made it over to the People to satisfy ritual requirements when he became High Priest in 12 B.C., and these religious connotations helped produce an ambiguity as to where his living-quarters stopped and the public buildings began. A hearth-temple of Vesta was part of the monumental approach to his moderate abode which was inseparable from the splendour of the *porticus* of the complex of Apollo Palatinus. When the Senate met in that temple, although the impropriety of meeting in the house of the *princeps* was avoided, symbolically that was indeed what they were doing. The grand row of ancient houses of patrician magistrates which lined the Via Sacra as it rose onto the slopes of the Palatine from the Forum until it was obliterated by the fire of A.D. 64, which forever wiped out this display of the antiquity of the Roman aristocracy, could now be regarded as leading up to the front door of Augustus' ambiguous home.[13] Their honours now consisted likewise not in contributing to the *monumenta* of Rome but in being subordinated to Augustus' new creations. When a prominent consular died in A.D. 56 this is how his outstanding honours were described: 'three triumphal statues, one bronze in the Forum Augustum, two marble in the new temple of the Divine Augustus; three consular statues, one in the temple of the Divine Julius, a second on the Palatine inside the Triple Gate, a third in the Precinct of Apollo in sight of where the Senate meets; one as Augur, at the Regia; one on horseback at the Speaker's Platform in the Forum; and one sitting in a curule chair in the Theatre of Pompey, in the Colonnade of the Lentuli' (*AE* 1972, 174). The regime now had total control of the symbolic topography of the

---

[12] Zanker 1988 (F 633) ch. 3 for the change; *id. Forum Augustum* n.d. [*c.* 1968] (F 625) (note the caryatids). Note however that Athenian craftsmen worked on the Pantheon (Pliny, *HN* XXXVI.38). For the politics – and the phrase 'Crisis in the Party and State' – Syme 1939 (A 93) ch. 23.

[13] For the platform under the Farnese gardens, Krause 1985 (F 458); on Augustus' house, Wiseman 1987 (F 81). The new discovery of the grand houses of the Via Sacra (Carandini) confirms his account strikingly. Houses too close to the Forum were already a risk politically in A.D. 20 (Tac. *Ann.* III.9, strikingly confirmed by the new *senatusconsultum* on the verdict on Piso); after the great fire those that survived could help destroy a consul (*Ann.* XV.69).

public space of the inner city; eight years after this display private space followed suit in the aftermath of the fire. But the Golden House, cutting a swathe through the city, for all its conceits and sheer offensive bulk, only made obvious a takeover of the city by the Caesars that had already happened when Augustus died.

Rome's periphery had undergone various evolutions with the changes in the nature and size of the population and the availability of wealth and food. One of the most striking was the tendency for the greatest men in the state to accumulate suburban property which they could convert into extraordinarily luxurious display-grounds for their wealth. The vocabulary was the same as we have seen in the buildings of the triumviral period – changing the face of nature, cultivating paradox. The proximity to seething Rome of evocations of the coast or countryside or wilderness was the most enjoyable feature, to emphasize which they called these estates 'kitchen gardens', *horti*. Even if the most extravagant Baroque taste of these whimsical pleasure-palaces was to be a creation of the first century A.D., they had already by this period attained considerable magnificence; in Augustus' own camp C. Maecenas was the creator of a particularly lavish example on the Esquiline.[14] The real singularity of Nero's Domus Aurea lay in extending inwards to the very heart of Rome the most opulent of these estates ever seen. By that time, the prestige attaching to the ownership of these pleasure-palaces was considered too great for anyone except the *princeps*. Claudius' reign had seen the fall of two great senators whose *horti* were thought to have contributed to their doom, and the suburban estates of the imperial patrimony had become a principal residence of the ruler from Caligula onwards.

Now the tone of this private luxury was, as we have seen, very close to the monarchic assertiveness which Augustus at first practised. So it was dangerous in the hands of other *primores* – and led many of them, in the reigns of Augustus' successors, to disaster. Nor was it, for the reasons outlined, even appropriate for the *princeps* himself. Augustus chose the path of benefaction as an alternative, and encouraged expenditure on more open public recreation places, not wholly different in their aesthetic language, but not exclusive or politically sensitive. The *proastion* of the hellenistic city had long been a potential place for this kind of architecture, and the repertoire of public walks, plantings, porticoes and waterworks had been tapped by Pompey and Caesar, whose admission of the populace into his own *suburbanum* in Transtiberim (across the Tiber) foreshadowed Augustus' activity in this area. A formal suburb of this kind was designed to be the location of the ceremonies of arrival and departure which had developed their standing during the Republic and became a feature of the public life of the *principes* (for an Augustan

[14] For *horti* Purcell 1987 (F 52), 1987 (F 51); gardens of Maecenas, Häuber 1990 (E 58).

example Dio LVI.1.1); it also provided a chance to pose as a second founder, building a new city alongside the old, as Hadrian was later to do at Athens. For Strabo the effect of the very numerous buildings of Augustus and his circle in the Campus Martius was to produce a suburb more beautiful than the city (v.3.8 (235–6C)). The process, again reminiscent of Caesar, was to make over to the public formally a building created on private land by private contract, as Dio makes clear in discussing the works of Agrippa; the effect was to tone down the unpleasant associations of *luxus* by making it a benefaction to all Romans, a sign of their status in the world. When Augustus demolished the house of Vedius Pollio, a byword for opulence, and Livia built a *porticus* there instead, the moral message was very clear. As early as 60 B.C. we find the son of the dictator Sulla pampering the plebs with baths and free oil as well as games and banqueting (Dio XXXVII.51.4). Nero's great gymnasium on the Campus Martius, expanding the Baths of Agrippa with a complex which set the tone for the later imperial Thermae, made explicit the Hellenic associations of this gesture. Part of what made luxury desirable was that it had the *cachet* of Greek civilization. But it was being made available not just to the ruling class, but to all inhabitants of the imperial city. We notice too that even Maecenas' *horti* seem first to have been accessible to the public and, second, to have had the purpose of reclaiming a frightful polluted stretch of suburban land for public and salubrious use.[15]

Thus it was that the prevailing architecture of Augustan Rome is not the concrete and vault, arch and terrace native to Rome and Italy, but the less boastful and more relaxed sequences of squares, courts and colonnades which the forty years of Augustan rule extended across much of Rome. Thus it was also that the utilitarian note was struck, in buildings like the Market of Livia, another of the improvements to the Esquiline fringe of the city. The old provision market of Rome, the Macellum, had had strong associations with the commercial with luxurious profit-making freedmen and over-indulgent customers, and the replacement of part of its district with the new Forum Augustum may have been the occasion for the new building and its banishment to the fringes of the city. Roman pragmatic utilitarianism is such a cliché, however, that we forget to notice the significance that it has in the actions of the first *princeps*. Rather than taking it on trust, we should attempt some explanation of what Augustus' attitude and intentions may have been in this field.

To attempt this, we need to move beyond the subject of large-scale

---

[15] For Rome's *proastion*, Purcell 1987 (F 52); on Agrippa's work, Roddaz 1984 (C 200) 231–305; for Nero's gymnasium, Tamm 1970 (F 591).

public building. Across the years of Augustus' Principate there are many other moments at which the affairs of the city as an entity received deliberate attention. Some such spirit may be discerned in the role played by Maecenas during Octavian's absence in the triumviral period and in the *diacheirisis* ('administration') of the city offered to Agrippa in 21 (Dio LIV.6.5); and, with greater certainty, in the evolution of a position of city prefect. During the Cantabrian War Messalla Corvinus took up this office, which was adapted in typical fashion from the immemorial practice of appointing a deputy for the consuls when they celebrated the Latin Festival on the Alban Mount: that he resigned it almost at once suggests that, for all that, the duties were quite unprecedented (Tac. *Ann.* VI.11). The experiment was tried again in 13 B.C. when Statilius Taurus became prefect, and from then on proved a great success. Like all Roman 'administrators', the city prefects spent most of their working time in judicial activity, with a particular reference to the unruliness of life among the urban populace: as Tacitus describes the officer's brief, he was 'a consular who could compel obedience among the slave element and the part of the citizen body which had the nerve to be riotous if there were no risk'.[16]

This involved the management of military personnel. As Ulpian, writing in the third century on the duties of the city prefect, puts it (*Dig.* 1.12.1.12) 'he often has to maintain soldiers on guard-duty to preserve quiet among the *populares* and for keeping him informed about what is happening where'. If there was a 'revolution' in the way Augustus ran Rome, it was in the making available to the relevant magistrates a larger and better organized body of manpower than had been available before. This transformed the executive capacity of the state in the city, even if the efficiency of the decision-makers was not particularly enhanced. Traditionally, the executive resources of the magistrates were limited to their *apparitores* and personal dependents; there are signs that Augustus left his mark on the decurial system by which these staffs were organized. But it was in the imposition on Rome of military units, the 1,500 men of the three *cohortes urbanae*, associated with the city prefect, and the *cohortes praetoriae* responsible directly to the *princeps* and, until Sejanus had built the great fortress on the Viminal outside the City, billeted around the urban area, that the revolution was really effected. The sources for the history of the early Empire time and again display these soldiers as the principal agents of state authority. An important side-effect of the establishment of these cohorts was to provide a prestigious channel by which Italians might move to Rome and rise in the social scale, a

---

[16] For the urban prefect, see Vitucci 1956 (E 136). Police duties, Nippel 1988 (A 71); Echols 1957–8 (D 187). Urban violence under the Principate: Moeller 1970 (C 376).

formalization of a common social pattern which was already in existence. Scores of thousands of Italians came to experience the life of Rome and convey its tendencies to their home towns through this machinery.[17]

Similar in its effects was the establishment of the city watch, the *cohortes vigilum*, by a series of steps which started with a force of 600 slaves set up in 22 B.C., when Augustus was surveying the city with a censor's eye (Dio LIV.2.3) and which were complete at a strength of 3,920 men by A.D. 55. Fire prevention, by means of brute force rather than technology, through the destruction of Rome's flimsy structures in the path of the fire with hooks and levers, was their principal duty. They were also, importantly, of help in maintaining order in other ways. Again, their *praefectus* came to play an increasing part in the running of the city; he too became a judge with considerable competence. Recruitment to the *vigiles*, limited as it was at first to the freedman population (later it rose in social prestige), also played an important part in the society of the city.[18]

The same spirit of the organization of manpower can also be seen in the regulation of the private *familia* owned by Agrippa for the maintenance of the aqueducts in 11 B.C. as a public institution. Further, the changes which we can dimly perceive in the management of the *collegium fabrorum tignuariorum*, the association of the building industry in Rome, may belong in this context. They adopted a parapolitical structure of some elaboration, and their own era dating from 7 B.C.; a parallel also for the organization of the city districts which is discussed below.[19]

The first sign that Augustus would involve himself in the running of the city was his tackling the question of corn distribution and the *annona* in 22 B.C. Here he had Pompey's precedent clearly behind him.[20] But most of the changes came in the decade after his return from Gaul and led up to the triumphant moment when he opened the Forum Augustum and was declared *pater patriae*, in 2 B.C. We find the *senatusconsultum* on the aqueducts in 11; an innovatory series of procedures for defining and maintaining the banks of the Tiber; concern for other public boundaries, and for the management of roads; the first establishment of the *vigiles*; the division of the city into fourteen *regiones* in 7 B.C., when the reform of the *compita* and *vici* which formed the smaller subdivisions of the city also took place. Also from that moment attention was paid to the boundary of the city, resulting in the ornamental rebuilding of the ancient city gates, though it probably did not involve a ritual extension of the sacred boundary, the *pomerium*.[21]

[17] Purcell 1983 (F 49); 1991 for movement to Rome. Durry 1938 (D 185).
[18] Reynolds 1926 (E 108); Rainbird 1986 (E 104); Freis 1967 (D 190).
[19] Pearse 1976–7 (B 261); Royden 1988 (F 58).   [20] Rickman 1980 (E 109) 60–6 and 179–85.
[21] Boatwright 1986 (E 5). City gates: Platner and Ashby 1929 (E 95) svv. 'Arcus Crispini et Lentuli', 'Arcus Dolabellae et Silani'; Nash 1968 (E 87) s.v. 'Arcus Dolabellae et Silani', 'Arcus Gallieni'.

These changes were not dramatic innovatory reforms based on policy. They were modified and evolved over the years. The delineation of the Tiber is a good example. A republican procedure, unused since 54 B.C., was deployed by the consuls in 8 B.C. and in 7 B.C. by Augustus himself; in A.D. 15 Tiberius changed the system again, with the appointment of a permanent board of *curatores* on the model of the body which saw to the aqueducts.[22] So these urban decisions are a matter of trial and error, but they do clearly have a general coherence, chronologically, and in that they all concern the good order of the city itself.

The wishes of the inhabitants of Rome were not without their political significance as Augustus knew from his experience of the triumviral period: it was amply confirmed. It may have been unwise for him to absent himself from the city so much in the years 27–24; certainly violence continued throughout the period, reaching a peak in 22, when the Senate was barricaded inside the Curia, and was not just a response to the natural disasters of famine, fire, pestilence and flood (see especially Dio LIII.33.4–5; LIV.1.1–2). The affection and favour of the people gave one Egnatius Rufus the base from which to attempt an illegal transfer from being praetor to the consulship in 19 B.C. His benefaction had been a successful fire-fighting programme, and he was only suppressed with difficulty.[23] Again in A.D. 6 the activities of P. Plautius Rufus, who built on the miseries of the people from famine and fire with a revolutionary pamphlet campaign, clearly constituted a serious political threat to the regime (Dio LV.27.1–3; Suet. *Aug.* 19). Not surprisingly, there is a clear link between particular crises and the various stages of Augustus' evolving solutions – impetus from outside was the normal source of governmental action in Antiquity. But Augustus' pose as the heir of Caesar – and indeed, by the time his Principate was at an end, of Clodius too – was relatively tardy compared to the vigour with which he cornered the market in military *gloria*, stabilizing legislation, and traditional *pietas*. So although his attention to the affairs of the city was not without its prudential, straightforwardly political aspect, we need not take such an attitude to be central to Augustus' response.

The tone of our principal sources for Augustus' activity, the *Res Gestae*, Suetonius and Dio, suggests that some ideal for the correct presentation of the city and its inhabitants was behind Augustus' measures – a general *cura Urbis* as it had come to be formulated by the end of the Republic. Augustus' boast about brick and marble has more to do with the overall effect of the changes which he had made at Rome than with the creation of individual triumphal *monumenta*, however spectacular. And considering what was available, the sumptuous regal display of individual magnificence was not at the centre of Augustan building

---

[22] Le Gall 1953 (E 73). [23] Lacey 1985 (C 150); for famine, Garnsey 1988 (A 33) 218–22.

projects after the middle of the twenties B.C. Instead there is a sense of decency and good order and good government, of responsibility, tidiness and justice about the new arrangements, which is reminiscent of the prescriptions of Cicero about how a city should be managed, and indeed has a long literary tradition. There is a flavour of the administrative sections of the Aristotelian *Constitution of Athens* in the care taken to distribute duties among competent authorities, and the same language of good public order and the right kind of official to maintain it is prominent in the descriptions of cities across the empire by Augustus' younger contemporary Strabo. The advantage of seeking such a background to the 'administrative reforms' of Augustus is that it saves us from the implausibility of attributing to Augustus either a reformer's zeal for a new policy, of which otherwise both he and his successors can be seen to have been almost entirely in default, or the intention of establishing a bureaucratic apparatus for solving technical organizational problems which seems on the evidence of the experience of the next hundred years to have been – if that were its aim – a singular failure, and which would also, in any case, be hard to parallel in the ancient world. And instead of this isolated specimen of bureaucratic creativity, hard to swallow and digest, we get a glimpse of a coherent, if rather optimistic, attitude to what befits a city which rules the world in the setting which Augustus had created for it.[24]

It is most important to this argument not to separate the 'hardware' of aqueducts and river banks and fire prevention from the people who moved in and around it. The remodelling of the *res publica*, moreover, had to include the *populus* and so could not avoid a social dimension: Augustus' Roman legislation concerned both the city and its inhabitants, and the regulations on manumission and the duties of the freedman should be seen alongside not just the corn distributions but also the maintenance of the roads, the laws on the height of buildings, and the provision of public spectacles. The intention was decency in behaviour and setting for the citizen of Rome, whose correct physical place in the polity on display in the theatres was laid down by the *lex Iulia theatralis*, and whose entitlement to the pleasures and conveniences and rights of a citizen of Rome was publicly to be made plain by the wearing of the *toga*.[25] This is why the burden of the Augustan legislation fell most heavily on the freedmen whose presence and activities actually made Rome what it was. We do not have to assume a long-lasting free poor to

---

[24] Purcell 1986 (D 107), for the assumptions of ancient administration; also Nicolet 1988 (A 69) advocating a much more positive view of the possibilities of ancient bureaucracy. Note that the benefits could, in general, be taxable; revenue was raised from Rome under the Empire in significant quantities, Le Gall 1979 (D 142).

[25] Rawson 1987 (F 56). By a noteworthy development, as the citizenship spread, the *toga* seems to have become characteristic of Roman citizens at *Rome*, and declined elsewhere: Mart. x.47.5; 51.6.

whom Augustus was showing favour, while the *liberti* were systematically coerced. The *plebs ingenua* of one generation derived from the *plebs libertina* of previous ones. The city population *was* in many ways the *plebs libertina*; the freeborn poor were despised as regularly and thoroughly by the Roman elite; and the largesses, the entertainments, the paramilitary garrison, the correct definition of public and private land, the water supply and the rules and privileges of the *magistri vicorum* were all part of a single attitude of defining how the *Urbs* and its people should best comport themselves. The 'Relief of the Vicomagistri', with the four *magistri* in charge of a city-district, in the shorter clothing (*stolae*) which shows their lowly status, self-consciously clutching the *lares* of their street in religious conclave with the group of aloof senators in their full togas, is the monument of this age.[26]

The populace was not entirely mute. From its expressive moments in the time of troubles a tradition of involvement in the doings of the elite continues through, and indeed does much to characterize, the whole Julio-Claudian period. Some have, however, argued powerfully to the contrary. 'The *populus*, decimated or terror-stricken, had disappeared in the whirlwind of civil war. All that was left were power-obsessed leaders on the one hand and a brutish multitude on the other, the centurion's sword and the irrational hero-worship of the urban plebs. Rome had already become the Empire.'[27] A city is people, not architecture; was Rome transformed in the terms of this ringing description during the Augustan age, or are there rather more continuities than historians of the Republic, gloomy about the demise of the institutions of liberty, traditionally accept?

Those who have wished to make the fall of the Republic the turning-point also of the history of the *plebs Romana* have usually done so for two reasons. The first is the 'golden age' view that there was at some stage in Roman history a moment when 'none was for a party; then all were for the State; then the rich man helped the poor and the poor man loved the great'. Even the 'revolution of violence' which the ancient historiographical tradition saw in the age of the Gracchi is mostly a construct of that tradition, and in any case is the result of change in the behaviour of the elite, not in that of the populace at large. As far back as our meagre evidence can be made to extend, we find the two salient characteristics of the life of the city, first the instability and insecurity in the precarious and passionate life of the urban nucleus caused by the constant process of exchange by which families and individuals on short and long time-scales moved in and out of Rome, and second the immemorial paradox between the constitutional inferiority which guaranteed the domination

---

[26] Freedmen in Augustan Rome: Treggiari 1969 (F 68) 73–6; 244–5.
[27] Nicolet 1980 (A 68) 352.

of the oligarchy and a real tradition of free expression, political engagement and actual practical influence. To this second tense dialogue the forms of personal power enshrined in the practice of the Principate were not alien; it made all the difference in the world to a junior patrician senator if the greatest men in the state had the position of Augustus or Vespasian rather than that of Cicero or Scipio Aemilianus; to the men and women of the Roman street the difference was much less palpable.[28]

The second ingredient in the traditional view of the final elimination of some democratic tradition is the constitutional moment at which the *comitia centuriata* were deprived of the reality of their electoral activity, directly after the accession of Tiberius in A.D. 14 (Tac. *Ann.* 1.15, cf. 81). This must be taken seriously: it was not a cosmetic change, a procedural recognition of a long-established reality. Augustus had found it necessary to enact legislation against *ambitus*; Caligula (Dio LIX.20.3) found it at least symbolically eloquent to reverse the change which ushered in the sole Principate of Tiberius. The process of election was not abolished; it was formally continued in the senate-house and a strong element of competition remained.[29] The *comitia centuriata*, moreover, continued to meet in the Saepta Iulia on the Campus Martius; their activities maintained some political consciousness of a constitutional kind, to judge by the association of Sejanus with an irregular assembly of some kind in the stone record of a speech to an assembly of the tribes (*ILS* 6044). Whether it is correct to see in Julio-Claudian times a surviving thread of public political behaviour which can be associated with the programmes of the *populares* of the end of the Republic remains uncertain. Certainly the behaviour of the supporters and opponents of Tiberius seems quite frequently to have a nuance which derives from the thought-world of that epoch.[30] It is hard not to see the move of A.D. 14 alongside the various other attempts by which Tiberius seems to have been determined to enhance the standing of the Senate and senators in the polity, and to read it as a judgment that the electoral function was too important for the crude and foreign plebs to be involved in.

To that extent, then, this is indeed the moment at which the Senate finally won the age-old 'struggle of the orders'. However, although the *comitia centuriata* had represented power for the small groups who dominated it, and provided a spectacular opportunity for the display of popular enthusiasm and dislike through less organized means than the

---

[28] Finley 1983 (A 28) 51–3 on the 'end of politics'.

[29] Elections under the Principate: Talbert 1984 (D 77) 341–5.

[30] Levick 1976 (C 366) 37–42. We may note also that the plebeian violence in A.D. 6 almost constituted popular revolution, if we are to credit the language of Dio LV.27.1–3. Ov. *Fast.* II.527–32 suggests that some truly archaic elements in the Roman constitution (the *curiae*) were no longer understood. Nicolet 1980 (A 68) 313–15; T. Siarensis. *ILS* 6049 shows the tribal structure being deployed to celebrate Vespasian's first *adventus* at Rome.

vote, it had rarely been a means of effective participation in politics for the plebs. Moreover, that informal participation survived, since the *comitia* continued to meet – hence one aspect of the Sejanus affair. Indeed it not only survived, it burgeoned. Enactments, to give one example, of A.D. 5, 19 and 21 – before and after, that is, the movement of the voting part of the election to the Senate – gave the display of favour by the thirty-five tribes at these occasions a respectable institutional link with the *ordines* of *equites* and senators, and a symbolic link with the fortunes of the *domus Caesarum* in the creation of *centuriae* linked with the names of the untimely dead of Augustus' household.[31] As late as A.D. 69 it was expedient for an emperor to proclaim the unity of Senate and plebs in supporting him at a formal *contio* (Tacitus *Hist.* 1.90.2). Maybe this worked too well: in A.D. 29 Tiberius had to respond with an edict to the agitation of the plebs on behalf of their imperial favourites, the family of Germanicus. Illicit *contiones*, like the public meetings of the past, were happening, and the *princeps* had to claim to the Senate that 'his majesty as *imperator* was mocked' (Tac. *Ann.* v.4–5, 'imperatoria maiestas elusa'). No mean success for the people.

The coming of the Principate enabled the personal attachments of the populace to become more stable and more deeply felt, richer as they were in raw material. So it is that, for example, the women of the *domus Caesarum* came to play a prominent part in the relationship between establishment and urban populace. The standing of Livia, the Iuliae, or Antonia or Claudius' daughters in the public eye is a phenomenon which could only be dimly foreshadowed in the Republic.[32] Similarly, the admiration felt and vigorously expressed for Gaius Caesar, Germanicus or Britannicus gives the impression of constituting a more developed personality-cult than the equivalent in the last years of the Republic; the projection of the personalities of the Principate offered new opportunities for the allegiance and disapproval of the urban populace which were abundantly taken up. The metaphor of language is a helpful one for the range of exchanges possible between the plebs and the rulers of Rome; with the Augustan Principate the richness and flexibility of that language became greater than it ever had been before.[33]

This process was closely linked with the steps which Augustus took to appropriate for himself the topography of the city, through the architectural initiatives which we have examined; and the chronology of the *res publica*, through his manipulation of the notion of history and, most important, of the passage of the months and years. The Roman calendar,

---

[31] Levick 1976 (C 366); Holladay 1978 (C 356); Brunt 1961(C 47).

[32] Flory 1984 (F 366); Purcell 1986 (F 50).

[33] In general, Yavetz 1969 (A 110); for messages about Rome's place in the world, Nicolet 1988 (A 69) esp. chs. 1, 2, 5, 9; also 1980 (A 68) 383–98.

with its slow progression of measured feasts and rites moving through the seasons and processionally among the temples and sacred places of the city and its neighbourhood, and recapitulating the progression of Rome's history, triumphs, deliveries and commemorations, as it did so, offered a wonderful opportunity for the self-presentation of the *princeps* and his family, and for the involvement of the populace. Caesar had done some exploration in this area, but the real harnessing of the potential of the calendars is an Augustan phenomenon. The great moments in the rise of Octavian to power, the dates of his life and career, the significant moments in his rule and in the lives of his relatives are inserted through the calendars first into the history of Rome, second into the divine life of the city – and we need postulate no cynicism on the part of Augustus and his advisers – third into the space of the town, with temples, altars, arches and statues, and fourth, and most relevant to our theme here, into the daily, yearly experience of the ordinary populace. So well did he succeed that the Feriae Augustae, the greatest dynastic feast of all, were still distracting the Romans from their Christian duties in the summer in the eighth century, and even though the feast has in an effort to clean it up since been postponed a fortnight and made to celebrate the Assumption, its name at least still remains, Ferragosto, the summer festival of Rome today.[34]

In the sections that follow we shall explore in more detail the nature of the 'occasions' which received their significance from being included in the Fasti. How did they provide a setting for dialogue between the *princeps* and the people? And what was the nature of the exchange and what its purpose? Let us begin with the 'purely religious'.

There has been an unfortunate tendency to omit the observance of public religious rites when considering the activities of the first *principes*, perhaps fuelled by a suspicion that such observance was somehow a sham, a perfunctory obedience to tradition. This is not the place to scrutinize the practicality of assessing the theological orientations of the Roman elite; it is enough to insist that the amount of time devoted to public cult by the *primores* at Rome was considerable, and that this provided the centre of the visibility of these people to the population of the city at large. Much of the activity was routine, and only finds mention in the sources when it was made singular by some other occurrence or observation. Augustus had a habit of sleeping at a friend's house as near as possible to the scene of a religious ceremony which involved a dawn start, because he disliked early rising (Suet. *Aug.* 78); on the morning of his assassination Gaius had just happened to be sacrificing a flamingo (Suet. *Calig.* 57) when he was splashed with blood; Claudius performed *obsecratio* in the Forum Romanum to counter ill omen in a ceremony

[34] Liebeschuetz 1979 (F 174) 79–81; Price 1996 (F 201).

which we are explicitly told involved the *populus*, though the *princeps* felt
it proper to exclude the 'herd of artisans and slaves' (Suet. *Claud.* 22); the
omen of Galba's fall (Suet. *Galba* 18–19) involved a whole set of public
religious acts all of which were clearly closely scrutinized for the kind of
significant accident that did in fact occur – as when on New Year's Day
69 his garland fell off during the sacrifice and the sacred chickens flew
away as he took the auspices. Not only did these activities inevitably take
up a considerable amount of the emperor's time and attention; but they
are, more importantly, part of a continuous dialectic of interpretation
between actor and audience, both parties explaining and expounding the
meaning they prefer in the unfolding interplay of casual circumstances
and prescribed cultic behaviour. It is necessary to insist that these
exchanges are indeed mutual. If we had only the literary evidence we
might, odd as it would seem, see the religious acts of the elite as mindless
posturing and inane traditionalism. But the reciprocity is very clear from
the evidence of epigraphy and archaeology. The altars, the statues, the
ex-votos, the buildings, offered by a very wide range of Romans, are the
contribution made by the audience to the exchange, an assurance of
complicity, engagement and loyalty to the relationship, a loyalty which
far transcends mere political obedience.[35]

The dialogue of public religion is the matrix which held together the
highly disparate elements of Roman society; I cannot establish that this
entails theological sincerity, but the dialogue very certainly mattered.

The religion of the city was quite literally urban: bridges, slopes,
statues, fountains and especially crossroads had their appropriate rites.
In 7 B.C. Augustus reconsidered the oppressive legislation which had
controlled the activities of the local assemblies which practised these
rites and celebrations – the 'uncountable associations cobbled together
from all the filth and slavery of the city', as Cicero had called them (*Pis.*
9). *Magistri* and *ministri* of the crossroads cults of each of the two or three
hundred *vici* or local districts of Rome were now regularly appointed; the
games which they performed were made legal again; the moment was
given historic recognition by the establishment of an era which began
with the measure of 7 B.C.; imperial generosity provided decoration for
the shrines from the loot of Greece, Apollo the Sandalmaker and – well-
suited to the *voluptates* of the people – Jupiter the Tragic Actor (Suet.
Aug. 57). The *magistri* were suitably inspired. Smart new *sacella* in the
latest taste for the *lares* of each district rose over the next years, the
dedication-inscriptions reflecting the sincere blend of old and new and
the combination of real religiosity with a sense of the civically appropriate: 'To Mercury, to the eternal God Jupiter, to Juno the Queen, to
Minerva; to the Sun, the Moon, Apollo and Diana; to [Anno]na, Ops,

[35] Examples: Zanker 1988 (F 633) chs. 6–8.

Isis and Pietas; to the Divine Fates: that it may go well, propitiously and prosperously for Imperator Caesar Augustus, for his [power] and that of the Senate and People of Rome, and for the Nations, at the propitious beginning of the consular year of Gaius Caesar and Lucius Paullus [A.D. 1] – Lucius Lucretius Zethus, Lucius' freedman, dedicated this Augustan Altar at the command of Jupiter. Victory of the People! Health in Seed-sowing!'[36] The Augustan religious changes were no sterile revivalism, but a part of the adaptability and creativity inherent in Roman religion.[37] On a more informal level the inscriptions of Rome show us how tutelary divinities were found for other new arrivals in the urban landscape as the imperial benefactions and building-projects progressed; the Bona Dea Veneris Cnidiae 'Good Goddess of the Venus of Cnidus', that statue being a well-known imported masterpiece, is a nice example. The Genius of the Corn Warehouses of Galba and the Venus of the Gardens of Sallust are further cases of how traditional responses were made to the new imperial complexes as much as to the tangled matrix of the unreformed city. 'You believe that there are gods to the places in the city - or even that the places themselves are gods', a critic of paganism was to say (Tert. *Ad. Nat.* 2.15).

Similarly, the new institutions of the imperial house were inserted into the traditional repertoire of Roman religiosity. The creation of the *sacerdotium sodalium Augustalium* on the model of the *Titiales* (Tac. *Ann* 1.54) in A.D. 14 did this at the top end of the social spectrum, interestingly adapting for the senatorial and equestrian elite a title which had already become current (at least since the last decade B.C.) among the poorer inhabitants, especially freedmen, of the Italian towns. The association of the *ordines* with the transformed state cult cannot, despite an influential view, be held to have excluded the poor and opened the way to religious influence from outside Italy. The new observances were important to the plebs too.[38] Nor was this limited to the self-consciously plebeian occasion like the *compitalia*: we should take into account also such occasions as their *ludi* founded by Livia within the *familia Caesaris* to commemorate Augustus, at which buffoons and actors performed, as much as on the great public occasions. Across the world of the Roman spectacles, the boundary between the religious and the entertaining cannot be clearly drawn by us any more than it could have been by the Romans themselves.

Augustus had been careful to involve the *populus* in the *ludi saeculares*, whose prescriptions ordain various forms of participation; but it need

---

[36] *CIL* VI 30705 = *ILS* 3090; Niebling 1956 (F 190); Boyancé 1950 (E 8). For Salus cf. Macrob. *Sat.* 1.16.8 'Salutem Semoniam Seiam Segetiam Tutilinam'. On the *compita* see also Liebeschuetz 1979 (F 174) 70–1, and for the Augustan shrines to the *lares*, Ladage 1980 (F 42).
[37] North 1976 (F 194); North 1986 (F 195).   [38] Altheim 1938 (F 84) 433f.

not be thought that this was unusual. The people were an important agent in Roman religion, not a passive congregation. The spates of individual *vota* and sacrifices which marked special occasions – such as the 890 days of *obsecrationes* decreed by the Senate for Augustus (*RG* 4) – are examples of this participation: and the involvement of the audience in the *ludi* is part of the same phenomenon. Thus the various expressions of opinion and demonstrations of disapproval or loyalty with which the audience in the theatre or the amphitheatre interrupted and adapted the words of the performers are not to be seen as a breaking for political purposes of a polite formal barrier of decorum between stage and *cavea*, but as part of a relationship of communication which goes both ways.

The presence of the *populus Romanus* at public spectacles, as at other religious rites, constituted a civic assembly. Ovid describes a popular rite in terms deliberately chosen to evoke the simple homespun life of Rome before its urban fabric grew so complex and monumental; 'On the ides of March is the jolly festival of Anna Perenna, above Rome and the Tiber and not far away from its bank. The populace comes and drinks, scattered at ease among the herbage, each person reclining with his partner. Some hold out in the open, a few set up tents, some build a bough-house out of branches, others use giant reed for stiff columns and stretch out their togas on top. Whatever they do, the sun and the wine heat them up . . . they sing all that they have picked up in the theatres and mime uninhibitedly along with the words' (*Fast.* III.523–42). The displays which the upper-class authors deride as the *voluptates* of the populace were embellishments of simpler festivals, given to show the status of donor and beneficiary. This is more easily seen if the other aspect of the religious assembly, the communal meal, is compared. These meals had increased in popularity in the late Republic (Varro, *Rust.* III.2.16), especially in the context of the triumphs of the dynasts. They were the object of censorial control by Augustus in 22 B.C. (Dio LIV.2.3), and became a monopoly of the *princeps*: as such they became a familiar part of life in Rome:

iam se, quisquis is est, inops, beatus,
convivam ducis esse gloriatur.

whoever he is, poor but happy, his boast is that he has been the guest of
    our Leader.

(Stat. *Silv.* 1.6.44–50)[39]

The *porticus*-architecture which was described above owes something to the need to be able to accommodate such occasions.

---

[39] For banqueting, D'Arms 1990 (F 24); Mrozek 1972 (F 46). For the 'associative urge' among inhabitants of Rome, cf. *CAH* IX², 671ff and Flambard 1981 (F 30).

The *spectacula* likewise demanded more and more lavish settings: even when such buildings were temporary they could be fantastically extravagant, like the theatre built by Aemilius Scaurus as aedile in 58 B.C. The great sequence of permanent structures – Pompey's Theatre, Caesar's Circus Maximus, the Theatre of Marcellus, and that of Balbus, Augustus' *naumachia* and Statilius Taurus' Amphitheatre, Gaius' Circus Vaticanus, Nero's Amphitheatre, Vespasian's greater Flavian Amphitheatre, Domitian's Odeon and Hippodrome, and Trajan's Circus Maximus – is a vivid reflection of the process.[40]

These buildings, above all the theatres, were political buildings as they had always been in the Hellenic world. To have statues or dedications in the theatres was a rare sign of achievement (cf. Tac. *Ann.* IV.7). This political life of the theatres was one of the many inheritances of Rome from Campania where urban politics had long been volatile and permanent buildings for both theatrical and gladiatorial spectacles were part of the repertoire of public architecture. The Romans were well aware of the resemblances between the orator's address in the Forum, the priest's sacred activity in the sanctuary, and the actor's performance on the stage – all witnessed and shared in by thousands of observers. We can set the long hostility towards permanent theatres, and towards providing seats at the *spectacula*, beside the great length of time it took before the *comitia* were given a permanent architectural setting – on the eve of their electoral emasculation.[41] The long series of responses to 'theatralis licentia' and 'immodestia histrionum' – expulsions, military presence, executions, prohibitions, warnings – should be compared with the ever vigorous campaign against the involvement of the men and women of the senatorial and equestrian orders in the performance of *spectacula*, which proves conclusively how much they wanted to be involved, and what was at stake. These occasions are not outlets, *faute de mieux*, for repressed political activity: the old formal political acts had been a single facet of an age-old political tradition which continued fervently and wildly in the public life of the face-to-face society. Indeed, when the relatively restrained formal politics of the Senate became completely overshadowed by Augustus' *novus status*, plebs and elite alike found an outlet for their various anti-establishment feelings in an expansion of the politics of the spectacle.[42] Finally, we may observe that the *princeps* himself constituted one of the main objects of spectacle; at triumphs, the formal entrances and exits from the city, and going about

---

[40] Spectacle-architecture, Frézouls 1984 (F 31), Humphrey 1986 (F 427), Rawson 1985 (F 55), Gros 1978 (F 398); Clavel-Lévêque 1984 (F 17).

[41] Cf. Coarelli 1985 (E 19) II 11–21; Gros 1987 (F 399).

[42] Bollinger 1969 (F 8); cf. Levick 1983 (C 369).

his daily business – or in attendance at other shows, himself nominally in the audience, but in reality an actor among actors.

There is no need here to rehearse the very long list of examples of the responses of emperors to the people at the games. Three typical examples are: the attack on Pompey by Diphilus in July 59 B.C. when the crowd took up the line 'it is by our wretchedness that thou art Great'; the moment when the audience mocked Galba by singing over and over again the passage from the Atellan farce 'Onesimus has come in from the country'; and, most memorably of all, the pastiche with which Datus the actor joked about Nero's murders of Claudius and Agrippina.[43] It would be wrong to take these as some form of resistance, as 'demonstrations' in the modern sense. Certainly the extent to which they were organized by the elite as deliberate disruptions must have been minimal – the difficulties would have been enormous, though we do hear of the managers of claques, like Percennius who fomented the Pannonian mutiny in A.D. 14. More importantly the absence of political pro-grammes even among the elite will have made it more difficult to build up continuous agitation: high politics were too mutable. On a more general level some perennial preferences and distastes there were, which are examined below, both the 'political' and the more selfish. But it is not enough to regard the urban populace as 'primitive rebels' living 'in an odd relationship with its rulers, equally compounded of parasitism and riot'. It is noteworthy that the poor of the city do not seem to have developed a counter-culture of the sort found in the Islamic cities of the Middle Ages, rich in criminal confraternities. The activities of the *populares* which the city prefect had to watch so carefully (above, p. 793) were very closely related to the legitimate forms of behaviour of the political elite.[44]

This is because the plebs was not parasitic; and its violence was not solely devoted to attaining selfish ends. The plebs was not wholly or even mostly dependent on state-managed largesse. Its economy was more vigorous than that. The benefits which the plebeians enjoyed were not charity to keep them alive, but a bonus to denote their status. Part of that status-symbolism was a degree of political licence, which stood beside the lavishness of the games and the grandeur of the buildings. The survival of that licence did credit to the *princeps* too, and was one of the elements in the presentation of Rome to the rest of the world as its

[43] Cameron 1976 (F 16); Millar 1977 (A 59) 368–75; Yavetz 1969 (A 110); Deininger 1979 (E 33); Kloft 1970 (D 138).

[44] Hobsbawm 1973; C. E. Bosworth *The Medieval Islamic Underworld* (Leiden, 1976) for the Islamic underworld. On the close cultural identification of plebeians and elite, cf. Jongman 1988 (E 62) 275–329.

uniquely favoured capital.[45] In return it elevated the emperor who could manage the relationship high on a wave of hysterical popularity which could not be managed anywhere else. But the violence of the invective and the cruelty of the wit involved in the exchange alongside the popularity are not wholly negative; there is an atmosphere of the licensed jester about the relationship, a curious pleasure in the luxury of being powerful enough not to need to mind or be diminished by scurrilous attacks. The anonymous buffoon who described himself on his tomb as 'in words and in dumb-play a mime of the emperor Tiberius; the man who first discovered the trick of imitating barristers' (*ILS* 5225) *may* have operated 'underground' but it is more likely that his art was part of the world of modish inversion and peculiar paradox which the elite of the Julio-Claudian empire found the height of luxury.[46] The emperors periodically found that the attacks had gone too far; but although some performers therefore suffered, their like remained a permanent part of the inevitable relationship of emperor with people in the gloriously hectic atmosphere of the most populous place in the world.

Within the phenomenon of this freedom of utterance various strands can be isolated. A consciousness of the tone of the political world of the elite is one: hostility to conspirators and traitors, and also to the *delatores*, or to individuals like the praetorian prefect Cleander under Commodus, is conspicuous. We are reminded that other senators and *equites* had public roles to play too; it will not do to represent the politics of Rome as being just a dialogue between plebs and *princeps*. The insecurity and danger of the political elite were things of which the populace was aware. Still more do they have a sense of the wrongs of the imperial family itself; the imperial women, above all, were objects of general affection and sympathy. Already we find the crowd in the Forum making it impossible for the triumvirs to reject the daring protest of Hortensia against an attempt to distrain on the resources of the noblest and richest women of the state (App. *BC* iv.5.32–4; Val. Max. viii.3.3). Their affection for Augustus' daughter and granddaughter is also very striking, and perhaps not wholly to be explained by the *civilitas* and popularity of their male relatives. For if Agrippina the elder gained in favour by association with her husband, and she was certainly highly popular, it is hard to explain politically the touching sympathy of the plebs for the tragic fate of Nero's wife, Claudius' daughter Octavia: Tacitus (*Ann.* xiv.60–4) recounts their dismay at the *princeps*' dismissal of her, and their enthusiastic response to the false rumour that he had changed his mind.

[45] On the ideology of *civilitas*, Wallace-Hadrill 1982 (D 21).

[46] Roueché 1984 (B 277) 184, for imperial acclamations; cf. *CIL* iv 1074, a graffito 'iudiciis Augusti Augustae feliciter!' Note also the performance of the *archimimus* Favor at Vespasian's funeral (Suet. *Vesp.* 19.2).

'They rushed to climb the Capitol without delay, and – belatedly – gave worship to the gods. Down they threw the statues of Poppaea; those of Octavia, borne shoulder-high, they decked with flowers and set up in Forum and temples'. The agitation was serious enough to provide Octavia's enemies with a believable case that her continued liberty and presence in Italy was a perpetual threat of civil war; at the same time, we are told, claiming that the rioting had been the work of 'clients and slaves of Octavia arrogating to themselves the name of plebs'. There was indeed a real political component: the plebeians who shouted Nero's praises in 68 when he made his grand return to Rome from his Greek tour, demolishing the city wall to enter a city garlanded and full of lamps and incense (Dio LXII.20.4), in only months were joining in the round of hysterical sacrifice and merrymaking, dressed in caps of liberty like freed slaves, to commemorate his suicide (*ibid.* LXIII.29.1). Within a year 50,000 had died in the civil war which ensued (*ibid.* LXIV.19.3).

In the end much of this popular feeling proceeds from the complex self-presentation of the *domus Caesarum* which we examined above; but this ingredient of sympathy for the underdog, the young and the helpless, with its sentimental flavour, is something separate. Marcus Oppius, who saved his father's life during the proscriptions, had been elected aedile in 37 B.C. on the wave of public approval, which even collected contributions to allow him to bear the expense. A group of wanted malefactors put on masks and made a theatre-show of adding their bit to the whip-round, in a revealingly dramatic and public way (Dio XLVIII.53.4). When Oppius died and was lionized even in death the Senate responded with significant spite. There are various other cases; we might cite the 'assembly of plebeians which verged on a riot' which formed to show solidarity with the condemned household of Pedanius Secundus, doomed because he had been murdered by a slave (Tac. *Ann.* XIV.42) or the pity they felt for elephants because of their appealing tricks in the arena on another well-known occasion. In A.D. 24 popular violence prevented a well-known prosecutor from proceeding with a case against his father (*Ann.* IV.29).

The plebs could also show conspicuous favour to the powerful, but that is less surprising. In one memorable instance, their humorous sentimentality combined with their loyalty to the *domus Caesarum*. 'Crows too have their share of esteem, as has been demonstrated by the moral attitude of the Roman plebs, or rather by their outrage. During the reign of Tiberius a young crow, hatched in a nest in the temple of Castor and Pollux, flew down to a cobbler's opposite, in the process winning the owner's approval, apart from anything else, as a religious bird. The crow quickly became familiar with human discourse, and every morning would fly along the Forum to the *rostra*, and would greet first Tiberius and then Drusus and Germanicus by name, and then the generality of the Roman crowd passing by. It would then return to the shop. The tenant of the next cobbler's, as ever jealous of his neighbour, or, as he preferred to put it, incensed by the droppings which stained the shoes he put out on display, killed the bird. The plebs went wild. The man was hustled out of the *regio* and before long made away with; for the fowl a funeral was put on with the most enormous elaboration, the bier decked out and carried between two negroes, with a flute player walking in front, garlands of every kind, all the way to the pyre which they had built at the second milestone of the Appia in the Campus called that of Rediculus ... this was done on 28 March in A.D. 35' (Pliny, *HN* x.121f). The public availability of members of the *domus Caesarum* – even if, given the date, it will be their effigies that received this unusual obeisance – is noteworthy. Germanicus is the prime example of a popular hero, but we may compare the delirious welcome to Rome of his son Caligula – 'star', 'chicken', 'baby', 'nurseling' they called him at his ceremonial arrival in the city, his *adventus* – and their defensive 'protection' of Claudius against his senatorial opponents. Titus later enjoyed the same approval – 'shortlasting and ill-omened' as Tacitus gloomily calls it.

Naturally enough, a strong streak of self-interest can be seen in the plebs' attitudes. Concern over prices and the availability of reasonably priced food – and drink – features prominently. It was the final blow for Nero's cause in 68 that a ship containing fine sand for a race-track docked from Alexandria at a moment when food was low and grain expected. But the riot over wine-prices which Augustus dismissed (Suet. *Aug.* 42.1) with an allusion to Agrippa's aqueducts shows that the demands are not only about subsistence. While it made economic sense to free slaves to qualify them for the *annona* (as in 56 B.C., when Pompey had to draw up a register of such recipients, Dio XXXIX.24.1), that did not mean that a provision for the destitute was being abused. The eager interest in the availability of *commoda* is part of the insatiable quest for the signs of status to which we have constantly referred and reflects appreciation of the provision of games, baths, beast-hunts, subsidized food, largesses. The building projects of the *principes* were triply useful: as a source of employment, for what they provided in a practical sense, and as a display of magnificence.[47] We see throughout the imperial period, accordingly, a steady escalation of the quality of the annonal food distributions and in the lavishness of the public buildings of the city. As Augustus saw, the grain dole might not be essential to the survival of the city, and it might not be a desirable thing to pamper the motley plebs – but even if he

---

[47] For the *commodum* of available employment, see Brunt 1980 (D 117). Thornton and Thornton 1989 (F 594) develop the idea of the dependence of the plebs on imperial buildings, but their quantitative methods are unreliable.

abolished the *annona* 'it could at any time be restored through *ambitio*' (Suet. *Aug.* 42.3). *Ambitio*, the pursuit of political support through the dealing out of favours, is the key to the world of *panem et circenses*. The vast population visible in Rome was the constituency which supported the early *principes*. Once they had ensured that they had no rivals in its support, it provided them, in return for the status their attentions gave it, with a visible position of ascendancy in the capital of the world which remained one of the key ingredients in their political position. That that ascendancy was in some sense freely granted by a free people was an important myth, because of the Roman past and because of the sensitivity of the interplay between the notions of freedom and subjection across the empire as a whole, especially in the East; and it was in the pursuit of that image of co-operative mutual freedom that the dialogue between plebs and *princeps*, with all its seeming disadvantages for the latter, was allowed to continue, indeed actively encouraged. The plebs was on display too, and the occasions such as the famous welcome given to the Armenian king Tiridates were meant to show off not just the luxury of Nero's court, which could be done in private, but something more unusual – the intricacy and reliability of the relationship between the ruler of the Roman world and the teeming cities of his homeland: the populousness is part of the point (Dio LXII.3.4), but the nature of the relationship, the element of freedom, is also significant.[48]

Cities, not city: it is important to remember that we are in fact not dealing with just the city of Rome. The social forms characteristic of the plebs in the first century B.C. had developed in a wide region which embraced both Rome and the wealthy and populous centres of Campania, and the milieu continued to exist for a very long time. Nero's display for Tiridates began at Puteoli, where Caligula's extravagant regal exhibition of a great procession along a temporary bridge across the sea had also been set. It was in Campania that Tiberius in A.D. 27 was overwhelmed by the 'assembling together of the inhabitants of the cities', so that he resolved to escape to Capri (Tac. *Ann.* IV.67). In the next year he was visited not just by the Senate but by 'magna pars plebis' (*Ann.* IV.74). The *principes* spoke to and reproved, favoured and checked, the people of these far-flung cities as they did the people gathered in Rome. An anecdote in Suetonius' life of Vitellius (12) gives us a glimpse of how the social contexts intermeshed. Vitellius' boyfriend and freedman Asiaticus decamped from Rome after their first *amour* and was later found employed in a cookshop at Puteoli, whence he was forcibly returned to Rome and his patron's favours. The audience of the *principes'* display in Campania overlapped considerably with that which he

---

[48] For the display of population see also Mithridates at Tac. *Ann.* XII.21, or Tiberius on the way to the *tribunal* 'conspicuous for the gathering of people from every side', *Ann.* II.34.

addressed in Rome; and the same is true of Ostia from the Julio-Claudian period on, and throughout of the old seats of Roman *villeggiatura*: Praeneste, Tibur, Tusculum and Antium. Quite apart from the slow currents of emigration, the people of our study were prepared to travel distances which surprise us for entertainment. They were quite at home throughout the region of the city. In A.D. 69 the populace, in a characteristic episode, poured out to the north up the Via Flaminia to meet Vitellius' legions on their *adventus* (Tac. *Hist.* 11.88). At the village of Saxa Rubra the *princeps* was treating the army to an *epulum*, at a safe distance from the city and with convenient imperial properties providing the necessary resources. But the plebs could not resist from teasing the soldiery with its 'vernacula urbanitas' and a massacre ensued. Similarly, the scores of thousands killed or maimed when the amphitheatre at Fidenae collapsed in A.D. 22 were not the population of that dormitory-town of the *Urbs* (Tac. *Ann.* IV.62); and the vast and disappointed audience of Claudius' attempt to drain the Fucine Lake did not derive from the villages and hamlets of the central Apennines (*ibid.* XII.56). From Campania the evidence shows clearly that people would go anywhere in the area for games, from Cumae and Capua to Pompeii and Nuceria; and on a handy table of market-days from that region all the local centres, even when they are 65–80 km apart, are present – and so is Rome itself.[49] The nature of the spectacles was to gather people like this; we have already insisted on the resemblance between the religious assembly at a spectacle and the political assembly of the same citizen-body, and it is important to remember that in the background of these great concourses in Roman Italy lies the dispersed citizen statuses of the middle Republic and before. Federal assemblies and their religious aspects underlie many of these imperial institutions, from the gods who are propitiated to the type of place where the gathering is held. A calendar of the end of the fourth century A.D. from Capua still shows how the festivals of the year wandered from significant place to significant place across the social landscape of the region (*ILS* 4918).

Nevertheless, the effect of the institution of the Principate was to increase the privileges of the part of the population which was present in the vicinity of the city of Rome. The republican aristocracy had spread its interests widely; the emperors needed an imperial city to be the location and symbol of their power.[50] It is not without significance that some at least thought that they might not choose old Rome for the job, and that from the second century onwards, they came increasingly to take other places as their long- or short-term bases. By that time the creation of the

[49] Markets: MacMullen 1970 (F 43), quoting *IItal* XII 2 (1963) 301–4. The connexion between markets and religious festivals should also be noted.

[50] For the formation of Rome as capital of the world, Nicolet 1988 (A 69); cf. Purcell 1990 (A 77).

imperial city was complete, so that many of the effects of the two centuries which we have been discussing proved remarkably tenacious. The appearance of the city and the notion of its privileges were two particularly long-lasting consequences. But the distribution of the evidence makes it dangerous to assume that the social patterns of the period from Sulla to Claudius lasted beyond the Severan period. The examination of Rome in that period and its relations with Italy, when the *princeps* was no longer there nearly so much, must be left for another occasion.

CHAPTER 16

THE PLACE OF RELIGION: ROME
IN THE EARLY EMPIRE

S. R. F. PRICE

Roman religion had always been closely linked with the city of Rome and its boundaries. The restructuring of a number of religious institutions in the Augustan period resulted in changes within Rome, and, beyond it, in the empire. The importance of the religion of place is illustrated by an episode from Livy's *History of Rome*, written in the early 20s B.C. After the sack of Rome by the Gauls in 390 B.C., there was a proposal that the Romans should migrate to the newly conquered Veii, rather than rebuild Rome. Livy put in the mouth of the Roman general Camillus a striking rejection of this proposal, which emphasized the religious foundation of the city, the necessity for the ancient cults to be located in Rome, and the significance of Rome's sacred boundary, the *pomerium* (v.52). Camillus' speech articulated issues of considerable topical importance.[1] There had been a fear that Caesar would move the seat of empire from Rome to the East, a fear that was revived by Antony's dalliance with Cleopatra. Augustus, however, was to promote Rome as the capital of the empire. Camillus' re-establishment of the ancestral rites neatly foreshadows the religious activity of Augustus himself and his argument about the indissoluble ties between Rome and her cults encapsulated the preoccupation of the imperial age with place and the associated issue of boundaries (see below, Section I).

Stress on the religious site of Rome was not an innovation of the Augustan age, but it did increase in this period and it formed the content within which the new political order was placed (see below, Section II). The Augustan restructuring of the earlier system was represented at the time as restoration: ancient cults had faded away, temples had fallen down, priesthoods were vacant. The 'restoration of the *res publica*' by Augustus necessarily involved 'restoration of the traditional cults'. Scholars used to hold that this view was indeed correct: religion, in decline in the late Republic, was revived under Augustus. They diverged from the Augustan view in arguing that, as the decline was real, the revival could be only artificial: meaningful religious energies were located in other contexts ('oriental cults' or, later, Christianity).[2] This old

[1] Liebeschuetz 1967 (F175).   [2] Warde Fowler 1911 (F 233); Latte 1960 (F 170).

orthodoxy now seems very fragile. Religion in the late Republic is best seen as suffering from disruption, not decline, while preoccupation with revival ignores the extent of change in the system.[3] But Augustan stress on restoration need not be treated as a cunning obfuscation. The age was fundamentally concerned to relate the present to the past.[4]

There were also rituals which focused more directly on the emperor himself, especially after his death. These are normally described as 'the imperial cult', and placed in a separate category from the 'restoration of religion'. But if the 'restoration' is to be seen as a restructuring around the person of the emperor, the rituals which alluded more specifically to him also belong in the context of restructuring (see below, Section III). Even the apotheosis of the dead emperor may be seen as rooted in 'tradition'.

The city of Rome also has to be located in the context of the empire (see below, Section IV). Roman cults were replicated outside Rome, in Italy and in the provinces in the army and colonies. Though the relations of the empire to Rome are normally seen in terms of 'the imperial cult', it is again necessary to stress not direct worship of the emperor, but the range of other Roman cults.[5]

The social and physical context of the changes in Rome in the Augustan period merits discussion. Rome was an enormous city, with a population which may at times have approached 1 million people, and yet the principal holders of religious offices were members of the Senate, which numbered around 600 in all. Does this mean that we are dealing with an official religious system which held no meaning in the popular religion of the city? In fact, the opposition between 'official' and 'popular' religion is somewhat deceptive. Official and popular manifestations are simply different aspects, on different levels, of a continuum of religious institutions and practices. Upper-class leadership does not mean that the system lacked significance for the lower classes, and we shall see some signs of the penetration of the Augustan system among the poorer citizens. But the population of Rome did not consist wholly

---

[3] On the Republic see Scheid 1985 (F 217); North, *CAH* vII.2², ch. 12; Beard, *CAH* IX², ch. 19. On the Augustan period see Nock 1934 (F 192). Liebeschuetz 1979 (F 174) 55–100, Kienast 1982 (C 136) 185–214.

[4] In addition to Livy, Dion. Hal. *Ant. Rom.* (published in 7 B.C.) is invaluable for its perspective on the past (cf. Gabba 1982 (B 56); Schultze 1986 (B 161)). Ovid's *Fasti*, perhaps composed in A.D. 1–4 but with later revisions, is a systematic account of the festivals of the first six months of the year. Despite the existence of two modern commentaries (J. G. Frazer, London 1929; F. Bömer, Heidelberg, 1958), the poem has been unjustly neglected in religious histories of the period (cf. however Schilling 1969 (F 219); Fauth 1978 (F 133)). Most of the relevant inscriptions are in *ILS*. Coarelli 1983 (F 116) offers a guide to the archaeological evidence; Nash 1968 (E 87) illustrates the major monuments. There are two collections of texts in English translation: Grant 1953 (F 149) and 1957 (F 150); see also M. Beard, J. North and S. Price *Religions of Rome* 2 (Cambridge, 1966). The main works of reference are Wissowa 1912 (F 241) and Latte 1960 (F 170).

[5] For such cults see Liebeschuetz, *CAH* XI².

of Roman citizens. Those of different ethnic groups, including some freedmen from the East, maintained cults from their places of origin. (See below, Section V.) However, it is very difficult to see how far the lower classes drew upon the Augustan religious system in constructing their own worlds.

I. MYTHS AND PLACE

Roman mythology, according to the traditional view, never existed: only under the influence of Greece in the last centuries B.C. did the gods acquire some kind of mythology.[6] A contrasting view holds that there was indeed a Roman mythology, which was in strict harmony with the mythology of the Vedic Indians, the Scandinavians or other Indo-European peoples, but that it was mainly swamped by the influx of Greek mythology in the middle Republic.[7] The outcome of both views for the imperial period is the same: the current mythology was an alien import without much significance for Roman religion, and thus works on late republican or early imperial religion have little or nothing to say about mythology.[8] The paradox is that the early books of Livy and Dionysius of Halicarnassus are full of mythological stories about early Rome, while Ovid's *Fasti* consists entirely of descriptions of festivals and their associated myths. These authors would have been perplexed to be told that their accounts were trivial foreign imports.

The Roman mythology current in the early Empire was very different from that of other peoples, including, surprisingly, the Greeks. The myths did not form a cosmogony like that of Hesiod, and several major deities, including Jupiter and Mars, do not take part in any divine adventures. Indeed the Greek Dionysius of Halicarnassus commends Romulus, whom he holds responsible for the establishment of Roman religion, for following 'the best customs in use among the Greeks', while rejecting traditional Greek myths which contained calumnies about the gods.[9] There had long been a debate in Greece about the propriety of certain myths, and Dionysius praises Romulus, and Roman religion of his own day, in the light of that debate. In the eyes of an educated Greek, Roman mythology was quite different from the traditional Greek stories

---

[6] Wissowa 1912 (F 241) 9; Latte 1926 (F 169); H. J. Rose, *Mnemosyne* 4th ser. 3 (1950) 281: 'It is as certain as any negative historical proposition can ever be that Rome had no myths, at least none of a kind which could possibly associate themselves with cult.' The traditional view also held that in the earliest period there were only primitive powers, undifferentiated by personal attributes. This is a separate issue, on which see North, *CAH* VII², ch. 12.

[7] See briefly Dumézil 1970 (F 124) 47–59, and also Koch 1937 (F 162) (with review by R. Syme, *JRS* 29 (1939) 108–10). Sabbatucci 1970–2 (F 210) discusses the general issue of the 'loss' of Roman myths.

[8] Grant 1973 (F 151) is the best introduction. See also Horsfall in Bremmer and Horsfall 1987 (F 105) ch. 1.   [9] Dion. Hal. *Ant. Rom.* II.18–20.

about their gods, contrary to the modern theories about the profound hellenization of Roman religion in the middle and late Republic.

Roman myths were in essence myths of place. They recounted the history of the area of Rome itself, a history that extended without interruptions or Dark Ages to the Augustan age and of which there were living tokens in the cults of Rome. Dionysius devotes the whole of his first book to the earliest populations of the area, especially the Arcadians, Greeks by origin, who were responsible for consecrating 'many precincts, altars and images of the gods and instituted purifications and sacrifices according to the custom of their own country, which continued to be performed in the same manner down to my day'.[10] The most striking of these was to Hercules, who passed through the area on one of his labours and killed a local bandit, Cacus. Evander, king of the Arcadians, wanted to offer divine honours to Hercules, knowing that he was destined for immortality. Hercules himself performed the initial rites and asked the Arcadians to perpetuate the honours by sacrificing at the spot each year with Greek rites. The altar at which Hercules sacrificed 'is called by the Romans the Greatest Altar (Ara Maxima). It stands near the place they call the Cattle Market (Forum Boarium) and is held in great veneration by the inhabitants'.[11]

The ritual of this altar was the subject of learned debate. The Greek nature of the sacrifices was satisfactorily explained by the story of Evander and Hercules, but there was a further peculiarity: women were barred from the altar. Various explanations were offered. A Roman annalist of the second century B.C. seems to have explained the ban through a story that the mother of Evander and her women were late for sacrifice.[12] Varro offered a different account: the priestess of the Bona Dea (whose shrine lay near the Ara Maxima) refused to allow Hercules to drink from the goddess' spring, and in turn Hercules banned all women from his altar.[13] The myth and ritual of the Ara Maxima were the subject of lively interest on the part of antiquarians, historians and poets of the late Republic and early Empire. Their accounts exemplify the focus of Roman myths on a particular place, and the elaboration of that focus in the Augustan age.[14]

The majority of Roman myths refer to the founding and early years of

---

[10] Dion. Hal. *Ant. Rom.* 1.33.3.

[11] *ibid.* 1.40. Cf. Wissowa 1912 (F 241) 273–5. Winter 1910 (F 239) and Bayet 1926 (F 88) 127–54 elucidate the different versions of the story; Coarelli 1988 (E 21) 61–77 notes the Greek design of the altar. Virgil too incorporated this story into his 'history': *Aen.* VIII.267–79.

[12] *Origo gentis Romanae* 6.7, from Cassius Hemina; cf. Plut. *Quaest. Rom.* 60.

[13] Macrob. *Sat.* 1.12.28. Prop. IV.9 follows Varro's account, not without a sense of humour.

[14] This perspective persisted through the imperial period. An inscription of the early third century, probably put up near the altar, commemorates the offering of the solemn sacrifice which Hercules had established at the time of Evander: *ILS* 3402.

Rome. So, for example, a myth related to the festival of the Parilia, the founding of Rome and the creation of its sacred boundary. According to Ovid, there was an ancient rural festival designed to purify the sheep and cattle by calling on the goddess Pales, from whose name that of the festival was derived.[15] Ovid goes on to describe the festival, in two parts. First, the contemporary urban festival, in which he says he had often taken part. 'I personally have often brought in handfuls the ashes of the calf and the beanstalks, pure means of expiation. I personally have leaped over the flames ranged three in a row, and been sprinkled with water by the moist laurel bough.'[16] After this, Ovid moves on to the rural festival of purification of sheep and cattle. 'Shepherd, you purify your well-fed sheep at fall of twilight, first sprinkle the ground with water and sweep it with a broom' and so on.[17] His account of the rural festival is much fuller than of the urban one, but he makes clear that the two do differ (there is no blood of a horse or ashes of a calf in the rural festival). In drawing this distinction Ovid is (allegedly) following the evidence of his own eyes, and also the work of Varro, who insisted on the distinction between the public and private festivals, that is the urban and the rural.[18]

Ovid goes on to discuss the origins and hence significance of the festival. The Parilia, like any Roman festival, permitted a multitude of competing explanations.[19] Ovid was faced with no less than seven: (i) fire is a natural purifier; (ii) fire and water were used together because everything is composed out of opposing elements; (iii) fire and water contain the source of life, as in the symbolism of exile and marriage; (iv) the festival alludes to Phaethon and Deucalion's flood, an explanation Ovid doubts; (v) shepherds once accidentally ignited straw; (vi) Aeneas' piety allowed him to pass through flames unscathed; (vii) when Rome was founded, orders were given to transfer to new houses; the country folk set fire to the old houses and leaped with their cattle through the flames. Ovid favours the last interpretation, commenting that it happens 'even to the present day on the birthday of Rome'.

Ovid elucidates his favoured interpretation by recounting the story of Romulus and the foundation of Rome, a story to which we shall return in the context of Augustus. Romulus chose the time of the celebration of the Parilia to found the city of Rome. He marked out the lines of the wall of the new city with a furrow, praying to Jupiter, Mars and Vesta; Jupiter responded with a favourable augury. Romulus then instructed one Celer to kill anyone who crossed the walls or the furrow, but Remus, in ignorance of the ban, leaped across them and was struck down by

---

[15] Ov. *Fast.* IV.820; Plut *Rom.* 12. Dion. Hal. *Ant. Rom.* 1.88.3 is uncertain whether it predated the foundation of the city. For testimonia on the Parilia see *IItal* XIII 2.443–5.

[16] Ov. *Fast.* IV.725–8.   [17] *Fast.* IV.735–6.   [18] Varro, *ap. schol.* Pers. 1.72.

[19] Cf. Beard 1987 (F 92).

Celer. In this common version, the Parilia, the founding of Rome, the creation of the *pomerium* and the killing of Remus all interconnect.[20]

In making his choice of interpretation Ovid was in good company. Though modern scholars are generally happy to treat the Parilia as a genuine, primitive agricultural ritual which survived into imperial Rome,[21] our only extant pre-Julian calendar marks against the entry Parilia 'Roma condita', and the association of the Parilia with the foundation of Rome only became more orthodox. When news of his decisive victory at Munda in 45 B.C. arrived in Rome at the time of the Parilia, the coincidence was exploited in favour of Caesar, the new Romulus: games were added to the Parilia, at which people wore crowns in Caesar's honour.[22] And the Romulan theme became dominant in A.D. 121 when Hadrian chose the date of the Parilia to found his new temple of Venus and Roma: the festival continued to have lively celebrations, but became known as the Romaea.[23]

The Parilia provide a perfect example of the way that competing interpretations of Roman festivals changed. The Parilia could be seen in all sorts of ways, as Ovid shows: in terms of natural science (fire as a natural purifier); philosophy (fire and water as opposing elements); Greek myths (Phaethon and Deucalion); accident (chance fire caused by shepherds); Roman myth (Aeneas and Troy). But the interpretation already offered by the pre-Julian calendar was the one Ovid favoured: that the festival was connected with the founding of Rome. For Ovid the ancient festival, at which Rome was founded, evokes the incorporation of the primitive golden age into the structures of imperial Rome.

The privileging of one, historicizing interpretation of the Parilia, which connects the festival and the site of Rome, is characteristic of the late Republic and early Empire. One might compare the contemporary accounts of Hercules and the Ara Maxima. Of course, since the early second century B.C. there had been 'histories' of Rome, which focused on the achievements of the Roman state, but, so far as we know, the preoccupation of Livy with the *place* of Rome is new, and Dionysius of Halicarnassus was able to recount Roman 'history' in a connected sequence from Hercules to Aeneas to Romulus to Camillus and so on to the present. Roman myths pertain almost exclusively to the site of Rome; the story of Romulus and Remus concerns the creation of the city and its sacred boundary.

[20] *Fast.* IV.833–48. There was another version of the killing of Remus: Livy 1.7.2; Dion. Hal. *Ant.Rom.* 1.87.2. Bremmer in Bremmer and Horsfall 1987 (F 105) ch. 3 discusses the myth of Romulus and Remus.
[21] Wissowa 1912 (F 241) 199–201; Scullard 1981 (F 223) 103–5. This view fails to exploit the differences between the urban and rural festivals. Dumézil 1969 (F 123) 283–7 and 1970 (F 124) 380–5 uses the festival to illuminate a cognate Indian deity.
[22] Weinstock 1971 (F 235) 184–6. Prop. IV.I.19–20 notes that the ritual had become more elaborate. [23] Ath. VIII.361ef; Beaujeu 1955 (F93) 128–33.

1. The pomerium

The importance of Rome's *pomerium* was manifold. At the mythical level, the conflict between Romulus and Remus over the foundation of the city was settled by the sight of six vultures by Remus on the Aventine and of twelve by Romulus on the Palatine: the Aventine was not included within the *pomerium* until the time of Claudius. And the killing of Remus was justified by his violation of the boundary of the new city.[24]

In the imperial period the *pomerium* was clearly marked by massive blocks of stone, 2 m tall and 1 m square.[25] Placed wherever the line of the *pomerium* changed direction, the precise distance in Roman feet between each marker stone was indicated on the stone itself and all the stones were numbered in sequence along the line of the *pomerium*. The markers ensured that there was no uncertainty about the precise line of the boundary, and no excuse for error. There had been various republican alterations to Romulus' *pomerium* but the extensions carried out by Claudius and Vespasian were the only ones in the imperial period; they took the area enclosed by the *pomerium* up from 325 ha to 665 and 745 ha respectively. In addition, when a dyke was built to control the Tiber floods, Hadrian ensured that new boundary stones were erected directly above the old ones. The right to extend the *pomerium* was sufficiently important to be specifically listed in the powers granted to Vespasian at his succession.[26] Such extensions were justified by a precise connexion between the boundary of Rome and the boundary of the Roman empire. The actual marker stones of Claudius and Vespasian include the formula: 'having increased the boundaries of the Roman people, he increased and defined the *pomerium*', and this was the generally accepted reason for the extension of the *pomerium*.[27] The *pomerium* was thus intimately bound up with the ultimate boundary of the Roman people.

The boundary was also reinforced at time of crisis. Following dire portents, the *pontifices* purified the walls with solemn lustrations, moving round the circuit of the *pomerium*. For example, the appearance on the Capitol in A.D. 43 of a horned owl, a bird considered to be particularly inauspicious, led to the lustration of the city.[28] The significance of such

[24] The execution of those who damaged city walls was justified in Roman law by the story of Remus: *Dig.* 1.8.11 (Pomponius). For sources on the *pomerium* see Lugli 1952 (E 82) 1116–31 and for Roman preoccupation with space see Rykwert 1976 (A 85), Meslin 1978 (F 188) ch. 2.

[25] Labrousse 1937 (E 68); Boatwright 1987 (F 289) 64–71. According to Varro, there were markers in the republican period, but they do not survive. The area enclosed by the *pomerium* was almost exactly that covered by the early third century A.D. official map of Rome, though the *pomerium* itself was not marked.   [26] *ILS* 244.14–16, citing Claudius as precedent.

[27] Tac. *Ann.* XII.24.2; Gell. *NA* XIII.14.3. The SHA claims that Augustus, Nero, Trajan and Aurelian extended the *pomerium*, but see Syme 1978 (F 225).

[28] Pliny, *HN* x.35. Cf. Tac. *Ann.* XIII.24, *Hist.* 1.87.1, IV.53, with Wissowa 1912 (F 241) 391. Such lustrations may be the origin of the alleged festival of the Amburbium: Wissowa 1912 (F 241) 142 and n.12; Scullard 1981 (F 223) 82–3.

lustrations is vividly depicted in Lucan's epic on the civil wars. He describes at length a fictitious lustration of the city along the line of the *pomerium* after Caesar's crossing of the Rubicon.[29] Lucan's retrojection of a contemporary practice is a perfect reflection of the preoccupations of the imperial period. Rome could not allow another Remus to cross the *pomerium*; at times of threat the boundary had to be purified and strengthened.

As in the republican period, the *pomerium* continued to be a significant dividing line, though some of the rules were redefined to accommodate the emperor. These changes foreshadow the more extensive alterations to be discussed in the next section. In one area, however, even emperors were no exception. The ancient prohibition on burial within the *pomerium* was reaffirmed by various emperors until the fourth century A.D. and seems to have been generally observed. And emperors themselves, with the solitary exception of Trajan, to whom we shall return (below, p. 820), were buried outside the *pomerium*. Indeed Claudius and Vespasian deliberately refrained in their extensions of the *pomerium* from including the area of the Campus Martius used for imperial cremations and burial.

Civil authority in the Republic had been defined and limited by the *pomerium*. The popular legislative assemblies could meet only within the *pomerium*; the favourable signs from the gods (*auspicia*) which were preconditions for the assemblies could be received by civil magistrates only within the *pomerium*.[30] With the shift in functions from the popular assemblies to the Senate and emperor, the significance of the assemblies waned in the first century A.D. but augury (i.e. the interpretation of *auspicia* from heaven) continued to be important: a list of auguries between the years 1 and 17 A.D. happens to survive on stone, and augurs were appointed until the end of the fourth century A.D. The augurs were the priests responsible for the interpretation of *auspicia* and for maintaining the *pomerium* itself.[31] The powers of a tribune of the people were likewise limited by the *pomerium*; when in 30 B.C. Octavian was given the powers of a tribune to aid those who appealed to him, they were restricted, in traditional manner, to the area within the *pomerium* and up to one Roman mile outside. But subsequently, with the grant of the tribunician power in 23 B.C. emperors ceased to be restricted by the *pomerium*.[32]

Military authority, which was traditionally valid only outside the *pomerium*, was partially redefined for the emperor. In the celebration of

[29] Luc. 1.584–604. Prop. IV.4.73 describes a threat to the boundary (by Tarpeia) at the Parilia, 'the day the city first got its walls'.

[30] Magdelain 1968 (F 180) 57–67; Magdelain 1977 (F 181); Catalano 1978 (F 110) 422–5, 479–91.

[31] *CIL* VI 36841 (auguries); Wissowa 1912 (F 241) 534 n.2 and Labrousse 1937 (E 68) 170 n.1 (*pomerium*). For an augur dealing with an Augustan *comitia*, see Torelli 1975 (B 291) 111–16, 131–2.

[32] Dio LI.19.6. Cf. Suet. *Tib.* 11.3.

triumphs emperors continued to follow the ancient rules. When Vespasian celebrated his victory over the Jews he spent the night before the triumph outside the *pomerium*, so as to start the triumph by crossing it at the Triumphal Gate.[33] The anomalous burial of Trajan within the *pomerium* is explained by the rules for a triumph. The ashes of Trajan, who had died in the East after conquering Parthia, were brought into Rome in triumphal procession and placed in the base of his column. Justification was found in an allegedly traditional right of those who held triumphs to be buried within the city.[34]

The scope of the emperor's *imperium*, which by now was broader than merely military authority, was redefined. From 23 B.C. onwards, emperors held *imperium*, both within and outside the *pomerium*.[35] They thus had command of troops in Rome, though the praetorian guard was actually stationed just outside the *pomerium*. Some emperors even appeared in the city in military dress[36] and in 2 B.C. Mars received for the first time a temple within the *pomerium* (below, p. 833). With the combination of civil and military power in the hands of the emperor, the *pomerium* ceased to exclude the military sphere, but it continued to be of central importance as the boundary of Rome. We turn now to other transformations of the traditional system as part of the establishment and definition of autocratic rule.

II. THE RE-PLACING OF ROMAN RELIGION

The Augustan period is conventionally viewed as one of restoration or renovation of traditional cults plus the addition of ruler cult. This dichotomy of restoration and innovation is quite false. The ancestral cults of Rome were not simply restored; they were restructured. Ruler cult in Rome was not a simple innovation; many aspects of it were deeply traditional. Thus the distinction between the two types of cults disappears. There were major changes in Rome in the Augustan period, which affected senatorial priesthoods and state temples; at the lower level, the ward cults; and the Secular Games. At the centre was Augustus, sometimes seen as the new Romulus, and round him the whole religion system was restructured.

The concern for the proper performance of religious rites is illustrated by a book entitled 'Memorable Acts and Sayings', which devoted the first chapter to religion.[37] The work, dedicated to Tiberius, notes

---

[33] Joseph. *BJ* VII.123. For the Younger Drusus see Tac. *Ann.* III.11.1, 19.4; for Trajan see the relief from Arch of Beneventum, Hassel 1966 (F 412) 19–20 and pls 15 and 17.

[34] Richard 1966 (F 204).

[35] Dio LIII.32.5. But note Tac. *Ann.* XII.41.1 on the young Nero.

[36] Alföldi 1935 (D 2) 5–8, 47–9.   [37] Val. Max. I.

examples of ancestral maintenance of religion even in the face of severe difficulties, of punishment meted out to those who ignored the claims of religion, and of the correct response to cases of superstition. These paradigmatic anecdotes neatly encapsulate the importance placed in the imperial period on the maintenance and even reinforcement of Roman religious practice.

An index of the energy put in the early Empire into the organization of religion is the production of books on religious law. Traditionally, sacred law had been the special preserve of the various priestly colleges, but from the second century B.C. various priests published books on the subject, and in the second half of the first century B.C. others also, both juriconsults and antiquarians, wrote further works. Jurists continued to write such works in the early Empire. Antistius Labeo wrote 'On Pontifical Law' in at least fifteen books, Ateius Capito 'On Pontifical Law' in at least six books, 'On Law of Sacrifices' and 'On Augural Law'; Veranius 'On Auspices' and 'Pontifical Questions'.[38] These treatises codified the basic framework of sacred law and made subsequent work unnecessary; after the early first century A.D. we hear of no further books on the subject, despite the fact that some leading jurists were also members of priestly colleges. The legal works of the Augustan and Tiberian periods are a neglected aspect of the religious and intellectual achievement of the age.

The need to pay particular attention to religion is stated by poets in the early 20s B.C. Horace, in an Ode composed before 28 B.C. associates the recent travails of Rome with religious neglect. This poem is sometimes used as evidence for the decline of religion in the late Republic, but it of course does not support that thesis.[39] Horace is here reflecting and creating an Augustan perspective on the previous period. Just as Livy, writing on early Rome, explained her misfortunes at the hands of the Gauls by religious neglect, so Horace is seeking to account in traditional fashion for the turmoil and near disasters of the previous generation.[40]

The solution, in the eyes of both Horace and Virgil, lay in the hands of one man.[41] Octavian, or to use his official Roman name, Imperator Caesar, held such a position of prominence that in 27 B.C. some proposed that his name should be changed to Romulus, as the new founder of Rome.[42] But others thought that Romulus was too regal a name and one that carried the taint of fratricide, and an alternative proposal won the

[38] Schulz 1946 (F 690) 40–1, 80–1, 89–90, 138.

[39] Hor. *Carm.* III.6, with Jal 1962 (F 158). Temples had been neglected by the rich in favour of their private luxury: *Carm.* II.15.17–20; *Sat.* II.2.103–4. Against the decline thesis see Beard, *CAH* IX², ch. 19.

[40] Compare Virg. *G.* I.501–2. Horace parallels the fate of Troy with that of Rome: *Carm.* III.3.

[41] Virg. *G.* I.498–501. Hor. *Carm.* I.2 with Bickerman 1961 (F 96) and Nisbet and Hubbard 1970 (B 133) *ad loc.*   [42] Suet. *Aug.* 7.2 and Dio LIII.16.7–8, with Scott 1925 (F 222).

day. His official name henceforth was Imperator Caesar Augustus. Both names indicated that the bearer was uniquely favoured by the gods for the service of Rome. The story was told that when Octavian was campaigning for his first consulship in 43 B.C. six vultures appeared, and that when he was elected six more appeared; this auspicy indicated that like Romulus he would (re)found the city of Rome.[43] This theme was maintained in the choice of the name 'Augustus', a word which was used of all places consecrated by augurs. The name carried evocations of the founding of Rome, without using the name of an actual king of Rome, and of the peculiar favour of the gods for its bearer.[44]

Augustus also awarded honours to the first founder of Rome. In 16 B.C. he rebuilt the temple to Quirinus, who had become identified in the late Republic as the deified Romulus. A fragment of a later relief depicts the pediment of the temple.[45] In the centre stand Victory and Mercury, with Jupiter and Hercules on either side, and beside them Vesta, Mars and Venus. This fine gathering of Augustan deities is impressive enough, but the important point is that these gods are connected with Romulus and Remus. They are at either end of the pediment sitting as augurs, and in the top centre are the vultures seen at the founding of Rome.

The depiction of both Romulus and Remus reflects an Augustan emphasis on fraternal harmony. The myth of Romulus presented above (pp. 816–17) simply gave one, Augustan, version of the myth, but there were other, earlier versions of the story with very different emphases. Horace, for example, condemned the renewed bloodshed in the civil wars, in the late 40s or early 30s B.C.: 'A bitter fate pursues the Romans, and the crime of a brother's murder, ever since blameless Remus' blood was spilt upon the ground, to be a curse upon posterity'. By contrast with this version, Ovid makes Romulus say to Remus: 'There is no need for strife. Great faith is put in birds; let us try the birds', and, as we have seen, he blames the death of Remus on his ignorance of Romulus' prohibition and the action of Celer.[46] Romulus himself is guiltless, the travails of Rome are ascribed to the sin of Laomedon, and Augustus can thus be seen as the new founder of Rome.

Augustus subsequently undertook a major administrative reorganiza-

---

[43] Obsequens, 69; Dio XLVI.46.1–3 gives six plus twelve. Suet. *Aug.* 95 and App. *BCiv.* III.94 give twelve only and treat them as a different type of auspicy.

[44] Suet. *Aug.* 7.2, drawing on the Augustan writer Verrius Flaccus, also used by Festus p. 2L; Ov. *Fast.* 1.608–16. Cf. Gagé 1930 (F 141); Erkell 1952 (F 129) 9–39; Dumézil 1957 (F 122).

[45] Hommel 1954 (F 425) 9–22; Koepel 1984 (F 164) 51–3. In the original temple the Senate had erected in 45 B.C. a statue of Caesar: Cic. *Att.* XII.45.3, XIII.28.3. On the Forum Augusti see below, p. 833.

[46] Hor. *Epod.* VII; Ov. *Fast.* IV.813–14. Cf. Wagenvoort 1956 (B 189); Koch 1954 (F 163); Grant 1973 (F 151) 101–47.

tion of the city, which created local analogues to the reformed religious system of the state. In the earlier system, ascribed to Servius Tullius, there were four regions and shrines to the *lares* at every crossroad, where annual sacrifices were offered. In 7 B.C. Augustus divided Rome into fourteen districts (*regiones*) and 265 wards (*vici*).[47] The importance of the wards lay primarily in the area of cults.[48] In the late Republic the colleges responsible for the cults at crossroads in the city had been a political danger and Caesar had attempted to suppress them, but, perhaps in 29 B.C. (among other occasions), Augustus had given theatrical performances in every ward of the city to celebrate a quadruple triumph, and the cults themselves seem to have continued in the early Augustan period.[49]

The Augustan reorganization transformed the cults of the wards: from 7 B.C. onwards they were of the *Lares Augusti* and the *Genius Augusti*. The traditional celebrations were also changed. To the old festival of the *lares* on 1 May was added a new celebration on 1 August, when the magistrates took up office, presumably in honour of the *Genius Augusti*.[50] The *lares* were ancient, but obscure beings, seen by some ancient writers as the deified spirits of the dead.[51] If this interpretation were dominant, the *Lares Augusti* would be the imperial ancestors, and the *Genius Augusti*, the Spirit of Augustus himself. The ward cults now consisted of cults previously located within the house of Augustus.[52]

The new cults involved building a shrine at the crossroads in each ward. The one excavated example is a small monument, 2.80 m by 2.38 m, with a flight of five steps running up to the shrine, which sheltered images of the *Lares Augusti* and the *Genius Augusti* as well as a small altar.[53] The reliefs on the various extant altars are of great interest. The most elaborately carved altar shows, on the two smaller sides, a sacrifice performed by the ward magistrates, and Victory with the shield of Virtue awarded to Augustus; and on the other two larger sides, Aeneas with the Laurentian sow and the apotheosis of Caesar. These reliefs clearly relate to the iconography of official Augustan art, but their style of carving and the wide range in the iconography of the altars is

[47] Cf. above, ch. 15, pp. 794, 801–02.

[48] Wissowa 1912 (F 241) 167–73; Alföldi 1973 (F 83) 18–36; Liebeschuetz 1979 (F 174) 69–71; Kienast 1982 (C 136) 164–7.

[49] Boyancé 1950 (F 102). Dion. Hal. *Ant. Rom.* IV.14.4; Degrassi 1965 (B 226) 269–71.

[50] Ov. *Fast.* V.129, 147–8; Suet. *Aug.* 31.4; Niebling 1956 (F 190) 324–5.

[51] Festus, p. 108L; Arn. *Adv. Nat.* III.41 (= Varro fr. 209 Cardauns).

[52] The only precedent for the *Lares Augusti* is a solitary dedication from Gallia Cisalpina: Degrassi, *ILLRP* 200 (59 B.C.), but the popular veneration of the Gracchi and Marius Gratidianus seems to have taken place at the neighbourhood shrines. For the relation between these cults and Augustus' cult of Vesta see below, p. 826–7.

[53] Nash 1968 (E 87) I 290–1. For full publication see Colini 1961–2 (F 334) and Tamassia 1961–2 (F 226); Dondin-Payre 1987 (F 350) gives further details. Cf. Holland 1937 (F 420).

very important. Though Augustus handed the cults of the *Lares Augusti* and of his *Genius* over to the wards,[54] the actual arrangements and the designs of the altars were the responsibility of the local officials.[55]

The Augustan reorganization of the ward cults placed the emperor within the life of the city of Rome. The shrines continued to be repaired (and used) through the third century and indeed still feature in the fourth-century catalogues of Roman monuments.[56] The cults were not a transient Augustan phenomenon. The running of the cults of a ward lay in the hands of the four annual magistrates, who were mainly ex-slaves, aided by four slave officials. They were responsible for the festivals, including the local games (*ludi compitalicii*), and the names of the magistrates were inscribed, just like the names of the consuls, on official lists (beginning in 7 B.C.). The public functions and forms of the magistracies gave a real status to the ex-slaves, who were debarred from holding state or municipal office. The Augustan system was not simply a sop for the senatorial class; it incorporated the emperor throughout the city and down to a lowly level of society. The ward cults are symptomatic of the changes in Roman religion under the Empire. Place continued to be important; indeed the creation of the new wards marks an increased emphasis on place. And within that framework the emperor was inscribed.

1. Priesthoods

The imperial focus on Rome continued in the sphere of priesthoods. Augustus, who held priesthoods only at Rome, gradually accumulated membership of all the major priestly colleges, becoming pontifex in 48 B.C., augur in 41–40 B.C., *XVvir sacris faciundis* in *c.* 37 B.C., and *VIIvir epulonum* by 16 B.C. To mark the cumulation of offices a coin issued in 16 B.C. featured the symbols of each of the four priesthoods.[57] In addition Augustus was also a member of three of the lesser priesthoods: *frater Arvalis, sodalis Titii* and *fetialis*. To hold more than one major priesthood was extremely unusual in the republican period. Caesar was both pontifex and augur, but Augustus went beyond even Caesar's precedent. Cumulation was established as a peculiarly imperial privilege; only emperors and their heirs held office in plurality.[58] When Nero was

---

[54] *IItal* XIII 2, p. 96; Ov. *Fast.* v.145–6.

[55] Zanker 1969 (F 243); Panciera 1987 (E 92) 73–8. For example, one altar turned the victory with the official shield of Virtue into a Victory with a purely military shield in front of a trophy.

[56] Panciera 1970 (E 89) 138–51; 1980 (E 90); 1987 (E 92) 61–73. *AE* 1975, 14: an attempt to avoid the duties of *vici magister*, which involved games with *venatio*.

[57] Sutherland and Carson, *RIC* I.69, nos 367–8. Cf. *RIC* I.73, no. 410, 13 B.C. Gagé 1931 (F 142); also Bayet 1955 (F 89). Gordon 1990 (F 148) stresses the emperor as the archetypal sacrificer.

[58] Weinstock 1971 (F 235) 28–34; Lewis 1955 (F 173) 23, 94–101.

adopted by Claudius, coins were issued with the same four symbols as had appeared on Augustus' coins and a legend indicating that Nero had been co-opted as a supernumerary into the four priestly colleges by decree of the Senate.[59] The co-optation into four colleges simultaneously was an innovation here, but it set a precedent for the later designation of the emperor's heir. The emperor and his heir embraced all religious activity in Rome. As a result, Roman religion was tied to a particular person as well as a particular place.

The first two of Augustus' offices, augur and pontifex, are worth consideration here: we shall return to the *XVviri sacris faciundis* later. The *lituus*, the symbol of the augurs, was regularly featured on the coinage of Octavian in the 30s B.C.[60] Octavian, like other republican leaders, emphasized that his military authority was properly founded on religious observance, but after Actium he stressed the peaceful over-tones of the office of augur. In 29 B.C. Octavian took the *augurium salutis*, at a time when no Roman forces were fighting; this was the 'greatest augury by which the safety of the Roman people is sought', in the words of an official record. Though the *augurium salutis* is treated as a tradition revived by Augustus, the practice had been carried out only once before (in 63 B.C.). The 'tradition' was, however, kept up subsequently.[61] In the early years of Augustus' career the office of augur had considerable importance, and later emperors continued to hold the office, but its significance was subsequently overshadowed by another priesthood.

Augustus had been pontifex since 48 B.C., but in 44 B.C. Lepidus was deviously appointed *pontifex maximus* in place of Caesar and held the office until his death in 13 B.C. Augustus gave considerable emphasis to the popularity of his election as *pontifex maximus* in 12 B.C. The date on which the election occurred was celebrated by an annual festival; and noted in Ovid's *Fasti*.[62] The event was indeed of central importance in the restructuring of Roman religion.

The *pontifex maximus* was traditionally obliged to live in an official house, which was in the Forum; even Caesar conformed. Augustus was unwilling to give up his own house on the Palatine, but followed the rule about the public house. Initially, he made a part of his own house public property and subsequently (A.D. 3) after a fire destroyed the house he rebuilt it and made it all public property.[63] Augustus also maintained, or rather enhanced, the connexion between the *pontifex maximus* and the

---

[59] *RIC* I.125, nos. 76–7, 129, no. 107, A.D. 50–4. For the history of this type see *BMCRE* III.xl–xliii.   [60] Gagé 1930 (F 141).

[61] Revival: Suet. *Aug.* 31.4; Dio LI.20.4. Repeated: *CIL* VI 36841; Tac. *Ann.* XII.23.1. For the semantic link with 'Augustus', see above, p. 822.

[62] *RG* 10.2; *IItal* XIII 2, p. 420; Ov. *Fast.* III.415–28.

[63] Dio LIV.27.3; LV.12.4–5. In 36 B.C. Octavian had been voted a house at public expense: XLIX.15.5. Cf. Weinstock 1971 (F 235) 276–81.

cult of Vesta. The republican official house of the *pontifex maximus* was adjacent to the precinct of the Vestal Virgins and among other responsibilities he oversaw the cult of Vesta by the Vestals. Just under two months after Augustus became *pontifex maximus* there was dedicated 'an image and shrine of Vesta in the house of Imperator Caesar Augustus *pontifex maximus*'.[64] The old shrine which contained the sacred flame and various secret objects remained on the Forum, but the creation of the new shrine in Augustus' house on the Palatine allowed a rearticulation of the position of *pontifex maximus*.

The relationship of Augustus to Vesta was much closer than that of any republican *pontifex maximus*. It was expressed by contemporary writers in two ways. First, by the stories of the origin of Vesta. Augustan writers stated that Aeneas had brought the fire of Vesta with him from Troy to Italy and that Romulus had transferred the cult, which his mother had served, from Alba Longa to Rome.[65] Secondly, they assert an actual kinship between Vesta and Augustus. In the words of Ovid, 'Gods of ancient Troy, the worthiest prize to him who bore you, you whose weight saved Aeneas from the foe, a priest of the line of Aeneas handles your kindred divinities: Vesta, you must guard his kindred head.'[66] Augustus was thus connected to Vesta both by blood and by the deeds of his ancestors.

The creation of the shrine on the Palatine was an important stage in the formation of a peculiarly imperial residence. What had been just one of many residences of the republican nobility on the Palatine was transformed into a palace. 'Vesta has been received into the house of her kinsman; so have the senators rightly decreed. Apollo has part of the house; another part has been given up to Vesta; what remains is occupied by Augustus himself ... A single house holds three eternal gods.'[67] Rather than Augustus going to live in the public residence near the shrine of Vesta he shared a house with her and Apollo (below, p. 832). The *pontifex maximus* could now be called 'priest of Vesta'[68] and Vesta had been replaced in a new imperial setting. The public hearth of the state, with its associations of the success of the Roman empire, was now confused with the private hearth of Augustus; in turn the private cult of

---

[64] *IItal* XIII.2, p. 452. The restoration of 'shrine' is controversial, but see Guarducci 1971 (F 153). There was already a ramp linking the old temple of Vesta to the Palatine: Coarelli 1983–5 (E 19) I 237, 248, II 156.

[65] Aeneas: Virg. *Aen.* II.296, 567; Ov. *Fast.* I. 527–8, III.29, VI.227; *Met.* XV.730–1; Prop. IV.4.69; Dion. Hal. *Ant. Rom.* II.65.2. Romulus: Plut. *Rom.* 22; Dion. Hal. *Ant. Rom.* II.64.5–69 argues at length for the (older?) alternative that Numa established the cult in Rome.

[66] *Fast.* III.423–6. Ovid does not spell out how they are related. For the various options see Bömer 1987 (F 98).   [67] Ov. *Fast.* IV.949–54. Cf. Wiseman 1987 (F 81).

[68] Ov. *Fast.* III.699, v. 573; *Met.* XV.778, retrospectively applied to Julius Caesar. In the third and fourth centuries the *pontifices* were also known as *pontifices Vestae*: *RE* VIII A.2, 1760.

the imperial *Lares* and the *Genius* of Augustus was established in all the wards of the city.

The new relationship with Vesta is one aspect of the transformation of the office of *pontifex maximus*. Scholars sometimes say that in 12 B.C. Augustus was appointed head of Roman religion, a pagan Archbishop of Canterbury or Pope, and they are inclined to date his religious reforms to the period after 12 B.C.[69] This attitude goes back to antiquity; Suetonius (*Aug.* 31) groups a series of religious reforms under the heading of Augustus as *pontifex maximus*, though some are demonstrably earlier. This conception of the office was the one established by Augustus, not the one current in the late Republic. The *pontifices* were, with the augurs, the most prestigious priestly colleges of the Republic, but they had distinct spheres of operation and the *pontifices* did not wield general authority over the augurs or the other priestly colleges.[70] Thus in the Republic the *pontifex maximus* was merely head of one of the priestly colleges. This changes with the emergence of dynasts in the late Republic. Caesar became *pontifex maximus* in 63 B.C., and had begun to convert the office into something new. Thus, in 44 B.C. it was decreed that his son or adopted son should become *pontifex maximus* after him.[71] The intrigues which led to the election of Lepidus rather than Octavian are hardly surprising. After the election of Augustus it was impossible for anyone but the emperor living on the Palatine to be *pontifex maximus* and all subsequent emperors took up the position soon after accession (usually in March) and regularly featured it among their official titles. Augustus had gradually accumulated membership of all four principal priestly colleges and was not hindered at all by Lepidus, a political nonentity. But once the office of *pontifex maximus* was in Augustus' hands, it did become the keystone of the religious system. 'From the fact that they are enrolled in all the priesthoods and moreover can grant most of the priesthoods to others, and that one of them, even if two or three emperors are ruling jointly, is *pontifex maximus*, they control all sacred and religious matters.'[72] From 12 B.C. onwards, for the first time, Roman religion had a head.

Under the guidance of Augustus, who increased the privileges of some priesthoods, the senatorial priesthoods remained extremely prestigious. Augustus noted that he had rewarded 170 of his senatorial supporters in the civil war with priesthoods and Dio says that in 29 B.C. Augustus was allowed to choose priests even beyond the regular number.[73] But despite Augustus' powers, the number of non-imperial

[69] Wissowa 1912 (F 241) 74; Wilheim 1915 (F 238); Liebeschuetz 1979 (F 174) 70.
[70] Beard and North 1990 (F 92A).   [71] Dio XLIV.5.3.   [72] Dio LIII.17.8.
[73] *RG* 25; Dio LI.20.3. Scheid 1978 (F 62) against Schumacher 1978 (F 63) on numbers. Millar 1977 (A 59) 357 n.15 on the first cumulation of major priesthoods.

members of the main four priestly colleges remained stable. As these priesthoods, unlike magistracies, were held for life, competition was fierce. For the first two centuries of the Empire it was not possible for a senator to be a member of more than one of the four main colleges. Indeed only a quarter to a third of senators (and a half of all consuls) could become priests. Some senators saw membership of one of the priestly colleges as the pinnacle of their career, ranking higher than being praetor or consul.

There were however problems with the appointment to two of the priesthoods. The case of the *flamen Dialis* is a clear case study in the flexibility of 'tradition'. The office of *flamen Dialis* had been vacant since 87 B.C., though the rites themselves had continued to be performed by the *pontifices* until Augustus as *pontifex maximus* had the post filled in 11 B.C. The *flamen Dialis* remained subject to unique restrictions: for example, 'the feet of the couch on which he sleeps must be coated with a thin layer of clay, and he must not sleep away from this bed for three nights in succession, and no other person must sleep in that bed'. But Augustus 'altered certain relics of a primitive antiquity to the modern spirit'.[74] The full details of the changes are lost to us, but the priest was now allowed to spend more nights outside Rome and there seem to have been changes in the status of his wife.[75] The debates over the restrictions continued. One *flamen Dialis* argued that he should be allowed to leave Rome to govern a province; Tiberius as *pontifex maximus* ruled against such a radical change. When this *flamen* died Tiberius argued that the restriction of the office to those married in an archaic and now rare manner should be lifted; this proved unnecessary as there was a suitable candidate, but some legal restrictions imposed on his wife were removed.[76] These changes in the rules governing the office of *flamen Dialis* are among the best examples of the malleability of Roman religious practice.

There had also been problems over the appointment of Vestal Virgins, which Augustus attempted to solve. He increased the privileges of the Vestals, including special seats in the theatre; later, distinguished imperial women sat among the Vestals in the theatre.[77] Many senators were reluctant to put their daughters forward to be Vestal Virgins (Vestals served for thirty years and subsequent marriage was unusual), but Augustus swore that if any of his granddaughters had been of the appropriate age, he would have proposed them. Such official encourage-

---

[74] Gell. *NA* XI.15.14. Tac. *Ann.* IV.16.3. Cf. Rohde 1936 (F 207) 136–7.

[75] Tac. *Ann.* III.71.3; Gai. *Inst.* 1.136, fragmentary. Cf. Gell. *NA* X.15.14 and 17 for other changes.

[76] Tac. *Ann.* III.58–59.1, 71 (A.D. 22); IV.16 (A.D. 24). Cf. Domitian's permission for a *flamen Dialis* to divorce his wife: Plut. *Quaest. Rom.* 50 = *Mor.* 276E.

[77] Suet. *Aug.* 31.3, 44.3. Tac. *Ann.* IV.16.4; Dio LIX.3.4, LX.22.2.

ment proved to be successful. Under Tiberius two senators vied with each other to have their daughters chosen as Vestal Virgins and the office remained in high prestige through the third into the fourth century.[78]

The Vestals in fact accumulated new, imperial functions in addition to their traditional ones. In the Republic they had been present with the other priests at the grand funeral of Sulla and it was voted that with the priests (*pontifices*) they should every five years offer up prayers for Caesar's safety.[79] After Actium the Vestals headed the procession greeting the returning Augustus; they were present at the dedication of the Ara Pacis and with the magistrates and priests were responsible for the annual sacrifices there. The Vestals were even put in charge of the cult of the deified Livia.[80] While Vesta gained a new shrine on the Palatine, the Vestals gained a concern for the emperor and his family. The emperor was thus further linked to the hearth of Rome and its tokens of the farmer of the gods for Rome.

The Arval Brethren illustrate in more detail the extent and nature of changes in priesthoods in the imperial period. They held a shadowy position among the numerous priesthoods of the Republic, but their sanctuary is attested archaeologically from the third century B.C. Augustus became a member of the college and, perhaps in 29 B.C., placed the body on a new footing.[81] Our only republican literary source on the Arvals explains that they perform rites to make the crops grow; their name (*fratres Arvales*) comes either from sowing (*ferendo*) and fields (*arvis*), or from the Greek *fratria* or brotherhood. By contrast, in the imperial period the name was explained differently. The nurse of Romulus had twelve sons, but one died and Romulus himself took his place, calling himself and the others 'Arval Brethren'.[82] This myth entirely suited a college which included Augustus, the new Romulus.

The revived college proudly inscribed a record of its ceremonies and membership. The extensive fragments that survive run from 21 B.C. to A.D. 304 and are the fullest extant record of any of the priesthoods of Rome.[83] The membership of the college was of some distinction from its first Augustan appointments to the end of Nero's reign. Thereafter the members were generally drawn from the middle ranks of the Senate

[78] Tac. *Ann* 11.86. Cf. IV.16.4: a grant of 2 million sesterces to a new Vestal, presumably in addition to the traditional salary.   [79] App. *BCiv.* 1.106; 11.106.

[80] Ara Pacis: Ryberg 1955 (F 209) 41, 43, 51–2, 71–4; Dio LI.19.2; *RG* 11–12. Livia: Dio LX.5.2.

[81] Scheid 1975 (F 61) 335–66; 1987 (F 218) Cf. Saulnier 1980 (F 215) and Wiedemann 1986 (F 237) for an Augustan reorganization of the *fetiales*.

[82] Varro, *Ling.* v. 85. Pliny, *HN* XVIII.6; Gell. *NA* VII.7.8, quoting Masurius Sabinus (*floruit* Tiberius–Nero), who drew on earlier historians.

[83] Texts mainly in Henzen 1874 (B 242) or *ILS* 229–30, 241, 5026–48. See in general Beard 1985 (F 91) with translation of selected documents.

which could not expect consulships or major priesthoods.[84] The records of the Arvals' ceremonies demonstrate clearly the extent to which the ancient (or allegedly ancient) cults of Rome were re-structured round the figure of the emperor.

The central, three-day festival of the Arval Brethren was in honour of Dea Dia, an obscure deity known only from these inscriptions. The festival was somewhat fluid, at least in the way it was recorded, but it never included imperial sacrifices. The emperor and his family were the focus of a range of quite separate sacrifices. There were annual vows and special vows for the emperor's safety, sacrifices to mark imperial birthdays, accessions, deaths or deifications, sacrifices because of the discovery of a conspiracy against the emperor or because he had returned safely to Rome. There was also in the sanctuary of Dea Dia a shrine to the emperors (a Caesareum) which contained imperial statues. But sacrifices for the emperor were never in the sanctuary of Dea Dia and almost never involved sacrifices to her. The vows were taken on the Capitol to the Capitoline triad, Jupiter, Juno and Minerva, and the other sacrifices were offered in various locations in Rome (mainly on the Capitol and at the temple of Divus Augustus) to the Capitoline triad and other deities, to the deified emperor and empress, to the *Genius* of the living emperor and the Juno of the empress.

After A.D. 69, with the exception of one offering to the *Genius* of the emperor and to the *divi* as part of a special ceremony of expiation in A.D. 224, there were no regular sacrifices to the *divi* nor sacrifices for imperial birthdays.[85] But sacrifices for special imperial events continued and vows for the emperor's safety were regular throughout the period. The records of the Arval Brethren thus demonstrate the range of religious activity focused on the emperor that was performed alongside their 'traditional' cult. Talk of 'restoration of ancient cults which had gradually fallen into disuse'[86] should not blind us to the fact that 'restoration' entailed a radical shift in focus.

2. Temples

The building or rebuilding of temples is another aspect of the restructuring of the religious system around the person of the emperor. Augustus was proud of his speed in repairing eighty-two temples in 28 B.C. and of building or repairing fourteen temples in Rome during his reign, but his account of the temples is interspersed with references to his work on

---

[84] Scheid 1975 (F 61); Syme 1980 (D 70).
[85] This change might be connected with a development in the function of the *sodales Augustales* and other imperial priesthoods in Rome itself, who may have taken over sacrifices to the *divi* previously carried out by the Arvals.   [86] Suet. *Aug.* 31.4.

other, secular buildings, such as the Senate-house, theatres, the water supply and a road.[87] That is, Augustus presented his temple construction within the tradition of building works carried out by victorious generals and other senators. There was, however, a profound difference. While senators continued to erect some secular buildings during the reign of Augustus, after 33 B.C. only Augustus and members of his family built temples in Rome. Senators, now excluded from their traditional opportunity for display in the capital, increased their munificence to their native cities in Italy and elsewhere. This shouldering of responsibility for temples in Rome increased the importance of the emperor.[88] Temple building placed the emperor in a unique relationship with the gods.

Almost all the nine state temples built in Rome between the death of Caesar and the accession of Vespasian refer directly or indirectly to the emperor. Two were dedicated to the officially deified ruler (Divus Julius; Divus Augustus). Three relate to official victories (Apollo; Neptune; Mars Ultor). Two stress imperial virtues (Concordia; Iustitia). One (Jupiter Tonans) was dedicated by Augustus in thanks for the fact that a thunderbolt just missed him. Only one (to Egyptian Isis) has no overt imperial associations, and may not be a real state temple. The reign of Augustus is the crucial period for the establishment of this imperial focus of temple building. Seven of the nine new temples date to his reign: in addition, some of the old temples rebuilt by Augustus gained new associations. Three temples built or rebuilt by Augustus may be taken as exemplary of the new system: Cybele, Apollo and Mars Ultor.

The temple of Cybele on the Palatine was a familiar peculiarity in the late Republic. The cult of the Mother of the Gods, introduced to Rome from Phrygia in 205 B.C., was noted for its barbaric exoticism. Even in Augustan Rome, at the festival of Cybele eunuchs preceded the goddess through the streets banging drums and clashing cymbals. But the goddess became in the Augustan period more Roman and more imperial. Her Phrygian homeland was now associated with the Trojan origins of Rome; according to Ovid, she almost followed Aeneas from neighbouring Troy to Italy but awaited a later date. Already in the *Aeneid* Cybele appears as a protectress of Aeneas on his journeys, and implicit association with Augustus was strengthened when he rebuilt the temple.[89]

---

[87] *RG* 19–21. Cf. Eck 1984 (D 39) 136–42. Wissowa 1912 (F 241) 596–7 lists the new temples, though that to Neptune was probably a restoration; see generally Gros 1976 (F 397).

[88] All temples 'would have fallen into complete ruins, without the far-seeing care of our sacred leader, under whom shrines feel not the touch of age; and not content with doing favours to humankind he does them to the gods. O holy one, who builds and rebuilds the temples, I pray the powers above may take such care of you as you of them': Ov. *Fast.* II.59–64. Cf. I.13–14, Livy, IV.20–7. Suet. *Aug.* 29–30.

[89] *Fast.* IV.251–4, 272. Virg. *Aen.* II.693–7, IX.7–9, X.252–5. The rebuilding may pre-date 2 B.C., with subsequent restoration after a fire in A.D. 3: Syme 1978 (B 179) 30.

The goddess herself gained prominence as the annual washing of the image took place from the early Empire onwards not in the temple, but after a grand procession down the river Almo, where the goddess had first arrived in Rome. In the Republic, though the praetors had overall responsibility for the sacrifices and games, no Roman citizen could take part in the festival and the priests and priestesses were Phrygians, but in the imperial period the rule changed and Roman citizens could become priests and priestesses. It was even possible to honour Drusilla posthumously with a festival modelled on the festival of Cybele.[90] The cult retained 'Phrygian' peculiarities – Cybele held precedence over the other gods, her children, and the offering to her of herbs, which the earth once grew without human labour, sacralizes the most primitive stage of human existence before the Greek Ceres introduced cereals[91] – but they obliquely emphasized the antiquity and pre-eminence of Rome.[92]

Adjacent to the temple of Cybele on the Palatine, Augustus also constructed a temple of Apollo, which with the temple of Vesta framed his own house. On the advice of *haruspices* he made public the part of his property which had been struck by lightning in 36 B.C., dedicating the temple itself in 28 B.C. The temple was of considerable grandeur, featuring statues of the Danaids in the surrounding colonnade, ivory carvings of Niobe and the Gauls on the door and statues of Apollo, his mother and sister inside the temple. These three cult images were indeed the works of three of the finest Greek sculptors of the Classical period.[93]

The location of the temple is very striking. As Apollo was a Greek god, his earlier temple was outside the *pomerium*, in the Circus Maximus. Augustus moved his cult in, and made Apollo, who had previously been a healing god of marginal importance, central to his new Rome.[94] The complex of Augustus' house and the two temples, to Vesta and Apollo, which was without precedent in Rome, subtly evoked the divine associations of Augustus. The iconography of the temple of Apollo, which highlighted the punishments meted out by Apollo to those who disobeyed him, reflects Augustan preoccupations. Apollo had helped Augustus to defeat Antony and Cleopatra at Actium in 31 B.C., and Augustus rebuilt the sanctuary of Apollo at Actium, founding prestigious games (and Nicopolis) there.[95] The new temple at Rome also received (probably in 23–19 B.C.) the ancient Sibylline Books from the temple of Jupiter which recorded the utterances of the prophetess under

[90] Dio LIX.11.3.   [91] Ov. *Fast.* IV.367–72 with Brelich 1965 (F 104).
[92] Lambrechts 1951 (F 167); Boyancé 1954 (F 103); Bömer 1964 (F 97); Wiseman 1984 (F 240). For later developments in the cult at Rome, see Wissowa 1912 (F 241) 319–27; Lambrechts 1952 (F 168); Van Doren 1953 (F 230).
[93] Lightning: Suet. *Aug.* 29.3; Dio XLIX.15.5. Grandeur: Prop. II.31; Pliny, *HN* XXXVI. 24, 25, 32.
[94] Liebeschuetz 1979 (F 174) 82–5; Zanker 1983 (F 630). Gros 1976 (F 397) 211–29 disposes of the alleged restoration of the earlier temple by Sosius in 34–32 B.C.   [95] Gagé 1936 (F 144).

the inspiration of Apollo.[96] And the focus of the Secular Games on Apollo and Diana (below, pp. 835–6) shows how Apollo had become a symbol of the new age.

The third major Augustan temple, which was later described as the most beautiful building in the world, is the summation of Augustan religious restructuring. The temple of Mars the Avenger formed the centrepiece of Augustus' new Forum, built next to the Forum of Caesar and dedicated in 2 B.C.[97] This was the first temple to the god of war within the *pomerium* and its location in the centre of Rome reflects the profound changes of the Augustan period in the rules governing the emperor's *imperium*.[98] Though the notion of the temple went back to a vow Augustus took in 42 B.C., when he defeated the murderers of his father, the emphasis on Mars as the Avenger also evoked Augustus' vengeance on the Parthians in 20 B.C.; the standards lost by Crassus were recovered and placed in the innermost shrine of the temple. This allusion to contemporary achievements against foreign foes was reinforced by the military functions prescribed for the temple. Military commanders were to set off from the temple, the Senate was to meet in it to vote triumphs, and victorious generals after the triumphs were to dedicate to Mars the symbols of their triumphs.[99] Thus military glory could be displayed only in a setting which explicitly evoked the emperor's authority.

The design of the Forum and temple articulates the relationship between Augustus, the gods and Rome, without directly glorifying Augustus.[100] Augustus was referred to overtly only by the dedicatory inscription on the architrave, and in the chariot which probably stood in the centre of the Forum, but the whole complex evoked him. The cult statues in the temple were of Mars, Venus and Caesar, referring both to Caesar's (and Augustus') descent from Venus, and to Augustus' piety in avenging Caesar. On the pediment were Mars, Venus and Fortune; Romulus as augur and victorious Roma flanked them, and on either side were representations of the Palatine, the setting of Romulus' augury, and the river Tiber. Augustus' own victories and restorations of Rome had here their mythical analogues. In the porticoes on either side of the temple stood balancing series of statues depicting Augustus' dual ancestry. On one side was Aeneas, the descendant of Venus, dutifully carrying his father from the flames of Troy (echoing Augustus' own filial

[96] Gagé 1931 (F 142) 99–101; 1955 (F 146), 542–55.
[97] Described in Ov. *Fast.* v. 545–98; Pliny, *HN* XXXVI.102.
[98] There was already within the *pomerium* a temple to Quirinus, who was associated with Mars, and Varro 'recorded' a primitive cult of Mars on the Capitol. Cf. Scholz 1970 (F 221) 18–33.
[99] Suet. *Aug.* 29; Dio LV.10.2–3. Cf. Bonnefond 1987 (F 293).
[100] Zanker n.d. [c. 1968] (F 625); Koeppel 1983 (F 454A) 98–101; Anderson 1984 (E 2) 65–100. For Romulus see Degrassi 1939 (B 223).

piety), and flanked by his descendants, the kings of Alba Longa and the Julii. Facing this series was a statue of Romulus, the son of Mars, victoriously bearing the armour of an enemy king whom he had slain in battle and round him other figures of Roman history, celebrated mainly for their military prowess. In all there were about 108 statues, each with a brief inscription itemizing their distinctions. To these famous predecessors and ancestors, stretching back to Aeneas, Romulus and through them to Venus and Mars, Augustus was the heir. The place of Rome, evoked by their achievements and by the representations of Palatine, Tiber and Roma herself, was now restructured around the figure of the emperor.

The restructuring connected with the temples of Apollo and Mars Ultor was not however because of animosity towards the existing cults. Both new temples did received functions previously part of the cult of Jupiter Optimus Maximus: the Sibylline Books were moved to the Palatine, and some military functions to the Forum Augustum. But Augustus himself rebuilt the Capitol and made lavish offerings to Jupiter. And the annual offering of vows on behalf of the emperor was always performed in the Capitol. The old system had now increased in complexity with the integration of the new temples into the life of Rome.

3. Secular Games

The celebration of the Secular Games in 17 B.C. neatly sums up the workings of religion under Augustus and the subsequent persistence and transformations of the Augustan system.[101] These games are uniquely well documented in a variety of sources: the Sibylline oracle ordaining the procedures, the inscribed record of the games, the hymn of Horace sung at the festival, and other scattered sources. The main location for the games was in the north-west Campus Martius beside the Tiber at an altar known as the Tarentum (or Terentum), where the records of the games were later set up. A story circulated from at least the first century B.C. onwards that in archaic times one Valesius, hoping to save his children from plague, was told by the gods to sail down the Tiber to Tarentum, a Greek colony in the 'instep' of Italy, and give his children water from the altar of Dis Pater and Persephone. Putting in at night at the Campus Martius, he gave water to his thirsty children, who were miraculously cured. He had unwittingly drawn water at a place called Tarentum from the altar of Dis Pater and Persephone, and in

---

[101] Nilsson 1920 (F 191); Pighi 1965 (B 263), who reprints the sources. There are two new fragments of the inscription in Moretti 1982–4 (B 256). La Rocca 1984 (F 165) 3–55 discusses the Tarentum.

thanks for the cure Valesius established three nights of sacrifices and games.[102] The Secular Games of Augustus were thus tied to this mysterious place.

The Augustan celebrations, however, differed substantially from any republican predecessors. Augustus and his heir Agrippa played leading roles, though not without traditional justification. Augustus, long a member of the *XVviri*, the board responsible for holding the games, initiated the celebrations by writing to the board as one of its four presidents. But in the festival the other three presidents stood aside in favour of Agrippa, an ordinary member of the board. Augustus himself offered the nocturnal prayers, and, with Agrippa, the diurnal ones. He also ended each prayer with a petition 'for me, my house and my family'. This was a traditional prayer formula,[103] but in Augustus' mouth the old words acquired a new resonance: it was in the same year that he adopted the sons of Agrippa as his ultimate heirs. The hymn sung on the third day alluded to the central importance of Augustus: 'May the illustrious descendant of Anchises and Venus obtain the help of you gods whom he worships with white oxen, superior to the enemy, merciful to the prostrate foe.' The old religion of place had acquired a new focus.

The celebrations themselves were also transformed. The preliminary distribution of torches, sulphur and asphalt to the entire free population of Rome (line 65; cf. line 8) had not been part of earlier Secular Games, but as with the cult of the *Lares Augusti*, there was an attempt to create widespread participation. The model for this general purification of the people of Rome was the Parilia; we recall Ovid's description of the purification by fire (above, pp. 816–17). As the Parilia was connected with the original founding of Rome, so the Secular Games marked the regular regeneration of Rome.

At the second stage of celebrations there were major changes to the old practices. The nocturnal rites remained, but Dis Pater and Persephone were replaced by the Fates, the Goddesses of Childbirth and Mother Earth, and three day-time celebrations were added, to Jupiter, Juno, and Apollo and Diana. Instead of a focus on the gloomy gods of the Underworld, marking the passing of an era, the Augustan games marked the birth of a new age. The fertility of Mother Earth, one of the themes on the Ara Pacis, was guarded by the Fates and the Goddesses of Childbirth. A prominent role was also played by 110 mothers, one for each year of the *saeculum*, and a chorus of boys and girls. The new temple of Apollo on the Palatine (above, pp. 832–3) was also incorporated: it

---

[102] Zosimus, II.1–3 (and Val. Max. II.4.5). Versnel 1982 (F 232) 217–28 discusses the relation of the story to the Valerii.

[103] The formula appears in Cato, *Agr.* 134, 139, 141. It is used by the matrons: Augustan *acta* line 130 (restored); Severan *acta* IV.12.

was one of the locations where the *XVviri* took in offerings of crops and gave out the material for purification, and where on the third day sacrifice and prayer were offered to Apollo and Diana and the saecular hymn was first sung.

The games are also worthy of comment.[104] They too reveal different layers. During the three days of the festival proper there were two quite different sorts of games: 'at night games were held after the sacrifices on a stage without a theatre and without seats'. This continued into the following day, but there were in addition 'games in a wooden theatre which had been built in the Campus Martius by the Tiber'. The second type of games formed the seven days of games that closed the festival; these were held in three locations, the theatre in the Campus Martius; the Greek musical games in the Theatre of Pompey and Greek theatrical games in the theatre in the Campus Martius. The first type of games, without theatre and without seats, was avowedly primitive (and un-popular – it was not repeated in the seven days at the end of the festival). Varro, writing on the origin of theatrical performances in Rome, associated them with the introduction of the *ludi Tarentini*.[105] Those who had read their Varro knew that quaint games of this type had to be incorporated into the new structure.

The rituals and their organization were based on traditional sources. The 'ancient books', perhaps the records of the *XVviri*, were searched for details (none was forthcoming on how to finance the Secular Games) and the organization of the rituals was in the hands of the eminent jurist Ateius Capito (above, p. 821), but the main shape of the rituals was pro-vided by a Sibylline oracle. Shortly before the Augustan celebration the Sibylline oracles were purged of spurious items and deposited beneath the statue of Apollo in the new temple on the Palatine (above, pp. 832–3), and perhaps in the process the oracle enjoining quite new rituals was discovered. In fact the oracle was probably an antiquarian product of the Augustan age, incorporating earlier material. Both the oracle and the prayers hope for the future obedience of the Latins to Rome, a notion that made little sense under the empire, and which must have evoked the troubles of the second century B.C.[106] The 'ancient books', legal expertise and the Sibylline oracle combined to create and sanction the new rites.

The timing of the celebrations also received due authority. The only well-attested republican celebrations were in 249 and 146 B.C., with a cycle of 100 years.[107] But, following the Sibylline oracle (and Varro), a cycle of 110 years was accepted as authentic and a sequence of earlier

---

[104] Erkell 1969 (F 130).   [105] *Ap.* Censorinus, *D.N.* 17.8 = Pighi 1965 (B 263) 37–8.

[106] Diels 1890 (F 120) 13–15; Gagé 1933 (F 143) 177–83; Momigliano 1941 (F 189) 165 and Momigliano 1966 (A 64) 625.

[107] Censorinus, *D.N.* citing Varro and Livy. Censorinus gives 146 B.C.; Livy, *Epit.* 49 gives 149 B.C.

republican games was established, beginning in 456 B.C. These were added after 17 B.C. to the official Calendar. This new history of the games, which ignored the two earlier authentic celebrations, authorized games in 16 B.C.; the puzzling choice of 17 B.C. is perhaps because of disagreement over the precise year of the foundation of Rome.[108]

The Augustan games formed the model for all subsequent celebrations. Claudius celebrated games in A.D. 47, receiving censure from modern scholars for his self-interested choice of date, but we tend to forget that A.D. 47 was 800 years from the foundation of Rome and a cycle of 100 years was perfectly reasonable (indeed the Greek translation of Augustus' *Res Gestae* (wrongly) translates *saecularis* as 'every hundred years'). Thereafter Domitian celebrated the games in A.D. 88 (six years ahead of the Augustan cycle) and Septimus Severus in A.D. 204 (exactly on the Augustan calculations). Both Domitian's and Severus' games followed the Augustan procedure extremely closely. There were of course some changes (a new hymn was written for 204, when the emperor and his family were also somewhat more prominent), but the basic structure of events was unaltered.

A second cycle of games was also celebrated under the Empire.[109] Taking its lead from Claudius' holding of Secular Games 800 years after the foundation of Rome, games were also held the following two centuries (A.D. 148 and 248). These were not counted in the official numbered sequence of Secular Games and, in the latter two cases, the ritual was quite different. The Tarentum seems to have been displaced in favour of rites in front of the temple of Venus and Rome, known as the Temple of the City, and the date was probably changed to 21 April, the birthday of Rome (above, p. 817). These anniversary celebrations, which developed from the Augustan framework, mark the emergence of a new consciousness of the importance of the city of Rome. While under the Republic such anniversaries of the foundation of Rome are unheard of, in the imperial period, the Secular Games, within which the emperor was inscribed, achieved a new importance.

III. IMPERIAL RITUALS

The religious position of the emperor was thus central and pervasive but also diffuse. There was no one major ceremony such as a coronation or new year's festival at which the emperor was the leading actor, nor did any one religious ritual sum up the religious position of the emperor.[110] Rather, a range of rituals incorporated the living emperor. From 30 B.C.

---

[108] For earlier plans to celebrate games in 23 B.C. see Virg. *Aen.* VI.65–70, 791–4, with Merkelbach 1961 (F 187) 91–9.   [109] Gagé 1933 (F 143A), 1936 (F 145).

[110] For such ceremonies elsewhere see Cannadine and Price 1987 (F 109).

games were celebrated every five years by one of the colleges of priests or the consuls in fulfilment of vows for Augustus' health; and in 28 B.C. Augustus' name was inscribed in the hymn of the Salii by a decree of the Senate.[111] His birthday was celebrated publicly, as we have seen in the case of the Arval Brethren (above, p. 830), and at banquets public and private libations were made to Augustus.[112] Images of Augustus and members of his family stood in household shrines, sometimes tended by 'worshippers of Augustus' organized on the model of private associations.[113]

Though there was no straightforward cult of the living Augustus in Rome, his *numen*, or divine power, did receive public honours there. In A.D. 6 (probably) Tiberius dedicated an altar at which the four main priestly colleges sacrificed to the *numen* of Augustus.[114] *Numen* was not shared by ordinary people, and had no resonances in family cult, which makes the establishment of an official cult in Rome the more striking.

Ovid's *Fasti* neatly encapsulates the invisible presence of Augustus. Interspersed with accounts of traditional festivals (such as the Parilia), Ovid mentioned every official festival of Augustan significance, such as the founding of the Ara Pacis (1.709–22) or the establishment of the cult of the *Lares Augusti* (v.129–46). Ovid has often been accused of poetical flattery, but in fact he merely reflects the emphases of the official state calendar. In addition, Augustus recurs in other contexts: the mother of Evander prophesies the rule of Augustus and his family (1.529–36); battles of Caesar and Augustus are recorded on otherwise blank dates (IV.377–84, 627–8); and the closing of the temple of Janus because of the Augustan peace (1.281–8); the disappearance of one temple leads to mention of Augustus' restoration of temples (II.55–66). In addition various interpretations reflect Augustan interests: Ovid's account of the establishment of the cult of Venus in Rome, in conflating two temples, ascribes the cult to Claudius Marcellus in 212 B.C. (IV.863–76). In earlier sources the first cult of Venus was established in Rome in 215 B.C. and not under the instigation of Marcellus, but Marcellus was the illustrious ancestor of Augustus' nephew and intended heir, who received high praise in Virgil (*Aen.* VI.855–6). Ovid also worked by suppression of awkward information. He offers three explanations of the etymology of 'June' and pleads his inability to decide among them (VI.1–100), but he makes no mention of the 'obvious' etymology, from Junius Brutus, the

[111] Dio LI.19.7 with Weinstock 1971 (F 235) 217–19; *RG* 9.1; Salii: *RG* 10.1; Dio LI.20.1. The same honour posthumously for members of the imperial family: EJ² 94a.4–5 and *AE* 1984, 508 IIc; Tac. *Ann.* II.83, IV.9.

[112] Dio LI.19.7; Petron. *Sat.* 60; Ov. *Fast.* II.637–8; cf. Hor. *Carm.* IV.5.31–2.

[113] Ov. *Pont.* IV.9.105–10; Tac. *Ann.* 1.73.2. Cf. Santero 1983 (F 214).

[114] *IItal* XIII.2, p. 401, restored with dating of Alföldi 1973 (F 83) 42–4. For examples from outside Rome see below, p. 845. See Fishwick 1969 (F 135) for the distinction between *Genius* and *numen*.

liberator of Rome from the kings (Macrob. *Sat*.1.12.31); after all, another Brutus had killed Iulius Caesar. The emperor and his achievements were formally celebrated throughout the year and his presence recurs throughout Ovid's *Fasti*, but there was no single, central religious institution devoted to the living emperor.

Emperors after death were seen in sharper focus.[115] The official cult of Caesar offered the obvious model for Augustus and subsequent emperors. Though some honours were probably voted for Caesar in his lifetime their posthumous consolidation was decisive for subsequent practice. In 42 B.C. the Senate passed the official consecration of Caesar, including the building of a temple; in 40 B.C. Antony was inaugurated as the first *flamen divi Iulii* (an office to which he had been appointed in 44 B.C.), and Augustus began to call himself *divi filius*. Finally, in 29 B.C. Augustus appointed a new *flamen* in place of Antony and dedicated the temple to Caesar, an event celebrated by lavish contests. The temple dominated the south side of the Forum Romanum and formed the backdrop for public speakers using the new tribunal in front of it. The posthumous status of Caesar was thus assured. Valerius Maximus, writing under Tiberius, related that Divus Iulius appeared to Cassius at Philippi, telling him that he did not actually kill Caesar as his *divinitas* could not be extinguished; and elsewhere Valerius prayed by Caesar's altars and temples that his divinity would favour and protect the human race (1.8.8; 6.13).

The transition of Augustus to the status long held by Caesar was smoothly managed. The expectation was expressed in his lifetime that he would ascend to his rightful place in heaven, and immediately after his death Augustus was made a *divus*. The funeral, cremation and burial in the Mausoleum were merely grand versions of the traditional funeral of the Roman nobility, but afterwards a senior senator declared on oath to the Senate that he had seen Augustus ascending to heaven. As a result, in the words of the official state calendar, 'on that day heavenly honours were decreed by the Senate to the divine Augustus'.[116] The main 'heavenly honours' were a temple, a *flamen*, who was to be a member of Augustus' own family, and a priestly college of *sodales Augustales*, leading members of the senatorial order. Augustus, like his ancestor Romulus, went to join the gods.

The practices of the Augustan age established the basic framework which prevailed for the rest of the imperial period. Emperors and members of their families were given divine honours only after their death and then only in recognition of the fact that they had, by their merits, actually become gods. This Augustan system marks a change from the tone of the triumviral period when Octavian was commonly

---

[115] Price 1987 (F 200).   [116] *IItal* XIII.2, p. 510.

thought to have held a dinner party of the Twelve Gods, himself appearing as Apollo, and when he erected a statue of himself on the Palatine in the guise of Apollo. In addition, official coins from the mint of Rome of the early 20s B.C. showed Octavian as Apollo, Jupiter and Neptune, and the original plan for the Pantheon was that it should be named after Augustus and have his statue inside it.[117]

After 27 B.C., Augustus no longer employed such imagery and his successors generally upheld his norms. There were, of course, some changes within the system. The *Genius*, or guardian spirit of Augustus had not entered the state calendar in his lifetime, though it had been honoured, mainly by freedmen, at the crossroads shrines in Rome (above, p. 823). Tiberius resisted oaths by his *Genius*, but Gaius despotically enforced them and they became standard from the reign of Nero or at least Vespasian.[118] For example, the official regulations for two towns in Spain enjoined an oath by Jupiter, various deified emperors and the *Genius* of the reigning emperor (Domitian).[119] Official sacrifices by the Arval Brethren to the *Genius* of the reigning emperor (or the Juno of the empress) are also to be found from Nero onwards. Such honours to the *Genius* were not an imperial peculiarity. Every man had his own *Genius*, and every woman her Juno, who received offerings at birthdays and also featured in oaths. But this was essentially a family matter and, despite the existence of a cult of the '*Genius* of the Roman People' by the first century B.C., official cult of the *Genius* of the emperor was slow to develop. The subordination of state to emperor implied in the public celebration of a family cult was only gradually acceptable.

The one major rejection of the Augustan norms in this period was by Gaius who, after a popular start to his reign, began to make claims to personal divinity. He is said to have sat between the statues of Castor and Pollux in their temple in the Forum, showing himself to be worshipped by those who entered; he wore the clothing or attributes of a wide range of deities, and established a temple to his own divinity.[120] Such behaviour was completely unacceptable in Rome. For his biographer it demonstrated that Gaius was no longer emperor or even king, but monster, and memory of Gaius' reign (however exaggerated) survived as a warning to subsequent emperors not to destroy the Augustan norms. Thus Claudius, by temperament a conservative with antiquarian interests, reverted to the maintenance of ancestral Roman customs. According to his biographer, 'he corrected various abuses, revived some

---

[117] Suet. *Aug.* 70. Coins: Burnett 1983 (F 108), discussing Sutherland and Carson, *RIC* I nos. 270–2. Pantheon: Coarelli 1983 (F 116) on Dio LIII.27.3.

[118] Tiberius: Dio LVII.8.3; LVIII.2.8. Gaius: Suet. *Calig.* 27.3; cf. *ILS* 192, Dio LIX.14.7.

[119] *ILS* 6088.i.30, 6089.iii.15. Cf. Weinstock 1971 (F 235) 205–6, 212–17.

[120] Suet. *Calig.* 22, 52. Cf. Philo, *Leg.* 78–113, Dio LIX.26–8.

old customs or even established some new ones'. For example, he always offered a supplication when a bird of ill omen was seen on the Capitol, and in making treaties he recited the ancient formula of the fetial priests.[121] Concern for the maintenance of the Augustan system recurs throughout the imperial period.

IV. ROME AND HER EMPIRE

The relations between Rome and her empire, to which we now turn briefly, reinforced the transformations visible in the religious system of Rome itself. These relations are normally analysed specifically as the spread of the imperial cult throughout the empire. That is, the worship of the Roman emperor is seen as the cement of empire. In fact, there was no such thing as 'the imperial cult', and in some important contexts imitation of the transformed system of Augustan Rome was of far greater significance than direct worship of the emperor.

Italy formed the core of the empire. All the freeborn population of the peninsula up to the Alps had been Roman citizens since the time of Caesar. Italy was not a province; it was not subject to Roman taxation, but remained in principle a collection of self-governing communities. But the authority of the religious institutions of Rome extended to Italy. The scope is neatly illustrated by an incident under Tiberius, when the equestrian order in Rome vowed a gift to the temple of Equestrian Fortune for the health of Livia, only to realize that there was no such shrine in Rome itself. But a temple was discovered at Antium, where the Senate decided that the gift could be placed, 'since all rituals, temples and images of the gods in Italian towns fall under Roman law and jurisdiction'. The case suits the tone of the imperial period. Expulsions of undesirables were normally from both Rome and Italy, and the Roman college of *pontifices* gave permissions to Italians on the repair of tombs or the moving of corpses.[122]

The unique position of Italy is visible most clearly in the calendar. There survive, often in small fragments, forty-four calendars dating to the reigns of Augustus and Tiberius (and one from the early first century B.C.)[123] Of thirty-eight calendars whose original location is known, twenty-five come from Rome itself, the others from towns in Italy, and only one from elsewhere, a colony in Sicily. The level of detail given in these calendars varies greatly, but all differ from earlier, Italian calendars and all are mutually compatible. They give no festivals peculiar to their

---

[121] Suet. *Claud.* 22, 25.5. Cf. Tac. *Ann.* XI.15 on *haruspices*.
[122] Tac. *Ann.* III.71.1. *Pontifices*: Millar 1977 (A 59) 359–61.
[123] Whatmough 1931 (F 236); *IItal* XIII 2; Panciera 1973–4 (E 93). The calendar from Cymae (*ILS* 108 = *IItal* XIII 2, p. 279) is very different and probably not civic.

own city, but only differing selections from the official festivals of the city of Rome. Towns in Italy, unlike those in the provinces, chose to adhere publicly to the official Roman religious calendar.

Even Italy, however, did not follow all the Roman rules. Some towns preserved their own religious institutions from pre-Roman days, even burying the dead within the town, which was impossible at Rome.[124] The ancient towns nearest Rome, who had been Rome's 'Latin' allies in the republican period, shared some of Rome's most particular practices; they claimed indeed that Rome had adopted them from the Latins. Thus Alba Longa, Lavinium, Tibur and other Latin towns had one or more of the following: *flamen Dialis*, Vestal Virgins, *rex sacrorum* and Salii.[125] The Salii and the *rex sacrorum* (and, once, the *flamen Dialis*) are also found in a few towns in northern Italy, but otherwise these offices appear almost nowhere else in the Roman empire. In addition, there was in the early empire a new flowering of (allegedly) ancient cults emphasizing the ancestral ties between the Latin towns and Rome.[126] For example, at Lavinium, where there was no settlement in the late Republic or early Empire, Italians of equestrian rank from Claudius on held a priesthood which continued the cult of the Lavinian *Penates*, participated at ceremonies of the Latin League on the Alban Hill, and renewed the treaty with Rome. In the second century A.D., with the renewal of civic life at Lavinium, local men began to hold the office, which is attested until the middle of the third century A.D. The Latin towns demonstrate in an extreme form the similarities between the religious practices of Rome and Italy.

Outside Italy replications of Roman practices were normal in the early Empire in two, related contexts: the army and colonies. The body of men which stood most clearly for Rome in the provinces was the legions, made up of Roman citizens, and with a religious life that was predominantly Roman. There was an official Roman calendar for both legions and auxiliaries that specified the year's religious festivals. The third-century archives of an auxiliary cohort, Twentieth Palmyrene, stationed on the Euphrates frontier included a copy of this calendar, which demonstrates how the restructured religious system of Augustan Rome was, in a modified form, repeated in the army.[127] On purely internal grounds it seems certain that the document is a third-century version of a calendar first issued to the legions under Augustus and subsequently also to the auxiliary forces. The first type of celebrations are in honour of the gods of Rome: Mars Pater Victor, the Quinquatria, the Neptunalia,

[124] Festus, p. 146L s.v. *municipalia sacra; Dig.* 47.12.3.5.
[125] Wissowa 1912 (F 241) 157 n.4, 519–21, 555 n.2; Ladage 1971 (F 166) 8–10.
[126] Wissowa 1915 (F 242); Purcell 1983 (F 49) 167–79; Saulnier 1984 (F 216). E.g. *ILS* 5004.
[127] Fink, Hoey and Snyder 1940 (B 368); Nock 1952 (F 193).

Salus. The circus-games in Rome founded by Augustus at the dedication of the temple of Mars Ultor in 2 B.C. were marked in the calendar, as was the festival of Vesta, another deity patronized by Augustus. The birthday of Rome was added to the calendar under Hadrian (perhaps replacing an earlier celebration of the Parilia). Secondly, there were the celebrations in honour of the reigning emperor, his family and pre-decessors. We cannot reconstruct the original version of the calendar, but there is no reason to think that there would have been few such entries. The marking of transient Augustan events, which were certainly celebrated in Rome, may easily have been pruned to make way for events of more contemporary relevance. But the birthdays of all the deified emperors and the eight deified empresses whose cult was still officially observed in Rome at this time remained in the calendar. (In fact only fifteen birthdays appear on the extant part; the others will have been in the missing section(s).) Only those deified empresses whose cult was no longer celebrated in Rome certainly do not appear on the Dura calendar. In other words, there is probably a complete correspondence between those honoured in the army and those honoured by the Arval Brethren in Rome. There were also commemorations of the accessions of at least five previous emperors, going back to Trajan, and of two other events in the reign of Septimus Severus; the legitimacy of Severus Alexander was thus strengthened by these ties to the Antonine dynasty to which Septimius Severus had linked himself. There were celebrations on at least four occasions of events in the life of the current emperor, all of which would have been in place under Augustus: for example, his first consulship and his appointment as *pontifex maximus*.

The structure of the Dura calendar is thus identical in type to the religious system of Rome itself. There were the festivals in honour of the gods, some of which now had clear imperial associations, and there were the celebrations of emperors past and present. Not that there was any opposition between the two: on 3 January vows were taken for the safety of the emperor and the eternity of the empire with sacrifices to the Capitoline triad. This was the religious system officially enjoined on the army. Nock argued that there was no official desire to see the soldiers worshipping the gods listed in the calendar rather than any other gods,[128] but this conclusion does not follow from the fact that officers and men also worshipped other gods. Rome chose to replicate its own religious system as the official basis of the Roman army.

Roman colonies were the other principal context in which the Roman religious system was replicated. This is hardly surprising as the colonists in the late Republic were landless citizens from Rome and in the early

---

[128] Nock 1952 (F 193) 223. MacMullen 1981 (F 179) 110–11 also denied that there was an official Roman religion of the army.

Empire were ex-soldiers who received land in return for their service. The regulations for the Caesarian colony at Urso in southern Spain provide our clearest evidence.[129] The extant copy of the regulations consists largely of the original rules, but with some additions of the Augustan period, and it was inscribed in the later first century A.D. The peculiarly Roman nature of Urso thus continued to provide a framework for her identity a century and more after the foundation of the colony, and may have been of particular importance at a time when other Spanish towns received another, subsidiary Roman status. The foundation of the colony began with rites that echoed those of the foundation of Rome itself. The auspices were taken and the founder ploughed a furrow round the site, lifting the plough where the gates were to be. The act was commemorated by cities on coin issues a century and more later.[130] The boundary of a colony, the equivalent of Rome's *pomerium*, was indicated by large marker stones; within it no burial could occur nor monuments to the dead be built; and the land immediately within the *pomerium* was public land which could not be expropriated even by the council.[131] Then the professional land-surveyors could proceed. One expert wrote that many surveyors positioned their sextant, after the taking of the auspices, perhaps in the presence of the actual founder, and oriented their land divisions in accordance with the direction of the sunrise.[132]

The colony at Urso celebrated its major games in honour of the Capitoline triad (sect. 70–1). This is the earliest evidence for the cult of the triad outside Italy and strongly suggests that Urso had an actual Capitolium. The building of a Capitolium, modelled on that at Rome, was certainly carried out at the creation of some early imperial military colonies. Both Cologne and Xanten in Lower Germany have Capitolia dating after their elevation to the rank of colony; the former was built not long after Cologne became a colony in A.D. 50; the latter was built perhaps 70 years after Xanten became a colony under Trajan, but in this case the entire town was rebuilt and work proceeded slowly. The great temple of Baalbek was begun in the Augustan period at a time when the town received some Roman colonists. Some of the design is purely Roman and the expenses of construction (128 monoliths of Egyptian granite) strongly suggest imperial financing. But the cults were a blend of Roman and Syrian: Jupiter Optimus Maximus Heliopolitanus, Venus and Mercury.[133]

---

[129] *ILS* 6087. Cf. D'Ors 1953 (B 222) 167–280; Mackie 1983 (E231) 222–3.

[130] Levick 1967 (E 851) 35–7, *SNG von Aulock*, Index pp. 224, 241.

[131] *ILS* 6308, Capua; Urso sect. 73; Frontin. *De controversiis* (Corpus agrimensorum Romanorum, ed. C. Thulin, p. 7; the section is misplaced in the text, but ancient).

[132] Hyginus Gromaticus, *Constitutio limitum* (ed. Thulin, p. 135; also pp. 10–11, 131–2). Cf. Le Gall 1975 (F 171) 301–8; Dilke 1988 (F 121).

[133] Bianchi 1949 (F 95); Barton 1982 (F 86). Cologne and Xanten: Ristow 1967 (F 205); Follmann-Schulz 1986 (E 579) 735–8, 766–9. Baalbek: Seyrig 1954 (E 1060); Liebeschuetz 1977 (E 1035) 485–9.

The priestly colleges, of *pontifices* and augurs, were established in colonies (and *municipia*) on Roman lines,[134] and some of the actual rituals of the colonies were also expressly modelled on Rome. Two colonies founded (or refounded) in the middle of the first century B.C. illustrate the point. Narbo in southern France dedicated an altar to the *numen* of Augustus in technically accurate religious formulae. Some of the precise regulations were spelled out; 'the other rules for this altar and inscriptions shall be the same as those for the altar of Diana on the Aventine'. The colony of Salona on the Dalmatian coast used almost identical formulae in dedicating an altar to Jupiter Optimus Maximus. This procedure is again strictly Roman, with a local pontifex reciting the words in advance of the presiding magistrate. The same details are given and the remainder are to follow the rules for the altar of Diana on the Aventine.[135] The temple of Diana on the Aventine hill in Rome was of great antiquity – allegedly founded by Servius Tullius *c.* 540 B.C. as a sanctuary common both to Rome and her Latin allies; inscriptions in archaic lettering certainly existed in the sanctuary down to the Augustan period.[136] This set of rules was not only ancient; it also governed the relations between Rome and the outside world, and was thus a singularly appropriate model for use in Roman colonies. The colonies made reference to Rome not only in the generation after they were founded (or refounded), but, in the case of Salona, some 170 years later. For some colonies at least, Roman rules provided a continuing framework for their religious identity.

Communities and associations not made up of Roman citizens did not seek to replicate the Roman system, but responded to Rome in their own fashions. In the East, Greek towns maintained their traditional religious systems, worshipping their own selection of the Olympic pantheon, as Pausanias was to describe in the second century A.D. They also commonly chose to establish cults of the living Augustus, sometimes in the context of their ancestral cults. For example, in one Macedonian town a local citizen volunteered to be priest of Zeus, Roma and Augustus, and he displayed extraordinary munificence in the monthly sacrifices to Zeus and Augustus and in the feasts and games for the citizens.[137] The text is a clear illustration of the integration of the worship of Augustus within local religious and social structures. In the Latin West too towns below colonial status sometimes established cults of the living Augustus, which did not correspond to practice in Rome but did express their position in the Roman hierarchy.[138]

---

[134] Ladage 1971 (F 166) 10–11, 32–5, 39–41, 51–4, 79–80, 103; Galsterer 1971 (E 221) 59–61.

[135] *ILS* 112 = *FIRA* III 73 (Narbo, A.D. 11) – the colony may have been founded originally in the late second century B.C.; *ILS* 4907 = *FIRA* III 74 (Salona, A.D. 137). Cf. *CIL* XI 361 (Ariminum).

[136] Dion. Hal. *Ant. Rom.* IV.26.5; Festus, p. 164.

[137] *Arch. Eph.* (1983) 75–84, A.D. 1. Cf Price 1984 (F 199).   [138] Fayer 1976 (F 134) 213–36.

The associations in both East and West which united these towns at the provincial level also established cults that referred to Rome. The practice began in the East when the Greeks of Asia and Bithynia-Pontus were given permission in 29 B.C. to establish cults of Roma and Augustus. Similarly the assembly of the province of Syria also acquired a priest of Augustus and games.[139] The Greeks thus expressed, in an entirely acceptable manner, their subordination to Rome. In barbarian areas of the West, which had just been conquered (as the Romans hoped), the Romans felt it appropriate to encourage similar institutions. For example, in north-west Spain soon after the Augustan conquest a governor established three altars to Augustus which were probably to serve as centres for three peoples in the north-west area; or, the three provinces of Gaul conquered by Caesar were united in 12 B.C. in a single provincial assembly at Lugdunum at an altar of Rome and Augustus, dedicated by Drusus, Augustus' step-son.[140] In the case of more 'civilized' western provinces, provincial cults were slow to appear, and followed strictly Roman models. In the two long-established Spanish provinces, after Augustus' official consecration in Rome, temples to the deified Augustus were built, with priests of the same name (*flamen*) as in Rome.

The place of religion was the city of Rome. Myths recounted aspects of the Roman past and related to features of Roman topography; individual festivals and cults were founded at a particular time and particular place. For example, the Ara Maxima was established at the time when Hercules passed through the area and the festival of the Parilia was associated with Romulus and the creation of Rome. Emphasis on the places at which cults had to be celebrated went together with an emphasis on the importance of a boundary round the site of Rome. At the Parilia Romulus defined a line, the *pomerium*, round the new city which was of crucial importance to Augustan consciousness of place, within it lay the key cults of Rome and only within it were civil auspices possible. Outside the *pomerium* were foreign cults, the sphere of military authority, and the burials of the dead.

The religion of place was adapted to accommodate the figure of the emperor, Augustus, seen as the second Romulus, and he expressed his religious position through the traditional priesthoods, through temple building, and through the celebration of the Secular Games. Though the individual elements had earlier parallels, their combination was novel and resulted in a new and remarkably coherent system centred on the emperor. The religion of place was now restructured round a person.

---

[139] Dio LI.20.6–7. Syria: *AE* 1976, 678; *I Magnesia* 149.

[140] Spain: Tranoy 1981 (E 244) 327–9. Gaul: Livy, *Epit.* 139. See further Fishwick 1987 (F 137) 97–168.

But it is misleading to categorize this as 'the imperial cult'. The term arbitrarily separates honours to the emperor from the full range of his religious activities, and it assumes that there was a single institution of cult throughout the empire. Within Rome, honours to the emperor have to be seen in the light of his holding of religious office, while outside Rome it is wrong to look only for honours to the emperor. In the context of the army and colonies, real clones of Rome, the copying of other Roman religious practices was at least as important. And when, as in Greek towns, religious honours to the emperor were of considerable significance, they were not replications of Roman honours. Indeed the Roman system was not designed to be replicated (except in the army and colonies). Its principal features were specific to the site of Rome, and the growing emphasis on those features served to distinguish Rome from other towns and to express the peculiar position of Rome as the capital of the empire.

CHAPTER 17

THE ORIGINS AND SPREAD
OF CHRISTIANITY[1]

G. W. CLARKE

I. ORIGINS AND SPREAD

Renewal and reform movements in Palestinian Judaism are well represented in the first-century generations preceding the fall of Jerusalem
and the destruction of the Temple A.D. 70; they flourished in a religious
context which lacked sharply defined doctrines and practices, where
there was no clearly accepted orthodoxy or authority. Not only was there
a range of distinguishable sects (the most notable being, of course, the
Pharisees, the Sadducees and the Essenes – but there were a number of
others, most prominent among which was the 'Philosophy of Judas'
with his politically active followers, the Sicarii and Zealots);[2] there was,
in addition, a bewildering array of individual ascetics, prophets and
preachers who frequently drew in great crowds and commanded
dedicated followings.[3] What they often shared in common was a passion
for the Torah and the Temple but what often distinguished them was
their precise definition, in ritual practice, of purity and sacrifice.
Messianic expectations were in the air – but they were by no means
shared equally by all, nor was there even agreement on the nature of
those messianic hopes.[4] Ethical debate went hand-in-hand with debate
over ritual and ceremony, diet and custom, oral law and written law, the
interpretation of the Torah; it was all part of the same process of drawing
the boundaries between purity and pollution, holiness and sin, in
defining for Israel the will of God. Doctrinal debate there certainly was,

---

[1] I have chosen a few generally non-controversial features of the ministry of Jesus: for these one
is necessarily reliant upon the evidence of the synoptic gospels (composed in their present form near
or generally after the destruction of the Temple, the chronological terminus of this study). But for
the most part I have preferred to follow as far as possible the contemporary witness of Paul and his
associates (supplemented, unavoidably, by the additional testimony of Acts). That way I hope to
eschew as much as I can the anachronistic perceptions of the early Christian past (embedded in the
Canon as it became later formed) as Christianity developed its own self-awareness and its own sense
of separate identity and sought legitimation for those developments in its preferred accounts of its
past.
[2] Josephus (*Vit.* 10) experienced all three major sects 'in order to select the best'. Some of the
smaller sects are registered by *inter alios* Hegesippus *ap.* Euseb. *Hist. Eccl.* 4.22.7, Justin, *Dial.* 80, not
to mention the Qumran sectarians. On the Philosophy of Judas see Schürer 1979 (E 1207) II 598ff.
[3] Some examples are to be found in Joseph. *Vit.* 11, BJ, II.4.1ff (55 ff) = *AJ* XVII.10.5 ff (271 ff);
BJ II.13.4 (258 ff) = *AJ* xx.8.6 (167 f).   [4] See Schürer 1979 (E 1207) 488ff ('Messianism').

especially centred on the after-life, immortality and resurrection, but the debates at least shared the same religious and cultural preoccupations.

Into such a religious context with its ferment of debate and diversity fit the movements of John the Baptist (urging a renewal of Israel in the wilderness and a new passage through the 'sea' of the Jordan), and of Jesus of Nazareth round about A.D. 30 (Christian sources being at pains, somewhat apologetically, to subordinate the former to the latter). Jesus' central activities of teaching in the synagogues, attending the Temple services, keeping the festivals – and disputing with other teachers (especially represented, at least in later tradition, as sharpening his views against those of the Pharisees) – these place him in the mainstream of contemporary religious occupations. And his central concerns fit comfortably into the continuing debate within the Judaism of the day, often characterized as they are with reformist tendencies: concerns for Temple purity and cleansing (Mark 11:15ff, Matt. 21:12f, Luke 19:45ff, John 2:14ff), concerns for intentional purity in worship as well as in morals (e.g. Matt. 5:21ff), concerns for the purity of the person (casting out of demons/curing the sick), concerns for love of neighbour (extended even to loving one's enemies, Matt. 5:43ff), concerns for regulating the sexual code of behaviour (with a restrictive view on divorce, Matt. 5:31f, 19:3ff), concerns for giving primacy to moral (as opposed to ceremonial) law (Mark 3:1ff (healing on the Sabbath)). The carpenter from Nazareth in Lower Galilee, with his chosen inner circle of fishermen (that is to say, drawn roughly from the 'small tradesman' class[5]) could certainly bluntly reject Mammon and outspokenly condemn the snares of riches (e.g. Matt. 6:24 = Luke 16:13), but this did not prevent him from fraternizing with wealthy tax-gatherers, worldly sinners, women of ill-repute and Gentiles[6] (and other social outcasts). For what he fervently preached was the urgent need for repentance before the impending *eschaton*[7] and the people to whom he spoke his message were not just the Torah-observant: sinners, the unrighteous, had even greater need of his call. There is an increasingly catholic sense of the definition of 'the children of Abraham', the true Israel who might enter upon the kingdom, and a continuous debate with contemporary 'Judaisms' about the sufficient and necessary conditions for entering upon that kingdom (now envisaged as so nigh). These are lines of debate which eventually opened the way to 'Gentile Christianity': did the twelve disciples come symbolically to represent the twelve tribes of this new Israel so soon to enter upon that

---

[5] Compare the story recorded by Hegesippus *ap.* Euseb. *Hist Eccl.* III.20.1ff (descendants of Jesus' family in the time of Domitian are small-holding farmers).

[6] Examples of contact with Gentiles are Mark 7:25ff (cf. Matt. 15:22ff), Matt. 8:5ff (cf. Luke 7:2ff).

[7] Was the scandalous prophecy of the destruction of the Temple intended as an indication of this coming End?

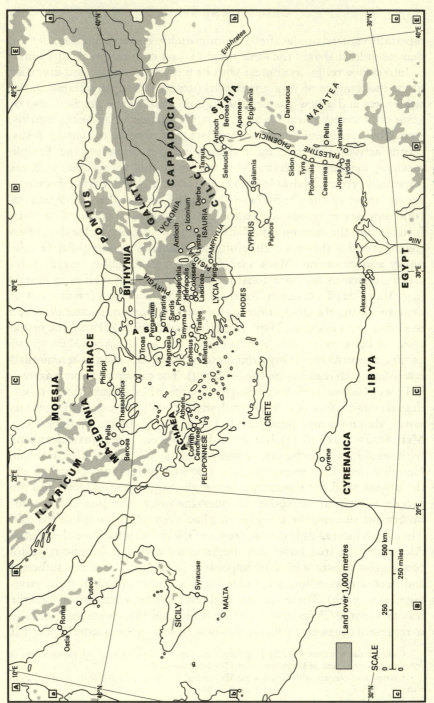

Map 21. The eastern Mediterranean in the first century A.D. illustrating the origins and spread of Christianity.

kingdom? But what Jesus demanded of his chosen disciples was a renunciation of family and worldly goods, a single-minded dedication and a proselytizing zeal to spread the word (e.g. Mark 10:28ff) which ensured that his movement did not remain confined just to sympathetic families and pious followers within Lower Galilee and Jerusalem even after his ignominious death (*c.* A.D. 30): their conviction of his resurrection became the decisive confirmation of his messiahship. The movement from these local Palestinian origins began to spread.

The Pentecostal scene in Jerusalem, as depicted in Acts 2:9ff, has Peter preaching to Jews who have gathered in Jerusalem from the Diaspora. There are 'Parthians, Medes, Elamites; inhabitants of Mesopotamia, Judaea and Cappadocia, of Pontus and Asia, of Phrygia and Pamphylia, of Egypt and the parts of Libya around Cyrene; visitors from Rome, both Jews and proselytes,[8] Cretans and Arabs ...'. This appears to be telling us in general terms that in the view of the writer the Christian message would be disseminated via these sojourners back to Rome and to the regions of the eastern Mediterranean beyond the Aegean (and to the islands of the Mediterranean) as well as along the north African littoral as far as Cyrenaica. After all, there were present at this scene 'devout Jews drawn from every nation under heaven' (2:5). But our information on the processes of this dissemination is fugitive and haphazard, leaving us with very little confidence in conceptualizing accurately the size and social configuration of the Christian communities formed down to the Flavian era. We can, of course, trace the work of one such emissary, viz. Paul, and whilst aware that his growing special sense of mission to the Gentiles will have dictated particular routes and contacts, particular missionary targets, we have basically to be content to take his missionary journeyings (their precise chronology and itineraries do not matter for this exercise) as roughly symptomatic of the types of community and area where Christian groups (in however minimal a gathering) became established in the first forty years after the death of Christ.

Indicative, however, of our general ignorance are Egypt and Cyrene, mentioned in Acts but lacking, in fact, any specific Pauline connexion.[9] Legend (but legend only) was required in later time to provide an

[8] The relative frequency of the appearance in the New Testament corpus of 'godfearers' (but more rarely 'proselytes') suggests awareness of the significance to the Christian movement of those non-Jewish sympathizers located more to the margins of Jewish communities. Among many discussions Schürer 1986 (E 1207) 160ff, Reynolds and Tannenbaum 1987 (E 1198) esp. 48ff, Goodman 1989 (D 132) 42f.

[9] Later, the Muratorian Canon (purportedly of the middle of the second century) can register a palpably fictitious epistle of Paul to the Alexandrians (*PL* 3.191f). There occurs incidentally in the Pauline following the learned Jew, Apollos of Alexandria (Acts 18:24), as well as the converted Jews from Cyrene (Acts 11:20) with whom Paul and Barnabas laboured at Antioch (Acts 11:22ff, 13:1–3: their number presumably included the Lucius of Acts 13:1).

apostolic-period pedigree for 'the Alexandrian churches'.[10] And despite geographical proximity to Jerusalem, despite second-century papyrological evidence for the remarkably early and remarkably penetrating spread of Christian literature between the Delta and Upper Egypt,[11] and despite the inherent likelihood that the Christian message would have found some sympathetic hearers, however few, in the region (given the well-documented Jewish communities of Cyrenaica and Alexandria, displaying a fair degree of permeability with their hellenistic cultural context),[12] despite all these factors we cannot go any further without blind conjecture. And we have to compound that conjecture with the surmise that such nascent Christian communities, still identified as Jewish, suffered virtual annihilation along with their parent communities in the later Jewish revolt under Trajan A.D. 115–17. And being without Pauline details also, we are similarly ignorant of Christian penetration into the land of the Arabs, let alone into the territory east of the Euphrates, among Medes and Parthians (despite the considerable Jewish Diaspora).[13] Paul seems to claim to have sojourned for some 'three years' in 'Arabia' (elastic term) according to Gal. 1:17f, but this could well have been in one or other of the southern hellenizing cities of the Decapolis (and the failure of churches in the area to claim Pauline foundation suggests that the sojourn may not even have been primarily missionary in intent).[14] Even so, we know the land was destined soon to become a richly Christianized area: already in the northernmost city of the Decapolis, Damascus, Christians were to be found in the Jewish community before the time of Paul's conversion (Acts 9:2ff),[15] that is to say, in the course of the thirties. This chance glimpse is a salutary reminder of our overall ignorance. Elsewhere in Syria proper (to which Damascus technically belonged)[16] we are relatively well informed about the rich and flourishing, as well as confidently independent, community established in the far north of the province, in the great urban complex of

[10] Thus, *inter alios*, Eus. *Hist. Eccl.* II.16.1, 2.24 (Mark the evangelist) along with the legendary *Acta Marci*: by the early fourth century a *martyrium* (with *tumba, coemeterium* and *sanctuarium*) could be located in Alexandria in Mark's memory (*Acta Petri, PG* 18.461, 462, 464) and was a site for later pilgrimage, Pallad. *Hist. Laus.* 45.4. (Philoromus).

[11] See Roberts 1979 (F 206).

[12] Note especially (on Cyrenaica) Lüderitz 1983 (B 250), cf. Applebaum 1979 (E 773), and (for Alexandria) the life and work of Philo (Schürer 1987 (E 1207) III.2 809ff) and more generally *CPJ* II (1960).

[13] The legends of Abgar and of Thaddaeus' mission (e.g. Eus. *Hist. Eccl.* I.13, II.1.6f) reflect the spread to Edessa and into Mesopotamia but it is well to remember that such spread was to be erratic in character (e.g. Carrhae, nearby to Edessa, was long to be a largely pagan stronghold, Theodoret *Hist. Eccl.* IV.15, Egeria 20).   [14] On Pella see below.

[15] Some notion of the size of the Jewish community can be derived from Josephus' figures for those claimed to have been slain in the Jewish revolt a generation later. BJ II.561 (10,500), VII.368 (18,000).

[16] In Paul's day (2 Cor. 2:32) Damascus had been under an ethnarch of the Nabataean king of Arabia, Aretas IV: by imperial concession?

Antioch (on the Orontes), thanks again to the Pauline connexion, for Paul seems to have spent some twelve years or so 'in the regions of Syria and Cilicia' according to Gal. 1:21, 2:1 (cf. Acts 11:25f, 13:1, 15:35) – this should include most or all of the decade of the forties. Notoriously, Antioch is depicted by Paul (Gal. 2:1ff) as well as by the author of Acts (11:20ff) as the *fons et origo* of 'Gentile Christianity': here the process of Christian self-identification is declared to have its beginning. But as for the rest of the country we have to be content to know that there were brethren of Gentile origin in Syria itself besides Antioch (Acts 15:23, cf. 15:41) – but whether these were to be found scattered among the village communities typical of the settlement pattern of the Syrian countryside or in the great Syrian cities like Apamea, Epiphania or Beroea we simply do not know.[17] All we can say is that if Paul was involved in their foundation[18] his practice was beyond doubt to bring his missionary efforts to bear on urban areas of concentration, particularly where (if we follow the narrative of Acts) there were Jewish synagogues (and Gentile Jewish-sympathizers). Certainly the Syrian Christian communities were soon to prove to be a rich source of extra-canonical texts.

By contrast, Palestine itself has more in the way of details recorded, not unnaturally given the nature of our evidence. But where we can, by means of incidental information, flesh out 'the churches in Judaea' (Gal. 1:22, cf. 1 Thes. 2:14, Acts 11:29 ('the brethren dwelling in Judaea'), we happen to find predominating the seaboard cities and ports (with their mobile and mixed populations, strongly under the influence of – if not dominated by – hellenistic culture) such as Sidon (Acts 27:3), Tyre (Acts 21:4), Ptolemais (Acts 21:7) – and Phoenicia in general (Acts 11:19, 15:3) – Caesarea (Acts 10, 21:8) and Joppa (Acts 9:36, 9:42f, 10:23).[19] In Caesarea, in fact, the procurator's headquarters, we are presented with an emblematic cameo, the miraculous conversion of Cornelius (a god-fearer), a centurion of the *cohors Italica*, symbol of Gentile authority (Acts 10) – along with his household (10:2, 10:44ff). But whilst our chance information certainly highlights such hellenized cities we cannot exclude the smaller towns and village communities dispersed throughout Galilee, Judaea and Samaria – in fact we have specific mention of villages in Samaria (Acts 8:25) evangelized by Peter and John following on the missionary activities of Philip and a more general scattering of preachers

[17] Our next information is not until the early second century when Ignatius, bishop of Antioch, can refer to churches (plural) with bishops, in the immediate neighbourhood of Antioch, *ad Philad.* 10 (? including the port of Seleucia, Acts 13:4).

[18] Other known missionaries at Antioch are converted Jews from Cyprus and Cyrene (Acts 11:20), Barnabas from Jerusalem but by birth a Cypriot (Acts 4:36, 11:22), the Gentile Titus (Gal. 2:2f), Simeon called Niger, Manaen, Lucius of Cyrene (Acts 13:1), John Mark (Acts 12:25, from Jerusalem) – as well as visitors from Jerusalem (Silas, Judas Barsabbas (Acts 15:22), Cephas (Gal. 2:11), Agabus (Acts 11:27f).   [19] For these cities see Schürer 1979 (E 1207), II §23.7, 9, 11.

of the Word through the country districts of Judaea and Samaria in the aftermath of Stephen's death (Acts 8:1, 8:4, 11:19, cf. Acts 15:3 (Paul and Barnabas travelling among the followers, through Samaria)). We can be precise only about the town of Lydda (close to Joppa), Acts 9:33, 9:35, on the road from Joppa to Jerusalem, and the coastal plain of Sharon, Acts 9:35, during a missionary tour of Peter's; inland Galilee, figuring so prominently in Christ's own mission, fades completely from our view (but note Mark 15:7 hinting at continuing evangelization: 'He [the risen Lord] will go on before you into Galilee and you will see him there'). Indeed if we are to judge from the cases where Christianity failed to establish itself with any significant presence even by the early fourth century – in, for example, such major inland towns as Sepphoris or Tiberias, Epiph. *Adv. Haeres.* 30:11[20] – then we must surmise that resistance could be strong, if not complete, in some of the more traditional Jewish towns and cities: we would do well to take with caution such jingoistic passages as Acts 21:20 ('myriads of believers among the Jews') and regard the following in Palestine as neither particularly numerous nor evenly distributed: agreed, our sources force us to view the expansion as basically an urban phenomenon but we must allow for at least some haphazard establishment in the countryside also. Even so, the holy city of Jerusalem is the focus of attention in our sources, firstly under the leadership of James, the brother of the Lord (Acts 15:13, Gal. 2:9), succeeded, according to tradition, by Simeon, son of Clopas, a cousin (Eus. *Hist. Eccl.* III.11, cf. IV.22.4). In Acts we are carefully provided with staggered statistics emphasizing the regular but spectacular growth of the church in the city, presented as the centre of Christendom: in 2:41 some 3,000 converts are added in a day, 2:47 sees daily increases, by 4:4 the numbers have reached about 5,000, there are more by 6:1, 6:7 attests to further rapid additions (including a large number of the priests), and general growth is recorded in 9:31 and yet again in 12:24, and by 15:5 we find some of the Pharisees are believers. So it comes as no surprise that in 21:20 it can be claimed that many thousands among the Jews have become believers. We do hear of (dissatisfied) Greek-speaking Jews (from the Diaspora?) in 6:1ff and it is Paul (it is emphasized) who talks and debates in Jerusalem with the Greek-speaking Jews in 9:28 – but these are pointedly exceptional, leaving us with the clear and deliberate impression of an overwhelmingly Jewish-Christian community, predominantly Hebrew-speaking, in which the many thousands among the Jews who have become believers are also 'all zealots for the Law' (Acts 21:20). Any Gentile converts are allowed to be visible only outside Jerusalem (Acts 10) and

---

[20] Though we must be aware of fluctuating populations over time, and changing levels of tolerance, Schürer 1979 (E 1207), II §23.31 and 33.

are made to be a cause for astonishment to Jewish believers from Jerusalem (Acts 10:45, 11:2ff) and for scandal (Acts 15:5): we are left in no doubt that until the 'Apostolic Decree' any such Gentile converts were obliged to submit to circumcision and to 'the observance of the Law' (Acts 15:1, 15:5) – however that was interpreted. We cannot go beyond the picture thus provided for us – and for what it is worth, the enigmatic Epistle of James (virtually a Jewish document) accords.[21] And it also accords with the whole tendency of Acts that despite the claims of growth for the Jerusalem church, the church in Antioch, with its clear-headed and divinely sanctioned Gentile mission, is represented as the more enterprising and the more prosperous (Acts 11:29): that may well have been the case.

So far we have been pressing into service for the most part the testimony of the Acts of the Apostles, itself composed possibly several generations after these events and composed moreover with a disarming tendency to telescope events and with a sharply focused historicizing agenda. From now on Paul himself, along with his associates and disciples, become our almost exclusive guide together with that (deceptively and tendentiously coherent) narrative of Acts. That is to say that we rely on the Paul of the seven indubitably genuine letters – though some of these may already be themselves composite documents (1 Thess., 1 Cor., 2 Cor., Gal., Rom., Phil., Philem.). The post-Pauline or deutero-Pauline epistles (2 Thess., Eph., Col. including the Pastorals, 1 Tim., 2 Tim., Titus) provide, on the whole, merely general and corroborative testimony.[22] And, notoriously, even of Paul's own missionary work we can glimpse but a partial view (though with some locations – such as Corinth – fortuitously visible to us under a disproportionately searching light). Thus even though Paul spent so long in the vicinity of his home city of Tarsus and its province of Cilicia – apparently some dozen years at least, Gal. 1:21, 2:1 – we are entirely without details of the centres of population he may have visited, of any success his mission may have had, let alone knowing with whom.[23] All we can say is that the Cilician churches are linked closely with Syrian Antioch. They share in the Pauline attitude towards Gentile salvation, their congregations definitely include Gentile Christians (Acts 15:23, cf. 15:41). If we move on westwards around the coastline in Pamphylia we find preaching only at

[21] Consult, for example, Evans 1970 (F 132) 264f.

[22] The Pastorals, for example, yield Corinth (2 Tim. 4:20), Troas (2 Tim. 4:13), Ephesus (1 Tim. 1:3, 2 Tim. 1:18, 2 Tim. 4:12), Miletus (2 Tim. 4:20) and Galatia (2 Tim. 4:10) – all otherwise attested. But they do record, additionally, Nicopolis (Titus 3:12), Dalmatia (2 Tim. 4:10) and Crete (Titus 1:5): on these see below.

[23] Three *syggeneis* ('kinsmen') of Paul's are sent greetings in Rome (from Corinth), Rom. 16:7, 16:11 (Andronicus, Junia[s], Heroidion) and three further *syggeneis* in Corinth send greetings to Rome, Rom. 16:21 (Lucius, Jason and Sosipatros). Are they fellow-Cilicians? Throughout I assume – though this is far from uncontested – that Rom. 16 is an integral part of the original letter to the Romans.

Perge (Acts 14:25, cf. 13:13), but for Lycia or Isauria we know nothing. Inland, however, in the Roman province of Galatia we reach Pauline country. In Lycaonia we encounter (in Acts) three cities. At Iconium (Acts 14:1–6, 21), a large number of converts are recorded among the Jews and Greeks as the result of a visit by Paul and Barnabas to the synagogue: the 'Greeks' are manifestly, in some sense, already 'god-fearers' (Acts 14:1). At the neighbouring town of Lystra (to the south west of Iconium) Paul and Barnabas are depicted amidst an initially adoring and enthusiastic native audience (Acts 14:8ff), with stalwart converts (Acts 14:20), and at Derbe (to the south east of Iconium) they are seen winning 'many converts' (Acts 14:21).[24] It is worth noting that this missionary journey of Paul and Barnabas included the surrounding country (*perichoros*) of these cities (Acts 14:6) and that they are able to report back to Antioch how God had 'opened up the gates of faith to the Gentiles' (Acts 14:27). Whilst this is all information carefully patterned for our benefit, it is worth registering that the mission seems to have reached tribal areas (and not only Jewish communities within hellenized cities – which could, indeed, boast of Roman colonial status). The return journey recorded in Acts 16:1–5 by Paul and Silas sees further increases.

In Pisidia we have instanced Antioch only (Acts 13:14ff), where Paul is made to address (successfully) in the synagogue a mixed audience of Jews and Gentile godfearers (Acts 13:26, 43).[25] Further northwards we have the journey 'through the Phrygian and Galatian country' towards Bithynia. No towns are specified and (though it is an insoluble conundrum) Paul's 'Galatians' may well refer to tribal communities and villages in this area[26] (rather than to the hellenized cities included in the Roman province of Galatia to the south and west). We have to allow that Pauline converts were not confined to such cities – though (to our knowledge) he would appear to have been most effective within them. As for Phrygia, though Acts is unspecific, we can reasonably rely on the three churches of the Lycus valley mentioned in the Letter to the Colossians, viz. Colossae (Col. 1:2), Laodicea (Col. 2:1, 4.12–17, cf. Apoc. 3:14ff) and nearby Hierapolis (Col. 4:13, 16) – and there may have been other communities (Col. 2.1). At the time of writing Paul is depicted as never having visited the congregations (Col. 2:1) but the

[24] Timothy is one named Christian, from Lystra (of mixed Jewish and Greek parentage), Acts 16:1–3 (2 Tim. 1:5 purports to record further family details): Gaius is another (Acts 20:4), from Derbe.

[25] Paul had made straight for Pisidian Antioch (via Perge) from Cyprus. Did the converted proconsul of Cyprus, Sergius Paulus, provide Paul with entrée into the colony (the family of Sergius Paulus having close links with that city)?

[26] The addressees of the Letter to the Galatians were once Gentile pagans, now tempted to revert to pagan ways (Gal. 4:8–11) and under pressure to submit to circumcision and other observances of the Law (e.g. Gal. 5:2ff). They did not easily fit with the Gentile godfearers and the Jews characterized as the converts (say) at Iconium or Pisidian Antioch.

churches are declared to have been founded (Col. 1:7–8) and supported (Col. 4:7ff) by his associates:[27] the addressees appear inclined to some form of Jewish-hellenistic syncretism (Col. 2:8, 15ff).

But further northwards again, in Bithynia and Pontus, we must remain in ignorance of any establishment, Paul being (mysteriously) thwarted of reaching there (Acts. 16:7). But the later evidence of 1 Pet. 1:1 (addressed to the elect dwelling in 'Pontus, Galatia, Cappadocia, Asia and Bithynia') as well as of Pliny, Ep. x.96.6 (Christian converts of over twenty years' standing in Pontus – that is, dating back to the eighties) is indication enough that evangelization cannot have been long thwarted.[28] Likewise for Cappadocia, to the east of Galatia. We need to recall that Jews from Pontus and Cappadocia are represented as witnesses at the Pentecostal scene in Acts 2:9.

It is clear that down towards the Asia Minor seaboard Paul made the great cosmopolitan city of Ephesus, the province's metropolis, his headquarters for missionary work along the Aegean littoral, whether in person or through his now growing following of associates (as in the Lycus valley).[29] We see him first at Ephesus on a brief visit (on his way back from Greece to Syria, in the early fifties) sounding out the vigorous and sizable Jewish population (Acts 18:19f). By the time he returns by the overland route (i.e. via Galatia and Phrygia) in about the mid-fifties we are given to believe that the Alexandrian Jew Apollos has already made converts in the synagogue (Acts 18:24ff). But Acts is careful to establish that they have been imperfectly instructed, they are without the Holy Spirit – and they number but a dozen (Acts 19:1–7): it is Paul who is shown to bring the full Faith. Acts is also at pains to emphasize that the Pauline mission was aimed initially at the Ephesian Jews but after three months of Jewish resistance and hostility, Paul opened his message (in the lecture hall of Tyrannus) to a more general audience and eventually it was heard by 'all the inhabitants of the province of Asia, Jew and Greek alike' (Acts 19:10), to the discomfiture of both diehard Jews (the story of the seven sons of Sceva, Acts 19:13ff) and diehard Greeks (the story of Demetrius and the silversmiths, Acts 19:23ff). Whilst Acts declares a missionary period of some two years, with evangelizing 'not only at Ephesus but also in practically the whole of the province of Asia' (Acts 19:26, cf. 19:10), we are not given details of other locations but we do learn, incidentally, of Christian communities at the ports of Miletus

---

[27] Ep. Philemon (certainly Pauline, unlike Col.) also records many of these same names. Consult Hemer 1986 (B 80) 178ff on these cities of the Lycus.

[28] Note, incidentally, the Christian Jew, Aquila of Pontus, Acts 18:2.

[29] They include, during this period, Priscilla and Aquila (Acts 18:26). Timothy and Erastus (Acts 19:22), Gaius and Aristarchus (Acts 19:29). Col 4:7ff preserves some further names (cf. Philem. 1f, 11, 23f).

(Acts 20:15ff, cf. 2 Tim. 4:20) and of Troas (Acts 20:5ff, 2 Cor. 2:12, cf. 2 Tim. 4:13). The focus remains for us Paul, and his work at Ephesus.

But the 'seven cities' of the *Apocalypse* should be guide enough to the sorts of other communities where Christians were soon to reside. Besides Ephesus (Apoc. 2:1ff) they included not only the large urban centres of Smyrna (Apoc. 2:8ff), Pergamum (Apoc. 2:12ff) and Sardis (Apoc. 3:1ff) but more minor towns such as Thyatira (Apoc. 2:18ff) and Philadelphia (Apoc. 3.7ff). And we could reasonably surmise that there were more.[30] Paul and his associates were not the only bearers of the message in Asia, whether it arrived via itinerant missionaries or mobile believers returning home.[31] Asia Minor was well on the way to becoming the heartland of Hellenic Christianity. And whilst Acts has Paul's mission in Asia aimed first at Jew, and then at Greek as well as Jew, the deutero-Pauline encyclical letter to Christians of Asia (known as the Letter to the Ephesians) is certainly addressed to an audience envisaged primarily as Gentile ('you, Gentiles as you are in the flesh, you called the uncircumcised', Eph. 2:11; 'I, Paul, who in the cause of you Gentiles am prisoner of Christ', Eph. 3.1). These Gentiles are seen in the *Haustafel* section of the letter (5:22ff, a section devoted to moral instructions on the proper ordering of the Christian household) as established families, as hierarchically structured Christian households, not only of husbands, wives and children but of masters and slaves as well (6:5ff): here Christianity has moved, at least for some, into the slave-owning levels of Hellenic society (cf. Ep. Philemon, at Colossae).

We now cross the Aegean to Macedonia and Achaea: it is a crossing and landfall which Acts makes into a significant and solemn moment (16:6ff), perhaps to be dated to the end of the forties. Here six communities are known to us. At his initial major landfall in Macedonia, at Philippi on the Via Egnatia, Paul, accompanied by Silas (and presumably Timothy), encounters for the first time a population predominantly Latin in character (it was a Roman colony which had received two groups of veteran settlers) – and he encounters the sort of reception and resistance that is to be characteristically Roman ('they are advocating customs which it is not lawful for us, being Romans, to adopt and follow', Acts 16:21, cf. Phil. 2:2). Physical assault by the city magistrates (*strategoi*) and temporary imprisonment follow – until, famously, Paul and Silas (= Silvanus) reveal their Roman citizenship (Acts 16:37ff). Acts has the new arrivals seek out on the Sabbath 'the

---

[30] Two strong candidates are, of course, Magnesia on the Meander and Tralles, to whom Ignatius writes early in the second century.

[31] One thinks, for example, of Lydia the purple-seller, from Thyatira but domiciled at Philippi at the time of Acts 16:14f, 40.

place of prayer'[32] outside the city gate – Jews are marginalized in this Romanized community – and, symbolically, they win over the household of a godfearer (Lydia) as they do later the household of their Gentile gaoler. Jewish converts go unmentioned; and they are absent from the hortatory Letter to the Philippians except for the attack (3.2ff) on those enemies ('those dogs') who insist on circumcision and other external observances. Here was formed a community notably generous in its contributions both to Paul (Phil. 4:15ff, cf. 2 Cor. 11:8f) and for the Jerusalem collection (2 Cor. 8:1f, 9:2ff ('the churches in Macedonia'), cf. Rom. 15:26), but there are no grounds for us to visualize it as a particularly sizable Christian group.

The missionary itinerary has Paul then aim for the next Jewish community, in the provincial headquarters and the large trading city of Thessalonica. Again Acts is careful to record Paul's habit of attending the synagogue and to note that a few (only) of the local Jews are persuaded (was Jason, and his household, one such?, Acts 17:5), whereas a great number of the Greek godfearers as well as a good number of the leading (Gentile) women (Acts 17:4)[33] are declared won over: indeed convert Jews go unaddressed in the Letters to the Thessalonians (note especially 1 Thess. 1:9, 2:14ff envisaging a Gentile readership). And we are left in no doubt of the virulent hostility roused in the Jewish community generally (Acts 17:5ff, cf. 1 Thess. 1:14ff, 3:2f), a hostility which hounds Paul, Silas and Timothy even at Beroea (reached via Pella?), their next halting-place, known to us only from Acts (17:10ff). And this, despite a warmer reception in the local synagogue of Beroea, with correspondingly, many Jewish converts as well as a considerable number of Greek women of high status and men[34] (Acts 17:12). It is well to be mindful of the rich variations in contemporary Judaism and hence in receptivity to Christian missionaries.

Apart from these three centres we have no knowledge of other locations to which Paul might be referring when he mentions (in 1 Thess. 4:10) 'all the brethren in the whole of Macedonia'. For our one source (Acts again, 17:14f) has Paul travel on hastily to Athens in the province of Achaea[35] where he is presented (as standard) speaking with Jews and godfearers (in the synagogue) and with passers-by (in the *agora*) before being given the celebrated Hellenic *apologia* for Christianity in the presence of the Areopagus, guardian council of the city's pagan religious traditions (Acts 17:21ff): two resulting converts are named (Dionysius,

---

[32] On the use of *proseuche* here see Schürer 1979 (E 1207) II 439f, 444f.

[33] Nevertheless the general injunction (paralleled elsewhere) of 2 Thess. 3:12 to work away quietly earning one's living suggests a predominantly *working* audience.

[34] Presumably Sopatros son of Pyrrhus (Acts 20:4) was one of these.

[35] 1 Thess. 3:1, 3:6 merely has Paul waiting in Athens for Timothy.

Damaris) representing the fledgling Athenian church (Acts 17:34) –
though it would be many centuries before Athens was to become in any
sense a major Christian centre.[36]

And so on to Corinth for a mission that was to last a year and a half
(Acts 18:11) and for what appears to be, on our information, Paul's most
penetrating evangelization, with high-status converts, Jews (the
archisynagogus Crispus,[37] Acts 18:8, 1 Cor. 1:14), godfearers (Titius Iustus,
Acts 18:7) as well as Gentiles (Gaius, 1 Cor. 1:15, Rom. 16:23; Erastus,
Rom. 16:23 – city *oikonomos* (administrator); Stephanas, 1 Cor. 1:16, 1
Cor. 16:15),[38] though it is well to bear in mind that Paul can characterize
the congregation as including 'not many men of wisdom by any human
standard, not many powerful, not many high-born', 1 Cor. 1:26. A later
and shorter return visit is recorded in Acts 20:1ff (cf. 2 Cor. 1:15f; with a
third visit projected in 2 Cor. 12:14, 13:1). The mission is represented in
Acts as being directed first to Jew and to Gentile godfearer and then,
with a conscious shift, concentrated upon the Gentile population after
repudiation by the Jewish community (the cameo scene before the
Roman governor of Achaea, Gallio, in Acts 18:12ff, datable to the very
early fifties, highlights the violence of the separation). And indeed the
Letters to the Corinthians address basically Gentile sensibilities ('you
know how when you were still pagans you were swept off to those dumb
heathen gods', 1 Cor. 12:2). The impression these letters give us is of a
sizable and diverse congregation clustering around the patronage of a
number of different households,[39] with local loyalties and rivalries
revealed when they all assemble together ('I heard that when you meet as
a congregation you fall into sharply divided groups', 1 Cor. 11:18): we
can discern a variety of preachers (for example, Apollos 1 Cor. 1:12, the
'super-apostles' 2 Cor. 11:5, 12:11), with Paul feeling under distinct
threat that his public performances are felt not to measure up to the
professional epideictic standards demanded of Hellenic rhetoric (2 Cor.
10:10ff) – clearly to the taste of some. We glimpse in Corinth a bustling
and turbulent trading and administrative centre, open to ideas and to
travellers – Paul is able to write to the church in Rome from Corinth well

---

[36] See Frantz 1988 (E 827) 18ff. In 1 Cor. 16:15 we meet Stephanas and his household as the 'first converts in Achaea': are we to suppose they were in Athens at the time of Paul's visit?

[37] On *archisynagogus* Schürer 1979 (E 1207) II 434ff.

[38] To judge from the reception they give Paul on his arrival in Corinth we probably ought to surmise that Prisca and Aquila, the much-travelled Jewish artisans recently come from Rome, are already Christians (Acts 18:1ff, cf. Acts 18:18, Rom. 16:3ff) – though it was not to the writer's purpose to emphasize this fact, and Paul feels free to boast in 2 Cor. 10:14 'we were the first to reach you [Corinthians] in preaching the gospel of Christ'.

[39] To the households of Stephanas, Titius Iustus, Gaius, Prisca and Aquila (already noted) we should probably add that of Chloe (1 Cor. 1:11). It was a fact worth recording that Gaius could act as 'host of the whole church' in Corinth, Rom. 16:23.

acquainted (whether in person or by reputation) with some twenty-eight individuals currently domiciled there (relying on Rom. 16:3ff). The Second Letter to the Corinthians is addressed to 'the church of God at Corinth together with all the saints throughout the whole of Achaea' (2 Cor. 1:1), but apart from Athens the only other Achaean Christian group known to us is nearby at Cenchreae, the port of Corinth on the Saronic Gulf (to which congregation belonged Phoebe, 'deacon of the church' and 'patroness (*prostastis*) of many', Rom. 16:1f). We know of no journey further to the south of Greece, into the Peloponnese, and whilst Paul can claim in Rom. 15:19 'I have completed the preaching of the gospel of Christ from Jerusalem as far round as Illyricum' we know of no voyaging into western Greece or the Adriatic.[40]

As for the Mediterranean islands, even Crete, mentioned at the Pentecostal scene, fails to score any mention save in the (later) Epistle to Titus. There Paul is claimed to have visited the island, leaving Titus temporarily behind 'to institute elders in each city' (1:5). At the very least we can say Crete is the type of island believed to have fallen within the Pauline missionary orbit, with urban Christian communities fully established and with converts amongst the Jewish population (1:10–14). Others of Paul's missionary entourage are expected to be calling by (3:13): Crete was a natural port of call on the sea-lanes for missionaries on the move just as was Cyprus (cf. Acts 27:4, 27:7–8). And at least for Cyprus we are on firmer ground in claiming an early missionary visit by Paul (in company with the Cypriot Barnabas, and John Mark) with the towns of Salamis and Paphos specified (Acts 13:5–6). The mission was aimed 'at the synagogues of the Jews'[41] and included, accordingly and pointedly, the confutation of a charlatan but influential Jewish sorcerer (13:6ff); Barnabas and Mark make a return missionary journey in Acts 15:39. But even (apparently) prior to Paul's mission, Jewish converts, scattering from Jerusalem after Stephen's death, had brought the good news to receptive Jews on the island (Acts 11:19).[42] But of the Aegean and Ionian islands generally, there is not a word, though Paul's voyaging brought him in passing contact with a number (e.g. Acts 20:14f, 21:1ff). And it is fortuitous that we learn of an enforced sojourn by Paul on Malta

[40] For what it is worth Titus 3:12 represents Paul as planning to winter at Nicopolis on the coast of Epirus and 2 Tim. 4:10 can report that Titus has gone to Dalmatia, further up the coastline. We have to wait until the early third century for the next Christian reference to Nicopolis: Origen found there a unique version of the Old Testament – which might suggest a somewhat early Christian connexion? (Eus. *Hist. Eccl.* VI.16.2).

[41] Note the convert Cypriot Jews who bring the message from Jerusalem to Gentiles at Antioch, Acts 11:20.

[42] One such could be 'Mnason of Cyprus, a disciple from the early days' later found domiciled in Jerusalem (Acts 21:16). As so often with the testimony of Acts, the chronology of events is controversial.

(Acts 28:1–11)[43] as well as an incidental landfall on Sicily (at Syracuse: Acts 28:12).[44] There, no Christians welcome Paul, unlike the reception accorded a little later at Puteoli (Acts 28:14) or earlier at Sidon (Acts 27:3): we should deduce that Christian communities were yet to be established. The impression to be gained is that whilst some regular ports – such as Troas (2 Cor. 2.12f, cf. Acts 16:11, 20:5ff), Cenchreae (Rom. 16:1–2) or Puteoli (Acts 28:14) – already had some Christian presence, this was not by any means yet a regular feature. And for all we know such major port-cities in the western Mediterranean as Carthage, Tarraco and Massilia, not to mention the western provinces of north Africa, Spain (despite Paul's declared aspiration, to reach the western limits of the Roman world, Rom. 15:24, 28),[45] and Gaul, still lay entirely outside any evangelization. After all Spain is mentioned by Paul in a context of 'places where the very name of Christ has not been heard' (Rom. 15:20). And were there by chance merchant travellers to these ports who were Christians or any early Christian pioneers in these provinces the memory of them faded fast, and completely: it would not be without significance that the western Mediterranean generally lacked established Jewish communities at this date.

And finally, Italy and Rome. By the time of Paul's arrival (very late fifties A.D.?), there was already formed a congregation at the port of Puteoli on the Gulf of Naples, the major Italian harbour for traffic with the Orient (Acts 28:14).[46] And of course Paul found in Rome itself a Christian community to welcome him (Acts 28:15): he had previous knowledge of or acquaintance with a number of its members (if we rely on Rom. 16:3ff) – and in his protreptic letter to the Roman brethren Paul had gone so far as to declare that the story of their faith was being told throughout all the world (Rom. 1:8). Acts is at pains to depict Paul making, once again, an initial effort – politely and patiently – to convince the Roman Jewish community (and it was a large one) but meeting with only mixed success (Acts 28:17ff). As we are given our final view of Paul teaching 'openly and unhindered' under house-custody awaiting trial, we are left with the deliberate impression that the two full years of waiting were spent largely with Gentile hearers (Acts 28:25ff). To a degree the letter to the Romans corroborates: it shows careful awareness

---

[43] Acts, typically, places emphasis on the respect Paul wins of 'the first man of the island, named Publius' and on Paul's wonder-working (Acts 28:78ff): of actual converts we hear nothing.

[44] It is characteristic of our patchy information that we have to wait until the middle of the third century for the first firm evidence of Christianity in Sicily, [Cyprian], Ep. 30.5.2.

[45] Later documents understand the aspiration to have been realized, Clem. *ad Cor.* 5.7, *Murat. Canon PL* 3.181, Jerome, *Comment. in Cap. xi. Isai. PL* 24.151.

[46] It would not be unreasonable to conjecture that in other similar Italian port-cities such as Ostia – with the same combination of resident Jewish community and exposure to frequent travellers – some Christian cell, however small, might also have been found. But it must remain conjecture.

of the mixed nature of the Roman congregation with its firm message that there is no longer distinction to be made between Jew and Greek. As for the size of this community, whilst we cannot go beyond Tacitus' *multitudo ingens* of Christian victims destined to fall in 64 A.D. we are left with the impression of a substantial community, probably grouped around a number of households as at Corinth[47] (not unreasonably given the urban sprawl) and, as at Corinth, themselves subject to rivalries and jealousies (or so Clement of Rome, *Ep. ad Corinth.* 6 obscurely implies, cf. Rom. 16:17ff).

Sporadic and fitful as our evidence manifestly is, adherents to this new religious movement had become, by the end of the sixties, as broadly spread in race and social class as they were scattered geographically. Being dispersed from Arabia in the East to Rome in the West, they spoke in a babel of tongues: Hebrew, Aramaic (and other Semitic languages), Greek, Latin (as at Philippi, Rome), local vernaculars (as in Galatia, Acts 14:11, and compare the Pentecostal scene of Acts 2:9ff). These reflected the range of country and nation of their origins, though Aramaic, Hebrew and Greek predominated (and our evidence is biased towards the latter). They dwelt not so much in country districts – villages and rural areas are not well represented (Palestine and Galatia providing the clearest examples, and rural penetration was to continue to be erratic, but not by any means unknown, over the succeeding centuries). The city, and the hellenized city at that, is where they characteristically dwelt, and the cities where we can see them – though they vary greatly in size and sophistication – for the most part (but not exclusively) lay on major routes of traffic and trade, or were reasonably accessible from them (as in the Lycus valley). And within those cities – to judge from the cases where we get status indicators – they appear to have formed congregations that might combine all but the highest levels of social stratification: that is not altogether surprising or radical when secular *collegia* can manifest similar combinations of class[48] and when the church-houses in which they characteristically met could operate under the prevailing patronage ethos, with comers able to find some familiar place or accepted social role. In all this it is easy to exaggerate the extent to which Christians might be located up the social scale – notoriously, the more socially prominent tend to be also the more visible in our sources. Nevertheless, in the city where we can form the most focused picture,

---

[47] There is a congregation at the Roman house of Prisca and Aquila and note the household groups of Aristobulus and Narcissus (Rom. 16:3f, 11) as well as the further two identifiable and separate groups in Rom. 16:14f. And some ethnic enclaves could be expected.

[48] For example, the association of fish-traders at Ephesus (*I. Eph.* 1a. 20, of Neronian date) attests some eighty-nine members ranging from Roman citizens (themselves both rich and poor), through Greeks of non-servile status, to slaves in proportions of *c.* 50 per cent, *c.* 45 per cent, *c.* 4 per cent.

viz. Corinth (though it, in turn, may well not be the most typical) we can discern not only men with households of notable substance (Gaius, as well as Crispus, Jason, Stephanus, Titius Iustus) and a local office-holder (Erastus) but converts with some social and intellectual pretensions (who clearly found Paul deficient on a number of counts, both in accomplishments and in deportment). But there were as well, equally clearly in this congregation, have-nots, dependants upon patronal largesse (1 Cor. 11:20ff) in addition to slaves (1 Cor. 7:21). And all these were caught up together in the same religious movement (all too obviously not without consequential tensions): even so, they have a remarkable appetite for, or at least they are thought capable of following, complex theological exposition and argumentation.[49] Paul himself does not seem to have aimed specifically at the proletarian down-and-outs as his missionary target – rather, the established households of the urban artisans and the middle-to-lower-range traders and businessmen. Even Paul's own tent-making smacks of a self-conscious act of making himself accessible to the public in the market-place (though his professed motives might be somewhat different).[50]

Whilst converts might range from Pharisees, still zealous for the observance of the Law, in Jerusalem to Greeks, sophisticated in the Hellenic philosophic traditions, in Athens (as perhaps Dionysius the Areopagite), nevertheless throughout, it is the Jewish sympathizers, godfearing Gentiles located somewhat to the margins of Judaism, who to our perception of things play a pivotal role: they appear to be found – and in significant numbers to be ready to lend an open ear – wherever synagogues flourished in the Diaspora: we must allow for a fair degree of interpenetration between Judaism and Gentile society around the Mediterranean at this period whilst aware, as always, that there will be regional differences (and sympathy with Judaism may diminish systematically as we move westwards, progressing deeper into a more Roman environment). Consequently, demarcation disputes with Judaism are perceived as endemic in this formative period as the processes of self-definition for the Christian movement get under way, processes which roused – and were to continue to rouse – much dissension and dispute within the movement itself: the Pauline formula for Gentile converts, involving as it did 'ritual invisibility', was manifestly not the only one nor was it necessarily acceptable either to them or to other (and especially Jewish) followers.

Some sort of control over our estimate of the social spread of Christianity in the generation between the thirties and the sixties might be sought in the onomastics of the Pauline connexion, from an examination of the sixty-six named individuals in the genuinely Pauline

---

[49] For a useful study, Theissen 1982 (F 229) 69ff.   [50] See Hock 1980 (F 156).

documents (plus thirteen more for the Pauline following provided by Acts) or of the full register of some ninety-seven names if we include in the tally the pastorals as well (treating bynames as separate entries). Caveats are obviously demanded not only in the field of onomastics itself (which name is exclusively, characteristically, sometimes, never Jewish?) but also in using the Pauline mission as a typical sample (which one can well imagine it may not have been). It is, however, the best sample we have.

What emerges, on analysis, is a mixed population, with a noticeably high proportion of Latin names (in a ratio 1:2 for Latin: Greek names), with no more than a dozen manifestly Semitic names altogether.[51] The Latin proportion may be accounted for, in part, by the adoption of Roman names (especially *praenomina* and *nomina*) in the Greek East, but the statistics still suggest an unusual proportion of travellers or immigrants whose traditional roots may not have been so deeply implanted in their local society of the eastern Mediterranean where Paul's mission had been concentrated – the more mobile may conceivably have been the more amenable to new ideas and to change. Actual mobility – or at least ability to travel – is a marked feature of many of the named figures in the Pauline corpus (nearly 50 per cent and rising to two-thirds if we assume that those greeted by name in Rom. 16 have encountered Paul personally). This may be partly a factor of secular occupation, partly of material support available to them (their own, or from the contributions of their brethren). This, too, may betoken a less fixed and traditional frame of mind on the part of the new adherents. At the least these members are not destitutes. And whilst fewer than 20 per cent of the named individuals in the Pauline connexion are women it is clear that they can play a prominent – though still circumscribed – role in prayer, prophecy, the ministry of teaching and of service and social support (note especially 1 Cor. 11:2ff, Phil. 4:2f, Rom. 16) – more so than is apparent to us in later generations (the pastorals e.g. 1 Tim. 2:8ff, already bearing testimony to a more traditional backlash).[52] On the evidence we have, they would appear to have had access, in this first generation, to more influential status than was available to them in contemporary Judaism.[53] But whatever may have been the personal and social factors which allowed minds to be receptive to the new message, it needs to be firmly recalled that the message they did receive was essentially theological: it was, in the Pauline version, an eschatological message of redemption and the *parousia* (the imminent Second Coming heralding final salvation), a message expressed as a *kerygma* (proclamation) of the crucified Jesus,

---

[51] Meeks 1983 (F 183) 47ff (Corinth), 55ff (other names in the Pauline churches) provides a useful survey.   [52] For careful analyses, Witherington 1988 (F 82).

[53] See Brooten 1982 (E 1098).

raised from the dead, construed as the new Passover sacrifice (1 Cor. 5:7f), the new Covenant sacrifice (1 Cor. 11:25), a sacrificial expiation for the new Israel consisting alike of Gentile (ritually freed of the Old Law) and of Jew (whether Law-observant or not): the Law of Christianity is proclaimed as a world religion. It was a message that manifested itself with superior spiritual powers, access to which was, importantly, open to all, not to a restricted elite: salvation was available universally. Above all we have that remarkable feature of Paul and his followers, viz. the vigour of their missionary zeal to bring both Jew and Gentile within the boundaries of the 'Israel of God', the *ecclesia*, the assembly of God where the cohesive factor would (ideally) be a combination of correct belief and right conduct, a combination unparalleled in the contemporary Gentile religious world.

II. CHRISTIANS AND THE LAW

1. Christ

The trial and condemnation of Christ 'as a criminal' (as pointedly observed by Tacitus, *Ann.* xv.44: 'Christus ... supplicio adfectus erat') certainly helped to cast a lengthy shadow of criminality over those who professed to be servants of his Name.[54] But the precise grounds for his sentence by the Roman procurator of Judaea have been, of course, endlessly disputed. The most plausible reconstruction – but reconstruction it is – is that whilst to the pious Jewish mind, and to the Sanhedrin, the essential crime may well have been blasphemy, to the Roman legal mind and to the governor's *consilium* it was as likely as not a charge of sedition, combined with the open threat of Jewish retaliation if Pilate refused to comply, that induced the condemnation. At all events it was Pilate who condemned whilst Jews accused – or that is what the sources, in retrospect, insist (e.g. Acts 3:13, 5:28ff, 13:28): such a combination of politics and theology was to dog the early followers in their relations with the society about them and with the Roman authorities.[55]

2. Sources

Sources are troublesome (here, as everywhere else). Acts is our major source for the early political relations between the Christian followers and the societies in which they lived. But Acts has amongst its

[54] The neologism *Christianus* being a derogatory epithet devised by their opponents, Acts 11:26 (Antioch) – still in vogue as a taunt there in the late second century, Theophilus, *ad Autol.* 1.12.

[55] Emblematically encapsulated in the words of Agabus in prophecy: 'Thus will the Jews in Jerusalem bind the man whose belt this is and hand him over to the Gentiles' (Acts 21:11).

underpinning themes the law-abiding nature of the Christian victims: the municipal and provincial administration, on the one hand, and, on the other, the Christian movement (growing as it is and spreading among the Gentiles, themselves of increasing dignity and status) need not live together in other than harmony, but (the document pointedly and persistently argues) it is the Jews (the 'unconverted Jews') who by their hostility have consistently stirred up trouble with the authorities for Christians[56] and have thereby forfeited their ancient claims to be the chosen race. Paul's personal spiritual history in Acts is patterned to reflect this progression, shifting from Jewish hostility to Christian conversion, and then, increasingly, dedicated to a mission away from the synagogues towards the Gentile world, leading, ultimately, as far as Rome. Paul's own retrospective views of his past life (both as persecutor and as persecuted) are notoriously unspecific and shifting in emphasis (Gal. 1:13f, 1:23; 1 Cor. 15:8f; 2 Cor. 11:23ff; Phil. 3:6): nevertheless, it remains clear that the initial followers of Jesus (whether from Paul himself or the author of Acts) in their perception of things were 'persecuted' – and in most cases persecuted by Jews, at times via urban or Roman authorities. It is an attitude encapsulated in the words given to Paul at Miletus to the Ephesian elders: 'In city after city the Holy Spirit assures me that imprisonment and hardships await me' (Acts 20:23); and, significantly, as the climax to the Beatitudes in the Matthaean version (5:10ff) figures the blessedness of those who suffer insults and persecution for Christ's sake. It is quite another matter to determine how exaggerated or indeed accurate a construing of events all this may be. But it is the mentality of this society which is crucial for its future: persecutions needs must come just as they had beset the prophets of old. The Christian prototype was on its way to be set not as the conforming

---

[56] Thus, in order, in the first dozen chapters (as a sample):

(1) 'the Chief Priests, the Controller of the Temple and the Sadducees' along with 'the Jewish rulers, elders and doctors of the law' (Peter and John, in Jerusalem, Acts 4:1–5)

(2) 'the High Priest and all his supporters, the Sadducean party' ('the Apostles', in Jerusalem, Acts 5:17)

(3) 'members of the Synagogue called the Synagogue of Freedmen' stirring up 'the [Jewish] people, the elders and the doctors of the law' (Stephen, in Jerusalem, Acts 6:9ff)

(4) (The pre-conversion) Saul, in Jerusalem, Acts 8:1ff (men and women)

(5) Saul, from the High Priest in Jerusalem to Damascus (via the synagogues of Damascus), Acts 9:1f (men and women)

(6) 'The Jews' (the converted Saul, in Damascus, Acts 9:23)

(7) Herod (pleasing the Jews) (James, the brother of John, and Peter, in Jerusalem, Acts 12:1ff)

In all the many instances of 'persecution' in the later chapters of Acts Jews fail to be implicated only in 16:20ff (Paul and Silas in Macedonian Philippi), in 17:18ff (Paul in Athens – but is this actually 'persecution'?) and in 19:23ff (Paul's companions Gaius and Aristarchus in Ephesus) – that is, in a Roman colony and in two of the great pagan cities of the eastern Mediterranean (with characteristic displays of pagan and self-interested prejudices).

householder but as the singular and suffering martyr, 2 Cor. 11:23ff, providing the *locus classicus* of the series of personal sufferings that might lie in store. By the time of the composition of the *Apocalypse* the attitude was firmly established (17:6: 'And I saw that the Woman [= Rome] was drunk with the blood of the Saints and with the blood of those who had borne witness to Jesus').

Accordingly, the death of Stephen, as Christian protomartyr, is highlighted in Acts 6 as the quintessential experience awaiting these Christian followers: the prophetic and inspired individual is depicted as the innocent victim of uncontrolled Jewish mob lynching, 6:54ff (though it is possible that legal condemnation by the Sanhedrin for violating the Temple precincts had been formally executed).[57] It is a scene which the unconverted Saul is tellingly made to approve (Acts 8:1, cf. 26:9ff – is Gal. 1:17 irreconcilable?). Whereas the encounters of (the later converted) Paul with Roman provincial authorities are contrived to represent him as unfairly accused by conniving enemies of Christianity, and accused of offences which are rightly judged by the Roman legal representatives as not punishable under the law – thus before Gallio, the proconsul of Achaea in 51/2 (Acts 18:12ff, cf. before Sergius Paulus, the proconsul of Cyprus, Acts 13:6ff) and before Felix and Festus, procurators of Judaea (Acts 24–6). Note the verdicts allegedly given after the – manifestly informal – hearing at Caesarea before Festus and Agrippa and his court: 'This man is doing nothing that deserves death or imprisonment'; 'This fellow could have been released had he not appealed to Caesar' (Acts 26:31f).

However apologetic and partial these accounts may be, two points still emerge clearly – individual Christians, for whatever circumstances, did keep falling foul of the law but no Roman law, nevertheless, specifically outlawed Christianity as such. The dealings of the Roman emperors themselves with Christians confirm this judgement.

3. Claudius

No certitude is possible that the incident recorded by Suetonius (*Claud.* 25.4) concerned Christians at all. All we know is that Claudius 'expelled from Rome Jews who were causing continual disturbances at the instigation of Chrestus' ('Judaeos impulsore Chresto assidue tumultuantis'). We can merely speculate whether this may register a garbled tradition of rioting within the Jewish community in Rome, between enthusiast converts to the recently arrived Christian *secta* and other Jews

---

[57] See, for example, Sherwin-White 1963 (D 109) 40ff.

of more traditional persuasions.[58] But the speculation must remain idle: we are otherwise ignorant of what occasioned the rioting and whether it was indeed basically domestic in character. And Claudius' reaction to Jewish turbulence in Rome follows imperial precedence (e.g. under Tiberius, Tac. *Ann.* 11.85, Suet. *Tib.* 36) and it is not inconsistent with his treatment of Jews elsewhere (e.g in Alexandria, *P. Lond.* 1912 coll. ivf. = *GCN* 370.73ff). Acts 18:2 blandly records that Aquila, a Pontic Jew, had arrived at Corinth from Italy 'because Claudius had issued an edict that all Jews should leave Rome': presumably Christians would have been affected insofar as they were also Jews. Certainly this incident is recorded as no general ideological pogrom: no more than a peace and order measure, and a local and temporary one that, it is implied, was involved.

4. Nero

Tacitus, an experienced and senior senator (consul A.D. 97), had been proconsular governor of the province of Asia early on in the second decade of the second century: there Christians were doubtless becoming a perceptible fact of life if not yet greatly numerous. He is our original source (*Ann.* XV.44) to connect the fire of Rome under Nero (July A.D. 64) with Christians. There is every reason to weigh seriously his account written under early Hadrian (though it would be prudent to take authorial attitudes in his account as reflecting more certainly those that prevailed in his class half a century after the events he is describing). He makes the connexion between fire and Christians in a narrative context in which dominant motifs are the destruction (much exaggerated, in fact) of the Rome of old and the present realities under Nero of a modern Rome of degraded immorality and irresponsibility in government (instanced by *inter alia* gratuitous cruelty and imperial spectacles).

As the Tacitean narrative runs, expiatory rites hallowed by traditional religion had failed to scotch the prevailing rumour of Nero's personal responsibility for starting the disastrous fire. So Nero provided Christians as scapegoats ('subdidit reos': the wording implies they were not, in Tacitus' view, in fact responsible for the fire); they were followers of a new-fangled superstition 'hated for their crimes' (typical, therefore, of the modern influx of depravity into the capital). Those who confessed

---

[58] Oros. VII.6.15f in fact reads *Christo*. He dates the incident to the ninth year of Claudius' reign (A.D. 49) but on that can be placed no firm reliance. Dio LX.6.6 (under A.D. 41, but in a generalizing context) possibly registers earlier measures taken by Claudius in an attempt to contain the Jewish turbulence in Rome, for 'he did not drive them out of the city but ordered them, whilst continuing their ancestral way of life, not to assemble'.

were arrested – the tense in Tacitus' wording ('qui fatebantur') implies they were confessing to being Christians – and they in turn revealed the names of others: a huge multitude was thus convicted 'not so much on the charge of arson as for their hatred of humankind'. Nothing is revealed by Tacitus of the actual processes of their legal conviction (did Nero delegate authority and if so, to whom?) but he does disclose a belief that whilst the charge of arson was false they undoubtedly deserved punishment anyway. In his view Christians are tainted with crime. But he manages nevertheless to create a haunting memory of their deaths, contrived (as he puts it) 'not for the public good but to glut one man's cruelty', a holocaust lit to indulge Nero's histrionic obsessions: 'Mockery of various kinds was added to their deaths: covered with the skins of wild beasts they were torn to pieces by dogs, they were nailed to crosses or were doomed to the flames: when daylight failed their burning served to illuminate the night. Nero had made available his gardens for the spectacle and provided a Circus show, dressed as a charioteer mingling with the crowd or driving on a chariot.' There is no good reason to disbelieve this account but there is room to suspect that Tacitus may have enhanced the numbers (*multitudo ingens*) in order to highlight Nero's monstrosities. Suetonius (*Ner.* 16.2) merely records the capital punishment ('afflicti suppliciis') of Christians amongst a heterogeneous catalogue of Nero's praiseworthy deeds. But the evidence does not warrant any credence in a persecution more widespread than Rome: there are no compelling grounds for positing any general enactment against Christians.[59] Neither are the arguments strong for accepting the speculation that it was through the influence of the imperial consort Poppaea that potential hostility against Jews was deflected onto their Christian rivals.[60] But the clear identification by people and Roman authorities alike of the separate existence of Christians is significant. Nero thus emerges in the Christian tradition as the very first of the imperial Persecutors (e.g. Tert. *Apol.* 5.3, cf. Melito *ap.* Eus. *Hist. Eccl.* iv.26.9).

5. Peter and Paul

There appears to be nothing except historical convenience to connect the deaths of Peter and Paul with these events of A.D. 64. Our last secure

---

[59] See the analysis of Barnes 1968 (F 85) and for examples of the connexion in the popular mind between dissident minority groups and the threat of urban incendiarism, Livy XXXIX.14.10 (Bacchanalians in Rome), Sall. *Cat.* 43.2 (Catilinarians in Rome), Joseph. BJ XLVII–LXI (Jews in Antioch).

[60] For the case see, for example, Frend 1965 (F 139) 164f: Poppaea undoubtedly shared in the fashionable fascination with Jewish rituals and customs (e.g. Joseph. BJ VII.45 (Greeks in Antioch) *Ap.* II.282f (Greeks and Barbarians everywhere)) but Josephus' enrolment of her among the *theosebeis* (worshippers of God) *AJ* xx.195, cf. *Vit.* xvi ought to be taken as non-technical and as honorific flattery (for the evidence and general discussion, Schürer 1986 (E 1207) III.1 78, 165)).

glimpse of Paul is that provided by the conclusion of Acts (28:16, 30) where he is depicted (in about A.D. 62) as being under house detention in Rome awaiting trial. The chances are high (but by no means absolute), given the delays of two full years already, that the trial was in the end aborted and that Paul secured some casual release.[61] Certainly the tone of the narrative in Acts and its whole tendency suggests (or at the very least is contrived to suggest) that at the time of writing the death of Paul at the hands of Roman authorities has not yet taken place – though admittedly Paul is made to foretell the permanence of his departure from Miletus and Ephesus (Acts 20:25, 38, at Miletus) along with forebodings of death (Acts 21:10–14, at Caesarea). And as for Peter, notoriously his Roman whereabouts are even more difficult to establish with any security.[62] On the other hand there can be no doubt about the reality of the *cultus* of Peter and Paul as martyrs located on the Vatican hill and by the Ostian Way, by no later than the course of the second century,[63] and of the tradition of their deaths as martyrs by the very end of the first.[64] But for all we know the incidents which encompassed their deaths in Rome may well have been quite separate from the Neronian fire.[65]

It would not be too long after these incidents that (inspired) Christians – if we are to believe a persistent story (and we need not) – took refuge from Jerusalem immediately before its siege and eventual destruction and fled to the safety of (Jordanian) Pella of the Decapolis. On this version of events providential protection did save Palestinian Christians from becoming victims in the devastation that was to befall Palestinian Jewry.[66]

III. CONCLUSION

Actual deaths may have been relatively few before A.D. 70.[67] But their heroic circumstances ensured that the lives of these charismatic indivi-

[61] For valuable discussion, Sherwin-White 1963 (D 109) 118f.

[62] On these, both the Pauline *corpus* and Acts are famously silent. 1 Pet. purports to be written from 'Babylon' (5:13: presumably = Rome, cf. Eus. *Hist. Eccl.* II.15.2), thereby witnessing a (?very late) first-century tradition of a Roman residence. For a convenient collection of the evidence, O'Connor 1969 (F 196).

[63] See Eus. *Hist. Eccl.* II.25.6ff (Gaius): discussion Toynbee and Ward Perkins 1956 (E 134) 128ff.

[64] For example 1 Clement 5.4f (late in the first century; Peter and Paul), cf. John 21:18f (Peter). Neither mentions the place of death.

[65] For what it is worth Eus. *Chron.* GCS (= *Die griechischen christlichen Schriftsteller der ersten Jahrhunderte*) 20.216 and Jerome GCS 47.185 record the deaths four years after the fire.

[66] The story (which suspiciously ensures an apostolic pedigree for the church of Pella) has disturbingly irreconcilable variants: Eus. *Hist. Eccl.* III.5.3 (implausibly making the migration not only of the full Jerusalem church but of all the 'holy men' in the land of Judaea besides), Epiph. *Adv. Haeres.* 29.7, 30.2, *Mens.* 15.2ff.

[67] Despite impressions Stephen and James, the brother of John, are the only two to die in Acts (7:60, 12:1f) along with the unsubstantiated Jerusalem victims whom Saul 'persecuted to the death' (if we are to place literal credence in the speech given him in Acts 22:4).

duals were to become the enduring models of behaviour and the focus of theological attention: characteristically these were outspoken missionaries, the zealous apostles, the staunch disciples and their descendants, often, as society and tradition expected of them, rootless men and professed celibates, or men who had sacrificed country and kin to their religious cause – and perceived, besides, as being direct descendants of one persistent lineage in Jewish tradition enshrined in the Book of Maccabees. Before their glittering examples the solid and dutiful householders of the secondary epistles ascribed to Paul, living out stable and orderly lives of domesticated Christianity, with loving wives, obedient progeny and submissive slaves, failed to capture the theological and spiritual imagination. Despite opponents, and despite the passage of the years, the spirit of the Pauline theology of imminent *parousia* – and his own potent example – was to maintain its hold on the high ground into the succeeding centuries. And it may well be that after the initial missionary successes (at least as highlighted for our benefit in Acts) the consolidation and spread of the Christian communities proceeded at a less spectacular pace in the following generations.

CHAPTER 18

SOCIAL STATUS AND SOCIAL LEGISLATION[1]

SUSAN TREGGIARI

The epoch of the destruction of the last great hellenistic monarchy which could challenge Rome in the Mediterranean world and of the addition of a *princeps* to the Roman constitutional system clarified the superiority of all Roman citizens to all others with whom they lived. Although political liberty was henceforth circumscribed, the privilege of citizens in private law and social status was apparent. Roman law applied only to citizens, but the spread of citizenship, the pervasive presence of a Roman administrative model and the symbiosis of Romans with non-Romans encouraged the imitation of Roman law and social institutions.[2] Nor was Rome immune to influences from outside: the migration of scholars after the conquest of Alexandria, the convenient Jewish idea of the sabbath, innovations in religion or cuisine. Roman social patterns and life must be seen against the mosaic of the empire.

I. LEGAL DISTINCTIONS

Gaius, writing his textbook on Roman law in the second century A.D., launches into the law of persons with a pithy classification of the human race, as far as it was relevant to Roman law: 'the primary distinction in the law of persons is this, that all men are either free or slaves. Next, free men are either *ingenui* (freeborn) or *libertini* (freedmen). *Ingenui* are those born free, *libertini* those manumitted from lawful slavery. Next, of freedmen there are three classes: they are either Roman citizens or Latins or in the category of *dediticii*.' (*Inst.* 1.3.9–12, de Zulueta's translation.)

To the mind of a Roman lawyer, legal status is the essential distinction. Although his first two sentences could be taken to refer to the whole human race, the third makes it clear that he is thinking of the community of Roman citizens and of slaves and *dediticii* within that context, those subject to Roman law ('the ... law observed by us',

---

[1] I am indebted to David Cherry, Colin Wells, members of Stanford seminars, and the editors for discussion and comments, and to James Rives for efficient verification of references.

[2] A Spanish inscription of 87 B.C. provides a striking early instance. See Richardson 1983 (B 271); Birks, Rodger and Richardson 1984 (D 247).

ibid. 8). His categories are not exhaustive for the whole of humanity. Division of humanity into slaves (born or made) and free implies that the free are subdivided into freeborn non-Roman and freeborn Roman (citizen-born or enfranchised aliens) on the one hand, and freed slaves on the other. Slaves freed by non-Romans become non-Roman free people; those freed by Romans fall into three classes. All the resulting classes need also to be subdivided by two other important variables, sex and age. Roman women are termed citizens, *cives Romanae*. They had no right to vote or stand for office, but in private law their rights were comparable to those of male citizens (with certain restrictions) and they could pass on citizenship to children or freed slaves. Boys attained the full public rights of citizens when judged mature for the Forum and military service (at about seventeen); they attained majority in private law at puberty or fourteen, a status which girls reached at twelve.[3]

Our focus, like that of our Roman sources, will be on that small proportion of inhabitants of the empire who, in 28 B.C., were free and Roman citizens, at most 5–6 million men, women and children, of whom not many more than 4 million lived in Italy.[4] But the masses of non-citizens of many disparate cities and tribes, who heavily outnumbered Roman citizens in the provinces, and the slaves, who made up a substantial proportion of the population in Rome and other cities and on the estates and cattle pastures of Italy, must not be forgotten. They sharpened Romans' perception of their own position of privilege. There is continuity between the humbly born traders who, as Cicero said (II *Verr.* 5.167), ought to have been able to trust to their citizen status to protect them in any province, among non-citizens as well as before Roman officials, even where they had no acquaintances to vouch for them, and the prosperous and scholarly Paul of Tarsus, who, when his zeal as a preacher came to the attention of the authorities, was able to claim citizen rights and convince officialdom that his own evidence on his status could be trusted.

Though the citizen's rights appear most strikingly when he is accused of a crime, they were usually important to his life because they dictated his capacity to act in private law. Roman civil law superimposed further regulations on the conventions generally accepted by mankind, the *ius gentium*. Free persons who were not Roman citizens had a legal personality through the laws of their own community, which were recognized by Rome. But slaves were chattels and had none. Slaves of Romans nevertheless had a role in Roman law, since they could function as extensions of their owners' personalities.[5] But any Roman who was on the point of making a contract or marriage ought to have taken the

---

[3] Buckland 1963 (F 646) 142f; Gardner 1986 (F 33) 14.
[4] Brunt 1971 (A 9) 12.   [5] Watson 1987 (F 703) ch. 6.

precaution of checking whether the other party was a slave or a non-citizen (*peregrinus/peregrina*). A man who unwittingly married a non-citizen or slave woman might find that he had begotten non-citizen (and in Roman law illegitimate) or slave children; anyone who left property to a slave enriched his or her owner; bequests to a non-citizen were void. Theoretically, the distinction between slave and free was sharp: a human being was either one or the other. In practice, status was fluid. A person might experience several changes of status in a lifetime. A Roman citizen might (through being captured in war for example) fall into slavery. A slave might be freed by a Roman and become a full citizen. Doubt and obscurity might exist. There were people wrongfully treated as slaves, foundlings for instance, whose free birth might be proved and whose status restored; persons thought to be slaves by current 'owners' acting in good faith (*bona fide servientes*); slaves who had been manumitted under a will, in the interval between the testator's death and the implementation of the provisions of a will (*statuliberi*); slaves informally manumitted, who did not become citizens or, in strict law, free people.

II. SOCIAL DISTINCTIONS

1. Ordines

Gradations of prestige, *gradus dignitatis*, might seem necessary for an equitable state (Cic. *Rep.* 1.43). Prestige was partly determined by constitutional function. Rome contained various orders or ranks, *ordines*.[6] Upper-class writers defined their society in constitutional terms as made up of Senate and People (plebs is used of the 'commons', e.g. D 1. 16.238 *pr.*) or, in more evocative language, of *patres* and *Quirites* (e.g. Hor. *Carm.* IV.14.1). These categories exclude or overlook the political nonentities, citizen women and children. For the late Republic, the membership of the senatorial order was defined by the current list of senators, men elected to the quaestorship and not subsequently demoted by censors or exiled by courts or a dictator or proscribed by triumvirs. (Close relatives of senators might be regarded as sharing their interests, but were not members of the order at this date.) Another stratum had gradually become defined. According to the Elder Pliny, an order had been inserted between the commons (plebs) and the senators (*patres*), when it became customary for wealthy men to wear a gold ring. The ring distinguished this 'second order' from the plebs, as the laticlave distinguished senators (who also wore gold rings) from them

---

[6] Cohen 1975 (F 18). For discussion of social structures over a longer period see Garnsey and Saller 1987 (A 34) ch. 6; Alföldy 1985 (F 1) ch. 5. MacMullen 1974 (F 44) ch. 4 gives a broader perspective on the economic basis of class. See also de Ste Croix 1981 (A 90) 350ff.

(HN XXXIII.29). Pliny's account is significant because it represents the views of an erudite administrator on the class to which he belonged. But it is imprecise in its chronology. The second order was in Pliny's day called *equites*, a title earlier enjoyed by the *equites equo publico* (cavalry) and gradually extended to jurors, although as late as the time of Augustus some jurors remained in the lower stratum of wearers of the iron ring rather than the gold one. It was now money, not the privilege of the public horse, which marked *equites*. What interests Pliny and has puzzled modern scholars is the fuzziness of the definition of the second class. But this is natural, since the class had evolved gradually over a couple of centuries. The growth of wealth and of the citizen body (as Pliny, a native of Comum in Transpadane Italy, recognized) meant that more men were qualified for various forms of public service and interested in achieving some public recognition without wanting a senatorial career. C. Gracchus in 123 B.C. first recruited them for honorific, influential and burdensome jury-service.[7] The class from which he drew was probably defined by the possession of capital of at least HS 400,000. By the 60s B.C. the title of *equites* was standard for non-senatorial jurors. Men whose property qualified them for jury service but who were not on the lists naturally claimed the title or were given it informally by their friends. But, because it was public function which defined an *ordo*, they could not strictly be regarded as members of the nascent equestrian order. Augustus, by holding the census efficiently and by expanding the number of administrative posts available, was to define the second order more formally and greatly increase its prestige. Five thousand *equites Romani* might in his time attend the parade which celebrated their official position (Dion. Hal. *Ant. Rom.* VI.13.4); there were 3,000 jurors. Tiberius was to unite jurors and holders of the public horse in one order, enjoying the title of *equites* and the gold ring.[8]

Equites in the broad sense might also remain entirely private gentlemen, managing their estates (the major form of investment for most of them) or sharing in financial ventures, especially banking and the larger scale forms of trade. Some local magnates qualified for equestrian rank. Strabo (III.5.3–5 (169C), V.1.6–7 (213C)) says Gades and Padua in the time of Augustus had 500 *equites* each. Whereas the Senate when swollen in the time of Caesar had had 900 members, the size of the equestrian order was very much greater. If Padua and Gades could show 1,000 whom their contemporaries regarded as equestrian, the order in its extended sense must have numbered in the tens of thousands by 44 B.C.

In the towns, the decurions formed an order just as the Senate did at Rome: local town councils included men who might also enjoy the status

---

[7] Sherwin-White 1982 (A 88), especially 28.
[8] Pliny, *HN* XXXIII.32. Cf. Wiseman 1970 (D 80) 76. See also Brunt 1988 (D 28).

of Roman *eques* (e.g. Cic. *Fam.* XIII.11). The decurionate was a channel to the equestrian and senatorial orders.[9] Members of disreputable professions were barred, as from the equestrian order; freedmen, allowed by Caesar, were later excluded; the qualification of a minimum capital may have varied according to local circumstances.[10] Certain .other groups whose status was legally defined or who performed public functions might also be termed *ordines*. Ex-slaves, *libertini*, were defined by their origin; the *ordo scribarum*, the most eminent of public servants, some of whom were also *equites*, were marked out because, like senators, they were registered.[11]

Other men who served the state were registered and distinguishable. Civil servants, *apparitores*, such as lictors and heralds, like the scribes bridged the gap between the upper classes and the freed slave.[12] Freeborn citizens in search of upward mobility were likely to join the army rather than the civil service. A private soldier might rise to the centurionate; a senior centurion was likely on retirement to become a prominent citizen in an Italian town. Augustus structured conditions of service and career-patterns: service became a road to upward mobility or to maintenance of a family's position. The successful make a transition to the decurionate or to equestrian administrative posts.[13] The gradual rise of families depended on a series of individual successes. Thus the historian Velleius Paterculus (praetor with his brother Magius Celer Velleianus in A.D. 15) was descended on his mother's side from a Campanian great-grandfather, Minatus Magius, who received Roman citizenship and his sons the praetorship after service in the Social War, and from a paternal grandfather who was an officer under Pompey and later M. Brutus and Ti. Nero, and killed himself in 41 B.C. The father was also an equestrian military man and Velleius himself reached the Senate via army service under the future emperor Tiberius, son of his grandfather's distinguished friend (Vell. Pat. II.16.2, 76.1). More dramatic stories of rags to riches in three generations or less circulated about new men, concerned to tie the senator as closely as possible to discreditable antecedents. Thus Cicero's grandfather was a fuller, Octavian was connected by Antony and others with grandfathers and great-grandfathers in low trade; P. Vitellius, *eques* and procurator of Augustus and father of four senators and grandfather of the emperor, was said to be son of an unsavoury speculator and a common prostitute and grandson of a freed cobbler and of a baker (Plut. *Cic.* 1, Suet. *Aug.* 2, 4, *Vit.* 2).

---

[9] Demougin 1983 (E 34); Wiseman 1971 (D 81) 86ff; on qualifications, Crook 1967 (F 21) 65ff.

[10] See Wiseman 1971 (D 81) 89–94; Garnsey 1970 (F 35) 242–5.

[11] Cicero regarded the tax-contractors as an *ordo*: *Planc.* 23; *Fam.* XIII.9.2. See Badian 1972 (D 84) 74.   [12] Purcell 1983 (F 49).

[13] Dobson 1970 (D 181) and 1974 (D 182); Breeze 1975 (D 167). On recruitment of the poor as common soldiers, Campbell 1984 (D 173) 8ff.

2. Wealth

But Roman class structure cannot be described solely by *ordines*. Economic distinctions modify the pattern imposed by constitutional function or legal status.[14] The most striking fact about society is the gap between rich and poor. At the top, senators and *equites* had, until the time of Augustus, the same census qualification of HS 400,000 (Dio LIV.17.3). But this is a minimum. Although misfortune could mean that a senator failed to maintain his qualification, many possessed capital far above that level. No totals are recorded for the Republic, but senators and *equites* could build vast fortunes through running and increasing estates and through financial investment and speculation (especially in the tax companies). The great generals and their friends dramatically increased their wealth through booty and the exploitation of financial opportunities in the provinces. Late republican data show the pattern for the beginning of our period. Pompey began with at least large estates in Picenum; by 51 the amount of interest actually paid (not as much as what was owed) to him by one foreign king was HS 792,000 per month (Cic. *Att.* VI.1.3). The disposable capital of Pompey in the fifties or Caesar in the forties was immense by the standards of ordinary senators. They could carry out public building schemes, and give games which put the munificence of lesser politicians in the shade. The enrichment and expenditure of the triumvirs and emperors followed the same pattern. But, though not comparable with the fortunes of such leaders, the property of the wealthier senators, enriched by civil war and conquest abroad, was huge. For Crassus a *bon mot*, for Domitius Ahenobarbus armies of tenants, for Lucullus luxurious dinners and gardens survive to attest wealth.[15] Cicero (with no public munificence on his record) collected villas and found some display necessary to the maintenance of his position (his critics thought a new man could have done with less): HS 3,500,000 (partly borrowed) bought his town house; HS 20 million came to him in inheritances, together with other honest, but short-lived, perquisites of an administrative career.

Setting himself up, in a sermon on true riches, as a senator of Stoic continence whose fortune would generally be considered modest, but who could adjust his expenditure to allow some surplus, Cicero mentions HS 100,000 as an income which would more than cover expenses, where an extravagant man would find 600,000 inadequate.[16] But he regarded 80,000 as an adequate allowance for young Marcus

[14] Wiseman 1971 (D 81) 65ff, 116ff. Cf. Harris 1988 (F 40).
[15] Crassus: Whitehead 1986 (F 80); Ahenobarbus: Brunt 1975 (F 13) 619ff, 634f; Lucullus: Shatzman 1975 (D 64) 378–81. For republican senatorial fortunes in general see Shatzman 1975 (D 64).
[16] *Parad.* 47ff, cf. Wiseman 1970 (D 80) 77.

when he was only a student in Athens – and in the first year travelling expenses brought the figure up to 100,000 (*Att.* xv.17.1, xvi.1.5 with Shackleton Bailey *ad loc.*). So 100,000 must not be taken seriously as representing Cicero's own budget. Some *equites* were as rich as wealthy senators; they could, if they wished, like Atticus, live with less display. Inheriting HS 10 million and an antique house on the Quirinal to add to his paternal (2 million) and other property, he lived with quiet good taste and such economy that he is *said* to have paid out only 3,000 a month for domestic expenses (Nep. *Att.* 5.2, 13, 14.2, 21.1).

The good man of course avoided disgraceful sources of enrichment (despoiling provinces, ejecting neighbours, going shares with unscrupulous freedmen and so on, Cic. *Parad.* 43, 46 etc.). Ranching on public land; the intensive exploitation of private land for cash crops or products such as oil and wine, bricks, pottery, timber, quarrying; rent from urban property such as housing or brothels; investment in transmarine commerce and small shops; usury; booty and the perquisites of office: these and other means of profit were usual and acceptable.[17] The largest attested senatorial fortune (from a rhetorical source) is that of Cn. Cornelius Lentulus the augur, probably the consul of 14 B.C. Seneca and Tacitus agree that he rose from poverty, but Tacitus claims that his money was made honourably and Seneca that he owed it to the generosity of Augustus. Seneca puts it at HS 400 million, a figure based perhaps on multiplication of the equestrian minimum and affection for 40 and 400, rather than on verification of records. But it is highly significant for upper-class perception, under Nero, of what a senator might be worth.[18] Seneca himself is said to have had 300 million sesterces.[19]

Lentulus had allegedly earlier scarcely supported the position of a *nobilis*. Other senators had difficulty maintaining the senatorial property qualification. This by 13 B.C. was fixed at HS 1 million.[20] Senators who dropped below the property qualification might resign or appeal to the emperor for a subvention: some are attested, especially if notable for ancestry or extravagance.[21]

Equites (who had to possess at least HS 400,000 and, usually, free birth)[22] might exceed the senatorial minimum, as Atticus had done, and

[17] For means of enrichment see Finley 1976 (A 27); D'Arms 1981 (F 22) ch. 3 and, for a later period, Duncan-Jones 1982 (A 24) ch. 1 on Pliny.

[18] Sen. *Ben.* II.27.1f; Tac. *Ann.* IV.44.1; Suet. *Tib.* 49. Appropriately, the money reverted to the emperor under his will (Suet. *Tib.* 49). Cf. *PIR* C 1379; Syme 1939 (A 93) 381, cf. 400f.

[19] Tac. *Ann.* XIII.42.4; Dio LXI.10.3, cf. Vibius Crispus; Tac. *Dial.* VIII; Brunt 1975 (F 13) 624 n.16. Duncan-Jones 1982 (A 24) App. 7 tabulates known fortunes under the Empire.

[20] Dio LIV.26.3–4, *pace* Suet. *Aug.* 41.1. Clear summary by Talbert 1984 (D 77) 47ff. See further Nicolet 1976 (D 53), 1984 (C 180) 90ff.

[21] Hopkins 1983 (A 46) 75f; Talbert 1984 (D 77) 47ff.

[22] Hor. *Epist.* I.1.57–9; *Ars P.* 383–4.

might rival the wealthiest senators. Virgil is said to have acquired nearly HS 10 million from friends (*Vita Verg.* 13). Maecenas must have far outclassed him. Moralists were more likely to focus on wealthy freedmen whose fortunes approached even that of Lentulus. The richest according to tradition were found under Claudius, the imperial freedmen Narcissus with over HS 400 million (Dio LXI.34.4) and M. Antonius Pallas with HS 300 million (Tac. *Ann.* XII.53.5). But already soon after the civil wars Caecilius Isidorus, despite losses, died possessed of 60 million in cash, besides estates estimated to bring him up to the level of L. Ahenobarbus (cos. 54 B.C.) and of the Claudian freedmen.[23] M. Aurelius Zosimus, freedman and *accensus* of Cotta Maximus (Messallinus, cos. 20), received several gifts equivalent to the equestrian census from his patron.[24]

Less than the equestrian census might make a family wealthy by the standards of a small community. The capital required of some municipal councillors is known to have been HS 100,000. Retired centurions or freedmen traders or even efficient farmers might attain solid wealth.[25] But ordinary artisans, shopkeepers and peasants were immeasurably removed from equestrian wealth. The pay of a private soldier, HS 900 annually, out of which he paid for food and equipment, was attractive and must have represented security compared with what an able-bodied man could have earned as a labourer, seasonally employed and with no compensation for injury. Cicero had argued in the 70s B.C. that an ordinary labourer would earn no more than HS 3 daily (*QRosc.* 28). Daily rates must have varied according to skill, demand, area and season; we cannot determine fluctuations over time.[26] Nor are costs of even basic essentials such as food and housing determinable over time or for any given moment. The precise economic situation of the small proprietor and the wage-earner eludes us. In the city of Rome and other urban centres, the craftsmen, shopkeepers and freed slaves (who often possessed a skill) distinguish themselves from the lower part of the population by their habit (which cost money) of commemorating themselves on tomb inscriptions. Some slaves, who might possess slaves of their own or other property, must also be counted among the relatively well-off.

[23] Pliny, *HN* XXXIII.135; Brunt 1975 (F 13).

[24] EJ² 358. Maximus' father, Messalla Corvinus, had probably gained from the civil wars (Syme 1958 (B 176) II 573). His mother was presumably the heiress of the Aurelii Cottae: Syme 1985 (A 95) 231–2.

[25] Wiseman 1971 (D 81) 91ff; Dobson 1974 (D 182) 392ff; Treggiari 1969 (F 68) 102ff, 109.

[26] On earnings, Wells 1984 (A 101) 203–5 for a succinct and judicious summary; Duncan-Jones 1982 (A 24) 54. For more general accounts of lower-class workers Garnsey 1980 (F 37); Brunt 1980 (D 117); de Ste Croix 1981 (A 90) 187ff; MacMullen 1974 (F 44) 42–5, on a later period, is suggestive. On soldiers, Campbell 1984 (D 173) 177ff.

3. Birth

'Though you strut in the pride of wealth, Fortune does not change your birth' (Hor. *Epod.* IV.5–6). Romans did not measure social position by census rating. Patrician lineage, descent from ancient consuls, descent from any man who had held the consulship or done great deeds, all these had varying weight. *Nobilitas* came to descendants in the male line from the first three. It might be difficult to discriminate between the scion of a patrician family which had achieved little in recent decades (e.g. Cic. *Mur.* 16) and the representative of a plebeian noble house, particularly as the female line might introduce other themes. Caesar could wring every last drop of value from descent from Alban kings and kinship with the new achiever, Marius. Octavian, a Iulius only by his maternal grand-mother and by an arrangement which even his stepfather for a time refrained from acknowledging (Cic. *Att.* XIV.12.2), became more accep-table to the nobles by his last marriage to an heiress of Claudii Nerones and Livii Drusi. Descent from mythical heroes or ancient kings might balance lack of recent and Roman public service. Maecenas, who remained an *eques*, drew real influence from his close friendship with Octavian and social status from his alleged descent from Etruscan princes (Hor. *Carm.* 1.1.1). Such genealogy could be alleged even in the minutes of the Senate (Tac. *Ann.* XII.53.3).[27]

Absence of real or fictitious distinctions of birth was not an insuper-able barrier to advancement. (If fictitious, they were normally invented after a man had succeeded.) The Senate had necessarily always been recruited from below, and although new men who rose to the consulship were rare, men of equestrian family steadily reached lower magistracies and their sons or grandsons might do better. New men, *novi homines*, whose families showed no previous senator, stand at the opposite end of the continuum from the *nobilis*. Between were various gradations.[28]

As the equestrian order was the seedbed of the Senate (Livy, XLII.61.5), closely linked to it by blood, intermarriage, friendship and similar interests and education, so lower strata of the propertied classes supplied recruits to the equestrian order. A man of modest means, *tenuis*, who knew how to make money, might end as a rich and influential *eques*.[29]

These various stratifications, themselves untidy, from senators and *equites* and local notables down through civil servants and centurions to

---

[27] Cf. Balsdon 1979 (A 2) 19f; Wiseman 1974 (D 82).
[28] Wiseman 1971 (D 81); Brunt 1982 (F 14); Hopkins 1983 (A 46) 56ff; Syme 1986 (A 95).
[29] Sen. *Ep.* 101.1f. For the topos on social mobility see Sen. *Controv.* 1.6.3f, with Winterbottom *ad loc.*

freed slaves and the common people, were interconnected by networks of patronage and friendship. The archaic patron–client relationship, sanctioned by the Twelve Tables, had evolved into a fluid situation in the late Republic, when ancestral ties of dependence were probably less relevant to a noble and a humble citizen than current economic ties (for instance Domitius Ahenobarbus could still control his tenants) and political advantage (*popularis* tribunes could attract voters and successful generals rely on their troops). But poets and scholars who needed to make their way as 'friends' of powerful men and the *domi nobiles* like the Roscii of Ameria still cultivated patrons of higher status than themselves. A Cicero could be useful, as senator and governor, to rich Greeks or Roman tax-contractors or businessmen, and they could be useful to him. Mutual interest was strengthened by a code which recommended reciprocity and strict repayment of *beneficia*. Between social equals the role of benefactor and beneficiary might rotate. Benefits might also be asked for third parties. Where there was inequality of status or influence, a humble *amicus* might request help from his patron who would ask his own patron to bring about the desired result.[30]

The troubles of the late Republic and triumviral period ruined many and promoted some. Territorial expansion and the civil wars of Caesar and the Pompeians increased the need for commanders and administrators; reliable and successful soldiers claimed rewards from the victor; despite casualties, the number of senators was inflated under Caesar. The wars which followed gave men of all classes further opportunities to rise. For example, Caesar's friendship secured the consulship of Cornelius Balbus of Gades (40 B.C.). The freedman's son Q. Horatius Flaccus would probably not have held an equestrian command if Brutus had not badly needed officers. Calvisius Sabinus (probably of Spoleto) was promoted by Caesar and rewarded by Octavian for attempting to defend the dictator against his assassins. He was consul in 39 and did Octavian good service in the navy and as governor of Spain during the war of Actium. A son and grandson follow him to the consulship. C. Carrinas (cos. suff. 43) is comparable. Young men of hitherto obscure Italian families came up with Octavian, for instance Salvidienus Rufus (who should have been consul in 39). M. Vipsanius Agrippa, who dropped the gentile name which revealed his un-Roman background, outshone them all. The piping days of peace gave fewer opportunities to soldiers, but reliability and efficiency might still win promotion through imperial favour and the eloquent new man might still rise through forensic oratory.[31]

---

[30] Brunt 1965 (F 11), 1988 (F 15); Wiseman 1971 (D 81) 35ff; Saller 1982 (F 59); Wallace-Hadrill 1989 (F 75).

[31] Tac. *Dial.* VIII.3. Curtius Rufus (cos. suff. A.D. 43, legate of Upper Germany 47) was alleged to

III. SOCIAL PROBLEMS AT THE BEGINNING
OF THE PRINCIPATE

The two themes of Romans who reflected on the twenty years after the murder of Caesar were social disruption and moral decay. The agony of the civil wars of the 80s and the shameful proscriptions of Sulla had been burned into the memory of Cicero's generation (Cic. *Cat.* II.20). Cicero himself perished in the second proscription, ordered by younger men. His elder, M. Terentius Varro (116–27), survived, but his book *On Peace* dates to the aftermath of Caesar's civil war, when his Pompeian sympathies had been forgiven, not to the peace dominated by the last and youngest of the triumvirs.[32]

C. Sallustius Crispus (?86–35), a new man from Sabine territory who reached the praetorship under Caesar (46), between 44 and 35 produced a series of works on the decline of the Republic, diagnosing its ills as avarice, luxury and selfish ambition. Since 146 B.C., *avaritia* had driven out good faith and replaced it with pride, cruelty, irreligion and venality. *Ambitio* taught deceit and treachery to friends. *Luxuria* came in with Sulla's eastern wars: conspicuous and reckless consumption included sexual and sensual indulgence of all kinds and a mania for building private houses, where the Romans of old had built simple temples. Sallust sounds notes which recur in Horace a decade later.[33]

Cornelius Nepos, from Cisalpina, friend of Cicero, Atticus and Catullus (*c.* 99 – *c.* 24 B.C.), made no sermons on civil war, but his assessment of Atticus' life defends the virtue of the able and rich *eques* who chose to take no part in politics, to be the friend simultaneously of Hortensius and Cicero, or of Brutus and Antony or Antony and Octavian, and (more remarkably) to succour the losers.[34] Since the second edition of this life appeared between Atticus' death in 32 and 27 B.C., it took courage to point out what wisdom Atticus had displayed in keeping the friendship of both Octavian and Antony when they were rivals for supreme power (20.5). Nepos preferred Atticus, who never lost a friend, to the warring princes who corresponded with him about literature. It was not many years later that one of Brutus' former officers, re-reading Homer, praised the peacemakers and criticized ruthless leaders. Achilles was ruled by passion, and both he and Agamemnon by

be the son of a gladiator. But Tiberius defended him by saying that 'he seemed to be his own father' (Tac. *Ann* XI.21.3, cf. Cic. *Phil.* VI.17: Cicero 'a se ortum').

[32] Varro's fragmentary early Satires include *Sexagesis*, about a Rip Van Winkle who went to sleep for fifty years and awoke *c.* 70 B.C. to find a great increase in greed, luxury and corruption (in Bücheler, *Petronii Saturae* 315ff, frr. 485–505).

[33] Sall. *Cat.* 10–13. The link between extravagance and civil war is explicitly made in Tacitus' version of a letter of Tiberius on the subject of a proposed sumptuary law (*Ann.* III.54.5).

[34] Nep. *Att.* 2.2, cf. 1.4, 8.6, 9.4f, 11.2, 4. See Horsfall 1989 (B 88).

anger: the parallel with Antony and Octavian is clear. Virtue and wisdom are personified by Ulysses, who tried to get his companions safely home and who resisted the harlot who tried to enslave him. Horace and his friends (he admits) follow bad leaders mindlessly, suppressing their anxieties and postponing the moral effort which is needed to save them.[35]

Sallust, Nepos and Horace were all conscious of the violent reversals of fortune which their age had witnessed. The fates of Pompey, Caesar and Antony were potent. Lesser men rose or fell. Octavian's admiral L. Tarius Rufus was said to have sprung from the lowest level of society (Pliny, *HN* XVIII.37: 'infima natalium humilitate'). Horace attacks an alleged ex-slave who became a military tribune (*Epod.* IV). Varying fortune raised men or ruined them, putting down the mighty and advancing the obscure.[36] Men were perturbed by the ambition of leaders, vices of generals, changes in the state, revolution, violent disaster, the fall of the great and the rise of the humble.[37] The Roman instinct was to get back to a mythical *status quo*, to a time when citizens were brave, hardworking, unselfish and harmonious.

Cicero had advised Caesar, when he controlled the state, to stabilize the Republic and so avoid further dissension (*Marcell.* 29); in particular he ought to set up courts, restore credit, repress self-indulgent vices, propagate children, and by means of severe laws tie up everything which had collapsed and run wild (*ibid.* 23). This vague and viticultural recipe represents a return to old values and discipline, imposed from outside. Caesar, as dictator like Sulla, could claim a mandate to rebuild the state. Sulla had systematized courts and magistracies and passed a sumptuary law (Gell. *NA* II.24.11); Caesar too tidied up the system, passed repressive measures, tackled the financial crisis and perhaps (Dio XLIII.25.2) offered rewards to fathers of large families. Sumptuary laws checked extravagance in meals, building and perhaps women's jewellery.[38]

The triumvirs, charged, like Sulla, with rebuilding, concerned themselves with the excision of their enemies from the body politic and other urgent measures. Once the emergency was advertised as over in 28,[39] Octavian had to take up the work of reconstruction. Before, Horace had prayed for the cessation of civil war, now he turns to a Sallustian diagnosis of problems to be solved. As Augustus, the ruler must aspire to be a father of cities (*Carm.* III.24). Founders were expected to construct a society as well as a constitution. It was in these years that Livy

---

[35] Hor. *Epist.* 1.2. especially 7–11, 12–16, 17–22, 25, 26–33. (Dated to 22 by Fraenkel 1957 (B 53) 316.)   [36] Nep. *Att.* 10.2; Hor. *Carm.* 1.34.12ff, 1.35.2f.   [37] Nep. *Att.* 16.4.
[38] Yavetz 1983 (C 252) 154f.   [39] Syme 1939 (A 93) 306f; Wells 1984 (A 101) 53ff.

was describing the work of Romulus and Numa. The date at which Dionysius of Halicarnassus worked on the same theme is obscure: it is tempting to associate his remarks on Romulus with the debate on whether it was worth attempting to legislate morality which took place between 28 and 18, but as his book began to be circulated in 7, its composition may well postdate the legislation of 18 B.C.[40]

Dionysius took the traditional philosophical view that the state depended on households, so the lawgiver should start by regulating marriages and sexual conduct. Romulus was an effective lawgiver. Instead of passing specific laws which allowed a husband to sue for adultery or desertion or a wife for ill-usage, desertion or recovery of dowry, he secured the good behaviour of wives by making marriage indissoluble and safeguarding their rights.[41] It was traditional that founders or constitution-makers regulated social behaviour. The Sicilian Diodorus (writing c. 60–30 B.C., died not earlier than 21) had recently given fresh currency to the legend that Zaleucus had enacted a law at Locri that a woman was not to leave the city at night, unless she was going to commit adultery, or to wear gold or purple unless she was a courtesan (XII.21.1). Charondas at Thurii was held to have legislated against adultery and remarriage for men (Stob. *Flor.* IV.2.24, cf. Diod. XII.12.1). Augustus would be expected to link sumptuary legislation and sexual behaviour.

The restoration of temples in 28[42] seems to have been accompanied by an effort to shore up sexual *mores*.[43] A remark of Livy's on Roman intolerance of necessary remedies (*Praef.* 9) and an ode of Horace (III.24) suggest that reaction was so unfavourable that Augustus dropped the proposal for the moment. Horace calls on an undefined man to restore old values of frugality and chastity to Rome: 'Oh whoever wishes to take away impious slaughter and civil madness, if he seeks to have the words "Father of cities" inscribed beneath his statues, let him dare to curb unbroken licence. He will be glorious to posterity.' The benefactor will need courage, but a later generation will be grateful to him. The link is made between the vices of parents and the corruption of children: fathers are avaricious and unscrupulous, mothers, thanks to their rich dowries, can control their husbands or take lovers. Surplus wealth should be given to Capitoline Jove (or thrown away). The horsebreaking or

---

[40] Cf. Balsdon 1971 (B 11).

[41] *Ant. Rom.* II.24–26.1. On this tendentious passage see Corbett 1930 (F 650) 219ff; Watson 1975 (F 701) 34.

[42] *RG* 19.2, 20.4, cf. App. 2; Nep. *Att.* 20.3 (temple of Iuppiter Feretrius restored on Atticus' advice).

[43] Prop. II.7. Cf. Flor. II.34; Oros. VI.22.3. The view given in the text is best presented by Williams 1962 (C 251). Badian 1985 (F 4) has recently challenged this reconstruction (with full bibliography).

pruning will not be pleasant: penalties will be needed, but legislation is useless without a fundamental change in behaviour.

Contemporary analysis of social problems focused on morality. Since a poor man or a slave might be thought to have deserved his lot because of bad character, we should not expect Romans to see poverty and slavery as social problems which required cure. But moderns, starting from their own presuppositions, diagnose slavery and the comparative stagnation of the Roman economy as the main causes of the top-heavy social system. The emperors palliated the insecurity of the poor of the city. They also propped up members of the senatorial class who were unable to maintain the economic base which public service and high position required. They sent aid in response to disasters. There was some 'humanitarian' legislation on the treatment of slaves, but this was dictated by concern for morality and the security of the free population rather than for the slaves: the result might be Claudius' decree that sick slaves abandoned by their owners were free, or the Silanian *senatusconsultum* of A.D. 10 providing for the torture of all slaves present in the house when the master was murdered.[44] The exceptionally high proportion of slaves in Italian society depressed the condition of the poorer Romans and their reproductivity.[45] Rome had once had great reserves of manpower: now, despite her admired generosity with the citizenship, the supply of soldiers was drying up. Augustus' preoccupation is indicated by his introduction of registration for legitimate children and enfranchised aliens.[46] If, as seems likely, it was Augustus himself who introduced the rule that soldiers could not marry, he must have been thinking only of military discipline and not of the usefulness of breeding citizens for the legions.[47]

IV. THE SOCIAL LEGISLATION OF AUGUSTUS AND THE JULIO-CLAUDIANS

The decade after 23 B.C. saw concentrated legislation in various areas. Augustus himself claimed that his laws re-introduced old standards and set an example to posterity. Like Horace, he harks back to a mythical past. Tiberius was in closer accord with the tradition of the republican aristocracy when he deprecated interference in private morality.[48]

---

[44] *D.* 40.8.2. Silanian decree: Barrow 1928 (F 5) 56. See also Watson 1983 (F 702).

[45] Tac. *Ann.* IV.27.3 for Rome. Brunt 1971 (A 9) 131–55 for Italy.

[46] Brunt 1971 (A 9) 114 (birth registration mentioned in both the Lex Aelia Sentia and the Lex Papia Poppaea, cf. *FIRA* III 2–3), *ibid.* 120 (aliens). See Gardner 1986 (F 34).

[47] Dio LX.24.3 shows that the ban on soldiers' marriage predates Claudius. Cf. Campbell 1978 (D 172).

[48] *RG* 8.5; Tac. *Ann* III.52–56.1, especially 54.5, on debate on sumptuary measures in A.D. 22, cf.

Augustus could not enforce his reforms without at least some measure of consensus: this he presumably achieved by 18, when the Senate and People approved the Julian law on the marriage of the orders.[49] The Julian law on adultery is convincingly dated to the same year. Some curbs on luxury had been introduced by sumptuary legislation regulating public banquets in 22, maximum expenditure on dinner parties, and perhaps other extravagances which may have included the building mania attacked by Horace.[50]

1. Marriage

Opposition to the marriage law was not stifled when it was passed: Augustus apparently had to make various modifications (Suet. *Aug.* 34, Dio LVI.10). Major revision (with some concessions) took place in the crisis year A.D. 9, when the suffect consuls Papius and Poppaeus updated the Julian law. Some complexities in the administration of the law seem to have been sorted out by a senatorial committee under Tiberius in A.D. 20 (Tac. *Ann.* III.28.6); refinements were introduced by juristic interpretation; later emperors restated or refined the law. The difference between the Julian and the Papio-Poppaean laws is obscured because the law as it stood from A.D. 9 is normally cited by the jurists as the Julian and Papian law. It seems clear that the original law had introduced penalties against men and women who were unmarried at an age at which they were expected to be married, or childless at an age when they could have been parents. It formulated rules about the intermarriage of people of various classes (which reflected previous custom) and introduced rewards to encourage parenthood.

The motive for the law seems to have been that Augustus perceived men as reluctant to marry: he read to the Senate the old speech of Metellus which contained the hackneyed *aperçu* that, though marriage had its inconvenient side it was necessary for the survival of state and family, through the production of children. He also perceived men as reluctant to father and rear children: Germanicus in A.D. 9 was presented as a model father (Suet. *Aug.* 34). This perception of the aristocracy goes back at least to the second century. Augustus, who held a census in 28, had hard evidence on the number of children claimed by citizen fathers.[51]

III.25–8, especially 28.6 on Lex Julia et Papia; Suet. *Tib.* 35.1 for family disciplining of adulteresses. The evidence on the texts of the marriage laws is conveniently assembled by B. Biondi in *ADA* no. 28, 166ff. The best account of the law is Brunt 1971 (A 9) App. 8. Cf. Treggiari 1991 (F 70) 277ff.

[49] *RG* 6.2, cf. Hor. *Carm. Saec.* 17f.

[50] *Carm.* III.1.33ff, 24.3f. For Augustus' law in 22 B.C. see Dio LIV.2.3; Suet. *Aug.* 34; Gell. *NA* II.24.14. For the aftermath, Tac. *Ann.* III.52–5 (A.D. 22): Tiberius' refusal to witch-hunt, although Augustus' law neglected. For previous laws see Gell. *NA* II.24; Macrob. *Sat.* III.13.13.

[51] Cf. Brunt 1971 (A 9) 113ff on the Augustan census.

Dio suggests that there was a known shortage of 'well-born' (which seems in this context to mean freeborn) women: 'Since males far outnumbered females among the freeborn, he encouraged anyone who wanted to marry even freedwomen, except the senators, and he ordered that their reproduction should be legitimate' (LIV.16.2). Moderns now generally agree that marriage between freeborn and freed had not (as Dio implies) been forbidden before: if he is muddled on this point it does not inspire faith in his views on the sex ratio.[52] Dio may be arguing back from the law to the situation.[53] But if contemporaries perceived a shortage of women, their best evidence would have been the census, in which fatherless unmarried women may have been under-reported (as women are in modern non-industrial populations). A real imbalance between the sexes might be caused by abandonment or malnutrition of girl babies. If Augustus saw this as a problem, we might expect measures against abandonment (which would constitute no greater invasion of privacy than did his adultery law). But he impartially encouraged the rearing of children of either sex. Nothing confirms Dio's alleged cause for the endorsement of hypergamy for freedwomen, nor did the text of the law speak only of freedwomen but of freedmen as well (*D* 23.2.44 *pr.*).

The law forbade intermarriage of senators, their sons, sons' sons and grandsons, their daughters, sons' daughters and sons' sons' daughters with freed persons, actors and actors' children. This is the first indication that the *liberi* of senators were to be regarded as sharing and affecting their status, although they are not yet called *senatorii*.[54] Freeborn Roman citizens were forbidden to marry infamous persons such as prostitutes. A person of higher rank was naturally barred from marriages forbidden to his inferiors (*D* 23.2.49). Forbidden marriages seem not originally to have been null but not to have conferred the advantages provided by the law.

The law was long and complicated. It invalidated provisions against marriage imposed by third parties. It laid down a series of penalties for the unmarried (*caelibes*), and for men over twenty-five and women over twenty who were childless (*orbi*).[55] A *caelebs* could not take under the will of anyone outside the sixth degree (unless he or she married within 100

---

[52] Watson 1967 (F 700) 33ff. For the interpretation of 'well-born' see Brunt 1971 (A 9) 558.

[53] Rawson 1986 (F 54) 49 n. 51.

[54] *D*. 23.2.44: 'qui senator est quive filiuis neposve ex filio proneposve ex filio nato cuius eorum est erit ...' Cf. Nicolet 1976 (D 53) 38.

[55] The prescribed ages for marriages were from twenty (or perhaps less, since this age is directly attested for parenthood: *Tit. Ulp.* 16.1) to fifty for women and twenty-five to sixty for men. (*Tit. Ulp.* 16.1; *Gnomon of the Idiologus* (*FIRA* I 99) 24–8; cf. Sen. fr. 119 Haase; Suet. *Claud.* 23.1; Tert. *Apol.* 4.8. There were grace periods for a woman who was widowed or divorced (two years and eighteen months from A.D. 9).

days: *Tit. Ulp.* 17.1); a married but childless person could only take half. Unclaimed property went to heirs or legatees who fulfilled the law's conditions or, failing that, to the treasury. The unmarried seem to have been debarred from public games (EJ[2] 30A, but cf. Suet. *Aug.* 34.2). The law offered rewards, for example, to parents of one child by allowing one year's seniority in public office[56] or the right to inherit each other's whole estate or to take under the wills of people outside the sixth degree; three children exempted a father from various legal duties in Rome (four in Italy, five in the provinces), three enabled a freedman worth HS 100,000 to exclude his patron from inheriting, two to get off services promised to his patron; three released a freeborn woman, four a freedwoman, from guardianship (Gai. *Inst.* III.44).

The law paid particular attention to the wealthier classes and freed persons. The reason was probably practical. Although he continued the grain-dole to adult male citizens in Rome, Augustus was in no position to finance family allowances for poor citizens (there was occasional largesse to fathers: Suet, *Aug.* 46), but he could release *libertini* who became parents from certain disabilities and duties (which cost him nothing) and he could interfere with the free transfer of property. In stopping *orbi* who had given no children to the state from enriching themselves with the property of strangers, and in seeing that property ultimately went to the community, he attacked the problems of avarice and childlessness. He was concerned to maintain the prestige of the senatorial class by checking marriage with people who might have dubious antecedents, but he was not concerned to delineate class boundaries or to favour native parents over freed.[57]

Augustus' laws responded to a complex situation and shifting political possibilities. It is a mistake to ask what his one motive was in inspiring the legislation of 18 B.C. and A.D. 9. The need to encourage nuptiality and reproductivity in order to supply Rome with soldiers and administrators appears to have been most prominent in the minds of Augustus and his advisers. The laws would also serve to encourage the upper classes to breed sons to succeed them in their dignities and property: it reinforced the executive measures which Augustus took to recruit qualified men to the service of the state and to encourage continuity, loyalty and *esprit de corps*.[58]

---

[56] Dio LIV.16.1. Seniority: Lex Malacitana (*FIRA* I 24) 56; Gell. *NA* II.15.3–6; cf. Suet. *Tib.* 35.2.

[57] Brunt 1971 (A 9) 561ff.

[58] Brunt 1971 (A 9) 104, 114 argues that Augustus' motive was demographic, but the law 'would at best have had little demographic effect' (154). Galinsky 1981 (F 32) concentrates on the need to maintain the morality and moral prestige of the ruling class. Wallace-Hadrill 1981 (F 73) stresses economic motives.

2. Adultery

The Julian law on adultery and extramarital sexual intercourse is intimately connected with the marriage law.[59] It covered adultery by married women and all kinds of fornication (*stuprum*) involving a person of respectable status. Slaves, prostitutes and women in low professions thought to involve sexual services (for instance, tavern waitresses) were outside the scope of the law.

Public sanctions against seduction of boys already existed. Adulterous wives had until now been dealt with by husbands or families, divorced and sometimes penalized by loss of one-sixth of their dowries or by relegation 200 miles from Rome. Rapists and seducers could be privately sued for damages. A permanent court was now set up to deal with adultery and *stuprum*. The law was exhaustive and complex; interpretation accrued. The most important of the known provisions are as follows. A husband who knew of his wife's adultery was to divorce her (with seven citizens as witnesses, *D* 24.2.9) and he or her father was then to prosecute her within sixty days. If he failed to prosecute, then an outsider might do so within the next four months, or if the husband failed to divorce, within five years from the alleged offence. A woman convicted by the court lost half her dowry and one-third of her other property and was relegated to an island. She could not form another fully valid marriage. The alleged adulterer might be brought to trial subsequently: the penalties were confiscation of half his property and relegation to a different island. A husband who failed to divorce risked the same penalties on a charge of pandering, as did anyone who married a convicted adulteress. A wife could not prosecute her husband for his adultery with a married woman, but if she connived at it she could be prosecuted, as could anyone who facilitated the affair. Detailed rules were laid down on the degree of violence which a husband or father who caught a woman in the act might subsequently justify. A husband could defend himself against a charge of having murdered the lover only if the latter was of low status; the wife's father could kill any lover caught in the act, but only in his own or the husband's house and if the woman was under his legal control or her husband's, but he had also at least to attempt to kill his daughter. Such murders seem to have been rare. The husband was forbidden to kill his wife.[60]

In describing the purpose and impact of the law, both ancient and modern writers tend to concentrate on the provisions about adultery, which was of interest to jurists because it caused divorce and loss of dowry. But the law may initially have been motivated not only by the

---

[59] *ADA* no 14, 112ff. Corbett 1930 (F 650) 133ff; Gardner 1986 (F 33) 127ff; Raditsa 1980 (F 53).
[60] There are traces of killings in second and third century rescripts: *D* 48.5.33 *pr.*, 39.8; *CJ* IX.9.4.

conviction that women were evading a commitment to chastity implicit in the marriage bond and that their adultery threatened the stability of the family and the production of legitimate children, but also by a conservative backlash against the *mores* of the fiercely individualistic aristocrats, whose conspiracies were allegedly cemented by homosexual bonds formed in adolescence and by collusion in heterosexual intrigue.[61] The lurid picture painted by Cicero for the entertainment of Atticus about procurement of an acquittal attests the deep conviction of old-fashioned Romans that some aristocrats were sexual *mafiosi* and that irregular sexual practices were at the root of political corruption.[62] It is difficult to separate slander from reality.

Realities of sexual conduct are comparatively inaccessible even through questionnaire and autobiography, harder to reach by way of political oratory or erotic verse. Latin literature had recently turned to exploration of emotional life; in law by about 100 B.C., marriages in which the husband had legal control of the wife had become uncommon; women had more independence in the bestowal of themselves and their property; wives, like husbands, could divorce unilaterally and without necessarily suffering severe economic consequences, scandal or complete separation from children. Men connected this social and legal emancipation with a sexual revolution. The evidence which reaches us is tendentious and it is impossible to measure the incidence of adultery and fornication in the society of Caelius and Clodia or of Ovid and Iulia. Augustus, who suffered not only the usual accusations of homosexuality but also circumstantial criticisms of adulteries with women of standing, and who had certainly married the divorced Livia with indelicate haste (Suet. *Aug.* 69, cf. his letter to Maecenas: *Ep.* fr. 32, Malcovati), was in a good position to assess the sexual morality of the upper classes, but can hardly have had statistical data.

The severe penalties ordained by the adultery law inflicted suffering on everyone concerned. A husband confronted with undeniable evidence stood at least to lose his wife (whom he might regret) and also most of her dowry. Although relegation was not always permanent and some social life must have developed on the islands, the lives of condemned women in particular were ruined. The system was (as for the marriage law) operated by private prosecutors, who, if successful, were rewarded by a percentage of the confiscated property. This opened the door to persecution of the wealthier members of society, while it was

---

[61] Suetonius lists the law on electoral bribery between marriage and adultery (*Aug.* 34; cf. Dio LIV.16.1).

[62] *Att.* 1.16.5. On the link between sexual immorality and subversion: Sall. *Cat.* 15. Homosexual bonding of conspirators or dangerous radicals: e.g. Cic. *Cat.* II.22f, *Dom.* 49, *Phil.* II.44f; heterosexual: *Dom.* 25, 83; Sall. *Cat.* 25. See Griffin 1977 (C 104) 21f on the 'stereotype of the man of action who lives a life of luxury', alternately admired and attacked.

hardly worth an outsider's while to pursue humbler adulterers. It also meant that a husband, to protect his wife, might divorce and prosecute her and hope that she would be acquitted (*D* 48.5.3). The law made some gestures towards preserving the stability of marriages: for instance, if a husband kept his wife a prosecutor would have to sue him first, for conniving (*D* 48.5.12.10, 48.5.27), and if a divorced woman remarried without having received notice of prosecution, the prosecutor was to sue her alleged lover first (*D* 48.5.18.6, 48.5.12.11), but its overall effect was to destabilize. Adultery cases could be brought by *delatores*, men who made money and a career by prosecution, and a charge of adultery (how well founded we naturally cannot tell) was routinely brought when someone wanted to ruin an imperial or senatorial woman (e.g. Gaius' sisters, Nero's wife Octavia).

3. Effectiveness of the laws on marriage and adultery

The laws were praised by Horace, in the *Secular Hymn* of 17 B.C., for producing children (17ff) and, in the *Odes*, for having curbed licence and restored old values (*Carm.* IV.15.9ff). Households were clear of *stuprum* and wives bore children who looked like their husbands (IV.5.20ff). Circumspection in recommending extramarital affairs was imposed on Ovid but perhaps morals were unaffected: Augustus and others in 2 B.C. discerned promiscuity in the heart of the governing class.

The marriage law of 18 B.C. does not seem to have impelled Horace to marry; the consuls who proposed the second law were *caelibes*, though it need not be assumed that they were lifelong bachelors. What was the situation before? Custom dictated that upper-class women married early in their reproductive years and, if necessary, often. Since a dowry provided income, a young Marcus or young Quintus Cicero might start considering matrimony in his early twenties; the rich *eques* Atticus married in his fifties; the normal age may have been in the late twenties. Men were not necessarily repelled by the idea of marrying: the demographic problem was that, while generally interested in breeding heirs to their name and property, they miscalculated by producing fewer than those needed to replace themselves and continue their lines.[63] Most men had wives through most of adult life. The law sought to make them marry younger – and here there is some visible impact in the careers of young senators, such as Agricola – and to rear more children. In setting the ages of parenthood at twenty for women and twenty-five for men, Augustus was not encouraging an unhealthy age of first pregnancy: this requirement suggested an age of marriage of about eighteen for women and twenty-two or twenty-three for men. Senators seem to have adopted

[63] Hopkins 1983 (A 46) chs. 2, 3, especially 69ff.

the latter.[64] There was no need for the upper classes to change their habits in marrying off their daughters. The most eligible girls probably continued to marry before eighteen. One child probably sufficed for entitlement to inheritances; a bigger family secured seniority in a political career.

The effect of the adultery law is hard to assess. Its deterrent effect might be demonstrated by the comparative rarity of known trials. Or did the upper class close ranks and discourage delation? Augustus himself invoked it in 2 B.C. and A.D. 8 and sharpened the penalties (Tac. *Ann.* III.24.2f). Later attested trials usually involved women of the highest position and the charge was often linked with treason.[65] Prosecutions for *stuprum* are rarely documented. Tiberius, perhaps deploring Augustus' interference in private life, as he found sumptuary legislation vain, encouraged reversion to domestic jurisdiction (Suet. *Tib.* 35.1), although he checked women who attempted to evade the law by registering as prostitutes.[66] Moralists continued to claim that adultery was rife.[67] Domitian revived the law, which may suggest that he thought the number of prosecutions insufficient. But professional prosecutors presented a threat to the rich: the law encouraged not only collusion and cover-up, but blackmail (*D* 4.2.7.1). Renewal and expansion of both marriage and adultery laws and the continuing interest of jurists suggest that, although the laws failed in their general aim and, as Tacitus says, corruption and legislation went together, they were sporadically enforced, especially against the rich and prominent.[68]

4. Manumission

Ambivalent traditions guarded the citizen body. Constant appeal was made to the ancestral virtues of Romans and Latins. But the extension of citizen rights to non-citizens was deep-rooted. The extension was grounded in practical needs, but justified by the moral qualities of the recipient – industry, loyalty, courage, eloquence. Men who would adopt the ancient customs of Romans deserved to be recruited. As the Senate was theoretically open to the good and rich, so the citizenship was to be open to the best men of allied states and to slaves and other non-citizens who deserved well (Cic. *Arch.* 19, 22ff, *Balb.* especially 24, 31). The

---

[64] Shaw 1987 (F 65), modifying Hopkins 1965 (F 41); Saller 1987 (F 60).

[65] Attested trials or punishments under Augustus and the Julio-Claudians usually concern members of the imperial family (e.g. the Iuliae, Appuleia Varilla, Aemilia Lepida, Claudia Pulchra, Livilla, Octavia).

[66] Suet. *Tib.* 35.2; Tac. *Ann.* II.8.5; *AE* 1978, 145 with Levick 1983 (C 369).

[67] E.g. Sen. *Ben.* I.9–10. Various scandals in Tacitus, e.g. *Ann.* XIII.21, 42, 44, 45, XIV.1, XV.68.

[68] *Ann.* III.27.5. Cf. Garnsey 1970 (F 35) 21ff. See further Bauman 1968 (F 6); Garnsey 1967 (D 258).

enfranchisement of slaves was effected chiefly by their owners by three formal methods: by the census, by the rod (a procedure before a magistrate with *imperium*) or posthumously by testament.[69] The increase in wealth in the late Republic meant a huge increase in the number an individual owner could enfranchise; slaves might be freed not as a reward for long or outstanding service, but in order to give their new votes or political support to their ex-owner (*patronus*) or relieve him of the direct burden of their support, by claiming the grain allowance in Rome. Private bodyguards and private armies increased the need for trusted *liberti*.[70] The right of a citizen man or woman to pass on full citizen rights to slaves is remarkable – especially when we remember that a *Romana* had no vote and could not secure citizen rights to her own children by a non-Roman husband. Augustus, as patron of the whole state could not shake this entrenched system, but he had reason to regulate the influx of citizens which any private owner could create at a time. Horace, the freedman's son, in a savage epode had attacked a former slave, scarred by public flogging, who sat in the fourteen rows with the *equites* (*Epod.* 4). Augustus, after advertising victory in a 'slave war' against Sextus Pompeius, may well have thought it necessary to regulate manumission (Cf. *RG* 25.1; Dio LVI.33.3). Dionysius explicitly connects the legislation with a need to keep out criminals (IV.24).

Manumission by will took effect on the owner's death, by census only at Rome and sporadically (and this method became obsolete under Augustus), by the rod only when a magistrate was available (but in the provinces as at Rome) (*Tit. Ulp.* 1.6–9). For convenience or haste, owners might free their slaves informally, by a written or verbal declaration. This method did not confer citizenship but allowed the slave temporary liberty, which might be protected by the praetor.[71] Any property, or children born to an informally freed woman, belonged to the master (*fr. Dos.* 5). Equity demanded that owners should not be encouraged to shrug off their responsibilities while retaining their privileges in this way.[72]

Three laws regulated manumission, the Lex Fufia Caninia of 2 B.C., the Lex Aelia Sentia of A.D. 4 and a Lex Iunia of uncertain date, which is associated with the Aelio-Sentian law and seems to precede it. It fits well with Augustus' social engineering (particularly with an urge to keep legal status tidy) and may tentatively be assigned to 17 B.C., the period of

---

[69] Cic. *Top.* 10; Watson 1967 (F 700) 185ff; Treggiari 1969 (F 68) 20ff.
[70] Treggiari 1969 (F 68) 11ff.
[71] Gai. *Inst.* III.56; *fr. Dos.* 5; Buckland 1908 (F 645) 444ff; Treggiari 1969 (F 68) 29ff.
[72] For a brief account of the history of manumission down to Justinian see Watson 1987 (F 703) 23ff. On the Augustan legislation, Buckland 1908 (F 645) 533ff; Bradley 1984 (F 10) 87ff.

Augustus' major efforts in this area.[73] The Lex Iunia recognized informally freed slaves and gave them freedom and a half-citizenship, as 'Junian Latins', like that of Latin colonists of an earlier age. The law specified that the owner must want the slave to be free and that he must be worthy of freedom in the opinion of the magistrate whose duty it would be to protect him; there were various details about the rights of owners.[74] The law proved useful and adaptable: further rulings were gradually added.[75]

Another area was regulated by the Fufio-Caninian law, which limited the numbers an owner could free by will. This method was popular because it displayed generosity at the expense of heirs. Augustus introduced a sliding scale: testators might free both slaves if they only had two, half the total if they had two to ten, a third if ten to thirty, a fourth if thirty to 100, one fifth if 100–500, and never more than 100. But they might always free as many as they would have been allowed if they had been in the category below (so an owner of thirty-two might free ten, rather than eight). This law applied only to will: an owner could still free as many as he liked in his lifetime.[76] Augustus had now regulated the two methods of manumission which had previously needed no specific ratification by public authority.

The Lex Aelia Sentia was a comprehensive law on manumission and the resulting rights of patrons and *libertini*. It required the freedman to show gratitude. It contained a requirement that the manumitter must be over twenty, but if he could prove a valid reason before a magistrate with *imperium* and a special council (five senators and five *equites* in Rome, or twenty citizens in the provinces) he could free by the rod (or informally).[77] The motive must be honourable: this was interpreted as meaning that the council might approve manumission of a blood relative or quasi-relative such as a nurse, a benefactor or a girl a master wanted to

[73] As Buckland 1908 (F 645) 534ff, Duff 1928 (F 28) 210ff and others argued, against those who, on the basis of a shaky late text (Just. *Inst*. 1.5.3) which names it the Lex Iunia Norbana, want to put it in A.D. 19 (when a pair of consuls had the requisite names). The positive argument for the Junian law antedating the Aelio-Sentian rests on Gai. *Inst*. 1.29 and 31, which suggest that slaves freed under thirty were Latins before the Aelio-Sentian law granted them the right to acquire full citizenship by claiming a one-year-old child. A suitable date would be 17 B.C., when C. Iunius Silanus was consul and Augustus was able to concentrate on social legislation. Also possible is 25 B.C., the consulate of M. Iunius Silanus, favoured by de Domenicis 1966 (F 27) and by Atkinson in her interesting reassessment, Atkinson 1966 (F 3) 366. Sherwin-White 1973 (A 87) 332ff argues for a Tiberian date. The evidence does not permit a sure solution.

[74] Gai. *Inst*. 1.17, 22ff; *fr. Dos*. 6–15; *Tit. Ulp*. 1.10, and other references in Buckland 1908 (F 645) 533f. The law is not in *ADA*.

[75] Atkinson 1966 (F 3) 362f argues that the Lex Aelia Sentia incorporated part of the Lex Iunia. For further rulings on Junian Latins see Gai. *Inst*. 1. 32bff.

[76] Gai. *Inst*. 1.43ff; *Tit. Ulp*. 1.24; Paulus, *Sent*. IV.14.4. See further *ADA* no. 35, 202ff.

[77] *ADA* no. 36, 205ff.

marry. The law also introduced a minimum age for the slave, thirty,
again with the possibility of justifying exceptions before a council.[78] A
younger slave did not become a citizen, but probably a Latin.[79] The law
also invalidated manumission which defrauded a creditor or a patron,
and it debarred from either citizen or Latin rights slaves previously
punished as criminals by their owners or the state, by whatever means
they were freed.[80] These were put in a pre-existing category of particularly recalcitrant surrendered enemies, the *dediticii*. They had to reside at
least 100 miles from Rome[81] and could not make a will[82] or inherit.[83]
Junian Latins were prohibited by the Junian law from making a will (*Tit.
Ulp.* 20.14). Unlike *dediticii*, they were encouraged to become full
citizens. For instance, a man freed under thirty who had become a Latin,
could prove that he had in accordance with the Aelio-Sentian Law
married a Roman or Latin woman and had a year-old child and claim
promotion to full citizenship for himself and his family.[84] The Visellian
Law, under Tiberius (?A.D. 24) gave Roman citizenship to Junians who
served six years in the *vigiles*; a Claudian edict to those who built a ship of
at least 10,000 measures and transported grain to Rome for six years, and
Nero to those who built a house in Rome costing at least HS 100,000.[85]
Formal repetition by *iusta manumissio* after thirty also gave full citizenship.[86] This law, among other things, laid down guidelines for magistrates who authorized a manumission.

Ancient sources thought Augustus aimed at checking the flow of
servile and foreign blood into the citizen body.[87] Though the Fufio-
Caninian law may have reduced the number of manumissions, the rest of
his legislation blocked only criminal ex-slaves and made access to
citizenship easier for others. He aimed to regulate, not to stop the
talented and energetic. Pollution by foreigners remained a favourite
theme of writers. But by the time of Nero it could be argued that most
senators and *equites* had ex-slaves in their family trees (Tac. *Ann.*
XIII.27.2).

Later emperors also intervened. The Visellian law regulated the
promotion of freedmen, pursuing those who sought offices reserved for
the freeborn, unless they obtained the gold ring by application to the

---

[78] Gai. *Inst.* 1.18–19, with details on *causae*; *Tit. Ulp.* 1.12.

[79] As *Tit. Ulp.* 1.12 says for one freed *testamento*. Gai. *Inst.* 1.16f seems to make this certain.

[80] *Tit. Ulp.* 1.11; cf. Gai. *Inst.* 1.13ff.

[81] Under penalty of re-enslavement: Gai. *Inst.* 1.27, 160.

[82] Either Roman, because they were foreign, or peregrine, because they had no citizenship (*Tit. Ulp.* 20.14).   [83] Gai. *Inst.* 1.25, III.74–6; *Tit. Ulp.* 22.2.

[84] Gai. *Inst.* 1.29–32b; if he died his wife could still claim, 32; later extended to other Junians *Tit. Ulp.* 3.3.

[85] *Tit. Ulp.* 3.5; cf. Gai. *Inst.* 1.32b, heavily restored; Gai. *Inst.* 1.32c, *Tit. Ulp.* 3.6; Gai. *Inst.* 1.33.

[86] Gai. *Inst.* 1.35, *Tit. Ulp.* 3.4.

[87] Suet. *Aug.* 40.3; cf. Dio LVI.33.3. Rejected by Atkinson 1966 (F 3) 357.

emperor (*CJ* IX.21), but also, as we have seen, assisting their rise in return for public service. Under Claudius, an important step was taken to channel talent into the service of the emperor himself, when Pallas the financial bureau chief excogitated a senatorial decree which ensured that if a slave lived in quasi-marriage with a free woman, his owner could, if he wished, take her and her children as his slaves. (The children would otherwise have been freeborn and illegitimate, and their father's owner have no rights over them.) The Senate may have thought they were repressing ambitious slaves and punishing perverse women, but the main motive was probably to allow the emperor to recruit back into his service the promising sons of his slave bureaucrats.[88] This system is introduced just when it seems that the upward mobility of slave 'civil servants' was recognized enough for them to become eligible husbands to freeborn women (although these were often daughters of imperial *liberti*).[89] We see in this later legislation nuanced measures designed for the state, not in the interests of any one group. It is unprofitable to expect general laws to be simple enough to be labelled as 'pro' or 'anti' a whole category of the population, let alone such a large and heterogeneous group as the slaves of Roman citizens.

V. THE IMPACT OF THE PRINCIPATE ON SOCIETY

Mixed 'marriages' (legally *contubernia*) between slave and freeborn persons are a striking indication of the fluidity of status which increases thanks to the dominant influence of great patrons and new opportunities for enrichment and influence which begin in the years of eastern and civil wars in the eighties B.C. and continue at least until the end of the Julio-Claudian period, vividly illustrated by the clients and freedmen of Sulla and Pompey and by the great Pallas and Felix. These brothers (so probably home-born slaves) were freed by the younger Antonia, daughter of Mark Antony and Octavia, and were employed, by her son Claudius, (probably) Pallas as *a rationibus* and Felix in such posts as the governorship of Judaea (52–60). Pallas' work and influence were acknowledged by the grant of praetorian insignia; Felix is alleged to have been married successively to three foreign princesses, including a granddaughter of Antony and Cleopatra.[90] The imperial slave or freed

---

[88] On 'civil servants' see above all Weaver 1972 (D 22). For this explanation of the SC Claudianum, 162ff. Cf. Weaver in Rawson 1986 (F 54) 145–69. Talbert 1984 (D 77) 441 lists the sources. The rule may also aim at acquisition of new slaves in general and avoidance of loss of patronal rights.   [89] Gai. *Inst.* 1.84, 91; Tac. *Ann.* XII.53.1; Weaver 1972 (D 22) 162ff.

[90] For Pallas, see Oost 1958 (C 383). For Felix, Weaver 1972 (D 22) 279. His name is proudly evoked by his daughter in commemorating his great-grandson, a boy of senatorial family (*CIL* V 34, Pola).

civil servants have rightly been seen as a 'symptom of the interpenetration of classes in Roman Imperial society'.[91]

Great freedmen consorted with senators and members of the imperial family (Pallas was an ally of Agrippina and accused of being her lover). Another of Antonia's ex-slaves, Antonia Caenis, was influential not only as a confidential secretary but as the mistress and later concubine of a future emperor, Vespasian. Claudia Acte in a similar role exercised influence and acquired wealth through Nero. Freedmen, barred normally from a public career, and freedwomen, barred, among other things, from marriage with *senatorii*, were partly dependent on their patrons, a dependence which could increase their usefulness and opportunities.

Imperial *liberti* provide a striking illustration of the difference the Principate made to Roman society. It was shocking to republican sentiment if dependent freedmen who were employed by patrons who held public office displayed their influence or wealth. Pompey caused offence; Cicero was discreet. Everyone needed the services of confidential administrators.[92] Augustus perforce continued the system, but on the whole succeeded in not publicizing the important role played by his own freedmen.[93] But while the freedmen of republican governors were important as long as their patrons were in office or power, the servants of Augustus who met the growing need for skilled subordinates could enjoy a longer and more secure career. For the first time, one man in control of Rome could evolve policy over a long period and needed a large and complex staff to supervise its administration. The beginnings of the 'civil service' under Augustus are obscure, for the surviving epigraphic data are thin. But it is clear that a staff of slaves and freedmen who belonged to the emperor himself and undertook specialized tasks which supported him in his public role gradually evolved during his Principate. Their legal status was that of his private household and individuals may have moved back and forth between functions which we would regard as domestic and those we would regard as public. They range from accountants and secretaries to the aqueduct workers recruited by Agrippa and bequeathed to the emperor, who remained as a distinct corps. Their social and economic position varied accordingly. These imperial civil servants parallel the *apparitores*. By the end of the Julio-Claudian period a (flexible) career structure had been established. The new minimum legal age of manumission seems to have been regarded as the norm. The death of an emperor implied no serious break

[91] Weaver 1964 (F 77) 315, quoted by Crook 1967 (F 21) 64.

[92] Treggiari 1969 (F 68) 152ff.

[93] Suet. *Aug.* 101.4 gives away the real importance of his servants. Augustus was scrupulous in refusing to invite freedmen to dinner (*ibid.* 74).

in continuity. The imperial bureaucracy functioned efficiently under a
Nero and only the most prominent freedmen might fail to survive a
change of dynasty. The most successful might be the ancestors of
senators; the ordinary freedmen of the emperor enjoyed advantages
unobtainable by the poorer freeborn citizen of the capital. It is the
patronage of the emperor and the administrative needs of the system
which fostered the growth of this bureaucracy. Just as Augustus shaped
the senatorial and equestrian orders to provide a pool from which
provincial administrators and army officers might be drawn, he created a
permanent substructure of lesser functionaries.

Senatorial sources, alert to detect that an emperor was swayed by non-
senators and people excluded from a constitutional position, would
attack wives, mothers and mistresses as well as ex-slaves. Women of the
imperial family were like freedmen in dependence and influence.
Antonia, Octavia's younger daughter by Antony, for instance, seems to
have endeared herself particularly to Augustus and Livia. She was kept
in reserve as a bride for Livia's son Drusus (they married when he was
twenty-two and she twenty), allowed to remain a widow on his death
(she had the requisite three children, but might normally have been
expected to remarry, since she was only twenty-seven) and held an
important position as the sister-in-law of Tiberius, the mother of
Germanicus (Tiberius' adopted son), the grandmother of Gaius and his
ill-fated brothers. She was a noted deployer of patronage, in the manner
of noble matrons, which had been expanded by Livia. Good fortune in
marriage alliances and motherhood and discreet conduct maintained and
enhanced the position of Livia[94] and Antonia; the fortunes of others
fluctuated. But the Principate gave the emperor's kinswomen opportunities richer than those enjoyed by republican ladies. Dynastic planning
by Augustus and his closest advisers brought noble families successively
into the imperial network, which was scarcely expanded by transient
marriages of later *principes*. The pattern remained that dictated by
Augustus, the descendants of his recruits providing new matches.
Emperors' wives whose position depended entirely on their husbands,
like Nero's Poppaea, could never attain the importance of the unrivalled
Agrippina, daughter of Germanicus, sister of Gaius, niece and then wife
of Claudius and mother of Nero.[95] Since influence depended on a
woman's position in relation to the current emperor, it often shifted.
Widowhood might push the elder Agrippina or Livia Julia to the
margins of power. Women had no lasting constitutional position. The
emperor might bestow the title 'Augusta'. But there were no empresses,
either as consorts or as mothers. Regnant women were even more
unthinkable. On the other hand, the position of women and children

94 See, e.g. Tac. *Ann.* v.1, Dio LVII.12.   95 Tac. *Ann.* XII.42.3.

related to Augustus was at once recognized by Romans and provincials.
Augustus' house was princely; the ladies might in the East be honoured
with the attributes of suitable goddesses, in the West have towns named
after them. Group portraits of the family set up by loyal towns may
include women and children.[96]

The independence and individuality of women (despite the restrictions of the marriage legislation and their deployment as brides) is
signalled by nomenclature. Few aristocrats in the Republic used a second
name for women. Practice becomes more flexible from Augustus on,
starting with the top. Livia Drusilla *dropped* her second name; her
stepdaughter Iulia's daughters were known as Iulia (a striking departure
from the rule that legitimate daughters take the father's name) and
Agrippina (from the father's *cognomen*). The daughter of Drusus and
Antonia was known not as Claudia, but by the two gentile names of Livia
(from her paternal grandmother) and Iulia (presumably from her step-
grandfather, Augustus). Maternal descent in a dynasty founded by a man
without a son acquires an importance unrecognized in old agnatic
theory. The upper class follows suit. There was also continued progress
in economic rights.[97] Accidents of survival and inheritance often
concentrated economic power in the hands of women in all the
propertied classes and no doubt down to the level of market-women.[98]

The existence of a 'court', with various nuclei (the circle of Iulia was
distinguishable on sight from that of Livia: Macrob. *Sat.* II.5.6) changed
the focus of society. Promotion was validated by the *princeps*, perhaps on
the recommendation of a Livia, a Maecenas or a Pallas.[99] Subventions to
enable a senator to maintain his status or dowries to protégées flowed
from the imperial family, who in turn were enriched by legacies from
foreign kings and wealthy Romans. Yet this was the last efflorescence of
the old aristocracy. The Julio-Claudians and their kin died out, the last
males wiped out by Nero, only one great-great-granddaughter of
Augustus, Iunia Calvina, surviving under Vespasian. Then unallied
republican nobles also disappeared; the newer families show little
continuity in senatorial status. The turnover accelerated as senators were
recruited from all over the empire.

The Flavii represent the gradual rise of an Italian family. T. Flavius
Petro, a *municeps* of Reate, after serving under Pompey in the civil war, is
said to have retired to his home town to earn his living as a debt-collector
(like Horace's father). His son Sabinus according to some was a
professional soldier who perhaps rose to be chief centurion of a legion,

---

[96] Cf. Syme 1984 (C 231). An arch at Pavia had statues of ten members of Augustus' family, including Livia and Germanicus' sons Nero and Drusus (*CIL* v 6416 = EJ² 61 = *AN* 28).

[97] Dixon 1984 (F 26).   [98] E.g. Setälä 1977 (F 64) 239; Treggiari 1979 (F 69).

[99] Cf. Syme 1939 (A 93) 365f; Sherwin-White 1973 (A 87) 225ff.

according to others first an excise-officer in Asia and then a banker in the Alps. His wife, Vespasia Polla, from a well-established family of Nursia, had more distinguished connexions: her father was an equestrian officer and her brother became praetor. Their two sons, Sabinus and Vespasian, both achieved a senatorial career, though Vespasian was late in embarking on it. Sabinus rose to be prefect of the city and Vespasian, through military ability and (it was alleged) the favour of the emperor Gaius and the imperial freedman Narcissus, to be proconsul of Africa and commander in the Jewish War, before he made his bid for the supreme power.[100] This was the culmination of the advancement of Italian families which Augustus had begun.[101]

A policy of enfranchizing suitable provincials and of promoting promising men from one level to another in the hierarchy of service is deduced from the emperor's reported actions and from the epigraphic records of individual careers. Comparatively few junior candidates can have been personally known to the emperor. Some were recommended to him by his advisers or their patrons. The system secured the controlled promotion of others, for instance the auxiliary troops who on discharge became citizens. By the end of the Julio-Claudian period the citizen body was much expanded and both *equites* and senators were of more diverse origin than in the late Republic. The Alexandrian Jew, Ti. Iulius Alexander, would not have been prefect of Egypt under Augustus as he was under Nero.[102] Roman society continued to show remarkable powers of absorption at all levels. Newcomers, says Tacitus, were assimilated through customs, liberal arts and marriage ties (*Ann.* XI.24.10). Despite their anxiety to conform, they contributed to the gradual changes of Roman culture. Though they might adopt Latin, new names, Roman cults, the practice of Greco-Roman rhetoric or the 'epigraphic habit', they might cling, for example, to non-classical ideas of visual art, to foreign deities and old customs. Enfranchized Jews, numerous in the city by the time of Caesar, communicated to Rome the idea of the week and a weekly day of renewal (e.g. Hor. *Sat.* 1.9.69; Ov. *Rem. Am.* 219f).

The imperial peace and Augustan reorganization meant that Roman citizens were spread over the old and newly annexed provinces as never before.[103] Veterans and some civilians were sent to colonies; peasants

---

[100] Suet. *Vesp.* 1ff. The significance of the account of the family's rise is independent of the precise accuracy of variant details. [101] Syme 1939 (A 93) 359ff, 383ff.

[102] Chastagnol 1973 (D 31); Brunt 1975 (E 906) and 1983 (D 26); Demougin 1982 (D 36).

[103] A pleasing example of the cultural mosaic is provided by EJ² 363, from Ithaca, in which a slave shopkeeper boasts of his passing there during the triumviral period and gives a trade address which the reader is expected to know refers to Rome: 'Epaphroditus (slave) of Novius, perfumer from the Sacred Way, was here on 1 October in the year when L. Cornificius and Sex. Pompeius were consuls' (35 B.C.).

displaced in the reallocations of Italian land in the civil war period emigrated to provinces; provincials, particularly the upper classes, were gradually enfranchized. The army provided continual geographical mobility for citizens and a route to citizenship for non-citizens. By the end of our period Italians were not joining up in such numbers as they had under Augustus: in part this may be an indication of the prosperity of Italy (so that their economic prospects in civilian life were now better). Augustus had done much to promote the standard of living of urban Italians, though nothing directly to solve the social problems caused by the agrarian economy.

The Roman plebs, losing political power, gained in material advantages, which ranged from a fire brigade to attractive places of public resort. The *esprit de corps* and energies of the guilds (*collegia*) were regulated and scope found for the ambitions of comparatively humble men for community service and social recognition. In Italian towns freedmen in particular enjoyed the office of *Augustales*. Such bodies directed loyalty to the emperor and created outlets for ambition, altruism and talent. The activity of guilds and boards of minor officials seems to have been a 'grassroots' phenomenon. The upper-class bias of our sources must not blind us to the strong sense of personal worth and of community which is often attested by the lower classes. The population of the capital was heterogeneous, including the poorest of native-born labourers, craftsmen and shopkeepers, the great households of the rich, foreign traders and envoys. But Rome could still elicit loyalty from the descendants of slaves. An actor and freedman of Claudius or Nero, with the pleasing name Tiberinus, is commemorated by his mother (presumably a freedwoman, but of another family), who makes him claim, 'Rome is my fatherland, my parents are from the heart of the plebs.'[104] Despite the insecurities and miseries of life, those plebeians who could afford to commemorate themselves show the vigour, independent spirit and cockney pride which Horace caught in his portrayal of the auctioneer Mena (*Epist.* 1.7.46ff). The type survives the Augustan revolution and the steady influx of freedmen and foreigners. At this social level, the impact of emperors is limited. But the institution of what, in contrast to republican *laissez-faire*, must be regarded as responsive government with some ability to plan ahead produced an Italian heyday.

The Roman world was opened up both physically and mentally. The Principate brought improved roads, made safer from brigands, sea-lanes at risk from weather rather than pirates. But more important was mental attitude. A new mood of optimistic imperialism encouraged Italians to

---

[104] *CIL* VI 33960 = 10097, Ti. Claudius Esquilina Aug(usti libertus) Tiberinus. Note that the tribe is given '... Roma mihi patria est, media de plebe parentes ...'. Brunt 1971 (F 12) 148ff draws up a balance-sheet of the socio-economic situation of the rural and urban plebs under the Empire.

enjoy that share in the empire which two generations earlier had been denied them and annexed new citizens to the service of Rome. Provincials recognized that they belonged to an empire ruled from Rome (Luke 2:1). As it was natural for a clever young man from Sulmo to make a career in Rome, whether he decided to be a senator or a poet, so humbler Italians marched out to all the frontiers, to war down the proud and exploit, bully, love or learn from the local people. If we look at the experience of the citizen of non-Italian descent, we see that by the time of Nero, Paul knows people he can write to not only in cities of the Greek East, but in Rome and the household of Caesar. It is hard to imagine that his opposite number in republican Rome would have had a similar mental map.

In upper-class life, Vespasian marks a sharper social break than Augustus. A change of taste, personified by the Sabine grandson of a Pompeian centurion, accomplished the switch in *mores* which Augustan legislation had been powerless to effect. People like Velleius or the Plinies now outnumbered survivors of a frivolous society like Ummidia Quadratilla. According to Tacitus' diagnosis, luxury and display, which lasted from Actium to the war of A.D. 68/9, gave way to parsimony, when they became dangerous and when new men of simpler tastes came to power. Or is there merely a cyclical pattern (Tac. *Ann.* III.55)? Cicero and Horace would perhaps have been disappointed by the change they had advocated. But the demographic problems remained. Rome never had hereditary monarchy or hereditary Senate. Some sons of senators lost their census qualification, some opted out, some families lacked sons. *Equites* might, like Ovid (*Tr.* IV.10.27ff, cf. Hor. *Sat.* II.3.168ff), refuse promotion. A trickle of the new rich, often freedmen, percolated into the higher strata: their sons were *equites*, their grandsons even senators. Members of the richest classes moved in and out of functions in high administration.

Society changed between 44 B.C. and A.D. 69. Some developments, such as the improved right of succession given to women, seem to have happened because views of the family continued to move further away from patriarchy and emphasis on agnatic relationships. Augustus merely hastened this trend. Others, such as greater social mobility up or down, were caused or increased by the major upheaval of the civil wars. Where before there had been a number of *principes viri* at the top of the social, economic and political pyramid, the emperor now stood alone and his kin and close associates occupied the strata below him. The whole of society felt the effect of his presence. For instance, his servants, particularly *Augusti liberti*, outranked other freedmen and might even, for wealth and influence, counterbalance senators. But no emperor could alter the basic social structures, even had he wished. The rights of citizens to own slaves and to enfranchize by manumission were unassailable. Marriage remained consensual. Reproductivity continued to be controlled by living conditions, not fiat. Planned legislation had less effect than the superimposition of an emperor on the constitutional, economic and social structure and the actions of the individual rulers. The effect of these was to unify the empire as never before; to draw in foreigners to the citizenship and recruits to the army and higher administration, and to produce a more broadly based and transient elite of officials within the upper classes. Beneath the *princeps*, Roman society remained a pyramid, but peace, prosperity and enfranchizement increased the relative size of the propertied classes within the citizen body. The social structure of the ruling elite survived the Julio-Claudian period, but its membership and tone were transformed.

Emperors affected society by legislation and the deliberate institution of certain practices, by individual acts of patronage (*beneficia*), by acquiescing in practices or institutions initiated by others, by the example which they set and by just 'being there'. Augustus deliberately undertook social engineering; his successors were normally concerned to continue what he had begun. Social legislation was effective in setting up a framework in which people should operate, but not in attacking perceived moral problems. The emperors stimulated social developments which were not the primary object of their actions or over which they had no direct control. It would be naive to expect otherwise.

CHAPTER 19

LITERATURE AND SOCIETY

GAVIN TOWNEND

I. DEFINITION OF THE PERIOD

While the age of Golden Latin is accepted as straddling the late republican and Augustan periods, the division between these two is particularly arbitrary, with no satisfactory date to set as the boundary – neither the death of Cicero in 43 B.C. nor the victory of Octavian in 31. Sallust survived into the 30s, but is properly classified as republican on the basis both of subject-matter and of attitudes; Nepos, still alive several years after Actium, likewise looks back to the last period of the Republic and shows no real affinity to the new age; Marcus Varro produced a great part of his work during Cicero's lifetime and his *De Re Rustica* in 37/36 B.C., although he was still writing when he died in 27, the year when the name 'Augustus' appeared, to distinguish the new era beyond doubt. On the other hand, within a year or two of 40 B.C. the emergence of Octavian Caesar as champion and saviour in the first *Eclogue* establishes Virgil as an Augustan from the start; while the fourth of the series, for all its puzzles, is already looking into a future of peace and prosperity. The dedication to Maecenas of both *Epodes* and *Satires* I attaches Horace openly to the imperial entourage, even if the decisive poems belong relatively late in the decade. The 30s are in every way a period of transition, in literature as in politics. The two previous decades had seen the great advances of Catullus, Lucretius and Cicero, the last with his expressed determination to make Latin literature the equal of Greek in every department. In the 20s a confident professionalism manifests itself, with the major theme of patriotism flowering in the Augustan peace and with unthreatened leisure for the romantic games of elegiac and lyric poetry. The lessons of Cicero's mastery of language for a whole range of literary purposes are available for application to poetry and prose alike, without yet becoming stereotyped as technique replaces original imagination, but with *ars* matching *ingenium* even more completely than Cicero had observed in the work of Lucretius.

Yet from the start imagination had its limitations. The emulation of Greek models so desired by Cicero was to lead inexorably to the summing-up by Quintilian towards the close of the following century, with parallel lists of writers in Greek and in Latin, carefully arranged according to their genres and set before the reader as models for *imitatio* in the pursuit of rhetorical excellence. This avoidance of innovation and failure to welcome the concept of change is paralleled in Roman politics and life in every period. Iulius Caesar had outraged the establishment, at least, by preparing to change the shape of the state as arbitrarily as he changed the Roman calendar. The 'Roman revolution' of Augustus owed much of its success to the extent to which change was concealed under the cover of 'restoration of the Republic', and insistence on precedent was emphasized at almost every stage under the early Principate. Throughout three centuries of imperial development, there was apparently never a moment when an emperor or a political theorist so much as contemplated the suitability of the machinery of government and society to its changing function and attempted to lay down the pattern for a fundamental revision. In a very similar way, literary criticism is essentially conservative, with *imitatio* as a basic presupposition: first the transference into Latin of forms and ideas derived from the Greeks; then the recognition of a Roman master in the relevant field, whether a Lucilius (one of the few genuine innovators), a Cicero, a Cornelius Gallus or a Virgil, and an attempt to adapt his achievements to new themes and new demands; and all the time compliance with the rules of the genre, one of a limited number with names revealing their Greek origins,[1] and on a lower level with the conventions of such forms of expression[2] as the *propemptikon* (farewell to a traveller), the *soteria* (thanksgiving for safety), the *kletikon* (invitation) and others less clearly named or defined.

Only the genre of satire has no formal Greek model and no Greek name – indeed no secure Latin name either, until the tradition started by Ennius' *satura* prevailed over Horace's preferred and clearer title of *sermones* (conversations). At the same time the rules of the genre were established almost as firmly as those of almost any other, allowing that an inherent formlessness was part of the tradition; so that dactylic hexameters were prescribed, as already sometimes in Ennius and always in Lucilius after his early experiments. This was at the cost of excluding that eccentric alternative tradition known as 'Menippean', characterized by the total lack of formal rules to the point of mixing prose with verse in all sorts of metre. Quintilian could not help recognizing this variant, as introduced by so reputable a writer as Varro; but the examples which have come down to us in fragmentary form from the Neronian age, under the uncertain titles of *Apocolocyntosis* and *Satiricon*, are not acknowledged by Quintilian or any other critic of the classical period.

---

[1] Quintilian gives a full list and discussion of the Greek genres at *Inst.* x.1.46–131.
[2] For a full list (perhaps unjustifiably full), see Cairns 1972 (A 13), esp. Ch. 3.

The exclusion of satire from the canon of regular genres is marked by its admission into Latin of Greek words and phrases, a licence shared by those two minor genres never fully recognized by the Greeks although invented by them, the epistle (whether in prose or in verse) and biography. The true Greek genres are accepted by the Latin writers without real question, and there are only minor attempts to cross the boundaries between them and to form such hybrids as Hamlet's 'tragical-comical-historical-pastoral', which still show the dominance of the classical categories. It is rare for a major writer to go as far as Virgil does in borrowing formal elements from tragedy to relate the story of Dido, and from Callimachean epyllion to describe Evander's reception of Aeneas on the Palatine. Once Cicero, Virgil and Horace were securely established as paragons in their different fields, their influence was paramount; and even in the Silver Age, starting with the death of Augustus and running on well after the disappearance of his descendants, reactions against the masters, such as those of Seneca and Lucan never escaped from dependence on the genre.

II. PATRONAGE AND ITS OBLIGATIONS

The social position of literature at Rome, never as fully integrated into the life of the city as it had been at Athens during the fifth and fourth centuries, changed markedly after Actium, when oratory lost its preeminence with its divorce from a genuine political function. Already at the end of the second century B.C. the function of drama, whether tragic or comic, seems to have been greatly diminished, as the population became too big and too cosmopolitan to provide the common cultural background necessary for a mass audience.[3] Drama survived, so far as it did, simply because of the major reputation of tragedy and comedy among classical genres, and revivals may have depended for their appeal largely on the spectacle.[4] There is virtually no evidence that the contemporary tragedies written by Q. Cicero, Caesar or Asinius Pollio ever reached the stage or were even intended to.

Instead, literature becomes more and more the property of an elite, as Horace repeatedly emphasizes.[5] Writers had never expected direct financial returns from the sale of their works, so long as there was no possible system of copyright or royalties; and men like Terence, of provincial origin and low rank, had attached themselves to prominent figures in society, without any apparent loss of creative independence. Even Lucilius, financially secure and proud of being his own man, took

---

[3] It is far from clear what sort of performance actually filled the theatre in Rome and outside. In Augustus' reign they certainly handled scripts in Greek and Oscan (Suet. *Aug.* 43.1, etc.); cf. Rawson 1985 (F 55) 97–113.   [4] E.g. Plut. *Luc.* 39.5.

[5] E.g. esp. *Sat.* 1.4.70–5, 137–9, 10.72–92.

pleasure also in being a close associate of Scipio Aemilianus, and did not object to devoting two or three of his satires to attacking his patron's political enemies, while confident of freedom from reprisals. Of the major writers of the last generation of the Republic, Cicero, Varro and Catullus had no need of literary patronage; the position of Lucretius and his possible dependence on C. Memmius remains mysterious.[6]

During the years from Philippi to Actium, political protection was perhaps more important; and the writer is traditionally pictured as dispossessed of his property and as welcoming the patronage of a great man for financial security at least. This tendency is perhaps accentuated by the fact that the great majority of writers, both in the Augustan period and throughout the following century, came from outside Rome, from the towns of Italy proper (Horace, Tibullus, Propertius, Ovid), from the old province of Cisalpine Gaul (several of the earlier neoteric poets, Cornelius Nepos, Virgil, Livy, and in due course the two Plinies), from southern Gaul (Cornelius Gallus and perhaps Tacitus a century later), or from Spain (the two Senecas, Lucan, Columella, Quintilian, Martial). But most of these men of letters appear to have enjoyed comfortable means and independent position, and to have fully assimilated into upper-class Roman society, with traditional Roman ideas and standards.

Not dissimilar was the position of Greeks, now rivalling Italians in the equestrian civil service, as the authors of extensive prose works in their own language. None of these comes from old Greece: Dionysius of Halicarnassus combines orthodox and respectable literary criticism with antiquarian history, evidently to present Rome to the Greek-speaking world, in Rome and in the provinces; Nicolaus of Damascus stands sufficiently close to Augustus to exploit the emperor's own apologia in the composition of his highly favourable biography, and then attaches himself to Herod the Great as a spokesman for the king and his people; Diodorus from Sicily writes voluminous if uninspired history, as does Strabo from Pontus, now known only from his geographical work. These men hardly need to be counted as 'Augustan writers', however important their work may have been in making the new era acceptable to the hellenistic world and cementing the unity of Greek and Roman after the rift in the 30s. Some time later, Philo of Alexandria, well known for his activities as a spokesman for the Jews under Caligula and Claudius, but mainly concerned with arguing the connexion between Greek and Jewish philosophy, belongs almost exclusively to his own hellenistic-Jewish society; but the Greek epigrammatist Lucillius, largely interested in music and drama, must have some claim as part of the literary scene of an emperor as philhellene as Nero. But, outside the field of diplomatic activity, where Greek oratory found a new and increasing role in the

[6] Cf. Wiseman 1974 (B 197A) 26–39.

mouths of envoys from provincial communities, the dependence of any of these men on the support, financial or otherwise, of Roman patrons is impossible to determine.

The picture is much clearer for the most prominent of the Augustan poets. Horace, son of a freedman and starting badly by fighting for the losing side at Philippi, became an accepted member of Maecenas' well-defined circle and was able in due course to give up his post as *scriba* and to settle down as a small country gentleman with a modest apartment in the capital. The later offer of the post of secretary to Augustus himself seems to have been rejected rather from aversion to regular employment than from any fear of subservience to the emperor's wishes (Suet. *Vita Hor.*). Virgil, losing his family estate near Mantua, sought and gained the support first of Pollio, a distinguished writer himself and an independent politician, and then of Maecenas to restore his position and presumably to promote his literary career. He appears to have given up his connexion with the north and lived for the most part near Naples (Suet. *Vita Ver.*). Financial considerations were to some extent involved in these and other cases, even if the claim to poetical poverty in Tibullus, as in Juvenal in the second century, is nothing but a literary convention. But the main objective appears to have been status and connexions.

It is hardly now believed that Maecenas (and still less Messalla, as patron of Tibullus and others) actually prompted the composition of particular works for quasi-political reasons, apart from such *pièces d'occasion* as Horace's *Carmen Saeculare*, written in 17 B.C. for a specific religious festival and with an obvious political aim; nor that Livy, close to the imperial family though he was and possibly financially rewarded for his help to the young Claudius in composing history, needed official direction to make him an active defender of ancient traditions and values, such as Augustus admired and wished to propagate.[7] In fact, Livy was notorious for his republican sympathies and particularly for his support of the memory of Pompey, which excited Augustus' comment but did not lead to the withdrawal of his friendship.[8] We certainly fail to find the sort of subservience which might have been expected of court poets. In the light of what we know of the war of propaganda which developed between Antony and Octavian during the late 30s, before Actium and probably earlier, it is noteworthy that there is no sign of the poets' involvement in this campaign. Even in Horace's *Satires*, where Lucilius had provided some precedent for attacking a patron's enemies, Antony appears only once (1.5.33), with an oblique reference four lines earlier to *aversos amicos* to be reconciled by the envoys, and there is no trace of criticism or hostility. In the diplomatic purpose of the trip to Brundisium, on which Horace and Virgil accompanied Maecenas,

[7] Syme 1959 (B 177); Walsh 1974 (B 191A) 5–6.   [8] Suet. *Claud.* 41.1, Tac. *Ann.* IV.34.3.

Horace assumes complete lack of interest. Again in the *Epodes* (VII and XVI) he twice laments the civil strife of the period without any suggestion of partisanship or idea of solution, while in the first of the series, whether written for the expedition against Sextus Pompeius or Antony, Horace gives no hint that the temptation to accompany Maecenas was due to anything but personal affection.[9]

The *Eclogues* were a less likely medium for expressing political views, and Virgil does no more than address Octavian, unnamed but unmistakable, as patron and protector in the first poem; while in the fourth contemporaries may have been more confident than we can be of the extent to which Octavian, or indeed any specific individual, was the subject of hopes or praise. In the *Georgics*, once peace had been established, Octavian can be hymned as the greatest of benefactors, deserving the title of godhead in the same way as Lucretius had honoured Epicurus for his blessings to mankind (v.7ff); and in III.16 Virgil promises a new poem centred on 'Caesar' as if on a god. Yet it is difficult to see how the four books, with their periodic outbursts of depression leading sometimes to despair, can be regarded as the sort of propaganda for an officially inspired revival of agriculture that historians used to claim they were.

When the next work came to be written, Virgil may have been aware that Augustus (as he now was) wanted a national epic to indicate the position of the *princeps* in a re-born Rome and an extended empire, together with an exposition of the moral values on which the new age was to be based; but it cannot be supposed that the *Aeneid* was in any way what had been suggested or expected. The term 'propaganda' fits awkwardly here,[10] despite the explicit recognition in three major passages (I. 286–96, with its notorious ambiguities, VI. 791–805, and VIII. 671–728); and there are all too many passages which appear to question the full worth of the leader's triumph. An epic intended simply to glorify and justify the character and victories of the ideal ruler, with Aeneas in some degree representing and prescribing the pattern of the just and self-sacrificing *princeps*, as Virgil's hero appears to do, could have reached the conclusion of the conflict against his rival without a savage killing, which, however acceptable in the context of heroic warfare and however justified in terms of statecraft, still has to be carried out in the madness of rage and revenge.[11] The great majority of contemporary readers, like the majority since then, will have been sufficiently carried along by the force of the narrative to accept the death of Turnus as dramatically and morally appropriate; everything we can infer about Virgil indicates that he can

---

[9] *Contra*, du Quesnay, in Woodman and West 1984 (B 204) 19–58.

[10] Cf. the dismissal of the dichotomy 'poetry or propaganda?' in the Epilogue to Woodman and West 1984 (B 204) 195.   [11] *Aen.* XII.946–7, 'furiis accensus et ira terribilis'.

never have been happy about this resolution of the problem. Likewise, the inflated praise of Augustus' young nephews and son-in-law can properly be seen as a tribute to the *princeps* and his bereaved sister Octavia, as if the poet might hope thereby to gain favour; but the fact that Marcellus' death concludes and crowns the long pageant of the glories of Rome suggests that what matters most to Virgil in the end is the price paid for military and political triumph and the irredeemable sorrow for the death of a young man.[12] A whole-hearted panegyric of the Augustan achievement, however full of hope for the future, did not require both its halves to end in such a minor key.

The failure of Horace to realize what might have been expected of the laureate, who could produce the *Carmen Saeculare* and hymn the victories of Drusus and his brother in *Carm.* iv.4, is more obvious and less demanding of explanation. The Roman odes of the third book are full of noble sentiments and an expression of true Roman virtues; but they hardly add up to the direct propaganda that has often been seen in them. All too often, as in iii.4, overt praise of Augustus drifts off into the poet's private reactions and his addiction to wine and girls; while private odes on themes of self-indulgence and the shortness of human life not only predominate in the collection but are commonly felt to reveal Horace at his most effective. We appear to have another Augustan spokesman who can hardly be held to have produced exactly what the Augustan age demanded.

This leads to a question which is especially pressing in connexion with the opening decades of the Principate: the tendency of poets to propound a set of values totally at variance with the major programme of moral reform whereby Augustus was hoping to bring Rome back to the greatness of earlier centuries. Respectable private and public behaviour, the marriage of Roman men to Roman women, the production of true Roman children to fight Rome's wars and carry on the traditions of 700 years – these are the most obvious of the ideas on which the Julian legislation and Augustus' own injunctions sought to base the new society of citizens. Of the poets who might be expected to promote these ideas, Virgil never married, and seems to have had homosexual inclinations, if any. Horace likewise remained celibate, although he gives the impression that he followed the Epicurean practice of sexual indulgence with women and boys indiscriminately to work off natural needs when they arose, as first Lucretius and then the satiric spokesman of *Sat.* i.2 had recommended. This may be merely the convention of the genre, but Horace nowhere attempts to suggest anything else – certainly not that he ever contemplated any sort of permanent union.

For the three elegists, things are no better. Tibullus and Propertius, as

---

12 vi.868–86, with Otis 1963 (B 135A) 303–4.

poets, are romantically inclined bachelors, Tibullus expressing affection
for boys no less than for girls; as men, they may have had wives and
children. The anonymous life of Tibullus is too fragmentary to establish
his marital status, unless by negative inference, although Pliny's friend
Passennus Paulus (*Ep.* VI.15) appears to have claimed direct descent
from Propertius. Whatever may be the truth of that, their love-poetry is
as extramarital as that of Catullus, without ever a hint of true love leading
to marriage or to possible divorce and the infringement of the rules of
class. The only claim to paternity in the whole of Augustan poetry is
Propertius' negative assertion (II.7.14) that he would produce no sons to
fight Rome's wars – no sons at all, indeed, for this is no pacifist manifesto
– and that the emperor's wishes have no validity in the context of love.
Ovid is even worse. He married three times and, like Augustus,
produced one daughter, the only attested child of any major republican
or Augustan poet; but his poetry reveals a still more irresponsible
rejection of the Augustan ideal. In the *Ars Amatoria*, as already in the
Amores, he describes a world devoted to philandering and promiscuity.
In particular, he pays what must have been a most unwelcome tribute to
the age of Augustus and its moral climate, when he declares (*Ars Am.*
III.121–2), 'I congratulate myself on being born now and no earlier: this
age is suited to my way of life.' On this reckoning, the new *pax Augusta*
had produced the circumstances for an unworried self-indulgence, quite
unaffected by the emperor's pronouncements and legislation aiming at
the restoration of old-fashioned values. This attitude of Ovid's ('prisca
iuvent aliis') must have been largely responsible, perhaps even more than
his questionable complicity in the intrigues of Augustus' granddaughter, the younger Iulia, for his banishment to the Black Sea in A.D. 8
– the clearest example known to us of a decisive punishment visited by
Augustus on an offensive writer, and one never revoked by his
successor.

In his attempts to secure his recall from exile, Ovid indulged to some
extent in the sort of flattery which becomes more and more noticeable as
the Julio-Claudian age advances. In Tiberius' reign, Velleius Paterculus,
while evidently paying due credit to the emperor's earlier successes as a
military leader, clearly expresses himself in stronger terms than the truth
required.[13] Poets in the following reigns were guilty of increasing
servility, often revealing a tendency to build up the achievements, or at
least the promise, of a new emperor by blackening the name of his
predecessor. There is some evidence that the same is true of some of the
lost historians of the Julio-Claudians, such as Servilius Nonianus and
Cluvius Rufus, if not of the more solid annalists, Aufidius Bassus and the

---

[13] E.g. II.94.1–3, 124.1–3; but see Woodman 1977 (B 202) 54–5, Goodyear in Kenney and Clausen
1982 (B 95) 639–40.

elder Pliny.[14] Certainly Seneca's *Apocolocyntosis* (if that is the proper name
of the *Ludus de morte Claudii*), mocks the dead Claudius and exalts the
young Nero in a way which appears to illustrate the development of the
historical tradition from reign to reign. Even the very fulsomeness of
flattery may sometimes have suggested an element of irony which rather
implies mockery – a device which many have seen in Catullus' praise of
Cicero in poem 49. The subtlety which this technique would require
means that today we can never confidently assess the poet's sincerity.

Flattery must necessarily have occupied a great amount of the oratory
which was delivered during the period, if Pliny's surviving *Panegyric*
provides a fair example for this earlier part of the century. But that
speech, delivered in A.D. 100 under Trajan, is the first we possess in full
since the death of Cicero. The considerable fragments of Claudius'
speech delivered in A.D. 48 on the admission of Gallic notables to the
Senate and preserved on a bronze tablet at Lyons, reveal the antiquarianism of the speaker, who knows that he does not need eloquence or
cogency to gain his point. Tacitus, who claimed that the role of oratory
had virtually ceased with the end of open discussion under the Republic
(*Dial.* 40–1), gives his own version of the same speech, with considerable
freedom, but reproducing the same qualities accurately enough (*Ann.*
XI.24). We cannot tell whether other speeches from the period inserted in
the *Annals* are as closely related to the speaker's recorded words; but it is
noticeable that the most powerful come from men of independent mind
upholding their own ideas of freedom – ideas which interested the
historian far more than any speeches which have simply approved of the
emperor's policy. Thus we have a speech from M. Terentius (VI.8),
protesting against the doctrine of guilt by association; from Cremutius
Cordus (IV.34–5), defending the rights of the historian; and from
Thrasea Paetus (XV.20–1), upholding the old values of Roman administration by Roman magistrates. The eloquence may be Tacitus' own,
interested to emphasize the voices of independent spirits. In any case,
there is a significant, and probably deliberate, link with the republican
ideal of unfettered rights to express one's beliefs and act according to
one's conscience, without ever proposing any genuine reform of the
imperial system or expressing concern for the great majority of people
whose interests might be affected.

This ideal, harking back to the heroic names of the younger Cato, of
Brutus and Cassius, appears to have provided a continuous focus for
discontent among senators throughout the first century. We lack
Tacitus' account of the debate which followed the murder of Caligula,
when the abolition of the Principate was allegedly debated for the first
and last time; but hostility to tyranny, if not to autocracy, plays an active

[14] G. B. Townend *Hermes* 88 (1960) 98–120, 89 (1961) 227–48.

part in the literature of the period. The actual expression of this hostility in the political field is regarded by Tacitus as fruitless and exhibitionist (*Agr*. 42.4–5); and he puts similar words into the mouth of Tigellinus, which he himself might not totally disclaim, blaming Stoicism for this truculence and mischief-making (*Ann*. XIV.57, supported by *Agr*. 4.4–5).[15]

Thanks to the loss of all of Livy's later books, we can form little idea of his treatment of the rise of Augustus to supremacy; but nothing suggests that he expressed hostility to the new settlement. Velleius Paterculus, to be discussed below, is too deeply devoted to Tiberius to reveal any reservations, and Curtius Rufus, writing his history of Alexander the Great apparently under Claudius, steers well clear of all but the most conventional reference to the contemporary world. Of the other main writers who recorded the reigns of the various Julio-Claudians within a few years of their deaths, Aufidius Bassus, Cluvius Rufus, Fabius Rusticus and the elder Pliny, we can infer little except that they provided a steady annalistic record of events and a great deal of highly hostile anecdotage to be used by Tacitus, Suetonius and Cassius Dio. There is no trace of any sort of republican sentiment, except in Cremutius Cordus, of whom we know at least that his remarks about the republican heroes, Brutus and Cassius, offended Tiberius enough to lead to prosecution and the ineffectual destruction of his works, which survived to gain a reputation for freedom of expression, and the surprising approval of Caligula (Tac. *Ann*. IV.34–5; Suet. *Calig*. 16.1). Titus Labienus, an outspoken orator and historian, shared the same fortune, without apparently expressing any positive republican views (Sen. *Controv*. x *pr*. 5–8).

In practice, the 'Stoic opposition', while confined to a small group of interrelated families, appears to have been sentimental and ineffectual, with Stoic language often playing no more significant a part than much of the traditional Christian language does in the literature of recent centuries in Britain. But Stoicism is still prominent in Latin literature of the Silver Age which follows Augustus. The Stoic concepts which feature in Manilius' astronomical poem are a feeble attempt to match the glowing Epicureanism of Lucretius, without any sort of credibility or cogency. More importance can be attached to expressions of hostility to Nero, as *dominus* rather than *rex*, found in Seneca and his nephew Lucan. Seneca produced a manifesto in favour of the just ruler in the *De*

---

15 The word 'Stoic', like the ancient literary terms 'lyric', 'tragic' and 'satiric', must be recognized as possessing a very precise sense in antiquity, deriving from the philosophical school of Zeno (335–263 B.C.) in the Stoa Poikile (painted portico) in Athens, with its rigid doctrines of absolute virtue and duty, of acceptance of divine destiny combined with involvement in public life. In particular, the Roman Stoics expressed opposition to tyranny and admired Caesar's opponents, Cato and M. Brutus.

Clementia, which he wrote for his pupil Nero early in his reign; and the same ideas appear scattered through his other works, particularly in the tragedies, where tyrants from Greek myth are employed presumably to cast light upon the contemporary situation, as some imitator of Seneca did more overtly in the play *Octavia*, written not long after Nero's death, with Nero as the stock tyrant and Seneca as the sage counselling restraint and justice. The whole tradition about Seneca has been bedevilled from the first by the paradox of the declared Stoic preacher, albeit of the new liberal type, who advocated the simple life but possessed immense wealth, which he was alleged to have increased by highly questionable financial practices, and who acted as tutor and then as minister to the unteachable and irresponsible Nero.

Seneca was driven to his death in A.D. 65 for his supposed complicity in the 'Pisonian conspiracy', if not its leadership. This plot certainly aimed at the assassination of the emperor (in the best tradition of the Athenian and republican tyrannicides) and at his replacement either by the unimpressive aristocrat Piso or by the elderly and ailing Seneca himself. So little was achieved that its true details cannot be discovered, if the conspirators indeed shared any common aim beyond that of murder.[16] To judge from Seneca's literary utterances, tyranny was abominable enough to warrant such an action, although he never actually recommends it. The link between philosophical theory and effective political action remains tenuous.

More certainly prominent in the same conspiracy was Lucan, described by his biographer as virtually the standard-bearer of the affair. His motive appears to have been that Stoic opposition to tyranny which features with increasing force in the books of his *Bellum Civile*, after the gross flattery of Nero with which the epic opens, closely matched by the panegyrics of contemporary poets and by Seneca himself in his *Apocolocyntosis* a few years earlier. Despite the claim in 1.33–45 that the civil war was justified as leading to the eventual accession of Caesar's descendant Nero, and despite the evident fascination of Caesar as the natural hero in comparison with the ineffectual Pompey, the poem turns into a clear indictment of Caesarism, with such phrases as 'Caesareae domus series' (iv.823) among the holders of bloody power pointing unmistakably at the latest of the line. But despite this ideological motive, there is reason to suppose that Lucan was primarily inspired by personal rancour from his loss of favour with Nero after he had been so rash as to surpass his patron in poetic skill. In the light of what follows, the flattery in the first book is a prime candidate to be considered from its very excess to be ironical in intention, even before the open break with Nero had taken place.

[16] Griffin 1984 (C 352), esp. 166–70.

It is difficult to know how much consistency we should look for in such a poet, or whether he was capable of any degree of subtlety. To judge by the evidence of Tacitus (*Ann.* xv.56–7), supported by Suetonius, Lucan's Stoicism did not establish his fortitude; for he turned state's evidence at the first threat and incriminated his own mother and several others, before recovering his philosophical principles and committing suicide in the tradition of the republican martyrs and his uncle Seneca. The biography by Vacca ignores all this story of cowardice; while Statius, in his commemorative poem (*Silv.* II.7), contrives to say nothing at all about the circumstances of Lucan's condemnation and death. There is incidentally no reference to his relationship to Stoics in any of these sources. The ancient biography of Persius, on the other hand, makes much of his training in Stoicism and his links with prominent exponents under Nero: he was much more deeply imbued with Stoic ideas and language than Lucan. But neither these ideological opponents of the establishment nor those most inclined to support the imperial system appear to have been able to exploit their convictions to the major advantage of their works, in prose or in verse. Only the two greatest of the Augustan poets found valid inspiration in some of the emperor's ideas and made a significant contribution to the new political order; but their reservations were always striking enough, as we have noted at the start of this section, to ensure that their independence never degenerated into subservience.

III. RHETORIC AND ESCAPISM

In a world where political comment was perilous and profitless and speech-making had no real political function, the development of rhetoric was at once natural and paradoxical. Cicero had not only provided a model for oratory; he had produced a series of treatises which could be the basis of training in all the necessary techniques. The establishment of rhetorical schools for young men of means is more or less contemporary with the rise of the Augustan age, as professionals took over where Cicero had left off in his coaching of aspirant politicians. Much of our knowledge of this training is contained in the *Controversiae* and *Suasoriae*, collections published by the elder Seneca during the reign of Tiberius of the rhetorical exercises performed by teachers and their pupils and preserved as examples of the craft. Stock themes were provided, whether of hypothetical legal problems or of situations from myth or history, which the student was required to develop in his own way, so as to catch and hold the attention of the listening audience and give them something to remember. Originality of expression was all-important, no matter how trite the material; and great value was attached to the *sententia* as the pithy and memorable phrase, often containing paradox and seldom concerned with real life or with the actual problems to be encountered in the courts or the Senate. Many listeners besides Petronius (*Sat.* 1–2) and Juvenal (I.15–17, VII.150–4) must have suffered from the *crambe repetita* of the same old material, whether served up by the inept or by the intolerably ingenious. But rhetorical training seems to have been more or less compulsory for any young man who wanted to make his way in public life and for many who had no such ambition.

Certainly it shows its influence in most of the surviving literature from the very beginning of the Augustan period. Not a little of Virgil's power can be seen to depend on his absorption of the Ciceronian rules for producing effective arguments, although the technique is never allowed to take precedence. Ovid's *Heroides* display most clearly the young poet's delight in all the devices of rhetoric, which he had learnt in the schools, gaining a distinction on which the elder Seneca comments. The *Heroides* are essentially similar compositions, depending for their success on immense dexterity in saying the same thing in an endless variety of different ways, as heroine after heroine laments her unhappy lot. Much the same is true of many elements in the *Metamorphoses*, particularly the actual descriptions of transformations of men or women into other creatures or plants. The ability to play this game with such unwearying freshness makes Ovid the perfect example of how the techniques of the schools could best be exploited in the most unlikely literary forms.

The vitality and originality which characterizes the literature of the Augustan age declines sharply during the succeeding reigns. In prose, Valerius Maximus, as much a devotee of the rhetorical schools as the elder Seneca himself, produces a series of books containing *exempla* of virtues and vices for the orator to exploit in his own compositions; but he has been unable to resist treating them in the fashionable rhetorical manner, often at the cost of clarity, in his attempt to avoid the monotony which such a catalogue might involve. It must have been very difficult for the aspiring speaker to incorporate such sophisticated material into his own speeches. At about the same time, Velleius Paterculus sets out to relate the history of the world in two books (an understandable reaction to Livy and Diodorus); but the need to cover the same stories, which generations of historians had dealt with in their own ways, constrains him to use all the devices of technique in pursuit of his own sort of originality. He is no master, as Ovid had been; and his account of the Battle of Actium (II.85) illustrates excellently the deployment of ingenious language which fails to leave any impression either of what really happened or of its historical significance. The battle had presumably been dealt with in Rabirius' lost epic and perhaps in Varius Rufus' panegyric of Augustus, as it was by the author of the *De Bello Actiaco*, which survives in papyrus fragments;[17] even Livy may have found it advisable to treat the subject as an excuse for rhetorical display rather than as an account of tactical moves and individual prowess. After these, and who knows how many other versions, there was little left for Velleius to do except to search for paradoxes as the schools had taught and the fashion demanded.

For the younger Seneca, trained in the manner illustrated by his father's works, the exposition of his chosen subject, philosophy, as a guide to life, a purpose of some weight and significance, continually tended to be dominated by the need to express the same doctrine again and again in striking and memorable phrases. The *Epistulae Morales*, generally regarded as the most successful and attractive of his voluminous works, suffer from something like the same fault as Ovid's *Heroides*: that, no matter how deeply felt, the subjects are so repetitive that they are kept going, up to the grand total of 124, by ingenuity rather than anything else. The same is true of the philosophical dialogues, enlivened though they are by striking *exempla*, as if to demonstrate how Valerius Maximus' anecdotes might be applied to a good purpose. Novelty of expression is the more necessary as Seneca is not searching for philosophical truth, as Plato does, so much as preaching an accepted code, enriched from Epicurus and elsewhere, to assist the reader in coping with the problems of life, and doing so in such a way as to seize and retain the attention by force of language. Apart from modifications of traditional Stoicism, Seneca, like most Silver Age writers, makes very little positive addition to what has been said before.

The nine tragedies which have come down to us under Seneca's name share enough of the characteristics of his prose works to make the slightly uncertain attribution of most, at least, virtually certain. Derived obliquely from Greek tragedies, mostly extant works by Euripides or Aeschylus, they have been totally adapted to the taste of the day, in which stage performance was a minor consideration, if indeed contemplated at all. Stoic doctrines, with the usual love of paradox, colour the speeches of kings, queens, commoners and choruses alike; and the dramatic flow is almost entirely sacrificed to the succession of telling *sententiae*, few of them appropriate to speaker or circumstances. Topics recur in speech after speech in different plays (freedom and tyranny, death as an escape, the wise man's invulnerability), but so skilfully organized that the sameness is at least masked at the first reading. Although limited by the settings of the plays, the ideas and expressions

---

[17] Cf. H. Benario, 'The *Carmen de Bello Actiaco*', in *ANRW* II, 30.3 (1983) 1656–62. The fragments preserved in fact deal with events in Egypt some time after the battle and exhibit a freedom in imaginative fictions which do not suggest a composition as early as the Augustan age proper.

are much the same as those of the prose works, only made more remote from the reader by transference to the unreal heroic world of Greek mythology.

The same combination of rhetoric and philosophy shows itself inevitably in Seneca's nephew, Lucan; although for him philosophy is not a major preoccupation, but simply a source for ideas and commonplaces, together with the accepted link of Stoicism with the republicanism which colours the narrative of the *Bellum Civile*. This story, already related in prose by Pollio and Livy, is made the field for the same sort of cleverness as we find in Seneca, with rather too many memorable phrases for more than a handful to deserve remembering, and with almost unlimited skill in making the same ideas sound fresh each time they occur. Lucan's originality lies partly in his choice of a subject from relatively recent history (although almost from the start poets had followed the laureates of Alexander the Great in writing short-lived accounts of Rome's glorious victories or of the achievements of the latest military hero, whether Marius or Caesar, Octavian or Germanicus), partly in his deliberate rejection of the conventional Homeric gods so busily employed by Virgil. This may be regarded as a concession to Stoicism, allowing Fate to play the dominant part rather than the eccentric and partial Olympians.

At least one can find in Lucan enough independence from tradition to grant him a degree of self-confidence hardly to be matched elsewhere in the derivative literature of the period. Our other surviving Silver Latin epics, by Silius Italicus, Valerius Flaccus and Statius, date from the Flavian dynasty; but they continue the general tendencies of the Julio-Claudian writers virtually unchanged, with the same desire for effect, which had begun as early as the major elegists, together with the same sensationalism and bloodthirstiness. All look back rather than forward, with Virgil always at hand as a model: the contemporary world or the future has no part in their scheme. It seems most unlikely that Statius' *German War* cut any new ground, in manner or subject-matter.

There may have been other important poets in the period from Tiberius to Nero, but even their names are lost. We do possess a number of minor poems, some falsely attributed to the young Virgil, perhaps to replace the master's lost juvenilia. These are commonly dated after the death of Augustus, but are essentially continuations of the practices of the great Augustans. None contains a hint of genuine creative potential. More interesting is the group of more or less court poems from the reign and perhaps from the circle, of Nero: pastorals from Calpurnius Siculus and from an anonymous poet preserved in a manuscript at Einsiedeln, quite competent but uninspired pastiches of Virgil's *Eclogues*, though hardly to be mistaken for Virgil, containing considerable florid emphasis on the golden age of the young Nero and no likelihood at all that their panegyric is ironical. Likewise, and possibly from the pen of these same writers, is the panegyric of Calpurnius Piso, perhaps the patron of Calpurnius Siculus, which essays to praise without relevant material to hand. This ineffectual praise points to a subject as dubious as the supposed leader of the Pisonian conspiracy of A.D. 65, and underlines the lack of valid themes for poetry during this period. What we know of Nero's own poetry on the Trojan War does not suggest that he was concerned with anything but the manipulation of words or hoped to establish any relevance of the Trojan War to his own day.

The reaction against these poetical fashions, especially epic as written by Nero himself, is found in Petronius, rather too intimate a member of the imperial clique for his esoteric criticisms of Lucan and others to be fully comprehensible to us[18] (neither as parody nor as models for improvement do they really make sense). And in Persius, whose charges of vapidity, affectation and effeminacy show at least that he has not got Lucan in mind, there is a strong protest against those who have nothing to say and use fanciful and contorted language to say it (1.32–5, *et alibi*). Yet Persius, setting out to write satire in the tradition of Lucilius and Horace, has chosen an almost impossible course. He declares his intention of using everyday language (v.14, *verba togae*), as his predecessors had done, but his complex allusiveness requires an intimate knowledge of Horace and probably of other writers no longer available to us. His dizzying switch of metaphors and his unexpected linking of words produce a texture which is anything but conversational (as satire or *sermo* had come to expect), straightforward or unaffected. And his material is all from stock: themes and phrases from Horace and the Stoic tradition make up a great part of it. But at least Persius comes closer to touching the heart than any other writer in a period when literature is tending to become a private pursuit to be practised and enjoyed in the sort of group of mutual admirers described by Persius in satire 1 and by Tacitus in *Ann.* XIV.16, as led by Nero and evidently supported by Lucan before the rupture. Horace and Virgil may to some extent have distanced themselves from all but a very select public by the complexity of their texture and their demands on the reader's knowledge and sensitivity; but they still provided plenty to engage a wide interest, with no reason for anyone to complain of the irrelevance of their poetry to the contemporary world.

One method of finding material for poetry without touching too

[18] The poet Eumolpus (apparently not intended to represent any living writer) utters in *Sat.* 89 sixty-five lines in iambics on the Sack of Troy, as if to combine the theme of Nero's main poem with his addiction to appearing on the tragic stage; and in 119–24 nearly 300 hexameters on the same civil war between Caesar and Pompey which Lucan took as his subject.

directly on the perilous issues of the day, a method already practised by Catullus and followed by the Augustans and on into the Silver Age, was the Alexandrine device of exploiting Greek mythology to provide either examples or actual subjects for poetry. Virgil's use of the Trojan War and the adventures of the Trojan Aeneas to provide an aetiology for Rome and for the Augustan settlement is on a different level (or series of levels) from any other borrowing we are aware of. The use of lesser myths, some of extreme obscurity, by Horace, Tibullus and Propertius to illuminate erotic and other topics in contemporary life, whether seriously or ironically, enriches their poetry immensely, without necessarily adding to the impact.[19] Ovid, after playing with Greek stories similarly in his early love-poetry, turns to myth as a subject in its own right for the *Metamorphoses* and the *Fasti*, largely in order to deal with erotic themes without causing further offence to the moral climate of Augustan reform. With very little serious intention and with all the apparatus of rhetorical mastery, he tells his stories for their own sake and with immense success.

Major Greek myth serves a much more solemn purpose in Seneca's tragedies, a field in which Roman subjects had hardly ever proved effective; although, as already remarked, some fairly close follower of Seneca was before long to devise in the *Octavia* a tragedy built round the efforts of Seneca himself to dissuade Nero from adopting the role of tyrant, and Tacitus (*Dial.* 2–3) reports the immediate impact of dramas on the themes of Domitius and Cato at about the same date. Epic, with the major exception of Lucan, depends likewise on myth, as we see it in the Flavian age with Valerius Flaccus' retelling of the Argonaut story and with Statius on the Theban and Trojan wars. For Silius Italicus the Punic War was very nearly as mythical as the legendary wars of Greece; and Curtius' version of the history of Alexander in prose is essentially part of the same process. Juvenal, in his first satire, laments the tedious dominance of the Greek cycles of mythology, in tragedy and epic alike, and he is supported by numerous epigrams of Martial. Their criticism evidently applies to almost the whole of the first century after Christ.

IV. THE JUSTIFICATION OF LITERATURE

Various reasons were advanced during the period for writing and for reading different sorts of books. For Quintilian, writing on the training of the young orator, almost all literature could contribute to the mastery of rhetorical techniques, even Catullus and Lucretius. He has no place for works which do not belong to the recognized genres, such as Phaedrus' fables or Petronius' picaresque novel.

---

[19] E.g. Hor. *Carm.* III.11 and 27; Prop. I.20 and *passim*.

Again, as Homer was often regarded by the Greeks as a repository of knowledge on all manner of practical matters, so a whole range of Latin works existed primarily as sources of information. Here Vitruvius *On Architecture* is an accepted example, with no literary pretensions, but demonstrating his practical value when he became a working handbook for Renaissance architects. Mela's *Geography*, limited though it is, could be of some use. Celsus *On Medicine*, as on other branches of knowledge in books now lost, seems to have been properly and exclusively concerned to impart information.

With the agricultural writers, however, Varro's practical application seems largely to be sacrificed to literary considerations, Columella's rather less so; but when Columella completes his treatise with a book in hexameter verse, he is deliberately placing himself beside Virgil's *Georgics*, the practical value of which, whether for constructing a plough, selecting a lucky day for various activities, or replacing a stock of bees, makes no claim at all for serious consideration. Likewise Manilius, following Cicero's translation of the hellenistic Aratus' astronomical poem, is concerned rather to write poetically than to provide genuine information; and it is noticeable that Tiberius' heir, Germanicus, during the same period chose to attempt an improvement on Cicero's *Aratea* as a purely literary challenge. For Quintilian, such didactic poets as Lucretius and Aemilius Macer are classified along with Virgil, as writers of epic, without concern for their subject-matter. It is certainly difficult to regard Grattius on hunting, Horace on poetry, or Ovid on the calendar (and perhaps on fishing) as allowing their subject to take precedence over their art.

The moral purpose of literature, taken over from the Greeks and emphasized in numerous apologias for the time spent on composition, is especially prominent in historiography, where there is a claim that reading about the past will enlighten and improve the quality of life, private and public, in the future; Cicero adds that this interest was not confined to the elite (*De Or.* II.59–61). There is a similar assumption that the main function of satire is moral, if not precisely didactic. Yet in Horace's *Satires* it is apparent that his primary purpose is neither to attack vice nor to advocate virtue: it is rather to discuss themes, ostensibly moral or not, in such a way as to involve the reader in a humane attitude to life and mankind. Only perhaps in the sequel, the first book of *Epistles*, can Horace be felt to provide specific moral admonishment to his addressee and thus to the reader, as when he encourages Tibullus to count his blessings and enjoy life as Horace does (4.12–16), or warns Celsus not to be too pleased with himself (8.15–17); and even in this book the majority of poems are concerned rather to play round quasi-philosophical commonplaces. Persius, Horace's successor in the Lucilian tradition, preaches with some fervour the urgent need for moral reform and for escaping from the ties which hinder moral freedom, but in such a way that everything takes second place to style and the striking expression. Seneca, whose philosophical works are certainly less theoretical than practical, uses the epistolary form to exhort his friend Lucilius, and so the general reader, often with a personal reference to his own circumstances and shortcomings which owes something to Horace and contributes a good deal to Persius. The moral dialogues are more remote and less immediately cogent; only the manifesto *De Clementia* appears seriously to aim at prescribing moral standards and political advice to the new emperor Nero. If moral impact is to be sought anywhere in the period, it is to be found most effectively in Virgil's *Georgics* and *Aeneid*, both ostensibly devoted to quite different objectives, but expressing a view of man's position in the universe and relationship to nature which goes well beyond Augustus' declared doctrine of restoring the morality of Roman life.

The overt declarations of poets and prose-writers alike seldom reveal their true objectives. Horace's division between the *utile* and the *dulce* (*Ars* 343) draws attention to the rarity with which it is claimed that literature exists to give pleasure to the reader – that is, that literature is virtually an end in itself. This view, already apparent in Catullus, ties in with the recognition, most explicit in Horace, that literature is for the elite, a limited number of devotees – for those few who are capable of appreciating the writer's artistry in whatever field he chooses to operate. From this point of view, the moral and erotic themes of Horace, the piety and patriotism of Virgil, the love-affairs in the elegists, the Stoicism and republicanism in Lucan, all form the material which the poet exploits to create different literary masterpieces.

There is a curious conflict concerning the writer's originality: poets continually claim to be the first to strike out a particular line, but this means for the most part a new line in Latin.[20] Explicitly or implicitly, there is always the assumption of accepted conventions within which a new work must develop, and the concept of *imitatio* of predecessors is seldom far away, together with the practice of allusiveness to recall the reader to the earlier masters, Greek or Latin, who have provided ideas for the new writer to play with and make his own. This is most evident in Virgil's deliberate evocation of (successively) Theocritus, Hesiod and Homer in his three great works; in Horace's use for the *Odes* of both the early lyricists and the Alexandrians; in the elegists' open acknowledgement of their debts to Callimachus, Philitas, Euphorion and others,

---

[20] Williams 1968 (A 103) 253–267, with (e.g.) Virg. *G.* III.10–12, Hor. *Carm.* III.30.13–14.

whose influence we should recognize if their works had not been wholly or mainly lost.[21]

Most contentious and debatable here is the role of Cornelius Gallus as in some sense the founder of the whole Augustan movement. The discovery in 1978 of a papyrus containing two tetrastichs and fragments of other lines, clearly belonging to Gallus, has done little to clarify the nature of his poetry and the limits of his influence on his successors.[22] His influence on the young Virgil especially cannot be doubted, but the precise part he plays in the sixth and tenth *Eclogues* still defies secure definition, while the pursuit of themes and phrases from Gallus in Propertius is a still-growing industry. One feature can be detected, in accordance with previous expectation: the emphasis on the poet's own personality and experience as a major element in his poetry and the development throughout a book of elegy of the course of a love-affair, which was to provide an important bridge between the personal poetry of Catullus (and very likely of other members of his circle) and the 'subjective love-elegy' of the Augustans. This autobiographical tendency in Latin poetry, not necessarily always based on reality, appears to take its origin in the satires of Lucilius, reporting 'the whole of life' according to Horace (*Sat.* II.1.32–4); and it developed in Horace's *Satires* and *Epistles* alongside the similar phenomenon in elegy and to a great extent in his own *Odes*. The personal and conversational becomes a characteristic of the greater part of Augustan poetry, although making little impact in Virgil.

An important issue here is the recognition that an intimate knowledge of the poetry of Gallus, and perhaps of other lost poets such as Cinna and Valerius Cato, could be taken for granted by the Augustan poets; and the alert reader would pick up many references and echoes which escape us today. This does not mean that Gallus was regarded as a completely satisfactory model for aetiological or erotic verse – certainly the surviving fragments contain usages which were totally rejected by the next generation. The concept of the master as model seems only to be fully developed after the climax of the Augustan age, when Virgil's pre-eminence is so universally recognized that epic poets feel obliged to follow him more or less closely, unless they take a positive step, as Lucan did, in abandoning all of Virgil's heroic machinery and writing a fundamentally different sort of historical epic. Horace's mastery in lyric poetry, on the other hand, appears virtually to have prevented later poets from attempting to operate within the genre at all; while Statius' two essays in Alcaic and Sapphic in the fourth book of *Silvae* (5 and 7) simply

[21] Cf. Hubbard 1974 (B 89A) 10–11, 70–81.
[22] Anderson, Parsons and Nisbet 1979 (B 4); cf. e.g. S. G. Hinds and R. Whitaker *Papers of the Liverpool Latin Seminar* 4 (1983) 43–54, 55–60; J. Fairbrother, *CQ* 24 (1984) 167–74.

demonstrate that nothing was left for an imitator to achieve. Whatever Caesius Bassus composed to deserve respectful comments from Persius (VI.1) and Quintilian (X.1.96), not a line of his lyrics has survived to show us whether his achievement was worth anything. However justified Gallus' reputation was among the Augustans, at least he never discouraged others from pursuing the tradition he had started.

The importance of earlier writers as sources for ideas and allusions of various sorts was expressly acknowledged in antiquity, as is shown by Macrobius' lists in the *Saturnalia* (especially V.2–22, VI.1–5), which were probably compiled by critics over several centuries, of Virgilian borrowings from Greek and early Latin poets; although it is not clear how concerned these critics were to assess the actual effect of some of these quotations. Modern scholarship has made considerable advances, handicapped by the loss of so many works which were evidently available to Virgil and others. But it has failed to find an altogether satisfactory explanation of the famous echo in Aeneas' address to the ghost of Dido, 'invitus, regina, tuo de litore cessi' (*Aen*. VI.460) from Catullus' burlesque, 'invita, o regina, tuo de vertice cessi' (56.39), which in turn presumably reflects a line, now lost, in Callimachus' original poem on the Lock of Berenice, on which Catullus' poem was based: it may be that both come from an unknown predecessor of enough solemnity for Virgil not to feel that the pathos of his own context might be spoiled by reminiscences of Catullus' parody.[23] On the other hand, Virgil strikingly quotes from his own *Georgics* to provide animal-similes for the *Aeneid*, evidently when he wants to sharpen the reader's attention and remind him of elements in the earlier context which have relevance to the later.[24]

There seems to be no comment in ancient criticism on the major Virgilian symbols which play a prominent and continuous part in certain books of the *Aeneid*, as the snakes and fire do in II, if not throughout all; but the presence and the effect of these symbols can hardly be denied once they are noticed. The reader's attention is likewise demanded, if scholars are right, by the occurrence of key words in Virgil (but also, it has been suggested, in Persius); and on a much larger scale by consideration of the overall architecture of the book of *Eclogues*, of the four *Georgics*, of the whole *Aeneid*, and increasingly complex diagrams have been produced for the books of the elegiac poets, for Horace's *Odes*, and for almost every other book of Latin poetry.[25] It may be significant that the greatest of the Augustans have lent themselves remarkably to the requirements of modern research, so that an endless succession of doctoral theses and published monographs can be extracted from more

[23] See R. G. Austin's note *ad loc*, in his edition of *Aen*. VI (1977).
[24] G. B. Townend, in *Laurea Corona* (1987) 84–8.
[25] E.g. Otis 1963 (B 135A) 129, 228, etc.

and more different ways of analysing language, metre, assonance, structure, symbolism and so on, suggesting that all these things were planted by Virgil and the others in their poetry in the expectation that the more appreciative reader would be equipped to observe them for himself and to gain the more from the work. There is little evidence, however, that this sort of awareness was encouraged by the *grammaticus* or the literary critic, who were more concerned with correct reading and the understanding of references, in the manner of a good nineteenth-century commentary. It is more credible, though unprovable, that the greatest artist may admit these elements unconsciously, and that the reader may equally unconsciously enjoy and value the work all the more on account of these qualities.

V. THE ACCESSIBILITY OF LITERATURE

The impact of major literature on the great public is hard to assess. The considerable production of tragedies seems never to have reached the theatres, the output of Asinius Pollio and Ovid evidently having little more success than Augustus' abortive *Ajax*; the *Medea* is one of Ovid's very few works not to be preserved for posterity (Quint. *Inst.* x.1.98; Tac. *Dial.* 12.6). Seneca's surviving plays contain elements of descriptions of their action suggesting that they did not need to be seen to be appreciated, but rather read aloud, perhaps to the accompaniment of dancing or mime. Mime itself, which under the late Republic retained some of the literary quality of Herondas and Sophron, still found no favour with Horace (*Sat.* 1.10.5–6). Under the Empire it came to depend more and more on the obscene and the spectacular, including real sex and real crucifixions, until it seems to have merged with pantomime. This never ranked as literature, despite the libretti derived from Virgil and Ovid and others specifically written by Lucan and Statius.

The most significant type of public performance becomes the *recitatio*, of poetry and prose alike. This seems to have been the regular way of launching a new work before the publication of an approved text.[26] Only after such an occasion, and the correction of faults which might have come to light, would the author make the work available to the public; and this, in the case of Virgil and Persius, and probably Lucan, might mean posthumous publication. Subsequent reading might also take the form of an oral performance, often by specifically trained slaves, to an individual or a group. In addition, we hear of public performances by professional *cantores*, as something quite distinct from Virgil's own reading of the *Georgics* and of three books of the *Aeneid* to the imperial household, as well as trials of various passages before a rather wider

---

[26] Kenney in Kenney and Clausen 1982 (B 95) 12.

audience (Suet. *Vita Ver.* 27, 32–3). Horace in particular (*Sat.* 1.4.73–7) emphasizes that he never recites his works except to selected friends and on their express insistence; while others take advantage of the crowds in the public baths to force their works on all sorts of listeners. The importance of all these readings will have been greatly increased by the extent of aural memory enjoyed by a society with far less written material than the modern world possesses, so that whole passages appear to have been retained by hearers, with varying degrees of accuracy.[27]

But apart from the fact that reading, like writing, was almost always carried out aloud, the general status of reading appears to have borne a considerable similarity to that of our own day, with bookstalls selling copies for personal enjoyment and most works available in the great public libraries, which begin almost exactly with the Augustan age and expanded rapidly in the following two centuries.[28] We still hardly know the extent of these collections, nor how far the different libraries duplicated each other. It would appear that readers would normally consult books inside the libraries, as in the British Library or the Bodleian. It may have been exceptional, and a matter of privilege, for Marcus Aurelius in the second century to report to Fronto that he has taken certain volumes of Cato out of the library of Apollo on the Palatine and advise him to bribe the librarian of the Tiberian collection to let him have copies from there.

Some works were evidently produced in fairly large numbers, with individuals having copies made by their own slaves from a borrowed text; others probably never merited marketing to any effective extent. Survival down to the Renaissance is little indication of the availability of works in antiquity: the fact that Velleius has come down to us largely complete cannot be proof of wide circulation. On the other hand, there is reason to suppose that Juvenal made so little impact in his own day that he survived only because of a surprising popularity in the fourth century, attested by Ammianus (28.4.14), when there was a sudden demand for improved texts, enriched with scholia and commenticious biographies of the author.[29] Gellius provides some interesting stories, not always plausible, of discovering rare texts in unlikely places (e.g. IX.4.1, XVIII.9.5); yet Quintilian can recommend for the student's reading a very wide range of authors as undistinguished as Rabirius and Albinovanus Pedo (e.g. X.1.90), who must at least have been available in one or more of the public libraries. It is a bolder assertion that the libraries in Rome also contained copies of all the obscure works cited only by Dionysius of

---

[27] Few can have rivalled the elder Seneca, who wrote down extensive passages from declamations he had listened to. There is no reason to suppose that he made use of shorthand reports, although both Greek and Latin systems existed by that date.

[28] Kenney in Kenney and Clausen 1982 (B 95) 24–5.   [29] Highet 1954 (B 84A) 186–7.

Halicarnassus or the elder Pliny. It may well be that these libraries were such easy victims of deliberate arson in later times of trouble that their collections would provide relatively few archetypes for transmission, and that the chances were better for books in private houses. Yet from Pompeii and Herculaneum together we have recovered only one library, consisting of Epicurean treatises otherwise lost, and not a single book from any other house. The element of hazard in the survival of books was so great that, apart from the evidence of wide circulation, largely dependent on use in the schools, of a few major writers like Virgil, Horace and Cicero, no safe conclusion can be drawn about the number of copies ever made. The total loss of Varius' poems or the histories of Cremutius Cordus (officially destroyed but preserved for subsequent distribution) and of the elder Pliny may indicate either a lack of quality or an excess of quantity, which made copying impracticable and allowed most of Livy to survive only in epitomes; but Pliny's *Natural History* has nevertheless survived, and so have the Neronian pastoralists.

The evidence for the familiarity of the great writers outside the educated elite is very small, almost limited to the few tags written on the walls of Pompeii, which do not extend far beyond *arma virumque* and *conticuere omnes* (the opening words of the first two books of the *Aeneid*) and a variety of odd lines from different parts of the same poem, evidently employed for writing exercises, from places as remote as Masada and Vindolanda.[30] Of specifically popular literature we have hardly any traces. When Horace wishes to contrast his own supposedly good taste with that of his down-to-earth slave (*Sat.* 11.7.95–101), he chooses painting, not literature, as the field of aesthetic expertise. But perhaps Davus could not afford books in any case, or could not read, at least well enough to do so with pleasure. His knowledge of Crispinus' philosophy he attributes to the oral teaching of Crispinus' porter. The press, providing the great majority of people with their main or sole reading today, was represented by the *Acta*, certainly not mass-produced and hardly likely to have a general appeal.

Where the modern world suggests fiction as the obvious type of literature to attract a wide public, we hear of little but 'the Milesian tale', suitably bawdy indeed and made available in Latin by Sisenna in the first half of the second century B.C. The Milesian tradition is certainly traceable in episodes of Petronius' *Satiricon*, such as the tale of the Widow of Ephesus, and may have played a considerable part in the origin of the whole of that work, with contributions from the Greek novel, evidently available to, and perhaps popular with, the large Greek-speaking element in the population of Rome and other Italian cities. The *Satiricon*, even in its mutilated state, is much too complex and sophisticated a work

---

[30] A. K. Bowman and J. D. Thomas, in *JRS* 76 (1986) 122, and in *Britannia* (1987) 125–142 with a useful list of such quotations and their provenances.

to have arisen from nothing,[31] although, as mentioned above, it fits awkwardly into the genre of Menippean satire and is totally ignored by Quintilian, who would have been hard pressed to recommend it for the training of the young orator, even if he had ever come across a copy of it. Although the low language and the low subject-matter might well appeal to a popular readership, a great deal of literary criticism and similar matter seems to be aimed only at a very limited circle; and the same is true of the other Menippean satire to survive, the *Apocolocyntosis*, patently written for circulation among a select group of readers at a particular point in time.

We do possess one writer, from the reign of Tiberius, who stands altogether apart from the fashion and attracted no attention from literary critics, although he may have been considerably more popular and widely read than many more imposing poets. Phaedrus was an imperial freedman, who was at one time involved in trouble with Sejanus. He versified a large number of supposedly Aesopian fables, adding some of his own, including a few on distinctively Roman contemporary topics. He is no master, but writes engagingly and unpretentiously, arousing the question as to how unusual his writing was in an age of great sophistication, and how far he was writing for a distinct level of reader. With his simple language and metre and his improving morals, he appears to be aiming at the younger pupils of the *grammaticus*; and these qualities probably contributed to his survival into the modern world. The fables would certainly have greater appeal to an elementary reader than the Twelve Tables of early law which at one time seem to have served this purpose; but we have no direct evidence of Phaedrus' use in the schools.

What is most striking in the Roman world is the lack of any basic text which was read by any who could read and listened to regularly by all, as the English bible was for at least 300 years, providing a common focus of language and knowledge. To a certain extent Homer had filled this place in some Greek cities at least in the classical period and probably later; although his language was far removed from colloquial Greek even in the fifth century B.C. and his very bulk made him difficult to assimilate. Virgil could make some claims to have become the bible of Rome, almost as soon as the *Aeneid* appeared; but the occasions of hearing him read cannot have been frequent, and an influence on Roman life which might have been a major force on the side of humanity and peace was never allowed to become really widespread. It is hard to imagine that any other writer of the period, even Horace or Seneca, can have had even that slight chance of exercising serious influence on the society to which they belonged.

---

[31] P. Parsons, in *BICS* 18 (1971) 53–66, sees some parallel to the *Satiricon* in a Greek papyrus, probably of the second century A.D. (*POxy.* 3010), suggesting the existence of a picaresque narrative tradition in Greek on which Petronius may have drawn.

CHAPTER 20

ROMAN ART, 43 B.C. TO A.D. 69

MARIO TORELLI

I. THE GENERAL CHARACTERISTICS
OF AUGUSTAN CLASSICISM

In the history of ancient art few changes are so dramatically apparent as that which unfolded, gradually yet unmistakably, during the first two decades of the reign of Augustus. This change came about under the banner of a Classicism inspired by the great Attic examples of the fifth and fourth centuries B.C. The origins of this Classicism were, however, remote. In the architectural and art-historical context of late republican 'Asiatic luxury' (*luxuria Asiatica*), both the Classical models, which were already present in the Hellenistic culture inspiring that *luxuria*, and the genuinely baroque practices, which were peculiar to middle and late Hellenistic art, had been enthusiastically welcomed by Roman patrons of the ruling class.[1] But in the Augustan and Julio-Claudian age, Classicism became an official artistic programme and one unique to the capital,[2] and from this centre emanated the models adopted by greater and lesser private patrons, as well as by Italian and provincial municipalities, especially in the West. Both taste and knowledge were so deeply affected that the history of Roman imperial art can to a large extent be seen as a series of variations on and interpretations of the Classicizing message.

In the age of Caesar, official architecture, sculpture and painting were still deeply imbued with a baroque and Hellenistic dramatic force, but they also recalled the distant experiences of the artistic culture common to the Etruscan and Italic world (the *koine*) of the third century B.C. This is especially discernable in the formal duality of the portrait. In portrait sculpture, an art deeply imbued with local ideology, the spare, incisive, 'realistic' aspects of the Italian portrait in fact co-existed with the distinctly psychological features, full of pathos, of the late-Hellenistic portrait. The point can be made quite simply by comparing the basic,

[1] F. Coarelli, *DArch* 2 (1968) 302ff; *id. DArch* 4–5 (1970–1) 241ff: *id. St. Miscell.* 15 (1970) 85ff; *id.* in Zanker 1976 (E 141) 21ff; *id.* in *L'art décoratif à Rome* (Rome, 1981) 229ff.

[2] Zanker 1988 (F 633); Simon 1987 (F 577); *Kaiser Augustus und die verlorene Republik* 1988 (F 443), the catalogue of an exhibition at Berlin.

linear countenances of the 'Arringatore' (The Orator, *c.* 100 B.C.)[3] and of Caesar (*c.* 50 B.C.)[4] on the one hand, with the soft, shaded features of the so-called Postumius Albinus (convincingly identified as Cato the Censor, *c.* 150 B.C.) and of Pompey (*c.* 60 B.C.) on the other.[5] The two formal approaches continued to co-exist in the second half of the first century B.C., but the 'Italic' modes tended increasingly to denote municipality or provincial patronage, and they spread eventually to the lowest social and cultural levels of so-called 'plebeian art'. We shall return to this later.

In the official art of the court and the great aristocracy of Rome, the moment of transition from this ambiguous coexistence of 'Italic' with late Hellenistic forms to the decisive selection of Classicism may be situated in a brief period of political and cultural settlement, that is, in the decade which followed the constitutional change of the year 27 B.C. Shortly before that date, characteristic late republican tendencies are still clearly in play. Portrait sculpture continues to produce masterpieces with a flavour of Hellenistic dynasticism, such as the 'Actium'-type portrait of Octavian[6] or the 'Gabii'-type of Agrippa.[7] Decorative painting continues to develop the long established themes of the Second Style, with its characteristic 'open walls' and wide scenic perspectives,[8] while public and private architecture operate within the framework of models developed between the end of the second and the middle of the first century B.C.[9] The last decade of the first century was, however, already dominated by the Classicizing language of the Augustan regime.[10] The 'Prima Porta'-type portrait of Augustus embodies the propaganda message of the new convictions of the Principate.[11] In painting, plain, undisturbed tapestries, across which run slender candelabras and minute friezes in the Third Style, support reproductions of the great Classical Greek panel paintings;[12] while architecture and architectural ornamentation in marble and stucco echo – in the context of consolidated building types – the Attic, or at least Classical, models of the fifth and fourth centuries B.C.[13] By now imperial Roman Classicism is completely formed and functioning.

As we have seen, the new style was not in fact entirely new: behind it

---

[3] T. Dohrn, *Der Arringatore* (Berlin 1968); M. Cristofani, *Bronzi Etruschi* I. *La plastica votiva* (Novara, 1985) no. 129.

[4] F. Johansen, *Ancient Portraits in the J. Paul Getty Museum* I (Malibu, 1987) 24ff.

[5] L. Giuliani, *Bildnis und Botschaft* (Frankfurt am Main, 1986).   [6] Zanker 1973 (F 627).

[7] M. Hofter, in *Kaiser Augustus* 1988 (F 443) no. 150, pp. 313f.

[8] The documentation is splendidly collected by Beyen 1938–60 (F 271). The highest urban level is that of the House of Augustus: Carettoni 1983 (F 316); also Barbet 1985 (F 262).

[9] P. Gros, G. Sauron, in *Kaiser Augustus* 1988 (F 443) 48ff. F. Coarelli, *ibid* (1988 (F 443)) 68ff.

[10] M. Torelli, *Index* 13 (1985) 589ff.   [11] Vierneisel and Zanker 1979 (F 605).

[12] Bastet and de Vos 1979 (F 265).

[13] *Kaiser Augustus* 1988 (F 443) *passim*, reviews the decoration of the principal Augustan monuments at Rome.

lay over 150 years of history. A work like the pediment in Via San Gregorio[14] sufficiently conveys with its decidedly classicizing character the antiquity of neoclassical experience in the city, under the stimulus of the strong classicizing element in the late Hellenism of Pergamum and Athens. What was new was the pervasive, all-embracing aspect of Classical forms, which freed buildings and their decoration, official sculptures, and urban planning from all that unrestrained baroque freedom (*licentia*) which came from the effrontery (*audacia*) of the Alexandrians. New also was the nostalgic recovery of a Roman and Italian national past onto which was grafted the formal, Classicizing message; and new too was the general and enthusiastic support of the Roman aristocracy and of the local magnates of Italy, the *domi nobiles*, for the unique programme developed in the capital. Baroque, Hellenistic experiences were thus pushed to the side, to be looked for in the narrow confines of private consumption of art, in silverware and fine pottery, and in the minor genre paintings, landscapes and still lifes, which were placed side by side with copies of classical or great classicizing paintings in the Arcadian gardens of urban villas.

Consistently with the assumptions of the Augustan programme for restoration, all these non-Classicizing forms were assigned to the representation of idylls and escapes, trifles (*nugae*) and erotic themes, that is, modes and fashions outside of reality, pseudo-messages void of content. But the very limiting of private and public *luxuria* imposed by the policy of the *princeps* ended by incorporating such developments, however devalued of meaning they may have been, so that often the Classicizing idiom, which tended to eliminate such risky departures from the austere and ubiquitous realm of official ideology, came to the surface even in the private consumption of art.

The ban on baroque language was accompanied by censure of any element that did not conform to the central plan of moral restoration. Once the military triumphs of the *nobilitas* were done away with (to be reserved for the *princeps* and his family), the great public building activity which had been financed by the generals' spoils of war (*ex manubiis*) came also to an end, along with all the dynastic ideology which it had carried in the last century of the Republic. The grandiloquent decorative programmes, both public and private, which had been aimed at individual glorification – using Hellenistic forms of self-representation – gave way in the public arena to imperial initiative alone, and in private to less compromising 'galleries' populated by the images of philosophers, or

---

[14] This pediment, like others of the second century B.C. (Rome, in the Via Latina; Luni; Volterra, etc.) needs reconsideration. See meanwhile, M. J. Strazzulla in M. Martelli, M. Cristofani, eds., I caratteri dell'ellenismo nelle urne etrusche (Florence, 1977) 41ff.

athletes or of gods, where *otium* (leisure) either had exclusively intellectual connotations or merely expressed a desire for escape.

This profound 'renewal', then, had its programmatic foundations in the ideology of the state. That was carefully fashioned by the great intellectuals within the circle of the *princeps*, from a singular mixture of Classicizing ideals, which were developed from the 'inimitable models' of the Greeks, and of national, Romano-Italian traditions, which were organized within the framework of a revival of Archaizing customs and native memories. The new figurative culture constituted a formidable vehicle for the propagation of the religious, political and symbolic elements of this revival in the most remote municipalities of Italy and among the lowest levels of society.

The instrument for the remarkable diffusion of this programme was above all a favoured group of sculptors in marble and bronze of the neo-Attic school. These men had already become established in Italy during the late Republic, working in Rome or Campania in a number of workshops, and controlled either directly or indirectly by such Roman aristocrats as Junius Damasippus, the Cossutii, or the notorious Gaius Verres. First among these workshops in both organization and quality was that directed by Pasiteles, who was head of a school which was well known for at least three generations.[15] There were, moreover, a large number of lesser, anonymous stone-cutters as well as legions of fresco-painters, also anonymous, to whom the whole of Italy, from the *princeps* to the humblest *municeps*, entrusted the decoration of their houses. Along with the even humbler crafters of small-scale work in metal and terracotta, these sculptors revived and developed Classical and Hellenistic models in the new spirit, operating within a capillary-like network of workshops, each with its own rules of apprenticeship and instruction, and within a no less capillary circulation of moulds, casts and clay models (*proplasmata*). Thanks to new discoveries, we now know far more about these than was revealed to us by the well-known anecdote about the plaster models used by Pasiteles.[16]

Thus the vein of formal inspiration began in a transplantation of neo-Attic craftsmen into a Roman environment which dates back to the middle of the second century B.C., with the activity of the school of

[15] On these ateliers, in addition to works cited in n. 1, see G. Becatti, 7 (1940) 7ff; M. Torelli, *MAAR* 36 (1980) 313ff; *id. Scienze dell' Antichità* 2 (1988) 403ff.

[16] Clay *proplasmata* intended to serve as models for moulds for bronze sculptures have been discovered by M. A. Tomei (*Archeologia laziale* 7 (1987) 73f, fig. 6) in the excavation of the *Domus Tiberiana*. These may be set beside the fragments of plaster casts of the Tyrannicides of Critios and Nesiotes discovered at Baiae with the well-known copy of the Sosandra (C. Landwehr, *Die antiken Gipsabgüsse aus Baiae* (1985)), in order to show the very close link between imperial residences and artisan activity in the replication and collage of works of art.

Timarchides, and it must have been re-invigorated under Augustus, thanks to the *pax Augusta* and the gradual extension of imperial monopoly over marble quarries. The very concentration of refined sculptors' studios around the palace, to which discoveries at the *Domus Tiberiana* on the Palatine and at Baiae bear witness, must have encouraged both centralization in the development of models and the creation of schools and workshops far more stable than those which had existed in the past, and thus the formation of an artistic tradition less sporadic and occasional than that of the late Republic. The proof of this is to some extent also offered by the solid fabric of Classicizing style which developed in the age of Augustus and which essentially continued into the reign of Domitian, when there probably occurred a new influx of artists and craftsmen from the eastern Mediterranean, in the wake of the pharaonic building programmes undertaken by that emperor.[17]

II. THE CREATION OF THE AUGUSTAN MODEL

The death of Julius Caesar put a sudden end to the grandiose projects of urban transformation cherished by the dictator.[18] It would fall to Octavian Augustus to resume, especially after Actium, the plans of his adoptive father, whose purpose it had been to imprint the Julian name (*nomen Iulium*) on the imperial capital. The first steps of the young *princeps* were informed by the same dynastic conception that had characterized Pompey's works in the Campus Martius and Caesar's own designs.

Typical of this is the choice of model for his own mausoleum, possibly begun in 27 B.C., which recalls that of the tomb of Alexander;[19] while both the public and the private activities of his appointed successor, Agrippa, between the Campus Martius and the right bank of the Tiber, carried out in the years from 33 to 19 B.C., were certainly inspired by great Ptolemaic models. This can especially be seen if we consider the close link between Agrippa's urban villa across the Tiber (*trans Tiberim*) – most likely the so-called Casa della Farnesina – and the *stagnum* (pool) and the *Euripus* (canal) located at the edge of the complex made up by the Pantheon, *saepta* (voting enclosure), baths, *campus Agrippae* and *porticus Vipsaniae*, all completed or planned by him.[20] This foreshadows the similar egyptianizing effects which Hadrian would recreate a century and

---

[17] Workshops were formed in the age of Domitian to respond to the demands of his colossal building programme, a phenomenon still little investigated (and responsible for the improbable Domitianic chronologies sometimes attributed to such works as the great Trajanic frieze). See the preliminary remarks of M. Torelli, in *L'Urbs – Espace urbain et histoire* 1987 (A 96) 576ff.

[18] On these projects and Caesarian town planning in general: Gros and Torelli 1988 (A 41) 117ff and 167ff; H. v. Hesberg, in *Kaiser Augustus* 1988 (F 443) 93ff.

[19] H. von Hesberg, in *Kaiser Augustus* 1988 (F 443) 121ff.

[20] F. Coarelli, *MEFR* 4 89 (1977) 816ff; *id.* in *Kaiser Augustus* 1988 (F 443) 71ff; Roddaz 1984 (C 200) 231ff (with useful bibliography).

a half later in his villa at Tivoli, with its evocative coupling of baths and Canopus; but it recalls above all the model of urban organization offered by Alexandria and repeated by the Augustan plan of *regiones* and *vici*. The tradition of the *viri triumphales* of the late Republic was also revived by Augustus with the theatre dedicated to his first heir Marcellus (23 B.C.) and with the restoration of the temple of Apollo *in Circo* attached to that theatre, thanks to which he was able to reinforce the Apollinian propaganda, launched after Actium, with a more traditional reference to the memory of the *nomen Iulium* which was associated with the first dedicator of the temple, Cn. Iulius (consul in 431 B.C.).[21] The construction of the temple of Palatine Apollo (36–28 B.C.) next to his house bore the same dynastic imprint. Watched over by the Magna Mater (an obvious symbol of the Trojan origins of both his *gens* and of Rome), and by his personal god, the prophet Apollo (who had been a reliable guide during the clash at Actium), the house evokes the model of the palaces of Hellenistic kings, which were likewise protected by the great personal deities of the *basileus*.[22] And another reminder of Egypt is offered by the *solarium*, the colossal sundial centred on the *obeliscus Augusti*, which he laid out on the extreme northern boundary of his city, a most unusual *horologium* set as it were in a gigantic garden (10 B.C.).[23]

In his other *opera triumphalis*, the Forum of Augustus,[24] which he vowed in 42 and inaugurated in 2 B.C., he follows yet again in Caesar's footsteps. On the pediment of the temple of Mars Ultor (Mars the Avenger), at the end of the Forum, Caesar's divine ancestress Venus Genetrix stood side by side with Augustus' Mars Ultor: a sacred marriage which was to be interpreted in a dynastic sense. To this Augustus added statues representing his own ancestors, mythical and historical, on one side of the Forum, and these faced a Romulean procession of the great men, the *summi viri*, of the city's history, on the other side. The *gens* of the new Aeneas and the new Romulus thus recapitulated the historical fortunes of Rome, a theme which was, as we shall see, developed in the Ara Pacis and which well displays the substance of the ideology of the Augustan Principate: the *princeps*, and he alone, had the right to mix or to juxtapose the public with the private. And indeed, in 19 B.C., Cornelius Balbus was the last triumphing general able to erect an edifice from his spoils, the *theatrum* with the *crypta Balbi*; after him there would be no more triumphs, save for those enjoyed by the emperor or his family, and consequently monuments would no longer be erected to celebrate the personal glories of the Roman aristocracy.

[21] E. La Rocca, in *Kaiser Augustus* 1988 (F 443) 121ff; A. Viscogliosi, *ibid.* 136ff.
[22] G. Carettoni, *ibid.* 263ff.   [23] E. Buchner, *ibid.* 240ff.
[24] J. Ganzert, V. Kockel, *ibid.* 149ff.

We may safely assert that, even if some works were completed a little later, in the course of the penultimate decade of the century the most complex and daring initiatives in architecture and urban planning of the Augustan period came to an end. Nevertheless, even where he did not erect new buildings or where the ideological interweaving of past and present was more subtle, Augustus imposed through his programme a new coherence on buildings which already existed, restoring a few – in his *Res Gestae* he claims to have restored eighty temples! – or adding some others, so as to compose a unified ideological design whose aim was the customary glorification of his own role as *princeps*. This is apparent above all in the old Forum Romanum. Here the reconstruction of the main temples and public buildings – the temples of Castor and Pollux, of Saturn, and of Concordia, the basilicas, the Curia, and the *regia* – have the evident objective of imposing the *nomen Iulium* as extensively as possible on the most majestic urban complex of the city, while at the same time 're-employing' all the venerable buildings within the context of his personal propaganda. Thus new messages were skilfully juxtaposed with or superimposed on ancient ones: his wife Livia was paired with Concord (A.D. 6); his grandsons the *principes iuventutis* were joined with Castor and Pollux (A.D. 7). But a quite different and crucial role was played by a few additions to the Forum which were statements of Augustan policy, that is, by the dynastic temple of the Divine Julius – which was set between two triumphal arches of Augustus, the one celebrating his victory at Actium (29 B.C., later tactfully transformed into a Dalmatian arch), the other his Parthian success (19 B.C.) – and by the Portico of Gaius and Lucius (A.D. 2). These monuments very elegantly exclude 'undesirable' buildings from the open space, undesirable either because they were associated with other aristocratic families, or because they could not be integrated into the new, Augustan ideological system: for example, the basilica Aemilia on the one hand, the *regia* and the *aedes Vestae*, which were replaced in the conception of the *princeps* by his residence on the Palatine, on the other.[25]

Although beset with continuous crises over the succession, the years of the consolidation of power were consistently devoted to these exercises in sophisticated urban 'inlay', which in fact destroyed or radically transformed earlier meanings as surely as his settlement of the constitution. But these years were also devoted to the reorganization of the administrative structure and functioning of the city, one similar to and as necessary as that enforced by Agrippa in his *cura aquarum*. In addition to their use in the collection of customs and the control of public order, the ancient, fourth-century city walls came again to mark

[25] Coarelli 1985 (E 19) II 211ff; with Gros 1976 (F 397).

the boundary between city and country through the systematic restoration of all the city gates (between A.D. 2 and 10), thus reaffirming the powerful symbolic value of both wall and gates which was to find a very special echo in the architecture and town planning of the Augustan cities of Italy and Gaul. In the years 8 and 7 B.C., the banks of the Tiber were set in order, the night watch (the *cohortes vigilum*) was established, and the city and the *continentia tecta* (the inhabited parts of the city and suburb) were divided into fourteen regions: together these completed in the organizational sphere the readjustment which Augustus had already begun between 12 and 7 B.C. in the religious sphere, with the institution of his personal cult in the sites of the *compita*, the shrines of the urban crossroads.[26]

In his *Res Gestae* Augustus placed great emphasis on his personal benefactions in the development of the city. Despite the customary official phrasing of the document, he goes far beyond the accepted practice of normal *elogia* and *commentarii*, not only in the boundless immensity of his achievements, but especially in the emphasis on the intensely urban character of his efforts, which did remain until the time of Domitian the grandest and most comprehensive in the history of the city: 'a city whose magnificence was not equal to the majesty of her empire, and which was exposed to floods and fires, he so improved that he might rightly boast that he left a city of marble which he had received made of brick' (Suet. *Aug.* 28). It is surprising then that the architectural expression of such a project should be essentially very limited and conventional. The great piazzas enclosed with porticoes and with temples at the end or in the centre, such as the Forum of Augustus and the *porticus Liviae* (A.D. 7), or open with temple at the centre of porticoes on three sides, as in the temple of Apollo Palatinus and perhaps in the Pantheon, are the most common elements of the Augustan contribution to the city. Perhaps its most novel and experimental aspect remains the work of Agrippa in the Campus Martius, with its intentional confusion of public and private, of dwellings, public parks, recreational spaces, boulevards and reflecting pools, a confusion which would reappear explicitly only in Nero's grand creation of 'private' buildings with strong dynastic connotations, from his villa at Subiaco to his Golden House. The Alexandrian model – which would then spread in private life, from the architecture of tombs to the Egyptian imagery of the late Second and Third Styles – is not merely mannerist exoticism, comparable to the chinoiseries of eighteenth-century Europe. It is also a recognition of the deep affinity between the realities of life at Alexandria and at Rome, both social and cultural, and at the same time of their

---

[26] F. Coarelli, in *Kaiser Augustus* 1988 (F 443) 75ff.

correspondingly deep diversity, which leads to the longing for, and the privatisation of, the models derived from that particular variant of Hellenism.

On the other hand, the programme of restoration required that the convictions of 'western' and 'national' values be defended, consolidated and reasserted within the framework of a pervasive *pietas*. Thus can we account for the systematic use of conventional architectural forms – temples on a podium at the end of a porticoed square – which had been the patrimony of Roman culture for over a century and a half, and which were now stripped of the late Hellenistic effronteries to be found in the great Latin and Campanian buildings between 120 and 50 B.C., and clothed again in neo-Attic forms. From the sculptor Diogenes, who was responsible for the decoration of the first Pantheon, to the extremely skilful stone-cutters, who created the elegant architectural partitions for the many sacred and public buildings ordered by Augustus, it was Athenian craftsmen who were the leaders in the neoclassical 'purification' of architectural decoration.

The dominant models are, as in all art forms, those of high Classicism, with a special and understandable predilection for the prototypes of Periclean Athens. The caryatids of the Attic neoclassicist Diogenes are not preserved for us, although we may suspect a Classicizing sculpture, caryatids of the Cherchell-Tralles or Venice-Mantua type.[27] But very clearly intended to evoke religious and revivalist memories are the copies of the *korai* from the portico of the Erechtheum in Athens, which were introduced into the upper storey of the Forum of Augustus and recopied in its replica at Emerita (Mérida, in Spain): these maidens, who are better understood in their role as *kanephoroi* (basket-carriers), encircled the shrines (*heroa*) of the *summi viri* and of the *nomen Iulium*, just as those at Athens are there to honour the tomb of the first king of Attica. All these architectural forms, from the mouldings of the temple podia to the Classical capitals, are crafted in a refined manner based on sharp and subtle lines, on a few projections from the representational plan which give a 'stiacciato' effect (that is, one of very low, flat surfaces) and on clear, undisturbed surfaces. The need for convictions, implicit in the search for the ideological models of Classicism, both shared and secure, asserts itself even in style, a style straining to evoke formal clarities and absolute definitions.

As to private architecture, innovations had already appeared in the culture of the late Republic, and the Augustan age added little to what had already been developed, other than its own neo-classical taste in decoration. Large mosaic pavements in black and white, walls painted in

---

[27] Documentation in E. Schmidt, *Ant. Plastik* 13 (1973); *id. Geschichte der Karyatide* (Wurzburg, 1982).

the Third Style, plain *impluvia*, and symmetric peristyles: these are the main contribution of an age concerned with returning to normal all that was bizarre or baroque in the domestic architecture of the late Republic.[28] Much broader was the spectrum of funerary typology, which reflects better than any other aspect of the culture the fundamental stratification of society, the ambitions of social ascent, the unifying force of the principles of the court in artistic culture.[29] *Columbaria* (tombs with niches for funerary urns) begin to proliferate to meet the needs of the less affluent social classes, while the late republican model of the *naiskos*, or shrine, was replaced in the preferences of the middle and upper classes of society by the tomb set on a tall, austere, archaizing cylinder: the most celebrated examples of this are the tomb of Caecilia Metella at Rome and that of Munatius Plancus at Gaeta, and that colossal *exemplum*, the mausoleum of Augustus. This taste for the exotic also provides a chance to indulge in such oddities as egyptianizing tombs in the form of pyramids. Above all the link – one derived from the practices of Hellenistic dynasts – between tombs and suburban estates, gardens or villas, grew even stronger than it had been, showing that these pyramids were not oddities, but that they too are to be included within the framework, already noted, of the 'bourgeoisification' of the royal cultural models of late Hellenism, a process increasingly evident as one penetrates the maze of private culture.

Naturally all this exists in delicate balance with the classicizing tradition, even in sculpture in the round. The programme of sculptural decoration of the Villa of the Papyri at Herculaneum[30] may have been due (as appears more likely) to a great intellectual of the Caesarian age such as L. Ateius Praetextatus, working for the patrician Claudii Pulchri, or (as some prefer) it may have been created a little later for the Calpurnii Pisones. Either way, it draws from a vast range of sculptural traditions in order to realize an articulated representation of the ideology and the ethical models of the leaders of society in the years of the civil wars. The classicizing formulae, which reach their peak in the ideal coupling of the Doryphorus/Achilles of Polyclitus with the Amazon/Penthesilea of Phidias, pass from the prototypes of the high fifth century B.C. through the late-classical – Lysippus' Hermes in Repose comes to mind – to end with the Hellenistic, found in garden sculpture. The choice of the prototype to be copied, developed and re-echoed is directly linked to the

---

[28] There is no standard work on Augustan domestic architecture and the relationship between it and painted, marble and stucco decoration. See in the meantime D'Arms 1970 (E 30); P. Zanker, *JDAI* 94 (1979) 460ff; Mielsch 1987 (F 502); Neudecker 1987 (F 513). Most interesting are the remarks of Leach 1982 (F 465).

[29] Eisner 1986 (F 357); von Hesberg and Zanker 1987 (F 418).

[30] M. R. Wojcik, *Ann. Fac. Lett. Filos. Perugia* 16/17 (1978/79–1979/80) 359ff; amplified in *La villa dei Papiri ad Ercolano* (Rome, 1986).

type of message which was intended: loftier and richer in ethical or political content, for sculptures copied from the Classical; lighter, more idyllic and epigrammatic, for works drawn from the Hellenistic repertory. Naturally in the public part of the house forms and messages are of a higher, Classicizing tone, while in the private area devoted to leisure the prevailing models are Hellenistic or at least escapist. The boundaries between these two levels are obviously very fluid, especially in houses, a fact which encouraged the mixing of genres and idioms in sculpture as well as in the other figurative arts.

The leading patrons called on the expertise of the neo-Attic masters, whom they bound to themselves as freedmen clients, as the above-mentioned case of the Cossutii shows. Already extensive under the late Republic, production expanded even further in order to furnish the town houses, country villas and suburban estates of the Roman aristocracy and the *domi nobiles* of Italy with candelabras, tables, seats, and neoclassical and archaizing reliefs.[31] These too express in concrete form the same atmosphere of idyll and escape which pervades architecture and painting. But to the same craftsmen and the same workshops are owed the last creations of Hellenistic culture on Italian soil, such as the Athlete of Stephanos, one of the masters of the school of Pasiteles, and above all the copies – either in bronze, with the technique of moulds and of clay models, or in marble, with the technique based on the pointing process – of great Classical originals: these are the key to the decoration of public and private buildings, with all the weight of traditional meanings or of meanings symbolically revived within the Roman context.[32]

Because of their talent for copying, these craftsmen had to contend with a series of operations of 'assembly' and 'disassembly' of their own creations. Particularly significant is the operation undergone by the 'Cavaspina', an epigrammatic sculpture which was certainly well known and is late Hellenistic in conception, as can be seen in the copy in London: all the same, in the bronze copy at Rome its head echoes the severe style.[33] The technical ability to reproduce sculpture relatively easily, when joined with a widespread 'culture of artistic canons' (modelled on that of literary canons), forged the opportunity for a whole series of formal tropes: archaistic heads on Classicizing torsoes, or Hellenistic draperies on naked limbs in a Classical manner, are to be read

---

[31] See the partial collections of K. Fuchs, *Die Vorbilder der neuattischen Reliefs* (Tübingen, 1953) and H. V. Cain, *Römische Marmorkandelaber* (Mainz, 1985). Still worth consulting are the pages of E. Pernice, *Die Hellenistische Kunst in Pompeji* IV–VI (Berlin, 1925–38), with J. Marcadé, *Au Musée de Délos. Étude sur la sculpture hellénistique en ronde-bosse découverte dans l'île* (Paris, 1969). On sculpture in general: N. Himmelmann, *Über Hirten – Genre in der antiken Kunst* (Opladen, 1980), and H. P. Laubscher, *Fischer und Landleute* (Mainz, 1982).

[32] Zanker 1974 (F 628); Bieber 1977 (F 283); Martin 1987 (F 495); *id.* in *Kaiser Augustus* 1988 (F 443) 251ff, 343ff.   [33] Zanker 1974 (F 628) 81ff.

as stylistic metaphors and transpositions meant to express *variationes*, rhetorical *elegantiae* which do not impair the content. In reality, as it is easy to see in Cicero's superficial remarks in commissioning the decoration for his Tusculan villa,[34] this new attitude prefigured that complete devaluation of the messages of the originals which would become typical from the later Julio-Claudian period. In that era copies of great Classical originals, such as the Mantua-type of Phidias' Apollo, are turned into banal lampstands in the townhouses of the Pompeian bourgeoisie, or reversed copies can be discovered facing each other to frame a doorway, as was the fate of the Pothos attributed to Scopas. From earlier symbolic 'translations' of their original content, the better to adapt it to the needs of the high Roman aristocracy, it is an imperceptible slide into pastiche and kitsch, a transformation which is also to be blamed on the gradual loss of coherence of formal values. The growing indifference to organic unity and stylistic coherence prefigures the indifference to content which would represent (with the exception of the great imperial complexes) the doctrine dominating decorations in the high empire.

However, the neo-Attic workshops had an even greater task than that of copying for public and private furnishings: this was to work out a sculpture in the round and in relief to exalt the *virtus* and the *pietas* of the *princeps*, to embody in another language the dynastic ambitions of Augustus and the climate of restoration of national values connected with them. Hence the aforementioned (and completely Hellenistic) concentration around the palace of intense activity in copying and development of the severe, Classical and late-Classical styles with models of terracotta or plaster, which were found at the *Domus Tiberiana* in Rome and the imperial complex at Baiae.[35] The Augustan programme called for the suppression of the highly visible phenomenon of self-glorification by aristocratic generals in favour of the restoration of *mos*, custom, and of the different degrees of dignity to which the typology of the statues was correlated. Thus, at the beginning of the Augustan age, Agrippa could still celebrate his own naval victories with an heroic statue inspired by images of Poseidon;[36] and this could be echoed, among the *domi nobiles*, by the heroic statue of the Ostian duumvir Cartilius Poplicola, commemorating *his* naval achievements, which were also extolled on the frieze of his sepulchre.[37] But the subsequent reduction of military and governing functions by the senatorial aristocracy favoured a rapid return to *mos*. Each function entailed a distinct type of portrait statue: *statuae augurales* and *pontificales* (*capite velato*, with *lituus*

[34] Cic. *Fam.* VII.23; *Att.* 1.4.3; 5.7; 6.2; 7; 8.2; 9.2; 10.3; 11.3.   [35] Cf. n. 16 above.
[36] G. Traversari, *Museo Archeologico di Venezia* I. *I ritratti* (Rome, 1986) 29, no. 13.
[37] Zevi 1976 (E 142) 56ff, fig. 13.

and sacrificial *patera*) to commemorate priests; *triumphales* (with *lorica*, *toga picta*, *hasta*) for recipients of triumphal honours; *loricatae* (with *lorica*) for military officers; *consulares* (with *toga* and *rotuli*) for consuls; *equestres* (with *tunica* and *paludamentum*) and *sella curuli sedentes*[38] for those governing with *imperium* military and civilian provinces, respectively.[39] Peripheral regions conformed relatively quickly to the urban model: the honours granted by the Cretans and the Herculaneans to Nonius Balbus[40] still reflect late-republican practices in the number and even the forms of the statues dedicated to him, but we soon meet the cuirassed statue of M. Holconius Rufus which celebrates, according to its appearance, his military tribunate *a populo*,[41] while such precious documents as the Barberini *togatus* illustrate both senatorial reassertion of the *ius imaginum* (the right to display the death-masks of ancestors who had held public office) and the power of the model of traditional political representation imposed by Augustus.[42]

Neither the *princeps* himself nor his family failed to observe these norms. Famous statues, such as that from the Via Labicana, depicting Augustus as *pontifex maximus*, or that recently discovered in the Euboean Sea,[43] reflecting his *imperium proconsulare maius* and his *ius gladii*, fit perfectly into the typology respectively of *statuae pontificales* and *statuae equestres*. But the profound sense of Augustan mystification is best felt in the most famous statue of the *princeps*, the Augustus of Prima Porta.[44] Probably intended as a *statua triumphalis* in connexion with the *honores* of the Parthian Arch, it celebrates through the figures on the cuirass deeds worthy of a triumph (*res triumphi dignae*), the return of the Parthian standards, an event which Augustus, with his accustomed skill, did not wish to be celebrated with a triumph. At the same time the statue presents a *princeps* uncharacteristically barefoot, in a heroic pose which is emphasized by the 'quotation' of Polyclitan *ponderatio*. Here as elsewhere, the transgression of *mos*, is confirmed by apparent reaffirmations of that very *mos* combined with marginal departures drawn from the tradition of Hellenistic monarchy. The creation of Augustus' official

[38] That is: augural and pontifical statues, head covered and with curved staff and sacrificial bowl; triumphal statues, with cuirass, embroidered toga, and spear; cuirassed statues; consular statues, with toga and scrolls; equestrian statues, with tunic and military cloak; and statues of magistrates sitting in chairs of office. For these concepts: M. Torelli, in A. M. Vaccaro and A. M. Sommella (eds.), *Marco Aurelio. Storia di un monumento e del suo restauro* (Milan, 1989) 83–102.

[39] As is shown beyond doubt in the series of statues granted to L. Volusius Saturninus (cos. 3 B.C.) in connexion with the *honores* he had received. See most recently S. Panciera, in *I Volusii Saturnini – Una famiglia romana della prima età imperiale* (Bari, 1982) 83ff.

[40] See most recently S. Adamo Muscettola, *Prospettiva* 28 (1982) 2ff; for the inscriptions, L. Schumacher, *Chiron* 6 (1976) 165ff.   [41] Zanker 1988 (F 633) 331, fig. 259.

[42] M. Torelli, *Index* 13 (1985) 589ff, with P. Zanker, *Wiss. Zeitschr. der Humboldt Univ. Berlin* 31 (1982) 307ff; *id.* 1983 (F 631) 251ff.

[43] M. Hofter, in *Kaiser Augustus* 1988 (F 443) no. 168, p. 323f; and E. Touloupa, *ibid.* no. 149, 311ff.   [44] See above, n. 7.

portrait and the parallel evolution of private portraiture in the second half of the first century B.C. take us over the same route. Portraits of the La Alcudia-type and the Actium-type, such as that of Agrippa, still follow the tradition of dynastic portraiture which flourished in the inflamed atmosphere of the Second Triumvirate. Echoes of this style are also to be found in private portraiture, even of women, as is shown by the extraordinary gallery of busts from the tomb of the Licinii.

The creation of the Prima Porta-type, which is dated by coins to the period when Octavian proclaimed himself Augustus (27 B.C.), but which ought perhaps to be associated with his triple triumph of 29, is the first consciously and decisively neoclassical step in portrait sculpture. Its success is witnessed by the number of copies, by its use over the whole span of Augustus' reign and beyond, and by its close connexion with the Augustan programme, stripped as it was of any glamorous dramatization of dynastic power, and lit from within by the aura of the *numen*, the divine nature. When we can glimpse in the better copies, such as that from the Via Labicana, the high level of the original, we can perfectly understand the sense of the message which permeates the extremely delicate workings of the surface, the accurate, almost academic, depiction of the hair, and the balance between a well-observed bone structure and a lightly shaded skin, that is to say, the successful distancing of the image from worldly concerns. In a word, on the formal level, the antithesis between the 'realistic' Roman portrait and its 'psychological' Hellenistic rival is resolved, through appeal to neoclassical modes of expression. The Classicizing assurance here becomes assurance of the rebirth of a charisma which is ancient, aristocratic, national, and therefore neither heroic nor Hellenizing, the aura of one who is 'leader', *princeps*, of a universal following, *clientela*, and confirmed as such by his divine origins: *numen adest*, a god is present.

Neo-Attic workmen were also engaged in the creation of the most important monument of Augustan sculpture, the Altar of Peace, Ara Pacis, which has come down to us in an exceptional state of preservation.[45] Voted (*constituta*) by the Senate on 4 July 13 B.C., the date of the *princeps'* return from Gaul and Spain, and consecrated (*dedicata*) on 30 January 9 B.C., the wedding anniversary of Augustus and Livia, the monument restated, but in a form much more grandiose and with the much more pronounced *maiestas*, majesty, of the *lex arae* (the sacred law concerning sacrifice at the altar), the motifs which had appeared in an altar dedicated to Fortuna Redux in 19, near the temples of Honos and Virtus outside the Porta Capena, to celebrate the return of Augustus from the East. Both altars wished to exalt in public forms a custom which was traditionally private and informal, the *ire obviam* (in Latin) or the

---

[45] Torelli 1982 (F 596) 27ff; S. Settis, in *Kaiser Augustus* 1988 (F 443) 400ff.

apantesis (in Greek), that is the going to meet a person of high rank outside the traditional boundaries of the city – here represented at the southernmost extremity by the Altar of Fortune Who Brings Back, and at the northernmost by the Altar of Peace. In fact both monuments were intended as substitutes for a triumph which Augustus no longer wanted (Flor. 11.34). However – and this is a typically Augustan trait – the renunciation of the triumph and of the excessive honours voted by the Senate was here rewarded with the establishment among the forms of state ceremony of a private custom with a dynastic flavour. The celebration of the return (*reditus*) became in this way an integral part of the prerogatives of the *princeps*, through a process in which the Ara Pacis is the basic point of both arrival and departure.

The placing of the monument, beside the Via Flaminia but open to the Campus Martius, is significant. In this case the northern boundaries of the city are imaginary (as is the 'realistic' depiction of the *reditus* on the reliefs), but setting the altar a Roman mile from the *pomerium* is a concrete representation of *mos*, insofar as it separates *imperium militiae* from *imperium domi*, the *imperia* of war and peace. According to juridical tradition, in passing this imaginary line the magistrate was obliged to take on the clothes and demeanour of *imperium domi*. Placing the altar at this point (where at that time the new pomerial line was drawn) is a clear announcement of peace, and at the same time it is the result of that choice and it alone (not of some obscure cabbalistic leanings), fully conforming to the Augustan habit of formally reviving traditional values, even though they may be introducing *nova exempla*.

Evocation of the past extends also to the shape of the monument, which is a traditional U-shaped altar set at the centre of a small enclosure. With its imitation of pillar posts at the four corners and of wooden panelling within, this enclosure is intended to reproduce a *templum in terris*, a space set aside for *auspicia* and *auguria*. At the same time, with the two doors (which are contrary to the norm for augural *templa*) and with the metallic appearance of the vegetal decoration on the exterior, it also recalls the shrine of Janus Quirinus in the Forum. Both suggestions serve to evoke the aura of augural charisma created by the *princeps* around his own person and the message of peace implicit in his return. The choice of the double model – augural temple and Janus Quirinus – is also reflected in the themes of the decorations in relief which embellish the exterior of the enclosure. The lower part of these reliefs presents swags of acanthus leaves populated with Apollinian swans, imitating metalwork and thus the bronze structure of the Janus Quirinus.

The upper parts of these exterior reliefs present friezes with human figures. On the long sides facing north and south these depict a procession. This cannot be a procession of 13 B.C., since that never took place, nor one of 9, which if it did occur would not have seen among its participants Agrippa, who is shown on the frieze but who had died in 12. It is rather a theoretical, idealized depiction of an imperial *reditus* for which it clearly aims to establish a norm. It means to depict the *reditus* of 13 B.C. not as it was but as it should have been, so that in future the return of the *princeps* might be marked by that same *ire obviam*, with the same participants and in the same order. An order of procession very carefully worked out by protocol embraces both sides: priests from the *ordo sacerdotum* in front (*pontifices* and *augures* on the south side, *XVviri* and *VIIviri*, on the north) are followed by members of the *domus Iulia* ranged according to the *ordo affinitatis*, their ranking by relationship to him, which was prescribed by *mos* and by Augustus' testamentary wishes. He himself is presented, significantly, in the robes of one sacrificing for his own return, a focal point between priests and relatives. The observation of details of protocol is extremely careful, as is shown, for example, by the presence of the *flamines* out of order at the shoulders of an Augustus presented in his role as *pontifex maximus* (another chronological 'imprecision'), or by the distribution of the two branches of the family on two sides, following firm genealogical logic. As usual, details appear on the frieze which have no relevance to protocol, but which allude rather to matters of status or propaganda, such as the elder Drusus shown in military costume, or the two children Gaius and Lucius Caesar dressed in the manner of participants in the *lusus Troiae*. The panels beside the doors depict the goddess Roma between Honos and Virtus, and Venus-Tellus-Pax among heavenly breezes (*aurae caelestes*), on the east side; those on the west, Mars and the *lupercal*, and Aeneas sacrificing the Laurentine sow, with a complex interweaving of meaning and structural responses between themes and iconographies.

Iconographical echoes among panels on the same side serve to confirm common meanings within the diversity of subjects. Aeneas and Mars, founders respectively of the *gens Iulia* and the *populus Romanus*, are paired – as would happen in the Forum of Augustus – by the omen of the discovery of a mythical animal (the sow and the she-wolf). This prodigy augurs the beginning of different heroic ages and different families, but these are united by the fact that Aeneas was the son of Venus while Mars was her husband, and she in her turn appears on the other side of the monument in the position of the *templum* which, according to augural law, is *sinistima*, or the most favourable of all, and rightly so. On this side the iconographical resemblances serve to establish the indivisibility of the pairing Roma–Venus (a couple later consecrated by Hadrian in his colossal temple) and Roma–Pax, a *pax Romana* in which Rome, flanked by Honos and Virtus, provides the ethical and political key to the monument, where Venus–Pax among the *aurae caelestes* provides the religious key. Here there is also a series of possible combinations, running from the formulaic 'pax terra marique parta' to the less ritual but more inclusive 'Aeneadum genetrix, hominum divomque voluptas' of Lucretian memory. These two goddesses, representing divine time (*aetas*) and successful conclusions (*res prospere gestas*), and Mars and Aeneas, embodiments of heroic ages (*aetates*) and of beginnings (*initia*) on the west side, correspond precisely with each other, symmetrical both directly and chiastically. With a perfect circularity of thought and expression, Rome and Mars represent the dimension of the *urbs*, Venus and Aeneas the dimension of the *gens*: the origins and fulfilment of both are evoked moving from west to east, their revivalist character in the opposite direction. Augustus proceeds from the Via Flaminia across the space of the templum, with the passage rich with omens (*augurium augustum*) over the central augural line, and peacefully celebrates the triumph offered and refused, moving between the two goddesses to leave the temple as the new Aeneas and the new Romulus (proceeding east to west). In the anniversary sacrifices of 30 January and 4 July, entering from the west and leaving from the east side, the *princeps* or the priests on his behalf experience anew the 'historic' sequence of the *primordia urbis* and the *primordia gentis* (the beginnings of the city of Rome and the Julian family), to bear witness to the fact that, thanks to the new Aeneas and the new Romulus, city and family are turning again to the perfection of a new age, *nova aetas*, a *novus ordo saeclorum*.

The style is rich in meanings, all of them playing within the purely traditional framework of augural law, of priestly ritual, of the *ius imaginum* – besides Augustus, only Agrippa and Appuleius Saturninus, as adult relatives and holders of curule magistracies, have a recognizable likeness on the southern frieze of the altar – and of the will of the *paterfamilias*. The style tries to underline the quality and unity of these diverse messages with the variety of languages and the generally Classicizing patina. The tiny frieze crowning the altar, which depicts the procession of the annual *sacrum* composed of the colleges of priests and Vestals with their appropriate victims, has however a didactic tone that has very little classicizing about it, being rather a faithful transcription of the *lex arae* and thus bound to traditional forms of thought and expression. Composed of single figures in fairly high relief, this style reappears in the small friezes on triumphal arches, such as those of Titus in Rome and of Trajan at Beneventum, and it is the most susceptible to 'plebeian involutions'. of which the style of the small frieze on the arch of Constantine is but the culmination. This level of discourse necessarily simplifies and rejects all tendencies of Hellenistic embellishment, but it co-exists with the loftier level of Classicizing abstraction in the great frieze of the procession, where the elimination of any reference to space and time (a function of the non-realistic character of the representation) corresponds to the fully neoclassical rendering of the faces and postures of the participants in the procession and the rite. A comparison is often made with the frieze on the Parthenon but this refers in a highly idealizing way to the subject-matter of the Ara Pacis: the style of the monument depends rather on late Hellenistic experiments of a classicizing nature, beginning with the great frieze on the altar at Pergamum. This distinction helps us to understand the more decidedly Hellenistic character of the minor panels, born of the same tradition (we can compare them with the Telephos frieze on the Pergamene altar), in which it is much easier to observe the composite nature of the representation, consisting of classicizing figures set against an idyllic Hellenistic landscape. The slight but perceptible difference of style between panels and processional frieze is closely tied to the diversity of genres in the two parts: in the frieze courtly, solemn, timeless and rhetorical in the grand style, but in the panels, seemingly contradictory but callimachean in flavour, that is, Classicizing and pathetic at the same time, as well as homerizing and grandiose in the style of the Hellenistic epyllion. In any case, these diverse stylistic realities, all of them part of the same monument and the same workshop, are perfectly understandable in terms of a neo-Attic culture – one whose strong propensity for elaborate toreutic models is so evident in the frieze of acanthus – a culture acclimatized for some time in Rome and now able to express in accomplished form the regime culture which was now fully functioning in the last decade of the first century B.C.

Painting, however, is even more revealing of the profound changes that occurred in the middle years of the Augustan Principate. The origins of the extremely baroque Second Style can be fixed chronologically at the turn of the second to the first century B.C., and ideologically in the yearning for the impressive spaces and the luxury of decor of late Hellenistic royal palaces. The years of Caesar's brief and brilliant career saw the highest level of *luxuria* expressed by the extraordinary painted architectures, conceived and executed by expert scene-painters on the walls of patrician town residences or of aristocratic villas in Latium and Campania. The decorations of the Roman house on the Esquiline (70 B.C.),[46] and in the villas of the Mysteries (60 B.C.),[47] at Boscoreale (60–50 B.C.),[48] and at Oplontis (50 B.C.),[49] count among the most significant examples of the high level of quality of this painting, which must be

---

[46] P. H. von Blanckenhagen, *MDAI(R)* 70 (1963) 106ff; Gallina 1964 (F 380).

[47] *Editio princeps* by A. Maiuri, *La Villa dei Misteri* (2nd edn, Rome, 1947).

[48] B. Andreae, in *Kaiser Augustus* 1988 (F 443) 273ff.

[49] A. De Franciscis, *PP* 1973, 453ff; *id.* in *La regione sotterrata del Vesuvio* (Naples, 1982) 907ff. (with earlier bibliography).

assigned to the period between 70 and 50 B.C., linked as it is to the baroque in all the other figurative arts between Sulla and Caesar.[50] Decorative painting under the Second Triumvirate and in the early years of the reign of Augustus shows the obvious signs of a crisis in this baroque. Augustus' house on the Palatine,[51] decorated after he acquired the property from the orator Hortensius in 36, is a precious document of that crisis and, more generally, of figurative art in the decade before Octavian assumed the title of Augustus. One of the two libraries of the *domus* is marked by a very traditional wall in an austere Second Style: without 'open walls', without effects or perspective, and without copies of famous classical paintings, it essentially offers only a false marble incrustation rendered illusionistically in paint. Other areas, such as the ramp connecting the *domus* with the temple of Palatine Apollo, the great tetrastyle hall (*oecus*), or the Room of the Garlands, show that 'open walls' are confined to the upper parts of the walls. This lesser austerity in decoration, compared to that of the library, indicates the less 'official' character of these rooms. But the 'open wall' with a perspective view and the loss of structural consistency in the decoration of one of the two small rooms (no. 11) to the sides of the reception hall (no. 10), and likewise the insertion of the central painting in bedroom no. 14, reveal the even more private character of these areas. This is most noticeable in the small and extremely private annexe (*diaeta*, no. 7) at the end of the north-west portico of the peristyle, where we find the greatest novelty of the time, a room entirely decorated with a monochrome black background, festoons hanging from small, non-architectural pillars and from very slender candelabras, and idyllic sacred landscapes painted in yellow colour, superimposed: technically we have already reached the Third Style, as in the Black Room in the House of the Farnesina a decade later. It is thus easy to understand why Vitruvius, writing in this very period before 27, penned his invective (VII.5.3) against just such effronteries, which threatened the physical consistency of painted buildings and with it the informing principle of Classical representation, *mimesis*, the imitation of reality.

The trend lamented by Vitruvius made giant strides in a relatively brief time. The House of the Farnesina (which was probably Agrippa's urban villa)[52] at this point features slender architectural forms and paintings imagined as centrally suspended on walls which are still Second Style, in contrast with the Black Room in full Third Style; whereas the so-called House of Livia, an extension of Augustus' House

---

[50] On the relationship between painting and royal architecture: Engemann 1967 (F 359); and K. Fittschen, in Zanker 1976 (E 141) 539ff.

[51] Carettoni 1983 (F 316); Carettoni, in *Kaiser Augustus* 1988 (F 443) no. 135, 287ff.

[52] Diagantini and de Vos 1982 (F 297).

on the Palatine, with its less realistic architecture, large paintings, monochrome friezes and candelabras, belongs about halfway between the House of Augustus and the Farnesina, that is to say, in 30–25 B.C.[53] In this particular period, marked by the conquest of Egypt and the Actian triumph, we find the triumphal entry into painting of egyptomania, which informs both the dying Second and the nascent Third Styles. Besides the well-known contemporary Isiac Hall belonging to a private house on the Palatine, the very recent restoration of the decoration of bedroom no. 15, the so-called 'studiolo', on the upper, private floor of the House of Augustus, a room decorated a little later than the one on the lower floor (c. 30–25), shows how rapidly the passion for these particular chinoiseries of Egyptian forms and decorations spread, mostly in the non-public parts of houses, and how a taste for both the floral and the filiform expanded, on which the transition to the Third Style was really based.

As we have already seen, the Third Style in theory took shape around the year 30 B.C. The reasons for its appearance and the paths it followed were completely independent of the conquest of Egypt and the consequent Alexandrianism, although these are often wrongly invoked to explain the beginnings of the Third Style.[54] However, the resistance shown in the passage cited from Vitruvius must have lasted at least fifteen years, for it is only around the year 15 B.C. that we find the first examples of the Third Style on a large scale, as in the pyramid of Gaius Cestius, built before 12 B.C., and the Auditorium of Maecenas, which certainly predated his death in 8 B.C.[55] In spite of its non-mimetic and therefore unrealistic and fundamentally anti-classical nature, the new style paradoxically responded perfectly to the expressive demands of Augustan neoclassicism; as such it is no accident that it was revived as the official decorative style for the First Napoleonic Empire. This style also helped to achieve a beneficial sumptuary effect, through the complete suppression of *luxuria*. Valuable objects such as vases of glass and precious metal, gold and silver shields, costly veils and fabrics, painted as if they had been forgotten among the flamboyant building fantasies of the Second Style, appear less and less frequently in the years between 30 and 20 B.C. They give way to values which are no longer sumptuary but ethical, and which are represented by imitations of famous panel paintings placed in a central position, copies or reworkings of classical originals, while the wealth which used to be set realistically

[53] *Editio princeps*: Rizzo 1937 (F 547).

[54] For problems of chronology, see most recently W. Ehrhardt, *Stilgeschichtliche Untersuchungen an römischen Wandmalerein* (Mainz 1987).

[55] Pyramid of C. Cestius: P. S. Bartoli, *Gli antichi sepolcri ovvero mausolei romani ed etruschi* (Rome, 1967); Ehrhardt, *Stilgeschichtliche* 53f, figs. 101–4. *Auditorium* of Maecenas: *ibid* 123f (with earlier bibliography).

among buildings is transformed into costly little objects painted within boards (*pinakes*) and therefore expressly 'false'. All these 'true' values were enhanced by the virtual disappearance of the architectural frames, which were too reminiscent of the *populi voluptas*, the popular pleasure of the theatre, and which were replaced by monochrome surfaces with narrow borders of minuscule friezes, essentially refined tapestries, in order to emphasize subjects or treatments which were either classicizing or purely escapist, bucolic idylls. The effect was remarkable, as witness the frescoes of the villa at Boscoreale (which is rightly thought to have belonged to Agrippa Postumus).[56]

The ancient relationship between a decorative style and the *dignitas* and *decorum* of its surroundings, the explicit link between the public and private function of the parts of the house and their furnishings and decor, which was so alive at the beginning of the Augustan age, began to deteriorate. This was due most probably to the clear 'death of politics', which rendered such links and distinctions obsolete, as well as to the consequent spread of a culture of escapism, one which was largely based on the pervasive diffusion of sacred and idyllic themes. Having passed from gardens and peristyles to reception halls and traditional rooms, these themes were thus translated into stucco for ceilings (the famous stuccoes of the House of the Farnesina come to mind), into large-scale paintings, into *pinakes* or friezes, into relief sculpture in the small neo-Attic panels to be inserted into the walls, and into genre groups or individual sculptures in the round, representing fishermen and priestesses, *erotes* and wild beasts, Apollos demoted to lampstands and Dionysiac figures. The intention was obviously to make sculptures and large paintings stand out against a background of monochrome walls and above mosaic floors which were basically a uniform black and white and devoid of ornamentation, but the devaluation of meaning in all of these scenes is only too evident, if not in purpose then in result.

Official culture having been monopolized by the *princeps*, the urban *nobilitas* or the *domi nobiles* who imitated urban models, the private sphere accounts for the great bulk of consumption of art. Hence there was a diffusion of motifs and themes, which originated at court, within the framework of a production for a more or less wide consumption, one favoured in this case by techniques of 'mechanical' reproduction. The highest quality could be found in relief work in metal and in the art of gem-cutting, where the intrinsic value of the material could not help but accentuate the high level of workmanship. There can be no doubt that for such works the contribution of Hellenistic craftsmen was not only great but decisive, as is the case for example in the cameos – perhaps the most Augustan of the minor arts – designed for the imperial house by

[56] Von Blanckenhagen and Alexander 1962 (F 287).

such Alexandrian artists as Dioscurides and his son Hyllos.[57] Extremely sophisticated silverware, from the exceptionally beautiful pieces from Hildesheim to the Hoby cups signed with the significant name of Cheirisophos ('Skilled-of-hand'), bear the imprint of great Hellenistic relief-work.[58] In the cups from Boscoreale it also grappled successfully with themes of official 'historical' representations,[59] and contributed no less than cameos and gems to establishing the official standards of good taste. From this there derived objects with a much larger circulation using less valuable materials. Glass and glass paste adopted forms and themes originally found in cameos, in gems, and in plate of precious stone and rock crystal, in order to create either such exceptional pieces as the famous Portland Vase[60] or vessels for daily use in transparent and coloured glass.[61] Toreutic works had even wider repercussions. On the one hand they inspired decoration, both vegetal and non-vegetal, for ceremonial bronzes (tripods, braziers, table vessels),[62] while on the other their style came to be engraved on the humblest terracotta, on the 'Campana' plaques used to decorate public and private porticoes and sometimes even temples (which abound in themes beloved of Augustan neoclassicism), and above all on the well-known and very widespread *terra sigillata*, which had been manufactured in the workshops at Arezzo since the age of Caesar, and then in their branch kilns in Italy, and later still in Gaul.[63]

These luxury goods are understandably linked very closely with the higher expressions of the figurative arts, specifically with bronze and marble sculpture in the round, and thanks to them a single cultural fabric developed which cut across virtually all the social classes capable of expressing artistic culture. From the aristocracy to the middle classes of the Italian towns, they could display their understanding of, and their ability to adapt to, both the formal and the ethical models prescribed by the *princeps*, through portrait sculpture and painting in their houses, through altars placed at crossroads and sculptures among their household furnishings, and through the use of bronzework, silverware and

---

[57] On gem-cutting, see the excellent synthesis by C. Maderna-Lauter, in *Kaiser Augustus* 1988 (F 443) 441ff (with earlier bibliography). On the imperial cameos, see especially H. Jucker, *JDAI* 91 (1976) 211ff. [58] E. Künzl, in *Kaiser Augustus* 1988 (F 443) 568ff.

[59] F. Baratte, *Le trésor d'orfèvrerie romaine de Boscoreale* (Paris, 1986).

[60] E. Simon, *Die Portlandvase* (Mainz, 1957); cf. Simon 1987 (F 577) 162ff.

[61] On this there is no modern, up-to-date synthesis. See the collection of C. Isings, *Roman Glass from Dated Finds* (Groningen, 1957).

[62] There is no standard work. See meanwhile E. Pernice, *JÖAI* 11 (1908) 212ff; M. Bieber, *Die antiken Skulpturen und Bronzen des königlichen Museum Fredericianum in Kassel* (Marburg, 1915); R. Thouvenot, *Catalogue des figurines et objets de bronze du Musée Archéologique de Madrid* 1 (Paris, 1927); C. Boube Picot, *Les bronzes antiques de Maroc* (Rabat, 1975); J. Petit, *Bronzes antiques de la collection Dutuit* (Paris, 1980).

[63] On all these kinds of materials, see A. Giardina, A. Schiavone (eds.), *Merci, mercati e scambi nel Mediterraneo* (Società romana e produzione schiavistica II, Bari, 1981).

pottery. The *tota Italia* of Augustus was expressed in calculated fashion through an unquestioned, capillary-like acceptance of the artistic culture promoted by the *princeps* for his own city, and spread by those who belonged to this historical bloc in the towns and colonies of the empire.

III. FROM TIBERIUS TO NERO: THE CRISIS OF THE MODEL

Basically the reign of Tiberius was a pedestrian repetition of the pattern laid down by the Principate of Augustus. Tiberius' amply documented lack of enthusiasm for public works lies at the root of the extremely modest innovations of the period in town planning and architecture. The only important work in relief in the city of Rome was the temple of the Divine Augustus, called the *templum novum divi Augusti*, situated between the Palatine and the Capitol in the area of the *vicus Jugarius*, and this is balanced by the 'private' works dedicated by Livia to the memory of her deceased spouse and now deified father by adoption, the Palatine temple of the Divus Augustus and the colossal statue of him near the Theatre of Marcellus.[64] These initiatives were of great importance, however, because it was undoubtedly in the early years of Tiberius, especially between A.D. 14 and 23, that the cult of the dynasty was spreading through Italy and the provinces along the path of the usual model of *imitatio Romae*. The effects of this diffusion are very striking, and they influenced both town planning and architecture, through the proliferation of temples of Augustus or of Rome and Augustus in Italy and the provinces, and of sculpture and decoration as well, with the endless commissions of statuary groups[65] depicting what was already in an inscription of A.D. 33 called the *domus divina*, the divine house.[66]

In fact a significant number of the portraits of the first imperial dynasty of Rome are Tiberian in date, and it is in the age of Tiberius that we even find new portrait-types of *Divus Augustus* (probably the so-called Forbes-type, which arguably comes from his colossal statue at the Theatre of Marcellus), as well as of Livia and of Tiberius himself.[67] On the whole, however, art in the Tiberian age followed in the path traced by Augustus, but it accentuates the traits of formal stiffness and the progressive loss of organic unity and ideological coherence of the Augustan model. Portrait-sculpture – as in the images of Germanicus and Drusus Minor – is increasingly hard and dry; wall-painting unimaginatively echoes the schemes of the Third Style; the decoration of

---

[64] On these works of Tiberius and Livia: Torelli 1982 (F 596) 63ff.

[65] Full bibliography in Hänlein-Schäfer 1985 (F408); also, *Le culte des souverains dans l'empire romain* (Geneva, 1973); and Price 1984 (F199).   [66] *AE* 1978, 295.

[67] P. Zanker, in Fittschen and Zanker 1985 (F 365) I no. 8, 7ff; Gross 1962 (F 401); Polacco 1955 (F 528).

buildings and of funerary altars retraces the forms worked out in the mid-Augustan period, but less lightly and brightly.

The last years of Tiberius and the ephemeral reign of Caligula show the first skirmishes of a structural crisis in the formal and ideological model established by Augustus, although output continued to develop with explicit or implicit citations of Augustan works; with Claudius and Nero the crisis was finally revealed. In town-planning and architecture,[68] the innovations which bore the richest implications for the future were those brought about by the definitive centralization in the hands of the *princeps* of all the machinery for carrying out public works, and by the huge, concomitant growth in the parasitic dependence of the urban plebs upon him. Augustus and Tiberius – but especially Augustus – had controlled this trend by diverting their investments into large works which bore witness to their own *pietas*. Claudius, on the other hand, constructed a large new port at the mouth of the Tiber, which joined with the great warehouses and similar edifices at Ostia to facilitate the supply of grain to Rome, and he reorganized the distributions of grain (*frumentationes*) at Rome, unifying in the *porticus Minucia frumentaria* the administrative offices for the distribution of food. Along the same lines of ever more grandiose intervention in the development of the city, are Nero's ambitious projects for urban renewal after the fire of A.D. 64. The very few works actually completed basically comprise the baths and gymnasium, which doubled the capacity of those of Agrippa (perhaps introducing a new type of bath plan, called 'imperial'), and the great market (*macellum magnum*), built on the Caelian Hill next to that dedicated to Livia on the Esquiline. However the triumph of the neo-baroque in this period is seen above all in the creativity of private architecture, especially in plans, and in the new conception of decorative elements. Among the latter, most noticeable is the predilection for rustic ashlar work, rich in chiaroscuro effects, which appears in more than one Claudian monument, from the grand pillared portico of the *Porticus Claudii* to the imposing façade of the Porta Maggiore, and to the substructures of the temple of the Divine Claudius which date from the earliest years of Nero. Even the decorative motifs on friezes and entablatures and on funerary altars and urns lose the stiff and severe execution of the Tiberian period to take on a new and accentuated interest in deep carving and shadows which enlivens garlands, bucrania (cattle skulls), heads of animals at corners, and so forth, thus setting the stage for the Flavian taste in decoration.

But it was in his Golden House that Nero wished to show off all of the advances which had been won in the period of late-republican *luxuria*

[68] On all Julio-Claudian architecture and town-planning in Rome, see P. Gros, in Gros and Torelli 1988 (A 41) 179ff (with earlier bibliography).

and then frozen in the age of Augustus and Tiberius, and thus to make them live again in the light of a century of experience in building and technology. First we may compare the plan of the *Domus Aurea* with the general conceptions lying behind some of the great private buildings of the emperor Tiberius, that is, the *Domus Tiberiana* at Rome and the Tiberian villas at Sperlonga and Capri. Beginning with the palace at Rome, which has been revealed by recent excavation and study, Tiberian buildings show strong tendencies to centralize spaces and corridors. Functional areas dominate, while only very small separate complexes, intended to enjoy the best panoramic views, seem to be spread about in asymmetrical fashion: the imperial loggia at Capri, for example, or the grotto of Sperlonga. But the *Domus Aurea*, a true and proper *villa urbana* with a baroque taste for painted scenery, has no real centre to its design. It appears rather to be conceived as a cluster of complexes and pavilions of varying character and importance, made up of imperial properties old and new which are unified around an ideal centre, the pool (*stagnum*) of the villa, on the site later to be occupied by the Colosseum. Thus can we in fact reconstruct the immense urban villa of the emperor, even if much of the original conception was later destroyed by the superimpositions of the Flavians, Trajan and Hadrian, which intentionally obliterated the designs developed for the tyrant prince by his *magistri et machinatores*, Severus and Celer (Tac. *Ann.* xv.42). However the thinking behind the project also involved a direct connexion between 'wild' nature (water above all, but also gardens and woods) and separate parts of the villa, which are made to fit in with that nature. That this is so, is confirmed by the embryonic design of Caligula with his ships on the Lake of Nemi – where we see a dramatically astonishing inversion of relationships and values between lake and dwellings – or by Nero's villa at Subiaco. As to the many pavilions and parts of the Golden House, the baroque stamp appears in the famous description of the revolving banquet hall (*cenatio rotunda*), which was set in motion by an appropriate machine and which was rich in symbolic implications (Suet. *Ner.* 31). It is also clear in the layout of its various parts, the best preserved of which is now visible under the Baths of Trajan, in the tendency to break up symmetry and rectilinearity, from the trapezoidal central hallway to the famous nympheum known as the Octagonal Room, where the central structure with its side areas designed according to a mixed-line plan reproduces a cupola with pavilions for the first time since the days of the late Republic.

The taste for a residence laid out in relation to a lake is entirely Hellenistic and Alexandrian – in particular, Caligula's idea of the ships on the Lake of Nemi is very Alexandrian, derived from the well-known *thalamegos* ship of Ptolemy IV. This taste is echoed even in the dwellings of the emerging classes in the Italian cities, where the old traditional plan of the Pompeian *domus*, which was already clearly in decline in the suburban villas of the late Republic and under Augustus, atrophies and quite disappears, to the benefit of areas intended for the *amoenitas* of gardens, of views of the sea, and of dining-rooms under pergolas. With his descendants and successors, the luxury driven from the door by Augustus returns through the window of opulent private consumption.

The baroque and dramatic form was the idiom of this revived *luxuria*. Imperial portraits, soon imitated by private portraits which often followed them slavishly not only in style but even in iconography, reflect the general longing for pathos and effect, by enlivening surfaces which were once so frigid, creating contrasts between scarcely shaded faces and turbulent hairstyles, in a word replacing rigid Tiberian 'fine art' with treatments which were softer and more pathetic and yet which did not – here as in other artistic media – break with the Classicizing essence of the plastic arts. This is especially noticeable in the Medici-Della Valle reliefs,[69] a splendid series of 'historical' reliefs from the early years of Claudius which were reworked in the Arcus Novus of Diocletian. The monument to which they had belonged was a 'copy' of the Ara Pacis and is generally identified with an Altar of Piety (Ara Pietatis), which is known only from an inscription recorded in a manuscript, although some see it as the Altar of the Julian *Gens* (Ara Gentis Iuliae), which is mentioned in military diplomas as standing on the Capitoline Hill. The parts which survive, and which can be assigned to the enclosure, show processions of magistrates, priests, sacrificers and victims passing in front of certain monuments in Rome, the temple of Magna Mater on the Palatine, the temple of the Divine Augustus also on the Palatine – or, according to some, that of Mars Ultor – and perhaps the temple of Fides on the Capitol. Regardless of who the divinities may be and where the altar stood, the *sacra* certainly refer to the imperial cult, and celebrate the deification of Livia ordered by Claudius immediately after his accession. The imitation of the Augustan model is extremely clear. The surviving fragments all pertain to the procession and they essentially reflect the paratactic composition of the processional frieze of the Ara Pacis. At the same time, in comparison, they innovate with noticeable hints of movement in the figures and especially with the disappearance of the Classicizing neutral background of the frieze: this is replaced by an almost 'plebeian' insistence on the painstakingly architectural depictions of the temples, which are inserted into the picture in order to locate the event precisely. The rendering also of the draperies, of the texture of the hair, and of the surfaces in general shows signs of the new stylistic climate, which appears to have been already active and widespread in A.D. 42–3, according to the dating of the monument which is universally

[69] Torelli 1982 (F 596) 70ff.

accepted. Comparison with Tiberian monuments, such as the so-called Altar of the Vicomagistri,[70] and with Augustan, such as the figured frieze on the temple of Apollo Sosianus,[71] shows the gradual abandonment by the Julio–Claudian figurative arts of the model created by Augustus. For the 'staccato' composition and the 'stiacciato' relief of the Augustan monument, we find substituted two finely distinguished planes of representation, with the precise appearance of 'natural perspective' in the full-bodied first plane of representation of the Tiberian altar, and with the rich chiaroscuro of the Claudian relief.

In decorative painting Tiberian Classicism carries on the Augustan heritage, especially in the obliteration of all use of the old Second Style, in order to achieve an air of *maiestas* and *gravitas* in individual reception areas. The old conception which linked the function of an area with the form and quality of its decoration gives way to a Third Style generalization and to the proliferation of copies of Classical paintings at the centre of walls. But, as in the developments which we have seen in architecture and sculpture, in the midst of uniform tapestries barely edged with extremely fragile friezes in the Augustan tradition, there spring up in the high Tiberian period extravagant architectural fantasies, filiform, theatrical wings, and almost metaphysical perspectives made of candelabras: between the end of the reign of Tiberius and the first years of Claudius, these prepare for the birth of the Fourth Style, an expression of the baroque renaissance in the field of decorative painting.[72] The Fourth Style in fact represents a conscious and deliberate revival of the great architectural paintings and dramatic views of the Second Style; but the revival manifests itself not as a restoration of the realistic values longed for by Vitruvius more than half a century earlier, but as a further accentuation of fantastic, non-realistic, theatrical effects, truly and properly surreal landscapes, in which room is found for candelabras and large paintings, together with figures leaning out which draw attention to and enliven the many superimposed stage-scenes.

The Fourth Style, which revives and mixes themes, elements and languages of the Second and Third Styles, is a 'pictorial asianism', in every way worthy to illustrate the verses of Seneca and Lucan, the coherent formulation of a taste which longed to surpass and to subsume the golden classicism of Augustus.

The nature of this phenomenon of the transformation of taste should be sought not so much in a regular, abstract swing between neoclassical and neobaroque periods in the figurative arts of Rome, although that dialectic did indeed exist, and not only in the Julio-Claudian age. It is

[70] T Hölscher, in *Kaiser Augustus* 1988 (F 443) no. 224, 396ff.
[71] A. Viscogliosi, 1988 (F 443) nos. 31–42, 144ff.
[72] W. Ehrhardt, *Stilgeschichtliche*, 85ff.

rather to be found above all in the deep crisis within the historical bloc of *tota Italia* which had arisen around Augustus.[73] This bloc essentially found its expression in what Bianchi Bandinelli very rightly termed 'the art of the centre of power',[74] the neoclassicism which gave shape to the accomplishments of the emperor and the upper and middle classes and to the more powerful works commissioned by them, which were closely tied to the workshops or to the architectural and technical models of the capital. But the unity showed cracks from the beginning. While the Augustan programme reached its fulfilment at Rome in the last two decades of the first century B.C., in the cities of northern and central Italy and in the more Romanized provinces of the West (Narbonensis, Baetica, and the eastern coasts of Spain) the old tradition – Hellenistic, baroque, pictorial and full of pathos – remained of central interest to important local patrons:[75] they continued to employ it in their own self-glorifying monuments and to mix it promiscuously with some of the Classicizing and courtly models from the capital. With the age of Tiberius the separation increases, as the old Hellenistic models of the Italian and provincial periphery lose their Hellenistic patina to reveal a schematic framework of Italic tradition. The 'plebeian' artistic tendencies of local workshops take on substance,[76] giving voice in a simple and often shapeless language, reminiscent of ancient, central-Italian experiences, to aspirations which were no longer those of the ruling classes of municipal Italy – they were already fully co-opted by 'the centre of power', or else extinct – but which were cherished by wealthy freedmen, now honoured as *augustales* – a concrete artistic counterpart to Trimalchio in Petronius' *Satiricon*. In their eyes this 'plebeian' art served to express aspirations of social ascent and political recognition.

In truth, this very conception of co-optation, which was inherent in the social structure by *ordines* in imperial Rome, undermined the apparently rocklike solidity of the historical Augustan bloc, which tried to model the portrait features of its members on those of the *princeps* and other members of the imperial house, and which meant with the assurance of Classicism to leave behind the uncertainties and the anguish of the overturning of *ordines* which was provoked by *luxuria*, by *lucrum* (avarice), and by the civil wars. With the age of Claudius the erosion of Augustus' social and economic order is quite clear, and the whole framework of the traditional society of *ordines* is in flux, as is shown by

---

[73] On this historical unity: M. Torelli, in *Kaiser Augustus* 1988 (F 443) 23ff.

[74] Bianchi Bandinelli 1970 (F 275).

[75] This development is well illustrated by the collective taste for funerary monuments with a doric frieze: Torelli 1969 (E 129).

[76] The definition is that of R. Bianchi Bandinelli, in *DArch* 1 (1967) 7ff = *Dall'Ellenismo al Medioevo* (Rome, 1978) 35ff (in which version the author adds an Introduction, pp. 3ff, with further definition of the concept).

the beginning of the rapid decline of the economy and social structure of Italian towns, and by the correspondingly rapid ascent of the provincial governing classes of Gaul and Spain. To this great turnover of governing classes is connected a dual and related phenomenon, that is, the rediscovery of formal baroque values in the culture of the court, both literary and artistic, and the formal birth of municipal 'plebeian' art, which lay in its turn at the roots of later provincial art. The cultural background of this new ruling class of Italian and provincial origin was in fact largely to be sought in the ancient formal experiences of its more remote origins, in the baroque and Asian artistic culture still dominant in their areas of origin two generations before, that is, in the world of Caesar and the triumvirs, a world which survived up to the early years of the first century A.D. and was not erased by the 'normalization' imposed by Augustus, as we can see in the art which spread quickly through Cisalpine Italy and Narbonensis in the first centuries B.C. and A.D.[77] At the same time, there were vacuums of power and of culture left behind by these former provincials in their swift social rise under Augustus and Tiberius, the local representatives of the historical bloc which was the base of the new Principate. These vacuums were filled by lower social classes, which were essentially of freedmen origin and which caused to flourish again even more remote conceptual, ideological and formal experiences, those of the artistic culture of the Romano-Italic *koine*, which expressed better than any other gesture the elements of affirmation of status which were necessary to the self-glorification of the new and powerful Trimalchios.

Therefore, the two greatest historians of Roman art in our century, G. Rodenwaldt and R. Bianchi Bandinelli, spoke rightly of the essentially bipolar nature of art at Rome. To the eternal formal bipolarity between Classicism and the baroque, within which was played out the Augustan experience of official, programmatic art and its crisis in the age of Claudius and Nero, there corresponds the no less eternal bipolarity of mentalities and idioms between 'art of the centre of power' and 'plebeian art'.

[77] M. Torelli, *Index* 13 (1985) 589ff.

CHAPTER 21

EARLY CLASSICAL PRIVATE LAW

BRUCE W. FRIER

With the establishment of the Augustan Principate, Roman private law enters its 'classical' period.[1] During the largely tranquil centuries that followed, Rome's jurists articulated and developed a body of law that is beyond doubt the most conspicuous and influential Roman contribution to Western civilization.[2] This chapter does not describe the system of Roman law itself,[3] but instead concentrates on the jurists and the Roman judicial system during the Julio-Claudian and Flavian eras.

I. THE JURISTS AND THE PRINCIPATE

Classical Roman law is based upon a distinctive procedural system, called formulary procedure.[4] Formulary procedure, like most other well-developed procedural systems, distinguishes between justiciability (*iur-isdictio*), the judicial determination that a plaintiff is stating a legally acceptable cause of action, and adjudication (*iudicatio*), the hearing and resolution of the plaintiff's claim. However, formulary procedure radicalizes this distinction: the trial is divided into two stages decided by separate persons.

At Rome, almost all suits between citizens were raised initially in the court of the urban praetor, an annually elected magistrate. The Praetor's Edict listed those causes of action that he was willing to accept during his term of office, as well as the general procedure to be followed in his court; already by the late Republic, the contents of the Edict varied little from year to year. If, in a given case, the plaintiff stated an acceptable cause of action, the praetor assigned a judge (*iudex*), or in some cases

---

[1] On defining classical law, see Wieacker 1961 (F 704) 161–86.

[2] See esp. Koschaker 1966 (F 664).

[3] On substantive law, see esp. Kaser 1971–5 (F 662) i–ii; on procedure, Kaser 1966 (F 661). The best general account in English is Buckland 1966 (F 646).

[4] It is described at length in Kaser 1966 (F 661) 107–338; see also Pugliese 1963 (F 680). The following account is necessarily inexact because of its brevity. The only surviving ancient description is Gai. *Inst.* IV. Formulary procedure is based on the Urban Praetor's Edict, reconstructed by Lenel 1927 (B 110); for the Edict's state in the early Empire, see Kaser 1984 (F 663) 65–73, 102–8. See also ch. 12 above, pp. 398–401.

multiple judges, to hear the case; the *iudex* was usually a layman acceptable as an arbiter to both sides.

In order to instruct the *iudex* on handling the case, the praetor embodied the cause of action, together with any legally acceptable defences from the defendant, in a brief statement called the *formula*. This *formula* officially appointed the *iudex*, named the parties to the suit, specified the legal issue between them, and ordered the *iudex* to decide the case.[5] In the second stage of the trial, the *iudex* heard argument from rhetorically skilled advocates on either side of the case; on the basis of this argument he returned a verdict that accorded with the *formula*. Although in practice the formulary procedure was complex and deviations from this simplified model were frequent, private trials under formulary procedure were in principle always highly arbitrational; as a rule the verdict of the *iudex* could be neither reviewed nor appealed.

The *formula*, which tied together the two stages of a typical trial, gives formulary procedure its name. This procedural system, introduced by urban praetors probably in the third century B.C., gradually supplanted the older and more formalistic *legis actio* system, until by the late Republic private litigation was normally initiated through formulary procedure.

The principal participants in the Roman judicial system (praetor, *iudex*, and advocates) normally had no special competence in law. The juristic movement began outside the judicial system. During the third century B.C., self-styled legal experts (*iurisconsulti* or *iurisperiti*) undertook to assist laymen with the drafting of legal instruments or with the procedural intricacies of trials. However, the juristic movement did not obtain real influence and intellectual strength until the first century B.C., when jurists like Q. Mucius Scaevola (cos. 95) and Ser. Sulpicius Rufus (cos. 52) began to study legal norms on a far more intensive, 'scientific' basis. Their efforts created a true legal science under the control of professionals. By the last years of the Republic, Roman jurists had come to exercise considerable influence over the conduct of private trials, particularly in resolving questions of law that arose in the course of trials. Although in the late Republic neither the praetor nor the *iudex* was legally obliged to accept the jurists' opinions as presumptively binding statements of law, in fact the jurists already determined large areas of law that had previously been discretionary.[6]

---

[5] The only completely preserved *formula* from an actual Roman trial runs, in part: 'The issue in this trial will be a formal promise (*sponsio*). Let C. Blossius Celadus be the *iudex*. If it appears that C. Marcius Saturninus ought to pay 6,000 sesterces to C. Sulpicius Cinnamus, which is the issue here, let C. Blossius Celadus the *iudex* condemn C. Marcius Saturninus for 6,000 sesterces to C. Sulpicius Cinnamus; if it does not appear, let him absolve him . . .' This claim for a specified sum of money (a *condictio*) was granted by a duumvir at Puteoli in A.D. 52; it illustrates the structure of a typical *formula*. See Bove 1979 (B 212) 97–111.

[6] These developments are further described in Frier 1985 (F 652) 261–6. See esp. Cic. *Top.* 65–6, written in 44 B.C.

The establishment of the Augustan Principate did not at first lead, as might have been expected, to a diminution of juristic independence and influence. On the contrary, the jurists, who in the late Republic derived chiefly from the Italian and equestrian stock that formed the core of Augustus' new oligarchy,[7] found themselves well positioned to interpret the aspirations of the new regime within the limited but important domain of private law. Likewise, emperors seem to have perceived the value in preserving private law's independence, as a symbol of legitimacy and continuity; accordingly, direct imperial intervention in the Roman judicial system was initially cautious and sporadic, at least as a rule. Only very slowly, over centuries, did the government move to control and centralize the administration of justice, and thus to give the Roman judicial system a more regularized form, one more familiar to modern eyes. This evolution hinged on two major changes: the gradual replacement of the formulary system with 'extraordinary cognition' under the control of imperial officials; and the rise of imperial rescripts as a major source of law eventually supplementing or replacing jurists' law. However, neither change was complete until after the end of the classical period of Roman jurisprudence, in the middle of the third century A.D.

During the classical period, Roman jurisprudence was more or less identical with the thought and writings of the great jurists of the city of Rome. Except for Gaius' *Institutes*, an introductory treatise, no classical writings survive except in fragmentary form; but Justinian's *Digest*, promulgated in A.D. 533, contains more than 800,000 words of lightly edited excerpts from the main works of the classical jurists, and other sources, mainly compilations of post-classical origin, supplement the *Digest*.[8] By working closely with these sources, modern legal historians have developed a reasonably reliable impression of how classical Roman law formed and evolved during the first three centuries of the Empire.

II. AUGUSTUS' PROCEDURAL REFORMS

Iulius Caesar, during his dictatorship, allegedly contemplated a complete codification of Roman private law; his attempts at legal reform, though never carried out, thus looked mainly to substantive law.[9] By contrast, three times during his long reign Augustus refused to accept any general grant of power to re-order the law and morals of the Roman people (*cura legum et morum*);[10] instead, he concentrated on careful

---

[7] Cf. Frier 1985 (F 652) 252–7.

[8] In addition to the *Digest*, the main juristic sources for Roman private law are collected in *FIRA* II. For a survey of surviving legal texts, see Schiller 1978 (F 689) 28–62.

[9] Suet. *Iul.* 44.2; Isid. *Etym.* 5.1.5.

[10] Augustus, *RG* 6.1; but contrast Suet. *Aug.* 27.5, and Dio LIV.10.5. It appears that Augustus only declined the express power; cf. Schiller 1978 (F 689) 467–8. On Augustus' moral legislation, see below at n. 76.

procedural reforms that actually consolidated the formulary system and strengthened the jurists' authority within it.

Probably in 17 B.C. Augustus proposed and carried a general statute reforming private procedure (*lex Iulia de iudiciis privatis*).[11] The text of the law does not survive, but its content is briefly described by Gaius and also often alluded to in juristic, literary and epigraphic sources. One portion of this law eliminated almost all surviving vestiges of archaic *legis actio* procedure. Henceforth, with the major exception of the centumviral court (which chiefly heard important inheritance cases), all private lawsuits brought at Rome had to be initiated through formulary procedure.[12]

The *Lex Iulia* also contained numerous provisions on the process of adjudication; it regulated the official panel (*album*) from which *iudices* were normally named, the conduct of judges in hearing trials, the legitimate excuses for avoiding service as a judge, and so on.[13] One fundamental distinction it introduced was between 'statutory trials' (*iudicia legitima*) and 'trials dependent on magisterial office' (*iudicia quae imperio continentur*). 'Statutory trials' included only suits brought at Rome between two Roman citizens, provided these were to be decided by a single *iudex*; the grant of such suits by the praetor remained effective for eighteen months, after which it lapsed if the *iudex* had not yet reached a verdict. By contrast, all other private lawsuits lapsed if they were undecided at the end of the granting magistrate's term of office.[14] Although this distinction probably resulted from delays in handling the large volume of lawsuits brought at Rome, its consequence was to give the urban praetor's court a special standing among all jurisdictions in the empire.

Perhaps at about the same date Augustus began granting to certain jurists the right to issue formal opinions on law (*responsa*) that were based on his own authority. Unfortunately, the two main sources on the *ius respondendi* are confused and difficult to interpret, and scholars have not reached consensus on the nature and operation of the right.[15] The likeliest view is that jurists with the *ius respondendi* could submit *responsa* that had very great, if not determinative, weight in settling questions of

---

[11] See Kaser 1966 (F 661) 115–16, with further literature; for references, see *Acta* 1945 (B 1) 143–8. The Lex Irnitana, a Flavian municipal charter from Spain, provides major new information on this law; it also may show that the Lex Iulia was supplemented by a second law extending Roman procedure to municipalities, see Gai. *Inst.* IV.30, with González 1986 (B 235) 150.

[12] Gai. *Inst.* IV.30–1, 35. Extraordinary cognition also comes to be an exception; see below, Section VI.

[13] See Suet. *Aug.* 32.3; Dio LIV.18.3; Modestinus, *D* 48.14.1.4; *Frag. Vat.* 197–8.

[14] Gai. *Inst.* IV.103–9.

[15] Pomponius, *D* 1.2.2.48–50; Gai. *Inst.* I.7. For a summary of scholarly views, see Schiller 1978 (F 689) 297–312; Wieacker 1985 (F 706). It is uncertain when the right was introduced, but Labeo probably had it (Gell. *N.A* IIII.10.1).

law within trials; even if the *responsa* of two such jurists diverged, the judge had to choose between them. Augustus is said to have created the right 'in order to increase the authority of law',[16] which implies that hitherto juristic opinions had not always been decisive in private trials. At the same time, however, the imperial grant of a *ius respondendi* isolated a privileged group of recognized legal experts, on whose authoritative opinions litigants would inevitably rely if possible; thus the emperor avoided having to determine questions of private law himself.

Augustus apparently granted the *ius respondendi* only to jurists who had also entered the Roman Senate; this probably remained normal throughout the first century A.D., though Tiberius bestowed the right also on the eminent equestrian jurist Masurius Sabinus.[17] It is likely, but cannot be proven, that almost all early classical jurists whose views are cited or reported in the *Digest* had received the *ius respondendi*. Grant of the right served the emperor in several ways: it increased legal security by limiting the number of jurists allowed to state law authoritatively, while simultaneously creating a new means of imperial patronage and reinforcing the link between the jurists and the empire's governing elite in the Senate. A jurist lacking the *ius respondendi* could still issue opinions, but his *responsa* were backed only by his own knowledge and personal authority;[18] such a jurist would inevitably tend to take his lead from more privileged jurists.

Augustus' thoughtful procedural reforms set the stage for classical Roman jurisprudence – which is, in essence, a protracted intellectual discussion of legal norms and principles conducted within a small circle of skilled professionals. The *lex Iulia de iudiciis privatis* gave Roman procedure a coherence and rationality it had not previously possessed, and thus narrowed and defined the framework of juristic discussion; the *ius respondendi* ensured that the best product of juristic discussion would have direct and immediate effect within the judicial system. The jurists thus came to occupy a commanding position in relation to the judicial system, even though they were not formally part of it. In the long history of Western law, this astonishing situation has seldom been replicated.

Yet almost at once the process began whereby the carefully balanced Augustan procedural system would be first eroded and then supplanted, although not before the Roman jurists had introduced changes which were permanently to affect Western understanding of what law is.

---

[16] Pomponius, *D* 1.2.2.49: 'ut maior iuris auctoritas haberetur'.
[17] Pomponius, *D* 1.2.2.48, 50; cf. Kunkel 1967 (F 666A) 272–89.
[18] Cf. Pomponius, *D* 1.2.2.49 (citing Hadrian); however, the meaning of this passage is uncertain.

III. LABEO

Servius Sulpicius Rufus, the great republican jurist, died in 43 B.C., while on a diplomatic mission for the Senate.[19] He left behind him a large and thriving juristic community, which dominated Roman private law until well into Augustus' reign; yet it lacked a leader comparable to Servius in influence and power of mind. During the triumviral period (43–31 B.C.), Servius' numerous students concentrated on compiling and editing their teacher's writings and *responsa*; the most prominent of these students was Alfenus Varus, one of Octavian's early partisans, who earned for his loyalty a consulate (39 B.C.) and a public funeral.[20] The only student of Servius who gained a reputation as an innovator was A. Ofilius, who wrote the earliest extended commentaries on the Praetor's Edict and on the corpus of existing statutes;[21] Ofilius remained a lifelong *eques* despite his former close ties to Julius Caesar. Ofilius also was the teacher of Q. Aelius Tubero, who turned to law only around the age of forty after a disappointing career as an orator; Tubero was later regarded as the most erudite of the early Augustan jurists in both public and private law, although his influence was diminished by his crabbed, archaizing prose.[22] Two eminent older jurists also survived into the early Principate: A. Cascellius, already very aged but still ferociously independent in his political views,[23] and C. Trebatius Testa, Cicero's sometime protégé, who like Ofilius remained an *eques*.[24]

Except for Alfenus, the early Augustan jurists were characterized by political caution or even quietism; they left almost no mark on the momentous events of their times. For his part, Augustus did not seek to bind them more closely to the new regime; the story that he offered a

---

[19] See esp. Cic. *Phil.* IX; Pomponius, *D* 1.2.2.43. Pomponius' *Enchiridion*, poorly preserved in *D* 1.2.2, is the only surviving history of the juristic movement; on its form and purpose, see Nörr 1976 (F 672). The work dates to *c.* A.D. 140.

[20] Pomponius, *D* 1.2.2.44; Scholiast on Hor. *Sat.* 1.3.130. The public funeral was perhaps accorded by Augustus. Alfenus, who cites no jurist after Servius, seems not to have participated in early Augustan discussions. Fragments: Lenel 1889 (B 109) I 37–54 (nineteen citations; eighty-one fragments from later epitomators). On the early Augustan jurists, see Bauman 1985 (F 642) 66–136 (speculative).

[21] Pomponius, *D* 1.2.2.44 (as emended). Fragments: Lenel 1889 (B 109) I 795–804 (fifty-eight citations, usually through Labeo). Ofilius survived until at least 20 B.C., since he taught C. Ateius Capito (cos. suff. A.D. 5): cf. n. 28.

[22] Pomponius, *D* 1.2.2.46. Fragments: Lenel 1889 (B 109) II 377–80 (thirteen citations, often through Labeo). On the family: Syme 1986 (A 95) 305–6. Tubero also wrote an annalistic history of Rome.

[23] Cascellius, a pupil of Q. Mucius, was quaestor by 73, but advanced no further; cf. Pomponius, *D* 1.2.2.45 (as emended). His independence: Val. Max. VI.2.12; Quint. *Inst.* V.3.87; Macrob. *Sat.* II.6.1. Fragments: Lenel 1889 (B 109) I 107–8 (thirteen citations, usually through Labeo).

[24] Pomponius, *D.* 1.2.2.45. Fragments: Lenel 1889 (B 109) II 343–52 (eighty-seven citations, often through Labeo). Trebatius was close to Julius Caesar: Cic. *Fam.* VII.14.2; Plut. *Cic.* 37.3; but cf. Suet. *Iul.* 78.1. Caesar probably made him an *eques*: Bauman 1985 (F 642) 126–7, 134–5.

consulate to Cascellius (who declined it) is of doubtful authenticity.[25] None of these jurists is expressly associated even with the drafting of major Augustan legislation, although Trebatius, at least, survived long enough to comment on some of it.[26]

Our impression of early Augustan jurisprudence derives mainly from the writings of M. Antistius Labeo, who was probably active as a jurist by about 30 B.C. A student of Trebatius, Labeo none the less closely attended the other senior jurists of his time, and he often reports on their agreement or disagreement concerning various technical questions.[27] Labeo clearly regards Trebatius and Ofilius, and to a lesser extent Cascellius, as constituting the juristic mainstream, while Tubero is more commonly aberrant in his views; but Labeo presents a general picture of consolidation and regulated contentiousness, with little in the way of major methodological or substantive innovation. However, by about 20 B.C. the generation of republican survivors was yielding before a new and more vigorous generation. According to literary and juristic sources, much of Augustus' reign was marked by the dominance and rivalry of two jurists: Labeo and C. Ateius Capito.[28]

Their rivalry was personal and political. Unlike their elders, both Labeo and Capito were politically active, but they diverged sharply in their attitude to the new regime. Capito, the grandson of a Sullan centurion and son of an obscure senator of praetorian rank, was widely considered a sycophantic courtier who prostituted his talent and knowledge in the service of his imperial masters.[29] Labeo, by contrast, was the son of a jurist who had conspired in Caesar's assassination and committed suicide after Philippi; Labeo himself soon acquired a reputation for his prickly insistence on constitutional details, often to the government's momentary discomfiture. After Labeo's death, Capito wrote of his rival that he had been driven by his excessive, foolhardy

---

[25] Pomponius, *D* 1.2.2.45; cf. Syme 1980 (F 697), but also Bauman 1985 (F 642) 120–2. On Augustus' relations with the jurists, see Wieacker 1969 (F 705).

[26] Cf. Paul, *D* 4.3.18.4 (on the *lex Iulia de iud. priv.* of 17 B.C.); Paul, *D* 32.29 *pr.* (on the *lex Iulia de marit. ord.* of 18 B.C.). A *responsum* concerning Maecenas' doubtful divorce from Terentia *c.* 15 B.C.: Javolenus *D* 24.1.64; consultation by Augustus (below, at n. 82) *c.* 20 B.C., see E. Champlin, *ZPE* 62 (1986) 249–51, more plausible than the traditional date of A.D. 4.

[27] Pomponius, *D* 1.2.2.47; on his expertise in language studies, see Gell. *NA* XIII.10.1, with Stein 1971 (F 694). Born *c.* 50, Labeo entered the Senate by 18 (Dio LIV.15.7–8) and died late in Augustus' reign (below, n. 44); the family stems from Ligures Baebiani in Samnium, cf. Kunkel 1967 (F 666A) 32–4, 114. Fragments: Lenel 1889 (B 109) I 299–315, 501–58 (367 citations and 109 fragments – more than all other Augustan jurists combined). Still invaluable on Labeo is Pernice 1873–1900 (F 678).

[28] On the rivalry: Tac. *Ann.* III.75; Pomponius, *D* 1.2.2.47 (noting that Capito was taught by Ofilius). Born *c.* 45, Capito entered the Senate by 17 B.C. (Zosimus, II.4.2: the legal date for the Secular Games) and died in A.D. 22 (Tac. *Ann* III.75). Of municipal origin: Kunkel 1967 (F 666A) 114–15. On Augustus' *consilium* in A.D. 13: Bowman 1976 (B 367) 154. Fragments: Strzelecki 1967 (B 172) (almost all from antiquarian works; he is cited once in the *Digest*).

[29] Capito's ancestors: Tac. *Ann.* III.75.1. His sycophancy, esp. to Tiberius: *ibid.* III.70, 75; Suet. *Gramm.* 22; but see also Rogers 1964 (F 682).

passion for *libertas*.[30] Augustus, keen to extend patronage to this new generation of jurists, offered both men a suffect consulate; and when Labeo, pleading the press of his legal studies, refused the honour, Augustus returned the snub (so we are told) by advancing the date of Capito's consulate (A.D. 5).[31] Literary sources on the two men are obviously biased by their typically senatorial outlook: contempt for the fawning Capito, admiration for the gruff and independent Labeo.

Jurists saw the rivalry quite differently. As Pomponius states, Capito clung narrowly to received views on law; but Labeo, more self-confident and daring, 'undertook numerous innovations' on the basis of his mastery of other branches of learning.[32] This judgment, which may seem innocuous enough, has a dramatic consequence in the juristic tradition: Capito is all but ignored by later jurists, whereas Labeo is cited more often than any jurist before the high classical period, his voluminous writings are frequently annotated or edited by later jurists, and his opinion is usually treated with great respect even when it fails to carry the day.[33] In short, Labeo is a commanding figure, the first indisputably 'classical' jurist.

To be sure, it is unclear what Pomponius means in saying that Labeo 'undertook numerous innovations'. The juristic tradition survives so fragmentarily that legal historians find it difficult to determine whether Labeo's position on a given question represents genuine innovation with respect to his predecessors. In any case, what modern scholars have chiefly discerned in Labeo's fragments are the traces of a defter and more conscious methodological approach to law, which Labeo may well have pioneered.[34] A description of this method is not easy since it must be based on evidence haphazardly preserved, but the following is thought to be more or less accurate.

First, Labeo stresses the importance of solving legal problems, if possible, through direct interpretation of fixed texts – either general norms such as can be found in statutes or edictal provisions, or self-

---

[30] Labeo's ancestors: Kunkel 1967 (F 666A) 32–4, 114. His independence: Tac. *Ann.* III.75; Suet. *Aug.* 54; Dio LIV.15.7–8. Capito on Labeo: Gell. *NA* XIII.12.1–4.

[31] Tac. *Ann.* III.75.2; Pomponius, *D* 1.2.2.47 (diverging on details). Pomponius also notes that Labeo spent half of each year 'with students' ('cum studiosis') in Rome: their names are lost.

[32] Pomponius, *D* 1.2.2.47. Nörr 1981 (F 674), discusses the paradox that the politically 'traditionalist' Labeo was the greater legal innovator. Capito's moral reputation may have adversely affected his standing among later jurists; compare the disreputable jurist C. Caninius Rebilus (cos. suff. A.D. 37; cf. Tac. *Ann.* XIII.30), not cited in the *Digest*.

[33] On Labeo's fragments, see n. 27. Labeo's *Posteriores* were excerpted by Proculus and Javolenus, annotated by Aristo and Paul; the *Pithana* were annotated by Paul. Examples of later respect for Labeo: Javolenus, *D* 40.7.39.4; Ulpian, *D* 8.5.2.3; Callistratus, *D* 49.14.1.1. Paul's acerbic *notae* may be a youthful work.

[34] Pomponius, *D* 1.2.2.47; 'plurima innovare instituit'. See Seidl 1971 (F 691); Stein 1972 (F 695) 9–16.

imposed norms contained in private documents like contracts or wills. Further, Labeo assumes that the wording of such a text is intended to express its author's intent fully, that the author's intent can be presumed rational, and that the author seeks primarily to communicate this intent (rather than, say, to express himself); therefore Labeo is usually reluctant to advance beyond the ordinary, 'objective' meaning of the words used in the text, even if the result is arguably harsh.[35] Two examples from contract law may illustrate this method of reasoning. If a contract clause clearly disadvantages one party, Labeo none the less enforces the clause if this interpretation corresponds with the apparent or 'objective' content of their agreement (*id quod actum est*); only if the overall agreement is unclear does Labeo resort to the externally more plausible interpretation of it. On the other hand, Labeo is also willing to construe an incurably ambiguous text against its author if he could have expressed himself more clearly.[36] Labeo's interpretations are not necessarily narrow, but they almost always are closely controlled by the text itself.

Second, if no text is available and law must be created, Labeo often relies on his belief that legal rules and institutions should be rationally purposive in their relation to society. This belief leads him to search for supervening principles that can be used to resolve doubtful cases. For example, if a minor child is old enough to understand his actions, should he be held liable for his wrongful damage to property (*damnum iniuria datum*)? Labeo says yes, simply because such a child is also held liable for his acts of theft (*furtum*); if law is rational, the child should be liable for both delicts unless there is a clear basis for distinguishing them. Labeo's fragments frequently display similar examples of reasoning by analogy.[37] Labeo's use of analogy is coupled with his insistence on sharp normative definition of legal institutions, so as to prevent their becoming blurred in practice.[38] For instance, when a legatee is left the 'use' (*usus*) of a farm, Labeo sets down clear rules allowing the legatee to bar the farm's owner (and, by analogy, the owner's domestic slaves) from residing on the farm; but Labeo does not allow him to prevent the owner's slaves or tenants from exploiting the farm; likewise, the legatee may use storage rooms for wine and olive oil, and may also forbid the owner from using them.[39] Labeo effortlessly generates these elaborate rules out of an

---

[35] A good example of close edictal interpretation is Ulpian, *D* 4.2.9 *pr.*: according to Labeo, the interdicts *unde vi* require physical, not just psychological violence (contrast Cic. *Caecin.* 46, 49). Compare: Ulpian, *D* 9.2.9 *pr.*, 17.4.1.5. If the result is too harsh, Labeo recommends that the Edict's wording be changed: Paul, *D* 42.1.4.3; or that the praetor use discretion in enforcing it: Paul, *D* 2.4.11, 3.3.43.6; Ulpian, *D* 4.8.15. Cf. Horak 1969 (F 658) 194–205, 212–16. [36] Javolenus, *D* 18.1.77; Paul, *D* 18.1.21; both citing Labeo. Compare, on wills, Labeo, *D* 32.30 *pr.* [37] Ulpian, *D* 9.2.5.2; cf. Horak 1969 (F 658) 242–61. [38] Martini 1966 (F 670) 137–48. [39] Ulpian, *D* 7.8.10.4.

implied definition of 'use', which his discussion is intended to illustrate; he obviously recognizes that, when vested property interests may conflict, certainty is all important.

Third, Labeo's decisions are often apparently influenced by an underlying belief that, in principle, no person should draw unjustified enrichment, even innocently, at another's expense, and that procedural law should if possible be construed to prevent this from occurring. Thus, for instance, if I lose a borrowed object and then pay the lender its value, and the lender later recovers the object, Labeo rules that I may sue the lender on the contract in order to recover (as the lender wishes) either the object or the payment for it. Labeo seemingly arrives at this decision through simple construction of procedural law, avoiding the fiction that the lender and I had ever 'tacitly' agreed on this outcome.⁴⁰ Likewise, Labeo rules that a plaintiff should have an action on fraud (*actio doli*) not only if, as the Praetor's Edict expressly provides, no other remedy is actually available, but also if it is unclear whether another remedy is available.⁴¹ In this context, it is no surprise that Labeo makes some of the earliest juristic decisions that impose on sellers a warranty of merchantability for the goods they sell, regardless of whether they are aware of major defects in these goods.⁴²

Labeo's various approaches to law are obviously not always compatible with one another, but he maintains an impressively productive tension between them. His influence with later jurists may thus result less from his specific substantive innovations than from the principled rigour of his decisions. In any case, his dominance of the Augustan era is so complete that his contemporaries are thrown into all but total obscurity. Fabius Mela, for example, was an able and penetrating jurist, to judge from surviving citations of his commentary on the Edict. It was Mela, for example, who concocted the famous hypothetical case of the slave whose throat was cut when an athlete's carelessly thrown ball struck the hand of a razor-wielding barber; this hypothetical case brilliantly illustrates several contrasting features of the law governing wrongful damage to property, including proximate cause and contributory negligence.⁴³ But Mela remains a shadowy figure within the juristic tradition; he may or may not have possessed the *ius respondendi*, but he was unable to compete on even footing with his more eminent contemporary, and Pomponius, in his history of Roman law, does not even mention Mela.

---

⁴⁰ Paul, *D* 13.6.17.5.   ⁴¹ Ulpian, *D* 4.3.7.3.   ⁴² Pomponius, *D* 19.1.64; 19.2.19.1.
⁴³ Ulpian, *D* 9.2.11 *pr.* Fragments: Lenel 1889 (B 109) I 691–6 (thirty-three citations). Mela's date and background (both uncertain): Kunkel 1967 (F 666A) 116. Other contemporary jurists, like Blaesus and Vitellius, are just names.

IV. PROCULIANS AND SABINIANS

Labeo's dominant position among the jurists ended only with his death, probably late in Augustus' reign.[44] No jurist could take his place, and in fact the reign of Tiberius (14–37) saw the more or less formal split of Rome's major jurists into two rival 'schools': the Proculians and the Sabinians or Cassians. This division would endure well into the second century; but its nature and the reasons for it remain controversial.[45] It is even unclear what our sources mean by 'school' (*schola* or *secta*) in this context: to what extent the two schools had an independent corporate existence, where and how often they met, how they recruited members and selected leaders, what role they played in legal education, and so on.[46] Later jurists concentrate on recording their disputes concerning particular legal questions; these disputes are reported not only in the *Digest* and other post-classical sources, but also in Gaius' *Institutes*.[47]

The emperor Tiberius, himself keenly interested in all branches of learning, extended political patronage to both schools; and whatever their earlier qualms, jurists now no longer declined the opportunity to obtain the consulate.[48] The Proculians owe their name to the brilliant jurist Proculus, who has been plausibly identified with Cn. Acerronius Proculus (cos. ord. 37).[49] However, Proculus did not derive from a socially prominent family, and during most of the Julio-Claudian era the Proculian school was also nominally led by two members of a far more influential family: first by M. Cocceius Nerva (cos. suff. 21/2), Tiberius' close friend who committed suicide in 33, and then by his homonymous son (cos. suff. 40), the emperor Nerva's father, who together with Proculus presided over the school from 33 until late in Nero's reign.[50]

[44] Labeo may have commented on the Lex Papia Poppaea of A.D. 9 (cf. Labeo, *D* 40.7.42), but receives no obituary from his admirer Tacitus (whose *Annales* begin with Augustus' death in 14).

[45] See Schiller 1978 (F 689) 327–30, summarising the scholarship. In any case, the division is not likely to be based on either political or philosophical disagreement.

[46] Cf. Liebs 1976 (F 668) 215–42 (very speculative).

[47] Liebs 1976 (F 668) 243–75, lists known controversies, not all of them certain; see also Falchi 1981 (F 651) 263–8.

[48] Tiberius, who preferred consuls distinguished in civilian arts (Tac. *Ann.* IV.6.2), also gave a consulate to the jurist Caninius Rebilus (see n. 32). Jurists serve him also in overseeing Rome's water supply: Capito from 13 to 22, the elder Nerva from 24 to 33 (Frontin. *Aq.* 2.102); see Syme 1986 (A 95) 220–3.

[49] On Proculus, see Pomponius, *D* 1.2.2.50, with Kunkel 1967 (F 666A) 123–9; Mayer-Maly 1957 (F 671); but also Honoré 1962 (F 656). Born *c.* 20 B.C., he probably lived until *c.* A.D. 60, when Pegasus succeeded him as head of the school (Pomponius, 53); Proculus may have been a pupil of Labeo, but wrote harshly critical notes on his writings and often disagrees with him. Fragments: Lenel 1889 (B 109) II 159–84 (179 citations); cf. Krampe 1970 (F 665), for a close analysis of his methods.

[50] The family, from Narnia in Umbria, first rose to notice in the triumviral period: Kunkel 1967 (F 666A) 120–30. Fragments: *pater*, Lenel, 1889 (B 109) I 787–90 (thirty-five citations); *filius, ibid.* 791–2 (eight citations).

Proculus, clearly a more brilliant jurist than either of the Nervae, appears to have relied on their prestige in order to secure a hearing for his views.

The history of the other school is similar but more complex. Masurius Sabinus, its first leader, was not by birth a member of Rome's status elite; indeed, at first he allegedly supported himself through honoraria from his students. At the advanced age of fifty Sabinus finally entered the equestrian order, doubtless through the patronage of Tiberius who also granted him the *ius respondendi* – the first time that a non-senator had received this honour.[51] Sabinus' writings, above all his brief but authoritative treatise on the *ius civile*, enjoyed very great eminence among later jurists, who frequently commented simply 'on Sabinus' (*ad Sabinum*).[52] However, Sabinus evidently shared leadership with one of his students, the extremely well-placed aristocrat C. Cassius Longinus (cos. suff. 30), whose direct ancestors included the jurists Servius and Tubero.[53] (This is a particularly clear example of the tendency of jurisprudence to 'run in families'.) In early sources the socially prominent Cassius is usually described as founding the 'Cassian' school (*Cassiani*); but the members of the school eventually came to be called 'Sabinians' (*Sabiniani*) after Sabinus, whom later jurists esteem more highly.[54] Both men survived into the 60s and probably ran the school jointly.

Since the Renaissance, legal historians have sought to isolate the underlying legal basis of the numerous doctrinal disputes between the two schools. A half-century ago it was widely argued that their differences resulted in large part just from the separate operation of the two schools; divergent solutions to various legal problems were formulated in each school and then transmitted from teacher to student, without a consistent pattern of larger dogmatic disagreement.[55] There is doubtless a measure of truth in this view. However, more recent scholars have re-emphasized a methodological line dividing the Proculians from the Sabinians.[56] According to Pomponius, the origin of the school

---

[51] Pomponius, *D* 1.2.2.48–50 (a troubled passage); cf. Kunkel 1967 (F 666A) 119–20. Sabinus, who may stem from Verona, was probably born *c.* 25 B.C. and survived into the reign of Nero (below, n. 66). Fragments: Lenel 1889 (B 109) II 187–216 (236 citations).

[52] Sabinus' three-book *ius civile* was annotated by Aristo, then commented on by Pomponius (in thirty-five books), Paul (sixteen) and Ulpian (fifty-one, but incomplete).

[53] Pomponius, *D* 1.2.2.51. Cassius is a collateral descendant of Caesar's assassin: Syme 1986 (A 95) Table XXIV. Born *c.* 5 B.C., he enjoyed a distinguished political career and is prominent in Tacitus' *Annales*; cf. Nörr 1984 (F 676), and also Nörr 1983 (F 675) on the speech in Tac. *Ann.* XIV.43–4. His character: Tac. *Ann.* XII.12.1. He studied with Sabinus (*D* 4.8.19.2); on his death, see n. 70. Fragments: Lenel 1889 (B 109) I 109–26 (143 citations).

[54] *Cassiani*: Pliny, *Ep.* VII.24.8; Pomponius, *D* 1.2.2.52; *et al.* The school is called *Sabiniani* first by Marcellus (cf. *D* 24.1.11.3), and often thereafter.

[55] For instance, Schulz 1946 (F 690) 119–23; and so still Schiller 1978 (F 689) 329–30, with bibliography.

[56] Stein 1972 (F 695); Liebs 1976 (F 668) 275–82; Falchi 1981 (F 651); Scacchetti 1984 (F 688). These authors differ in many details, implying that reconstruction is very difficult.

disputes was the earlier rivalry between Labeo and Capito; the two schools simply increased their differences, with the Proculians imitating Labeo and the Sabinians Capito.[57] And in fact the Proculians do frequently rely on an approach to law that somewhat resembles Labeo's principled rationality; by contrast, the Sabinians often adopt a freer, more heterodox position, though whether they are following Capito in this respect is unclear.

Thus the Proculians, like Labeo, normally prefer close objective interpretations of fixed texts, while the Sabinians allow interpretation based on the author's presumed 'subjective' intent. For example, if a debtor promises by stipulation to make a payment within a fixed interval of time, Sabinus holds that the creditor can claim payment on the first day of the period, while Proculus and his school rule that the claim is not legally effective until the entire period elapses.[58] Similarly, if someone promises by stipulation to pay money to both the promisee and a third party, both schools recognize that, owing to absence of privity, the third party acquires no enforceable right through the contract; but whereas the Sabinians hold that the entire payment is owed to the promissee, the Proculians rule that only half of it is owed to him and the rest of the promise is unenforceable.[59] The same differences recur in interpreting the Edict; for example, if the parties reach a settlement before the *iudex* renders judgment, the Sabinians require the *iudex* then to absolve the defendant in every case, but the Proculians require him to condemn in all trials not based on *bona fides*.[60] There are numerous similar examples of these contrasting methods of interpretation, both for statutory norms and for private instruments.

Likewise, the Proculians tend to uphold Labeo's rational conceptualism, while the Sabinians take a looser approach to law. Probably the most famous example of this difference concerns the law of sale (*emptio venditio*): the Sabinians hold that barter, the promised exchange of an object for an object, is a form of sale and enforceable as such; but the Proculians deny this and point out that since there is no money price, there is no clear way to distinguish buyer from seller.[61] Similarly, the Proculians often recognize the force of logical analogy in law, while the Sabinians play it down. For instance, the Proculians rule that the onset of puberty (and hence legal majority) should be legally presumed as of an age that is fixed for each sex, whereas the Sabinians insist on a physical inspection of boys even though this practice had long since been abandoned, for moral reasons, in the case of girls.[62] Again, if a legacy is

---

[57] Pomponius, *D* 1.2.2.48, 52. There is no evidence that Labeo himself founded a school, or that he taught Nerva *pater* or Proculus.

[58] Venuleius, *D* 45.1.128 *pr.*; cf. Papinian, *D* 45.1.115.2.   [59] Gai. *Inst.* III.103.

[60] Gai. *Inst.* IV.114; compare also III.168.   [61] Gai. *Inst.* III.141; Paul, *D* 18.1.1.1, 19.4.1 *pr.*

[62] Gai. *Inst.* I.196; Ulpian, *Lib. Sing. Reg.* 11.28.

left subject to an impossible condition (e.g. 'pay ten to Titius if he touches the sky'), the Sabinians read the legacy as if the condition had not been written, but the Proculians void the legacy on the ground that a contractual stipulation subject to an impossible condition is also void.[63]

By contrast, the Sabinians use analogy in a looser, more equitable fashion that arguably better captures the spirit of Labeo's style; their position on barter as a form of sale is a good example. Sabinus' expansive attitudes are at their most aggressive in the area of delict; for instance, he grants the direct Aquilian action for wrongful damage even when the plaintiff's property was not physically harmed (e.g. the defendant struck coins out of the plaintiff's hand and they fell down a sewer), and he also extends the action on theft even to the unauthorized sale of land.[64] Neither view was received by later jurists.

By and large, the Proculians emerge as the 'better lawyers', the Sabinians as the more flexible ones. Two central strains of Roman jurisprudence, formalism and equity, are momentarily divided from one another. However, in a number of respects it is misleading to lay too great a weight on these school controversies. First, even though the record of their controversies is incomplete, the school disputes seem to have centred mainly on technical details and do not necessarily imply a radically different stance on the nature and purposes of Roman private law. Second, the Proculians and Sabinians may not have represented all jurists then practising; the obscure jurist Atilicinus was clearly a Proculian, but other Julio-Claudian jurists may well have operated independently.[65] Third, by no means all of the attested controversies can be easily explained through a simple dichotomy in legal method; the theoretical basis of many disputes is extremely obscure. Fourth, the schools were in any case unable to enforce a narrow dogmatism on their members; the view of one school is not uncommonly adopted by one or more members of the other.[66]

Finally, the school debates must also be understood within the context of the Roman judicial system, in which a *iudex*, if confronted by dissenting *responsa* from two authorized jurists, was free to apply the opinion that seemed to him more plausible.[67] Juristic controversies,

---

[63] Gai. *Inst.* III.98, who admits that the Sabinian rule is hard to explain.

[64] See, respectively, Ulpian, *D* 9.2.27.31; and Gell. *NA* XI.18.13, with Gai. *Inst.* II.51.

[65] Fragments of Atilicinus: Lenel 1889 (B 109) I 71–4 (twenty-four citations, often with Proculus or Nerva *filius*); see also esp. Proculus, *D* 23.4.17, citing a letter from Atilicinus. Minicius may have been a student of Sabinus (cf. Julian, *D* 12.1.22); his writings were excerpted by Julian. Little or nothing is known of the jurists C. Caninius Rebilus (cf. n. 32), Longinus (pr. under Claudius?), Cartilius, and Servilius.

[66] Liebs 1976 (F 668) 210–11. Individual school jurists may also take extreme or eccentric positions; e.g. the view of Nerva *filius* on the physical nature of possession (Paul, *D* 42.1.1.1, 3, 14, 22, etc.).

[67] Gai. *Inst.* 1.7 (citing a rescript of Hadrian); so already Cic. *Caecin.* 69. The *iudex* is thus not free to create his own law.

whether or not they arose through school debate, will have tended in practice to increase the flexibility of law, at any rate until one or another opinion prevailed and became 'the law we use' (*ius quo utimur*).

The founders of the two schools had already achieved eminence under Tiberius; they continued to dominate Roman jurisprudence during the reigns of Caligula (37–41), Claudius (41–54), and Nero (54–68). Relations with these emperors did not always run smoothly. The demented Caligula reportedly threatened to revoke all previous grants of the *ius respondendi*, and Claudius drove the jurists into the shade by wilfully interfering with the independent administration of justice.[68] Still, Sabinus, Cassius and Proculus, and probably the younger Nerva as well, survived into Nero's reign.[69] The politically powerful Cassius held important positions under all three emperors, but in 65 Nero relegated him to Sardinia because of his allegedly suspect political views; Cassius was recalled by Vespasian in 69, but died soon thereafter.[70] As the great Julio-Claudian jurists passed from the scene, the way was cleared for a new generation.

V. LEGAL WRITING AND EDUCATION

Almost without exception, the attested writings of first-century jurists are directed primarily toward other jurists; these writings thus have an austere format that elevates technical discussion of rules and 'cases' above the didactic exposition of broad principles.[71] Two major types of juristic literature are attested. The first is the extended commentary on a set text: above all, the Urban Praetor's Edict (by Labeo, Mela, Sabinus and probably Plautius as well), but also the Twelve Tables (Labeo) and the edicts of the peregrine praetor (Labeo) and of the curule aediles (Caelius Sabinus). Such commentaries assemble and interpret all law pertinent to each provision of the object text. The second type is 'problem-oriented', assembling decisions on a wide range of legal questions; these writings may take the form of collected *responsa* (Labeo, Sabinus) or of disputes and investigations (Labeo, Capito, Proculus, Sabinus and Fufidius).

In addition to these basic types, some jurists devote monographs to particular areas of law; attested examples are Sabinus on theft and the younger Nerva on usucapion. Jurists also frequently develop law by

---

[68] Caligula: Suet. *Calig.* 34.2 (meaning disputed). Claudius: Sen. *Apocol.* 12.2; and below, at n. 90.

[69] Sabinus comments on an *sc* of Nero (from A.D. 55 or 60): Gai. *Inst.* II.218. Pegasus, consul probably in 76, cannot have succeeded Proculus much before 60: Pomponius, *D* 1.2.2.53.

[70] Tac. *Ann.* XVI.7, 9.1; Pomponius, *D* 1.2.2.51–52. Cassius was reportedly almost blind at the time of his exile.

[71] Still essential on forms of juristic writing is Schulz 1946 (F 690) 141–261, despite its dogmatism.

critically annotating the works of earlier jurists, especially those of Labeo and Sabinus.

This literature is not designed to be readily accessible to non-jurists, since it all presumes considerable prior knowledge of the institutions and principles of Roman private law. Yet literary sources show that demand was also growing among laymen for elementary handbooks.[72] Although there is no evidence that the more prominent first-century jurists offered instruction to beginners,[73] the need for a handbook was provisionally met by Sabinus' three books on the *ius civile*, an authoritative summary of the legal rules peculiar to Roman citizens. The arrangement and content of this work owe much to earlier republican treatises; like them, it introduces topics rather haphazardly and even omits some significant areas of law. None the less, by the reign of Nero it was already a standard elementary handbook.[74] So successful was it as a statement of the 'civilistic system' that in the following centuries it attracted lengthy commentaries from Pomponius, Ulpian and Paul. Cassius' treatise on the *ius civile*, in at least ten books, was similar in arrangement to Sabinus', but much less influential except among jurists. Deliberately designed handbooks for beginners (*Institutiones*) appear only in the second century A.D., contemporaneously with the emergence of professional law teachers.[75]

VI. IMPERIAL INTERVENTION

Although classical private law is chiefly a juristic creation, the Roman state did not surrender its power to create new legal norms through statute (*lex*). In the republican constitution, statutes were enacted through popular assemblies (*comitia*) upon a magistrate's initiative. During the Empire legislation was always initiated by the emperor or by a magistrate acting with his approval. Augustus had a large body of statutes enacted, a portion of which affected significant change in the private law of persons and succession; especially important is his extensive 'moral legislation' encouraging marriage and childbirth, imposing sanctions for adultery, and restricting testamentary manumissions.[76] Later Julio-Claudian emperors also utilized comitial statutes,

---

[72] Cf. Petron. *Sat.* 46.7, who refers to *libri rubricati* ('red-letter' handbooks). On legal education, see Atkinson 1970 (F 639), stressing its very late development at Rome.

[73] The pupils who 'supported' Sabinus (Pomponius, *D* 1.2.2.50: 'a suis auditoribus sustenatus') were probably men like Cassius; there is no evidence that the Sabinians and Proculians saw elementary instruction as a typical function of their 'schools'.

[74] Standard handbook: Pers. v.90 (the *rubricata Masuri*, probably a glossed edition of Sabinus' *ius civile*); cf. Fronto, *Ep. ad M. Caes.* 2.8.4 (p. 31 van den Hout); Arr. *Epict. Diss.* iv.3.12. Astolfi 1983 (F 638) attempts to reconstruct Sabinus' *ius civile*.

[75] Collections of legal maxims (*regulae*) first appear in the high classical period; the earliest is by Neratius. The relation of these works to legal education remains uncertain.

[76] Imperial statutes are collected in Rotondi 1912 (F 685). On Augustus' moral legislation, see esp. Nörr 1977 (F 673).

especially in matters concerning status or succession; the controversial social character of such laws may have made it desirable to obtain at least the formality of a popular vote.

However, legislation through the cumbersome popular assemblies soon became obsolete as new forms of law-making emerged to express a centralized government. These new forms had administrative origin and character; but they gradually created, alongside the *ius civile* (statutes, praetorian procedure and juristic interpretation), a body of law intended to supplement or replace older law. Eventually this law came to be called the 'new law' (*ius novum* or *ius extraordinarium*).[77]

Already in the Republic the Senate had often issued advisory directives to be executed by magistrates; but in the early Empire the decrees of the Senate (*senatusconsulta*) gradually emerged as a source of law in their own right, though how and when this occurred remain controversial.[78] During the first century A.D., *senatusconsulta* that significantly alter private law still often direct magistrates to execute their provisions; but in the following century this fiction is dropped and the Senate legislates directly – though always upon the emperor's initiative or at least with his express approval.[79]

The emperor, himself a magistrate, also gradually came to enunciate general legal norms through a variety of administrative channels, including proclamations (*edicta*), judicial decisions (*decreta*), answers to petitioners (*rescripta*), and instructions to other magistrates (*mandata*).[80] In the early second century these channels were formalized, and the rescript system emerged as the major channel for imperial pronouncements on private law; but earlier the channels have a much more casual, almost *ad hoc* quality. However, even as early as Augustus the emperor is occasionally described as proclaiming new rules of private law.[81] In most cases, he probably did so only after gathering advice from a specially summoned 'council' (*consilium*) consisting mainly of jurists. One such council, which led Augustus to approve the enforceability of codicils to a Senator's will, is described in Justinian's *Institutes*.[82] During the first

[77] Cf. Kaser 1971 (F 662) I 199, 208–9; Schiller 1978 (F 689) 533–7. The terms appear in a technical sense only from *c.* A.D. 150.

[78] See Schiller 1978 (F 689) 456–62, with bibliography. Most known *senatusconsulta* are listed by Talbert 1984 (D 77) 431–59.

[79] Directives to magistrates are found in *senatusconsulta* from the reign of Augustus (the earliest: A.D. 10) to as late as Vespasian. The legislative character of *senatusconsulta* is affirmed by Gai. *Inst.* 1.4 (acknowledging earlier uncertainty); cf. Papinian, *D* 1.1.7 *pr.*, and Ulpian, *D* 1.3.9.

[80] See Schiller 1978 (F 689) 480–506.

[81] E.g., Ulpian, *D* 16.1.2 *pr.* (*edicta* of Augustus and Claudius prohibiting women from assuming their husbands' debts); Paul, *D* 28.2.26 (*edictum* of Augustus forbidding disinheritance of a son serving as a soldier; later repealed).

[82] Just. *Inst.* II.25 *pr.* (Trebatius persuaded the emperor; on the date, see n. 26); compare *ibid.* II.23.1, on Augustus' recognition of informal bequests (*fideicommissa*). The *consilium principis* is, in the first century, an informal advisory gathering of the emperor's 'friends'; it acquires more formal status only in the second century. See Crook 1955 (D 10); Amarelli 1983 (D 4); and Schiller 1978 (F 689) 466–74, summarising the controversy.

century the emperor's legislative power may not yet have been recognized *de iure*, as an express function of his office; but it clearly existed *de facto*, and its importance steadily increased as the emperor's constitutional position was rationalized.[83]

The *ius novum*, insofar as it deviates significantly from older law, is often associated with a new form of procedure 'outside' the normal formulary system: extraordinary cognition (*cognitio extra ordinem*).[84] In the first century this new procedure still had a somewhat makeshift character, as various elements of administrative process were loosely combined. For example, when Augustus made informal testamentary requests (*fideicommissa*) legally enforceable in some instances, he ordered the consuls to supervise their implementation. Such *fideicommissa* proved popular and soon became more generally enforceable; in order to ease the burden on the consuls, Claudius created two new praetors (reduced to one by Titus) who did nothing but handle them.[85] In other instances the emperor relied on his own deputies; for example, Claudius gave legal force to the decisions of his procurators.[86]

Procedure before judges who had been delegated by the emperor differed markedly from the formulary system. Unlike the urban praetor, these judges took a much more active role in summoning the defendant, conducting the trial, determining the case and enforcing the verdict.[87] Unlike formulary procedure, which presumed a model in which adversary proceedings led to the binding arbitration of disputes, extraordinary cognition more resembled the inquisitorial procedure commonly associated with modern Continental law.

Extraordinary cognition implies the power of the emperor to hear and decide lawsuits, either personally or through delegates; Augustus and his successors used this power extensively, although its constitutional basis is once again elusive.[88] In turn, delegation implies at least the possibility of appeal (*appellatio, provocatio*) from the delegated judge to a higher authority. Appeal is also attested as early as Augustus, and it

---

[83] On the basis of the emperor's power to issue norms, see recently Sargenti 1984 (F 687), with literature. Not until the second century were imperial decisions recognized as sources of general norms: Gai. *Inst.* 1.5; Papinian, *D* 1.1.7 *pr.*; Ulpian, *D* 1.4.1 *pr.*-1. Gualandi 1963 (F 654) I, lists all juristic references to legislation by emperors.

[84] Kaser 1966 (F 661) 339–49. The expression does not occur in sources until the middle of the second century A.D.

[85] See esp. Just. *Inst.* 11.23.1; Pomponius, *D* 1.2.2.32; with Kaser 1966 (F 661) 354–5; Röhle 1968 (F 683). The consuls continued to handle important cases: Pomponius, *D* 40.5.44.

[86] Tac. *Ann.* XII.60.1; Suet. *Claud.* 12.1. See in general Millar 1977 (A 59) 158–74.

[87] Kaser 1966 (F 661) 371–409, based mainly on later sources. See also Jolowicz and Nicholas 1972 (F 660) 395–404; Buti 1982 (D 252).

[88] See generally Kaser 1966 (F 661) 349–53; Millar 1977 (A 59) 507–37. Cf. Dio LI.19.6–7, a garbled report of a law of 30 B.C. On Augustus, see esp. Val. Max. VII.7.3–4, 9.15 ext. 1. Caligula: Dio LIX.18.1; Ath. 148d. Claudius: Sen. *Apocol.* 7.4–5; Suet. *Claud.* 46; Dio LX.28.6.

seems to become steadily more frequent under later emperors.[89] Further, appeal was not confined, as might have been expected, only to extraordinary cognition; already Augustus is reported to have quashed the jurisdictional rulings of 'ordinary' magistrates, and Claudius and Domitian went still further by reforming the verdicts of *iudices*.[90]

Extraordinary cognition is a considerable advance in procedural rationality over formulary procedure; the ancient arbitrational system gradually gave way before a system with more modern characteristics – a striking instance of how legal modes of thought came gradually to pervade the Roman judicial system. Nevertheless, although the elements of this new system were in place by the first century A.D., formulary procedure remained the dominant form of civil procedure for Roman citizens throughout the empire (except in Egypt). Its continued preeminence is reflected in the numerous procedural documents buried by the ashes of Mount Vesuvius in A.D. 79,[91] as well as in the writings of first-century jurists who virtually ignore extraordinary cognition.

Another early imperial reform was also to be of lasting significance. By the Lex Cincia of 204 B.C., judicial advocates had been forbidden to accept honoraria for their services; Augustus reaffirmed this law, although it was already being widely flouted. In A.D. 47, however, Claudius had carried a *senatusconsultum* allowing payment of up to 10,000 sesterces to advocates; this measure was apparently confirmed, though with some restrictions, when Nero became emperor.[92] Ancient sources usually regard the change with distaste, because it eroded the position of oratory as a gentleman's pursuit. However, the possibility of pay undoubtedly encouraged an enlargement in the corps of orators, so that their services became more widely and easily available to litigants; and pay also promoted a more professional attitude on the part of advocates in their argument of cases. In Tacitus' *Dialogus* (set in the early 70s), speakers lament the displacement of lush oratory by legalism in the private courts;[93] what they basically resent is the emergence of truly professional lawyers, a major step in the rationalization of Roman civil procedure.

[89] Kaser, 1966 (F 661) 397–465; Litewski 1982 (F 669) 356–370. Of course, the emperor could also delegate the decisions of appeals; cf. Suet. *Aug.* 33.3. Nero allowed appeals from private judges to the Senate: Suet. *Ner.* 17; Tac. *Ann.* XIV.28.1.

[90] Augustus: Val. Max. VII.7.3–4. Claudius: Suet. *Claud.* 14. Domitian: *idem, Dom.* 8.1. By contrast, Caligula refused to allow appeals from republican magistrates: Suet. *Calig.* 16.2.

[91] See Bove 1979 (B 212) 123–6; also Bove 1984 (B 213). For a survey of surviving documents on private law, see Schiller 1978 (F 689) 86–8.

[92] Augustus: Dio LIV.18.2; cf. Gell. XII.12. Claudius: Tac. *Ann.* XI.6–7. Nero: *ibid.* XIII.5.1; Suet. *Ner.* 17; cf. Pliny, *Ep.* V.9.4, and in general Ulpian, *D* 50.13.1.10–13. Ancient reactions: e.g., Quint. *Inst.* XII.7.8–12; Mart. VIII.16–17.

[93] Tac. *Dial.* XIX.5–XX.2, XXXIX.1–3.

VII. THE FLAVIAN JURISTS

Probably even before Nero's overthrow in 68, the two juristic schools had changed leadership. The new heads, both closely associated with Vespasian, enjoyed little prestige within the later juristic tradition. Caelius Sabinus (cos. suff. 69), who headed the Sabinians, is all but ignored by later jurists.[94] His Proculian counterpart, Pegasus (cos. suff. 76?), fares only somewhat better; despite his reputation among contemporaries for vast learning, he is known to history mainly from Juvenal's biting description of his complacent behaviour while serving as Domitian's urban prefect.[95] Little is known about Pegasus, but he is perhaps the brother of a considerably more important jurist, Plautius, who may conceivably be D. Plotius Grypus (cos. ord. 88); Plautius' writings, also in the Proculian tradition, were frequently annotated and excerpted by later jurists.[96] By contrast, the elder Juventius Celsus, who succeeded Pegasus in the Proculian school, is an exceedingly dim figure.[97] The Flavian jurists in general maintained the standard school distinctions, with little major innovation in substance or method.[98]

The Flavian period was thus a disappointing one from the jurists' standpoint; talent was lacking, or the times were not right. However, by the end of Domitian's reign jurisprudence attracted several new personalities of major importance: Javolenus Priscus (cos. suff. 87), the successor of Caelius Sabinus among the Sabinians; Titius Aristo, who probably remained outside the Senate; and Neratius Priscus (cos. suff. 97) and the younger Celsus (pr. 106/107, cos. II 129), who jointly headed the Proculians after the death of the latter's father. The advent of these brilliant jurists marks the beginning of Roman private law's 'high classical' period, the apex of the juristic movement at Rome.[99]

---

[94] Fragments: Lenel, 1889 (B 109) I 77–82 (twelve citations, mostly from his commentary on the curule aediles' Edict). Pomponius, *D* 1.2.2.53, says he was influential with Vespasian; details are lacking.

[95] Juv. IV.75–81; cf. Pomponius, *D* 1.2.2.53, who says he held the post already under Vespasian. See also the gossipy scholion on Juv. IV.77. An inscription names him (Plo)tius Pegasus; cf. Champlin 1978 (F 648). See also Sturm 1981 (F 696). Fragments: Lenel 1889 (B 109) II 9–12 (twenty-eight citations, usually concurring with Proculus or Nerva *filius*). He presumably moved the two *senatusconsulta* bearing his name (Gai. *Inst.* 1.31, II.254); both concern private law.

[96] Fragments: Lenel 1889 (B 109) II 13–14 (two citations, seven fragments). His work was annotated by Javolenus and Neratius, and edited by Pomponius (*ibid.* II 79–85; forty-six fragments) and Paul (*ibid.* I 1147–78; 174 fragments). On Plautius, see Siber 1951 (F 693); Champlin 1978 (F 648) 271–2.

[97] Fragments: Lenel 1889 (B 109) I 127–8 (four citations, through his son or Neratius). He survived to at least A.D. 95: Celsus *filius*, *D* 31.29 *pr.*

[98] The other known Flavian jurists (Aufidius Chius, Fufidius, Fulcinius Priscus, Varius Lucullus) are little but names.

[99] This account of classical private law will continue in *CAH* XII².

APPENDICES

I. CONSULAR DATING FORMULAE
IN REPUBLICAN ITALY

Consular dating formulae *in series* are of extreme rarity in republican Italy; they occur on wine amphorae, roof-tiles, the so-called *tesserae nummulariae*, and also on the inscriptions of the Capuan *magistri*.

Dates on wine amphorae are readily intelligible:

CIL I² 2929, Falernian, 160 B.C. (A. Tchernia, *Le vin de l'Italie romaine*, Rome, 1986, 60–3, should not have rejected the testimony of Cic. *Brut.* 287; the absence of the term Falernian from the fragment Polyb. XXXIV.11.1 is manifestly without significance if one reads it in its context in Athenaeus)

ILLRP 1178, 121 B.C.

ILLRP 1180a, 107 B.C.

ILLRP 1181, Massican Falernian, 102 B.C.

ILLRP 1182, Falernian, 102 B.C.

IILRP 1179, 'O(pimian?)' Falernian, 101 B.C. (compare 1180, 'O(pimian?)' Falernian)

Hispania Epigraphica 2, 1990, no. 75, Dressel 1 amphora, 90 B.C.

E. Bucchi, in *Il Veneto nell'età romana* I, Verona, 1987, 157, Lamboglia 2 amphora, 46 B.C.

ILLRP 1185, Lucretian Falernian, 35 B.C.

Dates on roof-tiles, as on *ILLRP* 1151–70, 76–36 B.C., are to be explained by the fact that they were more valuable if weathered, see *Roman Statutes* 1995 (F 684) no. 15, Col. I, lines 32–8, with commentary.

The so-called *tesserae nummulariae* are discussed by J. Andreau, *La vie financière dans le monde romain*, Rome, 1987, 485–506, adopting the generally accepted view, which was originally propounded by R. Herzog, that they were labels attached to sacks of coin which had been checked and sealed. It remains completely unclear why it should be necessary to record not only the year, but also the month and the day, when coin had been inspected. A single example of course reads (*ILLRP* 1023, not accurate):

Anchial(us) Str < a > ti L. s.
specta < ui > t num(——)

979

mense Febr(uario)
M. Tul(lio) C. Ant(onio) co(n)s(ulibus)

But one may suspect that the labels were in general for perishables such as corn.

The inscriptions of the Capuan *magistri* are manifestly the result of the concession of some form of local administration to Capua in the late second century B.C.; they run from 112 or 111 B.C. to 71 B.C., with two gaps of ten years each, which allow us to regard the series as covering the period down to the Caesarian colony of 59 B.C. (see Frederiksen 1959 (E 41); the attempt of H. Solin, in *id.* and M. Kajava (eds.), *Roman Eastern Policy and Other Studies*, Helsinki, 1990, 151–62, 'Republican Capua', to minimize the role of the *magistri*, is unconvincing: the inscriptions of the Minturnensian *magistri* are quite unlike those of the Capuan.

The remaining relevant inscriptions are:

M. Cristofani, in *Archeologia nella Tuscia* II, Rome, 1986, 24–6, 'C. Genucius Cleusina pretore a Caere'; *Epigraphica* 48 (1986) 191; *Prospettiva* 49 (April 1987) 2–14, Caere, engraved in the wet plaster of a tomb chamber:

C. Cenucio Clousino prai(——)

It is unclear whether the text is to be regarded as in the nominative or in the ablative; whether the last word is to be restored as 'prai(fectus)/prai(fecto)' or 'prai(tor)/prai(tore)'; and whether in the latter case we have a praetor or the archaic term for a consul. But it is clear that the person is the consul of 276 and 270 B.C.; that his presence as authority or eponym is to be related to the status of Caere as a community with *civitas sine suffragio*; and that our text, although not certainly a consular dating formula, is to be related to those which follow.

ILLRP 1068; R. Frei-Stolba, *Jahresbericht 1983 des Rätischen Museums Chur*, 197–220; *Jahresbericht 1984*, 213–40, 'Die Erkennungsmarke (tessera hospitalis) aus Fundi im Rätischen Museum Chur'; ead., *ZPE* 63 (1986) 193–6, 'Zur "tessera hospitalis" aus Fundi', Fundi, 196, 183, 166, 155 or 152 B.C.

ILLRP 695, of uncertain origin, 171 B.C.

Supplementa Italica I, Rome, 1981, 156, no. 40 = *AE* 1982, 286, Falerii Novi, tombstone 'a.d. X K. Dec. C. Atilio Q. Seru < il > io co(n)s(ulibus)', 106 B.C.

ILLRP 518, Puteoli, 105 B.C.

A. Morandi, *ArchClass.* 36 (1984) 312–13 (inaccurate), Collemaggiore in territory of Cliternia of Aequi, building '[——C.] Claudio M. Perp[erna co(n)s(ulibus) ——], 92 B.C.

The Fasti Antiates may have begun to be inscribed before the Social War; if this is so, we have a phenomenon similar to the diffusion of consular dating formulae.

Where status is secure, it is always that of a community with citizenship, without or with the vote; this suggests that Falerii Novi possessed citizenship, not the Latin right, *contra*, I. di Stefano Manzella, l.c., pp. 105–6; for Falerii Novi note also A. Andrén, *SE* 48 (1980) 93–9, for a group of third- to second-century B.C. architectural terracottas from Falerii Novi, Caere, Lanuvium and Ostia, the others all being by this date communities with citizenship, with or without the vote. The combination of the likely status and anthroponymy should make it possible to locate *ILLRP* 695.

Cases after the Social War are:

ILLRP 1267, Cales, 86 B.C.

ILLRP 1123, Pompeii, 78 B.C.

ILLRP 911, Canusium, 67 B.C.

ILLRP 589, Ferentis, 67 B.C.

ILLRP 735, Minturnae, 65 B.C.

ILLRP 200, perhaps Cremona rather than Mantua, 59 B.C.

ILLRP 508, Furfo, 58 B.C.

ILLRP 608, Grumentum, 57 B.C.

ILLRP 152, Interamna Praetuttiorum, 55 B.C.

Forma Italiae I, 10 (1974), no. 382, Collatia, reservoir for oil, 55 B.C.

ILLRP 607, Grumentum, 51 B.C.

ILLRP 763, Pompeii, 47 B.C.

ILLRP 562a, Casinum, 40 B.C.

ILLRP 203, Verona, 38 B.C.

II. SURVIVAL OF GREEK LANGUAGE AND INSTITUTIONS

Funerary inscriptions, which may be of persons, often slaves or freedmen, of extraneous origin, are mostly excluded.

See in general F. Ghinatti, *Critica Storica* 11 (1974) 533–76, 'Riti e feste della Magna Grecia'; not I. R. Arnold, *AJA* 64 (1960) 245–51, 'Agonistic festivals in Italy and Sicily'.

Neapolis:

Varro, *Ling.* v.85; vi.15; Cic. *Balb.* 55; *Rab.Post.* 26–7; *Tusc.* 1.86; Dio LV.10.9; Strab. v.4.7 (246C), vi.1.2 (253C); Vell. Pat. 1.4.2; Suet. *Claud.* 11; *Ner.* 20 and 25; Tac. *Ann.* xv.33; Dio LX.6.1–2; HA, *Hadr.* 19.1.

F. de Martino, *PP* 7 (1952) 333–43, 'Le istituzioni di Napoli greco-romana'; F. Sartori, *Problemi di storia costituzionale italiota*, Rome, 1953, 46–55; F. Ghinatti, *Atene e Roma* n.s. 12 (1967) 97–109, 'Ricerche sui culti greci di Napoli in età romana imperiale'; J. Pinsent, *PP* 24 (1969) 368–72, 'The magistracy at Naples'; R. Merkelbach, *ZPE* 15 (1974) 192–3, 'Zu der Festordning für die Sebasta in Neapel'; E. Miranda, *Rend.Acc.Arch.Napoli* 57 (1982) 165–81, 'I cataloghi dei Sebasta di Napoli'; F. Costabile, *Istituzioni e forme costituzionali nelle città del Bruzio in età romana*, Naples, 1984, 126–8; E. Miranda, in *Napoli antica*, Naples, 1985, 386–97, 'Istituzioni, agoni e culti'.

Further inscriptions:

E. Miranda, in *Napoli antica*, Naples, 1985, 394, no. 117.1, a priestess of Athena Sicula

M. J. Osborne, *AncSoc* 19 (1988) 5–60, 'Attic epitaphs', at 27, no. 159, Λαελία 'Ρωμαία γυνὴ Πύρρου Νεαπολίτου (Roman period)

E. Miranda, *Epigr.* 50 (1988) 222–6, 'Tito a Napoli' (dedication to Titus)

C. Ferone, *Miscellanea Greca e Romana* XIII, Rome, 1988, 167–80, 'Sull'iscrizione napoletana della fratria degli Artemisi' (*AE* 1913, 134)

E. Miranda, *Miscellanea Greca e Romana* XIII, Rome 1988, 'Due nuove fratrie napoletane' (*IG* XIV, 730; *IGRR* I 436)

E. Miranda, *Puteoli* 12–13 (1988–9) 95–102, 'Un decreto consolatorio da Neapolis' (Augustan).

E. Miranda, *Iscrizioni greche d'Italia. Napoli* I, Rome, 1990, nos. 7, 17, 22, 26, 27

Dicaearchia (Puteoli):
Cic. *Tusc.* 1.86.

Velia:
Cic. *Balb.* 55.
Sartori, *Problemi*, 106–7 (unaware of the first inscription cited below); *id.*, 1976 (E 118) 113 nn. 119–20.
Further inscriptions:
ILS 6461, gymnasiarch
E. Miranda, *MEFRA* 94 (1982) 163–74, 'Nuove iscrizioni sacre di Velia', at 163–5, first-century B.C. to first-century A.D. dedication to Athena (Polias?)
J.-P. Morel, in E 77, 21–39, at 23 n. 14, Πόπλιος ἐπόησε.
SEG XXXVIII 1020; XXXIX 1078

Rhegium:
Strab. VI.1.2 (253C).
Sartori, *Problemi*, 136–42; F. Costabile, in Sartori 1976 (E 118) 466–7; F. Costabile, *Istituzioni e forme costituzionali nelle città del Bruzio in età romana*, Naples, 1984, 128–40; *SEG* XL 854–5, 858
Rediscovered inscription:
IG XIV 617 = B. F. Cook, *Antiquaries Journal* 51 (1971) 260–6, at 260–3.
Note that Rhegium had always gravitated more to Sicily than to Italy and that Sicily long remained an area of largely Greek culture under the Empire.

Locri:
F. Costabile, *Municipium Locrensium*, Naples, 1976, 73–5, with *SEG* XL 837.

Tarentum:
Cicero, II *Verr.* 4.135; *Arch.* 5; *Fin.* 1.7; Strab. VI.1.2 (253C).
Sartori, *Problemi* 89–90; L. Gasperini, in *Terza Miscellanea Greca e Romana*, Rome, 1971, 143–209, 'Il municipio tarentino' (note especially *prohedria* in first century A.D.); L. Gasperini, in *Settima Miscellanea Greca e Romana*, Rome, 1980, 365–84, 'Tarentina epigraphica'.
Further inscriptions:
M. Calvet, P. Roesch, *RA* (1966) 297–332 (Philon son of Philon of Taras at games in Tanagra between 90 and 80 B.C.)

L. Gasperini, *Ricerche e studi* 12 (1979) 141–51, 'Epitafio mistilingue di età imperiale a Taranto'.

E. Lippolis, *Taras* 4 (1984) 141–2 = *SEG* xxxiv 1020–1 = L. Gasperini, *Taras* 5 (1985) 311–14 = *SEG* xxxvi 943 (two second-century A.D. dedications)

L. Gasperini, *Studi A. Adriani* iii Rome, 1984, 476–9, 'Un buleuta alessandrino a Taranto' (third century A.D.).

Canusium:

Hor. *Sat.* 1.10.30, with Scholia.

Note also:

L. Moretti, *RFIC* 100 (1972) 180–2 = R. Gaeta *et al.*, *Le epigrafi romane di Canosa* i, Bari, 1985, no. 282 (visitor from Lycia). (The text of no. 193 is too uncertainly transmitted to form the basis of serious argument.)

III. INSCRIPTIONS IN LANGUAGES OTHER THAN LATIN AFTER THE SOCIAL WAR

ETRUSCAN

An oracle allegedly given to Romulus, reported by C. Fonteius Capito, claimed that Tyche would desert Rome when she had forgotten her πάτριος φωνή (John the Lydian, *De Mag.* II, 12 = III, 42 = *De Mens.* fr. 7, p. 180w); John certainly thought that this was Latin and it is very hazardous to argue that Etruscan was originally intended, as E. Gabba, in *Les origines de la république romaine*, Fondation Hardt, Entretiens 13, Geneva, 1967, 133–69, 'Considerazioni sulla tradizione letteraria sulle origini della Repubblica', at 148–9.

J. R. Wood, *MPhL* 5 (1981) 94–125, 'The Etrusco-Latin *liber Tageticus* in Lydus' *de ostentis*', may well be right to argue that John had got wind of a bilingual exposition of Etruscan lore; and his supplements for the gaps in the text are plausible. But John also claims that the Etruscan text had *never* been fully intelligible to foreigners; and there is no reason to swallow *that* claim.

W. V. Harris, *Rome in Etruria and Umbria*, Oxford, 1971, 172–5, discusses the limited evidence for Latin inscriptions in Etruria in Etruscan, as opposed to Roman or Latin, territory. In my view, the inscription from San Giuliano (173 n. 1) should be taken as evidence that the site formed part of the territory of Sutrium; and there is no certainty that the inscription on the statuette from Volsinii = Orvieto (175 n. 1) was engraved there. The tufa block from near Volsinii = Orvieto (175 n. 2, *NSc* (1932) 482–3), reading MAMIA, is mysterious. Note now the single Latin graffito ADON on an Arretine *coppetta*, second half of first century B.C., from the Etruscan and Greek sanctuary of Graviscae, M. Torelli, *Scavi e ricerche archeologiche 1976–9* ii, Quaderni di 'La Ricerca Scientifica', Rome: CNR, 1985, 355.

Bilinguals are discussed at Harris, *Rome in Etruria and Umbria* 175–7; note H. Rix, *Beiträge zur Namenforschung* 7 (1956) 147–72, 'Die Personnamen auf den etruskischen Bilinguen', for the striking case of Iuuentius constructed (mistakenly) from Iuppiter in replacement of *tinś* related to Tinia. There is a curious Etruscan inscription, engraved on a coarse-ware pot, before firing, in the Latin alphabet, from Limentra near Porretta on the way to the pass from the Po valley to Pistoia, G. Susini, *CRAI* 1965, 155 n. 1, citing Festus 17 L:

[——]AGI[——]
[——TIN] AFFNIN ARSE V[ERSE——]

I do not know what to make of a fragmentary and unintelligible inscription, partly in Etruscan, partly in Latin, engraved on a brick before firing, from a first- to second-century A.D. dump in Pisa, M. Cristofani, *SE* 38 (1970) 288.

Harris, *Rome in Etruria and Umbria*, 180–2, discusses the Latin inscriptions from after the Social War, 177–80, the last Etruscan inscriptions; note also:
Arretium:

G. Maetzke, *SE* 23 (1954) 353–6, 'Tomba con urnetta iscritta trovata in Arezzo': grave with Arretine ware and bilingual inscription; A. Cherici, *SE* 55 (1987–8) 331–2, no. 104, urn with second- to first-century B.C. inscription;

Caere:

M. Martelli, *SE* 55 (1987–8) 340–1, no. 118: Etruscan name in Latin script, second to first century B.C.; M. Cristofani, *ibid.*, 324–5, no. 95, Latin funerary inscription;

Clusium:

CIL XI 2146–57, 2185–9, 2190–5, 2196–2200, 2201–10, 2217–19, 2250–2; groups of funerary inscriptions which move from Etruscan to Latin, usually via Etrusco-Latin, between the second and first centuries B.C.

Perusia:

T. Rasmussen, *ArchRep* 1985–6, 113–14; tomb of *cutu* family, in use from the third to the first centuries B.C., one sarcophagus and fifty urns, Etruscan and then Latin inscriptions; add L. Cenciaioli, *SE* 55 (1987–8) 311–14; group of four urns, second to first century B.C. Etruscan and then Latin inscriptions.

Saena:

E. Mangani, *SE* 50 (1982) 103–46, 'Il tumulo dei *marcni* ad Asciano': two chambers, in use from the third century B.C. to Augustus; seventy-eight Etruscan inscriptions, one Latin (whence E. Mangani, *SE* 51 (1983) 425–6).

Volaterrae:

There is an enormous bibliography on the urns of Volaterrae, which may be pursued through A. Maggiani, *SE* 51 (1983) 247–8, no. 55 (urn of 100–50 B.C.); M. Pandolfini, *SE* 52 (1984) 310–11, no. 66 (urn of 100–50 B.C.); M. Nielsen, *J. Paul Getty Museum Journal* 1986, 43–58, 'Late Etruscan cinerary urns from Volterra at the J. Paul Getty Museum'; the consensus seems to be that they last for a generation or so after the Social War.

OSCAN

It is more than doubtful whether the plays and mimes of Strab. v. 3. 6 (233C); or the *Osci ludi* of Cic. *Fam.* VII.1.3 (= SB 24) are pieces in Oscan, rather than 'Atellan' farces, despite E. D. Rawson, *Intellectual Life in the Late Roman Republic*, London, 1985, 22 n. 12.

P. Poccetti, *Studi e Saggi Linguistici* 22 (1982) 183–7, 'Minima Paeligna' (Vetter, 217a-b), rejects the notion of an Italic 'revival'; his arguments are weak; but even if they are wrong, the texts which might document such a 'revival' cannot be closely dated. For Vetter 213 (Corfinium) as an example of such a 'revival', see A. L. Prosdocimi, in *Le iscrizioni pre-latine in Italia*, Atti dei Convegni Lincei 39, Rome, 1979, 119–214, 'Le iscrizioni italiche. Acquisizioni temi problemi', at 176–8.

A belief in the use of Oscan after the Social War has usually been supported by the painted inscriptions from Pompeii (Vetter, nos. 23–35; for a proper archaeological account it is necessary to go back to Conway), on the grounds that one should not posit too long an interval before A.D. 79; but the so-called *eituns* inscriptions, which are painted, are certainly no later than the Social War, A. L. Prosdocimi, in *Popoli e civiltà dell' Italia antica* VI, Rome, 1978, 825–912, at 874–8, 'Le "eituns"'; and in Montefusco near Benevento, a few years ago, a painted slogan 'Viva Badoglio' was perfectly legible nearly half a century on. None of the painted inscriptions from Pompeii need be even as late as Augustus.

For a group of Oscan graffiti on pottery from Pompeii, second to middle of the first centuries B.C., see C. Reusser, *SE* 50 (1982) 360–3.

M. L. Porzio Gernia, *MAL* 1973–4, 111–337, 'Contributi metodologici allo studio del latino arcaico. La sorte di M e D finali', at 151–2, shows that almost alone of Oscan cities, Pompeii sometimes abandons final M, under Latin influence, at the time of the Social War; a process of assimilation is evidently already taking place.

Capua:
The curse tablet, Vetter, no. 6, may belong after the Social War; it abandons final M on three out of twenty-six occasions, M. L. Porzio Gernia, *MAL* 1973–4.

Cumae:
The curse tablet, Vetter, no. 7, is conventionally placed between Sulla and Caesar; it is a strange mixture of Oscan and Latin.

MESSAPIC

C. de Simone, in H. Krahe, *Die Sprache der Illyrier* II, Wiesbaden, 1964, 36–7, discusses the possibility that Messapic survived for a time after the Social War.

IV. ITALIAN CALENDARS

Ov. *Fast.* III.87–98 (compare VI.59–63):

> quod si forte vacas, peregrinos inspice fastos:
> mensis in his etiam nomine Martis erit.
> tertius Albanis, quintus fuit ille Faliscis,
> sextus apud populos, Hernica terra, tuos.
> inter Aricinos Albanaque tempora constat
> factaque Telegoni moenia celsa manu.
> quintum Laurentes, bis quintum Aequiculus acer,

a tribus hunc primum turba Curensis habet;
et tibi cum proavis, miles Paeligne, Sabinis
convenit: huic genti quartus utrique deus.

So if you happen to have time, look at foreign calendars: in these too there will be a month with the name of Mars; it was the third month for the people of Alba, the fifth for the Falisci, the sixth for the Hernici; the people of Aricia and Alba have a calendar in common, just as they have high walls built by the hand of Telegonus; the Laurentes have Mars fifth, the fierce Aequi tenth, the people of Cures fourth; and the warriors of the Paeligni are in agreement with their Sabine ancestors, for Mars comes fourth in both cases.

Censorinus, *D.N.* 22.6:

apud Albanos Martius est sex et triginta, Maius viginti et duum, Sextilis duodeviginti, September sedecim; Tusculanorum Quintilis dies habet XXXVI, October XXXII, idem October apud Aricinos XXXVIIII.

March has thirty-six days among the people of Alba, May twenty-two, Sextilis eighteen, September sixteen, Quintilis of the people of Tusculum has thirty-six days, October thirty-two, yet October among the people of Aricia has thirty-nine.

Macrob. *Sat.* 1.15.18:

ut autem omnes Idus Iovi, ita omnes Kalendas Iunoni tributas et Varronis et pontificalis adfirmat auctoritas. quod etiam Laurentes patriis religionibus servant, qui et cognomen deae ex caerimoniis addiderunt, Kalendarem Iunonem vocantes...

The authority both of Varro and of the *pontifices* confirms that just as all the Ides are dedicated to Jupiter, so all the Kalends are dedicated to Juno. The Laurentes even preserve this fact in their ancestral cults, since they have actually adopted the name of the goddess from their liturgies, calling the day of the Kalends Juno ...

(Censorinus and Macrobius are clearly in error in supposing that the customs in question survived to their own day.)

Varro, *Ling.* VI.14:

Quinquatrus... ut ab Tusculanis post diem sextum Idus similiter vocatur Sexatrus et post diem septimum Septimatrus, sic hic quod erat post diem quintum Idus Quinquatrus.

Quinquatrus... Just as the sixth day after the Ides is called Sexatrus by the Tusculani on the same principle and the seventh day Septimatrus, so here Quinquatrus (was used) because it was the fifth day after the Ides.

Festus 304–6 L:

Quinquatrus... forma autem vocabuli eius exemplo multorum populorum Italicorum enuntiata est, quod post diem quintum Iduum est is dies festus, ut apud Tusculanos Triatrus et Sexatrus et Septematrus et Faliscos Decimatrus.

Quinquatrus... But the form of that word is adopted on the model of many Italic peoples, because it is a feast day the fifth day after the Ides, just as Triatrus and Sexatrus and Septematrus exist among the people of Tusculum and Decimatrus among the Falisci.

See in particular C. Ampolo, *CR* 38 (1988) 117–20, reviewing M. Torelli, *Lavinio e Roma*, Rome, 1984.

V. VOTIVE DEPOSITS

There is a general overall account by M. Fenelli, *ArchClass* 27 (1975) 206–52, 'Contributo per lo studio del votivo anatomico: i votivi anatomici di Lavinio': 'la diffusione di questa consuetudine si é avuta sopratutto dal IV al sec a.C.'

See *AJA* 1974, 25 = *Forma Italiae* III, 2, no. 19 for:

Volceii (San Mauro) – 200 down to 75–50 B.C. (there is no reason to blame the revolt of Spartacus; the site was converted to secular purposes in the first century A.D.).

See M. Torelli, E 130, 105 n. 49 for:

Veii (Porta Caere) – down to 50–40 B.C.

Gabii – down to 50–40 B.C. (see now M. A. Aubet, *Cuadernos* 14 (1980) 75–122, 'Catálogo preliminar de las terracottas de Gabii').

See A. La Regina, in P. Zanker (ed.) (E 141), 219–54, 'Il Sannio', at 237, for:

Schiavi d' Abruzzo – third century B.C. down to a miserable end some time after the Social War.

See *Sannio*, Rome, 1980, 249–50 for:

Capracotta – down to the middle of the first century A.D.

See *ibid.*, 269–81 for a site that almost dies at the end of the first century B.C. and then revives:

San Giovanni in Galdo.

The sanctuary of Mefitis in the Valle d'Ansanto is very imperfectly known; part of the votive deposit was discovered in circumstances which are for all practical purposes undocumented and was meticulously published by A. Bottini *et al.*, *NSc* 1976, 359–524, 'Valle d'Ansanto. Il deposito votivo del santuario de Mefite'; and part of the sanctuary was well excavated and published by I. Rainini, *Il santuario di Mefite in Valle d'Ansanto*, Rome, 1985. No more than a generic relationship can be established between the two sets of finds. That part of the votive deposit which is known just struggles down to the end of the Republic; and there was some building in the first half of the second century A.D. in the area of the sanctuary, which was thereafter abandoned until used for other purposes in the fourth century A.D.

VI. EPICHORIC FUNERARY PRACTICES

M. W. Frederiksen (n. 63), identified a group of Campanian funerary stelae with one or more full-length figures in an *aedicula* and dated it to the late Republic, say 150–50 B.C.; the stelae were replaced by *cippi* or mausolea. Apart from Capua, the stelae come from her dependency Atella (*CIL* x 3744, 3752); Caiatia (*CIL* x 4605); Sinuessa (*EE* VIII 563); Cales (Frederiksen, 103 n. 100: Vetter, no. 73, two Oscan stelae; Frederiksen, 100: *CIL* x 4696; *EE* VIII 540, 543, 551, 553, 555, 557; *CIL* x 4680, is uncertain); Teanum (Frederiksen, 102 n. 97: Vetter, nos. 123a, 123b + d (R. Antonini, in *Popoli e civiltà dell'Italia antica* VI, Rome, 1978, 825–912, 'L'Osco', at 874, 'Teano'), 123c, three Oscan stelae; Vetter, no. 123e = *NSc* 1913, 408, an Oscan stela; Frederiksen, 100, seven Latin stelae; A. Maiuri, *Passeggiate campane*[3], Florence, 1957, 182–4, a stela of a single woman brought from Teano to Casale di Carinola and intended for the Museo Provinciale

Campano); an example from Isola di Sora (*EE* VIII 609) has probably been transported there in modern times.

M. Eckert, *Capuanische Grabsteine* (Oxford: *BAR*, 1988), dates the stelae between 100 B.C. and A.D. 25; but his work is for all practical purposes unusable, since he is unaware that Atella is inseparable from Capua and he makes no attempt to relate his more limited corpus to that of Frederiksen; at no. 84, he randomly includes an Oscan stela from Teanum, which is a mis-read version of Poccetti, no. 137. Poccetti, nos. 137–8, are in fact two further examples of stelae in Oscan from Teanum.

H. Solin, in *id.* and M Kajava (eds.), *Roman Eastern Policy and Other Studies*, Helsinki, 1990, 151–62, 'Republican Capua', at 160–1, dates the stelae between 50 B.C. and A.D. 50, claiming that the letter forms, onomastic formulae and literary style are imperial; no support whatever is offered for these assertions, which ignore the much wider range of arguments adduced by Frederiksen; and note that Solin's assignation to the Empire of a substantial body of inscriptions of freedmen without *cognomina* has been disproved by M. Cébeillac-Gervasoni, *Annales Latini Montium Arvernorum* 16 (1989) 89–193 'Le *cognomen* des affranchis'.

P. Pensabene, *MDAI(R)* 82 (1975) 263–97 'Cippi funerari di Taranto', shows that at Tarentum traditional chamber and trench tombs virtually die out over the second and first centuries B.C.

id., *ibid.*, 285–6, nn. 110–18; M. W. Frederiksen, *loc. cit.*:

square herms of local stone, first aniconic, then iconic, at Pompeii, Stabiae, Surrentum, Nuceria Alfaterna, replaced by marble cippi; the change seems, with Frederiksen, against Pensabene, significant. (The herms are illustrated in *Un impegno per Pompei. Fotopiano e documentazione della necropoli di Porta Nocera*, Touring Club Italiano, 1983; V. Kockel, *Die Grabbauten vor dem Herkulaner Tor in Pompeji*, Mainz, 1983: the type appears in the second century B.C. and some examples may be as late as the last years of the town, 17–18.)

S. Diebner, *DArch* Terza serie, 1 (1983) 1, 63–78, 'Un gruppo di cinerari romani del Lazio meridionale':

square inscribed blocks with hole for ashes, covered with egg-shaped lids inscribed OSSA, from former Volscian territory, late Republic to early Empire.

G. D'Henry, in *Samnium*, Rome, 1991, 229–31, with earlier bibliography, eliminating Aesernia, where the lids are quite different and come in addition from a single tomb:

lids in the shape of money chests from Corfinium on the one hand and Amiternum and Foruli on the other hand.

For Etruria in general, see W. V. Harris, 177–80; G. Maetzke; T. Rasmussen; L. Cenciaioli; E. Mangani; A. Maggiani; M. Pandolfini; M. Nielsen, all cited in Appendix III; for Volsinii = Orvieto, see A. Andrén, *Il santuario della necropoli di Cannicella ad Orvieto*, Orvieto, 1968 3, nn. 4–5; *Mostra degli scavi archeologici alla Cannicella di Orvieto. Campagna 1977*, Orvieto, 1978, 103, for a cemetery that lasts just long enough to achieve a minimal presence of Arretine ware; for South Etruria, see E. di Paolo Colonna, in *Studi G. Maetzke* III, Rome, 1984, 513–26, 'Su una classe di monumenti funerari romani dell'meridionale'; F. Prayon, in *Atti Sec.Cong.Int.Etr.* 1, Florence, 1989, 441–9 'L'architettura funeraria etrusca.

La situazione attuale delle ricerche e problemi aperti', at 448–9, for stepped tombs drawing on earlier models and falling between the second century B.C. and Augustus.

VII. DIFFUSION OF ALIEN GRAVE STELAE

G. Ciampoltrini, *Prospettiva* 30 (1982) 2–12 'Le stele funerarie d'età imperiale dell'Etruria settentrionale': 'stele architettoniche', occurring largely between Luni and Florence, diffused under Augustus partly by veterans and partly by adoption of urban freedman ideology.

S. Diebner, *DArch* Terza serie, 5 (1987) 1, 29–42 'Aspetti della scultura funeraria tra tarda repubblica ed impero':

intrusion of urban decorative motifs in Umbria and Sabina under Augustus and Julio-Claudians.

I. Valdiserri Paoletti, *RAL* 1980, 193–216 'Cippi funerari cilindrici dal territorio di Marruvium':

monuments mostly of freedmen diffused from centre from late Republic to Augustus.

F. van Wonterghem, *Forma Italiae* IV, 1, Florence, 1984, 102–3:

a portrait stela of two freedmen from Superaequum modelled on those of Rome.

L. Todisco, *RAL*, serie ottava, 42 (1987) 145–55, 'Leoni funerari di Luceria', with earlier bibliography at 149 n. 12 :

'sculture del genere ebbero ampia diffusione nell'architettura dell' Italia romanizzata, con cronologia che s fa oscillare tra perlomeno la metà del I secolo a.C. ed il II d.C.'

F. van Wonterghem, *ActaArchLov* 21 (1982) 99–125 'Monumento funerario di un tribunus militum a Corfinio':

distribution map of round mausolea modelled on those of Rome (including that of C. Utianius C.f. at Polla, *IItal* III 1. 113, also discussed by F. Coarelli (n. 79)).

P. Pensabene, *MDAI(R)* 82 (1975) 263–97 'Cippi funerari di Taranto':

appearance of portrait *cippi* 25 B.C. to A.D. 50 in a Roman cemetery superimposed on the Greek one.

G. Chiesa, in *Studi... A. Calderini... E. Paribeni* III, Milan, 1956, 385–411 'Una classe di rilievi funerari romani a ritratti dell'Italia settentrionale:

a phenomenon surely to be explained in terms of diffusion from Rome to the Po valley rather than joint derivation from a 'tradizione italica'; see in general G. A. Mansuelli, *ibid.*, 365–84 'Genesi e caratteri della stele funeraria padana'; Dr Maurizio Harari draws my attention to funerary beds of central Italian type in early imperial graves in the Lomellina.

(I find it extraordinarily hard to accept the view of V. Kockel, cited in Appendix VI, that the late first-century B.C. herms from Adria, illustrated in G. Fogolari and B. M. Scarfi, *Adria antica*, Venice, 1970, pl. 54, 1–2, are not the result of diffusion via migrants from the region of Pompeii; the herms from Petelia, published by A. Capano, *Klearchos* 22 (1980) 15–69, 'Tombe romane da Strongoli', are admitted as a case of diffusion by Kockel, but are all of the very end of the first century and the second century A.D.)

I. DESCENDANTS OF AUGUSTUS AND LIVIA

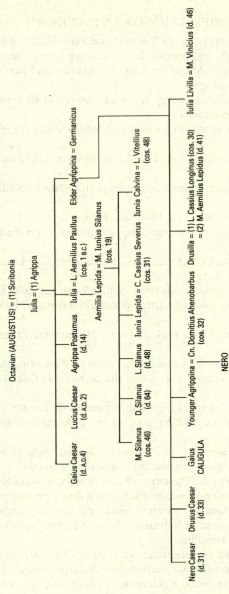

Octavian (AUGUSTUS) = (1) Scribonia

Iulia = (1) Agrippa

Gaius Caesar (d. A.D. 4)

Lucius Caesar (d. A.D. 2)

Agrippa Postumus (d. 14)

Iulia = L. Aemilius Paullus (cos. 1 B.C.)

Aemilia Lepida = M. Iunius Silanus (cos. 19)

M. Silanus (cos. 46)

D. Silanus (d. 64)

L. Silanus (d. 48)

Iunia Lepida = C. Cassius Severus (cos. 31)

Iunia Calvina = L. Vitellius (cos. 48)

Elder Agrippina = Germanicus

Nero Caesar (d. 31)

Drusus Caesar (d. 33)

Gaius CALIGULA

Younger Agrippina = Cn. Domitius Ahenobarbus (cos. 32)

NERO

Drusilla = (1) L. Cassius Longinus (cos. 30)
= (2) M. Aemilius Lepidus (d. 41)

Iulia Livilla = M. Vinicius (d. 46)

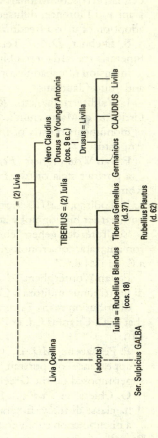

= (2) Livia

TIBERIUS = (2) Iulia

Livia Ocellina

(adopts)

Ser. Sulpicius GALBA

Iulia = Rubellius Blandus (cos. 18)

Rubellius Plautus (d. 62)

Tiberius Gemellus (d. 37)

Nero Claudius Drusus = Younger Antonia (cos. 9 B.C.)

Drusus = Livilla

Germanicus

CLAUDIUS

Livilla

—————— = distantly related to

II. DESCENDANTS OF AUGUSTUS' SISTER OCTAVIA AND MARK ANTONY

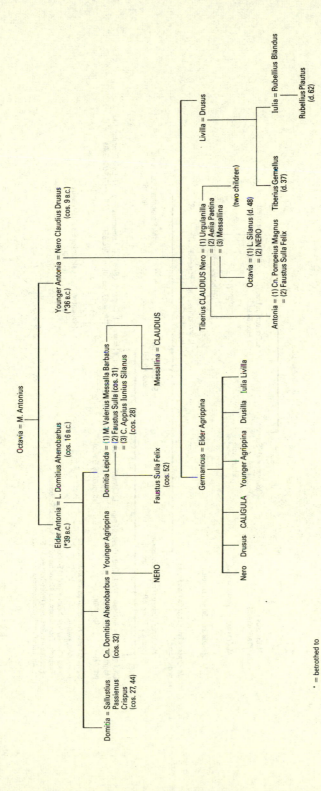

• = betrothed to

III. THE FAMILY OF M. LICINIUS CRASSUS FRUGI

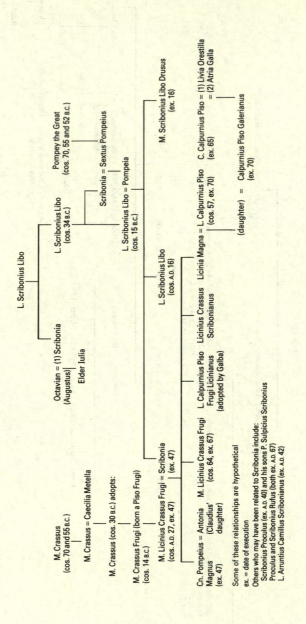

L. Scribonius Libo

Octavian = (1) Scribonia
(Augustus) |
Elder Iulia

L. Scribonius Libo
(cos. 34 B.C.)

Pompey the Great
(cos. 70, 55 and 52 B.C.)

Scribonia = Sextus Pompeius

L. Scribonius Libo = Pompeia
(cos. 15 B.C.)

M. Scribonius Libo Drusus
(ex. 16)

L. Scribonius Libo
(cos. A.D. 16)

Licinia Magna = L. Calpurnius Piso
(cos. 57, ex. 70)

C. Calpurnius Piso = (1) Livia Orestilla
(ex. 65) = (2) Atria Galla

(daughter) = Calpurnius Piso Galerianus
(ex. 70)

M. Crassus
(cos. 70 and 55 B.C.)

M. Crassus = Caecilia Metella

M. Crassus (cos. 30 B.C.) adopts:

M. Crassus Frugi (born a Piso Frugi)
(cos. 14 B.C.)

M. Licinius Crassus Frugi = Scribonia
(cos. A.D. 27, ex. 47)   (ex. 47)

Cn. Pompeius = Antonia
Magnus   (Claudius'
(ex. 47)   daughter)

M. Licinius Crassus Frugi
(cos. 64, ex. 67)

L. Calpurnius Piso
Frugi Licinianus
(adopted by Galba)

Licinius Crassus
Scribonianus

Some of these relationships are hypothetical
ex. = date of execution
Others who may have been related to Scribonia include:
Scribonius Proculus (ex. A.D. 40) and his sons P. Sulpicius Scribonius
Proculus and Scribonius Rufus (both ex. A.D. 67)
L. Arruntius Camillus Scribonianus (ex. A.D. 42)

IV. EASTERN CLIENTS OF ANTONIA, CALIGULA AND CLAUDIUS

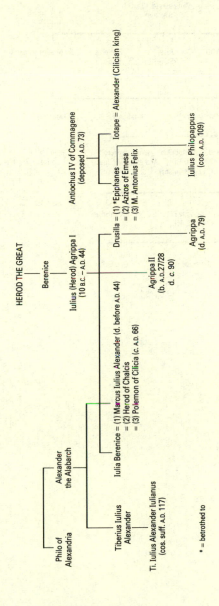

V. PRINCIPAL MEMBERS OF THE HERODIAN FAMILY

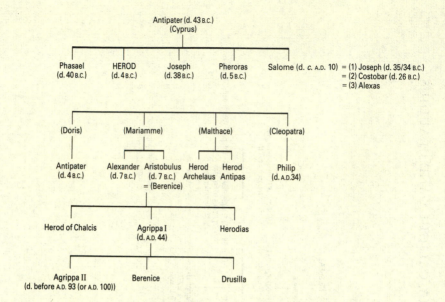

CHRONOLOGICAL TABLE

	Rome and Italy	The Provinces	Literature, Art and Architecture
B.C.			
44	Assassination of Iulius Caesar (15 March).		Cicero's *De Officiis*. Cicero's *Philippic* I (2 September), *Philippic* III (20 December).
43	Battle of Mutina, deaths of consuls Hirtius and Pansa. Octavian becomes consul (19 August). Lex Titia establishes the triumvirate (27 November).	Death of D. Brutus in Gaul.	Murder of Cicero. Birth of Ovid.
42	Deification of Iulius Caesar.	Sex. Pompeius controls Sicily. Naval battle with Salvidienus Rufus. Illyrian triumph of P. Vatinius (31 July). Battles of Philippi (first early in October, second on 23 October), followed by suicides of Brutus and Cassius.	Restoration of the temple of Saturn.
41		Antony in Asia. Herod and his brother Phasael appointed tetrarchs of Judaea. Antony meets Cleopatra at Tarsus in winter and proceeds to Alexandria.	Virgil, *Eclogue* IV written for Pollio's consulship of 40.
40	Surrender of Perusia to Octavian by L. Antonius (early spring). Octavian marries Scribonia (summer). Pact of Brundisium (September). Herod granted the throne of Judaea (autumn).	Parthian invasion of Syria led by Pacorus and Q. Labienus. Death of King Deiotarus of Galatia. Death of Calenus in Gaul (summer).	
39	Pact of Misenum (spring)	Ventidius defeats the Parthians. Agrippa campaigns in Gaul. Antony and Octavia at Athens (winter).	

B.C.	Rome and Italy	The Provinces	Literature, Art and Architecture
38	Renewal of triumviral powers for five years from 1 January. Marriage of Octavian and Livia (17 January). Triumph of Ventidius (27 November).	Second victory of Ventidius over Parthians and death of Pacorus. Antony captures Samosata. Sex. Pompeius' success against Octavian off Cumae and in Straits of Messina.	Publication of Virgil, *Eclogues*.
37	Pact of Tarentum (summer).	Capture of Jerusalem by Sosius and formal inauguration of the reign of Herod (July). Appointment of client kings: Archelaus in Cappadocia, Amyntas in Galatia, Polemo in Pontus. Marriage of Antony and Cleopatra at Antioch.	
37–36			Varro, *De Re Rustica*. Composition of Horace, *Satires* (37–30).
36	Removal of Lepidus from triumvirate. Octavian granted *sacrosanctitas* of a tribune.	After initial reverse (August), Octavian defeats Sex. Pompeius at Battle of Naulochus (3 September). Antony's Parthian offensive, failure at siege of Phraata and retreat through Armenia.	Reconstruction of the Regia.
35		Death of Sex. Pompeius in Asia.	Death of Sallust.
35–33		Octavian's campaigns in the Balkans.	
34	Sosius' triumph over Judaea (3 September).	Antony's invasion of Armenia and capture of Artavasdes. Triumph at Alexandria, followed by the 'Donations'.	
34–33			Agrippa restores aqueducts and adds a fifth (Aqua Iulia).
33	Octavian's second consulship. Powers of the triumvirate lapse at the end of the year.	Death of Bocchus of Mauretania. Antony remains in Armenia.	Agrippa as aedile revives *lusus Troiae*.
32	Divorce of Octavia by Antony. Publication of Antony's will by Octavian. Personal oath of loyalty sworn to Octavian in the towns of Italy and the West.		Restoration of Pompey's Theatre.
31	Octavian's third consulship.	Battle of Actium (2 September).	
30	Octavian offered tribunician *ius auxilii*.	Capture of Alexandria and suicide of Antony (1 August). Suicide of Cleopatra (10 August).	Publication of Horace, *Epodes*.
29	Closing of the doors of the temple of Janus (11 January). Octavian's triple triumph (13–15 August).		Dedication of the temple of Divus Iulius and the Curia Iulia (18 August) and the altar of Victory (28 August). Arch in the Forum
29–28		M. Licinius Crassus pacifies Thrace and defeats Bastarnae.	

Year BC		
		to commemorate the victory at Actium. Restoration of temples of Apollo and Hercules Musarum. Completion of Virgil, *Georgics* and Propertius, *Elegies* I.
28	Inscription of Cornelius Gallus commemorates defeat of revolt in the Egyptian Thebaid and penetration of Roman arms beyond the First Cataract.	Octavian and Agrippa share the consular *fasces* and begin *lectio senatus* with a grant of *censoria potestas* (or 29?). Return of control of *aerarium* to the praetors. Octavian becomes *princeps senatus*.
28	First celebration of the Actian Games (September). Dedication of the temple of Apollo on the Palatine (9 October). Mausoleum of Augustus begun. Composition of Vitruvius' *De Architectura* (28–23).	
27	Death of Varro. Agrippa's construction of the Pantheon.	Octavian appears before the Senate (13 and 16 January). He is given the name of Augustus, the oak wreath, the grant of a *provincia* for a period of ten years, with the right to govern it through *legati*. Triumph of M. Licinius Crassus (4 July).
27–24	Augustus in Gaul and Spain.	
26	Propertius, *Elegies* II–IV (26–16).	Dismissal and suicide of Cornelius Gallus (or in 27).
26–25		Campaign of Aelius Gallus to Arabia Felix.
25	Ovid begins writing the *Amores*.	Juba II made king of Mauretania. Campaigns of M. Terentius Varro in the Val d'Aosta. Death of Amyntas and annexation of Galatia.
25		Marriage of Iulia and Marcellus. Closing of the doors of the temple of Janus. Augustus falls ill.
24–23	Publication of Horace, *Odes* I–III.	
25–22	Campaigns of P. Petronius in Ethiopia (or 24–22).	
23	Maecenas falls out of favour in the imperial court.	Illness of Augustus. He resigns the consulship and on 1 July receives *imperium maius proconsulare* and *tribunicia potestas* for life, the latter renewed annually on 9 December. Death of Marcellus. Agrippa given a grant of *imperium proconsulare*.
23–21	Agrippa sent out to the East with *imperium*.	
22	Temple of Jupiter Tonans on Capitol (1 September).	Trial of Marcus Primus and conspiracy of Caepio and Murena. Augustus refuses dictatorship and consulship for life but accepts *cura annonae*.
22–19	Augustus in Greece and Asia.	
21		Marriage of Agrippa and Iulia.

Rome and Italy	The Provinces	Literature, Art and Architecture
B.C.	B.C.	B.C.
	20 Agrippa deals with trouble in Gaul. Recovery of Roman standards from Parthia. Tiberius crowns Tigranes as king of Armenia.	20 Dedication of temple of Mars Ultor on the Capitol (12 May). (? Or 19) Publication of Horace, *Epistles* I.
19 Augustus given a lifetime grant of the right to carry the consular *fasces* and to sit between the consuls.	19 Agrippa completes the pacification of Spain. Campaign of L. Cornelius Balbus against the Garamantes in Africa.	19 Deaths of Virgil (21 September) and Tibullus. Construction of the Aqua Virgo. Arch of Augustus in the Forum to commemorate the recovery of the Parthian standards. Dedication of Altar of Fortuna Redux (15 December).
18 Renewal of the grant of the *provincia* to Augustus. Agrippa's *imperium* is renewed for five years and he is granted *tribunicia potestas*. Another *lectio senatus*.		
18/17 ?Augustan moral legislation.		
17 Augustus adopts his grandsons, Gaius and Lucius, the children of Agrippa and Iulia. Celebration of the *ludi saeculares*.	17–16 Campaigns of P. Silius Nerva in north Italy and the Alps. Defeat of M. Lollius in Gaul.	17 Composition of Horace, *Carmen Saeculare*.
	16–13 Augustus in Gaul, Agrippa in the East.	
	15 Tiberius and Drusus invade Bavaria and reach the Danube. Agrippa visits Jerusalem.	
	14 Agrippa appoints Polemo king of Bosporus.	
13 Tiberius consul. Death of Lepidus the triumvir. Agrippa's *tribunicia potestas* and *imperium proconsulare* renewed, the latter made *maius*.	13 Agrippa campaigns in Pannonia.	13 Dedication of the Theatre of Marcellus (or, less probably, 11 B.C.). Inauguration of the Ara Pacis Augustae (4 July).
12 Augustus becomes *pontifex maximus* (6 March). Death of Agrippa (March).	12–9 Tiberius campaigns in the Balkans, Drusus in Germany. Rising in Thrace put down by L. Calpurnius Piso (*c.* 11–9).	12 Publication of Horace, *Epistles* II.1. Dedication of temple of Vesta on the Palatine (28 April). Bequest of the Baths of Agrippa to the Roman people.
	12 Dedication of the Altar of the Tres Galliae at Lugdunum (? or 10 B.C., see p.98). Inauguration of Caesarea by Herod.	

11	Tiberius made to divorce Vipsania and marry Iulia.
9	Death of Drusus the Elder (14 September).
8	Census held.
7	Tiberius' triumph over the Sugambri. Establishment of the fourteen *regiones* of Rome.
6	Tiberius granted *tribunicia potestas* for five years. He retires to Rhodes.
5	Augustus holds the consulship. C. Caesar assumes the *toga virilis* and is given the title *princeps iuventutis*. Beginning of regular appointment of suffect consuls.
2	Augustus holds the consulship again and is given the title of *pater patriae* (5 February). L. Caesar assumes the *toga virilis* and is given the title of *princeps iuventutis*. Iulia exiled. Appointment of first praetorian prefects. Lex Fufia Caninia.
A.D.	
2	Return of Tiberius from Rhodes.

9	Drusus reaches the Elbe but dies after an accident. Altar to Rome and Augustus established at Ara Ubiorum (probably in 9).
8	Tiberius campaigns against the Sugambri. Death of Polemo of Pontus.
7	Recall of Tiberius.
6	? Death of Tigranes II of Armenia.
5/3	?War of Sulpicius Quirinius against the Homonadenses.
4	Death of Herod. His kingdom divided between his sons Philip, Herod Antipas and Archelaus.
2	Death of Parthian king Phraates IV, succeeded by Phraates V (or Phraataces).
1	C. Caesar sent to the East with *imperium*.
A.D.	
2	Agreement between C. Caesar and Phraataces. Ariobarzanes installed as king of Armenia. L. Caesar dies at Massilia. End of Marmaric War in Cyrene (?).

9	Publication of first edition of Ovid, *Ars Amatoria*. End of Livy's history. Dedication of the Ara Pacis Augustae (30 January).
8	Deaths of Maecenas and Horace.
2	Dedication of the *Forum Augustum* and the temple of Mars Ultor (12 May). Second edition of Ovid, *Ars Amatoria*.
A.D.	
1–4	Composition of Ovid, *Fasti*.

Rome and Italy	The Provinces	Literature, Art and Architecture
B.C.	B.C.	B.C.
4 Another *lectio senatus*. Augustus adopts Agrippa Postumus and Tiberius (26 June), who in turn adopts Germanicus. Tiberius given a further grant of *tribunicia potestas* for ten years. Lex Aelia Sentia.	4 Death of C. Caesar. Tiberius invades Germany as far as the river Weser.	6 Rebuilding of the temple of Castor and Pollux by Tiberius.
6 Establishment of the *aerarium militare* and of the *vigiles*.	5 Tiberius reaches the Elbe.	8 Banishment of Ovid.
7 Agrippa Postumus banished to Planasia.	6 Outbreak of revolt in Pannonia and Illyricum. Banishment of Archelaus, son of Herod; Judaea turned into a province (census of Quirinius). Revolt in Isauria.	10 Restoration and dedication of the temple of Concordia by Tiberius.
8 Iulia the Younger banished.	9 End of the Pannonian revolt. Defeat of P. Quinctilius Varus and loss of three legions in the Teutoburg Forest.	
12 Tiberius' Illyrian triumph (23 October).	12 Germanicus takes command in Gaul and Germany.	
13 Tiberius given a further grant of *tribunicia potestas* for ten years and *imperium proconsulare maius* equal to that of Augustus. Germanicus given a grant of *imperium proconsulare*.	14 Army revolts in Pannonia and on the Rhine, dealt with by Drusus and Germanicus respectively (autumn).	
14 *Lustrum* held (11 May). Death of Augustus at Nola (19 August). Tiberius becomes *princeps*. Augustus is granted a public funeral (early September) and voted divine honours (17 September). Death of Agrippa Postumus.	15–16 Germanicus' campaigns in Germany, from which he is recalled by Tiberius.	
15 Tiberius becomes *pontifex maximus* (10 March).		
16 Conviction for treason (*maiestas*) of Libo Drusus, great-grandson of Pompey and great-nephew of Augustus' first wife, Scribonia (3 September).		

17	Death of Archelaus of Cappadocia. Triumph of Germanicus (26 May).	
18	Consulship of Tiberius and Germanicus.	
19/20	Twin sons born to the younger Drusus, of whom only Tiberius Gemellus survives.	
20	Trial and suicide of Cn. Calpurnius Piso. Triumph of Drusus (28 May).	
21	Consulship of Tiberius and Drusus. Tiberius retires temporarily to Campania.	
22	Grant of *tribunicia potestas* for Drusus.	
23	Death of Drusus (14 September).	
25	Sejanus' request to marry Livilla (Livia Iulia), widow of Drusus, is refused.	
26	Tiberius leaves Rome for Capreae.	
28	Death of Iulia the Elder. Marriage of Agrippina the Younger to Cn. Domitius Ahenobarbus.	
29	Death of Livia. Banishment of Agrippina and of Nero, son of Germanicus and Agrippina.	
30	Suicide of Nero.	
31	Consulship of Tiberius and Sejanus. Denunciation and death of Sejanus (18 October). Appointment of Sutorius Macro as praetorian prefect. Gaius Caligula assumes *toga virilis*.	
33	Death of Agrippina (18 October). Death of Drusus. Suicide of Asinius Gallus. Quaestorship of Gaius.	

17	Outbreak of war against Tacfarinas in Numidia. Germanicus sent to the East with *imperium*. Cappadocia becomes a province. Commagene also annexed.	
18–19	Germanicus visits Egypt.	
19	Death of Germanicus at Antioch (10 October). Death of Arminius.	
21	Revolt of Florus and Sacrovir in Gaul.	
24	Defeat and death of Tacfarinas.	
26	(?) Pontius Pilate becomes *praefectus* of Judaea.	
28	Revolt of the Frisii.	
33	(?) Death of Philip, son of Herod; his tetrarchy is taken under direct rule.	
34	Death of Artaxias of Armenia.	

17	Death of Livy. Death of Ovid (?). Dedication of temple of Janus (18 October) and Fors Fortuna.
21–2	Building of *castra praetoria*.
30	Publication of Velleius Paterculus' history.

	Rome and Italy	The Provinces	Literature, Art and Architecture
	B.C.	B.C.	B.C.
36		Pontius Pilate removed from his post for maladministration by L. Vitellius, governor of Syria.	
37	Death of Tiberius at Misenum (16 March). Gaius Caligula acclaimed *princeps* (18 March), confirmed by the Senate (28 March). Death of Antonia the Younger (1 May). Claudius consul with Gaius (1 July–31 August). Suicide of Tiberius Gemellus. Illness of Gaius (autumn). Birth of Nero (15 December).	Herod Agrippa I given Philip's kingdom.	Dedication of the temple of Divus Augustus.
38	Death and deification of Drusilla (10 June, 23 September). Gaius marries Lollia Paulina.	Trouble between the Jewish and Greek communities in Alexandria.	
39	Gaius divorces Lollia Paulina and marries Milonia Caesonia. Leaves Rome (September). Claudius marries Messallina.	Herod Antipas deposed. Gaius visits the Rhineland (October). Conspiracy and execution of Gaetulicus.	
40	Gaius returns to Rome (31 August).	Herod Antipas' ethnarchy given to Herod Agrippa I. Gaius in Gaul (winter). Preparations for an invasion of Britain. Outbreak of rebellion in Mauretania. Gaius orders his statue to be placed in the Temple at Jerusalem.	
40–4		Conquest of Mauretania and organization of provinces of Tingitana and Caesariensis.	
41	Murder of Gaius (24 January). Proclamation of Claudius (25 January). Birth of Britannicus.	Claudius' letter to the Alexandrians.	Beginning of the construction of a new harbour at Ostia and of the draining of the Fucine Lake. Seneca sent into exile.
42	Claudius proclaimed *pater patriae* (12 January).	Conspiracy and death of Scribonianus.	
43		Invasion of Britain. Lycia-Pamphylia made a province.	
44	*Aerarium* transferred from praetors to quaestors. Claudius' triumph for conquest of Britain.	Death of Herod Agrippa I.	

47 Ovation of Aulus Plautius for conquest of Britain.

47–8 Censorship of Claudius and L. Vitellius. Celebration of *ludi saeculares*.

48 'Marriage' and execution of Messallina and C. Silius.

49 Marriage of Claudius and Agrippina the Younger (1 January). Extension of the *pomerium* of Rome. Seneca returns from exile and becomes praetor and tutor of Nero.

50 Claudius adopts Nero (25 February). Agrippina becomes Augusta.

51 Burrus becomes praetorian prefect. Nero given the title of *princeps iuventutis*.

53 Nero marries Octavia.

54 Death of Claudius (13 October), accession of Nero.

55 Death of Britannicus.

56 Nero given the title of *pater patriae*. *Aerarium* transferred from quaestors to *praefecti*.

58 Rejection of proposal that Nero should be *consul perpetuus*.

59 Murder of Agrippina. Institution of *Iuvenalia*.

60 Institution of the *Neronia*.

---

46 Annexation of Thrace.

47 Corbulo in the Rhineland.

49 Agrippa II given the kingdom of Chalcis.

51 Ostorius Scapula defeats Caratacus. Death of Gotarzes of Parthia, succeeded by Vonones and then Vologaeses.

53 Parthians take control of Armenia and Tiridates is appointed to the throne.

55 Corbulo appointed to an eastern command against Parthia and Armenia.

58 Corbulo attacks Tiridates and captures Artaxata.

59 Capture of Tigranocerta by Corbulo.

60 Completion of the subjugation of Armenia and appointment to the throne of Tigranes, great-grandson of Herod and of Archelaus of Cappadocia. Corbulo appointed governor of Syria. Revolt of Boudica and the Iceni.

51–2 Dedication of the Triumphal Arch of Claudius, forming part of the Aqua Virgo.

54 Publication of Seneca, *Apocolocyntosis*.

55 Publication of Seneca, *De Clementia*.

56–7 Dedication of the Macellum Magnum.

B.C. Rome and Italy	B.C. The Provinces	B.C. Literature, Art and Architecture
	61 Tigranes invades Adiabene. Vologaeses threatens Syria.	
62 Nero divorces Octavia and marries Poppaea Sabina. Execution of Octavia (9 June). Death of Burrus, retirement of Seneca. Introduction of *maiestas* charges.	62 Caesennius Paetus sent to Cappadocia. Surrenders to Vologaeses at Rhandeia.	62 Construction of the Thermae Neronianae (or possibly 64).
63 Birth and death of daughter of Nero and Poppaea, deified as Claudia Augusta.		
64 Outbreak of fire in Rome (18/19 July). Victimization of the Christians. Reform of the currency.	64–5 Incorporation of kingdom of Pontus into Galatia.	64 Destruction of the *Domus Transitoria*. 64–8 Building of the *Domus Aurea*, rebuilding of the Circus Maximus and reconstruction of Rome.
65 *Neronia* held again. Conspiracy of Piso (April). Death of Seneca. Death of Poppaea Sabina.		65 Deaths of Seneca and Lucan.
66 Deaths of Thrasea Paetus and Barea Soranus. Conspiracy of Vinicianus. Nero marries Statilia Messallina. Tiridates crowned king of Armenia in Rome.	66 Nero proclaims the freedom of Greece (? or 67, see p.664). Conspiracy and deaths of the Scribonii brothers. Corbulo instructed to commit suicide. Outbreak of revolt in Judaea.	66 Death of Petronius.
	67 Vespasian appointed as legate in command of the war in Judaea (February).	
68 Nero returns to Italy and while in Naples receives news of the revolt of Vindex. Death of Nero (9 or possibly 11 June). Proclamation of Galba as *princeps*. Galba arrives at Rome (autumn).	68 Vespasian reduces Samaria and Idumaea and prepares to attack Jerusalem. Revolt of Vindex in Gaul. Galba acclaimed by his troops in Spain (2 or 3 April). Battle of Vesontio and suicide of Vindex (late spring). Revolt of Clodius Macer in Africa.	
69 Otho proclaimed *princeps* by the praetorian guard (15 January). Murder of Galba. Otho defeated by Vitellius' troops at Bedriacum (14 April) and commits suicide (16 April). Vitellius granted imperial powers by the Senate (19 April) and enters Rome (June).	69 German legions in revolt against Galba. Vitellius proclaimed emperor by the German legions. Revolt of Civilis and the Batavians. Vespasian proclaimed emperor at Alexandria (1 July) and then by the army in Syria and Judaea.	

Second battle of Cremona (24/25 October). Antonius Primus enters Rome, murder of Vitellius (20 or 21 December)

70 Mucianus arrives in Rome (January). Vespasian confirmed by the Senate as *princeps*. Publication of the *lex de imperio Vespasiani*. Domitian made urban praetor with the *imperium* of a consul. Arrival of Vespasian in Rome (summer).

70 *Imperium Galliarum* of Iulius Classicus and Iulius Tutor. Petilius Cerialis defeats the Batavian revolt. Titus attacks and captures Jerusalem and destroys the Temple (August).

BIBLIOGRAPHY

ABBREVIATIONS

AA	*Archäologischer Anzeiger*
A&A	*Antike und Abendland*
AAES	*Publications of an American Archaeological Expedition to Syria 1899–1900.* New York
AAntHung	*Acta Antiqua Academiae Scientiarum Hungaricae*
AArchHung	*Acta Archaeologica Academiae Scientiarum Hungaricae*
AAS	*Annales archéologiques arabes syriennes*
AAWM	*Abhandlungen der Akademie der Wissenschaften in Mainz, geistes- und sozialwissenschaftliche Klasse*
ABAW	*Abhandlungen der Bayerischen Akademie der Wissenschaften*
ABSA	*Annual of the British School at Athens*
AC	*L'Antiquité classique*
AClass	*Acta Classica. Proceedings of the Classical Association of South Africa*
ActaArchLov	*Acta Archaeologica Lovanensia*
ADA	S. Riccobono, *Acta Divi Augusti*. Rome, 1945
AE	*L'année épigraphique*
AEA	*Archivo Español de Arqueología*
AFLN	*Annali della Facoltà di Lettere e Filosofia della Università di Napoli*
AHB	*Ancient History Bulletin*
AHDE	*Anuario de Historia del Derecho Español*
AION (Archaeol.)	*Annali dell'Istituto Universitario Orientale di Napoli. Seminario di Studi del Mondo classico. Sezione di Archeologia e Storia antica.*
AJ	F. F. Abbott, A. C. Johnson, *Municipal Administration in the Roman Empire*. Princeton, 1926
AJA	*American Journal of Archaeology*
AJAH	*American Journal of Ancient History*
AJPh	*American Journal of Philology*
AJS Review	*Journal of the Association for Jewish Studies*
AN	D. C. Braund, *Augustus to Nero: A Sourcebook on Roman History 31 B.C. – A.D. 68*. London and Sydney, 1985

AncSoc	*Ancient Society*
AncW	*Ancient World*
Annales ESC	*Annales (Economies, Sociétés, Civilisations)*
AnnDeptAntiqJordan	*Annual of the Jordan Department of Antiquities*
ANRW	H. Temporini, W. Haase (eds.), *Aufstieg und Niedergang der römischen Welt. Geschichte und Kultur Roms im Spiegel der neueren Forschung.* Berlin and New York, 1972–
AntAfr	*Antiquités africaines*
APF	*Archiv für Papyrusforschung*
AR	*Africa romana*
ArchCant	*Archaeologia Cantiana*
ArchClass	*Archaeologia Classica*
ArchIug	*Archaeologia Iugoslavica*
ArchLaz	*Archaeologia Laziale*
ArchRep	*Archaeological Reports.* London, Council of the Society of Hellenic Studies and Management Committee of the British School of Archaeology at Athens
ArchS	*Archäologie der Schweiz*
ArhVestnik	*Arheološki Vestnik*
ARID	*Analecta Romana Instituti Danici*
ARS	A. C. Johnson *et al., Ancient Roman Statutes.* Austin, 1961
ASAA	*Annuario della Scuola Archeologica di Atene e delle Missioni Italiane in Oriente*
ASAW	*Abhandlungen der Sächsischen Akademie der Wissenschaften zu Leipzig*
ASNP	*Annali della Scuola Normale di Pisa, classe di lettere e filosofia*
ASS	*Archivio Storico Siciliano*
AU	*Der altsprachliche Unterricht*
AW	*Antike Welt*
BAA	*Bulletin d'archéologie algérienne*
BABesch	*Bulletin Antieke Beschaving*
BAGB	*Bulletin de l'Association Guillaume Budé*
BAR	British Archaeological Reports
BASOR	*Bulletin of the American Schools of Oriental Research in Jerusalem and Baghdad*
BASP	*Bulletin of the American Society of Papyrologists*
BayVorgeschichtsbl	*Bayerische Vorgeschichtsblätter*
BCAR	*Bullettino della Commissione Archeologica Comunale in Roma*
BCH	*Bulletin de correspondance hellénique*
BdA	*Bollettino d'Arte del Ministero per i beni culturali e ambientali*
BEFAR	*Bibliothèque des écoles françaises d'Athènes et de Rome*
BGU	*Ägyptische Urkunden aus den Staatlichen Museen zu Berlin, Griechische Urkunden.* Berlin, 1895–

BIAL	Bulletin of the Institute of Archaeology of the University of London
BiAr	The Biblical Archaeologist
BICS	Bulletin of the Institute of Classical Studies of the University of London
BIDR	Bullettino dell'Istituto di Diritto Romano
BJ	Bonner Jahrbücher
BMCPhoenicia	Catalogue of Greek Coins in the British Museum, Phoenicia. London, 1910
BMCRE	H. Mattingly et al., Coins of the Roman Empire in the British Museum. London, 1923–
BMCRR	H. A. Grueber, Coins of the Roman Republic in the British Museum. London, 1910
BRGK	Bericht der Römisch-Germanischen Kommission des Deutschen Archäologischen Instituts
BSAO	Bulletin de la société des antiquaires de l'Ouest
BSEAA	Boletín del Seminario de Estudios de Arte y Arqueología, Valladolid
BSNAF	Bulletin de la société nationale des antiquaires de France
Bull.ép	J. and L. Robert, Bulletin épigraphique. Paris, 1972–
BzN	Beiträge zur Namenforschung
CAH	The Cambridge Ancient History
CAR	Cahiers d'archéologie Romande
CBA ResRep	Council for British Archaeology, Research Reports
CBQ	Catholic Biblical Quarterly
CCG	Cahiers du Centre G. Glotz
CE	Chronique d'Egypte
ChLA	A. Bruckner, R. Marichal, Chartae Latinae Antiquiores. Olten and Lausanne, 1954–
CHM	Cahiers d'histoire mondiale
CIA	W. Dittenberger, A. Kirchhoff, J. Kirchner, U. Koehler, Corpus Inscriptionum Atticarum. Berlin, 1873–95
CIG	A. Boeckh, Corpus Inscriptionum Graecarum. Berlin, 1828–77
CIJ	J. B. Frey, Corpus Inscriptionum Judaicarum. Rome, 1936–75
CIL	T. Mommsen et al., Corpus Inscriptionum Latinarum. Berlin, 1863–
CIS	Corpus Inscriptionum Semiticarum. Paris, 1881–1951
CISA	Contributi dell'Istituto di Storia Antica dell'Università del Sacro Cuore, Milano
CJ	P. Krüger, Codex Justinianus, 1877
ClAnt	Classical Antiquity
ClassJ	Classical Journal
C&M	Classica et Mediaevalia
CPh	Classical Philology

CPJ	V. A. Tcherikover *et al.*, *Corpus Papyrorum Judaicarum.* Jerusalem, 1957–64
CPL	R. Cavenaile, *Corpus Papyrorum Latinarum.* Wiesbaden, 1958
CQ	*Classical Quarterly*
CR	*Classical Review*
CRAI	*Comptes rendus de l'Académie des inscriptions et belles lettres*
CRR	E. A. Sydenham, *The Coinage of the Roman Republic.* London, 1952
CSCA	*California Studies in Classical Antiquity*
CSDIR	*Centro Studi e Documentazione sull'Italia Romana*
CSSH	*Comparative Studies in Society and History*
CTh	T. Mommsen, *Codex Theodosianus.* Berlin, 1905
CV	*Classical Views* [= EMC]
D	T. Mommsen, *Digesta Justiniani Augusti.* Berlin, 1870
DAF	*Documents d'archéologie française*
DArch	*Dialoghi di archeologia*
DE	E. de Ruggiero, *Dizionario Epigrafico di antichità romana*, Rome, 1895–1988
DHA	*Dialogues d'histoire ancienne*
Diadora	*Glasilo arheološkoga Muzeja u Zadru*
EA	*Epigraphica Anatolica*
EAA	*Enciclopedia d'arte antica.* Rome, 1958–85
EE	*Ephemeris Epigraphica. Corporis inscriptionum Latinarum supplementum, edita iussu Instituti Archaeologici Romani.* Berlin, 1872–9, 1903–13
EJ²	V. Ehrenberg, A. H. M. Jones, *Documents Illustrating the Reigns of Augustus and Tiberius.* 2nd edn. Oxford, 1975
EL	*Etudes de lettres. Bulletin de la Faculté des Lettres de l'Université de Lausanne et de la Société des Etudes et Lettres*
EMC	*Echos du monde classique* [= *CV*]
Entretiens Hardt	*Entretiens sur l'antiquité classique*, Fondation Hardt. Vandoeuvres-Geneva 1952 –
EPRO	*Etudes préliminaires aux religions orientales dans l'empire romain*
EpStud	*Epigraphische Studien*
EtPap	*Etudes de Papyrologie*
ESAR	T. Frank *et al.*, *An Economic Survey of Ancient Rome.* 5 vols. Baltimore, 1933–40
FGrH	F. Jacoby, *Die Fragmente der griechischen Historiker.* Berlin and Leiden, 1923 –
FHG	C. Müller, *Fragmenta Historicorum Graecorum.* Paris, 1841–70
FIRA	S. Riccobono *et al.*, *Fontes Iuris Romani Anteiustiniani.*

	2nd edn. Florence 1940–3
GB	*Grazer Beiträge*
GCN	E. M. Smallwood, *Documents Illustrating the Principates of Gaius, Claudius and Nero*. Cambridge, 1967
GGA	*Göttingische gelehrte Anzeigen*
GJ	*Geographical Journal*
G&R	*Greece and Rome*
GRBS	*Greek, Roman and Byzantine Studies*
GWU	*Geschichte in Wissenschaft und Unterricht*
GZMS	*Glasnik zemaljskog muzeja Bosne i Hercegovine: Arhelogija*
HABES	*Heidelberger althistorische Beiträge und epigrapische Studien*
Habis	*Habis: arqueología, filología clásica. Sevilla, Universidad*
HSCP	*Harvard Studies in Classical Philology*
HTR	*Harvard Theological Review*
ICS	*Illinois Classical Studies*
IDR	D. M. Pippidi, I. I. Russu, *Inscriptiones Daciae Romanae*. Bucharest, 1977–
IEJ	*Israel Exploration Journal*
IFAO Mémoires	*Institut français d'archéologie orientale, Mémoires*
IG	A. Kirchhoff *et al.*, *Inscriptiones Graecae*. Berlin 1873–
IGBulg	G. Mihailov, *Inscriptiones Graecae in Bulgaria repertae*. Sofia, 1956–66
IGLS	L. Jalabert, R. Mouterde *et al.*, *Inscriptions grecques et latines de la Syrie*. Beirut, Paris, 1929– [see also *IJord*]
IGRR	R. Cagnat *et al.*, *Inscriptiones Graecae ad res Romanas pertinentes*. Paris, 1901–27
IItal	V. Bracco *et al.*, *Inscriptiones Italiae*. Rome, 1931–
IJ	*Irish Jurist*
IJord	P.-L. Gatier, *Inscriptions de la Jordanie, 2, Amman, Ammanitis et Jordan central*, Paris, 1986 [= *IGLS* vol. XXI]
ILAfr	R. Cagnat, A. Merlin, L. Chatelain, *Inscriptions latines d'Afrique (Tripolitanie, Tunisie et Maroc)*. Paris, 1923
ILAlg	S Gsell, H.-G. Pflaum, *Inscriptiones latines de l'Algérie*. Paris, 1922–
ILER	J. Vives, *Inscripcions latinas de la España romana*. Barcelona, 1971–2
ILGN	*Inscriptiones latines de la Gaule Narbonnaise* I, J. Gascou, M. Janon. Fréjus, 1985
ILGR	M. Šašel Kos, *Inscriptiones Latinae in Graecia repertae: additamenta ad CIL III*. Faenza, 1979
ILIug	A. and J. Šašel, *Inscriptiones Latinae quae in Iugoslavia . . . repertae et editae sunt. Inter annos MCMXL et MCMLX* (Situla 5, 1963); *Inter MCMLX et MCMLXX* (Situla 19, 1978); *Inter MCMII et MCMXL* (Situla 25, 1986). Ljubljana

ILLRP	A. Degrassi, *Inscriptiones Latinae Liberae Rei Publicae.* 2nd edn. 2 vols. Florence, 1957–63
ILS	H. Dessau, *Inscriptiones Latinae Selectae.* 3 vols. Berlin 1892–1916
ILTG	P. Wuilleumier, *Inscriptions latines des Trois Gaules* (*Gallia* suppl. XVII, Paris, 1963)
ILTun	A. Merlin, *Inscriptions latines de la Tunisie.* Paris, 1944
IMagnesia	O. Kern, *Die Inschriften von Magnesia am Maeander.* Berlin, 1900
IMS	F. Papazoglu, *Inscriptions de la Mésie supérieure.* Belgrade, 1976–
InscrCret	M. Guarducci, *Inscriptiones Creticae.* Rome, 1935–50
IPhil	A. and E. Bernand, *Inscriptions grecques de Philae.* Paris, 1969
IRB	S. Mariner-Bigorra, *Inscripciones romanas de Barcelona lapidarias y musivas.* Barcelona, 1973
IRC	G. Fabre, M. Mayer, I. Roda, *Inscriptions romaines de Catalogne I: Barcelone sauf Barcino.* Paris, 1984–5
IRPC	J. González, *Inscripciones romanas de la Provincia de Cádiz.* Cádiz, 1982
IRT	J. M. Reynolds, J. B. Ward-Perkins, *The Inscriptions of Roman Tripolitania.* Rome, 1952
ISM	D. M. Pippidi, I. I. Russu, *Inscriptiones Scythiae Minoris Graecae et Latinae,* 1–. Bucharest, 1980–
JACTJ	*Journal of the Joint Association of Classical Teachers*
JAOS	*Journal of the American Oriental Society*
JbAW	*Jahrbuch der Bayerischen Akademie der Wissenschaften*
JBL	*Journal of Biblical Literature*
JDAI	*Jahrbuch des Deutschen Archäologischen Instituts*
JEA	*Journal of Egyptian Archaeology*
JFA	*Journal of Field Archaeology*
JHS	*Journal of Hellenic Studies*
JJP	*Journal of Juristic Papyrology*
JJS	*Journal of Jewish Studies*
JNG	*Jahrbuch für Numismatik und Geldgeschichte*
JÖAI	*Jahreshefte des Österreichischen Archäologischen Instituts in Wien.* Vienna 1898–
JR	*Journal of Religion*
JRA	*Journal of Roman Archaeology*
JRGeogS	*Journal of the Royal Geographical Society*
JRS	*Journal of Roman Studies*
JS	*Journal des Savants*
JSJ	*Journal for the Study of Judaism*
JSNT	*Journal for the Study of the New Testament*
JTS	*Journal of Theological Studies*
LA	*Libya Antiqua*
LCM	*Liverpool Classical Monthly*

LEC	*Les études classiques*
LF	*Listy Filologické*
LS	*Libyan Studies*
MAAR	*Memoirs of the American Academy in Rome*
MAI	*Mémoires de l' Académie des inscriptions et belles-lettres*
MAL	*Memorie dell' Accademia Nazionale dei Lincei, classe di scienze morali e storiche*
MAMA	W. M. Calder, *Monumenta Asiae Minoris Antiquae.* Manchester, 1928–
MChr	L. Mitteis, *Grundzüge und Chrestomathie der Papyruskunde, Juristischer Teil,* 11. Leipzig–Berlin, 1912
MDAI (D)	*Mitteilingen des Deutschen Archäologischen Instituts (Station Damaskus)*
MDAI (I)	*Mitteilungen des Deutschen Archäologischen Instituts (Abteilung Istanbul)*
MDAI (M)	*Mitteilungen des Deutschen Archäologischen Instituts (Abteilung Madrid)*
MDAI(R)	*Mitteilungen des Deutschen Archäologischen Instituts (Römische Abteilung)*
MdI	*Mitteilungen des Deutschen Archäologischen Instituts*
MEFRA	*Mélanges d'archéologie et d'histoire de l'école française de Rome*
MH	*Museum Helveticum*
Milet	*Milet* 1. Berlin, 1908–28
MMAI	*Monuments et mémoires publiés par l' Académie des inscriptions et belles lettres*
MonArtAnt	*Monumenta artis antiquae*
MPhL	*Museum Philologicum Londiniense*
MPAA	*Atti della Pontificia Accademia romana di Archeologia, Ser. IIIa, Memorie*
MRR	T. R. S. Broughton, *The Magistrates of the Roman Republic* (Philological Monographs of the American Philological Association, no. 15, Cleveland, 1951–86)
MUSJ	*Mélanges de l'Université St Joseph*
MW	M. McCrum and A. G. Woodhead, *Select Documents of the Principates of the Flavian Emperors.* Cambridge, 1961
MZ	*Mainzer Zeitschrift*
NC	*Numismatic Chronicle*
NSc	*Notizie degli Scavi di Antichità*
NTH	E. M. Smallwood, *Documents Illustrating the Principates of Nerva, Trajan and Hadrian.* Cambridge, 1966
NTS	*New Testament Studies*
OGIS	W. Dittenberger, *Orientis Graeci Inscriptiones Selectae.* 4 vols. Leipzig, 1903–5
ORF	H. Malcovati, *Oratorum Romanorum fragmenta,* 3rd edn. Turin, 1967

OR*om*	*Opuscula Romana: Acta Instituti Romani Regni Seuciae*
P*AAJR*	*Proceedings of the American Academy for Jewish Research*
P*ACA*	*Proceedings of the African Classical Associations*
P*AES*	*Syria: Publications of the Princeton University Archaeological Expedition to Syria in 1904–5 and 1909.* Leiden
P*APhs*	*Proceedings of the American Philosophical Society*
P*BA*	*Proceedings of the British Academy*
P*BSR*	*Papers of the British School at Rome*
P*CPhS*	*Proceedings of the Cambridge Philological Society*
P*Dura*	C. B. Welles, R. O. Fink, J. F. Gilliam, *The Excavations at Dura-Europos, Final Report* v, Part I, *The Parchments and Papyri*. New Haven, 1959.
P*ECS*	R. Stillwell, W. L. MacDonald, M. H. McAllister, *Princeton Encyclopedia of Classical Sites*. Princeton, 1976
P*EQ*	*Palestine Exploration Quarterly*
P*Fay*	B. P. Grenfell, A. S. Hunt, D. G. Hogarth, *Fayum Towns and their Papyri*. London, 1900
P*IR*	E. Klebs *et al.*, *Prosopographia Imperii Romani*. Berlin 1897–8; 2nd edn, 1933–
P*Köln*	*Die Kölner Papyri*. Opladen 1975–
P*Mich*	C. C. Edgar, A. E. R. Boak, J. G. Winter *et al.*, *Papyri in the University of Michigan Collection*. Ann Arbor, 1931–
P*Oxy*	*The Oxyrhynchus Papyri*. London, 1898–
P*P*	*La parola del passato*
P*&P*	*Past and Present*
P*Ryl*	A. S. Hunt, J. de M. Johnson, V. Martin, C. H. Roberts, E. G. Turner, *Catalogue of the Greek Papyri in the John Rylands Library, Manchester*. Manchester, 1911–52
P*Yadin*	N. Lewis, Y. Yadin, J. C. Greenfield, *The Documents from the Bar Kokhba Period in the Cave of Letters: Greek Papyri (including Aramaic and Nabataean Signatures and Subscriptions)*. Jerusalem, 1989
Q*AL*	*Quaderni di Archeologia della Libia*
Q*S*	*Quaderni di Storia*
Q*Tic*	*Quaderni Ticinesi*
R*A*	*Revue archéologique*
R*AC*	*Revue archéologique du centre de la France consacrée aux antiquités nationales de Auvergne etc.*
R*AL*	*Rendiconti dell' Accademia dei Lincei, Classe di Scienze morali, storiche e filologiche*
R*AN*	*Revue archéologique de Narbonnaise*
R*BPh*	*Revue belge de philologie et d'histoire*
R*CCM*	*Rivista di cultura classica e medioevale*
R*DGE*	R. K. Sherk, *Roman Documents from the Greek East*. Baltimore, 1969

RDM	*Revue des Deux Mondes*
RE	A. F. von Pauly *et al.*, *Real-Encyclopädie der klassischen Altertumswissenschaft*. Stuttgart 1894–
REA	*Revue des études anciennes*
REG	*Revue des études grecques*
REL	*Revue des études latines*
RevAfr	*Revue africaine*
RevArchOuest	*Revue archéologique de l'Ouest*
RFIC	*Rivista di Filologia e di Istruzione Classica*
RG	*Res Gestae Divi Augusti*
RHD	*Revue de l'histoire du droit* (= *Tijdschrift voor Rechtsgeschiedenis*)
RHDFE	*Revue historique de droit français et étranger*
RhM	*Rheinisches Museum für Philologie*
RIB	R. G. Collingwood, R. P. Wright, *Roman Inscriptions of Britain*. Oxford, 1965–
RIC	H. B. Mattingly, E. A. Sydenham, *Roman Imperial Coinage*. London, 1923–
RIDA	*Revue internationale des droits de l'antiquité*
RIG	*Recueil des inscriptions gauloises* (*Gallia*, Suppl. 45, Paris, 1985 -: P.-M. Duval, G. Pinault, *Les Calendriers*, 1985; M. Lejeune, *Textes gallo-étrusques, Textes gallo-latins sur pierre*, 1988)
RIL	*Rendiconti del Istituto Lombardo di scienze e lettere, Classe di lettere*
RIU	L. Barkóczi, A. Mócsy, *Die römische Inschriften Ungarns*. Budapest, 1972–
RivArchCr	*Rivista di Archeologia Cristiana*
RMD	M. M. Roxan, *Roman Military Diplomas, 1954–77* and *1977–84* (University of London, Institute of Archaeology, Occasional Publications, nos. 2 and 9, 1978 and 1985)
RMR	R. O. Fink, *Roman Military Records on Papyrus* (Philological Monographs of the American Philological Association, no. 26, Cleveland, 1971)
RN	*Revue numismatique*
RPAA	*Rendiconti della Pontificia Accademia Romana di Archeologia*
RPh	*Revue de Philologie*
RRC	M. H. Crawford, *Roman Republican Coinage*. Cambridge, 1976
RSA	*Rivista storica dell'antichità*
RSI	*Rivista storica italiana*
RVV	*Religionsgeschichtliche Versuche und Vorarbeiten*
SB	F. Preisigke, F. Bilabel, *Sammelbuch griechischer Urkunden aus Ägypten*. Strassburg 1915–
SBAW	*Sitzungsberichte der Bayerischen Akademie der Wissenschaften, philos.-hist. Klasse*

SCI	*Scripta Classica Israelica*
SCO	*Studi Classici e Orientali*
SDHI	*Studia et documenta historiae et iuris*
SE	*Studi Etruschi*
SEG	*Supplementum Epigraphicum Graecum*
*SIG*³	W. Dittenberger, *Sylloge Inscriptionum Graecarum*, 3rd edn. 4 vols. Leipzig 1915–24
SMSR	*Studi e Materiali di Storia delle Religioni*
SNG von Aulock	*Sylloge Nummorum Graecorum, Deutschland, Sammlung von Aulock*
SP	A. S. Hunt, C. C. Edgar, *Select Papyri*. London and New York, 1932–4
StClasice	*Studii Clasice*
SymbOsl	*Symbolae Osloenses*
SZ	see ZRG
TabPomp	L. Bove, *Documenti processuali dalle Tabulae Pompeianae di Murecine*. Naples, 1979
TabVindol	A. K. Bowman, J. D. Thomas, *Vindolanda: the Latin Writing-Tablets* (Britannia Monograph Series no. 4, London, 1983)
TAM	E. Kalinka *et al.*, *Tituli Asiae Minoris*. Vienna, 1901–
TAPA	*Transactions of the American Philological Association*
TLL	*Thesaurus Linguae Latinae*, Leipzig 1890–
TransPhilSoc	*Transactions of the Philological Society*
UBHJ	*University of Birmingham Historical Journal*
VAHD	*Vjesnik za arheologiju i historiju dalmatinsku (continuation of Bull. Dalm.)*
VerhandAkWet	*Verhandelingen van de Koninklijke Akademie voor Wetenschappen, Letteren en Schone Kunsten van België, Klasse der Letteren*
WChr	U. Wilcken, *Grundzüge und Chrestomathie der Papyruskunde, Historischer Teil*, II. Leipzig–Berlin, 1912
WJA	*Würzburger Jahrbücher für die Altertumswissenschaft*
WS	*Wiener Studien*
YCS	*Yale Classical Studies*
ZDPalV	*Zeitschrift des Deutschen Palästina-Vereins*
ZPE	*Zeitschrift für Papyrologie und Epigraphik*
ZRG	*Zeitschrift der Savigny-Stiftung für Rechtsgeschichte*

A. GENERAL STUDIES

1. Abaecherli Boyce, A. 'The origin of ornamenta triumphalia', *CPh* 37 (1942) 130–41
2. Balsdon, J. P. V. D. *Romans and Aliens*. London, 1979
3. Beard, M. and Crawford, M. H. *Rome in the Late Republic*. London, 1985
4. Beloch, K. H. *Die Bevölkerung der griechisch-römischen Welt*. Leipzig, 1886
5. Béranger, J. *Recherches sur l'aspect idéologique du principat*. Basel, 1953

6. Blagg, T. and Millet, M. (eds.) *The Early Roman Empire in the West.* Oxford, 1990
7. Bradford, J. S. *Ancient Landscapes.* London, 1957
8. Braund, D. C. *Augustus to Nero: a Sourcebook on Roman History 31 B.C.–A.D. 68.* London and Sydney, 1985
9. Brunt, P. A. *Italian Manpower 225 B.C.–A.D. 14.* Oxford, 1971
10. Brunt, P. A. Review of Syme, R. *Roman Papers* III (Oxford, 1984), *CR* 34 (1984) 349–50
11. Brunt, P. A. *The Fall of the Roman Republic and Related Essays.* Oxford, 1988
12. Brunt, P. A. *Roman Imperial Themes.* Oxford, 1990
13. Cairns, F. *Generic Composition in Greek and Roman Poetry.* Edinburgh, 1972
14. Charles-Picard, G. *Augustus and Nero. The Secret of Empire* (transl. by L. Ortzen). London, 1966
15. Chaumont, M. 'L'Arménie entre Rome et l'Iran. 1. De l'avènement d'Auguste a l'avènement de Dioclétien', *ANRW* II, 9.1 (1976) 71–194
16. Chisholm, K. and Ferguson, J. *The Augustan Age.* Oxford, 1981
17. Clark, C. G. and Haswell, M. R. *The Economics of Subsistence Agriculture.* 4th edn. London, 1970
18. Corradi, G. *Studi ellenistici.* Turin, 1929
19. Debevoise, N. C. *A Political History of Parthia.* Chicago, 1938; repr. 1968
20. Deroux, C. (ed.) *Studies in Latin Literature and Roman History* (Coll. Latomus 164, 168, 180, 196) Brussels, 1979–86
21. Dilke, O. A. W. *The Roman Land Surveyors.* Newton Abbot, 1971
22. Dudley, D. R. *Urbs Roma.* London, 1967
23. Dudley, D. R. (ed.) *Silver Latin:* 1. *Neronians and Flavians.* London, 1972
24. Duncan-Jones, R. *The Economy of the Roman Empire. Quantitative Studies.* Cambridge 1974, 2nd edn 1982
25. Dyson, S. L. 'Native revolts in the Roman Empire', *Hist.* 20 (1971) 239–74
26. Esser, A. *Cäsar und die julisch-claudischen Kaiser im biologisch-ärtztlichen Blickfeld* (*Janus* Suppl. 1). Leiden, 1958
27. Finley, M. I. (ed.) *Studies in Roman Property.* Cambridge, 1976
28. Finley, M. I. *Politics in the Ancient World.* Cambridge, 1983
29. Fraser, P. M. and Matthews, E. (eds.) *A Lexicon of Greek Personal Names,* 1. Oxford, 1987
30. Friedlaender, L. *Darstellungen aus der Sittengeschichte Roms.* 10th edn. 4 vols. Leipzig, 1922
31. Gabba, E. 'The historians and Augustus', in C 176 61–88
32. Gapp, K. S. 'Famine in the Roman world from the founding of Rome to the time of Trajan'. Diss., Princeton, 1934
33. Garnsey, P. *Famine and Food Supply in the Graeco-Roman World: Responses to Risk and Crisis.* Cambridge, 1988
34. Garnsey, P. and Saller, R. *The Roman Empire. Economy, Society and Culture.* London, 1987
35. Garzetti, A. *From Tiberius to the Antonines* (English transl.). London, 1974
36. Gaudemet, J. 'A propos d'un "héritage" romain des monarchies

hellénistiques', *Ktema* 3 (1978) 165–75 (= *Les gouvernants à Rome* (Antiqua 31) 133–43. Naples, 1985)

37. Gianfrotta, P.-A. and Pomey, P. *Archeologia subacquea.* Milan, 1981
38. Gilbert, R. *Die Beziehungen zwischen Prinzeps und stadtrömischer Plebs im frühen Prinzipat.* Bochum, 1976
39. Giovannini, A. *Consulare Imperium* (Schweiz. Beiträge zur Altertumswissenschaft 16). Basel, 1983
39A. Gold, B. K. (ed.) *Literary and Artistic Patronage in Ancient Rome.* Austin, TX, 1982
40. Greene, K. *The Archaeology of the Roman Economy.* London, 1986
41. Gros, P. and Torelli, M. *Storia dell'urbanistica. Il mondo romano.* Bari, 1988
42. Hackett, J. *Warfare in the Ancient World.* London, 1989
43. Hammond, M. *The Antonine Monarchy.* Rome, 1959
44. Hatzfeld, J. *Les trafiquants italiens dans l'orient hellénique.* Paris, 1919
45. Hopkins, K. *Conquerors and Slaves. Sociological Studies in Roman History* I. Cambridge, 1978
46. Hopkins, K. *Death and Renewal. Sociological Studies in Roman History* II. Cambridge, 1983
47. Jones, A. H. M. *Studies in Roman Government and Law.* Oxford, 1960
48. Jones, A. H. M. *The Roman Economy, Studies in Ancient Economic and Administrative History* (ed. P.A. Brunt). Oxford, 1974
49. Juster, J. *Les Juifs dans l'empire romain.* 2 vols. Paris, 1914
50. Kähler, H. *Rom und seine Welt.* 2 vols. Munich, 1958–60
51. Kähler, H. *Rom und sein Imperium.* Baden-Baden, 1962 (= *Rome and her Empire.* London, 1963)
52. Kloft, H. 'Aspekte der Prinzipatsideologie im frühen Prinzipat', *Gymn.* 91 (1984) 307–26
53. Kraft, K. *Gesammelte Aufsätze zur antiken Geschichte und Militärgeschichte.* Darmstadt, 1973
54. Kroll, W. *Die Kultur der ciceronischen Zeit.* 2 vols. Stuttgart, 1933 (reissued in 1 vol., 1963)
54A. *Die Kultur der augusteischen Zeit* (collected papers of a conference) *Klio* 67.1 (1985)
55. Kunkel, W. *Kleine Schriften.* Weimar, 1974
55A. Lefèvre, E. (ed.) *Monumentum Chiloniense. Studien zur augusteischen Zeit* (Festschr. Burck). Amsterdam, 1975
56. Lloyd, G. E. R. *Greek Science after Aristotle.* New York–London, 1973
57. Luttwak, E. *The Grand Strategy of the Roman Empire.* Baltimore, 1976
58. Martino, F. de. *Storia della costituzione romana* IV,1. Naples, 1974
59. Millar, F. *The Emperor in the Roman World (31 B.C.–A.D. 337).* London, 1977
60. Millar, F. 'The Mediterranean and the Roman revolution: politics, war and the economy', *P & P* 102 (1984) 3–24
61. Millar, F. *The Roman Empire and its Neighbours.* 2nd edn. London, 1981
62. *Misurare la terra. Centuriazione e coloni nel mondo romano. L'organizzazione del territorio in epoca romana.* Modena, 1983

63. Momigliano, A. D. *Alien Wisdom: the Limits of Hellenization.* Cambridge, 1975
64. Momigliano, A. D. *Terzo contributo alla storia degli studi classici e del mondo antico* (Storia e Letteratura 108/9). Rome, 1966
65. Mommsen, T. *Römisches Staatsrecht.* Vols. I and II 3rd edn, Leipzig, 1887; vol. III, Leipzig 1888
66. Nicolet, C. *Le métier de citoyen dans la Rome républicaine.* Paris, 1976; transl. as A 68
67. Nicolet, C. *Rome et la conquête du monde méditerranéen.* 2 vols. Paris, 1977; 2nd edn. I vol. Paris, 1979
68. Nicolet, C. *The World of the Citizen in Republican Rome.* London, 1980
69. Nicolet, C. *L'inventaire du monde. Géographie et politique aux origines de l'Empire romain.* Paris, 1988; transl. as A 70
70. Nicolet, C. *Space, Geography and Politics in the Early Roman Empire.* Ann Arbor, 1991
71. Nippel, W. *Aufruhr und 'Polizei' in der römischen Republik.* Stuttgart, 1988
72. Ogilvie, R. M. *Roman Literature and Society.* Brighton, 1980
73. Peters, F. E. *The Harvest of Hellenism.* London, 1972
73A. Pippidi, D. M. (ed.) *Assimilation et résistance à la culture gréco-romaine dans le monde ancien.* Bucharest–Paris, 1976
73B. 'Politics and art in Augustan literature', *Arethusa* 5.1 (1972)
74. Premerstein, A. von *Vom Werden und Wesen des Principats* (*ABAW* 15). Munich, 1937
75. *Princeton Encyclopedia of Classical Sites.* Princeton, 1975
76. *Prosopographia Imperii Romani* I–IV edited by E. Groag and A. Stein; V edited by L. Petersen. Berlin–Leipzig, 1933–
77. Purcell, N. 'Maps, lists, money, order and power', *JRS* 80 (1990) 178–82
78. Quinn, K. 'Poet and audience', *ANRW* II, 30.1 (1982) 75–180
79. Rawson, E. D. *Intellectual Life in the Late Roman Republic.* London, 1985
80. Reinhold, M. *The Golden Age of Augustus.* Toronto, 1978
81. Rich, J. W. *Declaring War in the Roman Republic in the Period of Transmarine Expansion* (Coll. Latomus 149). Brussels, 1976
82. Ridley, R. T. 'Pompey's command in the 50s: how cumulative?', *RhM* 126 (1983) 136–48
82A. *La rivoluzione romana: inchiesta tra gli antichisti* (Biblioteca di Labeo 6). Naples, 1982
83. Rostovtzeff, M. I. *Social and Economic History of the Roman Empire.* 2nd edn. 2 vols. Oxford, 1957
84. Rowell, H. T. *Rome in the Augustan Age.* Norman, OK, 1962
85. Rykwert, J. *The Idea of a Town. The Anthropology of Urban Form in Rome, Italy and the Ancient World.* Princeton, 1976
86. Sherk, R. K. *The Roman Empire: Augustus to Hadrian* (Translated Documents of Greece and Rome 6). Cambridge, 1988
87. Sherwin-White, A. N. *The Roman Citizenship.* 2nd edn. Oxford, 1973
88. Sherwin-White, A. N. 'The Lex Repetundarum and the political ideas of Gaius Gracchus', *JRS* 72 (1982) 18–31
89. Sherwin-White, A. N. *Roman Foreign Policy in the East.* London, 1984

90. Ste Croix, G. E. M. de *The Class Struggle in the Ancient Greek World.* London, 1981

91. Stier, H. E. 'Augustusfriede und römische Klassik', *ANRW* II, 2 (1975) 3–54 (= *Kleine Schriften*, Beiträge zur klassischen Philologie 109, Meisenheim, 1979)

92. Sullivan, J. P. *Literature and Politics in the Age of Nero.* Ithaca, NY, 1985

93. Syme, R. *The Roman Revolution.* Oxford, 1939

94. Syme, R. *Roman Papers.* 7 vols. Oxford, 1979–91 (I, II: 1979; III: 1984; IV, V: 1988; VI, VII: 1991)

95. Syme, R. *The Augustan Aristocracy.* Oxford, 1986

95A. *Thought* 55.216 (1980). (Roman Empire anniversary issue)

96. *L'Urbs. Espace urbain et histoire (Ier siècle av. J.-C.–IIIe siècle ap. J.-C.)* Collection de l'école française de Rome 98). Rome, 1987

97. Versnel, H. *Triumphus.* Leiden, 1970

98. Veyne, P. *Le pain et le cirque.* Paris, 1976

99. *Villes et campagnes de l'Empire romain, Actes du colloque d' Aix-en-Provence 1980.* Aix, 1982

100. Wallace-Hadrill, A. 'The emperor and his virtues', *Hist.* 30 (1981) 298–323

101. Wells, C. M. *The Roman Empire.* London, 1984

102. Wickert, L. 'Neue Forschungen zum römischen Prinzipat', *ANRW* II, 1 (1974) 3–76 (with bibliography, 5–8)

103. Williams, G. W. *Tradition and Originality in Roman Poetry.* Oxford, 1968

104. Williams, G. W. *Change and Decline in Roman Poetry* (Sather Classical Lectures 45). Berkeley–Los Angeles, 1978

105. Williams, G. W. *Figures and Thought in Roman Poetry.* New Haven, 1980

106. Wilson, A. J. N. *Emigration from Italy in the Republican Age of Rome.* Manchester–New York, 1966

107. Wirszubski, C. *Libertas as a Political Idea at Rome during the Late Republic and Early Principate.* Cambridge, 1950

107A. Wirth, G. (ed.) *Romanitas-Christianitas. Untersuchungen zur Geschichte und Literatur der römischen Kaiserzeit* (Festschr. Straub). Berlin, 1982

108. Wiseman, T. P. (ed.) *Roman Political Life 90 B.C.–A.D. 69.* Exeter, 1985

109. Wiseman, T. P. *Roman Studies Literary and Historical.* Liverpool, 1987

110. Yavetz, Z. *Plebs and Princeps.* Oxford, 1969; 2nd edn. New Brunswick, NJ, 1988

111. Yuge, T. and Doi, M. (eds.) *Forms of Control and Subordination in Antiquity.* Leiden, 1988

B. SOURCES

I. WORKS ON ANCIENT AUTHORS

1. *Acta diui Augusti* I (only this volume published), edited by S. Riccobono *et al.* Rome, 1945

2. Albrecht, M. von 'Properz als augusteischer Dichter', *WS* 16 (1982) 220–36

3. Ambrose, J. W. 'Horace on foreign policy. Odes 4.4', *CJ* 69 (1973/4) 26–33

4. Anderson, R. D., Parsons, P. J. and Nisbet, R. G. M. 'Elegiacs by Gallus from Qaṣr Ibrîm', *JRS* 69 (1979) 125–55

5. André J. *La vie et l'œuvre d'Asinius Pollion*. Paris, 1949

6. Anna, G. d'. 'Cornelio Gallo, Virgilio e Properzio', *Athenaeum* 59 (1981) 284–98

7. Armstrong, D. 'Horatius eques et scriba: Satires 1.6 and 2.7', *TAPA* 116 (1986) 255–88

8. Badian, E. 'Nobiles amici: art and literature in an aristocratic society', *CP* 80 (1985) 341–57

9. Baldwin, B. *Suetonius*. Amsterdam, 1983

10. Ball, R. J. 'The politics of Tibullus: Augustus, Messalla, and Macer', *GB* 10 (1981) 135–42

11. Balsdon, J. P. V. D. 'Dionysius on Romulus: a political pamphlet?', *JRS* 61 (1971) 18–27

12. Beaujeu, J. 'Le frère de Quirinus (à propos de Virgile, Enéide I 292 et de Properce IV 1, 9)', *Mélanges Boyancé*, 57–72. Rome, 1974

13. Bellemore, J. *Nicolaus of Damascus, Life of Augustus*. Bristol, 1984

14. Bilde, P. *Flavius Josephus between Jerusalem and Rome. His Life, his Works, and their Importance*. Sheffield, 1988

15. Bowersock, G. W. 'Historical problems in late Republican and Augustan classicism', *Le classicisme à Rome* (Entretiens Hardt 25) 57–78. Vandoeuvres, 1978

16. Bowersock, G. W. 'The addressee of the eighth eclogue. A response', *HSCP* 82 (1978) 201–2

17. Brink, C. O. *Horace on Poetry* III. Cambridge, 1982

18. Broshi, M. 'The credibility of Josephus', *JJS* 33 (1982) 379–84

19. Brunt, P. A. 'Marcus Aurelius in his Meditations', *JRS* 64 (1974) 1–20

20. Bultmann, R. *The History of the Synoptic Tradition*. 2nd edn. London, 1972

21. Burck, E. 'Die Rolle des Dichters und der Gesellschaft in der augusteischen Dichtung', *A & A* 21 (1975) 12–35

22. Cairns, F. 'Propertius on Augustus' marriage law (II, 7)', *GB* 8 (1979) 185–204

23. Cairns, F. 'Propertius and the battle of Actium (4.6)', in B 204, 129–68

24. Carter, J. M. (ed.) *Suetonius, Diuus Augustus*. Bristol, 1982

25. Charles, R. H. *The Apocrypha and Pseudepigrapha of the Old Testament*. 2 vols. Oxford, 1913

26. Charlesworth, J. H. *Old Testament Pseudepigrapha*. 2 vols. London, 1983–5

27. Chilver, G. E. F. *A Historical Commentary on Tacitus' Histories, 1 and 2*. Oxford, 1979; *4 and 5*, edited by G. B. Townend. Oxford, 1985

28. Christ, K. 'Tacitus und der Prinzipat', *Hist.* 27 (1978) 449–87

29. Claassen, J. M. 'Error and the imperial household; an angry god and the exiled poet's fate', *AClass* 30 (1987) 31–47

30. Coffey, M. *Roman Satire*, 2nd edn. Bristol, 1989

31. Cohen, S. J. D. *Josephus in Galilee and Rome: his Vita and Development as a Historian*. Leiden, 1979

32. Curran, L. C. 'Transformation and anti-Augustanism in Ovid's "Metamorphoses"', *Arethusa* 5.1 (1972) 71–91

33. Daly, L. J. 'Livy's veritas and the spolia opima. Politics and the heroics of A. Cornelius Cossus', *AncW* 4 (1981) 49–63

34. Deininger, J. 'Livius und der Prinzipat', in A54A, 265–72

35. Desch, W. 'Horazens Beziehung zu Maecenas', *Eranos* 79 (1981) 33–45

36. Dobesch, G. 'Nikolaos von Damaskus und die Selbstbiographie des Augustus', *GB* 7 (1978) 91–174

37. Du Quesnay, I. M. le M. 'Virgil's first eclogue', *Papers of the Liverpool Latin Seminar* 3 (1981) 29–182

38. Duckworth, H. T. F. *A Commentary on the Fifty Third Book of Cassius Dio's Roman History* (University of Toronto Studies, Philological Series 4). Toronto, 1916

39. Duret, L. 'Dans l'ombre des plus grands: I. Poètes et prosateurs mal connus de l'époque augustéenne', *ANRW* II, 30. 3 (1983) 1447–560

40. Eisenhut, W. 'Deus Caesar. Augustus in den Gedichten des Properz', in A 107A, 98–108

41. Elia, S. d'. 'L'esilio di Ovidio e alcuni aspetti della storia Augustea', *AFLN* 5 (1955) 95–157

42. Fadinger, V. *Die Begründung des Prinzipats. Quellenkritische und staatsrechtliche Untersuchungen zu Cassius Dio und der Parallelüberlieferung.* Berlin, 1969

43. Fairweather, J. 'Ovid's autobiographical poem, *Tristia* 4.10', *CQ* 37 (1987) 181–96

44. Fantham, R. E. 'Ovid, Germanicus, and the composition of the Fasti', *Papers of the Liverpool Latin Seminar* 5 (1985) 243–81

45. Farron, S. 'Aen. VI 826–35 (the vision of Julius Caesar and Pompey) as an attack on Augustan propaganda', *AClass* 23 (1980) 53–68

46. Farron, S. 'The Aeneas–Dido episode as an attack on Aeneas' mission and Rome', *G & R* 27 (1980) 34–47

47. Farron, S. 'Aeneas' revenge for Pallas as a criticism of Aeneas', *AClass* 29 (1986) 69–93

48. Feldman, L. H. *Josephus and Modern Scholarship, 1937–1980.* Berlin, 1984

49. Feldman, L. H. 'Flavius Josephus revisited: the man, his writings, and his significance', *ANRW* II, 21.2 (1984) 763–862

50. Feldman, L. H. *Josephus: a Supplementary Bibliography.* New York, 1986

51. Fitton-Brown, A. D. 'The unreality of Ovid's Tomitan exile', *LCM* 10 (1985) 18–22

52. Fornaro, P. *Flavio Giuseppe, Tacito et l'Impero.* Turin, 1980

53. Fraenkel, E. *Horace.* Oxford, 1957

54. Gabba, E. 'Progetti di riforme economiche e fiscali in uno storico dell'età dei Severi', *Studi Fanfani* I, 39–68. Milan, 1962

55. Gabba, E. *Appiani Bellorum Civilium Liber Quintus.* Florence, 1970

56. Gabba, E. 'La "Storia di Roma arcaica" di Dionigi d'Alicarnasso', *ANRW* II, 30.1 (1982) 799–816

57. Gabba, E. 'Political and cultural aspects of the classical revival in the Augustan age', *ClAnt* I (1982) 43–65

58. Galinsky, G. K. 'Some aspects of Ovid's golden age', *GB* 10 (1981)
    193–205
59. Gascou, J. *Suétone historien*. Rome, 1984
60. Getty, R. J. 'Romulus, Roma, and Augustus in the sixth book of the
    Aeneid', *CPh* 45 (1950) 1–12
61. Ginsburg, J. *Tradition and Theme in the Annals of Tacitus*. Salem, NH, 1981
62. Goodyear, F. R. D. *The Annals of Tacitus I (Annals 1, 1–54)*. Cambridge,
    1972; *II (1, 55–11)*. Cambridge, 1981
63. Goold, G. P. 'The cause of Ovid's exile', *ICS* 8 (1983) 94–107
64. Gosling, A. 'Tibullus 2.5 and Augustan propaganda', *EMC* 31 (1987)
    333–9
65. Gow, A. S. F. and Page, D. L. *The Garland of Philip*. Cambridge, 1968
66. Grant, R. M. *Eusebius as Church Historian*. Oxford, 1980
67. Green, P. 'Carmen et error. Πρόφασις and αἰτία in the matter of Ovid's
    exile', *ClAnt* 1 (1982) 202–20
68. Griffin, J. 'Augustan poetry and the life of luxury', *JRS* 66 (1976) 87–105
69. Griffin, J. 'Propertius and Antony', *JRS* 67 (1977) 17–26
70. Griffin, J. 'The fourth Georgic, Virgil and Rome', *G & R* 26 (1979)
    61–80
71. Griffin, M. *Seneca. A Philosopher in Politics*. Oxford, 1976
72. Grimal, P. 'Poésie et "propagande" au temps d'Auguste', *CHM* 8 (1964)
    54–75
73. Grimal, P. 'Jupiter, Anchise et Vulcain: trois révélations sur le destin de
    Rome', in Diggle, J., Hall, J. B. and Jocelyn, H. D. (eds.) *Studies in Latin
    Literature . . . in Honour of C. O. Brink* (Camb. Phil. Soc. Suppl. Vol. 15),
    1–14. Cambridge, 1989
74. Hahn, H. 'Untersuchungen zur Autobiographie des Kaisers Augustus'.
    Diss., Leipzig, 1957
75. Hahn, H. 'Neue Untersuchungen zur Autobiographie des Kaisers
    Augustus', *La Nouvelle Clio* 10 (1958–60) 137–48
76. Hanslik, R. 'Die Augustusvita Suetons', *WS* 67 (1954) 99–144
77. Harrison, S. J. 'Augustus, the poets, and the *spolia opima*', *CQ* 39 (1989)
    408–14
78. Harvey, F. D. '"Cognati Caesaris": Ovid *Amores* I 2, 51–2', *WS* 17 (1983)
    89–90
79. Hellegouarc'h, J. 'Les buts de l'œuvre historique de Velleius Paterculus',
    Latomus 23 (1964) 669–84
80. Hemer, C. J. *The Letters to the Seven Churches of Asia in their Local Setting*.
    Sheffield, 1986
81. Hemer, C. J. *The Book of Acts in the Setting of Hellenistic History*. Tübingen,
    1989
82. Hermes, J. C. 'Cornelius Gallus und Vergil. Das Problem der
    Umarbeitung des vierten Georgica-Buches'. Diss., Münster, 1977
83. Herter, H. 'Das Concilium Deorum im 1. Metamorphosenbuch Ovids',
    in A 107A, 109–24
84. Heubner, H. *P. Cornelius Tacitus: die Historien*. 5 vols. Heidelberg,
    1963–82

84A. Highet, G. *Juvenal the Satirist*. Oxford, 1954
85. Holleman, A. W. J. 'Ovid and politics', *Hist.* 20 (1971) 458-66
86. Hollis, A. S. *Ovid, Ars Amatoria, Book 1*. Oxford, 1977
87. Horsfall, N. 'Maecenas, Horace and the Georgics once more', *Macquarie Ancient Hist. Association* 3, 1981
88. Horsfall, N. *Cornelius Nepos. A Selection, Including the Lives of Cato and Atticus*. Oxford, 1989
89. Horsfall, N. 'Virgil and Marcellus' education', *CQ* 39 (1989) 266–7
89A. Hubbard, M. *Propertius*. London, 1974
90. Hurst, A. 'Un critique grec dans la Rome d'Auguste: Denys d'Halicarnasse', *ANRW* II, 30.1 (1982) 839–65
91. Janssen, O. 'De verbanning van Ovidius: waarheid of fictie?', *Coll. Francisc. Neerlandica* 5.3 (1981) no. 3, 77–105
92. Jeffreys, E., Jeffreys, M. and Scott, R. *The Chronicle of John Malalas. A Translation*. Melbourne, 1986
93. Johnson, W. R. 'The emotions of patriotism: Propertius, 4.6', *CSCA* 6 (1973) 151–80
94. Jones, C. P. *Plutarch and Rome*. Oxford, 1971
95. Kenney, E. J. and Clausen, W. (eds.) *The Cambridge History of Classical Literature*, II: *Latin Literature*. Cambridge, 1982
96. Koester, H. *Introduction to the New Testament*. 2 vols. Berlin, 1982
97. Koester, H. *Ancient Christian Gospels: their History and Development*. London, 1990
98. Koestermann, E. *Cornelius Tacitus: Annalen*. 4 vols. Heidelberg, 1963–8
99. Korfmacher, W. C. 'Vergil, spokesman for the Augustan reforms', *CJ* 51 (1955/6) 329–34
100. Kragerrud, S. 'Perusia and the Aeneid', *SymbOsl* 62 (1987) 77–87
101. Kühnert, F. 'Augusteische Dichtung und Dichtung der augusteischen Zeit', in A 54A, 118–29
102. La Penna, A. *Orazio e l'ideologia del Principato*. Turin, 1963
103. Lambrecht, U. *Herrscherbild und Prinzipatsidee in Suetons Kaiserbiographien. Untersuchungen zur Caesar- und zur Augustusvita*. Bonn, 1984
104. Lana, I. *Velleio Patercolo o della propaganda*. Turin, 1952
105. Lasserre, F. 'Strabon devant l'empire romain', *ANRW* II, 30.1 (1982) 867–96
106. Leach, E. W. 'Seneca's *Apocolocyntosis* and *De Clementia*', *Arethusa* 22 (1989) 197–230
107. Lefèvre, E. 'Horaz und Maecenas', *ANRW* II, 31.3 (1981) 1987–2029
108. Lefèvre, E. 'Die *laudes Galli* in Vergils Georgica', *WS* 20 (1986) 183–92
109. Lenel, O. *Palingenesia Iuris Civilis*. Leipzig, 1889; repr. 1960
110. Lenel, O. *Das Edictum Perpetuum*. 3rd edn. Leipzig, 1927; repr. 1974
111. Little, D. 'Politics in Augustan poetry', *ANRW* II, 30.1 (1982) 254–370
112. Lüdemann, G. *Early Christianity According to the Traditions in Acts: a Commentary*. Minneapolis, 1989
113. Lundström, S. *Ovids Metamorphosen und die Politik des Kaisers* (Stud. Lat. Upsal. 12). Stockholm, 1980
114. Lyne, R. O. A. M. 'Virgil and the politics of war', *CQ* 33 (1983) 188–203

115. Mack, B. L. *A Myth of Innocence: Mark and Christian Origins*. Philadelphia, 1988

116. McKechnie, P. 'Cassius Dio's speech of Agrippa. A realistic alternative to imperial government?', *G & R* 28 (1981) 150–5

117. McKeown, J. C. '*Fabula proposito nulla tegenda meo*: Ovid's *Fasti* and Augustan politics', in B 204, 169–87

118. Malcovati, E. (ed.) *Imperatoris Caesaris Augusti operum fragmenta.* 5th edn. Turin, 1969

119. Malcovati, E. 'Augusto fonte di Svetonio', *WS Beiheft* 8 (Festschr. R. Hanslik), 187–95. Vienna, 1977

120. Malherbe, A. J. *Paul and the Popular Philosophers.* Minneapolis, 1989

121. Manuwald, B. *Cassius Dio und Augustus.* Wiesbaden, 1979

122. Mehl, A. 'Bemerkungen zu Dios und Tacitus' Arbeitsweise und zur Quellenlage im "Totengericht" über Augustus', *Gymn.* 88 (1981) 54–64

123. Mehl, H. *Tacitus über Kaiser Claudius.* Munich, 1974

124. Mendelson, A. *Philo's Jewish Identity.* Atlanta, 1988

125. Mensching, E. 'Livius, Cossus und Augustus', *MH* 24 (1967) 12–32

126. Merkelbach, R. 'Augustus und Romulus (Erklärung von Horaz, *Carm.* 1 12, 37–40)', *Philologus* 104 (1960) 149–53

127. Mette, H. J. 'Livius und Augustus', *Gymn.* 68 (1961) 269–85

128. Millar, F. *A Study of Cassius Dio.* Oxford, 1964

129. Moehring, H. R. 'Joseph ben Matthia and Flavius Josephus: the Jewish prophet and Roman historian', *ANRW* II, 21.2 (1984) 864–944

130. Nagle, B. R. *The Poetics of Exile. Program and Polemic in the Tristia and Epistulae ex Ponto of Ovid* (Coll. Latomus 170). Brussels, 1980

131. Nikiprowetzky, V. *La troisième Sibylle.* Paris, 1970

132. Nisbet, R. G. M. 'Horace's *Epodes* and History', in B 204, 1–20

133. Nisbet, R. G. M. and Hubbard, M. *Horace, Odes Book* I. Oxford, 1970; *Book* II. Oxford, 1978

134. Norberg, D. 'La divinité d'Auguste dans la poésie d'Horace', *Eranos* 44 (1946) 389–403

135. Ogilvie, R. M. *A Commentary on Livy 1–5.* Oxford, 1965

135A. Otis, B. *Virgil: a Study in Civilized Poetry.* Oxford, 1963

136. Paladini, M. L. 'A proposito della tradizione poetica sulla battaglia di Azio', *Latomus* 17 (1958) 240–69, 462–75

137. Paratore, E. 'Letteratura pagana nella Gallia romana', *Atti del colloquio sul tema La Gallia romana (1971)*, 53–86. Rome, 1973

138. Pelling, C. B. R. *Plutarch, Life of Antony.* Cambridge, 1988

139. Petersman, G. 'Cornelius Gallus und der Papyrus von Qaṣr Ibrîm', *ANRW* II, 30 (1983) 1649–55

140. Phillips, C. R. 'Rethinking Augustan poetry', *Latomus* 42 (1983) 780–818

141. Poma, G. 'Provvedimenti augustei su debiti e schiavi nell'interpretazione di Orosio', *RSA* 16 (1986) 155–64

142. Pöschl, V. *Horaz und die Politik* (SB Heidelberg 1956.4) (= *Kleine Schriften* I, 145–77. Heidelberg, 1979)

143. Pöschl, V. 'Virgil und Augustus', *ANRW* II, 31.2 (1981) 707–27

144. Putnam, M. C. J. 'The Virgilian achievement', *Arethusa* 5.1 (1972) 53–70

145. Quinn, K. 'The poet and his audience in the Augustan age', *ANRW* II, 30.1 (1982) 75–180
146. Rahn, H. 'Zum Carmen saeculare des Horaz', *Gymn.* 77 (1970) 467–79
147. Rajak, T. *Josephus: the Historian and his Society*. London, 1983
148. Reckford, K. J. 'Horace and Maecenas', *TAPA* 90 (1959) 195–208
149. Reinhold, M. 'The unhero Aeneas', *C & M* 27 (1966) 195–207
150. Reinhold, M. *From Republic to Principate: an Historical Commentary on Cassius Dio Books 49–52 (36–29 B.C.)* (American Philological Association Monographs 34). Atlanta, 1988
151. Ritter, H. W. 'Cluvius Rufus bei Josephus?', *RhM* 115 (1972) 85–91
152. Roddaz, J. M. 'De César à Auguste: l'image de la monarchie chez un historien du siècle des Sévères. Réflexions sur l'œuvre de Dion Cassius, à propos d'ouvrages récents', *REA* 85 (1983) 67–87
153. Rostagni, A. (ed.) *Svetonio 'de poetis' e biografi minori*. Turin, 1956
154. Rudd, W. J. N. 'Ovid and the Augustus myth', in *id. Lines of Enquiry*, 1–31. Cambridge, 1976
155. Rudd, W. J. N. 'The idea of empire in the Aeneid', *Hermathena* 134 (1983) 35–50
156. Saller, R. P. 'Anecdotes as evidence for Roman imperial history', *G & R* ser. 2, 27 (1980) 69–83
157. Sanders, E. P. and Davies, M. *Studying the Synoptic Gospels*. London, 1989
157A. Santirocco, M. *Unity and Design in Horace's Odes*. Chapel Hill, 1986
158. Scardigli, B. and Delbianco, P. *Nicolao di Damasco, Vita di Augusto*. Florence, 1983
159. Schäfer, P. 'New Testament and hekhalot literature', *JJS* 38 (1984) 19–35
160. Schalit, A. *Namenwörterbuch zu Flavius Josephus*. Leiden, 1968
161. Schultze, C. 'Dionysius of Halicarnassos and his audience', in Moxon, I. S., Smart, J. D. and Woodman, A. J. (eds.) *Past Perspectives*, 121–41. Cambridge, 1986
162. Schwartz, D. R. 'Josephus and Nicolaus on the Pharisees', *JSJ* 14 (1983) 157–71
163. Scott-Kilvert, I. (transl.). *Cassius Dio. The Roman History: the Reign of Augustus*. Harmondsworth, 1987
164. Stahl, H. P. *Propertius: 'Love' and 'War'. Individual and State under Augustus*. Berkeley–Los Angeles, 1985
165. Stambaugh, J. E. and Balch, D. L. *The New Testament in its Social Environment*. Philadelphia, 1986
166. Starr, C. G. 'Horace and Augustus', *AJPh* 90 (1969) 58–64 (= *Essays on Ancient History*, 241–7. Leiden, 1979)
167. Steidle, W. 'Beobachtungen zum Geschichtswerk des Cassius Dio', *WJA* 14 (1988) 203–24
168. Stern, M. *Greek and Latin Authors on Jews and Judaism*. 3 vols. Jerusalem, 1974–84
169. Stone, M. E. (ed.) *Jewish Writings of the Second Temple Period. Apocrypha, Pseudepigrapha, Qumran Sectarian Writings, Philo, Josephus* (Compendia Rerum Iudaicarum ad Novum Testamentum, Sect. II). Assen, 1984

170. Strack, H. L. and Stemberger, G. *Introduction to the Talmud and Midrash* (transl. by M. Bockmuehl). Edinburgh, 1991
171. Stroh, W. 'Tröstende Musen: zur literarhistorischen Stellung und Bedeutung von Ovids Exilgedichten', *ANRW* II, 31.4 (1981) 2638–84
172. Strzelecki, W. *C. Atei Capitonis Fragmenta.* Leipzig, 1967
173. Sullivan, J. 'The politics of elegy', *Arethusa* 5.1 (1972) 17–34
174. Sumner, G. V. 'The truth about Velleius Paterculus: Prolegomena', *HSCP* 74 (1970) 257–97
175. Swan, P. M. 'Cassius Dio on Augustus: a poverty of annalistic sources?', *Phoenix* 41 (1987) 272–91
176. Syme, R. *Tacitus.* Oxford, 1958
177. Syme, R. 'Livy and Augustus', *HSCP* 64 (1959), 27–87 (= A 94, I, 400–54)
178. Syme, R. *Ten Studies in Tacitus.* Oxford, 1970
179. Syme, R. *History in Ovid.* Oxford, 1978
180. Syme, R. 'Janus and Parthia in Horace', in Diggle, J., Hall, J. B. and Jocelyn, H. D. (eds.) *Studies in Latin Literature . . . in Honour of C. O. Brink.* (Camb. Phil. Soc. Suppl. Vol. 15), 113–24. Cambridge, 1989 (= A 94, VI, 441–50)
181. Tarrant, R. J. 'The addressee of Virgil's eighth eclogue', *HSCP* 82 (1978) 197–9
182. Thollard, P. 'La notion de civilisation dans les livres III et IV de Strabon', *Annales littéraires de la Faculté de Besançon* (1987)
183. Thorley, J. 'The nativity-census. What does Luke actually say?'. *G & R* 26 (1979) 81–4
184. Toher, M. 'The date of Nicolaus' βίος Καίσαρος', *GRBS* 26 (1985) 199–206
185. Torelli, M. 'Contributi al Supplemento del *CIL* IX', *RAL* 8, 24 (1969) 9–48
186. Traill, D. A. 'Horace C. 1 3. A political ode?', *CJ* 78 (1982/3) 131–7
187. Voit, L. 'Horaz-Merkur-Augustus (zu Horaz, C. II 17, I 10, I 2)', *Gymn.* 89 (1982) 479–96
188. Wacholder, B. Z. *Nicolaus of Damascus.* Berkeley, 1962
189. Wagenvoort, H. 'The crime of fratricide (Horace *Epode* 7, 18)', in Wagenvoort, H. (ed.) *Studies in Roman Literature, Culture and Religion,* 169–83. Leiden, 1956
190. Wallace-Hadrill, A. *Suetonius: the Scholar and his Caesars.* London, 1983
191. Wallace-Hadrill, A. 'Time for Augustus: Ovid, Augustus, and the *Fasti*', in Whitby, L. M., Hardie, P. R. and Whitby, M. (eds.) *Homo Viator* (Classical Essays for John Bramble), 221–30. Bristol–Oak Park, IL, 1987
191A. Walsh, P. G. *Livy* (New Surveys in the Classics 8). Oxford, 1974
192. Watson, L. '*Epode* 9, or The Art of Falsehood', in Whitby, L. M., Hardie, P. and Whitby, M. (eds.) *Homo Viator* (Classical Essays for John Bramble), 119–30. Bristol–Oak Park, IL, 1987
193. Wellesley, K. *Cornelius Tacitus: the Histories, Book* III. Sydney, 1972
194. Wickert, L. 'Horaz und Augustus', *WJA* 2 (1947) 158–72
195. Wiedemann, T. 'The political background to Ovid's *Tristia* II', *CQ* 25 (1975) 264–71

196. Williams, G. 'Horace Odes I 12 and the succession to Augustus', *Hermathena* 118 (1974) 147–55

197. Williams, G. *Technique and Ideas in the Aeneid.* New Haven–London, 1983

197A. Wiseman, T. P. *Cinna the Poet and other Roman Essays.* Leicester, 1974

198. Wiseman, T. P. 'Calpurnius Siculus and the Claudian civil war', *JRS* 72 (1982) 57–67 (= A 109, 86–96)

199. Wiseman, T. P. 'Cybele, Virgil and Augustus', in B 204, 117–28

200. Wistrand, E. *Horace's Ninth Epode and its Historical Background.* Göteborg, 1958

201. Witke, C. *Horace's Roman Odes. A Critical Examination (Mnemosyne* Suppl. 77). Leiden, 1983

202. Woodman, A. J. *Velleius Paterculus: the Tiberian Narrative.* Cambridge, 1977

203. Woodman, A. J. *Velleius Paterculus: the Caesarian and Augustan Narrative.* Cambridge, 1983

204. Woodman, A. J. and West, D. (eds.) *Poetry and Politics in the Age of Augustus.* Cambridge, 1984

205. Zecchini, G. *Il carmen de bello actiaco. Storiografia e lotta politica in età augustea (Historia* Einzelschr. 51). Stuttgart, 1987

2. EPIGRAPHY

206. Arangio-Ruiz, V. 'Testi e Documenti VI, L'iscrizione leidense di Augusto', *BIDR* 64 (1961) 323–42

207. Atkinson, K. M. T. '*Restitutio in integrum* and *iussum Augusti Caesaris* in an inscription at Leyden', *RIDA* 7 (1960) 228–72

208. Badian, E. 'Notes on some documents from Aphrodisias concerning Octavian', *GRBS* 25 (1984) 157–70

209. Balland, A. 'Q. Veranius cos. ord. 49 et sa famille', *Fouilles de Xanthos* VII (*Inst. français d'études anatoliennes*) 79–102. Paris, 1981

210. Bivona, L. *Iscrizioni latine lapidarie del Museo di Palermo.* Palermo, 1970

211. Bogaers, J. E. 'King Cogidubnus: another reading of *RIB* 91', *Britannia* 10 (1979) 243–54

212. Bove, L. *Documenti processuali dalle tabulae Pompeianae di Murecine.* Naples, 1979

213. Bove, L. *Documenti di operazioni finanziarie dall'archivio dei Sulpici.* Naples, 1984

214. Brunt, P. A. 'C. Fabricius Tuscus and an Augustan dilectus', *ZPE* 13 (1974) 161–85

215. Brunt, P. A. and Moore, J. M. (eds.) *Res Gestae divi Augusti: the Achievements of the Divine Augustus.* Oxford, 1967

216. Carter, J. M. 'A new fragment of Octavian's inscription at Nicopolis', *ZPE* 24 (1977) 227–30

217. Cavallaro, M. A. 'Economia e religio nei ludi secolari augustei. Per una nuova interpretazione di *CIL* VI 32324; 32323, 59', *RhM* 122 (1979) 49–87

218. Coli, U. 'Nuove osservazioni e congetture sulla Tabula Hebana', *Iura* 3 (1952) 90–131

219. Collingwood, R. G. and Wright, R. P. *The Roman Inscriptions of Britain*. I: *Inscriptions on Stone*. Oxford, 1965. II: *Instrumentum Domesticum*. Fasc. 1. Gloucester, 1990

220. Crook, J. A. 'An Augustan inscription in the Rijksmuseum at Leyden, *SEG* XVIII 555', *PCPhS* 8 (1962) 23–9

221. D'Agata, A. R. M. *Decreta Pisana, CIL* XI, 1420–21. Pisa, 1980

222. D'Ors, A. *Epigrafía jurídica de la España romana*. Madrid, 1953

223. Degrassi, A. 'Frammenti di elogi e di una dedica a Romolo del Foro d'Augusto', *BCAR* 67 (1939) 5–12

224. Degrassi, A. (ed.) *Inscriptiones Italiae* XIII. Rome, 1947 and 1963

225. Degrassi, A. 'Il sepolcro dei Salvii a Ferento e le sue iscrizioni', *RPAA* 34 (1961–2) 59–77 (= *Scritti vari di antichità* III, 155–72. Venice–Trieste, 1967)

226. Degrassi, A. 'Epigraphica II', *Memorie dell'Accademia Nazionale dei Lincei*, Classe de Sc. mor., stor. e filol., 8th ser., 11 (1965) 233–47 (= *Scritti vari di antichità* III, 35–87. Venice–Trieste, 1967)

227. Ehrenberg, V. and Jones, A. H. M. *Documents Illustrating the Reigns of Augustus and Tiberius*. 2nd edn. Oxford, 1955; repr. with Addenda, 1976 and 1979

228. Engelmann, H. and Knibbe, D. 'Das Monumentum Ephesenum. Ein Vorbericht', *Epigraphica Anatolica* 8 (1986) 19–32

229. Engelmann, H. and Knibbe, D. 'Das Zollgesetz der Provinz Asia', *Epigraphica Anatolica* 14 (1989) 1–206

230. Frey, J. B. *Corpus Inscriptionum Iudaicarum*. 2 vols. Vol. I, 2nd edn with prolegomenon by B. Lifshitz, New York, 1975; vol. II, Rome, 1952

231. Frisch, P. 'Zu den Elogien des Augustusforums', *ZPE* 39 (1980) 91–8

232. Frova, A. 'L'iscrizione di Pontio Pilato a Cesarea', *RIL* 95 (1961) 419–34

233. Gagé, J. (ed.) *Res Gestae Divi Augusti*. 3rd edn. Paris, 1977

234. González, J. 'Tabula Siarensis, Fortunales Siarenses et Municipia Civium Romanorum', *ZPE* 55 (1984) 55–100

235. González, J. 'The Lex Irnitana: a new copy of the Flavian municipal law', *JRS* 76 (1986) 147–243

236. Gordon, A. E. 'Notes on the Res Gestae of Augustus', *CSCA* 1 (1968) 125–38

237. Griffin, M. T. 'The Lyons tablet and Tacitean hindsight', *CQ* 32 (1982) 404–18

238. Guarducci, M. 'Ancora una volta sul frammento dell'*Edictum de pretiis* di Diocleziano trovato a Pettorano sul Gizio', *Athenaeum* 63 (1985) 491–4

239. Habicht, C. 'New evidence on the province of Asia', *JRS* 65 (1975) 64–91

240. Hall, A. 'New light on the capture of Isaura Vetus', *Akten des VI internationalen Kongresses für griechische und lateinische Epigraphik* (Vestigia 17), 568–71. Munich, 1972

241. Hartmann, E. 'Die Gallus-Inschrift auf dem Vatikanischen Obelisken', *Gymn.* 72 (1965) 1–8

242. Henzen, W. *Acta fratrum Arvalium quae supersunt*. Berlin, 1874

243. Hoffmann, W. 'Der Widerstreit von Tradition und Gegenwart im Tatenbericht des Augustus', *Gymn.* 76 (1969) 17–33

244. Kroemer, D. 'Textkritisches zu Augustus und Tiberius (Res gestae c. 34–Tac. Ann. 6,30,3)', *ZPE* 28 (1978) 127–44

245. Kunkel, W. 'Über die Leidener Augustus-Inschrift aus Kyme', *Studi Betti* II, 591–620. Milan, 1962

246. Laffi, U. 'Le iscrizioni relative all'introduzione nel 9 a.C. del nuovo calendario della Provincia d'Asia', *SCO* 16 (1967) 5–98

247. Lauffer, S. 'Annos undeuiginti natus', *Historia* Einzelschr. 40 (Studies H. Bengtson), 174–7. Wiesbaden, 1983

248. Lesuisse, L. 'La clause transitoire de la lex de imperio Vespasiani', *RBPh* 40 (1962) 51–75

249. Levi, M. A. 'La composizione delle Res gestae diui Augusti', *RFIC* (1947) 189–210

250. Lüderitz, G. (ed.) *Corpus jüdischer Zeugnisse aus der Cyrenaica.* Wiesbaden, 1983

251. McCrum, M. and Woodhead, A. G. *Select Documents of the Principates of the Flavian Emperors* A.D. *68–96.* Cambridge, 1961

252. Manni Piraino, M. T. *Iscrizioni greche lapidarie del museo di Palermo.* Palermo, 1973

253. Millar, F. 'Imperial ideology in the Tabula Siarensis', in González, J. and Arce, J. (eds.) *Estudios sobre la Tabula Siarensis*, 11–19. Madrid, 1988

254. Michelsen, E. 'The palaeographical interference as reflected in the Latin inscriptions of Clusium and Perusia', in Bruun, P. *et al. Studies in the Romanisation of Etruria*, 247–67. Rome, 1975

255. Mitchell, S. 'Requisitioned transport in the Roman empire: a new inscription from Pisidia', *JRS* 66 (1976) 106–31

256. Moretti, L. 'Frammenti vecchi e nuovi del Commentario dei Ludi secolari', *RPAA* 55–6 (1982–4) 361–79

257. Mourgues, J.-L. 'The so-called letter of Domitian at the end of the Lex Irnitana', *JRS* 77 (1987) 78–87

258. Oliver, J. H. 'The main problem of the Augustan inscription from Cyme', *GRBS* 4 (1963) 115–22

259. Oliver, J. H. 'Octavian's inscription at Nicopolis', *AJPh* 90 (1969) 178–82

260. Paci, G. 'Possibili tracce di statuti municipali in alcune iscrizioni d'Italia concernenti un particulare tipo di munificenza privata', in *Epigrafia Juridica Romana*, 125–33. Pamplona, 1989

261. Pearse, J. L. D. 'Three *alba* of the *Collegium Fabrum Tignariorum* of Rome', *BCAR* 85 (1976–7) 163–76

262. Pekáry, T. 'Statuae meae ... argenteae steterunt in urbe xxx circiter, quas ipse sustuli. Interpretationen zu Res gestae diui Augusti 24', in A 55A, 96–108

263. Pighi, J. B. *De ludis saecularibus ... libri sex.* 2nd edn. Amsterdam, 1965

264. Pleket, H. W. *The Greek Inscriptions in the Rijksmuseum van Oudheden at Leyden.* Leiden, 1958

265. Ramage, E. S. *The Nature and Purpose of Augustus' 'Res Gestae'. (Historia Einzelschrift* 54). Wiesbaden, 1987

266. Ramage, E. S. 'The date of Augustus' Res Gestae', *Chiron* 18 (1988) 71–82

267. Rehm, A. in Kawerau, G. and Rehm, A. (eds.) *Das Delphinion in Milet*, *Milet* I. 3. Berlin, 1914

268. Rengen, W. van 'L'épigraphie grecque et latine de Syrie. Bilan d'un quart de siècle de recherches épigraphiques', *ANRW* II, 8 (1978) 31–53

269. Rey-Coquais, J.-P. 'Inscriptions grecques d'Apamée', *AAS* 23 (1973) 39–84

270. Reynolds, J. *Aphrodisias and Rome* (*JRS* Monographs 1). London, 1982

271. Richardson, J. S. 'The Tabula Contrebiensis. Roman law in Spain in the early first century B.C.', *JRS* 73 (1983) 33–41

272. Ritter, H. W. 'Überlegungen zur Inschrift des Augustusbogens auf dem Forum Romanum', *MDAI(R)* 85 (1978) 371–84

273. Robert, J. and L. *Bulletin épigraphique* in *REG* (1934–84)

274. Robert, L. *Études épigraphiques et philologiques*. Paris, 1938

275. Robert, L. *Hellenica, recueil d'épigraphie, de numismatique et d'antiquités grecques*, I–XIII. Limoges–Paris, 1940–65

276. Robert, L. 'Discussion of a place-name in the Leiden inscription', *REG* 86 (1973) 135–6

277. Roueché, C. 'Acclamations in the later Roman Empire: new evidence from Aphrodisias', *JRS* 74 (1984) 181–99

278. Salvaterra, C. 'Forum Iulium nell'iscrizione di C. Cornelius Gallus sull'obelisco Vaticano', *Aegyptus* 67 (1987) 171–81

279. Schachermeyr, F. and Merkelbach, R. *Inschriften griechischer Städten aus Kleinasien*. Bonn, 1972–

280. Seston, W. 'Le clipeus virtutis d'Arles et la composition des Res gestae divi Augusti', *CRAI* 1954, 286–97

281. Seyfarth, W. 'Potitus rerum omnium. Ein Beitrag zur Deutung der *RGDA*, Kapitel 34', *Philologus* 101 (1957) 305–23

282. Sherk, R. K. *Roman Documents from the Greek East: Senatus Consulta and Epistulae to the Age of Augustus*. Baltimore, 1969

283. Sherk, R. K. *Rome and the Greek East* (Translated Documents of Greece and Rome, 4). Cambridge, 1984

284. Smallwood, E. M. *Documents Illustrating the Principates of Gaius, Claudius and Nero*. Cambridge, 1967; Bristol, 1984

285. Solin, H. 'Ricerche epigrafiche in Ciociaria', *Epigraphica* 50 (1988) 87–104

286. Sotgiu, G. *Iscrizioni latine della Sardegna* I. Padua, 1961

287. Stiehl, R. *Die Datierung der Kapitolinischen Fasten*. Tübingen, 1957

288. Syme, R. 'Sejanus on the Aventine', *Hermes* 84 (1956) 257–66 (= A 94, 1 305–14)

289. Taylor, L. R. 'The date of the Capitoline Fasti', *CPh* 41 (1946) 1–11

290. Taylor, L. R. 'New indications of Augustan editing in the Capitoline Fasti', *CPh* 46 (1951) 73–80

291. Torelli, M. *Elogia Tarquiniensia*. Florence, 1975

292. Vassileiou, H. 'Drusus imperator appellatus in Germania (Ergänzung des Drususelogiums auf dem Forum Augusti)', *ZPE* 51 (1983) 213–14

293. Visscher, F. de *Les édits d' Auguste découverts à Cyrène*. Louvain, 1940; repr. Osnabrück, 1965

294. Volkmann, H. 'Bemerkungen zu den Res gestae diui Augusti', *Hist.* 3 (1954) 81–6

295. Volkmann, H. 'Zur Gallus-Inschrift auf dem Vatikanischen Obelisken', *Gymn.* 72 (1965) 325–30 (= *id. Endoxos Duleia* (Berlin, 1975) 191–3)

296. Weber, E. 'Zur Inschrift des Pontius Pilatus', *BJ* 171 (1971) 194–200

297. Wigtil, D. N. 'The ideology of the Greek Res Gestae', *ANRW* II, 30.1 (1982) 624–38

298. Wigtil, D. N. 'The translator of the Greek Res Gestae of Augustus', *AJPh* 103 (1982) 189–94

299. Wuilleumier, P. *Inscriptions latines des Trois Gaules. Gallia.* Suppl. 17 (1984)

300. Yavetz, Z. 'The Res Gestae and Augustus' image', in C 176, 1–36

301. Zecchini, G. 'La Tabula Siarensis e la "Dissimulatio" di Tiberio', *ZPE* 66 (1986) 23–9

3. NUMISMATICS

302. Alföldi, M. R. *Die Fundmünzen der Römischen Zeit in Deutschland* IV.3/1. Berlin, 1970

303. Allen, D. 'The Belgic dynasties of Britain and their coins', *Archaeologia* 90 (1944) 1–46

304. Allen, D. 'A study of the Dobunnic coinage', in Clifford, E. M. (ed.) *Bagendon: a Belgic Oppidum*, 75–149. Cambridge, 1961

305. Allen, D. 'The origins of coinage in Britain: a reappraisal', in Frere, S. S. (ed.) *Problems of the Iron Age in Southern Britain*, 97–308. London, 1958

306. Aulock, H. von *Münzen und Städte Lykaoniens (MDAI(I)* 16). Tübingen, 1976

307. Aulock, H. von *Münzen und Städte Pisidiens 1 and 2 (MDAI(I)* 19 and 22). Tübingen, 1977, 1979

308. Aulock, H. von. *Münzen und Städte Phrygiens 1 (MDAI(I)* 25). Tübingen, 1980

309. Bay, A. 'The letters SC on Augustan aes coinage', *JRS* 62 (1972) 111–22

310. Belloni, G. G. 'Monete romane (repubblica e impero) in quanto opera d'artigianato e arte. Osservazioni e impostazione di problemi', *ANRW* II, 12. 3 (1985) 89–115

311. Burnett, A. 'Sicily', in B 312, 165–81

312. Burnett, A., Amandry, M. and Ripollès, P. P. *Roman Provincial Coinage.* 1: *From the Death of Caesar to the Death of Vitellius (44 B.C.–A.D. 69).* London–Paris, 1992

313. Burnett, A. M. 'The authority to coin in the late Republic and early Empire', *NC* 17 (1977) 37–63

314. Buttrey, T. V. 'Studies in the coinage of Marc Antony'. Diss., Princeton, 1953

315. Buttrey, T. V. 'Roman coinage of the Cyrenaica, first century B.C. to first century A.D.', in Brooke, C. N. L. (ed.) *Studies in Numismatic Method presented to Philip Grierson* 23–46. Cambridge, 1983

315A. Buttrey, T. V. 'Crete and Cyrene', in A. M. Burnett and M. H. Crawford (eds.), *The Coinage of the Roman World in the Late Republic* (BAR International Series 326), 165–74. Oxford, 1987

316. Carson, J. *Principal Coins of the Romans: II. The Principate 31 B.C.–A.D. 296.* London, 1980

316A. Chapman, A. E. 'Some first century B.C. bronze coins of Cnossos', *NC* 8 (1968) 13–26

317. Collis, J. R. 'Functional and theoretical interpretations of British coinage', *World Archaeology* 3 (1971) 71–84

318. Crawford, M. H. *Roman Republican Coin Hoards.* London, 1969

319. Crawford, M. H. *Roman Republican Coinage* I–II. Cambridge, 1974

320. Crawford, M. H. *Coinage and Money under the Roman Republic: Italy and the Mediterranean Economy.* London, 1985

321. Ercolani Cocchi, E. *Metodi di ricerca numismatica e problemi della prima monetazione imperiale, I: Augusto* (Studi di storia antica 2). Bologna, 1978

322. Grant, M. *From Imperium to Auctoritas: a Historical Study of Aes Coinage in the Roman Empire 49 B.C.–A.D. 14.* Cambridge, 1946; repr. 1969

323. Grant, M. 'A step toward world-coinage, 19 B.C.', in P. R. Coleman-Norton (ed.) *Studies in Roman Economic and Social History in Honour of A. C. Johnson*, 88–112. Princeton, 1951

324. Grant, M. *The Six Main Aes Coinages of Augustus. Controversial Studies.* Edinburgh, 1953

325. Howgego, C. J. *Greek Imperial Countermarks. Studies in the Provincial Coinage of the Roman Empire.* Roy. Num. Soc. Special Publ. 17. London, 1985

326. Imhoof-Blumer, F. *Kleinasiatische Münzen.* Sonderschr. des Öst. Arch. Inst. in Wien I, III. Vienna, 1901–2

327. Jucker, A. 'Apollo Palatinus und Apollo Actius auf augusteischen Münzen', *MH* 39 (1982) 82–100

328. Kadman, L. *The Coins of the Jewish War of 66–73 C.E.* Tel Aviv, 1960

329. Kadman, L. *The Coins of Akko Ptolemais.* Jerusalem, 1961

330. Kent, J. P. C. *Roman Coins.* London, 1978

331. Kindler, A. *The Coinage of Bostra.* Warminster, 1983

332. Kraay, C. M. *The Aes Coinage of Galba.* New York, 1956

333. Kraft, K. 'Zur Datierung der römischen Münzmeisterprägung unter Augustus', *MZ* 46/47 (1951–2) 28–35 (= *Gesammelte Aufsätze zur antiken Geldgeschichte und Numismatik* I (*Kleine Schriften* II), 42–56. Darmstadt, 1978)

334. Kraft, K. 'S(enatus) C(onsulto)', *JNG* 12 (1962) 7–49. (Repr. in Schmitthenner, W. (ed.) *Augustus*, 336–403. Darmstadt, 1969) (= *Gesammelte Aufsätze* II (*Kleine Schriften* III), 143–210. Darmstadt, 1985)

335. Kraft, K. *Zur Münzprägung des Augustus* (SB Frankfurt 7, no. 5), Wiesbaden, 1969 (= *Gesammelte Aufsätze* I (*Kleine Schriften* II), 291–337. Darmstadt, 1978)

336. Kunisz, A. *Recherches sur le monnayage et la circulation monétaire sous le règne d'Auguste.* Warsaw, 1976

337. Levick, B. M. 'Mercy and moderation on the coinage of Tiberius', in Levick, B. M. (ed.) *The Ancient Historian and his Materials*, 123–38. Farnborough, 1976

338. Levick, B. M. 'Propaganda and the imperial coinage', *Antichthon* 16 (1982) 104–16

339. Liegle, J. 'Die Münzprägung Oktavians nach dem Sieg von Actium und die augusteische Kunst', *JDAI* 56 (1941) 91–119

340. *Masada I: The Yigael Yadin Excavations 1963–1965. Final Reports. The Coins of Masada*, edited by Y. Meshorer. Jerusalem, 1989

341. Mattingly, H. and Carson, R. A. G. *Coins of the Roman Empire in the British Museum*. 6 vols. London, 1932–62

342. Mattingly, H., Sydenham, E. A., Webb, P. H. *et al. The Roman Imperial Coinage* I–V; VII; IX. London, 1923–66

343. Meshorer, Y. *Nabataean Coins*. Quedem 3. Jerusalem, 1975

344. Meshorer, Y. *Ancient Jewish Coinage*. 2 vols. New York, 1982

345. Mirnik, I. *Coin Hoards in Yugoslavia* (BAR International Series 95). Oxford, 1981

346. Newby, J. D. *A Numismatic Commentary on the Res Gestae of Augustus*. London, 1938

347. Panvini Rosati, F. 'Le emissioni in oro e argento dei "tresviri monetales" di Augusto', *ArchClass* 3 (1951) 66–85

347A. Robinson, E. S. G. *Catalogue of the Greek Coins of Cyrenaica (in the British Museum)*. London, 1927

348. Rodewald, C. *Money in the Age of Tiberius*. Manchester, 1976

349. Scheer, R. 'Vindex libertatis', *Gymn.* 78 (1971) 182–8

350. Seyrig. H. 'Le monnayage de Ptolemais en Phénice', *RN* n.s. 4 (1962) 25–50

351. Shear, J. P. 'Athenian Imperial coinage', *Hesperia* 5 (1936) 285–332

352. Smith, H. R. W. 'Problems historical and numismatic in the reign of Augustus', *University of California Publications in Classical Archaeology* II, 4. Berkeley, 1951

353. Spijkerman, A. *The Coins of the Decapolis and Provincia Arabia*. Jerusalem, 1978

354. Sutherland, C. H. V. *Coinage in Roman Imperial Policy*. London, 1951; repr. 1971

355. Sutherland, C. H. V. *The Cistophori of Augustus*. London, 1970

356. Sutherland, C. H. V. *The Emperor and the Coinage. Julio-Claudian Studies*. London, 1976

357. Sutherland, C. H. V. *The Roman Imperial Coinage*. I. Rev. edn. London, 1984

358. Sutherland, C. H. V. *Roman History and Coinage 44 B.C.–A.D. 69*. Oxford, 1987

359. Sutherland, C. H. V. and Kraay, C. M. *Catalogue of the Coins of the Roman Empire in the Ashmolean Museum* I. Oxford, 1975

360. Sydenham, E. A. *The Coinage of the Roman Republic*. London, 1952

361. Walker, D. R. *The Metrology of the Roman Silver Coinage* I *From Augustus to*

Domitian (British Archaeological Reports, Supplementary Series 5). Oxford, 1976

362. Wallace-Hadrill, A. 'Image and authority in the coinage of Augustus', *JRS* 76 (1986) 66–87

363. Wruck, W. *Die syrische Provinzialprägung von Augustus bis Traian.* Stuttgart, 1931

364. Zehnacker, H. *Tensions et contradictions dans l'empire au 1ᵉʳ siècle: les témoignages numismatiques* (Entretiens Hardt 33) 321–57. Vandoeuvres–Geneva, 1987

4. PAPYROLOGY

365. Badian, E. 'Notes on the Laudatio of Agrippa', *CJ* 76 (1980/1) 97–109

366. Balconi, C. 'Documenti greci e latini d'Egitto di età augustea', *Aegyptus* 56 (1976) 208–86

367. Bowman, A. K. 'Papyri and Roman imperial history, 1960–1975', *JRS* 66 (1976) 153–74

368. Fink, R. O., Hoey, A. S. and Snyder, W. F. 'The *Feriale Duranum*', *YCS* 7 (1940) 1–222

369. Gray, E. W. 'The imperium of M. Agrippa, a note on P. Colon. inv. No. 4701', *ZPE* 6 (1970) 227–38

370. Gronewald, M. 'Ein neues Fragment der Laudatio Funebris des Augustus auf Agrippa', *ZPE* 52 (1983) 61–2

371. Haslam, M. W. 'Augustus' funeral oration for Agrippa', *CJ* 75 (1979/80) 193–9

372. Koenen, L. 'Die laudatio funebris des Augustus für Agrippa auf einem neuen Papyrus (P. Colon. inv. Nr. 4701)', *ZPE* 5 (1970) 217–83 (see also 6 (1970) 239–43)

373. Lewis, N. 'P. Oxy. 2820. Whose preparations?', *GRBS* 16 (1975) 295–303

374. Lewis, N. 'P. Oxy. 2820: Gallus … Vous dites Gallus?' *CE* 123/124 (1987) 219–22

375. Lewis, N., Yadin, Y. and Greenfield, J. C. (eds.) *The Documents from the Bar Kokhba Period in the Cave of Letters: Greek Papyri (including Aramaic and Nabatean Signatures and Subscriptions).* Jerusalem, 1989

376. Luppe, W. 'P. Oxy. 2820. Ein Bericht über die politische Tätigkeit des Cornelius Gallus?', *APF* 26 (1978) 33–8

377. *Masada I: The Yigael Yadin Excavations 1963–1965. Final Reports. The Aramaic and Hebrew Ostraca and Jar Inscriptions,* edited by Y. Yadin and J. Naveh. Jerusalem, 1989

378. *Masada II: The Yigael Yadin Excavations 1963–1965. Final Reports. The Latin and Greek Documents,* edited by H. M. Cotton and J. Geiger. Jerusalem, 1989

379. Mitteis, L. and Wilcken, U. *Grundzüge und Chrestomathie der Papyruskunde.* 4 vols. Leipzig–Berlin, 1911–12

380. Montevecchi, O. *La Papirologia.* 2nd edn. Milan, 1988

381. Musurillo, H. *The Acts of the Pagan Martyrs: Acta Alexandrinorum.* Oxford, 1954

382. Musurillo, H. (ed.) *Acta Alexandrinorum*. Leipzig, 1961
383. Reinhold, M. 'Marcus Agrippa's son-in-law, P. Quinctilius Varus', *CPh* 67 (1972) 119–21
384. Sherk, R. K. 'The last two lines of the Laudatio Funebris for Agrippa', *ZPE* 41 (1981) 67–9
385. Skeat, T. C. 'The Augustan era in Egypt. A note on P. Oxy. xii 1453', *ZPE* 53 (1983) 241–4
386. Tcherikover, V. A., Fuks, A., Stern, M. *Corpus Papyrorum Judaicarum*. 3 vols. Cambridge, MA, 1957–64
387. Treu, M. 'Nach Kleopatras Tod (P. Oxy. 2820)', *Chiron* 3 (1973) 221–33
388. Wilcken, U. *Griechische Ostraka aus Ägypten und Nubien*. 2 vols. Leipzig–Berlin, 1899

C. POLITICAL HISTORY

I. THE TRIUMVIRAL PERIOD AND THE REIGN OF AUGUSTUS

1. Adcock, F. E. 'The interpretation of *Res gestae diui Augusti* 34,1', *CQ* 45 (1951) 130–5 (and in German in c 208, 230–40)
2. Adcock, F. E. 'A note on *Res gestae diui Augusti* 34, 3', *JRS* 42 (1952) 10–12
3. Aigner, H. *Die Soldaten als Machtfaktor in der ausgehenden Republik*. Innsbruck, 1974
4. Alföldy, G. 'Die Ablehnung der Diktatur durch Augustus', *Gymn.* 79 (1972) 1–12
5. André, J. M. *Mécène. Essai de biographie spirituelle*. Paris, 1967
6. André, J. M. *Le siècle d'Auguste*. Paris, 1974
7. André, J. M. 'Mécène écrivain', *ANRW* II, 30.3 (1983) 1765–87
8. Anello, P. 'La fine del secondo triumvirato', Φιλίας Χάριν (*Miscellanea in onore di Eugenio Manni*) 1 103–14. Rome, 1980
9. Arangio-Ruiz, V. 'La legislazione', in c 12A, 101–46
10. Astin, A. E. 'Augustus and *censoria potestas*', *Latomus* 22 (1963) 226–35
11. Atkinson, K. M. T. 'The governors of the province Asia in the reign of Augustus', *Hist.* 7 (1958) 300–30
12. Atkinson, K. M. T. 'Constitutional and legal aspects of the trials of Marcus Primus and Varro Murena', *Hist.* 9 (1960) 440–73
12A. *Augustus: Studi in occasione del bimillenario augusteo*. Rome, 1938
13. Badian, E. 'The quaestorship of Tiberius Nero', *Mnemosyne* 27 (1974) 160–72
14. Badian, E. '"Crisis theories" and the beginning of the principate', in A 107A, 18–41
15. Badot, P. 'A propos de la conspiration de M. Egnatius Rufus', *Latomus* 32 (1973) 606–15
16. Barnes, T. D. 'The date of Herod's death', *JTS* 19 (1968) 204–9
17. Barnes, T. D. 'Julia's child', *Phoenix* 35 (1981) 362–3
18. Bastomsky, S. J. 'Proculeius and Augustus. A note on a friendship turned sour', *Latomus* 36 (1977) 129–31

19. Bauman, R. A. 'Tiberius and Murena', *Hist.* 15 (1966) 420–33
20. Bauman, R. A. 'Tribunician sacrosanctity in 44, 36 and 35 B.C.', *RhM* 124 (1981) 166–83
21. Benario, H. W. 'Augustus Princeps', *ANRW* II, 2 (1975) 75–85
22. Bengtson, J. *Zum Partherfeldzug des Antonius, SBAW* I (1974) 1–48
23. Bengtson, H. *Kaiser Augustus.* Munich, 1981
24. Béranger, J. 'A propos d'un imperium infinitum: histoire et stylistique', *Mél. Marouzeau*, 1948, 19–27 (= C 27A, 98–106)
25. Béranger, J. 'La démocratie sous l'empire romain: les opérations électorales de la Tabula Hebana et la "destinatio"', *MH* 14 (1957) 216–40 (= C 27A, 209–42)
26. Béranger, J. 'L'accession d'Auguste et l'idéologie du "priuatus"', *Palaeologia* 7 (1958) 1–11 (= C 27A, 243–58)
27. Béranger, J. 'Diagnostic du principat: l'empereur romain, chef de parti', *REL* 37 (1959) 151–70 (= C 27A, 259–80)
27A. Béranger, J. *Principatus: Etudes de notions et d'histoire politiques dans l'Antiquité gréco-romaine.* Geneva, 1973
28. Béranger, J. 'Imperium, expression et conception du pouvoir impérial', *REL* 55 (1977) 325–54
29. Bicknell, P. J. 'Caesar, Antony, Cleopatra, and Cyprus', *Latomus* 36 (1977) 325–42
30. Birch, R. A. 'The correspondence of Augustus. Some notes on Suetonius, *Tiberius* 21.4–7', *CQ* 31 (1981) 155–61
31. Birch, R. A. 'The settlement of 26 June A.D. 4 and its aftermath', *CQ* 31 (1981) 443–56
32. Bleicken, J. *Zwischen Republik und Prinzipat: zum Charakter des Zweiten Triumvirats* (Abh. d. Akad. Wiss. Gött. Phil. – Hist. klasse, 3 Folge, nr. 185). Göttingen, 1990
33. Boatwright, M. T. 'The Pomerial extension of Augustus', *Hist.* 35 (1986) 13–27
34. Bosworth, A. B. 'Asinius Pollio and Augustus', *Hist.* 21 (1972) 441–73
35. Bosworth, A. B. 'Augustus and August: some pitfalls of historical fiction', *HSCP* 86 (1982) 151–70
36. Botermann, H. *Die Soldaten und die römische Politik in der Zeit von Caesars Tod bis zur Begründung des Zweiten Triumvirats* (Zetemata 46). Munich, 1968
37. Boucher, J. P. *Caius Cornelius Gallus.* Paris, 1966
38. Bowersock, G. W. 'Augustus on Aegina', *CQ* 14 (1964) 120–1
39. Bowersock, G. W. *Augustus and the Greek World.* Oxford, 1965
40. Bowersock, G. W. 'Augustus and the East: the succession', in C 176, 169–88
41. Braunert, H. 'Zum Eingangssatz der *Res gestae Divi Augusti*', *Chiron* 4 (1974) 343–58 (= C 44, 238–54)
42. Braunert, H. 'Die Gesellschaft des römischen Reiches im Urteil des Augustus', in A 55A, 9–54 (= C 44, 255–93)
43. Braunert, H. '*Omnium prouinciarum populi Romani ... fines auxi*: ein Entwurf', *Chiron* 7 (1977) 207–17 (= C 44, 294–304)

44. Braunert, H. *Politik, Recht und Gesellschaft in der griechisch-römischen Antike, Gesammelte Aufsätze und Reden.* Stuttgart, 1980

45. Bretone, M. 'Il "diritto antico" nella polemica antiaugustea', *QS* 4, 8 (1978) 273–91

46. Bringmann, K. '*Imperium proconsulare* und Mitregentschaft im frühen Principat', *Chiron* 7 (1977) 219–38

47. Brunt, P. A. 'The lex Valeria Cornelia', *JRS* 51 (1961) 71–83

48. Brunt, P. A. '"Augustus" e la "respublica"' in A 82A, 236–44 (in English)

49. Buchheim, H. *Die Orientpolitik des Triumvirn M. Antonius.* Heidelberg, 1960

50. Carcopino, J. *Passion et politique chez les Césars.* Paris, 1958

51. Carter, J. M. *The Battle of Actium. The Rise and Triumph of Augustus Caesar.* New York, 1970

52. Cartledge, P. 'The second thoughts of Augustus on the res publica in 28/ 7 B.C.', *Hermathena* 119 (1975) 30–40

53. Castritius, H. *Der römische Prinzipat als Republik* (Historische Studien 438). Husum, 1982

54. Ceauşescu. G. 'Augustus, der "Hellenisator" der Welt (Kommentar zu Philo, Legatio ad Gaium, 143–147)', *Klio* 69 (1987) 46–57

55. Ceauşescu, P. 'Das programmatische Edikt des Augustus (Suet. *Aug.* 28, 1) – eine missverstandene Stelle', *RhM* 124 (1981) 348–53

56. Cerami, P. 'Ideologie, terminologie e realtà costituzionale', in A 82A, 66–73

57. Chamoux, F. 'Gaius Caesar', *BCH* 74 (1950) 250–64

58. Champlin, E. 'The testament of Augustus', *RhM* 132 (1989) 154–65

59. Charbonnel, N. 'A propos de l'inscription de Kymé et des pouvoirs d'Auguste au lendemain du règlement de 27 av. n. è.', *RIDA* 26 (1979) 177–225

60. Charlesworth, M. P. 'Some fragments of the propaganda of Mark Antony', *CQ* 27 (1933) 172–7

61. Chilver, G. E. F. 'Augustus and the Roman constitution 1939–50', *Hist.* 1 (1950) 408–35

62. Christ, K. 'Zur Beurteilung der Politik des Augustus', *GWU* 19 (1968) 329–43

63. Combès, R. *Imperator. Recherches sur l'emploi et la signification du titre d'imperator dans la Rome républicaine.* Paris, 1966

64. Consigliere, L. '*Slogans' monetarie e poesia augustea.* Genoa, 1978

65. Corbett, J. H. 'The succession policy of Augustus', *Latomus* 33 (1974) 87–97

66. Corte, F. della. 'La breve *praefectura urbis* di Messalla Corvino', Φιλίας Χάριν (*Miscellanea in onore di Eugenio Manni*) II Rome, 1980. 667–77

67. Crook, J. A. 'Some remarks on the Augustan constitution', *CR* 3 (1953) 10–12

68. Crook, J. A. 'A legal point about Mark Antony's will', *JRS* 47 (1957) 36–8

69. Csillag, P. 'Das Eherecht des augusteischen Zeitalters', *Klio* 50 (1968) 111–38

70. Cuff, P. J. 'The settlement of 23 B.C. A note', *RFIC* 101 (1973) 466–77

71. Daly, L. J. 'Varro Murena, cos. 23 B.C., [magistratu motu]s est', *Hist.* 27 (1978) 83–94

72. Daly, L. J. 'The report of Varro Murena's death (Dio 54.3.5). Its mistranslation and his assassination', *Klio* 65 (1983) 245–61

73. Daly, L. J. 'Augustus and the murder of Varro Murena (cos. 23 B.C.)', *Klio* 66 (1984) 157–69

74. Daly, L. J. and Reiter, W. L. 'The Gallus-affair and Augustus' *lex Iulia maiestatis*: a study in historical chronology and causality', in A 20, I 289–311

75. De Coninck, L. *Suetonius en de Archivalia* (Verhand. Ak. Wet., Kl. der Lett. 45 (1983) no. 104). Brussels, 1983

76. Degrassi, A. 'I nomi dell'imperatore Augusto: il "praenomen imperatoris"', *Studi Volterra* v (Milan, 1971) 573–92 (= *Scritti vari di antichità* III, 353–71), Venice-Trieste, 1967

77. Deininger, J. 'Von der Republik zur Monarchie: die Ursprünge der Herrschertitulatur des Prinzipats', *ANRW* I, 1 (1972) 982–97

78. Detweiler, R. 'Historical perspectives on the death of Agrippa Postumus', *CJ* 65 (1970/1) 289–95

79. Dominguez-Sanchez, B. *La politica de Augusto*. Bogota, 1960

80. Dorey, T. A. 'Adultery and propaganda in the early Roman empire', *UBHJ* 8 (1961) 1–6

81. Earl, D. *The Age of Augustus*. London, 1968

82. Eck, W. 'Augustus' administrative Reformen: Pragmatismus oder systematisches Planen?', *AClass* 29 (1986) 105–20

83. Erkell, H. *Augustus, Felicitas, Fortuna. Lateinische Wortstudien*. Gothenburg, 1952

84. Espinosa Ruiz, U. *Debate Agrippa–Mecenas en Dion Cassio*. Madrid, 1982

85. Fabbrini, F. *L'impero di Augusto come ordinamento sovrannazionale*. Milan, 1974

86. Fabre, G. and Roddaz, J. M. 'Recherches sur la familia de M. Agrippa', *Athenaeum* 60 (1982) 84–112

87. Ferrabino, A. 'L'imperatore Cesare Augusto', in C 12A, 1–59

88. Ferrill, A. 'Prosopography and the last years of Augustus', *Hist.* 20 (1971) 718–31

89. Ferrill, A. 'Augustus and his daughter: a modern myth', in A 20, II 332–46

90. Flach, D. 'Destinatio und nominatio im frühen Prinzipat', *Chiron* 6 (1976) 193–203

91. Francisci, P. de 'La costituzione Augustea', in C 12A, 61–100

92. Frei-Stolba, R. *Untersuchungen zu den Wahlen in der römischen Kaiserzeit*. Zurich, 1967

93. Gabba, E. 'The Perusine War and Triumviral Italy', *HSCP* 75 (1971) 139–60

94. Gabba, E. 'Sesto Pompeo a Naulocho', *RCCM* 19 (1977) 389–92

95. Gardthausen, V. *Augustus und seine Zeit*. Leipzig: I, 1891; II, 1904

96. Geiger, J. 'An overlooked item of the war of propaganda between Octavian and Antony', *Hist.* 29 (1980) 112–14

97. Girardet, K. M. 'Der Rechtsstatus Oktavians im Jahre 32 v. Chr.', *RhM* 133 (1990) 322–50

98. Girardet, K. M. 'Die Entmachung des Konsulates im Übergang von der Republik zur Monarchie', *Festgabe für Peter Steinmetz* (Palingenesia 30), ed. Görler, W. and Koster, S., 89–126. Stuttgart, 1990

99. Giua, M. A. 'Augusto nel libro 56 della storia romana di Cassio Dione', *Athenaeum* 61 (1983) 439–56

100. Grant, M. 'The Augustan "constitution"', *G & R* 18 (1949) 97–112

101. Grant, M. *Cleopatra.* St Albans, 1974

102. Gray, E. W. 'The crisis in Rome at the beginning of 32 B.C.', *PACA* 13 (1975) 15–29

103. Grenade, P. *Essai sur les origines du principat.* Paris, 1961

104. Griffin, J. 'Propertius and Antony', *JRS* 67 (1977) 17–26 (= *Latin Poets and Roman Life*, 32–47. London, 1985)

105. Griffiths, J. G. 'The death of Cleopatra VII', *JEA* 49 (1961) 113–18

106. Grimal, P. 'Le promenade d'Evandre et Enée', *REA* 50 (1948) 348–51

107. Grimal, P. 'Enée à Rome et le triomphe d'Octave', *REA* 53 (1951) 51–61

108. Hadas, M. *Sextus Pompey.* New York, 1930

109. Hallett, J. P. 'Perusinae glandes and the changing image of Augustus', *AJAH* 2 (1977) 151–71

110. Hammond, M. *The Augustan Principate.* Cambridge, MA, 1933; repr. with appendix, 1968

111. Hammond, M. 'Hellenistic influences on the structure of the Augustan principate', *MAAR* 17 (1940) 1–25

112. Hammond, M. 'The sincerity of Augustus', *HSCP* 69 (1965) 139–52

113. Hanell, K. 'Kaiser Augustus', *Gymn.* 78 (1971) 188–200

114. Hanslik, R. 'Horaz und Varro Murena', *RhM* 96 (1953) 282–7

115. Hanslik, R. 'M. Vipsanius Agrippa', *RE* IX, 1 (1961) 1226–75

116. Hanson, A. E. 'Juliopolis, Nicopolis, and the Roman camp', *ZPE* 37 (1980) 249–54

117. Herrmann, P. *Der römische Kaisereid* (Hypomnemata 20). Göttingen, 1968

118. Heuss, A. 'Zeitgeschichte als Ideologie. Komposition und Gedankenführung der Res gestae diui Augusti', in A 55A, 55–95

119. Hohl, E. 'Augustus', *Altertum* 2 (1956) 224–41

120. Hornblower, S. 'Another suggestion about 'Varrones Egnatios Iullos' (Tac. Ann. 1 10)', *LCM* 12 (1987) 114

121. Horsfall, N. 'Labeo and Capito', *Hist.* 23 (1974) 252–4

122. Huzar, E. G. *Mark Antony: a Biography.* Minneapolis, 1978

123. Instinsky, H. U. 'Consensus uniuersorum', *Hermes* 75 (1940) 265–78

124. Instinsky, H. U. 'Augustus und die Adoption des Tiberius', *Hermes* 44 (1966) 324–43

125. Jameson, S. '22 or 23?', *Hist.* 8 (1969) 204–29

126. Jameson, S. 'Augustus and Agrippa Postumus', *Hist.* 24 (1975) 287–314

127. Jeffreys, R. 'The date of Messalla's death', *CQ* 35 (1985) 140–8

128. Johnson, J. R. 'The authenticity and validity of Antony's will', *AC* 47 (1978) 494–503
129. Jones, A. H. M. 'The imperium of Augustus', *JRS* 41 (1951) 112–19 (= A 47, 1–17)
130. Jones, A. H. M. 'The censorial powers of Augustus', in A 47, 19–26
131. Jones, A. H. M. *Augustus*. London, 1970
132. Judge, E. 'Res publica restituta. A modern illusion?', in *Polis and Imperium* (Studies in honour of E. T. Salmon), 279–311. Toronto, 1974
133. Keddie, J. N. 'The identity of Aelius Gallus (Tacitus, *Ann.* v, 8, 1)', in A 20, I 312–16
134. Kennedy, D. F. Review of Woodman and West 1984 (B 204), *LCM* 9.10 (1984) 157–60
135. Kienast, D. 'Horaz und die erste Krise des Prinzipats', *Chiron* 1 (1971) 239–51
136. Kienast, D. *Augustus. Prinzeps und Monarch*. Darmstadt, 1982
137. Kienast, D. '*Corpus imperii*. Überlegungen zum Reichsgedanken der Römer', in A 107A, 1–17
138. Knibbe, D. 'Quandoque quis trium virorum rei publicae constituendae', *ZPE* 44 (1981) 1–10
139. König, I. 'Der doppelte Geburtstag des Augustus: 23, 24 September (Suet. Aug. 51, 1 [*sic*])', *Epigraphica* 34 (1972) 3–15
140. Kraft, K. 'Zu Sueton *Divus Augustus* 69.2', *Hermes* 95 (1967) 496–9
141. Kromayer, J. *Die rechtliche Begründung des Prinzipats*. Marburg, 1888
142. Kromayer, J. 'Kleine Forschungen zur Geschichte des zweiten Triumvirats, IV: Der Partherzug des Antonius', *Hermes* 31 (1896) 70–104
143. Kromayer, J. 'Kleine Forschungen zur Geschichte des zweiten Triumvirats, VI: Die Vorgeschichte des Kriegs von Actium', *Hermes* 33 (1898) 13–70
144. Kromayer, J. 'Der Feldzug von Actium und der sogenannte Verrath der Cleopatra', *Hermes* 34 (1899) 1–54
145. Kunkel, W. 'Über das Wesen des augusteischen Prinzipats', *Gymn.* 68 (1961) 353–70 (= *Kleine Schriften* (1974) 383–404)
146. Lacey, W. K. 'Octavian in the senate, January 27 B.C.', *JRS* 64 (1974) 176–84
147. Lacey, W. K. 'Summi fastigii uocabulum. The story of a title', *JRS* 69 (1979) 28–34
148. Lacey, W. K. '2 B.C. and Julia's adultery', *Antichthon* 14 (1980) 127–42
149. Lacey, W. K. '19 B.C.', *Classicum* 23 (1983) 30–5
150. Lacey, W. K. 'Augustus and the senate, 23 B.C.', *Antichthon* 19 (1985) 57–67
151. Laet, S. J. de 'Où en est le problème de la juridiction impériale?', *AC* 14 (1945) 145–63
152. Last, H. M. '*Imperium maius*: a note', *JRS* 37 (1947) 157–64
153. Last, H. M. 'On the "tribunicia potestas" of Augustus', *RIL* 84 (1951) 93–110 (= C 208, 241–6, in German)
154. Leon, E. F. 'Scribonia and her daughters', *TAPA* 82 (1951) 168–75

155. Levick, B. M. 'Drusus Caesar and the adoptions of A.D. 4', *Latomus* 25 (1966) 227–44

156. Levick, B. M. 'The beginning of Tiberius' career', *CQ* 21 (1971) 478–86

157. Levick, B. M. 'Abdication and Agrippa Postumus', *Hist.* 21 (1972) 674–97

158. Levick, B. M. 'Atrox fortuna', *CR* 22 (1972) 309–11

159. Levick, B. M. 'Tiberius' retirement to Rhodes in 6 B.C.', *Latomus* 31 (1972) 779–813

160. Levick, B. M. 'Julians and Claudians', *G & R* 22 (1975) 29–38

161. Levick, B. M. 'Primus, Murena, and *fides*: notes on Cassius Dio 54.3', *G & R* 22 (1975) 156–63

162. Levick, B. M. 'The fall of Julia the Younger', *Latomus* 35 (1976) 301–39

163. Liebeschuetz, J. H. W. G. 'The settlement of 27 B.C.', in A 20, IV 345–65

164. Linderski, J. 'Rome, Aphrodisias and the *Res Gestae*: the *Genera Militiae* and the status of Octavian', *JRS* 74 (1984) 74–80

165. Linderski, J. 'Julia in Regium', *ZPE* 72 (1988) 181–200

166. Mackie, N. K. '*Res publica restituta*. A Roman myth', in A 20, IV 303–40

167. Magdelain, A. *Auctoritas Principis*. Paris, 1947

168. Malcovati, E. 'Il nuovo frammento augusteo della Laudatio Agrippae', *Athenaeum* 50 (1972) 142–51 (also 389)

169. Malitz, J. 'Caesars Partherkrieg', *Hist.* 33 (1984) 21–59

170. Manfredini, A. D. 'Ottaviano l'Egitto i senatori e l'oracolo', *Labeo* 32 (1986) 7–26

171. Mannsperger, D. 'Apollo gegen Dionysos', *Gymn.* 80 (1973) 381–404

172. Martin, P. M. 'A propos de l'exil d'Ovide et de la succession d'Auguste', *Latomus* 45 (1986) 609–11

173. Maschkin, N. A. *Zwischen Republik und Kaiserreich. Ursprung und sozialer Charakter des augusteischen Prinzipats* (transl. by M. Brandt). Leipzig, 1954

174. Millar, F. 'Two Augustan notes', *CR* 18 (1968) 263–6

175. Millar, F. 'Triumvirate and principate', *JRS* 63 (1973) 50–67

176. Millar, F. and Segal, E. (eds.) *Caesar Augustus: Seven Aspects*. Oxford, 1984

177. Mitchell, T. N. 'The inevitability of the Principate', *Thought* 55. 216 (1980) 18–35

178. Nenci, G. 'Gaio e Lucio Cesari nella politica Augustea', *Introduzione alle guerre persiane e altri saggi di storia antica* (Studi e Testi 15), 310–47. Pisa, 1958

179. Newman, J. K. *Augustus and the New Poetry* (Coll. Latomus 88). Brussels, 1967

180. Nicolet, C. 'Augustus, government and the propertied classes', in C 176, 89–128

181. Oliver, J. H. 'On the Hellenic policy of Augustus and Agrippa in 27 B.C.', *AJPh* 93 (1972) 190–7

182. Orestano, R. 'Rivisitazione di Augusto', in A 82A, 270–316

183. Paladini, M. L. 'I poteri di Tiberio Cesare dal 4 al 14 d.C.', in *Hommages Renard* II (Coll. Latomus 102) 573–99. Brussels, 1969

184. Palmer, R. E. A. 'Octavian's first attempt to restore the constitution (36 B.C.)', *Athenaeum* 56 (1978) 315–28

185. Pani, M. *Tendenze politiche della successione al principato di Augusto*. Bari, 1979

186. Pelling, C. B. R. 'Puppes sinistrorsum citae', *CQ* 36 (1986) 177–81

187. Piganiol, A. 'Les pouvoirs constitutionnels et le principat d'Auguste', *JS* (1937) 150–66

188. Polverini, L. 'L'aspetto sociale del passaggio dalla repubblica al principato', *Aevum* 38 (1964) 241–85, 439–67; 39 (1965) 77–100

189. Pouilloux, J. 'Deux amis: le Stratège Diogenes fils de Noumenios et le Gymnasiarche Stasicrates fils de Stasicrates', Πρακτικὰ τοῦ 1ου Διεθνοῦς Κυπρολογικοῦ Συνεδρίου, 141–50. Lefkosia, 1972

190. Raaflaub, K. A. 'The political significance of Augustus' military reforms', in Hanson, W. S. and Keppie, L. J. F. (eds.) *Roman Frontier Studies 1979*, III (BAR International Series 71), 1005–25. Oxford, 1980

191. Raaflaub, K. and Toher, M. *Between Republic and Empire: Interpretations of Augustus and his Principate*. Berkeley, 1990

192. Raepsaet-Charlier, M.-Th. 'Clarissima femina', *RIDA* 28 (1981) 189–212

193. Rapke, T. T. 'Julia and C. Proculeius. A note on Suetonius, *Augustus* 63, 2', *LCM* 9 (1984) 21–2

194. Rapke, T. T. 'Varrones Egnatios Iullos: Tacitus Annals 1 10, 4', *LCM* 12 (1987) 99

195. Rapke, T. T. 'Some unexpected consulships', *AncW* 20 (1989) 47–56

196. Reinhold, M. 'Augustus' conception of himself', *Thought* 55. 216 (1980) 36–50

197. Rich, J. W. 'Agrippa and the nobles. A note on Dio 54.29.6', *LCM* 5 (1980) 217–21

198. Rieks, R. 'Sebasta und Aktia', *Hermes* 98 (1970) 96–116

199. Roddaz, J.-M. 'Un thème de la "propagande" augustéenne. L'image populaire d'Agrippa', *MEFRA* 92 (1980) 947–56

200. Roddaz, J.-M. *Marcus Agrippa* (*BEFAR* 253). Rome, 1984

201. Roddaz, J.-M. 'Lucius Antonius', *Hist.* 37 (1988) 317–46

202. Rowland, R. J. 'The conspiracy of Varro Murena', *CJ* 62 (1966/7) 362–3

203. Ruikes, P. W. *Samenzweringen en Intriges tegen Octavianus Augustus Princeps* (Diss., Nijmegen, 1966). Maastricht, 1976

204. Salmon, E. T. 'The evolution of Augustus' principate', *Hist.* 5 (1956) 456–78

205. Salmon, E. T. 'Augustus the patrician', in Dunston, A. J. (ed.) *Essays on Roman Culture: the Todd Memorial Lectures*, 3–33. Toronto, 1976

206. Samuel, A. E. 'The joint regency of Cleopatra and Caesarion', *Études de Papyrologie* 9 (1971) 73–9

207. Scheid, J. 'Scribonia Caesaris et les Julio-Claudiens. Problèmes de vocabulaire de parenté', *MEFRA* 87 (1975) 349–75

208. Schmitthenner, W. (ed.) *Augustus*. Darmstadt, 1969

209. Schumacher, L. 'Die imperatorischen Akklamationen der Triumvirn und die Auspicia des Augustus', *Hist.* 34 (1985) 191–222

210. Schwartz, J. 'Recherches sur les dernières années du règne d'Auguste (4–14)', *RPh* 19 (1945) 21–90

211. Scott, K. 'Octavian's propaganda and Antony's *De sua ebrietate*', *CP* 24 (1929) 133–41

212. Scott, K. 'The political propaganda of 44–30 B.C.', *MAAR* 11 (1933) 7–49

213. Shotter, D. C. A. 'Julians, Claudians, and the accession of Tiberius', *Latomus* 30 (1971) 1117–23

214. Siber, H. *Das Führeramt des Augustus*. *ASAW* 44, no. 2. Leipzig, 1940

215. Signon, H. *Agrippa. Freund und Mitregent des Augustus*. Frankfurt, 1978

216. Simpson, C. J. 'The change in *praenomen* of Drusus Germanicus', *Phoenix* 42 (1988) 173–5

217. Sirago, V. A. *Il principato di Augusto: concentrazione di proprietà*. Bari, 1978

218. Sirago, V. A. 'L'aspetto economico dell'opera di Augusto', *Labeo* 26 (1980) 378–89; repr. in A 82A, 258–69

219. Skeat, T. C. 'The last days of Cleopatra', *JRS* 43 (1953) 98–100

220. Starr, C. G. 'How did Augustus stop the Roman revolution?', *CJ* 52 (1956/7) 107–12 (= *Essays on Ancient History*, 222–7. Leiden, 1979)

221. Stockton, D. L. 'Primus and Murena', *Hist.* 14 (1965) 18–40

222. Stockton, D. L. 'Augustus *sub specie aeternitatis*', *Thought* 55. 216 (1980) 5–17

223. Suerbaum, W. 'Merkwürdige Geburtstage. Der nicht-existierende Geburtstag des M. Antonius, der doppelte Geburtstag des Augustus, der neue Geburtstag der Livia und der vorzeitige Geburtstag des älteren Drusus', *Chiron* 10 (1980) 327–55

224. Sumner, G. V. 'Germanicus and Drusus Caesar', *Latomus* 26 (1967) 413–35

225. Sumner, G. V. 'Varrones Murenae', *HSCP* 82 (1978) 187–95

226. Swan, M. 'The consular fasti of 23 B.C. and the conspiracy of Varro Murena', *HSCP* 71 (1966) 235–47

227. Swan, M. 'Προβάλλεσθαι in Dio's account of elections under Augustus', *CQ* 32 (1982) 436–40

228. Syme, R. 'Imperator Caesar: a study in nomenclature', *Hist.* 7 (1958) 172–88 (= A 94, I, 361–77)

229. Syme, R. 'The crisis of 2 B.C.', *SBAW* 7 (1974) 3–34 (= A 94, III, 912–36)

230. Syme, R. 'Some imperatorial salutations', *Phoenix* 33 (1979) 308–29 (= A 94, III, 1198–219)

231. Syme, R. 'Neglected children on the *Ara Pacis*', *AJA* 88 (1984) 583–9 (= (with improvements) A 94, IV, 418–29)

232. Tarn, W. W. 'The Battle of Actium', *JRS* 21 (1931) 173–99

233. Tarn, W. W. 'Alexander Helios and the Golden Age', *JRS* 22 (1932) 135–60

234. Thibault, J. C. *The Mystery of Ovid's Exile*. Berkeley–Los Angeles, 1964

235. Tibiletti, G. *Principe e magistrati repubblicani*. Rome, 1953

236. Timpe, D. 'Die Bedeutung der Schlacht von Carrhae', *MH* 19 (1962) 104–29

237. Valvo, A. 'M. Valerio Messalla Corvino negli studi piu recenti', *ANRW* II, 30. 3 (1983) 1663–80

238. Vassileiou, A. 'Sur les dates de naissance de Drusus, de Caius et Lucius César', *RPh* 58 (1984) 45–52

239. Vittinghoff, F. *Römische Kolonisation und Bürgerrechtspolitik unter Caesar und Augustus* (Akad. Mainz Abh. Geistes und Sozialwissensch. Kl. Jhrg. 1951 no. 14). Wiesbaden, 1952

240. Vittinghoff, F. *Kaiser Augustus*. Göttingen, 1959

241. Volkmann, H. 'Mos maiorum als Grundzug des augusteischen Prinzipats', in Berve, H. (ed.) *Das neue Bild der Antike* II, 246–64. Leipzig, 1942 (= (with certain omissions) *Endoxos Duleia*, 173–90. Berlin, 1975)

242. Wallmann, P. 'Zur Zusammensetzung und Haltung des Senats im Jahre 32 v. Chr.', *Hist.* 25 (1976) 305–12

243. Wallmann, P. *Triumviri rei publicae constituendae*. Frankfurt, 1989

244. Watkins, O. D. 'Horace, Odes 2.10 and Licinius Murena', *Hist.* 34 (1985) 125–7

245. Weigel, R. D. 'Augustus' relations with the Aemilii Lepidi: persecution and patronage', *RhM* 128 (1985) 180–91

246. Weller, J. A. 'Tacitus and Tiberius' Rhodian exile', *Phoenix* 12 (1958) 31–5

247. Welwei, K. W. 'Augustus als vindex libertatis. Freiheitsideologie und Propaganda im frühen Prinzipat', *AU* 16 (1973) 29–41

248. Wickert, L. 'Der Prinzipat und die Freiheit', in *Symbola Coloniensia* (Festschr. Kroll) 111–41. Cologne, 1949

249. Wieacker, F. 'Zur Verfassungsstruktur des augusteischen Prinzipats', (Festschr. Grewe) 639–53. Baden-Baden, 1981

250. Wilinski, A. and Kurylowicz, M. 'Dalla repubblica al principato', in A 82A, 217–22

251. Williams, G. 'Poetry in the moral climate of Augustan Rome', *JRS* 52 (1962) 28–46

252. Yavetz, Z. *Julius Caesar and his Public Image*. London, 1983

2. THE EXPANSION OF THE EMPIRE, 43 B.C.–A.D. 69

253. Barnes, T. D. 'The Victories of Augustus', *JRS* 64 (1974) 21–6

254. Braund, D. *Rome and the Friendly King: the Character of Client Kingship.* London–Canberra–New York, 1984

255. Braunert, H. '*Omnium provinciarum populi Romani fines auxi*', *Chiron* 7 (1977) 207–17

256. Brunt, P. A. Review of Meyer, H. *Die Aussenpolitik des Augustus* (= C 288), *JRS* 53 (1963) 170–6 (= A 12, 96–109)

257. Brunt, P. A. '*Laus Imperii*', in Garnsey, P. D. A. and Whittaker, C. R. (eds.) *Imperialism in the Ancient World*, 159–91. Cambridge, 1978 (= A 12, 288–323)

258. Burstein, S. M. 'Cornelius Gallus and Aethiopia', *AHB* 2 (1988) 16–20

259. Christ, K. 'Zur römischen Okkupation der Zentralalpen und des nördlichen Alpenvorlandes', *Hist.* 6 (1957) 416–28

260. Christ, K. 'Zur augusteischen Germanienpolitik', *Chiron* 7 (1977) 149–205

261. Deman, A. 'Matériaux et réflexions pour servir à une étude du développement et du sous-développement dans les provinces de l'empire romain', *ANRW* II, 3 (1975) 3–97

262. Desanges, J. 'Le triomphe de Cornelius Balbus', *RevAfr* (1957) 1–43
263. Desanges, J. 'Les relations de l'empire romain avec l'Afrique nilotique et érythréene, d'Auguste à Probus', *ANRW* II, 10.1 (1988) 3–43
264. Dobias, J. 'King Maroboduus as a politician', *Klio* 38 (1960) 155–66
265. Doblhofer, E. 'Horaz und Augustus', *ANRW* II, 31.3 (1981) 1922–86
266. Dyson, S. L. 'Native revolt-patterns in the Roman Empire', *ANRW* II, 3 (1975) 138–75
267. Fears, J. R. 'The cult of virtues and Roman imperial ideology', *ANRW* II, 17.2 (1981) 827–948
268. Fears, J. R. 'The theology of victory at Rome: approaches and problems', *ANRW* II, 17.2 (1981) 737–825
269. Griffin, J. 'Augustus and the poets: "Caesar qui cogere posset"', in C 176, 189–218
270. Grosso, F. 'La Media Atropatene e la politica di Augusto', *Athenaeum* 35 (1957) 240–56
271. Gruen, E. S. 'Augustus and the ideology of war and peace', in *The Age of Augustus* (Archaeologica Transatlantica, v) 51–72. Louvain, 1986
272. Grummond, N. de. 'Pax Augusta and the Horae on the Ara Pacis Augustae', *AJA* 94 (1990) 663–77
273. Harris, W. V. *War and Imperialism in Republican Rome, 327–70 B.C.* Oxford, 1979
274. Hartley, B. and Wacher, J. (eds.) *Rome and her Northern Provinces* (Papers presented to Sheppard Frere in honour of his retirement from the Chair of the Archaeology of the Roman Empire, University of Oxford, 1983). Gloucester, 1983
275. Hoffman, M. 'Ptolemaios von Mauretania', *RE* XXIII, 3 (1959) 1780–82
276. Horrent, J. 'Nota sobre el desarrollo de la guerra Cántabra del año 26 a.C.', *Emerita* 21 (1953) 279–90
277. Huzar, E. 'Augustus, heir of the Ptolemies', *ANRW* II, 10.1 (1988) 343–82
278. Isaac, B. *The Limits of Empire: the Roman Army in the East.* Oxford, 1990. 2nd edn. 1992
279. Jal, P. 'L'impérialisme romain: observations sur les témoignages littéraires latins de la fin de la République romaine', *Ktema* 7 (1982) 143–50
280. Kneissl, P. 'Zur Entstehung der Provinz Noricum', *Chiron* 9 (1979) 261–73
281. Koestermann, E. 'Der pannonisch-dalmatische Krieg 6–9 n. Chr.', *Hermes* 81 (1953) 345–78
282. Koestermann, E. 'Die Feldzüge des Germanicus, 14–16 n. Chr.', *Hist.* 6 (1957) 429–79
283. Letta, C. 'La dinastia dei Cozii e la romanizzazione delle Alpi occidentali', *Athenaeum* 64 (1976) 37–76
284. Luce, T. J. 'Livy, Augustus, and the Forum Augustum', in C 191, 123–38
285. Magie, D. 'Augustus' War in Spain', *CPh* 15 (1920) 323–39
286. Mann, J. C. 'The frontiers of the Principate', *ANRW* II, 1 (1974) 508–33
287. Martino, E. *Roma contra Cántabros y Astures. Nueva lectura de las fuentes.* Santander, 1982

288. Meyer, H. *Die Aussenpolitik des Augustus und die augusteische Dichtung* (Kölner hist. Abhandlungen 5). Cologne, 1961

289. Mócsy, A. 'Der vertuschte Dakerkrieg des M. Licinius Crassus', *Hist.* 15 (1966) 511–14

290. Momigliano, A. '*Panegyricus Messalae* and "Panegyricus Vespasiani": two references to Britain', *JRS* 40 (1950) 39–42

291. Moynihan, R. 'Geographical mythology and Roman imperial ideology', in *The Age of Augustus* (Archaeologica Transatlantica, v), 149–62. Louvain, 1986

292. Negev, A. 'The Nabataeans and the Provincia Arabia', *ANRW* II, 8 (1978) 520–686

293. Ober, J. 'Tiberius and the political testament of Augustus', *Hist.* 31 (1982) 306–28

294. Oldfather, W. A. and Canter, H. V. *The Defeat of Varus and the German Frontier Policy of Augustus*. Urbana, IL, 1915

295. Pani, M. *Roma e i re d'Oriente da Augusto a Tiberio*. Bari, 1972

296. Pavis d'Escurac, H. 'L'impérialisme romain en Maurétanie de 33 av. J.-C. à 40 ap. J.-C.', *Ktema* 7 (1982) 221–33

297. Rachet, M. *Rome et les Berbères. Un problème militaire d'Auguste à Dioclétien*. Brussels, 1970

298. Raschke, M. 'New studies in Roman commerce with the East', *ANRW* II, 9.2 (1978) 604–1378

299. Ritter, H. W. *Rom und Numidien*. Lüneburg, 1987

300. Romer, F. E. 'A numismatic date for the departure of C. Caesar', *TAPA* 108 (1978) 187–202

301. Romer, F. E. 'Gaius Caesar's military diplomacy in the East', *TAPA* 109 (1979) 199–214

302. Romer, F. E. 'A case of Client Kingship', *AJP* 106 (1985) 75–100

303. Santos, F. D. 'Die Integration Nord- und Nordwestspaniens als römische Provinz in der Reichspolitik des Augustus. Von der konsularischen zur hispanischen Ära', *ANRW* II, 3 (1975) 523–71

304. Schmitthenner, W. 'Octavians militarische Unternehmungen in den Jahren 35–33 v. Chr.', *Hist.* 7 (1958) 189–236

305. Schmitthenner, W. 'Augustus' spanischer Feldzug und der Kampf um den Prinzipat', *Hist.* 11 (1962) 29–85 (= C 208, 404–85)

306. Schmitthenner, W. 'Rome and India. Aspects of universal history during the principate', *JRS* 69 (1979) 90–106

307. Scholz, U. W. 'Herculis ritu – Augustus – consule Planco', *WS* 84 (1971) 123–37

308. Seager, R. 'The return of the standards in 20 B.C.', *LCM* 2 (1977) 201–2

309. Seager, R. '*Neu sinas Medos equitare inultos*: Horace, the Parthians and Augustan foreign policy', *Athenaeum* 58 (1980) 103–18

310. Sidebotham, S. E. *Roman Economic Policy in the Erythra Thalassa, 30 B.C.–A.D. 217* (*Mnemosyne* supplement 91). Leiden, 1986

311. Sidebotham, S. E. 'Aelius Gallus and Arabia', *Latomus* 45 (1986) 590–602

312. Syme, R. 'The northern frontiers under Augustus', *CAH* x¹, 340–81. Cambridge, 1934

313. Syme, R. 'The Spanish war of Augustus', *AJP* 55 (1934) 293–317

314. Syme, R. 'The conquest of northwest Spain', in *Legio VII Gemina*, 83–107. Leon, 1970

315. Telschow, K. 'Die Abberufung des Germanicus (16 n. Chr.). Ein Beispiel für die Kontinuität römischer Germanienpolitik von Augustus zu Tiberius', in A 55A, 148–82

316. Timpe, D. 'Drusus' Umkehr an der Elbe', *RhM* 110 (1967) 289–306

317. Timpe, D. 'Zur Geschichte und Überlieferung der Okkupation Germaniens unter Augustus', *Saeculum* 18 (1967) 278–93

318. Timpe, D. *Der Triumph des Germanicus. Untersuchungen zu den Feldzügen der Jahre 14–16 n. Chr. in Germanien.* Bonn, 1968

319. Timpe, D. *Arminius-Studien.* Heidelberg, 1970

320. Timpe, D. 'Zur augusteischen Partherpolitik zwischen 30 und 20 v. Chr.', *WJA* 1 (1975) 155–69

321. Timpe, D. 'Zur Geschichte der Rheingrenze zwischen Caesar und Drusus', in A 55A, 124–47

322. Vulic, N. 'The Illyrian war of Octavian', *JRS* 24 (1934) 163–7

323. Welwei, K. W. 'Römische Weltherrschaftsideologie und augusteische Germanienpolitik', *Gymn.* 93 (1986) 118–37

324. Whittaker, C. R. *Les frontières de l'Empire romain* (Ann. Litt. Univ. Besançon 390). Paris, 1989

325. Williams, G. 'Did Maecenas "fall from favor"? Augustan literary patronage', in C 191, 258–75

326. Wissman, H. von. 'Die Geschichte des Sabäerreichs und der Feldzug des Aelius Gallus', *ANRW* II, 9.1 (1978) 308–544

327. Ziegler, F. H. *Die Beziehungen zwischen Rom und dem Partherreich. Ein Beitrag zur Geschichte des Völkerrechtes.* Wiesbaden, 1964

3. THE JULIO-CLAUDIANS AND THE YEAR A.D. 69

328. Alföldy, G. 'La politique provinciale de Tibère', *Latomus* 24 (1965) 824–44

329. Ameling, W. 'Tyrannen und schwangere Frauen', *Hist.* 35 (1986) 507–8

330. Baldwin, B. 'Executions under Claudius', *Phoenix* 18 (1964) 39–48

331. Balsdon, J. P. V. D. *The Emperor Gaius.* Oxford, 1934

332. Barrett, A. A. 'Chronological errors in Dio's account of the Claudian invasion', *Britannia* 11 (1980) 31–3

333. Barrett, A. A. *Caligula: the Corruption of Power.* London, 1989

334. Brunt, P. A. 'The revolt of Vindex and the fall of Nero', *Latomus* 18 (1959) 531–59 (= A 12, 9–32)

335. Brunt, P. A. 'Lex de Imperio Vespasiani', *JRS* 67 (1977) 95–116

336. Burr, V. *Tiberius Iulius Alexander.* Bonn, 1955

337. Ceauşescu, P. 'Caligula et le legs d'Auguste', *Hist.* 22 (1973) 269–83

338. Chandler, D. C. 'Quaestor Ostiensis', *Hist.* 27 (1978) 328–35

339. Chilver, G. E. F. 'The army in politics, A.D. 68–70', *JRS* 47 (1957) 29–36

340. Cizek, E. *L'Epoque de Néron et ses controverses idéologiques.* Leiden, 1972

341. Cizek, E. 'L'expérience néronienne', *REA* 84 (1982) 105–15

342. Daly, J. L. 'Verginius at Vesontio', *Hist.* 24 (1975) 75–100
343. Ehrhardt, C. 'Messalina and the succession to Claudius', *Antichthon* 12 (1978) 51–77
344. Gallivan, P. A. 'Some comments on the *fasti* for the reign of Nero', *CQ* 24 (1974) 290–311
345. Gallivan, P. A. 'The *fasti* for the reign of Claudius', *CQ* 28 (1978) 407–26
346. Gallivan, P. A. 'The fasti for the reign of Gaius', *Antichthon* 13 (1979) 66–9
347. Gallivan, P. A. 'The fasti for A.D. 70–96', *CQ* 31 (1981) 186–220
348. Gallotta, B. *Germanico*. Rome, 1988
349. Gapp, K. S. 'The universal famine under Claudius', *HTR* 28 (1935) 258–65
350. Gordon, A. E. *Quintus Veranius Consul A.D. 49* (University of California Publications in Classical Archaeology 11. 5). 1952
351. Greenhalgh, P. A. L. *The Year of the Four Emperors*. London, 1975
352. Griffin, M. T. *Nero: the End of a Dynasty*. London, 1984
353. Hennig, D. 'Zur Ägyptenreise des Germanicus', *Chiron* 2 (1972) 349–65
354. Hennig, D. *L. Aelius Seianus* (Vestigia 21). Munich, 1975
355. Hind, J. G. F. 'The middle years of Nero's reign', *Hist.* 20 (1971) 488–505
356. Holladay, J. 'The election of magistrates in the early principate', *Latomus* 37 (1978) 874–93
357. Houston, G. W. 'Tiberius on Capri', *G & R* 32 (1985) 178–96
358. Jakobson, A. and Cotton, H. M. 'Caligula's recusatio imperii', *Hist.* 34 (1985) 497–503
359. Jones, B. W. *The Emperor Titus*. London, 1984
360. Jones, B. W. 'Agrippina and Vespasian', *Latomus* 43 (1984) 581–3
361. Jung, H. 'Die Thronerhebung des Claudius', *Chiron* 2 (1972) 367–86
362. Koestermann, E. 'Die Feldzüge des Germanicus 14 – 16 n. Chr.', *Hist.* 6 (1957) 429–79
363. Koestermann, E. 'Die Mission des Germanicus im Orient', *Hist.* 7 (1958) 331–75
364. Kokkinos, N. *Antonia Augusta: Portrait of a Roman Lady*. London, 1992
365. Levick, B. M. 'Imperial control of elections under the early principate', *Hist.* 16 (1967) 207–30
366. Levick, B. M. *Tiberius the Politician*. London, 1976
367. Levick, B. M. 'Antiquarian or revolutionary? Claudius Caesar's conception of his principate', *AJP* 99 (1978) 79–105
368. Levick, B. M. 'Nero's Quinquennium', in A 20, III, 211–25
369. Levick, B. M. 'The *Senatus Consultum* from Larinum', *JRS* 73 (1983) 97–115
370. Levick, B. M. 'L. Verginius Rufus and the four emperors', *RhM* 128 (1985) 318–46
371. Levick, B. M. 'The politics of the early Principate', in A 108, 45–68
372. Levick, B. M. *Claudius*. London, 1990
373. McAlindon, D. 'Senatorial opposition to Claudius and Nero', *AJPh* 77 (1956) 113–32
374. McAlindon, D. 'Claudius and the senators', *AJPh* 78 (1957) 279–86
375. Meise, E. *Untersuchungen zur Geschichte der Julisch-Claudischen Dynastie*. Munich, 1969

376. Moeller, W. O. 'The riot of A.D. 59 at Pompeii', *Hist.* 19 (1970) 84–95
377. Momigliano, A. *Claudius: the Emperor and his Achievement.* Oxford, 1934; 2nd edn. Cambridge, 1961
378. Murison, C. L. 'Some Vitellian dates', *TAPA* 109 (1979)187–97
379. Murison, C. L. 'Galba in Germany A.D. 43', *Hist.* 34 (1985) 254–6
380. Murray, O. 'The Quinquennium Neronis and the Stoics', *Hist.* 14 (1965) 41–61
381. Nicols, J. *Vespasian and the Partes Flavianae.* Wiesbaden, 1978
382. Oliver, J. H. 'The descendants of Asinius Pollio', *AJPh* 68 (1947) 147–60
383. Oost, S. J. 'The career of M. Antonius Pallas', *AJPh* 79 (1958) 113–39
384. Orth, W. *Die Provinzialpolitik des Tiberius.* Munich, 1970
385. Pippidi, D. M. *Autour de Tibère.* Rome, 1965
386. Raaflaub, K. A. 'Grundzüge, Ziele und Ideen der Opposition gegen die Kaiser im 1. Jh. n. Chr.: Versuch einer Standortbestimmung', *Opposition et résistances* (Entretiens Hardt 33) 1–55. Vandoeuvres–Geneva, 1987
387. Reece, B. R. 'The date of Nero's death', *AJPh* 90 (1969) 72–4
388. Rogers, R. S. *Studies in the Reign of Tiberius.* Baltimore, 1943
389. Roper, T. K. 'Nero, Seneca and Tigellinus', *Hist.* 28 (1979) 346–57
390. Sancery, J. *Galba.* Paris, 1983
391. Schmitt, H. H. 'Der Pannonische Aufstand d. J. 14 n. Chr.', *Hist.* 7 (1958) 378–83
392. Seager, R. *Tiberius.* London, 1972
393. Shotter, D. C. A. 'Tiberius and Asinius Gallus', *Hist.* 20 (1971) 443–57
394. Simpson, C. J. 'The "conspiracy" of A.D. 39', in A 20 II, 347–66
395. Swan, M. 'Josephus, A. J. XIX 251–252: Opposition to Caius and Claudius', *AJPh* 91 (1970) 149–64
396. Syme, R. 'Piso Frugi and Crassus Frugi', *JRS* 50 (1960) 12–20 (= A 94, II, 496–509)
397. Syme, R. 'Domitius Corbulo', *JRS* 60 (1970) 27–39 (= A 94 II, 805–24)
398. Syme, R. 'History or biography: the case of Tiberius Caesar', *Hist.* 23 (1974) 481–96 (= A 94 III, 937–52)
399. Syme, R. 'The march of Mucianus', *Antichthon* 11 (1977) 78–92 (= A 94, III, 998–1013)
400. Syme, R. 'Partisans of Galba', *Hist.* 31 (1982) 460–83 (= A 94, IV, 115–39)
401. Syme, R. 'The marriage of Rubellius Blandus', *AJPh* 103 (1982) 62–85 (= A 94, IV, 177–98)
402. Timpe, D. 'Römische Geschichte bei Flavius Josephus', *Hist.* 9 (1960) 474–502
403. Timpe, D. *Untersuchungen zur Kontinuität des frühen Prinzipats.* Wiesbaden, 1962
404. Townend, G. 'Some Flavian connections', *JRS* 51 (1961) 54–62
405. Turner, E. G. 'Tiberius Julius Alexander', *JRS* 44 (1954) 54–64
406. Urban, R. *Der 'Bataveraufstand' und die Erhebung des Julius Classicus* (Trierer historische Forschungen 8). Trier, 1985
407. Wallace, K. G. 'The Flavii Sabini in Tacitus', *Hist.* 36 (1987) 343–58
408. Wankenne, J. 'Encore et toujours Néron', *AC* 53 (1984) 249–65
409. Warmington, B. H. *Nero: Reality and Legend.* London, 1969
410. Waters, K. H. 'The character of Domitian', *Phoenix* 18 (1964) 49–77

411. Weinrib, E. J. 'The family connections of M. Livius Drusus Libo', *HSCP* 72 (1967) 247–78
412. Wellesley, K. *The Long Year A.D. 69*. London, 1975
413. Wellesley, K. 'What happened on the Capitol in December A.D. 69?', *AJAH* 6 (1981) 166–90
414. Wilkes, J. J. 'A note on the mutiny of the Pannonian legions in A.D. 14', *CQ* 56 (1963) 268–71

D. GOVERNMENT AND ADMINISTRATION

I. THE IMPERIAL COURT

1. Alföldi, A. 'Die Ausgestaltung des monarchischen Zeremoniells am römischen Kaiserhofe', *MDAI(R)* 49 (1934) 1–118 (= D 3, 119–276)
2. Alföldi, A. 'Insignien und Tracht der römischen Kaiser', *MDAI(R)* 50 (1935) 3–158 (= D 3, 3–171)
3. Alföldi, A. *Die monarchische Repräsentation im römischen Kaiserreiche*. 3rd edn. Darmstadt, 1970
4. Amarelli, F. *Consilia Principum*. Naples, 1983
5. Bang, M. 'Die Freunde und Begleiter der Kaiser', in A 30, IV, 56–76. Leipzig, 1921
6. Boulvert, G. *Esclaves et affranchis impériaux sous le haut-empire romain, rôle politique et administratif*. Naples, 1970
7. Boulvert, G. *Domestique et fonctionnaire sous le haut-empire romain: la condition de l'affranchi et de l'esclave*. Paris, 1974
8. Burton, G. Review of Boulvert 1970 (D 6) and 1974 (D 7), *JRS* 67 (1977) 162–6
9. Chantraine, H. *Freigelassene und Sklaven im Dienst der römischen Kaiser: Studien zu ihrer Nomenklatur*. Wiesbaden, 1967
10. Crook, J. A. *Consilium Principis: Imperial Councils and Counsellors from Augustus to Diocletian*. Cambridge, 1955
11. Frézouls, E. 'Les Julio-Claudiens et le Palatium', in Levy, E. (ed.) *Le système palatial en Orient, en Grèce, et à Rome* (Actes du colloque de Strasbourg 19–22 juin 1985) 445–62. Leiden, 1987
12. Herman, G. 'The "friends" of the early hellenistic rulers: servants or officials', *Talanta* 12–13 (1980–1) 103–49
13. Hirschfeld, O. *Die Kaiserlichen Verwaltungsbeamten bis auf Diocletian*. 2nd edn. Berlin, 1912
14. Millar, F. 'Epictetus and the imperial court', *JRS* 55 (1965) 141–8
15. Millar, F. 'Emperors at work', *JRS* 57 (1967) 9–19
16. Mooren, L. *La hiérarchie du cour ptolemaique*. Louvain, 1977
17. Parsi, B. *Désignation et Investiture de l'Empereur Romain*. Paris, 1963
18. Pavis d'Escurac, H. 'La *familia Caesaris* et les affaires publiques: *discretam domum et rempublicam*' in Levy, E. (ed.) *Le système palatial en Orient, en Grèce, et à Rome* (Actes du colloque de Strasbourg 19–22 juin 1985) 393–410. Leiden, 1987

19. Rogers, R. S. 'The emperor's displeasure – amicitiam renuntiare', *TAPA* 90 (1959) 224–37

20. Turcan, R. *Vivre à la cour des Césars d'Auguste à Dioclétien* (Coll. études anciennes 57). Paris, 1987

21. Wallace-Hadrill, A. 'Civilis princeps: between citizen and king', *JRS* 72 (1982) 32–48

22. Weaver, P. R. C. *Familia Caesaris. A Social Study of the Emperor's Freedmen and Slaves.* Cambridge, 1972

2. THE SENATE AND THE *EQUITES*

23. Alföldy, G. 'Die Stellung der Ritter in der Führungsschicht des Imperium Romanum', *Chiron* 11 (1981) 169–215 (= *Die römische Gesellschaft*, 162–207. Stuttgart, 1981)

24. Bonnefond-Coudry, M. *Le sénat de la république romaine de la guerre d'Hannibal à Auguste: pratiques délibératives et prise de décision* (BEFAR 273). Rome, 1989

25. Bowersock, G. W. 'Roman senators from the Near East', in D 42, 651–68

26. Brunt, P. A. 'Princeps and equites', *JRS* 73 (1983) 42–75

27. Brunt, P. A. 'The role of the senate in the Augustan regime', *CQ* 34 (1984) 423–44

28. Brunt, P. A. 'The equites in the Late Republic', in A 11, 144–93

29. Cadoux, T. J. Review of Vitucci, G. *Ricerche sulla Praefectura Vrbi, JRS* 49 (1959) 152–60

30. Chastagnol, A. 'Les modes d'accès au sénat romain au début de l'empire. Remarques à propos de la table claudienne de Lyon', *BSNAF* (1971) 282–309

31. Chastagnol, A. 'La naissance de l'ordo senatorius', *MEFRA* 85 (1973) 581–607. (= D 54, 175–98)

32. Chastagnol, A. 'Les sénateurs d'origine provinciale sous le règne d'Auguste'. *Mélanges Boyancé*, 163–71. Rome, 1974

33. Chastagnol, A. '"Latus clavus" et "adlectio"; l'accès des hommes nouveaux au sénat romain sous le haut-empire', *RHD* 53 (1975) 375–94 (= D 54, 199–27)

34. Chastagnol, A. 'Le laticlave de Vespasien', *Hist.* 25 (1976) 253–6

35. Chastagnol, A. 'La crise de recrutement sénatorial des années 16–11 av. J.-C.', Φιλίας Χάριν. *Miscellanea in onore di Eugenio Manni* II, Rome, 1980, 463–76

36. Demougin, S. '*Uterque ordo*: les rapports entre l'ordre sénatorial et l'ordre équestre sous les Julio-Claudiens', in D 42, 73–104

37. Demougin, S. *L'Ordre équestre sous les Julio-Claudiens* (Collection de l'école française de Rome 108). Rome, 1988

38. Devreker, J. 'Les orientaux au Sénat romain d'Auguste à Trajan', *Latomus* 41 (1982) 495–516

39. Eck, W. 'Senatorial self-representation: developments in the Augustan period', in C 176, 129–67

40. Eck, W. 'Die Ausformung der ritterlichen Administration als

Antisenatspolitik?', in *Opposition et Résistances* (Entretiens Hardt 33) 249–83. Vandoeuvres, 1986

41. Ensslin, W. 'Praefectus Praetorio', *RE* xxii (1954) 2391–502

42. *Epigrafia e ordine senatorio*: *Atti del Colloquio Internazionale AIEGL, Roma, 14–20 Maggio 1981* (ed. Panciera, S.). Rome, 1982

43. Frei-Stolba, R. *Untersuchungen zu den Wahlen in der römischen Kaiserzeit*. Zurich, 1967

44. Halfmann, H. *Die Senatoren aus den östlichen Teilen des Imperium Romanum bis zum Ende des 2. Jh. n. Chr.* (Hypomnemata 58). Göttingen, 1979

45. Hammond, M. 'Curatores tabularum publicarum', in Jones, L. W. (ed.) *Classical and Medieval Studies in Honor of E. K. Rand*, 123–31. New York, 1938

46. Henderson, M. I. 'The establishment of the equester ordo', *JRS* 53 (1963) 61–72

47. Jones, A. H. M. 'The elections under Augustus', *JRS* 45 (1955) 9–21 (= A 47, 27–50)

48. Laet, S. J. de. *De Samenstelling van den romeinschen Senaat gedurende de eerste Eeuw van het Principaat (28 vóór Chr.–68 na Chr.)*. Antwerp, 1941

49. Millar, F. 'Some evidence on the meaning of Tacitus, Annals xii. 60', *Hist.* 13 (1964) 180–7

50. Millar, F. 'The development of jurisdiction by imperial procurators: further evidence', *Hist.* 14 (1965) 362–7

51. Morris, J. 'Leges annales under the Principate, i. Legal and constitutional', *LF* 87 (1964) 316–37; 'ii. Political effects', *ibid.* 88 (1965) 22–31

52. Nicolet, C. *L'Ordre équestre* i–ii. Paris, 1966, 1974

53. Nicolet, C. 'Le cens sénatorial sous la république et sous Auguste', *JRS* 66 (1976) 20–38. (Repr. with revisions in D 54, 143–74)

54. Nicolet, C. (ed.) *Des Ordres à Rome*. Paris, 1984

55. Pavis d'Escurac, H. *La Préfecture de l'annone: service administratif impérial d'Auguste à Constantin*. Rome, 1976

56. Pflaum, H.-G. *Les procurateurs équestres sous le haut-empire romain*. Paris, 1950

57. Pflaum, H.-G. 'Procurator', *RE* xxiii (1957) 1240–79

58. Pflaum, H.-G. *Abrégé des procurateurs équestres*. Paris, 1974

59. Pflaum, H.-G. *Les carrières procuratoriennes équestres sous le Haut-Empire Romain*. 3 vols. Paris, 1960–1, with *Supplément*. Paris, 1982

60. Pistor, H.-H. 'Prinzeps und Patriziat in der Zeit von Augustus bis Commodus'. Diss., Freiburg, 1965

61. Raepsaet-Charlier, M. T. *Prosopographie des femmes de l'ordre senatorial*. Louvain, 1987

62. Saller, R. P. 'Patronage and promotion in equestrian careers', *JRS* 70 (1980) 44–63

63. Sattler, P. *Augustus und der Senat. Untersuchungen zur römischen Innenpolitik zwischen 30 und 17 v. Chr.* Göttingen, 1960

64. Shatzman, I. *Senatorial Wealth and Roman Politics* (Coll. Latomus 142). Brussels, 1975

65. Sherwin-White, A. N. 'Procurator Augusti', *PBSR* 15 (1939) 11–26

66. Stein, A. *Der römische Ritterstand*. Munich, 1927
67. Syme, R. 'Who was Decidius Saxa?', *JRS* 27 (1937) 127–37 (= A 94, I, 31–41)
68. Syme, R. 'Caesar, the senate and Italy', *PBSR* 14 (1938) 1–31 (= A 94, I, 88–119)
69. Syme, R. 'Who was Vedius Pollio?' *JRS* 51 (1961) 23–30 (= A 94, II, 518–29)
70. Syme, R. *Some Arval Brethren*. Oxford, 1980
71. Syme, R. 'The sons of Piso the Pontifex', *AJPh* 101 (1980) 333–41 (= A 94, III, 1226–32)
72. Syme, R. 'Clues to testamentary adoption', *Tituli* IV (1984) 397–410 (= A 94, IV, 159–73)
73. Syme, R. 'Marriage ages for Roman senators', *Hist.* 36 (1987) 318–32 (= A 94, VI, 232–46)
74. Syme, R. 'Paullus the censor', *Athenaeum* 75 (1987) 7–26 (= A 94, VI, 247–68)
75. Szramkiewicz, R. *Les gouverneurs de province à l'époque augustéenne* (Etudes Prosopographiques III–IV). Paris, 1975 and 1976
76. Talbert, R. J. A. 'Augustus and the senate', *G & R* 31 (1984) 55–63
77. Talbert, R. J. A. *The Senate of Imperial Rome*. Princeton, 1984
78. Talbert, R. J. A. 'Commodus as diplomat in an extract from the acta senatus', *ZPE* 71 (1988) 137–47
79. Thompson, D. L. 'The meetings of the Roman senate on the Palatine', *AJA* 85 (1981) 335–9
80. Wiseman, T. P. 'The definition of "Eques Romanus" in the late Republic and early Empire', *Hist.* 19 (1970) 67–83 (= A 109, 57–73)
81. Wiseman, T. P. *New Men in the Roman Senate*. Oxford, 1971
82. Wiseman, T. P. 'Legendary genealogies in late Republican Rome', *G & R* 21 (1974) 153–64 (= A 109, 207–18)

3. PROVINCIAL ADMINISTRATION

83. Abbott, F. F. and Johnson, A. C. *Municipal Administration in the Roman Empire*. Princeton, 1926
84. Badian, E. *Publicans and Sinners. Private Enterprise in the Service of the Roman Republic*. Ithaca, 1972
85. Braunert, H. 'Der römische Provinzialzensus und der Schätzungsbericht des Lukas-Evangeliums', *Hist.* 6 (1957) 192–214 (= *Gesammelte Aufsätze*, 213–37)
86. Brunt, P. A. 'Charges of provincial maladministration under the early Principate', *Hist.* 10 (1961) 189–223 (= A 12, ch. 4)
87. Brunt, P. A. 'Procuratorial jurisdiction', *Latomus* 25 (1966) 461–87 (= A 12, ch. 8)
88. Burton, G. P. 'Proconsuls, assizes and the administration of justice under the Empire', *JRS* 65 (1975) 92–106
89. Burton, G. P. 'The issuing of mandata to proconsuls and a new inscription from Cos', *ZPE* 21 (1976) 63–8
90. Cardinali, G. 'Amministrazione territoriale e finanziaria', in C 12A, 161–94

91. Deininger, J. *Die Provinziallandtage der römischen Kaiserzeit von Augustus bis zum Ende des dritten Jahrhunderts n. Chr.* (*Vestigia* 6). Munich, 1965

92. Galsterer, H. 'La loi municipale des romains: chimère ou réalité?' *RHD* 65 (1987) 181–203

93. Isaac, B. 'The Decapolis in Syria, a neglected inscription', *ZPE* 44 (1981) 67–74

94. Jones, A. H. M. *The Greek City from Alexander to Justinian.* Oxford, 1940

95. Jones, A. H. M. 'Procurators and prefects in the early empire', in A 47, 115–25

96. Jones, A. H. M. *Cities of the Eastern Roman Provinces.* 2nd edn. Oxford, 1971

97. Laffi, U. *Attributio e contributio: problemi del sistema politico-amministrativo dello stato romano.* Pisa, 1966

98. Levick, B. M. *The Government of the Roman Empire.* London, 1985

99. Lintott, A. W. *Imperium Romanum: Politics and Administration.* London, 1993

100. Millar, F. 'The emperor, the senate and the provinces', *JRS* 56 (1966) 156–66

101. Millar, F. 'Empire and city, Augustus to Julian: obligations, excuses, and status', *JRS* 73 (1983) 76–96

102. Millar, F. 'State and subject: the impact of monarchy', in C 176, 37–60

103. Millar, F. ' "Senatorial provinces": an institutionalised ghost', *ANCW* 20 (1989) 93–7

104. Nicolet, C. *Tributum: recherches sur la fiscalité directe sous la république romaine.* Bonn, 1976

105. Nörr, D. *Imperium und Polis in der hohen Prinzipatszeit* (Münchener Beiträge zur Papyrusforschung und antiken Rechtsgeschichte 50). Munich, 1966: 2nd edn 1969

106. Nörr, D. 'Die Städte des Ostens und das Imperium', *ANRW* II, 7.1 (1979) 3–20

107. Purcell, N. 'The arts of Government', in Boardman, J., Griffin, J. and Murray, O. *The Oxford History of the Classical World*, 560–91. Oxford, 1986

108. Pflaum, H.-G. 'De nouveau sur les *agri decumates* à la lumière d'un fragment de Capoue, CIL x. 3872', *BJ* 163 (1963) 224–37

109. Sherwin-White, A. N. *Roman Society and Roman Law in the New Testament.* Oxford, 1963

110. Thomasson, B. *Laterculi Praesidum* I–II. Gothenburg, 1975–84

111. Weaver, P. R. C. 'Freedmen procurators in the imperial administration', *Hist.* 14 (1965) 460–9

4. THE IMPERIAL WEALTH

112. Bellen, H. 'Die "Verstaatlichung" des Privatmögerns der römischen Kaiser im I. Jahrhundert n. Chr.', *ANRW* II, 1 (1974) 94–112

113. Bolin, S. *State and Currency in the Roman Empire to 300 A.D.* Stockholm, 1958

114. Boulvert, G. 'Tacite et le fiscus', *RHD* 48 (1970) 430–8

115. Bourne, F. C. *The Public Works of the Julio-Claudians and Flavians.* Princeton, 1946

116. Brunt, P. A. 'The fiscus and its development', *JRS* 56 (1966) 75–91 (= A 12, ch. 7)

117. Brunt, P. A. 'Free labour and public works at Rome', *JRS* 70 (1980) 81–100

118. Brunt, P. A. 'The revenues of Rome', review of Neesen 1980 (D 151), *JRS* 71 (1981) 161–72 (= A 12, ch. 15)

119. Brunt, P. A. 'Publicans in the Principate', (= in A 12, ch. 17)

120. Cimma, M. R. *Reges socii et amici populi romani.* Milan, 1976

121. Cimma, M. R. *Ricerche sulle società di publicani.* Milan, 1981

122. Corbier, M. *L'Aerarium Saturni et l'Aerarium Militare: administration et prosopographie sénatoriale.* Rome, 1974

123. Corbier, M. 'L'aerarium militare', in *Armées et fiscalité dans le monde antique,* 197–234. Paris, 1977

124. Corbier, M. 'Fiscalité et dépenses locales', in *L'origine des richesses dépensées dans la ville antique,* 219–32. Aix-en-Provence, 1985

125. Crawford, D. 'Imperial estates', in A 27, ch. 3

126. Crawford, M. H. 'Money and exchange in the Roman world', *JRS* 60 (1970) 40–8

127. Dodge, H. and Ward-Perkins, B. (eds.) *Marble in Antiquity. Collected Papers of J. B. Ward-Perkins.* London, 1992

128. Frank, T. *Economic Survey of Ancient Rome* i–v. Baltimore, 1933–40

129. Gàbrici, E. 'La monetazione di Augusto', in C 12A 379–404

130. Garnsey, P., Hopkins, K. and Whittaker, C. R. (eds.) *Trade in the Ancient Economy.* Cambridge, 1983

131. Garzetti, A. 'Aerarium e fiscus sotto Augusto. Storia di una questione in parte di nomi', *Athenaeum* 31 (Studi Fraccaro) (1953) 298–327

132. Goodman, M. 'Nerva, the *Fiscus Judaicus*, and Jewish Identity', *JRS* 79 (1989) 40–4

133. Hopkins, K. 'Taxes and trade in the Roman empire (200 B.C.–A.D. 400)', *JRS* 70 (1980) 101–25

134. Howgego, C. J. 'Coinage and military finance: the imperial bronze coinages of the Augustan east', *NC* 142 (1982) 1–20

135. Howgego, C. J. 'The supply and use of money in the Roman world 200 B.C. to A.D. 300', *JRS* 82 (1992) 1–31

136. Jones, A. H. M. 'The aerarium and the fiscus', *JRS* 40 (1950) 22–9 (= A 47, ch. 6)

137. Jones, A. H. M. 'Taxation in antiquity', in A 48

138. Kloft, H. *Liberalitas Principis. Herkunft und Bedeutung.* Cologne, 1970

139. Laet, S. J. de. 'Note sur l'organisation et la nature juridique de la "uicesima hereditatum"', *AC* 16 (1947) 29–36

140. Laet, S. J. de. *Portorium. Etude sur l'organisation douanière chez les romains surtout à l'époque du Haut-Empire.* Bruges, 1949

141. Last, H. M. 'The *Fiscus*: a note', *JRS* 34 (1944) 51–9

142. Le Gall, J. 'Les habitants de Rome et la fiscalité sous le haut-empire', in van Effenterre, H. (ed.) *Points de vue sur la fiscalité antique* (Centre G. Glotz), 113–26. Paris, 1979

143. Lo Cascio, E. 'La riforma monetaria di Nerone: l'evidenza dei ripostigli', *MEFRA* 92 (1980) 445–70

144. Lo Cascio, E. 'State and coinage in the late republic and early empire', *JRS* 71 (1981) 76–86

145. Lo Cascio, E. 'La struttura fiscale dell'impero romano', in Crawford, M. H. (ed.) *L'impero romano e le strutture economiche e sociali delle province*, 29–59. Como, 1986

146. MacMullen, R. 'The Roman Emperor's army costs', *Latomus* 43 (1984) 571–80

147. MacMullen, R. 'Tax-pressure in the Roman empire', *Latomus* 46 (1987) 737–54

148. Millar, F. 'The fiscus in the first two centuries', *JRS* 53 (1963) 29–42

149. Millar, F. 'The aerarium and its officials under the empire', *JRS* 54 (1964) 33–40

150. Mitchell, S. 'Imperial building in the eastern Roman provinces', in F 479, 18–25

151. Neesen, L. *Untersuchungen zu den direkten Staatsabgaben der römischen Kaiserzeit (27 v. Chr.–284 n. Chr.).* Bonn, 1980

152. Noè, E. 'La fortuna privata del Principe e il bilancio dello Stato romano: alcune riflessioni', *Athenaeum* 65 (1987) 27–65

153. Pflaum, H.-G. 'Essai sur le Cursus Publicus sous le Haut-Empire romain', *MAI* 14 (1940) 189–390

154. Rogers, R. S. 'The Roman emperors as heirs and legatees', *TAPA* 78 (1947) 140–58

155. Rodríguez Alvarez, L. 'Algunas precisiones in materia de impuestos indirectos de la época augustea', *RIDA* 33 (1986) 189–208

156. Thornton, M. K. (ed.) *Julio-Claudian Building Programs: A Quantitative Study in Political Management.* Wauconda, 1989

157. Wesener, G. 'Uicesima hereditatum', *RE* VIII, A (1958) 2471–7

5. THE ARMY AND THE NAVY

158. Adcock, F. E. *The Roman Art of War under the Republic.* Cambridge, MA, 1940

159. Alföldy, G. *Römische Heeresgeschichte. Beiträge 1962–85.* Amsterdam, 1987

160. Bellen, H. *Die germanische Leibwache der römischen Kaiser des julisch-claudischen Hauses.* Wiesbaden, 1981

161. Birley, E. B. 'A note on the title Gemina', *JRS* 18 (1928) 56–60

162. Birley, E. B. 'Alae and cohortes milliariae', in *Corolla memoriae Erich Swobodae dedicata*, 54–67. Graz, 1966 (= D 164, 349–64)

163. Birley, E. B. '*Alae* named after their commanders', *AncSoc* 9 (1978) 257–74 (= D 164, 368–84)

164. Birley, E. B. *The Roman Army, Papers 1929–1986.* Amsterdam, 1988

165. Boren, H. C. 'Studies relating to the stipendium militum', *Hist.* 32 (1983) 427–60

166. Breeze, D. J. 'The organisation of the legion: the First Cohort and the *Equites Legionis*', *JRS* 59 (1969) 50–5

167. Breeze, D. J. 'The career structure below the centurionate during the Principate', *ANRW* II, 1 (1975) 435–51

168. Brisson, J. P. (ed.) *Problèmes de la guerre à Rome*. Paris, 1969
169. Brunt, P. A. 'Pay and superannuation in the Roman army', *PBSR* 18 (1950) 50–71
170. Brunt, P. A. 'The army and the land in the Roman Revolution', *JRS* 52 (1962) 69–86 (= A 11 240–80)
171. Brunt, P. A. 'Conscription and volunteering in the Roman imperial army', *SCI* 1 (1974) 90–115 (= A 12, ch. 9 (with 512–13))
172. Campbell, B. 'The marriage of soldiers under the Empire', *JRS* 68 (1978) 153–66
173. Campbell, J. B. *The Emperor and the Roman Army 31 B.C.–A.D. 235*. Oxford, 1984
174. Cheesman, G. L. *The Auxilia of the Roman Imperial Army*. Oxford, 1914
175. Connolly, P. *Greece and Rome at War*. London, 1981
176. Davies, R. W. 'The daily life of the Roman soldier under the Principate', *ANRW* II, 1 (1974) 299–380
177. Davies, R. W. *Service in the Roman Army* (ed. D. J. Breeze and V. A. Maxfield). Edinburgh, 1989
178. Devijver, H. 'Suétone, *Claude* 25 et les milices équestres', *AncSoc* 1 (1970) 69–81
179. Devijver, H. 'Equestrian officers from the East', in Freeman, P. and Kennedy, D. (eds.) *The Defence of the Roman and Byzantine East* (BAR International Series 297), 109–225. 2 vols. Oxford, 1986
180. Devijver, H. *The Equestrian Officers of the Roman Army*. Amsterdam, 1989
181. Dobson, B. 'The centurionate and social mobility', in Nicolet, C. (ed.) *Recherches sur les structures sociales dans l'antiquité classique*, 99–115. Paris, 1970
182. Dobson, B. 'The significance of the centurion and "primipilaris" in the Roman army and administration', *ANRW* II, 1 (1974) 392–434
183. Dobson, B. *Die Primipilares*. Cologne–Bonn, 1978
184. Domaszewski, A. von *Die Rangordnung des römischen Heeres*. Rev. by B. Dobson. Cologne, 1967
185. Durry, M. *Les cohortes prétoriennes* (*BEFAR* 146). Paris, 1938
186. Durry, M. 'Praetoriae cohortes', *RE* XXII (1954) 1607–34
187. Echols, E. 'The Roman city police: origins and development', *CJ* 53 (1957–8) 377–84
188. Forni, G. *Il reclutamento delle legioni da Augusto a Diocleziano*. Milan–Rome, 1953
189. Forni, G. 'Estrazione etnica e sociale dei soldati delle legioni nei primi tre secoli dell'impero', *ANRW* II, 1 (1974) 339–91
190. Freis, H. *Die cohortes urbanae* (Epigraphische Studien 2). Cologne–Graz, 1967
191. Gabba, E. 'Le origini dell'esercito professionale in Roma: i proletari e la riforma di Mario', *Athenaeum* 27 (1949) 173–209 (= 'The origins of the Professional Army at Rome: the "proletarii" and Marius' Reform', in *Republican Rome: the Army and the Allies*, 1–19. Oxford, 1976)
192. Gilliam, J. F. *Roman Army Papers*. Amsterdam, 1986
193. Harmand, J. *L'armée et le soldat à Rome de 107 à 50 avant notre ère*. Paris, 1967

194. Harmand, J. *Une campagne césarienne: Alésia.* Paris, 1967
195. Holder, P. A. *Studies in the Auxilia of the Roman Army from Augustus to Trajan* (BAR International Series 70). Oxford, 1980
196. Ilari, V. *Gli Italici nelle strutture militari romane.* Milan, 1974
197. Johnson, A. *Roman Forts of the 1st and 2nd centuries A.D. in Britain and the German Provinces.* London, 1983
198. Kennedy, D. L. 'Some observations on the Praetorian Guard', *AncSoc* 9 (1978) 275–301
199. Kennedy, D. L. 'Milliary cohorts: the evidence of Josephus *BJ* 4.2 (67) and of epigraphy', *ZPE* 50 (1983) 253–63
200. Keppie, L. 'Vexilla veteranorum', *PBSR* 41 (1973) 8–17
201. Keppie, L. Review of Schneider, H.-C. *Das Problem der Veteranenversorgung* (Bonn, 1977), *Latomus* 40 (1981) 141–3
202. Keppie, L. *The making of the Roman Army: from Republic to Empire.* London, 1984
203. Keppie, L. 'Legions in the East from Augustus to Trajan', in Freeman, P. and Kennedy, D. (eds.) *The Defence of the Roman and Byzantine East* (BAR International Series 297), 411–29. 2 vols. Oxford, 1986
204. Kienast, D. *Untersuchungen zu den Kriegsflotten der römischen Kaiserzeit.* Bonn, 1966
205. Kromayer, J. 'Die Entwicklung der römischen Flotte von Seeräuberkriege des Pompeius bis zur Schlacht von Aktium', *Philologus* 56 (1897) 426–91
206. Kromayer, J. and Veith, G. *Heerwesen und Kriegführung der Griechen und Römer.* Munich, 1928
207. Kubitschek, W. 'Legio', *RE* XII (1925) 1186–1210
208. Le Bohec, Y. *L'armée romaine sous le Haut-Empire.* Paris, 1989
209. Le Bohec, Y. *La Troisième Légion Auguste.* Paris, 1989
210. Le Gall, J. 'Evocatio', in *Mélanges Jacques Heurgon*, 519–24. Paris, 1976
211. Le Glay, M. 'Le commandement des *cohortes voluntariorum* de l'armée romaine', *AncSoc* 3 (1972) 209–22
212. MacMullen, R. 'The legion as a society', *Hist.* 33 (1984) 440–56
213. Mann, J. C. 'The raising of new legions during the Principate', *Hermes* 91 (1963) 483–9
214. Mann, J. C. 'The development of auxiliary and fleet diplomas', *EpStud* 9 (1972) 233–41
215. Mann, J. C. *Legionary Recruitment and Veteran Settlement during the Principate* (Univ. London, Inst. Arch. Occasional Papers 7). London, 1983
216. Maxfield, V. A. *The Military Decorations of the Roman Army.* London, 1981
217. Momigliano, A. 'I problemi delle istituzioni militari di Augusto', in c 12A, 195–215
218. Paget, R. F. 'The ancient ports of Cumae', *JRS* 58 (1968) 152–69
219. Parker, H. M. D. *The Roman Legions.* Oxford, 1928. Rev. by G. R. Watson, 1971
220. Passerini, A. *Le coorti pretorie.* Rome, 1939
221. Passerini, A. 'Legio', *DE* 4 (1949) 549–627
222. Reddé, M. *Mare Nostrum* (*BEFAR* 260, Paris, 1986)

223. Ritterling, E. 'Legio', *RE* XII (1925) 1211–829

224. Roxan, M. M. 'The distribution of Roman military diplomas', *EpStud* 12 (1981) 265–86

225. Royen, R. A. van. 'Colonia Augusta Praetoria and Augustus' Cohortes Praetoriae', *Talanta* 5 (1973) 48–71

226. Saddington, D. B. 'Prefects and lesser officers in the auxilia at the beginning of the Roman Empire', *PACA* 15 (1980) 20–58

227. Saddington, D. B. *The Development of the Roman Auxiliary Forces from Caesar to Vespasian (49 B.C.–A.D. 79)*. Harare, 1982

228. Saxer, R. *Untersuchungen zu den Vexillationen des römischen Kaiserheeres von Augustus bis Diokletian* (= *EpStud* 1). Cologne–Graz, 1967

229. Schleussner, B. *Die Legaten der römischen Republik*. Munich, 1978

230. Schmitthenner, W. C. G. 'The armies of the Triumviral period: a study of the origins of the Roman imperial legions'. D. Phil. thesis, University of Oxford, 1958

231. Schneider, H.-C. *Das problem der Veteranenversorgung in der späteren römischen Republik*. Bonn, 1977

232. Smith, R. E. *Service in the Post-Marian Roman Army*. Manchester, 1958

233. Speidel, M. P. 'The pay of the auxilia', *JRS* 63 (1973) 141–7 (= D 235, 83–9)

234. Speidel, M. P. 'Citizen cohorts in the Roman imperial army', *TAPA* 106 (1976) 339–48 (= D 235, 91–100)

235. Speidel, M. P. *Roman Army Studies* I. Amsterdam, 1984

236. Speidel, M. P. 'Germani corporis custodes', *Germania* 62 (1984) 31–45

237. Starr, C. G. *The Roman Imperial Navy 31 B.C.–A.D. 324*. New York, 1941. 2nd edn. Cambridge, 1960

238. Syme, R. 'Some notes on the legions under Augustus', *JRS* 23 (1933) 14–33

239. Vendrand-Voyer, J. *Normes civiques et métier militaire à Rome sous le Principat*, Clermont-Ferrand, 1983

240. Watson, G. R. *The Roman Soldier*. 2nd edn. London, 1983

241. Webster, G. *The Roman Imperial Army*. 3rd edn. London, 1985

242. Wierschowski, L. *Heer und Wirtschaft. Das römische Heer der Prinzipatszeit als Wirtschaftsfaktor*. Bonn, 1984

6. THE ADMINISTRATION OF JUSTICE

243. Bauman, R. A. 'The "leges iudiciorum publicorum" and their interpretation in the Republic, Principate and Later Empire', *ANRW* II, 13 (1980) 103–233

244. Bauman, R. A. 'Hangman, call a halt!', *Hermes* 110 (1982) 102–10

245. Behrends, O. *Die römische Geschworenenverfassung*. Göttingen, 1970

246. Behrends, O. Review of Jones 1972 (D 264), *ZRG* 90 (1973) 462–75

247. Birks, P., Rodger, A. and Richardson, J. S. 'Further aspects of the *Tabula Contrebiensis*', *JRS* 74 (1984) 45–73

248. Bleicken, J. *Senatsgericht und Kaisergericht. Eine Studie zur Entwicklung des Prozessrechtes im frühen Prinzipat*. (Abh. Ak. Göttingen, phil.-hist. Klasse, ser. 3, 53) Göttingen, 1962

249. Bringmann, K. 'Zur Gerichtsreform des Kaisers Augustus', *Chiron* 3 (1973) 235–44
250. Brunt, P. A. Review of Kunkel 1962 (D 268) *RHD* 32 (1964) 440–9
251. Brunt, P. A. Review of Jones 1972 (D 264), *CR* 88 (1974) 265–7
252. Buti, I. 'La "Cognitio extra Ordinem": Da Augusto a Diocleziano', *ANRW* II, 14 (1982) 29–59
253. Cuq, E. *Manuel des institutions juridiques des Romains.* 2nd edn. Paris, 1928
254. Frezza, P. 'Storia del processo civile in Roma fino all'età di Augusto', *ANRW* I, 2 (1972) 163–96
255. Galsterer, H. Review of Behrends, 1970 (D 245), *GGA* 225 (1973) 29–46
256. Galsterer, H. Review of Simshäuser 1973 (D 275), *GGA* 229 (1977) 64–81
257. Garnsey, P. D. A. 'The *lex Iulia* and appeal under the empire', *JRS* 56 (1966) 167–89
258. Garnsey, P. D. A. 'Adultery trials and the survival of the *quaestiones* in the Severan age', *JRS* 57 (1967) 56–60
259. Garnsey, P. D. A. 'The criminal jurisdiction of governors', *JRS* 58 (1968) 51–9
260. Greenidge, A. H. J. *The Legal Procedure of Cicero's Time.* London, 1901
261. Guarino, A. 'La formazione dell'editto perpetuo', *ANRW* II, 13 (1980) 62–102
262. Jones, A. H. M. '"I appeal unto Caesar"', *Studies D. M. Robinson* II, 918–30. Saint Louis, MS, 1953 (= A 47, 51–65)
263. Jones, A. H. M. 'Imperial and senatorial jurisdiction in the early Principate', *Hist.* 3 (1955) 464–88. (= A 47, 67–98)
264. Jones, A. H. M. *The Criminal Courts of the Roman Republic and Principate.* Oxford, 1972
265. Kelly, J. M. *Princeps Iudex.* Weimar, 1957
266. Kelly, J. M. *Roman Litigation.* Oxford, 1966
267. Kelly, J. M. *Studies in the Civil Judicature of the Roman Republic.* Oxford, 1976
268. Kunkel, W. 'Untersuchungen zur Entwicklung des römischen Kriminalverfahrens in vorsullanischer Zeit', *ABAW* 56 (1962)
269. Kunkel, W. 'Über die Entstehung des Senatsgerichts', *SBAW* (1969) no. 2 (= *Kleine Schriften* (1974) 267–323)
270. Laffi, U. 'La lex Rubria de Gallia Cisalpina', *Athenaeum* 64 (1986) 5–44
271. Lintott, A. W. 'Provocatio. From the struggle of the orders to the principate', *ANRW* I, 2 (1972) 226–7
272. Luzzatto, G. I. *La procedura civile romana* I–III. Bologna, 1946–50
273. Mommsen, T. *Römisches Strafrecht.* Berlin, 1899
274. Polay, E. 'Der Kodifizierungsplan des Julius Caesar', *Iura* 16 (1965) 27–51
275. Simshäuser, W. *Iuridici und Munizipalgerichtsbarkeit in Italien.* Munich, 1973
276. Stroux, J. 'Eine Gerichtsreform des Kaisers Claudius (BGU 611)' *JbAW* 8 (1929)
277. Torrent, A. *La 'Iurisdictio' de los Magistrados Municipales.* Salamanca, 1970
278. Wolff, H.-J. 'Römisches Provinzialrecht in der Provinz Arabia', *ANRW* II, 13 (1980) 763–806

E. ITALY AND THE PROVINCES

I. ITALY

1. Ampolo, C. Review of Torelli, M. *Lavinio e Roma* (Rome, 1984), *CR* 38 (1988) 117–20
2. Anderson, J. C. *The Historical Topography of the Imperial Fora* (Coll. Latomus 182). Brussels, 1984
3. Bermond Montanari, G. 'Monumenti funerari atestini', *RIA* 8 (1959) 111–40
4. Bleicken, J. 'Vici magister', *RE* 2, VIII (1958) 2480–3
5. Boatwright, M. T. 'The pomerial extension of Augustus', *Hist.* 35 (1986) 13–27
6. Boethius, A. Review of Shipley, F. W. *Agrippa's Building Activities in Rome* (St Louis, 1933), *Athenaeum* 12 (1934) 431–5
7. Bonjour, M. *Terre natale. Etudes sur une composante effective du patriotisme romain.* Paris, 1975
8. Boyancé, P. 'Properce aux fêtes de quartier', *REA* 52 (1950) 64–71
9. Braunert, H. 'Verfassungsnorm und Verfassungswirklichkeit im spätrepublikanischen Rom', *AU* 9 (1966) 51–73
10. Briquel, D. 'Le témoignage de Claude sur Mastarna/Servius Tullius', *RBPh* 68 (1990), 86–108
11. Carettoni, G., Colini, A. M., Cozza, L. and Gatti, G. *La pianta marmorea di Roma antica.* Rome, 1960
12. Castrén, P. *Ordo Populusque Pompeianus.* Rome, 1975
13. Castrén, P. 'Cambiamenti nel gruppo dei notabili municipali dell'Italia centro-meridionale nel corso del I secolo a.C.', in E 77, 91–7
14. Cébeillac Gervasoni, M. 'Problématique de la promotion politique pour les notables des cités du Latium à la fin de la République', *Ktema* 3 (1978) 227–42
15. Chevallier, R. *La romanisation de la Celtique du Pô* (*BEFAR* 249). Rome, 1983
16. Ciampoltrini, G. 'Note sulla colonizzazione augustea nell'Etruria settentrionale', *SCO* 31 (1981) 41–55
17. *La città nell'Italia settentrionale in età romana. Morfologia, strutture e funzioni dei centri urbani delle Regiones X e XI* (Collection de l'école française de Rome 130) Trieste–Rome, 1990
18. Coarelli, F. 'Il Vallo di Diano in età romana. I dati dell'archeologia', in D'Agostino, B. (ed.) *Storia del Vallo di Diano I*, 217–77. Salerno, 1981
19. Coarelli, F. *Il Foro Romano.* 2 vols. Rome, 1983–5
20. Coarelli, F. *Roma* (Guide archeologiche Laterza). 3rd edn. Rome and Bari, 1985
21. Coarelli, F. *Il Foro Boario.* Rome, 1988
22. Coleman, R. G. 'The central Italic languages in the period of Roman expansion', *TransPhilSoc* (1986) 100–31
23. Conway, R. S. *The Italic Dialects* I–II. Cambridge, 1897
24. Cornell, T. J. 'Etruscan historiography', *ASNP* 3, 6 (1976) 411–39

25. Cornell, T. J. '*Principes* of Tarquinia', *JRS* 68 (1978) 167–73
26. Crawford, M. H. 'Italy and Rome', *JRS* 71 (1981) 153–60
27. Crawford, M. H. 'Early Rome and Italy', in Boardman, J., Griffin, J. and Murray, O. (eds.) *The Oxford History of the Classical World* ch. 17. Oxford, 1986
28. Crawford, M. H. 'Ateste and Rome', *QTic* 18 (1989) 191–200
29. Crawford, M. H. 'Rome and Italy after the Social War', forthcoming
30. D'Arms, J. H. *Romans on the Bay of Naples. A Social and Cultural Study of the Villas and their Owners from 150 B.C. to A.D. 400.* Cambridge, MA, 1970
31. D'Arms, J. H. 'Upper-class attitudes towards *uiri municipales* and their towns in the early Roman Empire', *Athenaeum* 62 (1984) 440–67
32. David, J.-M. 'Les orateurs des municipes à Rome: intégration, réticences et snobismes', in E 77, 309–23
33. Deininger, J. 'Brot und Spiele; Tacitus und die Entpolitisierung der *plebs urbana*', *Gymn.* 86 (1979) 278–803
34. Demougin, S. 'Notables municipaux et ordre équestre à l'époque des dernières guerres civiles', in E 77, 279–98
35. Devijver, H. and Wonterghem, F. van. 'Il *campus* nell'impianto urbanistico delle città romane', *ActaArchLov* 20 (1981) 33; 21 (1982) 93
36. Dumont, J. C. 'Les gens de théâtre originaires des municipes', in E 77, 333–45
37. Duthoy, R. 'Les Augustales', *ANRW* II, 16.2 (1978) 1254–309, esp. 1293–306
38. Eck, W. *Die staatliche Organisation Italiens in der hohen Kaiserzeit* (Vestigia 28). Munich, 1979
39. Emiliozzi, A. 'Sull'epitaffio del 67 a.C. nel sepolcro dei Salvii a Ferento', *MEFRA* 95 (1983) 701–17
40. Franciscis, A. de. 'Sculture connesse con la scuola medica di Elea', *PP* 25 (1970) 267–84
41. Frederiksen, M. W. 'Republican Capua. A social and economic study', *PBSR* 27 (1959) 80–130
42. Frederiksen, M. W. 'Changes in the pattern of settlement', in E 141, II, 341–55
43. Frederiksen, M. W. *Campania*. London, 1984
44. Gabba, E. 'Urbanizzazione e rinnovamenti urbanistici nell'Italia centro-meridionale del I sec. a.C.', *SCO* 21 (1972) 73–112
45. Gabba. E. 'Il problema dell' "unità" dell'Italia romana', in Campanile, E. (ed.) *La cultura italica*. 11–27. Pisa, 1978
46. Gabba, E. 'Proposta per l'elogio tarquiniese de Velthur Spurinna', *QTic* 8 (1979) 143
47. Gabba, E. 'La rifondazione di Salapia', *Athenaeum* 61 (1983) 514–16
48. Gabba, E. 'Ticinum: dalle origini alla fine del III sec. d.C.', in Gabba, E. (ed.) *Storia di Pavia* I, 205–47. Pavia, 1984
49. Gabba, E. 'Le città italiche del I sec. a.C. e la politica', *RSI* 98 (1986) 653–63
50. Gaggiotti, M. *et al. Umbria Marche* (Guide Archeologiche Laterza.) Bari, 1980

51. Vacat

52. Galsterer, H. *Herrschaft und Verwaltung im republikanischen Italien.* Munich, 1976

53. Gely, E. '*Terra patria* et *societas hominum*', *REL* 52 (1974) 149–67

54. Hammond, M. 'Germana patria', *HSCP* 60 (1951) 147–74

55. Harris, W. V. *Rome in Etruria and Umbria.* Oxford, 1971

56. Harris, W. V. 'The era of Patavium', *ZPE* 27 (1977) 283

57. Harvey, P. B. '*Socer Valgus, Valgii* and C. Quinctius Valgus', in Borza, E. N. and Carrubba, R. W. (eds.) *Classics and the Classical Tradition. Essays presented to R. E. Dengler,* 79–94. Pennsylvania State University, 1973

58. Häuber, R. C. 'Zur Topographie der Horti Maecenatis und der Horti Lamiani auf dem Esquilin in Rom', *Kölner Jahrbücher* 73 (1990) 11–107

59. Heurgon, J. 'La vocation étruscologique de l'empereur Claude', *CRAI* 1953, 92

60. Homo, L. *Rome impériale et l'urbanisme dans l'antiquité.* Paris, 1971

61. Humbert, M. '*Municipium' et 'civitas sine suffragio'.* Rome, 1978

62. Jongman, W. *The Economy and Society of Pompeii.* Amsterdam, 1988

63. Jordan, H. and Hülsen, G. *Topographie der Stadt Rom im Alterthum.* 2 vols. Berlin, 1878–1907

64. Kaimio, J. 'The ousting of Etruscan by Latin in Etruria', in Bruun, P. *et al. Studies in the Romanisation of Etruria,* 85–245. Rome, 1975

65. Keppie, L. *Colonisation and Veteran Settlement in Italy, 47–14 B.C.* London, 1983

66. Keppie, L. 'Colonisation and veteran settlement in Italy in the first century A.D.', *PBSR* 39 (1984) 77–114

67. Keuls, E. C. 'Aspetti religiosi della Magna Grecia nell'età romana', in *La Magna Grecia nell'età romana. Atti del quindicesimo Convegno di Studi sulla Magna Grecia,* 439–58. Naples, 1976

68. Labrousse, M. 'Le *pomerium* de la Rome impériale', *MEFRA* 54 (1937) 165–99

69. Laffi, U. 'La *lex aedis* Furfensis', in Campanile, E. (ed.) *La cultura italica,* 121–44. Pisa, 1978

70. Lampe, P. *Die stadtrömischen Christen in den ersten beiden Jahrhunderten: Untersuchungen zur Sozialgeschichte.* 2nd edn. Tübingen, 1989

71. Lanciani, R. *The Destruction of Ancient Rome.* London, 1906

72. Lavizzari Pedrazzini, M. P. *Ceramica romana di tradizione ellenistica in Italia settentrionale. Il vasellame 'tipo Aco'.* Florence, 1987

73. Le Gall, J. *Le Tibre, fleuve de Rome, dans l'antiquité.* Paris, 1953

74. Lejeune, M. *L'anthroponymie osque.* Paris, 1976

75. Lepore, E. 'Geografia del modo di produzione schiavistica e modi residui in Italia meridionale', in Giardina, A. and Schiavone, A. (eds.) *Società romana e produzione schiavistica* I, 79–85. Bari, 1981

76. Lepore, E. 'Roma e le città greche o ellenizzate nell'Italia meridionale', in E 77, 347–54

77. *Les bourgeoisies municipales italiennes aux IIᵉ et Iᵉʳ siècles av. J.-C.* (Colloques internationaux du Centre national de la recherche scientifique n. 609). Paris–Naples, 1983

78. Linderski, J. 'Natalis Patavii', *ZPE* 50 (1983) 227–32
79. Lo Cascio, E. 'I *greges oviarici* dell'iscrizione di Sepino', in *Scritti offerti a Ettore Paratore ottuagenario* (= *Abruzzo* 23–8 (1985–90) 557–69)
80. Lugli, G. *I monumenti antichi di Roma e suburbio.* 3 vols. Rome, 1931–40
81. Lugli, G. *Roma antica: Il centro monumentale.* Rome, 1946
82. Lugli, G. *Fontes ad Topographiam veteris urbis Romae pertinentes* Vols. I–VII. Rome, 1952; Vols. VIII, XIX–XX. Rome, 1962
83. Martino, F. de 'Note sull'Italia augustea', *Athenaeum* 53 (1975) 245–61
84. Meiggs, R. *Roman Ostia.* 2nd edn. Oxford, 1973
85. Moreau, P. 'Structures de parenté et d'alliance à Larinum', in E 77, 99–123
86. Nash, E. *Bildlexicon zur Topographie des antiken Rom.* 2 vols. Tübingen, 1961–2. Translated as E 87
87. Nash, E. *Pictorial Dictionary of Ancient Rome.* 2nd edn. London, 1968
88. Pais, E. 'Cittadinanza romana e cittadinanza attica', in *Dalle guerre puniche a Cesare Augusto I*, 349–61. Rome, 1918
89. Panciera, S. 'Tra epigrafia e topografia – I', *ArchClass* 22 (1970) 131–63
90. Panciera, S. 'Nuovi luoghi di culto a Roma dalle testimonianze epigrafiche', *ArchLaz* 3 (1980) 202–13
91. Panciera, S. 'In operis publicis esse', in Broilo, F. (ed.) *Xenia: Scritti in onore P. Treves*, 129. Rome, 1985
92. Panciera, S. 'Ancora tra epigrafia e topografia', *L'urbs* (1987) 61–86
93. Panciera, S. 'Due nuovi frammenti di calendario romano', *Arch Class* 25/26 (1973/1974) 481–90
94. Picard, G. C. *Rome et les villes d'Italie des Gracques à la mort d'Auguste.* Paris, 1978
95. Platner, S. and Ashby, T. *A Topographical Dictionary of Ancient Rome.* Oxford–London, 1929
96. Poccetti, P. 'Romani e Italici a Delo', *Athenaeum* 62 (1984) 646–56
97. Poccetti, P. 'Per una definizione delle iscrizioni "bilingui" in area etrusca ed italica', in Campanile, E. *et al.* (eds.) *Bilinguismo e biculturalismo nel mondo antico*, 127. Pisa, 1988
98. Potter, T. W. *Roman Italy.* London, 1986
99. Prontera, F. 'L'Italia meridionale di Strabone. Appunti tra geografia e storia', in Maddoli, G. (ed.) *Strabone e l'Italia antica* 93–109. Naples, 1988
100. Prosdocimi, A. 'Contatti e conflitti di lingue nell'Italia antica: l'elemento greco', in *Popoli e civiltà dell'Italia antica* VI, 1029–88. Rome, 1978
101. Pucci, G. 'La ceramica italica', in Giardina, A. and Schiavone A. (eds.) *Società romana e produzione schiavistica* II, 99–121. 1981
102. Purcell, N. 'The city of Rome and the Plebs Urbana in the late Republic', in *CAH* IX², 644–88. Cambridge, 1994
103. Purcell, N. 'The capital of Italy and the world: Rome from Vespasian to Constantine', in *CAH* XI². Forthcoming
104. Rainbird, J. S. 'The fire stations of Imperial Rome', *PBSR* 54 (1986) 147–69
105. Ramage, C. T. *The Nooks and Byways of Italy. Wanderings in Search of Its Ancient Remains and Modern Superstitions.* Liverpool, 1868

106. Rawson, E. D. 'Caesar, Etruria and the *disciplina Etrusca*', *JRS* 68 (1978) 132–52
107. Rawson, E. D. 'Cicero and the Areopagus', *Athenaeum* 63 (1985) 44–67
108. Reynolds, P. K. B. *The Vigiles of Imperial Rome*. Oxford, 1926
109. Rickman, G. *The Corn Supply of Ancient Rome*. Oxford, 1980
110. Robinson, O. 'The water supply of Rome', *SDHI* 46 (1980) 44–86
111. Rodriguez Almeida, E. *Forma Urbis Marmorea. Aggiornamento generale 1980*. Rome, 1980
112. *Roma, Archeologia nel centro urbano* I–II. Rome, 1985–6
113. *Roma Capitale 1870–1911. L'archeologia di Roma Capitale tra sterro e scavo*. Exhibition Catalogue, 1983
114. *La romanizzazione della Basilicata*. Forthcoming
115. Rossignani, M. P. 'Gli edifici pubblici nell'Italia settentrionale fra l'89 a.C. e l'età augustea', in *La città nell'Italia settentrionale*, 305–39. Trieste–Rome, 1990
116. Sablayrolles, R. 'Espace urbain et propagande politique: l'organisation du centre de Rome par Auguste (Res Gestae 19 à 21)', *Pallas* 28 (1981) 59–77
117. Sachers, E. 'Praefectus urbi', *RE* XXII (1954) 2502–34
118. Sartori, F. 'Le città italiote dopo la conquista romana', in *La Magna Grecia nell'età romana. Atti del quindicesimo Convegno di Studi sulla Magna Grecia*. 83–137. Naples, 1976
119. Sena Chiesa, G. 'Frammenti con fregio dorico al Museo Archeologico di Milano', in *Scritti G. Massari Gaballo and U. T. Pollini*, 131–40. Milan, 1986
120. Sensi, L. 'Assisi: aspetti prosopografici', in E 77, 165–73
121. Simone, C. de 'Italien', in Neumann, G. and Untermann, J. (eds.) *Die Sprachen im römischen Reich der Kaiserzeit*, 65–81. Bonn, 1980
122. Sommella, P. *Italia antica. L'urbanistica romana*. Rome, 1987
123. *Studi Lunensi e prospettive sull'Occidente romano* (Atti del Conv. di Lerici). La Spezia, 1987
124. Susini, G. 'I profughi della *Sabatina*', *Convegno in memoria di Plinio Fraccaro*, 172–6. Pavia, 1976
125. Tagliaferri, A. *Coloni e legionari romani nel Friuli celtico*. Pordenone, 1986
126. Tchernia, A. *Le vin de l'Italie romaine*. Rome, 1986
127. Thomsen, R. *The Italic Regions from Augustus to the Lombard Invasion*. Copenhagen, 1947
128. Tibiletti, G. 'Italia Augustea', *Mélanges J. Carcopino*, 917–26. Paris, 1966
129. Torelli, M. 'Monumenti funerari romani con fregio dorico', *DArch* 2 (1969) 1, 32–54
130. Torelli, M. 'La situazione in Etruria', in E 141, 1, 97–109
131. Torelli, M. 'Una nuova epigrafe di Bantia e la cronologia dello statuto municipale bantino', *Athenaeum* 61 (1983) 252–7
132. Torelli, M. 'Gesellschaft und Wirtschaftsformen der augusteischen Zeit: der *Consensus Italiae*', in *Kaiser Augustus und die verlorene Republik*, 23–48. Berlin, 1984

133. Torelli, M. '"Tribuni Plebis" municipali?', in *Sodalitas: scritti in onore di Antonio Guarino* III, 1397–402. Naples, 1984
134. Toynbee, J. and Ward Perkins, J. *The Shrine of St Peter and the Vatican Excavations*. London, 1956
135. Visscher, F. de *Le droit des tombeaux romains*. Milan, 1963
136. Vitucci, G. *Ricerche sulla praefectura urbi in età imperiale*. Rome, 1956
137. Wiseman, T. P. 'The census in the first century B.C.', *JRS* 59 (1969) 59–75
138. Wiseman, T. P. '*Domi nobiles* and the Roman cultural élite', in E 77, 299–307
139. Wiseman, T. P. *Catullus and his World*. Cambridge, 1985
140. Wiseman, T. P. 'Reading the city: history, poetry and the topography of Rome', *JACTJ* 2 (1987) 3–6
141. Zanker, P. (ed.) *Hellenismus in Mittelitalien*. Göttingen, 1976
142. Zevi, F. 'Monumenti e aspetti culturali di Ostia repubblicana', in E 141, I, 52–63

2. SICILY, SARDINIA AND CORSICA

143. Acquaro, E., Barreca, F., Gecchini, S. M., Fantar, D. and M., Guzzo Amadasi, M. G. and Moscati, S. *Ricerche Puniche ad Antas*. Rome, 1969
144. Angiolillo, S. *L'arte della Sardegna romana*. Milan, 1987
145. Ascari, M. C. *La Corsica nell'antichità*. Rome, 1942
146. Balmuth, M. S. and Rowland, R. J. Jr. (eds.) *Studies in Sardinian Archaeology* I. Ann Arbor, 1984
147. Bejor, G. 'Ricerche di topografia e di archeologia romana nella Sicilia sud-occidentale', *Annali della Scuola normale superiore di Pisa* 5 (1975) 1275–1303
148. Bejor, G. 'Aspetti della romanizzazione della Sicilia', in *Forme di contatto e processi di trasformazione nelle società antiche* (Atti Convegno di Cortona, 1981) 354–74. Pisa–Rome, 1983
149. Beloch, K. J. 'La popolazione antica della Sicilia', *ASS* 14 (1889) 1–83
150. Belvedere, O. 'Opere pubbliche ed edifici per lo spettacolo nella Sicilia di età imperiale', *ANRW* II, 11,1 (1988) 346–413
151. Boninu, A., Le Glay, M. and Mastino, A. *Turris Libisonis Colonia Iulia*. Sassari, 1984
152. Bouchier, E. S. *Sardinia in Ancient Times*. Oxford, 1917
153. Brown, P. J. 'Malaria in Nuragic, Punic and Roman Sardinia: some hypotheses', in E 146, 209–35
154. Clemente, G. 'La Sicilia nell'età imperiale', in Gabba, E. and Vallet, G. (eds.) *Sicilia Antica* II, 463–80. Naples, 1980
155. Clemente, G. 'Considerazioni sulla Sicilia nell'impero romano (III sec. a.C.–V sec. d.C.)', *Kokalos* 26–7 (1980–1) 192–219
156. Cuntz, O. 'Zur Geschichte Siciliens in der cäsarisch-augusteischen Epoche', *Klio* 6 (1906) 466–76
157. Dyson, S. L. *The Creation of the Roman Frontier*. Princeton, 1985
158. Finley, M. I. *Ancient Sicily*. 2nd edn. London, 1979
159. Fraschetti, A. 'Per una prosopografia dello sfruttamento: romani e italici

in Sicilia (212–44 a.c.)', in Giardina, A. and Schiavone, A. (eds.) *Società romana e produzione schiavistica: L'Italia: insediamenti e forme economiche*, 51–77. Bari, 1981

160. Gabba, E. 'La Sicilia romana', in Crawford, M. H. (ed.) *L'Impero Romano e le strutture economiche e sociali delle province* (Biblioteca di Athenaeum 4). Como, 1986

161. Goldsberry, M. *Sicily and its Cities in Hellenistic and Roman Times*. (Diss., Chapel Hill (Univ. of N. Carolina) 1973) Ann Arbor, 1982

162. Guzzo Amadasi, M. G. *Iscrizioni fenicie e puniche delle colonie in Occidente*. Rome, 1967

163. Holm, A. *Geschichte Siziliens im Alterthum* III. Leipzig, 1878

164. Jéhasse, J. 'La Corse antique d'après Ptolemée', *Archeologia Corsa. Études et Memoires* I. Ajaccio, 1976

165. Jéhasse, J. and L. 'La Corse romaine', in Arrighi, P. (ed.) *Histoire de la Corse*, 97–128. Toulouse, 1971

166. Jéhasse, J. and L. *Aléria antique*. Aléria, 1982

167. Kahrstedt, U. 'Die Gemeinden Siziliens in der Römerzeit', *Klio* 35 (1942) 246–67

168. Maetzke, G. 'Architettura romana in Sardegna', *Atti del XIII Congresso di Storia dell' Architettura*, 155–69. Rome, 1966

169. Manganaro, G. 'Per una storia della Sicilia romana', *ANRW* I, 1 (1972) 442–61

170. Manganaro, G. 'La provincia romana', in Gabba, E. and Vallet, G. (eds.) *La Sicilia Antica* II, 411–61. Naples, 1980

171. Manganaro, G. 'I senatori di Sicilia e il problema del latifondo', *Epigrafia e ordine senatorio* II (= *Tituli* 5, 1982), 369–85

172. Manganaro, G. 'La Sicilia da Sesto Pompeio a Diocletiano', *ANRW* II, 11, 1 (1988) 3–89

173. Manni, E. *Geografia fisica e politica della Sicilia antica*. Rome, 1981

174. Meloni, P. *L'amministrazione della Sardegna da Augusto all'invasione vandalica*. Rome, 1958

175. Meloni, P. *La Sardegna romana*. Sassari, 1975

176. Michon, E. 'Administration de la Corse sous la dominion romaine', *MEFRA* 8 (1888) 411–25

177. Moracchini-Mazel, G. *Les Fouilles de Mariana (Corse)*. 1. *La nécropole de Palazzetto-Murotondo* (= *Cahiers Corsica* 4–7). Bastia, 1971

178. Moracchini-Mazel, G. *Les Fouilles de Mariana (Corse)*. 6. *La nécropole d'i ponti* (= *Cahiers Corsica* 37–9). Bastia, 1974

179. Pace, B. *Arte e civiltà della Sicilia antica*. 4 vols. Rome–Naples, 1936–49. 2nd edn. vol. I, 1958

180. Pais, E. 'Alcune osservazioni sulla storia e sulla amministrazione della Sicilia durante il dominio romano', *ASS* 13 (1888) 113–256

181. Pais, E. *Storia della Sardegna e della Corsica durante il dominio romano*. Rome, 1923

182. Rowland, R. J. Jr. *I ritrovamenti romani in Sardegna*. Rome, 1981

183. Rowland, R. J. Jr. 'The case of the missing Sardinian grain', *AncW* 10. 1–2 (1984) 45–8

184. Rowland, R. J. Jr. 'The countryside of Roman Sardinia', in E 146, 285–300

185. Rowland, R. J. Jr. 'The Roman invasion of Sardinia', in Malone, C. and Stoddart, S. (eds.) *Papers in Italian Archaeology* IV.iv, 99–117. Oxford, 1985

186. Sartori, F. 'Appunti di storia siceliota: la costituzione di Tauromenio', *Athenaeum* 32 (1954) 356–83

187. Scramuzza, V. M. 'Roman Sicily', in D 128, III, 225–377

188. Stone, S. C. 'Sextus Pompey, Octavian and Sicily', *AJA* 87 (1983) 11–22

189. Tarn, W. W. 'Sicily and the end of Sextus Pompeius', *CAH* x¹, 55–62. Cambridge, 1934

190. Thomasson, B. E. 'Zur Verwaltungsgeschichte der Provinz Sardinia', *Eranos* 70 (1972) 72–81

191. Tronchetti, C. 'The cities of Roman Sardinia', in E 146, 237–83

192. Vismara Pergola, C. 'Prima miscellanea sulla Corsica romana', *MEFRA* 92 (1980) 303–28

193. Wilson, R. J. A. 'Sardinia and Sicily during the Roman Empire: aspects of the archaeological evidence', *Kokalos* 26–7 (1980–1) 219–42

194. Wilson, R. J. A. 'Changes in the pattern of urban settlement in Roman, Byzantine and Arab Sicily', in Malone, C. and Stoddart, S. (eds.) *Papers in Italian Archaeology* IV.i, 313–44. Oxford, 1985

195. Wilson, R. J. A. 'Un insediamento agricolo romano a Castagna (Comune di Cattolica Eraclea)', *Sicilia Archeologia* xviii, 57–8 (1985) 11–35

196. Wilson, R. J. A. 'Towns of Sicily during the Roman Empire', *ANRW* II, 11, 1 (1988) 90–206

197. Wilson, R. J. A. *Sicily under the Roman Empire: the Archaeology of a Roman Province 36 B.C.–A.D. 535*. Warminster, 1990

3. SPAIN

198. Albertini, E. *Les divisions administratives de l'Espagne romaine*. Paris, 1923

199. Albertos Firmat, M. L. *La onomástica personal primitiva de Hispania Tarraconense y Bética*. Salamanca, 1966

200. Albertos Firmat, M. L. *Organizaciones suprafamiliares en la Hispania antigua*. Valladolid, 1975. – II: *BSEAA* 47 (1981) 208–14

201. Alföldy, G. *Fasti Hispanienses. Senatorische Reichsbeamte und Offiziere in den spanischen Provinzen des römischen Reiches von Augustus bis Diokletian*. Wiesbaden, 1969

202. Alföldy, G. 'Tarraco', *RE* Suppl. xv (1978) 570–644

203. Alföldy, G. 'Zur Geschichte von Asturia et Callaecia', *Germania* 61 (1983) 511–28

204. Alföldy, G. 'Drei städtische Eliten im römischen Hispanien', *Gerión* 2 (1984) 193–238 (= *id. Die römische Gesellschaft* (HABES 1), 239–84. Stuttgart, 1986)

205. Alföldy, G. *Römisches Städtewesen auf der neukastilischen Hochebene. Ein Testfall für die Romanisierung* (Abh. Heidelberger Akad. Wiss., phil.-hist. Kl., 1987, 3. Abh.). Heidelberg, 1987

206. Blázquez, J. M. 'Estado de la romanización de Hispania bajo César y Augusto', *Emerita* 30 (1962) 71–129

207. Blázquez (Martínez), J. M. *Religiones primitivas de Hispania* 1. *Fuentes literarias y epigráficas.* Madrid, 1962

208. Blázquez (Martínez), J. M. *Ciclos y temas de la Historia de España: la Romanización.* 11. *La Sociedad y la Economía en la Hispania Romana.* Madrid, 1975

209. Blázquez (Martínez), J. M. *Economía de la Hispania romana.* Bilbao, 1978

210. Blázquez (Martínez), J. M. *et al. Historia de España antigua* 11. *Hispania romana.* Madrid, 1982

211. Brancati, A. *Augusto e la guerra di Spagna.* Urbino, 1963

212. Broughton, T. R. S. 'The Romanization of Spain. The problem and the evidence', *PAPhS* 103 (1959) 645–51

213. Castillo García, C. 'Städte und Personen der Baetica', *ANRW* II, 3, 601–54. Berlin–New York, 1975

214. Castillo García, C. 'Los senadores béticos. Relaciones familiares y sociales', *Epigrafia e ordine senatorio* II *(Tituli* 5), 465–519. Rome, 1982

215. Diego Santos, F. 'Die Integration Nord- und Nordwestspaniens als römische Provinz in der Reichspolitik des Augustus', *ANRW* II, 3 (1975) 523–71

216. Domergue, C. *Les mines de la péninsule ibérique dans l'antiquité romaine.* Rome, 1990

217. Etienne, R. *Le culte impérial dans la péninsule ibérique d'Auguste à Dioclétien.* Paris, 1958

218. Etienne, R. 'Sénateurs originaires de la province de Lusitanie', *Epigrafia e ordine senatorio* II *(Tituli* 5), 521–9. Rome, 1982

219. Fabre, G., Mayer, M. and Rodà, I. 'A propos du pont de Martorell: la participation de l'armée à l'aménagement du réseau routier de la Tarraconnaise orientale sous Auguste', *Épigraphie hispanique*, 282–8. Paris, 1984

220. Fishwick, D. 'The altar of Augustus and the municipal cult of Tarraco', *MDAI(M)* 23 (1982) 222–33

221. Galsterer, H. *Untersuchungen zum römischen Städtewesen auf der Iberischen Halbinsel (Madrider Forschungen* 8). Berlin, 1971

222. Galsterer, H. 'Bemerkungen zur Integration vorrömischer Bevölkerungen auf der Iberischen Halbinsel', *Actas del II Coloquio sobre lenguas y culturas prerromanas de la Península ibérica*, 453–64. Salamanca, 1979

223. García y Bellido, A. 'Las colonias romanas de Hispania', *AHDE* 29 (1959) 447–517

224. García y Bellido, A. 'Die Latinisierung Hispaniens', *ANRW* I, (1972) 462–500 (cf. *id. AEA* 40 (1967) 3–29)

225. González Rodríguez, Mª. Cruz *Las unidades organizativas indígenas del area indoeuropea de Hispania.* Vitoria a Gasteiz, 1986

226. Jones, R. F. J. 'The Roman military occupation of north-western Spain', *JRS* 66 (1976) 45–66

227. Keay, S. J. *Roman Spain.* London, 1988

228. Le Roux, P. *L'armée romaine et l'organisation des provinces ibériques d'Auguste à l'invasion de 409*. Paris, 1982
229. Le Roux, P. 'Les sénateurs originaires de la province d'Hispania citérieure au Haut-Empire romain', in D 42, 439–64
230. Lomas Salmonte, F. J. *Asturia prerromana y altoimperial*. Seville, 1975
231. Mackie, N. *Local Administration in Roman Spain A.D. 14–212* (BAR International Series 172). Oxford, 1983
232. Maluquer de Motes Nicolau, J. *et al. Ciudades augusteas de Hispania*. 2 vols. Saragossa, 1976
233. Montenegro Duque, A. *et al. Historia de España* II. *España romana (218 a. de J. C.–414 de J. C.)*. 2 vols. Madrid, 1982
234. Palomar Lapesa, M. *La onomástica personal pre-latina de la antigua Lusitania*. Salamanca, 1957
235. Roldán Hervás, J. M. *Hispania y el ejército romano. Contribución a la historia social de la España antigua*. Salamanca, 1974
236. Roldán Hervás, J. M. *Itineraria Hispana. Fuentes antiguas para el estudio de las vías romanas en la Península Ibérica*. Madrid, 1975
237. Santos Yanguas, N. 'La conquista romana del N. O. de la Peninsula Ibérica', *Latomus* 41 (1982) 5–49
238. Schulten, A. *Los Cantabros y los Astures y su guerra con Roma*. Madrid, 1943
239. Solana Sainz, J. M. *Los Cantabros y la ciudad de Iuliobriga*. Santander, 1981
240. Sutherland, C. H. V. *The Romans in Spain 217 B.C.–A.D. 117*. London, 1939
241. Syme, R. 'The conquest of north-west Spain', *Legio VII gemina*, 83–107. León, 1970 (= A 94, II, 825–54)
242. Thouvenot, R. *Essai sur la province romaine de Bétique*. Paris, 1940
243. Tovar, A. *Iberische Landeskunde* II. *Die Völker und die Städte des antiken Hispanien*. 2 vols. Baden-Baden, 1974–6
244. Tranoy, A. *La Galice romaine. Recherches sur le nord-ouest de la péninsule ibérique dans l'antiquité*. Paris, 1981
245. Wiegels, R. *Die Tribusinschriften des römischen Hispanien. Ein Katalog* (*Madrider Forschungen* 13). Berlin, 1985

4. GAUL

246. *Actes du colloque: Mines et fonderies antiques de la Gaule, 1980*. Toulouse, 1982
247. *Actes du colloque: La patrie gauloise, 1981*. Lyons, 1983
248. *Actes du colloque: Le vicus gallo-romain* (Caesarodunum XI). Paris, 1976
249. Agache, R. 'Détection aérienne de vestiges protohistoriques gallo-romains et médiévaux dans le bassin de la Somme et ses abords'. *Bulletin de la Société de Préhistoire du Nord*, Special Number 7. Amiens, 1970
250. Agache, R. 'La villa gallo-romaine dans les grandes plaines du nord de la France', *Archeologia* 55 (1973) 37–52
251. Agache, R. 'La campagne à l'époque romaine dans les grandes plaines du Nord de la France', *ANRW* II, 4 (1975) 658–713
252. Agache, R. *La Somme préromaine* (Mémoires de la Société des Antiquaires de Picardie 24). Amiens, 1978
253. Amy, R. and Gros, P. *La Maison Carrée de Nîmes* (*Gallia* Suppl. 38). Paris, 1979

254. Ancien, B. and Tuffreau-Libre, M. *Soissons gallo-romain, découvertes anciennes et récentes.* Soissons, 1980

255. *Archéologie et rapports sociaux en Gaule* (Actes de la table ronde de Besançon 1982, CNRS). Besançon, 1984

256. *Archéologie urbaine, Actes du colloque international de Tours 1980.* Paris, 1982

257. *Architecture domestique de terre et de bois dans les provinces occidentales de l'Empire romain, Actes du 2e congrès de Gaule méridionale.* Lyons, 1983

258. *Aspects de la construction de bois en Normandie du Ier au XIVe siècle*, ed. P. Halbout and J. Le Maho. Caen, 1984

259. Aubin, G. 'L'or romain dans l'ouest de la Gaule, circulation et stagnation', *Revue Archéologique de l'Ouest* 1 (1984) 89–119

260. Audin, A. *Lyon, miroir de Rome.* Fayard, 1979

261. Audin, A. and Burnand, Y. 'Le marché lyonnais de la pierre sous le Haut-Empire romain', *Actes du 98e congrès national des Sociétés Savantes, Saint-Étienne 1973.* Paris, 1975

262. Audin, A. and Reynaud, J.-F. 'Le mur de bord de Saône et ses inscriptions antiques', *Bulletin Musées et Monuments Lyonnais* 6 (1977–81) 457–77

263. *Autun-Augustodunum, capitale des Eduens.* Exhibition catalogue. Autun, 1985

264. Badian, E. 'Notes on Provincia Gallia in the late Republic', in Chevallier, R. (ed.) *Mélanges d'Archéologie et d'Histoire offerts à André Piganiol*, 901–18. Paris, 1966

265. Balty, J.-Ch., 'La basilique de Bavay et les basiliques de forum', *Revue du Nord* 71 (1989) 5–65

266. Barbet, A. 'Peintures de second style schématique en Gaule et dans l'Empire romain', *Gallia* 26 (1968) 145–76

267. Barbet, A. 'Glanum', *Gallia* Suppl. 27 (1974)

268. Barbet, A. 'La diffusion du 3e style pompéien en Gaule', *Gallia* 40 (1982)

269. Barbet, A. 'L'introduction de la peinture murale romaine en Transalpine', *Études languedociennes, CTHS* (1985) 181–204

270. Barraud, D. *et al.* 'Le site de "la France": origines et évolution urbaine de Bordeaux antique', *Aquitania* 6 (1988) 3–59

271. Barruol, G. 'Les peuples préromains du Sud-Est de la Gaule', *RAN* Suppl. 1 (1969)

272. Barruol, G. 'La résistance des substrats préromains en Gaule méridionale', *6e congrès international des études classiques.* Paris, 1976

273. Bayard, D. and Massy, J.-L. 'Amiens romain. Samarobriva Ambianorum', *Revue archéologique de Picardie* (1983)

274. Bémont, C. and Jacob, J.-P. (eds.) *La terre sigillée gallo-romaine.* (*DAF* 6). 1986

275. Benoît, F. *Fouilles de Cemelenum* 1. *Cimiez, la ville antique.* Paris, 1977

276. Benoît, J. 'Nîmes: études sur l'urbanisme antique', *Bulletin de l'École antique de Nîmes*, 16 (1981) 69–90

277. Berchem, D. van 'Avenches, colonie latine', *Chiron* 11 (1981) 221–8

278. Berchem, D. van *Les routes et l'histoire.* Geneva, 1982

279. Bloemers, J. H. F. 'Acculturation in the Rhine/Meuse basin in the

Roman period', in Brandt, R. and Slofstra, J. (eds.) *Roman and Native in the Low Countries* (BAR International Series 64) (Oxford, 1983) 159–209

280. Bögli, H. and Weidmann, D. 'Nouvelles recherches à Aventicum', *Archäologie der Schweiz* 1 (1978) 71–4

281. Boiron, R., Landuré, C. and Nin, N. 'Les fouilles de l'aire du Chapitre', *Documents d'archéologie aixoise* 2 (1986)

282. *Bordeaux, Saint-Christoly, sauvetage archéologique et histoire urbaine.* Bordeaux, 1982–3

283. Bost, J.-P. 'Spécificité des villes et effets de l'urbanisation dans l'Aquitaine augustéenne', *Actes du colloque Villes et Campagnes dans l'Empire romain, Aix-en-Provence 1980*, 61–76. Aix, 1982

284. Bost, J.-P. and Fabre, G. 'Aux origines de la province de Novempopulanie. Nouvel examen de l'inscription d'Hasparren', *Aquitania* 6 (1988) 167–78

285. Bridel, P. 'Le nouveau plan archéologique de Nyon', *Archéologie Suisse* V (1982) 178–83

286. Broise, P. *Genève et son territoire dans l'antiquité.* (Coll. Latomus). Brussels, 1974

287. Broise P. 'L'urbanisme vicinal aux confins de la Viennoise et de la Séquanaise', *ANRW* II, 5. 2 (1976) 602–29

288. Brulet, R. *Braives gallo-romain.* 1: *La zone centrale.* Louvain-la-Neuve, 1981

289. Brulet, R. 'Les origines du *vicus* à la lumière des recherches récentes en Belgique méridionale', *LEC* 53 (1985) 51–60

290. Brun, J.-P. 'L'oléiculture antique en Provence', *RAN* Suppl. 15 (1986)

291. Burnand, Y. *Domitii Aquenses.* Paris, 1975

292. Burnand, Y. 'Sénateurs et chevaliers romains originaires de la cité de Nîmes', *MEFRA* (1975) 681–791

293. Burnand, Y. 'Le rôle des communications fluviales dans la genèse et le développement des villes antiques du Sud-Est de la Gaule', in Duval, P.-M. and Frézouls, E. (eds.) *Thèmes de recherche sur les villes antiques d'Occident*, 279–305. Paris, 1977

294. Burnand, Y. 'Primores Galliarum, Sénateurs et chevaliers romains originaires de la Gaule de la fin de la République au IIIᵉ siècle'. Diss., Paris, 1985

295. *Cadastres et espace rural, approches et réalités antiques* (Actes de la table ronde de Besançon 1980, éd. CNRS). Paris, 1983

296. Cadoux, J.-L. 'Amiens dans l'Antiquité: Samarobriva Ambianorum', in Hulschen, R. (ed.) *Histoire d'Amiens*, 7–46. Toulouse, 1986

297. Cambon, C. 'Les thermes romains dans le Sud de la Gaule', *Mélanges M. Labrousse, Pallas* 32 (1986) 259–82

298. Chapotat, G. 'Le problème des enceintes successives de Vienne', *Bull. Soc. des amis de Vienne* (1976) 7–30

299. Chevallier, R. 'Gallia Lugdunensis. Bilan de vingt-cinq ans de recherches historiques et archéologiques', *ANRW* II, 3 (1975) 860–1060

300. Chevallier, R. 'Gallia Narbonensis', *ANRW* II, 3 (1975) 686–828

301. Chevallier, R. 'Cité et territoire: solutions romaines aux problèmes de l'organisation de l'espace', *ANRW* II, 1 (1974) 649–784

302. Chossenot, F. *et al.* 'Metz antique', in E 364, 1, 235–350
303. Chouquer, G. and Favory, F. *Contribution à la recherche des cadastres antiques.* Paris, 1980
304. Christie, F. and Morel, J. 'Un nouveau quartier romain de Nyon: fouilles de Bel-Air, 1978–1980', *EL* 1 (1982) 105–25
305. Christol, M. 'Réflexions sur le provincialisme gallo-romain', *Centralismo y Decentralizacion 1983*, 79–99. Madrid, 1985
306. Christol, M. and Goudineau, C. 'Nîmes et les Volques Arécomiques', *Gallia* 45 (1987–8) 87–103
307. Clavel-Lévêque, M. 'Pour une problématique des conditions économiques de l'implantation romaine dans le Midi gaulois', *Cahiers ligures de Préhistoire et Archéologie* 24 (1975) 35–75
308. Clavel-Lévêque, M. *Marseille grecque.* Marseilles, 1977
309. Clavel-Lévêque, M. *Puzzle gaulois, les Gaules en mémoire.* Paris, 1989
310. Clavel-Lévêque, M. and Lévêque, P. 'Impérialisme et sémiologie. L'espace urbain à Glanum', *MEFRA* 94, 2 (1982) 675–98
311. Cüppers, H. 'Die Stadt Trier und die verschiedenen Phasen ihres Ausbaus', in Duval, P. M. and Frézouls, E. (eds.) *Thèmes de recherches sur les villes antiques l'Occident*, 223–8. Paris, 1977
312. Dangréaux, B. 'Recherches sur les origines de Grenoble d'après l'étude du mobilier archéologique', *Gallia* 46 (1989) 71–102
313. Daubigney, A. 'Reconnaissance des formes de la dépendance gauloise', *DHA* 5 (1979) 145–89
314. Delplace, C. 'Les villes de la Gaule Belgique au Haut-Empire', *RA* (1983) 345–78
315. Deman, A. 'Germania Inferior et Gallia Belgica: état actuel de la documentation épigraphique', *ANRW* II, 1 (1974) 300–19
316. Desbat, A. and Martin-Kilcher, S. 'Les amphores sur l'axe Rhin–Rhône à l'époque d'Auguste', *Anfore romane e storia economica: un decennio di ricerche, Atti del colloquio di Siena (1986)* (Coll. de l'école française de Rome 114), 339–65. Paris, 1989
317. Desbordes, J.-M. 'Jalons pour l'étude des noyaux urbains dans l'antiquité gallo-romaine: exemples régionaux', *Cahiers archéologiques de Picardie* (1974) 97–102
318. Desbordes, J.-M. 'Les origines de la vie urbaine en Limousin: ébauche d'une problématique', *RAC* XVI (1977) 221–42
319. Dion, R. 'La ville en Gaule à l'époque impériale romaine', *RDM* Jan–Feb 1954
320. Doreau, J. Girardy, C. and Pichonneau, J.-F. 'Contribution à l'étude du forum de Vésone (Périgueux, Dordogne)', *Aquitania* 3 (1985) 91–104
321. Doreau, J. Golvin, J.-C. and Maurin, L. *L'amphithéâtre gallo-romain de Saintes.* Paris, 1982
322. Drinkwater, J.-F. 'Lugdunum: "natural capital" of Gaul?', *Britannia* 6 (1975) 133–40
323. Drinkwater, J.-F. 'The rise and fall of the Gallic Iulii', *Latomus* 37 (1978) 817–50

324. Drinkwater, J.-F. 'A note on local careers in the Three Gauls under the early Empire', *Britannia* 10 (1979) 89–100

325. Drinkwater, J.-F. 'Gallic personal wealth', *Chiron* 9 (1979) 237–42

326. Drinkwater, J.-F. *Roman Gaul: the Three Provinces, 58 B.C.–A.D. 260*. London–Canberra, 1983

327. Duby, G. *Histoire de la France urbaine* 1. *La ville antique*. Paris, 1980

328. Duncan-Jones, R.-P. 'The wealth of Gaul', *Chiron* 11 (1981) 217–20

329. Duval, P.-M. *La vie quotidienne en Gaule pendant la paix romaine*. Paris, 1952

330. Duval, P.-M. *Paris antique, des origines au IIIe siècle*. Paris, 1960

331. Duval, P. M. *Les dieux de la Gaule*. Payot, 1970. Rev. edn 1976

332. Duval, P.-M. *Les sources de l'histoire de France* 1. *La Gaule jusqu'au milieu du Ve siècle*. 2 vols. Paris, 1971

333. Duval, P.-M. 'Bilan et perspectives des études sur la Gaule romaine', *Atti del colloquio sul tema La Gallia romana (1971)*, 7–16. Rome, 1973

334. Ebel, C. *Transalpine Gaul, the Emergence of a Roman Province*. Leiden, 1976

335. Ebel, C. 'Southern Gaul in the triumviral period: a critical stage of romanization', *AJPh* 109 (1988) 572–90

336. *Les enceintes augustéennes dans l'Occident romain, Actes du colloque de Nîmes 1985*. École Antique de Nîmes, 1987

337. Es, W. A. van 'Das niederländische Flussgebiet von der Römerzeit bis ins Forschungsprogramm', *Beiheft zum Bericht der R.-G. Kommission* 58 (1977) 105–26

338. Etienne, R. *Bordeaux antique*, Féd. Hist. du Sud-Ouest. Bordeaux, 1962

339. Ettlinger, E. 'Die italische Sigillata von Novaesium', *Novaesium* IX (1983)

340. Euzennat, M. 'Les fouilles de la Bourse à Marseille', *CRAI* (1976) 529–52

341. Euzennat, M. 'Ancient Marseilles in the light of recent excavations', *AJA* 74 (1980) 133–40

342. Faider-Feytmans, G. 'Les vici du Nord de la Gaule à l'époque romaine', *Annales de la Fédération historique et archéologique de Belgique* (1953) 11–16

343. Favory, F. 'L'esclavage en Narbonnaise et en Lyonnaise', *Actes du colloque sur l'esclavage*, 317–38. Besançon, 1974

344. Ferdière, A. 'Organisation et contrôle de l'espace rural par la ville', *Actes du colloque Villes et Campagnes dans L'Empire romain, Aix-en-Provence 1982*, 95–100. Marseilles, 1982

345. Feugère, M. *Les fibules en Gaule méridionale de la conquête à la fin du Ve siècle après J.-C.* Paris, 1985

346. Février, P.-A. 'Les villes et campagnes des Gaules sous l'Empire', *Ktema* 6 (1981) 359–72

347. Février, P.-A., Fixot, M. and Rivet, L. *Au coeur d'une ville épiscopale, Fréjus*. Fréjus, 1988

348. Février, P.-A., Janon, M. and Varoqueaux, C. 'Fouilles au Clos du Chapitre à Fréjus', *CRAI* (1972) 335–81

349. Février, P.-A., Janon, M. and Varoqueaux, C. 'The origins and growth of the cities of southern Gaul', *JRS* 63 (1973) 1–28

350. Fiches, J.-L. 'Processus d'urbanisation indigène dans la région de Nîmes', *DHA* 5 (1979) 35–57

351. Fiches, J.-L. *L'oppidum d'Ambrussum: le pont romain, le quartier bas.* Caveirac, 1982

352. Fiches, J.-L. 'Les transformations de l'habitat autour de Nîmes au Haut-Empire', *Actes du colloque Villes et Campagnes dans l'Empire romain, Aix-en-Provence 1982*, 111–23. Marseilles, 1982

353. Fiches, J.-L. *Les maisons gallo-romaines d'Ambrussum (Villetelle-Hérault). La fouille du secteur IV 1976–1980 (DAF 5).* Paris, 1986

354. Fiches, J.-L. 'L'espace rural antique dans le Sud-Est de la France: ambitions et réalités archéologiques', *Annales ESC* (1987) 219–38

355. Fischer, F. *Der Heidengraben bei Grabenstetten.* Stuttgart, 1971

356. Fishwick, D. 'The temple of the Three Gauls', *JRS* 62 (1972) 46–52

357. Fishwick, D. 'L'autel des Trois Gaules: le témoignage des monnaies', *BSNAF* (1986) 90–111

358. Fixot, M., Guyon, J., Pelletier, J.-P. and Rivet, L. *Les fouilles de la cour de l'Archevêché, Documents d'archéologie aixoise* 1 (1985)

359. Formigé, J. *Le trophée des Alpes (La Turbie) (Gallia* Suppl. 2). Paris, 1949

360. *Los foros romanos de las provincias occidentales.* Madrid, 1987

361. Frere, S. S. 'Town planning in the western provinces', *Beiheft zum Bericht der R. G. Kommission* 58 (1977) 87–103

362. Frézouls, E. 'Metodo per lo studio dell'urbanistica, strutture e infrastrutture delle città antiche d'Occidente', *Atti CSDIR* III (1970–1) 79–100

363. Frézouls, E. 'Études et recherches sur les villes en Gaule', *Atti del colloquio sul tema La Gallia romana (1971)*, 153–66. Rome, 1973

364. Frézouls, E. *Les villes antiques de France*: 1: *Belgique* (1982) II: *Germanie Supérieure 1* (Strasbourg, 1988)

365. Frézouls, E. 'Évergétisme et construction urbaine dans les Trois Gaules et Germanies', *Mélanges E. Will, Revue du Nord* (1984) 27–54

366. Frézouls, E. 'L'empire romain et la cité. Réflexions sur la politique d'urbanisation', *Actes du 95e congrès national des Sociétés Savantes, Reims 1970.* Paris, 1974 43–8

367. Furger-Gunti, A. 'Die Ausgrabungen in Basler Muster', *Basler Beitr. Ur- und Frühgeschichte* 6 (1979)

368. Galinié, H. *et al. Les archives du sol à Tours. Survie et avenir de l'archéologie de la ville.* Tours, 1979

369. Galliou, P. *L'Armorique romaine.* Braspars, 1983

370. Galliou, P. *Les tombes romaines d'Armorique, (DAF* 17) 1989

371. Gascou, J. 'Quand la colonie de *Forum Julii* fut-elle fondée?', *Latomus* 41 (1982) 132–45

372. Gayraud, M. 'Narbonne aux trois premiers siècles après J.-C.', *ANRW* II, 3 (1975) 829–59

373. Gayraud, M. *Narbonne antique des origines à la fin du IIIe siècle (RAN* Suppl. 8). 1981

374. Giard, J.-B. 'La pénurie de petite monnaie en Gaule au début du Haut-Empire', *JS* (1975) 81–102

375. Goudineau, C. 'Le statut de Nîmes et des Volques Arécomiques', *RAN* 9 (1976) 105–14

376. Goudineau, C. 'Les fouilles de la Maison au Dauphin, recherches sur la romanisation de Vaison-la-Romaine', *Gallia* Suppl. 37 (1979)

377. Goudineau, C. 'Note sur la fondation de Lyon', *Gallia* 44 (1986) 171–3

378. Goudineau, C. (ed.) *Aux origines de Lyon*. Lyons, 1989

379. *Le goût du théâtre à Rome et en Gaule romaine*. Musée archéologique de Lattes, 1989

380. Grenier, A. 'Le recrutement des légionnaires romains en Narbonnaise', *BSNAF* (1956) 35–42

381. Gros, P. 'Traditions hellénistiques de l'Orient dans le décor architectural des temples romains de Gaule Narbonnaise', *Actes du colloque sur la Gaule romaine*, 167–80. Rome, 1973

382. Gros, P. 'Les arcs de triomphe de Gaule Narbonnaise', *Gallia* 37 (1979) 55–83

383. Gros, P. 'Les temples géminés de Glanum, étude préliminaire', *RAN* 14 (1981) 125–58

384. Gros, P. 'L'*Augusteum* de Nîmes', *RAN* 17 (1984) 123–34

385. Gros, P. 'Un programme augustéen: le centre monumental de la colonie d'Arles', *JDAI* 102 (1987) 339–63

386. Guild, R., Guyon, J. and Rivet, L. 'Les origines du baptistère de la cathédrale Saint-Sauveur, étude de topographie aixoise', *RAN* 16 (1983) 171–232

387. Harmand, J. *Les origines des recherches françaises sur l'habitat rural gallo-romain* (Coll. Latomus 51). Brussels, 1961

388. Hatt, J.-J. *Celtes et gallo-romains*. Geneva, 1970

389. Heinen, H. 'Auguste en Gaule et les origines de la ville romaine de Trêves', *Hommages L. Lerat*, 1, 329–48. Paris, 1984

390. Hesnard, A. *et al. L'épave du Grand Ribaud D* (Archaeonautica, 8). 1988

391. Hiernard, J. 'La topographie historique de Poitiers dans l'antiquité', *Bull. Soc. des Antiquaires de l'Ouest* (1987) 163–88

392. Hirschfeld, O. 'Die Organisation der drei Gallien durch Augustus', *Klio* 8 (1908) 464–76

393. *Histoire de Nîmes*. Aix-en-Provence, 1982

394. Kaenel, G., Klausener, M. and Fehlmann, S. *Lousonna 2: nouvelles recherches sur le vicus gallo-romain*, *CAR* 18 (1980–)

395. Kisch, Y. de 'Tarifs de donation en Gaule romaine d'après les inscriptions', *Ktema* 4 (1979) 259–80

396. Kleiner, F. S. 'Artists in the Roman world: an itinerant workshop in Augustan Gaul', *MEFRA* (1972) 661–95

397. Labrousse, M. *Toulouse antique des origines à l'établissement des Wisigoths*. Paris, 1968

398. Laet, S.-J. de 'Esquisse de la naissance et du développement des agglomérations urbaines en Gaule septentrionale à l'époque romaine', *Pamatky archeologicke* 52 (1961) 450–8

399. Laet, S.-J. de. 'Claude et la romanisation de la Gaule septentrionale', *Mélanges A. Piganiol* II, 951–61. Paris, 1966

400. Lafon, X. 'Sur quelques représentations iconographiques des habitants de Narbonnaise de César à Auguste', *Ktema* 9 (1984) 89–95

401. Langouet, L. *Les Coriosolites.* St Malo, 1988

402. Lasfargues, J. and Vertet, H. 'L'atelier de potiers augustéen de la Muette à Lyon, la fouille de sauvetage de 1966', *Notes d'Épigraphie et d'Archéologie lyonnaise,* 61–80. Lyons, 1976

403. Lasfargues, J. and Le Glay, M. 'Découverte d'un sanctuaire municipal du culte impérial à Lyon', *CRAI* (1980) 394–414

404. Laubenheimer, F. *La production des amphores en Gaule Narbonnaise.* Paris, 1985

405. Laubenheimer, F. 'Production et fonction des amphores en Gaule sous l'Empire', *Céramiques hellénistiques et romaines* II, 191–9. Paris 1987

406. Laubenheimer, F. 'Les amphores gauloises sous l'Empire: recherches nouvelles sur leur production et leur chronologie', *Anfore romane e storia economica: un decennio di ricerche, Atti del colloquio di Siena (1986)* (Coll. de l'école française de Rome 114), 105–38. Paris, 1989

407. Laur-Belart, R. *Führer durch Augusta Raurica.* Basle, 1948

408. Lauxerois, R. 'Le Bas-Vivarais à l'époque romaine', *RAN* Suppl. 9 (1983)

409. Le Gall, J. *Alésia.* Paris, 1963

410. Le Glay, M. and Tourrenc, S. 'L'originalité de l'architecture domestique à Vienne d'après les découvertes récentes de Saint-Romain-en-Gal', *CRAI* (1972) 764–74

411. Leday, A. 'Trois vici du Cher', *Caesarodunum* 11 (1976) 237–55

412. Leday, A. 'La campagne à l'époque romaine dans le Centre de la Gaule' (BAR International Series). Oxford, 1980

413. Leman, P. 'Les villes gallo-romaines de la région Nord/Pas-de-Calais à la lumière des fouilles récentes', *RA* (1979) 168–76

414. Lerat, L. 'Vesontio. Besançon antique', *Histoire de Besançon* (1964) 27–241

415. Lerat, L. *La Gaule romaine, textes choisis et présentés.* Paris, 1977

416. Lewuillon, S. 'Histoire, société et lutte des classes en Gaule', *ANRW* II, 4 (1975) 427–583

417. Loustaud, J.-P. *Limoges gallo-romain.* Limoges, 1980

418. *Lutèce-Paris de César à Clovis.* Catalogue of the Musée Carnavalet. Paris, 1984

419. MacKendrick, P. *Roman France.* New York, 1972

420. Mandy, B. *et al.* 'Un réseau de fossés défensifs aux origines de Lyon', *Gallia* 45 (1987–8) 49–66

421. Mangin, M. *Un quartier de commerçants et d'artisans d'Alésia. Contribution à l'histoire de l'habitat urbain en Gaule.* Paris, 1981

422. Mangin, M. *Artisanat et commerce dans les agglomérations romaines du Centre-Est sous l'Empire. Origine des richesses, dépenses dans la ville antique.* Aix-en-Provence, 1984

423. Mangin, M., Jacquet, R. and Jacob, J.-P. *Les agglomérations secondaires en Franche-Comté* (Ann. Litt. Univ. Besançon 337). Paris, 1987

424. Martin, R. 'Formation et développement de l'habitat urbain en Gaule romaine', in *Actes du colloque international du CNRS, thèmes de recherches sur les villes antiques d'Occident, Strasbourg 1971,* 173–83. Paris, 1977

425. Martin, R. and Varène, P. 'Le monument d'Ucuetis à Alésia', *Gallia* Suppl. 26 (1973)

426. Martin-Kilcher S. *Die römischen Amphoren aus Augst und Kaiseraugst* (Forschungen in Augst, 7). Augst, 1987
427. Maurin, L. *Saintes antique des origines à la fin du VIe siècle après J.-C.* Saintes, 1978
428. Maurin, L. 'Gaulois et Lyonnais', in *REA* 88 (1986) 109–24
429. Maurin, L. (ed.) *Les fouilles de 'Ma Maison', Études sur Saintes antique, (Aquitania* Suppl. 3). Bordeaux, 1988
430. *Mediolanum, une bourgade gallo-romaine.* Exhibition catalogue. Dijon, 1988
431. *Mélanges offerts à Roger Dion.* Paris, 1974
432. *Mélanges offerts à E. Will. (Revue du Nord* 46) 1984
433. Mertens, J. 'Réflexions sur le rapport ville-campagne dans le Nord de la Gaule', *Actes du colloque L'archéologie du paysage urbain, Paris, ENS, 1979, Caesarodunum* 15 (1980) 75–8
434. Mertens, J. L'armée romaine en Belgique', *Histoire et Archéologie. Les dossiers* 86 (Aug–Sept 1984) 59–64
435. Middleton, P. 'Army supply in Roman Gaul', *Invasion and Response,* 81–97 (BAR British Series 73). Oxford, 1979
436. Moreau, J. *Dictionnaire de la géographie historique de la Gaule et de la France.* Paris, 1972
437. Moreau, J. *Supplément au dictionnaire de la géographie historique de la Gaule et de la France.* Paris, 1983
438. Nash, D. 'Plus ça change: currency in Central Gaul from Julius Caesar to Nero', in Carson, R. A. G. and Kraay, C. M. (eds.) *Scripta Nummaria Romana. Essays Presented to Humphrey Sutherland,* 12–31. London, 1978
439. Neiss, R. 'Reims gallo-romain. Ébauche de l'histoire d'un site urbain', *Congrès archéologique de France, 135e session, 1977, Champagne,* 52–78. Paris, 1980
440. Neiss, R. *Le développement urbain de Reims dans l'antiquité.* Reims, 1977
441. Neiss, R. 'Une dédicace de la cité des Rèmes à C. César et L. César', *Bull. Soc. Arch. Champenoise* 4 (1982) 3–8
442. Nicolini, G. 'Les sanctuaires ruraux de Poitou-Charentes: quelques exemples d'implantation et de structure interne', *Caesarodunum* 11 (1976) 256–72
443. Nicolini, G. 'Stratigraphie et histoire de Poitiers aux 1er et IIe siècles', *Actes du 111e congrès national des Sociétés savantes, Poitiers* 1986, 7–24. Paris 1987
444. Oliver, J. H. 'North, South, East, West in Arausio and elsewhere', *Mélanges Piganiol* (Paris, 1966) 1075–9
445. Pailler, J-M. 'Domitien et la cité de Pallas, un tournant dans l'histoire de Toulouse antique', *Pallas* 34 (1988) 99–109
446. *Palladia Tolosa, Toulouse romaine.* Musée Saint-Raymond, Toulouse, 1988
447. Pape, L. 'Villes et urbanisme dans l'extrême ouest de l'Armorique à l'époque gallo-romaine', *RA* (1975) 177–91
448. Pape, L. *La civitas des Osismes à l'époque gallo-romaine.* Paris, 1978
449. Passelac, M. 'Le vicus Eburomagus', *RAN* 3 (1970) 71–101
450. Paunier, D. 'L'archéologie gallo-romaine en Suisse romande; bilan et perspectives', *EL* 1 (1982) 5–28

451. Paunier, D. *et al. Le vicus gallo-romain de Vidy-Lausanne*. Lausanne, 1989
452. *Peinture murale en Gaule (Actes des séminaires de Limoges (1980) de Sarrebourg (1981)*. Nancy, 1984; *de Lisieux (1982) de Bordeaux (1983)* (BAR International Series 240). Oxford, 1985; *de Vaison-la-Romaine (1987)*. Vaison, 1990
453. Pelletier, A. 'La superficie des exploitations agraires dans le cadastre d'Orange', *Latomus* 25 (1976) 582–5
454. Pelletier, A. *Vienne antique*. Roanne, 1982
455. Pelletier, A. *Vienne antique* II. Lyons, 1983
456. Petrikovits, H. von 'Kleinstädte und nichtstädtische Siedlungen im Nordwesten des römischen Reichs', in *Das Dorf der Eisenzeit und des frühen Mittelalters*, 86–135. Göttingen, 1977
457. Pétry, F. 'Observations sur les vici explorés en Alsace', *Caesarodunum* 11 (1976) 273–95
458. Pétry, F. 'La culture gallo-romaine des sommets vosgiens', *RA* (1981) 161–7
459. Pétry, F. 'La ville romaine: Argentoratum', in Livet, G. and Rapp, F. (eds.) *Histoire de Strasbourg*. Toulouse, 1987
460. Pflaum, H.-G. 'Les fastes de la province Narbonnaise', *Gallia* Suppl. 30 (1978)
461. Picard, G.-C. 'Le trophée augustéen de La Turbie', *RA* 34 (1949) 151–6
462. Picard, G.-C. 'La mythologie au service de la romanisation', *Mythologie gréco-romaine, échos d'iconographie*, CNRS, 41–52. Paris, 1981
463. Picard, G.-C. 'La république des Pictons', *CRAI* 1982, 532–62
464. Picard, G.-C. 'Les centres civiques ruraux dans l'Italie et la Gaule romaines', *Architecture et société*, 415–22. Rome, 1983
465. Pilet, C. 'Vieux antique (Araegenuae, Viducasses)', *Rev. Arch. Ouest* 1 (1984) 63–84
466. Py, M. *L'oppidum des Castels à Nages (fouilles 1958–1974)*. (*Gallia* Suppl. 35) 1978
467. Py, M. 'Recherches sur Nîmes préromaine', *Gallia* Suppl. 41 (1981)
468. Raepsaet-Charlier, M.-T. and Raepsaet, G. 'Gallia Belgica et Germania. 1. Vingt-cinq années de recherches historiques et archéologiques', *ANRW* II, 4 (1975) 3–299
469. Rambaud, M. 'L'origine militaire de la colonie de Lugdunum', *CRAI* (1965) 252–77
470. Reddé, M. 'Le camp militaire romain d'Arlaines et l'aile des Voconces', *Gallia* 43 (1985) 49–79
471. Richard, J. C. M. 'Le problème des origines de Montpellier', *RAN* 2 (1969) 49–62
472. Rivet, A. *Gallia Narbonensis*. London, 1988
473. Roblin, M. 'Les limites de la *civitas* des Silvanectes', *BSNAF* 1963, 27–9
474. Roblin, M. 'Les limites de la *civitas* des Silvanectes', *JS* 1963, 68–85
475. Rolland, H. 'Fouilles de Glanum (Saint-Rémy-de-Provence)', *Gallia* Suppl. 1 (1946)
476. Rolland, H. 'L'arc de Glanum', *Gallia* Suppl. 31 (1977)
477. Roman, D. 'Apollon, Auguste et Nîmes', *RAN* 14 (1981) 207–14

478. Roth-Congès, A. and Gros, P. 'Le sanctuaire des eaux à Nîmes', *RAC* 22 (1983) 131–46

479. Rouanet-Liesenfelt, A.-M. *La civilisation des Pictones.* Brest, 1980

480. Sabrié, M. and Solier, Y. *La Maison à portiques du Clos de la Lombarde à Narbonne et sa décoration murale,* (*RAN* Suppl. 16). 1987

481. Salviat, F. 'Marseille grecque', and Euzennat, M. 'Marseille romaine', in Baratier, E. (ed.) *Histoire de Marseille.* Toulouse, 1973

482. Salviat, F. 'Orientation, extension et chronologie des plans cadastraux d'Orange', *RAN* 10 (1977) 107–18

483. Schnurbein, S. von *Die Römer in Haltern.* Münster, 1979

484. Schnurbein, S. von 'Die Unverzierte Terra Sigillata aus Haltern', *Bodenaltertümer Westfalens* 19 (1982)

485. Simpson, C. J. 'The birth of Claudius and the date of dedication of the altar *Romae et Augusti* at Lyon', *Latomus* 46 (1987) 186–92

486. Syme, R. 'Tacitus on Gaul', *Latomus* 12 (1953) 23–37

487. Syme, R. 'La richesse des aristocraties de Bétique et de Narbonnaise', *Ktema* 2 (1977) 373–80 (= A 94, III, 977–85)

488. Syme, R. 'More Narbonensian senators', *ZPE* 65 (1986) (= A 94, VI, 209–31)

489. Tardy, D. *Le décor architectonique de Saintes antique* (*Aquitania* Suppl. 5). 1990

490. Tasseaux, D. and F. 'Aulnay-de-Saintonge: un camp augusto-tibérien en Aquitaine', *Aquitania* 1 (1983) 49–95; 2 (1984) 105–57

491. Ternes, C.-M. *Das römische Luxemburg.* Zurich, 1973

492. Ternes, C.-M: 'Le vicus d'époque gallo-romaine en pays trévire et rhénan', *Caesarodunum* 11 (1976) 18–31

493. Ternes, C.-M. 'Recherches concernant la Gaule et les Germanies', *REL* 56 (1978) 226–71

494. *Trier, Augustusstadt der Treverer.* Mainz, 1984

495. Turcan, R. 'L'autel de Rome et d'Auguste ad Confluentem', *ANRW* XII (1982) 607–44

496. Turcan, R. 'L'arc de Carpentras: problèmes de datation et d'histoire', *Hommages L. Lerat*, 809–19. Paris, 1984

497. *Ugernum, Beaucaire et le Beaucairois à l'époque romaine.* Caveirac, 1987

498. *Ur- und frühgeschichtliche Archäologie der Schweiz 5, Die Römerzeit,* Société suisse de Préhistoire et d'Archéologie. Basle, 1976

499. Vaginay, M. and Valette, P. 'Recherches sur les origines de l'urbanisme antique de Feurs', *Cahiers archéologiques de la Loire* 2 (1982) 39–72

500. *Le vicus gallo-romain* (*Caesarodunum* 11). Tours, 1976

501. Vidal, M. 'Note préliminaire sur les puits et fosses funéraires du Toulousain aux IIᵉ et Iᵉʳ siècle avant J.-C.', *Aquitania* 4 (1986) 55–65

502. *Villes augustéennes de Gaule, Actes du colloque d'Autun 1985*

503. *Les villes de la Gaule Belgique au Haut-Empire, Actes du colloque de Saint-Riquier 1982.* (*Revue archéologique de Picardie* 3–4) 1984

504. *Vingt ans d'archéologie à Vienne.* Société des amis de Vienne, 1981

505. Walker, S. 'Récentes recherches en archéologie gallo-romaine et paléochrétienne sur Lyon et sa région' (BAR International Series 1980). Oxford, 1981

506. Walter, H. *La Franche-Comté romaine. Histoire de la Franche-Comté* 11. Weholsheim, 1979

507. Walthew, C. V. 'A note on the street plan and early growth of Roman Amiens', *Britannia* 12 (1981) 298–302

508. Werner, K.-J. *Histoire de France, les origines*. Paris, 1984

509. Wiblé, F. *Forum Claudii Vallensium, la ville romaine de Martigny*. Martigny, 1981

510. Wiblé, F. 'Nouvelles découvertes de Martigny. Forum Claudii Vallensium', *ArchS* 5 (1982) 2–14

511. Wightman, E. M. *Roman Trier and the Treveri*. London, 1970

512. Wightman, E. M. 'La Gaule Chevelue entre César et Auguste', *Actes du IXᵉ congrès international d'études sur les frontières romaines*, 473–83. Bucarest-Köln-Vienne, 1974

513. Wightman, E. M. 'Rural settlement in Roman Gaul', *ANRW* II, 4 (1975) 584–647

514. Wightman, E. M. 'Le vicus dans le contexte de l'administration et de la société gallo-romaine: quelques réflexions', *Caesarodunum* 11 (1976) 59–64

515. Wightman, E. M. 'Il y avait en Gaule deux sortes de Gaulois. Assimilation et résistance à la culture gréco-romaine', *Travaux du VIᵉ congrès international d'études classiques, Madrid 1974*, 407–19. Bucarest–Paris, 1976

516. Wightman, E. M. 'Soldier and civilian in early Roman Gaul', *Akten des XIᵉ internationalen Limeskongresses, Budapest*, 59–64. 1976

517. Wightman, E. M. 'Military arrangements, native settlements and related developments in early Roman Gaul', *Helinium* 17 (1977) 105–26

518. Wightman, E. M. 'Peasants and potentates', *AJAH* 3 (1978) 97–128

519. Wightman, E. M. 'Imitation ou adaptation? Une note sur les inscriptions dans le Nord de la Gaule romaine', *Mélanges E. Will, Revue du Nord* (1984) 69–72

520. Wightman, E. M. *Gallia Belgica*. London, 1985

521. Wiseman, A. and Wiseman, P. *Julius Caesar: the Battle for Gaul*. London, 1980

533. Will, E. *Bavay, cité gallo-romaine*. Douai, 1957

523. Will, E. 'Recherches sur le développement urbain sous l'Empire romain dans le Nord de la France', *Gallia* 20 (1962) 79–101

524. Witt, N. de. *Urbanization and the Franchise in Roman Gaul*. Lancaster, PA, 1940

525. Wolff, H. 'Kriterien für lateinische und römische Städte in Gallien und Germanien und die "Verfassung" der gallischen Stammesgemeinden', *BJ* 176 (1976) 45–121

526. Wuilleumier, P. *L'administration de la Lyonnaise sous le Haut-Empire*. Paris, 1948

527. Wuilleumier, P. *Lyon, métropole des Gaules*. Paris, 1953

5. BRITAIN

528. Bennett, P. 'The topography of Roman Canterbury: a brief reassessment', *ArchCant* 100 (1984) 47–56

529. Birley, A. R. 'Petillius Cerialis and the conquest of Brigantia', *Britannia* 4 (1973) 179–90

530. Burnham, B. C. and Johnson, H. B. (eds.) *Invasion and Response: the Case of Roman Britain.* Oxford, 1979

531. Burnham, B. C. and Wacher, J. *The Small Towns of Roman Britain.* London, 1990

532. Crummy, P. 'The origins of some major Romano-British towns', *Britannia* 13 (1982) 125–34

533. Cunliffe, B. W. (ed.) *Fifth Report of the Excavations of the Roman Fort at Richborough, Kent.* Oxford, 1968

534. Fishwick, D. 'Templum Divo Claudio Constitutum', *Britannia* 3 (1972) 164–81

535. Frere, S. 'Civitas – a myth?', *Antiquity* 35 (1961) 29–36

536. Frere, S. *Verulamium Excavations* I. Oxford, 1972. *Verulamium Excavations* II. London, 1983

537. Frere, S. *Britannia.* 3rd edn. London, 1987

538. Frere, S. and St Joseph, J. K. S. *Roman Britain from the Air.* Cambridge, 1983

539. Fulford, M. *Silchester Defences 1974–80.* London, 1984

540. Fulford, M. *Guide to the Silchester Excavations: the Forum Basilica.* Reading, 1985

541. Fulford, M. *The Silchester Amphitheatre: Excavations of 1979–85.* London, 1989

542. Greene, K. 'Imported fine wares in Britain to A.D. 250: a guide to identification', in Arthur, P. and Marsh, G. (eds.) *Early Fine Wares in Roman Britain.* Oxford, 1978

543. Grew, F. and Hobley, B. (eds.) *Roman Urban Topography in Britain and the Western Empire.* London, 1985

544. Hanson, W. S. and Campbell, D. B. 'The Brigantes: from clientage to conquest', *Britannia* 17 (1986) 73–89

545. Hawkes, C. F. C. 'History of the Belgic Dobunni, their division and subjection', in Clifford, E. M. *Bagendon, a Belgic oppidum: a record of the excavations of 1954–6,* 62–7. Cambridge, 1961

546. Jones, G. D. B. and Mattingly, D. *An Atlas of Roman Britain.* Oxford, 1990

547. Margary, I. D. *Roman Roads in Britain.* 3rd edn. London, 1973

548. Millett, M. *The Romanization of Britain, an Essay in archaeological Interpretation.* Cambridge, 1990

549. Milne, G. 'Further evidence for Roman London Bridge?', *Britannia* 13 (1982) 271–6

550. Ordnance Survey. *Map of Roman Britain.* Southampton, 1978

551. Piggott, S. *The Druids.* Harmondsworth, 1974

552. Rivet, A. L. F. and Smith, C. *The Place-Names of Roman Britain.* London, 1979

553. Rodwell, W. 'Coinage, oppida and the rise of Belgic power in south-eastern Britain', in Cunliffe, B. and Rowley, T. (eds.) *Oppida: the Beginnings of Urbanisation in Barbarian Europe*, 181–367. Oxford, 1976

554. Rodwell, W. and Rodwell, K. 'The Roman villa at Rivenhall, Essex', *Britannia* 4 (1973) 115–27

555. Ross, R. *Pagan Celtic Britain*. London, 1974

556. Salway, P. *Roman Britain*. Oxford, 1982

557. Todd, M. (ed.) *Studies in the Romano-British Villa*. Leicester, 1978

558. Todd, M. (ed.) *Research on Roman Britain: 1960–89*. Gloucester, 1989

559. Wacher, J. S. (ed.) *The Civitas Capitals of Roman Britain*. Leicester, 1966

560. Wacher, J. S. *Towns of Roman Britain*. London, 1995

561. Wacher, J. S. *The Coming of Rome*. London, 1981

562. Wacher, J. S. *Roman Britain*. London, 1978

563. Walthew, C. V. 'The town house and the villa house in Roman Britain', *Britannia* 6 (1975) 189–205

564. Webster, G. *Boudica: the British Revolt against Rome, A.D. 60*. London, 1978

565. Webster, G. (ed.) *Fortress into City*. London, 1988

566. Whittick, G. C. 'The earliest Roman lead-mining on Mendip and in North Wales: a reappraisal', *Britannia* 13 (1982) 113–24

6. GERMANY

567. Alföldy, G. *Die Legionslegaten der römischen Rheinarmeen. EpStud* 3. Köln, 1967

568. Alföldy, G. *Die Hilfstruppen der römischen Provinz Germania Inferior. EpStud* 6. Düsseldorf, 1968

569. Baatz, D. and Herrmann, F.-R. *Die Römer in Hessen*. 2nd edn. Stuttgart, 1982

570. Bogaers, J. E. 'Civitates und Civitas-Hauptorte in der nördlichen Germania Inferior', *BJ* 172 (1972) 312–33

571. Brandt, R. and Slofstra, J. (eds.) *Roman and Native in the Low Countries, Spheres of Interaction* (BAR International Series 71). Oxford, 1983

572. Capelle, W. (ed.) *Das alte Germanien. Die Nachrichten der griechischen und römischen Schriftsteller*. 2nd edn. Jena, 1937

573. Chevallier, R. *Rome et la Germanie au premier siècle de notre ère*. (Coll. Latomus 53) Brussels, 1961

574. Cüppers, H. *Die Römer in Rheinland-Pfalz*. Stuttgart, 1990

575. Cüppers, H. and Rüger, C. B. *Römische Siedlungen und Kulturlandschaften, Geschichtlicher Atlas der Rheinlände* III. 1–2. Cologne, 1985

576. Doppelfeld, O. and Held, O. *Der Rhein und die Römer*. 2nd edn. Cologne, 1976

577. Eck, W. *Die Statthalter der germanischen Provinzen vom 1–3. Jahrhundert. EpStud* 14. Köln, 1985

578. Fingerlin, G. 'Dangstetten, ein augusteisches Legionslager am Hochrhein', *BRGK* (1972) 197–232

579. Follmann-Schulz, A.-B. 'Die römischen Tempelanlagen in der Provinz Germania Inferior', *ANRW* II, 18.1 (1986) 672–793

580. Heinen, H. *Trier und das Trevererland in römischer Zeit*. Trier, 1985

581. Horn, H.-G. (ed.) *Die Römer in Nordrhein-Westfalen*. Stuttgart, 1987

582. Klinghoffer, H. *Germania Latina. Sammlung literarischer, inschriftlicher und archäologischer Zeugnisse zur Geschichte und Kultur Westdeutschlands in der Römerzeit.* Dusseldorf, 1955

583. Krüger, B. *et al. Die Germanen, Geschichte und Kultur der germanischen Stämme in Mitteleuropa* 1. 4th edn. Berlin, 1983

584. Petrikovits, H. von *Das römische Rheinland. Archäologische Forschungen seit 1945.* Cologne, 1960

585. Petrikovits, H. von 'Der Wandel römischer Gefässkeramik in der Rheinzone', *Landschaft und Geschichte: Festschrift für H. Petri*, 383–404. Bonn, 1970

586. Petrikovits, H. von *Die Rheinlande in römischer Zeit.* Dusseldorf, 1978

587. Raepsaet-Charlier, M.-T. and Raepsaet-Charlier, G. 'Gallia Belgica et Germania Inferior, Vingt-cinq années de recherches historiques et archéologiques', *ANRW* II, 4 (1975) 3–299

588. Roymans, N. 'Tribale samenlevingen in Noord-Gallie'. Diss., Amsterdam–Utrecht, 1987

589. Rüger, C. B. *Germania Inferior. Untersuchungen zur Territorial-und Verwaltungsgeschichte Niedergermaniens in der Prinzipatszeit (BJ* Beih. 30). 1968

590. Schlippschuh, O. *Die Händler im römischen Kaiserreich in Gallien, Germanien und den Donauprovinzen Rätien, Noricum und Pannonien.* Amsterdam, 1974

591. Schönberger, H. 'The Roman frontier in Germany, an archaeological survey', *JRS* 59 (1969) 144–97

592. Schönberger, H. 'Die römischen Truppenlager der frühen und mittleren Kaiserzeit zwischen Nordsee und Inn', *BRGK* 66 (1985) 321–495

593. Schönberger, H. and Simon, H. G. *Das augusteische Römerlager Rödgen.* Berlin, 1976

594. Stein, E. *Die kaiserlichen Beamten und Truppenkörper im römischen Deutschland unter dem Prinzipat.* Vienna, 1932

595. Ternes, C. M. *La vie quotidienne en Rhénanie romaine (Ier–IVe siècles).* Paris, 1972

596. Ternes, C. M. 'Die provincia Germania Superior im Bilde der jüngeren Forschung', *ANRW* II, 5. 2 (1976) 721–1260

597. Todd, M. *The Northern Barbarians.* London, 1975

598. Vittinghoff, F. 'Die politische Organisation der römischen Rheingebiete in der Kaiserzeit', *Rhenania Romana, Atti dei Convegni Lincei* 23 (1976) 73ff

599. Weisgerber, J. L. *Die Namen der Ubier.* Cologne–Opladen, 1968

600. Weisgerber, J. L. *Rhenania Germano-Celtica.* Bonn, 1969

601. Wells, C. M. *The German Policy of Augustus. An Examination of the Archaeological Evidence.* Oxford, 1972

602. Wild, J. P. *Textile Manufacture in the Northern Roman Provinces.* Cambridge, 1970

7. RAETIA

603. *Archäologie in Württemberg, Ergebnisse und Perspektiven archäologischer Forschung von der Altsteinzeit bis zur Neuzeit*, ed. D. Planck. Stuttgart, 1988

604. *Die Ausgrabungen in Manching*, 11 vols. Wiesbaden, 1970–89
605. Berchem, D. van. 'La conquête de la Rhétie', *MH* 25 (1968) 1–10
606. Bilgeri, G. *Geschichte Vorarlbergs* 1: *Vom freien Rätien zum Staat der Monforter*. 2nd edn. Vienna–Cologne–Graz, 1976
607. Chantraine H. 'Zu den neuen Fasten der raetischen Statthalter', *Bay Vorgeschichtsbl* 38 (1973) 111–15
608. Czysz, W., Dietz, K., Fischer, T. and Kellner, H.-J. *Die Römer in Bayern*. Stüttgart, 1995
609. Drack, W. and Fellmann, R. *Die Römer in der Schweiz*. Stuttgart–Jona SG, 1988
610. Eck, W. 'Senatorische Amtsträger und Rätien unter Augustus', *ZPE* 70 (1987) 203–9
611. Fischer, F. 'P. Silius Nerva, zur Vorgeschichte des Alpenfeldzuges 15 v. Chr.', *Germania* 54 (1976) 147–55
612. Fischer, T. *Das Umland des römischen Regensburg*. 2 vols. (Münchn. Beiträge z. Vor- u. Frühgeschichte 42). Munich, 1990
613. *Forschungen zur provinzialrömischen Archäologie in Bayerisch-Schwaben*, ed. J. Bellot, W. Czysz and G. Krahe (Schwäbische Geschichtsquellen u. Forschungen 14). Augsburg, 1985
614. Frei, B. *et al. Das Räterproblem in geschichtlicher, sprachlicher und archäologischer Sicht* (Schriften d. Rätischen Museums Chur 28). Chur, 1984
615. Frei-Stolba, R. 'Die römische Schweiz: ausgewählte staats- und verwaltungsrechtliche Probleme im Frühprinzipat', *ANRW* II, 5.1 (1976) 288–403
616. Frei-Stolba, R. 'Die Schweiz in römischer Zeit: der Vorgang der Provinzialisierung in rechtshistorischer Sicht', *Hist.* 25 (1976) 313–55
617. Frei-Stolba, R. Review of Schön 1986 (E 635), *Gnomon* 60 (1988) 137–42
618. Gottlieb, G. *et al.* (eds.) *Geschichte der Stadt Augsburg von der Römerzeit bis zur Gegenwart*. Stuttgart, 1984
619. *Geschichte der Stadt Kempten*, ed. V. Dotterweich *et al.* Kempten, 1989
620. Haider, P. W. 'Tirol unter römischer Herrschaft', *Geschichte des Landes Tirol* 1, ed. J. Fontana *et al.*, 127–88; 238ff. Bozen, 1985
621. Heuberger, R. *Rätien im Altertum und Mittelalter, Forschung und Darstellung*. Innsbruck, 1932
622. Keller, E. *Die frühkaiserzeitlichen Körpergräber von Heimstetten bei München und die verwandten Funde aus Südbayern* (Münchn. Beiträge z. Vor- u. Frühgeschichte 37). Munich, 1984
623. Kellner, H.-J. 'Zur römischen Verwaltung in den Zentralalpen', *Bay Vorgeschichtsbl* 39 (1974) 92–104
624. Kellner, H.-J. *Die Römer in Bayern*. 4th edn. Munich, 1978
625. Kellner, H.-J. 'Die Zeit der römischen Herrschaft', *Handbuch der bayerischen Geschichte*, ed. M. Spindler, 65–96. 2nd edn. Munich, 1981
626. Kellner, H.-J. 'Ein Jahrzehnt Römerforschung in Bayern (1974–1983)', in Kraus, A. (ed.) *Land und Reich, Stamm und Nation. Probleme und Perspektiven bayerischer Geschichte* (Festgabe für Max Spindler zum 90. Geburtstag 1) 147–62. Munich, 1984

627. Laffi, U. 'Sull'organizzazione amministrativa dell'area alpina nell'età giulio-claudia', *CSDIR* 7 (1975–6) 391–420

628. Laffi, U. 'Zur Geschichte Vindeliciens unmittelbar nach der römischen Eroberung', *Bay Vorgeschichtsbl* 43 (1978) 19–24

629. Laffi, U. 'L'organizzazione dei distretti alpini dopo la conquista', in Vacchina, M. (ed.) *La Valle d'Aosta e l'arco alpino nella politica del mondo antico*, 62–78. Aosta, 1988

630. Mackensen, M. *Frühkaiserzeitliche Kleinkastelle bei Nersingen und Burlafingen an der oberen Donau* (Münchn. Beiträge z. Vor- u. Frühgeschichte 41). Munich, 1987

631. Meyer, E. 'Römische Zeit', *Handbuch der Schweizer Geschichte* I, 55–92. Zurich, 1972

632. Overbeck, B. *Geschichte des Alpenrheintals in römischer Zeit auf Grund der archäologischen Zeugnisse.* 2 vols. (Münchn. Beiträge z. Vor- u. Frühgeschichte 20/1). Munich, 1973–82

633. Overbeck, B. 'Raetien zur Prinzipatszeit', *ANRW* II, 5.2 (1976) 658–89

634. *Die Römer in Schwaben* (Jubiläumsausstellung 2000 Jahre Augsburg ... Bay. Landesamt f. Denkmalpflege, Arbeitsheft 27). Munich, 1985

635. Schön, F. *Der Beginn der römischen Herrschaft in Rätien.* Sigmaringen, 1986

636. Staehlin, F. *Die Schweiz in römischer Zeit.* 3rd edn. Basle, 1948

637. Ulbert, G. *Der Lorenzberg bei Epfach, die frührömische Militärstation* (Münchn. Beiträge z. Vor- u. Frühgeschichte 9). Munich, 1965

638. Untermann, J. 'Alpen-Donau-Adria', *Die Sprachen im römischen Reich der Kaiserzeit* (BJ Beih. 40), 45–63. Cologne–Bonn, 1980

639. Waasdorp, J. A. 'Immanes Raeti. A hundred years of Roman defensive policy in the Alps and Voralpenland', *Talanta* 14–15 (1982/3) 33–89

640. Walser, G. *Die römischen Strassen und Meilensteine in Raetien.* Stuttgart, 1983

641. Werner, J. (ed.) *Studien zu Abodiacum-Epfach* (Münchn. Beiträge z. Vor- u. Frühgeschichte 7). Munich, 1964

642. Winkler, G. 'Die Statthalter der römischen Provinz Raetien unter dem Prinzipat', *Bay Vorgeschichtsbl* 36 (1971) 50–101; 38 (1973) 116–20

643. Wolff, H. 'Einige Probleme der Raumordnung im Imperium Romanum, dargestellt an den Provinzen Obergermanien, Raetien und Noricum', *Ostbairische Grenzmarken* 28 (1986) 152–77

644. Wolff, H. 'Zu den Anfängen des römischen Raetien' (Review of Schön 1986 (E 635)), *JRA* 3 (1990) 407–14

8. THE BALKANS

645. Alföldy, G. 'Die Auxiliartruppen der römischen Provinz Dalmatien', *AArchHung* 14 (1962) 259–96 (=D 159, 239–97)

646. Alföldy, G. 'Des territoires occupés par les Scordisques', *AAntHung* 12 (1964) 107–27

647. Alföldy, G. 'Die Namengebung der Urbevölkerung in der römischen Provinz Dalmatia', *BzN* 15 (1964) 55–104

648. Alföldy, G. 'Eine römische Strassenbauinschrift aus Salona', *AArchHung* 16 (1964) 247–56

649. Alföldy, G. 'Veteranendeduktionen in der Provinz Dalmatien', *Hist.* 13 (1964) 167–79 (= D 159, 298–312)

650. Alföldy, G. 'Rider', *RE* Suppl. 11 (1968) 1207–14

651. Alföldy, G. 'Senatoren in der römischen Provinz Dalmatien', *EpStud* 5 (1968) 99–144

652. Alföldy, G. *Noricum.* London, 1974

653. Batović, S. 'Investigation of the Illyrian settlement at Radovin', *Diadora* 4 (1968) 53–70. In Serbo-Croat

654. Batović, S. 'Les vestiges préhistoriques sur archipel de Zadar', *Diadora* 6 (1973) 5–165. In Serbo-Croat

655. Clairmont, C. W. *Excavations at Salona, Yugoslavia, 1969–72.* Park Ridge, NJ, 1975

656. Crişan, I. H. *Burebista and his Time.* Bucharest, 1978

657. Curk, I. Mikl. *Poetovio I* (Katalogi et Monographiae Mus. Nat. Labac. 13). Ljubljana, 1976

658. Daicoviciu, H. *Dacia de la Burebista la cucerirea Romana.* Cluj, 1972

659. Danoff, C. M. 'Zur Geschichte des westpontischen *koinon*', *Klio* 31 (1938) 436–9

660. Danov, C. M. 'Die Thraker auf dem Ostbalkan von der hellenistischen Zeit bis zur Gründung Konstantinopels', *ANRW* II, 7.1 (1979) 21–185

661. Dušanić S. 'Aspects of Roman mining in Noricum, Pannonia, Dalmatia and Moesia Superior', *ANRW* II, 6 (1977) 52–94

662. Egger, R. *Die Stadt auf dem Magdalensberg: ein Grosshandelsplatz* (Denkschr. Ost. Akad. phil.-hist. Kl. 79). Vienna, 1961

663. Fitz, J. 'La division de l'*Illyricum*', *Latomus* 47 (1988) 13–25

664. Gajdukević, F. *Das Bosporanische Reich.* Berlin, 1971

665. Garašanin, M. 'The early Iron Age in the central Balkan area', *CAH* III².1, 582–618. Cambridge, 1982

666. Gerov, B. 'Römische Bürgerrechtsverleihung und Kolonisation in Thrakien von Trajan', *St Clasice* 3 (1961) 107–16 (= E 669, 83–92)

667. Gerov, B. 'Epigraphische Beiträge zur Geschichte des moesischen Limes in vorclaudischer Zeit', *AAntHung* 15 (1967) 85–105 (= E 669, 147–67)

668. Gerov, B. 'Die Grenzen der römischen Provinz Thracia bis zur Gründung des aurelianischen Dakien', *ANRW* II, 7.1 (1979) 212–40

669. Gerov, B. *Beiträge zur Geschichte der römischen Provinzen Moesien und Thrakien. Gesammelte Aufsätze.* Amsterdam, 1980

670. Hoddinott, R. F. *The Thracians.* London, 1981

671. Klemenc, J. and Saria, B. *Archaeologische Karte von Jugoslavien: Blatt Ptuj.* Belgrade–Zagreb, 1936

672. Kraft, K. *Zur Rekrutierung der Alen und Kohorten an Rhein und Donau* (Diss. Bernenses ser. 1, fasc. 3) Berne, 1951

673. Marić, Z. 'Archaeologische Forschungen auf der Akropolis der illyrischen Stadt DAORS . . . in Ošanići bei Stolać', *GZMS* 30/31 (1977) 5–99

674. Matijasić, R. 'La produzione ed il commercio di tegole ad Aquileia', *Vita sociale, artistica e commerciale di Aquileia romana* II (Antichità Altoadriatiche 29). Udine, 1987

675. Mócsy, A. 'Pannonia', *RE* Suppl. IX (1962) 516–776
676. Mócsy, A. *Gesellschaft und Romanisation in der römischen Provinz Moesia Superior.* Budapest, 1970
677. Mócsy, A. *Pannonia and Upper Moesia.* London, 1974
678. Mócsy, A. 'Die Einwanderung der Iazygen', *AAntHung* 25 (1977) 439–36
679. Mócsy, A. 'The civilized Pannonians of Velleius', in C 274, 169–75. Gloucester, 1983
680. Novak, G. 'La province Illyricum était-elle au temps d'Octavien Auguste et de Tibère divisée en Superior provincia Illyricum et Inferior provincia Illyricum?', in Chevallier, R. (ed.) *Mélanges Piganiol* III, 1359–66. Paris, 1966
681. Papazoglu, F. *The Central Balkan Tribes in Pre-Roman Times.* Amsterdam, 1978
682. Papazoglu, F. 'Quelques aspects de l'histoire de la province de Macédoine', *ANRW* II, 7. 1 (1979) 302–69
683. Piccottini, G. 'Die Stadt auf dem Magdalensberg – ein spätkeltisches und frührömisches Zentrum im südlichen Noricum', *ANRW* II, 6 (1977) 263–301
684. Piccottini, G. and Vetters, H. *Führer durch die Ausgrabungen auf dem Magdalensberg.* 2nd edn. Klagenfurt, 1981
685. Pippidi, D. M. *Epigraphische Beiträge zur Geschichte Histrias in hellenistischer und römischer Zeit.* Berlin, 1962
686. Pippidi, D. M. *Contributii la istoria veche a Romaniei.* Bucharest, 1967
687. Polomé, E. C. 'Balkan Languages (Illyrian, Thracian and Daco-Moesian)', *CAH* III².1, 866–88. Cambridge, 1982
688. Rapanić, Z. (ed.) *La vallée du fleuve Neretva depuis la préhistoire jusqu'au début du Moyen Age* (Réunion scientifique Metković, 4–7, X 1977, Soc. Arch. Croat.). Split, 1980
689. Šašel, J. 'Keltisches Portorium in den Ostalpen', *Corolla Memoriae Erich Swoboda Dedicata*, 198–204. Graz–Vienna, 1966
690. Šašel, J. 'Hüldigung norischer Stämme am Magdalensberg in Kärnten', *Hist.* 16 (1967) 70–4
691. Šašel, J. 'Emona', *RE* Suppl. XI (1968) 540–78
692. Šašel, J. 'Trajan's canal at the "Iron Gate"', *JRS* 63 (1973) 80–5
693. Šašel, J. 'Siscia', *RE* Suppl. XIV (1974) 702–41
694. Šašel, J. and Weiler, I. 'Zur Augusteisch-Tiberischen Inschrift von Emona', *Carnuntum Jahrbuch 1963/4*, 40–2. Graz, 1965
695. Stiglitz, H., Kandler, M. and Jobst, W. 'Carnuntum', *ANRW* II, 6 (1977) 583–730
696. Stipčević, A. *The Illyrians: History and Culture.* Park Ridge, NJ, 1977
697. Suić, M. *Antički Grad na istočnom Jadranu.* Zagreb, 1976
698. Sullivan, R. D. 'Thrace in the eastern dynastic network', *ANRW* II, 7.1 (1979) 186–211
699. Svoljšak, Dr. 'The prehistoric settlement at Most na Soči', *ArchIug* 17 (1976) 13–20
700. Swoboda, E. *Octavian and Illyricum.* Vienna, 1932

701. Swoboda, E. *Forschungen am obermoesischen Limes* (Schriften der Balkankommission: Ant. Abt. 10). Vienna–Leipzig, 1939

702. Syme, R. *Danubian Papers*. Bucharest, 1971

703. Velkov, V. *Cities in Thrace and Dacia in Late Antiquity*. Amsterdam, 1977

704. Vulpe, R. and Barnea, I. *Din istoria Dobrogei* II. Bucharest, 1968

705. Wilkes, J. J. 'Σπλαυνον – Splonum again', *A AntHung* 13 (1965) 111–25

706. Wilkes, J. J. *Dalmatia*. London, 1969

707. Wilkes, J. J. 'Boundary stones in Roman Dalmatia: I. The inscriptions', *ArhVestnik* 25 (1974) 258–74

708. Wilkes, J. J. 'Romans, Dacians and Sarmatians in the first and early second centuries', in C 274, 255–89

709. Winkler, G. 'Noricum und Rom', *ANRW* II, 6 (1977) 183–262

710. Zabehlicky-Scheffenegger, S. and Kandler, M. *Burnum I. Erster Bericht über die Kleinfunde der Grabungen 1973 und 1974 auf dem Forum* (Schriften der Balkankommission, Antiqu. Abt. 14). Vienna, 1979

711. Zaninović, M. 'The Economy of Roman Dalmatia', *ANRW* II, 6 (1977) 767–809

712. Zaninović, M. 'The territory of the Neretva valley as a foothold of Roman penetration', in E 688, 173–80

9. AFRICA

713. Aranegui, C. and Hesnard, A. 'Magon et les amphores à huile à Lepcis', forthcoming

714. Bénabou, M. 'Proconsul et légat; le témoignage de Tacite', *AntAfr* 6 (1972) 129–36

715. Bénabou, M. *La résistance africaine à la romanisation*. Paris, 1976

716. Benseddik, N. *Les troupes auxiliaires de l'armée romaine en Maurétanie Césarienne*. Alger, 1982

717. Benseddik, N. and Potter N. 'Excavations at the forum site at Cherchel, 1977–81', *BAA* forthcoming

718. Beschaouch, A. 'Mustitana', *Recueil des nouvelles inscriptions de Mustis, cité romaine de Tunisie*. I (Karthago 14). Paris, 1968

719. Beschaouch, A. 'Le territoire de Sicca Veneria (El Kef), nouvelle Cirta, en Numidie Proconsulaire (Tunisie)', *CRAI* (1981) 105–22

720. Broughton, T. R. S. *The Romanization of Africa Proconsularis*. Repr. New York, 1968

721. Broughton, T. R. S. 'The territory of Carthage', *Mélanges Marcel Durry, REL* 47 bis (1971) 265–75

722. Cagnat, R. *L'armée romaine d'Afrique et l'occupation militaire de l'Afrique sous les empereurs*. Paris, 1913

723. Carcopino, J. 'L'inscription d'Ain el-Djemala. Contribution à l'histoire des "saltus" et du colonat partiaire', *MEFRA* 26 (1906) 365–81

724. Chevallier, R. 'Essai de chronologie des centuriations romaines de Tunisie', *MEFRA* 70 (1958) 61–128

725. Daniels, C. *The Garamantes of Southern Libya*. New York, 1970

726. Debbasch, Y. '"Colonia Julia Karthago". La vie et les institutions municipales de la Carthage romaine', *RHD* 30–53 (1953) 335–77

727. Desanges, J. 'Le triomphe de Cornelius Balbus', *RevAfr* 101 (1957) 5–43
728. Desanges, J. 'Les territoires gétules de Juba II', *REA* 66 (1964) 33–47
729. Desanges, J. 'Un drame africain sous Auguste. Le meurtre du proconsul L. Cornelius Lentulus par les Nasamons', in *Hommages Renard* II (Coll. Latomus 102) 197–213. Brùssels, 1969
730. Faur, J.-C. 'Caligula et la Maurétanie, la fin de Ptolémée', *Klio* 55 (1973) 249–71
731. Février, P.-A. 'Le culte des Cereres en Afrique', *BSNAF* (1975) 39–43
732. Fishwick, D. 'The annexation of Mauretania', *Hist.* 20 (1971) 467–87
733. Fishwick, D. and Shaw, B. D. 'The era of the Cereres', *Hist.*27 (1978) 343–54
734. Flach, D. 'Inschriftenuntersuchungen zum römischen Kolonat in Nordafrika', *Chiron* 8 (1978) 441–92
735. Gascou, J. *La politique municipale de l'empire romaine en Afrique proconsulaire de Trajan à Septime-Sévère.* Rome, 1972
736. Gascou, J. 'Les curies africaines: origine punique ou italienne?' *AntAfr* 10 (1976) 33–48
737. Gascou, J. 'Les *pagi* Carthaginois' in Février, P.-A. and Leveau, P. (eds.) *Villes et campagnes dans l'empire romain*, 139–75. Aix-en-Provence, 1980
738. Gascou, J. 'La politique municipale de Rome en Afrique du Nord: 1. De la mort d'Auguste au début du IIIᵉ siècle', *ANRW* II, (1982) 136–229
739. Gascou, J. 'Pagus et castellum dans la confédération cirtéenne', *AntAfr* 19 (1983) 175–207
740. Gascou, J. 'Les *sacerdotes Cererum* de Carthage', *AntAfr* 23 (1987) 95–128
741. Gsell, S. *Histoire de l'Afrique du Nord*, VIII. 2nd edn. Paris, 1930
742. Gutsfeld, A. *Römische Herrschaft und einheimischer Widerstand in Nordafrika. Militärische Auseinandersetzungen Roms mit den Nomaden.* Stuttgart, 1989
743. Haywood, R. M. 'Roman Africa'. Part I of *ESAR* IV. Reprint. New Jersey, 1959
744. Heurgon, J. 'L'agronome Carthaginois Magon et ses traducteurs en latin et en grec', *CRAI* (1976) 441–56
745. Hurst, H. 'Fouilles britanniques au port circulaire et quelques idées sur le développement de la Carthage romaine', *Cahiers des Etudes Anciennes* 17 (1985) 143–56
746. Kehoe, D. P. *The Economics of Agriculture on Roman Imperial Estates in North Africa.* Göttingen, 1988
747. Kotula, T. *Les curies municipales en Afrique romaine.* Warsaw, 1968
748. Lancel, S. (ed.) *Histoire et archéologie de l'Afrique du Nord. IIᵉ Colloque International. Grenoble. 1983. Bull. Arch. du Comité des Trav. Hist.* 19 B. Paris, 1985
749. Lassère, J.-M. *Ubique populus.* Paris, 1977
750. Le Glay, M. *Saturne africain. Histoire.* Paris, 1966
751. Leschi, L. *Etudes d'épigraphie, d'archéologie et d'histoire africaines.* Paris, 1957
752. Leveau, P. *Caesarea de Maurétanie: une ville romaine et ses campagnes.* Rome, 1984
753. Mackie, N. 'Augustan colonies in Mauretania', *Hist.* 32 (1983) 332–58

754. Nerom, C. van 'Colonia Julia Concordia Karthago', *Hommages M. Renard* (Coll. Latomus 102), II 767–76. Brussels, 1969

755. Pflaum, H.-G. 'La romanisation de l'ancien territoire de la Carthage punique à la lumière des découvertes épigraphiques récentes', *AntAfr* 4 (1970) 75–118

756. Picard, G. C. 'Néron et le blé d'Afrique', *Cahiers de Tunisie* 14 (1956) 163–73

757. Picard, G. C. *Les religions de l'Afrique antique.* Paris, 1954

758. Picard, G. C. 'L'administration territoriale de Carthage', *Mélanges Piganiol* III 1257–65. Paris, 1966

758A. Picard, G. C. *Historie et archéologie de l'Afrique du Nord.* Ière College International, 1981. *Bull. Arch. du Comité des Trav. Hist.* 17 B. Paris, 1984

759. Poinssot, C. *Les ruines de Dougga.* Tunis, 1958

760. Romanelli, P. *Storia delle provincie romane dell' Africa.* Rome, 1959

761. Salama, P. 'La colonie de Rusguniae', *MEFRA* 67 (1955) 127–48

762. Saumagne, C. 'Colonia Julia Karthago', *Cahiers de Tunisie* 10 (1962) 463–71

763. Smadja, E. 'Remarques sur les débuts du culte impérial en Afrique sous le règne d'Auguste', in *Religions, pouvoir, rapports sociaux* (Ann. Litt. Univ. Besançon 237) 151–69. Paris, 1980

764. Syme, R. 'Tacfarinas, the Musulami and Thubursicum', in *Studies in Honor of A. C. Johnson*, 113–30. Princeton, 1951. (= A 94, I, 218–30)

765. Teutsch, L. *Das römische Städtewesen in Nordafrika in der Zeit von C. Gracchus bis zum Tode des Kaisers Augustus.* Berlin, 1962

766. Thébert, Y. 'La romanisation d'une cité indigène d'Afrique', *MEFRA* 85 (1973) 247–312

767. Thompson, L. A. and Ferguson, J. *Africa in Classical Antiquity.* Ibadan, 1969

768. Trousset, P. 'Les bornes du Bled Segui nouveaux aperçus sur la centuriation romaine du sud Tunisien', *AntAfr* 12 (1978) 125–77

769. Werff, J. H. van der. 'Amphores de tradition punique à Uzita', *BABesch* 52/53 (1977/8) 171–98

770. Whittaker, C. R. 'Land and labour in North Africa', *Klio* 60 (1978) 331–62

10. CYRENE

771. Alföldi, A. 'Commandants de la flotte romaine stationnée à Cyrène sous Pompée, César et Octavien', *Mélanges J. Carcopino*, 2225–43. Paris, 1966

772. Anti, C. *Sculture greche e romane di Cirene.* Padua, 1959

773. Applebaum, S. *Jews and Greeks in Ancient Cyrene.* Leiden, 1979

774. *Area Handbook for Libya.* Washington, 1969

775. Bacchielli, L. *L'Agorà di Cirene*: II.1. *L'area settentrionale del lato ovest della platea inferiore.* Rome, 1981

775A. Barker, G., Lloyd, J. A. and Reynolds, J. (eds.) *Cyrenaica in Antiquity* (BAR International series 236). Oxford, 1985

776. Bowsky, M. Baldwin, '*M. Tittius Sex. f. Aem.* and the Jews of Berenice', *AJPh* 108 (1987) 494–510
777. Chamoux, F. *Cyrène sous la monarchie des Battiades*, Part II, chs. 1, 2. Paris, 1953
778. Desanges, J. 'Un drame africain sous Auguste, le meurtre du proconsul L. Cornelius Lentulus par les Nasamons', *Hommages Renard* II (Coll. Latomus 102) 197–213. Brussels, 1969
779. *Economic Development of Libya.* Baltimore, 1960
780. Ermeti, A. L. *L'Agorà di Cirene*: III. 1 *Il monumento navale.* Rome, 1981
780A. Gadullah, F. (ed.) *Libya in History* (Historical conference held at Benghazi, March 1968)
781. Goodchild, R. G. 'Roman milestones in Cyrenaica', *PBSR* 18 (1950) 83–91
782. Goodchild, R. G. *Tabula Imperii Romani*, sheet H.1.34. *Cyrene.* London, 1954
783. Goodchild, R. G. *Cyrene and Apollonia, an Historical Guide.* Cyrene, 1963
784. Goodchild, R. G. *Kyrene und Apollonia.* Zurich, 1971
785. Humphrey, J. H. (ed.) *Apollonia, the Port of Cyrene, Excavations by the University of Michigan 1967–7.* Tripoli, 1976
786. Huskinson, J. *Roman Sculpture from Cyrenaica in the British Museum.* London, 1975
787. Johnson, D. L. *Jabal al-Akhdar, Cyrenaica: an Historical Geography of Settlement and Livelihood.* Chicago, 1973
788. Jones, G. D. B. and Little, J. H. 'Coastal settlement in Cyrenaica', *JRS* 61 (1971) 64–79
789. Kraeling, C. H. *Ptolemais, City of the Libyan Pentapolis.* Chicago, 1962
790. Laronde, A. *Cyrène et la Libye hellénistique*, chs. 13, 14, 18. Paris, 1987
791. Laronde, A. 'La Cyrénaïque romaine des origines à la fin des Sévères, 96 av. J.-C.–235 ap. J.-C.', *ANRW* II, 10. 1 (1988) 1006–2064
792. Laronde, A. *Greeks and Libyans in Cyrenaica* (Proceedings of the 1st Australian Congress of Classical Archaeology 1985), 169–80. Canberra, 1990
793. Lloyd, J. A. (ed.) *Excavations at Sidi Khrebish, Benghazi (Berenice) Tripoli*: I. *Buildings, Coins, Inscriptions, Architectural Decoration* (1977); II. *Economic Life at Berenice, Sculpture and Terracottas, Coarse Pottery* (1979); III. 1. *Fine pottery* (1985); III. 2. *Lamps* (1985). Tripoli
793A. Lüderitz, G. *Die Juden der Cyrenaika: Zeugnisse zur Sozial-und Kulturgeschichte einer religiösen Minderheit in der Antike.* Tübingen, 1993
794. Masson, O. 'Grecs et Libyens en Cyrène, d'après les témoignages de l'épigraphie', *AntAfr* 10 (1976) 49–62
795. Mingazzini, P. *L'Insula di Giasone Magno.* Rome, 1966
796. Paribeni, E. *Catalogo delle sculture di Cirene; statue e rilievi di carattere religioso.* Rome, 1959
797. Perl, G. 'Die römischen Provinzbeamten in Cyrenae und Creta', *Klio* 52 (1970) 319–54; 53 (1971) 370–9
798. Pernier, L. *Il tempio e l'altare di Apollo a Cirene.* Bergamo, 1935
799. Pesce, G. *Il Palazzo delle Colonne in Tolemaide di Cirenaica.* Rome, 1950

800. Reddé, M. *Prospection des vallées du nord de la Libye (1979–80)*. *La région de la Syrte à l'époque romaine* (Armée romaine et les provinces 4). Paris, 1988
801. Reynolds, J. (ed.) *Libyan Studies*. London, 1976
802. Reynolds, J. M. 'Senators originating in the provinces of Egypt and of Crete and Cyrene', in D 42, 671–83
803. Romanelli, P. *La Cirenaica Romana*. Verbania, 1935. (See also his translated résumé in *CAH* x¹ (1936) 667–75)
804. Rosenbaum, E. *A Catalogue of Cyrenaican Portrait Sculpture*. London, 1969
804A. Smith, R. M. and Porcher, E. A. *A History of the Recent Discoveries at Cyrene*. London, 1864
805. Stucchi, S. *L'Agorà di Cirene*: I. *I lati Nord e Est della platea inferiore*. Rome, 1965
805A. Stucchi, S. (ed.) *Cirene 1957–66. Un decennio di attività della missione archeologica italiana a Cirene*. Tripoli, 1967
806. Stucchi, S. '*L'Architettura Cirenaica*. Rome, 1975
806A. Stucchi, S. (ed.) *Giornata Lincea sulla Archeologia Cirenaica*. Rome, 1990
807. Stucchi, S. and Bacchielli, L. *L'Agorà di Cirene*: II. 4. *Il lato sud della platea inferiore e il lato nord della terrazza superiore*. Rome, 1983
807A. Thrige, J. P. *Res Cyrenensium*. Reprinted Verbania, 1940
808. Vitali, L. *Fonti per la storia della religione cirenaica*. Padua, 1932
809. White, D. *The Extramural Sanctuary of Demeter and Persephone at Cyrene, Libya, Final Reports*: I (1984); II (1985); III (1987). Philadelphia

11. GREECE AND ASIA MINOR

810. Alcock, S. E. 'Archaeology and imperialism: Roman expansion and the Greek city', *Journal of Mediterranean Archaeology* 2 (1989) 87–135
811. Alcock, S. E. *Graecia Capta: The Landscapes of Roman Greece*. Cambridge, 1993
812. Baladié, R. *Le Péloponnèse de Strabon: Étude de géographie historique*. Paris, 1980
813. Bean, G. E. *Aegean Turkey, an Archaeological Guide*. London, 1966
814. Bean, G. E. *Turkey's Southern Shore, an Archaeological Guide*. London, 1968
815. Bean, G. E. *Turkey Beyond the Maeander, an Archaeological Guide*. London, 1971
816. Bintliff, J. and Snodgrass, A. 'The Cambridge/Bradford Boeotia Expedition: the first four years', *JFA* 12 (1985) 123–61
817. Bowersock, G. W. 'Eurycles of Sparta', *JRS* 51 (1961) 212–18
818. Bowersock, G. W. 'Zur Geschichte des römischen Thessaliens', *RhM* 108 (1965) 277–89
819. Box, H. 'Roman citizenship in Laconia', *JRS* 21 (1931) 200–14
820. Broughton, T. R. S. 'Roman landholding in Asia Minor', *TAPA* 65 (1934) 207–39
821. Broughton, T. R. S. 'Roman Asia', in D 128, IV
822. Chaumont, M. L. 'Armenia', *ANRW* II, 9 (1976) 73–84
823. Daux, G. 'Les Empereurs romains et l'Amphictionie pyléo-delphique', *CRAI* (1975) 348–62

824. Day, J. *An Economic History of Athens under Roman Domination*. New York, 1942
825. Erim, K. T. *Aphrodisias. City of Venus Aphrodite*. London, 1986
826. Fossey, J. M. 'The cities of the Kopäis in the Roman period', *ANRW* II, 7.1 (1979) 549–91
827. Frantz, A. *The Athenian Agora*: XXIV. *Late Antiquity: A.D. 267–700*. Princeton, 1988
828. Fraser, P. M. and Bean, G. E. *The Rhodian Peraea and Islands*. Oxford, 1954
829. French, D. H. 'The Roman road system of Asia Minor', *ANRW* II, 7.2 (1980) 698–729
830. Geagan, D. J. *The Athenian Constitution after Sulla* (*Hesperia* Suppl. 12). Princeton, 1967
831. Geagan, D. J. 'Roman Athens, some aspects of life and culture: I. 86 B.C.– A.D. 267', *ANRW* II, 7.1 (1979) 371–437 (bibliography)
832. Graindor, P. *Athènes sous Auguste*. Cairo, 1927
833. Graindor, P. *Athènes de Tibère à Trajan*. Cairo, 1931
834. Groag, E. *Die römischen Reichsbeamten von Achaia bis auf Diokletian*. Ak. Wiss. Wien, Schriften der Balkankommission, Ant. Abt. 9. Vienna, 1939
835. Gwatkin, W. E. *Cappadocia as a Roman Procuratorial Province*. Univ. Missouri Stud. V, 4. Columbia, 1930
836. Halfmann, H. 'Die Senatoren aus den kleinasiatischen Provinzen des römischen Reiches vom 1. bis 3. Jahrhundert (Asia, Pontus-Bithynia, Lycia-Pamphylia, Galatia, Cappadocia, Cilicia)', in D 42, 603–50
837. Hanfmann, G. M. A. *Sardis from Prehistoric to Roman Times: Results of the Archaeological Exploration of Sardis 1958–1975*. Cambridge, MA, 1983
838. Harris, B. F. 'Bithynia: Roman sovereignty and the survival of Hellenism', *ANRW* II, 7.2 (1980) 857–901
839. Hellenkemper, H. 'Zur Entwicklung des Stadtbildes in Kilikien', *ANRW* II, 7.2 (1980) 1262–83 (bibliography)
840. Hoben, W. *Untersuchungen zur Stellung kleinasiatischer Dynasten in den Machtkämpfen der ausgehenden Republik*. Mainz, 1969
841. Hoff, M. C. 'Civil disobedience and unrest in Augustan Athens', *Hesperia* 58 (1989) 267–76
842. Holtheide, B. *Römische Bürgerrechtspolitik und römische Neubürger in der Provinz Asia*. Diss., Heidelberg, 1983
843. Jameson, S. A. 'Lycia and Pamphylia, an historical review', in Campbell, A. C. (ed.) *History of Turkey*, 11–31. Tripoli, 1971
844. Jameson, S. A. 'The Lycian League: some problems in its administration', *ANRW* II, 7.2 (1980) 832–55
845. Kahrstedt, U. 'Die Territorien von Patrai und Nicopolis in der Kaiserzeit'. *Hist.* 1 (1950) 549–61
846. Kahrstedt, U. 'Zwei Probleme im kaiserlichen Griechenland', *SymbOsl* 28 (1950) 70–5
847. Kahrstedt, U. *Das wirtschaftliche Gesicht Griechenlands in der Kaiserzeit: Kleinstadt, Villa, und Domän* (Diss. Bern I, 7). Berne, 1954
848. Knibbe, D. and Alzinger, W. 'Ephesos vom Beginn der römischen Herrschaft in Kleinasien bis zum Ende der Prinzipatszeit', *ANRW* II,

7.2 (1980) 748–830

849. Larsen, J. A. O. 'The policy of Augustus in Greece', *AClass* (1959) 123ff
850. Larsen, J. A. O. 'Roman Greece', in D 128 III, 259–498
851. Levick, B. *Roman Colonies in Southern Asia Minor.* Oxford, 1967
852. Macro, A. D. 'The cities of Asia Minor under the Roman Imperium', *ANRW* II, 7.2 (1980) 658–97
853. Magie, D. *Roman Rule in Asia Minor to the end of the Third Century after Christ.* Princeton, 1950
854. Mitchell, S. 'Legio VII and the garrison of Augustan Galatia', *CQ* 26 (1976) 298–305
855. Mitchell, S. 'Roman residents and Roman property in southern Asia Minor', *Congresso internazionale di archeologia classica X: Ankara-Izmir 1973* 3, 311–18. Ankara, 1978
856. Mitchell, S. 'Archaeology in western and southern Asia Minor 1971–8: 1979–84' in *Archaeological Reports: Soc. Promotion of Hell. Stud. and British School at Athens,* 59–90. London, 1979, 1985
857. Mitchell, S. 'Iconium and Ninica: two double communities in Roman Asia Minor', *Hist.* 28 (1979) 409–38
857A. Mitchell, S. *Anatolia: Law, Men and Gods in Asia Minor.* 2 vols. Oxford, 1993
858. Mitford, T. B. 'A Cypriot oath of allegiance to Tiberius', *JRS* 50 (1960) 76–9
859. Mitford, T. B. 'Roman Cyprus', *ANRW* II, 7.2 (1980) 1286–384 (bibliography)
860. Mitford, T. B. 'Roman Rough Cilicia', *ANRW* II, 7.2 (1980) 1230–61
861. Oliver, J. H. 'Panachaeans and Panhellenes', *Hesperia* 47 (1978) 185–91
862. Oliver, J. H. 'Roman Senators from Greece and Macedon', in D 42, 583–602
863. Olshausen, E. 'Pontos und Rom (63 v. Chr.–64 n. Chr.)', *ANRW* II, 7.2 (1980) 903–12
864. Pekáry, T. 'Kleinasien unter römischer Herrschaft', *ANRW* II, 7.2 (1980) 595–657 (bibliography)
865. Radt, W. *Pergamon. Geschichte und Bauten, Funde und Erforschung einer antiken Metropole.* Cologne, 1988
866. Rawlinson, H. C. 'Memoir on the site of the Atropenian Ecbatana', *JRGeogS* 10 (1841) 65–158
867. Rigsby, K. J. 'Cnossus and Capua', *TAPA* 106 (1976) 314–30
868. Robert, L. *Villes d'Asie Mineure.* 2nd edn. Paris, 1962
869. Robert, J. and L. *La Carie* II. Paris, 1952
870. Rostovtzeff, M. 'Augustus und Athen', *Festschrift O. Hirschfeld, Klio* 3 (1903) 303–11
871. Sanders, I. F. *Roman Crete.* Warminster, 1982
872. Schmitt, H. H. *Rom und Rhodos.* Munich, 1957
873. Shear, T. L. 'Athens: from city state to provincial town', *Hesperia* 50 (1981) 356–77
874. Sherk, R. K. *The Legates of Galatia from Augustus to Diocletian.* Johns Hopkins Univ. Stud. in Hist. and Pol. Science 69, 2. Baltimore, 1951

875. Sherk, R. K. 'Roman Galatia: the governors from 25 B.C.–A.D. 114', *ANRW* II, 7.2 (1980) 954–1052

876. Speidel, M. 'Legionaries from Asia Minor', *ANRW* II, 7.2 (1980) 730–46

877. Strubbe, J. 'A group of imperial estates in central Phrygia', *AncSoc* 6 (1975) 228–50

878. Sullivan, R. D. 'The dynasty of Commagene', *ANRW* II, 8 (1977) 732–98

879. Sullivan, R. D. 'Dynasts in Pontus', *ANRW* II, 7.2 (1980) 913–30

880. Sullivan, R. D. 'The dynasty of Cappadocia', *ANRW* II, 7.2 (1980) 1125–68

881. Syme, R. 'Galatia and Pamphylia under Augustus: the governorships of Piso, Quirinius and Silvanus', *Klio* 27 (1934) 122–48

882. Syme, R. 'Pamphylia from Augustus to Vespasian', *Klio* 30 (1937) 227ff (= A 94, 1, 42–6)

883. Teja, R. 'Die römische Provinz Kappadokien in der Prinzipatszeit', *ANRW* II, 7.2 (1980) 1083–124

884. Travlos, J. *Pictorial Dictionary of Ancient Athens.* London, 1971

885. Vogel-Weidemann, U. *Die Statthalter von Africa und Asia in den Jahren 14–68 n. Chr.: eine Untersuchung zum Verhältnis Princeps und Senat. Antiquitas* I, 31. Bonn, 1982

886. Wallace, P. W. 'Strabo's description of Boiotia, a commentary', *Bibl. der Klass. Altertumswissenschaften* n.s. 2, 65. Heidelberg, 1979

887. Wiseman, J. 'Corinth and Rome', *ANRW* II, 7.1 (1979) 438–548

12. EGYPT

888. el-Abbadi, M. A. H. 'The Alexandrian citizenship', *JEA* 48 (1962) 106–23

889. Bagnall, R. S. 'Publius Petronius, Augustan prefect of Egypt', *YCS* 28 (1985) 85–93

890. Barns, J. W. B. *Egyptians and Greeks* (Papyrologica Bruxellensia 14). Brussels, 1978

891. Bastianini, G. 'Lista dei prefetti d'Egitto dal 30a al 299p', *ZPE* 17 (1975) 263–328

892. Bastianini, G. 'Aggiunte e correzioni', *ZPE* 38 (1980) 75–89

893. Bell, H. I. 'Alexandria ad Aegyptum', *JRS* 36 (1946) 130–2

894. Bell, H. I. *Cults and Creeds in Graeco-Roman Egypt.* Liverpool, 1953

895. Bell, H. I. *Egypt from Alexander the Great to the Arab Conquest.* Oxford, 1956

896. Bingen, J. 'L' Égypte gréco-romaine et la problématique des interactions culturelles', *Proceedings of the XVI International Congress of Papyrology* (American Studies in Papyrology 22), 3–18. Toronto, 1981

897. Bonneau, D. *La crue du Nil, divinité égyptienne à travers mille ans d'histoire (332 av.–641 ap. J.-C.).* Paris, 1964

898. Bonneau, D. *Le fisc et le Nil.* Paris, 1971

899. Bowman, A. K. 'A letter of Avidius Cassius?', *JRS* 60 (1970) 20–6

900. Bowman, A. K. *The Town Councils of Roman Egypt* (American Studies in Papyrology 11). Toronto, 1971

901. Bowman, A. K. *Egypt after the Pharaohs*. 2nd edn. Oxford, 1990

902. Bowman, A. K. 'Public buildings in Roman Egypt,' *JRA* 5 (1992) 495–503

903. Bowman, A. K. and Rathbone, D. W. 'Cities and administration in Roman Egypt', *JRS* 82 (1992) 107–27

904. Braunert, H. 'IDIA: Studien zur Bevölkerungsgeschichte des ptolemäischen und römischen Ägypten', *JJP* 9–10 (1955–6) 211–328

905. Braunert, H. *Die Binnenwanderung: Studien zur Sozialgeschichte Ägyptens in der Ptolemäerzeit und Kaiserzeit* (Bonner Historische Forschungen 26). Bonn, 1964

906. Brunt, P. A. 'The administrators of Roman Egypt', *JRS* 65 (1975) 124–47 (= (with addenda) A 12, 215–54, 514–15)

907. Butzer, K. W. *Early Hydraulic Civilisation in Egypt*. Chicago, 1976

908. Cavenaile, R. 'Prosopographie de l'armée romaine d'Égypte d'Auguste à Dioclétien', *Aegyptus* 50 (1970) 213–320

909. Chalon, G. *L'édit de Tiberius Julius Alexander*. Olten–Lausanne, 1964

910. Criniti, N. 'Supplemento alla prosopografia dell'esercito romano d'Egitto da Augusto a Diocleziano', *Aegyptus* 53 (1973) 93–158

911. Criniti, N. 'Sulle forze armate romane d'Egitto: osservazioni e nuove aggiunti prosopografiche', *Aegyptus* 59 (1979) 190–261

912. Daris, S. 'Le truppe ausiliarie romane in Egitto,' *ANRW* II, 10. 1 (1988) 724–42

913. Davies, R. W. 'Minicius Iustus and a Roman military document from Egypt', *Aegyptus* 53 (1973) 75–92

914. Devijver, H. 'The Roman army in Egypt (with special reference to the militiae equestres)', *ANRW* II, 1 (1974) 452–92

915. Devijver, H. *De Aegypto et exercitu romano sive prosopographia militiarum equestrium quae ab Augusto ad Gallienum seu statione seu origine ad Aegyptum pertinebant* (Studia Hellenistica 22). Louvain, 1975

916. Devijver, H. 'L'Égypte et l'histoire de l'armée romaine', in Criscuolo, L. and Geraci, G. (eds.) *Egitto e storia antica dall'ellenismo all'età araba, Atti del colloquio internazionale, Bologna, 31 Agosto–2 Settembre, 1987*, 37–54. Bologna, 1989

917. Dobson, B. 'The praefectus castrorum Aegypti – a reconsideration', *CE* 57 (1982) 322–37

918. Duncan-Jones, R. P. 'The price of wheat in Egypt under the Principate', *Chiron* 6 (1976) 241–62

919. Evans, J. A. S. 'A social and economic history of an Egyptian temple in the Greco-Roman period', *YCS* 17 (1961) 145–283

920. Foti Talamanca, G. *Ricerche sul processo nell'Egitto greco-romano*: I. *L'organizzazione del 'Conventus' del 'Praefectus Aegypti'*: II. 1 *L'introduzione del giudizio*. Milan, 1974–9

921. Fraser, P. M. *Ptolemaic Alexandria*. 3 vols. Oxford, 1972

922. Gara, A. *Prosdiagraphomena e circolazione monetaria*. Milan, 1976

923. Gara, A. 'Aspetti di economia monetaria dell'Egitto romano,' *ANRW* II, 10. 1 (1988) 912–51

924. Geraci, G. *Genesi della provincia romana d'Egitto*. Bologna, 1983
925. Geraci, G. 'Publio Petronio, il genetliaco di Augusto e il "Faraone Cesare"', *ZPE* 65 (1986) 195–6
926. Geraci, G. "Ἐπαρχία δὲ νῦν ἐστί. La concezione augustea del governo d'Egitto', *ANRW* II, 10.1 (1988) 383–411
927. Grimm, G., Heinen, H. and Winter E. (eds.) *Alexandrien* (Aegyptiaca Treverensia 1). Trier, 1981
928. Grimm, G., Heinen, H. and Winter E. (eds.) *Das römisch-byzantinische Ägypten, Akten des internationalen Symposions 26–30 September 1978 in Trier* (Aegyptiaca Treverensia 2). Trier, 1983
929. Hagedorn, D. 'Zum Amt der *dioiketes* im römischen Ägypten', *YCS* 28 (1985) 167–210
930. Hanson, A. E. 'Publius Ostorius Scapula. Augustan Prefect of Egypt', *ZPE* 47 (1982) 243–53
931. Hanson, A. E. 'Two copies of a petition to the Prefect', *ZPE* 47 (1982) 233–43
932. Hanson, A. E. 'The keeping of records at Philadelphia in the Julio-Claudian period and the "Economic Crisis" under Nero', *Proceedings of the XVIII International Congress of Papyrology* II, 261–77. Athens, 1988
933. Haycock, B. G. 'The later phases of Meroitic civilization', *JEA* 53 (1967) 107–20
934. Hobson, D. W. 'Women as property owners in Roman Egypt', *TAPA* 113 (1983) 311–21
935. Hobson, D. W. 'The role of women in the economic life of Roman Egypt: a case study from first century Tebtunis', *CV* 28, n.s. 3 (1984) 373–89
936. Hohlwein, N. *Le stratège du nome* (Papyrologica Bruxellensia 9). Brussels, 1969
937. Hopkins, K. 'Brother–sister marriage in Roman Egypt', *CSSH* 22.3 (1980) 303–54
938. Humbert, M. *La Juridiction du préfet d'Égypte d'Auguste à Dioclétien*. Paris, 1964
939. Jameson, S. 'Chronology of the campaigns of Aelius Gallus and C. Petronius', *JRS* 58 (1968) 71–84
940. Johnson, A. C. *Roman Egypt to the Reign of Diocletian*. (= D 128, II)
941. Kennedy, D. L. 'The composition of a military work party in Egypt (*ILS* 2483, Coptos)', *JEA* 71 (1985) 156–60
942. Kirwan, L. P. 'Rome beyond the southern Egyptian frontier', *PBA* 53 (1977) 13–31
943. Lesquier, J. *L'armée romaine d'Égypte d'Auguste à Dioclétien* (*IFAO Mémoires* 41). Cairo, 1918
944. Lewis, N. 'Graeco-Roman Egypt: fact or fiction?', *Proceedings of the XII International Congress of Papyrology, Ann Arbor 1968* (American Studies in Papyrology 7), 3–14. Toronto, 1970
945. Lewis, N. *The Compulsory Public Services of Roman Egypt* (Papyrologica Florentina 11). Florence, 1982
946. Lewis, N. *Life in Egypt under Roman Rule*. Oxford, 1983

947. Lewis, N. 'The romanity of Roman Egypt: a growing consensus', *Atti del XVII Congresso Internazionale di Papirologia*, 1077–84. Naples, 1984

948. Maehler, H. G. T. 'Egypt under the last Ptolemies', *BICS* 30 (1983) 1–16

949. Meredith, D. 'The Roman remains in the eastern desert of Egypt', *JEA* 38 (1952) 94–111; 39 (1953) 95–106

950. Milne, J. G. *A History of Egypt under Roman Rule*. London, 1924

951. Modrzejewski, J. 'La règle de droit dans l'Égypte romaine', *Proceedings of the XII International Congress of Papyrology, Ann Arbor, 1968* (American Studies in Papyrology 7), 317–77. Toronto, 1970

952. Montevecchi, O. 'L'amministrazione dell'Egitto sotto i Giulio-Claudi,' *ANRW* II, 10.1 (1988) 412–71

953. Nelson, C. A. *Status Declarations in Roman Egypt* (American Studies in Papyrology 9). Toronto, 1979

954. Oertel, F. *Die Liturgie*. Leipzig, 1917

955. Pack, R. A. *The Greek and Latin Literary Texts from Greco-Roman Egypt*. 2nd edn. Ann Arbor, 1965

956. Parássoglou, G. M. *Imperial Estates in Roman Egypt* (American Studies in Papyrology 18). Toronto, 1978

957. Pflaum, H.-G. 'Un nouveau diplome militaire d'un soldat de l'armée d'Égypte', *Syria* 44 (1967), 339–62 (= *Scripta Varia* II, 269–94. Paris, 1981)

958. Porter, B. and Moss, R. L. B. *Topographical Bibliography of Ancient Egyptian Hieroglyphic Texts, Reliefs and Paintings* I–VII. Oxford, 1927–51; 2nd edn. of vols. I–III, Oxford, 1960–78

959. Préaux, C. 'L'attache à la terre: continuités de l'Égypte ptolémaïque à l'Égypte romaine', in E 928, 1–5

960. Rathbone, D. W. 'The ancient economy and Graeco-Roman Egypt', in Criscuolo, L. and Geraci, G. (eds.) *Egitto e storia antica dall'ellenismo all'età araba, Atti del colloquio internazionale, Bologna, 31 Agosto–2 Settembre, 1987*, 159–76. Bologna, 1989

961. Rathbone, D. W. 'Villages, land and population in Graeco-Roman Egypt,' *PCPhS* (1990) 103–42

962. Rathbone, D. W. 'Egypt, Augustus and Roman taxation', *CCG* 4 (1993) 81–112

963. Rowlandson, J. L. *Landowners and Tenants in Roman Egypt: the Social Relations of Agriculture in the Oxyrhynchite Nome*. Oxford, 1996

964. Seidl, E. *Rechtsgeschichte Ägyptens als römische Provinz: die Behauptung des ägyptischen Rechts neben den römischen*. St Augustin, 1973

965. Sijpesteijn, P. J. *Customs Duties in Graeco-Roman Egypt*. Amsterdam, 1987

966. Skeat, T. C. 'The Augustan era in Egypt', *ZPE* 53 (1983) 241–4

967. Stead, M. 'The high-priest of Alexandria and all Egypt', *Proceedings of the XVI International Congress of Papyrology* (American Studies in Papyrology 23), 411–18. Chico, 1981

968. Speidel, M. 'Nubia's Roman garrison', *ANRW* II, 10. 1 (1988) 767–98

969. Speidel, M. P. 'Augustus' deployment of the legions in Egypt', *Chronique d'Égypte* 57 (1982) 120–4 (= D 235, 317–21)

970. Straus, J. A. 'L'esclavage dans l'Égypte romaine,' *ANRW* II, 10. 1 (1988) 841–911

971. Strocka, V. M. 'Augustus als Pharao', *Eikones: Studien . . . H. Jucker gewidmet* (*Antike Kunst* Beih. 12) 177–80. Bern, 1980

972. Swarney, P. R. *The Ptolemaic and Roman Idios Logos* (American Studies in Papyrology 8). Toronto, 1970

973. Thomas, J. D. *The Epistrategos in Ptolemaic and Roman Egypt*: I. *The Ptolemaic Epistrategos*; II. *The Roman Epistrategos* (Papyrologica Coloniensia 6). 1975–82

974. Thomas, J. D. 'Compulsory public service in Roman Egypt', in E 928, 35–9

975. Tomsin, A. 'Étude sur les *presbyteroi* des villages de la *chora* égyptienne', *Academie royale de Belgique, Classe des Lettres et des Sciences morales et politiques, Bulletin* 38 (1952) 95–130, 467–532

976. Török, L. 'Geschichte Meroes. Ein Beitrag über die Quellenlage und den Forschungsstand', *ANRW* II, 10.1 (1988) 107–341

977. Turner, E. G. 'Roman Oxyrhynchus', *JEA* 38 (1952) 78–93

978. Turner, E. G. 'Oxyrhynchus and Rome', *HSCP* 79 (1975) 1–24

979. Wallace, S. L. *Taxation in Egypt from Augustus to Diocletian*. Princeton, 1938

980. Weingärtner, D. G. *Die Ägyptenreise des Germanicus* (Papyrologische Texte und Abhandlungen 11). Bonn, 1969

981. West, L. C. and Johnson, A. C. *Currency in Roman and Byzantine Egypt*. Princeton, 1944

982. Whitehorne, J. E. G. 'More about L. Pompeius Niger, legionary veteran', *Proceedings of the XVIII International Congress of Papyrology* II, 445–50. Athens, 1988

983. Whitehorne, J. E. G. 'Recent research on the *strategi* of Roman Egypt (to 1985)', *ANRW* II, 10. 1 (1988) 598–617

984. Wolff, H.-J. *Das Recht der griechischen Papyri Ägyptens in der Zeit der Ptolemäer und des Prinzipats*: II. *Organisation und Kontrolle des privaten Rechtsverkehrs* (Handbuch der Altertumswissenschaft 10). Munich, 1978

13. SYRIA

985. Balty, J. and J. C. 'Apamée de Syrie, archéologie et histoire, 1. Des origines à la Tétrarchie', *ANRW* II, 8 (1978) 103–34

986. Bawden, G. 'Khief El-Zarah and the nature of the Dedonite hegemony in the al- 'Ula oasis', *Atlal* 3 (1399 A.H.–1979 A.D.), 63–72

987. Berchem, D. van. 'Le plan de Palmyre', *Palmyre. Bilan et Perspectives*, 165–73. Strasburg, 1976

988. Bietenhard, H. 'Die syrische Dekapolis von Pompeius bis Traian', *ANRW* II, 8 (1977) 220–61

989. Bintliff, J. L. 'Climatic change, archaeology and Quaternary science in the eastern Mediterranean region', in Harding, A. (ed.) *Climatic Change in Later Prehistory*, 143–61. Edinburgh, 1982

990. Bowersock, G. W. *Roman Arabia*. Cambridge, MA, 1983

991. Bowsher, J. 'The Nabataean army', in E 1008 B, 19–30

992. Brown, J. P. *The Lebanon and Phoenicia*; 1 *The Physical Setting and the Forest*. Beirut, 1966

993. Cantineau, J. 'Textes Palmyréniens provenant de la fouille du Temple de Bel', *Syria* 12 (1931) 116–41

994. Colledge, M. A. R. 'Le temple de Bêl à Palmyre: qui l'a fait, et pourquoi?' in *Palmyre. Bilan et Perspectives*, 45–52. Strasburg, 1976

995. Colledge, M. A. R. 'Interpretatio Romana: the semitic populations of Syria and Mesopotamia', in Henig, M. and King, A. (eds.) *Pagan Gods and Shrines of the Roman Empire*, 221–31. Oxford, 1986

996. Cumont, F. 'The population of Syria', *JRS* 24 (1934) 187–90

997. Dayton, J. E. 'A Roman/Byzantine site in the Hedjaz', *Proc. Seminar Arabian Studies* 1–3 (1972) 21–5

998. Dentzer, J.-M. 'Sondages près de l'arc nabatéen à Bostra', *Berytus* 32 (1984) 163–74

999. Dentzer, J.-M. *Hauran*, I, 1: 1, 2, Paris, 1985; 1986

1000. Dentzer, J.-M. 'Développement et culture de la Syrie du Sud dans la période préprovinciale (1er siècle avant J.-C.–1er siècle après J.-C.)', in E 999, 1, 2, 387–420

1001. Dentzer, J.-M. 'Les sondages de l'arc nabatéen et l'urbanisme de Bostra', *CRAI* (1986) 62–87

1002. Dentzer, J.-M. and J. 'Les fouilles de Sì et la phase hellénistique en Syrie du Sud', *CRAI* (1981) 78–102

1003. DeVries, B. 'Umm el-Jimal in the first three centuries A.D.', in E 1008 A, 227–41

1004. Dihle, A. 'Das Datum des Periplus des Roten Meeres', in *Umstrittene Daten*, 9–35. Cologne, 1965

1005. Downey, G. 'The size of the population of Antioch', *TAPA* 89 (1958) 84–91

1006. Downey, G. *A History of Antioch in Syria from Seleucus to the Arab Conquest*. Princeton, 1961

1007. Dussaud, R. *La pénétration des Arabes en Syrie avant l'Islam*. Paris, 1955

1008. Evenari, M., Shanan, L. and Tadmor, N. *The Negev*. 2nd edn. Cambridge, MA, 1982

1008A. Freeman, P. and Kennedy, D. (eds.) *The Defence of the Roman and Byzantine East* (BAR Int. Series 297). 2 vols. Oxford, 1986

1008B. French, D. H. and Lightfoot, C. S. (eds.) *The Eastern Frontier of the Roman Empire* (BAR Int. Series 553). Oxford, 1989

1009. Gatier, P.-L. 'Philadelphie et Gerasa, du royaume nabatéen à la province d'Arabie', *Géographie historique au Proche-Orient*. Forthcoming

1010. Gracey, M. H. 'The Roman army in Syria, Judaea and Arabia'. 2 vols. Diss., Oxford, 1981

1011. Graf, D. 'The Nabataeans and the Decapolis', in D 1008 A, 785–96

1012. Heichelheim, F.M., 'Roman Syria', in D 128 IV, 121–258

1013. Hütteroth, W.-D. and Abdulfattah, K. *Historical Geography of Palestine. Transjordan and Southern Syria in the Late 16th Century*. Erlangen, 1977

1014. Ingraham, M. L., Johnson, T. D., Rihani, B. and Shatla, I. 'Preliminary report on a reconnaissance survey of the Northwestern Province (with a note on a brief survey of the Northern Province)', *Atlal* 5 (1981) 59–84

1015. Isaac, B. 'Trade routes to Arabia and the Roman army', *Roman Frontier Studies, 1979* (1980) 889–901

1016. Isaac, B. 'The Decapolis in Syria. A neglected inscription', *ZPE* 44 (1981) 67–74

1017. Janssen, A. and Savignac, R. *Mission archéologique en Arabie*. 2 vols. Paris, 1909–14

1018. Jones, A. H. M. 'The urbanisation of Palestine', *JRS* 21 (1931) 78–85

1019. Jones, A. H. M. 'The urbanisation of the Ituraean principality', *JRS* 21 (1931) 265–75

1020. Jones, C. P. 'Three foreigners in Attica', *Phoenix* 32 (1978) 222–34

1021. Kennedy, D. L. 'Parthians in the Roman army', in Fitz, J. (ed.) *Limes, Akten des XI. Internationalen Limeskongresses*, 521–31. Budapest, 1977

1022. Kennedy, D. L. 'The auxilia and numeri raised in the Roman Province of Syria', Diss., Oxford, 1980

1023. Kennedy, D. L. 'C. Velius Rufus', *Britannia* 14 (1983) 183–96

1024–6 Vacant

1027. Kennedy, D. L. and Riley, D. *Rome's Desert Frontier from the Air*. London, 1990

1028. Kirwan, L. 'A Roman shipmaster's handbook', *GJ* 147 (1981) 80–5

1029. Kirwan, L. 'Where to search for the ancient port of Leuke Kome', *Studies in the History of Arabia*: II. *Pre-Islamic Arabia*, 55–61. Riyadh, 1984

1030. Kraeling, C. H. 'The Jewish community at Antioch', *JBL* 51 (1932) 130–60

1031. Kraeling, C. H. *Gerasa. City of the Decapolis*. New Haven, CT, 1938

1032. Lassus, J. *Les portiques d'Antioche. Antioch on the Orontes*, 5. Princeton, 1972

1033. Lauffray, J. 'Beyrouth I', *ANRW* II, 8 (1978) 135–63

1034. Lewis, N. N. *Nomads and Settlers in Syria and Jordan, 1800–1980*. Cambridge, 1987

1035. Liebeschuetz, J. W. H. G. 'Epigraphic evidence on the Christianization of Syria', *Limes. Akten des XI internationalen Limeskongresses*, 485–508. Budapest, 1977

1036. Lindner, M. *Petra und das Königreich der Nabatäer*. 2 vols. Munich, 1974

1037. Matthews, J. F. 'The tax law of Palmyra. Evidence for economic history in a city of the Roman East', *JRS* 74 (1984) 157–80

1038. McKenzie, J. *The Architecture of Petra*. British Institute at Amman for Archaeology and History. Oxford, 1990

1039. Millar, F. G. B. 'Empire, community and culture in the Roman Near East: Greeks, Syrians, Jews and Arabs', *JJS* 38 (1987) 143–64

1040. Millar, F. G. B. 'The Roman *coloniae* of the Near East: a study of cultural relations', in Solin, H. and Kajava, M. (eds.) *Roman Eastern Policy and Other Studies in Roman History*, 7–58. Helsinki, 1990

1041. Miller, D. S. 'Bostra in Arabia: Nabataean and Roman city of the Near East', in Marchese, R. T. (ed.) *Aspects of Graeco-Roman Urbanism* (BAR International Series 188), 110–37. Oxford, 1983

1042. Miller, J. I. *The Spice Trade of the Roman Empire, 29 B.C. to A.D. 641*. Oxford, 1969

1043. Mouterde, R. 'Tyr, les agoranomes de l'an 60', *MUSJ* 26 (1944–6) 60–3

1044. Muhly, J. D. 'Copper and tin', *Trans. Conn. Acad. Arts and Sciences* 43 (1973) 155–535

1045. Negev, A. *The Nabataean Potter's Workshop at Oboda*. Bonn, 1974

1046. Negev, A. 'The Nabataeans and the Provincia Arabia', *ANRW* II, 8 (1978) 520–686

1047. Negev, A. *Nabataean Archaeology Today*. New York, 1986

1048. Parr, P. J., Harding, G. L. and Dayton, J. E. 'Preliminary survey in NW Arabia, 1968', *BIAL* 8/9 (1968/9) 193–242; 10 (1971) 23–60

1049. Peters, F. E. 'The Nabataeans in the Hauran', *JAOS* 97 (1977) 263–77

1050. Peters, F. E. 'City planning in Greco-Roman Syria; some new considerations', *MDAI(D)* 1 (1983) 269–77

1051. Ploug, G. *Hama: Fouilles et recherches de la Fondation Carlsberg 1931–1938:* III, 1. *The Graeco-Roman Town*. Copenhagen, 1985

1052. Ragette, F. *Baalbek*. London, 1980

1053. Raikes, R. 'The climate and hydrological background to the post-glacial introduction of farming in the Middle East and its subsequent spread, with examples from Jordan', in Hadidi, A. (ed.) *Studies in the History and Archaeology of Jordan* II, 267–72. Amman, 1985

1054. Rey-Coquais, J.-P. 'Syrie romaine, de Pompée à Dioclétien', *JRS* 68 (1978) 44–73

1055. Richmond, I. A. 'Palmyra under the aegis of Rome', *JRS* 53 (1963) 43–54

1056. Sartre, M. *Trois études sur l'Arabie romaine et byzantine* (Coll. Latomus 178). Brussels, 1982

1057. Sartre, M. *Bostra. Des Origines à l'Islam*. Paris, 1985

1058. Schlumberger, D. 'Bornes frontières de la Palmyrène', *Syria* 20 (1939) 43–73

1059. Schmidt-Colinet, A. 'Nabatäische Felsarchitektur: Bemerkungen zum gegenwärtigen Forschungsstand', *BJ* 180 (1980) 189–230

1060. Seyrig, H. 'Questions héliopolitaines', *Syria* 31 (1954) 80–98 (= *Antiquités syriennes* 5 (1958) 99–177)

1061. Sourdel, D. *Les Cultes du Hauran*. Paris, 1952

1062. Starcky, J. 'Pétra et la Nabatène', *Suppl. au Dict. du Bible* VII, 886–1017. Paris, 1966

1063. Strong, E. 'Sulle tracce della Lupa Romana', in Paribeni, R. (ed.) *Scritti in onore di B. Nogara*, 475–501. Rome, 1937

1064. Sullivan, R. D. 'Papyri reflecting the eastern dynastic network', *ANRW* II, 8 (1978) 908–39

1065. Sullivan, R. D. 'The dynasty of Emesa', *ANRW* II, 8 (1977) 198–219

1065A. Teixidor, J. *The Pantheon of Palmyra*. Leiden, 1979

1066. Teixidor, J. *Un port romain du désert. Palmyre*. (*Semitica* 34). Paris, 1984

1067. Tirpan, A. 'Roman masonry techniques at the capital of the Commagenian kingdom', in E 1008B, 519–36

1068. Vita-Finzi, C. *The Mediterranean Valleys. Geological Changes in Historical Times*. Cambridge, 1969

1069. Wenning, R. *Die Nabatäer – Denkmäler und Geschichte.* Göttingen, 1987
1070. Winnett, F. V. and Reed, W. L. *Ancient Records from North Arabia.* Toronto, 1970
1071. Wright, G. R. H. 'The Khazneh at Petra: a review', *AnnDeptAntiqJordan*, 6–7 (1962) 24–54

14. JUDAEA

1072. Alon, G. *Jews, Judaism and the Classical World.* Jerusalem, 1977
1073. Applebaum, S. 'The Zealots: the case for revaluation', *JRS* 61 (1971) 156–70
1074. Applebaum, S. 'Judaea as a Roman province; the countryside as a political and economic factor', *ANRW* II, 8 (1977) 355–86
1075. Applebaum, S. *Judaea in Hellenistic and Roman Times.* Leiden, 1989
1076. Archer, L. J. 'The role of Jewish women in the religion, ritual and cult of Graeco-Roman Palestine', in Cameron, A. and Kuhrt, A. (eds.) *Images of Women in Antiquity*, 273–87. London, 1983
1077. Archer, L. J. *Her Price is Beyond Rubies. The Jewish Woman in Graeco-Roman Palestine.* Sheffield, 1990
1078. Avi-Yonah, M. and Stern, E. (eds.) *Encyclopedia of Archaeological Excavations in the Holy Land.* 4 vols. Jerusalem–London, 1975–8
1079. Avi-Yonah, M., Baras, Z. and Peli, A. (eds.) *The World History of the Jewish People:* VII. *The Herodian Period.* Jerusalem, 1975
1080. Avigad, N. *Discovering Jerusalem.* Oxford, 1984
1081. Avigad, N. *et al.* 'The expedition to the Judaean desert, 1961', *IEJ* 12 (1962) 167–262
1082. Baer, Y. 'Jerusalem in the times of the Great Revolt', *Zion* 36 (1971) 127–90; 37 (1972) 120. In Hebrew
1083. Bammel, E. 'Die Rechtsstellung des Herodes', *ZDPalV* 84 (1968) 73–9
1084. Bammel, E. and Moule, C. F. D. (eds.) *Jesus and the Politics of his Day.* Cambridge, 1984
1085. Bar-Adon, P. 'Another settlement of the Judaean desert sect at 'En el-Ghuweir on the shores of the Dead Sea', *BASOR* 277 (1977) 1–25
1086. Bar-Kochva, B. 'Seron and Cestius at Beith Horon', *PEQ* 108 (1976) 13–21
1087. Barnes, T. D. 'Trajan and the Jews', *JJS* 40 (1989) 145–62
1088. Barnett, P. W. 'Under Tiberius all was quiet', *NTS* 21 (1975) 564–71
1089. Barnett, P. W. 'The Jewish sign prophets A.D. 40–70 – their intentions and origin', *NTS* 27 (1981) 679–97
1090. Baron, S. W. *A Social and Religious History of the Jews:* I. *Ancient Times: to the Beginning of the Christian Era.* New York–London, 1952
1091. Baumann, U. *Rom und die Juden: die römisch-jüdischen Beziehungen von Pompeius bis zum Tode Herodes, 63 v. Chr.–4 v. Chr.* Frankfurt, 1983
1092. Ben-Shalom, I. 'The Shammai school and its place in the political and social history of Eretz Israel in the first century A.D.'. Ph.D. thesis, Tel Aviv, 1980. In Hebrew

1093. Benoît, P., Milik, J. T. and De Vaux, R. *Les Grottes de Murabba'at. Discoveries in the Judaean Desert*, ii. Oxford, 1960

1094. Bilde, P. 'The causes of the Jewish War according to Josephus', *JSJ* 10 (1979) 179–202

1095. Blenkinsopp, J. 'Prophecy and priesthood in Josephus', *JJS* 25 (1974) 239–62

1096. Brandon, S. G. F. *The Fall of Jerusalem and the Christian Church*. 2nd edn. London, 1957

1097. Brandon, S. G. F. *Jesus and the Zealots: a Study of the Political Factors in Primitive Christianity*. Manchester, 1967

1098. Brooten, B. J. *Women Leaders of the Ancient Synagogue: Inscriptional Evidence and Background Issues*. Chico, 1982

1099. Brunt, P. A. 'Josephus on social conflicts in Roman Judaea', *Klio* 59 (1977) 149–53

1100. Busink, T. A. *Der Tempel von Jerusalem von Salomo bis Herodes*. 2 vols. Leiden, 1980

1101. Cohen, S. J. D. 'The origins of the matrilineal principle in rabbinic law', *AJS Review* 10 (1985) 19–53

1102. Cohen, S. J. D. 'Was Timothy Jewish (Acts 16:13)? Patristic exegesis, rabbinic law and matrilineal descent', *JBL* 105 (1986) 251–68

1103. Cohen, S. J. D. 'Crossing the boundary and becoming a Jew', *HTR* 82 (1989) 13–33

1104. Collins, J. J. *Between Athens and Jerusalem. Jewish Identity in the Hellenistic Diaspora*. New York, 1983

1105. Corbishley, T. 'Quirinius and the census: a re-study of the evidence', *Klio* 29 (1936) 81–93

1106. Crook, J. A. 'Titus and Berenice', *AJPh* 72 (1951) 162–75

1107. Davies, P. S. 'The meaning of Philo's text about the gilded shields', *JTS* n.s. 37 (1986) 109–14

1108. De Lange, N. R. M. 'Jewish attitudes to the Roman Empire', in Garnsey, P. D. A. and Whittaker, C. R. (eds.) *Imperialism in the Ancient World*, 225–81. Cambridge, 1978

1109. Dimant, D., Mor, M. and Rappaport, U. (eds.) *Bibliography of Works on Jewish History in the Persian, Hellenistic and Roman Periods. Publications of the Years 1981–1985*. Jerusalem, 1987

1110. Dupont-Sommer, A. 'Exorcismes et guérisons dans les récits de Qoumran', *Vetus Testamentum Supplement* 7 (1960) 246–61

1111. Epstein, L. M. *Marriage Laws in the Bible and the Talmud*. Cambridge, MA, 1942

1112. Farmer, W. R. *Maccabees, Zealots and Josephus, an Inquiry into Jewish Nationalism in the Greco-Roman Period*. New York, 1956

1113. Farmer, W. R. 'Judas, Simon and Athronges', *NTS* 4 (1958) 147–55

1114. Fasola, U. M. 'Le due catacombe ebraiche di Villa Torlonia', *RAC* 52 (1976) 19–20

1115. Freyne, S. *Galilee from Alexander the Great to Hadrian, 323 b.c.e. to 135 c.e.* Notre Dame, 1980

1116. Fuks, G. 'Again on the episode of the gilded Roman shields at Jerusalem', *HTR* 75 (1982) 503–7

1117. Gabba, E. 'The finances of King Herod', in Kasher, A., Rappaport, U. and Fuks, G. (eds.) *Greece and Rome in Eretz Israel: Collected Essays*, 160–8. Jerusalem, 1990

1118. Gager, J. G. *The Origins of Anti-Semitism: Attitudes towards Judaism in Pagan and Christian Antiquity*. New York, 1985

1119. Ghiretti, M. 'Lo "status" della Giudea dall'età Augustea all'età Claudia', *Latomus* 44 (1985) 751–66

1120. Gichon, M. 'Idumea and the Herodian limes', *IEJ* 17 (1967) 27–45

1121. Gichon, M. 'Cestius Gallus' campaign in Judaea', *PEQ* 113 (1981) 39–62

1122. Golb, N. 'The problem of origin and identification of the Dead Sea Scrolls', *PAAJR* 124 (1980) 1–24

1123. Goodblatt, D. 'The place of the Pharisees in first century Judaism: the state of the debate', *JSJ* 20 (1989) 12–30

1124. Goodenough, E. R. *The Jurisprudence of the Jewish Courts in Egypt: Legal Administration by the Jews under the Early Roman Empire, as Described by Philo Judaeus*. New Haven, 1929

1125. Goodenough, E. R. *By Light, Light: the Mystic Gospel of Hellenistic Judaism*. New Haven, 1935

1126. Goodenough, E. R. *Jewish Symbols in the Greco-Roman Period*. 13 vols. New York, 1953–68

1127. Goodman, M. D. 'The first Jewish revolt: social conflict and the problem of debt', *JJS* 33 (1982) 417–27

1128. Goodman, M. D. *State and Society in Roman Galilee, A.D. 132–212*. Totowa, 1983

1129. Goodman, M. D. 'A bad joke in Josephus', *JJS* 36 (1985) 195–9

1130. Goodman, M. D. *The Ruling Class of Judaea. The Origins of the Jewish Revolt against Rome, A.D. 66–70*. Cambridge, 1987

1131. Gracey, M. H. 'The armies of the Judaean client-kings', in E 1008 A, 311–23

1132. Hachlili, R. and Killebrew, A. 'Jewish funerary customs during the Second Temple period, in the light of the excavations at the Jericho necropolis', *PEQ* 115 (1983) 109–39

1133. Hamel, G. *Poverty and Charity in Roman Palestine, First Three Centuries C.E.* Berkeley, 1990

1134. Hengel, M. 'Proseuche und Synagoge: Jüdische Gemeinde, Gotteshaus und Gottesdienst in der Diaspora und in Palästina', in Jeremias, G., Kuhn, H. W. and Stegemann, H. (eds.) *Tradition und Glaube. Das frühe Christentum in seiner Umwelt*, 157–84. Göttingen, 1971

1135. Hengel, M. *Judaism and Hellenism: Studies in their Encounter in Palestine during the Early Hellenistic Period*. 2 vols. London, 1974

1136. Hengel, M. *Die Zeloten: Untersuchungen zur jüdischen Freiheitsbewegung in der Zeit von Herodes I. bis 70 n. Chr.* 2nd edn. Leiden, 1976; transl. as E 1138

1137. Hengel, M. *The 'Hellenization' of Judaea in the First Century after Christ*. London, 1989

1138. Hengel, M. *The Zealots: Investigations into the Jewish Freedom Movement in the Period from Herod I until 70 A.D.* Edinburgh, 1989

1139. Hoehner, W. W. *Herod Antipas.* Cambridge, 1972

1140. Holum, K. G. *et al. King Herod's Dream. Caesarea on the Sea.* New York, 1989

1141. Horsley, R. A. 'Josephus and the bandits', *JSJ* 10 (1979) 37–63

1142. Horsley, R. A. 'The sicarii: ancient Jewish "terrorists"', *JR* 52 (1979) 435–58

1143. Horsley, R. A. 'Ancient Jewish banditry and the revolt against Rome, A.D. 66–70', *CBQ* 43 (1981) 409–32

1144. Horsley, R. A. 'Menahem in Jerusalem: a brief messianic episode among the Sicarii – not "Zealot Messianism"', *Novum Testamentum* 27 (1985) 334–48

1145. Horsley, R. A. 'High Priests and the politics of Roman Palestine. A contextual analysis of the evidence in Josephus', *JSJ* 17 (1986) 23–55

1146. Horsley, R. A. 'Popular prophetic movements at the time of Jesus', *JSNT* 26 (1986) 3–27

1147. Horsley, R. A. 'The Zealots: their origin, relationship and importance in the Jewish revolt', *Novum Testamentum* 28 (1986) 159–92

1148. Horsley, R. A. and Hanson, J. S. *Bandits, Prophets and Messiahs. Popular Movements in the Time of Jesus.* Minneapolis, 1985

1149. Isaac, B. 'Bandits in Judaea and Arabia', *HSCP* 88 (1984) 171–203

1150. Isaac, B. 'Judaea after A.D. 70', *JJS* 35 (1984) 44–50

1151. Jeremias, J. *Jerusalem in the Time of Jesus.* London, 1969

1152. Jones, A. H. M. *The Herods of Judaea.* Oxford, 1938

1153. Kasher, A. (ed.) *The Great Jewish Revolt: Factors and Circumstances Leading to its Outbreak.* Jerusalem, 1983. In Hebrew

1154. Kasher, A. *The Jews in Hellenistic and Roman Egypt. The Struggle for Equal Rights* (Texte und Studien zum antiken Judentum 7). Tübingen, 1985

1155. Kasher, A. *Jews, Idumaeans and Ancient Arabs: Relations of the Jews in Eretz-Israel with the Nations of the Frontier and the Desert.* Tübingen, 1988

1156. Kasher, A. *Jews and Hellenistic Cities in Eretz-Israel:Relations of the Jews in Eretz-Israel with the Hellenistic Cities during the Second Temple Period (332 B.C.E.–70 C.E.).* Tübingen, 1990

1157. Kingdon, H. P. 'The origins of the Zealots', *NTS* 19 (1972–3) 74–81

1158. Klausner, J. *The Messianic Idea in Israel.* London, 1956

1159. Kloner, A. 'Underground hiding complexes from the Bar Kochba war in the Judaean Shephelah', *BiAr* 46.4 (December 1983) 210–21

1160. Kloner, A. and Tepper, Y. *The Hiding Complexes in the Judaean Shephelah.* Tel Aviv, 1987. In Hebrew

1161. Kochavi, M. (ed.) *Judaea, Samaria and the Golan: Archaeological Survey 1967–1968.* Jerusalem, 1972. In Hebrew

1162. Kokkinos, N. 'A fresh look at the gentilicium of Felix, procurator of Judaea', *Latomus* 49 (1990) 126–41

1163. Kraabel, A. T. 'The Roman diaspora: six questionable assumptions', *JJS* 33 (1982) 445–64

1164. Kraft, R. A. 'The multiform Jewish heritage of early Christianity', in

Neusner, J. (ed.) *Christianity, Judaism and Other Greco-Roman Cults*, III, 174–99. Leiden, 1975

1165. Kreissig, H. 'Die landwirtschaftliche Situation in Palästina vor dem Judäischen Krieg', *Acta Antiqua* 17 (1969) 223–54

1166. Kreissig, H. *Die sozialen Zusammenhänge des judäischen Krieges: Klassen und Klassenkampf im Palästina des I. Jahrhunderts v.u.Z.* Berlin, 1970

1167. Levine, L. I. *Caesarea under Roman Rule* (Studies in Judaism in Late Antiquity 3). Leiden, 1975

1168. Levine, L. I. (ed.) *Ancient Synagogues Revealed.* Jerusalem, 1981

1169. Levine, L. I. (ed.) *The Synagogue in Late Antiquity.* Philadelphia, 1987

1170. Lieberman, S. *Hellenism in Jewish Palestine* (Texts and studies of the Jew. Theol. Sem. of America 18). New York, 1950

1171. Lieberman, S. *Greek in Jewish Palestine.* 2nd edn. New York, 1965

1172. Linder, A. *The Jews in Roman Imperial Legislation.* Detroit–Jerusalem, 1987

1173. McEleney, N. J. 'Orthodoxy in Judaism of the first Christian century', *JSJ* 9 (1978) 83–8

1174. McKnight, S. *A Light among the Gentiles: Jewish Missionary Activity in the Second Temple Period.* Minneapolis, 1991

1175. Mantel, H. P. *Studies in the History of the Sanhedrin.* Cambridge, MA, 1961

1176. Michel, O. 'Studien zu Josephus: Simon bar Giora', *NTS* 14 (1968) 402–8

1177. Millar, F. G. B. 'The background to the Maccabean revolution', *JJS* 29 (1978) 1–21

1178. Momigliano, A. D. *Ricerche sull'organizzazione della Giudea sotto il dominio romano, 63 aC–70 dC.* Bologna, 1934

1179. Moore, G. F. *Judaism in the First Centuries of the Christian Era.* 3 vols. Cambridge, MA, 1927–30

1180. Netzer, E. 'Miqvaot (ritual baths) of the Second Temple period at Jericho', *Qadmoniot* 11 (1978) 54–9. In Hebrew

1181. Netzer, E. *Greater Herodium* (Qedem 13). Jerusalem, 1981

1182. Neusner, J. *A History of the Jews in Babylonia* I. 2nd edn. Leiden, 1969

1183. Neusner, J. *A Life of Yohanan ben Zakkai A.D. 1–80.* 2nd edn. (Studia Postbiblica 6). Leiden, 1970

1184. Neusner, J. *The Rabbinic Traditions about the Pharisees before 70.* 3 parts. Leiden, 1971

1185. Neusner, J., Green, W. S. and Frerichs, E. S. (eds.) *Judaisms and their Messiahs at the Turn of the Christian Era.* Cambridge, 1987

1186. Nickelsburg, G. W. E. *Resurrection, Immortality and Eternal Life in Intertestamental Judaism.* Cambridge, MA, 1972

1187. Oppenheimer, A. *The 'Am Ha-aretz: a Study in the Social History of the Jewish People in the Hellenistic-Roman Period.* Leiden, 1977

1188. Oppenheimer, A., Rappaport, U. and Stern, M. (eds.) *Jerusalem in the Second Temple Period.* Abraham Schalit memorial volume. Jerusalem, 1980

1189. Piattelli, D. 'Ricerche intorno alle relazioni politiche tra Rome e l'Ἔθνος τῶν Ἰουδαίων dal 161 a.C. al 4 a.C.', *BIDR* 74 (1971) 219–340

1190. Pucci, M. *La Rivolta Ebraica al tempo di Traiano*. Pisa, 1981

1191. Rahmani, L. Y. 'Ancient Jerusalem's funerary customs and the tombs: part three', *BiAr* 45.1 (Winter 1982) 43–53

1192. Rahmani, L. Y. 'Some remarks on R. Hachlili's and A. Killebrew's "Jewish funerary customs"', *PEQ* 118 (1986) 96–100

1193. Rajak, T. 'Justus of Tiberias', *CQ* n.s. 23 (1973) 345–68

1194. Rajak, T. 'Was there a Roman charter for the Jews?' *JRS* 74 (1984) 107–23

1195. Rappaport, U. 'Jewish–pagan relations and the revolt against Rome in 66–70 c.e.', *The Jerusalem Cathedra* 1 (1981) 81–95

1196. Rappaport, U. 'John of Gischala: from Galilee to Jerusalem', *JJS* 33 (1982) 479–93

1197. Rappaport, U. and Mor, M. *Bibliography of Works on Jewish History in the Hellenistic and Roman Period, 1976–1980*. Jerusalem, 1982

1198. Reynolds, J. and Tannenbaum, R. *Jews and God-Fearers at Aphrodisias* (*PCPhS*, Supp. vol. 12). Cambridge, 1987

1199. Rhoads, D. M. *Israel in Revolution: 6–74 c.e.: a Political History Based on the Writings of Josephus*. Philadelphia, 1976

1200. Rivkin, E. *A Hidden Revolution. The Pharisees' Search for the Kingdom Within*. Nashville, 1978

1201. Roth, C. 'The historical implications of the Jewish coinage of the First Revolt', *IEJ* 12 (1962) 33–46

1202. Roth, C. 'The constitution of the Jewish republic of 66–70', *JJS* 9 (1964) 304–19

1203. Rowland, C. *The Open Heaven: a Study of Apocalyptic in Judaism and Early Christianity*. London, 1982

1204. Safrai, S. and Stern, M. (eds.) *The Jewish People in the First Century* (Compendia Rerum Iudaicarum ad Novum Testamentum, Sect. 1) 2 vols. Assen, 1974–6

1205. Sanders, E. P. *Jewish Law from Jesus to the Mishnah: Five Studies*. London–Philadelphia, 1990

1206. Schalit, A. *König Herodes: der Mann und sein Werk*. Berlin, 1969

1207. Schürer, E. *The History of the Jewish People in the Age of Jesus Christ*. Revised by G. Vermes, F. Millar, M. Black and M. Goodman. 3 vols. Edinburgh, 1973–87 (I: 1973; II: 1979; III. 1 (pp. 1–704): 1986; III. 2 (pp. 705–1015): 1987)

1208. Schwartz, D. R. 'Ishmael ben Phiabi and the chronology of Provincia Judaea', *Tarbiz* 52 (1983) 177–200. In Hebrew

1209. Schwartz, D. R. *Agrippa I, the Last King of Judaea*. Jerusalem, 1987. In Hebrew

1210. Shanks, H. *Judaism in Stone: the Archaeology of Ancient Synagogues*. New York, 1979

1211. Smallwood, E. M. 'High priests and politics in Roman Palestine', *JTS* n.s. 13 (1962) 14–34

1212. Smallwood, E. M. *The Jews under Roman Rule from Pompey to Diocletian: a Study in Political Relations*. Leiden, 1976

1213. Smith, M. 'Zealots and sicarii: their origins and relations', *HTR* 64 (1971) 1–19

1214. Sparks, H. F. D. (ed.) *The Apocryphal Old Testament*. Oxford, 1984

1215. Speidel, M. P. 'The Roman army in Judaea under the procurators', *AncSoc* 13/14 (1982/3) 233–40

1215A. Stemberger, G. *Einleitung in Talmud und Midrasch*. 8th edn. Munich, 1992

1216. Stern, M. 'Herod's policy and Jewish society at the end of the Second Temple period', *Tarbiz* 35 (1966) 235–53. In Hebrew

1217. Stern, M. 'The status of Provincia Judaea and its governors in the Roman Empire under the Julio-Claudian dynasty', *Eretz Israel* 10 (1971) 274–82. In Hebrew

1218. Stern, M. 'Aspects of Jewish society: the priesthood and other classes', in E 1204, II, 561–630

1219. Stern, M. 'Sicarii and Zealots', in Avi-Yonah, M. and Baras, Z. (eds.) *Society and Religion in the Second Temple Period. The World History of the Jewish People* 1.8, 263–301. London, 1977

1220. Stern, M. 'The expulsion of Jews from Rome in antiquity', *Zion* 44 (1980) 1–27. In Hebrew

1221. Stern, M. 'Social and political realignments in Herodian Judaea', *The Jerusalem Cathedra* 2 (1982) 40–62

1222. Stern, M. 'The suicide of Eleazar ben Jair and his men at Masada, and the "Fourth Philosophy"', *Zion* 47 (1982) 367–98. In Hebrew

1223. Stone, M. E. *Scriptures, Sects and Visions: a Profile of Judaism from Ezra to the Jewish Revolt*. Oxford, 1982

1224. Sullivan, R. D. 'The dynasty of Judaea in the first century', *ANRW* II, 8 (1978) 262–94

1225. Tcherikover, V. A. *Hellenistic Civilization and the Jews*. Philadelphia–Jerusalem, 1961

1226. Tcherikover, V. A. 'Was Jerusalem a Polis?', *IEJ* 14 (1964) 61–78

1227. Theissen, G. *The First Followers of Jesus: a Sociological Analysis of the Earliest Christians*. London, 1978

1228. Urbach, E. E. *The Sages: their Concepts and Beliefs*. 2 vols. Jerusalem, 1975

1229. Vaux, R. de *Archaeology and the Dead Sea Scrolls*. London, 1973

1230. Vermes, G. *The Dead Sea Scrolls: Qumran in Perspective*. London, 1977

1231. Vermes, G. *The Dead Sea Scrolls in English*. 3rd edn. Harmondsworth, 1987

1232. Vidal-Naquet, P. 'Du bon usage de la trahison', in Josephus, *De Bello Judaico*, trans. by P. Savinel. Paris, 1977

1233. Wilkinson, J. 'Ancient Jerusalem: its water supply and population', *PEQ* 106 (1974) 33–51

1234. Winter, P. *On the Trial of Jesus*. Revised by T. A. Burkill and G. Vermes. 2nd edn. Berlin–New York, 1974

1235. Yadin, Y. *Masada: Herod's Fortress and the Zealots' Last Stand*. London, 1966

1236. Yadin, Y. (ed.) *Jerusalem Revealed: Archaeology in the Holy City 1968–1974*. Jerusalem, 1975

1237. Zeitlin, S. *The Rise and Fall of the Judaean State. A Political, Social and*

Religious History of the Second Commonwealth. 3 vols. Philadelphia, 1962–78

F. SOCIETY, RELIGION AND CULTURE

I. SOCIETY AND ITS INSTITUTIONS

1. Alföldy, G. *The Social History of Rome*. London, revd edn. 1988
2. Astolfi, R. *La lex Iulia et Papia*. 2nd edn. Padua, 1986
3. Atkinson, K. M. 'The purpose of the manumission laws of Augustus', *IJ* n.s. 1 (1966) 356–74
4. Badian, E. 'A phantom marriage-law', *Philologus* 129 (1985) 82–98
5. Barrow, R. H. *Slavery in the Roman Empire*. London, 1928
6. Bauman, R. A. 'Some remarks on the structure and survival of the *quaestio de adulteriis*', *Antichthon* 2 (1968) 68–93
7. Besnier, R. 'Properce (Elégies II, vii et viiA) et le premier échec de la législation démographique d'Auguste', *RHD* 57 (1979) 191–203
8. Bollinger, T. *Theatralis licentia: die Publikumsdemonstrationen an den öffentlichen Spielen im Rom*. Winterthur, 1969
9. Bouvrie, S. des 'Augustus' legislation on morals. Which morals and what aims?' *SymbOsl* 59 (1984) 93–113
10. Bradley, K. R. *Slaves and Masters in the Roman Empire. A Study in Social Control* (Coll. Latomus 185). Brussels, 1984; repr. New York, 1987
11. Brunt, P. A. '"Amicitia" in the late Roman Republic', *PCPhS* n.s. 11 (1965) 1–20 (= Seager, R. (ed.) *The Crisis of the Roman Republic*. Cambridge, 1969 = revd in A 11, 351–81)
12. Brunt, P. A. *Social Conflicts in the Roman Republic*. London, 1971
13. Brunt, P. A. 'Two great Roman landowners', *Latomus* 34 (1975) 619–35
14. Brunt, P. A. '*Nobilitas* and *novitas*', *JRS* 72 (1982) 1–17
15. Brunt, P. A. 'Clientela', in A 11, 382–442
16. Cameron, A. *Circus Factions: Blues and Greens at Rome and Byzantium*. Oxford, 1976
17. Clavel-Lévêque, M. *L'Empire en Jeux*. Paris, 1984
18. Cohen, B. 'La notion d'"ordo" dans la Rome antique', *BAGB* 1975, 259–82
19. Corte, F. della. 'Le leges Iuliae e l'elegia romana', *ANRW* II, 30. 1 (1982) 539–58
20. Crawford, M. H. 'Greek intellectuals and the Roman aristocracy in the first century B.C.', in Garnsey, P. D. A. and Whittaker, C. R. (eds.) *Imperialism in the Ancient World*, 193–207. Cambridge, 1978
21. Crook, J. A. *Law and Life of Rome*. London, 1967
22. D'Arms, J. H. *Commerce and Social Standing in Ancient Rome*. Cambridge, MA, 1981
23. D'Arms, J. H. 'Control, companionship and clientela: some social functions of the Roman communal meal', *CV* 28 (1984) 327–48

24. D'Arms, J. H. 'The Roman *convivium* and equality', in Murray, O. (ed.) *Sympotica: a Symposion on the Symposion*. Oxford, 1990

25. De Ruyt, C. *Macellum, marché alimentaire des romains*. Louvain, 1985

26. Dixon, S. 'Infirmitas sexus: womanly weakness in Roman law', *TvR* 52 (1984) 343–71

26A. Dixon, S. *The Roman Mother*. London, 1988

27. Domenicis, M. de. 'La *Latinitas Iuniana* e la legge Elia Senzia', *Mélanges d'Archéologie et d'Histoire offerts à André Piganiol* III, 1419–31. Paris, 1966

28. Duff, A. M. *Freedmen in the Early Roman Empire*. Cambridge, 1928; 2nd edn. 1958

29. Duncan-Jones, R.-P. 'Demographic change and economic progress under the Roman Empire', in *Tecnologia, economia e società nel mondo romano* (= Proceedings of the Como conference of 1979), 67–80. Como, 1980

30. Flambard, M. '*Collegia compitalicia*: phénomène associatif, cadres territoriaux et cadres civiques dans le monde romain à l'époque républicaine', *Ktema* 6 (1981) 143–66

31. Frézouls, E. 'Le theatrum lapideum et son contexte politique', in *Théâtre et spectacles dans l'Antiquité, Actes du colloque de Strasbourg (1981)*, 193–214. Leiden, 1983

32. Galinsky, G. K. 'Augustus' legislation on morals and marriage', *Philologus* 125 (1981) 126–44

33. Gardner, J. F. *Women in Roman Law and Society*. London, 1986

34. Gardner, J. F. 'Proofs of status in the Roman world', *BICS* 33 (1986) 1–14

35. Garnsey, P. *Social Status and Legal Privilege in the Roman Empire*. Oxford, 1970

36. Garnsey, P. 'Urban property investment', in A 27, 123–36

37. Garnsey, P. (ed.) *Non-Slave Labour in the Greco-Roman World*. Cambridge, 1980

38. Garnsey, P. 'Descendants of freedmen in local politics: some criteria', in Levick, B. M. (ed.) *The Ancient Historian and his Materials. Essays in Honour of C. E. Stevens on his Seventieth Birthday*, 167–80. Farnborough, 1975

39. Hands, A. R. *Charities and Social Aid in Greece and Rome*. London, 1968

40. Harris, W. V. 'On the applicability of the concept of class in Roman history', in A 111, 598–610

41. Hopkins, M. K. 'The age of Roman girls at marriage', *Population Studies* 18 (1965) 309–27

42. Ladage, D. 'Soziale Aspekte des Kaiserkultes', in Eck, W. *et al.* (eds.) *Studien zur antiken Sozialgeschichte* (= *Festschrift F. Vittinghoff*), 377–88. Köln, 1980

43. MacMullen, R. 'Market days in the Roman Empire', *Phoenix* 24 (1970) 333–41

44. MacMullen, R. *Roman Social Relations 50 B.C. to A.D. 284*. New Haven, 1974

45. Montagna Pasquinucci, M. (ed.) *Terme romane e vita quotidiana*. Modena, 1987

46. Mrozek, S. 'Crustulum et mulsum dans les villes italiennes', *Athenaeum* 50 (1972) 294–300

47. *Nécropoles à incinération du Haut-Empire, Actes de la table ronde de Lyon 1986.* Lyons, 1987

48. Nicolet, C. 'Plèbe et tribus. Les statues de Lucius Antonius et le testament d'Auguste', *MEFRA* 97 (1985) 799–839

49. Purcell, N. 'The *apparitores*: a study in social mobility', *PBSR* 51 (1983) 125–73

50. Purcell, N. 'Livia and the womanhood of Rome', *PCPhS* 212 (1986) 78–105

51. Purcell, N. 'Town in country and country in town', in MacDougall, E. B. (ed.) *The Ancient Roman Villa Garden*, 188–203. Washington, DC, 1987

52. Purcell, N. 'Tomb and suburb', in Hesberg, H. von and Zanker, P. (eds.) *Römische Gräberstrassen*, 25–41. Munich, 1987

53. Raditsa, L. F. 'Augustus' legislation concerning marriage, procreation, love-affairs and adultery', *ANRW* II, 13 (1980) 278–339

54. Rawson, B. *The Family in Ancient Rome. New Perspectives.* London, 1986

55. Rawson, E. D. 'Theatrical life in Rome and Italy', *PBSR* 53 (1985) 97–113

56. Rawson, E. D. 'Discrimina ordinum: the Lex Iulia Theatralis', *PBSR* 55 (1987) 83–114

57. Robert, L. *Les gladiateurs dans l'orient grec.* Limoges, 1940; repr. Amsterdam, 1971

58. Royden, H. *The Magistrates of the Roman Professional Collegia in Italy from the First to the Third Centuries A.D.* Pisa, 1988

59. Saller, R. *Personal Patronage under the Early Empire.* Cambridge, 1982

60. Saller, R. 'Men's age at marriage and its consequences in the Roman family', *CPh* 82 (1987) 21–34

61. Scheid, J. *Les frères Arvales. Recrutement et origine sociale sous les empereurs julio-claudiens.* Paris, 1975

62. Scheid, J. 'Les prêtres officiels sous les empereurs julio-claudiens', *ANRW* II, 16.1 (1978) 610–54

63. Schumacher, L. 'Die vier höhen römischen Priesterkollegien unter den Flaviern, den Antoninen und den Severern (69–235 n. Chr.), *ANRW* II, 16.1 (1978) 655–819

64. Setälä, P. *Private Domini in Roman Brick Stamps of the Empire. A Historical and Prosopographical Study of Landowners in the District of Rome* (Annales Academiae Scientiarum Fennicae. Dissertationes humanarum litterarum 10). Helsinki, 1977

65. Shaw, B. D. 'The age of Roman girls at marriage: some reconsiderations', *JRS* 77 (1987) 30–46

66. Spruit, J. E. *De lex Iulia et Papia Poppaea. Beschouwingen over de bevolkingspolitiek van Augustus* (Univ. of Leiden Inaugural Lecture). Deventer, 1969

67. Toynbee, J. *Death and Burial in the Roman World.* London, 1971

68. Treggiari, S. *Roman Freedmen During the Late Republic.* Oxford, 1969

69. Treggiari, S. 'Lower-class women in the Roman economy', *Florilegium* 1 (1979) 65–86

70. Treggiari, S. *Roman Marriage. Iusti Coniuges from the Time of Cicero to the Time of Ulpian.* Oxford, 1991

71. Veyne, P. *Le pain et le cirque. Sociologie historique d'un pluralisme politique.* Paris, 1976 (Translated and abridged as *Bread and Circuses: Historical Sociology and Political Pluralism.* London, 1990)

72. Wacke, A. 'Manumissio matrimonii causa: le mariage d'affranchies d'après les lois d'Auguste, *RD* 67 (1989) 413–28

73. Wallace-Hadrill, A. 'Family and inheritance in the Augustan marriage laws', *PCPhS* 207, n.s. 27 (1981) 58–80

74. Wallace-Hadrill, A. 'Propaganda and dissent? Augustan moral legislation and the love-poets', in A 54A, 180–4

75. Wallace-Hadrill, A., ed. *Patronage in Ancient Society.* London, 1989

76. Wallace-Hadrill, A. 'Patronage in Roman society', in F 75, 63–87

77. Weaver, P. R. C. '*Cognomina ingenua,* a note', *CQ* 14 (1964) 311–15

78. White, P. '*Amicitia* and the profession of poetry in early imperial Rome', *JRS* 68 (1978) 74–92

79. White, P. 'Positions for poets in early imperial Rome', in A 39A, 50–66

80. Whitehead, D. 'The measure of a millionaire: what Crassus really said', *LCM* 11 (1986) 71–4

81. Wiseman, T. P. 'Conspicui postes templaque digna deo: the public image of aristocratic and imperial houses in the late Republic and early Empire', in A 96, 393–413

82. Witherington, B. *Women in the Earliest Churches.* Cambridge, 1988

2. RELIGION

83. Alföldi, A. *Die zwei Lorbeerbäume des Augustus.* Bonn, 1973

84. Altheim, F. *A History of Roman Religion* (transl. by H. Mattingly). London, 1938

85. Barnes, T. D. 'Legislation against the Christians', *JRS* 58 (1968) 32–50

86. Barton, I. M. 'Capitoline temples in Italy and the Provinces (especially Africa)', *ANRW* II, 12.1 (1982) 259–342

87. Bauer, W. *Orthodoxy and Heresy in Earliest Christianity.* Philadelphia, 1971

88. Bayet, J. *Les origines de l'Hercule romain (BEFAR* 132). Rome, 1926

89. Bayet, J. 'Les sacerdoces romains et la pré-divinisation impériale', *Bull. Acad. royale de Belgique, cl. des lettres* 41 (1955) 453–527 (= *Croyances et rites dans la Rome antique,* 275–336. Paris, 1971)

90. Beard, M. Review of McBain 1982 (F 177), *Gnomon* 55 (1983) 510–13

91. Beard, M. 'Writing and ritual: a study of diversity and expansion in the Arval Acta', *PBSR* 53 (1985) 114–62

92. Beard, M. 'A complex of times: no more sheep on Romulus' birthday', *PCPhS* n.s. 33 (1987) 1–15

92A. Beard, M. and North, J. *Pagan Priests.* London, 1990

93. Beaujeu, J. *La religion romaine à l'apogée de l'empire* 1. Paris, 1955

94. Becher, I. 'Tiberüberschwemmungen. Die Interpretation von Prodigien in augusteischer Zeit', *Klio* 67 (1985) 471–9

95. Bianchi, A. 'Disegno storico del culto Capitolino nell'Italia romana e nelle provincie dell'Impero', *Atti Accademia Nazionale dei Lincei* (Memorie, Sc. morali, 8th ser., II. 7). Rome, 1949

96. Bickerman, E. J. 'Filius Maiae (Horace, Odes, 1.2.43)', *PP* 16 (1961) 5–19 (= *Religions and Politics in the Hellenistic and Roman Periods*, 453–69. Como, 1985)

97. Bömer, F. 'Kybele in Rom', *MDAI(R)* 71 (1964) 130–51

98. Bömer, F. 'Wie ist Augustus mit Vesta verwandt?', *Gymn.* 94 (1987) 525–8

99. Bornkamm, G. *Jesus of Nazareth*. London, 1960

100. Bousset, W. *Kyrios Christos*. London, 1970

101. Bowker, J. *Jesus and the Pharisees*. Cambridge, 1973

102. Boyancé, P. 'Properce aux fêtes de quartier', *REA* 52 (1950) 64–70 (= *Etudes sur la religion romaine* (Collection de l'école française de Rome 11), 291–7. Rome, 1972)

103. Boyancé, P. 'Cybèle aux Mégalésies, *Latomus* 13 (1954) 337–42 (= *Etudes sur la religion romaine* (Collection de l'école française de Rome 11), 195–200. Rome, 1972)

104. Brelich, A. 'Offerte e interdizioni alimentari nel culto della Magna Mater a Roma', *SMSR* 36 (1965) 27–42

105. Bremmer, J. and Horsfall, N. *Roman Myth and Mythography* (*BICS*, Suppl. 52). London, 1987

106. Brind'amour, P. 'L'origine des jeux séculaires', *ANRW* II, 16 (1978) 1353–71

107. Brunt, P. A. 'Stoicism and the principate', *PBSR* 43 (1975) 7–35

108. Burnett, A. Review of Rainer, A. *Das Bild des Augustus auf den frühen Reichsprägungen, Gnomon* 55 (1983) 563–5

109. Cannadine, D. and Price, S. (eds.) *Rituals of Royalty: Power and Ceremonial in Traditional Societies*. Cambridge, 1987

110. Catalano, P. 'Aspetti spaziali del sistema giuridico-religioso romano. Mundus, templum, urbs, ager, Latium, Italia', *ANRW* II, 16.1 (1978) 440–553

111. Cerfaux, L. and Tondriau, J. *Un concurrent du Christianisme. Le culte des souverains dans la civilisation gréco-romaine*. Tournai, 1957

112. Chadwick, H. *The Early Church*. Harmondsworth, 1968

113. Charlesworth, J. H. *Jesus Within Judaism*. New York, 1988

114. Charlesworth, M. P. 'The virtues of the Roman emperor. Propaganda and the creation of belief', *PBA* (1937) 105–33

115. Charlesworth, M. P. 'The refusal of divine honours, an Augustan formula', *PBSR* 2 (1939) 1–10

116. Coarelli, F. 'Il Pantheon, l'apoteosi di Augusto e l'apoteosi di Romolo', *Città e architettura nella Roma imperiale* (*Analecta Romana*, Suppl. 10), 41–6. Odense, 1983

117. Collins, J. J. *The Apocalyptic Imagination: an Introduction to the Jewish Matrix of Christianity*. New York, 1987

118. Daniélou, J. *The Theology of Jewish Christianity*. London, 1964

119. Davies, W. D. *Paul and Rabbinic Judaism*. 4th edn. London, 1980

120. Diels, H. *Sibyllinische Blätter*. Berlin, 1890

121. Dilke, O. A. W. 'Religious mystique in the training of Agrimensores', *Hommages à Henri Le Bonniec* (Coll. Latomus 201) 158–62. Brussels, 1988

122. Dumézil, G. 'Augur', *REL* 35 (1957) 126–51 (= F 123, 79–102)

123. Dumézil, G. *Idées romaines*. Paris, 1969

124. Dumézil, G. *Archaic Roman Religion*. 2 vols. Chicago, 1970

125. Dumézil, G. *Fêtes romaines d'été et d'automne*. Paris, 1975

126. Dunn, J. D. G. *Christology in the Making*. 2nd edn. London, 1990

127. Duthoy, R. 'Recherches sur la répartition géographique et chronologique des termes *sevir augustalis, augustalis* et *sevir* dans l'Empire romain', *EpStud* 11 (Köln, 1976) 143–214

128. Duthoy, R. 'Les Augustales', *ANRW* II, 16. 2 (1978) 1254–309

129. Erkell, H. *Augustus, Felicitas, Fortuna. Lateinische Wortstudien.* Gothenburg, 1952

130. Erkell, H. 'Ludi saeculares und ludi Latini saeculares', *Eranos* 67 (1969) 166–74

131. Esler, P. F. *Community and Gospel in Luke-Acts: the Social and Political Motivations of Lucan Theology*. Cambridge, 1987

132. Evans, C. F. 'The New Testament in the making', *The Cambridge History of the Bible*, 1, 232–84. Cambridge, 1970

133. Fauth, W. 'Römische Religion im Spiegel der "Fasti" des Ovid', *ANRW* II, 16.1 (1978) 104–86

134. Fayer, C. *Il culto della dea Roma*. Pescara, 1976

135. Fishwick, D. '*Genius* and *Numen*', *HTR* 62 (1969) 356–67

136. Fishwick, D. 'The development of provincial ruler worship in the western Roman empire', *ANRW* II, 16.2 (1978) 1201–53

137. Fishwick, D. *The Imperial Cult in the Latin West* 1 (*EPRO* 108). Leiden, 1987

138. Fredriksen, P. *From Jesus to Christ: the Origins of the New Testament Images of Jesus*. New Haven, 1988

139. Frend, W. H. C. *Martyrdom and Persecution in the Early Church*. Oxford, 1965

140. Frend, W. H. C. *The Rise of Christianity*. London, 1984

141. Gagé, J. 'Romulus-Augustus', *MEFRA* 47 (1930) 138–81

142. Gagé, J. 'Les sacerdoces d'Auguste et ses réformes religieuses', *MEFRA* 48 (1931) 75–108

143. Gagé, J. 'Recherches sur les jeux séculaires II. Ce que nous apprennent les nouveaux fragments épigraphiques', *REL* 11 (1933) 172–202 (= *Recherches sur les Jeux Séculaires*, 45–75. Paris, 1934)

143A. Gagé, J. 'Recherches sur les jeux séculaires III. Jeux séculaires et jubilés de la fondation de Rome', *REL* 11 (1933) 400–35 (= *Recherches sur les Jeux Séculaires*, 77–111. Paris, 1934)

144. Gagé, J. 'Actiaca', *MEFRA* 53 (1936) 37–100

145. Gagé, J. 'Le "Templum Urbis" et les origines de l'idée de "Renovatio"', *Mélanges F. Cumont* 1, 151–87. Brussels, 1936

146. Gagé, J. *Apollon romain. Essai sur le culte d'Apollon et le développement du 'ritus Graecus' à Rome des origines à Auguste*. Paris, 1955

147. Gager, J. G. *Kingdom and Community: the Social World of Early Christianity*. Englewood Cliffs, 1975

148. Gordon, R. L. 'The veil of power: emperors, sacrificers, and benefactors', in F 92A, 201–31

149. Grant, F. C. *Hellenistic Religions*. New York, 1953
150. Grant, F. C. *Ancient Roman Religion*. New York, 1957
151. Grant, M. *Roman Myths*. Harmondsworth, 1973
152. Grant, R. M. *Gods and the One God*. Philadelphia, 1986
153. Guarducci, M. 'Enea e Vesta', *MDAI(R)*. 78 (1971) 73–118 (= *Scritti scelti sulla religione greca a romana e sul cristianesimo*, 198–243. Leiden, 1983)
154. Habicht, C. 'Die augusteische Zeit und das erste Jahrhundert nach Christi Geburt', *Le culte des souverains dans l'empire romain* (Entretiens Hardt 19) 39–99. Vandoeuvres, 1973
155. Harvey, A. E. *Jesus and the Constraints of History*. London, 1982
156. Hock, R. F. *The Social Context of Paul's Ministry: Tentmaking and Apostleship*. Philadelphia, 1980
157. Holladay, A. J. and Goodman, M. D. 'Religious scruples in ancient warfare', *CQ* n.s. 36 (1986) 151–71
158. Jal, P. 'Les dieux et les guerres civiles dans la Rome de la fin de la République', *REL* 40 (1962) 170–200
159. Judge, E. A. *The Social Pattern of Christian Groups in the First Century*. London, 1960
160. Kee, H. C. *Medicine, Miracle and Magic in New Testament Times*. Cambridge, 1986
161. Knoche, U. 'Die augusteische Ausprägung der Dea Roma', *Gymn.* 59 (1952) 324–49 (= *Vom Selbstverständnis der Römer, Gesammelte Aufsätze* (*Gymn.* Beiheft 2 (Heidelberg, 1962) no. 5), 145–73)
162. Koch, C. *Der römische Juppiter*. Frankfurt, 1937)
163. Koch, C. 'Der altrömische Staatskult im Spiegel augusteischer und spätrepublikanischer Apologetik', in *Convivium. Festschrift Konrat Ziegler*, 85–120. Stuttgart, 1954 (= *Religio. Studien zu Kult und Glauben der Römer*, 176–204. Nuremberg, 1960)
164. Koeppel, G. M. 'Die historischen Reliefs der römischen Kaiserzeit II', *BJ* 184 (1984) 1–65
165. La Rocca, E. *La riva a mezzaluna. Culti, agoni, monumenti funerari presso il Tevere nel Campo Marzio occidentale*. Rome, 1984
166. Ladage, D. 'Städtischer Priester- und Kultämter im lateinischen Westen des Imperium Romanum zur Kaiserzeit'. Diss., Cologne, 1971
167. Lambrechts, P. 'Cybèle, divinité étrangère ou nationale?', *Société royale belge d'anthropologie et de préhistoire* 62 (1951) 44–60
168. Lambrechts, P. 'Les fêtes "phrygiennes" de Cybèle et d'Attis', *Bulletin de l'Institut historique belge de Rome* 27 (1952) 141–70
169. Latte, K. 'Über eine Eigentümlichkeit der italischen Gottesvorstellung', *Archiv für Religionswissenschaft* 24 (1926/7) 244–58 (= *Kleine Schriften*, 76–90. Munich, 1968)
170. Latte, K. *Römische Religionsgeschichte*. Munich, 1960
171. Le Gall, J. 'Les Romains et l'orientation solaire', *MEFRA* 87 (1975) 287–320
172. Levi, M. A. 'Il ciclo religioso augusteo e il superamento delle guerre civili', *CISA* 10 (1984) 181–93
173. Lewis, M. W. H. *The Official Priests of Rome under the Julio-Claudians* (Papers and Monographs of the Amer. Acad. Rome 16). Rome, 1955

174. Liebeschuetz, J. H. W. G. *Continuity and Change in Roman Religion.* Oxford, 1979

175. Liebeschuetz, J. H. W. G. 'The religious position of Livy's History', *JRS* 57 (1967) 45–55

176. Lüdemann, G. *Opposition to Paul in Jewish Christianity.* Minneapolis, 1989

177. McBain, B. *Prodigy and Expiation: a Study in Religion and Politics in Republican Rome* (Coll. Latomus 177). Brussels, 1982

178. MacDonald, M. Y. *The Pauline Churches: a Socio-Historical Study of Institutionalization in the Pauline and Deutero-Pauline Writings.* Cambridge, 1988

179. MacMullen R. *Paganism in the Roman Empire.* New Haven–London, 1981

180. Magdelain, A. *Recherches sur l''Imperium', la loi curiate et les auspices d'investiture.* Paris, 1968

181. Magdelain, A. 'L'inauguration de l'*urbs* et l'*imperium*', *MEFRA* 89 (1977) 11–29

182. Malherbe, A. J. *Social Aspects of Early Christianity.* 2nd edn. Philadelphia, 1983

183. Meeks, W. A. *The First Urban Christians. The Social World of the Apostle Paul.* New Haven, 1983

184. Meeks, W. A. *The Moral World of the First Christians.* Philadelphia, 1986

185. Meeks, W. A. and Wilkens, R. L. *Jews and Christians in Antioch in the First Four Centuries of the Common Era.* Missoula, MT, 1978

186. Mellor, R. ΘΕΑ ΡΩΜΗ: *the Worship of the Goddess Roma in the Greek World* (Hypomnemata 42). Göttingen, 1975

187. Merkelbach, R. 'Aeneas in Cumae', *MH* 18 (1961) 83–99

188. Meslin, M. *L'homme romain, des origines au Iᵉʳ siècle de notre ère. Essai d'anthropologie.* Paris, 1978

189. Momigliano, A. D. Review of Sherwin-White, A. N. *The Roman Citizenship* (Oxford, 1939), *JRS* 31 (1941) 158–65

190. Niebling, G. 'Laribus Augustis magistri primi. Der Beginn des Compitalkultes der Lares und des Genius Augusti', *Hist.* 5 (1956) 303–31

191. Nilsson, M. P. 'Saeculares ludi', *RE* I A (1920) 1696–720

192. Nock, A. D. 'Religious developments from the close of the Republic to the reign of Nero', *CAH* x¹, 465–511. Cambridge, 1934

193. Nock, A. D. 'The Roman army and the Roman religious year', *HTR* 45 (1952) 186–252 (= *Essays on Religion and the Ancient World*, 736–90. 2 vols. Oxford, 1972)

194. North, J. 'Conservatism and change in Roman religion', *PBSR* 44 (1976) 1–12

195. North, J. 'Religion and politics, from Republic to Principate', *JRS* 76 (1986) 251–8

196. O'Connor, D. W. *Peter in Rome. The Literary, Liturgical and Archaeological Evidence.* New York–London, 1969

197. Pettazzoni, R. 'La religione', in C 12A, 217–49

198. Pötscher, W. '"Numen" und "Numen Augusti"', *ANRW* II, 16.1 (1978) 355–92

199. Price, S. R. F. *Rituals and Power: the Roman Imperial Cult in Asia Minor*. Cambridge, 1984

200. Price, S. R. F. 'From noble funerals to divine cult: the consecration of Roman emperors', in F 109, 56–105

201. Price, S. R. F. 'The City of Rome', in Beard, M., North, J. and Price, S. (eds.) *Religions of Rome* 1. Cambridge, 1996

202. Raubitschek, A. E. 'Octavia's deification at Athens', *TAPA* 77 (1946) 146–50

203. Rawson, E. D. 'Scipio, Laelius, and the ancestral religion', *JRS* 63 (1973) 161–74

204. Richard, J.-C. 'Les funérailles de Trajan et le triomphe sur les Parthes', *REL* 44 (1966) 351–62

205. Ristow, G. 'Götter und Kulte in den Rheinlanden', in *Römer am Rhein*, 57–69. Cologne, 1967

206. Roberts, C. H. *Manuscript, Society and Belief in Early Christian Egypt*. London, 1979

207. Rohde, G. *Die Kultsatzungen der römischen Pontifices*. RVV 25 (Berlin, 1936)

208. Rowland, C. *Christian Origins: from Messianic Movement to Christian Religion*. London, 1985

209. Ryberg, I. S. *Rites of the State Religion in Roman Art (MAAR* 22). Rome, 1955

210. Sabbatucci, D. 'Mito e demitizzazione nell'antica Roma', *SMSR* 41 (= *Religione e civiltà* 1 (1970–2) 539–89)

211. Sanders, E. P. *Paul and Palestinian Judaism: a Comparison of Patterns of Religion*. London, 1977

212. Sanders, E. P. *Jesus and Judaism*. London, 1985

213. Sanders, E. P. *et al.* (eds.) *Jewish and Christian Self-Definition*. 3 vols. Philadelphia, 1980–2

214. Santero, J. M. 'The "Cultores Augusti" and the first worship of the Roman emperor', *Athenaeum* 61 (1983) 111–25

215. Saulnier, C. 'Le rôle des prêtres fétiaux et l'application du "ius fetiale" à Rome', *RHDFE* 58 (1980) 171–90

216. Saulnier, C. 'Laurens Lavinas. Quelques remarques à propos d'un sacerdoce équestre à Rome', *Latomus* 43 (1984) 517–33

217. Scheid, J. *Religion et piété à Rome*. Paris, 1985

218. Scheid, J. 'Les sanctuaires de confins dans la Rome antique', in A 96, 583–95

219. Schilling, R. 'Ovide interprète de la religion romaine', *REL* 46 (1969) 222–35. (= *Rites, cultes, dieux de Rome*, 11–22. Paris, 1979)

220. Schippman, K. *Die iranischen Feuerheiligtümer*. Berlin, 1971

221. Scholz, U. W. *Studien zum altitalischen und altrömischen Marskult und Marsmythos*. Heidelberg, 1970

222. Scott, K. 'The identification of Augustus with Romulus-Quirinus', *TAPA* 56 (1925) 82–105

223. Scullard, H. H. *Festivals and Ceremonies of the Roman Republic*. London, 1981

224. Segal, A. F. *Rebecca's Children: Judaism and Christianity in the Roman World.*
Cambridge, MA–London, 1986
225. Syme, R. 'The *pomerium* in the Historia Augusta', *Bonner Historia Augusta
Congress 1975–6* (1978) 217ff (= *Historia Augusta Papers*, 131–45. Oxford,
1983)
226. Tamassia, A. M. 'Iscrizioni del Compitum Acili', *BCAR* 78 (1961–2)
158–63
227. Teixidor, J. *The Pagan God. Popular Religion in the Greco-Roman Near East.*
Princeton, 1977
228. Theissen, G. *The First Followers of Jesus: a Sociological Analysis of the
Earliest Christians.* London, 1978
229. Theissen, G. *The Social Setting of Pauline Christianity.* Philadelphia, 1982
230. Van Doren, M. 'L'évolution des mystères phrygiens à Rome', *AC* 22
(1953) 79–88
231. Vermes, G. *Jesus the Jew.* London, 1976
232. Versnel, H. S. 'Die neue Inschrift von Satricum in historischer Sicht',
Gymn. 89 (1982) 193–235
233. Warde Fowler, W. *The Religious Experience of the Roman People.* London,
1911
234. Watson, F. *Paul, Judaism and the Gentiles.* Cambridge, 1986
235. Weinstock, S. *Diuus Iulius.* Oxford, 1971
236. Whatmough, J. 'The calendar in ancient Italy outside Rome', *HSCP* 42
(1931) 157–79
237. Wiedemann, T. 'The *Fetiales*: a reconsideration', *CQ* 36 (1986) 478–90
238. Wilhelm, J. 'Das römische Sakralwesen unter Augustus als Pontifex
Maximus'. Diss., Strasburg, 1915
239. Winter, J. G. 'The myth of Hercules at Rome', in Sanders, H. A. (ed.)
Roman History and Mythology, 171–273. London, 1910
240. Wiseman, T. P. 'Cybele, Virgil and Augustus', in B 204, 117–28.
Cambridge, 1984
241. Wissowa, G. *Religion und Kultus der Römer.* 2nd edn. Munich, 1912; repr.
1971
242. Wissowa, G. 'Die römischen Staatspriestertümer altlateinischer
Gemeindekulte', *Hermes* 50 (1915) 1–33
243. Zanker, P. 'Der Larenaltar im Belvedere des Vatikans', *MDAI(R)* 76
(1969) 205–18

3. ART AND ARCHITECTURE

244. Albert, R. *Das Bild des Augustus auf den frühen Reichsprägungen. Studien zur
Vergöttlichung des ersten Prinzeps* (Diss., Mannheim, 1980). Speyer, 1981
245. Albertson, F. C. 'An Augustan temple represented on a historical relief
dating to the time of Claudius', *AJA* 91 (1987) 441–50
246. Alföldi, A. *Der Vater des Vaterlandes im römischen Denken.* (Contains his
papers 'Die Geburt der kaiserlichen Bildsymbolik' from *MH* 7 (1950) 1–
13; 8 (1951) 190–215; 9 (1952) 204–43; 10 (1953) 103–24; 11 (1954) 133–
69.) Darmstadt, 1971

247. Alföldi, A. *Die monarchische Repräsentation im römischen Kaiserreiche*. 3rd edn. (Contains his papers 'Die Ausgestaltung des monarchischen Zeremoniells am römischen Kaiserhofe', *MDAI(R)* 49 (1934) 3–118 and 'Insignien und Tracht der römischen Kaiser', *MDAI(R)* 50 (1935) 3–158.) Darmstadt, 1970

248. Alzinger, W. *Augusteische Architektur in Ephesos*. Vienna, 1974

249. Amelung, W. and Lippold, G. *Die Skulpturen des Vaticanischen Museums*. 4 vols. Berlin, 1903–56

250. Anderson, M. L. 'The portrait medallions of the imperial villa at Boscotrecase', *AJA* 91 (1987) 127–35

251. Anderson, W. J., Spiers, R. P. and Ashby, T. *The Architecture of Ancient Rome*. London, 1927

252. Andreae, B. 'Der Zyklus der Odysseefresken im Vatikan', *MDAI(R)* 69 (1962) 106–17

253. Andreae, B. *Römische Kunst*. Freiburg, 1973

254. *Architecture et société de l'archaïsme à la fin de la république romaine* (Atti del Colloquio di Roma). Rome, 1983

255. Arias, P. E. 'Teatro e odeon', s.v. in *EAA* VII. Rome, 1966

256. *L'art décoratif à Rome à la fin de la République et au début du Principat*. Rome, 1981

257. Ashby, T. *The Aqueducts of Ancient Rome*. Oxford, 1935

258. Astolfi, F., Bauer, H., Guidobaldi, F. and Pronti, A. 'Horrea Agrippiana', *ArchClass* 30 (1978) 31–146

259. Aymard, A. and Auboyer, J. *Rome et son empire*. Paris, 1954

260. Bacchielli, L. 'Le porte romane ad ordini sovrapposti e antecedenti greci', *MDAI(R)* 91 (1984) 79ff

261. Barbet, A. *Recueil général des peintures murales de la Gaule*: 1 *Province de Narbonnaise* 1, *Glanum (Gallia* Suppl. 27). Paris, 1974

262. Barbet, A. *La peinture murale romaine. Les styles décoratifs pompéins*. Paris, 1985

263. Bartels, H. *Studien zum Frauenporträt der augusteischen Zeit. Fulvia, Octavia, Livia, Julia*. Munich, 1963

264. Bastet, F. L. 'Domus transitoria. I', *BABesch* 46 (1971) 144–72; II, *BABesch* 47 (1972) 61–87

265. Bastet, F. L. and Vos, M. de. *Proposta per una classificazione del terzo stile pompeiano*. The Hague, 1979

266. *Bauplanung und Bautheorie der Antike* (Deutsches Archäol. Inst., Diskussionen zur archäologischen Bauforschung 4). Berlin, 1984

267. Becatti, G. 'Le varie correnti artistiche dei periodi sillano e cesariano e la formazione dell'arte romana', in *L'età classica*, 291–385. Florence, 1965

268. Becatti, G. *L'arte romana*. Milan, 1962

269. Bejor, G. 'L'edificio teatrale nell'urbanizzazione augustea', *Athenaeum* 57 (1979) 126–38

270. Bernoulli, J. J. *Römische Ikonographie* I–III. Stuttgart, 1882–94; repr. Hildesheim, 1969

271. Beyen, H. G. *Die pompeianische Wanddekoration vom zweiten bis zum vierten Stil* I (1938); II. 1 (1960). Haag

272. Beyen, H. G. 'Pompeiani, Stili', s.v. in *EAA* vi. Rome, 1965
273. Bianchi Bandinelli, R. *Storicità dell'arte classica*. Florence, 1943; repr. Bari, 1973
274. Bianchi Bandinelli, R. 'Romana Arte', s.v. in *EAA* vi. Rome, 1965
275. Bianchi Bandinelli, R. *Rome, le centre du pouvoir*. Paris, 1969 (= *Roma. L'arte romana nel centro del potere*. Milan, 1969; = *Rome, the Centre of Power: Roman Art to A.D. 200*. London, 1970)
276. Bianchi Bandinelli, R. 'Noterella in margine ai problemi della pittura antica', in F 273, 245ff
277. Bianchi Bandinelli, R. 'Tradizione ellenistica e gusto romano nella pittura pompeiana', in F 273, 273ff
278. Bianchi Bandinelli, R. *Dall'Ellenismo al Medioevo*. Rome, 1978
279. Bianchi Bandinelli, R. 'Sulla formazione del ritratto romano', in *Archeologia e cultura*, 164ff. Rome, 1979
280. Bianchi Bandinelli, R. *La pittura antica*. Rome, 1980
281. Bianchi Bandinelli, R. and Torelli, M. *L'arte dell'antichità classica, Etruria–Roma*. Turin, 1976
282. Bieber, M. *The History of the Greek and Roman Theater*. Princeton, 1961
283. Bieber, M. *Ancient Copies. Contributions to the History of Greek and Roman Art*. New York, 1977
284. Blake, M. E. 'The pavements of the Roman Republic and the early Empire', *MAAR* viii (1930) 5ff
285. Blake, M. E. *Ancient Roman Construction in Italy from Tiberius through the Flavians*. Washington, 1959
286, Blanck, H. *Wiederverwendung alter Statuen als Ehrendenkmäler bei Griechen und Römern*. Rome, 1969
287. Blanckenhagen, H. von, and Alexander, C. *The Paintings from Boscotrecase*. Heidelberg, 1962
288. Bloch, H. *I bolli laterizi e la storia edilizia romana*. Rome, 1947
289. Boatwright, M. T. *Hadrian and the City of Rome*. Princeton, 1987
290. Boethius, A. *The Golden House of Nero: Some Aspects of Roman Architecture*. Ann Arbor, 1960
291. Boethius, A. and Ward-Perkins, J. B. *Etruscan and Roman Architecture*. Harmondsworth, 1970
292. Bonanno, A. *Portraits and Other Heads on Historical Reliefs up to the Age of Septimius Severus* (BAR Supplementary Series 6). Oxford, 1976
293. Bonnefond, M. 'Transferts de fonctions et mutation idéologique: le Capitole et le Forum d'Auguste', in A 96, 251–78
294. Borbein, A. H. 'Die Ara Pacis Augustae. Geschichtliche Wirklichkeit und Programm', *JDAI* 90 (1975) 242–66
295. Borchhardt, J. 'Ein Kenotaph für Gaius Caesar', *JDAI* 89 (1974) 217–41
296. Borda, M. *La pittura romana*. Milan, 1958
297. Bragantini, I. and Vos, M. de *Museo Nazionale Romano. Le pitture*: ii. 1. *Le decorazioni della villa romana della Farnesina*. Rome, 1982
298. Breckenridge, J. D. 'Roman Imperial portraiture from Augustus to Gallienus', *ANRW* II, 12. 2 (1981) 477–92
299. Brendel, O. *Prolegomena to the Study of Roman Art*. New Haven–London, 1979

300. Brilliant, R. *Gesture and Rank in Roman Art. The Use of Gesture to Denote Status in Roman Sculpture.* New Haven, 1963

301. Brommer, P. 'Zur Datierung des Augustus von Primaporta', in F 356A, 78–80

302. Brown, F. E. *Roman Architecture.* New York, 1961

303. Brunn, H. and Arndt, P. *Griechische und römische Porträts,* edited by F. Bruckmann and G. Lippold. Munich, 1891–1942

304. Buchner, E. 'Solarium Augusti und Ara Pacis', *MDAI(R)* 83 (1976) 319–65

305. Buchner, E. 'Horologium Solarium Augusti', *MDAI(R)* 87 (1980) 355–73

306. Buchner, E. *Die Sonnenuhr des Augustus.* Mainz, 1982 (Contains E 304 (pp. 7–55) and E 305 (pp. 57–77))

307. Buchner, E. 'Horologium Augusti: Neue Ausgrabungen in Rom', *Gymn.* 90 (1983) 494–508

308. Cagiano de Azevedo, M. 'I *capitolia* dell'impero romano', *MPAA* ser. 3 (1940)

309. Cagnat, R. and Chapot, V. *Manuel d'archéologie romaine.* 2 vols. Paris, 1916–20

310. Calci, C. and Messineo, G. *La villa di Livia a Prima Porta.* Rome, 1984

311. Camodeca, G. 'Una nuova fonte sulla topografia del foro di Augusto', *Athenaeum* 74 (1986) 505–8

312. Carandini, A. 'Domus e insulae sulla pendice settentrionale del Palatino', *BCAR* 91.2 (1986) 263–78

313. Carandini, A. and Ricci, A. (eds.) *Settefinestre. Una villa schiavistica nell'Etruria romana.* Modena, 1985

314. Carettoni, G. 'Nuove pitture del Palatino', *BdA* 40 (1955) 210ff

315. Carettoni, G. 'Roma. Le costruzioni di Augusto e il tempio di Apollo sul Palatino' (*ArchLaz* 1), *Quaderni del centro di studi per l'archeologia etrusco-italica* 1 (1978) 72–4

316. Carettoni, G. *Das Haus des Augustus auf dem Palatin.* Mainz, 1983

317. Carettoni, G. 'La decorazione pittorica della casa di Augusto sul Palatino', *MDAI(R)* 90 (1983) 373–419

318. Castagnoli, F. (ed.) *Studi di urbanistica antica.* Rome, 1966

319. Castagnoli, F. 'Sul tempio "italico"', *MDAI(R)* 73–4 (1966–7) 10–14

320. Castagnoli, F. *Orthogonal Town-Planning in Antiquity.* Cambridge, MA, 1971

321. Cavalieri Manasse, G. *La decorazione architettonica romana d'Aquileia, Trieste, Pola:* 1. *L'età repubblicana, augustea e giulio-claudia.* Padua, 1978

322. Cerulli Irelli, G. 'Le pitture della Casa dell'Atrio a mosaico', *MonPitt* III, vol. Ercolano I. Rome, 1971

323. Chamoux, F. 'Un portrait de Thasos, Lucius Caesar', *MMAI* 44 (1950) 83–96

324. Chamoux, F. 'Nouveaux portraits des fils d'Agrippa', *RA* 37 (1951) 218–20

325. Chamoux, F. 'Un nouveau portrait de Gaius César découvert à Mayence', *BSNAF* (1963) 205–6

326. Charbonneaux, J. *L'art au siècle d'Auguste.* Paris, 1948

327. Charbonneaux, J. 'Un portrait présumé de Marcellus', *MMAI* 51 (1960) 53–72

328. Cima, M. and La Rocca, E. *Le tranquille dimore degli dei; la residenza imperiale degli horti Lamiani.* Venice, 1986

329. *La città di fondazione* (Atti del II Congresso internaz. di studi di urbanistica). Vicenza, 1978

330. *Città e architettura della Roma imperiale* (*ARID* Supplement 10). Odense, 1983

331. Clavel, M. and Lévêque, P. *Villes et structures urbaines dans l'Occident romain.* Paris, 1971

332. Coarelli, F. *Guida Archaeologica di Roma.* Milan, 1981

333. Coarelli, F. 'Il Panteon, l'apoteosi di Augusto e l'apoteosi di Romolo', in F 330, 41–6

334. Colini, A. M. 'Compitum Acili', *BCAR* 78 (1961–2) 47–57

335. Colledge, M. A. R. *The Art of Palmyra.* London, 1976

336. Corlaita Scagliarini, D. 'Spazio e decorazione nella pittura pompeiana', *Palladio* 23–5 (1974–6) 3ff

337. Crema, L. *Architettura romana.* Turin, 1959

338. Cristofani, M. 'Sul rinvenimento dell'Arringatore', *Prospettiva* 45 (1986–7) 56–7

339. Croisille, J. M. *Les natures mortes campaniennes.* Brussels, 1965

340. *Les cryptoportiques dans l'architecture romaine* (Collection école française de Rome 14) 1973

341. Curtius, L. 'Ikonographische Beiträge zum Porträt der römischen Republik und der julisch-claudischen Familie', *MDAI(R)* 47 (1932) 202–68; 48 (1933) 182–243; 49 (1934) 119–56; 50 (1935) 260–320; 54 (1939) 112–44; 55 (1940) 36–64; *MdI* 1 (1948) 53–94

342. Dacos, N. 'Fabullus et l'autre peintre de la Domus Aurea', *MEFRA* 80 (1968) 85ff

343. Danson, C. M. *Romano-Campanian Mythological Landscape Painting.* Yale, 1944

344. Darmon, J. P. 'Les mosaïques en Occident, I', *ANRW* II, 12. 2 (1981) 266–319

345. Daut, R. *Imago. Untersuchungen zum Bildbegriff der Römer.* Heidelberg, 1975

346. Degrassi, A. 'Virgilio e il foro di Augusto', *Epigraphica* 7 (1945) 88–103 (= *Scritti vari di antichità* 1, 283–97. Rome, 1962)

347. Degrassi, N. 'La dimora di Augusto sul Palatino e la base di Sorrento', *RPAA* 39 (1966–7) 77–116

348. Deman, E. B. van *The Building of the Roman Aqueducts.* Washington, 1934

349. Deppert-Lippitz, B. 'Römischer Goldschmuck. Stand der Forschung', *ANRW* II, 12. 3 (1985) 117–26

350. Dondin-Payre, M. 'Topographie et propagande gentilice: le *compitum Acilium* et l'origine des *Acilii Glabriones*', in A 96, 87–109

351. Drerup, H. *Zum Ausstattungsluxus in der römischen Architektur.* Münster, 1957

352. Drerup, H. 'Die römische Villa', in *Marburger Winckelmann-Programm*, 1–24. Marburg, 1959

353. Drerup, H. 'Architektur als Symbol', *Gymn.* 73 (1966) 181–96
354. Ducati, P. *L'arte in Roma dalle origini al secolo VIII.* Bologna, 1938
355. Duval, P.-M. and Frézouls, E. (eds.) *Thèmes de recherches sur les villes antiques d'Occident.* Paris, 1977
356. Eck, W., Fittschen, K. and Naumann, F. *Kaisersaal. Porträts aus den kapitolinischen Museen in Rom.* Rome, 1986
356A. *Eikones. Studien zum griechischen und römischen Bildnis* (Studien Hans Jucker) (*Antike Kunst* Beiheft 12). Berne, 1980
357. Eisner, M. *Zur Typologie der Grabbäuten im Suburbium Roms.* Mainz, 1986
358. Elia, O. *Pitture di Stabia.* Naples, 1957
359. Engemann, J. *Architekturdarstellungen des frühen Zweiten Stils. Illusionistische römische Wandmalerei der ersten Phase und ihre Vorbilder in der realen Architektur.* Heidelberg, 1967
360. Evans, H. B. 'Agrippa's water plan', *AJA* 86 (1982) 401–11
361. Fabbrini, L. 'Marco Vipsanio Agrippa. Concordanze e discordanze iconografiche. Nuovi contributi', in F 356A, 96–107
362. Felletti Maj, B. M. *La tradizione italica nell'arte romana.* Rome, 1977
363. Felletti Maj, B. M. and Moreno, P. C. 'Le pitture della casa delle Muse', *MonPitt* III, vol. Ostia III. Rome, 1967
364. Fittschen, K. *Katalog der antiken Skulpturen in Schloss Erbach.* Berlin, 1977
365. Fittschen, K. and Zanker, P. *Katalog der römischen Porträts in den Capitolinischen Museen und den anderen kommunalen Sammlungen der Stadt Rom:* I. *Kaiser- und Prinzenbildnisse.* Mainz 1985; III. *Kaiserin- und Prinzessinnenbildnisse.* Mainz, 1983
366. Flory, M. B. '"Sic exempla parantur": Livia's shrine to Concordia and the Porticus Liviae', *Hist.* 33 (1984) 309–30
367. Forni, G. 'Anfiteatro', s.v. in *EAA* I. Rome, 1958
368. Forni, G. 'Teatro', s.v. in *EAA* Suppl. Rome, 1970
369. Franciscis, A. de *La villa romana di Oplontis.* Recklinghausen, 1977
370. Fraschetti, A. 'La mort d'Agrippa et l'autel du Belvédère. Un certain type d'hommage', *MEFRA* 92 (1980) 957–76
371. Fraschetti, A. 'Morti dei "principi" ed "eroi" della famiglia di Augusto', *AION (Archeol)* 6 (1984) 151–89
372. Freyer-Schauenburg, B. 'Augustus capite uelatus. Zu einer unpublizierten Porträtbüste von Samos', in A 55A, 1–8
373. Frézouls, E. 'Aspects de l'histoire architecturale du théâtre romain', *ANRW* II, 12. 1 (1982) 343–441
374. Frova, A. *L'arte di Roma e del mondo romano.* Turin, 1961
375. Fuchs, M. *Untersuchungen zur Ausstattung römischer Theater.* Mainz, 1987
376. Fullerton, M. D. 'The Domus Augusti in imperial iconography of 13–12 B.C.', *AJA* 89 (1985) 473–83
377. Gabelmann, H. 'Römische Grabbauten in Italien und den Nordprovinzen', in *Festschr. F. Brommer*, 101–17. Mainz, 1977
378. Gabriel, M. M. *Livia's Garden Room at Prima Porta.* New York, 1955
379. Gagé, J. 'L'era del principato e le speculazioni astrologiche', in A 82A, 223–35

380. Gallina, A. *Le pitture con paesaggi dell'Odissea dall'Esquilino* (*Studi Misc.* 6 (1960–1)). Rome, 1964

381. Ganzert, J. 'Der Mars-Ultor-Tempel auf dem Augustusforum in Rom', *MDAI(R)* 92 (1985) 200–19

382. Garcia y Bellido, A. *Arte romano.* Madrid, 1957

383. Gasparri, C. 'Le pitture della caupona del pavone', *MonPitt* III, vol. Ostia IV. Rome, 1970

384. Gazzola, P. *I ponti romani* I–II. Florence, 1963

385. Gercke, W. B. 'Untersuchungen zum römischen Kinderporträt von den Anfängen bis in hadrianische Zeit'. Diss., Hamburg, 1968

386. Gerkan, A. von 'Griechische und Römische Architektur', *BJ* 152 (1952) 21–6

387. Giuliani, C. F. 'Note sull'architettura delle residenze imperiali dal I al III secolo d. Cr.', *ANRW* II, 12.1 (1982) 233–58

388. Giuliano, A. *Catalogo dei ritratti romani del Museo Profano Lateranense.* Vatican City, 1957

389. Gnoli, R. *Marmora romana.* Rome, 1971

390. Goethert, F. W. 'Studien zur Kopienforschung', *MDAI(R)* 54 (1939) 176ff

391. Golvin, J.-C. *L'amphithéâtre romain*, CNRS. Paris, 1988

392. Grieco, G. 'A propos de la statue d'Auguste de Prima Porta. Confirmation de la thèse de la création Tibérienne...', *Latomus* 38 (1979) 147–64

393. Grimal, P. *Les jardins romains.* Paris, 1969; repr. 1984

394. Grimm, G. 'Die Porträts der Triumvirn ... Überlegungen zur Entstehung und Abfolge der Bildnistypen des Kaisers Augustus', *MDAI(R)* 96 (1989) 347–64

395. Gros, P. 'Trois temples de la Fortune des I et II siecles de notre ère. Remarques sur l'origine des sanctuaires romains à abside', *MEFRA* 79 (1967) 503–66

396. Gros, P. 'Hermodoros et Vitruve', *MEFRA* 85 (1973) 137–61

397. Gros, P. *Aurea templa: recherches sur l'architecture religieuse de Rome à l'époque d'Auguste* (*BEFAR* 231). Paris, 1976

398. Gros, P. *Architecture et société à Rome et en Italie centro-méridionale aux deux derniers siècles de la république* (Coll. Latomus 156). Brussels, 1978

399. Gros, P. 'La fonction symbolique des édifices théâtraux dans le paysage urbain de la Rome augustéenne', in A 96, 319–46

399A. Gros, P. and Torelli, M. *Storia dell'urbanistica antica. Il mondo romano.* Rome–Bari, 1988

400. Gross, W. H. *Zur Augustusstatue von Primaporta.* Göttingen, 1959

401. Gross, W. H. *Iulia Augusta. Untersuchungen zur Grundlegung einer Livia-Ikonographie.* Göttingen, 1962

402. Gusman, P. *L'art décoratif de Rome.* 2 vols. Paris, 1912

403. Hafner, G. *Späthellenistische Bildnisplastik.* Berlin, 1954

404. Hammond, M. *The City in the Ancient World.* Cambridge, MA, 1972

405. Hanell, K. 'Das Opfer des Augustus an der Ara Pacis. Eine archäologische und historische Untersuchung', *ORom* 2 (Lund, 1960) 33–123

406. Hanfmann, G. M. A. *Römische Kunst.* Wiesbaden, 1964; transl. as E 407
407. Hanfmann, G. M. A. *Roman Art: a Modern Survey of the Art of Imperial Rome.* Greenwich–New York, 1964
408. Hänlein-Schäfer, H. *Veneratio Augusti. Eine Studie zu den Tempeln des ersten römischen Kaisers* (Archaeologica 39). Rome, 1985
409. Hannestad, H. *Roman Art and Imperial Policy.* Aarhus, 1986
410. Hanson, J. A. *Roman Theater-Temples.* Princeton, 1959
411. Harden, D. B. (ed.) *Glass of the Caesars.* Milan, 1987
412. Hassel, F. J. *Der Trajansbogen in Benevent. Ein Bauwerk des römischen Senates.* Mainz, 1966
413. Hausmann, U. 'Zur Typologie und Ideologie des Augustus-Porträts', *ANRW* II, 12.2 (1981) 513–98
414. Heintze, H. von *Die antiken Porträts in Schloss Fasanerie bei Fulda.* Mainz, 1968
415. Heintze, H. von *Römische Kunst.* Stuttgart, 1969
416. Heintze, H. von (ed.) *Römische Porträts.* Darmstadt, 1974
417. Helbig, W. *Führer durch die öffentlichen Sammlungen klassischer Altertümer in Rom* I–IV. 1963–72
418. Hesberg, H. von and Zanker, P. (eds.) *Römische Gräberstrassen.* Munich, 1987
419. Himmelmann, N. 'Das Hypogäum der Aurelier am Viale Manzoni', *AAWM* 7 (1975)
420. Holland, L. A. 'The shrine of the *Lares Compitales*', *TAPA* 68 (1937) 428–41
421. Holloway, R. R. 'The tomb of Augustus and the princes of Troy', *AJA* 70 (1966) 171–3
422. Hölscher, T. *Victoria Romana.* Mainz, 1967
423. Hölscher, T. 'Zu römischen historischen Denkmälern', *AA* (1979) 337–48
424. Hölscher, T. *Staatsdenkmal und Publikum. Xenia (Konstanzer alt-historische Vorträge und Forschungen)* 9. Konstanz, 1984
425. Hommel, P. *Studien zu den römischen Figurengiebeln der Kaiserzeit.* Berlin, 1954
426. Hönle, A. and Henze, A. *Römische Amphitheater und Stadien.* Zurich, 1981
427. Humphrey, J. *Roman Circuses: Arenas for Chariot-Racing.* London, 1986
428. Inan, J. and Rosenbaum, E. *Roman and Early Byzantine Portrait Sculpture in Asia Minor.* London, 1966
429. Ingholt, H. 'The Prima Porta statue of Augustus. The interpretation of the breastplate', *Archaeology* 22 (1969) 176–87, 304–18
430. Instinsky, H. U. *Die Siegel des Kaisers Augustus.* Baden-Baden, 1962
431. Johansen, F. S. 'Ritratti marmorei e bronzei di Marco Vipsanio Agrippa', *ARID* 6 (1971) 17–48
432. Jones, Stuart H. *A Catalogue of the Ancient Sculptures Preserved in the Municipal Collections of Rome:* I. *The Sculptures of the Museo Capitolino.* Oxford, 1926; II. *Palazzo dei Conservatori.* Oxford, 1926; repr. Rome, 1968
433. Jucker, H. *Vom Verhältnis der Römer zur bildenden Kunst der Griechen.* Frankfurt, 1950
434. Jucker, H. *Das Bildnis im Blätterkelch.* Olten, 1961

435. Jucker, H. 'Römische Herrscherbildnisse aus Ägypten', *ANRW* II, 12. 2 (1981) 667–97
436. Jucker, H. 'Iulisch-claudische Kaiser- und Prinzenporträts als "Palimpseste"', *JDAI* 96 (1981) 236–316
437. Jucker, H. and Willers, D. (eds.) *Gesichter: Griechische und römische Bildnisse aus Schweitzer Besitz.* Berne, 1982
438. Kähler, H. 'Triumph- und Ehrenbogen', s.v. in *RE* VIIA I. Stuttgart, 1939
439. Kähler, H. 'Die Ara Pacis und die augusteische Friedensidee', *JDAI* 69 (1954) 67–100
440. Kähler, H. 'Der Augustus von Primaporta', *Gymn.* 63 (1956) 345–50
441. Kähler, H. *Die Augustusstatue von Prima Porta.* Cologne, 1959
442. Kähler, H. *Der römische Tempel.* Berlin, 1970
443. *Kaiser Augustus und die verlorene Republik. Eine Ausstellung im Martin-Gropius-Bau. Berlin, 7 Juni–14 August 1988.* (No editor stated.) Mainz, 1988
444. Kaschnitz von Weinberg, G. *Ausgewählte Schriften* II. *Römische Bildnisse*, edited by G. Kleiner and H. von Heintze. Berlin, 1956
445. Kaschnitz von Weinberg, G. *Zwischen Republik und Kaiserreiche.* Hamburg, 1961
446. Kaschnitz von Weinberg, G. *Römische Kunst.* 4 vols. Hamburg, 1961–3
447. Kersauson, K. de *Musée du Louvre. Catalogue des portraits romains*: 1. *Portraits de la République et d'époque Julio-Claudienne.* Paris, 1986
448. Kiss, Z. *L'iconographie des princes julio-claudiens aux temps d'Auguste et de Tibère.* Warsaw, 1975
449. Kleiner, D. E. E. *Roman Group Portraiture. The Funerary Reliefs of the Late Republic and the Early Empire.* New York, 1977
450. Kleiner, D. E. E. 'The great friezes of the Ara Pacis Augustae: Greek sources, Roman derivatives, and Augustan social policy', *MEFRA* 90,2 (1978) 753–85
451. Kluge, K. and Lehmann-Hartleben, K. *Die antiken Grossbronzen.* Berlin, 1927
452. Kockel, V. 'Beobachtungen zum Tempel des Mars Ultor und zum Forum des Augustus', *MDAI(R)* 90 (1983) 421–48
453. Koeppel, G. 'Official state reliefs of the city of Rome in the Imperial age. A bibliography', *ANRW* II, 12. 1 (1982) 480–9
454. Koeppel, G. 'The grand pictorial tradition of Roman historical representation during the early empire', *ANRW* II, 12. 1 (1982) 507–35
454A. Koeppel, G. 'Die historischen Reliefs der Römischen Kaiserzeit', *BJ* 183 (1983) 61–144
455. Koeppel, G. 'Die historischen Reliefs der römischen Kaiserzeit V, Ara Pacis Augustae', Pt. 1, *BJ* 187 (1987) 101–57; Pt. 2, *BJ* 188 (1988) 97–106
456. Kraft, K. 'Der Sinn des Mausoleums des Augustus', *Hist.* 16 (1967) 189–206 (= *Kleine Schriften* I (Darmstadt, 1973), 29–46)
457. Kraus, T. 'Das römische Weltreich', in *Propyläen Kunstgeschichte* II. Berlin, 1967
458. Krause, C. 'Rapporti di lavoro', in *Domus Tiberiana: nuove ricerche, studi di restauro*, 73–136. Zurich, 1985

459. La Rocca, E. 'Sculture frontonali del tempio di Apollo Sosiano: notizia preliminare', *BCAR* 87 (1980–1) 57–73
460. La Rocca, E. *L'età d'oro di Cleopatra. Indagine sulla tazza Farnese.* Rome, 1984
461. Lahusen, G. *Untersuchungen zur römischen Ehrenstatue in Rom.* Rome, 1983
462. Lambrechts, P. 'Auguste et la religion romaine', *Latomus* 6 (1947) 177–91
463. Lambrechts, P. 'La politique apollinienne d'Auguste et le culte impérial', *NClio* 5 (Mélanges Carnoy) (1953) 65–82
464. Lancha, J. *Mosaïques géometriques. Les ateliers de Vienne.* Rome, 1977
465. Leach, E. W. 'Patrons, painter and patterns', in A 39A
466. Lefèvre, E. *Das Bild-Programm des Apollo-Tempels auf dem Palatin* (Konstanzer althistorische Vorträge und Forschungen 24). Constance, 1989
467. Levi, M. A. 'Il regno degli api e la "domus Augusta"', *PP* 38 (1983) 327–46
468. Licht, K. de Fine. *The Rotunda in Rome.* Copenhagen, 1966
469. Ling, R. J. 'Studius and the beginnings of Roman landscape painting', *JRS* 67 (1977) 1–16
470. Ling, R. *Roman Painting.* Cambridge, 1991
471. Lippold, G. *Gemmen und Kameen des Altertums und der Neuzeit.* Stuttgart, 1922
472. Lippold, G. *Kopien und Umbildungen griechischer Statuen.* Munich, 1923
473. Little, A. M. G. *Roman Perspective Painting and the Ancient Stage.* Kenneburk, ME, 1971
474. Lloyd, R. B. 'The Aqua Virgo, Euripus and Pons Agrippae', *AJA* 83 (1979) 193–204
475. Lugli, G. *La tecnica edilizia romana con particolare riguardo al Lazio.* Rome, 1957
476. Lyttleton, M. *Baroque Architecture in Classical Antiquity.* London, 1974
477. MacDonald, W. L. *The Architecture of the Roman Empire*: I. *An Introductory Study*, 1965, rev. 1982; II. *An Urban Appraisal*, 1986. New Haven-London
478. McKay, A. G. *Houses, Villas and Palaces in the Roman World.* London, 1975
479. Macready, S. and Thompson, F. H. (eds.) *Roman Architecture in the Greek World.* Society of Antiquaries Occasional Papers, n.s. 10. London, 1987
480. Maiuri, A. *Roman Painting.* Geneva, 1953
481. Mansuelli, G. A. 'El arco honorifico en el desarrollo de la arquitectura romana', *AEA* 27 (1954) 93–178
482. Mansuelli, G. A. *Le ville del mondo romano.* Milan, 1958
483. Mansuelli, G. A. *Galleria degli Uffizi. I ritratti.* Rome, 1961
484. Mansuelli, G. A. *Architettura e città. Problemi del mondo classico.* Bologna, 1970
485. Mansuelli, G. A. 'Programmi funerari e monumentalizzazione suburbana. Esempi di urbanistica romana' *St Romagnoli* 29 (1978) 347ff
486. Mansuelli, G. A. *Studi sull'arco onorario romano.* Rome, 1979
487. Mansuelli, G. A. *Roma e il mondo romano.* 2 vols. Turin, 1981

488. Mansuelli, G. A. 'Forme e significati dell'architettura di Roma nell'età del principato', *ANRW* II, 12. 1 (1982) 212–32

489. Mansuelli, G. A. 'La città romana nei primi secoli dell'impero. Tendenze dell'urbanistica', *ANRW* II, 12. 1 (1982) 145–78

490. Mansuelli, G. A. in *Rasenna: Storia e civiltà degli Etruschi*, 679–713. Milan, 1986

491. Mansuelli, G. A., Arslan, E. A. and Scagliarini, D. *Urbanistica e architettura della Cisalpina romana.* Brussels, 1971

492. Marconi, P. *La pittura dei Romani.* Rome, 1929

493. Maria, S de 'Metodologia per una rilettura dei fornici di Roma antica', *Parametro* 20 (1973) 41ff

494. Marini Calvani, M. M. 'Urbanizzazione e programmi urbanistici nel settore occidentale della Cispadana Romana', *Caesarodunum* 20 (1985) 349–73

495. Martin, H. *Römische Tempelstatuen.* Rome, 1987

496. Massner, A.-K. *Bildnisangleichung, Untersuchungen zur Entstehungs- und Wirkungsgeschichte der Augustusporträts (43 v. Chr.–68 n. Chr.).* Berlin, 1982

497. Mau, A. *Geschichte der decorativen Wandmalerei in Pompeji.* Berlin, 1882

498. Megow, W.-R. *Kameen von Augustus bis Alexander Severus.* Berlin, 1987

499. Memel, R. *Das Odeion.* Frankfurt, 1980

500. Mielsch, H. *Römische Stuckreliefs.* Heidelberg, 1975

501. Mielsch, H. 'Funde und Forschungen zur Wandmalerei der Prinzipatszeit von 1945 bis 1975, mit einem Nachtrag 1980', *ANRW* II, 12. 2 (1981) 158–203, 247–56

502. Mielsch, H. *Die römische Villa, Architektur und Lebensform.* Munich, 1987

503. Mitchell, S. 'Imperial building in the eastern Roman provinces', in F 479, 18–25

504. Möbius, H. 'Sinn und Typen der römischen Kaiserkameen', *ANRW* II, 12. 3 (1985) 32–88

505. Moretti, G. *Ara Pacis Augustae.* Rome, 1948

506. Morricone Matini, M. L. *Mosaici antichi in Italia. Regione prima. Roma: Reg X. Palatium,* 1967

507. *La mosaïque gréco-romaine.* Paris, 1965

508. *Mostra Augustea della Romanità: Bimillenario della nascità di Augusto.* Exhibition Catalogue. Rome, 1938

509. Müller, V. 'The Roman basilica', *AJA* 41 (1937) 250–61

510. Mustilli, D. 'L'arte augustea', in C 12A, 307–77

511. Napoli, M. *Pittura antica in Italia.* Bergamo, 1960

512. Neppi Modona, A. *Edifici teatrali greci e romani: teatri, odei, anfiteatri, circhi.* Florence, 1961

513. Neudecker, R. *Die Skulpturenausstattung römischer Villen in Italien.* Mainz, 1987

514. Neuerburg, N. *L'architettura delle fontane e dei ninfei nell'Italia antica.* Naples, 1965

515. Niemayer, H. G. *Studien zur statuarischen Darstellung der römischen Kaiser.* Berlin, 1968

516. Pallottino, M. *Arte figurativa e ornamentale.* Rome, 1940

517. Pallottino, M. 'Arco onorario e trionfale', s.v. in *EAA* I. Rome, 1958
518. Paribeni, R. 'Le opere pubbliche', in c 12A, 405–13
519. Parra, M. C. 'Per la definizione del rapporto fra teatri e ninfei', *SCO* 25 (1976) 89–118
520. *La peinture murale romaine dans les provinces de l'Empire* (BAR International Series 165). Oxford, 1983
521. *La peinture murale antique* (*Actes du séminaire de Paris 1985*, *DAF* 10, 1987)
522. Pekáry, T. *Das römische Kaiserbildnis in Staat, Kult und Gesellschaft. Dargestellt anhand der Schriftquellen.* Berlin, 1985
523. Peters, W. J. T. *Landscape in Romano-Campanian Mural Painting.* Assen, 1963
524. Phillips, E. J. 'The Roman law on the demolition of buildings', *Latomus* 32 (1973) 86–95
525. Picard, G.-C. *Les trophées romains. Contribution à l'histoire de la religion et de l'art triomphal de Rome.* Paris, 1957
526. Picard, G.-C. *L'art romain.* Paris, 1962; transl. as F 527
527. Picard, G.-C. *Roman Painting.* London, 1970
528. Polacco, L. *Il volto di Tiberio.* Rome, 1955
529. Polaschek, K. *Porträttypen einer claudischen Kaiserin.* Rome, 1973
530. Polaschek, K. *Studien zur Ikonographie der Antonia Minor.* Rome, 1973
531. Pollini, J. 'Studies in Augustan "historical" reliefs'. Diss., Berkeley, 1978
532. Pollitt, J. J. *The Art of Rome (753 B.C.–337 A.D.).* Sources and Documents. New York, 1966; reissued Cambridge, 1983
533. Poulsen, *Greek and Roman Portraits in English Country Houses.* Oxford, 1923
534. Poulsen, F. *Porträtstudien in norditalienischen Provinzmuseen.* Copenhagen, 1928
535. Poulsen, F. *Römische Privatporträts und Prinzenbildnisse.* Copenhagen, 1939
536. Poulsen, F. *Claudische Prinzen. Studien zur Ikonographie des ersten römischen Kaiserhauses.* Baden-Baden, 1960
537. Poulsen, V. H. *Les portraits romains:* I. *République et dynastie julienne.* Copenhagen, 1962
538. Rakob, F. 'Römische Architektur', in *Propyläen Kunstgeschichte* II, 153ff. Berlin, 1967
539. Ramage, E. S. 'Augustus' treatment of Julius Caesar', *Hist.* 34 (1985) 223–45
540. *Recueil général des mosaïques de la Gaule.* Paris, 1957
541. Richard, J. C. 'Mausoleum. D'Halicarnasse à Rome, puis à Alexandrie', *Latomus* 29 (1970) 370–88
542. Rickman, G. 'Porticus Minucia', in F 330, 105–8
543. Riemann, H. 'Pons Agrippae', *RE* xxi, 2 (1952) 2455–61
544. Rizzo, G. E. *La pittura ellenistica-romana.* Milan, 1929
545. Rizzo, G. E. 'Le pitture della "Casa dei Grifi"', in *MonPitt* III, vol. Roma I. Rome, 1936
546. Rizzo, G. E. 'Le pitture dell'Aula Isiaca di Caligola', in *MonPitt* III, vol. Roma II. Rome, 1936

547. Rizzo, G. E. 'Le pitture della "Casa di Livia"', in *MonPitt* III, vol. Roma III. Rome, 1937

548. Roccos, L. J. 'Apollo Palatinus: the Augustan Apollo on the Sorrento base', *AJA* 93 (1989) 571–88

549. Rodenwaldt, G. *Kunst der Antike (Propyläen Kunstgeschichte* III). Berlin, 1927

550. Rodenwaldt, G. *Kunst um Augustus.* Berlin, 1942

551. *Roman Urban Defences in the West.* London, 1983

552. Roques de Maumont, H. von *Antike Reiterstandbilder.* Berlin, 1958

553. Rowell, H. T. 'Vergil and the forum of Augustus', *AJPh* 62 (1941) 261–76

554. Rumpf, A. 'Römische historische Reliefs', *BJ* 155–6 (1955–6) 122–35

555. Ryberg, I. S. 'The procession of the Ara Pacis', *MAAR* 19 (1949) 77–101

556. Ryberg, I. S. *Rites of the state religion in Roman art (MAAR* 22). Rome, 1955

557. Ryberg, I. S. 'Clupeus uirtutis', *The Classical Tradition* (Studies Caplan) (1966) 232–8

558. Sadurska, A. 'L'art d'Auguste: progrès, regrès, ou transformation?', in A 54A, 70–3

559. Santoro Bianchi, S. 'Alcune riflessioni su scuole e tipologie urbanistiche nell'Italia centro-settentrionale', *Caesarodunum* 20 (1985) 375–92

560. Sauron, G. 'Le message symbolique des rinceaux de l'Ara Pacis Augustae', *CRAI* (1982) 81–101

561. Sauron, G. 'Le message esthétique des rinceaux de l'Ara Pacis Augustae', *RA* (1988) 3–40

562. Schefold, K. *La peinture pompéienne. Essai sur l'évolution de sa signification.* Brussels, 1972

563. Schefold, K. 'Caesars Epoche als goldene Zeit römischer Kunst', *ANRW* I, 4 (1973) 945–69

564. Schmidt Colinet, A. *Antike Stützfiguren.* Frankfurt, 1977

565. Schneider, B. *Studien zu den kleinformatigen Kaiserporträts von den Anfägen der Kaiserzeit bis ins dritte Jahrhundert.* Munich, 1976

566. Schumacher, W. N. *Basilika: Untersuchungen zur antiken und frühmittelalterlichen Baukunst.* Berlin, 1928

567. *Sculture municipali dell'area Sabellica tra l'età di Cesare e quella di Nerone. (Studi Miscellanei* 10 (1963–1964)). Rome 1965

568. Sear, F. B. *Roman Wall and Vault Mosaics.* Heidelberg, 1977

569. Sena Chiesa, G. and Facchini, G. M. 'Gemme romane di età imperiale: produzione, commerci, committenza', *ANRW* II, 12. 3 (1985) esp. 3–31

570. Settis, S. '"Esedra" e "ninfeo" nella terminologia architettonica del mondo romano', *ANRW* I, 4 (1973) 661–745

571. Shipley, F. 'Chronology of the building operations in Rome from the death of Caesar to the death of Augustus', *MAAR* 9 (1931) 17–60

572. Shipley, F. *Agrippa's Building Activities in Rome.* St Louis, 1933

573. Sichtermann, H. 'Gemalte Gärten in pompeianischen Zimmern', *AW* 5 (1974) vol. 3, 41–51

574. Simon, E. 'Zur Augustusstatue von Prima Porta', *MDAI(R)* 64 (1957) 46–68

575. Simon, E. 'Das neugefundene Bildnis des Gaius Caesar in Mainz', *MZ* 58 (1963) 1–18

576. Simon, E. *Ara Pacis Augustae.* Tübingen, 1967

577. Simon, E. *Augustus: Kunst und Leben in Rom um die Zeitenwende.* Munich, 1986

578. Simpson, C. J. 'The date of the dedication of the temple of Mars Ultor', *JRS* 67 (1977) 91–4

579. Sjöqvist, E. 'Kaisareion. A study in architectural iconography', *ORom* 1 (1954) 86–108

580. Smith, R. R. R. 'The Imperial reliefs from the Sebasteion at Aphrodisias', *JRS* 77 (1987) 88–138

581. Speyer, W. 'Das Verhältnis des Augustus zur Religion', *ANRW* II, 16.3 (1986) 1777–805

582. Stemmer, K. *Untersuchungen zur Typologie, Chronologie und Ikonographie der Panzerstatuen.* Berlin, 1978

583. Stewart, A. F. 'To entertain an emperor: Sperlonga, Laokoon and Tiberius at the dinner-table', *JRS* 67 (1977) 76–90

584. Strong, E. *La scultura romana da Augusto a Costantino.* 2 vols. Florence, 1923–6

585. Strong, E. *Art in Ancient Rome.* London, 1929

586. Strong, E. 'The art of the Augustan age', in *CAH* x¹ (1934) 545ff

587. *Studi sulla città antica.* Rome, 1983

588. Taeger, F. *Charisma. Studien zur Geschichte des antiken Herrscherkultes.* Stuttgart, 1957 and 1960

589. Tamassia, A. M. 'La pittura nell'età di Augusto', *Arte antica e moderna* 4 (1958) 319–33

590. Tamm, B. *Auditorium and Palatium. A Study on Assembly-Rooms in Roman Palaces During the 1st Century B.C. and the 1st Century A.D.* Stockholm, 1963

591. Tamm, B. *Neros Gymnasium in Rom.* Stockholm, 1970

592. Technau, W. *Die Kunst der Römer* (Geschichte der Kunst, das Altertum). Berlin, 1940

593. Thompson, H. 'The impact of Roman architects and architecture on Athens: 170 B.C.–A.D. 170', in Macready, S. and Thompson, F. H. (eds.) *Roman Architecture in the Greek World* (The Society of Antiquaries Occasional Papers n.s. 10) London, 1987

594. Thornton, M. K. and R. L. *Julio-Claudian Building Programs, a Quantitative Study in Political Management.* Wauconda, 1989

595. Todd, M. 'Forum and capitolium in the early Empire', in Grew, F. and Hobley, B. (eds.) *Roman Urban Topography in Britain and the Western Empire* (*CBA ResRep.* 59), 55–66. London, 1985

596. Torelli, M. *Typology and Structure of Roman Historical Reliefs* (Jerome Lectures, 14th Ser.). Ann Arbor, 1982

597. Toynbee, J. M. C. 'The Ara Pacis reconsidered and historical art in Roman Italy', *PBA* 39 (1953) 67–95

598. Toynbee, J. M. C. 'The Ara Pacis Augustae', *JRS* 51 (1961) 153–6

599. Toynbee, J. M. C. *The Art of the Romans*. London, 1963

600. Tram Tan Tinh. *Catalogue des peintures romaines du Musée du Louvre*. Paris, 1974

601. Treves, P. *Il mito di Alessandro e la Roma d'Augusto*. Milan and Naples, 1953

602. Tufi, S. R. 'Frammenti delle statue dei *summi viri* nel foro di Augusto', *DArch* 3.1 (1981) 69–84

603. Vermeule, C. C. *Roman and Imperial Art in Greece and Asia Minor*. Cambridge, 1968

604. Vermeule, C. *The Cult Images of Imperial Rome*. Rome, 1987

605. Vierneisel, K. and Zanker, P. *Die Bildnisse des Augustus. Herrscherbild und Politik im kaiserlichen Rom*. Munich, 1979

606. *La villa romana*. Bologna, 1971

607. Vos, M. de 'Due monumenti di pittura postpompeiana a Roma', *BCAR* 81 (1968–9) 149ff

608. Vos, M. de *L'egittomania in pitture e mosaici romano-campani della prima età imperiale*. Leiden, 1980

609. Walker, S. and Burnett, A. *The Image of Augustus* (British Museum Publications). London, 1981

610. Walker, S. and Burnett, A. *Augustus* (Handlist of the exhibition and supplementary studies) (British Museum Occasional Papers 16). London, 1981

611. Wallace-Hadrill, A. 'The golden age and sin in Augustan ideology', *P & P* 95 (1982) 19–36

612. Ward-Perkins, J. B. 'From Republic to Empire: reflections on the early provincial architecture of the Roman west', *JRS* 60 (1970) 1–19

613. Ward-Perkins, J. B. *Architettura romana*. Milan, 1974 (transl. as *Roman Architecture*. New York, 1977)

614. Ward-Perkins, J. B. *Cities of Ancient Greece and Italy. Planning in Classical Antiquity*. London, 1974

615. Ward-Perkins, J. B. *Roman Imperial Architecture*. Harmondsworth, 1981

616. Wardman, A. *Religion and Statecraft among the Romans*. London, 1982

617. Weinstock, S. 'Pax and the "Ara Pacis"', *JRS* 50 (1960) 44–58

618. West R. *Römische Porträtplastik* I–II. Munich, 1933–41

619. Wheeler, M. *Roman Art and Architecture*. London, 1964

620. White, P. 'Julius Caesar in Augustan Rome', *Phoenix* 42 (1988) 334–56

621. Williams Lehmann, P. *Roman Wall Painting from Boscoreale in the Metropolitan Museum of Art*. Cambridge, MA, 1953

622. Wilson-Jones, M. 'Designing the Roman Corinthian Order', *JRA* 2 (1989) 35–69

623. Winckes, R. *Clipeata Imago. Studien zu einer römischen Bildnisform*. Bonn, 1969

624. Winckes, R. 'Zum Illusionismus römischer Wandmalereien der Republik', *ANRW* I, 4 (1973) 927–44

625. Zanker, P. *Forum Augustum. Das Bildprogramm*. Tübingen, n.d. [*c.* 1968]

626. Zanker, P. *Forum Romanum. Die Neugestaltung durch Augustus*. Tübingen, 1972
627. Zanker, P. *Studien zu den Augustus-Porträts*, 1: *Der Actium-Typus* (Abh. Gött. Ak. Wiss. 3). Göttingen, 1973
628. Zanker, P. *Klassizistische Statuen. Studien zur Veränderung des Kunstgeschmacks in der römischen Kaiserzeit*. Mainz, 1974
629. Zanker, P. *Provinzielle Kaiserporträts. Zur Rezeption der Selbstdarstellung des Princeps*. Munich, 1983
630. Zanker, P. 'Der Apollontempel auf dem Palatin', in F 330, 21–40
631. Zanker, P. 'Zur Bildnisrepräsentation führender Männer in mittelitalischen und campanischen Städten zur Zeit der späten Republik und der julisch-claudischen Kaiser', in E 77, 251–66
632. Zanker, P. *Augustus und die Macht der Bilder*. Munich, 1987
633. Zanker, P. *The Power of Images in the Age of Augustus* (Jerome Lectures, 16th Ser.) (transl. of 'Augustus und die Macht der Bilder', by A. Shapiro). Ann Arbor, 1988
634. Zazoff, P. *Die antiken Gemmen*. Munich, 1983
635. Zevi, F. *La casa Reg, IX, 5, 18–21 a Pompei (Studi Misc.* 5 (1960–1)). Rome, 1964
636. Zinserling, G. 'Der Augustus von Primaporta als offiziöses Denkmal', *Acta Antiqua* 15 (1967) 327–39

4. LAW

637. Allison, J. E. and Cloud, J. D. 'The *lex Iulia maiestatis*', *Latomus* 21 (1962) 711–31
638. Astolfi, R. *I 'Libri Tres Iuris Civilis' di Sabino*. Padua, 1983
639. Atkinson, K. M. T. 'The education of the lawyer in ancient Rome', *The South African Law Journal* 87 (1970) 31–59
640. Bauman, R. A. *The Crimen Maiestatis in the Roman Republic and Augustan Principate*. Johannesburg, 1967
641. Bauman, R. A. *Impietas in Principem*. Munich, 1974
642. Bauman, R. A. *Lawyers in Roman Transitional Politics*. Munich, 1985
643. Bauman, R. A. *Lawyers and Politics in the Early Roman Empire: a Study of Relations Between the Roman Jurists and the Emperors from Augustus to Hadrian* (Münchener Beiträge zur Papyrusforschung und antiken Rechtsgeschichte, 82), Part 1, chs. 1 and 2. Munich, 1989
644. Brunt, P. A. 'The legal issue in Cicero, *pro Balbo*', *CQ* n.s. 32(1982) 136–47
645. Buckland, W. W. *The Roman Law of Slavery. The Condition of the Slave in Private Law from Augustus to Justinian*. Cambridge, 1908; repr. 1970
646. Buckland, W. W. *A Textbook of Roman Law from Augustus to Justinian*. 3rd edn revised by P. Stein. Cambridge, 1966
647. Cancelli, F. 'Il presunto "ius respondendi" istituito da Augusto', *BIDR* 29 (1987) 5–31
648. Champlin, E. 'Pegasus', *ZPE* 32 (1978) 269–78

649. Cloud, J. D. 'The Augustan authorship of the lex Iulia de vi publica (*Digest* 46.6)', *LCM* 12 (1987) 82–5

650. Corbett, P. E. *The Roman Law of Marriage*. Oxford, 1930; repr. Aalen, 1979

651. Falchi, G. L. *Le controversie tra Sabiniani e Proculiani*. Milan, 1981

652. Frier, B. W. *The Rise of the Roman Jurists: Studies in Cicero's pro Caecina*. Princeton, 1985

653. Girard, P. F. 'Les leges Iuliae iudiciorum publicorum et priuatorum', *ZRG* 34 (1913) 295–371

654. Gualandi, G. *Legislazione imperiale e giurisprudenza*. 2 vols. Milan, 1963

655. Hennig, D. 'T. Labienus und der erste Maiestätsprozess *de famosis libellis*', *Chiron* 3 (1973) 245–54

656. Honoré, A. M. 'Proculus', *RHD* 30 (1962) 472–509

657. Honoré, A. M. *Emperors and Lawyers*. London, 1981

658. Horak, F. *Rationes Decidendi: Entscheidungbegründungen bei den älteren römischen Juristen bis Labeo* 1. Innsbruck, 1969

659. Johnston, D. *The Roman Law of Trusts*. Oxford, 1988

660. Jolowicz, H. F. and Nicholas, B. *Historical Introduction to the Study of Roman Law*. 3rd edn. Cambridge, 1972

661. Kaser, M. *Das römische Zivilprozessrecht*. Munich, 1966

662. Kaser, M. *Das römische Privatrecht*. 2nd edn. Vol. 1 Munich, 1971; Vol. 11 Munich, 1975

663. Kaser, M. '"Ius Honorarium" und "Ius Civile"', *ZRG* 101 (1984) 1–114

664. Koschaker, P. *Europa und das römische Recht*. 4th edn. Munich, 1966

665. Krampe, C. *Proculi Epistulae: eine Frühklassische Juristenschrift*. Karlsruhe, 1970

666. Kunkel, W. 'Das Wesen des *ius respondendi*', *ZRG* 66 (1948) 423–57

666A. Kunkel, W. *Herkunft und Soziale Stellung der römischen Juristen*. 2nd edn. Graz–Vienna–Cologne, 1967

667. Kunkel, W. *An Introduction to Roman Legal and Constitutional History* (transl. by J. M. Kelly) 2nd edn. Oxford, 1973

668. Liebs, D. 'Rechtsschulen und Rechtsunterricht im Principat', *ANRW* II, 15 (1976) 197–286

669. Litewski, W. 'Die römische Appellation in Zivilsachen', *ANRW* II, 14 (1982) 60–96

670. Martini, R. *Le definizioni dei giuristi romani*. Milan, 1966

671. Mayer-Maly, T. 'Proculus', *RE* s.v. (1957) 1234–40

672. Nörr, D. 'Pomponius: oder "Zum Geschichtsverständnis der römischen Juristen"', *ANRW* II, 15 (1976) 497–604

673. Nörr, D. 'Planung in der Antike: Über die Ehegesetze des Augustus', in Baier, H. (ed.) *Freiheit und Sachzwang: Beiträge zu Ehren H. Schelskys*, 309–34. Opladen, 1977

674. Nörr, D. 'I giuristi romani: tradizionalismo o progresso?', *BIDR* 84 (1981) 9–33

675. Nörr, D. 'C. Cassius Longinus: der Jurist als Rhetor (Bemerkungen zu Tacitus, Ann. 14.42ff.)', in Heine, H. (ed.) *Althistorische Studien H. Bengtson*, 187–222. Wiesbaden, 1983

676. Nörr, D. 'Zur Biographie des Juristen C. Cassius Longinus', in *Sodalitas:*

Scritti in Onore di A. Guarino VI, 2957–78. Naples, 1984

677. Orestano, R. *Il potere normativo degli imperatori e le costituzioni imperiali.* Rome, 1937; repr. Turin, 1962

678. Pernice, A. *Labeo: Römisches Privatrecht im Ersten Jahrhundert der Kaiserzeit.* 3 vols. Halle, 1873–1900

679. Provera, G. 'Ancora sul "ius respondendi"', *SDHI* 28 (1962) 342–60

680. Pugliese, G. *Il Processo Civile Romano* II: *Il processo formulare* I. Milan, 1963

681. Riccobono, S. 'La giurisprudenza dell'impero', in C 12A, 147–59

682. Rogers, R. S. 'Ateius Capito and Tiberius', in *Synteleia V. Arangio-Ruiz* I, 123–7. Naples, 1964

683. Röhle, R. 'Praetor Fideicommissarius', *RIDA* 15 (1968) 399–428

684. *Roman Statutes.* London, 1995

685. Rotondi, G. *Leges publicae populi romani.* Milan, 1912; repr. with appendix, 1962

686. Ruggiero, E. de *La patria nel diritto pubblico romano.* Rome, 1921

687. Sargenti, M. 'Considerazioni sul potere normativo imperiale', in *Sodalitas: Scritti in Onore di A. Guarino* VI, 2625–51. Naples, 1984

688. Scacchetti, M. G. 'Note sulle differenze di metodo fra Sabiniani e Proculiani', in *Studi in Onore di A. Biscardi* V, 369–404. Milan, 1984

689. Schiller, A. A. *Roman Law: Mechanisms of Development.* The Hague–Paris–New York, 1978

690. Schulz, F. *History of Roman Legal Science.* Oxford, 1946

691. Seidl, E. 'Labeos geistiges Profil', in *Studi in Onore di E. Volterra* I, 63–81. Milan, 1971

692. Sherwin-White, A. N. 'Poena legis repetundarum', *PBSR* 17 (1949) 5–25

693. Siber, H. 'Plautius', *RE* s.v. (1951) 45–51

694. Stein, P. 'The relations between grammar and law in the early principate: the beginning of analogy', *La Critica del Testo* II, 757–69. Florence, 1971

695. Stein, P. 'The two schools of jurists in the early principate', *Cambridge Law Journal* 31 (1972) 8–31

696. Sturm, F. 'Pegaso: un giureconsulto dell'epoca di Vespasiano', *Atti del Congresso Internazionale di Studi Vespasianei*, 105–36. Rieti, 1981

697. Syme, R. 'Fiction about Roman jurists', *ZRG* 99 (1980) 78–104 (= A 94, III, 1393–1414)

698. Thomas, J. A. C. 'Lex Iulia de adulteriis coercendis', *Etudes J. Macqueron*, 637–44. Aix-en-Provence, 1970

699. Volkmann, H. *Zur Rechtsprechung im Prinzipat des Augustus* (Historische Beiträge). Munich, 1935

700. Watson, A. *The Law of Persons in the Later Roman Republic.* Oxford, 1967

701. Watson, A. *Rome of the XII Tables.* Princeton, 1975

702. Watson, A. 'Roman slave law and Romanist ideology', *Phoenix* 37 (1983) 53–65

703. Watson, A. *Roman Slave Law.* Baltimore, 1987

704. Wieacker, F. *Vom römischen Recht.* 2nd edn. Stuttgart, 1961

705. Wieacker, F. 'Augustus und die Juristen seiner Zeit', *RHD* 37 (1969) 331–49

706. Wieacker, F. 'Respondere ex auctoritate principis', in J. A. Ankum *et al.* (eds.) *Satura Roberto Feenstra oblata*, 71–94. Fribourg, 1985

INDEX

References in italics are to maps (by map number) and illustrations (by page number).
   Arrangement of material within entries is predominantly chronological, though some material of a topical nature is alphabetically ordered. Footnotes are referred to only where the subject is not mentioned in the corresponding page of text.

Aba, ruler of Olba 650
Abbaeitae *16 Cc*, 659
Abila, tetrarchy of 745
Abodiacum (Epfach) *10 Db*, 540, 543
abortion 769
Absortium *11 Bb*, 575
Abuzza 611
Acarnania *15 Bb*, 648, 653
Acci (Guadix) 453, 457
Acerronius Proculus, Cn. (*cos.* A.D. 37) 969
Achaea, province of *1 Ec*, *15 Bb-Cb*, *21 Cb* 445,
   549; annexation 644; administration 346n9,
   369, 555–6, 567, 633–4, 648, 655–6
Achaean League 656
Acilius Strabo, L. 639–40
Acmonia 674
Acrae *4 Cb*, 439
Acruvium (Kotor) *11 Cb*, 574
actiones: iudicati 401; *Publiciana* 399
Actium campaign *1 Ec*, *2 Cb*, *15 Bb*, 54–9, *60*,
   66, 376, 384, 651; commemoration 75, 76,
   77, 189–90, 829, 832, 936; defections to
   Octavian 56–7, 61, 152, 550; literary
   treatments 917–18; symbolism 73, 189–90,
   191, 658, 832; veterans 61–2, 73, 375, 573
actors 669, 888
Acts of the Alexandrian Martyrs 701
Acts of the Apostles 737, 854, 855, 866–7
Acts of the Pagan Martyrs 779
Ad Castores 271
Ad Fines (Martorell) 454
adaeratio (cash payment of wheat-dues) 314
Adiabene 248, 780
Adiatorix, prince of Heraclea Pontica 29, 649
adiutores 341, 342
administration 145; *ad hoc* development 70,
   112, 117–18; under Augustus 128, 898; local
   145, 421; senatorial class 337–40; *see also
   individual officers*, secretariat, *and under
   individual regions and* equites; provinces;
   Rome
Adminius (son of Cunobelin) 228, 506
adoption in imperial family 93–4, 201, 240
Adria 989

adultery 304, 334; *lex Iulia* 93, 132, 887, 890–2,
   893, 974; private jurisdiction 890, 893;
   quaestio de adulteriis 122, 409, 890
adventus 791–2, 798n30, 804, 808, 943–4, 945
Aedemon's revolt in Mauretania 597–8
aediles: curule 125, 327, (Agrippa) 47–8, 82,
   788–9, (games) 206–7, 222, (jurisdiction)
   398, 406, 973; Italian 422; provincial 456
Aedui *7 Cc*, *9 Cd*, 488, 490, 491, 493, 498
Aegina *2 Cb*, *15 Cc*, 11, 651, 654
Aegis(s)us (Tulcea) *11 Ea*, 555
Aegium *15 Cb*, 666
Aelia Paetina 233, 240, 991
Aelius Catus, Sex. 175–6, 350, 553
Aelius Gallus, M. 149, 150, 155, 196, 680, 711, 722
Aelius Gracilis, M. 460
Aelius Lamia, L. 165
Aelius Plautius Silvanus, Ti. (*cos.* A.D. 45, 74) 350
Aelius Seianus, L. (Sejanus): in Pannonia 208;
   ascendancy 213–16, 301, 303, 304, 384, 798,
   799; fall 216–17, 218–19, 229, 305, 307, 639;
   and *castra praetoria* 393, 793
Aelius Tubero, Q. 218, 964, 965, 970
Aemilia Lepida 224
Aemilius Lepidus, M. (*cos.* 46 B.C., *triumvir*);
   areas of responsibility 1, 5, 9, 18, 457, 470,
   589; a *triumvir* 18, 25, 34, 35–6, 435, 590;
   pontifex maximus 825, 827
Aemilius Lepidus, M. (son of *triumvir*) 62, 74
Aemilius Lepidus, M. (*cos.* A.D. 6) 129, 177,
   178, 204–5, 206, 212, 215
Aemilius Lepidus, M. (son of above) 204–5,
   224, 226, 990
Aemilius Lepidus, M'. 219
Aemilius Lepidus Paullus, L. (*cos.* 34 B.C.) 47
Aemilius Macer 922
Aemilius Paullus, L. (*cos.* 1 B.C.) 108, 990
Aemilius Rectus (prefect of Egypt) 220
Aemilius Scaurus (*aedile* 58 B.C.) 804
Aenaria *2 Ba*, 20
Aenona *11 Cb*, 552n9, 581, 584
Aequiculi 421
Aequum *11 Cb*, 575, 584
aerarium militare 320, 321, 338, 378

Colchester *see* Camulodunum
Colchis 647, 649
Collatia 981
collega imperii, collegiate rule 121, 221; *see also under* Augustus; Tiberius
collegia (guilds) 143, 513, 794, 902; 'Augustales' 135, 902, 957
Cologne (Ara Ubiorum Agrippinensis, Colonia Agrippina) *1 Ca, 7 Db*, 391, 395, 500, 525, 528; altar of Ubii 134, 182, 187, 350, 524, 527, 530; army revolt (A.D. 14) 208–9; *colonia* status (A.D. 50) 240, 491, 530–1; buildings 266, 524, 844
colonies: Augustan 587, 589, 603, 604, 605; reasons for 130, 477; religious rituals 813, 843–5, 847; see also individual colonies, *incolae*; *ius Italicum*; *ius Latinum*; *and under individual provinces and*: Iulius Caesar, C; veterans
Colossae *21 Cb*, 856, 858
columbaria (type of tomb) 939
Columella 461, 908, 922
Comana Pontica *2 Da, 16 Gb*, 29, 154, 644, 649
comedy 907
comitia 333, 974–5, 804, 819; *centuriata* 206, 798–9
Commagene *2 Db, 16 Gd-Hd, 19 Ca-Da*, 729–30; under Antiochus I 23–4, 709, 729, 731; Ventidius' and Antony's campaign 23–4, 729; Augustus and dynasts 154, 159, 195, 650; under Antiochus III 650, 731; incorporated in Syria 650, 670, 709, 711, 712, 713, 729; returned to Antiochus IV 670, 731; Vespasian eliminates 730 army 708, 716, 730–1; festival of Claudius 669; royal burials 731
commendatio 126
Commius, king of Atrebates 503, 505
Comoiscus, king of Dacia 549
compita 794, 801, 802, 823–4, 937
concilia, provincial 348, 356, 359, 499, 500; see also *koina*
Concordia *3 Ba*, 431
concrete 718–19, 784
Condate, altar of *see* Lugdunum (Altar)
Condrusi 517
Consolatio ad Liviam 142, 171
constitution, Roman: Principate as restoring Republican 76–7, 99, 324, 412, 906; triumvirs and 1, 19–20, 26–7, 37, 42, 48; *see also individual elements and* Augustus (constitutional powers)
construction methods 548n1, 584, 718–19, 782, 784, 785
consular power, Augustus, 91–2, 347
consulship 327; Augustus' use of 94–5, 100, 113, 117, 126, 327; dating formulae 415,

979–81; Fasti 72; jurisdiction 398, 407, 408–9; ordinary and suffect 99–100, 125, 327, 333; perpetual 88, 246, 273; provincials 460, 612; repeated 327; sculptural typology 942; triumviral period 18, 20, 48–9, 68; social distinction 85–6, 99, 125, 881; *see also under individual emperors*
contiones, formal 799
contract law 874–5
Contrebia *6 Ca*, 404–5
contubernia (mixed 'marriages') 897
contubernium principis 283, 290, 292
Convenae 471, 498
conventus (assize circuits) 366, 405, 452–3, 649; Egypt 691–2; Gaul 471, 500; Illyricum 576, 577; Spain 452–3, 463
conventus civium Romanorum 455, 574
convivia et circuli 295
copper mines 447, 458, 477, 648, 653, 722n85, 735, 747
Coptos *17 Bb*, 679, 680, 688, 692
Corbières 477
Corbulo *see under* Domitius
Corcyra *1 Dc, 2 Bb, 15 Ab-Bb*, 54, 56, 648, 655
Corcyra Nigra *11 Cb, 12 Cb*, 574
Corduba *1 Bc, 6 Cb*, 452, 457, 460, 461
Corfinium 984, 988
Corieltavi *8 Da*, 503
Corinium, Dalmatia *11 Cb*, 575
Corinth *1 Ec, 2 Cb, 15 Cc, 21 Cb*, 254, 647, 666; Caesarian colony 573, 653; capital of Achaea 567, 583, 648; Christianity 367, 855, 860, 863–4; coinage 655; in triumviral period 54, 56
corn distribution 47, 238, 251, 794, 808, 894; Augustus' 88, 104, 130, 794, 808–9, (to Greek cities) 651, 654; see also *praefecti (frumenti dandi)*
corn supply: Caesar and 586, 587, 617; disruption (41–38 B.C.) 14, 19, 20, 24, 435, 440, (A.D. 69) 259, 263, 276, 440; emperors' responsibility 88, 311, 322, 617, (Augustus) 88, 97, 104, 117, 130, 651, 794, 808–9, (Claudius) 235, 238, 953, (Nero) 251, 599; procurators *de Minucia* 238; sources 440, 458, 480, 557, 721, (*see also under* Africa; Cyrene; Egypt; Sardinia; *see also* corn distribution; *curae (frumenti)*; famine; *praefecti (annonae)*; *and under* taxation
Cornelius Balbus, L. the Elder 1, 460, 882
Cornelius Balbus, L. the Younger: African campaigns 91, 139, 167, 168, 591, 592; theatre in Rome 139, 804, 935
Cornelius Celsus, A.; *On Medicine* 922
Cornelius Dolabella, P. (*cos.* 44 B.C.) 6, 10, 709
Cornelius Dolabella, P. (*cos.* A.D. 10) 556, 568, 594, 595